Professiona
Adobe® Flex® 3

Professional
Adobe® Flex® 3

Joseph Balderson
Peter Ent
Jun Heider
Todd Prekaski
Tom Sugden
Andrew Trice
David Hassoun
Joe Berkovitz

WILEY

Wiley Publishing, Inc.

Professional Adobe® Flex® 3

Published by
Wiley Publishing, Inc.
10475 Crosspoint Boulevard
Indianapolis, IN 46256
www.wiley.com

ISBN: 978-0-470-22364-2

Manufactured in the United States of America

10 9 8 7 6 5 4 3 2 1

Library of Congress Cataloging-in-Publication Data is available from the publisher.

To my love, my light, my precious wife Joanne. And to my Grade 13 English teacher, Mr. Barrs,
who always said I'd be a published author someday. :)
— Joseph Balderson

I could not, and would not, have done this without the support of my partner, Joseph.
Thanks for listening to me and encouraging me to press on.
— Peter Ent

I would like to dedicate my portion of this book and give immense love and thanks to my son Kobi,
daughter Mia, father Robert, aunt Kathryn, sisters Lisa, Hiromi, and Mayumi, and mother Masako,
and most of all my wife Michelle. Without their love, support, and encouragement throughout
the writing process, I would not have had the energy and time to complete my chapters.
— Jun Heider

This book is dedicated to all the technology geeks out there who shunned social activity in college
in order to dedicate themselves to the higher art of software engineering.
— Todd Prekaski

Dedicated to my dear wife, Romola, and our delightful, mischievous children, Minna and Lorimer.
— Tom Sugden

To my wife Marta, for her unconditional love and support.
— Andrew Trice

For my friends and family; you know who you are and I hope you know how much you all mean to me.
— David Hassoun

To my wife, Max.
— Joe Berkovitz

About the Authors

Joseph Balderson has been fascinated by computers and programming since picking up LEGOs and disassembling nearly every appliance he could find as a child, progressing on to electronics, microcontrollers, and robotics as a teen. This interest took a detour in his college years, when he attended art school and studied poetry, philosophy, and graphic design. When he discovered Flash 4 in 1999, Joseph found his true vocation, one that would allow him to combine his passions for art and science, design, and programming under one roof.

That passion has led Joseph through an evolution of roles throughout his career, from graphic designer to web designer, to Flash designer, to Flash developer, and finally, today, as a Flex and ActionScript developer. Joseph has held various positions throughout this time, from a jack-of-all-trades for a dot-com in the early days of the Web to a bank employee, Flash freelancer, and hired temp.

Joseph's interests in communication and writing also led him to a position as staff writer and authoring partner at Community MX in 2005, writing biweekly tutorials on Flash and Flex technologies to this day. Joseph also served as Professor of Multimedia Studies at Humber College in 2005–2006, teaching Flash and ActionScript. After a stint as an Adobe-certified corporate instructor in 2006–2007, Joseph resumed his freelance career to focus on consulting and writing. He has since participated as contributor and technical editor on a number of book projects, and has been involved in the construction of Flex and AIR rich Internet applications for a number of startups and consulting agencies.

Joseph is now a freelance Flex and Flash platform developer living in central Ontario, Canada, in the Georgian Bay area. He spends most of his time in his home studio dreaming up ways of making cool stuff with Adobe technologies. Joseph's work and blog can be viewed at `http://www.joeflash.ca`.

Peter Ent is a Computer Scientist at Adobe, working with the LiveCycle team. Prior to this, Peter worked for Adobe Customer Care as a Flex support engineer and then as a technical account manager. Before joining Adobe, Peter worked in the financial services industry at State Street and Fidelity Investments. He also has experience at two startups, building software applications doing imaging and molecular modeling. Peter holds a BS in Computer Science from Syracuse University.

Jun Heider is a senior developer and technical trainer with RealEyes Media, an Adobe partner company based in Denver, Colorado, with a focus in rich Internet applications. Jun graduated from Regis University with a BS in Computer Networking and has a number of technical certifications.

Jun has worked with ColdFusion since 4.5, Flex since Flex 2 beta, and AIR since it was first available in prerelease. Projects that Jun has worked on have ranged from a large clustered ColdFusion application for a global home-based business organization to internal Flex-based business applications for companies such as Chase Manhattan to large-scale Flex-based online businesses such as Beatport.com, and also AIR-based utility applications such as the Beatport downloader.

In addition to development and training, Jun loves to speak at conferences such as those on Adobe MAX, 360|Flex, and Flexmaniacs. Jun also loves to write; he is an active blogger on O'Reilly Inside RIA and has written articles for the Fusion Authority and Flex Authority.

In his free time, Jun loves to sing for his band Bucket, play his Xbox 360, snowboard, and hang out with his son, Kobi, daughter, Mia, and wife, Michelle, in colorful Colorado.

Todd Prekaski has been building software since 1993 (not including his youthful days programming an Apple IIc and TRS-80). He's been leading application development and strategy for Web-based startups and Fortune 100/500 enterprises ever since, using a panoply of technologies and platform, including Java, .NET, and LAMP. Todd is currently the chief technical architect at Beacon Street Software, based in Boston, Massachusetts. Occasionally, his thoughts show up in his blog at www.simplifiedchaos.com.

When he's not in front of a computer, Todd can be found racing his bicycles around New England, especially in early winter during cyclocross season.

Tom Sugden is a technical architect for Adobe Professional Services. His interest in computers began in the 1980s, programming sport simulators and beep-music on the ZX Spectrum 48k. When the keyboard broke from too much Dailey Thompson, Tom upgraded to the Commodore Amiga and continued to create amateur games (but with multi-channel sound) in AMOS, before dabbling in the black art of Assembly language.

With these foundations laid, Tom studied Computer Science, picking up C++, Java, and Flash 3 along the way. After graduation, Tom freelanced for Domino Record Company, building its first website and encoding music videos. This led Tom to Realise, an early Scottish Internet café turned web company, where he wrote components for a search engine and document classifier known as Glowworm (later disastrously rebranded to KM-Bridge).

The bubble burst. No more Hoegaarden on school nights. Tom escaped to the safe haven of EPCC, a software consultancy and high-performance computing center within the University of Edinburgh. There he worked on various data integration projects, helping astronomers to analyze objects in space, linking biological and pharmaceutical databases, and correlating late bus arrivals with angry customers. During this time, Tom became interested in design patterns and agile methods, and he began lecturing on the Masters Course in High Performance Computing.

When the opportunity came to join Adobe, Tom saw a more commercial setting for the same kind of creative programming that he'd always loved. Flex and the Flash Player were evolving fast and the possibilities seemed endless, as they had done years earlier on the Commodore Amiga. Tom joined Steven Webster's crack team in Edinburgh, Scotland, where he learned Flex 2 and LiveCycle Data Services from the experts, and began delivering rich Internet applications for Adobe's many enterprise customers.

Andrew Trice is the principal architect for Flex and AIR for Cynergy Systems, based in Washington, DC. He specializes in data visualization, client/server architectures, object-oriented principles, and rich application development. He has been developing for the Web for more than a decade, with more than eight years in development for the Flash platform. Andrew has developed with Flex since version 1.5, and thrives off the creativity and rich experience that the Flex/Flash platform enables. Andrew is also a regular author for Adobe Devnet and other industry weblogs. He is known not only for Flex expertise but is also a Microsoft Certified Application Developer and possesses a wide range of knowledge regarding relational databases, AJAX/JavaScript, ColdFusion, .NET, and Java-based Web applications.

David Hassoun is the founder of RealEyes Media, LLC, a digital media firm based in Colorado that focuses on interactive motion media and advanced Flash and Flex platform applications. David has always had a passion for motion media, the power of video, and the challenges of usability and interactivity. David is an Adobe Certified Master Instructor, teaches advanced RIA classes at the University of Denver, serves as the Rocky Mountain Adobe user group manager, and has taught and developed advanced Flash and Flex application courses. As a consultant or while employed with other firms, he has worked for a wide range of companies such as American Express, Chase Manhattan, Qwest, Boeing,

Macromedia, Adobe, the U.S. Air Force, Bechtel/Bettis, and many more. David regularly performs advanced code and technical best practices reviews, and has provided directional advice for international industry leaders over the past years — including many technical, courseware, and application reviews as an industry expert.

Joe Berkovitz is president of Noteflight LLC, maker of the world's first online music notation editor, and is a senior software architect with consulting shop Infrared5. With almost three decades of designing and building world-class software, Joe brings creativity and discipline to his work in Flash and Flex. He is a frequent speaker at conferences and is the originator of the popular MVCS architecture for complex Flex applications. Joe has published several ambitious open-source projects, most recently the Moccasin graphical editing framework and Flexcover, a code coverage tool for AS3. Joe is an active pianist and composer, and performs frequently in the Boston area.

Credits

Acquisitions Editor
Scott Meyers

Development Editors
John Sleeva
Gus Miklos

Technical Editors
Campbell Anderson
Charles Bihis
Matthew Fabb
Greg Jastrab
Douglas Knudsen

Production Editor
Rebecca Coleman

Copy Editor
Foxxe Editorial Services

Editorial Manager
Mary Beth Wakefield

Production Manager
Tim Tate

Vice President and Executive Group Publisher
Richard Swadley

Vice President and Executive Publisher
Barry Pruett

Associate Publisher
Jim Minatel

Project Coordinator, Cover
Lynsey Stanford

Compositor
James D. Kramer, Happenstance Type-O-Rama

Proofreader
Word One New York

Indexer
J & J Indexing

Acknowledgments

This book is made possible by all the hard work of my colleagues and coauthors, Andrew Trice, Peter Ent, Jun Heider, Todd Prekaski, Tom Sugden, David Hassoun, and Joe Berkovitz, who have slaved and poured their passion and their life into this text for over a year to create one helluva book. I want to thank you, dear sirs, for making this dream possible. It has been an incredible privilege to have shared this space with such truly talented and awesome people.

And a special thanks to all the tech editors who believed in this project enough to give up their weekends just to help us authors keep true to the course. Thanks also goes out to Steve Webster at Adobe for writing the Foreword and believing in this book enough to lend us one of his brainiacs for the last fifth of this book, without which this project would not have been possible. And thanks to all the Adobe people I've spoken with who have encouraged me to write this book and have patiently answered my poignant and esoteric technical questions.

A big thank you goes to my agent David Fugate at LaunchBooks, who has put up with my incessant questions about the tech publishing industry and shepherded me through the process of finding this, one of the coolest of writing projects I have participated in to date. I'd also like to thank my esteemed colleague Tom Green for introducing me to David and mentoring me during my start in tech writing.

And, of course, a thank you to my editors at Wrox Publishing, Chris Webb and John Sleeva, for believing in this project. And who have patiently put up with my trying to buck procedure time and again to try new things, resulting in the use of some interesting collaborative tools such as Google Docs, Buzzword, and Subversion in the creation and organization of this project.

My biggest and heartfelt thanks goes to the love of my life, my wife Joanne. With her love and support through the long days and nights, I have achieved things in my career I would have never thought possible 10 years ago when I started down this road. We are truly of stardust and the stuff of dreams made manifest.

Finally, a big thank you to Adobe Systems Incorporated for helping generate such a creative industry of passionate professionals, and for being a shining example of the Cluetrain Manifesto at work, and without whose efforts neither this book nor my entire career would have been possible.

— *Joseph Balderson*

I'd like to thank my Adobe colleagues, Kyle Quevillon and the entire Flex Support Team, for their help and tips. I'd also like to thank the many Adobe customers for their suggestions that continue to make Flex a great product.

— *Peter Ent*

I would like to dedicate my portion of this book and give immense love and thanks to my son, Kobi; daughter, Mia; father, Robert; aunt, Kathryn; sisters, Lisa, Hiromi, and Mayumi; mother, Masako, and, most of all, my wife Michelle. Without their love, support, and encouragement throughout the writing process, I would not have had the energy and time to complete my chapters.

— *Jun Heider*

I would like to thank Joseph Balderson for organizing the team for this book and for having the vision to write such an in-depth book on Adobe Flex. I would also like to thank John Sleeva, whose editing skill and keen eye for clarity helped me through the process. Thanks, also, to all the technical editors who reviewed my work and kept me sharp — Campbell Anderson, Charles Bihis, Matthew Fabb, Greg Jastrab, and Douglas Knudsen. Finally, thanks to Chris Webb for providing the way to make writing this hefty and ambitious tome possible.

— *Todd Prekaski*

I'd like to thank Joseph Balderson and John Sleeva for taking me onboard, and Steven Webster for pointing the ship in my direction to begin with. The waters were sometimes choppy, but the destination was worth the journey.

I'm also grateful to my colleagues and friends at Adobe, EPCC, and Realise for teaching me so much, and to all those who provided feedback and improvements. Thank you, Jeff Vroom and Seth Hodgson, for your LCDS wisdom; David Coletta and Allan Padgett, for the insider knowledge on Buzzword and the Tour Tracker; and especially the Bing Street Bunch, Alex, Paul, Dianne, James, JP, George, and Xavier, for the great company and curries over the last year. May there always be lime pickles at your table.

I am much indebted to the Flex community for their infectious spirit of invention and continuous knowledge sharing. My apologies for not acknowledging everyone individually; if your trick is in this book, please consider me grateful, and pinch one of mine any time you like.

I'd also like to thank my parents, Chris and Celia, for sparking my interest in computers, my brother and sister, Graham and Kate, for their friendship and phone calls, and my friend, Johnny, for lending me his Gang of Four book a decade ago and never seeing it again. I promise to return it now, along with a copy of *Professional Adobe Flex 3!*

— *Tom Sugden*

First and foremost, I thank my wife Marta. She has endured the writing process at my side, and without her encouragement and support, this book would never have been possible. I also would like to say thank you to my parents for always encouraging me to pursue my dreams and never give up.

Thank you to everyone involved in making this project a reality — my fellow authors, Joseph Balderson, Peter Ent, Jun Heider, Todd Prekaski, Tom Sugden, and Joe Berkovitz; our editing team lead by John Sleeva; our technical reviewers; and our publisher John Wiley & Sons.

— Andrew Trice

Thanks to my friends and colleagues on the RealEyes team. Special thanks to Nils Thingval and John Crosby.

— David Hassoun

I'd like to thank Todd Rein for involving me in the messy fun of deep linking in the first place, and also express my gratitude to my very, very patient family.

— Joe Berkovitz

Contents

Contents

Contents

Contents

Contents

Contents

Contents

Contents

Contents

Contents

Contents

Contents

Contents

Contents

Contents

Contents

Contents

Contents

Contents

Contents

Contents

Contents

Contents

Contents

Contents

Contents

Contents

Contents

Contents

Contents

Foreword

Wherever there is a piece of glass, there is an opportunity to deliver a rich and immersive user experience upon Adobe technology.

In 2005, my own RIA consultancy, iteration::two, was acquired by Macromedia and then Adobe, creating a tremendous opportunity for me to meet with our customers, partners, and community around the world to understanding the challenges that they face and the manner by which Adobe technology is uniquely positioned to address these challenges. Whether these are the innovative start-ups or hundreds-of-year-old financial services institutions, governments or peacekeeping organizations, or organizations managing clinical trial processes or salesforce automation, the value that we can deliver them with Adobe technology remains the same.

Innovate on Both Sides of the Glass

I like to describe this opportunity to customers as the opportunity to "Innovate on Both Sides of the Glass."

Behind the glass, complex enterprise architectures, manual paper-based processes with electronic processing and business workflows where people are intermingled with electronic business processes are the order of the day — the server-side infrastructure and enterprise architectures that are the engines for our economy.

In front of the glass, we can hide all of the complexity of these underlying systems with screamingly simple, elegant, rich and immersive user experiences that are useful, usable and desirable, and consistent across platforms and devices, where the medium of delivery is matched to the moment of interaction. Whether it is the glass display of a mobile device, a car dashboard, a touch-screen kiosk, an ATM, a desktop computer, or a conventional web browser, there is an opportunity to deliver a user-centric experience, leveraging the ubiquity of the Flash Player and Adobe Integrated Runtime (AIR) that is consistent to all.

As a software developer, this is an incredibly compelling juncture we find ourselves at — able to create software that, through the effectiveness of the user experience, can remove the day-to-day frustrations that permeate so much of the applications that we endure day-to-day in our own lives.

I trust that the opportunity to participate in this revolution, the chance to innovate on both sides of the glass in the projects that you deliver, is why you are holding this book now.

Developing Rich Internet Applications with Adobe Flex

Like many of the authors, my first attempts at building rich Internet applications (RIAs) were with Flash rather than Flex; in fact, my first book, *Reality J2EE: Architecting for Flash MX*, documented my first attempts at creating an online banking solution using Flash MX, remoting technology, which is now part of the plumbing of Flex, and J2EE. I had the privilege of working with some incredibly talented designers and developers to apply that knowledge to building some real-world enterprise-grade RIAs, but the development experience was left wanting.

However, that experience matured as I wrote *Developing Rich Clients with Macromedia Flex*, the first book to accompany the launch of the Flex development platform. During the course of writing that book, I learned one of the most incredible things about Adobe technology, and particularly about the technologies around the Flash platform — the depth, talent, expertise, diversity, and passion of the community of designers and developers who have chosen to base their livelihood upon these technologies.

What's exciting about the book that you are holding in your hands is that the authors themselves reflect that depth, talent, expertise, diversity, and passion and are indeed a tremendous cross-section of the community they participate in. I know many of these authors personally, whether as peers in the industry who have become friends, friends who have become colleagues, or community leaders who have gained my respect and the respect of their peers through their tireless contributions around the Adobe platform.

Furthermore, this team of authors reflects the ecosystem itself, whether they are individual contractors for hire, product developers working in product teams, or consultants belonging to professional services organizations. This team of authors has been responsible for delivering some of the most innovative and complex solutions across all industries; what you have encapsulated in this book is not just thought leadership but lessons learned in the field, on projects that have spanned weeks of effort to, in many cases, several man-years of effort.

Joseph Balderson and Peter Ent are community leaders, known to the Flash community before transferring their knowledge and expertise to delivering more complex experience upon Adobe Flex. Between them, Joe and Peter will ensure that you lock in the fundamentals of working with Flex and Flex Builder, MXML, and ActionScript, developing with containers and controls and the underlying event-programming model that underpins each and every application you will develop.

Andrew Trice has been a tireless advocate of Flex in the community, working with Cynergy Systems, one of our Adobe partners who have hugely invested in applying their software engineering heritage to the user-experience approaches that RIAs so clearly benefit from. To this end, Andrew really focuses in his contributions on helping you understand the techniques necessary to translate a user-experience designer's vision into the code that breathes life into it, with skinning, choreographic effects, and the seamless blending of rich media into your digital experiences. David Hassoun contributes also, helping you understand how to bring content in from Flash authoring, as well as integrate video and sound more effectively. Thereafter, Andrew will help you understand how to ensure that these experiences can sit atop mission-critical applications, introducing you to design patterns and application development strategies such as those related to security and performance.

Another enterprise software developer who found his way from Java and .NET to the Adobe platform is Todd Prekaski. Todd has already written several articles on Adobe.com about Flex and AIR, and his contributions to this work will really help you think about the extra steps you need to take to break your applications out of the browser and target the Adobe Integrated Runtime (AIR) on the desktop.

If you have followed the O'Reilly Inside RIA community, I'd be surprised if you haven't been following the work of Jun Heider. Jun contributes some great chapters on data management, which I highly recommend that you supplement by checking out his O'Reilly column.

Finally, there are two authors in this book whom I know most of all, and who compelled me to write this foreword in the first place — Joe Berkovitz and Tom Sugden.

Joe Berkovitz is an incredibly prolific developer and one of those people who just seems to be incredibly talented at whatever he chooses to invest his time and energy in, and the Adobe and Flex communities are indeed the better for it. Joe has been instrumental in shaping the direction of the platform itself. I participated with Joe in the Customer Advisory Boards for the very first versions of Flex, and many of the features and specifications you see in place today are the result of Joe's contributions. Since Flex was released to the open-source community, Joe has offered not only ideas but also code — he is an incredibly trusted advisor to the engineering teams at Adobe. As lead architect at Allurent, Joe has been responsible for creating one of the most complex e-commerce platforms upon Flex. His most recent venture — Noteflight — combines Joe's passion and talent for music with an incredible score editor, a beautifully simple immersive user experience for writing and sharing music.

Tom Sugden works within the Technical Services organization beside me at Adobe; indeed I hired Tom to join our consulting team, and since that time, he has most certainly not disappointed, leading some of our largest delivery teams of customers, partners, and Adobe Consultants in the delivery of some of the most beautiful, immersive, industry-changing, and complex enterprise applications I've seen in my career. Along the way, Tom has absorbed, iterated, and innovated in the engineering practices applied to these projects and has been instrumental in bringing best-in-industry software discipline to the development of applications upon Adobe technology. As Tom has contributed his chapters, he has continually sought me out to review them to ensure that he wasn't disclosing too much intellectual property. However, we have erred on the side of ensuring that he capture and present the most current thought leadership with the Adobe Professional Services organization, as few are more articulate and clear at presenting this leadership as Tom. For me, Tom's chapters on unit testing, test-driven development, logging and debugging, advanced development with Cairngorm, data management services and messaging, stress testing, and automation testing are the chapters I would have liked to have written in my Flex book, had I the depth of project knowledge under my belt at the time of writing that Tom does now. I will be referring my own development teams to these chapters as the price of admission into any team I am responsible for.

What Lies Ahead

And so there you have it: a team of community leaders with a maturity and depth of industry experience gained since the phrase "rich Internet application" was first coined by Macromedia, a team of community leaders who bring with them a depth of expertise developing with Adobe Flex and AIR.

Most important, however, is you. By absorbing the information this book contains, by building relationships and rapport with the authors through their guidance in this book, and by engaging with them in the community, you are investing in yourself and enabling yourself to make a fundamental difference to the world that we are living in through your software development craft.

There is a tremendous opportunity for you to participate in a revolution, where designers and developers organize themselves around human beings and Adobe technology, and create truly differentiated solutions that "Innovate on Both Sides of the Glass."

Wherever there is a piece of glass, there is an opportunity for you to participate in this innovation.

I look forward to seeing your fingerprints everywhere I look.

— Steven Webster

Steven Webster is director of technology and experience innovation at Adobe Systems. Working within the Technical Services organization — an organization that brings together over 700 customer-facing technology and design professionals in technical sales, technical enablement, professional services, technical account management, customer care, and technical response and support — Steven and his team are responsible for driving best practices around technology implementations and user-experience design across the organization, helping to ensure that whenever someone engages with a solution built upon Adobe technology, it is "Innovative on Both Sides of the Glass."

In 2002, Steven was at the forefront of rich Internet application (RIA) development as the field emerged. He wrote the first book on creating RIAs for the enterprise, Reality J2EE: Architecting for Flash MX, *showcasing at the time how Flash and J2EE technologies could be combined with software engineering disciplines such as agile development, unit testing, Test-Driven Development, and continuous integration, as well as introducing the RIA community to many of the J2EE design patterns that have been adopted for RIA development.*

At the same time, Steven cofounded iteration::two, one of the first consultancies to specialize in delivering RIAs upon enterprise infrastructures. Through iteration::two, Steven and the team delivered many firsts: introducing the prevalent Cairngorm framework to the open-source community and the FlexUnit testing framework (both now available on Adobe Labs), delivering the first-ever production deployment of Flex in Europe and the first-ever Flex-based RIA for a financial services organization in Europe.

With his cofounder, Alistair McLeod, Steven wrote the first Flex book to accompany the launch of the product, Developing Rich Internet Applications with Macromedia Flex.

Since joining Macromedia and Adobe in 2005, Steven first led the worldwide consulting team and later the wider technical services team, in driving best practices and implementations across Adobe technologies. He is recognized as a passionate and evangelical speaker who has spoken all over the world at analyst conferences, internal events to Adobe customers, and community events such as the Adobe MAX events.

Steven travels across Europe and the United States, meeting with development teams and senior business leaders across Adobe's enterprise customers and media and broadcasting customers.

Steven is most passionate when he is helping customers to marry best-in-industry user-experience design with best-in-industry software-engineering methods, seamlessly blending Adobe technologies "on both sides of the glass" with existing architectures and infrastructures.

Introduction

Flex has, in recent years, become the leader in rich Internet applications (RIA) development technologies based on the Flash Platform. There is a growing excitement about Flex and the Flash platform in creating unique experiences on the Internet and on the desktop that were simply not possible in the same way just a few years ago. The book you are now holding in your hands is an extensive guide to understanding and mastering this technology.

The Flash Platform has become so encompassing in its capabilities, its technologies, and its reach into the world of web and desktop rich application development, that it can be very challenging keeping up with all the changes, while still finding a comprehensive reference on Flex development. The Adobe Flex documentation does a superb job as a language reference, and a starting point for general development techniques, but we felt that there was considerable room to expand upon and document usage of some of Flex's more advanced capabilities. At the same time, it was felt at the time that altogether too many books merely "scratched the surface" of exposing the technology, forcing developers to round out their knowledge through online tutorials and blogs. So, this book is also an attempt to bring a little more in-depth information to those topics that form the basis of the technology.

Lead author Joseph Balderson describes his reasons for embarking on this project:

> *In the summer of 2007, I was asked a question from one of my former Flex students, enquiring whether there was just "one book" he should read that would give him a comprehensive grasp of the technology. And that made me really think: there was no such book at the time–it all depended on the specific topic and your level of experience. Coincidentally, I had just been approached by Wrox about the possibility of assuming the* Professional Flex *series. What a golden opportunity! Now I could write the Flex book I wish I had read when I was first migrating from Flash to Flex development only a few years before. So I sent a call out to my most admired colleagues, and gradually a crack team of Flex developer-writers and tech editors was assembled to co-create this book.*

Who This Book Is For

If you are a Flash or ActionScript 3.0 developer looking to expand your knowledge and experience in the world of Flex, this is the book for you. The early chapters of this book will expose you to what Flex Builder can do and how to develop simple Flex applications. Later, you'll learn about using the Flex framework classes and components. And when you're ready, the last third of the book will expose you to some advanced topics to really make your applications rock.

If you are an enterprise applications developer experienced in other languages such as Java, ColdFusion, or C#, the early chapters of this book will give you a comprehensive idea of what Flex is and how all the technologies fit together. After spending a short time familiarizing yourself with the Flex framework classes and components, you can jump to the last third of the book, which will expose you to some of the advanced tools, frameworks, and data integration techniques, which will have you building enterprise applications in no time.

If you are a Flex developer, this book will serve to give you a comprehensive in-depth understanding of the foundations of the technology, techniques for intermediate and advanced client-side and the server-side development, as well as some exposure to best practices and usage of advanced tools.

Whether you consider yourself a Flex novice, an intermediate developer, or an advanced enterprise programmer, this book has something in it for you.

What This Book Covers

This book aims to provide exhaustive, comprehensive coverage of what we have come to name as "the Flex 3 ecosystem" of technologies. In doing so, the aim has been to cover not only the foundations of the technology and distinguish the relationships between various aspects of Flex and the Flash Platform, and a firm coverage of client-side Flex applications development, development best practices, and the development environment, but also an in-depth look at more advanced and "enterprise" topics such as data integration, architectural frameworks, and advanced tools that traditionally have not received adequate coverage in Flex reference.

And for those still on the fence about using Flex for their RIA development, the aim is to show them how to take the plunge and go for it — the water is just fine.

This book also aims to provide a balance between theory and practice. In doing so, the book may be used as a companion reference guide or as an active learning tool by following the various exercises throughout the text. In some chapters, such as those in "Section 8: Server Integration," some of the exercises have been fashioned to be as similar to other chapters as possible, allowing you to compare a server-side data integration done in one language with an implementation in another language. If you're familiar with how to integrate Flex and Java, for example, simply compare it with the PHP implementation, and you'll be up and running in no time. This lets you pick up certain topics with a minimum of fuss.

The book is also peppered liberal with tips, tricks. and "gotchas" that are more commonly found in community blogs and lists than in the Adobe documentation, in an effort to relieve the frustrations of some Flex developers that a particular topic has rather scattered coverage, has not been covered clearly enough, or is not documented much at all.

A Word on AIR

Although other books, such as *Adobe AIR: Create – Modify – Reuse* and *Beginning Adobe AIR: Building Applications for the Adobe Integrated Runtime*, may delve into much greater depth on developing AIR applications, this book takes a unique approach to AIR documentation. *Professional Adobe Flex 3* introduces the topic of AIR development not as a standalone technology or topic but within the larger context of Flex development. In doing so, the reader can learn to create Flex applications both for browser and desktop deployment, a topic seldom found outside of AIR-specific texts. In fact, AIR is treated as merely another "add-on" framework, and the distinction is made within this text between the "Flash-AIR" framework and the "Flex-AIR" framework, further increasing the reader's knowledge of interoperability between the various Flex- and Flash-related technologies.

How This Book Is Structured

This book could be considered to be divided into three main "sections," each with its own "parts" and chapters. In brief these are:

❑   Parts I and II — Describe the foundations of the Flex technology

❑   Parts III to VII — Describe client-side applications development

❑   Parts VIII to XII — Describe server-side integration and advanced tools

The book is divided into 12 parts, each of which conforms to a particular theme, which are further divided into chapters for specific topics:

❑   **Part I, "Introduction to Flex 3,"** explains the foundations of the Flex and Flash platform technology ecosystem, the fundamentals of the ActionScript language, and the Flex development environment.

❑   **Part II, "Developing with Flex 3,"** delves into using the Flex Builder IDE to create applications, including specifics on the MXML language.

❑   **Part III, "Working with Components,"** introduces the basics of building applications with the Flex and AIR frameworks.

❑   **Part IV, "Advanced Component Development,"** covers some more advanced Flex framework development topics.

❑   **Part V, "Visual Effects and Multimedia,"** delves into skinning and styling Flex components, visual effects, and using sound and video with Flex, including integrating Flash-built assets into Flex applications.

❑   **Part VI, "Data Management,"** examines components in the Flex framework whose primary task is to manipulate or display data in the application. Drag and drop functionality in Flex and AIR is also examined, along with resource and data localization.

❑   **Part VII, "Client Communications,"** takes a look at client-side data communications between the Flash Player and the browser, and between the AIR and the desktop environment.

❑   **Part VIII, "Server Integration,"** gets into server-side communication using HTTP requests and Web Services involving a range of server-side technologies, as well as building online video applications with Flash Communications Server, and a look at local data store communication in AIR.

❑   **Part IX, "Data Services,"** takes an in-depth look at LiveCycle Data Services and BlazeDS.

❑   **Part X, "Using Cairngorm,"** delves into the Cairngorm micro-architecture framework, from an introductory to an advanced application development perspective.

❑   **Part XI, "Application Development Strategies,"** examines various techniques, strategies, and best practices in building efficient and high-performance Flex applications.

❑ **Part XII, "Testing and Debugging,"** provides an in-depth look at more advanced and comprehensive features of the Flex toolset, such as the debugger, the profiler, the unit testing framework, the logging framework, and the automation framework.

❑ **Appendix A, "ActionScript 3 Language Comparison,"** provides a reference for developers migrating to ActionScript and Flex from other languages, examining the differences between ActionScript, Java, and C++.

What You Need to Use This Book

The examples in this book can be run on any of the operating systems supported by the Flash Player and AIR — Windows, OS X, and Linux. Although the chapters on Flex Builder have been created on the Windows operating system, the exercises will work just as well in Flex Builder for OS X. If you want to use a development environment other than Windows or OS X, such a Linux or Ubuntu, you will need to use the open-source Flex SDK along with your editor of choice.

For best results, you will need a copy of Flex Builder for either PC or Mac, which can be purchased online at the Adobe Store or at a licensed retailer. Since Flex Builder ships with the Flex SDK and Flash and AIR, this is all you will need to get started.

Some of the more advanced chapters in Parts VIII–XII may require access to an Adobe server product such as LiveCycle Data Services or Flash Media Server, some of which may be available as a free developer license. See the relevant chapters for details.

Conventions

To help you get the most from the text and keep track of what's happening, we've used a number of conventions throughout the book.

> **Boxes like this one hold important, not-to-be forgotten information that is directly relevant to the surrounding text.**

Notes, tips, hints, tricks, and asides to the current discussion are offset and placed in italics like this.

As for styles in the text:

❑ We *highlight* new terms and important words when we introduce them.

❑ We show keyboard strokes like this: Ctrl+A.

❑ We show filenames, URLs, and code within the text like so: `persistence.properties`.

❑ We present code in two different ways:

```
We use a monofont type with no highlighting for most code examples.
```

```
We use gray highlighting to emphasize code that's particularly important in
the present context.
```

Source Code

As you work through the examples in this book, you may choose either to type in all the code manually or to use the source code files that accompany the book. All of the source code used in this book is available for downloading at www.wrox.com. Once at the site, simply locate the book's title (either by using the Search box or by using one of the title lists) and click the Download Code link on the book's detail page to obtain all the source code for the book.

All the code for this book is also available from a public Subversion repository, so you can pick and choose which code to download. See Chapter 9, "Customizing Flex Builder 3," for more information on using Subversion with Flex Builder 3.

> ### The Professional Adobe Flex 3 Code Repository
>
> All the code for this voluminous book can be accessed and downloaded from the Assembla hosting page for the Professional Adobe Flex 3 book code.
>
> ❑ Project Page: www.assembla.com/wiki/show/proFx3BookCode
>
> ❑ Repository URL: http://svn.assembla.com/svn/proFx3BookCode/trunk
>
> You can also browse the repository in your browser at this URL: https://code.assembla.com/proFx3BookCode/subversion/nodes /trunk

Because many books have similar titles, you may find it easiest to search by ISBN; this book's ISBN is 978-0-470-22364-2.

Once you download the code, just decompress it with your favorite compression tool. Alternately, you can go to the main Wrox code download page at www.wrox.com/dynamic/books/download.aspx to see the code available for this book and all other Wrox books.

Errata

We make every effort to ensure that there are no errors in the text or in the code. However, no one is perfect, and mistakes do occur. If you find an error in one of our books, such as a spelling mistake or faulty piece of code, we would be very grateful for your feedback. By sending in errata, you may save another reader hours of frustration and at the same time you will be helping us provide even higher-quality information.

To find the errata page for this book, go to www.wrox.com and locate the title using the Search box or one of the title lists. Then, on the Book Search Results page, click the Errata link. On this page you can view all errata that has been submitted for this book and posted by Wrox editors.

A complete book list including links to errata is also available at www.wrox.com/misc-pages/booklist.shtml.

If you don't spot "your" error on the Errata page, click the Errata Form link and complete the form to send us the error you have found. We'll check the information and, if appropriate, post a message to the book's errata page and fix the problem in subsequent editions of the book.

p2p.wrox.com

For author and peer discussion, join the P2P forums at p2p.wrox.com. The forums are a Web-based system for you to post messages relating to Wrox books and related technologies and interact with other readers and technology users. The forums offer a subscription feature to email you topics of interest of your choosing when new posts are made to the forums. Wrox authors, editors, other industry experts, and your fellow readers are present on these forums.

At http://p2p.wrox.com you will find a number of different forums that will help you not only as you read this book but also as you develop your own applications. To join the forums, just follow these steps:

1. Go to p2p.wrox.com and click the Register link.

2. Read the terms of use and click Agree.

3. Complete the required information to join as well as any optional information you wish to provide, and click Submit.

4. You will receive an email with information describing how to verify your account and complete the joining process.

   You can read messages in the forums without joining P2P, but in order to post your own messages, you must join.

Once you join, you can post new messages and respond to messages other users post. You can read messages at any time on the Web. If you would like to have new messages from a particular forum emailed to you, click the Subscribe to this Forum icon by the forum name in the forum listing.

For more information about how to use the Wrox P2P, be sure to read the P2P FAQs for answers to questions about how the forum software works as well as many common questions specific to P2P and Wrox books. To read the FAQs, click the FAQ link on any P2P page.

Part I: Introduction to Flex 3

Chapter 1: Why Flex?

Chapter 2: The Flex 3 Ecosystem

Chapter 3: ActionScript 3.0 Fundamentals

Chapter 4: Using ActionScript 3.0

Chapter 5: Introduction to Flex Builder 3

1

Why Flex?

It seems like nearly every programming book I have ever read starts off with the obligatory "Introduction to [whatever]" chapter, which basically regurgitates the essentials that everyone knows, and hence is the one chapter nearly every reader skips. In this first chapter of the book, I thought we'd start things off with a different approach, one that takes you, the reader, through the reasons that you might want to use Flex, what Flex is for, bursting some myths about Flex and the Flash platform, and, finally, ending up with a "Top 10" of Flex's strong points. Enjoy!

What Is Flex?

Often this is either the first presciently asked question for someone new to the Adobe Flex ecosystem and the Flash Platform, or it is the last question asked after many hours of wrestling with how all of this "stuff" fits together in the scheme of things. Read on: the first two chapters in this book will make it all crystal clear.

In a nutshell, Flex is a rich Internet application (RIA) development toolkit based on the ActionScript 3.0 and MXML languages that can be deployed for the Web using the Flash Player plug-in, or to the desktop using the Adobe Integrated Runtime (AIR).

As Adobe Evangelist James Ward puts it in his article "How I Overcame My Fear of Flash" (www.jamesward.com/wordpress/2007/02/21/how-i-overcame-my-fear-of-flash/),

> "[the] Flash Player is a ubiquitous, cross-browser, cross-OS virtual machine enabling next generation web experiences. Flex is a simple tool for developers to build applications that execute in the Flash virtual machine."

What Is an RIA?

No introductory discussion of Flex would be complete without at least a cursory examination of the rich Internet application, or RIA.

Although the concept of RIAs had been around for quite some time, it wasn't until 2002 when Macromedia (now Adobe Systems Inc.) coined the term from a Flash MX white paper, that the idea began catching on in web development. You can read the white paper, "Macromedia Flash MX — A next-generation rich client," at www.adobe.com/devnet/flash/whitepapers/richclient.pdf.

The RIA's predecessor could be called a "Web 1.0 application," which is based on a linear, hypertext-centric architecture written in HTML, JavaScript, and CSS, which for the purposes of this text we will call a "hypertext application." An RIA, which has also come to be known as a "Web 2.0 application," is unique and differs from a hypertext application in several important ways:

❑ **Rich media** — Although it could be argued that a hypertext application can have and use what is known as "rich media," it is not its defining characteristic. An RIA, on the other hand, is typified by the presence-rich content. This usually involves custom designed interfaces in a highly branded and/or expressive visual environment, which may use sounds, video, graphics, and motion that cannot be reproduced in a hypertext environment. One could say that a hypertext application is defined by a textual paradigm, whereas an RIA is defined by a visual paradigm.

❑ **Resides on the client** — More importantly, a hypertext application follows a page-oriented architecture, where an application interface is created on the server and downloaded to the client in "pages." An RIA, on the other hand, is a self-contained solid-state machine that runs on the client, usually with the help of a dedicated runtime, such as a browser plug-in.

❑ **Asynchronous communication and data persistence** — The browser page makes an HTTP GET request to the server each and every time the application must refresh its functional state, which uses a *synchronous* method of communication. The state and logic of the application must be tracked on the server, as each page cannot easily manage application logic across other pages. So, it is left up to the server scripting, typically coded in a language such as PHP, ASP, or JSP, to manage the application state for each and every client connected to the server.

Whereas a hypertext application communicates or "downloads" each page to the browser as the user traverses the application, the RIA need only be downloaded once, since it manages the creation of its own UI and internal logic. Because the client maintains full control over application state and functionality, and can communicate with the server independently of user interaction with the application, it is said to use *asynchronous* server communication.

❑ **Lower network consumption** — And because an RIA does not need to communicate its state to the server, it is free to communicate to the server only if and when the online functionality is required, such as when retrieving or uploading a file, saving or retrieving data to and from the user's account, or performing some task the client is unable to process on its own. This has the potential of considerably reducing bandwidth and server load, often translating into a huge financial savings.

❑ Developers must take care not to overuse the pre-fetching of assets and/or data, which can eliminate any bandwidth or server load savings that might have been gained. Some RIAs actually consume a lot more network resources, but these are typically applications that make heavy use of streaming media, which would simply not be possible in a hypertext application.

❏ **Acts like software** — Most RIAs distinguish themselves from simple embedded rich content by the presence of a standard user interface and a certain level of complexity that categorizes it as an application and not simply a rich media animation or video delivery medium. For instance, a video player on YouTube is not an RIA, but an online video editing application could be considered one.

Since most RIAs are developed according to object-oriented principles and not a page state model, their architecture can be more flexible; states can be set asynchronously by different parts of the application as a whole. This allows the application to act more like traditional software than a website. In other words, what determines where the user is in the application can be fluid and prone to many different variables, depending on the task being performed at any given moment. Therefore, RIAs have the advantage of increased responsiveness, as there is no waiting for a page refresh, which increases user productivity in accomplishing the task at hand.

❏ **Increased security protocols** — However, that flexibility and fluidity comes at a price. Maintaining the application on the client means increased vigilance in communications security must be taken to avoid abuse, and some RIA technologies have developed some very specific and sophisticated security "sandboxes" that allow data to be communicated to and from the application only in very specific ways, which is mostly a good thing.

❏ **Browser-opaque** — One of the typical drawbacks to RIAs over traditional hypertext applications is that because they act as a closed system (i.e., their application states are managed internally), they are "browser-opaque." That is, they cannot be navigated with browser controls (i.e., history states, the Back button), are not search engine indexable, and are not visible to accessible devices. This is a failing of all RIAs by any technology, including AJAX, Flash, AIR, Silverlight, WPF, and JavaFX.

This means that just as hypertext applications are not very good at rich interactive content, RIAs are not very good at large volumes of search engine–accessible hypertext content, which is why many applications such as text-heavy websites, blogs, and social networks still use the traditional hypertext application paradigm. Some RIA technologies have made great inroads to mitigate this disadvantage, but at the moment these kinds of solutions require conscious implementation on the part of the developer to bridge the browser divide. No RIA technology is currently browser-transparent, and probably will not be until browsers start integrating an RIA runtime as part of their native rendering model and search engines change their indexing schemes to include certain state-dependant standards, which given the current rate of browser evolution may be a long time in coming. The irony is that even as RIAs are redefining the way we use the Web, they are accused of "breaking the Web paradigm." Perhaps it is a matter of finding the right balance.

See Chapter 40 for more information on deeplinking in Flex applications.

❏ **Can be desktop-enabled** — Until recently, the term "RIA" implied that the application would be run from within a browser context, which typically limits access and interaction with the operating system. But now, certain technologies, such as Adobe AIR, allow for the creation of RIAs that break out of the browser paradigm and onto the desktop. An RIA that resides on the desktop is differentiated from a traditional software application in that it still requires a runtime sandbox to execute the application, is usually built on web technologies and their derivatives, and has direct access to the Internet. A desktop-enabled RIA may function similarly to both an Internet browser and an installed application. At the moment, no RIA technology has the same level of system interaction with the operating system that typifies installed software, but this line is becoming ever more indistinct as the technologies driving RIAs continue to evolve.

❑ **"Sometimes connected" applications** — Since the RIA can often choose when it is connected to the server, certain applications — whether in a browser or on the desktop — can operate in a "sometimes connected" mode unique to web applications, although the term is mostly used when referring to desktop RIAs. This can allow users to work offline for a period, and reconnect to the server if and when they need to save their work or update the application. A "sometimes connected" application is not necessarily independent of the server, as would be traditional network-enabled desktop software, but it allows a degree of flexibility in application usage that was impossible to accomplish just a few years ago.

❑ **Enables new business models** — Since RIAs are redefining the way we use the Web, enabling applications that act more like software than web pages, new business models are possible, such as the software as a service (SaaS) model. This more than anything is the current thrust driving the Web 2.0 revolution, which is seen as the promises of the dot-com years finally coming home to roost.

For instance, Adobe has launched Acrobat.com, a rich service portal built into Flex that allows users to convert documents to PDF, upload documents and files to their account through Adobe Share, create real-time online meetings through the ConnectNow service (an online version of Adobe Connect), and author, save and download documents using Buzzword, a full-featured word processor application. Adobe has also released an online version of Photoshop that allows users to process images with a subset of the features of the original application, as well as a video delivery portal called Adobe TV, which features video tutorials on myriad Adobe technologies. Gmail and Google Docs, built with an AJAX development model, are also immensely powerful and popular applications. Other sites, too numerous to mention here, leverage the RIA advantage to offer users everything from personal scheduling and organization, to social networking and media creation tools. Using RIA technologies such as Adobe Flash and AIR in tandem, *some applications can even leverage simultaneous browser and desktop-enabled versions of their online service,* or create a product developed exclusively for desktop deployment.

Clarifying the Competition

Before we get into the specifics of Flex and the Flash platform, let us enumerate some of the current RIA technologies available. As of this writing, primary contenders in the current market are considered to be AJAX, Adobe Flash and Adobe AIR. Secondary contenders are considered to be Microsoft Silverlight, Sun JavaFX, OpenLaszlo, Mozilla Prism, Google Gears, Curl, and Adobe Flash Lite.

Since there is some confusion in tech reporting circles and the blogosphere as to competing equivalencies between certain of these technologies, without getting into too much detail on specific capabilities, some clarifications are in order.

❑ AJAX, Adobe Flash, Microsoft Silverlight, OpenLaszlo, and Curl run in a browser environment, so they can be considered to be comparable competitors.

❑ Adobe AIR, Google Gears, and Mozilla Prism are desktop-enabled RIA runtime environments, so they can be considered to be comparable competitors. Although Microsoft WPF is often compared with Adobe AIR, some do not consider it an RIA technology because it is not intended to be connected to an Internet server, but to be used as a high-level Windows development platform.

To clarify, Silverlight does not compete with AIR, and WPF does not compete with Flash, because they are deployed in completely different environments.

❑ Flash Lite and Silverlight applications can be deployed in a mobile environment, so they can be said to be comparable competitors. Many mobile RIAs are developed for the native device operating system instead of through a mobile browser, so there is some ambiguity as to whether certain mobile technologies can be considered to be RIA-centric. For instance, Java is currently the language used by the majority of mobile applications, and by itself is not considered an RIA-specific technology. Google Android is a mobile operating system, which is sometimes confused as an RIA platform.

❑ JavaFX competes with all of these, since it can be deployed to the browser, on the desktop, or in a mobile environment.

For the Love of Flex

Without getting into a blow-by-blow comparison between the previously mentioned technologies, let's examine some of the misconceptions about Flex and the Flash platform, and some compelling reasons why Flex, Flash, and AIR are extremely powerful solutions for building engaging, next-generation RIAs. Since you're reading this book, like me you're probably already convinced. But if you still have concerns, or you're still on the fence, let us be of help.

Bursting Myths about Flash and Flex

The majority of misconceptions and concerns about Flash and Flex fall into the following categories:

❑ **Flash is proprietary** — Many people immersed in traditional open-source development environments using Linux, PHP, Java have the following concerns:

❑ *Can I author a SWF application without Adobe software?*

Yes. To write software you need three things: an editor, a compiler, and a runtime. The SWF format is open, and there are third-party utilities that enable you to compile ActionScript into SWF bytecode. The ActionScript API itself is built into the Flash player, and the Flash Player and AIR runtimes are not open source. The Flex compiler is an open-source, free command-line utility that can be used with any third-party editor. The Flex framework and many of the Adobe specifications and tools are open source. Some of Adobe's other tools (such as BlazeDS, a communications server for the AMF binary protocol), are open source, and for those that are not there are usually open-source versions (such as Red5, an open-source version of Flash Media Server). Some of the elements in the Flex SDK are not open source, such as the Flash Player, the font encoding libraries, and the Data Visualization components. More information on what aspects of the Flex SDK are open and which are free are available here: http://opensource.adobe.com/wiki/display/flexsdk/Downloads. There are also some great proprietary tools for Flex development, such as Adobe Flex Builder, but if you need to go completely open source with your tools as well as your framework, there is the option.

❑ *Can I deconstruct a SWF application without Adobe software?*

Yes. There are third-party utilities that enable the deconstruction of SWF files. The resulting ActionScript is not in its originally written format, but reverse-interpreted from the SWF bytecode, so markup code such as compiler metadata, MXML, and CSS will be shown as their

ActionScript equivalents. For those people for which this is a negative, who wish to protect their distributed software, there are obfuscation and encryption schemes that make reverse-engineering SWFs difficult-to-impossible.

❑   *Do I have to use an Adobe runtime to run my software?*

Yes. The Flash Player itself is not open source, and even though the SWF format is open, Adobe controls the SWF specification. This means that although third parties can build software that can create SWF files, no one else but Adobe can create a new Flash Player. This is actually one of its strengths. The Flash Player's ubiquity at over 97.7% market distribution across popularly used browsers is because there has only ever been one Flash Player (albeit different versions). The Flash Player is able to achieve such a small download footprint, and the incredible number-crunching speeds of 100–1000% the execution speed of JavaScript primarily due to the presence of the JIT compiler, which converts ActionScript bytecode directly into system-level machine code at runtime. This level of precision engineering would be very difficult if not impossible without the dedicated Adobe Flash Player engineers who have done nothing but advance and perfect the Flash virtual machine for more than 12 years. If users had to choose between competing Flash Players for their browser space, the ubiquity of the Flash Platform would be diluted and meaningless. So, open sourcing the Flash Player would actually be incredibly damaging to the stability of the platform. However, the ActionScript virtual machine within the Flash Player, which is called Tamarin, has been open sourced to Mozilla, which opens the door for future runtime solutions.

❑   **It's used to create annoying content** — One could say that about nearly any Web technology. As Aral Balkan, Flash Platform developer extraordinaire, puts it in his article "Bare-naked Flash: Dispelling Myths and Building Bridges" (`http://aralbalkan.com/1305`), "Usability is not an inherent property of a platform … is HTML '99% bad' because of MySpace?" (Uh, no, in case you were wondering, although it is a tempting thought.) And we've come a long way since the "skip intro" days. Through YouTube and other video portals, Flash revolutionized video on the Internet in 2003, and one has only to examine the plethora of RIAs present and on the market because of Adobe Flash, such as Buzzword, Adobe TV, Blist, Aviary, or SlideRocket, to name but a few, to know that Flash, used to its potential, is far from just a media plug-in for quirky content.

❑   **It's not browser-integrated or SEO-capable** — This is true of all RIAs, due to the nature of the architecture, and is not unique to Flash applications. See "What Is an RIA?" above for details.

However, Google can index SWF files and introspect their metadata, which can be set at compilation, even if state introspection must be manually included. Adobe has made some great advances in search engine indexing in cooperation with Google and Yahoo! and is in ongoing discussions with these two search engine companies to improve SEO capability and the overall search experience.

Flash natively allows for ActionScript-to-JavaScript communication, and the Flex framework brings application deep linking and full browser integration to Flash applications. This allows the browser URL to change as the user navigates through the application, which enables browser history states, bookmarking and the back button. See Chapter 40, "Deep Linking," for details. And these same tools allow Flash applications to be fully accessible to screen readers.

AIR, Adobe's desktop RIA solution, allows seamless script bridging between JavaScript and ActionScript, with the ability to treat Flash objects as native JavaScript objects, and vice versa. This means that AIR can develop solutions that leverage both DHTML and Flash seamlessly in the same application, which is simply not possible in a browser environment.

So, yes, Flash is mostly browser-opaque natively, but the tools exist to develop solutions that enable full browser- and accessibility-enabled Flash solutions.

❑ **It's a browser plug-in** — This is actually a good thing, as it allows the technology to advance independently of the snail's pace of browser languages. Consider that the Flash Player adoption has moved through versions 3 to 10, Flex through versions 1 to 3, and ActionScript through versions 1.0, 2.0 and now 3.0. Although some browsers have adopted more up-to-date standards, as far as overall browser adoption is concerned, JavaScript and CSS have barely moved one version ahead after nearly a decade, and updates to HTML 4 have been incredibly slow in coming.

❑ **It's not secure** — *This is perhaps one of the greatest misconceptions of Flash-based applications, and is patently and unequivocally not true.* Adobe continues to improve security sandboxing specifications multiple times over the course of any Flash Player version and is quick to issue an upgrade when a critical vulnerability has been found, to keep pace with new use cases, security scenarios and capability. In fact, a common complaint nowadays in the community is that the Flash Player security sandbox requirements are often too strict! In fact they are a judicious balance between robust security and strong capability. The security protocols prevent everything from cross-domain or illegal security domain communication, script injection and other common issues. The Flash Player is in fact the most secure, capable, and powerful RIA runtime on the market today. See Chapter 65, "The Security Model," for details.

For example, the security vulnerability known as "clickjacking" was identified in late September 2008 as a security flaw in all browsers, and within weeks a security advisory was issued for the Flash Player, and a security patch for Flash Player 10 issued a few weeks after in mid-October. Although Microsoft has issued a patch for IE 8 RC1 beta, to this date IE 7 continues to be vulnerable, and Firefox, Safari, and Chrome continue to be affected. This is perhaps an extreme example, but in general, security updates to the Flash Player occur as fast if not faster than all the leading browsers.

❑ **The Flex Framework bloats my application filesize** — This is also a valid concern. Flex is an incredible toolset for creating component-based RIAs (the rest of this book is testament to this fact). But that toolset comes at a price. Flex adds between approximately 120 to 600 KB of filesize to your SWF file upon compilation, which means that the user will need to download at least that much on top of your own development footprint to view your application.

One way to mitigate this added footprint is to use persistent framework caching, covered in Chapter 66, "Modular Applications Development." This allows the application to be compiled with only your code additions. Upon running your application in the browser, the Flash Player downloads a signed Runtime Shared Library (RSL) file containing the Flex Framework from an Adobe server, which is cached on the client. So your user only ever has to download it once, reducing the total download in subsequent sessions.

RSLs are compiled code libraries that can be used in many scenarios. They are typically common groups of logic that can be reused in multiple projects, and they can be cached on the client side to help make your applications smaller in compiled file size.

If you're looking to develop something very lightweight, as is the case for mobile or interactive ad development, then using the Flex framework may not be the solution for you. You can still author a bare-bones ActionScript 3.0 project in Flex Builder, using either the Flash IDE or Flex as the compiler. See Chapter 26, "Flash Integration," for use case scenarios.

❑ **Doesn't easily integrate with my CMS** — The fact that a Flash or Flex application may or may not integrate well with a preexisting CMS has more to do with the lack of a consumable web service or an ActionScript API on the part of the CMS than it has to do with an incompatibility of the technology. A Flex RIA can be made to do nearly anything with regard to organizing and consuming web content. The Flash Player has the ability to launch a system dialog allowing the user to browse the local filesystem for the purposes of uploading a file to the server, or download a manipulated vector or bitmap as an image file. All that remains is to build the client side of the CMS interface. There exist third-party solutions that facilitate this process, offering a convenient applications framework for building Flash-based CMS solutions.

❑ **Flex is hard to learn and to use** — Flex is in fact very easy to learn and use. But seeing is believing, so try this experiment:

   1. Install and launch Flex Builder, which is the Eclipse-based Flex-integrated development environment (IDE) (we'll get into that later in this book).

   2. Create a new workspace, and a new Flex project in that workspace.

   3. In the default MXML application for that project, add the code in Listing 1-1:

Listing 1-1: A simple Flex RSS reader

```
<?xml version="1.0" encoding="utf-8"?>
<mx:Application xmlns:mx="http://www.adobe.com/2006/mxml" layout="absolute"
  creationComplete="RSSFeed.send();">
    <mx:HTTPService id="RSSFeed" url="http://www.joeflash.ca/blog/feed/"/>
    <mx:List id="postTitles" labelField="title" left="20" right="20" top="20"
  dataProvider="{RSSFeed.lastResult.rss.channel.item}"/>
    <mx:TextArea htmlText="{postTitles.selectedItem.description}" left="20"
       right="20"
  top="190" height="200"/>
    <mx:Button label="Go to page" click="navigateToURL(new URLRequest
  (postTitles.selectedItem.link));" left="20" top="400" />
</mx:Application>
```

   4. Run the application.

In less than a dozen lines of code, using only four tags, you have created a fully functional RSS reader application that can grab an RSS feed, parse the XML, display the blog titles and their descriptions, and navigate to the page URL at the touch of a button. Easy, wasn't it? That is the power of Flex. We'll get more into building Flex applications throughout this book.

❑ **Requires the Flex Player** — There is no such thing. Flex is a development toolkit with a component framework for developing RIAs aimed at the Flash Player or AIR.

❑ **Requires a special server which is very expensive, and it's slow** — You may be thinking of Flex 1.0 or 1.5, which was a Macromedia product (now owned by Adobe) that existed between 2004 and 2005. This first iteration of Flex needed to be compiled on the proprietary Flex Server, which had a considerable financial barrier, and used the Dreamweaver engine as the IDE, which was considerably slower. It was a component architecture built in ActionScript 2.0 aimed at Flash Player 7, an earlier version of the language and the runtime, which did not have the capabilities nor the speed of the current version. Adobe has since reinvented the ActionScript language, the Flash runtime, and the Flex 2 SDK in 2006. Flex 3 is based on ActionScript 3.0, which is a much more robust, JIT-compiled language that runs up to 100 times faster than ActionScript 2.0. The Flex SDK, which includes the framework and the compiler, is open source and does not require a server model for compilation (although that option is available through another Adobe product), and the Flex IDE is based on Eclipse.

❑ **Flex does not have a mature development community** — That depends on your definition of a "mature development community," but I and many others believe this statement to be patently untrue. The recent iteration of the Flex community, started mostly by Flash developers migrating to the (then) new ActionScript 3.0 language and the Flex 2.0 beta, began developing and sharing open-source code back in early 2005. And since ActionScript 3.0 is, according to many developers, at least as powerful as other languages such as C# and Java, developers coming to Flex from other languages add their experience in advanced programming architectures to the Flex community, which can be seen by the active discussions on Design Patterns and J2EE architectures that have been evolving on lists such as Flexcoders since 2004 (`http://tech.groups.yahoo.com/group/flexcoders/`).

The development community for the Flash Platform, upon which Flex is based, has an even longer history. Adobe (then Macromedia) coined the very term RIA back in 2002 in a white paper on Flash MX development. Since Flex is built on top of the ActionScript language, one could argue that the Flex development community is built upon a community at least that mature. The ActionScript development community has a history of open-source collaboration going back to the late 1990s (OSFlash, Prototype). As Aral Balkan, Flash platform developer extraordinaire, puts it,

"The vibrant and eclectic open-source community is one of the major legitimizing factors of the Flash Platform as a mature platform and thriving ecosystem and not some marketing construct."

The "maturity" of a development community is not just about how long its been around, despite the fact that application development in Flash and Flex predates the very term "rich Internet application" by several years. It's also about the diversity and vibrancy of that community. And there is no question that Flash and Flex developers are a passionate and open-minded lot sharing and participating in the ongoing evolution of the technology on a daily basis. Therefore, many would say that Flex has a very mature development community indeed.

❑ **Flex is not geared towards enterprise development** — *This is also untrue.* Flex is built upon a robust, ECMAScript-compliant, strongly typed OOP language, using an IDE based on Eclipse, a proven and tested enterprise development tool. Flex can interface with any Web-based service, protocol, or language, and Adobe has a dedicated Data Services server product that uses the AMF protocol, allowing the asynchronous or real-time passing of native ActionScript objects to the server with full Java interoperability. Verify for yourself the speed of this messaging protocol, by taking a look at Census, an application built by Adobe Evangelist James Ward that benchmarks about a dozen different protocols and communications formats in Flex (`www.jamesward.org/census`).

Other third-party products on the market implement .NET or PHP data services for Flex frontends, and Adobe has several server products that enable scalable, real-time streaming media solutions for video encoding and playback. The Flex ecosystem, which will be covered in the next chapter, also features Adobe Cairngorm, a J2EE-compliant, enterprise-level applications framework that has become the gold standard for deploying enterprise-level Flex applications and development teams. See Part X, "Using Cairngorm," for more information.

Adobe was voted "One of the 12 companies that will matter the most to the intelligent enterprise in 2008" by the Intelligent Enterprise 2008 Editors' Choice Awards (`www.intelligententerprise.com/channels/performance_management/showArticle.jhtml?articleID=205207028&pgno=2`). And in December 2007, NATO adopted Adobe Flex and LiveCycle Data Services to deliver an enterprise-capable, highly data-intensive RIA for its Mission Support System (MSS), built to "help improve NATO's operational readiness, by reducing the time to prepare for missions, and improve the delivery of information to flight crew members" (`www.adobe.com/aboutadobe/pressroom/pressreleases/200712/121107adobenato.html`). See Part IX, "Data Services," for more information on LiveCycle Data Services.

10 Reasons to Love Flex

Now that you may be convinced of a few things that are and are not true about Flash and Flex, let's take a look at the top 10 reasons to love to develop RIAs in Flex.

1.   **Flash is everywhere** — The Adobe Flash 9 Player has about 98% market penetration across browsers. This means that when you launch an application on the Web, you are virtually guaranteed that anyone will be able to use it. Compared to the distribution statistics of other RIA runtimes, there is simply no contest.

Flash is cross-OS, or "platform-agnostic": it runs in Windows, Mac and Linux. It is also installed in every type of browser, making it the only RIA technology that can truly claim to be a "write once, run everywhere" platform.

As Kevin Merritt put it when considering AJAX for the development of blist (`http://blog.blist.com/2008/02/23/why-blist-chose-flex-and-flash/`):

I met these guys for coffee, described it, and asked if AJAX was up to the task. They confirmed my suspicion. One of them commented something along the lines of "You could probably get 80% to 90% of that functionality with AJAX, but not 100%. More important, in order to make this work across browsers and OS's, you're going to have a gargantuan JavaScript payload with all sorts of browser-specific hacks. The end result is you're going to have a buggy, fragile mess."

Flash does not have this problem.

2.   **Flex = Flash on steroids** — Flex is Flash and Flash is ActionScript 3.0 (or more specifically, Flex runs on the Flash Player, and the Flash Player's language is ActionScript 3.0.)

In ActionScript 3.0 you have all the aspects of a mature, robust programming language: strong runtime typing, class inheritance, interfaces, error handling, a built-in event model, sealed classes, method closures, custom namespace accessors, regular expressions, E4X. The Flash Player incorporates the Tamarin ActionScript 3.0 Virtual Machine with the power of a Just in Time (JIT) compiler, which interprets SWF application bytecode into machine-level instructions so that your code runs as fast as the processor can handle. Warp speed, Scotty!

And since Flex is built on top of Flash, you have the full power of the Flash APIs to draw in real time with lines, gradients and fills and manipulate and animate vectors, bitmap data, and visual assets, complete with matrix transformations, programmatic Photoshop-like filters, and blends. Flash allows communication using a dizzing array of data formats, but if you don't find the format that suits your needs, create your own using a binary socket and custom interpreter! You also get high-definition, full-screen, hardware-accelerated video capabilities, supported by enterprise-capable video encoding and streaming server products.

Flex 3 adds another layer of power onto the Flash runtime: a visual markup language called MXML, and a full-featured compiler that includes compiler metadata and data binding. The Flex framework adds class libraries for natively managing HTTP requests, RPC services, and Web Services, a dizzying array of visual UI components, a deep linking framework for browser integration, an API for AIR applications that can interact natively with the desktop, logging and unit testing frameworks, and much much more, all of which will be covered in this book. Not to mention an IDE based on Eclipse, and a whole suite of server tools for your application to communicate with the backend using native ActionScript class objects.

3. **Flex is open source** — The Flex Software Development Kit (SDK), which comprises the compiler, the component framework, and several other tools, is a free, open-source development platform. Although Flex Builder is neither free nor open source, it is built upon Eclipse, and can be installed standalone (with Eclipse built in) or as an Eclipse plug-in alongside other Eclipse development environments. In fact, Adobe Flex Builder has been voted Best Open Source Developer Tool for RIAs by *InfoWorld*'s Best of Open Source Software Awards (www.infoworld.com/slideshow/2008/08/166-best_of_open_so-7.html).

4. **Interoperability** — ActionScript 3 has XML baked into it as a native format with E4X parsing capability, facilitating JSON and XML data transfer. The Flash Player is able to interface directly with JavaScript in the browser through a native JavaScript communications API, and is able to recognize SWF filename query name-value pairs. Two great examples of Flash-AJAX interoperability are Google Finance and Yahoo! Maps Canada, both of which combine the versatility of an enhanced hypertext application with the interactive power of the Flash runtime.

   The Flash Player also includes XML and binary sockets capability, including traditional GET and POST HTTP requests.

   The Flash Player natively supports image file formats GIF, JPG, PNG, media file formats MP3, FLV, F4P, F4A, and F4V, including the AAC, MP4, M4V, M4A, 3GP, and MOV multimedia container formats, encoded in Sorenson Spark, On2VP6, H.264, MPEG-4, MP3, or AAC.

   The Flash Platform also enables some unique RIA communications protocols. Connected to the Flash Media Server, the Flash Player is also able to stream video and audio using the RTMP protocol, and its rights-encrypted cousin RTMPE, as well as the new RTMFP format in Flash 10. Using the Adobe AMF protocol, the Flash Player is able to communicate complex ActionScript objects directly with data services applications on the server. Adobe LiveCycle Data Services and its open-source cousin BlazeDS enable bidirectional ActionScript-to-Java object transfer, and the ColdFusion server allows for ActionScript-to-CFC object transfer. Third-party data service implementations such as WebOrb, AMFphp, and Zend enable native ActionScript object communication with the .NET and PHP server languages. Other third-party data services solutions exist for languages such as Ruby and Python.

   The Flex framework contains APIs that allow very easy deployment for HTTP requests, Web Services, and RPC services data transfers. So needless to say, a Flex application can communicate a wide variety of web technologies, allowing for a plethora of server integration options with an impressive array of interoperability with many data formats, languages, and protocols.

5. **The community** — Conceived with the same spirit as the Flash community, the Flex community is passionate, generous, and vibrant, always coming up with new ways to alert each other of the latest quirks, share their discoveries, their tips, their components, and their experiments, helping Adobe make a better product. And Adobe does an incredible job of feeding that fire: it actually listens to the community, and rewards them with changes to product development that directly reflect what designers and developers has been asking for, going so far as to organize events and surveys that elicit feedback for the sole purpose of making Flash and Flex better and better. One has only to look at all the new features in Flash Player 10 and those planned for Flex 4 to know that Adobe has listened to and cares about its community. Many Flash and Flex designers and developers, including the writers of this book, really enjoy what they do for a living, and thrive on that energy. And this level of passion and commitment to each other and to the evolution of the platform shows through in every Flash and Flex conference, every technical blog, every community forum and list this author has ever visited.

6. **Creative Suite integration** — When Adobe purchased Macromedia in 2005, it brought to the Flash and Flex development scene the possibility of the full force of its Creative Suite of applications. As of Creative Suite 3, we can now experience the fruits of that promise, as we now have seamless integration between Flash and Illustrator, Fireworks and After Effects. This opens up a vast sea of creative possibilities for Flex development, enabling even "richer media" applications than ever before. See Chapters 26 and 29, which cover Flash and Flex workflow integration in greater detail.

7. **Flex is easy to learn** — *for Flash developers* — For Flash developers with experience with ActionScript 3.0 and OOP principles, Flex can be considered merely another component framework with some new authoring tools. Most ActionScript developers already use a third-party coding editor such as FlashDevelop or FDT, so migrating to Flex Builder is easy, especially for those already using Eclipse for JavaScript, PHP, Java, or ColdFusion development. And for those comfortable with their existing tools, both FlashDevelop and FDT work well with the open-source Flex SDK (framework + compiler). Many Flash developers also use Flex Builder for coding ActionScript projects compiled with the Flash CS3 compiler, so there is much cross-workflow potential (see Chapters 26 and 29 for more detail on Flash-Flex integration) Flex has better GUI components, a better debugger, a memory profiler, a more versatile compiler, and there's no timeline to complicate your project structure or code execution. And that's just for starters.

   And, contrary to the popularly held belief among some Flash developers, Flex does not make Flash and pure ActionScript development obsolete. Far from it. In fact, the sheer explosion in RIA development in Flex in recent years has only increased the need for rich asset creation only a Flash developer can provide, and the deep knowledge of ActionScript that is common to experienced Flash developers. As Adobe Evangelist Ely Greenfield puts it in her article "Why the Flex in FlexBook, or … Why a Flash Author should care (a lot!) about Flex" (www.quietly scheming.com/blog/2007/03/14/why-the-flex-in-flexbook-orwhy-a-flash-author -should-care-a-lot-about-flex),

   "There's a lot of incredibly talented individuals out there who know how to create amazing visual effects with ActionScript and the timeline. There's a whole lot more incredibly talented developers out there who really do not have the skill-set to create those effects, but would really like to use them in their Flex applications. … I believe talented Flash dev-igners could make good money selling their services into the Flex community. … if the Flash community considers bringing some of that creativity to bear on the growing Flex ecosystem."

   for Java developers — I've heard it said how uncanny is the resemblance between ActionScript and Java. To such an extent that after a brief learning curve (and I do mean very brief), many Java developers find themselves building fully functional Java-enabled Flex apps in no time at all. Flex Builder is an Eclipse plug-in, which fits right at home in a traditional Java workflow. In addition, Adobe's LiveCycle Data Services and BlazeDS are both Java-based server solutions, enabling a high degree of interoperability between ActionScript and Java objects. Adobe also has a developer resource page dedicated to Flash-Java integration articles, tutorials, and white papers. See Parts VIII, "Server Integration," and IX, "Data Services," for an in-depth look at Flex, Java, and data services. Appendix A, "ActionScript 3 Language Comparison," also provides a comparison table between ActionScript and Java.

   and for anyone else used to the Eclipse-based environment or enterprise-level applications development.

8. **Flex enables modular, rapid application development (RAD)** — Flex natively encourages a Model-View-Controller (MVC) separation of application parts through the use of MXML, which is an XML-based visual layout markup language that facilitates rapid prototyping and development (see Listing 1-1 for details). In the simplest Flex MVC pattern, the *View* or interface layout is typically coded in CSS and MXML, and the *Controller* or application logic is typically coded in ActionScript, though one is not constrained to these norms. This will be covered in greater detail in Chapter 60, "MVC Frameworks." Flex Builder also has a *Design View*, which allows for the visualization of MXML layouts, and a Properties View, which allows for the setting of inspectable component properties directly in the IDE (see Chapter 5, "Introduction to Flex Builder 3," for details).

   Flex also enables a variety of modular compilation and deployment methods. You can precompile application modules or class libraries to increase compilation efficiency, code distribution, or asset management. By compiling all your fonts into one module, and all your skins into another module, for example, you cut down overall application compilation time and increase asset management efficiency. You can compile SWFs to be compiled in the main application as embedded assets, which can be easier to use than Flex modules, or you can opt to load SWF application subcomponents at runtime, decreasing the initial application filesize.

   The application footprint can also be mitigated by the use of *persistent framework caching*, where you can compile your application sans the Flex framework, allowing the Flash Player runtime to preload and cache the framework as a separate class library on the client. This means that after the Flex framework has been downloaded once, it is cached on the client, and your application will load much quicker for the user. See Chapter 66, "Modular Application Development," for details.

9. **Adobe AIR** — AIR brings the power of Flash and Flex to a whole other level. With AIR, AJAX applications can be deployed to the desktop, or a Flash/Flex application can be deployed to the desktop, in either the PC, Mac or Linux OSs, with access to system windowing and local file system interactivity. Or even more powerfully, both AJAX *and* Flash can be leveraged together in the same application, in ways that could never be done in a conventional browser environment. You can apply Flash bitmap filters and tweens directly onto an HTML object, or have a JavaScript object communicate directly with an ActionScript object without the intermediary of a communications format. This enables the development of flexible, "sometimes connected," desktop solutions that have not previously been possible in the realm of RIAs.

10. **Seeing is believing** — But don't take our word for it. Check out some Flex and AIR applications yourself. Have a look at some of the showcased applications, and you'll see exactly what we mean:

    ```
    www.flex.org/showcase
    www.adobe.com/products/air/showcase
    ```

Summary

Hopefully throughout this chapter, you have gained an increased understanding of what Flex is and where it sits in the overall scheme of RIA development. In this chapter, we also looked at clearing up several misconceptions you might have about the Flash Platform and Flex, including some very compelling reasons for using Adobe Flex for all your RIA development requirements. The delight is in the details, of course, as the rest of this book will show you.

2

The Flex 3 Ecosystem

Before diving into the specifics of any technology, it helps to know the terrain. You may have heard terms such as the Flash Player, Flash runtime, Flex, Flex framework, virtual machine, Flash Platform, Flex ecosystem, and various Adobe server products. The previous chapter defined a few aspects of this ensemble of technologies but perhaps not enough for the uninitiated to get a grasp of how they are related. What else is there? And how do they all fit together? This chapter will attempt to categorize and enumerate as many aspects of the ensemble of Adobe and related technologies that we call "the Flex ecosystem" as possible. These technologies are divided into the following categories:

❏ Runtimes

❏ Languages

❏ Development tools

❏ Frameworks and APIs

❏ Data communications

❏ Servers

A (Not So) Brief History of Flex

Before Flex, there was (and still is) Flash. Flash started as SmartSketch in 1995, which was changed to FutureSplash Animator, which was then acquired by Macromedia in 1996 and rebranded as Flash (www.adobe.com/macromedia/events/john_gay/page04.html). Flash got its start as a timeline-based animation vector tool in 1996, which published .swf files, which was short for ShockWave Flash.

As the tools and its player grew, the extension name stuck even though what it stood for lost significance. At the time, Flash only had proto-scripting capability, and it wasn't until Flash 4 in 1999 that it acquired anything approaching a language. In 2000, Flash 5 was released, which catapulted Flash into the object-oriented programming arena with the birth of what is now known as ActionScript 1.0, based on the same ECMAScript-262 standard as JavaScript. And with it came dot syntax and dynamic asset manipulation, meaning that you didn't have to do everything on the timeline if you didn't want to. Flash saw some significant upgrades in 2002 with Flash MX and Flash Player 6, which catapulted the Web into a revolution in online video with the FLV format and Flash Communications Server (which was later renamed Flash Media Server).

But it wouldn't be until 2003 with Flash MX 2004 and Flash Player 7 when Flash and ActionScript would get another facelift in the form of ActionScript 2.0, a new development methodology, and some impressive new video capabilities. The Flash integrated development environment (IDE) now allowed classes to be coded in external files, whereas before they were confined to the Flash timeline, which opened up the platform to a growing developer community. ActionScript 2.0 allowed for an inheritance-based syntax and class-based programming. But since the compiler reduced AS 2.0 into AS 1.0 bytecode in the SWF, the language itself was still prototype-based. This meant that you could instantiate classes directly on the prototype chain, and circumvent private class members at runtime with the right syntax. This had its uses, as the Flash component library was closed source and often the only way of extending component functionality was to circumvent the compiler syntax. Ah, the good old days of hacking your way through the prototype chain.

It was also in this year that Flex was born. In 2002, Macromedia foresaw a future need for a new type of Internet application and wrote a white paper where it coined the term "rich Internet application" (RIA) in anticipation of that need (www.adobe.com/devnet/flash/whitepapers/richclient.pdf). In 2004, it made good on that promise and created a new development-oriented platform called Flex 1, which soon after became Flex 1.5. Flex used the Dreamweaver authoring engine to lay out applications in an XML-based language called MXML, with ActionScript 2.0 files supporting the application logic and component architecture. It was a marvelous first attempt at creating a completely code-centric Flash development platform. Developers could concentrate on the code and the structure of the application without worrying about design metaphors such as scenes, layers, and an animation timeline, enabling the compilation of component-driven, Flash-based applications.

But Flex 1 had some serious limitations. SWFs could be compiled only on the Flex Server, which created some unique debugging difficulties. The component library and authoring tool were also packaged together with the Flex Server, which was priced for enterprise, well outside the reach of small web shops, let alone individual developers — so adoption was very slow. And because the component architecture was based on the default Flash components, a fair amount of highly specialized Flash knowledge was required to work around the quirks in the framework, which was not a skillset possessed by the typical enterprise-level programmer. The components also lacked any significant skinning capability, which made every Flex application look pretty much the same, negating the wild and creative appeal that drew people to Flash as a technology in the first place. And because Flex 1 ran very much like Flash under the hood (given that they used the same runtime), many developers at that time grudgingly admitted that Flash 7 and ActionScript 2.0 ran way too slow to build enterprise-level applications.

Macromedia knew the way forward, but the current technology would not support what it was designed to achieve. So, they did the only thing they could do: they reinvented Flash as a technology from the ground up, starting with the runtime, then the language, and finally, Flex itself. Meanwhile, Flash evolved into version 8, which added some significant dynamic graphics-handling capabilities and video enhancements to the platform.

In 2005, Macromedia released the Flash Player 8.5 beta and the Flex 2 beta. In December 2005, Adobe Systems Incorporated acquired Macromedia (www.adobe.com/aboutadobe/pressroom/press releases/200512/120505AdobeAcquiresMacromedia.html), and shortly thereafter, Adobe released Flash Player 9 and Flex 2.0. And the Flex RIA revolution was born.

While conceiving these changes, Macromedia (now Adobe) knew at the time it would have to reinvent the Flash runtime to significantly push the technology forward, but there were also literally millions of web pages with Flash 7- and 8-compatible content (and earlier) on the Internet. So, the Flash Player, considered a part of the "Flash Platform" umbrella of technologies since 2005, was split into two separate runtimes, or virtual machines (VMs), to maintain compatibility with legacy content. One virtual machine would play all the old ActionScript 2.0, Flash Player 8-equivalent content, which would thereafter only ever be updated with security patches, not new features. The other virtual machine would be the "new hotness," crunching the new ActionScript 3.0 code up to 100 times faster than its predecessor, including other incredible, game-changing features. Built into this new Flash 9 runtime is ActionScript 3.0, which was also re-created, not evolved from the old, and the change was nothing less than revolutionary.

Flex as a development toolset also changed. The Flex software development kit (SDK) is now free and (with exception of certain elements, such as the compiler) is open source. Before this, Flash developers were used to sharing code, creating their own component sets and class libraries. This was due in part to the closed-source nature of the Flash 7/Flex 1 components, partly because in many cases, collectively the community could do it better. Now with Flex 2, the Flash and Flex community had a robust, enterprise-level component architecture that could actually be skinned in Flash. This was like a dream come true for many Flash Platform developers, and it got a lot of programmers from other languages such as ColdFusion, Java, and C# suddenly very interested in what Adobe was doing. Fed up with trying to shoehorn RIA frameworks into hypertext-based application paradigms, many developers have converted to Flex as their RIA technology of choice.

In February 2008, Adobe released Flex 3 and AIR 1.0, further expanding the Flash Platform with native desktop applications development, improved skinning, new server models, and improved tools. Adobe also open sourced the Flex 3 SDK, starting the trend we see today at Adobe of releasing new technologies under an open-source initiative, which was a radical departure from its closed-source roots in the days of Flex 1.

In October 2008, Adobe released Flash Player 10, introducing a host of powerful new capabilities to the Flash runtime, and in November it released AIR 1.5 and Flex 3.2 to include Flash Player 10 support.

Flex and the Flash runtime are in an ever-evolving state of technological enhancement and will continue to grow and expand as better and more improved capabilities are developed.

The Adobe Flex 3 Ecosystem

The "Adobe Flex 3 ecosystem" is an umbrella term used to describe technologies such as the Flash Platform, the Flex SDK, and Adobe server products are a part of the Flex development and deployment workflow.

Runtimes

The Flash Platform consists of three runtimes: the Flash Player, AIR, and Flash Lite.

Flash Player

The Adobe Flash Player is a browser plug-in that runs .swf files, which are written in a binary format known as ActionScript Byte Code (ABC). The Flash Player executes the ABC data in one of two virtual machines based on the nature of its content. The SWF file format right up to Flash 9 was a fairly well-guarded (or at least well-licensed) secret, until May 2008, when Adobe launched the Open Screen Project (www.adobe.com/openscreenproject/faq/), which made the SWF specification available with a minimum of restrictions.

There are two types of Flash Player browser plug-ins: a *Release version*, which is what the majority of users will download from Adobe. For developers, a *Debug version* allows errors and exceptions to appear in a browser dialog box for debugging. The Debug version also enables remote debugging over TCP on port 7935. The Debug version is included in the default Flex Builder installation and the free Flex 3 SDK, or it can be downloaded from Adobe (www.adobe.com/support/flashplayer/downloads.html).

The Flash Player follows a single-threaded execution model, with the exception of specific advances related to Flash Player 10. This means that event handling is synchronous, which may take some getting used to for users of multithreaded languages. A single-threaded model has the advantage of simplified event propagation and debugging, and since there are no race conditions or deadlocks to worry about, it simplifies the coding of certain class structures such as the Singleton design pattern. The disadvantage of a single-threaded environment, of course, is in performing certain processor-intensive tasks, like sorting and processing a large data set, which may cause UI responsiveness to degrade. Which is why it is paramount for the developer to optimize the performance of the application to ensure that the responsiveness and usability of the application is taken into consideration. See Chapter 67, "Application Performance Strategies," for details.

In Flash Player 9 and above, the Flash Player has been forked into two separate runtimes: ActionScript Virtual Machine 1 (AVM1) and ActionScript Virtual Machine 2 (AVM2).

ActionScript Virtual Machine 1 (AVM1)

The ActionScript Virtual Machine 1 (AVM1) is the old Flash Player 8 runtime reserved exclusively for rendering legacy SWF files, sequestered in its own sandbox. The AVM1 plays SWF files written in ActionScript 1 and 2. Since ActionScript 2.0 is merely a compiler-based syntax that is compiled down to ActionScript 1.0 bytecode, the AVM1 runtime is actually an ActionScript 1.0 virtual machine. The AVM1 cannot play ActionScript 3 SWFs or Flex 2+ applications.

Functionality access problems arise when attempting to load AVM1 SWFs into an AVM2 application because of sandboxing restrictions, which is not recommended. Since the Flash 9 player includes the capability to run legacy content, designers can still create new ActionScript 1 or 2 content in the Flash IDE (i.e., Flash CS4) targeted for Flash Player 9 or 10.

ActionScript Virtual Machine 2 (AVM2)

The ActionScript Virtual Machine 2 (AVM2) in the Flash Player is designed to run ActionScript 3.0 SWFs in a completely different manner than its predecessor. Some of the major changes include:

❑   Addition of the Just-in-Time (JIT) compiler, which converts ActionScript bytecode into machine-native PPC and X86 machine code at runtime. This allows for incredible speed increases of up to approximately 100 times faster than the AVM1, and up to approximately 1000 times faster than traditional browser JavaScript.

With certain recent improvements to browsers such as Firefox, Safari, and Chrome, some of which use a dedicated JavaScript JIT compiler such as SquirrelFish, the execution speed difference between ActionScript 3.0 and JavaScript has closed significantly, but browser applications must still be built to take advantage of such new capabilities.

❑ Several changes to the ActionScript language itself have made code execution much more efficient. ActionScript 3.0 has been remade from a loosely typed, prototype-based scripting language into a strongly typed, true inheritance-based language, which has been incorporated into the VM language runtime system. (See the section "ActionScript 3.0" later in this chapter for details.)

In broad strokes, the AVM2 runtime components are:

❑ ABC parser

❑ Bytecode verifier

❑ Interpreter

❑ Runtime system for AS3 language and core APIs

❑ Garbage Collector and memory manager

❑ JIT compiler

Flash APIs in the Virtual Machine

Flash Player 9 introduced several improvements to the Flash APIs on which ActionScript 3.0 is based.

❑ A new Display List API makes working with display objects much more robust and consistent. See Chapters 3 and 5 for details.

❑ A standardized DOM 3 event model, which makes object communication very simple, without the need for a separate event framework. The Flex framework uses the same event model as the Flash API.

❑ Low-level binary data access allows ActionScript to have direct control over data manipulation in the runtime, which was never before available in ActionScript. This allows for cross-format data interpretation and the possibility of custom data formats and protocols, making the Flash VM extremely flexible and powerful.

For instance, the URLStream class provides access to raw binary data as it is downloaded, the ByteArray class allows direct manipulation of binary data, and binary sockets allow the VM to write binary data to a server socket, allowing for the creation of custom data protocols. See Chapter 4, "Using ActionScript 3.0," for more information on the Flash APIs.

Flash Player 9 Releases

Since the release of Flash Player 9, which first made it possible to author ActionScript 3.0-enabled Flex applications, there have been a few notable releases with significant additions in capability.

❑ **Flash Player 9.0.16** — First official release of the Flash 9 Player with AVM2 and ActionScript 3.0.

❑ **Flash Player 9.0.28** — Vista support, fullscreen capability.

- **Flash Player 9.0.115** (Player 9 Update 3 "MovieStar"):

  - H.264/HE-AAC CODEC support; can play back MP4, M4A, MOV, MP4V, 3GP and, 3G2 content.

  - Multi-core support for up to four CPUs for visual rendering, and image scaling for bitmap images through mipmapping, leading to huge performance increases for bitmap handling.

  - Hardware scaling for fullscreen video enables true 1080p HD video, and multithreaded video decoding for both On2VP6 and H.264 CODECS, ensuring flawless playback in fullscreen.

  - Persistent Framework Caching in the Flash Player, allowing signed .swz library files such as the Flex framework to be pre-cached on the client, significantly reducing the application footprint. See Chapter 66, "Modular Application Development," for details.

  - Improved security enhancements, retroactively dubbed "Phase 1," such as stricter policy file rules. This affects policy file control, DNS hardening, within-domain redirects, Content-Type whitelisting, strict sockets, and improved meta-policies. See Chapter 65, "The Security Model," and the following Adobe article for details: www.adobe.com/ devnet/flashplayer/articles/fplayer9_security.html.

- **Flash Player 9.0.124** — Introduced significant security enhancements, dubbed "Phase 1.5."

  - A socket policy file, introduced in 9,0,115,0, will always be required for all socket connections.

  - A policy file will be required to send headers across domains.

  - The allowScriptAccess default will always be "sameDomain".

  - "javascript:" URLs will be prohibited in networking APIs, except for getURL(), navigateToURL(), and HTML-enabled text fields. *Note in FP 10 this is now disallowed altogether.*

  - See Chapter 65, "The Security Model," and the following Adobe article for details: www.adobe.com/devnet/flashplayer/articles/flash_player9_security_ update.html.

Flash Player 10 Releases

In October 2008, Adobe released Flash Player 10.0.12.36, introducing many extraordinary new features to the Flash Platform

- **Flash Player 10.0.12.36** — Public launch of Flash Player 10.

  - 3D Effects using a new Drawing API, including a third axis of rotation.

  - Custom filters and effects using Adobe Pixel Bender (codenamed Hydra or Adobe Image Foundation). Pixel Bender is a high-performance image-processing language and a multithreaded visual transformation engine, which allows for real-time custom Photoshop-like effects to be used for the first time in Flash.

❏ New display modes that allow for GPU hardware acceleration for graphics, effects, and fullscreen video playback using DirectDraw or Direct3D for the PC and OpenGL for the Mac. GPU blitting, or surfacing, extends the hardware-scaled fullscreen view introduced in Flash Player 9 Update 3 and applies it to the browser window.

❏ Flash Text Engine (FTE), which allows for multidirectional text, multi-column text flow and support for font ligatures. An update to the Saffron anti-aliasing text engine has also been added, allowing for bitmap transformations on system fonts, which can now be rotated and have text applied, previously only possible with embedded fonts. Context menus now also support rich text.

Although FTE enhancements have not been natively implemented in the Flex 3 text components, by extending these components the developer can enable these improved features, which will be natively included in the Flex 4 component set.

❏ ActionScript 3.0 additions such as typed arrays, called *vectors*.

❏ Dynamic sound creation in the Sound APIs.

❏ New streaming media improvements and protocols (see the sections "Data Communications" and "Flash Media Server" later in this chapter).

❏ Improved media unloading with the unloadAndStop() method, ensuring that all media ceases playing upon being unloaded, without waiting for the runtime Garbage Collector (GC) to end playback.

❏ Large bitmap support allows for 4096×4096 pixel bitmaps with a maximum length of 8191 pixels per side, expanding the previous 2888-pixel limit.

❏ Better Linux support. Among certain performance and stability improvements, the Linux version of Flash Player 10 now supports the Video4Linux v2 (V4L2) camera API.

❏ Enhanced system access, such as improved uploading and downloading capability and system clipboard access.

❏ AIR 1.5 is released, which includes Flash Player 10 (see the "Adobe AIR" section).

Note this applies to the browser version of the Flash player. The Flash VM in AIR already has more advanced desktop system integration.

❏ **Flash Player 10.0.22.xx and later**:

   ❏ Implementation of Phase 2 security restrictions for the Flash Player. In Phase 2, all the warnings of Phase 1 become errors and the transition to stricter security rules is complete. See Chapter 65, "The Security Model," and the following Adobe articles for details: www.adobe.com/devnet/flashplayer/articles/fplayer9_security.html and www.adobe.com/devnet/flashplayer/articles/fplayer10_security_changes.html

- ❏ AIR 1.5.1 is released with Flash Player v10.0.22 (see the "Adobe AIR" section), in addition to a few new APIs. See the Adobe AIR 1.5.1 Release Notes for details (`www.adobe.com/support/documentation/en/air/1_5_1/releasenotes_developers.html`).

- ❏ Normalization of the versioning for the Flash Player. Instead of tracking Flash Player versions according to "Flash Player X Update Y," which does not intuitively correspond with the minor Flash Player version number, all version numbers will now follow a more intuitive versioning system. The first, second, and third versioning digits now actually mean Major, Minor, and Bugfix, respectively. More details on this change can be found at `http://weblogs.macromedia.com/emmy/archives/2008/10/a_small_improvement _to_our_version_numbering_aka_why_there_wont_be_a_flash_player_10_ update_1.html`.

For further Flash Player release information, see the Flash Player Release Notes, at `www.adobe.com/support/documentation/en/flashplayer/releasenotes.html`.

Tamarin

In November of 2006, Adobe contributed a significant amount of scripting-engine source code from the Flash ActionScript 3 virtual machine to the Mozilla Foundation. With some minor exceptions, Tamarin is considered to be the same as the Flash AVM2, although Tamarin is *not* the Flash Player, as it does not include the AVM1 and non-language-specific capabilities. As the Flash Player virtual machine advances, Adobe continues to contribute code to the Tamarin project (`www.mozilla.org/projects/tamarin`). This also means that a significant portion of the Flash Player is now open source.

This was done to encourage future Mozilla applications such as Firefox to contain a native ActionScript virtual machine. It was hoped that if JavaScript 2 and ActionScript 3 were to share the same ECMAScript-262 Edition 4 (ES4) standard, both would be able to run on the same high-performance, JIT-powered engine, which would bring performance improvements for AJAX applications as well.

Since work on ECMAScript 4 was halted in favor of working on ECMAScript 3.1 (codenamed "Harmony") in October 2008, JavaScript 2 will most likely adhere to this standard, while ActionScript 3.0 will not be scaled back in favor of the 3.1 standard, so it is currently unlikely that JavaScript and ActionScript will natively run in the same browser-integrated JIT. Newer browsers such as Google Chrome, and AIR 1.5, use the Squirrelfish JIT for improved JavaScript performance.

Flex applications cannot natively be compiled to run in Tamarin.

The Flash Player is not *open source. Adobe has no plans of open sourcing the AVM1, which was kept in the Flash Player for legacy SWF playback. Although there is a Flash 7 SDK, and a version of the Flash Player 8 in the Flash Lite 3 SDK, which runs what is now known as the AVM1, there is currently no Flash Player 9 SDK for third-party licensing. This is most likely due to the fact that the Flash Player AVM2 has been open sourced through the Mozilla Tamarin project, which has made the necessity of a Flash Player 9 SDK obsolete. Adobe has revised its Flash Player licensing model and made it available for Flash Player 10 through the Open Screen Project (`www.openscreenproject.org`). This removes many prior licensing restrictions, encouraging its use for multiple devices and technologies.*

Adobe AIR

The Adobe Integrated Runtime (AIR) is a cross-OS desktop runtime environment allowing RIAs to be deployed to a desktop environment. AIR was released in beta on Adobe Labs in mid-2006, under the name of "Apollo," and was released along with Flex 3 in February 2008.

Technologies

The Adobe Integrated Runtime is a composite of several web technologies intermarried together to create unique desktop experiences:

❑ **Flash Player** — The Flash Player Tamarin virtual machine enables the deployment of Flash and Flex applications.

AIR applications can be authored in Flash CS4 using the core Flash AIR API, or they can be authored in Flex Builder using the Flex AIR APIs, which include extended components built upon the Flex framework.

The AIR file format (.air) is designed according to the ZIP format, and contains all the images, JavaScript, Flash, and XML metadata files necessary for the runtime to install and execute the application.

AIR 1.0 and 1.1 contains the Flash Player 9 VM, whereas AIR 1.5 has the Flash Player 10 VM at its core, with all the progressive enhancements from Flash Player versions 9 through 10 (see the "Flash Player 9 Releases" and "Flash Player 10 Releases" sections above).

Although AIR includes the full Flash Player, some hardware acceleration capabilities, such as GPU rendering, are not yet available as of AIR 1.5.

Since AIR includes a "full" Flash Player, applications programmed in ActionScript 1 and 2, which run in the AVM1, can be created, although they do not have access to the AIR APIs, so they must either be loaded at runtime into an AS3 AIR application or displayed in an HTML AIR application.

❑ **WebKit Browser** — The WebKit browser is used for rendering HTML and JavaScript-based content. WebKit is an open-source browser, which is the same engine used in the Apple Safari and Google Chrome browsers. The advantage of having the WebKit browser within AIR is that it is a lightweight, industry-standard HTML engine that doesn't add a considerable footprint to the AIR installation. Adobe does not have to maintain its own proprietary HTML engine, and developers do not have not code for the quirks of yet *another* web browser. Adobe also contributes to the WebKit open-source project.

Since AIR has a full-featured browser, applications can be authored exclusively as HTML/JavaScript or AJAX desktop applications.

As of AIR 1.5, the SquirrelFish JavaScript VM is integrated into the Webkit HTML engine, meaning higher performance for JS/AJAX applications in AIR, although experimental features from the current WebKit builds are not included.

❑ **Acrobat Reader** — Acrobat Reader facilitates the viewing of PDF documents in AIR through the WebKit engine.

Users must have Acrobat Reader 8.1 or higher installed on their machine in order to view PDF content in AIR. Although Adobe AIR does not install Adobe Reader, the latest version of Adobe Reader currently includes an optional install for Adobe AIR.

❑ **SQLite Database** — AIR also includes a SQLite database for local data storage, which presents some unique opportunities to store data locally during offline periods for sometimes-connected applications, or even as a mainstay of the application's business logic.

AIR 1.5 also enables encryption in the local SQLite database.

For further AIR release information, see the Adobe AIR Release Notes, at www.adobe.com/support/ documentation/en/air/releasenotes.html.

Cross-Rendering Capabilities

Under the hood, AIR uses the WebKit engine for rendering browser content, and the Acrobat Reader plug-in for rendering PDF content in WebKit. The AIR runtime then renders HTML/JS/PDF objects from the WebKit engine as Flash objects to be displayed in the Flash VM. This means that HTML/JS or PDF objects can be treated as ActionScript objects and vice versa, allowing for an incredible cross-development to occur between the two technologies.

> *It is to be noted that there are some limitations for accessing PDF content in AIR. See the AIR 1.5 documentation for details:* http://help.adobe.com/en_US/AIR/1.5/devappshtml/WS5b3ccc5 16d4fbf351e63e3d118666ade46-7eb4.html.

Since web pages interpreted by the WebKit browser may also host Flash content, rendering recursion can occur. For example, if a Flex AIR application includes an <HTML> object in a Flex Panel, that "browser" object may load a URL containing a Flash site, which is also rendered in the Flash VM without difficulty.

This enables "script bridging" between Flash and JavaScript, meaning that HTML objects and JavaScript APIs can be natively accessed in ActionScript, and Flash objects and APIs can be natively accessed in JavaScript. For instance, JavaScript or AJAX AIR applications can access Flash APIs for XML parsing or sockets, and Flash or Flex AIR applications can apply a blur filter, a color transformation, and a tween to an HTML-native object at runtime. The developer can also merge an HTML web page right into a Flex application as if it were a native object, or control a Flash asset natively in JavaScript.

System Access

An AIR application also has access to certain features of the native operating system, such as file drag and drop, custom application window chrome, system tray or doc presence, and custom launch icons. AIR can open certain file types, and if you don't find the file type you need, create an interpreter or parser for that data format. AIR can also capture bitmap and other data and save it to the desktop as a file. See Chapter 15, "Getting Started with AIR," for details.

The Power of AIR

This unique cross-rendering of different web technologies has never existed before Adobe AIR. It has even been called a "superbrowser," even though AIR does not aim at replacing the browser in any way. Because AIR consists of two main rendering technologies, AIR applications can be authored in HTML/ JS or by using an AJAX framework for rendering for the WebKit browser engine, or in ActionScript 3.0 or by using a Flex framework for rendering in the Flash Player VM.

AIR also has the power to merge the two main technologies that make up most RIAs seamlessly and effortlessly, hybridizing the full capabilities of Flash, Flex, HTML, JavaScript, AJAX, PDF, and any other compatible web formats and protocols.

See Chapter 15 for more detail on building AIR applications in Flex.

Although not available for Flex, the Flash IDE enables compilation for another type of Flash Player, the Flash standalone player. This is an executable (.exe) version of the Flash Player plug-in that can play SWF files outside the browser. This is the Flash Player bundled with the Flash CS4 installation that allows for the Test Movie *compilation preview. Flash CS4 can also create a desktop-enabled application called a* projector, *where the Flash standalone player is bundled with the application SWF into an executable file that can be launched on the desktop. Until the existence of the AIR alpha (codenamed "Apollo") and AIR 1.0, this was the only way that Flash applications could run on the desktop. Projectors are usually created for CD-ROM and kiosk distribution of Flash applications, although interfacing with the desktop is primitive and extremely limited. Third-party software allows for the creation of a wrapper for a SWF or Projector file for developing applications, screensavers, and widgets with improved desktop interfacing, although these solutions do not possess script-bridging and other advanced desktop integration capabilities of Adobe AIR. Apart from some very specific use case scenarios, the Flash Projector as desktop application is considered to have been made obsolescent by Adobe AIR.*

Languages

Flex 3 can compile applications using ActionScript 3.0 as the base language, with two additional helper languages, MXML and CSS.

ActionScript 3.0

ActionScript 3.0 is an imperative, true inheritance-based, strongly typed OOP language that conforms to the ECMA-262 Edition 4 (or ES4) standard, which is the same standard as the evolving JavaScript 2 language.

*The Edition 4 standard was canceled by the ECMA in August 2008 in favor of developing the "Harmony," or ES3.1, standard. Adobe representatives have stated that ActionScript 3.0 is "still based on ECMAScript 3 and will now be treated as an extension with some additional functionality" (*http://blog.digital backcountry.com/?p=1375*). Adobe will not devolve the existing ActionScript specification as a result of this decision.*

All Flash and Flex applications are compiled using ActionScript as a base language, which is considered to be a scripting language, even though it is compiled into a binary SWF or AIR file containing ABC bytecode. But it can also be considered a compiled language because of the JIT compiler within the Tamarin VM, converting the ActionScript into machine-native code at runtime. So, there's a bit of a debate into which camp ActionScript 3.0 falls. One could say that it's a scripting language operating at the efficiency of a compiled language.

Some of the highlights of ActionScript 3.0 as a language include:

❑   ActionScript 3 is a true inheritance-based language, while the prototype chain, which was the predominant inheritance model in previous versions, takes a backseat. This allows for mature OOP constructs, architectures, and design patterns.

❑   Method closures make the event model simple and possible, ensuring that functions are scoped to the defining class, removing the necessity of listener delegates.

❑   Sealed classes ensure that only class members that were defined upon compilation exist at runtime. This facilitates strong typing, improving performance and type integrity.

❑ Strong typing and runtime type-checking ensure type safety, enabling data-robust applications. Dynamic types and untyped objects (*) are possible but must be explicitly declared. Type information is also used in native machine code representations, improving performance and memory usage.

❑ Runtime exceptions, supported by strong typing, ensure that critical errors will be handled in a robust fashion and not fail silently, improving debugging performance.

❑ Primitive types `int` and `uint` are signed and unsigned 32-bit integers that take advantage of native math processing capabilities of the CPU. 64-bit integers do not yet exist, as the AVM2 is a 32-bit runtime, and have not yet been ported for 64-bit environments. Adobe is currently planning development of a 64-bit Flash Player able to handle 64-bit integers, although, as of this writing, there is no planned release date.

❑ Other *primitive types* are `Boolean`, `Null`, `Number`, `String` and `void`, and other *complex types* are `Object`, `Array`, `Date`, `Error`, and `Function`, in addition to those mentioned below.

❑ ECMAScript for XML (E4X) establishes `XML` and `XMLList` as a native complex data types, dramatically improving XML parsing and processing.

❑ Regular expressions are also supported in the native `RegExp` data type, allowing for very efficient parsing of data.

❑ Class and method access specifiers include `dynamic`, `static`, `public`, `private`, `internal`, `protected`, `override`, and `final` namespaces. The `native` keyword is also present, which is similar to the AS2 `intrinsic` specifier, although it is only available for the Flash Player APIs and cannot be used by developers.

❑ Namespaces can also be defined as custom access specifiers, allowing new ways of controlling visibility to class members, offering an alternative to *interface programming*. Namespaces are given a URI as a unique identifier. They can also be used with E4X for XML namespaces, allowing for the parsing of complex XML formats.

❑ The Flex framework uses the custom `mx_internal` namespace for its internal data, allowing for semi-privatization of class members without completely restricting access to developers who wish to tinker with the framework.

❑ Flash Player 10 has enabled a powerful new feature in ActionScript 3.0 from the disbanded ECMA ES4 specification: typed arrays (or "generics"), which are called *vectors*.

ActionScript 3.0 does not currently allow for private constructors, method overloading, or multiple inheritance. Some of these and other features are in the proposed ES4 spec and may be implemented in future releases of the Flash Player or in the next version of ActionScript.

MXML and CSS

MXML is an XML-based markup language used for the visual layout and display of Flex components. Rather than instantiating components with ActionScript and calculating spatial relationships with code, MXML allows for rapid development of applications with a minimum of code. As a part of the MXML specification, certain nonvisual classes and even data binding between components can be declared in MXML. ActionScript can also be written within a script block for added functionality. Flex also recognizes Cascading Style Sheets (CSS), utilizing a subset of the CSS 2 specification for the purposes of styling and skinning of components. See Chapter 7, "MXML Fundamentals," for more information.

MXML and CSS are considered to be a part of Flex, and not Flash (i.e., Flash Player APIs), because the interpreter is built into the Flex compiler. Upon compilation, the Flex compiler reduces all ActionScript, MXML, CSS, and compiler metadata into ActionScript bytecode.

CSS markup used to style Flex components is different from CSS, which can be used to implement rudimentary text formatting in ActionScript.

Pixel Bender

Pixel Bender is a scripting language used to create Pixel Bender (.pbj) filters for use in Flash Player 10. It is based on the OpenGL Shading Language (GLSL), which is based on the C language. Pixel Bender filters, called *kernels*, are written and compiled using the Adobe Pixel Bender Toolkit, which can be embedded into an ActionScript or Flex application and accessed by using the Shader class.

Flex Builder 3

Flex Builder is the IDE for Adobe Flex that is based on the Eclipse platform. Flex Builder can be installed as a standalone application (i.e., bundled as a branded Eclipse application), or it can be installed as an Eclipse plug-in so that it can run alongside other Eclipse environments. See Chapters 5, 6, and 8 for more information on Adobe Flex Builder.

Installing Flex Builder, either as a standalone application or as an Eclipse plug-in, automatically installs the Flex 3 SDK. Although Flex Builder is a paid-for product, the Flex SDK is free and may be downloaded and used separately with your own IDE of choice.

Since the FDT ActionScript editor is also based on Eclipse, some Flex developers also prefer this IDE as an alternative to Flex Builder.

The Flex SDK

The Flex SDK contains everything you need to compile Flex applications aimed at the Flash Player or AIR runtime. It comprises open-source and free closed-source elements.

The Flex SDK can be downloaded as both free and open-source elements (Free Adobe Flex SDK), just the open-source elements (Open Source Flex SDK), or just the free closed-source elements (Adobe Add-ons for Open Source Flex SDK). See www.adobe.com/products/flex/flexdownloads and http://opensource.adobe.com/wiki/display/flexsdk/Downloads for more information.

- ❑ Open Source Flex SDK
    - ❑ The compilers
    - ❑ The debugger
    - ❑ The Flex framework
- ❑ Free (closed-source) Flex SDK
    - ❑ Flash Player runtime (debug version)
    - ❑ AIR runtime
    - ❑ Advanced font-encoding libraries
    - ❑ Licensing and codebase for charting and data visualization components

Pixel Bender (AIF) Toolkit

The Pixel Bender Toolkit, formerly known as the Adobe Image Foundation (AIF) Toolkit (whose beta was codenamed "Hydra"), is an application that enables you to author pixel bender filters (.pbj files) for use with Flash Player 10. For details about embedding Pixel Bender filters in Flex, see www.mikechambers .com/blog/2008/09/17/creating-re-distributable-actionscript-libraries-of-pixel-bender-filters/ and www.gotoandlearn.com/play?id=84.

Frameworks and APIs

The Flash Platform, specific to the Flex ecosystem, encompasses a multitude of APIs and frameworks.

Flash Player APIs

The Flash Player APIs are considered to be the base framework necessary to compile an ActionScript 3.0 application and include the core ActionScript 3.0 classes and functionality built into the VM, and the playerglobal.swc class library, which is required by both the Flash and the Flex compiler. See Chapter 4, "Using ActionScript 3.0," for more details on the Flash Player APIs.

The Flex Framework

The Flex framework is a composite of the core visual components, enhancements to the event flow, metadata tags for compiler declarations, and utility and communications classes. It is also composed of several "subframeworks" or APIs offering specialized functionality. Among these are the following:

❑   **Flex charting and data visualization components** — Although not a part of the open-source Flex SDK, the charting components are licensed with Flex Builder and are considered to be a part of the Flex Framework. See Chapter 36, "Using the Charting Components," for details.

❑   **Deep linking framework** — This enables enhanced state-integration functionality in the browser (see Chapter 40, "Deep Linking").

❑   **Logging framework** — This allows an application to capture and log messages to text components, class objects, or text files, functioning like an enhanced trace() method. See Chapter 74, "The Logging Framework," for details.

❑   **Automation framework** — This allows for automated testing, gathering metrics on application performance, and multiple client application synchronization and browsing. See Chapter 75, "The Automation Framework," for details.

❑   **Messaging API** — These classes are used to communicate with BlazeDS data services. See Chapter 59, "Using BlazeDS" for details.

The AIR APIs

Adobe AIR consists of two main APIs:

❑   The **Flash AIR API**, which extends the core Flash Player APIs, enabling AIR applications to be authored in Flash CS4 (which are also available in Flex). See Chapter 4 for more information.

❑   The **Flex AIR API**, which is a part of the Flex Framework, available for Flex AIR application compilation. See Chapter 15 for more information.

Other Adobe Frameworks

Other Adobe frameworks that can assist in the development of Flex or AIR applications include the following:

- ❑ **as3corelib** is an ActionScript 3.0 library that contains a number of helper classes and utilities for working with MD5 and SHA 1 hashing, image encoding, and JSON serialization, as well as extensions to the String, Number and Date APIs. See `http://code.google.com/p/as3corelib/` for more information.

- ❑ **Cairngorm** is an architectural framework or "micro-architecture," composed of several recognizable J2EE design patterns, that encourages best practices in Flex application development, as endorsed by Adobe Consulting. Cairngorm is considered to be a standard for coding enterprise-level architectures in Flex. See Part X, "Using Cairngorm," for details. See `http://opensource .adobe.com/wiki/display/cairngorm/Cairngorm` for more information.

- ❑ **FlexUnit** is a unit-testing framework for Flex and ActionScript 3.0 applications and libraries. It mimics the functionality of JUnit, a Java unit-testing framework, and comes with a graphical test runner. See Chapter 73, "Unit Testing and Test-Driven Development with FlexUnit," and `http://opensource.adobe.com/wiki/display/flexunit/FlexUnit` for more information.

- ❑ **Adobe AIR Update Framework** is a collection of best practices and APIs that assist in the development of AIR application autoupdate functionality, which includes checking for downloadable updates to the AIR application, alerting the user of a newer version of the application, and displaying information about the application version and the opt-in choices for updating the application. See `http://labs.adobe.com/wiki/index.php/Adobe_AIR_Update_Framework` for more information.

- ❑ **Adobe Spry Framework**, although slightly outside of the scope of the Flex ecosystem, is an AJAX framework noteworthy for its use in AJAX AIR applications. See `http://labs.adobe .com/technologies/spry/home.html` for more information.

- ❑ **Adobe Data Services Stress-Testing Framework** helps developers using LiveCycle Data Services ES 2.6 load test the server-side implementation of their LCDS applications. This framework is not currently compatible with BlazeDS, although BlazeDS support is planned for future versions of the tool. See Chapter 58, "Using the Flex Stress Testing Framework," and `http://labs.adobe .com/wiki/index.php/Flex_Stress_Testing_Framework` for more information.

Third-Party Frameworks and Components

Popular third-party components and frameworks for Flex include:

- ❑ **ILOG Elixir** is a set of advanced data visualization components. Built in partnership with Adobe, ILOG offers high-performance visualization components with unique and rich UI for Adobe Flex applications. See `www.ilog.com/products/ilogelixir` for more information.

- ❑ **Zend PHP Framework** brings together the flexibility and enterprise reliability of the Zend PHP platform with the advantages of Adobe technologies such as an AMF implementation for PHP. This is the result of a collaboration between Adobe and Zend to add Adobe technologies to the open-source Zend Framework Project. See `http://framework.zend.com` for more information.

- ❑ **FlexLib** is an impressive open-source community effort to create additional UI components for Flex 2 and 3. Adobe has contributed a few components and libraries, such as the Flex Scheduling Components, to FlexLib. See `http://code.google.com/p/flexlib` for more information.

❑ **OpenFlux** is an open-source component framework for Flex that offers a radically different way of building components in Flex. Inspired by the upcoming Flex 4 beta ("Gumbo") specification, OpenFlux is a component framework that uses intrinsic view and controller properties to control each component's display and behavior, respectively. This offers a very flexible MVC approach to component usage for Flex 3 applications. See http://code.google.com/p/openflux for more information.

❑ **Other architectural frameworks** include the EasyMVC framework (http://projects.simb .net/easyMVC), the PureMVC framework (http://puremvc.org), the Mate framework (http://mate.asfusion.com), and the Swiz framework (http://code.google.com/p/ swizframework/), to name but a few.

❑ **Papervision3D** (www.papervision3d.org) is an impressive 3D rendering framework for ActionScript 3.0 and is considered the gold standard of 3D frameworks in Flash; it is popular with Flash and Flex developers alike. Other popular 3D "engines" for ActionScript include Away3D (http://away3d.com), Sandy (www.flashsandy.org), and Alternativa3D (http://alternativaplatform.com/en/alternativa3d/).

❑ **Degrafa**, which stands for Declarative Graphics Framework, is an open-source initiative that enables Flex developers to create shapes with the Flash Drawing API in MXML using an intuitive XML-based declarative markup similar to the SVG format. See www.degrafa.com for more information.

Degrafa has made such innovative strides in creating this format that Adobe is consulting with the project leaders to get feedback and ideas for the FXG graphics format coming up in Flex 4, at which time Degrafa will become a superset of the FXG specification.

The Tour de Flex Application

Other frameworks can be found listed in the Tour de Flex application, which showcases many third-party frameworks, APIs, services, and components for Flex developers, including a visual reference (or "explorer") for what's possible in Flex. See www.adobe.com/devnet/flex/tourdeflex for details.

Data Communications

The Flash Player and AIR can communicate using a range of data formats over specific networking protocols.

Protocols

Communications protocols unique to the Flash Platform include the "RTMP"-family used by Flash Media Server and related technologies.

❑ **RTMP** — RTMP, which stands for Real-Time Messaging Protocol, is the standard communications protocol for Adobe Flash Media Sever, which allows for real-time streaming of video, audio or data communications over TCP to and from the Flash Player VM, whether it be the Flash Player plug-in, AIR, or Flash Lite. Variations of the RTMP protocol allow for other communications methods.

❑ The **RTMPT** protocol is a version of RTMP that is tunneled over HTTP. RTMPS is a version of the RTMP protocol sent over SSL for secure communications. RTMPE is an enhanced and encrypted version of RTMP that is faster than SSL.

❑ The **RTMPTE** protocol was introduced in Flash Player 9,0,115,0 and AIR 1.1. It adds 128-bit AES encryption tunneled over HTTP for both streaming and non-streaming downloads. This protocol is required to use the DRM features added in Flash Media Server 3.5.

❑ **RTMFP** — Flash Player 10 includes support for the RTMFP protocol, which stands for (Real-Time Media Flow Protocol), a UDP-based secure network transport alternative to RTMP-over-TCP. This allows, for the first time in Flash, peer-to-peer communications between Flash Player installations, with Flash Media Server 4 arbitrating connection identification and authorization. See www.adobe .com/devnet/flashmediaserver/articles/overview_streaming_fms3_02.html for more information.

Data Formats

The Flash platform also uses a number of data formats for messaging and media. See Figure 2-1 for a complete list of data formats.

❑ **The Action Message Format (AMF)** — AMF is a compact binary format used to serialize typed ActionScript objects. The first version of AMF, referred to as AMF 0, supports sending complex objects, and the recent version, AMF 3, includes support for newer AVM2 native data types. This has the advantage of being a very compact ActionScript-native communications format, reducing the need for parsing and interpretation at either end of the transmission. This format is used in Flash Media Server, LCDS ES, BlazeDS, and the Adobe-sponsored Zend PHP framework.

In late 2007, Adobe opened up the AMF 3 format (http://opensource.adobe.com/wiki/ download/attachments/1114283/amf3_spec_05_05_08.pdf?version=1), allowing open-source implementations of AMF to proliferate. To date, AMF implementations have been ported to PHP, Python, Java, .NET, and Ruby.

The main advantage of using AMF, apart from being able to send native ActionScript object to and from the server, is that is very fast compared to other data formats. James Ward, technical evangelist for Flex at Adobe, has a useful RIA data-loading benchmarking application called *Census* (www.jamesward.com/census), which demonstrates the power of the AMF format.

❑ **Video formats and CODECs** — The main video format for Flash video uses the FLV specification (.flv file format) for encoding synchronized audio and video streams and progressively loaded video. The FLV format is reserved for encoding by the Sorenson Spark H.263 and the On2 VP6-E CODECs. The Flash Player also supports the ADPCM, MP3, and Nellymoser audio CODECs.

Support for the H.264 (MPEG-4 Part 10) and On2 VP6-S video CODECs, and the HE-AAC (MPEG-4 Part 3) audio CODEC was added in Flash Player 9 Update 3 (v.9.0.115). This allows for the playback of MP4, M4A, MOV, MP4V, and 3GP files using the same NetStream API used to load FLV files. Preference is sometimes given for such files renamed to the new F4V format (.f4v) extension, which will be natively supported in a future version of Flash Media Server. The F4V format implements parts of ISO 14496-12 specification. Flash Player 10 added encoding support for the Speex audio CODEC.

Other video extensions, .f4p, .f4a and .f4b, are currently unused and are reserved for as yet undetermined Adobe video products.

Thanks to binary sockets, the Flash Player can connect to any server with an open TCP/IP port using virtually any protocol, such as POP3 or IMAP email server, FTP, Telnet, SVN, and more, using virtually any data format for which one can create a binary data parser. In this way, the Flash Player can be made to be truly "data agnostic." For instance, one can employ a zip compression algorithm to send, receive, compress, and decompress files in real-time, to name but one use. Other code libraries allow for encryption protocols to be applied to custom applications.

Servers

Following are a few of the Adobe server products likely to be used by Flex applications and the development workflow.

Flash Media Server

Flash Media Server (FMS), previously known as Flash Communications Server, is a streaming media hub that connects Flash Player installations to server-side streaming media over some flavor of RTMP. Clients can also make remote procedure calls (RPCs) to the server, which can delegate real-time communications between clients by means of the AMF format, or a SharedObject can be used to synchronize data on multiple clients. While these data services are still available in Flash Media Server, their functionality is considered to be feature-final and may be deprecated in future versions of FMS, while more featured implementations are assumed by Adobe data services products.

Flash Media Server 3 adds several new communications protocols, including DRM capability through RTMPE and token authentication, and unlimited load-balancing scalability through Edge/Origin server configurations. It also includes support for dynamic streaming in Flash Player 10. Flash Media Server 3.5 includes support for the RTMFP protocol, including native support of the new F4V format, which is an MPEG "wrapper" format allowing for future Adobe-specific metadata.

A popular open-source alternative is the Red5 Server, which includes support for playback and recording of video streams, shared objects, and AMF.

The Flash Media Server family currently includes four different products:

❏ **Flash Media Interactive Server** is what was simply known as "Flash Media Server," or FMS for short, and is the fully featured media-streaming server product mentioned above. The Flash Media Development Server is an unlimited trial version of FMS limited to 10 simultaneous users.

❏ **Flash Media Streaming Server** is a more cost-effective version of the Flash Media Interactive Server, without data communications, video recording/publishing, or Edge/Origin server options.

❏ **Flash Media Encoding Server** is a real-time, server-side encoding tool for conversion of uploaded video files from virtually any digital video format into FLV/F4V formats.

❏ **Flash Media Rights Management Server** provides encrypted video encoding and key authentication support for the DRM capabilities in Flash Media Server.

ConnectNow

ConnectNow (formerly codenamed "Brio") is the next generation of Adobe Acrobat Connect (formerly named Macromedia Breeze). Acrobat Connect is a videoconferencing and real-time document-sharing tool that has been very popular with online training and distance learning providers. Acrobat Connect is actually a Flash application built upon a specialized implementation of Flash Media Server. Acrobat Connect allows for special screensharing capability through a proprietary add-on for the Flash Player unique to this product. The Acrobat Connect application, previously built upon Flex 1.5, is actually a Flex-built AIR application sold as a major software product. The ConnectNow application contains a subset of Acrobat Connect capabilities and is actually Acrobat Connect, rebuilt as a Flex browser application. Combined with the Acrobat.com Document Service's APIs, ConnectNow as Acrobat Connect's successor is not so much a server product as it is an RIA combined with a Web Services API.

ColdFusion

ColdFusion is an application server, a software development framework, and an XML-based markup language. Originally a product of Allaire in July 1995, Allaire was acquired by Macromedia in 2001, which was in turn acquired by Adobe Systems in 2005.

The ColdFusion server is a JRun server application that may also be run on WebSphere or Apache and produces HTML pages in a similar fashion to many other server-side languages. ColdFusion allows for seamless integration with Java or .NET server objects and allows for native generation of FlashPaper and PDF forms in addition to HTML pages. ColdFusion is preferred over other server-side languages in that it is coded in CFML, an object-oriented and tag-based markup language allowing for rapid server-side development. ColdFusion applications can be written to include Server-Side ActionScript (SSAS) and CFScript.

Flex applications can make use of ColdFusion's ease of server-side coding by employing ColdFusion Services and integrated Flash Remoting, which enables communication between the Flash client and a ColdFusion application using AMF. See Chapter 54, "LCDS and ColdFusion," for details.

LiveCycle Data Services ES

LiveCycle Data Services Enterprise Suite (formerly "Flex Data Services"), or LCDS ES for short, is a functional subset of LiveCycle Data Services for use with Flex technologies. LCDS ES is a J2EE application that installs on the integrated JRun server, which may also be run on JBoss, WebSphere, or Apache.

The advantage of using LCDS ES includes native support for the AMF format through LiveCycle Remoting, data conflict resolution, data paging, client-server synchronization, data push and subscribe messaging, server-side PDF generation, automated testing, server-side Flex compilation, AJAX data services, native Java and ColdFusion object integration, proxy services, and RTMP tunneling.

BlazeDS

BlazeDS is an open-source version of LiveCycle Data Services ES, with a functional subset of LCDS ES, including the open-source AMF format. See Chapter 59 for more detail. A comparison between LCDS and BlazeDS can also be found here: `www.adobe.com/products/livecycle/dataservices/compare.html`.

The Adobe Flex RIA Process Flow

Now that you've seen the various technologies and processes involved in the Flex 3 ecosystem — runtimes, languages, editors, formats, protocols, and servers — how do they all fit together?

Figure 2-1 traces (and the following sections describe) the process tiers of various technologies involved in the Flex 3 ecosystem.

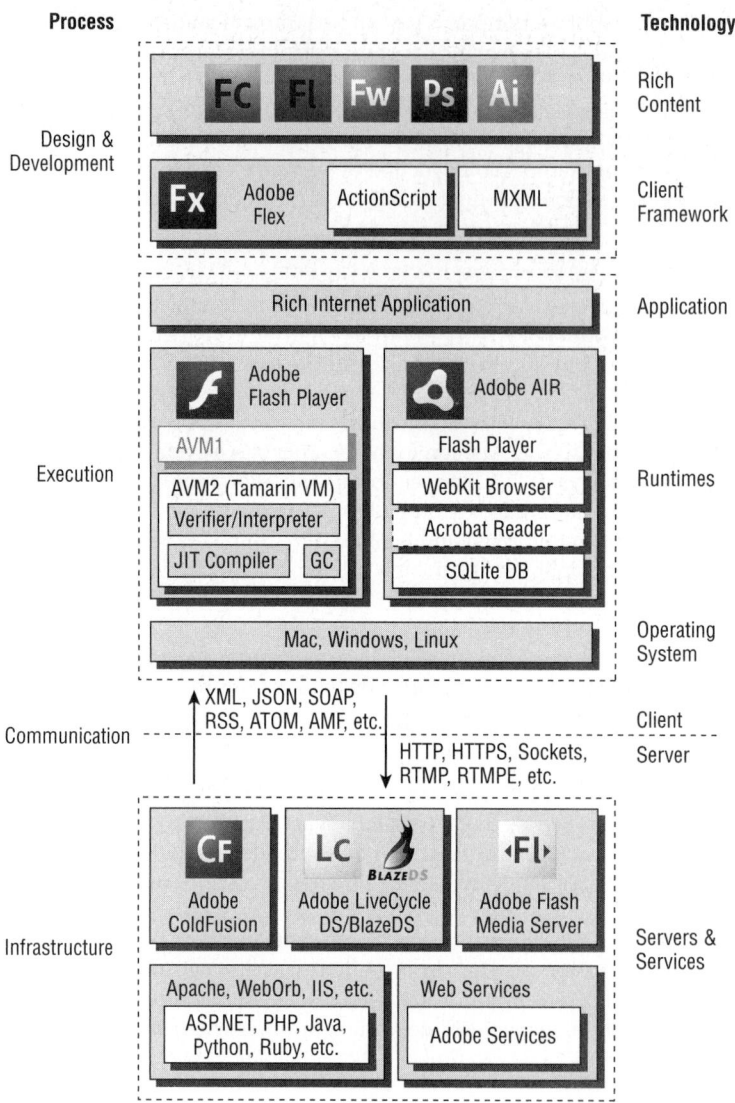

Figure 2-1

Design and Development

The Flex 3 design and development process involves:

❑   Creating the UI design for component skinning, including embedded and loaded rich media for the Flex application, through the use of Adobe authoring applications such as Illustrator,

Photoshop, Fireworks, Flash, and others (not shown). These and other authoring applications are used to create bitmap and vector images for skinning and graphics, and audio and video for content.

❏ The coding and compilation of the application involves the use of Flex Builder or a third-party editor using the open-source Flex SDK. The files created depend on whether the RIA is being launched for the Flash Player, AIR, or both.

❏ In some cases, other authoring applications can be used to create smart assets or Flex components that will be incorporated into the Flex Builder workflow. This can be done in Flash with the help of the Flex Skin Design Extension or the Flex Component Kit for Flash CS4.

When released in 2009, Flash Catalyst will enable an even closer bridge in the Flex workflow between design and development, allowing for the direct creation of a functional Flex UI from a static design proof.

❏ Server-side technologies such as the Flash Media Encoding Server (not shown) may be involved in the creation of some application content prior to compilation.

Developing Flash Platform RIAs without Flex

It is worth mentioning that although we are covering the Flex 3 RIA ecosystem deployment process, it is also possible to create RIAs with the Flash IDE. Although RIAs developed in the Flash IDE do not have the advantage of the Flex framework or the code-editing intelligence of Flex Builder, prior to the release of ActionScript 3/Flash Player 9/Flex 2, most Flash RIAs were created in Flash authoring, with a small percentage developed with Flex 1.

For the Flash developer of today, there are many options for RIA creation. These options typically involve using the Flash CS4 component set or a third-party component set in Flash, in addition to using a third-party ActionScript editor, such as FlashDevelop or FDT. (Because the FDT ActionScript editor is also based on Eclipse, some Flex developers also prefer this as an alternative to Flex Builder.)

A Flash application can be created for the Flash Player, of course, but it can also be deployed for AIR using the core (non-Flex) AIR API available in the Adobe AIR update for Flash CS4 Professional. The core Flash and AIR APIs will be covered in Chapter 4.

Execution

Executing a Flex 3 RIA can be achieved through one of two runtimes: the Adobe Flash Player or Adobe AIR. If the Flex application is executed in the Flash Player runtime, it will be in the AVM2.

If the Flex application is executed in AIR, it will be rendered in the Flash Player VM inside AIR. The Flex AIR application will have access to HTML objects through script bridging, to PDFs rendered through the WebKit browser (providing the user has Acrobat Reader 8.1 or higher installed separately), to data in the SQLite database, and to the system functionality through the Flash and Flex AIR APIs.

Communication

Communication involves the actual exchange of data between client and server. The client runtime can accept data from the server in a variety of formats, and establishes a communication with the server using a number of different protocols.

The runtime can establish a connection to the server over HTTP or HTTPS, which is more common with server applications returning string or XML-based data. The runtime can also create a persistent binary or XML socket connection for the return of binary or XML data, or establish a streaming RTMP or RTMPE connection for AMF data transfer from a data services tier or media and data streamed to and from the Flash Media Server.

Infrastructure

Infrastructure is considered to be any server-side technology that lends support to the client application. This can use a number of different technologies, depending on application requirements, such as the ColdFusion Server, LiveCycle Data Services, Flash Media Server, server-side applications, or Web Services.

Future Additions to the Flex Ecosystem

At the time of this chapter's writing, here some of the up-and-coming releases that will soon be added to the Adobe ecosystem of technologies.

❑ **Flex 4** (codename "Gumbo"), which will be released in 2009, includes a radical recursive MVC approach to the component architecture, including the new FXG format, MXML improvements, and greater visual support and development options in Flex Builder. Because of certain enhancements to the Flex 4 component set, Flex 4 will only be compatible with Flash Player 10. See `http://opensource.adobe.com/wiki/display/flexsdk/Gumbo` for more information.

❑ **FXG** will be an XML-based graphics interchange format for the Flash platform based on the SVG format. See `http://opensource.adobe.com/wiki/display/flexsdk/FXG+1.0+Specification` for more information on the FXG specification.

❑ **Flash CS4** offers several new authoring features integrated with Flash Player 10 capabilities, including:

  ❑ Object-based animation with inverse kinematics (IK).

  ❑ Native 3D animation on the timeline, and a complex motion editor similar to the graphical controls in After Effects.

  ❑ New XFL file support, which allows Flash source documents to be saved as ZIP archives with all source file metadata encoded in XML files, which can be dynamically read by a Flash, Flex, or AIR application.

  ❑ Native authoring for AIR applications without requiring an extension.

  ❑ Adobe Pixel Bender authoring and filter integration support.

❑ **Flash Catalyst** is intended to be a boundary-crossing design and development tool that will allow static proofs to be turned into fully functional Flex component UIs, ready to be wired up with application functionality and business logic in Flex Builder. See `http://labs.adobe.com/technologies/flashcatalyst` for more information.

❑ **Adobe Flash Collaboration Service SDK** (AFCS), formerly codenamed "CoCoMo," will be a Flash-based Web Services platform for development of real-time collaboration and social media applications to be used in conjunction with Acrobat.com Document Services APIs, built upon the next generation of Adobe Acrobat Connect, which is currently available in beta as Adobe ConnectNow. It will make collaboration components such as those used in ConnectNow available for the first time to developers, allowing for the rapid creation of collaboration-based Flex applications with whiteboarding, videoconferencing and chat, to name a few. See `http://labs .adobe.com/technologies/afcs` for more information.

❑ **Pacifica** will be a product similar to AFCS, only it will enable real-time collaboration via P2P communications with the new RTMFP protocol, allowing for high-quality voice-over-IP (VOIP) in Flash and AIR, without depending on the ConnectNow infrastructure. Pacifica will likely compete with existing VOIP-for-Flash technologies such as Ribbit. See `http://pac.ifica.net` for more information.

❑ **Stratus** will be a free RTMFP client connector service that matches RTMFP end-point (Flash Player client) peer IDs using the new peer-to-peer capabilities of the Flash Player, without requiring the use of Flash Media Server to make the introductory handshake. See `http://labs.adobe.com/ technologies/stratus` for more information.

❑ **Adobe Wave** will be an AIR framework and Hosted Service for creating opt-in desktop notifications from the system dock or task bar.

❑ **Alchemy** is a C++ to AS3 bytecode converter, which allows users to compile C and C++ code that is targeted to run on the ActionScript Virtual Machine (AVM2). This will allow C and C++ code libraries to be used natively in ActionScript or Flex applications. See `http://labs.adobe.com/ wiki/index.php/Wave` for more information.

Summary

This chapter introduced a major concept in understanding Flex: the Flash platform and the Flex ecosystem — what these are, what technologies they comprise, and how they can be used with other parts of the system. You learned how the Flex ecosystem is divided into runtimes, programming languages, dev tools, frameworks and APIs, data communications, and servers. You also got an in-depth look at how all the parts fit together in a typical development process. And finally, you got a look at some of the technologies coming up for the Flex ecosystem.

3

ActionScript 3.0 Fundamentals

In the previous chapter, you saw how Flex is a development toolkit, a development framework, an IDE, and a way of architecting rich Internet applications targeted at the Flash platform. The Flex framework is built upon the Flash Player APIs, which are in turn built upon the ActionScript 3.0 language. ActionScript 3.0 is an imperative, true inheritance-based, strongly typed object-oriented (OOP) language that conforms to the ECMA-262 Edition 4 (or ES4) draft standard (www.ecmascript.org/es4/spec/overview.pdf).

This chapter takes a condensed look at the following aspects of the ActionScript language:

- ❏ Core language concepts
- ❏ Control structures
- ❏ Data types
- ❏ Object-oriented programming
- ❏ ActionScript 3.0 best practices

Core Language Concepts

To begin describing a language and expose its methodologies, one must begin with a discussion of three core concepts:

- ❏ Basic syntax
- ❏ Reserved keywords
- ❏ Variables and data types

Basic Syntax

The following syntax defines the way that ActionScript is written:

❑ **Type declaration** — All variables and properties are usually typed, identified by a colon (:) after the identifier, followed by the data type or class object:

```
var myVar:Number;
```

❑ **Case sensitivity** — Identifiers of the same name but of different case are considered to be different. For example, the two following variables are considered to be different properties:

```
var myVar:String;
var myvar:String;
```

❑ **Dot syntax** — When properties and methods are accessed, inheritance, display object, and XML parent/child hierarchies are all identified with the dot (.) syntax. For example, we know by looking at this code that myVar is a property of myClass:

```
var myClass:SomeClass = new SomeClass();
myClass.myProp = "hello";
```

Slash syntax, which was a part of earlier versions of ActionScript, is no longer supported.

❑ **Comments** — Can be single line comments (//) or block comments (/* */):

```
var myVar:int = 2; // this is an integer
/* this code is not in use
var myVar2:int = 3; */
```

Comments which begin with /** are like block comments, only they can be picked up by the ASDoc tool to create online documentation. Rich text can also be used and recognized by the ASDoc tool. See Chapter 68, "Project Documenting With ASDoc," for details.

```
/**
 * <p>This is internal documentation</p>
 */
```

❑ **Parentheses** — Are used to reorganize the order of an expression from operator precedence to user precedence:

```
trace(4 + 5 * 2);// returns 14
trace((4 + 5) * 2);// returns 18
```

To evaluate a series of expressions and return the last one:

```
var a:int = 4;
var b:int = 5;
trace((a++, b++, a+b)); // returns 11
```

Or to define the parameters or arguments of a function:

```
trace("hello world!"); // returns hello world
```

Reserved Keywords

With every language, there are certain keywords that are either reserved and cannot be used, or are keywords that mean something in a specific context. The following lists both the reserved and special context keywords. It is good practice to not use these keywords in your code:

as	final	namespace	switch
break	finally	native	this
case	for	native	throw
catch	function	new	to
class	get	null	try
const	if	override	typeof
continue	implements	package	use
default	import	private	var
delete	in	protected	void
do	include	public	while
dynamic	instanceof	return	with
each	interface	set	false
else	internal	static	true
extends	is	super	

The following keywords are considered to be reserved for future use. It is recommended that you not use these words in your code either:

abstract	double	long	transient
boolean	enum	prototype	type
byte	export	short	virtual
cast	float	synchronized	volatile
char	goto	throws	
debugger	intrinsic	to	

Variables and Data types

A variable is, at its most basic level, a data container declaration. Since ActionScript is a typed language, all variables must have a type declaration, that is, associated with a "kind" of information, whether it be a number, a string of characters, or others:

```
var myVar:Number;
```

This declares the variable, or "data container" myVar as being able to store numbers, or said another way, information of the "Number" data type.

Although all variables must have a type declaration, that does not mean that all variables must be strongly typed. Variables can also be declared as untyped by omitting the typing or by using the asterisk (*) notation:

```
var myNum:Number; // strongly typed
var myVar;        // untyped
var myVar:*;      // untyped
```

Loose typing (i.e., not declaring the data type of a variable) is available as an option if strict type checking (i.e., strict mode) is disabled in the compiler settings. As a best practice, it is recommended to strongly type variables as a way of avoiding compiler and runtime errors through mismatched types, and to speed up application efficiency.

Control Structures

There are two main types of logic or control structures in ActionScript: conditional statements and loops.

Conditional Statements

Conditionals can be written using three different statements:

❑   The if/if..else/if..else if statements (which could be called the if[..else [if]] statement group for short)

❑   The switch statement

❑   The conditional operator (?:)

The if[..else [if]] Statement

This statement allows a block of code to execute depending on whether the initial conditions exist, and if not (else), the second block of code runs. Alternately, the second conditional can be an else if statement, continuing the chain of inquiry. This "compound conditional" statement can be used in the following ways:

```
if (x < 5){
    trace("x is smaller than 5");
}
```

You can also add an `else` conditional to make it an `if..else` statement:

```
if (x < 5){
    trace("x is smaller than 5");
} else {
    trace("x is larger than 4");
}
```

You can also add an `else if` conditional to make it an `if..else if` statement:

```
if (x < 5){
    trace("x is smaller than 5");
} else if (x > 9){
    trace("x is larger than 9");
} else {
    trace("x is between 5 and 9");
}
```

The `else if` statements can even be chained together to achieve a desired control structure:

```
if (x < 5){
    trace("x is smaller than 5");
} else if (x > 9){
    trace("x is larger than 9");
} else if (x == 7){
    trace("x is 7");
} else {
    trace("x is between 5 and 9, but not 7");
}
```

If you anticipate needing many `else if` statements in a conditional, you may want to look at more efficient control structures such the switch statement, or even using regular expressions, which is covered in Chapter 31, "Formatters and Validators."

The switch Statement

The `switch` statement is useful if you have several values to be compared with the same expression, and can serve as shorthand for a long series of `if..else if` statements:

```
switch(productTypeNum)
{
case 0:
        trace("shoes");
        break;
case 1:
case 2:
        trace("scooter or bike");
        break;
case 3:
        trace("skateboard");
        break;
default:
        trace("no product selected");
}
```

In this example, the `switch` statement first checks equality (==) between the expression (`productTypeNum`) and the case clause 0; if the result is true, it executes the code. The `break` statement prevents a fall-through to the next `case` expression. In some situations, you may want a fall-through, in which case you would simply omit the `break` statement, as in the `case 1:` and `case 2:` statements in the preceding example. A `default` statement is akin to using `else` at the end of an `if` statement, and is executed if none of the case expressions in the `switch` statement evaluate.

The Conditional Operator

The conditional operator (`?:`) is a shorthand form of conditional expression, used to evaluate conditional expressions on one line of code in the following syntax:

```
expression1 ? expression2 : expression3
```

where `expression2` is called if `expression1` is true, and `expression3` is called if `expression1` is not true. Expressions using the conditional operator are used in the following fashion:

```
var greetingMsg:String = (isAdmin) ? "Hello Admin" : "Hello User";
```

Loops

A loop could be defined as an iterative statement, where a block of code repeats depending on a series of initially defined parameters.

The for Statement

The `for` statement could be summarized as being composed of four parts:

```
for ([initialization];[conditional];[iteration])
{
[statement body]
}
```

And that is: the initialization statement, the conditional statement, the iteration statement, and the statement body. The following `for` loop statement will run a block of code 10 times:

```
for (var i:int = 0; i < 10; i++) {
    trace('Current value of i is: ' + i);
}
```

This statement will initialize the counter for the loop at zero (`var i:int = 0`), and increment the iterator variable by one each time (`i++`), running the block of code in curly braces until the conditional (`i < 10`) is no longer true.

The while/do..while Statements

The `while` statement is like a simpler version of a loop, where the initialization statement is declared outside the loop statement, and the iterator variable is incremented within the statement body:

```
[initialization]
while ([conditional])
```

```
{
[iteration]
}
```

As in the following example:

```
var i:int = 0;
while (i < 10)
{
    trace(i);
    i++;
}
// result: 1,2,3…10
```

Most times it is a good idea to place your iterator statement at the end of the statement body, although the while loop has the advantage of being able to iterate at any place in the statement body. The drawback of the while statement is that it is easier to inadvertently write infinite loops, since the for statement requires an iterator statement for compilation, but the while statement does not.

The do..while statement is like the while statement, only the conditional is checked at the end of the statement body, guaranteeing that the statement body will execute at least once:

```
var i:int = 10;
do
{
    trace(i);
    i++;
} while (i < 10);
// result: 10
```

Other control structures involving introspecting (or "looking into") objects with the use of an iteration statement will be covered in the "Introspection" section later in this chapter.

Using Classes and Data types

Value Types

There are three categories of native data types in ActionScript: primitive, special and complex data types.

Primitive data types are:

- ❏ Boolean
- ❏ Number
- ❏ int
- ❏ uint
- ❏ String

And special data types are:

- ❏ Null
- ❏ void

The Boolean data type can have one of two values, `true` or `false`, which can also be cast from values 1 and 0. The Null data type, containing only the value `null`, is the default value for all complex objects. Primitive data types cannot have the value `null`, with exception to `String`. The `void` data type, containing only the value `undefined`, is the default value for all untyped objects, and it is used mostly as a return type annotation for method declarations.

Complex data types are:

- ❏ Object
- ❏ Array
- ❏ Date
- ❏ Error
- ❏ Function
- ❏ RegExp
- ❏ XML
- ❏ XMLList

Numbers

Number data types in ActionScript are `Number`, `int`, and `uint`, which represent floating point numbers, integers, and unsigned integers, respectively.

The maximum and minimum values that the `Number` type can represent are stored in static properties of the `Number` class called `Number.MAX_VALUE` and `Number.MIN_VALUE`, respectively.

The NaN (Not a Number) value is used as the default for `Number` variables, and to represent results that should return a number but don't, such as the square root of a negative number.

```
var a:Number = Math.sqrt(-1);
trace(a);
// result: NaN
```

The `Infinity` and `-Infinity` values are also used to represent a divide-by-zero operation:

```
var a:Number = 1/0;
trace(a);
// result: Infinity
```

The `Math` class in ActionScript contains methods allowing for many mathematical operations beyond the base arithmetic operators (`-`, `+`, `*`, `/`).

Strings

The String data type represents a sequence of 16-bit characters, internally stored as Unicode UTF-16. An undefined string has a value of null, which is not the same as an empty string (" ").

Three basic operators allow for the creation and manipulation of strings:

❑   The string delimiter (") defines string values:

```
var str:String = "hello";
```

❑   The concatenation operator (+) adds string values or string variables:

```
var str1:String = "hello";
var str2:String = " wor" + "ld";
var str3:String = str1 + str2
trace(str3);// returns: hello world
```

❑   The concatenation assignment (+=) adds the value of one string to itself plus another:

```
var str:String = "hello";
str += " world";
trace(str); // returns: hello world
```

The String class contains several methods for character manipulation, as shown in the following table:

Method	Description
charAt()	Returns the character in the position specified by the index parameter
charCodeAt()	Returns the numeric Unicode character code of the character at the specified index
fromCharCode()	Returns a string comprising the characters represented by the Unicode character codes in the parameters
indexOf()	Searches the string and returns the position of the first occurrence of the parameter found at or after the starting index within the calling string
lastIndexOf()	Searches the string and returns the position of the last occurrence of the parameter found at or after the starting index within the calling string
localeCompare()	Compares the sort order of two or more strings and returns the result of the comparison as an integer
match()	Matches the specified pattern against the string
replace()	Matches the specified pattern against the string and returns a new string in which the first match of pattern is replaced with the content specified by the second parameter
search()	Searches for the specified pattern and returns the index of the first matching substring

Continued

Continued

Method	Description
slice()	Returns a string that includes the startIndex character and all characters up to, but not including, the endIndex character
split()	Splits a String object into an array of substrings
substr()	Returns a substring consisting of the characters that start at the specified startIndex and with a length specified by the length parameter
substring()	Returns a string consisting of the character specified by startIndex and all characters up to endIndex - 1
toLowerCase() toUpperCase()	Returns a copy of this string, with all uppercase characters converted to lowercase, or all lowercase characters converted to uppercase

Arrays

The Array class lets you create and manipulate arrays. The Array is a complex data type, representing an untyped, zero-index list of elements, defined by the array access operator ([ ]). Elements of an Array can be of any class, and multiple class/data types can be present in the same array. Arrays are considered to be dynamic, in that the size and number of elements in the array can be manipulated at runtime.

Arrays can be declared in three different ways:

1.   Using the constructor function, and assigning values by individual element:

```
var myArray:Array = new Array();
myArray[0] = true;
myArray[1] = 43;
myArray[2] = "hello";
```

2.   Using the constructor function, and assigning values with an array literal:

```
var myArray:Array = new Array([true,43,"hello"]);
```

3.   Using simply an array literal, as shorthand:

```
var myArray:Array = [true,43,"hello"];
```

You can also instantiate an Array object with the array literal syntax for short:

```
var arr:Array = [];
```

Associative arrays can be created by using a string as a key instead of an unsigned integer in the array access operator:

```
var myArray:Array = new Array();
myArray["key1"] = true;
```

Although in this case you are actually not creating an array element; what you are really doing is creating a dynamic property on the `Array` class instance, for the array access operator is also used to declare object properties on a dynamic class. Because of the lack of typing on arrays in Flash Player 9, it is considered a best practice to create associative arrays by using the `Object` class. If you need a true key-based list, it is recommended that you use the `Dictionary` class. See Chapter 30, "Working with Data," for more information on associative arrays and the `Dictionary` class. Strong typing for arrays is possible in Flash Player 10 using Vector postfix type syntax. See "Vectors" later in this chapter for details.

Simple two-dimensional arrays can be created by combining the arrays:

```
var arr0:Array = [1,2,3];
var arr1:Array = [2,3,4];
var arr2:Array = [5,6,7];
var multiArray:Array = [arr0, arr1, arr2];
trace(multiArray[0][2])// array 0, index 2
// result: 3
```

Declaring multidimensional arrays of complex data is also possible using the array syntax:

```
var multiArray:Array = new Array();
multiArray[0] = new Array();
multiArray[0][2] = new Array();
multiArray[0][2][1] = new Array();
multiArray[0][2][1][0] = new Array();
multiArray[0][2][1][0][2] = new Array();
multiArray[0][2][1][0][2][3] = "multidimensional array";
trace(multiArray[0][2][1][0][2][3]);
// result: multidimensional array
```

Unlike in some other languages, a multidimensional array in ActionScript is not considered to be a matrix construct. ActionScript has a `Matrix` class in the `flash.geom` package specifically for this purpose. See Chapter 4, "Using ActionScript 3.0," for more details on this class package.

Because an `Array` is a complex primitive inherited directly from `Object`, and ActionScript 3.0 does not have watch points like ActionScript 2.0 did, using data binding and change watchers with `Array` is not possible. If you require this functionality, it is recommended that you use the `ArrayCollection` class instead, which is a member of the Flex framework, also covered in Chapter 11, "Using Data Binding and Events."

The `Array` class contains several methods for element manipulation, as shown in the following table:

Method	Description
`every()`	Executes a test function on each item in the array until an item is reached that returns `false` for the specified function
`filter()`	Executes a test function on each item in the array and constructs a new array for all items that return true for the specified function, similarly to the `String.replace()` method
`forEach()`	Executes a code block or function on each item in the array

Continued

Continued

Method	Description
indexOf() lastIndexOf()	Searches for an item in an array by using strict equality (===) and returns the index position of the item
join()	Converts the elements in an array to strings, inserts the specified separator between the elements, concatenates them, and returns the resulting string
map()	Executes a code block or function on each item in an array, and constructs a new array of items corresponding to the results of the function on each item in the original array; considered to be a type of clone() method for the Array class
pop()	Removes the last element from an array and returns the value of that element
push()	Adds one or more elements to the end of an array and returns the new length of the array
reverse()	Reverses the array in place
shift()	Removes the first element from an array and returns that element
slice()	Returns a new array that consists of a range of elements from the original array, without modifying the original array
some()	Executes a test function on each item in the array until an item is reached that returns true
sort() sortOn()	Returns a substring consisting of the characters that start at the specified startIndex and with a length specified by the length parameter
splice()	Adds elements to and removes elements from an array
unshift()	Adds one or more elements to the beginning of an array and returns the new length of the array

Vectors

New to ActionScript 3.0 in Flash Player 10 is the Vector class, which is a typed array having a syntax similar to vectors in other languages, such as C++ and Java, which run at a much greater efficiency than Arrays. A vector is by definition also a sparse array, which means that it can only contain elements that are defined to be all of the same data type, and that type is declared at the time of object instantiation by using postfix type parameter syntax(. <>), which is also new to ActionScript 3. A vector is also a dense array, meaning that all elements must have a value. If empty, the value must be null.

Optionally, you can declare the vector to be a static array (fixed-size), by specifying the number of elements in the first parameter of the constructor, and assigning a Boolean value of `true` to the second parameter of the constructor:

```
// creating a vector that contains a fixed number of 7 String elements
var daysOfTheWeek:Vector.<String> = new Vector.<String>(7, true);
daysOfTheWeek[0] = "Monday";
daysOfTheWeek[1] = "Tuesday";
daysOfTheWeek[2] = "Wednesday";
daysOfTheWeek[3] = "Thursday";
daysOfTheWeek[4] = "Friday";
daysOfTheWeek[5] = "Saturday";
daysOfTheWeek[6] = "Sunday";
```

The `Vector` class has much the same methods as the `Array` class.

Objects

The `Object` class is considered to be at the top of the inheritance chain for all complex objects, including other native complex data types. The `Object` class is a dynamic class, meaning that properties may be declared on instances at runtime.

Object instances can be declared in three different ways, similar to the `Array` class:

1.   Using the constructor function, and assigning values by individual element:

```
var myObj:Object = new Object();
myObj.var1 = true;
myObj.var2 = 43;
myObj.var3 = "hello";
```

2.   Using the constructor function, and assigning values with an object literal:

```
var myObj:Object = new Object({var1:true, var2:43, var3:"hello"});
```

Note that using this syntax in the default *strict mode* will cause a compile error, as the `Object` constructor does not accept arguments unless the compiler is in *standard mode*.

3.   Using simply an array literal, as shorthand:

```
var myObj:Object = {var1:true, var2:43, var3:"hello"};
```

You can also instantiate an `Object` object with the object literal syntax for short:

```
var abj:Object = {};
```

Because `Object` is the top class in the inheritance chain in ActionScript, it has but a small number of methods. For more information on using objects as an associative array, see Chapter 30.

Casting

Casting is the process of converting or transforming one data type or class into another. Type conversions can be either implicit or explicit.

Implicit Casting

Implicit casting relies on type coercion, that is, the ability for a class to be upcast (cast to a superclass or type) or downcast (cast to a subclass or type) by treating one class object the same as another class object:

```
// SomeClass is a subclass of Object
var obj:Object = new Object();
var cls:SomeClass = new SomeClass();
cls = obj;
```

Implicit casting can generate a type mismatch error in strict mode if the coercion fails.

Explicit Casting

Explicit casting uses type conversion as opposed to type coercion and is a much safer form of casting. Explicit casting uses the following syntax:

```
type(expression)
```

The following example casts a string to an integer:

```
var product:String = "35";
var prodNum:int = int(product);
```

If we attempted to use type coercion as in the previous example, (that is, `prodNum = product`), the casting would fail in strict mode.

The as Operator

The `as` operator will evaluate whether casting of an expression as a certain data type would succeed, and if so, return the original expression. The `as` operation syntax is as follows:

```
expression as type
```

For example, if you want to upcast a Flex component as a generic `DisplayObject`, you might use the following:

```
var parent:DisplayObject = rootApp.parent as DisplayObject;
```

The `as` operation has the same advantage as a cast operation, except that it returns the value `null` if the cast fails, instead of a runtime error. For this reason, using the `as` operator is considered a best practice over straight casting.

Introspection

The following language constructs exist to help in manual type checking and object introspection at runtime:

- ❑   The `in` operator
- ❑   The `is` operator
- ❑   The `instanceof` operator
- ❑   The `typeof` operator
- ❑   The `for..in` operator
- ❑   The `for each..in` operator

The in Operator

This operator evaluates whether a property is a part of an object:

```
var obj:Object = {prop:true};
trace("prop" in obj); // result: true;
```

The is Operator

This operator evaluates whether an object belongs to particular data type or class. One use of this is identifying the subclass of event dispatched to a listener method, which allows the application to reuse the same listener method for different event types, and make the appropriate response based on the specific event subclass being dispatched:

```
private function loadHandler(event:Event):void {
    if(event is IOErrorEvent){
        trace("IO error")
    } else if(event is SecurityErrorEvent){
        trace("Security Error");
    } else if(event is ProgressEvent){
        trace("Loading…");
    }
}
```

The instanceof Operator

The `instanceof` operator functions like the `is` operator, except that it evaluates whether a particular object's prototype chain (which is secondary to the inheritance chain) includes the prototype for that class. This operator is intended for backward compatibility with previous versions of ActionScript, which were prototype-based. And while the `is` operator works for interfaces, the `instanceof` operator does not, because interfaces are not a part of the prototype chain:

```
var mySprite:Sprite = new Sprite();
trace(mySprite instanceof Sprite);          // true
trace(mySprite instanceof DisplayObject);   // true
trace(mySprite instanceof IBitmapDrawable); // false
```

Here you can test this by looking at the preceding code: the `Sprite` class inherits from `DisplayObject`, which implements the `IBitmapDrawable` interface. If you used the `is` operator instead, you would get an equality:

```
trace(mySprite is IBitmapDrawable);          // true
```

Unless you have need to connect with the prototype chain of a class, it is recommended that you use the `is` operator instead of the `instanceof` operator, as use of this operator has been deprecated.

The typeof Operator

This operator evaluates the expression and returns a string specifying the expression's data type, from one of six possible values: `boolean`, `function`, `number`, `object`, `string`, and `xml`. Note that all results are lowercase. If you apply this operator to any class other than the data types previously listed, it will return the string `object`. The `typeof` operator is included for backward compatibility. If you require more specific type or class identification for an object, use the `flash.utils.getQualifiedClass-Name()` method. See Chapter 4 for details.

The for . . in Operator

The `for..in` operator iterates through the dynamic properties of an object or elements in an array. This statement uses the following syntax; note that `iterant` can be untyped:

```
for each (iterant:String in object){
    // statement(s)
}
```

The following example iterates through the values in an object:

```
var myFruit:Object = {apple:2, pear:0, plum:3};
for (var prop:String in myFruit)
{
    trace("I have "+ myFruit [prop]+" "+prop+"s.");
}
// result:
// I have 2 apples.
// I have 0 pears.
// I have 3 plums.
```

You can only iterate through the properties of a dynamic class (i.e., not a sealed class), and even then you can only iterate through the dynamically added properties for that class, not properties defined as part of the class definition (i.e., fixed properties).

The for each . . in Operator

The `for each..in` operator iterates through the items in a collection, whether they be properties in an `Object`, the elements of an `Array`, or the tags in an `XML` or `XMLList` object. This statement uses the following syntax; note that `iterant` can be untyped:

```
for each (iterant in object){
    // statement(s)
}
```

The following example iterates through the values in an array:

```
var myNums:Array = ["one", "two", "three"];
for each (var item:* in myNums)
{
    trace(item);
}
// result:
// one
// two
// three
```

As with the `for each..in` operator, you can only iterate through the properties of a dynamic class (i.e., not a sealed class), and even then you can only iterate through the dynamically added properties for that class, not properties defined as part of the class definition (i.e., fixed properties).

The `for in` and `for each..in` statements are very useful for parsing complex data objects.

Object-Oriented Programming

ActionScript is first and foremost an object-based language. Every distinct language construct or "building block" you create, whether it be a variable, a method, or a class, are all objects. ActionScript is very much like other object-oriented programming (OOP) languages such as Java and C++, with the exception that every object is simply a collection of properties, as opposed to an object being a kind of module defining two kinds of members (property or method).

Another subtle difference between ActionsScript and other languages is that a class in ActionScript is not just an abstract entity; it is actually a class object, represented by its own property data type. In other words, when you write:

```
var myObject:SomeClass = new SomeClass();
```

you are storing a reference to the `SomeClass` class in the `myObject` property, data typed as a `SomeClass` object. Thus, parent-child (compositional) relationships are simple: all objects contain properties, and all objects are properties of some other object. Although a method is defined in the class body in a different way than a variable, it is of the `Function` data type, which means that a function is actually a class object, which can be treated as any other property.

Thus, all classes in ActionScript except the primitive data types owe the origin of their inheritance chain to one of the native complex data types, as listed in the previous "Value Types" section. The `Object` class is considered to be at the top of the inheritance chain for all complex objects, including other native complex data types, and serves as the base class for all other class definitions in ActionScript.

In previous versions of ActionScript, class objects called prototypes are linked together into inheritance structures by way of prototype chains, served as the entire foundation of the inheritance hierarchy. The inheritance chain could also be manipulated at runtime with certain built-in language elements. ActionScript 3.0 classes still have a prototype object to reference the inheritance chain, but it is no longer the dominant construct to establish inheritance. Since the current version of ActionScript is now a true inheritance-based language and not a prototype-based OOP language, certain virtual machine performance improvements and language changes disallow for manipulation of the inheritance hierarchy.

The Class Object

Although the `Object` class is the base class for all classes, all user-defined class definitions are of the top-level `Class` class, which is a subclass of `Object` and has no distinct properties or methods of its own, except those inherited from `Object`. In most situations, you will never need to refer to the `Class` object, but it is useful in certain advanced techniques, such as assigning an instance to a particular class at runtime:

```
var myClass:Class = SomeUserClass;
trace(getQualifiedClassName(myClass));
// result: SomeUserClass
```

Packages and Classes

A package is considered to be the location of a class, in a folder structure containing the actual class file, starting from a codebase root. For instance, if the root of the project source were the `src/` folder, the `com.foo.utils` package would be located in the `src/com/foo/utils/` folder. A class is considered to be a template or abstraction for a kind of object. An object belonging to a type of class is called a *class instance*, and the process of creating objects from classes is called *instantiation*.

In a text file defining a class, the package comes first, followed by any import statements, followed by the class definition containing the class keyword. As a convention and best practices, all classes are named in capitalized camel-case (i.e., `FooClass`):

```
package com.foo
{
    public class FooClass
    {

    }
}
```

To use a class inside a particular package, you need to use the import directive to list the class or class package. The import directive opens a public namespace reference for use in the current scope (i.e., class body) and all nested scopes (i.e., method bodies), provided the class's access attributes can be referenced from the current scope (see the following). To use a property of `FooClass` from another class, that class would need to reference that class through the following import directive:

```
import com.foo.FooClass
```

You can also create a public namespace reference to a package by using a wildcard:

```
import com.foo.*
```

Although you can only use wildcards in `import` statements and only for the immediate package scope. In other words, you could not access the `com.foo.utils.SomeFoo` class using:

```
import com.foo.*
```

but you could if you declared:

```
import com.foo.utils.*
```

Class Attributes

ActionScript 3.0 allows for four different types of class attributes:

❑ The `internal` class attribute is the default for undeclared class attributes, and allows the class to be visible to other classes inside the current package.

❑ The `public` class attribute allows the class to be visible to every other class.

❑ The `dynamic` class attribute allows the class to add properties to instance objects at runtime.

❑ The `final` class attribute disallows the class from being subclassed. If another class attempts to subclass this class, a compiler error will occur.

These attribute can be used in combination with others to achieve the desired behavior. For example, you could write:

```
package com.foo
{
    public dynamic final class FooClass
    {

    }
}
```

This would create a dynamic class that can be publicly referenced and cannot be subclassed.

There is no such thing as a `static` *class attribute in ActionScript 3.0, which was present in ActionScript 2.0.* `static` *class members are defined individually in ActionScript 3.0. See the upcoming section "Static versus Instance Members."*

Class Members

A class property or method is called a *class member*. A variable is another word for a class property, although it usually refers to a property with a constrained scope such as a loop or a method. As a convention and best practices, all class members are named in uncapitalized camel-case (i.e., `myCountProp`).

Properties and Methods

A function is usually another word for a class method, although in the context of ActionScript 3.0 the term *function* actually refers to a property whose data type is `Function`. There are three ways to declare a function in ActionScript 3.0:

❑ As a class method using an access modifier:

```
public function someMethod(argument:SomeClass):returnType { … }
```

❏ As a function literal, otherwise known as an anonymous function:

```
someProp = function(argument:SomeClass):returnType { … };
```

A function literal has the advantage of being handy for dynamic or runtime method construction, but has the disadvantage of not being a referenced function. So, defining function literals as event listeners, for example, prevents dereferencing and subsequent cleanup by the garbage collector.

❏ Nested within another function:

```
public function nestedFunction():void
{
    function internalFunction():String
    {
        return "internal function";

    }
    trace(internalFunction());
}
```

The internally nested function is available only within its parent function unless a reference to the internal function is passed externally, either via a class property or return value.

Method Parameters

ActionScript 3.0 allows you to define a default value for a parameter by writing the parameter type as an expression. In this example, the first argument requires a value, while the second and third arguments can be omitted:

```
function objPosition(x:int, y:int = 3, z:int = 5):void
{
    trace(x, y, z);
}
objPosition(1); // result: 1 3 5
```

A method in ActionScript 3.0 may also accept a variable number of arguments, using a method defined with the …(rest) parameter. This parameter allows you to specify an array as a parameter that accepts any number of comma-delimited arguments. The variable name of the array can be any unreserved word:

```
function objValuesArray(… args):void
{
    trace(args);
}
objValuesArray(1,2,3); // result: 1, 2, 3
```

Method overloading is not allowed in ActionScript 3.0, although it can be simulated with a combination of the …(rest) parameter and some if statements, using the is operator.

Constructor Methods

Class constructor methods can only be declared as public and never take a return data type. Private constructors were allowed in ActionScript 2.0, but were left out in ActionScript 3.0 because of the draft nature of the ES4 specification. If a constructor is not defined in the class body, an empty class method will be automatically created by the compiler:

```
package com.foo
{
    public dynamic final class FooClass
    {
        public function FooClass()
        {
            // something
        }
    }
}
```

Access Modifiers

ActionScript 3.0 allows for the following four different access modifiers, or access specifier class members (i.e., properties or methods), which determines their visibility to other references:

❑ The `public` attribute allows any reference visible to the class to access the class member.

❑ The `private` attribute makes the member visible only to other members internally in that class. In ActionScript 2.0, private access could be circumvented at runtime using the bracket operator. This is no longer possible for a nondynamic class in ActionScript 3.0 due to sealed classes. Using the bracket (`[]`) operator in ActionScript 3.0 (i.e., `myClass["someProp"]`) will always result in a runtime error. Using the dot (`.`) operator, (i.e., `myClass.someProp`) will likewise result in a compile-time error in strict mode, and a runtime error in standard mode. Private dynamic class members will generally return `undefined` instead of generating an error, unless the dot operator is used in strict mode, in which case a compiler error will result.

❑ The `protected` attribute makes the class member visible to any references in the same class and other subclasses. This is useful for hiding members from outside the inheritance chain.

❑ The `internal` attribute makes a class member visible to any reference within the same package. This is the default attribute, meaning an absence of an attribute declaration, or that which does not contain one of the three modifiers described earlier (or a custom namespace) defaults the access modifier to `internal`. Despite being the default, the purpose of this modifier is to allow for explicit declaration of the intent that the member be accessed in the same namespace.

Namespaces

A namespace is essentially a custom access modifier, allowing for more precise control over which code has access to certain parts of other code.

One use case in point is the Flex framework, which contains millions of lines of code. In any framework of that size, there will be the need for class members to access each other across packages, but for those class members to be considered internal to the framework. Because there are multiple packages involved in the Flex framework, simply using the `internal` access specifier is not adequate. Which is why the `mx_internal` namespace was created. Here's a snippet of that declaration from the Flex framework source code:

```
package mx.core
{
```

```
public namespace mx_internal =
    "http://www.adobe.com/2006/flex/mx/internal";
}
```

If you dig through the Flex framework code, you will notice that the namespace is defined in its own file, named the same as the namespace mx_internal. This is a common occurrence for namespace declarations and is considered a best practice.

The mx_internal.as *file is located in the Flex SDK under* {Flex Builder program folder}/ sdks/{sdk version number}/frameworks/projects/framework/src/mx/core/.

To create your own custom namespace, follow these steps:

1. Define the namespace within a package or class. As a best practice, namespaces are named as lowercase with underscore separators (i.e., foo_reserved), in their own separate file, with the same name as the namespace.

2. Give it an optional Uniform Resource Identifier (URI) as a unique identifier. A URI is usually a fictional URL using the same domain name as the company issuing it.

3. Define an access specifier for the namespace.

These steps have been used to create the following namespace in the foo_reserved.as file:

```
package com.foo
{
    public namespace foo_reserved = "http://www.foocompany.com/foo/reserved";
}
```

To apply the namespace, simply import it for use in that class:

```
package com.foo
{
    import com.foo.foo_reserved;

    public class FooClass
    {
        foo_reserved var reservedVar:int;

        foo_reserved function reservedMethod():void
        {
            trace("reserved state achieved");
        }
    }
}
```

To use a class member defined as controlled by the namespace, employ the use keyword, followed by the namespace name:

```
use namespace foo_reserved;
trace(reservedMethod());
```

Static versus Instance Members

Static properties and methods, otherwise known as class properties and methods, are declared with the static keyword, and define properties and methods that are accessed on the class itself, not on an instance of a class. The static keyword comes after the access modifier in the member declaration:

```
package com.foo
{
    public class FooClass
    {
        public static var statusCount:int = 0;

        public function FooClass(){}

        public static function doCount():void
        {
            trace("Count done.");
        }
    }
}

// usage:
import com.foo.FooClass;
trace(FooClass.statusCount); // result: 0
FooClass.doCount(); // result: Count done.
```

Constants

To create a constant in ActionScript, which is to say a property with a fixed value defined in the class definition, you use the const keyword. By convention, constants in ActionScript use all capital letters, with words separated by the underscores. You can create a static constant, similar to properties on the Math class, by using the static keyword:

```
package com.foo
{
    public class FooClass
    {
        public const MAXIMUM:int = 50;
        public static const ERROR_MSG:String = "An error.";
    }
}
```

Getters and Setters

A *getter* is a special kind of function that returns a value when used like a property, and a *setter* is a special function that accepts the input of a value when set like a property. This allows property calls to function as methods, and allows you to create a public interface for private properties. A getter method is defined using the get keyword, and a setter method is defined using the set keyword. To create a read/write "property," create a separate get and set for the same function name.

```
package com.foo
{
    public class FooClass
```

```
    {
        private var _size:Number;

        public function FooClass()

        public function get size():Number
        {
            return _size;
        }

        public function set size(s:Number):void
        {
            _size = s;
        }
    }
}

// usage
var foo:FooClass = new FooClass();
foo.size = 10; // set _size
trace(foo.size) // get _size
```

Interfaces and Inheritance

Class inheritance is the process of code reuse that enables functionality from one class to extend to a descendant, or child class, called a *subclass*. The class lending its code to the subclass is called the *base* or *superclass*. A subclass is defined by using the extends keyword.

An interface is a template defining class members that must be present in the class definition. Interfaces can be subclassed using the same extends keyword as classes. Although it is possible to implement multiple interfaces on a class, multiple inheritance is not allowed in ActionScript 3.0.

To call the superclass's constructor function, call the super() method from the constructor of a subclass. Static properties cannot be inherited. To redefine an existing inherited class member, use the override keyword before any access modifiers:

```
public interface IFooAnimal
{
    function size():Number;
}

public class FooAnimal implements IFooAnimal
{

    public function size():Number
    {
        return NaN;
    }
}

public class FooGlob extends FooAnimal
{
```

```
        public var squishiness:String = "very squishy";

        public function FooGlob()
        {
            super();
        }

        override public function size():Number
        {
            return 20;
        }
    }

    public class FooJabberwok extends fooAnimal
    {
        public var fearsomeness:String = "very fearsome";

        public function FooJabberwok()
        {
            super();
        }

        override public function size():Number
        {
            return 50;
        }
    }

    // usage:

    var glob:FooGlob = new fooGlob();
    trace("The glob's "+glob.squishiness+" size is "+glob.size()+".");
    // returns: The glob's very squishy size is 20.

    var jabberwok:FooJabberwok = new fooJabberwok();
    trace("The jabberwok's "+jabberwok.fearsomeness+" size is "+jabberwok.size()+".");
    // returns: The jabberwok's very fearsome size is 50.
```

Summary

This chapter has covered a brief overview of the ActionScript 3.0 language. For more in-depth information on the specifics of various aspects of the ActionScript language, consult the Adobe Flex ActionScript 3.0 reference, either online (http://livedocs.adobe.com/flex/3/langref) or included with your Flex Builder or Flex SDK installation.

In the next chapter, you'll learn some specifics about using ActionScript 3.0 within the context of the classes and functionality in the Flash Player and AIR.

4

Using ActionScript 3.0

In Chapter 3, "ActionScript 3.0 Fundamentals," you saw how the core ActionScript 3.0 language works, including some core language APIs. This chapter will expand on this by exploring the Flash APIs underlying the Flex framework.

To find out how to build an ActionScript application in Flex Builder, see Chapter 6, "Using Flex Builder."

The Flash Platform Framework

In the Flash platform, or one could say the "Flex ecosystem" as was coined previously, several blocks of APIs, classes, packages, and frameworks distinguish how one builds Flash-based rich Internet application (RIA) applications (see Figure 4-1).

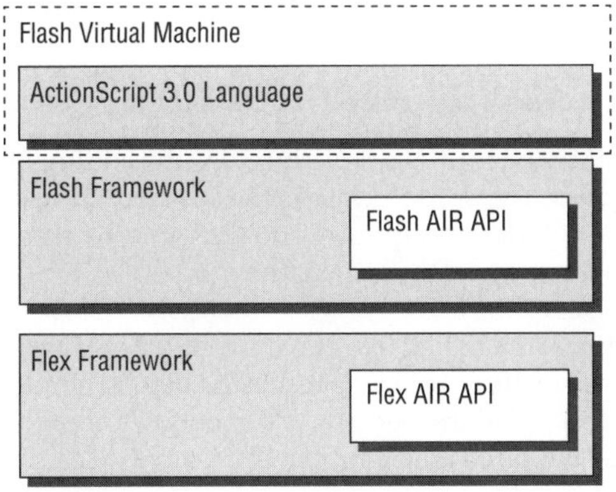

Figure 4-1

1. First, there are the core ActionScript 3.0 language elements, constructs, and classes. These classes reside at something Adobe calls the *top level*, or *base*, and are called the *top-level classes*. ActionScript 3.0 elements and top-level classes reside in the Flash Player or Tamarin virtual machine.

2. Next, there are the Flash APIs belonging to the `flash.*` package. All these classes could actually be considered a framework of their own, although no one really calls it that. Although the hooks into the display and event Document Object Model (DOM) reside in the Flash Player, the classes themselves reside in the `playerglobal.swc` precompiled "framework," which must be used by any Flash or Flex compiler. Said another way, the actual classes for the top-level properties and methods, and the Flash APIs, are *defined* in the `playerglobal.swc` library, but the system hooks that account for some of their functionality are located in the virtual machine.

   Although you do need to include any custom frameworks in an application build, you will never have to manually include the Flash framework in any application you build, as it is automatically referenced by and is a requirement for the Flex compiler. The Flash framework is considered to be a closed source.

3. A subset of these classes contains the core AIR APIs required to author basic AIR applications with the Flash compiler, or from the Flex compiler not using the Flex framework (such as an ActionScript project, which will be covered in Chapter 6).

4. The Flex framework builds on top of these classes.

5. A subset of the Flex framework builds on top of the Flash AIR classes, and these we call the Flex AIR APIs.

This chapter covers an overview of the Flash and Flash AIR APIs and classes, and how some of the core functionality of the Flash Platform works.

Display Programming

ActionScript 3.0 introduces a different concept and approach to working with objects living on the Flash Player stage. Along with the new class structure, new methods and classes have been created to program how the visual elements of an SWF application are organized and manipulated.

Understanding the Display Architecture

One of the major architectural changes in ActionScript 3.0 is the addition to a non-timeline `MovieClip`-like class called the `Sprite` class. The `Sprite` class is the basic building block of display objects under the assumption that most user interface components do not typically use a timeline. There is a bit that goes on structurally to get that button on the screen, though.

Each ActionScript 3.0 application has a nested tree of parent-child containers in a compositional relationship of objects that are displayed on the screen, one inside the other. The resulting object structure is called the *display list*. The `DisplayObject` defines methods and properties needed by leaf or parent objects on the display list. All classes that can be placed on the display list extend the `DisplayObject` class.

When using the Flex compiler to create ActionScript 3.0 applications, the resulting SWF has a display list built from two basic blocks: a stage object and a main class. The *stage* is the root of the display list.

The main class file's constructor is called and an instance is added to the stage. All display objects and display containers are then attached to the main class's instance, as shown in Figure 4-2.

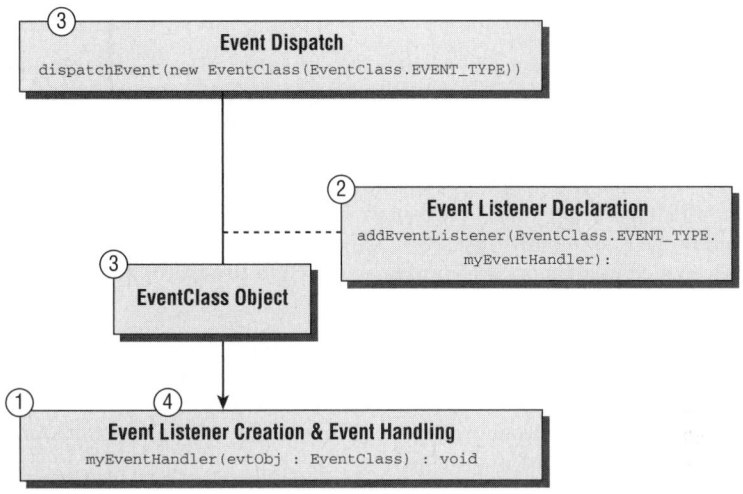

Figure 4-2

The Event Model

In ActionScript 3.0, the event model allows for class objects to communicate with each other without direct method calls, as a form of "communication system" between objects that loosely ties them to each other. The event process in ActionScript is modeled after the Observer design pattern and is based on the Document Object Model (DOM) Level 3 Events Specification, an industry-standard event-handling architecture.

Because this interobject communications process is baked right into the core language capability itself, this adds to the object-oriented nature of the language and facilitates loosely coupled component designs.

Event Classes and Types

The `flash.events.Event` class is the base class for all events in your application. Any time an event occurs and is dispatched in an application, this class or one of its subclasses is implicitly created. It contains properties with information about the event that occurred.

Contained within the event object being dispatched is information about the *type* of event dispatched and the target that dispatched the event. Said another way, the `Event` class has a `type` property that contains information about the specific event occurrence. Event types are defined as constants or fixed strings within the `Event` class.

When you declare an event listener, you call the `addEventListener` method, passing to it a string indicating the type of event and the designated listener function. You can use the event type string directly, but it is a best practice to use the event type constant belonging to the same `Event` class from which the event object will be created.

For example, the `MouseEvent` class, which extends `Event`, includes a few properties such as `stageX` and `stageY`, which are common to all events that have to do with user interaction from the mouse. The `type` property of the `Event` class contains information about the specific mouse interaction that occurred, such as a mouse click or a mouse rollover. When the `MouseEvent.MOUSE_MOVE` event is declared, and the event dispatched, a listener method listening for this event will receive a `MouseEvent` class object in its first parameter, which has a `type` property containing the "click" type string identifier, which is the same as what's stored in the `MouseEvent.MOUSE_MOVE` class constant. The function can then proceed with application logic, which uses the `stageX` and `stageY` properties to, for instance, position a custom cursor image on screen as the user moves the mouse.

Event Process

As illustrated in Figure 4-3, the event process, or the means by which information passes from one class object to another, can be described in four steps:

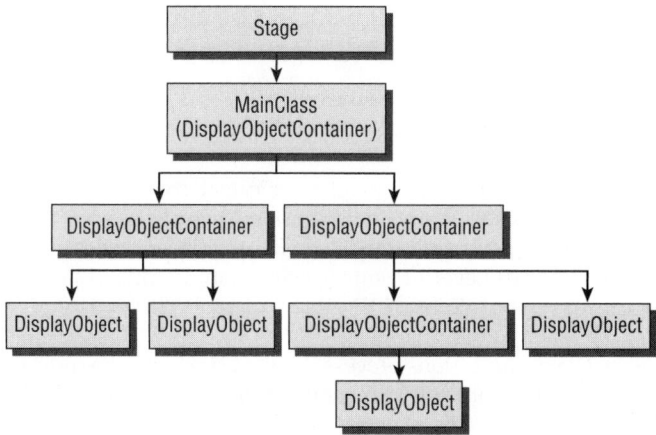

Figure 4-3

1. **Listener creation**

Class methods are declared to receive the event object when it is dispatched. These methods can be called any one of the following interchangeable terms:

- ❏ Listeners
- ❏ Event listeners
- ❏ Listener methods
- ❏ Event handlers
- ❏ Handler methods

The following is an example of an event method for receiving the event from a button click:

```
public function clickHandler(evtObj:Event):void
{
    trace("button clicked");
}
```

The event listener method must have the first parameter declared to receive the event object, and should be typed as an Event class, with no return type.

A best practice for the naming of event listeners is to suffix the method name with the word "handler," although you could also use the word "listener".

2.   Listener declaration

The listener method must then be associated with the object dispatching the event, using the addEventListener method:

```
btnObj.addEventListener(MouseEvent.CLICK, clickHandler);
```

3.   Event dispatch

When an event is triggered by the application as a result of user interaction or in response to an internal occurrence, an event object containing information about the type of event and other specific data about the occurrence is created and "broadcast" or dispatched (see the upcoming section "The EventDispatcher Class" for more information).

In this case, you do not have to code the event dispatching, since the event is triggered by the Flash Player itself. But if you were to manually dispatch a MouseEvent event, you would use the following code:

```
dispatchEvent(new MouseEvent(MouseEvent.CLICK))
```

4.   Event handling

The event handling is the process by which the event listener is called by the event dispatcher. Passing an Event object to the event listener is optional, meaning that your listener method can contain no parameters. Though is it a best practice to at least declare the event parameter in the listener method in case you might need to reference the event object in the function body. This is useful for referencing the target dispatching the event instead of referencing the target directly, in order to create loosely coupled components. More information on using events with Flex components can be found in Chapter 11, "Using Data Binding and Events."

```
public function clickHandler(evtObj:Event):void
{
    trace(evtObj.target.id + " has dispatched a " + evtObj.type + " event.");
}
// returns: Button1 has dispatched a mouseClick event.
```

Event Flow

The event system also allows for event bubbling, which is the propagation of an event in a compositional relationship from parent to child and back in display objects. The flow of an event starts when an object of type Event (or one of its subclasses) is dispatched. It then makes a journey from the root of the display list to the target node, checking for registered listeners. The *target node* is the node where the event originated from (for example, a user clicks a `Button` control named `Button1`). The `Event` object's target node holds a reference to `Button1`. (See the following section for more details on the display list.)

The `Event` object is only created once on every dispatch. During the bubbling and capturing phases, the values on the `Event` object change as it moves up or down the display list. This is much more efficient than creating a new `Event` object for each node.

Event flow consists of the following three phases:

❑ **Capturing phase** — This phase comprises of all the nodes from the root node to the parent of the target node. Once this phase is executed, the Flash Player starting at the root examines each node to see if there is a listener registered to handle the event. If it finds registered listeners, it will set the values of the `Event` object and then call the listener function. The Flash Player stops after it has reached the target node's parent and called the registered event listeners.

❑ **Targeting phase** — This phase consists only of the target node. The Flash Player sets the values on the `Event` object, looks at the target node for any registered event listeners, and then calls those listeners.

❑ **Bubbling phase** — This phase consists of all the nodes from the target node's parent to the root node. It begins at the target node's parent where the Flash Player sets the values on the `Event` object and then calls the event listeners on each of these nodes. The Flash Player will stop after any listeners on the root node are called.

For more information on the event flow and event bubbling, see Chapter 11.

The EventDispatcher Class

The `EventDispatcher` class implements the `IEventDispatcher` interface, and it is the base class for all classes that dispatch events, which include every class that subclasses `DisplayObject`. Since all visually displayed classes extend `DisplayObject`, all UI elements or components can be an event target.

The inheritance model for event dispatching (skipping a few intermediary classes) is:

`IEventDispatcher` ➔ `EventDispatcher` ➔ `DisplayObject` ➔ `Sprite` ➔ `UIComponent Class`

When you are declaring an event listener using the `addEventListener` method, you are using a method from the `EventDispatcher` class that your class has inherited.

If you need to use event dispatching in a custom class that does not inherit from `DisplayObject` (i.e., it is not a display object), you can simply subclass the `EventDispatcher` class. Events and event types listed in the Flash or Flex APIs are already dispatched as a result of user or system interaction. If you wish to manually dispatch a custom event, you use the `dispatchEvent` method.

Although specific discussion of this technique is outside the scope of this book, if extending `EventDispatcher` is not possible because your custom class already extends another class, you can implement the `IEventDispatcher` interface. Simply implement `addEventDispatcher` and other `IEventDispatcher` methods that use `EventDispatcher` through composition as opposed to inheritance.

The Flash Player APIs

The classes included by default in the Flash framework can be divided into several principal class packages, or APIs, which encompass the capabilities of the Flash Player. This will give you an overview of how the capabilities of the Flash Player are structured.

Package	Description
flash. accessibility	Contains classes for supporting accessibility in Flash content and applications.
flash.display	Contains the core classes that the Flash Player uses to build visual displays. See the upcoming section "The Display API" for details.
flash.errors	Contains a set of commonly used error classes.
flash.events	Supports the DOM event model and includes the EventDispatcher base class.
flash.external	Contains the ExternalInterface class API, which can be used to communicate with the Flash Player's HTML container.
flash.filters	Contains classes for bitmap filter effects.
flash.geom	Contains geometry classes, such as points, rectangles, and transformation matrices, to support the BitmapData class and the bitmap caching feature.
flash.media	Contains classes for working with multimedia assets such as sound and video.
flash.net	Contains classes for sending and receiving from the network, such as URL downloading and Flash Remoting which uses the AMF format (see the "Data Formats" section in Chapter 2).
flash.printing	Contains classes for printing content displayed in the Flash runtime.
flash.profiler	Contains functions used for debugging and profiling ActionScript code.
flash.sampler	Contains methods and classes for tracking procedure calls so that you can profile memory usage and optimize applications.
flash.system	Contains classes for accessing system-level functionality, such as security domains, multilanguage content (regionality), and system interactions such as camera, microphone, and clipboard.
flash.text	Contains classes for working with text fields, text formatting, text metrics, style sheets, and layout. Note that this is not the API for the new Flash Text Engine introduced in Flash Player 10. See the flash.text.engine package in the "Flash 10 APIs" section later in this chapter for details.
flash.ui	Contains user interface classes for interacting with the mouse and keyboard.
flash.utils	Contains utility classes, such as advanced class introspection functions and data structures like ByteArray.
flash.xml	Contains support for Flash Player's legacy XML classes, and other Flash Player-specific XML functionality.

The Display API

In ActionScript 3.0, all visual and graphical content is created and manipulated using the classes in what is known as the Display API. The classes in this API are located in the `flash.display.*` package.

The hierarchy of the objects is based on the `DisplayObject`, `InteractiveObject` and `DisplayObjectContainer` classes. These act as pseudo-abstract classes, which cannot be directly instantiated.

The `DisplayObjectContainer` is the base class for objects that can contain other objects on the display list. The `Sprite` class inherits from `DisplayObjectContainer` and provides the most basic needs of the application component display structure. Not all display objects on the tree need to have children (for example, the `Shape` class or the `TextField` class). Both the `Shape` and `TextField` class extend the `DisplayObject` class and not the `DisplayObjectContainer`.

Figure 4-4 illustrates the hierarchy of the display list classes.

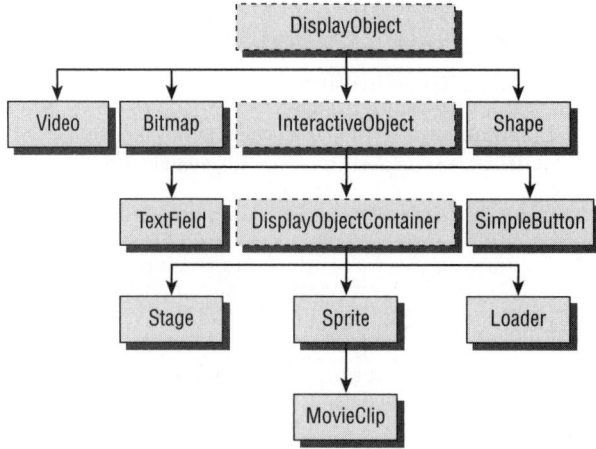

Figure 4-4

The following table briefly describes the core display classes.

Class	Description
Video	Found in the `flash.media` package, all video-related functionality must use the `Video` class to render the media on screen.
Bitmap	Handles bitmap objects. ActionScript 3.0 allows for the following bitmaps to be loaded externally by using the `Loader` class: GIF, JPG, and PNG. The `bitmap` class can also be used in connection with the `BitmapData` class to manipulate images. Some of the current uses include taking pictures from a webcam, reading barcodes from a webcam, thumbnail application components, and many other image-related ideas.
Shape	This object is the canvas for vector graphics.

Continued

Continued

Class	Description
Loader	Used to load external assets, including SWFs and images.
TextField	Found in the flash.text package, this class is the display object that handles user input and displaying text.
SimpleButton	Previously known simply as "Button" in previous versions of ActionScript, this simple interactive object defines three states: up, over, and down.
Sprite	This class provides the most basic needs of the application component display structure, and is the class many Flex UI components indirectly inherit from.
MovieClip	This is like a Sprite class with an added timeline. This is mostly used for Flash-authored content that is embedded or imported into the application. See Chapter 26 for more information on using Flash-authored assets.

The functionality of both the DisplayObject and DisplayObjectContainer class can be broken up into four loosely defined categories:

- **Manipulation of display list structure** — This covers the methods and properties used to add, remove, and move display objects around on the display list.

- **Appearance and spatial properties** — The DisplayObject class defines number of properties for placement, size, and other appearance-related functionality.

- **Finding display objects** — This covers methods relating to retrieving display objects off the display list by name or index, up and down the parent and child display list structure.

- **Event handling** — The EventDispatcher class is inherited by all the classes to provide all display objects with access to the event model.

Manipulating the Display List

The following table shows the methods and properties that fall under this category and are exclusive to the DisplayObjectContainer class.

Method	Description
addChild() addChildAt()	These methods add the display object to the container class, either at the end of the containers child list or inserted at a specific index.
removeChild() removeChildAt()	These methods remove the display object from the container class, either by providing a reference to the child display object or a specific index.
setChildIndex()	This method is used to change the index in the children list of the provided display object.
swapChildren() swapChildrenAt()	These are other methods of changing the position of children in the container's specific display list. The swapping can be done with two display objects or two index values.

Appearance and Spatial Properties

The following table shows the methods and properties that fall under this category and are defined in both the `DisplayObject` and the `DisplayObjectContainer` class.

A new feature to Flash Player 10 is the ability to transform the special perspective of the `DisplayObject` in three dimensions.

Method/Property	Description
accessibilityProperties cacheAsBitmap loaderInfo stage	These properties provide functionality to specific Flash Player information and capabilities. There will always be a root stage object that can be referenced here. The `loaderInfo` is specific to loading external resources and provides low-level information. The accessibility and cache of bitmaps are features specific to the Flash Player.
alpha blendMode filters mask opaqueBackground scale9Grid transform visible	This group of properties covers the basic appearance features available in the Flash Player. These are some of the most powerful properties when it comes to creating custom, visually appealing components. See the Adobe documentation to learn the more specific uses of each of these properties.
height width rotation scaleX scaleY x y	This group of properties defines the specific spatial characteristics of the display object. This is the basic positioning of all display objects.
scrollRect getBounds() getRect()	These methods and properties are used to retrieve rectangles that define specific bounds of the display object.
hitTestObject() hitTestPoint()	These methods determine if the specific objects intersect spatially on screen.
mouseX mouseY globalToLocal() localToGlobal()	These methods and properties relate to specific points in pixels on the screen. Using the `mouseX` and `mouseY` values, you can move between the stage's `Point` and the `Point` specific to the display object.

Continued

Continued

Method/Property	Description
rotationX rotationY rotationZ scaleZ z globalToLocal3D local3DToGlobal	These methods are new to Flash Player 10, and allow for manipulation of 3D perspective.

Finding Display Objects

The following table shows the methods and properties that fall under this category and are defined in both the DisplayObject and the DisplayObjectContainer class.

Method	Description
name parent root	These properties define who the display object is, specific to its relationship with other display objects located in the display list.
contains()	This determines if the display object is present in this container.
getChildAt() getChildByName() getChildIndex() getObjectsUnderPoint()	The get functions provide methods to retrieve the index to a display object or the objects themselves. The display objects can be retrieved by index, name, or using a Point class.

Event Handling

The following table shows some of the methods and properties that fall under this category and are defined in both the DisplayObject and the DisplayObjectContainer class.

Method	Description
activate deactivate	These events are fired when the Flash Player gains and loses focus from the operating system.
added removed	These events fire when every display object is added or removed from a display container.
enterFrame render	These two methods are events that relate to the execution cycle of the Flash Player.

Continued

Continued

Method	Description
click	
doubleClick	
focusIn	
focusOut	
keyDown	
keyFocusChange	
keyUp	
mouseDown	This long list defines all the events caused by client interaction with the
mouseFocusChange	application. Either through mouse or keyboard the events handle all the
mouseMove	typical display objects interaction states. See the constants listed under the
mouseOut	MouseEvent class in the Flex Language Documentation for more
mouseOver	information.
mouseUp	
mouseWheel	
rollout	
rollover	
tabChildrenChange	
tabEnabledChange	
tabIndexChange	

The Flash AIR APIs

The Flash API includes distinct packages specific for Flash AIR-specific functionality.

Package	Description
flash.data	Contains classes used for working with the AIR local SQLite database.
flash.desktop	Contains classes used for copy and paste and drag and drop operations, as well as the Icon class, used to define system icons used by a file.
	As of Flash Player 10, this package's Clipboard-related classes are native to the Flash framework and not exclusive to the AIR API.
flash.filesystem	Contains classes used in accessing the filesystem from the AIR runtime.
flash.html	Contains classes used for including HTML content in an AIR application, using script bridging with objects in the WebKit browser.
flash.security	Includes classes for validating XML signatures in the AIR runtime.

In addition, several classes located in other `flash.*` packages provide AIR-specific functionality:

```
flash.display.FocusDirection              flash.events.FileListEvent
flash.display.NativeMenu                  flash.events.HTMLUncaughtScriptExceptionEvent
flash.display.NativeMenuItem              flash.events.InvokeEvent
flash.display.NativeWindow                flash.events.NativeDragEvent
flash.display.NativeWindowDisplayState    flash.events.NativeWindowBoundsEvent
flash.display.NativeWindowInitOptions     flash.events.NativeWindowDisplayStateEvent
flash.display.NativeWindowResize          flash.events.OutputProgressEvent
flash.display.NativeWindowSystemChrome    flash.events.ScreenMouseEvent
flash.display.NativeWindowType            flash.events.SQLErrorEvent
flash.display.Screen                      flash.events.SQLEvent
flash.errors.DRMManagerError             flash.events.SQLUpdateEvent
flash.errors.SQLError                    flash.net.URLRequestDefaults
flash.errors.SQLErrorOperation
flash.events.BrowserInvokeEvent
flash.events.DRMAuthenticateEvent
flash.events
    .DRMAuthenticationCompleteEvent
flash.events
    .DRMAuthenticationErrorEvent
flash.events.DRMErrorEvent
flash.events.DRMStatusEvent
```

Flash 10 APIs

Flash Player 10 introduced several new classes to the Flash APIs. See Chapter 2, "The Flex 3 Ecosystem," for an overview of these features. New functionality has also been added to existing classes, which are too numerous to mention here.

For a complete list of the new methods and properties added to Flash Player 10, see the Adobe Flash Platform ActionScript reference for RIA development available in PDF at www.adobe.com/devnet/actionscript/articles/atp_ria_guide.html.

3D Graphics and Pixel Bender

The following packages have been included in Flash Player 10 to take advantage of the new graphics capabilities of the Flash Player.

flash.geom

Class	Description
Matrix3D	Represents a transformation matrix that determines the position and orientation of a three-dimensional (3D) display object.
Orientation3D	An enumeration of constant values for representing the orientation style of a Matrix3D object.

Continued

Continued

Class	Description
PerspectiveProjection	Provides an easy way to assign or modify the perspective transformations of a display object and all its children.
Utils3D	Contains static methods that simplify the implementation of certain three-dimensional matrix operations.
Vector3D	Represents a point or a location in the three-dimensional space using the Cartesian coordinates x, y, and z.

flash.display

Class	Description
Graphics GraphicsBitmapFill GraphicsEndFill GraphicsGradientFill GraphicsPath GraphicsPathCommand GraphicsPathWinding GraphicsShaderFill GraphicsSolidFill GraphicsStroke GraphicsTrianglePath	The new graphics classes handle the filling and drawing of shapes and bitmaps in 3D space, as well as UV texture mapping. Most of these features have the option of being either CPU- or GPU-accelerated, depending on the WMODE setting in HTML.
Shader ShaderData ShaderInput ShaderJob ShaderParameter ShaderParameterType ShaderPrecision TriangleCulling	The shader classes allow for the execution and manipulation of Pixel Bender engine shader kernels, which are written in the Pixel Bender language and run in their own threaded JIT in the virtual machine. Note that on PowerPC-based Macs, Pixel Bender code does not run in a JIT but is interpreted.

flash.filters

Class	Description
ShaderFilter	Applies a filter by executing a shader on the object being filtered. ShaderFilter extends BitmapFilter, which is the base class for all image filter effects.

flash.events

Class	Description
ShaderEvent	Dispatched when a shader operation by the Pixel Bender engine launched from a ShaderJob finishes.

Flash Text Engine

A new package known as the flash.text.engine has been created in Flash Player 10 specifically for the capabilities of the improved text engine, called the Flash Text Engine (FTE).

flash.text.engine

Class	Description
BreakOpportunity CFFHinting ContentElement DigitCase DigitWidth EastAsianJustifier ElementFormat FontDescription FontLookup FontMetrics FontPosture FontWeight GraphicElement GroupElement JustificationStyle Kerning LigatureLevel LineJustification RenderingMode SpaceJustifier TabAlignment TabStop TextBaseline TextBlock TextElement TextJustifier TextLine TextLineCreationResult TextLineMirrorRegion TextLineValidity TextRotation TypographicCase	These new classes account for the capability enhancements in the Flash Text Engine (FTE), which include advanced text ligatures, case control, kerning, tab stops, (and other text metrics), formatting, bidirectional text and multilingual capabilities. The FTE is primarily designed as a foundation for the creation and support of text-handling components.

System Integration

Previous to Flash Player 10, the flash.desktop package was exclusively for the Flash AIR API. Recent additions to this package add enhanced clipboard capabilities to the Flash Player.

flash.desktop

Class	Description
Clipboard ClipboardFormats ClipboardTransferMode	These classes represent the enhanced cut and paste and rich text clipboard handling capabilities in Flash 10.

flash.ui

Class	Description
ContextMenuClipboardItems	The ContextMenuClipboardItems class determines which items are enabled or disabled on the clipboard context menu.
MouseCursor	The MouseCursor class is an enumeration of constant values used in setting the cursor property of the Mouse class. New functionality in the mouse class allows the cursor to be changed to system default arrow, button, hand or I-beam cursors. This allows developers the ability to control the appearance of the text input cursor, for instance, without using skinned graphics for a custom cursor, which usually incurs a slight performance penalty.

Media

Several new media enhancements were introduced in Flash 10, including dynamic sound, improved streaming media capabilities, and a new audio codec.

flash.events

Class	Description
SampleDataEvent	Dispatched when the player requests new audio data. Useful for managing dynamically generated sound.

flash.media

Class	Description
SoundCodec	Previous to Flash Player 10, there was only ever one sound codec available in the Flash Player. Now that there are two to choose from, the SoundCodec class provides an enumeration of constant values used in setting the codec property of the Microphone class.

flash.net

Class	Description
NetStreamInfo NetStreamPlayOptions NetStreamPlayTransitions	These classes provide additional functionality enabled by dynamic stream switching capability, enabled by the new NetStream.play2() method.

flash.system

Class	Description
JPEGLoaderContext	The JPEGLoaderContext class extends the LoaderContext class, which provides options for loading SWF files and other media by using the Loader class.

Summary

The intent of this chapter was not to provide "cookbook-style" coverage of specific use cases and class applications; rather, it was to provide a comprehensive overview of the major programming models, APIs, and functionality groupings in Flash and AIR. This will enable you to develop your own low-level custom applications in ActionScript 3.0, and arm you with a firm grasp of the basics as you prepare to develop Flex applications.

5

Introduction to Flex Builder 3

This chapter covers the basic Flex Builder Workbench layout and areas, as well as how to customize the workbench experience. It also teaches you how to learn more about Flex Builder from within the Flex Builder Help resources.

If you're already well familiar with the Flex Builder 3 Workbench, but you'd like to know only what has been improved or added in Flex Builder 3, you can skip the "Getting Started with Flex Builder" and "The Flex 3 Workbench" sections and jump right to "What's New in Flex Builder 3" at the end of this chapter.

Getting Started with Flex Builder

The Flex Builder is a fully integrated development environment (IDE). It provides tools to assist you in creating, debugging, packaging, and compiling code into SWF applications. Following are just a few of the features:

❑ **Text editor** — Flex Builder 3 provides separate editors for MXML, ActionScript, and CSS code. You do not need to keep track of which editor is for which file type. This is because the Flex Builder automatically handles it for you. The editors also provide features that will be discussed in this chapter, including code hinting, navigation, formatting, commenting, and others.

❑ **Design editor** — The design view editor is specific to the MXML editor. It provides a collection of views to help create components and applications visually by placing user-interface and data-access controls on the design mode stage.

❑ **Navigation features** — The Navigator and the Outline Views provide the ability to navigate not only projects, but also components. Flex Builder also provides the functionality to open code through definition links and view editors with line numbers to help locate specific code.

❑ **Build tools** — The mxmlc compiler does all compiling of the applications, but what Flex Builder does is provide the ability to manage the process. You can configure projects to build automatically as you write code and save the file, or to be built manually. Configuration settings are also set per project to give you full control of the compilation and deployment process.

❑ **Integrated debugger** — Flex Builder integrates the mxmlc compile-time errors with the Console View for easy access to error locations. Runtime debugging is handled through the Flex Debugging perspective and the associated console, debug, variables, breakpoints, and expressions views.

❑ **Integrated profiler** — This enables you to see how much memory is allocated to instances, force Garbage Collection, and see what the internals of your applications are doing with tons of information. See Chapter 72, "Using The Flex Profiler," for details.

❑ **Integrated Adobe Flex 3 Help** — Flex Builder Help system provides eight main categories from how Flex works to the Flex 3 language reference. It also provides a list of links to other online Flex resources.

❑ **Eclipse plug-ins and third-party tools** — Eclipse provides a plug-in architecture embraced by the community with many well-done projects to support other development requirements. Most common are development and version control plug-ins such as Ant, Tomcat, CVS, Subversion, and ColdFusion (www.CFEclipse.org). Along with the plug-in architecture, Eclipse allows you to configure external tools from within the Flex Builder. See Chapter 9, "Customizing Flex Builder 3," for more information on using other Eclipse plug-ins.

Many other features have been added to Flex Builder 3 since the last release. See "What's New In Flex Builder 3" later in this chapter for details.

Flex Builder and Eclipse

If you have built applications with other comparable development environments, you will find that the Flex Builder and Eclipse platform provides extensive capabilities.

Flex Builder 3 comes in two installation options. The first is the standalone Flex Builder with the prepackaged Eclipse environment included. The second option is to install Flex Builder as an Eclipse plug-in into an existing Eclipse installation.

Flex Builder 3 is based on the Eclipse workbench and can be installed in one of two ways:

❑ **Standalone Configuration**, which is a prepackaged installation of both Eclipse and the Flex Builder.

❑ **Plug-in Configuration**, which adds Flex Builder to an existing Eclipse installation.

Installing Flex Builder in the standalone configuration has the advantage of not requiring a prior installation of Eclipse to function, and its feature set is preconfigured to work with Flex development. Flex Builder standalone is in fact a branded and preconfigured Eclipse installation, so it may not work intuitively with other language plug-ins. Developers who already have eclipse installed with another language plug-in such as Java, PHP, or ColdFusion may want to install Flex Builder as a plug-in, which lends flexibility to the Eclipse workbench in allowing for multiple language environments. When installing the Flex Builder Eclipse plug-in into an installation with other ActionScript or MXML plug-ins, you must resolve editor conflicts through the Eclipse Preferences window.

Although this chapter uses the standalone Flex Builder in its examples, the information is still pertinent to the plug-in edition as well, although some menus may be labeled differently in the Eclipse workbench.

Learning Flex and Getting Help

Some of the most useful tools in learning Flex and Flex Builder are the resources built into the Flex Builder installation. You can get assistance with help or documentation in one of four ways:

1. **The Flex Start Page** — One of the most overlooked places to start learning about Flex Builder is the Flex Start Page (see Figure 5-1). If you are like most developers, you probably vaguely remember seeing it the first time you opened up Flex Builder. Do not worry if you did skip over it; you can bring the Flex Start Page back up by selecting Help ➪ Flex Start Page.

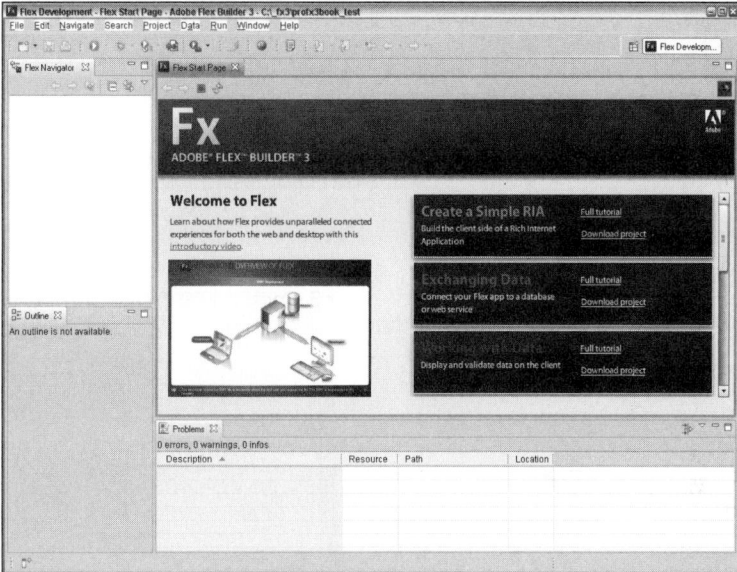

Figure 5-1

On the first screen of the Flex Start Page, there are three tutorials to get you started. Click on the link to the first tutorial, and it will take you to a web page where, in addition to the tutorial, links in the left-hand menu will take you to other Flex documentation and resources.

2. **The Flex 3 Help Documentation** — The next step to finding extensive information on Adobe Flex 3 and related technologies is Flex Help itself. Figure 5-2 shows the Flex Builder Help system, which opens as a windowed application outside of the Eclipse workbench when you select Help ➪ Help Contents from the Flex Builder menu system.

Figure 5-2 also shows the name of the eight main titles in the Flex Help library. The library is quite extensive, and many times you'll want to narrow your search to specific sections of the library. You do this by clicking on the blue "Search scope" link found on the top-middle area of Figure 5-2. The search mechanism uses groups of topics as named search lists that can be selected as the current search scope. Figure 5-3 shows the two dialog windows used to create and select a search list for just the "Using Flex Builder 3" section of the Flex library.

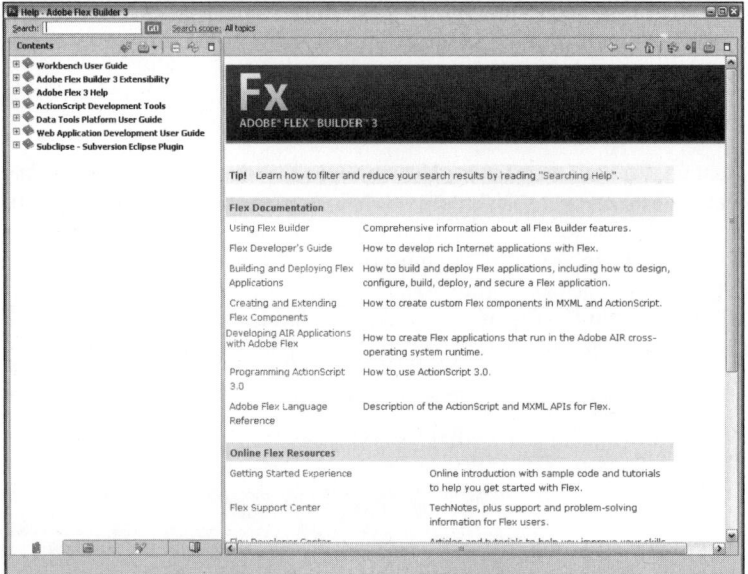

Figure 5-2

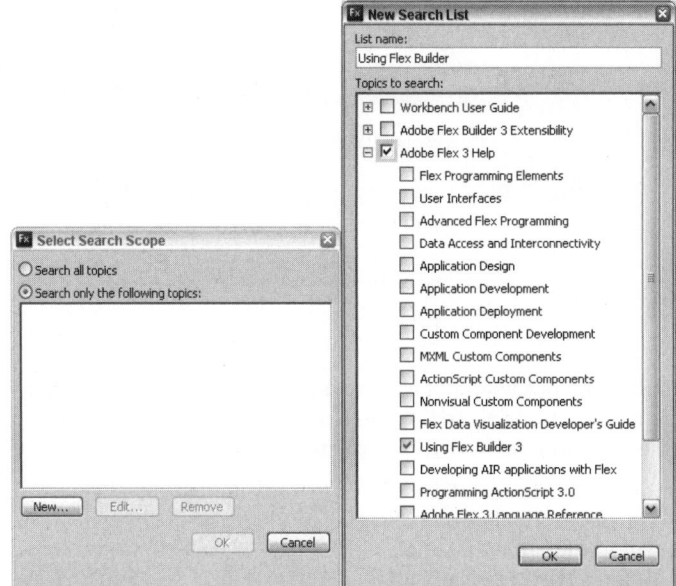

Figure 5-3

The selection of scope will now filter all search results to only pull information from the "Using Flex Builder 3" Help section. The search scope not only affects the external Help system, but also affects the Help View search mode available inside Flex Builder. You can see that in Figure 5-4, which demonstrates a search result on the term "debugging." The search returns the same filtered results as Help View search mode, shown in Figure 5-5.

A second and often overlooked way to search the Flex 3 Help documentation is to select the Help View search mode from the Help menu, which allows you to search the documentation in a side panel (or view), displaying the results in the editor part of the workbench instead of opening up a new window.

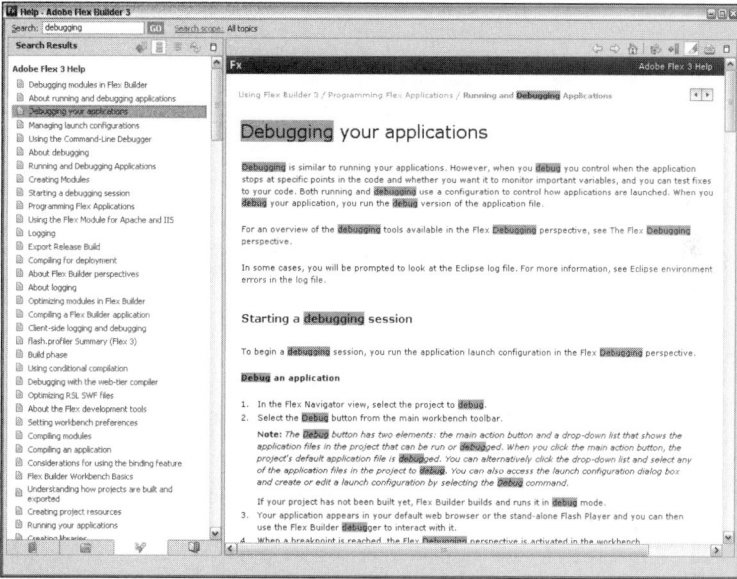

Figure 5-4

Those of you astute in the ways of Eclipse will notice that both the windowed Help application and the inline Help View are custom implementations of the Eclipse internal web browser, which runs on the Internet Explorer engine. Each new Flex Builder session creates a new port connection to a local Java servlet, which runs the documentation application, so bookmarking Flex Help pages using right-click ⇨ Add To favorites is not very reliable, since those port-specific bookmarks will not work the moment you restart Flex Builder. Unfortunately, the bookmarking feature built into the Flex Builder Help application itself is not very well integrated either, since bookmarks do not carry over between workspaces. If you need to bookmark Flex 3 documentation pages, it is recommended that you use the online documentation instead.

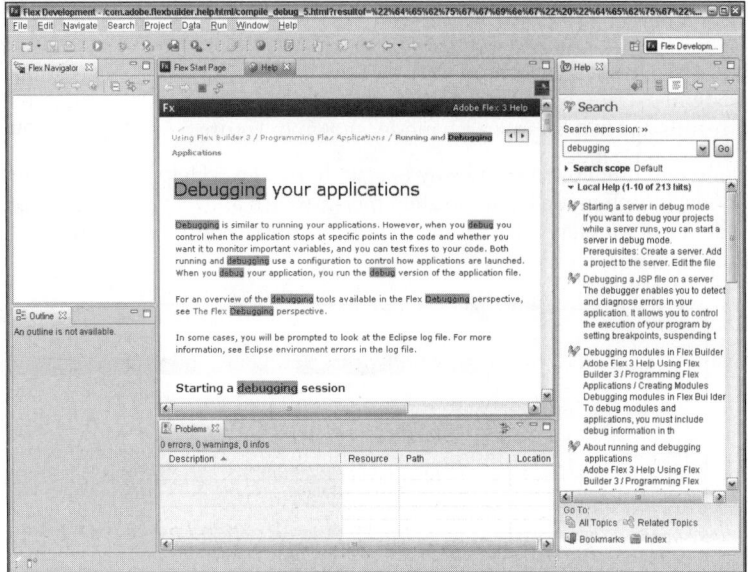

Figure 5-5

3. **Contextual Assistance** — Contextual assistance can be obtained in one of a few ways:

  ❑ The Dynamic Help View available from the Help menu provides real-time contextual help as you write your code.

  ❑ A list of keyboard shortcuts can be obtained using the Key Assist pop-up list containing a quick view to all the shortcuts, which can be seen by clicking Ctrl+Shift+L(Win)/Option+Shift+L(OSX), or by selecting Help ⇨ Key Assist.

  ❑ When in the Code Editing View, control/option+clicking a class in the Flex Framework sends you to that class file within the Flex framework itself. Clicking F3 works much the same way, and will find the source for a particular object reference.

4. **Online Documentation** — The Flex 3 online documentation can be found at `www.adobe.com/go/flex_documentation`.

If you need to bookmark Flex Builder Help documentation pages, it is recommended that you do so from the online documentation. Some pages within the Flex Builder help documentation include a link named "Submit Feedback on LiveDocs." Clicking this link will open the online version of this page in your default browser.

The Flex 3 Workbench

The *workbench* refers to the whole of the Flex Builder development environment, including all menus and UI elements, and is made up of perspectives, editors, and views. The following table provides definitions to better explain the basics of the Flex Builder Workbench and other related topics.

Term	Definition
Workspace	A defined area on your file system that defines project resources for your applications.
Editor	A view where source files of various types are edited in either Source mode or Design mode.
View	Supplies tools when modifying a file in an editor. They are like panels in Adobe CS3 applications.
Perspective	A group of views and editors laid out in a certain configuration.

Figure 5-6 illustrates all the parts of the Flex 3 workbench.

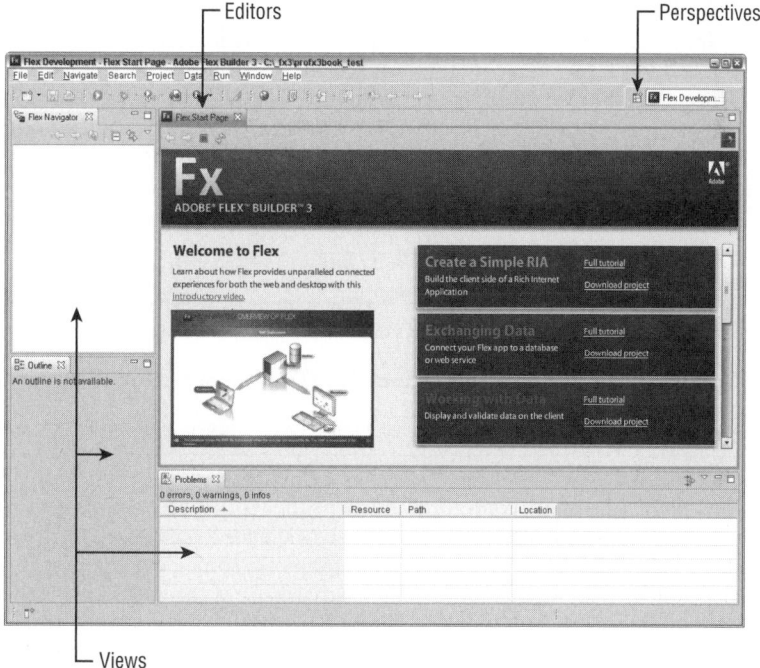

Figure 5-6

Workspaces

A *workspace* is a defined area on your file system that defines the resources that make up your application projects. A Flex application is always built within the context of a *project*, which is a grouping of application files plus metadata that defines not only the source files for your application but also compiler settings and other metadata specific to the editing and compilation of that application. The files and folders within a project folder are called *resources*. You will learn how to create a Flex project in the next chapter.

Creating and Switching Workspaces

Flex Builder opens up to a blank workspace by default, which may not point to the location you want your project assets to reside on your file system by default. To create a new workspace, simply select File Switch Workspace ⇨ Other, and then browse to the location where you want the workspace metadata to reside. To switch to another existing workspace, simply select the workspace to change to in the Switch Workspace dropdown menu. If the existing workspace is not in the list, select Other.

Many developers new to the Eclipse or Flex Builder workflow often wonder how they could ever need more than one workspace, given that a workspace can hold any number of projects containing applications. Having more than one workspace is useful for keeping certain types of projects separate, such as a personal and a work workspace, or having different workspaces for projects belonging to different clients, or if certain groups of projects are located on different networked filesystems.

Workspace Configurations

Although the metadata files defining the workspace are usually located in the workspace folder containing your project folders, the metadata for your workspaces and the project folders can be in different locations. Generally, there are three ways in which workspace and project locations may be set up on your local file system:

1. The *default setting* is to have the workspace metadata reside in the same workspace folder where your project folders reside. Thus, we would have the locations shown in the following table.

Item	Location
Workspace metadata	{main drive}/myFlexWorkspace
Workspace folder	{main drive}/myFlexWorkspace
Project	{main drive}/myFlexWorkspace/projectName

2. A *lightly coupled* workspace configuration keeps the workspace metadata in a separate folder within the workspace folder. In this case, the workspace folder is actually distinct from the workspace metadata folder. This is common usage for some developers who prefer a cleaner workspace folder without metadata. The disadvantage of this technique is that creation of new project locations may default to the workspace metadata folder, not the workspace folder, requiring the developer to remember to change it when setting up a new project.

Item	Location
Workspace metadata	{main drive}/myFlexWorkspace/_workspace
Workspace folder	{main drive}/myFlexWorkspace
Project	{main drive}/myFlexWorkspace/projectName

3. A *loosely coupled* workspace configuration keeps the workspace metadata completely separate from the actual project folder locations. This allows the same project to be a part of different workspaces without being tied to the same workspace folder location, and it may be implemented in networked filesystem environments.

Item	Location
Workspace metadata	{main drive}/someOtherLocation/
Workspace folder	{main drive}/myFlexWorkspace
Project	{main drive}/myFlexWorkspace/projectName

Editors

An *editor* is where files of various types are edited in Source mode or Design mode. Source code in ActionScript (.as), MXML and CSS files are edited in Source mode. While editing an MXML file, you can use Design mode to position UI elements visually in that container. When editing a CSS file, Design mode enables you to edit the states or skins of the UI component. Design mode cannot be used for an ActionScript file. The Source and Design Mode buttons, as shown in Figure 5-7, can only be used for MXML and CSS files.

Figure 5-7

The Source Mode editor has certain language intelligence features that allow for autocompletion and other features, which will be covered in subsequent chapters.

Views

Flex Builder includes the following views for debugging and development, The table does not cover views specific to the Profiling perspective. See Chapter 72, "Using the Flex Profiler," for more details.

View	Description
Navigator	Shows all the projects and project resources available in the workspace. Project settings files are hidden by default, although they can be made visible in the Navigator view.
Outline	For an MXML file, shows the component container hierarchy. For an ActionScript file, shows the class members in the file. For a CSS file, shows the CSS style hierarchy.
Editor	Allows for editing of code for an ActionScript file. For an MXML file, allows for editing code in Source mode, and the visual layout of display components in Design mode.
Problems	Shows a compilation of warnings and errors.
Components	Presents a list of available Flex components.
States	Shows the presently configured states in the selected file.

Continued

Continued

View	Description
Properties	Available only in Design mode, this allows for a GUI-style editing of component properties.
Debug	Displays the call stack, that is, the order of called methods in the application, in its currently suspended state.
Variables	Displays information about the properties available for a particular object in the call stack.
Breakpoints	Presents a list of all set breakpoints in the application.
Expressions	Monitors particular variables earmarked from the Variables View.
Search	Displays the current and previous code searches.
Console	Displays the Flash Player trace log from trace statements used in the code, and runtime feedback from the debugger.
Tasks	Useful for assigning and tracking line-specific tasks associated with the project.
Bookmark	Displays the markers used for earmarking particular locations in your application code.

Perspectives

A *perspective* is a group of views and editors laid out in a certain configuration. There are three default perspectives in Flex Builder 3, shown in the following table.

Perspective	Description
Development	Shows tools available while in the course of code development
Debugging	Shows tools available while debugging the application
Profiling	Allows you to examine real-time properties of the running application, such as memory usage, performance, and object instantiation, in addition to having control over virtual machine internals such as garbage collection

The following tables show the default view configurations for each perspective, as well as which Flex Development perspective the view appears in. To open any view in the current perspective, select Window ⇨ Other Views, and a pop-up of all the available views will open.

Default Development views

View Name	Group	Typical Layout Area
Navigator	Source/Design	Left Side
Outline	Source/Design	Left Side
Editor	Source/Design	Middle
Problems	Source/Design	Bottom
Components	Design	Left Side
States	Design	Right Top
Properties	Design	Right Bottom

Figure 5-8 shows the default layout of views in the Development perspective.

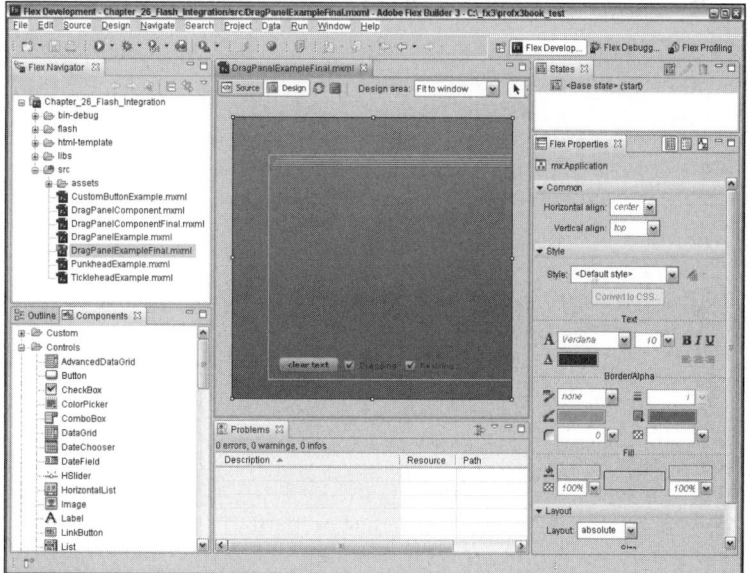

Figure 5-8

Default Debugging Views

View Name	Group	Typical Layout Area
Navigator	Debugging	Left Side
Debug	Debugging	Middle Top
Editor	Debugging	Middle
Variables	Debugging	Right Top
Breakpoints	Debugging	Right Top
Expressions	Debugging	Right Top
Console	Debugging	Bottom
Problems	Debugging	Bottom

Figure 5-9 shows the default layout of views in the Debugging perspective.

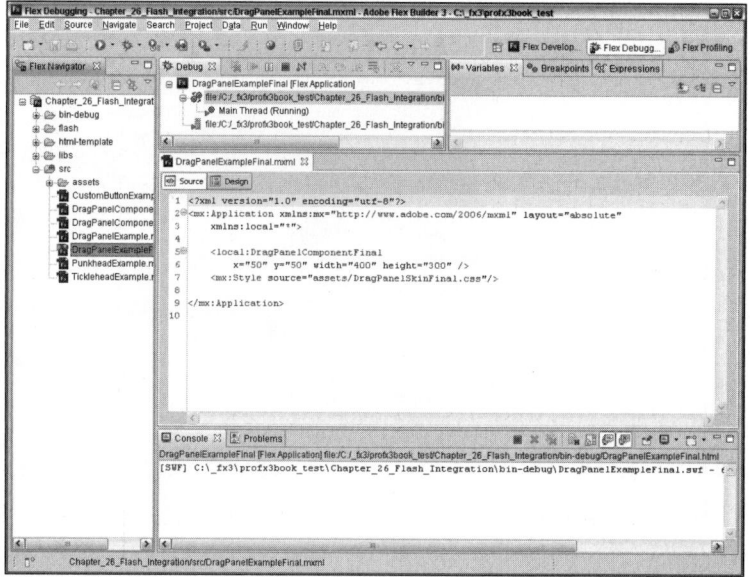

Figure 5-9

Default Profiling Views

View Name	Group	Typical Layout Area
Profile	Profiling	Left Top
Saved Profiling Data	Profiling	Left Top
Console	Profiling	Right Top
Live Objects	Profiling	Bottom
Memory Snapshot	Profiling	Bottom
Performance Profile	Profiling	Bottom
Object References	Profiling	Bottom

Figure 5-10 below shows the default layout of views in the Profiling perspective.

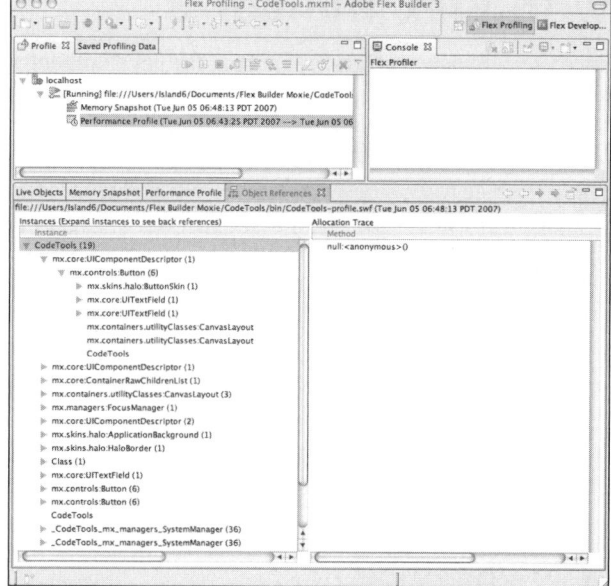

Figure 5-10

Default Optional Views

View Name	Group	Typical Layout Area
Search	Any	Bottom
Console	Any	Bottom
Tasks	Any	Bottom
Bookmark	Any	Bottom

Creating a Custom Perspective

When you switch workspaces, the workbench changes to the default perspective layouts. To save your favorite arrangement of views and editors across workspaces, you need to save a custom perspective. To create a custom perspective, select Window ➪ Perspective ➪ Save Perspective As.

What's New in Flex Builder 3

Flex Builder 3 introduced several new features, enhancing the development toolset, and increasing productivity and integration with other tools.

New Wizards

❑ **Import Skin Artwork Wizard** — This feature enables you to select a folder of images, Flash SWFs and SWCs, and import them into a Flex Project. The wizard allows you to map assets to skinnable elements of Flex components, and helps you to write the resulting CSS code. See Chapter 26, "Flash Integration," for details on using the Import Skin Artwork wizard.

❑ **Import Web Service Wizard** — This automatically generates the connection code for invoking SOAP-based Web Service (WSDL) operations, which includes client-side ActionScript Web Service proxy classes that return strongly typed objects.

❑ **Create Application from Database Wizard** — This allows you to generate an application that uses a PHP/MySQL, J2EE, or ASP.NET database.

Design Mode Enhancements

❑ **Design View Zoom/Pan** — You can zoom and pan your stage in Design mode, making component layout easier.

❑ **Design mode support for ItemRenderers** — `Tree` and `DataGrid` components populated with static data and custom `itemRenderers` can now be previewed in Design View. This feature allows you to see what custom `itemRenderers` look like at design time and greatly simplify the design process for data-driven elements.

❑ **CSS Design View** — You can now view the CSS states of a component directly in Design View and edit them using the Flex Properties panel.

Development Enhancements

❑ **Advanced Constraints** — Flex now allows you to specify constraint-based relational positioning based on constraint parameters rather than absolute-versus-relational positioning. See Chapter 13 for more information on enhanced layout constraints.

❑ **CSS Outline View** — The Outline view is now able to introspect CSS files with full language intelligence support.

❑ **CSS Subcomponent Selectors** — These allow you to inherit certain CSS properties based on component relationships. See Chapter 22, "Styles," for more information.

❑ **Compilation** — The MXMLC/COMPC/ASC compiler performance has been improved and will be about 30–40% faster than Flex 2.

❑ **Language Intelligence** — Refactoring, Code Search, Code Outline, Syntax highlighting, and Code completion have been added and improved in this version, leading to incremental but very important development performance improvements.

❑ **Flex Profiler** — This a release-defining addition to Flex Builder that allows you to see how much memory is allocated to instances, force Garbage Collection, and see what the internals of your applications are doing with tons of information. See Chapter 72 for details.

❑ **Module Support** — Module support for `Module` and `ModuleLoader` has been fully integrated into Flex Builder.

❑ **Multiple SDK Support** — Flex Builder now allows you to switch between versions of the Flex SDK you wish to compile to. So if you're still coding applications in Flex 2.01 or want to try out nightly builds of an upcoming framework release, this feature allows you to switch your compilation source.

❑ **New Advanced Components** — New advanced components such as the `AdvancedDataGrid` and the `OLAPDataGrid`, along with new collection classes, have been added in this release.

❑ **Deep Linking** — This API has been added to the Flex framework to allow for more seamless integration between the browser and the Flex application in the Flash Player. See Chapter 40, "Deeplinking," for details.

❑ **Resource Bundles and Runtime Localization** — Support for the creation of resource bundle compile-time shared libraries (CSLs) and runtime-shared libraries (RSLs) allow you to extend multilingual support in your Flex applications. See Chapter 37, "Resource Bundles and Data Localization," for details.

❑ **Persistent Framework Caching** — This has been added in the Flash Player 9 and RSL support in the Flex framework to enable the optional usage of a cached version of the Flex framework on the client machine, so you don't have to compile the Flex framework itself into the application SWF, dramatically cutting down subsequent client load times for your Flex application. See Chapter 27, "Loading External Assets," for details.

CS3 Suite Integration

❑ **Flash, Illustrator, Photoshop, and Fireworks CS3 Skinning** — Each of these respective applications can export assets as static skins. And Flash, Fireworks, and Illustrator allow you to publish your artwork as a SWF file that serves as a compile-time library for Flex components. See Chapter 26, "Flash Integration," for details on using Flash for component skinning.

❑ **Completely Skinned Components in Fireworks CS3** — Fireworks CS3 is able to save component designs as both assets, MXML and CSS. See the Adobe Developer Center article "Designing Flex 3 skins and styles using Creative Suite 3 and Flex Builder 3." (`www.adobe.com/devnet/flex/articles/skins_styles.html`) for more information on Fireworks skinning.

❑ **Building Flex Components in Flash CS3** — Using the Flex Component Kit for Flash CS3, you can build a Flex component in Flash with improved animation and skinning and use it in your Flex application. See Chapters 26 and 29 for more information.

Summary

In this chapter, we covered the basics of the Flex Builder IDE, including a look at what is new in this release of Flex Builder. The next chapter looks at using Flex Builder 3 to build simple Flex applications.

Part II: Developing with Flex 3

## 6

Using Flex Builder 3

Learning how to build applications using Flex Builder is the first step in understanding the power of Flex. Once you begin, whether you are a seasoned Eclipse user or a first-time developer, you will realize just how easy and rewarding it is. This chapter takes you through some basics of the Flex application compilation process, followed by a walkthrough of developing a Flex application in the Flex Builder Design View. And, finally, you will learn to develop and compile a pure ActionScript project using only the code-editing tools in Flex Builder.

The Flex Compilation Process

Before you begin building your first Flex application, it is helpful to get a bigger picture of the development process. Without going into details about Flex Builder settings (which we will get to in Chapter 8, "Developing with Flex Builder"), the compilation and publishing process for Flex 3 is as follows and as illustrated in Figure 6-1.

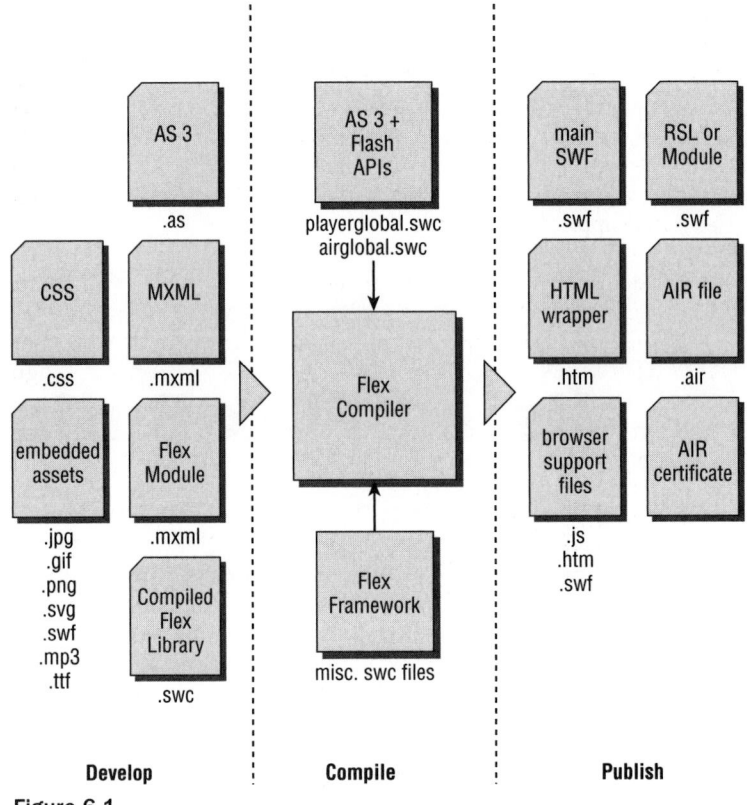

Figure 6-1

Development

The main source code of a Flex application uses the MXML, CSS, and ActionScript languages, in .mxml, .css, and .as files, respectively. You can develop a Flex application using all three languages or just MXML or just ActionScript. As you will see in Chapter 7, "MXML Fundamentals," an MXML file can contain MXML, CSS, and ActionScript code, whereas .css style sheets and .as class files can contain only CSS and ActionScript, respectively.

You can also develop with ActionScript libraries or .swc files. These are Zip archives containing either raw source code or precompiled SWF class libraries, including asset files and XML metadata. These files are compiled with the application and later accessed as a Runtime Shared Library (RSL), which will load dynamically at runtime. See Chapter 21, "Using Libraries," for more information on compiling SWC libraries.

Flex Builder can also compile *modules*, which are like RSLs, except they include a class factory framework that allows critical parts of the application to be abstracted separate of the main application, allowing them to be loaded and unloaded at runtime without requiring that the module be compiled with the rest of the Flex application. See Chapter 66, "Modular Application Development," for more information on creating modular applications.

In addition, other assets such as images, Flash SWF files, sound files, and fonts may be embedded directly into the application by the Flex compiler.

Compilation

The Flex compiler, otherwise known as the MXMLC, is an application file mxmlc.exe located in the Flex SDK directory in your Flex Builder installation. The MXML and CSS languages are convenient markup languages that are interpreted by the Flex compiler into pure ActionScript. The Flex compiler takes the code from the .mxml, .css and .as files and compiles them down to ActionScript 3 bytecode (ABC), which is binary format that can be read by the Flash virtual machine. It also compiles all non-code assets into the final application file.

Flex Builder also checks the code for import statements and other language constructs and compiles the appropriate classes and frameworks into the final bytecode. If you were to open an active Flex project in Flex Builder and take a look at the Project properties, under the Build path ➪ Library path option you would see where the Flex compiler gets the code to build Flex applications (see Figure 6-2).

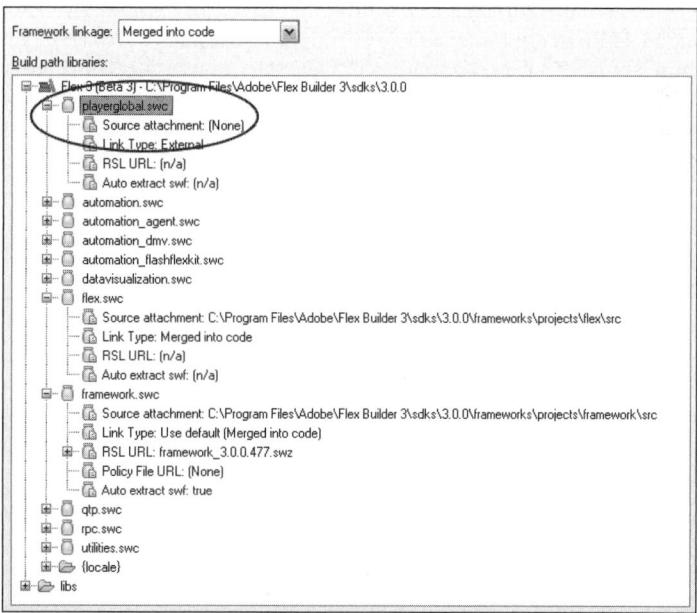

Figure 6-2

Note the SWC file named playerglobal.swc in Figure 6-2. This is the base ActionScript 3 and Flash API framework required to author an application for the Flash runtime. It has a "Source attachment" of "none" because the AS3/Flash API is stored as a precompiled class library, so there is no source code to reference. All the other SWC libraries are collectively part of the Flex framework, flex.swc and framework.swc containing the core Flex framework classes. They indicate a "Source attachment" because the source code is part of that SWC.

If you are publishing for AIR (not shown in Figure 6-2), you will see airglobal.swc in the preferences window, as illustrated in Figure 6-1. This is a compiled class library containing all the AS3 classes, Flash APIs, and the Flash AIR API. Instead of framework.swc, there is a airframework.swc file, which contains Flex framework classes plus the Flex AIR API.

Publishing

Once the compiler interprets all the source into bytecode, it publishes a series of files according to whether you are compiling a Flex or ActionScript project, a Library project, or a Flex AIR project.

If you are publishing a Flex or ActionScript project, you might see the following files:

❑ **The main application SWF**, which is the core Flex application file that will run in the Flash Player.

❑ **Runtime Shared Library (RSL) or Module SWFs** (if applicable), which the main application SWF will load into itself at runtime.

❑ **Supporting browser integration files** are comprised of HTML wrapper files which enables the main SWF to be played in a browser. This includes support HTML and JavaScript files, and SWF files for history state caching and full browser integration. For more information on the HTML wrapper files, see the Adobe Flex documentation under "About The Flex Builder Wrapper" (`http://livedocs.adobe.com/flex/3/html/wrapper_03.html`). For more information on the browser integration capabilities in Flex, see Chapter 40, "Deep Linking."

Later in this chapter you will learn how to compile a Flex project and an ActionScript project that follow this process.

About Projects

There are four types of projects you can create in Flex Builder:

❑ A **Flex project**, which you will creating shortly, contains MXML files and optional CSS style sheet and ActionScript class files — in addition to other optional source files listed in the "development" column in Figure 6-2 — to create a Flex application. A Flex project is published to run in the Flash Player.

❑ An **ActionScript project** does not contain any MXML or CSS files, just ActionScript classes. It is commonly used to compile an application that does not use the Flex framework or a purely ActionScript-based Flex project. Interpreting MXML and CSS into ActionScript by the compiler requires the Flex framework, which is why MXML-based projects cannot be coded with an ActionScript project. You will learn to build an ActionScript project that does not use the Flex framework later in this chapter. An ActionScript project is published to run in the Flash Player.

❑ An **AIR project** is created just like a Flex project, except that in the New Flex Project Wizard, you select the Desktop Application type, which indicates to Flex Builder that you will be publishing for AIR instead of the Flash Player.

❑ Instead of publishing SWFs and supporting files, an AIR project would publish to an AIR application file (`.air`) — which contains the application SWF — and perhaps also an AIR certificate file. For more information on Flex AIR projects, see Chapter 15, "Getting Started with AIR."

❑ A **Library project** is used to compile class libraries into a SWC (.swc) file, which may be added to an application as a class library at compile time, or referenced as a Runtime Shared Library (RSL) at runtime. See Chapter 21, "Using Libraries," for more information on creating library projects.

All four types of projects can be compiled for the Flash Player, which is the default, or for AIR, which adds the necessary Flex AIR libraries. Figure 6-1 illustrates the publishing process for a Flex, ActionScript, or AIR project.

> ### Publishing ActionScript Applications for AIR
>
> Currently there is no way to publish ActionScript-only projects for AIR in Flex Builder, since the Flex AIR API is required to publish an AIR application from Flex Builder. To publish AIR applications using only the Flash AIR API and not the Flex AIR API (see Chapter 4, "Using ActionScript 3.0"), you will need to use the Flash CS3 authoring tool with the "AIR 1.1 Update for Flash CS3" (www.adobe.com/go/kb403682), or the Flash CS4 authoring tool, which natively includes AIR publishing capability. To publish AIR 1.5 applications in Flash CS4, you may need to download and install the "Adobe AIR 1.5 Update for Flash CS4 Professional" (http://kb.adobe.com/selfservice/viewContent.do?externalId=b62ce659&sliceId=2#air_15_11_17_2008).

Creating New Projects

You can create new projects a few different ways:

- ❏ You can select a wizard by right-clicking in the Navigator View and selecting New ➪ Project, or from the main menu, clicking File ➪ New ➪ Other, as illustrated in Figure 6-3.

- ❏ You can choose a specific project wizard type straight from the main menu by selecting File ➪ New ➪ *<specific type>*, or from the context menu in the Navigator View New ➪ *<specific type>*. The specific type options are Flex Project, ActionScript Project, or Flex Library Project.

- ❏ You can import a previous project by selecting from the main menu File ➪ Import or by selecting Import from the context menu in the Navigator View. See Chapter 8, "Using Flex Builder 3," for more information on importing projects.

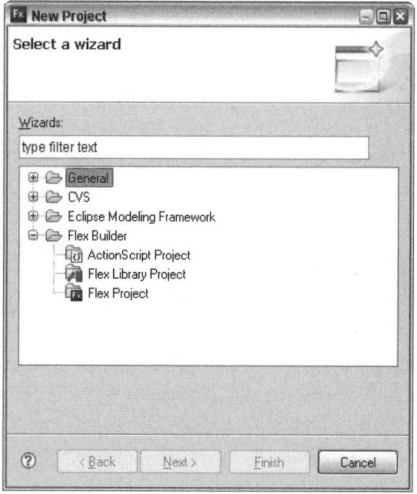

Figure 6-3

Each project type has a specific wizard for creating a project. The wizard for creating a new Flex project walks you through the application data access setup, project file location, and build path setup dialog windows.

Creating a Flex Application

Flex Builder is the integrated development environment (IDE) for Flex. To start creating applications in Flex, you need to create a workspace that points to folder locations on your filesystem that contain projects, which are assemblies or resources necessary to code your project. In the last chapter, you learned how to create a workspace in Flex. In this chapter, you'll take that one step further and create a basic Flex application in Flex Builder.

1. If you have not yet created a workspace, open Flex Builder, select File ⇨ Switch Workspace ⇨ Other, and browse to where your workspace folder will be located in {root}/profx3book/. This will be your workspace folder for all the exercises in this book. We will be using the default workspace metadata location (configuration #1), which was mentioned in the last chapter.

{root} *is the root folder of whatever hard drive you are currently using for your project files. In the case of Windows or any operating system with a 256-character limit on file paths, it is a good idea not to nest workspace folders too deeply or you may find that large projects with a complex nested package structure may get corrupted because your operating system has reached its maximum file path character limit.*

Creating a Flex Project

Now that you've created your workspace, you need to create a project.

2. Right-click in the empty Navigator View, and select New ⇨ Flex Project.

3. In the New Flex Project dialog, fill in the name of the project as **Chapter_06_Flex_Project**, as shown in Figure 6-4.

Flex Builder will not let you use any characters in the name other than letters, numbers, underscores (_), hyphens (-), or dollar signs ($). Although it lets you use spaces, it is not recommended that you use spaces in the project name, as this may cause problems if you attempt to rename the project later.

> **If you have just opened Flex Builder after installation and have not yet created a workspace,** *do not accept the Default location entry.* **Upon installation, this will by default point to the My Documents folder deep in the folder structure of your hard drive. For simplicity's sake and to safeguard against the file path character limitation, place project workspaces on the root of the drive.**

Notice that "Use Default location" is checked and fills in the rest of the field when you enter the name of the project. Had you selected Workspace configuration #2 from the previous chapter (i.e., your workspace metadata is in a different location than the workspace folder), you would want to uncheck this box so that the project folder was not created in your workspace metadata directory c:\profx3book_workspace.

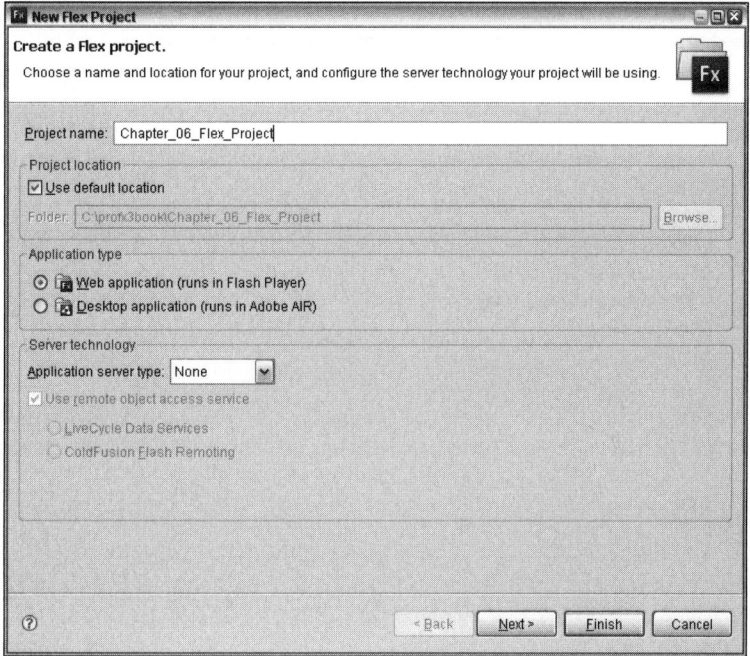

Figure 6-4

You also have the option here of selecting whether you will be compiling to a Web application (Flash Player) or a Desktop application (AIR). For this exercise, you will keep the setting at Web application.

Keep the Application Server type as None. You would select one of the options in this menu only if you wanted to deploy your Flex application compilation directly to a server environment. For more information on creating Flex server projects, see the Adobe Flex documentation at http://livedocs.adobe.com/flex/3/html/projects_3.html. For additional information on building server-based Flex projects, see Part VIII, "Server Integration," and Part IX, "Data Services" later in this book.

4. Click Next.

5. This is the screen for determining the output folder that the Flex compiler will publish the final files to. Keep the default at `bin-debug`, for this is a standard name for the output folder, and click Next.

6. The screen shown in Figure 6-5 is used to set the build paths for the Flex application.

The Source path tab links any source locations that are external to the project folder. There are none for this project, so leave this blank. The Library path tab sets build paths for any additional library SWCs you wish to compile with our project. There are none for this example, so leave the default here as well.

The Main source folder field indicated the folder name where all of your project code will go. Leave it at the default of src, which is a common convention.

The Main application filename field will default to the name of the project folder. This is a little long for a filename, so change it to Main.mxml.

Since you are not compiling the application on a server, leave the Output folder URL field blank, per the default.

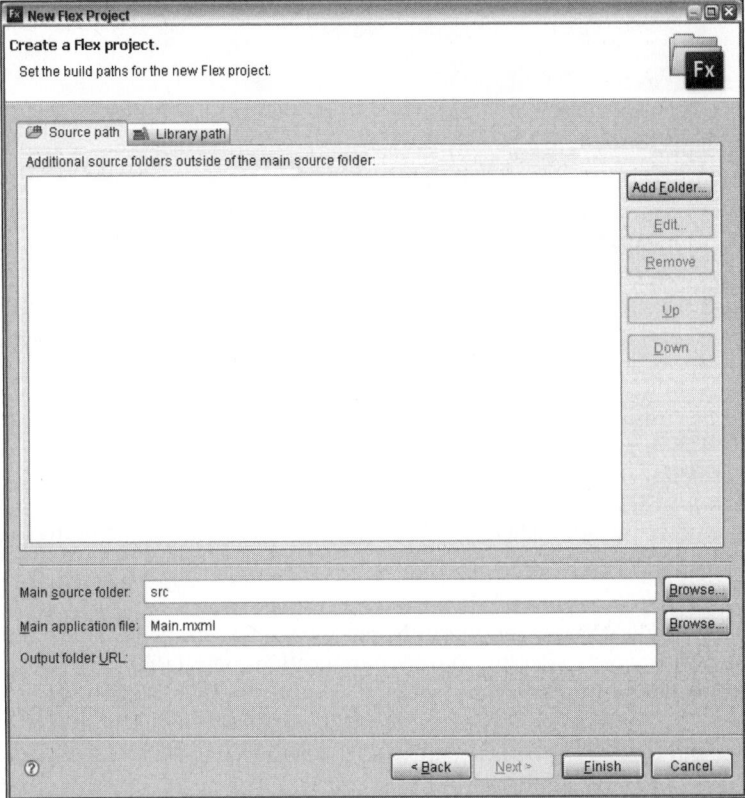

Figure 6-5

It is a good idea to use the same character restrictions on the main source filename as you did for the project name. In addition, as a best practice, always name the MXML file with a capital letter. As will be explained in the next chapter, an MXML file resolves to an ActionScript class, and since class names by convention start with uppercase letters, so should MXML filenames.

7. Click Finish.

You should now see the project in the Flex Navigator View, and the `Main.mxml` file loaded in the editor (see Figure 6-6).

By default, the editor defaults to the Source Mode Editor. For now, let's use the Design Mode Editor.

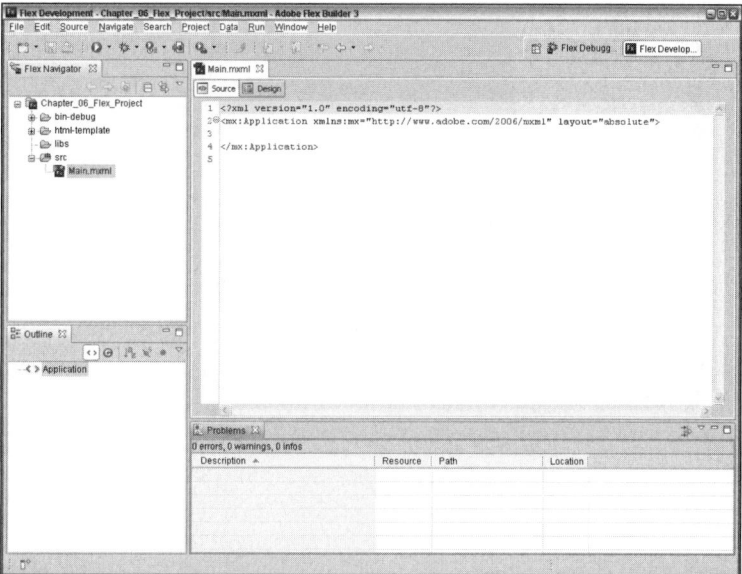

Figure 6-6

Using Design Mode

8. Click the Design button on the editor. If the Problems View is visible, click the minimize button on that view panel to hide it in order to maximize the working area. Minimize the States View, as you won't be needing that view for this exercise either.

    As shown in Figure 6-7, on the bottom left you should now see the Components View, which contains a list of all Flex UI components available. And on the right, the Flex Properties View, which allows you to edit component properties.

    For Flash developers, much of this is looking familiar by now, as the Flash IDE has many of the same layout tools, in addition to others. The Components View of Flex Builder is like the Components panel in Flash, and the Properties View in Flex is like the Properties panel in Flash. Although the Flex Builder Design mode is only for layout, the Flash IDE allows for the creation of graphical content via its drawing and animation tools. So if you need to create and animate graphical content, use Flash Professional. See Chapters 26 and 29 for more information on integrating Flash content into Flex applications.

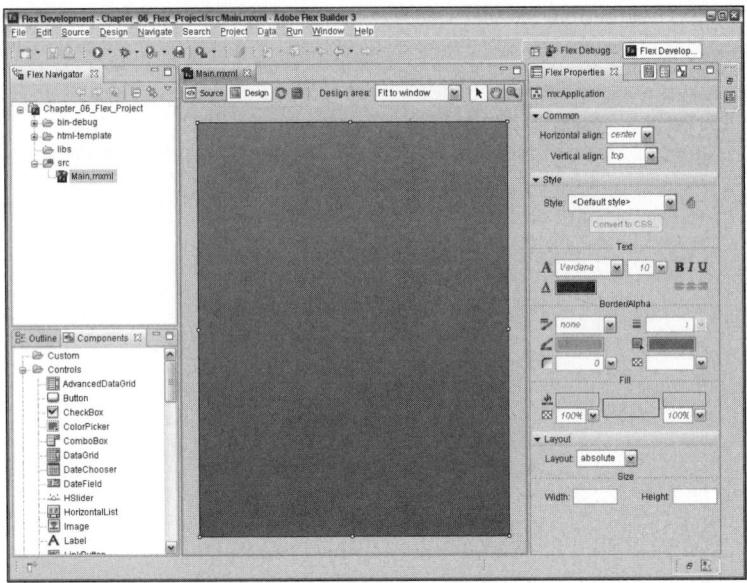

Figure 6-7

9. Click on the blank canvas in the editor. What appears in the Flex Properties View are the prop-
    erties of the application, which is the main layout container component for the rest of your
    application. Under the Layout section, notice that Layout is set to `absolute` by default.

    An *absolute layout* means that objects can be positioned either by their absolute x and y pixel
    locations on the stage, or according to *layout constraints*, which is new in Flex 3. More in-depth
    information on layout techniques in Flex can be found in Chapter 12, "Layout Strategies."

Using the Components and Properties Views

10. In the Components view ➪ Layout folder, drag a Panel component onto the design canvas.

    Drag the `Panel` component until two cyan snap guides appear in the design canvas to indicate
    that the component is aligned vertical top and horizontal center, as illustrated in Figure 6-8.

    These snap guides allow you to position components in relation to one another given default
    style settings. In this case, you are positioning the `Panel` component in relation to the root
    application container visible in the design area.

11. In the Common pane of the Flex Properties View, give the Panel set the ID property to `textPanel`.
    You have now set the instance name for an object of the `Panel` component class.

    The ID property of a Flex component is the class object's instance name.

12. Double-click on the top part of the `Panel`, type **Design Mode Is Cool** (or whatever you would
    like to type there), and then press Enter.

    If you look at the value of the Title property, it now contains the text you just typed. This dem-
    onstrates that you can edit a component's text through a property listed in the Flex Properties

View, or by *context editing* in the design canvas as you have just done, by double-clicking the component text. This applies to any component whose text or label is visible in Design mode.

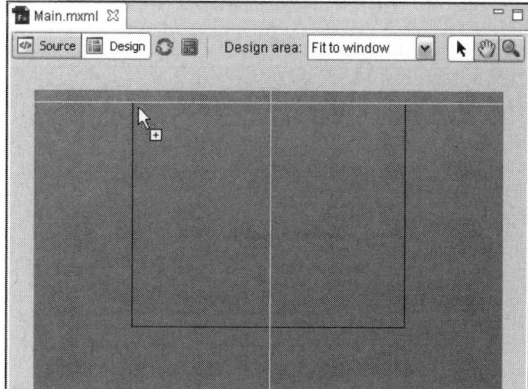

Figure 6-8

13.   If you cannot see the whole Layout pane, collapse the Style pane in the Flex Properties View so that the Layout pane is visible without scrolling.

Observe that although you may think you positioned the `Panel` in the center of the design canvas, looking at the Layout pane, it seems it is not. How do you get the `Panel` to align itself to the center of the canvas by default? By using a horizontal layout constraint.

Using Layout Constraints

14.   In the Layout pane, select the top middle check box. You will see a vertical green line and a number appear in the bottom text field. Change that number to 0. This "zeros in" the `Panel` with the center of the design canvas or stage. Notice that in the editor your `Panel` is now in the center of the design canvas.

Figure 6-9 illustrates what you should now see in your Flex Properties View.

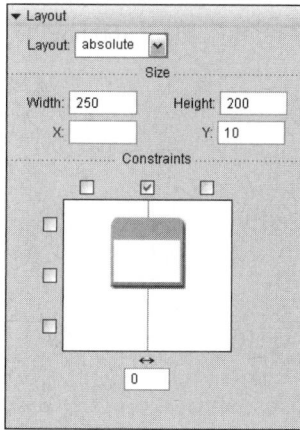

Figure 6-9

Now you're going to set up the alignment for components *inside* the `Panel` container.

15. Make sure that the `Panel` component is still selected. In the Common pane, set the "Horizontal align" to `center`, and the "Vertical align" to `middle`.

16. In the Layout pane, set the Layout property to `vertical`. This assigns a proportional layout to the inside of the `Panel` component.

Constraint-based layouts only work when the parent container has its `layout` *property set to* `absolute`.

17. From the Controls folder in the Components View, drag a Label component into the center of the `Panel`.

18. Double-click the Label in the design canvas, and give it a short phrase of text, such as **Hello Flex 3!!**, and then press Enter.

19. In the Flex Properties View Style pane, set the font weight to bold, with a font size of 16.

20. From the Controls folder in the Components View, drag a Button under the Label text.

21. In the Flex Properties View Common pane, set the Label property to Click Me and press Enter. Your in-progress Flex application should look like Figure 6-10.

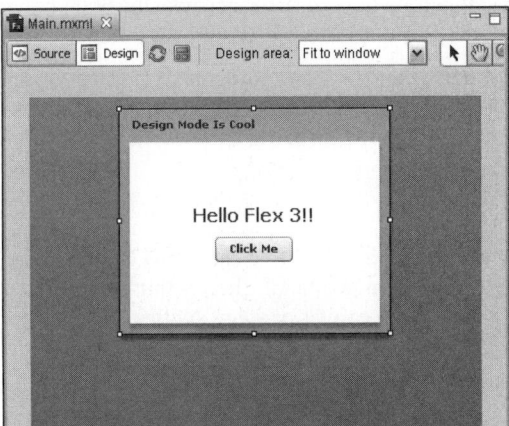

Figure 6-10

Navigating the Design Area

Now you'll explore some of the design tools.

22. Collapse the Flex Properties View by selecting the minimize button at the top right of the view so that you can see all of the Design mode controls at the top of the Editor View.

23. In the Design Area drop-down, you should see a few default options: fit to window, 1024×768, 800×600, and Custom size. Select Custom size. You will now see the options window shown in Figure 6-11.

24. In the Width and Height fields, enter 640 and 480, respectively, and then press OK.

You should now see the design canvas shrink down to 640×480 pixels (see Figure 6-12). This feature allows you to preview a static representation of your application at different sizes, which is handy to know if your design is to adapt to or look good at certain screen resolutions.

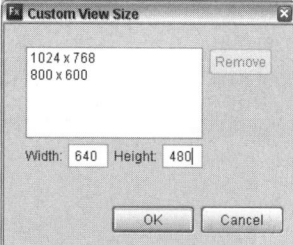

Figure 6-11

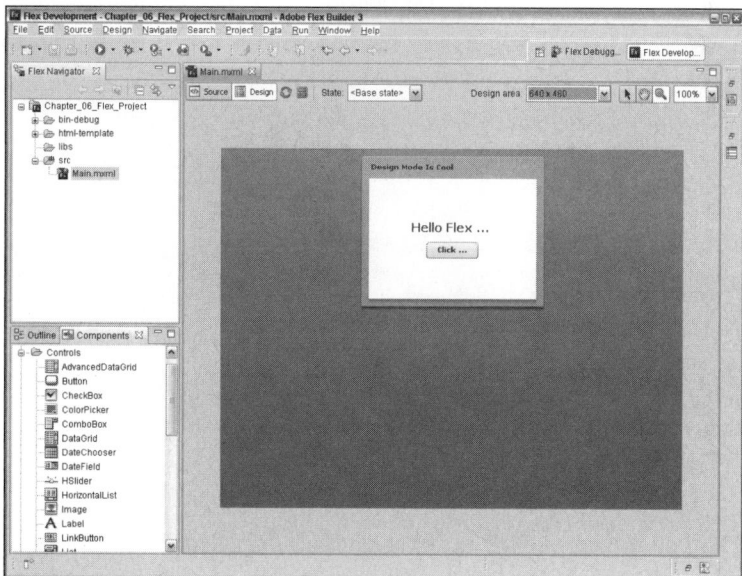

Figure 6-12

25. Experiment with the selection, pan and zoom tools on the right of the Design mode toolbar. You'll find there are keyboard shortcuts for these tools: *V* for the selection tool, *H* for the pan tool, and *Z* for the zoom tool. You can also zoom in with Ctrl+= and zoom out with Ctrl+-.

26. Click the Refresh button, which is the button in the Design mode toolbar that looks like a circular recycle icon. This will refresh the design canvas layout in the application.

The Refresh button is also useful for viewing changes in a CSS file in Design mode. Note that child components are not updated in Design mode.

Viewing the Display Hierarchy

27. Click the Panel component on the stage.

28. In the Design mode toolbar, click the Show Surrounding Containers button immediately to the right of the Refresh button.

You will now see how the container components nest inside one another, as shown in Figure 6-13.

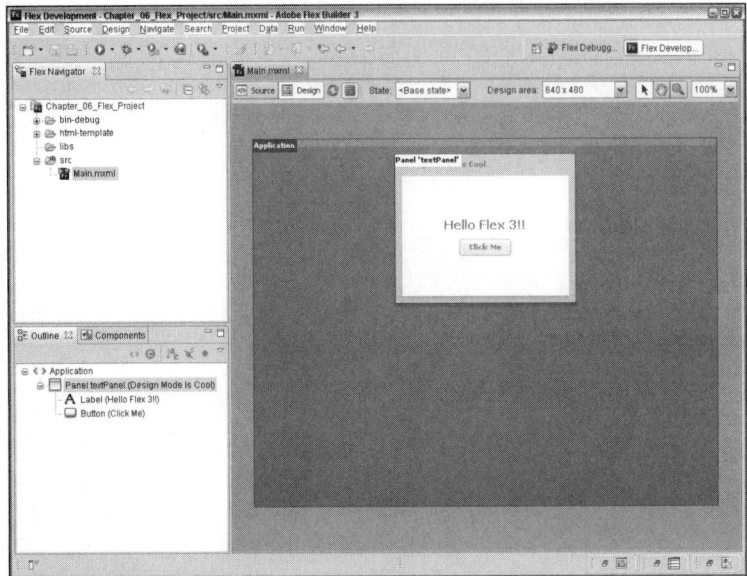

Figure 6-13

29. Click on the Outline View. This will show you the layout order of your components in the application.

The Outline View has three parts: MXML View, Class View, and CSS View. Here we're using the Outline MXML View. Chapter 8 takes a look at the two other kinds of Outline Views.

You can now clearly see that the `Application` container is the main application component. Contained within is a `Panel` with an instance name of `textPanel` and within the `textPanel` object lie the `Label` and `Button` components. This is a very useful tool once your application reaches a certain complexity, enabling you to find containers and components no matter where they are located in the display hierarchy. For more information on the `Application` class, see Chapter 7, "MXML Fundamentals," and Chapter 10, "The Component Life Cycle."

Working with Fast Views

30. Select the Components panel, open the Controls folder and scroll down until you get to the `TextInput` component.

31. Drag a `TextInput` component under the button in the `Panel`.

Now say you want to make a quick adjustment to a property in the Flex Properties View, but you don't want to keep the view there. This is where Fast Views come in.

A fast view is a quick way to interact with a minimized view so that it doesn't take up a lot of room in the workbench.

32. If you didn't collapse your Flex Properties View in step 22, minimize this view now.

33. Click the Flex Properties icon (not the Restore icon to its left) where it lies in its minimized state in the workbench taskbar. This activates fast view for Flex Properties, as shown in Figure 6-14.

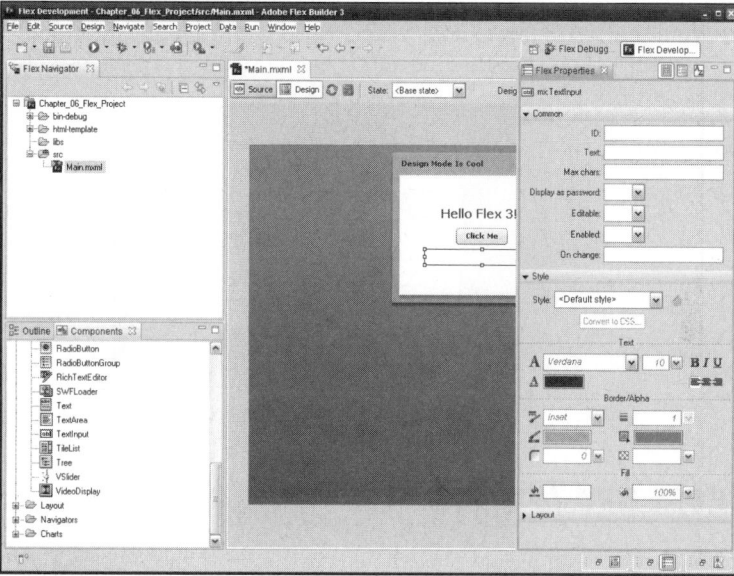

Figure 6-14

34. Give the mx:TextInput component an ID value of labelInput. This will allow you to refer specifically to the component later on.

35. Now click on the design canvas, or anywhere else in the workbench. You should see the Flex Properties View return to its minimized state.

Using Data Binding

Now let's get the application to accept user input.

36. Select the Label component above the button, and open the Flex Properties View.

37. Give the component a Text value of {labelInput.text}. Be sure to include the curly braces "{}".

You should see the value "{labelInput.text}" appear in the Label component.

38. In the main toolbar, press the green arrow button whose tooltip says "Run Main."

You can also use the shortcut Ctrl/Option+F11 to run the compilation of your application.

You should see your application compiled and displayed in your default browser.

39. Type something in the input text field.

You will find that the text that appears in the label above mirrors the text you type into the field. In Figure 6-15, the user has typed in "hello world!!" which shows up in the label.

This is what is known as *data binding*. Data binding is the process of "binding" or associating a data *source* (the TextInput component) with a data *destination* (the Label component), which is declared with the curly bracket ({ }) syntax. Think of data binding as a special kind of event dispatcher/listener declaration. Data binding is a core feature of the Flex framework and will be used time and again throughout this book. For more specific information on data binding, see Chapter 11, "Using Data Binding and Events."

Figure 6-15

Using Triggers and Effects

This example would not be complete without a demonstration of Flex's visual effects capabilities.

40. Select the Button component on the stage, and click on the Category subview button, which is the middle of the three buttons in the upper-right corner of the Flex Properties View. This will get you access to other properties of the component.

41. Change the label property in the Common category to "Glow Baby Glow!"

42. Open the Effects category folder, if it's not already open, and beside mouseDownEffect, type **Glow** (see Figure 6-16). This calls the Glow effect class when the mouseDown event is dispatched from the Button. The mouseDownEffect property is called a *trigger*.

There may be some confusion about what an effect is, since the Flex documentation states that a trigger is not an event, even though triggers act somewhat like event handlers. In fact, a trigger is a placeholder reference to a specific event listener method. When the MouseEvent.MOUSE_DOWN event is called, the mouseDownEffect property is called as a function. If the property contains a reference to an event handler function, that event handler is called. If not, nothing happens. So a trigger is a proxy reference to an internal event listener method that calls the effect class stored in the trigger property.

43. Run your application. You will see the final application in your browser. Click on the button, and it will glow blue and fade.

Figure 6-16

Compiling Your Application

You can compile your application in one of a few ways:

❑ Click the green Run button in the main toolbar or select another Flex application from the menu beside it.

❑ Select the Run menu, and under the Run submenu, select the application to compile.

❑ Selecting the Run option compiles, publishes, and displays your application in your default browser.

❑ Using the keyboard shortcut Ctrl/Option+F11, which is the same as selecting the Run button.

❑ By default Flex Builder will automatically compile your project every time you save a file. If you do not want Flex Builder to compile automatically, uncheck Project ➪ Build Automatically.

Creating an ActionScript Application

In this exercise, you're going to learn a bit more about Flex Builder 3 by creating an ActionScript application in Source mode.

> *Most of the time you spend in Flex Builder will probably be creating code in Source mode, using Design mode only for quick mockups or prototypes, or to check the layout of certain UI.*

Creating an ActionScript Project

Creating an ActionScript project means that using the Flex framework is optional, and must be explicitly imported for the application to be compiled with the Flex framework. This means you can, if you wish, create SWF applications with a small file size footprint that depend solely on the ActionScript 3.0 and Flash API classes.

1. Right-click in the empty Navigator View, and select New ⇨ Flex Project.

2. In the resulting screen, shown in Figure 6-17, fill in the name of the project as **Chapter_06_AS_Project**.

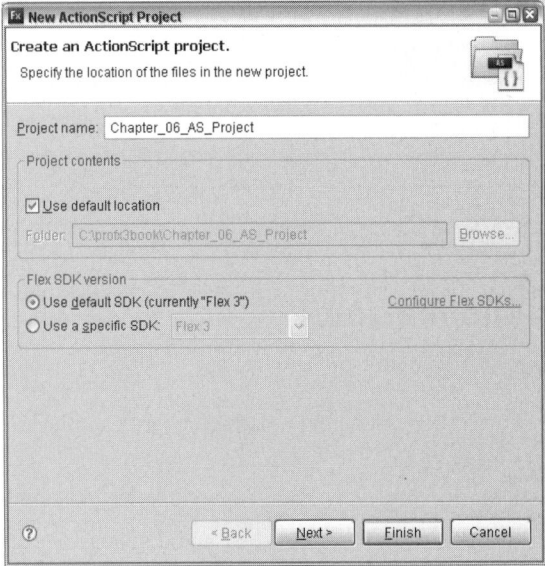

Figure 6-17

3. Click Next.

4. This screen will set the build paths and the application filename for the ActionScript project (see Figure 6-18). Set the Main source folder as src (short for "source"), and the Main application file as DrawCircles.as. Leave the other fields as per their defaults.

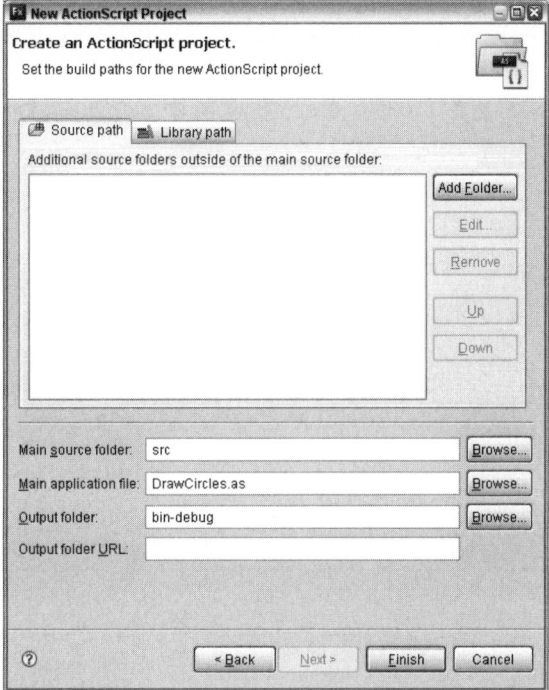

Figure 6-18

5. Click Finish.

As shown in Figure 6-19, you should now see the project in the Flex Navigator View, and the DrawCircles.as file loaded in the editor containing the following default code:

```
package {
    import flash.display.Sprite;

    public class DrawCircles extends Sprite
    {
        public function DrawCircles()
        {
        }
    }
}
```

Notice that DrawCircles extends Sprite by default and not a Flex framework class. By default the editor defaults to the Source Mode Editor, since you can only use Design mode when working on an MXML file.

Notice that the Outline View now displays the default class structure for the DrawCircles class you just created.

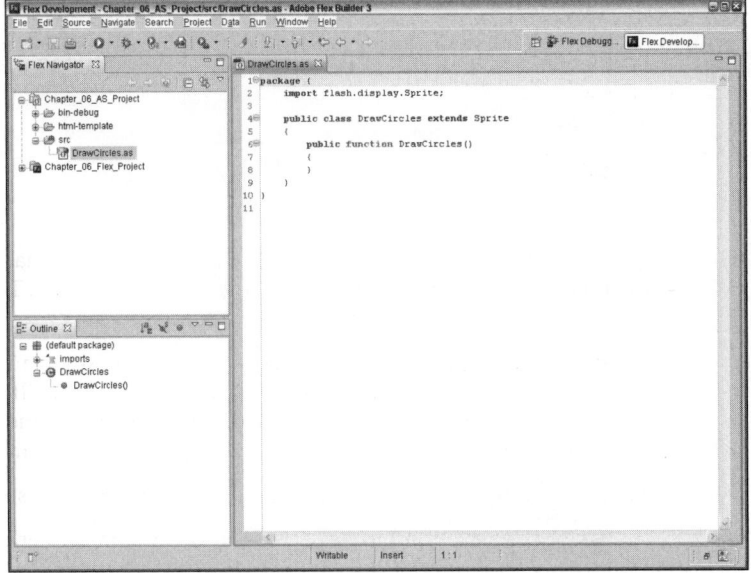

Figure 6-19

6. Add the source code shown in Listing 6-1 to the file.

Listing 6-1: DrawCircles.as

```
package {
    import flash.display.Graphics;
    import flash.display.Shape;
    import flash.display.Sprite;
    import flash.display.StageScaleMode;
    import flash.display.StageAlign;

    public class DrawCircles extends Sprite
    {
        public function DrawCircles()
        {
            stage.scaleMode = StageScaleMode.NO_SCALE;
            stage.align = StageAlign.TOP_LEFT;
            doDrawCircle( 0x336699 );
            doDrawCircle( 0x993333 );
            doDrawCircle( 0x339933 );
        }

        private function doDrawCircle( color:uint ):void
        {
            var child:Shape = new Shape();
            child.graphics.beginFill( color );
            child.graphics.lineStyle( 2, 0xCCCCCC );
```

```
                child.graphics.drawCircle( 30, 40, 30);
                child.graphics.endFill();
                child.x = (this.numChildren * 65) + 10;
                child.y = 0;
                addChild(child);
            }
        }
    }
```

The first two lines in the constructor function set the stage properties so that the SWF will appear at the top left and will be resized rather than scaled in the browser. The constructor then calls the doDrawCircle method, passing a hex color number for the new circle.

The doDrawCircle method uses the Flash drawing API (you could say the "Flash 6 Drawing API," not the new "Flash 10 Drawing API") to draw a gray circle with a fill, the color that has been passed to its argument. It then positions the new circle according to the current number of circles already created and adds the object to the stage with the addChild method.

7. Run the application. You should see a blue, a red, and a green circle on the stage.

   See Chapter 8 for more information on using the code editor in Flex Builder.

Now let's compare file sizes between the two applications from this chapter.

Comparing File Sizes

8. Navigate to the bin-debug folder in the Flex project, and right-click ⇨ Properties on the Main.swf file. You will observe that the Main.mxml application is about 276KB.

9. Navigate to the bin-debug folder in this ActionScript project, and right-click ⇨ Properties on the DrawCircles.swf file. You will find that the file size is an astounding 1KB.

   This demonstrates just how much the Flex framework adds to a SWF file. If the file size of your SWF is a concern, such as the development of small embedded Flash widgets or online Flash advertising, it pays not to use the Flex framework. (Shhh! Don't tell anyone I told you that! This is a Flex book, after all!) For more information about the class APIs available without the Flex Framework, see Chapter 4, "Using ActionScript 3.0." For a review of where Flex fits into Flash platform development, see Chapter 1, "Why Flex?"

The (Undocumented) [SWF] Metadata Tag

In Flash authoring, you have a multitude of publishing options for controlling the actual width and height of the stage in the SWF application, the frame rate, and so on. In Flex, these settings can be configured in properties of the Application MXML tag. For an ActionScript application in Flex Builder, some compiler settings can be configured using the undocumented [SWF] metadata tag.

You can also configure publishing settings via the compiler options in the project properties settings. See Chapter 8 for more information on common Flex compiler settings.

Let's go back to the last example, and add a few steps to the end of that exercise:

10. Add the following highlighted line after the import statements and before the class declaration:

```
package {
    import flash.display.Graphics;
    ...
        [SWF(width="320", height="240", frameRate="31", backgroundColor="#33FF99")]

    public class DrawCircles extends Sprite
    ...
```

11. Run the application. You should see a blue, a red, and a green circle on a stage that measures only 320×240 pixels, having a blue background instead of the default blue-gray. Figure 6-20 shows the before and after implementations of the [SWF] metadata tag (albeit in black and white).

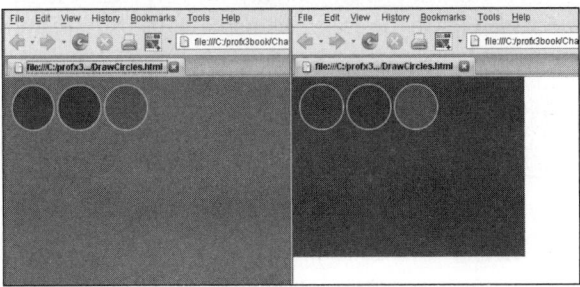

Figure 6-20

[SWF] Metadata Properties

The [SWF] metadata tag has the properties shown in the following table:

Property	Description
backgroundColor	The background color of the stage shown in the browser.
pageTitle	A string representing the title of the HTML page shown in the browser.
frameRate	The frame rate of the SWF.
width	The width of the SWF displayed in the browser in pixels.
height	The height of the SWF displayed in the browser in pixels.
widthPercent	The width of the SWF in proportion to the inner browser width in pixels. *Be sure to use the percent (%) sign in the value.*
heightPercent	The height of the SWF in proportion to the inner browser width in pixels. *Be sure to use the percent (%) sign in the value.*

Continued

Continued

Property	Description
scriptRecursionLimit	The maximum depth or stack overflow limit of the Flash Player call stack, which is to say how many times a recursive script will run before the Flash Player stops.
scriptTimeLimit	The maximum duration, in seconds, that an ActionScript event listener can execute before the Flash Player assumes that it has stopped processing and aborts it. The default value is 60 seconds, which is also the maximum allowable value.

These properties convey instructions to the Flex compiler about how to publish your SWF application. The backgroundColor, pageTitle, width, height, widthPercent, and heightPercent properties set values that are used in the creation of the HTML wrapper file. The frameRate, scriptRecursionLimit and scriptTimeLimit properties determine some of the compiler parameters for the creation of the SWF itself.

Summary

In this chapter, you have learned some valuable things about the basics of the Flex Builder compilation process, as well as how to author and compile Flex and ActionScript projects. In the first exercise, you learned how to create a Flex Project and a Flex application using Design mode editing. Along the way you learned how to use other views, navigating the design area, the basics of data binding and effects. In the second exercise, you built an application in ActionScript with Flex Builder without using the Flex framework, and learned a few things about configuring SWF attributes with the [SWF] metadata tag.

In the next chapter, you'll learn everything you need to know about the Flex MXML language.

MXML Fundamentals

MXML is an XML-based, presentational markup language intended for laying out Flex components much like one would lay out HTML elements on a page. MXML markup may be combined with both CSS styles and ActionScript in the same file to create complete applications. This chapter explores the underlying principles of MXML, its syntax, and the ways in which it can be used with other languages in the Flex ecosystem.

The term "MXML" is not in fact an acronym, even though it is obviously derived from the term "XML". Although Adobe, and Macromedia before it, has never ascribed a definition to this term, the likeliest meaning for a possible acronym is "Macromedia eXtensible Markup Language," or the "M" is a remnant from the Macromedia "MX" line of products when Flex was first under development.

Language Principles

In this section, we'll explore the basic principles of the MXML language.

MXML Is XML

Since an MXML document is in XML, it must conform to the following guidelines:

❏ It must start with an XML declaration, like so:

```
<?xml version="1.0" encoding="utf-8"?>
```

❏ It must be a well-formed XML document, which means that each element is closed properly, each element is nested properly, attributes are declared with single or double quotation marks, and comments adhere to XML standards.

❏ The document must contain a root node. For the main application file for instance, this would be either `<mx:Application />` for a Flex application or `<mx:WindowedApplication />` for an AIR application.

Naming Conventions

When you create new MXML files, you must adhere to the following naming conventions:

❑   Filenames can only start with a letter or an underscore (_), and they can only contain alphanumeric and underscore characters after that.

❑   Filenames cannot be the same name as ActionScript class names, component id values, or reserved keywords such as the word "application." See the list of reserved keywords in Chapter 3, "ActionScript 3.0 Fundamentals." Likewise, MXML filenames cannot be the same as MXML component names in the Flex framework.

❑   All filenames are required to end with the lowercase .mxml file extension.

Each MXML file is compiled into an ActionScript class by the Flex compiler, and from there into SWF bytecode. The MXML filename represents a portion of the actual ActionScript class name as rendered by the MXML interpreter in the Flex compiler.

Flex applications are compiled with the MXMLC (mxmlc.exe) compiler. AIR applications are compiled with the AMXMLC (amxmlc.exe) compiler, which converts the main MXML file and related source into an AIR application instead of a web application. Both are considered to be the "Flex Compiler" for the purposes of this text.

MXML Syntax

MXML is written in the form of an XML tag with the following syntax:

```
<namespace:Component [classMember="someValue"]/>
```

or

```
<namespace:Interpreted [setting="value"]/>
```

The namespace of the component determines its class or framework origins. The name identifies the function of the tag, which may be a component class or an interpreted directive.

If the tag represents a component, the component name represents the ActionScript class identified as belonging to that namespace. Values for component properties and events can be defined by tag attributes:

```
<mx:Button label="Click me" id="myButton" />
```

This tag declares the Button component in MXML, which creates an instance of the Button class. The mx namespace identifies this component class as belonging to the Flex framework. And the label attribute declares the label property of the component class with a string value. The id value of a component tag always represents the instance name of the class object being created.

If the tag is an interpreted or "MXML-only" component, tag attributes will represent additional settings as opposed to class members:

```
<mx:Script source="code.as" />
```

In the preceding MXML code, the `Script` tag represents a compiler directive to add the ActionScript source code contained in the filename defined by the `source` property to the MXML code at compile time. An interpreted or MXML-only tag may only be associated with the Flex framework namespace.

Display Hierarchy

Since MXML is written in an XML format, the tag hierarchy makes it easy to specify parent-child container relationships.

In the last chapter, you created a Flex project, and with it an application built in Design Mode, as shown in Figure 7-1.

Figure 7-1

Open up that same project, and switch to Source Mode in the editor. You will see the following code:

```
<?xml version="1.0" encoding="utf-8"?>
<mx:Application xmlns:mx="http://www.adobe.com/2006/mxml" layout="absolute">
    <mx:Panel y="10" width="250" height="200" layout="vertical"
        id="textPanel" title="Design Mode Is Cool"
        horizontalCenter="0" horizontalAlign="center" verticalAlign="middle">
        <mx:Label fontWeight="bold" fontSize="16" text="{labelInput.text}"
            id="daLabel"/>
        <mx:Button label="Glow Baby Glow!" mouseDownEffect="Glow"/>
        <mx:TextInput id="labelInput"/>
    </mx:Panel>
</mx:Application>
```

When you look at XML hierarchy of the code, you can clearly identify that a `Panel` component is contained within the main `Application`. Within that `Panel` is a `Label`, a `Button`, and a `TextInput` component.

The XML hierarchy of the MXML tags represents the display relationships that the components have with each other, their spacing and their layout on the stage.

MXML Namespaces

In XML, namespaces are used to avoid potential naming conflicts with other components that have the same name but a different class package or API. Each MXML tag in the Flex framework is interpreted as a compiler action or is mapped to a class by the Flex compiler.

When you create an MXML document, the root tag defines the namespaces to be used in that document. Some of the ways this can be written, depending on the root container class, are:

```
<mx:Application xmlns:mx="http://www.adobe.com/2006/mxml" …
```

```
<mx:WindowedApplication xmlns:mx="http://www.adobe.com/2006/mxml" …
```

```
<mx:Canvas xmlns:mx="http://www.adobe.com/2006/mxml" …
```

In the first example, the mx namespace identifies the Application class as belonging to the Flex framework. This namespace is defined by the xmlns attribute, which stands for "XML namespace." The namespace declaration syntax for an MXML document is as follows:

```
xmlns:namespace="[URI or class package]"
```

The value of the namespace declaration may be either a URI (Universal Resource Indicator) or a class package.

Namespaces and URIs

In the case of the mx namespace, this is identified with a URI. A URI is like a generic form of a URL, and is written very much like one, except that it does not point to a real web address. If you type http://www.adobe.com/2006/mxml into your browser, you will get an invalid URL.

This URI serves two purposes: to identify the company that created the namespace, and to provide a reference for all the tags using the same prefix.

These are the steps for Flex Builder to associate the mx namespace with its associated component classes:

1. The Application (or WindowedApplication) tag is written as follows:

    ```
    <mx:Application xmlns:mx="http://www.adobe.com/2006/mxml" …
    ```

    This associates the mx namespace with the http://www.adobe.com/2006/mxml URI.

2. The Flex MXMLC compiler looks in the flex-config.xml file, and the AIR AMXMLC compiler looks in the air-config.xml file for compiler settings; both are located in the installation directory \Flex Builder 3\sdks\{sdk#}\frameworks.

3. The flex-config.xml and air-config.xml files both contain the following XML:

    ```
    <namespaces>
        <namespace>
            <uri>http://www.adobe.com/2006/mxml</uri>
            <manifest>mxml-manifest.xml</manifest>
        </namespace>
    </namespaces>
    ```

    This associates the http://www.adobe.com/2006/mxml URI with the mxml-manifest.xml file.

4. The mxml-manifest.xml file helps the compiler associate all the MXML component tag names with their fully qualified class names. For instance, the <mx:Button> MXML tag would have the following mxml-manifest definition:

    ```
    <component id="Button" class="mx.controls.Button"/>
    ```

This is how the compiler knows which tag resolves to which class in the Flex framework. Although core ActionScript data type classes are not a part of the Flex framework, the mx namespace is still used when declaring them in MXML. See "Core Data Type Objects in MXML" later in this chapter.

By adding new </namespace> definitions in the config file, indicating a unique URI string and a manifest file, custom component classes and APIs can be identified with the new URI.

For example:

Defining Namespaces for Custom Components

flex-config.xml:

```
<namespace>
    <uri>http://www.foocompany.com/uri/mxml</uri>
    <manifest>foo-manifest.xml</manifest>
</namespace>
```

foo-manifest.xml:

```
<componentPackage>
    <component id="CustomButton" class="foo.components.CustomButton"/>
    ...
</componentPackage>
```

Namespaces and Packages

A namespace can also be associated directly with a class package, without the necessity of defining a hard-coded URI and associated configuration XML files. Since the Flex framework components are already defined in this fashion, this technique is most commonly used for custom classes.

The code for defining the namespace for custom classes with a class package is written similarly to the way you would write an import statement with a wildcard:

```
<mx:Application ... xmlns:profx3book="com.wrox.profx3book.*" ...
```

Similar to how an import statement works, the package declaration may only apply to the immediate folder, not its subfolders. For it to be applicable to a subfolder, each subpackage must be identified with a different namespace:

```
<mx:Application ...
    xmlns:profx3Utils="com.wrox.profx3book.utils.*"
    xmlns:profx3Comp="com.wrox.profx3book.components.*"
    xmlns:profx3Data="com.wrox.profx3book.data.*"
    ...
>
```

Once a namespace is identified with a class package, and a component class is present in the pertinent class package (whether it be in MXML or ActionScript), the component can be instantiated in MXML:

```
<pfx3Comp:CustomComponent id="myCustomComponent" />
```

The preceding code creates a `com.wrox.profx3book.components.CustomComponent` class object with an instance name of `myCustomComponent`.

> *The advantage of associating a namespace with a URI as opposed to a package now becomes apparent: if a namespace is associated with a URI, many classes in different packages composing a framework or API library may be associated with that namespace. Whereas associating a namespace with a class package confines the definition to that class package and no other. The package-defined namespace is quicker to code and does not require modifying a configuration file, which makes it easier to distribute code. But a URI-defined namespace has the flexibility to encompass a greater number of classes and packages in one namespace. A package-defined namespace is traditionally used for custom Flex components, whereas a URI/config file–defined namespace is mostly used for third-party APIs or frameworks.*

For more information on creating custom MXML components, see Chapter 17, "Custom MXML Components."

The Local Namespace

You can also refer to component classes in the root application package, which is to say the same package as the main MXML application file, by what is known as the *local namespace*. The syntax when using this namespace is:

```
xmlns:{ns name}="*"
```

which can be used as follows:

```
<mx:Application xmlns:mx="http://www.adobe.com/2006/mxml"
    xmlns:myLocal="*">
    <myLocal:LocalComponent/>
</mx:Application>
```

For the `myLocal` namespace to work, the `LocalComponent` component class file must reside in the same root directory as the main application. See Chapters 16 and 17 for more information on creating custom Flex components.

The Null Namespace

A *null namespace* can be used with a URI or class package, enabling the instantiation of MXML components without requiring a namespace declaration. When you use the "null namespace," the `xmlns` remains undeclared:

```
<mx:Application …
    xmlns="com.foo.*">
```

Assuming, for example, that the `com.foo.CustomComponent` class has been defined, this component tag can then be written in MXML without a namespace declaration:

```
<CustomComponent/>
```

If you choose to associate a null namespace with the Flex framework by declaring:

```
xmlns="http://www.adobe.com/2006/mxml"
```

all Flex component tags in that MXML document must be written without a namespace.

Although it is more common to change the default namespace for the Flex framework from mx *to a null namespace, this namespace can in fact be a string of your choosing, such as* xmlns:flex="http://www.adobe.com/2006/mxml", *for example.*

Since Flex Builder's code intelligence can fill in the namespace for all component tags, this technique is used by developers more out of personal preference than productivity. For more information on Flex Builder's code intelligence features, see Chapter 8, "Developing with Flex Builder 3."

Using MXML

There are two main considerations for using MXML in your application: the tag structures, and the properties within the MXML markup, which can be expressed in a number of ways which are covered next.

MXML Tags

There are three main types of MXML tags in Flex, loosely categorized as component tags, interpreted tags, and core data type tags.

Component Tags

Components make up the majority of tags in MXML. There are considered to be two types of component tags, representing visual and nonvisual components.

Visual components are the user interface components of the Flex framework. They may be viewed in Design Mode, and obey all the rules of the Flex layout engine. All Flex visual components inherit from the UIComponent class.

Nonvisual components in the Flex framework are classes such as effects, validators, collections, view states or utility classes, which have no visual representation on the stage at runtime.

To use MXML for instantiating non–Flex framework components and classes, *the class must inherit from* UIComponent *somewhere in the inheritance chain.*

Custom classes that do not inherit from UIComponent can be instantiated in MXML, providing that they implement the IMXMLObject *interface. Otherwise, certain interfaces must be implemented for the object to work with other visual Flex components and the Flex layout engine. So this is most often used for nonvisual components, which may not necessarily need to rely on the Flex framework. See the* IMXMLObject *entry in the Flex 3 Language Reference for details.*

For more information on the class hierarchy for visual components, see Chapter 10, "The Component Life Cycle and Class Hierarchy."

Interpreted Tags

Most MXML tags resolve directly to an ActionScript class, either in the Flex framework or elsewhere, as you saw previously. But there are other component tags for which there is an indirect relationship between the MXML tag and the class they represent, and yet others have no class equivalent at all. Otherwise known as *MXML-only components*, these MXML tags are interpreted by the compiler for specific functionality.

MXML Tag	Description
`<mx:Binding>`	Creates an event-based "binding" between a source and a destination. Used mostly for manually declaring bindings in MXML that cannot easily be declared using the {} syntax: `<mx:Binding source="Obj1.prop" destination="Obj2.prop"/>`
`<mx:Component>`	This defines an inline item renderer or item editor for a list-based component. Allows you to define a component class inline without creating a new MXML file.

`<mx:Metadata>`	Allows you to insert compiler metadata that would normally be declared in the ActionScript class definition in MXML:
	
	`<mx:Metadata>`
	`    [Event("enableChange")]`
	`</mx:Metadata>`

`<mx:Model>`	This allows you to declare an XML-like structure of data that is converted into a tree of ActionScript objects:
	
	`<mx:Model id="modelID">`
	`    <root>`
	`        <node1>some data</node1>`
	`        <node2>other data</node1>`
	`    </root>`
	`</mx:Model>`

`<mx:XML>`	Resolves indirectly to either an `XML` or an `XMLNode` class object.
`<mx:XMLList>`	Is parsed by the compiler into an `XMLList` object.
`<mx:Script>`	This tag allows for the injection of ActionScript into the MXML code or creates an include-like reference to external ActionScript, which becomes that MXML object's class members. See "MXML and ActionScript" later in this chapter for details.
`<mx:Style>`	This tag allows for the injection of CSS-style markup into the MXML file, or a reference to externally defined CSS markup. See "MXML and CSS" later in this chapter for details.

The two most commonly used interpreted tags are `<mx:Script>` and `<mx:Style>`, which allow you to add ActionScript and CSS code, respectively, to the MXML file. We will take a closer look at these two specific tags later in this chapter.

The `<mx:Model>` tag is unique in that it does not provide purely compiler-based functionality like `<mx:Script>` and `<mx:Style>`, nor does it have any class equivalent. This tag resolves to a tree struc-ture of user-anonymous objects resembling XML, but is not an XML object.

The lack of a direct class equivalent for the `<mx:Model>` tag makes it ill-suited for any dynamic data applications because it has no class code to introspect and no class-based documentation on its inner workings. Which is why it is mostly used in small prototypes and in training seminars to represent the Model in a basic MVC pattern for MXML-based applications.

Although most core ActionScript 3.0 data type classes can be instantiated in MXML (see Listing 7-1 below), the `<mx:XML>` and `<mx:XMLList>` tags are considered to be interpreted tags or "MXML-only components" rather than component tags because they do not resolve directly to their respective XML and XMLList classes. The `<mx:XML>` tag can resolve either to the E4X-compatible XML class using a value of `"e4x"` for the format property attribute, or the legacy XMLNode class using a `format` value of `"xml"`. Although the `<mx:XMLList>` tag would seem to resolve directly to an XMLList object, it is also considered to be a compile-time tag because it requires interpretation by the Flex compiler into an equivalent XMLList class object.

Core Data types in MXML

The XML and XMLList classes are the only core ActionScript 3.0 data types that require interpreted or compile-time tags in order to be instantiated with MXML. This is why you will not find the XML and XMLList class definitions in the `mxml-manifest.xml` file.

The rest of the data type classes can be expressed in MXML and are considered to be "component tags" because they have a direct class equivalency listed in the `mxml-manifest.xml` file.

When instantiating a core ActionScript data type class object in MXML, the id attribute is used to define the instance name for that class object, even though the equivalent class has no id property. Only the Error data type cannot be expressed in MXML. Although technically Class is not a core data type, it is included in the following list as a top-level class that is supported in MXML.

Listing 7-1: Core Datatype MXML tags

```
<mx:Array>
<mx:Boolean>
<mx:Class>
<mx:Date>
<mx:Function>
<mx:int>
<mx:Number>
<mx:Object>
<mx:RegExp>
<mx:String>
<mx:uint>
<mx:XML>
<mx:XMLList>
```

MXML Properties

Most of time, MXML component tags represent the component classes, and the attributes represent the public class members for those classes, be they properties or event listener methods.

Property Attributes

MXML properties are most commonly represented as tag attributes, using the following syntax:

```
<ns:Component property="value" […property="value"]/>
```

Some of the rules for MXML attributes are very much the same as for any well-formed XML tag:

❑   All attributes, or properties, must start and finish with double or single quotation marks.

❑   If double quotation marks are used, only single quotation marks may be used within them, and vice versa.

❑   XML markup, such as "<" or ">" symbols, may not be used within attribute quotation marks, and may not be escaped with the "\" character.

❑   Certain reserved symbols such as curly braces "{ }" (reserved for data binding) may be escaped with the "\" character.

Typing in MXML Properties

MXML property attributes do not use typing syntax. But since MXML properties map to class members at compilation, typing exists but is not readily apparent in the MXML code. For example, the following component declaration defines five properties of the `TextArea` class: two are typed as strings and three are typed as numbers. But this data typing is only apparent if you mistype the x property with a string, which would generate a compiler error:

```
<mx:TextArea id="textBox" x="150" y="50" width="20%"
    htmlText="The quick onyx goblin&lt;br&gt;jumps over the lazy dwarf." />
```

This lack of typing declaration has the advantage of allowing MXML property attributes a greater amount of flexibility than their class member counterparts. In the preceding code, we have used a legal value of `20%` for the `width` property, which is clearly a string, even though the `width` property of the `TextArea` class is typed as `Number`. If we attempted to use a percentile value for the `width` property in ActionScript, we would get a compiler error. Although we must use the `percentWidth` property in ActionScript to define the width of the component in percentile, in MXML the `width` property allows for percentages. This flexibility is a major contributing factor to MXML's rapid development potential.

Text Properties

The following code shows a simple application containing a solitary `TextArea` component that can accept multi-line text with basic HTML formatting:

PropAttributes.mxml

```
<?xml version="1.0" encoding="utf-8"?>
<mx:Application xmlns:mx="http://www.adobe.com/2006/mxml" layout="absolute">
    <mx:TextArea id="textBox" x="150" y="50" width="20%"
        htmlText="The quick onyx goblin jumps over the lazy dwarf." />
</mx:Application>
```

The id of the component is the class object instance name, the x, y and `width` properties contain layout positioning information, and the `htmlText` property instructs the component which characters to display.

To have the `htmlText` property truly live up to its name, it would be logical to place some HTML markup in the text, say a line break:

```
<mx:TextArea id="textBox"
    htmlText="The quick onyx goblin<br>jumps over the lazy dwarf." />
```

The only problem with the preceding code is that it violates one of the cardinal rules of property attributes:

> *You cannot have XML tag markup located within an attribute.*

This means no smaller-than or greater-than symbols are allowed within the attribute. So how do you get around this?

To solve the problem of using HTML markup in an MXML property attribute, you can use HTML entities instead. Using HTML entity names, your code would look like this:

```
PropAttributes.mxml
    <mx:TextArea id="textBox"
        htmlText="The quick onyx goblin&lt;br&gt;jumps over the lazy dwarf." />
```

Alternatively, you can use HTML entity numbers:

```
PropAttributes.mxml
    <mx:TextArea id="textBox"
        htmlText="The quick onyx goblin&#60;br&#62;jumps over the lazy dwarf." />
```

Unfortunately, URL encoding will not be properly interpreted as HTML markup for text components.

The problem with using HTML entities is that your code can get messy real fast, making it difficult to distinguish between the actual text content and the "escaped" HTML markup. But there is a solution.

> *If you define the `htmlText` property of the component dynamically, say from an external XML file, you will not have this problem, because the HTML markup is not defined in the MXML itself.*

Property Tags

You can also represent MXML properties as tags by using the following syntax:

```
<ns:Component>
    <ns:property>value</ns:property>
</ns:Component>
```

Escaping HTML Markup

A property tag comes in very handy in a few situations. If you were to modify the code in `PropAttributes.mxml`, an easy solution to the problem of HTML markup within an `htmlText` value can be achieved by using property tags:

PropAttrTag.mxml

```
<?xml version="1.0" encoding="utf-8"?>
<mx:Application xmlns:mx="http://www.adobe.com/2006/mxml" layout="absolute">
    <mx:TextArea id="textBox" x="150" y="50" width="20%">
        <mx:htmlText>
            <![CDATA[The quick onyx goblin<br>jumps over the lazy dwarf.]]>
        </mx:htmlText>
    </mx:TextArea>
</mx:Application>
```

Notice that you can now place the <br> tag in the HTML text without any problems. Using the htmlText property as a subtag allows you to place the actual HTML text inside of CDATA tags, allowing you to use HTML markup without incident. Using CDATA tags is an effective way to escape XML or HTML markup within MXML.

Any line breaks inside the CDATA may be interpreted as line breaks without requiring <br> tags, so be aware of whitespace characters in your HTML text.

The great thing about using Flex Builder in this example is that its code intelligence senses what you are about to do and creates the CDATA tags for you. You find out more information on Flex Builder's code intelligence in Chapter 8.

Objects as Values

Another reason to use property tags is when a property value is actually a class object reference rather than a data type such as a string, number or Boolean. Consider the following example where you need to an Array object as the dataProvider for a List component:

```
PropAttrTagObj.mxml<?xml version="1.0" encoding="utf-8"?>
<mx:Application xmlns:mx="http://www.adobe.com/2006/mxml" layout="absolute">
    <mx:Array id="authors">
        <mx:Object label="Joseph Balderson"/>
        <mx:Object label="Peter Ent"/>
        <mx:Object label="Jun Heider"/>
        <mx:Object label="Todd Prekaski"/>
        <mx:Object label="Tom Sugden"/>
        <mx:Object label="Andrew Trice"/>
        <mx:Object label="David Hassoun"/>
        <mx:Object label="Joe Berkovitz"/>
    </mx:Array>
    <mx:List id="authorList" x="150" y="50" width="20%"
        dataProvider="{authors}"/>
</mx:Application>
```

This illustrates an important concept for MXML properties: An object as a value for a property attribute must be surrounded by curly braces, otherwise known as the data-binding syntax in MXML.

In the preceding example, you have an Array named authors, which serves as the reference value for the dataProvider property of the authorList component.

This `Array` object can be also written as a subtag within the `dataprovider` property tag:

```
PropAttrTagObj2.mxml<?xml version="1.0" encoding="utf-8"?>
<mx:Application xmlns:mx="http://www.adobe.com/2006/mxml" layout="absolute">
    <mx:List id="authorList" x="150" y="50" width="20%">
        <mx:dataProvider>
            <mx:Array>
                <mx:Object label="Joseph Balderson"/>
                <mx:Object label="Peter Ent"/>
                <mx:Object label="Jun Heider"/>
                <mx:Object label="Todd Prekaski"/>
                <mx:Object label="Tom Sugden"/>
                <mx:Object label="Andrew Trice"/>
                <mx:Object label="David Hassoun"/>
                <mx:Object label="Joe Berkovitz"/>
            </mx:Array>
        </mx:dataProvider>
    </mx:List>
</mx:Application>
```

Declaring objects as values within a property tag allows you to declare object values within the component tag itself.

Using MXML and CSS

Style information in the form of CSS markup can be written and referenced in MXML in one of four ways:

- ❑ As a component property of an MXML tag
- ❑ Within a `<mx:Style>` tag
- ❑ Linked from an external CSS file
- ❑ In ActionScript 3.0

In this section. we will explore the first three of these possibilities. See Chapter 22, "Styles," for more information on defining CSS styles in ActionScript 3.0.

Inline CSS

Component styles can be defined by component property attributes, otherwise known as *component styles*, as follows:

CSSInline.mxml

```
<?xml version="1.0" encoding="utf-8"?>
<mx:Application xmlns:mx="http://www.adobe.com/2006/mxml" layout="absolute">
    <mx:Label text="This is Inline CSS"
        fontSize="72"
        fontFamily="Futura, Helvetica, Arial"
        fontWeight="bold"/>
</mx:Application>
```

Here you can see the `Label` component with three styles applied: a font size of 72, boldfaced, using either the Futura, Helvetica, or Arial font.

The Style Tag

Within an MXML document, styles are more commonly defined with a `<mx:Style>` tag. The style tag is an interpreted or MXML-only tag, which allows component styling information to be inserted into an MXML document using standard CSS syntax:

CSSStyleTag.mxml

```
<?xml version="1.0" encoding="utf-8"?>
<mx:Application xmlns:mx="http://www.adobe.com/2006/mxml" layout="absolute">
    <mx:Style>
        Label {
            fontSize: 72;
            fontFamily: Futura, Helvetica, Arial;
            fontWeight: bold;
        }
    </mx:Style>
    <mx:Label text="This Uses the Style Tag" />
</mx:Application>
```

The preceding example applies the same three styles to the `Label` component using a CSS class selector. See Chapter 22 for more information on using styles in Flex applications.

Linking External CSS

The `<mx:Style>` tag has a `source` property that allows an external style sheet to be associated with the application. The following is a Flex application that displays a `Label` component, using an external style sheet defined in `csslinked.css`.

CSSLinked.mxml

```
<?xml version="1.0" encoding="utf-8"?>
<mx:Application xmlns:mx="http://www.adobe.com/2006/mxml" layout="absolute">
    <mx:Style source="csslinked.css"/>
    <mx:Label text="This Uses Linked CSS" />
</mx:Application>
```

The `csslinked.css` file in turn contains the following style information:

csslinked.css

```
Label {
    fontSize: 72;
    fontFamily: Futura, Helvetica, Arial;
    fontWeight: bold;
}
```

Linking external CSS files to an application is a good way to increase styling reusability and to separate styling concerns within the application. For instance, you may have one CSS file for text styling in the application and yet another to define component skinning.

Note that core Flash Player functionality allows for CSS styling defined in ActionScript or an external CSS file to be used for text field formatting, which should not be confused for a CSS style sheet defining styles for Flex components. Details on using CSS styles for low-level text field formatting is outside the scope of this book. Consult the `StyleSheet` *class and "Loading an external CSS file"* (`http://livedocs.adobe.com/flex/3/html/Working_with_Text_15.html`) *in the Adobe Flex documentation for details.*

Using MXML and ActionScript

ActionScript can be written and referenced in MXML in one of four ways:

1. Within a component property attribute

2. Within a component property tag

3. Within a `<mx:Script>` tag

4. Linked from an external ActionScript file

In this section, you'll see how to incorporate ActionScript into MXML files using the above methods.

Inline ActionScript

The first two techniques are often called "inline ActionScript" because ActionScript syntax is written within an MXML component tag.

Data Binding

One way to express inline ActionScript is within a component property attribute. The simplest expression of using ActionScript within a property attribute is through data binding, where an ActionScript object reference is used to bind the data of one component to another:

ASinMXMLDatabinding.mxml

```
<?xml version="1.0" encoding="utf-8"?>
<mx:Application xmlns:mx="http://www.adobe.com/2006/mxml" layout="vertical">
    <mx:TextInput id="myInput" width="150"/>
    <mx:Label id="myLabel" width="150"
        text="{myInput.text}"/>
</mx:Application>
```

In the preceding example, the `text` property (data-binding source) of the `myInput` component is bound to the `text` property (data-binding destination) of the `myLabel` component. More information on data binding can be found in Chapter 11, "Data Binding and Events."

Inline Event Script

MXML component property attributes that represent class properties, as in the preceding example, cannot reference script, only values and objects, which is why it must be enclosed in data binding or function closure syntax { }. Component property attributes that represent class methods, such as events, can use more complex ActionScript without requiring the data-binding or method closure syntax {}.

In ActionScript, when you declare an event, you must create declare the event listener method, and then associate the event listener with the dispatching object through an event type with the `addEventListener()` method. An MXML component event property does most of the work of declaring an event for you; it is actually a placeholder for an anonymously named listener method associated with that event type, and as such any script within is treated as if it is declared within an event method, without the need for any function declaration syntax. For example, if you take the preceding application and add a button with an event using inline ActionScript, you will have the following:

ASinMXMLInlineEvent.mxml

```
<?xml version="1.0" encoding="utf-8"?>
<mx:Application xmlns:mx="http://www.adobe.com/2006/mxml" layout="vertical">
    <mx:TextInput id="myInput" width="150"/>
    <mx:Label id="myLabel" width="150"/>
    <mx:Button id="myButton"
        label="Enter Text"
        click="myLabel.text = myInput.text;mx.controls.Alert.show('Text Entered
    is:\n'+myInput.text, 'Alert Box', mx.controls.Alert.OK);"/>
</mx:Application>
```

In this example, when you press the button, an event listener causes the text entered in the `TextInput` component to show up in an `Alert` window and in the `Label` below.

Declaring a `click` event property in this example causes the MXML interpreter in the Flex compiler to create an anonymous event listener method containing the code within that tag attribute, of the `flash.events.MouseEvent.CLICK` event type, dispatched by the `myButton` object. As such, the code within this anonymous event listener method is separated by semicolons just like ActionScript code declared in a class method, providing that the rules for well-formed MXML tag attribute values are followed. So, you could not use unescaped double quotation marks or HTML markup in the inline script.

Because the code in between quotation marks is regular ActionScript, white space does not affect the compilation of the code. So, you could rewrite the preceding code in a slightly more legible fashion:

ASinMXMLInlineEvent2.mxml

```
<?xml version="1.0" encoding="utf-8"?>
<mx:Application xmlns:mx="http://www.adobe.com/2006/mxml" layout="vertical">
    <mx:TextInput id="myInput" width="150"/>
    <mx:Label id="myLabel" width="150"/>
    <mx:Button id="myButton"
        label="Enter Text"
        click="
            myLabel.text = myInput.text;
            mx.controls.Alert.show(
                'Text Entered is:\n' + myInput.text,
                'Alert Box',
                mx.controls.Alert.OK
            );"
    />
</mx:Application>
```

Notice that you did not need to use an import statement for the Alert *class in the preceding code. As covered in Chapter 3, if you use a fully qualified class name, you do not need to import the class package in the class definition or MXML file.*

Although no event object argument has been declared, because there is no formal function definition syntax, the event object is still available as event. *If you replace the first line of ActionScript in the click event for the preceding example with the following, you will see the event object in action:*

```
myLabel.text = event.type;
```

Script in a Property Tag

Just as text can be expressed in an MXML component property tag as you saw earlier, ActionScript may also be defined in an event property tag. The preceding example could be expressed in the following fashion:

ASinMXMLInlineTag.mxml

```
<?xml version="1.0" encoding="utf-8"?>
<mx:Application xmlns:mx="http://www.adobe.com/2006/mxml" layout="vertical">
    <mx:TextInput id="myInput" width="150"/>
    <mx:Label id="myLabel" width="150"/>
    <mx:Button id="myButton"
        label="Enter Text">
        <mx:click>
            <![CDATA[
                myLabel.text = myInput.text;//event.type;
                mx.controls.Alert.show(
                    "Text Entered is:\n" + myInput.text,
                    "Alert Box",
                    mx.controls.Alert.OK
                );
            ]]>
        </mx:click>
    </mx:Button>
</mx:Application>
```

When you build this application yourself, you'll notice that the moment you complete the opening click tag, Flex Builder inserts the CDATA tags for you.

Since the code is contained within an XML node and not an attribute, you can use CDATA to disregard any otherwise illegal characters in the code, such as double quotation marks or dynamic XML object declarations, which is a major advantage of this technique. Wrapping ActionScript within an MXML tag in a CDATA node is almost a requirement, which is why Flex Builder auto-inserts them for you; your code may compile fine without it, but you run a big risk of compilation failure if you do.

The disadvantage of using inline ActionScript within an event property attribute or tag is that you cannot refer to the method script outside of this component, preventing code reuse and encouraging tight component coupling. It is for this reason that these techniques are considered to be against best practices, and they are used mostly for rapid prototyping and instructional purposes. Since the listener method is anonymously named, it cannot be explicitly removed by the application at runtime, making Garbage Collection (GC) difficult. If you find the need to place more than very short scripts inside an event property attribute or tag, consider referencing an event method defined in a <mx:Script> *tag, which is explained next.*

The Script Tag

Placing ActionScript code within a `<mx:Script>` tag allows for the greatest flexibility in your coding and is considered the best way to define ActionScript within an MXML document.

By placing the ActionScript in the event property in a `<mx:Script>` tag, the code from the preceding application could look like the following:

ASinMXMLScr.mxml

```
<?xml version="1.0" encoding="utf-8"?>
<mx:Application xmlns:mx="http://www.adobe.com/2006/mxml" layout="vertical">
    <mx:Script>
        <![CDATA[
            import mx.controls.*;
            private function clickHandler(event:MouseEvent):void
            {
                myLabel.text = event.type + ": " + myInput.text;
                Alert.show("Text Entered is:\n" + myInput.text, "Alert Box",
                    Alert.OK);
            }
        ]]>
    </mx:Script>
    <mx:TextInput id="myInput" width="150"/>
    <mx:Label id="myLabel" width="150"/>
    <mx:Button id="myButton"
        label="Enter Text"
        click="clickHandler(event)"/>
</mx:Application>
```

In this example, the `clickHandler` named listener method is associated with the `click` event for the `myButton` object.

One advantage of defining the event listener as a named function is code reusability. If you were to modify the preceding application, two buttons could call the same event handler:

ASinMXMLScr2.mxml

```
<?xml version="1.0" encoding="utf-8"?>
<mx:Application xmlns:mx="http://www.adobe.com/2006/mxml" layout="vertical">
    <mx:Script>
        <![CDATA[
            import mx.controls.*;
            private function clickHandler(event:MouseEvent):void
            {
                myLabel.text = event.type + ": " + myInput.text;
                Alert.show("Text Entered by the\n" + event.target.id + " button.",
                    "Alert Box", Alert.OK);
            }
        ]]>
    </mx:Script>
    <mx:TextInput id="myInput" width="150"/>
    <mx:Label id="myLabel" width="150"/>
    <mx:Button id="myButton1"
        label="myButton1"
```

```
                click="clickHandler(event)"/>
         <mx:Button id="myButton2"
              label="myButton2"
              click="clickHandler(event)"/>
    </mx:Application>
```

In this example, two different buttons, `myButton1` and `myButton2`, are using the same event handler method for the `click` event. `event.target.id` gets the instance name of the dispatching button though the event object defined as `event` in the listener method parameters. So when either button is pressed, an `Alert` window opens displaying the name of the button instance that dispatched the `click` event to the `clickHandler` method.

Functions in MXML

In addition to declaring functions in ActionScript inside a `Script` block, as covered in the previous section, you can also express functions in MXML to approximate ActionScript programming structures. Although seldom used in most real-world projects, the two following examples illustrate two interesting techniques for coding methods in MXML.

Property Tag as Anonymous Function

As seen above in `ASinMXMLInlineTag.mxml`, you can place code in a property tag if that property represents an event or other class method that may be inspected in MXML. Placing a code in a property tag is essentially assigning an anonymous function declaration as the event handler method:

```
<mx:Button id="myButton">
    <mx:click>
        <![CDATA[
            myLabel.text = event.type+" event dispatched.";
        ]]>
    </mx:click>
</mx:Button>
```

In the preceding property tag event method declaration, the `event` variable is the default spelling for the anonymous event handler method argument. The following ActionScript equivalent uses an anonymous function declaration to serve as the click event handler for `myButton`, where the event handler argument is spelled `event`.

```
myButton.addEventListener(MouseEvent.CLICK, function(event:MouseEvent):void {
    myLabel.text = event.type+" event dispatched.";
});
```

The Function Tag

As you saw in Listing 7-1, the `Function` class is a core data type, which means you can also compose a method declaration in MXML using the `Function` tag. Thus, instead of declaring the event handler method in a named function, as seen in the preceding `ASinMXMLScr.mxml` example, you could declare the event method in a `Function` tag, as follows:

```
<mx:Function id="clickHandler">
<![CDATA[
    function (event:MouseEvent):void
    {
```

```
                myLabel.text = event.type + ": " + myInput.text;
                //...
        }
    ]]>
</mx:Function>

<mx:Button id="myButton1"
    label="myButton1"
    click="clickHandler(event)"/>
```

The ActionScript equivalent of using the Function tag as just shown is to assign an anonymous function to a function object in an expression:

```
var clickHandler:Function =
function(event:MouseEvent):void
{
    myLabel.text = event.type + ": " + myInput.text;
    //...
};
```

```
myButton1.addEventListener(MouseEvent.CLICK, clickHandler);
```

Best Practices for MXML Functions

The preceding two examples are but possible uses of MXML language convention and do not constitute good programming practices, for the simple reason that declaring anonymous functions does not allow for the explicit runtime removal of event handler methods. Since anonymous functions cannot be referenced, they can neither be removed nor marked for deletion by the Garbage Collector in the ActionScript virtual machine (AVM), or the Flash Player. This can, if used frequently in a large project, impact AVM memory usage and performance. Therefore, it is recommended that event handlers be declared as named methods in ActionScript, in either a Script block or a class file.

Linking External ActionScript

You can also reference ActionScript code that would otherwise be defined in the MXML file in an external ActionScript file. Very similarly to how the <mx:Style> tag works, instead of placing the code within the <mx:Script> tag, you point the source property to the filename:

ASinMXMLExtScr.mxml

```
<?xml version="1.0" encoding="utf-8"?>
<mx:Application xmlns:mx="http://www.adobe.com/2006/mxml" layout="vertical">
    <mx:Script source="ASinMXMLExtScrCode.as"/>
    <mx:TextInput id="myInput" width="150"/>
    <mx:Label id="myLabel" width="150"/>
    <mx:Button id="myButton1"
        label="myButton1"
        click="clickHandler(event)"/>
```

```
    <mx:Button id="myButton2"
        label="myButton2"
        click="clickHandler(event)"/>
</mx:Application>
```

The `ASinMXMLExtScrCode.as` file in turn contains the following ActionScript:

ASinMXMLExtScrCode.as

```
import mx.controls.*;
private function clickHandler(event:MouseEvent):void
{
    myLabel.text = event.type + ": " + myInput.text;
    Alert.show("Text Entered by the\n" + event.target.id + " button.",
        "Alert Box", Alert.OK);
}
```

This is exactly the same as what was in the `<mx:Script>` tag in the previous example.

The `source` property of the `<mx:Script>` tag functions exactly the same way as the include compiler directive: the ActionScript contained in the external file is treated as if it were declared within the MXML document, not as a class definition. File location references for the `source` property may be absolute or relative.

Since the code file referenced by the `source` *property is more like an extension of the MXML document than a class definition, it's a good idea to use the same name as the MXML file, with a prefix of something similar to "Code" on the end. So the external AS for an MXML file named "ASinMXMLExtScr. mxml" becomes "ASinMXMLExtScrCode.as" Using external ActionScript is a simple and common technique for employing code behind for MXML files without resorting to inheritance patterns.*

Rules of Usage

The following are some rules about defining ActionScript in the `<mx:Script>` tag of an MXML document (whether inline or external), as opposed to using an ActionScript class file:

❑ All ActionScript code with an `<mx:Script>` tag observes the same class access modifiers such as `public`, `private`, `protected`, and so on, and the same class syntax as a class file.

❑ Since there is no package declaration to place import statements outside the class definition, import statements are placed within the `<mx:Script>` tag but outside of any method definition.

❑ You cannot define the constructor of the class defined by the MXML. Most MXML documents use a `creationComplete` event listener method as suitable replacement for a constructor function.

❑ Since there is no class declaration for an MXML file, you cannot define the interfaces implemented by the MXML document class nor the classes inherited.

MXML or ActionScript?

So, which language or combination of languages should you use for your application — an MXML document, an MXML document with ActionScript, or ActionScript class files?

The short answer is, probably all three. MXML is intended to serve visual component layout classes, including the main application class. And undoubtedly you'll have ActionScript within those pages to have your components interact with the application logic. With ActionScript class files to serve as the application logic and control, which may inherit from a Flex framework class, or a core ActionScript class, it's your choice, and there are many possibilities, quite a few of which are covered in this book.

As a rule of thumb, MXML embeds values and component layouts at compile time. ActionScript is used more for runtime functionality, although most component properties and styles can also be defined and set at runtime.

Summary

In this chapter, you learned some important fundamentals of using MXML. We covered the basics of MXML syntax and usage, including some in-depth discussions and examples on techniques for using MXML with both CSS and ActionScript code in the same application. In the next chapter, you'll learn how to use specific development tools in Flex Builder.

8

Developing with Flex Builder 3

Chapter 6 looked at creating Flex and ActionScript projects, including some basics of using Flex Builder, the Flex 3 integrated development environment (IDE). In this chapter, you'll delve further into the topic and learn how to use all the unique development features that make Flex Builder such a powerful development tool, including managing projects, building applications, and using Flex Builder's code-assist features.

Flex Builder is based on Eclipse, so if you're already familiar with the Eclipse's toolset, this chapter may be merely a refresher for you, although there are some features unique to Flex Builder that may not be present in other Eclipse-based IDEs. For more advanced details on using Flex Builder, see Chapter 9, "Customizing Flex Builder 3."

Managing Projects

Creating a project in Flex Builder, writing code, and compiling the application, as you did in Chapters 6 and 7, are just a small part of the development story. To manage your assets and your code effectively, it helps to be aware of the options present for any given project.

Project Properties

When you create a Flex, AIR, or ActionScript project, several options are available for configuring project settings in Flex Builder.

You can access a project's preferences by selecting an open project folder and selecting File ➡ Properties, or by selecting [project folder] ➡ right click ➡ Properties. The following sections describe some of the most commonly used preference settings.

Project Settings Files

Project settings are stored primarily in three files in the root of the project folder: `.project`, `.flexProperties`, and `.actionScriptProperties`. Although these are actually XML files, editing them directly is not recommended. Direct manipulation of these files is recommended only for advanced users who may need to automate project builds with server scripts, a discussion of which is beyond the scope of this book. See the "Subclipse for Subversion Source Management" section in Chapter 9 for details on ignoring these files for repository-based projects. Although not all tags contained in these files are documented, information on certain tags can be obtained under compiler settings in the Flex 3 documentation or in the standalone compiler help (`mxmlc -help`).

Flex Applications Settings

The Flex Applications settings, shown in Figure 8-1, determine which applications are recognized as buildable by Flex Builder — that is, which applications can form the root file for a Flex or ActionScript application.

Flex project applications will be MXML files with a root `<mx:Application>` tag. AIR project applications will be MXML files containing a root `<mx:WindowedApplication>` tag. ActionScript project applications will be ActionScript (`.as`) files defining a class that extends a `DisplayObject`, usually `Sprite`.

The MXML or ActionScript file listed as "(default)" indicates which application will be compiled by default when you press the Run button in Flex Builder. All "runnable" applications are indicated with a green arrow added to the icon in the Flex Navigator View.

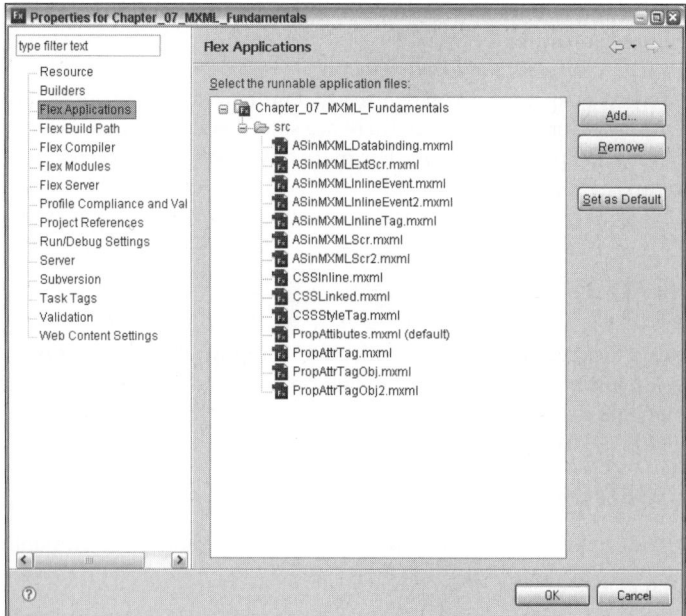

Figure 8-1

The Applications List

When you create a new application file in Flex Builder, that application is automatically added to the "runnable applications" list. So why would you need to edit this list?

- ❏ If you create a copy of an application file, it is not automatically added to the applications list in the Applications settings, and the application file will not, by default, appear in the Run menu. You will have to manually add the application file to the list by selecting the Add button and navigating to the file in question.

- ❏ If the application file in question is not in the list, right-clicking on the file and selecting "Run Application" will cause the file to be automatically added to the applications list.

- ❏ If the most current application file changes to another file, as in the case of filename-based project versioning (which is only recommended for spikes and prototypes), you may also want to change the default application by selecting a file and clicking Set as Default.

- ❏ You can also set a file as default by right-clicking on the file and selecting Set as Default.

> **Renaming an application file in Flex Builder is not recommended, as it may cause build problems with untraceable compilation errors. Rather than renaming an existing application file, copy and rename an application file, then delete the original and clean your project. This is not recommended if you are using a version control system in your Flex project.**

Flex Build Path Settings

The Flex Build Path settings, shown in Figure 8-2, enable you to configure source file settings.

These settings can be divided into three main sections:

- ❏ The Source Path tab enables you to configure local and external source code libraries.

- ❏ The Library Path tab enables you to configure local and external SWC libraries. Included in this list are libraries that make up the Flash, Flex, and AIR frameworks.

- ❏ The project folder settings indicate locations for source code and compilation output. The "Main source folder" field indicates the name of the folder where the source code for the project is located. The "Output folder" field indicates the name of the folder where the compiler will place its debug builds. The "Output folder" field indicates the URL directory to build resulting application files, and applies only if the server-side compilation option is used (see the upcoming section "Other Settings").

See the "Building Applications" section for more information on using these settings in configuring different kinds of builds.

Flex Compiler Settings

Flex Compiler settings are divided into three sections, each of which allows you to configure aspects of the Flex Builder compilation process (see Figure 8-3).

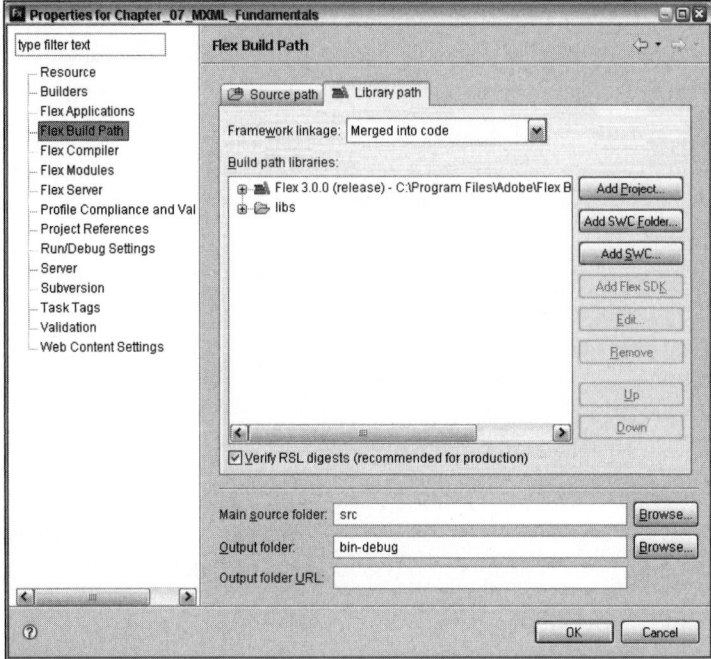

Figure 8-2

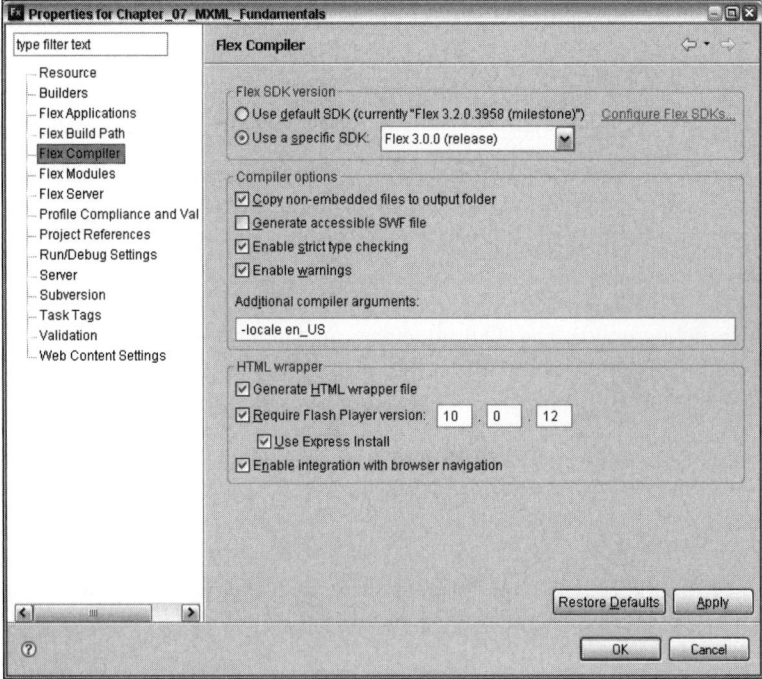

Figure 8-3

❏ The "Flex SDK version" section enables you to assign the version of the Flex SDK used by the Flex compiler. For more information on importing and configuring SDKs, see Chapter 9.

❏ The "Compiler options" section allows you to configure the arguments Flex Builder sends to the MXML or AMXMLC compiler. Certain compiler arguments can be configured with check boxes:

   ❏ The "Copy non-embedded files to output folder" option causes the compiler to copy all non-embedded assets into the output folder.

   ❏ The "Generate accessible SWF file" option enables accessibility features in the Flex application. This is equivalent to using the `-accessible` command-line compiler argument, which is `false` by default.

   ❏ The "Enable strict type checking" option enforces strict typing in the ActionScript language and reports any errors at compile time. This is equivalent to the `-strict` command-line compiler argument, which is `true` by default.

   ❏ The "Enable warnings" option enables Warnings mode, which has Flex Builder show compiler warnings related to fonts, CSS, bindings and others. This is equivalent to the `-warnings` command-line compiler argument, which is `true` by default. You can configure more specific warning display options for the command-line compiler in the "Additional compiler arguments" field. A complete list of these warning options can be obtained from the advanced command-line compiler help or in the `flex-config.xml` file.

   ❏ The "Additional compiler arguments" field allows you to specify additional arguments that get sent to the command-line compiler. Write these arguments as you would on the command line. See "Building Applications" later in this chapter for more information on common compiler arguments.

❏ The "HTML wrapper" section determines which HTML support files will be included in the Flex or ActionScript project build. This option is not available for AIR projects. Upon project creation, and after any change in these settings, the relevant support files are copied from the Flex SDK located in one of the folders located in the `{Application Root}\Flex Builder 3\sdks\{SDK number}\templates` directories, into the `html-template` project folder, depending on the wrapper options selected. Upon compilation, these support file templates located in the `html-template` folder are used to create the support files for the Flex or ActionScript application.

For information on additional compiler settings using command-line compiler arguments, consult the Adobe Flex 3 Help Documentation, at `http://livedocs.adobe.com/flex/3/html/compilers_14.html`.

Other Settings

Other settings that can be configured in the Project Properties window include:

❏ The Builders settings enable you to configure external build scripts such as Apache Ant tasks. See Chapter 70, "Dual Deployment for Flex and AIR," and Chapter 73, "Unit Testing and Test-Driven Development with FlexUnit," for details on using build scripts.

❏ Library projects have access to the Flex Build Path and Flex Compiler settings that are slightly different than for Flex, AIR, and ActionScript projects. Consult Chapter 21, "Using Libraries," for details on Library project settings and the COMPC compiler.

❑   Project settings for modules are discussed at length in Chapter 66, "Modular Application Development."

❑   The Flex Server settings option applies for server-side compilation, such as LiveCycle Data Services ES. See Chapter 53, "Introduction to LCDS," for details. This option will be disabled if server-side compilation has not been enabled.

Exporting Projects

One way to share projects between developers is to export the entire project folder as a zipped archive. To do so, perform the following steps:

1.   Select the project folder and then select either File ➪ Export ➪ Flex Project Archive or [Project Folder]+right-click ➪ Export ➪ Flex Builder ➪ Flex Project Archive.

2.   Click Browse and navigate to the directory to export the archive. By default, Flex Builder will fill in the project name as the filename of the archive.

3.   Click OK.

Importing Projects

Having received a Flex Builder project from another developer, you can import it into your workspace in one of two ways: from a folder or from a ZIP archive.

Importing Single Projects

Importing a single project into a workspace is very simple.

1.   Select the project folder and then select either File ➪ Import ➪ Flex Project or [Project Folder]+right-click ➪ Import ➪ Flex Builder ➪ Flex Project.

2.   Select either the Archive file or Project folder options, and browse to the folder or ZIP file location of the project to import.

> If you have set your workspace metadata to be located in a folder other than your main workspace folder (see "Workspace Configurations" in Chapter 5, "Introduction to Flex Builder 3"), you may have to uncheck "Use default location," and select your workspace folder to copy/unpack the imported project. When importing to a non-default project location, Flex Builder may not automatically create the project folder, so you may have to manually create the project folder in the OS prior to importing.

Flex Builder cannot import a multiple project archive using the Import Flex Project option as indicated above. This only works for single project archives. If you want to import a multiple project archive, see "From a ZIP Archive" in the next section.

Importing Multiple Projects

You can also import multiple projects at the same time by using a different import selection.

From a ZIP Archive

Perform the following steps to import multiple projects from a ZIP archive:

1. Select the project folder and then select File or Right-click ➪ Import ➪ Other ➪ General ➪ Existing Projects Into Workspace.

If you are using the Flex Builder as an Eclipse plug-in and not as a standalone installation, the Other menu option may not be present. As a reminder, all menu options indicated in this chapter are for the Flex Builder standalone installation. Flex Builder plug-in menu options may differ slightly.

2. In the Import Projects window, select the "Select archive file" option, and check the projects in the archive you want to import (see Figure 8-4). When importing multiple projects from an archive, the "Copy projects into workspace" option is checked by default, since it must unpack those files into the host workspace directory.

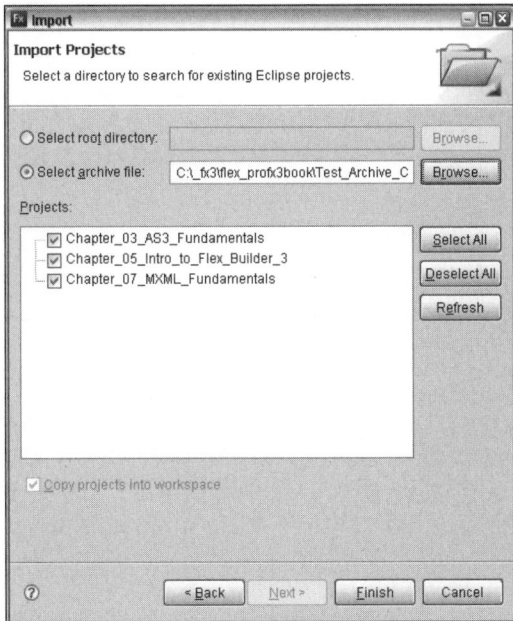

Figure 8-4

3. Click Finish.

Flex Builder is unable to export a ZIP archive containing more than one project at a time. To create a multi-project archive, simply use a ZIP archiving utility to manually package multiple project folders into one ZIP file.

From a Directory

To import multiple projects from a directory, perform the following steps:

1. Select the project folder, and then select File or right-click ⇨ Import ⇨ Other ⇨ General ⇨ Existing Projects Into Workspace.

2. In the Import Projects window, select the "Select root directory" option and check the projects in the archive you want to import (see Figure 8-5).

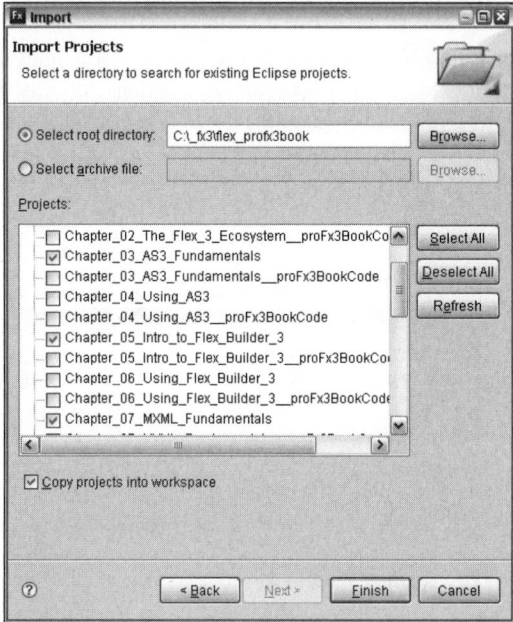

Figure 8-5

3. Select or deselect the "Copy projects into workspace" option. Deselecting it merely creates named references to projects located externally to the current workspace location. Selecting this option actually copies all the projects from the external workspace location to the current workspace location.

4. Click Finish.

In Flex Builder 2, importing references to external projects would cause Flex Builder to wrap the project name in square brackets to indicate that they are located outside the current workspace. Although Flex Builder 3 does not change referenced project folder names from the originals, wrapping the new project folder names in square brackets (or prefixing them with an underscore) is still a good idea. This indicates which projects are located in the host workspace and which are located elsewhere, avoiding confusion as to where the actual files are located.

From a Repository

For information on importing projects from a Subversion code repository, see the "Subclipse for Subversion Source Management" section in Chapter 9.

Navigating Projects

Several features in Flex Builder allow you to manage projects in an efficient manner. Here are some tips on some of these techniques.

Creating a Folder Structure

Creating a new folder in your source code may be necessary for custom class packages, or simply to store media assets and other non-code source files. For example, if you want to create a folder structure for a new class package, perform the following steps:

1. Select File/right-click ➪ New ➪ Folder.

2. In the New Folder window, select the root folder where you want the new folder to go, if it is not already selected. In the case of creating a class package, select the "src" or equivalent folder, as shown in Figure 8-6. You should see a nested folder structure created, similar to Figure 8-7.

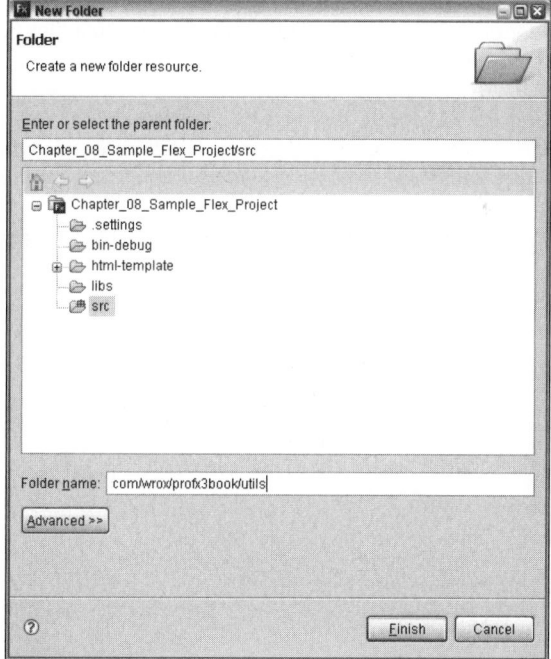

Figure 8-6

If you want to create multiple directories at once, rather than repeating these steps for every subfolder, create a nested folder structure by separating them with a forward slash, as indicated in Figure 8-6.

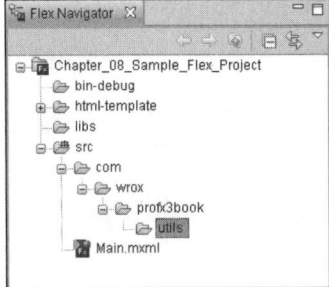

Figure 8-7

Creating Folder Linkages

Creating a linkage to a directory or file external to the project folder location is extremely useful for referencing code and assets outside of the project. The steps are similar to creating a new folder:

1. Select File/right-click ⇨ New ⇨ Folder

2. In the New Folder window, shown in Figure 8-8, click the Advanced button, and then select "Link to folder in the file system."

3. Browse to a folder on the file system. This example links to a Flex SDK folder located in the Flex Builder installation directory.

   Linking to a Flex SDK folder, or even the frameworks folder within, is a great way to keep a reference to the Flex framework within your projects, to provide a ready reference and increase your comprehension of Flex. Just be careful not to alter any of these files unless you have an advanced understanding of Flex.

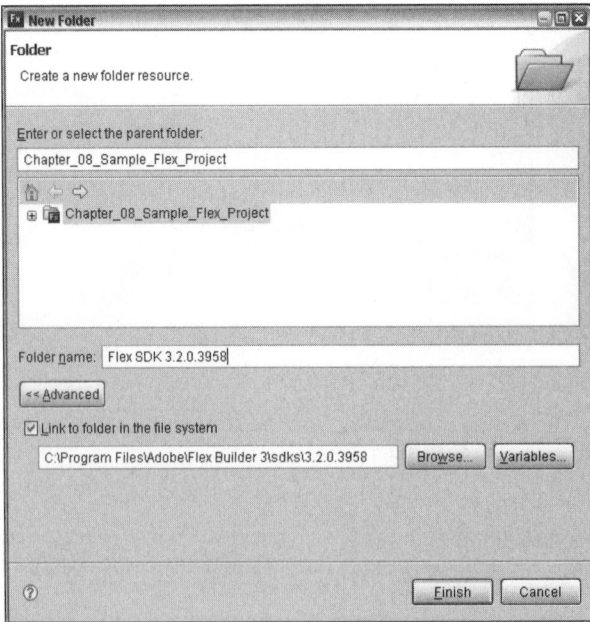

Figure 8-8

You should now see a folder appear in your project with an arrow in the corner, indicating it is a linked folder (see Figure 8-9).

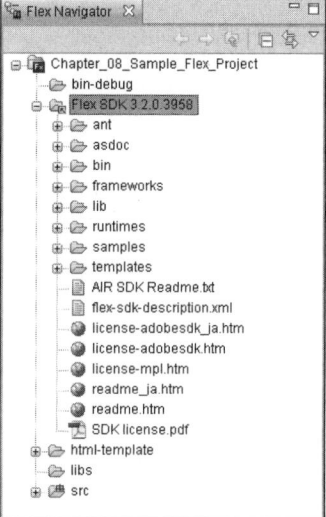

Figure 8-9

Bear in mind that if you export a project archive with linked folders or files, this may cause your project to be corrupted when imported into another workspace. If this happens, use the Import Existing Projects into Workspace feature instead.

Creating File Linkages

Creating a linkage to a file outside the project folder location is extremely useful in referencing specific files outside of the project. The steps are similar to creating a new folder:

1. Select File/right-click ⇨ New ⇨ File.

2. In the New File window, shown in Figure 8-10, click the Advanced button, and then select "Link to file in the file system."

3. Browse to an external file. This example links to the `flex-config.xml` file located in the Flex SDK. See Chapter 7, "MXML Fundamentals," for information on the significance of this file.

You should now see a folder appear in your project with an arrow in the corner, indicating it is a linked folder (see Figure 8-11).

Linking to an external file is useful for things like changing configuration settings, making notes, or peering at log files, without leaving the Flex Builder IDE.

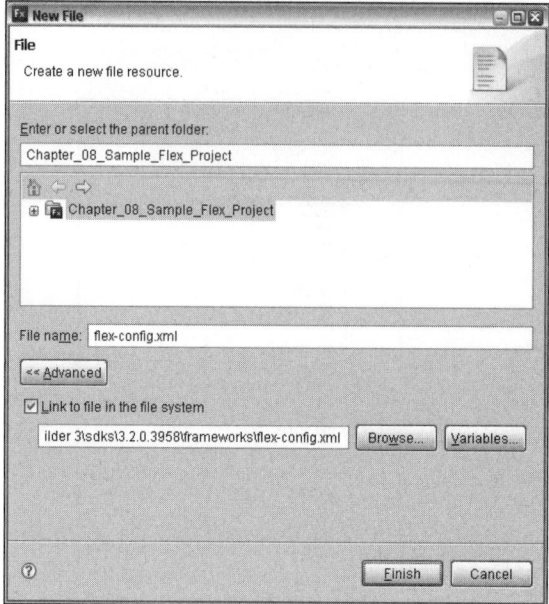

Figure 8-10

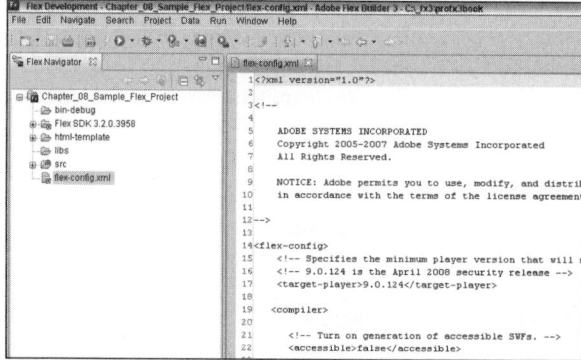

Figure 8-11

"Go Into" Browsing

This is a very useful feature if you find your workspace has become cluttered with too much detail such that you have to vertically scroll a lot to get to the information you need, and you want to temporarily navigate into a project directory or subdirectory without all the other stuff appearing in the Flex Navigator view. Simply right-click on a folder and select the "Go into" menu option. Then use the three navigation icons in the top left of the Flex Navigator view to move up and down the directory tree.

The "Go into" option even works for linked folders. Figure 8-12 illustrates navigating into an externally linked folder pointing to the Flex SDK created earlier.

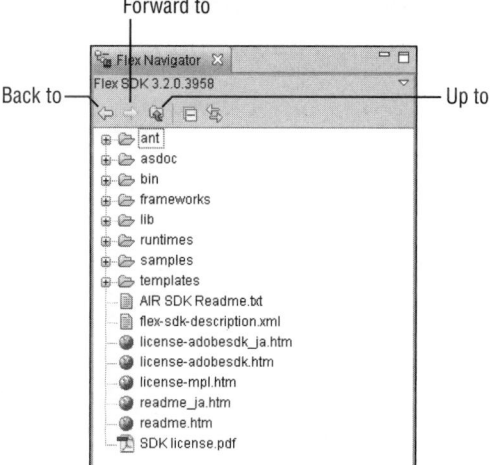

Figure 8-12

Working Sets

Flex Builder allows you to view a subset of the total number of projects in the workspace, showing only those projects in the Flex Navigator view. This displayed subset of the total workspace is called a *working set*. Using working sets comes in very handy if you have many projects in a given workspace and want to work with a smaller number of them at a time, saving you from a lot of potential scrolling in the Flex Navigator View.

To create a working set, perform the following steps:

1.   Select the projects you want to include in the working set. Whether these projects are open or closed doesn't matter, as you will still be able to add them to the working set in a later screen.

2.   In the top-right of the Flex Navigator View, click the down arrow marked with the "menu" tool-tip, and select Select Working Set, as shown in Figure 8-13.

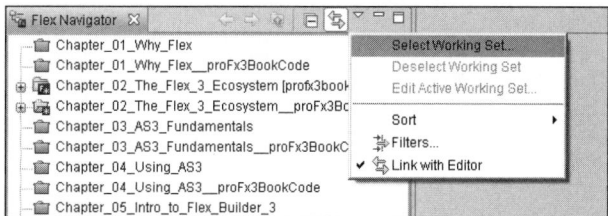

Figure 8-13

3.   Click New.

4.   In the New Working Set window, select Resource and then click Next (see Figure 8-14).

Figure 8-14

5. In the Resource Working Set window, give the working set a name, and check the projects to include in the working set (see Figure 8-15). In this example, I'm checking the two projects for Chapter 8 out of my total workspace. Click Finish.

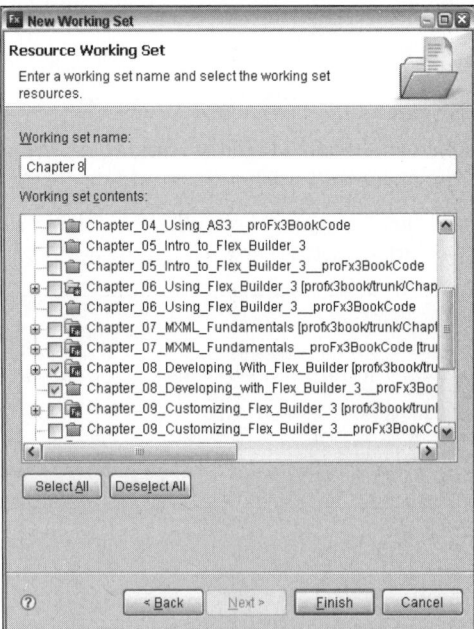

Figure 8-15

6. In the Select Working Set window, as shown in Figure 8-16, check the working set just created, and then select OK. You should see the new working set in the workspace, as shown in Figure 8-17.

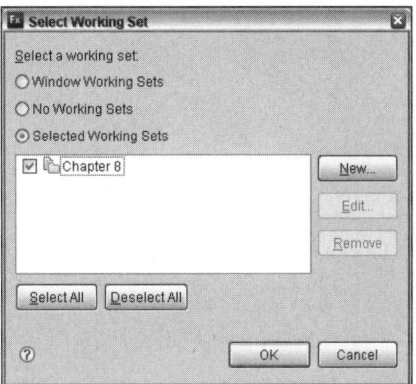

Figure 8-16

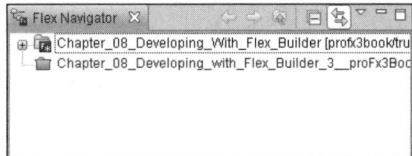

Figure 8-17

7. To navigate back to the workspace showing all projects, select Flex Navigator ⇨ Menu ⇨ Deselect Working Set.

Navigator Filters

Navigator filters specify which project files shall remain hidden in the workspace. These are usually project settings files that do not need to be shown in the Flex Navigator View.

In the top-right of the Flex Navigator view, click the down arrow marked with the "menu" tooltip, and select Filters (refer to Figure 8-13). This will open the Navigator Filters window, shown in Figure 8-18, which allows you to select or "filter out" the file types you don't want to see in the workspace.

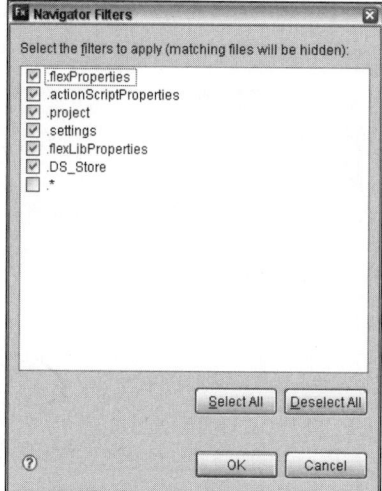

Figure 8-18

Link With Editor

The Link With Editor button is an icon with two arrows situated in the Flex Navigator toolbar (refer to Figure 8-17). When this button is selected, navigating between documents in the editor will highlight and select the corresponding file in the workspace; it is a particularly effective tool for finding your place in a project.

Building Applications

There are two methods of application deployment in Flex Builder: debug release and export release builds. Which build method you choose will depend on whether you are actively building (hence debugging) your application or whether you are compiling it for final release.

Creating a Debug Release

When you build a Flex, AIR, or ActionScript project, Flex Builder will by default compile a *debug SWF*, also known as a *debug build*. This enables debugging capability within your application using the Flash Debug Player, which must be installed in your browser. The Flash Debug Player is then able to relay trace and debugging information to the Debugging Perspective and the Flex Profiler. More information on using these perspectives and capabilities can be found in Chapters 71 and 72. The Debug Player is also able to dump stack traces into a log file and show uncaught runtime exception errors in a browser dialog window.

The default debug build folder name is `bin-debug`, which can be named differently upon project creation or through the Flex Build Path settings in Project Properties. See the "Project Properties" section previously in this chapter for details on configuring your debug release compilation.

To create a debug release for your application, simply select Run in the workbench toolbar for the default application, or select a file from the Run menu for a particular application file in your project, as illustrated in Figure 8-19.

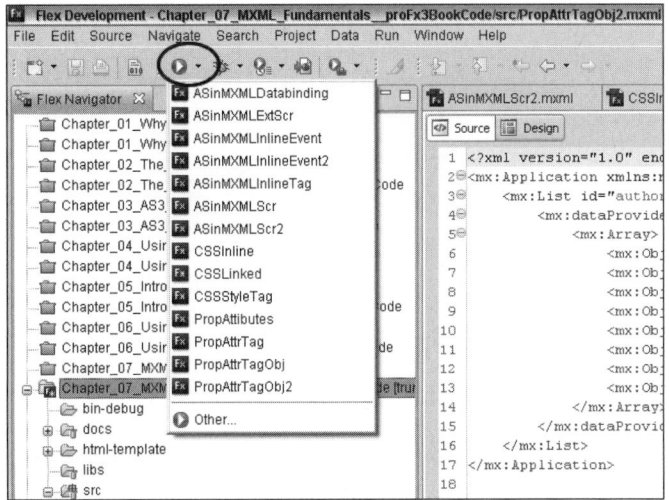

Figure 8-19

Creating a debug release of your application is not the same as using the Flex Builder Debugging Perspective. Whether you press Run to compile your application or Debug to introspect the live application with the Flex Builder Debugging Perspective, both options produce a debug build SWF. Consult Chapter 71 for more information on the Flex Builder Debugging Perspective.

Creating an Export Release

A release build compiles a SWF that does not include all the extra information that allows it to take advantage of the Flash Debug Player capabilities. Another name for a release build is an *export release*.

In Flex Builder 2, when you pressed the Run button to build your application, both a debug and a release build would be created in the export folder (named `bin` by default), named `[appname].swf/html` for the release build, and `[appname]-debug.swf/html` for the debug build. In Flex 3, you must initiate a release build separately, and the debug build does not have a `-debug` suffix appended to the application filenames. This change enables increased compilation efficiency in Flex Builder.

Although it is very easy to press Ctrl+F12 (Windows)/Option+F12 (OS X) to create a debug build of your application, it is considered a best practice to create an Export Release Build when deploying your application. When you export a debug SWF, a lot of extra bytecode is added to the SWF for debugging and profiling capabilities, and can add up to 35% in file size). An export release SWF may also run significantly faster and more efficiently than a debug release.

Unlike the Flash IDE, Flex Builder (and by extension the Flex Compiler) has no option to "remove" or "disable" trace statements from the final build SWF.

You can create an export release in one of three ways:

- ❑ Click the Export Release Build button in the workbench toolbar, as indicated in Figure 8-20.
- ❑ Select File ➪ Export ➪ Release Build.
- ❑ Right-click in Flex Navigator ➪ Export ➪ Flex Builder ➪ Release Build.

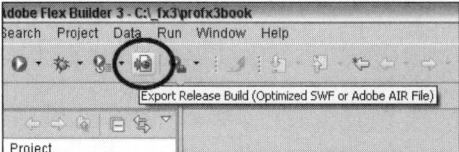

Figure 8-20

Flex Builder will then ask you which application from which project you want to export, and will create a new default folder named bin-release, where it will place the optimized files. Figure 8-21 illustrates creating the Flex Project from Chapter 6 as an export build.

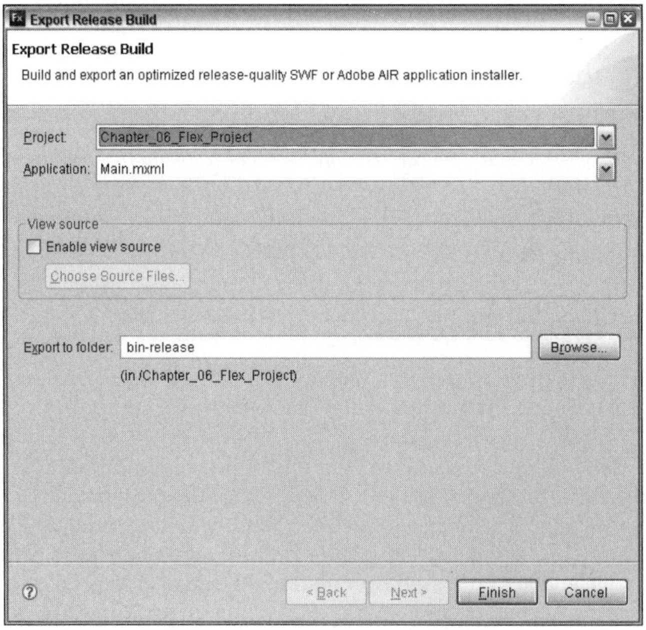

Figure 8-21

There are several other techniques available to optimize your application speed, memory consumption and build footprint (i.e., your main application SWF file size), such as loading assets versus embedding them, optimizing for garbage collection, and using persistent framework caching. These techniques are covered in Chapter 27, "Loading External Assets," Chapter 66, "Modular Application Development," and Chapter 67, "Application Performance Strategies."

You can also turn off debugging and optimize the SWF by setting the compiler arguments `-debug=false -optimize=true`. *This allows you to compile an optimized build in the default build folder. As previously stated, this will not remove trace statements from your SWF, as you are able to with the Flash IDE.*

Enabling Source View

Flex Builder has a feature that allows you export the source files along with the application, making sharing open-source projects or prototypes extremely easy.

To enable source view in your application:

1. Select Export Release Build, as per the previous section.

2. In the Export Release Build window, check the Enable view source option. For this example, you can use the project from Chapter 28, as shown in Figure 8-22.

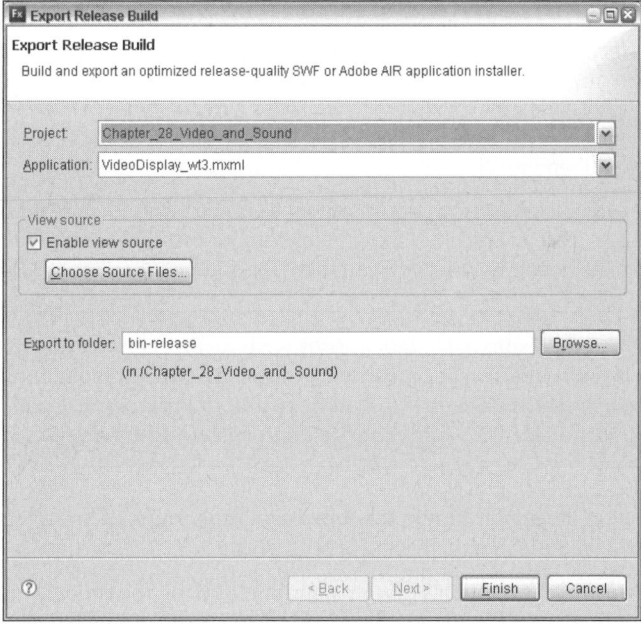

Figure 8-22

3. Click the Choose Source Files button.

4. In the Publish Application Source window, select which files in the project specifically to export, and the name of the source folder, as seen in Figure 8-23.

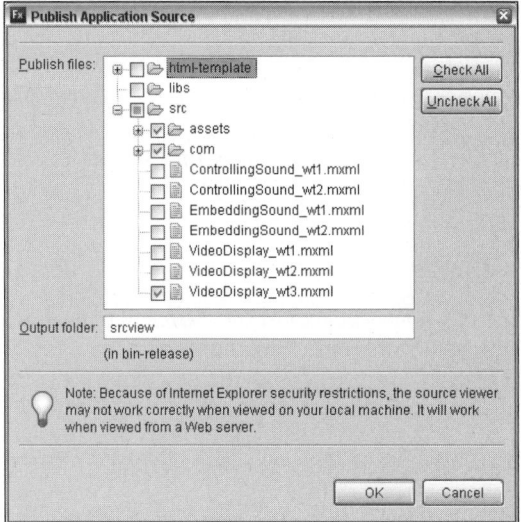

Figure 8-23

You cannot specify an absolute URL for the source folder for a release build from the Publish Application Source window. For a workaround to this limitation, see "Using a Custom Source View URL" later in this chapter.

5.   Click OK and then Finish.

As shown in Figure 8-24, you should now see a `srcview` folder created in both `bin-debug` and `bin-release` folders. Since the Export Release Build created source files for both the export release and the debug release, you can view the source for either application build.

> **If you have linked resource folders or files with incorrect links (such as may occur if you download them from a repository or import a project from another drive), you may get a mysterious error: "Could not publish project source: null" Simply delete the erroneous linked folder or file and you should be able to export.**

6.   When viewing the application in the browser, simply right-click anywhere in the application and select View Source in the Flash Player menu.

This will launch a new tab or browser window showing the source view. Flex Builder actually creates an HTML application complete with Flash menu on the left, a link to the zipped source code at the bottom, and a code browser frame on the right, as shown in Figure 8-25.

When exporting the source for an application, Flex Builder adds a property to the `Application` tag:

```
viewSourceURL="srcview/index.html"
```

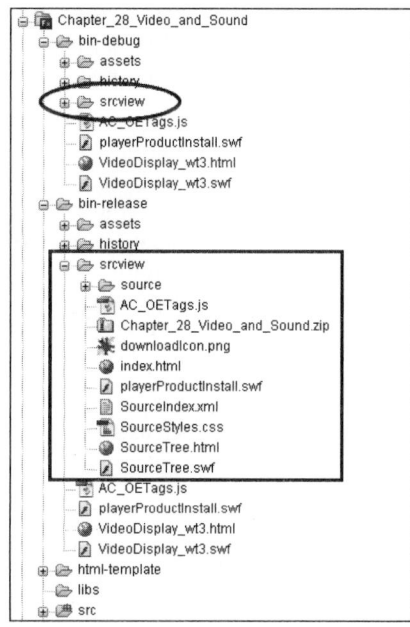

Figure 8-24

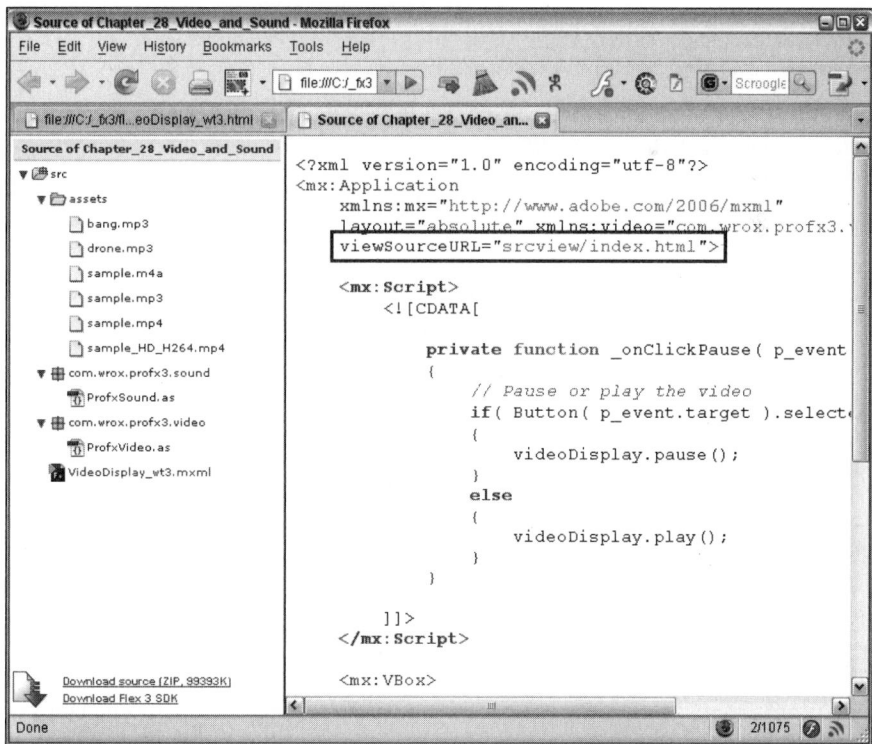

Figure 8-25

The `viewSourceURL` *property of the* `Application` *tag merely enables the View Source right-click menu in the Flash Player; it does not add the source files to the build. So, if you want to enable source view for a debug build, you need to create an export release first.*

> Keep in mind that when you export a release build with view source enabled, it adds the `viewSourceURL` property to your application tag. But when you export a release build a second time with view source disabled, it does not always remove the code in your application. If this happens, your "View Source" right-click link will still be active, but now there's no source in the build folder. To correct this, you have to manually remove the added `viewSourceURL` property in your `Application` tag.

Using a Custom Source View URL

If you have your own reference to project source, such as a web-based repository browser, you cannot presently specify a custom URL for the Source View, such as an absolute link to a website, in a release build. But you can for a debug build. Here's how:

1. If you have previously created an export release, you must first export a release build with View Source disabled to erase the local source files. Then add the following line to your `Application` tag:

   ```
   viewSourceURL="http://www.foo.com/mySourceView.html"
   ```

2. From here you can only build a debug application, because a release build with View Source disabled may erase that line in your code.

When you run the debug application build, the View Source right-click menu item will appear, which will take you to your custom source URL.

Keep in mind that specifying a custom view source URL for a domain other than the location of your application may cause cross-domain errors.

You can also build your own Flash Player right-click context menu to enable the user to navigate to a URL, including a custom source page. For more information on creating custom context menus, see Chapter 41, "System Interactions in Flex."

Language Intelligence

While you were typing the code for the exercises in the previous two chapters, you may have noticed a few things about the editor that help you to code more efficiently. Let's take a look at some of Flex Builder's code intelligence features with the code from these examples in mind.

Code Editing

Flex Builder contains several important features to assist in editing code more efficiently.

ActionScript Code Assist

If you place your cursor to the right of the dot syntax in one of the import statements and then press Ctrl+Space (Windows)/Option+Space (OS X), you'll activate the code assist functionality in Flex Builder, which shows you either the classes in a package, as shown in Figure 8-26, or the class members belonging to an object, as shown in Figure 8-27, so you don't have to guess at what's available in the language.

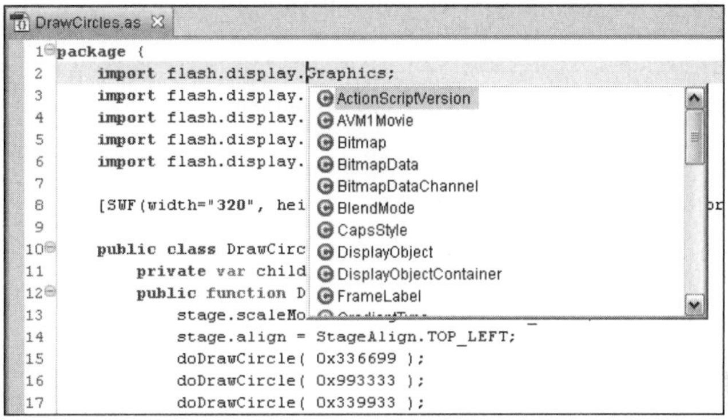

```
DrawCircles.as ⊠
1⊖package (
2      import flash.display.Graphics;
3      import flash.display. ⓒActionScriptVersion
4      import flash.display. ⓒAVM1Movie
5      import flash.display. ⓒBitmap
6      import flash.display. ⓒBitmapData
7                            ⓒBitmapDataChannel
8      [SWF(width="320", hei ⓒBlendMode
9                            ⓒCapsStyle
10⊖     public class DrawCirc ⓒDisplayObject
11        private var child   ⓒDisplayObjectContainer
12⊖       public function D   ⓒFrameLabel
13           stage.scaleMo
14           stage.align = StageAlign.TOP_LEFT;
15           doDrawCircle( 0x336699 );
16           doDrawCircle( 0x993333 );
17           doDrawCircle( 0x339933 );
```

Figure 8-26

```
19
20⊖        private function doDrawCircle( color:uint ):void (
21            var child:Shape = new Shape();
22            child.graphics.beginFill( color );
23            child.   ◇ constructor
24            child.   ○ accessibilityProperties
25            child.   ● addEventListener(type:String, listener:Function, use
26            child.   ○ alpha
27            child.   ○ blendMode
28            addChi   ○ cacheAsBitmap
29            childC   ● dispatchEvent(event:Event):Boolean
30          )        ○ filters
31      )            ● getBounds(targetCoordinateSpace:DisplayObject):
32  )
33
```

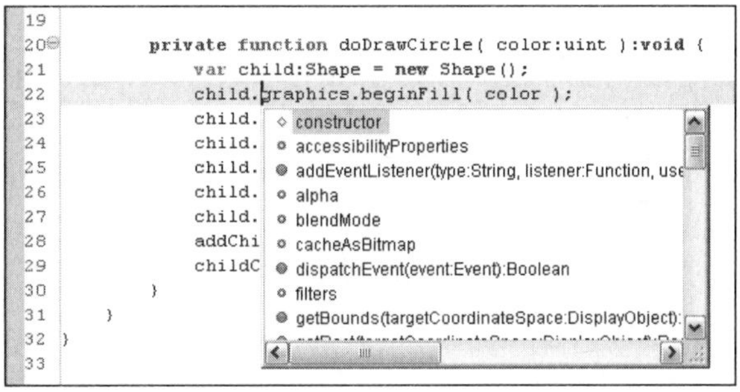

Figure 8-27

Syntax Highlighting

After having defined a class method, calling that method will trigger syntax highlighting, which indicates the syntax for calling that method and is another very useful tool to save you from having to remember everything about your code (see Figure 8-28).

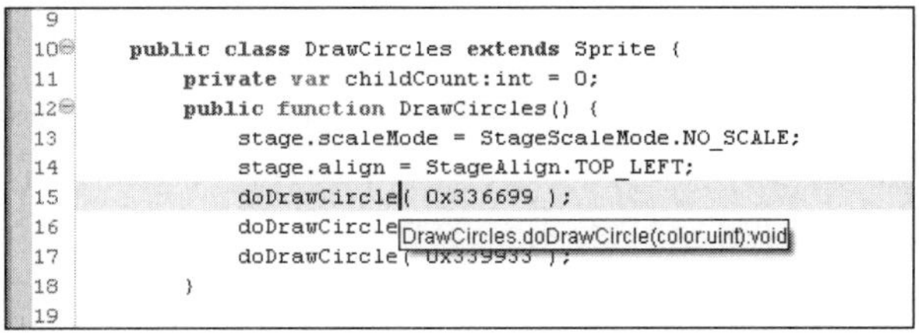

```
9
10⊖   public class DrawCircles extends Sprite (
11        private var childCount:int = 0;
12⊖       public function DrawCircles() (
13           stage.scaleMode = StageScaleMode.NO_SCALE;
14           stage.align = StageAlign.TOP_LEFT;
15           doDrawCircle( 0x336699 );
16           doDrawCircle
17           doDrawCircle DrawCircles.doDrawCircle(color:uint):void
18         )
19
```

Figure 8-28

MXML Code Assist

In addition, if you go back to the Flex project in Chapter 6 and switch to Source Mode, you will see the MXML used to build that application. If you were to type a new MXML component from code, you would find that you don't have to *ever* type the mx: namespace for that component (no, really, please don't); the code assist will type it for you, as shown in Figure 8-29. Attributes for that MXML tag are also indicated in code assist, so you don't have to guess what's available for any given tag, as shown in Figure 8-30.

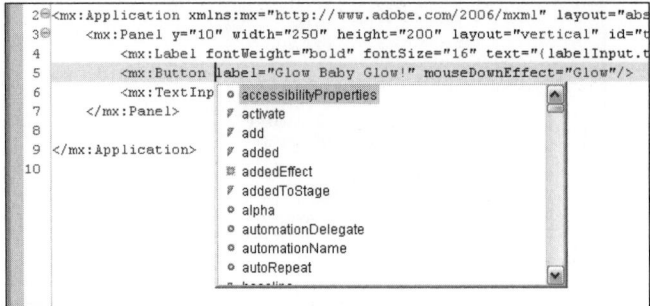

Figure 8-29

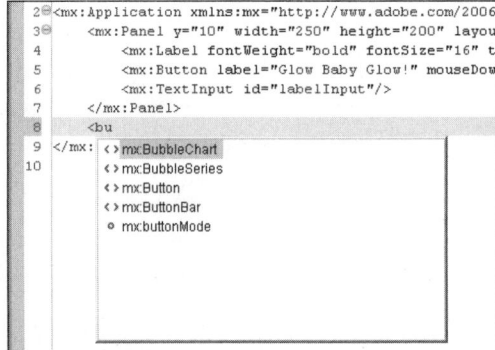

Figure 8-30

You can also get code assist on namespace packages located in the root tag of the MXML document (not shown). For more information about namespaces and coding in MXML, see Chapter 7.

Mark Occurrences

When the Mark Occurrences button in the workbench toolbar is selected, as shown in Figure 8-31, placing your cursor on a known class member or MXML property will highlight all other occurrences of that word in the document.

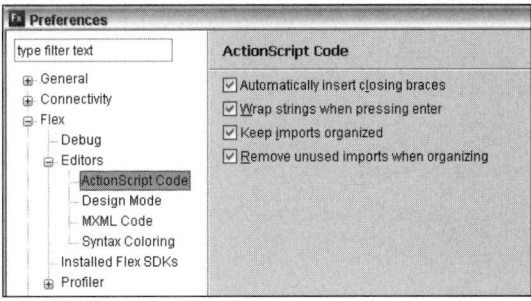

```
/Circles.as - Adobe Flex Builder 3 - C:\_fx3\profx3book
Window  Help

                                    SVN Repositor...   Fx Flex Developm...
DrawCircles.as
  1 package {
  2      import flash.display.Graphics;
  3      import flash.display.Shape;
  4      import flash.display.Sprite;
  5      import flash.display.StageScaleMode;
  6      import flash.display.StageAlign;
  7
  8      [SWF(width="320", height="240", frameRate="31", backgroundColo
  9
 10      public class DrawCircles extends Sprite {
 11          private var childCount:int = 0;
 12          public function DrawCircles() {
 13              stage.scaleMode = StageScaleMode.NO_SCALE;
 14              stage.align = StageAlign.TOP_LEFT;
 15              doDrawCircle( 0x336699 );
 16              doDrawCircle( 0x993333 );
 17              doDrawCircle( 0x339933 );
 18          }
 19
 20          private function doDrawCircle( color:uint ):void {
 21              var child:Shape = new Shape();
 22              child.graphics.beginFill( color );
 23              child.graphics.lineStyle( 2, 0xCCCCCC );
 24              child.graphics.drawCircle( 30, 40, 30);
```

Figure 8-31

Code Preferences

Flex Builder also enables you to configure the default language behavior for how ActionScript code is organized in a file. To pull up the ActionScript Preferences screen, as shown in Figure 8-32, select Window ➪ Preferences ➪ General ➪ Flex ➪ Editors ➪ ActionScript Code.

```
Fx Preferences
┌─────────────────┐  ActionScript Code
│ type filter text │
├─────────────────┤  ☑ Automatically insert closing braces
│ ⊞ General       │  ☑ Wrap strings when pressing enter
│ ⊞ Connectivity  │  ☑ Keep imports organized
│ ⊟ Flex          │  ☑ Remove unused imports when organizing
│    Debug        │
│    ⊟ Editors    │
│       ActionScript Code │
│       Design Mode │
│       MXML Code │
│       Syntax Coloring │
│    Installed Flex SDKs │
│    ⊞ Profiler   │
└─────────────────┘
```

Figure 8-32

Code Introspection

The Outline View provides several tools to introspect the code shown in the current editor document.

The Class Outline View

The class outline in the Outline View is invaluable for an at-a-glance inspection of a class file opened in the editor. Each member shown in the class outline has a colored symbol next to it for quick reference. Figure 8-33 illustrates the class outline for the UIComponent class (compressed to demonstrate the different symbols).

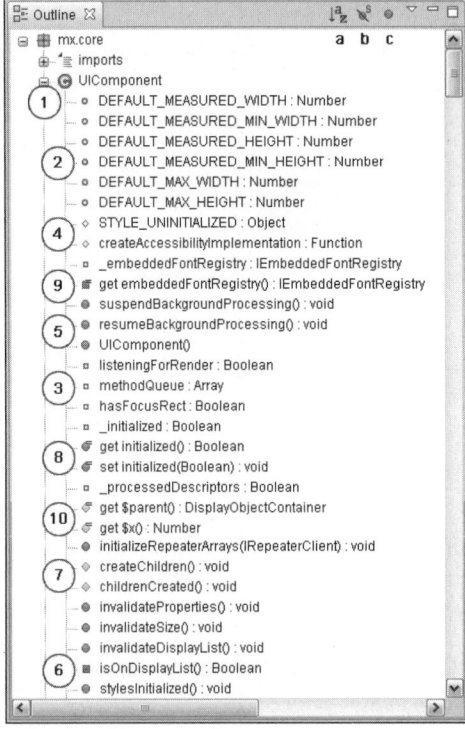

Figure 8-33

1. The class constructor function is indicated by a green C.

2. Public properties are indicated by a hollow green circle.

3. Private properties are indicated by a hollow red square.

4. Custom namespace properties are indicated by a hollow yellow diamond.

5. Public methods are indicated by a solid green circle.

6. Private methods are indicated by a solid red square.

7. Custom namespace methods are indicated by a solid yellow diamond.

8. Public getter and setter methods are indicated by a solid green circle and an equal sign.

9. Private getter and setter methods are indicated by a solid red square and an equal sign.

10. Custom namespace getter and setter methods are indicated by a solid yellow diamond and an equal sign.

Other access modifiers, such as `override` or `static`, do not affect the symbols used.

Class Outline Sort Options

The default view shows you all class members in the order in which they appear in the file. Three options are available in this view's toolbar to refine the display of class members in this view (indicated as a, b, and c in Figure 8-33):

❑ **(a) Sort (alphabetically)** — Sorts class members and imports in alphabetic order

❑ **(b) Hide Static Functions and Variables** — Hides static class members from the list

❑ **(c) Hide Non-Public Members** — Hides all class members that are not public, showing only members associated with green symbols

Other Outline Views

The Outline view can serve two other purposes, depending on what kind of file is currently displayed in the editor:

❑ If an MXML file is selected in the editor, the Outline View shows the component hierarchy, including nonvisual component organization (see Figure 8-34). You can switch from the default MXML view to the Class View, which shows the class outline for the MXML file.

❑ If a CSS file is selected in the editor, the Outline view shows the CSS selectors and properties (see Figure 8-35).

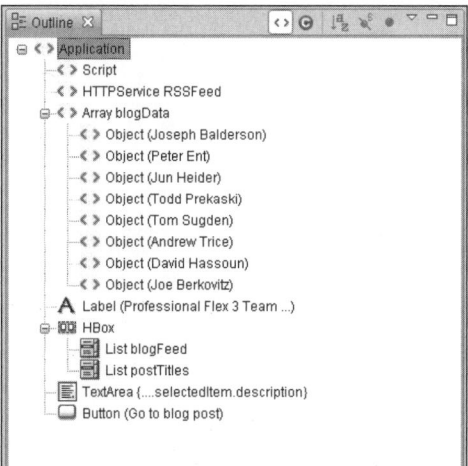

Figure 8-34

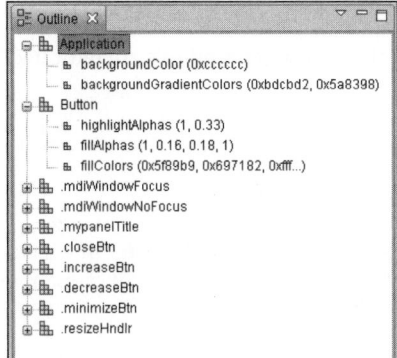

Figure 8-35

Keyboard Shortcuts

The most important productivity tool in Flex Builder is shortcuts: knowing them, using them, exploring them. The most important shortcut you should remember is the shortcut to pull up the list of all shortcuts, Ctrl+Shift+L (Windows)/Option+Shift+L (OS X), as shown in Figure 8-36.

Activate Editor	F12
Add Other Comment	Ctrl+Shift+D
Align Baselines	Ctrl+Alt+8
Align Bottom	Ctrl+Alt+6
Align Horizontal Centers	Ctrl+Alt+5
Align Left	Ctrl+Alt+1
Align Right	Ctrl+Alt+3
Align Top	Ctrl+Alt+4
Align Vertical Centers	Ctrl+Alt+2
Backward History	Alt+Left
Breakpoints	Alt+Shift+Q, B
Build All	Ctrl+B
Cheat Sheets	Alt+Shift+Q, H
Close	Ctrl+F4
Close All	Ctrl+Shift+F4
Collapse	Ctrl+Numpad_Subtract
Collapse All	Ctrl+Shift+Numpad_Divide
Console	Alt+Shift+Q, C
Content Assist	Ctrl+Space
Context Information	Ctrl+Shift+Space
Copy	Ctrl+C
Copy Lines	Ctrl+Alt+Down
Cut	Ctrl+X
Debug Adobe AIR Application	Alt+Shift+D, L
Debug Flex Application	Alt+Shift+D, F
Debug Last Launched	F11
Delete	Delete
Delete Line	Ctrl+D
Delete Next Word	Ctrl+Delete
Delete Previous Word	Ctrl+Backspace
Delete to End of Line	Ctrl+Shift+Delete
Duplicate Lines	Ctrl+Alt+Up
Expand	Ctrl+Numpad_Add
Expand All	Ctrl+Numpad_Multiply
Find All Declarations In Workspace	Ctrl+G

Press "Ctrl+Shift+L" to open the preference page.

Figure 8-36

Some Useful Shortcuts

Here is a partial list of a few useful shortcuts for Flex Builder.

Shortcut Keys*	Name	Description
Ctrl+Shift+T	Open Type	Opens a full list of types dialog box.
F3/Ctrl+click	Go to Definition	Jumps to identifier's declaration code. Useful for exploring code references.
Ctrl+O	Quick Outliner	Opens outline view with filtering ability.
Shift+F2	Find in Language Reference	Opens context-sensitive help.
Ctrl+Space	Content Assist	Opens code-hinting pop-up window.
Right-click in gutter	Folding	Folds/unfolds code and shows gutter options.
Ctrl+Alt+Up	Copy Lines	Duplicates the current line above the selection.
Ctrl+Alt+Down	Duplicate Lines	Duplicates the current line below the selection.
Ctrl+Shift+Enter	Insert Line Above	Inserts a line above the current line.
Ctrl+Enter	Insert Line Below	Inserts a line below the current line.
Ctrl+/	Toggle Comment	Selected line is (un)commented.
Ctrl+Shift+C	Toggle Block Comment	Selected lines are (un)commented.
Ctrl+[Shift+]Tab	Next/Previous Editor	Navigates through opened editors.
Ctrl+[Shift+]F8	Next/Previous Perspective	Navigates through opened perspectives.
Ctrl+Shift+O	Organize Imports	If "Keep Imports Organized" is disabled in the ActionScript Code preferences, this triggers Flex Builder to organize import statements. Window ⇨ Preferences ⇨ Flex ⇨ Editors ⇨ ActionScript Code ⇨ Keep Imports Organized*
Alt+Enter	Properties	Opens the project's properties window.
F5	Refresh	Refreshes the file list in Workspace Navigator View.

*Windows only. Consult the Flex documentation for Mac OS X shortcuts.

Summary

In this chapter, you have learned how to use just some of the many features to develop applications with Flex Builder. This chapter also provided a good overview of how to manage project preferences, importing and exporting projects, including techniques for navigating projects and use techniques to enhance your project workflow. A solid coverage of creating builds was also provided, ending up with a look at the code intelligence features of Flex Builder to enable faster, more efficient coding.

In the following chapter, you'll learn how to really maximize your productivity in Flex Builder by customizing the workbench environment.

9

Customizing Flex Builder 3

There are many things you can do to work more efficiently in Flex Builder. These techniques fall into two main categories: working faster and working smarter. The first section of this chapter will look at techniques to optimize the efficiency of the Flex Builder environment. In the following section, you will learn how to optimize your workflow through workbench customization. And finally, a detailed tutorial on using the Subclipse repository plug-in.

Optimizing Flex Builder Performance

There are times when developing a large project in Flex Builder that the performance of the IDE can be a little slow. But there are many things you can do to work faster and more efficiently. One is to employ certain best practices in your workflow, and another is to tweak the Eclipse environment itself.

Project Development Best Practices

There are a number of things you can do in Flex Builder to ensure that your code compiles faster, the workbench updates sooner, and the workflow is more efficient that have to do with *how* you use Flex Builder:

- ❑ **Turn off "Build Automatically."** This is a great feature for small projects, spikes, and prototypes, as it saves you from pressing that Run button all the time. Just refresh the browser after saving and *voila*! But the moment your project begins to take on a medium size (thousands of lines of code versus hundreds), having Flex Builder recompile every time you save one small change in one file is a huge time sink. Turning this off should be the very first performance optimization you do.

- ❑ **Don't have too many projects open at once.** This is another one of those "of course" tips that you'll be using more and more when you realize how much time it saves. Every time Flex Builder creates a build or conducts a file action such as copy-paste/rename, Flex

Builder refreshes the document tree for every open project. If you have several projects open, and each has hundreds of files, this can take up to a few minutes of precious time. It's okay to have a lot of projects open, as long as you're not doing a lot of compiles. But if you're like me, saving and recompiling constantly during development, you want that process to go as fast and smoothly as possible. Even an added half minute for refreshing every project every time you do a build, over the course of dozens of compiles, over the course of a day, can add up. This is one of the principal causes of premature baldness from tearing out your hair because the compile is too slow.

❑ **Don't embed too many assets.** Not only does this bloat your SWF file size, but it increases your compile times as well. If you find you absolutely need to embed that 1001-icon set plus a dozen fonts, for example, embed them in a module that is loaded into your application at runtime, or a library SWC.

Better yet, if you're embedding a lot of fonts for multilingual purposes, use resource bundles. Either option will dramatically decrease your compile times if you have a lot of embedded assets. In one large project this author has participated in, we decreased our compile times from more than five minutes to just under a minute simply by placing all our embedded assets into modules. See Chapter 21, "Using Libraries," Chapter 37, "Resource Bundles and Data Localization," and Chapter 66, "Modular Application Development" for more information.

If your reason for embedding many fonts is to enable transformations or bitmap effects on text, consider using device fonts and compiling for Flash 10, an option now available for Flex Builder 3.0.2 and Flex SDK 3.2.

❑ **Turn off "Copy non-embedded files to source folder" when compiling.** Similar to the last tip, copying files to the build folder your application will never reference is a waste of compilation time. You can turn this off in the Compiler options window in the project preferences/properties.

❑ **Clean your project if you run into trouble.** If you find you're getting mysterious build errors such as "file not found" when you try to compile (Run) the application, it usually means that your current changes are breaking the build, and Flex Builder is trying to run the last application built in the debug build directory. Only the file may not be there if you have not had a successful build yet, or if you renamed some application files. You want Flex Builder to show you a compiler error so that you know what's wrong, but maybe Flex Builder doesn't get that far, in which case the solution to this and other build-oriented problems is to clean your project. This will reset the `html-template` folder and erase all the files in the debug directory, so you can start fresh. It also cleans any cached code, so any incremental compilation (which is the default unless you set a compiler argument) starts from new.

To clean your project, select Project ⇨ Clean from the workbench menu. As shown in Figure 9-1, you will be prompted for whether you want to clean all open projects or just the ones you select. The "Start a build immediately" option will attempt to recompile these projects. If this is unchecked, it will clear the debug build directory. If you are cleaning the project to get out of a tough spot, and cleaning with this option checked does not work, uncheck "Start a build," so you can start fresh.

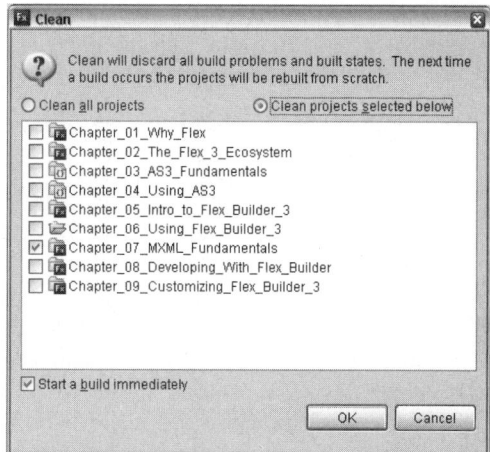

Figure 9-1

Eclipse Performance Management

Since Flex Builder, whether as a plug-in or standalone installation, is built on Eclipse, there are also ways to tweak the Eclipse settings themselves to squeeze out more performance from the application.

The Heap Status Indicator

The easiest way to tell if Flex Builder (or Eclipse) could use some tweaking is to launch the Heap View. This enables you to see the memory consumption of Eclipse in real time.

It can be a challenging little feature to find if you don't know where to look. Go to Window ⇨ Preferences ⇨ General, and check "Show heap status" to turn on this feature. If you are running Flex Builder as a plug-in, you may be able to access this feature in Eclipse by selecting Window ⇨ Preferences ⇨ Workbench ⇨ Memory Indicator.

If neither of these items is present, you might need to download the plug-in from the Eclipse project website (http://dev.eclipse.org/viewcvs/index.cgi/platform-ui-home/dev.html?revision=1.38). Scroll down to Utilities ⇨ Heap Status on the page, and follow the installation instructions.

> *You can obtain the Heap Status plug-in via the Platform UI team's update site. Use Help ⇨ Software Updates ⇨ Find and Install ⇨ Search for new features to install ⇨ New Remote Site, and give the following as the URL:* http://dev.eclipse.org/viewcvs/index.cgi/%7Echeckout%7E/ platform-ui-home/updates.
>
> *When prompted, choose Yes to restart. If you don't see the status indicator in the status line, or if the preference window is missing, restart Eclipse with the* -clean *command-line option.*

This plug-in will show you the current state of memory consumption for the Java Virtual Machine (JVM) which runs Eclipse. If you want to force the Garbage Collection of the memory, click the blue garbage can icon (see Figure 9-2).

Figure 9-2

Why Compilation Slows Down

When you run a process in Eclipse that consumes memory, the heap memory will fill up with data as the action is processed in virtual memory. As the heap stack fills up, the amount of free memory becomes less and less, sometimes reaching a critical mass, forcing Eclipse to do Garbage Collection to free up more memory.

As you can see by the progression of the heap stack in Figures 9-3 to 9-5, the heap fills up, comes close to overflow, and empties as the Garbage Collector kicks in. This process may happen a dozen times or more over the course of a large build. And each time the Garbage Collector empties the stack, it takes precious time from your build.

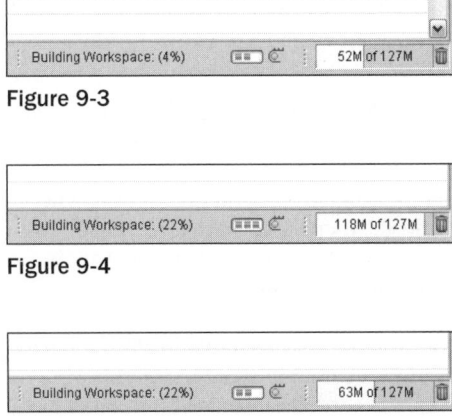

Figure 9-3

Figure 9-4

Figure 9-5

Fortunately, there is a way around this: assign more memory to the JVM upon startup. See the -vmargs command in the next section for details.

Command-Line Startup Options

Several options can be applied on the command line while starting up Flex Builder to ensure better performance. For example, the following command-line arguments increase the memory allocated to the Eclipse JVM (more details are given later):

```
FlexBuilder -vmargs -Xms958m -Xmx958m
```

You can also define these arguments in your Windows or OS X shortcut for launching the application. For example, the Target field in my Windows shortcut for Flex Builder (Flex Builder Shortcut ➪ Properties) contains the following string, as shown in Figure 9-6:

```
"C:\Program Files\Adobe\Flex Builder 3\FlexBuilder.exe" -clean -refresh
-showlocation -vmargs -Xms958m -Xmx958m -XX:PermSize=64m -
XX:MaxPermSize=64m
```

Figure 9-6

For an example of adding command arguments to your Flex Builder executable, see http://weblogs.java.net/blog/davidrupp/archive/2004/09/ibm_web_tools_p.html.

Workbench Optimizations

Let's examine each of these arguments and what they mean to Eclipse functionality and performance:

❑ -clean — This argument flushes the registry caches and clears the Eclipse settings and framework cache (see www.eclipsezone.com/eclipse/forums/t61566.html for details.)

If you find that your Search functionality doesn't work, code hinting or completion no longer works when you press Ctrl+Space (Cmd+Space for Mac), or certain plug-ins don't work or give you strange results, it could be that you need to use this command. It is usually considered a one-time flag, meaning that you only have to run it once until it is needed again, sometimes after installing a new plug-in or feature. Setting it may increase startup times, but I keep it set by default on my startup shortcut to save myself the trouble of having to remember to use it.

❑ -refresh — This argument instructs Eclipse to refresh the file list in the local workspace.

When Eclipse starts, it does not by default refresh the workspace file tree until the workbench auto refreshes the workspace or a file action is taken. Using this argument is roughly equivalent to pressing the Refresh button in the Flex Navigator View.

This command is useful if many file changes have occurred between Eclipse startups, if Eclipse has shut down unexpectedly, or if you have problems restarting Eclipse/Flex Builder after a crash. Used judiciously, it can improve stability. Note that this command can also increase startup times, so if you find that startup or switching workspaces takes a long time, disable this option until you need it.

❏ `-showlocation` — This command gives the current location of the workspace in the window title bar, as shown in Figure 9-7.

If you're like me, and you have more than a few workspaces, this is a cool hack to keep track of which workspace you're currently in.

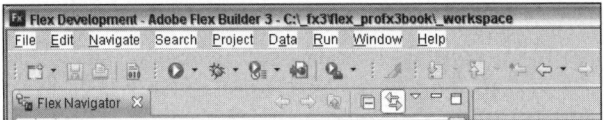

Figure 9-7

Memory Tuning

❏ `-vmargs` — This argument enables you to customize the operation of the JVM that runs Eclipse (For more information, see `www.eclipsezone.com/eclipse/forums/t61618.html` and `http://help.eclipse.org/stable/topic/org.eclipse.platform.doc.user/tasks/running_eclipse.htm`).

The following parameters for this argument involve tweaking the memory allocation for the JVM:

❏ `-Xms[memory]`

❏ `-Xmx[memory]`

By default Eclipse will allocate up to 256MB of Java heap memory. If this is not enough, you can assign more memory. The `Xms` parameter determines the minimum assigned memory, and the `Xmx` parameter determines the maximum assigned memory.

In general, you should assign as much memory to the JVM as your system will allow. Although many people set these values differently, you should set these two values to be the same to avoid memory resizing, or part of the assigned memory may be gobbled up by another application.

Not only will this allocate more memory to the JVM heap, it may in some cases drastically increase performance of the Eclipse workbench, and by extension Flex Builder.

❏ `-XX:MinPermSize=[memory]`

❏ `-XX:MaxPermSize=[memory]`

The above values set the JVM's permSpace requirements, which is the area of memory it uses to store data structures and class information in real-time. Even if you increase Eclipse's heap allocation, you may still get an `OutOfMemoryException` from the workbench if you're driving the workbench particularly hard. Rare though this error can be, if it happens, it's because the JVM does not have enough memory to run its internal processes. Generally, a value of 64m will help solve this problem, but if not, increase it to 128m or even 256m. Again, set both parameters to the same value to avoid memory resizing.

For instance, you could use the following values:

```
-vmargs -Xms768m -Xmx768m -XX:PermSize=64m -XX:MaxPermSize=64m
```

Experiment a little and see what values work for your particular machine.

> **Keep in mind that certain values will crash the Eclipse Flex Builder startup routine, returning an error window such as that shown in Figure 9-8. If this happens, don't panic. It's just letting you know that your system won't allow that much memory to be assigned to the JVM. All you need to do is turn down those values a little, and try again. For example, the following startup** vmargs **will crash the Flex Builder startup routine on my machine:**
>
> ```
> -vmargs -Xms1024m -Xmx1024m -XX:PermSize=128m -XX:MaxPermSize=128m
> ```
>
> **But when I turn them down a notch, Flex Builder starts up with the following values just fine:**
>
> ```
> -vmargs -Xms958m -Xmx958m -XX:PermSize=64m -XX:MaxPermSize=64m
> ```
>
> **As a recommendation, assign as much memory as your system will allow to the JVM: in my experience, it's between a quarter and a third of the total available RAM for your particular machine. This will enable your workbench to run as efficiently as possible.**

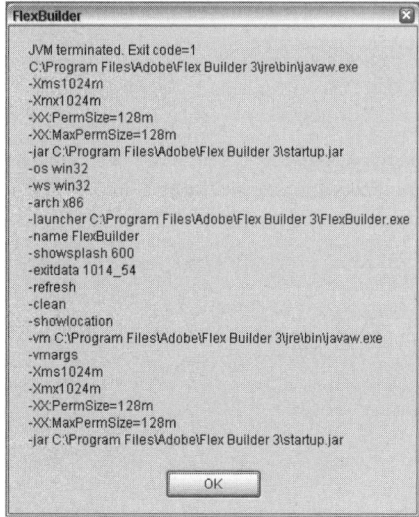

Figure 9-8

Other Startup Arguments

❏ `-nosplash` — This argument tells Eclipse not to show the start screen upon startup. Personally, I like to see the splash startup screen because it tells me that something is happening while I wait. But it is a matter of personal preference and does not impact Eclipse performance.

❏ `-vm` — This argument specifies the precise location of the JVM application. This is an advanced setting that most users will not need to employ. Flex Builder automatically looks for the JVM application (`javaw.exe`) in the `/jre` folder of the Flex Builder installation directory. If your Java runtime is located elsewhere, you might use something like this:

```
"C:\Program Files\Adobe\Flex Builder 3\FlexBuilder.exe" -vm
C:\Java\jre1.6.0_05\bin\javaw.exe
```

All the settings described in this section and others can be found in the Eclipse online documentation (`http://help.eclipse.org/stable/topic/org.eclipse.platform.doc.user/tasks/running_eclipse.htm`).

Customizing the Workbench

Another way to get the most out of your Flex Builder experience is to customize the workbench. Here are just a few techniques for increasing the productivity of your Flex Builder workflow.

Editing the Workspaces List

When you have moved or deleted workspaces a few times, the Switch Workspace "cache" (which is really just a list) may contain workspaces that no longer exist. To delete items from that list (and even add others), perform the following steps:

1. Find the `org.eclipse.ui.ide.prefs` file.

❏ **Windows location:** `C:\Documents and Settings\{user}\My Documents\Flex Builder 3\configuration\.settings`

❏ **Mac OS X location:** `Applications\Flex Builder` ⇨ [Right click - Show Package Contents] ⇨ `Contents\MacOS\@user\{Default workspace location}\configuration\.settings`

2. Back up this file. In Windows I recommend creating a copy with a `.bak` extension.

3. Close Flex Builder if you have it opened.

4. Open the file in a plain text editor.

You should see something like the following:

```
#Sun Nov 02 03:53:47 EST 2008
RECENT_WORKSPACES_PROTOCOL=3
MAX_RECENT_WORKSPACES=5
SHOW_WORKSPACE_SELECTION_DIALOG=false
eclipse.preferences.version=1
RECENT_WORKSPACES=C\:\\flex_workspace1\nC\:\\flex_workspace2\nC\:\\flex_workspace3\n ↵
C\:\\flex_workspace4\nC\:\\flex_workspace5
```

Here is what the settings mean:

❑ RECENT_WORKSPACES_PROTOCOL — This stores the version of the protocol used to decode/encode the list of recent workspaces. *Do not edit this setting*, or you risk corrupting your workspaces.

❑ MAX_RECENT_WORKSPACES: This allows you to set a maximum of how many workspaces are shown in the list. If you have a lot of workspaces and find yourself constantly switching between them, set this number to 10 or more.

❑ SHOW_WORKSPACE_SELECTION_DIALOG: Setting this to true will cause a workspace selection dialog window to appear every time you start Flex Builder, to allow you to pre-select the workspace Flex Builder uses upon startup. If false (by default), Flex Builder will open the first workspace in the list, which is always the last workspace opened.

❑ eclipse.preferences.version: This stores a reference to the metadata version used to store Eclipse preferences. *Do not edit this setting*, or you risk corrupting your workspaces.

❑ RECENT_WORKSPACES: This is a list of absolute paths for all the workspace locations in the list. This is the entry you will edit either to delete an item or to increase MAX_RECENT_WORKSPACES and add items to the list.

The first location in the list, which is by default the last workspace opened, does not appear in the Switch Workspace list in the workbench. So if you edit this list completely, by default whichever location is the first in the list is the one which will open next time Flex Builder is launched.

The \n characters are a line return separating each location. Each colon and each backslash is escaped with the backslash character. So a list of workspaces such as this:

```
C:\flex_workspace1
C:\flex_workspace2
C:\flex_workspace3
C:\flex_workspace4
C:\flex_workspace5
```

becomes this in the file:

```
C\:\\flex_workspace1\nC\:\\flex_workspace2\nC\:\\flex_workspace3\n ↵
C\:\\flex_workspace4\nC\:\\flex_workspace5
```

When you start up Flex Builder, your "Switch Workspace" menu will look something like Figure 9-9.

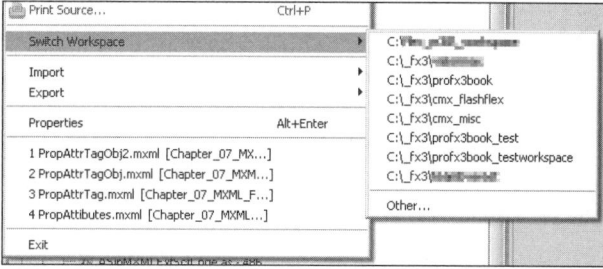

Figure 9-9

Using Custom Shortcuts

Even though I spend most of my time in Flex Builder nowadays developing Flex applications, years ago before Flex 2, I was a Flash developer. And no matter how much I use Flex Builder, it still seems a little counter-intuitive for me to type Ctrl+F12 (Cmd+F12 for Mac) to build my application, when I am so used to pressing Ctrl+Enter (Cmd+Enter for Mac), which is the shortcut for building a SWF application in Flash Authoring. So I customized the shortcut list so that in my workspace preferences, Ctrl+Enter (Cmd+Enter for Mac) runs a build instead of Ctrl+F12 (Cmd+F12 for Mac).

Here's how to do it:

1. Select Windows ⇨ Preferences ⇨ General ⇨ Keys in the workbench menu, or Eclipse ⇨ Preferences ⇨ General ⇨ Keys for Macintosh.

2. Type **run** in the search field. This narrows down the list somewhat.

3. Find the Run Last Launched command, which is the equivalent to the Run button in the workbench toolbar, as shown in Figure 9-10.

4. Select the Remove Binding button to reset the keypress for that command.

5. Click in the Binding field, and hit the Control and Enter keys.

6. Make sure that the When drop-down menu has "In Windows" selected.

7. Select Apply and OK to save your changes.

8. Restart Flex Builder for the changes to take effect.

Now when you press Ctrl+Enter (Cmd+Enter for Mac), it will do the same thing that Ctrl+F12 (Cmd+F12 for Mac) used to do.

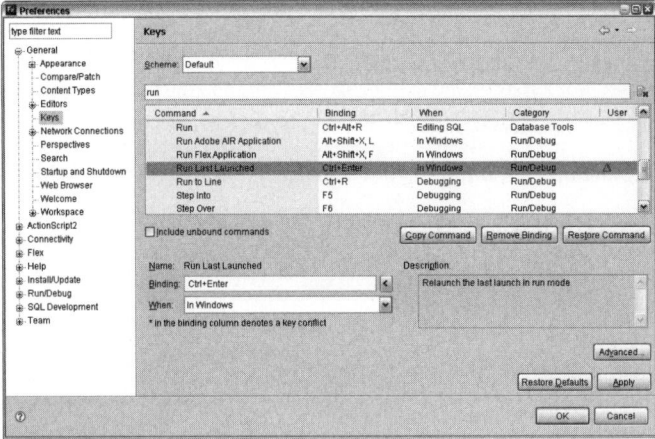

Figure 9-10

The term *unbound command* refers to commands that do not have keyboard shortcuts assigned to them. A *binding* is the keystrokes assigned to a command. You can copy a command and assign different keystrokes to the same command, which will respond according to where in the workbench the user is currently situated, as determined by the "When" drop-down menu.

You may have other uses or reasons for creating or modifying shortcuts in Flex Builder. Just repeat the preceding steps but for different commands.

Layouts for Productivity

Essential to customizing Flex Builder is the layout of the workbench.

Repositioning Views

One of the most obvious ways to customize your Flex Builder workflow is to reposition the views. You can move view panels by clicking and dragging the view's tab. A ghost outline of the new position of the view will appear before you let go of the mouse, allowing you to situate it in the workbench.

One of the most effective ways to reposition views involves docking Editor views horizontally side by side, allowing you to view and edit two documents at once (see Figure 9-11). Because I use a large monitor with 1920×1200 resolution, I have the space to do so. This is different from doing a Diff of two documents (Flex Navigator ⇨ {file(s)} ⇨ Compare With), because you're in the editing mode, not in a Diff mode, allowing for full syntax coloring and code assist. And each of the two view positions allow for multiple Editor view tabs, creating further flexibility. I have also seen developers with 30-inch monitors dock editor views four-by-each, enabling them to view and edit four documents at once.

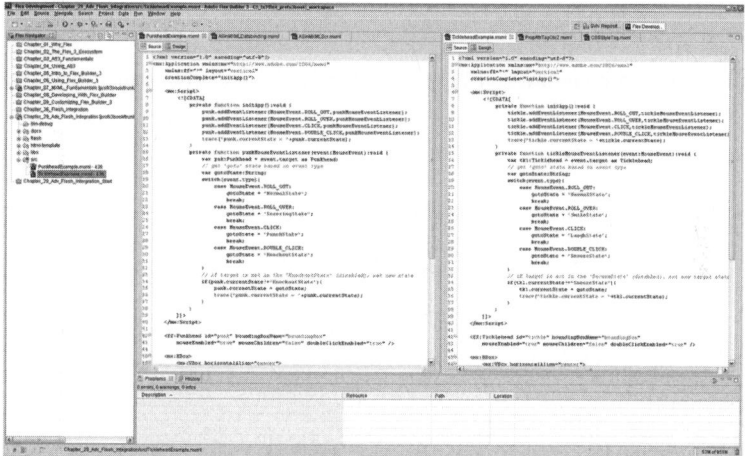

Figure 9-11

Other possible layouts include:

- ❏ Docking the Variables Debugging view vertically across the entire workbench. When intro-specting complex objects, this enables you to get a good look at the tree structure of the object without needing to scroll as much.

- ❏ Docking the Problems view vertically instead of horizontally, if there are a lot of warnings, so you can get a firm grasp of the status of the build warnings and errors without scrolling.

- ❏ If there is a view missing from a particular perspective, open it by selecting Window ⇨ Other Views, and then move it where you will in the workbench.

Creating Custom Perspectives

Creating a custom perspective is one way to save your layout changes. To do so, select a default perspective, make your layout changes, and then select Window ⇨ Perspective ⇨ Save Perspective As.

To recall the custom perspective, select Window ⇨ Perspective ⇨ Other.

Managing Workspace Preferences

So you've created some custom shortcuts, maybe changed the font size or the syntax coloring in the workbench preferences, and created a few custom perspectives. Problem is, the moment you switch to a different workspace, you're back to square one, no customizations. That's because workbench and preferences changes, with few exceptions, are actually stored in the workspace, not in the Eclipse installation.

To transfer any change in the default preferences to a different workspace, you need to save your preferences from one workspace, switch workspaces, and import them into the other.

To save preferences, perform the following steps:

1. Select File ⇨ Export ⇨ Other ⇨ General ⇨ Preferences.
2. Click Next.
3. Check Export all.
4. Give the file a name in the To preferences file field. I usually name mine something like `FB3_prefs_2008-12-16`.
5. Browse to the directory in which to save the file.

To import preferences, perform the following steps:

1. Select File ⇨ Import ⇨ Other ⇨ General ⇨ Preferences.
2. Click Next.
3. Browse to the preferences file.
4. Check Import All.
5. Click Finish.
6. Restart Flex Builder for the new preferences to take effect.

Using Code Repositories in Flex Builder

Many developers regard a code repository to be one of the most essential tools for programming workflow. A code repository is not just for backing up files; it's used for code versioning, team collaboration, and project planning. Code versioning is a system implemented by the repository to keep track of the version history of every single file uploaded or "checked in" to the system. But you don't need to use an OS-specific repository client, which can seem a little daunting for those who have not used a repository system. Although a general discussion of versioning systems and their use is outside the scope of this book, this section will introduce you to a few ways to get access to code-versioning capabilities right in Flex Builder.

Using the Local History

Little do many programmers know that Eclipse comes with its own repository, complete with local data store, which is actually a self-contained CVS repository (www.nongnu.org/cvs). You can access this repository through the History View, as shown in Figure 9-12, by selecting Window ⇨ Other Views ⇨ Team ⇨ History.

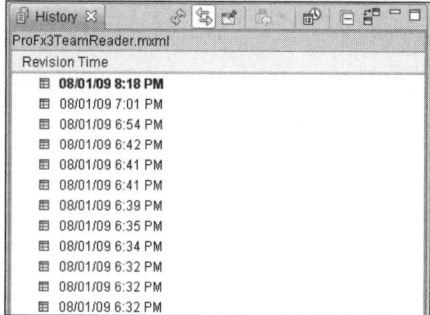

Figure 9-12

❑ If you right-click an entry and select Open, or double-click a time entry in the History View, you open the file in the state it was at that time and date.

❑ If you right-click the entry and select Get Contents, you will be prompted whether you wish to rewrite the current state of the file with the previous history state.

Compare with Local History

There are two ways to use the Diff tool with the Local History:

❑ Right-click an entry in the History View, and select Compare Current With Local.

❑ Right-click on a file in the Flex Navigator View, and select Compare With ⇨ Local History. Then double-click on an entry in the History view.

Local History Preferences

Some of the preferences for the Local History are not actually intuitive to find: they are located in Preferences ⇨ General ⇨ Workspace ⇨ Local History. In this window are options that determine how many days records are kept of files, how many maximum "commits" or history entries per file, and what is to be the maximum file size of the data store (see Figure 9-13).

Recovering Deleted Files

Using the Local History, you can also recover deleted files, if the file was removed within the time frame set in the preferences. Simply right-click an open project folder in the workspace (Flex Navigator View), and then select Restore from Local History. You will then be prompted with a window that enables you to select the files to restore and the history state of each file, showing the contents of the file at that time (see Figure 9-14).

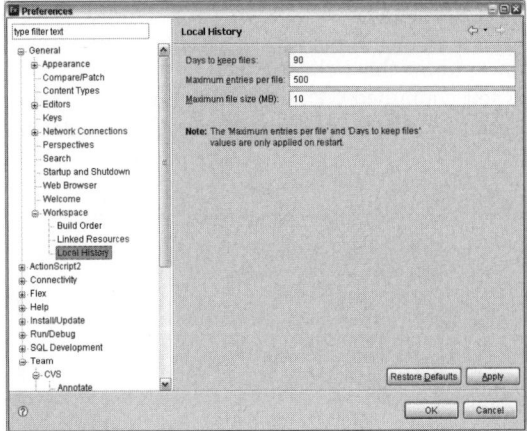

Figure 9-13

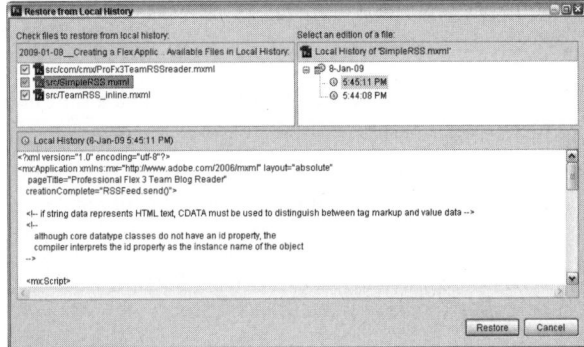

Figure 9-14

Subclipse for Subversion Source Management

Many developers use some form of source version control. In fact, with more complex projects, it is almost a prequisite: filename-based versioning works, to a point. And the Local History is a nice feature if no repository is available, but its features are limited. At some point you're going to want to use source control with your projects. The three in most common version control systems seem to be CVS, Subversion (http://subversion.tigris.org), and Git (http://git.or.cz).

We could show you how to use CVS in Flex Builder (see www.flashmagazine.com/tutorials/detail/setting_up_cvs_in_adobe_flex for details), but it is mostly already implemented in the default Eclipse installation and requires no plug-in to install (which is what the Local History is based on). However, CVS is considered by many to be an older repository system that is a little more temperamental than recent versioning systems. Since Subversion is considered to be the predecessor to CVS, we will take a look at installing the Subclipse plug-in for Subversion in this chapter.

There are two well-known Subversion plug-ins for Eclipse: Subclipse and Subversive. Of the two, Subclipse in my opinion is the easier to use and slightly more stable, although it is largely a matter of personal preference.

This section will not teach you how to use a Subversion repository. You should already be familiar with the concepts of tags, branches, trunk, commits, updates, and synchronization. For more information on using Subversion, see the online Subversion documentation (`http://svnbook.red-bean.com`*), also available as a free PDF book by O'Reilly Media.*

Installing Subclipse

To download and install the Subclipse plug-in, perform the following steps:

1. Select Help ➪ Software Updates ➪ Find and Install.

2. In the Feature Updates window, select "Search for new features to install," and then click Next.

3. In the Update sites to visit window, click New Remote Site. In the resulting New Update Site dialog, shown in Figure 9-15, fill in the Name **"Subclipse"** and the URL `http://subclipse.tigris.org/update_1.4.x`, click OK, and then click Next.

If the download link above does not work, the latest "Eclipse update site URL" can be obtained at `http://subclipse.tigris.org/servlets/ProjectProcess?pageID=p4wYuA`*.*

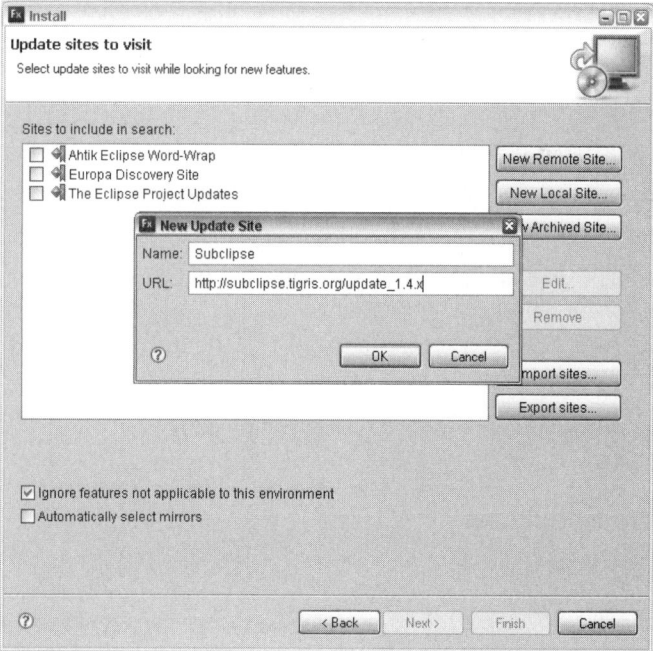

Figure 9-15

4. In the Search Results window, shown in Figure 9-16, deselect features like "Integrations (optional)" and "Revision Graph (optional)" (not shown) until the warning notification disappears. Click Next.

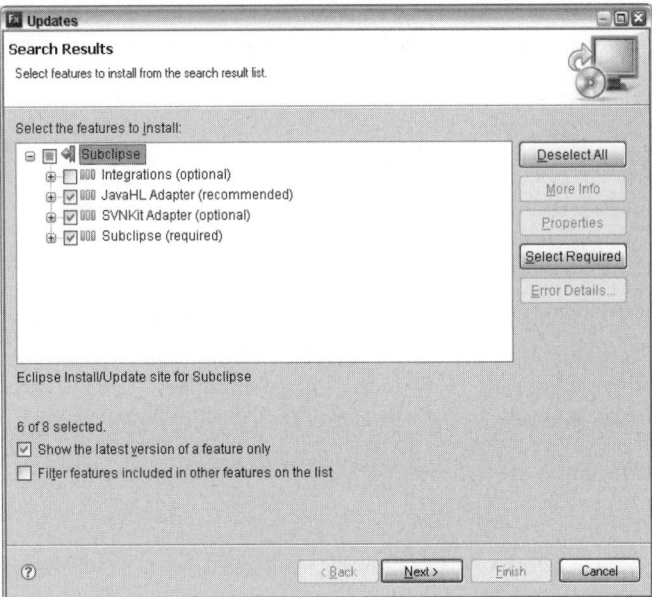

Figure 9-16

5. In the Feature License window, accept the license agreement, and then click Next.

6. In the Optional features window, leave the default checked, and then select Next.

7. In the Installation window, leave the locations per their defaults, and then select Finish.

The Download window will then appear, showing the software download progress from the Subclipse project repository.

8. The Feature Verification window then asks you to verify the installation. Click Install All (see Figure 9-17).

9. After a short-lived progress bar, you'll be prompted to restart Flex Builder. Click Yes to ensure that the changes take effect.

The Subclipse Perspectives

Now that you've installed Subclipse, two perspectives become available: the SVN Repository Exploring perspective and the Team Synchronizing perspective, both of which you can access from the Window ⇨ Perspective ⇨ Other ⇨ SVN menu. In addition, you can access the Team Synchronizing perspective by right-clicking a resource in the workspace navigator, and selecting Team ⇨ Synchronize with Repository.

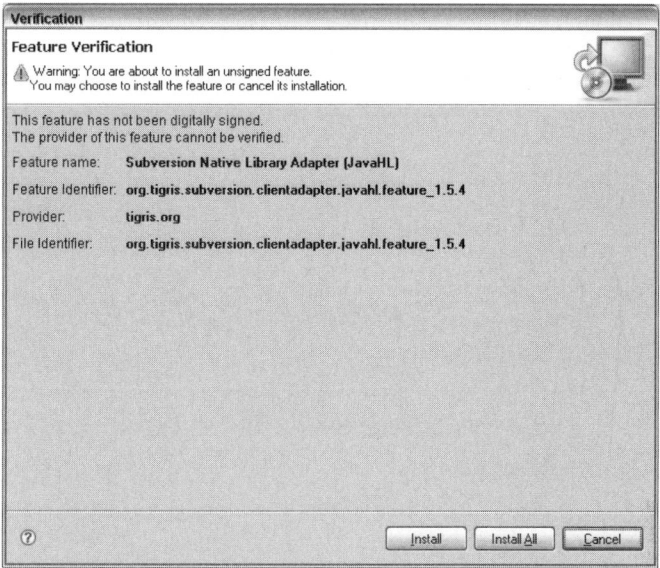

Figure 9-17

Establishing a Repository

Before you begin using Subclipse, you need a repository on a remote server to store your Subclipse versioned files. Although you can install Subversion on your own server and use that, most developers register with a site that offers Subversion repository hosting. Some regular web hosting providers even have Subversion hosting capability for personal accounts, though the sharing capabilities of these accounts are usually quite limited. If you are launching an open source project, you can register your project on Google Code (`http://code.google.com/hosting/createProject`), which uses Subversion.

Creating a Repository Location in Subclipse

Before you can access the repository either for upload or download, you need to create a repository location that Subclipse can access.

1. Open the SVN Repository Exploring perspective.

2. In the SVN Repositories view, right-click and select New ➪ Repository Location.

3. Enter the location for the Professional Flex 3 Book Repository: `http://svn.assembla.com/svn/proFx3BookCode/trunk`.

If you're creating a location for a nonpublic repository, or logging in as a user to your own public repository, you may need to enter your login and password at this stage.

The location should now appear in the SVN Repositories View.

4. Click the main folder to browse the folders and files within (see Figure 9-18).

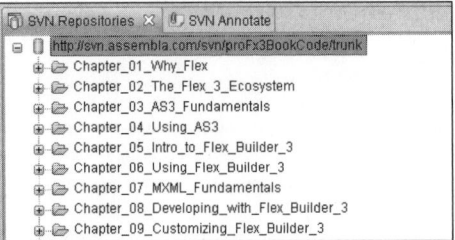

Figure 9-18

The Professional Flex 3 Book Repository

All the code for this voluminous book can be accessed and downloaded from the Assembla hosting page for the Professional Flex 3 book code.

- ❑ Project Page: `www.assembla.com/wiki/show/proFx3BookCode`

- ❑ Repository URL: `http://svn.assembla.com/svn/proFx3BookCode/trunk`

You can also browse the repository in your browser at this URL:
`http://code.assembla.com/proFx3BookCode/subversion/nodes`

The Adobe Open-Source Flex SDK Repository

Adobe places the open-source part of the Flex SDK — the Flex framework, the compiler, and other tools — on its own public repository, located at `http://opensource.adobe .com/svn/opensource/flex/sdk`. Adding this location to your repository location list is a great way to have every version of the Flex framework source at your fingertips, including upcoming alpha and beta releases. This is actually the place where Adobe releases its nightly builds for upcoming Flex releases (see `http://opensource.adobe .com/wiki/display/flexsdk/Flex+SDK`). You can peek inside previous releases of the Flex SDK by way of the `/branches` and `/tags` and directories, or browse the latest build in `/trunk`. You can also get more information on using the SDKs in the source repository at `http://blog.flexexamples.com/2008/08/01/downloading-and-installing-flex-sdk-builds-from-opensourceadobecom`.

A word of caution: this repository is *massive*, so don't download the entire `/trunk` or an entire `/branches` or `/tags` version folder unless you have a day to spare and a lot of space on your hard drive. I usually download pieces at a time for just what I need, say a specific version of the framework, or even a class package within a particular framework version, not the whole SDK.

There are two possible scenarios to connect local workspace files with a repository: one is to download a project from the repository, and the other is to upload a project to the repository.

Sharing a Project with the Repository

In this situation, you have an existing project in the workspace, and you want to upload it or create it on the repository for the first time. You must have a Subversion repository space already established in order to accomplish this.

1. Create a new Flex project. For this example, name your project Chapter_09_Customizing_Flex_Builder_3_TESTPROJECT.

2. Add a few project files, and then create the resources code you want versioned.

This example has copied over a few files from Chapter 26, "Flash Integration."

3. Right-click on the project folder and select Team ➪ Share Project (see Figure 9-19).

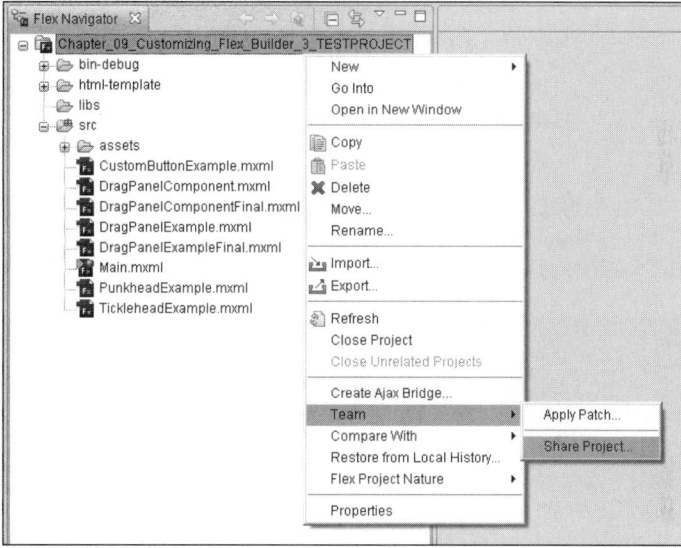

Figure 9-19

4. Any project metadata files visible in the workspace will also be shared with the repository. To avoid sharing these files, in the Share Project window, shown in Figure 9-20, select the SVN repository type, and then click Next.

5. In the Share Project with SVN Repository window (see Figure 9-21), selecting "Create a new repository location" is the same as creating a repository location from the SVN Repositories View described previously, and it takes you to a similar window where you specify the URL of the repository. Selecting "Use existing repository location" will use a location already established, which would be your own repository. In my case, I'll upload the test project to the book repository for the purposes of this exercise.

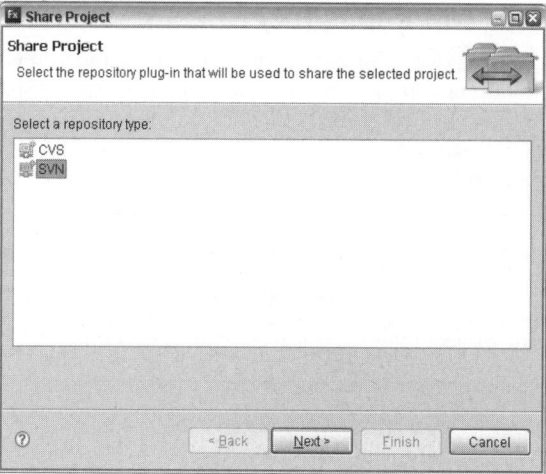

Figure 9-20

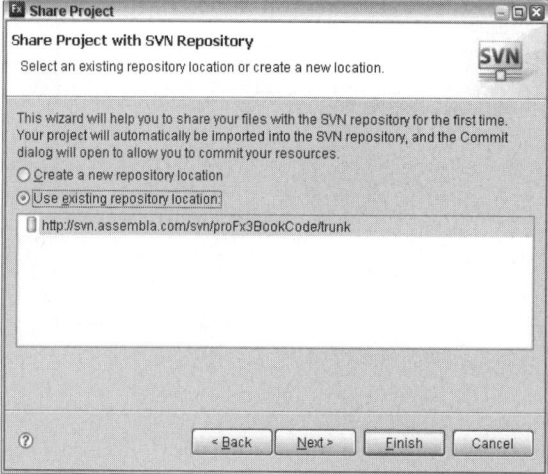

Figure 9-21

6.   In the Enter Folder Name window, as shown in Figure 9-22, either use the current project folder name as the folder name that will appear in the repository, or create a new one. My recommendation is that you keep the folder names the same for consistency.

7.   In the Ready to Share Project window (see Figure 9-23), choose a comment for the repository commit, and then click Finish.

The Ready to Share Project window also enables you to configure comment templates. You also can find this option by selecting Window ⇨ Preferences ⇨ Team ⇨ SVN ⇨ Comment Templates.

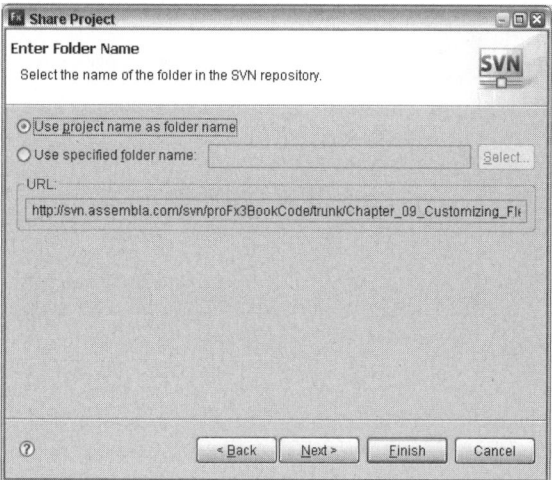

Figure 9-22

If you get an error at this screen that says "Folder [name] exists in the repository," you must specify a folder name that does not already exist.

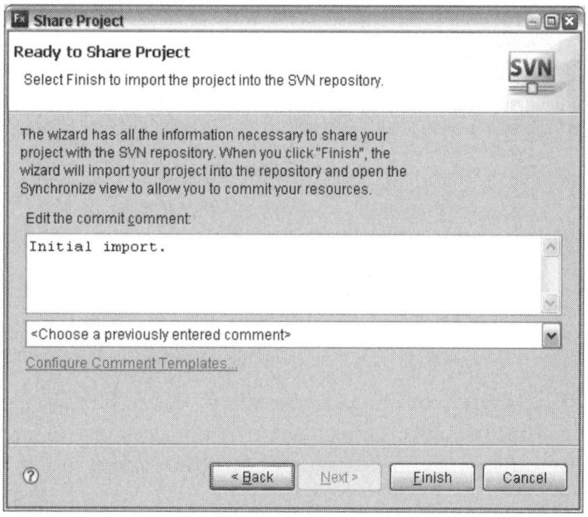

Figure 9-23

You may at first see a red warning notification in the Console View. Don't worry; this is just the repository telling Subclipse that the folder does not yet exist. After the upload progress bar, Flex Builder may display the Confirm Open Perspective dialog, as shown in Figure 9-24.

8. Flex Builder now wants to switch to a new perspective to show you the uploaded folder, but it needs your permission first. Click Yes.

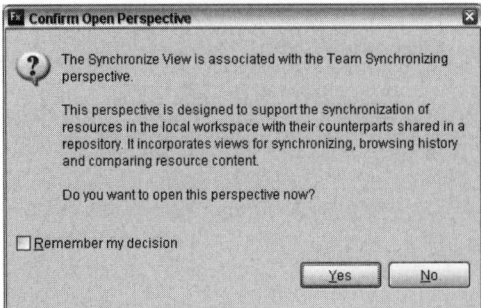

Figure 9-24

9. If Flex Builder takes you to the Team Synchronizing perspective, switch to the SVN Repository Exploring perspective for a moment. Click to expand the project you just uploaded (see Figure 9-25).

What happens? There's nothing there… yet. You still have to commit the changes to upload them. All you've done thus far is create the folder in the repository. This is why it took you to the synchronization perspective first — so that you could commit those changes.

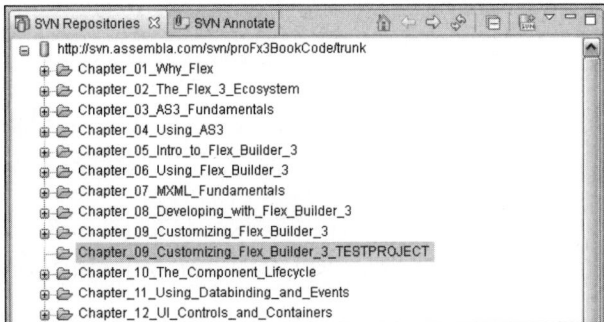

Figure 9-25

10. Switch to the "Team Synchronizing" perspective, where Flex Builder wanted to take you in the first place. Here you can commit (i.e., upload) the files in one of two ways: either by clicking the Commit All Outgoing Changes button, or by right-clicking the project folder and selecting Commit (see Figure 9-26). Don't worry, you'll be able to pick and choose which ones to include or exclude in the next screen.

As you will see later, you can select individual resources to commit from the right-click Team menu in the workspace navigator.

11. In the "Commit to: Multiple targets selected" window (see Figure 9-27), specify which resources to share with (i.e., commit to) the repository, and edit the comment that will be associated with the timestamp and revision number for each file.

The files will then begin uploading to the repository, as shown in Figure 9-28.

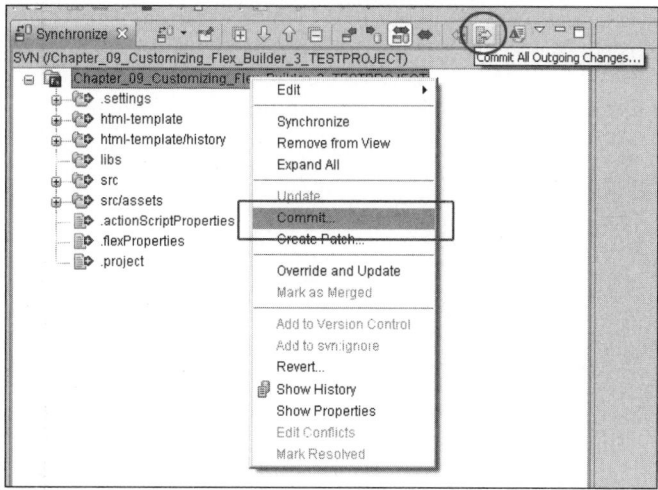

Figure 9-26

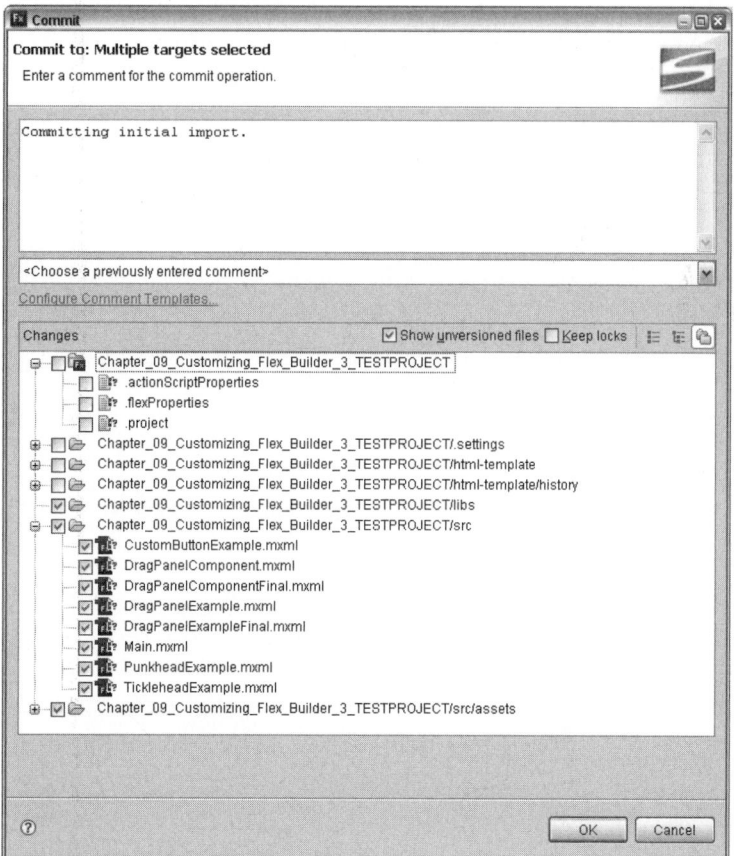

Figure 9-27

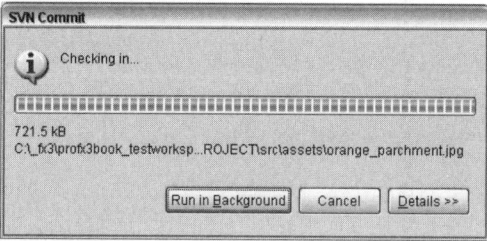

Figure 9-28

Best Practices for Flex Builder Project Commits

Generally speaking, I don't share my `html-template` folder, my `bin-debug` folder, or my project settings files with the repository. The `bin-debug` files change too often, depending on debugging parameters and test builds, and the `html-template` folder gets rewritten when you change certain compiler settings, so it's no use to archive it either.

If you need to archive custom HTML templates, keep them in a separate folder named something like `html-template-bak` so that you can restore the folder if it ever gets overwritten and, more importantly, so that you don't have to worry about other people's project commits overriding your custom HTML template when you update your files from the repository.

If you commit the `.project` settings file, it may be easier for people to download the folder as a Flex Builder project later on (see step 5 in the following section, "Creating a Project from the Repository").

You may also want to commit the `.actionScriptProperties` file if the project requires certain compiler settings, but this can be a dicey proposal and may corrupt other people's projects if you're not careful. So again I'd recommend keeping a copy of the file in a backup folder like `settings-bak` and committing that folder so that other developers can review it, instead of committing the actual settings file used by Flex Builder.

12. When the upload is complete, switch to the Flex Development perspective to see the files in the workbench. Figure 9-29 shows my workbench with the Console View next to it, which will show you a complete log of the repository actions.

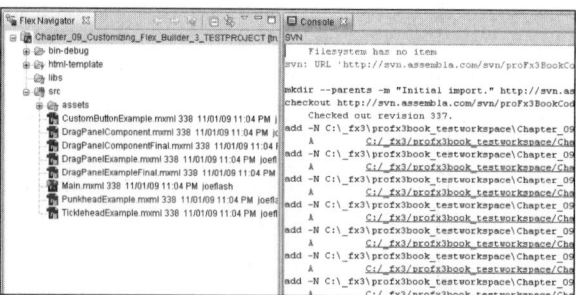

Figure 9-29

Notice that in Subclipse, all the successfully committed files have an orange square in the bottom right of the icon. The folders and files you choose not to commit will have a question mark in them.

Certain Flex Builder icons override the Subclipse icons, such as the default application, so the file may be committed and not show it visually.

Creating a Project from the Repository

In this situation, you have a project in the repository, perhaps as a part of a team project, that you need to download to a local copy. Or you want to download the code from an open-source project, say from Google Code or from the Adobe Flex SDK repository.

For this exercise, you'll download a project from the Professional Flex 3 book repository.

1. From the workbench menu or workspace navigator, right-click and select New ⇨ Other.

2. In the Select a Wizard window (see Figure 9-30), select SVN ⇨ Checkout Projects from SVN, and then click Next.

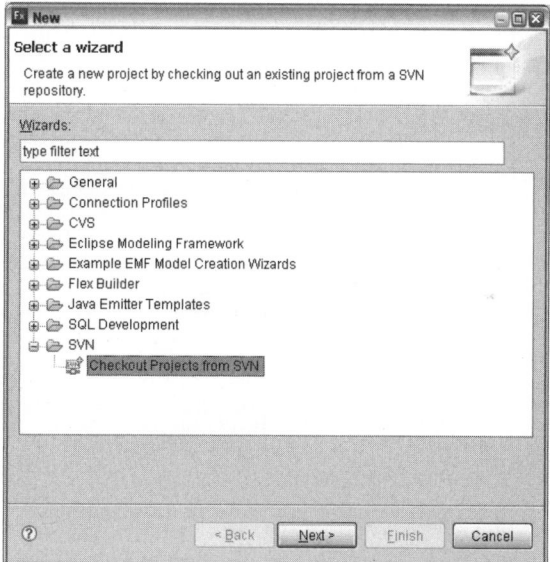

Figure 9-30

3. In the Select/Create Location window (see Figure 9-31), since you've already created the Professional Flex 3 repository location, select that location in the list, and then click Next.

4. In the Select Folder window (see Figure 9-32), select a folder in the repository to download, and then click Next.

5. In the Check Out As window, shown in Figure 9-33, you need only be concerned with the first two options. Leave the others at their defaults.

You have two possible options here, only one of which may be available:

❑   Check out as a project configured using the New Project Wizard

❑   Check out as a project in the workspace

Now here's where things get interesting. If only the second option is available, it means that the folder in the repository has a .project settings file that will tell Flex Builder what kind of project to create. All you need to worry about is what name you will give the project in the local workspace.

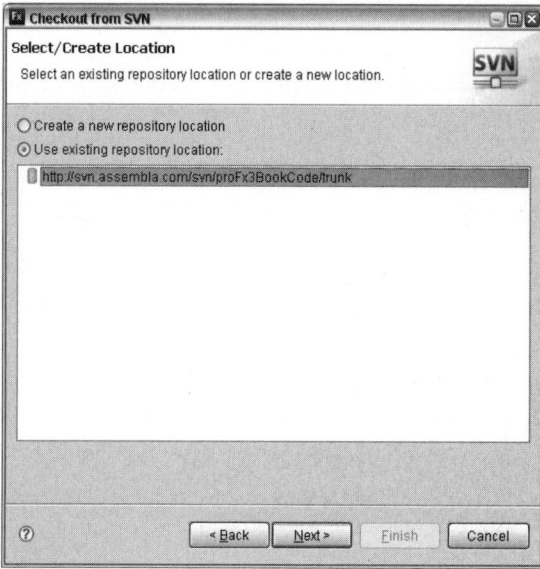

Figure 9-31

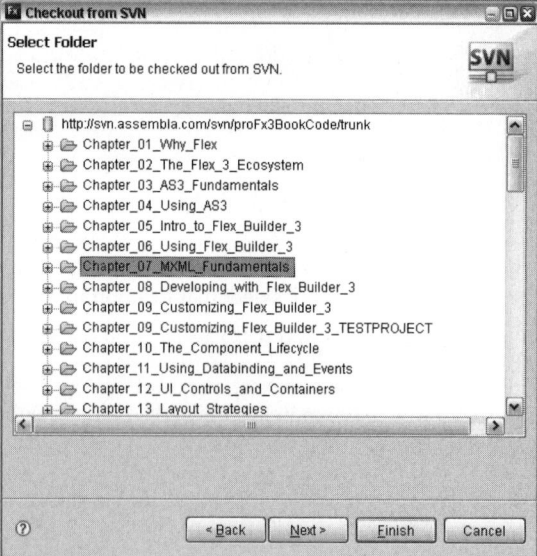

Figure 9-32

Downloading Projects from the Professional Flex 3 Repository

Take note that not all chapter folders in the repository will map directly to projects in the workspace. Some chapter folders have two or more project folders contained within, and some chapter folders are project folders themselves. The telltale sign is whether the folder in question has a "src" folder within it. If it does, it's a project folder. If it doesn't, drill deeper into the folder structure to find the project folder in question. If you don't select a project folder, you risk creating a Flex Builder project with the source in the wrong location for the applications to compile. So be sure that the folder in the repository you're selecting has a src folder directly within.

Some chapters have two project folders because one contains the starting files to complete exercises in the book, and the other contains the completed source files. Check with the instructions in that particular exercise for details.

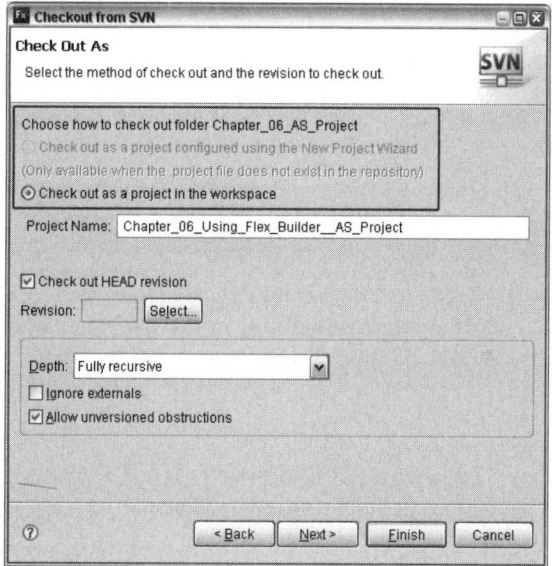

Figure 9-33

If both options are available, as shown in Figure 9-34, it means that the project folder in the repository is lacking a .project settings file to tell Flex Builder what kind of project folder to create. So if you select the second option "Check out as a project in the workspace," and both options are available, Flex Builder will create a generic Eclipse project because it doesn't know what kind of project to create. This is not what you want, since you cannot compile a Flex application from a generic Eclipse project. So if the first option, "Check out as a project configured using the New Project Wizard," is available, take the first option. This will send you to a second wizard that will enable you to determine what kind of project to create in Flex Builder.

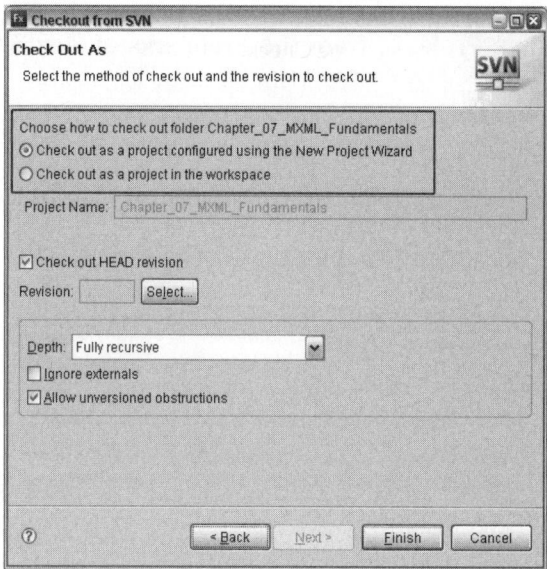

Figure 9-34

If you picked the second option "Check out as a project in the workspace," skip ahead to the "Check Out As Flex Builder Project" section.

If you picked the first option "Check out as a project configured using the New Project Wizard," make a note of the spelling of the chapter folder for later, and proceed to the following "Check Out As New Project" section.

Check Out As New Project

6. Click Finish. A New Project wizard window will open.

7. In the Select a Wizard window, select the type of Flex Builder project under the Flex Builder menu, and then click Next (see Figure 9-35).

In most cases in this book, the projects will be Flex projects, but there are a few ActionScript and library projects around, so be sure to pay attention to the instructions of that particular chapter to find out what kind of project you need to be creating.

8. In the Create a Flex Project window, type the name you want the project folder in your local repository to have (see Figure 9-36). Unfortunately, this is not filled in for you, so consult the notes you made in step 5 on the spelling of the folder if you want them to match. Click Next.

9. Leave the Configure Output window at the default, and then click Next.

10. In the Create a Flex Project window, leave the Main source folder at the default.

Normally when you're creating a Flex Builder project where application files already exist, you'd browse to define a Main application file. But this time, when you do so, what happens?

As shown in Figure 9-37, there are no files to browse to!

This happens because the New Flex Project Wizard has only created the project folder, and you have not gone far enough yet for the Checkout from SVN Wizard to have downloaded any files from the repository yet. So leave the Main application file entry per the default for now. This will take care of itself later on.

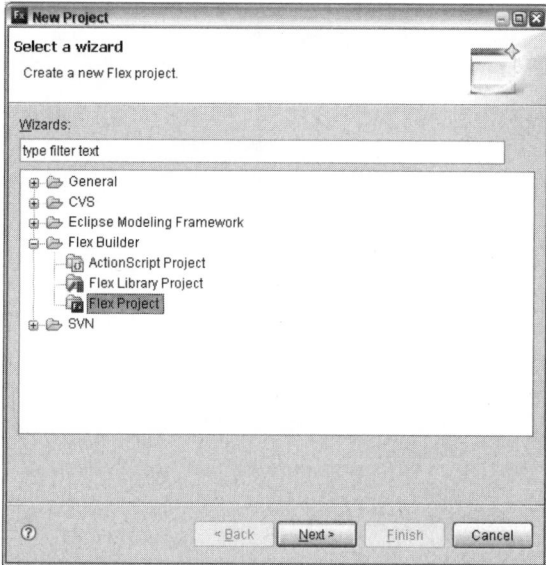

Figure 9-35

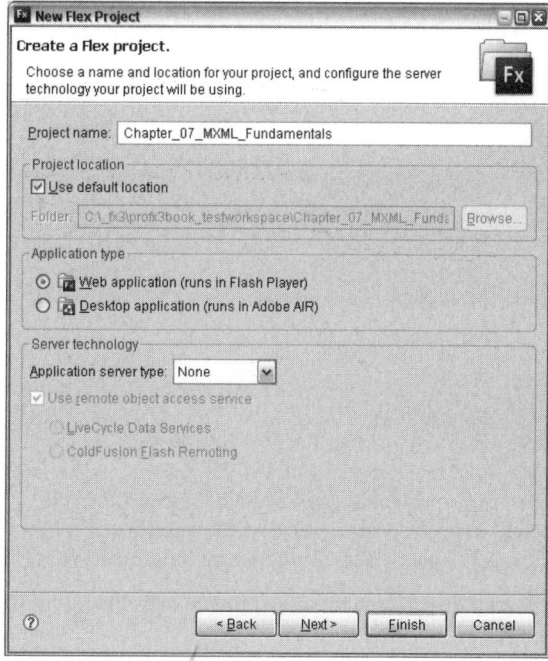

Figure 9-36

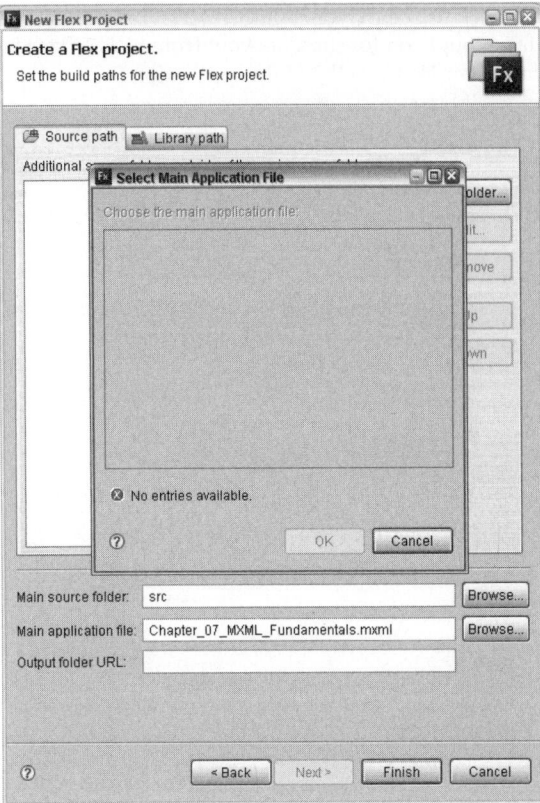

Figure 9-37

11. Click Finish. You will see a progress bar as the repository files are being accessed, as shown in Figure 9-38.

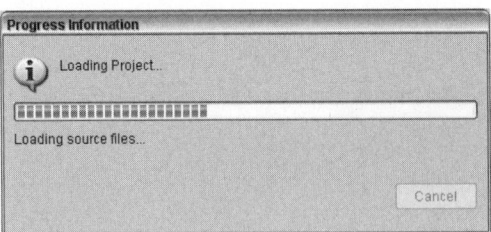

Figure 9-38

12. When the progress bar completes, the Confirm Overwrite dialog will appear (see Figure 9-39). Select OK. This will overwrite the default MXML application that was created in the last step, which you don't need anyway. The files will now download from the repository (see Figure 9-40).

After the download, you will see the new project, complete with files from the repository in your workspace (see Figure 9-41).

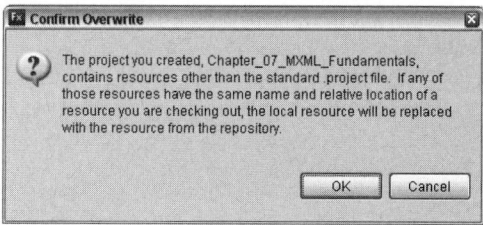

Figure 9-39

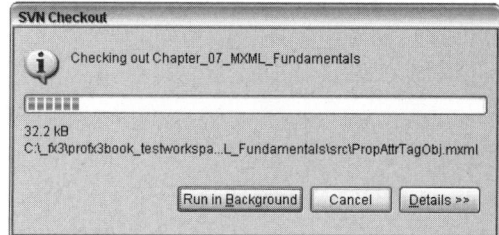

Figure 9-40

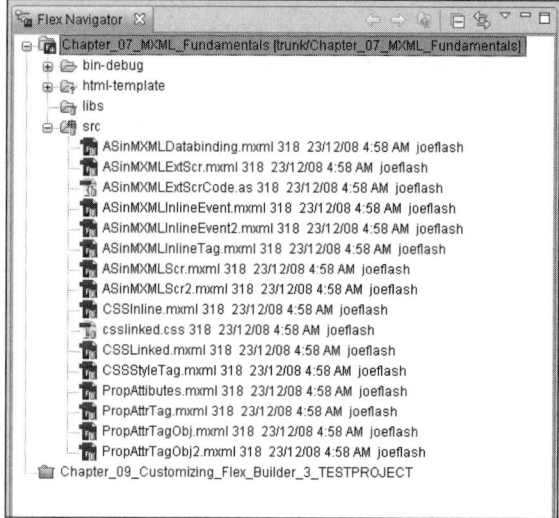

Figure 9-41

Check Out As Flex Builder Project

This section is continued from step 5.

6. Click Finish.

7. Leave the Check Out As window per the default, assuming that your workspace's metadata is located in the same directory as your project folders (as per the default), and then click Finish (see Figure 9-42).

Figure 9-42

The files will download from the repository, and you should then see your ActionScript project in the workspace, as shown in Figure 9-43.

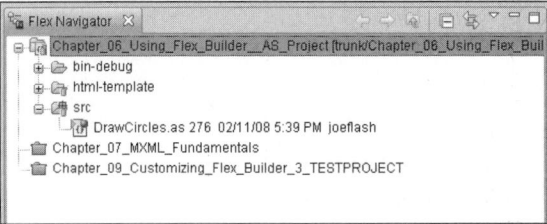

Figure 9-43

Project Management for Multiple Repositories

If you have identical project folder names in different repositories, you might want to establish different project names in the workspace. For example, for the writing of this book I kept one project folder linked to my own personal repository, which contains all the draft and research files I used to write the various chapters, and another project in the repository linked to the official book repository for the final files. When I am working on a client project, I keep prototype projects linked to my personal repository, and projects with nearly identical naming linked to the client's team repository. You may want to create a similar setup.

Disconnecting a Local Project

If you have a local project in the workspace that you no longer want connected to its repository, simply right-click on the open project folder in the workspace, and select Team ⇨ Disconnect. You will be prompted whether you want to delete the SVN metadata or leave it as is. The only time you would disconnect a project in the workspace but leave the Subversion metadata is if you no longer want Subclipse to manage the repository linkage, and have a Subversion client located on the system you're using instead, such as TortoiseSVN (http://tortoisesvn.net) for Windows, or SCPlugin (http://scplugin.tigris.org) for Mac OSX. Otherwise, delete the SVN metadata.

Using Subclipse

Once you've established a connection between a local project and a remote repository, you can begin doing file-specific actions and using the real power of the Subclipse plug-in. Each side, local and repository, has its own right-click menu for resource manipulation, as shown in Figure 9-44. (Note that this is a composite image that you would never find in reality.)

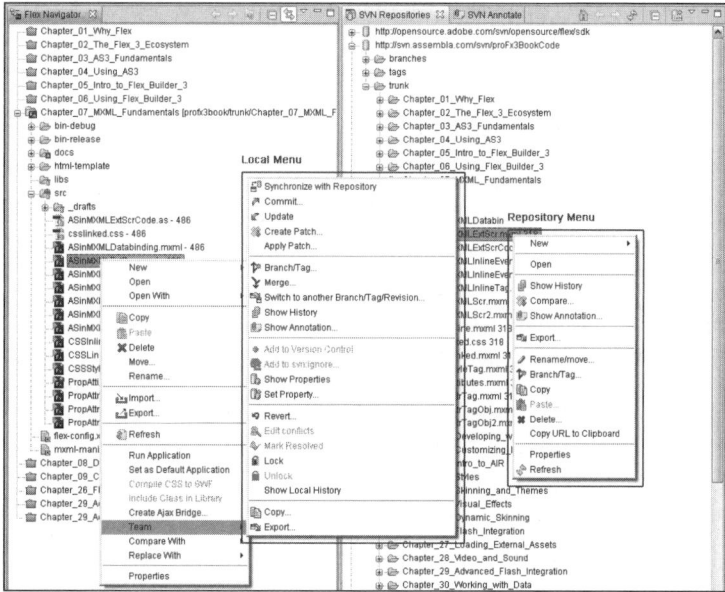

Figure 9-44

Deleting, Moving, and Renaming Files in Subclipse

Although this section is not meant to be a tutorial on using Subversion, there are a few things to keep in mind specific to Subclipse usage. When deleting, moving, or renaming a file in Subclipse, it's always a better idea to do it in the SVN Repositories View (where you define locations and browse the repositories) and then update the files in the workspace. By doing any of these operations in the workspace, you may risk repository synchronization issues, which could cause no end of headaches. This is probably due to the fact that the navigator takes time to refresh its file list and synchronize the changes back with the repository to change the file status icons. Many people refuse to use Subclipse for this reason, but it isn't the fault of the plug-in; it's the Eclipse workbench. To save yourself many possible headaches, do these operations in the repository browser in Subclipse, not the workspace navigator.

Committing Unversioned Files

On a similar topic, although you can directly commit unversioned files from the work-space, you're taking a chance, since you may get synchronization errors. Better to first add files to the versioning system, wait for the workspace to refresh, and then commit them, in two distinct steps.

Although we would love to give you further guidance on using the specific features present in Subclipse and Subversion, such a discourse could easily fill an entire book on its own. For more information on using Subversion in Subclipse, I would recommend you download and familiarize yourself with the Subclipse documentation at `http://svn.collab.net/subclipse/help/index.jsp`, and the Subversion documentation at `http://svnbook.red-bean.com`.

Subclipse Settings

After installing Subclipse, go to Window ⇨ Preferences ⇨ Team ⇨ SVN, and under SVN interface, select SVNKit. For the Mac Flex Builder Plugin, select Eclipse ⇨ Preferences ⇨ Team ⇨ SVN.

Secure Connectivity Made Simple

If you're accessing a repository over a secure connection, this allows you to enter your username and password once, without using an SSH key created through Putty or a similar program; otherwise, you may be entering your name and password for each operation, which is hardly feasible. If you're experienced with Subversion server settings, you can use a generated SSH key, but I have found changing the SVN interface to SVNKit to be more user-friendly. Although some more experienced folks would disagree with this method, it is much easier to implement for team members who don't necessarily have extensive Subversion experience.

Customizing Labels

After a while, some of those verbose filename labels can get cumbersome. To customize the labels or annotations that appear beside each filename in the workspace, go to Window ⇨ Preferences ⇨ Team ⇨ SVN ⇨ Label Decorations, and select the Text Tag, as shown in Figure 9-45. For the Mac Flex Builder Plugin, select Eclipse ⇨ Preferences ⇨ Team ⇨ SVN ⇨ Label Decorations. This will allow you to edit the text templates that determine Subclipse labeling for your files in Flex Builder.

For instance, I changed the default File Format text from:

```
{added_flag}{dirty_flag}{name} {revision}  {date}  {author}
```

to:

```
{added_flag}{dirty_flag}{name} - {revision}
```

which creates a less cluttered workspace.

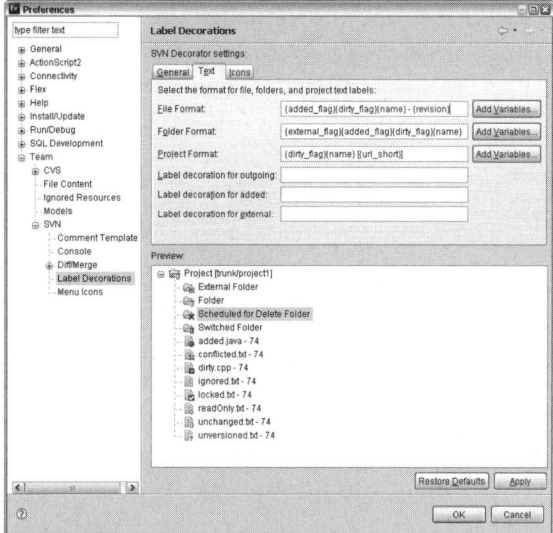

Figure 9-45

Migrating Subclipse Preferences

The most annoying thing about switching workspaces is the loss of preference settings. In the last chapter, you learned how to get around this by saving and importing preferences from one workspace to another. Unfortunately, Subclipse settings, such as custom labels and repository locations, do not seem to export with the rest of the workspace preferences. But there is a way around this.

1. Close Flex Builder if it is open.

2. In your workspace folder containing the Subclipse settings you want to save, browse to:

   ```
   [workspace folder]\.metadata\.plugins
   ```

   In this folder, you will find two directories:

   ```
   org.tigris.subversion.subclipse.core
   org.tigris.subversion.subclipse.ui
   ```

3. Copy these two folders into the `\.metadata\.plugins` folder in the workspace you want to transfer these settings to. Overwrite the existing Subclipse folders, if present. Make sure that there are no Subversion locations in the second workspace you want to keep, or they will get overwritten.

4. Open Flex Builder in your second workspace, and you will find all your Subclipse settings have been transferred.

Bug Tracking and Subclipse in Flex Builder

The next step in this evolution in developer tools is to use a bug-tracking system. Wouldn't it be great if you could view the details of your issues-tracking system right inside Flex Builder?

In the Search Results installation window (refer to the earlier "Installing Subclipse" section), you may have had to disable the Integrations ⇨ Subclipse Integration for Mylyn module to properly install Subclipse. The reason is that this module could not be installed before having first installed Mylyn. (You can go back and install the missing module later once you install Mylyn.) So what is Mylyn?

Mylyn (www.eclipse.org/mylyn) essentially enhances the tasks-tracking abilities of Eclipse (see Window ⇨ Other Views ⇨ General ⇨ Tasks) and integrates this functionality with a number of issues-tracking systems, including Bugzilla (www.bugzilla.org), Trac (www.trac.edgewall.org), and JIRA (www.atlassian.com/software/jira), which is what Adobe uses for its open source Flex repository.

Using the Adobe Bug Database

If you find a mysterious issue with either Flex Builder or the Flex SDK, there is a slight chance it may be a known bug. You can search for and participate in reporting bugs by browsing the Adobe Bug and Issue Management System, dubbed "Adobe JIRA" for short, at https://bugs.adobe.com/jira. You can also report a bug from within Flex Builder by clicking "Help ⇨ Report A Bug."

Summary

This chapter described a number of advanced topics related to Flex Builder performance and workflow optimization, and repository usage. You learned how to tweak the Eclipse settings for both performance and stability, how to use the customize the workbench for maximum productivity, and a lot of fine details on using Flex Builder's built-in repository, including setting up and using the Subclipse plug-in for Subversion repository interaction.

The next chapter begins a new section of this book, which takes a detailed look at developing with the Flex framework, starting with the basics of the Flex framework component life cycle.

Part III: Working with Components

10

The Component Life Cycle and Class Hierarchy

Adobe Flex is built on the Adobe Flash platform. Understanding the relationship between Flex and Flash can help you write better and more engaging applications. Understanding how Flex works and the relationship between the Flex classes will make it easier to write applications and make them easier to maintain.

The Role of Flash in Flex Applications

The line between Flex and Flash can appear at first to be blurry. In fact, you might not even be aware of how Flash influences Flex. In short, the Flash Player provides the environment in which Flex applications run. This is also true of Adobe AIR applications, as the AIR runtime is analogous to the Flash Player runtime. The AIR runtime provides a desktop environment, whereas the Flash Player runtime provides a browser environment.

The basis of Flash is animation. If you know Flash or have even toyed with it for a bit, you'll know that you develop animations frame by frame on a timeline, exactly as a cartoonist does when creating a motion picture cartoon. On one frame you have a figure of bird, on the next frame the bird's wings move a bit, on the next frame they move a bit more, and so forth. The animation of a bird flapping its wings is then placed on the stage (the background of the movie) in one frame. On the next frame the bird (with wings flapping) is moved a bit, on the next frame it is moved a bit more, and so forth until the bird has moved from one side of the stage to the other. When the movie is played you see a bird flying from one side to the other and flapping its wings all the way.

This animation-within-animation concept is what makes the Flash player so expressive. More important, is the frame-by-frame mentality of the Flash Player that provides the engine to make it all work.

The Flash Player also holds the interface to the outside world. Flex applications communicate with server applications by using the built-in networking classes of the Flash Player. Early in its life, the Flash Player had the ability to communicate and this seemingly small ability gave developers the tools to build dynamic, and animated, applications. Being able to accept user input through the mouse and keyboard provided developers the means to engage users with business applications in ways that were not possible before.

Flex makes use of these Flash Player resources simply because Flex is just another way to create Flash animations. Your Flex source files — MXML and ActionScript files — are compiled into a SWF file just as if you had used the Flash integrated design environment (IDE) to make an SWF. What all this means is that Flex *is* Flash, and knowing that gives you the ability to create wonderful and out-of-the-box applications.

The Flex Framework Life Cycle

The Flex framework is the name given to the collection of classes that make the Flex user interface possible. The framework also includes the manner in which instances of these classes are created, used, and destroyed — the *life cycle* of Flex.

The Flex framework uses the Flash Player frame-by-frame engine to create and render the visual aspects of the user interface. Take the `Button` class as an example. Putting `<mx:Button label="Push Me" />` in a Flex application illustrates how the Flex framework works, as discussed in the next section.

Frame-by-Frame

When the SWF that contains this `Button` has been loaded by the Flash Player, the Flash Player begins executing the code inside of the SWF. Keep in mind the frame-by-frame nature of the Flash Player as you read this.

1.   The code in the SWF creates the instances of all the objects. In this case, it will be the `Application` and the `Button`.

     Next frame.

2.   The code in the SWF creates the visual aspects of the `Application` and `Button`.

     Next frame.

3.   The code in the SWF listens for keyboard or mouse events or any event handlers that have been queued.

     Next frame.

4.   Repeat previous frame until a mouse or keyboard event happens.

     You move the mouse over the button.

5.   The code in the SWF changes the visual appearance of the `Button`.

6.   Go back to Frame 3.

     You press the mouse down.

7. The code in the SWF changes the visual appearance of the `Button`.

8. Go back to Frame 3.

You release the mouse.

9. The code in the SWF changes the visual appearance of the `Button`. Code in the SWF queues an event handler for the click on the `Button`.

10. Go back to Frame 3.

11. The queued event handler is executed.

Basically, after executing a bit of ActionScript code, the Flash Player returns to listening for input events (mouse and keyboard) or for any code queued up from another frame. During the time between frames, the Flash Player renders the graphics on the screen. For example, when you press the mouse down over a button, the code associated with that action creates graphic instructions to recolor the button. When the Flash Player finishes that frame, the Flash Player's rendering engine takes those instructions and redraws the button with its "mouse down" appearance.

It is never the case that your ActionScript code has an immediate visual effect. Whenever your code, no matter how explicitly you write it, makes visual changes to the screen, that information is simply placed onto a list (called the Display List, as shown in Figure 10-1). Only after the Flash Player finishes executing a frame does the rendering engine update the display. Suppose that your code draws a blue line. Then your code erases that line and draws a red line. Then your code erases that line and draws a green line. When the code is executed, all you will see is the green line.

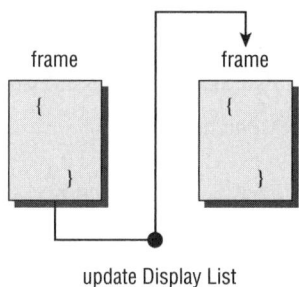

Figure 10-1

Anything you draw in your code will not appear on the display until after the current frame has completed.

This is an important concept and can help you write better and more efficient code. You'll see how to make use of this later in the book in Part IV, "Advanced Component Development." For the moment, understand that your code is building and modifying the Display List. When your code has finished executing on a frame, the Flash Player rendering engine then presents the Display List. Many updates to the Display List are optimized and then drawn as efficiently as possible. This is what gives the Flash Player its speed.

The Life Cycle

Consider this slightly more advanced Flex application:

```
<mx:Application …>
    <mx:Panel title="Employee Data">
        <mx:DataGrid …>
            …
        </mx:DataGrid>
        <mx:ControlBar>
            <mx:Button label="Submit" />
        </mx:ControlBar>
    </mx:Panel>
</mx:Application>
```

The Flex framework life cycle uses the nesting nature of the components (DataGrid is a child of Panel, which is a child of Application). The cycle begins by creating instances of the components, then it tells the components to create their children, then the children report their status to their parent, and so on (the word in parentheses is the name of the function that is called at that point in the framework and is explained below):

Start of Frame (initialize)

❑   The Application is created, dispatches an initialize event, and is instructed to create its children.

❑   The Panel is created, dispatches an initialize event, and is told to create its children.

❑   The DataGrid is created, dispatches an initialize event, and is told to create its children.

❑   The ControlBar is created, dispatches an initialize event, and is told to create its children.

❑   The Button is created and dispatches an initialize event; it has no children.

End of Frame

Start of Frame (createChildren)

❑   The Button reports that it has been created by dispatching a creationComplete event.

❑   The ControlBar, having created its children, dispatches a creationComplete event.

❑   The DataGrid, having created its children, dispatches a creationComplete event.

❑   The Panel, having created its children, dispatches a creationComplete event.

❑   The Application, having created its children, dispatches a creationComplete event.

End of Frame

Start of Frame (commitProperties)

❑   The Application applies properties to itself and its children.

❑   The Panel applies properties to itself and its children.

❑   The DataGrid applies properties to itself and its children.

❑   The ControlBar applies properties to itself and its children.

❑   The `Button` applies properties to itself.

End of Frame

Start of Frame (`measure`)

❑   The `Application` is told to measure itself and its children.

❑   The `Panel` is told to measure itself and its children.

❑   The `DataGrid` is told to measure itself and its children.

❑   The `ControlBar` is told to measure itself and its children.

❑   The `Button` measures itself.

End of Frame

Start of Frame (`updateDisplayList`)

❑   The `Application` is told to position its children.

❑   The `Panel` is told to position its children.

❑   The `DataGrid` is told to position its children.

❑   The `ControlBar` is told to position its children.

End of Frame

Start of Frame (`updateDisplayList`)

❑   The `Button` is positioned and dispatches a render event.

❑   The `ControlBar` is positioned and dispatches a render event.

❑   The `DataGrid` is positioned and dispatches a render event.

❑   The `Panel` is positioned and dispatches a render event.

❑   The `Application` is positioned and dispatches a render event.

End of Frame

The progression from parent component down to child component and back up, with events reporting the progress, is the Flex framework life cycle.

It is important to understand just when these events occur. As you can see from the cycle above, multiple passes are made through the application. For example, if you have several buttons in a `ControlBar`, the `ControlBar` cannot position the buttons properly without knowing how large they are. Once the buttons have been measured, the `ControlBar` can apply its layout algorithm to position them. Likewise, the `Panel` cannot position the `ControlBar` until the `ControlBar` is measured. The height of the `ControlBar` depends on the height of its children.

The multiple passes ensure an accurate layout of the application. Further, changes to components — such as adding another `Button` to a `ControlBar` at runtime or even simply resizing the application — cause some of the Flex framework to be invoked again.

As you write your applications you may run into a situation where things are not happening as you planned. For example, you may create a button and try to get its size and position it all in one place.

Knowing about the Flex framework's multiple passes, you realize that the Flash Player will not have had the opportunity to render the button inside of the function creating the button. Nor will the `Button`'s parent have had an opportunity to measure the `Button`. What you wind up doing is breaking the creation of the `Button` and the positioning of the `Button` into separate functions.

In fact, the Flex framework has accounted for this, and there are specific functions that are called on the Flex components throughout the life cycle of the application as follows:

❑   When a component is told to create its child components, the component's `createChildren()` function is called.

❑   When a component has had its properties set and when its children have been created, the component's `commitProperties()` function is called.

❑   When a component is told to measure itself, the component's `measure()` function is called.

❑   When a component is told to position its children, the component's `updateDisplayList()` function is called.

You'll learn more about these functions in the section on Flex components, as the Flex framework life cycle is an important factor when creating custom Flex components.

Flex Class Hierarchy

The Adobe Flex documentation contains a complete list of all the Flex classes and their inheritance. Rather than reprinting that information, this section points out the more salient parts.

Flash and Flex Class Packages

Continuing with the theme of Flash and its impact on Flex, you should know how to distinguish between the Flash and Flex classes.

All Flash classes are in packages that begin with `flash`, such as `flash.display.Display` or `flash.net.NetConnection`. All Flex classes are in packages that begin with `mx` such as `mx.collections.ArrayCollection` and `mx.controls.Button`.

Further, the basic data types such as `Number`, `String`, and `Array`, are also Flash classes. The Flash classes are built into the Flash Player and are not part of the SWF file your Flex application is compiled into. This makes your SWF file smaller, although it does limit the versions of the Flash Player your application will be able to use.

UIComponent

All user interface components inherit from `mx.core.UIComponent`. In other words, `UIComponent` is the base class and contains members common and useful to all Flex components.

UIComponent forms the boundary between Flex and Flash classes. If you are familiar with Flash CS3, you know about the Shape, Sprite, and MovieClip classes. These classes are progressively more complex in their ability to render and describe Flash objects that are displayed on the stage.

Only classes that extend UIComponent can be part of the Flex framework life cycle.

UIComponent is itself a Flash Sprite and as such can have other Flash classes as children. UIComponent can also have other Flex classes as children, such as Button and HBox. However, other Flex components, such as Canvas and HBox, cannot have Flash objects as children. In other words, if you try to make a Shape a child of an HBox, you will get an error.

Because all Flex classes extend UIComponent, it means that nearly any Flex component that is a container can hold any other Flex class because those container classes expect their children to be UIComponents. This is why you can have a Panel with an HBox child that has a Button for a child. This nesting of visual objects is perfectly normal for Flash (MovieClips may have other MovieClips as children), and this carries over to Flex as well.

One interesting aspect of UIComponent is that it implements the interface IUIComponent. You see, the Flex components do not always know, nor even care, what type of component their children might be. Take a VBox for example. It can have any Flex component as a child. Whenever the VBox works with its children, it refers to them by using the IUIComponent interface, which defines the requirements for a component to be a member of a Flex container.

UIComponent also implements the IEventDispatcher interface. The EventDispatcher is the mechanism by which the Flex framework communicates — components send messages, *events*, to each other. This is true even when the components are being created, as you have seen above. Events are discussed in detail later in this book. However, having UIComponent implement IEventDispatcher means that every Flex component is capable of sending (dispatching) events and listening for events.

UIComponent also implements the IBitmapDrawable interface. This means that any Flex component can be rendered off-screen into a bitmap, which can be printed, saved, or sent to a server.

Finally, UIComponent implements IFlexDisplayObject. This interface allows a component to act as a skin for another component. Skins are the visual appearance of a component (a Button has an up skin, a down skin, etc. for each of its states). UIComponent implementing this interface means you can use one component as the skin for another component. Skinning is covered in detail later in this book.

Here is a partial list of the classes that extend UIComponent and some of their subclasses:

- Button
    - AccordionHeader
    - CheckBox
    - LinkButton
    - RadioButton
- Container (see next section)
- DateChooser

- ❏ HRule
- ❏ Label
    - ❏ FormItemLabel
    - ❏ Text
- ❏ MenuBar
- ❏ NumericStepper
- ❏ ProgressBar
- ❏ Repeater
- ❏ ScrollBar
    - ❏ HScrollBar
    - ❏ VScrollBar
- ❏ Slider
    - ❏ HSlider
    - ❏ VSlider
- ❏ SWFLoader
    - ❏ Image
- ❏ TextInput
- ❏ VRule

Notice, for example, that Image extends SWFLoader and Text extends Label. You'll find that related classes have a common base class, and therefore share properties, interfaces, functions, events, and even styles. Knowing this can help you locate documentation quickly.

Container Classes

Flex classes such as HBox, Panel, and even Application are considered *container* components, because they can have other Flex components as children. Nesting containers is very common and lets you create very elaborate layouts.

You may already be familiar with container classes such as Application, HBox, and Panel, but it is interesting to see how those classes fit into the Flex class hierarchy. For example, Application seems like such a big and important class, but in fact, it extends LayoutContainer. Here is list of container classes and their subclasses:

- ❏ Accordion
- ❏ Box
    - ❏ ControlBar
        - ❏ ApplicationControlBar

- ❑ DividedBox
    - ❑ HDividedBox
    - ❑ VDividedBox
- ❑ Grid
- ❑ HBox
    - ❑ GridItem
    - ❑ GridRow
- ❑ NavBar
    - ❑ ButtonBar
    - ❑ ToggleButtonBar
    - ❑ LinkBar
- ❑ VBox
- ❑ ModuleLoader
- ❑ Canvas
- ❑ Form
- ❑ FormItem
- ❑ LayoutContainer
    - ❑ Application
        - ❑ WindowedApplication
    - ❑ Module
    - ❑ Window
- ❑ Panel
    - ❑ Alert
    - ❑ RichTextEditor
    - ❑ TitleWindow
- ❑ Tile
    - ❑ Legend
- ❑ ViewStack
    - ❑ TabNavigator

List Classes

More complex Flex classes are built from the simpler classes. For example, a DataGrid does not directly extend UIComponent. DataGrid is a member of the "list" classes — List, DataGrid, AdvancedDataGrid, and Tree. These classes are based on ListBase, which provides common elements.

The `mx.controls.listClasses.ListBase` class is the base class for all the list controls. This class gives uniform capabilities to all the list types. For example, all lists have `itemRenderers`, which are handled by the `ListBase` class. All lists have a selection model, also handled by the `ListBase` class. Here is a list of the list classes and their subclasses:

- ❑ `DataGridBase`
  - ❑ `DataGrid`
  - ❑ `FileSystemDataGrid`
  - ❑ `PrintDataGrid`
- ❑ `List`
  - ❑ `FileSystemList`
  - ❑ `Menu`
  - ❑ `Tree`
    - ❑ `FileSystemTree`
- ❑ `TileBase`
  - ❑ `HorizontalList`
  - ❑ `TileList`

Formatters, Validators, and Collection Classes

In addition to the controls and containers, Flex contains a number of helper classes. These include the formatters, validators, and other classes that you can use to make writing your applications simpler.

The formatter classes include `DateFormatter`, `NumberFormatter`, and `CurrencyFormatter`. The formatters are designed to be included in MXML, as shown here:

```
<mx:DateFormatter id="dfmt" formatString="DD-MMM-YYY JJ:NN:SS" />
...
<mx:Label text="Expiration Date: {dfmt.format(data.expirationDate)}" />
```

or created in ActionScript:

```
import mx.formatters.DateFormatter;
...
var dfmt = new DateFormatter();
[Bindable] private var expDate:String;
dfmt.formatString = "DD-MMM-YYYY JJ:NN:SS";
...
expDate = dfmt.format(data.expirationDate);
```

The base class for the formatters is `mx.formatters.Formatter`. Its subclasses are:

- ❑ `CurrencyFormatter`
- ❑ `DateFormatter`

❑   NumberFormatter

❑   PhoneFormatter

❑   ZipCodeFormatter

The validator classes include DateValidator, CreditCardValidator, and NumberValidator. These classes may also be used in MXML or ActionScript. The validation classes provide a way to check input and provide the user with a visual cue (a red border) that something is incorrect:

```
<mx:NumberValidator source="{quantity}" property="text"
minValue="1" maxValue="100"
exceedsMaxError="Quantity must not exceed 100"
lowerThanMinError="Quantity cannot be less than 1" />
```

or

```
import mx.validators.NumberValidator;
…
var numVal:NumberValidator = new NumberValidator();
numVal.source = quantity;
numVal.property = "text";
numVal.minValue = 1;
numVal.maxValue = 100;
numVal.exceedsMaxError = "Quantity must not exceed 100";
numVal.lowerThanMinError = "Quantity cannot be less than 1";
```

The base class for the validators is mx.validators.Validator. Its subclasses are:

❑   CreditCardValidator

❑   CurrencyValidator

❑   DateValidator

❑   EmailValidator

❑   NumberValidator

❑   PhoneNumberValidator

❑   RegExpValidator

❑   SocialSecurityValidator

❑   StringValidator

❑   ZipCodeValidator

Another group of highly useful, but nonvisual, classes are the collections found in the mx.collections package. The individual classes in this package are covered in detail elsewhere in this book, but to give you an idea of what is available, here is brief list:

❑   ArrayCollection — This class makes it possible use arrays as dataProviders to the List components (see Chapter 30, "Working with Data").

❑ HierarchicalData — This class is useful for structuring data for use with the AdvancedDataGrid, Tree, and other components that use ordered data.

❑ XMLListCollection — This class makes it possible to create XML nodes as dataProviders to the List components.

❑ Sort — This class lets you place a sorting order on a collection.

Framework Functions and Events

Now that you have an idea of what the Flex classes are like and a basic understanding of the Flex framework life cycle, it is time to put the two together.

The first part of the life cycle is the object creation and instantiation phase. For this example, consider the example above, repeated here, with a couple of modifications:

```
<mx:Application initialize="initApp()"…>
    <mx:Panel title="Employee Data">
        <mx:DataGrid …>

            …

        </mx:DataGrid>
        <mx:ControlBar>
            <mx:Button label="Submit" />
        </mx:ControlBar>
    </mx:Panel>
    <mx:Script>
    <![CDATA[
        import mx.collections.ArrayCollection;
        [Bindable] private var listData:ArrayCollection;
        private function initApp() : void {
            listData = new ArrayCollection();
        }
    ]]>
    </mx:Script>
</mx:Application>
```

The Flex framework begins by using the ActionScript new operator to make an instance of the Application object. Then the Application's initialize() function is called. This is followed by the dispatching of the initialize event. You can see in the example where the initialize event has been caught (by the initialize attribute on the <mx:Application> tag) and handled (by the initApp() function).

The Flex framework causes each child of the Application to be created by invoking the createChildren() method of the Application. The children (Panel, etc). are created and initialized following the same pattern, having their createChildren() functions called along the way. When each child has been created, it dispatches the childAdd event.

Once all the components have been created and initialized, the Flex framework starts again with the Application and invokes its commitProperties() function. This function can now apply property value settings to the children components. When commitProperties() is called, you know that both your properties have been set and your children are created and ready to be modified.

Once everyone's commitProperties() function has been called, the Flex framework invokes the measure() function on the Application, which, in turn, invokes it on its children and so forth. The measure step makes it possible to position the children.

Once measured, the `updateDisplayList()` function can be called, and the process continues until every component is positioned and no further measurement takes place.

Finally, when each component has finished its creation, it dispatches the `creationComplete` event.

One thing about the Flex framework — it is flexible, no pun intended here. It is possible that during the course of laying out a component's children, the size of the component changes. That would prompt a remeasure step. This is perfectly normal, and it allows the Flex application to have very dynamic layout possibilities.

The dispatching of events throughout the cycle gives you the opportunity to intercede and add your own modifications. This is an important part of Flex component development and is covered in detail later in this book.

Summary

Understanding how Flex relates to Flash can make a big impact on your applications. The relationship between Flex and Flash means that you can use Flash animation within your Flex applications. It also means you can create Flash graphics using ActionScript within your Flex applications. Take time to understand the Flex class hierarchy so that you know how best to use these classes in your application.

The next chapter covers data binding, which makes it easy to associate variables' values with Flex controls.

## 11

Using Data Binding and Events

Data binding is one of the most powerful features of Flex. This is a mechanism whereby an ActionScript object instance is associated with another ActionScript object instance so that changes in one object are reflected in the other object.

The Flex compiler can detect data binding in MXML tags or you can set up data binding explicitly by using ActionScript classes. In either case, Flex classes are used to watch the value of a variable and dispatch events when the variable's value changes. It is this coupling of variable watching and events that makes data binding work so well.

Using {Curly Braces}

You are probably familiar with data binding in MXML tags using curly braces. This is where a property of a Flex control has been bound to a variable or property of another control. For example:

```
<mx:Script>
<![CDATA[
    [Bindable] private var userName:String;
    …
]]>
</mx:Script>
<mx:TextInput id="inputUserName" text="{userName}" />
<mx:HBox>
    <mx:HSlider id="ageSlider" snapInterval="0.1"/>
    <mx:Label text="{ageSlider.value}" />
</mx:HBox>
```

The TextInput control's text property is bound to the value of the variable, userName. The Label control's text property is bound to the value property of the HSlider, ageSlider.

Only ActionScript statements may appear within curly braces.

In this type of data binding, the Flex compiler recognizes the data binding because of the presence of curly braces in the MXML tags.

The Flex compiler generates code to make data binding work. The generated code sets up a `ChangeWatcher` on the source of the binding (the variable, `userName`, and the property value on `ageSlider` in this example), which monitors the content of those objects. The `ChangeWatcher` dispatches events when the variables change. The Flex compiler also generates code for the target, or destination, of the data binding (the text properties in this example), which listens for these events and copies the new values into the bound properties.

Using variables, or properties of objects, as the source for data binding is the most common use. But you can also use ActionScript expressions. Here are a few examples:

```
<mx:Text text="Good morning, {userName}" />
```

In this example, the `userName` binding is part of a string being used for the `Text` control:

```
<mx:Text text="{firstName + '\n' + lastName}" />
```

In this example, the expression is a string concatenation with a newline character between the parts. This is necessary because `{firstName}\n{lastName}` will not make two lines in the Text control, as the Flex compiler does not recognize the `\n` as being a newline, since that is an ActionScript construct and not part of XML. Only items appearing within the curly braces are taken to be ActionScript.

```
<mx:Canvas backgroundColor="{bgColor}" ... >
```

In this example, the `backgroundColor` style is bound to the `bgColor` variable. You can use data binding with styles as well as properties, on MXML tags.

```
<mx:Text text="{calculateResult()}" />
```

In this example, the binding is to the result of a function. This is not a real data binding because the function cannot be invoked spontaneously. In other words, when you bind to a variable, the variable can be changed elsewhere in the program. This triggers the event to grab the new value and put it into a control. When you use a function, there is no way for the function to be invoked from anywhere else, which would cause it to produce a value detectable by the `ChangeWatcher`. Thus, this binding is weak and will only be called once.

However, if you include one or more arguments to the function, which can be changed, then the function will be called each time its argument(s) change.

The most common type of data binding is that between MXML tags and variables or object properties, but there are other ways to use data binding, as follows:

- ❑ You can create "reverse" bindings, where the value of a control is copied to a variable or object property.
- ❑ You can set up data binding in ActionScript.

Setting up a "reverse" binding is simple using the `<mx:Binding>` MXML tag. Imagine that you are allowing the `userName` to be changed by the `TextInput`, and you'd like the change to wind up back in the `userName` variable. Right now, the binding copies the value from the `userName` variable to the `TextInput` control. You can also copy the value back to the `userName` variable, for example:

```
<mx:Binding source="inputUserName.text" destination="userName" />
```

As soon as the `TextInput` control changes, the `userName` variable is also updated. This will not set up an infinite data-binding loop; having a binding from a variable to a control and a binding from a control to a variable is perfectly safe and quite useful.

Here is a complete example of reverse binding using MXML tags:

```
<mx:Script>
<![CDATA[
    [Bindable] private var userName:String = "Charles";

    private function editUserName(newName:String):void
    {
        userName = newName;
    }
]]>
</mx:Script>

<mx:TextInput id="userNameInput" text="{userName}"/>
<mx:Label text="{userName}"/>
```

This example shows one-way binding, where any change to the `TextInput`, `userNameInput` does not actually change the `userName` variable:

```
<mx:Script>
<![CDATA[
    [Bindable] private var userName:String = "Charles";

    private function editUserName(newName:String):void
    {
        userName = newName;
    }
]]>
</mx:Script>

<mx:Binding source="userNameInput.text" destination="userName"/>
    // new line

<mx:TextInput id="userNameInput" text="{userName}"/>
<mx:Label text="{userName}"/>
```

This example uses the `<mx:Binding>` tag to bind the `userNameInput`'s text property to the variable `userName`. Now when there are changes in the `TextInput`, they are reflected in the variable.

Setting up data binding in ActionScript is almost as simple as if you were using data binding with MXML tags. In this example, the `TextInput` control is being created in ActionScript and the `userName` variable is being bound to it:

```
inputUserName = new TextInput();
addChild(inputUserName);
BindingUtils.bindProperty( inputUserName, "text", this, "userName" );
```

The `mx.binding.utils.BindingUtils` class has a static function, `bindProperty`, which creates a `ChangeWatcher` for the binding. You can use this `ChangeWatcher` if you would like to know when the property is updated. For example, you may want to change other controls or send data to a Web Service.

```
var cw:ChangeWatcher = BindingUtils.bindProperty( inputUserName,
        "text",
        this,
        "userName");
cw.setHandler( handleUserNameChange );
...
private function handleUserNameChange( event:PropertyChangeEvent ) : void
{
    // do something with the value
}
```

When the event handler, `handleUserNameChange`, is called, the event contains information about the change as follows:

❑ `.type` is "propertyChange".

❑ `.kind` is "update", meaning that the value has been changed or updated.

❑ `.oldValue` is the former value or null if it was never set.

❑ `.newValue` is the value to be set.

❑ `.property` is the name of the property being changed.

❑ `.source` is the owner of the property.

If you decide to handle the event, you must copy the value to the destination yourself. Setting the handler replaces the default function, which copies the value for you.

What you might want to do instead of setting the handler function is to simply watch for changes in the value while allowing the normal flow of copying the value to the intended target. You do this with the `ChangeWatcher.watch()` function, as shown here:

```
ChangeWatcher.watch( inputUserName, "text", watchUserName );
...
private function watchUserName( event:Event ) : void
{
// do something
}
```

Here, the watch() static function is set to examine the text property on the inputUserName TextInput control for any changes. This includes data-binding changes when the userName variable changes, but it also includes changes made by the end user as he or she types into the control.

You can also watch the source of the data binding, userName:

```
ChangeWatcher.watch( this, "userName", watchUserName );
```

Whenever the value of userName changes, the watchUserName function will be called.

> *Using the* ChangeWatcher.watch() *function does not require data binding to be used on the property being watched — you can use it for any variable or property.*

[Bindable] Metadata

In the first example, the variable, userName, was prefixed by the metadata, [Bindable]. The [Bindable] metadata is a hint to the Flex compiler that this variable may be used in data-binding expressions. The Flex compiler only generates the ChangeWatcher code when [Bindable] is present. This keeps the size of the SWF to a minimum and improves overall performance.

Sometimes you may see this warning message from the Flex compiler:

```
Data binding will not be able to detect assignments to "address".
```

where address is a property of some object.

This message appears because the source of the data binding does not have the ability to dispatch change events from the ChangeWatcher. Suppose that you have a simple ActionScript class representing a person:

```
public class Person
{
public var name:String;
public var address:String;
public var city:String;
public var state:String;
public var phone:String;
}
```

and you use this as a source in data binding, such as:

```
[Bindable] private var person:Person;
...
<mx:TextInput text="{person.address}" />
```

This will cause the warning mentioned above.

To remedy this, add [Binding] metadata to the class itself. You can either add the metadata to each variable or you can tell the compiler that all of the public variables are binding candidates by placing the [Bindable] metadata above the class definition:

```
[Bindable]
public class Person
{
    ...
}
```

The appearance of the [Bindable] metadata in the class definition instructs the compiler to generate code that enables the Person class to dispatch events when its properties change.

Events

As you have been developing Flex applications, you have been handling events. You cannot write a useful Flex application without event handlers. At some point in your application, you will have a Button to cause some action to take place or you will receive data from a server and have to present it when it arrives. The controls and data services dispatch events and the actions you take in response to those events are the *event handlers*.

The Flex framework is event driven. There is a specific flow to the events, and if you know how the event system works, you can capitalize on that to make better and more engaging applications.

There are three phases to the event system: capture, target, and bubbling. To illustrate this, consider an application structured like this:

```
Application
    HDividedBox
        ViewStack
            Panel id="medical"
                    Button label="Submit"
            Panel id="dental"
                    Button label="Submit"
```

Notice that there are two Submit Buttons — one in the medical Panel and the other in the dental Panel. You can imagine an application that has many forms and many Submit Buttons.

When the user clicks the Submit Button in the medical Panel, a click event (data type MouseEvent .CLICK) begins its journey within the event framework.

Capture Phase

The capture phase works from the outermost component downward toward the Button. This means the click event is first given to the Application to handle. If the click event is not consumed by the Application, it is given to the HDividedBox. It is then given to the ViewStack and then to the medical Panel (and not to the dental Panel since that is not in the hierarchy with the medical Panel's Submit Button).

You might want to capture an event before it reaches the item that actually sent the event out. For example, if you have a condition where the click on the Submit Button should not be allowed (perhaps you are waiting for data from the server to confirm the user is authorized to submit the form), you can intercept the MouseEvent.CLICK and prevent it from reaching its event handler (more on this later in the chapter).

Setting up a capture phase event handler must be done in ActionScript — there is no MXML equivalent way to do this. Suppose that you want to prevent the click event from reaching its intended target at the Application level, as shown here:

```
<mx:Application creationComplete="initApp()" >
<mx:Script>
<![CDATA[
private function initApp() : void
{
    addEventListener( MouseEvent.CLICK, authorizeClickEvent, true );
}
private function authorizeClickEvent( event:MouseEvent ) : void
{
    // check to see if this event should be allowed if not,
    // stop it from propagating further
    if( not_authorized ) event.stopPropagation();
}
]]>
</mx:Script>
```

In this example, the third argument to addEventListener() is true — this means the event handler (the authorizeClickEvent function) is a capture phase event handler.

Target Phase

If the event reaches the object that dispatched it, the event is in the target phase. This is the most commonly used event phase, where most events are handled, such as this:

```
<mx:Panel id="medical">
    <mx:Script>
    <![CDATA[
        private function handleSubmit() : void
        {
            // submit the form
        }
    ]]>
    </mx:Script>
    ....
    <mx:Button label="Submit" click="handleSubmit()" />
</mx:Panel>
```

When the event reaches the Button, it looks to see if there is an event handler on the Button itself. In this example there is, so the event handler is executed.

Bubbling Phase

The third and final phase is the bubbling phase, where the event reverses course and moves up the hierarchy. The `MouseEvent.CLICK` event is given to the `Panel` to handle, then to the `ViewStack`, then to the `HDividedBox`, and finally to the `Application`.

Bubbling is a very handy way to work with similar events from multiple sources. In this fictional application, there are many Submit `Button`s that all do the same thing: submit data. You would be tempted to handle each Submit `Button` locally, as shown previously in the target phase example.

A cleaner way to do this would be at a higher level, perhaps in the `Application` itself. Each Submit `Button` could gather the information from its form fields and dispatch an event with the intention of the event to bubble upward until it reached the `Application`, where it could be handled and sent to the data service; it would not be unheard of to have a single point of contact with the data services.

Setting up an event to bubble is done when creating the event itself. Here is an example of a `SubmitEvent` (a custom event, described later) that is set to bubble when dispatched:

```
var event:SubmitEvent = new SubmitEvent( SubmitEvent.SUBMIT, true );
```

The setting of the bubbles argument to `true` is all that is necessary. Some events naturally bubble such as `MouseEvent` and `KeyboardEvent`. For most others you have to set the bubbles argument to `true`.

Stopping Events

Sometimes you will want to interrupt the journey and stop the event. One example is event handling in `itemRenderers` for the list controls (`List`, `DataGrid`, `AdvancedDataGrid`, `Tree`). Suppose that you have an `itemRenderer` that contains a `Button` (perhaps a Buy `Button` or a Play `Button`). Any click within the `itemRenderer` automatically selects the row or item in the list. When you have a `Button` inside of an `itemRenderer`, you do not want the click of the `Button` to select the item.

The way to avoid that is to stop the propagation of the mouse-down event from reaching the list which is what causes the selection to happen. Here is an example of a `Button` `itemRenderer` that prevents the item from being selected:

```
<mx:itemRenderer>
    <mx:Component>
        <mx:Button label="Buy" click="outerDocument.makePurchase(event)"
                   mouseDown="event.stopPropagation()" />
    </mx:Component>
</mx:itemRenderer>
```

The use of `event.stopPropagation()` allows the `mouseDown` event to affect the `Button` but will prevent the event from reaching the control and making the selection.

Another case of stopping the normal event flow is found in the list `itemEditors`. Suppose that you have an `itemEditor` for a column and want to prevent someone from entering an invalid value. By handling the list's `itemEditEnd` event, you can examine the data and prevent the user from leaving the item if the value is incorrect, for example:

```
<mx:DataGrid editable="true" itemEditEnd="verifyEdit(event)" …>
private function verifyEdit( event:DataGridEvent ) : void
{
    if( event.dataField == "price" ) {
        var editor:TextInput = (event.currentTarget as DataGrid).itemEditorInstance
            as TextInput;
        var newValue:Number = Number(editor.text);
        if( newValue <= 0 || newValue > 100 ) event.preventDefault();
    }
}
```

Within the event handler, the new value is tested, and if it meets the condition, the default behavior of the event is prevented by using `event.preventDefault()`. Of course, you need to know what the default behavior of a specific event is, and in this case, the behavior is to commit the value to the data-Provider and move to the next cell.

The `Event` class has several functions to handle these special cases:

❑ `stopPropagation()` — This function stops the event from going to the next level of its journey.

❑ `stopImmediatePropagation()` — This function not only stops the event from going to the next level of its journey but also prevents any other functions from being called on the current level. Suppose that you have a `Panel` with several `Button`s and you register a "click" event handler on the `Panel` itself:

```
<mx:Panel click="handleAllClicks(event)" …>
    <!-- other MXML components and ActionScript code -->
    <mx:Button label="Modify" id="modifyButton" />
    <mx:Button label="Remove" id="removeButton" />
    <mx:Button label="Clear All" id="clearButton" />
</mx:Panel>
```

❑ This function will be called whenever any of the `Button` children of the `Panel` are clicked. If the event handler calls `event.stopImmediatePropagation()`, none of the other event handlers for the `Button` will be called.

❑ `preventDefault()` — This function stops the default behavior of a control from happening.

Event Listeners

This section describes event listeners, using both MXML and ActionScript examples. Remember, MXML is compiled into ActionScript, which means that the event listener code within an MXML tag causes an ActionScript function to be generated. Still, adding event listeners to MXML tags can make the application easier to write.

Using MXML

You have already seen how to add event listeners in MXML tags where you simply give an ActionScript expression to the event handler. This ActionScript expression can be a function call or other expression. Here, for example, is a ComboBox that changes a Label control:

```
<mx:ComboBox change="price.text=event.currentTarget.selectedItem.price" … />
```

The ComboBox dispatches the change event whenever the user makes a selection from its drop-list. Rather than calling a function, the event handler expression takes the selectedItem from the ComboBox (event.currentTarget) and sets the price Label control's text property.

Notice there are no curly braces here — this is event handling and not data binding.

When using MXML, event is a variable automatically created that contains the event data. Here is how you might assign the result and fault events on a RemoteObject:

```
<mx:RemoteObject id="ro" result="handleResult(event)"
                        fault="handleFault(event)" … >
```

Using ActionScript

Event handlers are added to a component in ActionScript by using the addEventListener() function. You might add event listeners to a RemoteObject this way:

```
ro.addEventListener( ResultEvent.RESULT, handleResult );
ro.addEventListener( FaultEvent.FAULT, handleFault );
```

Not only can you add event listeners in ActionScript, but you can remove them as well. The event type and handler function must be identical to what was passed to addEventListener.

```
ro.removeEventListener( ResultEvent.RESULT, handleResult );
ro.removeEventListener( FaultEvent.FAULT, handleFault );
```

There are a couple of key differences between event handlers added with ActionScript and those added with MXML:

❑   Event listeners added with ActionScript must be written to accept a single parameter — the event to be handled. With MXML, you can pass whatever parameters you like.

❑   Event listeners added with ActionScript can only be functions. With MXML the event listener can be any ActionScript expression.

❑   It is very difficult to remove MXML event handlers since you must match the function name given to addEventListener and the Flex compiler generates code to handle the event.

Event Types

There are literally dozens and dozens of event types in Flex and the Flash Player. Events from the flash.events package are part of the Flash Player; events from the mx.events package are from the Flex framework. When writing event handlers, it is important to get the event type correct since the event object carries useful data.

The flash.events.MouseEvent, for example, contains the state of the mouse button, the x and y location of the mouse, and the type of MouseEvent — CLICK, MOUSE_DOWN, MOUSE_UP, and so forth.

Consult the Flex documentation for the specific class and see the event data type for each event the class dispatches.

Custom Events

Of course, you can create your own event classes. Using the previous example, there are many Submit Buttons, each of which is supposed to submit a form containing data. If you decide to handle all of the Submit Button clicks in one location, you need a way to get to the data being submitted. The easiest way to do that is to create your own event type and include the form data in the event.

Creating Custom Events

The first step in creating custom events is to determine why you need the event and what information it will convey. The MouseEvent, for instance, carries mouse-specific information. The event for the Submit Button will need to include the information from each form. That information varies of course, so a simple Object property on the event can be used to handle that.

All events should be derived from flash.events.Event:

```
package book.ch11
{
    import flash.events.Event;

    public class SubmitEvent extends Event
    {
        public static const SUBMIT:String = "submit";

        public function SubmitEvent(type:String, bubbles:Boolean=true,
                                    cancelable:Boolean=false)
        {
            super(type, bubbles, cancelable);
        }

        public var formData:Object;

    }
}
```

A best practice is to use constants to define event types. You can either define the constants in the event class (as shown here) or in a different class.

Since this SubmitEvent is intended to bubble, the default value of the bubbles parameter in the class constructor is set to true.

The next step is to set up the event listener function to handle the event. The SubmitEvent is not a standard event and so cannot be set from MXML tags; you must use ActionScript. In the Application, you can set this from the creationComplete event handler:

```
<mx:Application creationComplete="initApp()" … >
<mx:Script>
<![CDATA[
    private function initApp() : void
    {
        addEventListener( SubmitEvent.SUBMIT, handleFormSubmit );
    }
    private function handleFormSubmit( event:SubmitEvent ) : void
    {
        // use the event.target to determine which component dispatched the event
        // event.formData is the data to send
    }
]]>
</mx:Script>
```

Finally, you must dispatch the event. Here is how it might be done from the medical Panel:

```
<mx:Panel id="medical">
    <mx:Script>
    <![CDATA[
        private function sendSubmit() : void
        {
            var event:SubmitEvent = new SubmitEvent( SubmitEvent.SUBMIT );
            event.formData = … // set from all of the fields in this panel
            dispatchEvent( event );
        }
    ]]>
    </mx:Script>
    ….
    <mx:Button label="Submit" click="sendSubmit()" />
</mx:Panel>
```

Because the event bubbles and because there is an event handler at the Application level, all of the SubmitEvents, from wherever they are dispatched, will be received and processed.

If your application uses custom components, having custom events will make them easier to use and reusable by others.

[Event] Metadata

Suppose that you have a component that is a shopping cart. You may want to know when items are added to or removed from the cart. The easiest way to do that is with events. You do not need a custom event for this. Rather, you can declare a custom event using [Event] metadata.

The first step is deciding what the events should be. For this example, `addToCart` and `removeFromCart` seem like reasonable event types. You can picture using these events like this:

```
<cart:ShoppingCart addToCart="handleAdd(event)"
                   removeFromCart="handleRemove(event)" />
```

To put custom event names in the MXML tag, the Flex compiler must know about them. You tell the compiler about these new events using metadata in the component definition file.

For ActionScript components, set the metadata above the class definition:

```
package cart
{
    [Event(name="addToCart",type="flash.events.Event")]
    [Event(name="removeFromCart",type="flash.events.Event")]

    public class ShoppingCart extends UIComponent
    {
        ...
    }
}
```

For MXML components, use the `<mx:Metadata>` tag:

```
<mx:Canvas ... >
    <mx:Metadata>
        [Event(name="addToCart",type="flash.events.Event")]
        [Event(name="removeFromCart",type="flash.events.Event")]
    </mx:Metadata>
...
</mx:Canvas>
```

The `Event` metadata names the event and associates a type with it. If you are not creating a custom event type, then use `flash.events.Event` as the type or reduce the `Event` metadata to simply `[Event("addToCart")]` and `[Event("removeFromCart")]`.

Using the name and type options of the `Event` metadata makes your intentions clear.

Strategies for Using Custom Events

There are two approaches when using custom events: the event contains data or the component contains the data.

When events contain data, the event handler has all of the information it needs to process the event. For example, when you handle a `MouseEvent.MOUSE_DOWN` event, the event data contains the position of the mouse and state of the mouse buttons. The same is true for the `PropertyChange` event — you know what changed and what the old and new values are.

Many events are like that throughout Flex. But some events do not contain useful data. This is true of any event that uses the base class, `flash.events.Event`. The `Event.CHANGE` event is the most common. When you select something from a `ComboBox`, a change event is dispatched. The event does not contain any information about what was selected. For that, you must return to the component itself. For instance, the `ComboBox` has a `selectedItem` property, which is what the user picked and the event handler would access that property since the event does not contain the information.

You can use either strategy when developing your own components. Using the latter technique, the event simply signals that something is happening. The event handler can access the component via `event.target` or `event.currentTarget` and then examine the component's properties for the information it needs.

This technique is fine to a point and is especially useful when there is a large amount of data involved. But the technique does not work well when the component may disappear or may otherwise not be available when the event handler needs to address it.

Take the case of a pop-up. You present the user with a form, and they make adjustments. When they click the OK button, the information on the pop-up has to be communicated. In all likelihood, the pop-up will be gone when the event handler is called. This is a good reason to use a custom event with the data from the pop-up contained in the event itself.

Summary

Complex Flex applications are simpler and easier to maintain when the code is clear and obvious. While data binding using curly braces may not seem clear at first, the simplicity of the code you write should make your application more reliable and easier to enhance in the future.

Likewise, custom events not only fit with the Flex framework event model, custom events make your application easier to understand and follow. By passing data along with events, you will use less contrived means to reach data needed by event handlers. Understanding the Flex event model also gives you more opportunities to be creative when developing applications.

The next chapter covers Flex controls and containers. Controls are the on-screen elements that you click or type into, whereas containers are used to position those elements.

12

User Interface Controls and Containers

This chapter describes the Flex components used to present data, accept input, and define the application's layout. Rather than duplicating the Flex documents of the components, with their properties, methods, events, and styles, this chapter gives you some practical tips and ideas for using the components in your applications.

Static Controls

These controls present information and are not normally used for any input.

mx.controls.Label and mx.controls.Text

These controls display static text. Although both controls will display a string of characters, the Label control can display only one line of text and will truncate the string if necessary, whereas the Text control will word-wrap the string and automatically increase its height to accommodate the text.

Both controls use the same styles and methods. Figure 12-1 provides an example for each of these controls.

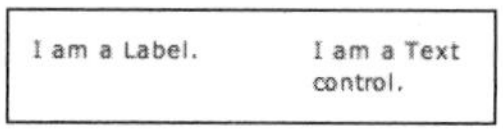

Figure 12-1

The following shows the code behind the controls:

```
<mx:Label text="Hello" />
<mx:Text text="World" />
```

Tips:

❑ The `selectable` property for the `Text` control is set to `true` by default, which allows you to highlight the text displayed within the component; it is `false` for `Label`. If you use `Text` and `Label` interchangeably, you may want to set the `Text` control's `selectable` property to `false`.

❑ When a `Label` control is not wide enough to contain all its text, the remainder is truncated and replaced with an ellipsis (...). The `Text` control will word-wrap its content and automatically change its height. However, if you set the `Text` control's height explicitly the content will be truncated and end with an ellipsis.

mx.controls.Image

This control displays static images, as shown in Figure 12-2. The Flash Player supports PNG, GIF, and JPG (nonprogressive) image formats. The image data may be embedded into the SWF or loaded dynamically.

Figure 12-2

The following shows the code behind the `Image` control:

```
<mx:Image source="/assets/catalog.jpg" />
<mx:Image source="@Embed('/icons/help_icon.gif')" />
```

Tips:

❑ Data that is loaded dynamically is subject to security settings. For example, if the image data is coming from a domain other than the one loading the SWF, the image data may be viewed, but you cannot manipulate it. This includes performing many effects on the image as the image's data may be altered by the effect. If you try this, you will get a security sandbox error. Be sure the other domain has a crossdomain.xml security file in place.

❑ You can make an image clickable by adding an event handler for the `MouseEvent.CLICK` event.

❑ You can change the cursor to the "hand" cursor by adding the following properties to the `Image`: `buttonMode="true"`, `mouseChildren="false"`, and `useHandCursor="true"`.

mx.controls.SWFLoader

This control is used to display SWFs — either SWFs created by Flash or by Flex. SWFLoader is similar to Image and in fact, uses the same underlying technology in the Flash Player. SWFLoader is specifically designed to work with SWFs because it is geared toward the security requirements of external SWFs.

The following shows the code behind the SWFLoader control:

```
<mx:SWFLoader source="http://mydomain.com/shopping.swf" />
```

Tips:

❑   As with images, SWFs are subject to security settings. Because SWFs are potentially interactive there are even more precautions in place. For example, if your main SWF is loaded from domain A.com and it then loads a SWF from domain B.com, one of several things may happen:

   ❑   There may be an immediate security error if B.com does not have a crossdomain.xml security file in place.

   ❑   If the SWF from B.com attempts to access any variables or functions in the main SWF's realm, there will be a security error. You can allow SWFs from B.com to have access to the data in the main SWF by having the main SWF execute a Security .allowDomain("B.com") function.

   ❑   Similarly, if the main SWF attempts to access variables and functions in the SWF from B.com, there will be a security error. The SWF from B.com must also execute an allowDomain("A.com") to authorize the main SWF to have access to its data and methods.

❑   If the SWF being loaded uses classes already defined in the Flash Player (because the main SWF has loaded them, for example), the classes in the loading SWF will be ignored. Errors can result if the loading SWF expects a class to be defined a certain way and it is not.

mx.controls.HRule and mx.controls.VRule

These controls produce horizontal and vertical lines, respectively, typically used as separators (see Figure 12-3).

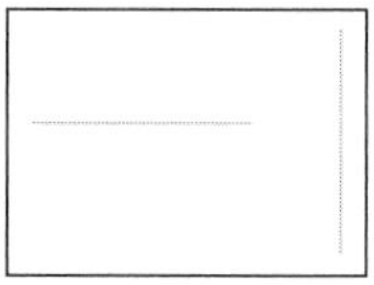

Figure 12-3

The following shows the code behind the controls:

```
<mx:HRule width="80%" />
<mx:VRule height="50%" />
```

Tip:

❏   The HRule and VRule have default sizes. For example, if you make a container that's 25 pixels high and insert a VRule, the VRule's default height may resize the container larger than 25 pixels. When using these controls, add 100% width (HRule) or height (VRule) to ensure they size properly to fit the container.

mx.controls.ProgressBar

This control's purpose is to provide the user with feedback during a long operation. The ProgressBar has two modes: determinate and indeterminate. The determinate mode is the default, and the ProgressBar progresses from 0 to 100%; indeterminate mode shows the ProgressBar as a spinning barber pole (see Figure 12-4).

Figure 12-4

The following shows the code behind this control:

```
<mx:ProgressBar id="pBar" source="{swfLoader}" />
```

Tips:

❏   In determinate mode, the ProgressBar can be controlled by another Flex control that dispatches progress and complete events. Typical controls to use with ProgressBar are Image or SWFLoader.

❏   A ProgressBar can be used for long ActionScript operations, but be careful: control must return to the Flex Framework (and Flash Player) periodically to update the display. The ProgressBar won't move if you fail to do this.

❏   In indeterminate mode, the ProgressBar simply "spins" until told to stop. A typical use is when a remote data call is being made and you do not have any idea of how long the server will take to respond. You can also mix the modes by switching back to determinate mode once the data arrives and you begin to process it with a known number of steps.

Input Controls

These controls enable users to enter data in one form or another. All these controls dispatch events when they are changed. All controls dispatch a valueCommit event when they are changed either by the user or through ActionScript. All controls dispatch a change event only when changed by the user. Each control may also have additional events it dispatches.

You can write ActionScript inline for any control's event handling if you do not want to call a function in a Script block. Here is how a `Button` could dispatch a custom event inline with the MXML tag:

```
<mx:Button label="Submit">
    <mx:click>  <![CDATA[
        var event:SaveEvent = new SaveEvent( SaveEvent.SAVE );
        event.data = data;
        dispatchEvent( event );
    ]]>  </mx:click>
</mx:Button>
```

This may not be the best of coding practices, but is an interesting artifact of MXML nonetheless.

mx.controls.Button and mx.controls.LinkButton

These simple controls allow the user to click them to trigger ActionScript code. `Button` and `LinkButton` differ only in their visual appearance. As shown in Figure 12-5, `Button` has the traditional border and background, whereas `LinkButton` is simply the label.

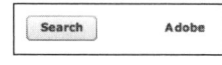

Figure 12-5

The following shows the code behind the controls:

```
<mx:Button label="Submit" click="onSubmit()" />
<mx:LinkButton label="Adobe"
    click="navigateToURL(new URLRequest('http://www.adobe.com'))" />
```

Tips:

❑ You can turn a `Button` (or `LinkButton`) 90° by setting its `rotation` property, but you will lose the label unless you use an embedded font. Embedded fonts are converted to vectors so that the Flash Player can render them at any angle.

❑ You can change the cursor to the "hand" cursor by adding the following properties to the image: `buttonMode="true"`, `mouseChildren="false"`, and `useHandCursor="true"`.

mx.controls.TextInput and mx.controls.TextArea

The `TextInput` control accepts a single line of text; the `TextArea` control accepts multiple lines, as shown in Figure 12-6.

Figure 12-6

The following shows the code behind the controls:

```
<mx:TextInput id="phoneNumber" />
<mx:TextArea htmlText="{data.content}" />
```

Tips:

❑ You can restrict the characters these controls will accept. For example, if you want to get some-one's telephone number you can restrict the characters to '0' through '9', space, and '-':

```
<mx:TextInput restrict="0-9 \-" />
```

❑ Use the `enter` event on the `TextInput` control and tie it to the same event handler as a Submit or Save button. That way, when a user clicks Enter while in an input control, it will trigger the same event as the Submit or Save button.

❑ If you do not want to use a `Form` container, you can achieve the same alignment by using `Labels` and `TextInput` or `TextArea` controls if you use advanced constraints.

❑ Display HTML content with the `TextArea` control by setting its `htmlText` property instead of its `text` property. The Flash Player has limited HTML capabilities, and many tags simply do not work (e.g., `<table>`).

mx.controls.NumericStepper

This control (see Figure 12-7) accepts only numeric input. The input is restricted to a range defined by the control's `minimum` and `maximum` properties.

Figure 12-7

The following shows the code behind the `NumericStepper` control:

```
<mx:NumericStepper minimum="-5" maximum="5" stepSize="0.25" />
```

Tips:

❑ The `NumericStepper` is not limited to positive integers. `NumericStepper` can display both positive and negative values as well as decimals (e.g., setting the `stepSize` to `0.25`).

❑ The `NumericStepper` is a good candidate for use as an `itemEditor` in a list control such as `DataGrid`. Be sure to set the `DataGridColumn`'s `editorDataField` to "value" since that is the `NumericStepper`'s property containing the value selected by the user.

mx.controls.DateChooser and mx.controls.DateField

These controls allow you to select dates. The `DateChooser` presents a full month calendar, whereas the `DateField` resembles a `TextInput` control with a pop-up of a month calendar. The `DateChooser` allows the selection of multiple dates; the `DateField` does not. Both controls disable dates (e.g., weekends).

Figure 12-8 shows the DateChooser (left) and DateField (right) with the calendar button selected.

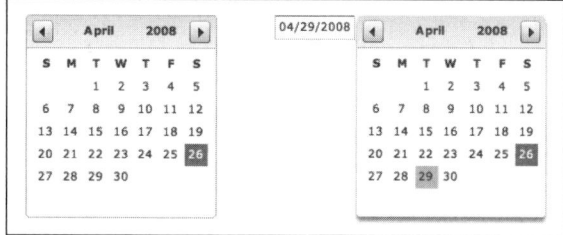

Figure 12-8

The following shows the code behind the controls:

```
<mx:DateChooser />
<mx:DateField />
```

Tip:

❑ If a date has been selected and the user selects it again, the DateChooser's or DateField's selectedDate value will be null.

mx.controls.CheckBox

This control presents a label and a box the user can select to indicate a true/false choice. Figure 12-9 shows a typical Checkbox.

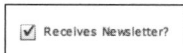

Figure 12-9

The following shows the code behind the CheckBox control:

```
<mx:CheckBox label="Receives Newsletter?" selected="true" />
```

Tips:

❑ When using the CheckBox in a Form, use data binding to inspect its value rather than handling events. For example, a CheckBox for receiving email newsletters could have a click event handler, which changes a value in a record. Instead, bind the value of the record to the CheckBox's selected property. This will save time on coding and streamline the component.

❑ The CheckBox is a common choice as both an itemRenderer and itemEditor in list controls when displaying Boolean data.

mx.controls.ComboBox

This control, shown in Figure 12-10, presents a drop-down list of choices where the user can pick a single item from the list. The ComboBox is a fairly complex component. The data displayed in the list is formed from a collection and is displayed using an itemRenderer.

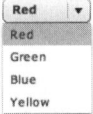

Figure 12-10

The following shows the code behind this control:

```
<mx:ComboBox dataProvider="{Colors}" />
```

Tips:

❑ The ComboBox control has a prompt property, which is a string that shows when nothing has been selected. For example, <mx:ComboBox prompt="Select Color" ... /> shows "Select Color" when the ComboBox first appears. The prompt does not appear in the drop-down list. When the ComboBox is showing the prompt string, the ComboBox's selectedIndex property is -1. You can reset the ComboBox to show the prompt string by programmatically setting the selectedIndex property to -1. Many people find this feature useful for forms to give the user instruction without the instruction being part of the data.

❑ The dataProvider for the ComboBox must be a collection as with any list control. However, you can also give the ComboBox an array when defining the ComboBox in MXML, and the Flex compiler will generate the ArrayCollection for you.

mx.controls.RadioButton and mx.controls.RadioButtonGroup

The RadioButton control is typically used in groups of two or more (see Figure 12-11). RadioButtons differ from CheckBoxes in that RadioButtons work in groups. The RadioButtonGroup is a nonvisual component that associates the RadioButtons with the same group name into a single control. In other words, a RadioButtonGroup presents a single choice but displayed as separate controls (RadioButton).

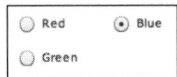

Figure 12-11

The following are examples of the RadioButton tag:

```
<mx:RadioButton label="Red" groupName="colorGroup" />
<mx:RadioButton label="Blue" groupName="colorGroup" />
<mx:RadioButton label="Green" groupName="colorGroup" />
```

Tips:

❑ The easiest way to set up `RadioButton` controls is to use a `RadioButtonGroup`, give each `RadioButton` a value (using the value property), and add an event listener to the `RadioButton Group` instead of the individual `RadioButtons`. When the event is triggered, simply use the `RadioButtonGroup`'s selectedValue property to know which `RadioButton` was selected.

❑ The `RadioButtonGroup` tag has the event handler, rather than the individual `RadioButton` tags:

```
<mx:RadioButtonGroup id="colorGroup" itemClick="handleClick(event)" />
<mx:RadioButton label="Red" groupName="colorGroup" />
<mx:RadioButton label="Blue" groupName="colorGroup" />
<mx:RadioButton label="Green" groupName="colorGroup" />
```

❑ If you want to process events from each `RadioButton` separately, there is no need to create a `RadioButtonGroup`. Instead, set each `RadioButton`'s groupName property to the same string value.

```
<mx:RadioButton label="Red" groupName="colorGroup" change="handleRed(event)"/>
<mx:RadioButton label="Blue" groupName="colorGroup" change="handleBlue(event)"/>
<mx:RadioButton label="Green" groupName="colorGroup" change="handleGreen(event)"/>
```

mx.controls.HSlider and mx.controls.VSlider

These controls present a bar (horizontal or vertical, respectively) with one or more thumb controls to change its value(s), as shown in Figure 12-12. The slider controls are similar to the `NumericStepper` in that they are governed by `minimum` and `maximum` properties and work exclusively with numeric data.

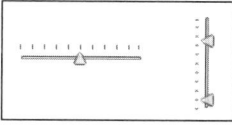

Figure 12-12

The following shows the code behind these controls:

```
<mx:HSlider minimum="-32" maximum="212" />
<mx:VSlider thumbCount="2" values="[3,52]" />
```

Tips:

❑ By default the slider determines the value a thumb can have by dividing the size of the slider between its `minimum` and `maximum` values. This does not always translate to integer values. You might want to include a `snapInterval` property when setting up a slider.

❑ The slider controls dispatch change events whenever the user changes the position of its thumb controls. If you set `liveDragging` to true, change events will be dispatched while the thumb is sliding to its final position. This may adversely affect performance if the change event handler is doing anything computationally intensive. Instead of using the change event, consider using the `thumbRelease` event.

mx.controls.RichTextEditor

This control provides a text editor with additional controls, much as you would expect in a modern text editor (see Figure 12-13). You can change the font, the font size, color, paragraph spacing, and more.

Figure 12-13

The following shows the code behind the RichTextEditor control:

```
<mx:RichTextEditor width="100%" id="commentEditor" />
```

Tips:

- ❑ The RichTextEditor (sometimes written as *RTE*) is really a composite control. It is made up of a Panel, a TextArea, and several ButtonBars.

- ❑ The RichTextEditor has both text and htmlText properties. The htmlText property is a string with embedded style tags. The text property is simply the text minus the style tags.

- ❑ The RichTextEditor has the same HTML limitations as the TextInput and TextArea controls.

- ❑ You can remove the toolbars programmatically. For example, to remove the alignment buttons: editor.toolbar.removeChild(editor.alignButtons); remember to remove the items from the RichTextEditor's toolbar or toolbar2 child and not from the RichTextEditor itself.

- ❑ You can add your own buttons or tools. To add Save and Cancel buttons, create them in ActionScript and add them to one of the RichTextEditor's toolbars (toolbar or toolbar2).

mx.controls.PopUpButton

This control is similar to a Button and ComboBox. As shown in Figure 12-14, part of this control is a down arrow, which when clicked, pops up another control.

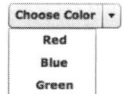

Figure 12-14

The following shows the code behind the `PopUpButton` control:

```
<mx:PopUpButton label="Choose Color" id="popUpButton"
        creationComplete="initPopUpButton()">
```

Tips:

❑ Nearly any Flex control may be used as the pop-up. It is typically a `Menu`, but you can pop-up a `List`, a `DataGrid`, or your own custom Flex control.

❑ The pop-up cannot be created with MXML tags. Create a function for `PopUpButton`'s `creation Complete` event, and create the pop-up and assign it to the `PopUpButton`'s `popUp` property.

mx.controls.PopUpMenuButton

This control (see Figure 12-15) provides a button-like control but will spring open a menu when clicked.

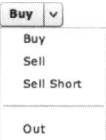

Figure 12-15

The following shows the code behind this control:

```
<mx:PopUpMenuButton dataProvider="{cmds}"
        labelField="@label"
        showRoot="false"
        creationComplete="initPopUpMenu();"/>
```

Tips:

❑ When you specify XML as the `dataProvider` for a `PopUpMenuButton`, be sure to set `showRoot="false"` so that the XML root structure is not shown in the menu.

❑ It is also a good idea to either specify a label for the `PopUpMenuButton` if the `dataProvider` is XML (because the root tag will be displayed) or set the label from the `creationComplete` event listener.

mx.controls.ColorPicker

This control lets the user pick a color from a palette of standard web colors, as shown in Figure 12-16.

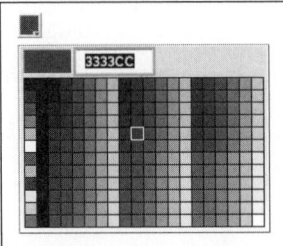

Figure 12-16

The following shows the code behind the ColorPicker control:

```
<mx:ColorPicker id="picker" />
```

Tips:

❑ The selectedColor property is a number and represents the value of the color selected. To display this value as a hexadecimal value, use the Number class's toString() function with a value of 16. For example:

```
<mx:Text text="0x{Number(picker.selectedColor).toString(16)}" />
```

displays "0xff0000" if the user has picked pure red.

❑ Use data binding to associate the selected color of the ColorPicker with another control or container. This changes the background color of a Canvas:

```
<mx:Canvas backgroundColor="{picker.selectedColor}">
...
</mx:Canvas>
```

Layout Containers

Building a Flex application requires you to position the controls on the screen. Placement of the controls is managed by other Flex components called *containers*.

Containers expand to fit their contents unless they are given a width and/or height. The width or height may be specified explicitly or with constraints.

mx.containers.Canvas

The Canvas container allows its children — other controls and containers — to be positioned in a number of ways. Component children can be positioned by (x,y) coordinates, with the upper-left corner of the Canvas being (0,0). Component children can also be positioned relative to the edges of the Canvas by using constraints. The constraints are styles each Flex component possesses: left, right, top, and bottom. The values of the constraints are relative to their respective edges. For example:

```
<mx:TextInput left="10" right="10" />
```

stretches the TextInput control so that its left edge is 10 pixels from the left edge of the Canvas and its right edge is 10 pixels from the right edge of the Canvas. If the Canvas changes size, the left and right constraints are maintained, resizing the TextInput control.

```
<mx:Canvas width="400" height="300">
```

Tips:

❑   It is tempting to use the Canvas whenever you need to place components by location. This is fine in most instances but can be a performance problem if a Canvas is used for an itemRenderer in a list control. A Canvas is a container and has overhead; for an itemRenderer, it would be best to create a custom component based on UIComponent, where you have control of sizing and placement of children and can improve the list control's performance.

❑   The Canvas, along with Panel, Application, and TitleWindow, can also position children using advanced constraints — See Chapter 13, "Layout Strategies."

❑   Any drawing you do using the Canvas's graphics property (for example, drawing a blue circle) will always appear behind any component children of the Canvas. If you want to have custom drawings appear mixed with other component children, create a new UIComponent child and draw into its graphics property.

❑   By default the Canvas has no background color, which means that any mouse clicks will not be intercepted by the Canvas. If you want to receive mouse clicks but do not want a background color, set the backgroundColor style and set the backgroundAlpha style to 0 (zero). The zero value will make the background present but transparent.

mx.container.VBox and mx.container.HBox

As shown in Figure 12-17, these components automatically position their children vertically (VBox — right) or horizontally (HBox — left), respectively, without overlap.

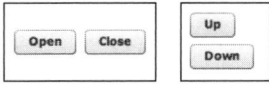

Figure 12-17

```
<mx:VBox>
    <mx:Button label="Up" />
    <mx:Button label="Down" />
</mx:VBox>
```

Tips:

❑ If you know you will need three `Button`s in a row, for example, you can do the following:

```
<mx:HBox>
    <mx:Button label="Open" />
    <mx:Button label="Close" />
</mx:HBox>
```

❑ These containers are designed to grow to accommodate their children. If you want scrollbars to appear, you must fix the size of the container. If that is not possible in your design, place the children inside of another container and allow that container to grow.

❑ Using a `<mx:Spacer>` control with `width="100%"` (for HBox) or `height="100%"` (for VBox) is a simple way to push a container's children to its edges. For example:

```
<mx:HBox width="100%">
    <mx:Button label="Save" />
    <mx:Button label="Cancel" />
    <mx:Spacer width="100%" />
    <mx:Button label="Discard" />
</mx:HBox>
```

causes the Discard button to be on the far right. Note that the HBox must also be given a width so that it spreads out.

mx.containers.HDividedBox and mx.containers.VDividedBox

These containers (see Figure 12-18) mimic HBox and VBox, respectively, but have a control between each child, allowing the user to resize them. For example, an HDividedBox with three children will have two dividers (between the first and second and between the second and third children). The user can slide the first divider to the right, making the width of the first child larger, while making the width of the second child smaller.

Figure 12-18

The following shows the code behind the VDividedBox control:

```
<mx:VDividedBox width="100%" height="500">
    <mx:Canvas width="400" minWidth="400" height="100%">
    ...
    </mx:Canvas>
    <mx:Panel width="100%" minWidth="200" height="100%">
```

```
    ...
    </mx:Panel>
</mx:VDividedBox>
```

Tips:

❑ If possible, give each child a minWidth (for HDividedBox) or minHeight (for VDividedBox). This will prevent the user from making the children too small.

❑ If you want to have one or more children present, but not visible, setting their visible property to false will leave not only a gap on the display but also a corresponding divider. Use includeIn Layout="false" along with visible="false" for each child that you do not want seen. This way the divider is not displayed.

mx.core.Application, mx.containers.Panel, mx.containers.TitleWindow

These containers are similar in their layout features in that they all have a layout property that can be set to either absolute, vertical, or horizontal. This property enables them to act like a Canvas, VBox, or HBox without the need to embed one of those containers to get the layout you need. Figure 12-19 shows a Panel.

Figure 12-19

Here is the code for the Panel control:

```
<mx:Panel x="776" y="62" width="265" height="200" layout="absolute"
    title="Welcome">
        <mx:Form x="10" y="10">
            <mx:FormItem label="User:">
                <mx:TextInput width="127"/>
            </mx:FormItem>
            <mx:FormItem label="Password:">
                <mx:TextInput width="127" displayAsPassword="true"/>
            </mx:FormItem>
        </mx:Form>
        <mx:ControlBar>
            <mx:Button label="Login"/>
            <mx:Button label="Clear"/>
        </mx:ControlBar>
    </mx:Panel>
```

And here are other examples of the `Application`, `Panel`, and `Title` window tags:

```
<mx:Application xmlns:mx="http://www.adobe.com/2006/mx" layout="vertical" >
<mx:Panel title="Shopping Cart" layout="absolute" >
<mx:TitleWindow title="Themes" showCloseButton="true" >
```

Tips:

❑ The default layout for these controls is vertical — they will act like a `VBox`. Setting the `layout` to `absolute` makes them act like a `Canvas`. This gives you the opportunity to use constraints when positioning their children.

❑ Using a `layout` of `horizontal` or `vertical`, these containers will automatically grow to accommodate their children. If you want to have scrollbars appear, either fix the size of the container or place the children inside of another container and fix its size to the `Panel`, `Application`, or `TitleWindow`.

mx.containers.Grid

This container provides a grid-like layout where its child components are divided into rows and columns (see Figure 12-20).

Figure 12-20

The following shows the code behind the `Grid` control:

```
<mx:Grid left="10" right="10" top="10" bottom="10">
    <mx:GridRow width="100%" >
        <mx:GridItem>
            <mx:Label text="Name:"/>
        </mx:GridItem>
        <mx:GridItem width="100%" >
            <mx:TextInput/>
        </mx:GridItem>
        <mx:GridItem>
            <mx:CheckBox label="default?"/>
        </mx:GridItem>
    </mx:GridRow>
    <mx:GridRow width="100%">
        <mx:GridItem>
            <mx:Label text="Address:"/>
        </mx:GridItem>
        <mx:GridItem width="100%">
            <mx:TextInput/>
        </mx:GridItem>
        <mx:GridItem >
```

```
                <mx:CheckBox label="default?"/>
            </mx:GridItem>
        </mx:GridRow>
        <mx:GridRow width="100%">
            <mx:GridItem>
                <mx:Label text="Phone:"/>
            </mx:GridItem>
            <mx:GridItem width="100%">
                <mx:TextInput/>
            </mx:GridItem>
            <mx:GridItem>
                <mx:CheckBox label="default?"/>
            </mx:GridItem>
        </mx:GridRow>
    </mx:Grid>
```

Tips:

❑   The Grid is one of the most tedious containers to set up, as it requires rigorous attention to the GridRow and GridItem tags, much like the <tr> and <td> tags of an HTML table. Consider using Flex Builder Design View to set up the Grid, or use a Repeater to fill out a Grid from a data source.

❑   When sizing a Grid container, make sure you also size the GridRow and GridItem children. For example, if you want a column to be 50% of the width of the Grid, set the GridRow's width to be 100% and set the width of the second GridItem to be 50%. The GridRow will then span the width of the Grid and the GridItem will take up 50% of that.

mx.containers.Tile

This container positions its children in rows and columns (see Figure 12-21), but does so on an as-needed basis, depending on the Tile's size and the size of its children. For example, you can have a Tile with 6 children that might be 3 columns of 2 rows, and when made larger, 5 columns on 2 rows but with the second row having only one child.

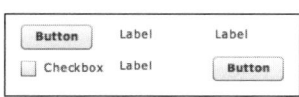

Figure 12-21

The following shows the code behind the Tile control:

```
<mx:Tile width="100%">
    <mx:Repeater id="rep" dataProvider="{ro.lastResult}">
        <mx:VBox width="100" height="100">
            <mx:Label text="{rep.currentItem.title}" />
            <mx:Image source="{rep.currentItem.image}" />
        </mx:VBox>
    </mx:Repeater>
</mx:Tile>
```

Tips:

❑ The `Tile` container and the `TileList` control have similar functions — which you use depends on what type of data you have. The `TileList` however, does not provide smooth scrolling, but doesn't require that all its children be created at once. If you do want smooth scrolling, consider using a `Tile` with a `Repeater`. You can set the `Repeater`'s `dataProvider` to be the same as a `TileList` and use the `TileList`'s `itemRenderer` as the child of the `Tile` within the `Repeater`; set the `itemRenderer`'s `data` property to the `Repeater`'s `currentItem`:

```
<mx:TileList dataProvider="{listOfBooks}"
        itemRenderer="bookView" />
```

to

```
<mx:Tile>
    <mx:Repeater dataProvider="{listOfBooks}" id="rep">
        <renderers:BookView data="{rep.currentItem}" />
    </mx:Repeater>
<mx:Tile>
```

❑ It comes down to performance. A `TileList` can handle hundreds of records but scrolling can be irregular; a `Tile` will scroll smoothly but will take a long time to appear if there are a significant number of items.

mx.containers.Form

This container arranges its children vertically and makes it easy to construct a typical data-entry form. Each child is a `FormItem` whose label appears to the left of the `FormItem`'s own child, which might be a `TextInput` control.

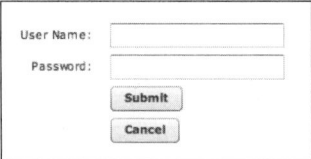

Figure 12-22

The following shows the code behind these controls:

```
<mx:Form x="76" y="70">
    <mx:FormItem label="User Name:">
        <mx:TextInput/>
    </mx:FormItem>
    <mx:FormItem label="Password:">
        <mx:TextInput displayAsPassword="true"/>
    </mx:FormItem>
    <mx:FormItem>
        <mx:Button label="Submit"/>
        <mx:Button label="Cancel"/>
```

```
    </mx:FormItem>
  </mx:Form>
```

Tips:

❑ When using Flex Builder's Design View to make a `Form`, there is no `FormItem` control per se. Instead, drag a control, such as `TextInput`, into the `Form` and the `FormItem` is automatically created. You can change the label on the `FormItem` by clicking the label and changing its properties in the Flex Builder Design View Property Inspector.

❑ You can add additional children to a `FormItem`, and they will arrange themselves vertically. You can change that by setting the `FormItem`'s direction property to `horizontal`.

mx.containers.ControlBar

This container, shown in Figure 12-23, is used with `Panel` or `TitleWindow` and appears at the bottom of these containers as an enlarged border.

Figure 12-23

The following shows the code behind the control:

```
<mx:Panel title="Login">
    …
    <mx:ControlBar>
        <mx:Button label="Login" />
        <mx:Button label="Clear" />
    </mx:ControlBar>
</mx:Panel>
```

Tips:

❑ Treat the `ControlBar` like an `HBox`. Use the `Spacer` component to add white space in the `ControlBar`. For example, use `<mx:Spacer width="100%"/>` to push some controls to the left edge of the `ControlBar` and other controls to the right edge.

```
<mx:ControlBar>
    <mx:Button label="Login" />
    <mx:Button label="Clear" />
    <mx:Spacer width="100%" />
    <mx:Label text="{data.pageCount}" />
    <mx:Button label="Help" />
</mx:ControlBar>
```

❑ You do not need to size the `ControlBar`; the `Panel` or `TitleWindow` will take care of that. The `ControlBar`'s contents will dictate its height.

mx.containers.ApplicationControlBar

The ApplicationControlBar (see Figure 12-24) is an area into which you can put other controls, such as Buttons, LinkButtons, Labels, Menus, and so forth. The most common placement of the Application ControlBar is at the top of the application and spanning the width of it, although it can be placed anywhere.

Figure 12-24

The following shows the code behind the control:

```
<mx:ApplicationControlBar y="20" left="20" right="20" styleName="BlueAppBar">
    <mx:Label text="Real Estate To-Go" styleName="TitleStyle"/>
    <mx:Spacer width="100"/>
    <mx:TextInput/>
    <mx:Button label="Search"/>
    <mx:Spacer width="100%"/>
    <mx:LinkButton label="Logout"/>
</mx:ApplicationControlBar>
```

Tips:

❑   Treat the ApplicationControlBar like an HBox.

❑   Use Spacers to add white space (for example, a Spacer with width="100%" to push component children to the left and right sides of the ApplicationControlBar).

Navigation Components

The Flex navigation components (Accordion, TabNavigator, and ViewStack) all show a single child at a time. The children of the navigation components must be containers. Since only a single child is visible at any one time, the actual creation of the children is deferred until the user visits the child. This speeds up the overall initialization time of your application, since those controls are not created.

creationPolicy

Having only the first child created may present a problem if you need to reference controls that have not yet been created. For example, if the second child of a TabNavigator displays a Form for an employee profile, your application may want to fill in the Form's children's controls when data is returned from a server. If the user has not yet visited that child, those Form controls will not yet exist and the program will fail.

You can change that child creation policy by setting the creationPolicy property to all (the default is auto). Doing this ensures that every control is created, but your application may take longer to start and become usable.

For other ways to work around this using data binding, refer to Chapter 11, "Using Data Binding and Events."

mx.containers.Accordion

As shown in Figure 12-25, the Accordion control presents its children vertically with a horizontal Button for each child. Only one child is visible at a time; the rest are represented by their Button header. Clicking the Button header switches to the selected child.

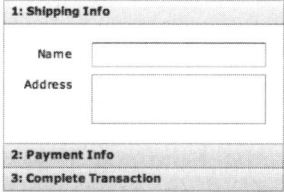

Figure 12-25

The following shows the code behind the Accordion control:

```
<mx:Accordion >
    <mx:Form label="1: Shipping Info" width="100%" height="100%">
        ...
    </mx:Form>
    <mx:Form label="2: Payment Info" width="100%" height="100%">
        ...
    </mx:Form>
    <mx:Form label="3: Complete Transaction" width="100%" height="100%">
        ...
    </mx:Form>
</mx:Accordion>
```

Tips:

❑   The Accordion works with the Flex HistoryManager. This enables the browser's Back button to return to a previous Accordion child.

❑   The Accordion arranges its children vertically, although several horizontally oriented Accordion controls are available from non-Adobe sources.

mx.containers.TabNavigator

The TabNavigator shows a single child at a time with a row of tabs for each child (see Figure 12-26). Clicking a tab switches to the selected child.

Figure 12-26

The following is an example of the `TabNavigator` tag:

```
<mx:TabNavigator >
    <mx:Form label="Profile" width="100%" height="100%">
    ...
    </mx:Form>
    <mx:Form label="Account Status" width="100%" height="100%">
    ...
    </mx:Form>
    <mx:Form label="Administration" width="100%" height="100%">
    ...
    </mx:Form>
</mx:TabNavigator>
```

Tips:

❑ The `TabNavigator` is really a composite control, consisting of a `ViewStack` and a `TabBar`.

❑ The `TabNavigator` works with the Flex `HistoryManager`. This enables the browser's Back button to return to a previous `TabNavigator` child.

❑ If you want to remove a tab from the `TabNavigator`, use the `removeChild()` method. Setting the child's `includeInLayout` property to `false` has no effect with the `TabNavigator`. You can restore the child by using the `TabNavigator`'s `addChild()` or `addChildAt()` functions.

❑ Style the tabs by setting the `TabNavigator`'s `tabStyleName` style to the name of a style defined in a `<mx:Style>` block or an external CSS file.

mx.containers.ViewStack

The `ViewStack` shows a single child at a time without any additional controls. All children occupy the same location. Switching between children is done either with ActionScript or by associating another navigation control with the `ViewStack` such as `TabBar` or `LinkBar`.

The following is an example of the `ViewStack` tag:

```
<mx:ViewStack x="358" y="103" id="pages" width="200" height="200">
    <mx:Canvas label="Outline" width="100%" height="100%">
    ...
    </mx:Canvas>
    <mx:Canvas label="Pages" width="100%" height="100%">
    ...
    </mx:Canvas>
    <mx:Canvas label="Web" width="100%" height="100%">
    ...
    </mx:Canvas>
    <mx:Canvas label="Images" width="100%" height="100%">
    ...
    </mx:Canvas>
</mx:ViewStack>
```

Tips:

- ❏ The ViewStack works with the Flex HistoryManager. This enables the browser's Back button to return to a previous ViewStack child.

- ❏ You can add visual interest to the ViewStack by including Flex effects such as mx.effects .WipeRight and mx.effects.Dissolve. The effects are used to switch between the children. For example, if a child's hideEffect style is set to an instance of WipeRight, switching to another child will cause the current child to disappear from left to right. Including a showEffect controls how the child appears.

- ❏ All children of the ViewStack must be containers.

mx.controls.LinkBar

The LinkBar presents a horizontal array of LinkButton controls with vertical separators between them (see Figure 12-27). The LinkBar is typically associated with a ViewStack.

Outline | Pages | **Web** | **Images**

Figure 12-27

The following shows the code behind the LinkBar control:

```
<mx:LinkBar x="50" y="119" dataProvider="{pages}">
</mx:LinkBar>
```

Tip:

- ❏ To remove a LinkButton from the LinkBar, use removeChild() on the LinkBar's dataProvider (e.g., a ViewStack). Restore the LinkButton by using either the addChild() or addChildAt() functions of the LinkButton's dataProvider.

mx.controls.TabBar

The TabBar control presents a horizontal array of tab controls and is typically associated with a ViewStack (see Figure 12-28).

Outline | Pages | Web | Images

Figure 12-28

The following shows the code behind the TabBar control:

```
<mx:TabBar x="50" y="157" dataProvider="{pages}">
</mx:TabBar>
```

Tip:

❑ To remove a tab from the `TabBar`, use `removeChild()` on the `TabBar`'s `dataProvider` (e.g., a `ViewStack`). Restore the tab by using either the `addChild()` or `addChildAt()` functions of the `TabBar`'s `dataProvider`.

mx.containers.MenuBar and mx.controls.Menu

The `MenuBar`, shown in Figure 12-29, presents a label that, when clicked by the user, displays a list of `Menu` controls in a drop-down list. You can also use `Menu` by itself and make it pop up in response to user clicks anywhere in the application.

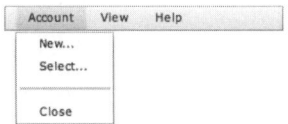

Figure 12-29

The following shows the code behind the `MenuBar` tag:

```
<mx:MenuBar width="100%" dataProvider="{mainMenus}"
    labelField="@label"/>
```

Menus (`mx.controls.Menu`) cannot be created in MXML. You must create them in ActionScript. This example creates a simple menu in response to a click on a button:

```
private function handleMousePress( event:MouseEvent ) : void
{

    popupMenu = Menu.createMenu(null,popupData,false);
    popupMenu.labelField = "@label";
    popupMenu.show( event.stageX, event.stageY );
    popupMenu.addEventListener(MenuEvent.ITEM_CLICK, handleMenuSelect);

}
```

Tips:

❑ When using XML to describe the menus, make sure that you include a `labelField` property and name the attribute to use for the label using E4X syntax. For example, `labelField="@label"` is necessary when you have an item described as `<menuItem label="File" >`.

❑ The `Menu` will dispatch `change` events for every item — even for the top-level menus on a `MenuBar` (e.g., the "File" part of a File menu) and separators. You might want to use `itemClick` events instead of `change`, which is only dispatched when the user picks a normal, radio, or check type item.

❑ The `MenuEvent` contains an `item` property, which is the item describing the item selected. If your `dataProvider` to the `Menu` or `MenuBar` is XML, this item will be an XML node.

❑ When positioning a pop-up menu, use the event's stageX and stageY properties in the Menu's show(x,y) function. The x and y values should be in the stage coordinate space, not in the coordinate space of the component.

mx.controls.ButtonBar and mx.controls.ToggleButtonBar

These controls present groupings of buttons. The buttons are packed tightly, with the leftmost and rightmost buttons given a different style (slightly rounded). The ToggleButtonBar sets its Button children into toggle mode and operates like a RadioButtonGroup in that only a single Button can be selected. Selecting another Button in a ToggleButtonBar causes the previous selection to be removed.

Figure 12-30 illustrates the ButtonBar control.

Figure 12-30

The following shows the code behind the ButtonBar control:

```
<mx:ButtonBar x="50" y="55" dataProvider="{favorites}">
</mx:ButtonBar>
```

And Figure 12-31 shows the ToggleButtonBar control.

Figure 12-31

The following shows the code behind the ToggleButtonBar control:

```
<mx:ToggleButtonBar x="358" y="55" dataProvider="pages">
</mx:ToggleButtonBar>
```

Tips:

❑ Both of these controls can be associated with a ViewStack and automatically control which child of the ViewStack is presented.

❑ Both controls can use an array of ActionScript objects to define the buttons. Use the labelField and iconField properties of the controls to indicate which fields of the data should be used for the label and icon of the buttons, respectively.

❑ Set the ToggleButtonBar's toggleOnClick property to true if you want to click on a selected Button to deselect it.

269

List Controls

List controls are Flex components that display data in some format of a list — either a vertical list of one or more columns, a horizontal list, or tile of list elements. All list controls present data in a Flex `Collection` class.

More details about the list controls and data services are presented in Part IX.

A Flex component called an `itemRenderer` displays the data. A limited number of `itemRenderers` are created for a list control — usually one for every visible item. Those items that are scrolled out of view are assigned an `itemRenderer` as they become visible; the `itemRenderers` are then recycled to reduce memory consumption. All the list controls have default `itemRenderers`, but you can write own custom `itemRenderers`.

- ❑ `mx.controls.List` — This control presents a vertical, scrollable, list of items.

- ❑ `mx.controls.DataGrid` — This control presents data in a scrollable arrangement of rows and columns with headers for each column. You can assign a Flex component to render the contents of a cell by associating the renderer with a column. The display is similar to a spreadsheet or table.

- ❑ `mx.controls.Tree` — This control presents nested or hierarchical data. The information is displayed as nodes and branches.

- ❑ `mx.controls.TileList` — This control arranges data into rows and columns without headers.

- ❑ `mx.controls.HorizontalList` — This control presents a horizontal, scrollable list of items.

- ❑ `mx.controls.AdvancedDataGrid` — This control is similar to the `DataGrid`, but uses the Flex hierarchical `Collection` classes. You must also have a Flex Charting license to use `AdvancedDataGrid`.

- ❑ `mx.controls.OLAPDataGrid` — This version of the `DataGrid` is useful for presenting complex data sets.

Summary

There are a lot of controls and containers in the Flex framework. This chapter has given you a taste of those controls along with some ideas as to how to use them. The Flex documentation contains the complete description of the controls' and containers' API (application programming interface).

The next chapter covers ways to size and position the controls and containers.

13

Layout Strategies

This chapter covers the many ways you can position Flex components. Once you have chosen the components you need, you have to place them on the page. Flex offers a variety of ways to do that, from using explicit coordinates to alignment relative to other components. Flex comes with a set of container components to help you lay out your application. Some containers help you align your components, whereas others let you position them as you see fit. Keeping in mind the nesting nature of Flex, you'll find that the container components (e.g., Canvas, VBox) can be placed inside of each other for more complex layouts.

Coordinate Positioning

The simplest way to position a component is to use (x,y) coordinates. All Flex components have x and y properties. The container determines if these properties will be honored, so you need to either use a Canvas container or set the layout property of Panel, Application, or TitleWindow to "absolute" when you want to use (x,y) positioning.

Here is an example of placing a TextInput and a Label, using their x and y properties:

```
<mx:Panel layout="absolute">
    <mx:Label text="Your Name:" x="10" y="25" />
    <mx:TextInput x="70" y="25" />
</mx:Panel>
```

Coordinate positioning is fine for a small number of components. It is also best done using Flex Builder's Design View because you can drag the components to position them. When the number of components increases, it becomes time-consuming to reposition them to change the layout. Flex has more flexible ways to handle your layout requirements.

Constraint Positioning

Another way to position components uses styles called *constraints*. There are six constraint styles: top, left, bottom, right, horizontalCenter, and verticalCenter. The values of these constraints are the number of pixels from their respective edges, as shown in Figure 13-1.

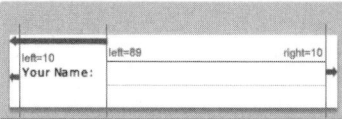

Figure 13-1

Here is the code for this example:

```
<mx:Panel layout="absolute" height="100%" width="100%">
    <mx:Label text="Your Name:" left="10" top="25" />
    <mx:TextInput left="89" top="25" right="10" />
</mx:Panel>
```

Notice that the TextInput control not only has left and top constraints but also has a right constraint. This ensures that the TextInput's right edge is always 10 pixels from the right side of the Panel. That is, as the Panel's width changes, so does the TextInput's width.

Here is another layout:

```
<mx:Panel layout="absolute" width="100%" height="100%">
    <mx:Label text="First Name:" left="10" top="10" />
    <mx:TextInput left="89" top="10" right="10" />
    <mx:Label text="Address:" left="10" top="45" />
    <mx:TextArea left="89" top="45" right="10" bottom="10" />
</mx:Panel>
```

The TextArea not only has its right constraint set to 10, but it has its bottom constraint set to 10 as well. This means that as the Panel changes size, the TextArea will expand vertically and horizontally, maintaining a 10-pixel margin with the Panel's right and bottom edges.

The centering constraints work like the others, with their values being relative to the horizontal or vertical center of the container. To center a Label precisely in the middle of a container, you can do the following:

```
<mx:Label text="Congratulations!" horizontalCenter="0" verticalCenter="0" />
```

Positioning two Labels, one 15 pixels above the vertical center and one 15 pixels below the vertical center, works like this:

```
<mx:Label text="Hello" verticalCenter="-15" horizontalCenter="0" />
<mx:Label text="World" verticalCenter="15" horizontalCenter="0" />
```

Note that the coordinate (0, 0) is located in the top-left corner of your application, so positive values position components below the verticalCenter and to the left of the horizontalCenter. Negative values position components above the verticalCenter and to the right of the horizontalCenter.

You can also use these constraints with the other constraints mentioned earlier. Here, an HBox has its bottom 10 pixels above the bottom edge of its parent and is also horizontally centered:

```
<mx:Panel layout="absolute">
    <mx:HBox horizontalCenter="0" bottom="10">
        <mx:Label text="Status" />
        <mx:ComboBox dataProvider="{statusData}" />
    </mx:HBox>
</mx:Panel>
```

Since constraints are styles, they can also be set with ActionScript, using the setStyle() function on the component being positioned. This example shows a TextArea being created and positioned:

```
var address:TextArea = new TextArea();
address.setStyle("left", 70);
address.setStyle("right", 10);
address.setStyle("top", 30);
address.setStyle("bottom", 10);
… other settings …
addChild(address);
```

Positioning by Percentage

Although not technically a positioning technique, you can use a combination of coordinate positioning and percentage sizes to achieve similar effects to constraint positioning.

For example, if the TextArea were positioned at x="70" and y="30", setting its width="100%" and height="100%" would yield nearly the same result as including right and bottom constraints. The main difference is that the TextArea's right and bottom edges would be directly adjacent to and touching the Panel's edges, since there would be no way to indicate a gap using the percentage values.

You could add paddingRight="10" *and* paddingBottom="10" *to the* Panel *to get those margins in this case.*

Percentage sizing works best in containers that do not use absolute positioning — containers such as HBox, VBox, HDividedBox, VDividedBox, or Application, Panel, and TitleWindow with their layout properties set to either vertical or horizontal.

Here is an example of a ControlBar with two Buttons on the left and a third Button on the far right:

```
<mx:ControlBar>
    <mx:Button label="Save" />
    <mx:Button label="Cancel" />
    <mx:Spacer width="100%" />
    <mx:Button label="Help" />
</mx:ControlBar>
```

The `Spacer` component with its `width` set to 100% will always take up the remainder of the horizontal space of the `ControlBar`, forcing the Help Button to the right side of the `ControlBar`.

So, you can set the percentage width and the percentage height of a component by modifying the `width` and `height` properties of the MXML component. Here is an example of creating a `Canvas` that is 100% wide and 50% high:

```
<mx:Canvas id="myCanvas" width="100%" height="50%">
...
</mx:Canvas>
```

However, you can also set a component's width or height to a percent value explicitly in ActionScript as well. The `width` and `height` properties themselves do not accept percent values, so you use the `percentWidth` and `percentHeight` properties instead. Here is the example of creating the same canvas, except that we create it and set its width and height programmatically:

```
var canvas:Canvas = new Canvas();
canvas.percentWidth = 100;
canvas.percentHeight = 50;
...
```

When this `Canvas` is added to its parent's display list, the parent will query the `Canvas` for its size and the percentage values will return the parent's full width and half of its height, thus giving you a `Canvas` that is 100% wide and 50% high.

Positioning by Alignment

Box containers (`HBox`, `VBox`, `Panel`, `Application`, and `TitleWindow`) have another way they can position their children: by alignment.

The alignment properties also apply to `Panel`, `Application`, *and* `TitleWindow` *when their layout property is set to "vertical" or "horizontal."*

The `horizontalAlign` and `verticalAlign` styles of the box containers automatically align all of the container's children. For example, to center a `Label` and `ComboBox` in the middle of an `HBox`, no matter how wide the `HBox` becomes, you set the `HBox`'s `horizontalAlign` style to "center", as shown here:

```
<mx:HBox left="10" right="10" horizontalAlign="center">
    <mx:Label text="Status:" />
    <mx:ComboBox dataProvider="{statusData}" />
</mx:HBox>
```

Likewise, to keep all of a `VBox`'s children floating in its middle, set its `verticalAlign` style to "middle", for example:

```
<mx:HBox>
    <mx:Image source="{data.image}" width="100" height="100" />
    <mx:VBox verticalAlign="middle">
        <mx:Label text="{data.productName}" />
        <mx:Label text="{data.productPrice}" />
```

```
        </mx:VBox>
    </mx:HBox>
```

Notice in the first example that the Label and ComboBox were aligned to the top of the HBox. This is because all container components' default verticalAlign is "top" (their default horizontalAlign is "left").

```
<mx:HBox left="10" right="10" horizontalAlign="center" verticalAlign="middle">
    <mx:Label text="Status:" />
    <mx:ComboBox dataProvider="{statusData}" />
</mx:HBox>
```

Box containers that do not have explicit sizes expand to fit their children. Giving horizontalAlign= "right" *to an* HBox *that has no width set has no effect. There has to be enough white space in the container for the alignment to make sense.*

The alignment fields are styles and can also be set and changed using ActionScript, for example:

```
var hBox:HBox = new HBox();
hbox.setStyle("horizontalAlign","center");
```

Because the alignments are styles, they can be set from CSS as well, as shown here:

```
HBox {
    horizontalAlign: right;
    verticalAlign: bottom;
}
```

This sets the default alignment for *all* HBoxes to be right and bottom.

Advanced Constraints

Previously, you saw how to use the top, left, bottom, and right constraint styles to position components relative to the edge of their parent container.

Advanced constraints allow you to create constraint columns and rows and position controls relative to these columns. An example is easier to understand. Suppose that you have set up a Panel like a form using constraints, as shown in Figure 13-2.

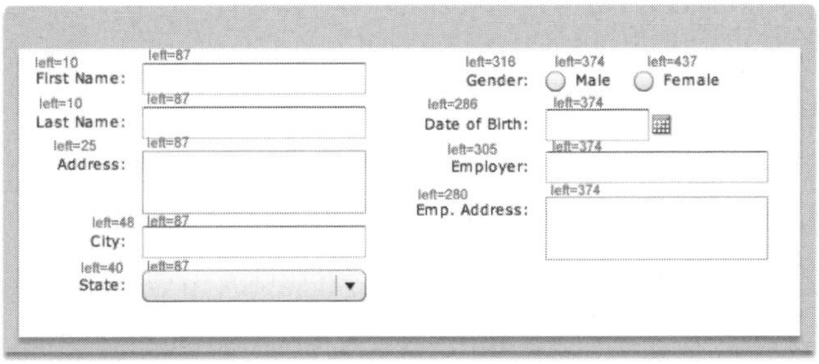

Figure 13-2

Figure 13-2 shows a `Panel` with a number of `Label`, `TextInput`, `RadioButton`, and `DateField` controls. You can see by the annotations where the components were placed, using the `left` constraint style.

Now suppose that you were asked to insert another element into the first column, this new element having a label longer than the others already in position, as shown in Figure 13-3.

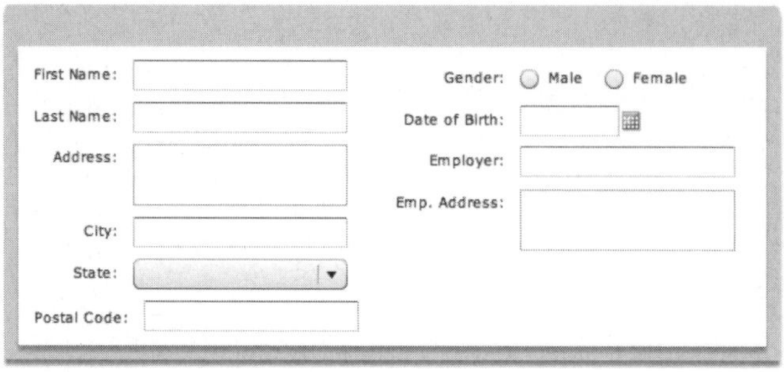

Figure 13-3

You can see that the new Postal Code `Label` and `TextInput` field are not easily (or nicely) aligned with the rest of the fields on the form. Using the normal constraints, you would have to adjust the other components until the form was aligned and then do it again when another field was added.

Flex Builder does not have a way to create or set advanced constraints in Design View. However, if your MXML file has advanced constraints, they will be honored in Design View and be rendered correctly.

ConstraintColumns

With normal constraints, you would have to adjust the left edge of the `TextInput` fields to align with the new `TextInput` field as well as adjusting the right edges of the `Labels`. Note that in this example the `Labels` of the first column do not use `right` constraint styles, as this would change their positions if the `Panel` is resized.

With advanced constraints this is much simpler. First, you set up your constraint columns:

```
<mx:constraintColumns>
        <mx:ConstraintColumn id="leftLabelCol" width="95"/>
        <mx:ConstraintColumn id="leftFieldCol" />
        <mx:ConstraintColumn id="rightLabelCol" width="135"/>
        <mx:ConstraintColumn id="rightFieldCol" />
</mx:constraintColumns>
```

Then you set the `Label` and `TextInput` fields' positions to be relative to these columns:

```
<mx:Label right="leftLabelCol:0" y="18" text="First Name:"/>
<mx:Label right="leftLabelCol:0" y="48" text="Last Name:"/>
<mx:TextInput id="firstName" left="leftFieldCol:0" y="16"/>
<mx:TextInput id="leftName" left="leftFieldCol:0" y="46"/>
```

As you can see in Figure 13-4, the Label fields now use a right constraint style, so their right edges are always aligned. The input fields align their left edges to the next ConstraintColumn.

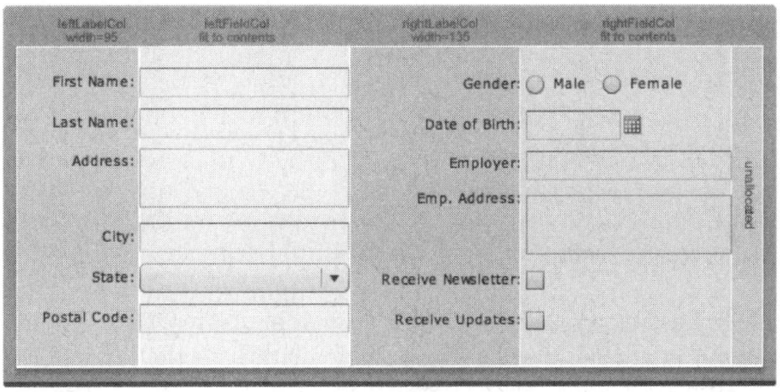

Figure 13-4

The ConstraintColumns are laid out consecutively without overlapping. The first column is given an explicit width so the labels leave a margin with the left edge. The second column has no width specified, so it shrinks to fit its contents. The third column is also given a width to provide a gap with the second column. The fourth column also has no explicit width and it too sizes itself to fit its contents. Since the sum of the widths of the ConstraintColumns does not fill the width of the Panel, a portion of the space is left unallocated.

Adding a new Label and TextInput field is simple: insert the Label and TextInput field and adjust the position of the ConstraintColumn — all the components attached to that ConstraintColumn will be positioned accordingly.

Now you can have a hundred fields, and inserting a new one is as simple as adjusting one constraint.

ConstraintRows

ConstraintRows works the same way as ConstraintColumns. Here is an example of keeping a Button 25% up from the bottom of a Canvas:

```
<mx:constraintRows>
    <mx:ConstraintRow height="75%" id="filler" />
    <mx:ConstraintRow height="25%" id="bottomRow" />
</mx:constraintRows>
<mx:Button left="10" top="bottomRow:0" label="Button" />
```

You can combine ConstraintRows with ConstraintColumns, too. In this example, the Button is not only 25% up from the bottom of the Canvas; it is also centered in the middle of half the width of the Canvas:

```
<mx:Canvas width="100%" height="100%">
    <mx:constraintRows>
        <mx:ConstraintRow height="75%" id="filler" />
        <mx:ConstraintRow height="25%" id="bottomRow" />
    </mx:constraintRows>
```

```
            <mx:constraintColumns>
                <mx:ConstraintColumn width="50%" id="leftCol" />
            </mx:constraintColumns>
            <mx:Button horizontalCenter="leftCol:0" top="bottomRow:0"
                label="Button" />
    </mx:Canvas>
```

Constraints in ActionScript

So far you've seen how to create `ConstraintColumns` and `ConstraintRows` in MXML. It is also possible to create and change advanced constraints in ActionScript.

The constraints are kept as array properties of the container classes. Notice that you use `<mx:constraint Columns>` to denote the `<mx:ConstraintColumn>` elements. Use the same property from ActionScript. Here is an example of creating some `ConstraintColumns`:

```
var pop:TitleWindow = PopUpManager.createPopUp(this,TitleWindow) as TitleWindow;
pop.layout = "absolute";
pop.width = 500;
pop.height = 300;
PopUpManager.centerPopUp(pop);

var leftLabelCol:ConstraintColumn = new ConstraintColumn();
leftLabelCol.id = "leftLabelCol";
leftLabelCol.width = 95;
var leftFieldCol:ConstraintColumn = new ConstraintColumn();
leftFieldCol.id = "leftFieldCol";
var rightLabelCol:ConstraintColumn = new ConstraintColumn();
rightLabelCol.width = 135;
var rightFieldCol:ConstraintColumn = new ConstraintColumn();
```

After creating the `ConstraintColumns`, you can assign them to the `constraintColumns` property of the container as an array of the `ConstraintColumns`:

```
pop.constraintColumns = [ leftLabelCol, leftFieldCol,
    rightLabelCol, rightFieldCol ];
```

Constraint Sizes

The `width` and `height` properties of the `ConstraintColumn` and `ConstraintRow` elements may be one of three values:

❏ **An explicit size** — The column or row will be that absolute size. This is the case for the example where the `leftLabelCol` and `rightLabelCol` were given exact sizes.

❏ **A percentage** — The column or row will occupy that percent of the size of the container as the container changes its size. You can also add `maxWidth` and `maxHeight` properties to prevent the column or row from getting any larger.

❏ **No value** — If you do not give a value, the column or row will be sized to fit its content. This is the case with the `leftFieldCol` and `rightFieldCol` ConstraintColumns in the previous example.

Using includeInLayout

When using MXML, each child you add to a container component is adding to the container's display list — the list of components to be rendered by the Flex framework at the appropriate time.

Likewise, adding a child in ActionScript using the container's addChild() function also places the child onto the container's display list.

If you do not wish a child to appear (or wish to make it disappear later), you can set the child component's visible property to false. Doing so leaves a hole or empty space where the child should be. Consider this example:

```
<mx:HBox>
    <mx:Button label="Open" />
    <mx:Button label="Close" visible="false" />
    <mx:Button label="Exit" />
</mx:HBox>
```

What you see in Figure 13-5 are two buttons with a big space between them where the Close button should be. That's because the Close button is really still there — just invisible (like the *Invisible Man's* footprints in the snow).

Open   Exit

Figure 13-5

To remove a child — temporarily — from its parent's display list, you can set the child component's includeInLayout property to false. For example:

```
<mx:HBox>
    <mx:Button label="Open" />
    <mx:Button label="Close" visible="false" includeInLayout="false" />
    <mx:Button label="Exit" />
</mx:HBox>
```

Now the HBox appears to have just two buttons (see Figure 13-6). The Close button exists but is not rendered. You can switch the includeInLayout property back to true at any time to have it rendered.

Open Exit

Figure 13-6

Here is another example using TabNavigator. There are three children, but the last one will not produce a tab on the TabNavigator because its includeInLayout property is false.

```
<mx:TabNavigator width="100%" height="100%">
    <mx:Canvas label="Profile">

    ...
    </mx:Canvas>
    <mx:Canvas label="Strategies">
```

```
        ...
      </mx:Canvas>
      <mx:Canvas label="Accounts" includeInLayout="false">
        ...
      </mx:Canvas>
    </mx:TabNavigator>
```

Performance Considerations

The `Canvas` container is considered to be the "lightest" container because it has no logic to impose a layout onto its children. If you have an `HBox`, for example, adding a new child or resizing an existing child causes the `HBox` to recalculate the layout of its children to accommodate the new child.

A `Canvas`, on the other hand, does not care how large its children become or where they are placed. Positioning by absolute coordinates is the most efficient method. Constraints (normal or advanced) impose just a little more overhead.

Anything that causes a recalculation of the layout of components will affect performance of the application.

If you are concerned about increasing your application's performance, create your own container class by extending `UIComponent` and position the child components in the `updateDisplayList()` function.

Summary

Building a Flex application not only means selecting the controls, but positioning them as well. This chapter showed the variety of positioning and aligning options you have as a Flex developer. Some techniques yield the same result, so you should choose the method based on how comfortable you are with it. Bear in mind that if your layout needs to be changed, some options make it easier to do that than others.

The next chapter covers a hodgepodge of Flex components focused on input and feedback.

14

User Interface Integration

This chapter covers creating forms in MXML and uses an example of dynamically creating forms from sources such as XML data.

Pop-ups are common ways to get input from users. Flex is unique in that nearly every Flex control or container can be used as a pop-up. Examples of some common and not so common uses are shown. This chapter also shows how to exchange data with pop-ups in the Flex asynchronous event model.

The custom styling of tooltips and error strings, and using custom cursors created with Flash are also covered.

Creating Forms

A *form* is a neatly arranged collection of labeled input fields. HTML has had a tag to create forms since its beginning. Flex also has the ability to lay out forms using the `Form` class, either as the MXML `<mx:Form>` tag or the ActionScript class `mx.containers.Form`.

A Flex form makes it easy to line up the labels. Figure 14-1 is an example of part of an insurance claim form.

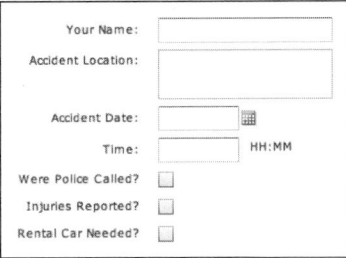

Figure 14-1

You can see that the labels are aligned by their right edges, and the input controls are aligned to their left edges. If you add another field, the labels and input controls realign themselves automatically.

The Flex application code for this example is shown here:

```
<mx:Form x="47" y="368">
        <mx:FormItem label="Your Name:">
            <mx:TextInput/>
        </mx:FormItem>
        <mx:FormItem label="Accident Location:">
            <mx:TextArea/>
        </mx:FormItem>
        <mx:FormItem label="Accident Date:">
            <mx:DateField/>
        </mx:FormItem>
        <mx:FormItem label="Time:" direction="horizontal">
            <mx:TextInput width="74"/>
            <mx:Label text="HH:MM"/>
        </mx:FormItem>
        <mx:FormItem label="Were Police Called?">
            <mx:CheckBox/>
        </mx:FormItem>
        <mx:FormItem label="Injuries Reported?">
            <mx:CheckBox/>
        </mx:FormItem>
        <mx:FormItem label="Rental Car Needed?">
            <mx:CheckBox/>
        </mx:FormItem>
</mx:Form>
```

Flex forms differ from HTML forms in a number of ways. A Flex form can contain any Flex control or container — you can even nest forms, if necessary. You can use states (shown in the code block below) to display and hide parts of the forms, depending on how the user fills in the input controls. When the state changes to InjuryState, two additional fields appear in the form: one for the name of the hospital and one for the name of the doctor.

```
<mx:states>
        <mx:State name="InjuryState">
            <mx:AddChild relativeTo="{injuryField}" position="after">
                <mx:FormItem label="Hospital:">
                    <mx:TextInput/>
                </mx:FormItem>
            </mx:AddChild>
            <mx:AddChild relativeTo="{injuryField}" position="after">
                <mx:FormItem label="Doctor:">
                    <mx:TextInput/>
                </mx:FormItem>
            </mx:AddChild>
        </mx:State>
</mx:states>

<mx:Form x="440" y="368" id="form1">
        <mx:FormItem label="Your Name:">
            <mx:TextInput/>
```

```
            </mx:FormItem>
            <mx:FormItem label="Accident Location:">
                <mx:TextArea/>
            </mx:FormItem>
            <mx:FormItem label="Accident Date:">
                <mx:DateField/>
            </mx:FormItem>
            <mx:FormItem label="Time:" direction="horizontal">
                <mx:TextInput width="74"/>
                <mx:Label text="HH:MM"/>
            </mx:FormItem>
            <mx:FormItem label="Were Police Called?">
                <mx:CheckBox/>
            </mx:FormItem>
            <mx:FormItem id="injuryField" label="Injuries Reported?">
                <mx:CheckBox change="currentState=event.target.selected?
                    'InjuryState':''"/>
            </mx:FormItem>
            <mx:FormItem label="Rental Car Needed?">
                <mx:CheckBox/>
            </mx:FormItem>
</mx:Form>
```

The Flex Form container has several specific tags:

❑   <mx:Form> is the Form container itself.

❑   <mx:FormItem> surrounds the input control and has a label property. You can have several input controls per FormItem:

```
<mx:FormItem label="Open Windows:" direction="horizontal">
    <mx:RadioButton label="All" groupName="sample2"/>
    <mx:RadioButton label="Favorites" selected="true" groupName="sample2"/>
    <mx:RadioButton label="None" groupName="sample2"/>
</mx:FormItem>
```

❑   <mx:FormHeading> is a title you can use to separate parts of your form:

```
<mx:Form>
<mx:FormHeading label="Identification" />
<mx:FormItem label="Name:">
    <mx:TextInput … />
</mx:FormItem>
<mx:FormItem label="Address:>
    <mx:TextInput … />
</mx:FormItem>
<mx:FormHeading label="Account" />
<mx:FormItem label="SSN:">
    <mx:TextInput … />
</mx:FormItem>
<mx:FormItem label="Password:">
    <mx:TextInput … />
</mx:FormItem>

…
</mx:Form>
```

Submitting Form Content

There are several ways to submit the content of a form to a server. The hard part is extracting the values from the input controls and making them ready to submit to the server. Here is one scenario to do this task.

Suppose that you are making a form to let the user control the appearance of your application. You have fields that contain the background color, the size of the font, if the user wants items stacked vertically or horizontally, and so forth.

The developers of the server-side portion of the application provide you with an ActionScript class, AppSettings, that encapsulates all these settings. They want you to create a new AppSettings object, fill it from the fields on your form, and send it to the server using a RemoteObject stored in the main application file.

Your approach is to create a new custom event that has an AppSettings member, and the main application can catch this event — which you will set to bubble — and then the developer for the main application file can send it to the server.

The first thing you do is lay out your form as follows:

```
<mx:Form>
    <mx:FormItem label="Color">
        <mx:ColorPicker id="appBackgroundColor" />
    </mx:FormItem>
    <mx:FormItem label="Font Size">
        <mx:NumericStepper id="appFontSize" minimum="8" maximum="36" />
    </mx:FormItem>
    <!-- etc -->
</mx:Form>
```

You need to copy the values from the form to an instance of AppSettings. You decide to do this with data binding and set up the bindings from a creationComplete event handler:

```
private var appSettings:AppSettings = new AppSettings();
private function handleCreationComplete() : void
{
    BindingUtils.bindProperty(appSettings,"appBackgroundColor",
        appBackgroundColor, "selectedColor");
}
```

Finally, you set up a function to be called from the Submit button's click event handler:

```
private function handleSubmitClick() : void
{
    var newEvent:AppEvent = new AppEvent();
    newEvent.settings = appSettings;
    dispatchEvent( newEvent );
}
```

Because `BindingUtils.bindProperty()` was used to link the UI controls to the members of `AppSettings`, the `AppSettings` variable already contains the values from the form fields. All you need to do is dispatch some event that notifies the rest of the application that the user has made some changes.

Another approach would be to not use data binding, but to create a new instance of `AppSettings` in the click event handler function and then copy the values from the input controls to the matching `AppSettings` properties. Both approaches have their merit, so you should use whichever method you feel comfortable with.

Building Forms with Flex Builder Design View

An easy way to create forms is to use Flex Builder's Design View. Start out by picking the `Form` container. When you drop it onto the application, you see a dialog box asking for the initial size of the form, as shown in Figure 14-2.

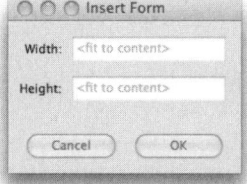

Figure 14-2

The default is to size the form based on its children. This is the easiest method to use.

When you are ready to add children, you will see that there is no `FormItem` listed in the component list for Design View. That is because a `FormItem` is automatically created for you when you drop a control into the form, as shown in Figure 14-3. For example, drag and drop the `ColorPicker` into the form. You should see the dialog shown in Figure 14-4.

Figure 14-3

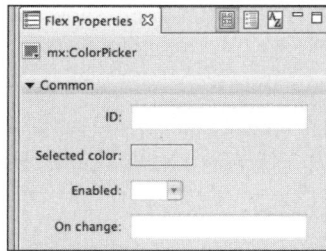

Figure 14-4

285

The `FormItem` is created and selected. You can use the Design View Property Inspector to change the label. If you want to change the `ColorPicker`, just select it with the mouse.

If you drop multiple controls into the same form label, such as the radio buttons (refer to Figure 14-1), you can have them appear vertically (which is the default) or set them to be horizontal. Select the `FormItem` (pick its label), and then switch the Property Inspector to list view and change the `direction` property from `vertical` to `horizontal`.

Setting the defaultButton on the Form

It is often convenient for users to be able to press the Enter (or Return) key when filling out a form to submit it. This feature is not automatically enabled in Flex, but it is pretty easy to set up.

First, make sure that the `Button` control you want to be activated when the user presses the Enter key has an ID. For example, `submitButton` is a good choice.

Next, add `defaultButton="{submitButton}"` to the `Form` container, for example:

```
<mx:Form defaultButton="{submitButton}" ...>
```

When the form is displayed, the `defaultButton` (`submitButton`, in this case) will have a highlight around it. The click event on the `Button` will be invoked when users press the Enter key when they are editing a field on that form.

Customizing Tooltips

Tooltips are small, static controls that pop up when the user hovers the mouse over a control. Tooltips appear automatically. All you do is set their values. You can create tooltips on the fly or you can set them statically in MXML tags. Tooltips can also be styled. They cannot be styled individually, although you can change the global tooltip style at runtime using the `StyleManager`.

Normally, tooltips contain text — an explanation of a control, although you can create your own tooltip class if you want to do something special.

Custom ToolTips

You can create your own custom tooltip if you want to show something more complex than text. For example, here is a tooltip that displays a colored bar indicating a temperature when over a `NumericStepper`.

The first step is to create a class that implements the `mx.core.IToolTip` interface. This is simply a Flex component that has a set and get function for a text property. Here is the `ColoredBarTip` ActionScript class that does this:

```
package tooltips
{
    import mx.core.IToolTip;
```

```
import mx.core.UIComponent;

public class ColoredBarTip extends UIComponent implements IToolTip
{
    public function ColoredBarTip()
    {
        super();
    }

    // Implement the IToolTip interface
    private var _text:String;

    public function get text() : String
    {
        return _text;
    }

    public function set text(value:String) : void
    {
        _text = value;
    }

    // the temperature property value used to determine color
    public var temperature:Number;

    // draw the colored bar with coloring based on temperature

    override protected function updateDisplayList(unscaledWidth:Number,
            unscaledHeight:Number):void
    {
        var color:uint = 0xFFFFFF; // white by default
        if( 0 <= temperature && temperature <= 20 ) color = 0x0000FF;
        if( 20 < temperature && temperature <= 40 ) color = 0x00FF00;
        if( 40 < temperature && temperature <= 60 ) color = 0xFFFF00;
        if( 60 < temperature && temperature <= 80 ) color = 0xFF8800;
        if( 80 < temperature && temperature <= 100 ) color = 0xFF0000;

        graphics.clear();
        graphics.lineStyle(1,0);
        graphics.beginFill( color );
        graphics.drawRect(0,0,unscaledWidth,unscaledHeight);
        graphics.endFill();
    }
}
}
```

Now, you must substitute your custom tooltip for the standard tooltip. You do this by handling the `toolTipCreate` event on the control that has this new custom tooltip and then creating an instance of the new tooltip class:

```
<mx:Script>
    <![CDATA[
        import tooltips.ColoredBarTip;
```

```
            import mx.events.ToolTipEvent;

            private function createCustomTip( temp:Number, event:ToolTipEvent ) : void
            {
                var cbt:ColoredBarTip = new ColoredBarTip();
                cbt.width = 50;
                cbt.height = 20;
                cbt.temperature = temp;
                event.toolTip = cbt;
            }

        ]]>
    </mx:Script>

    <mx:NumericStepper id="stepper" toolTip=" " maximum="100"
            toolTipCreate="createCustomTip(stepper.value,event)" />
```

Notice that the `NumericStepper` has a blank `toolTip` property — you must set this in order for the `toolTipCreate` event to be dispatched. Once the event handler function has been called, an instance of the object being used for the `toolTip` is created and given a size (or it can determine its own size) and value. The text property will be set with whatever is set for the `toolTip` property (which is blank in the code block above) or you can set it in this event handler function if you are using the property (this example is not using it).

Once the new object has been created, set the event's `toolTip` property to this new instance. You will see this instance appear as the tooltip when used with this control.

Creating Pop-Ups

When you need to gather additional information from the user, or when something extraordinary happens, you need a way to grab the user's attention. This has been the traditional role of the *pop-up*. When your application calls for this, Flex gives you many choices.

Flex has an object that controls, or manages, pop-ups: the `PopUpManager`. The `PopUpManager`'s job is to provide controls with an input context that is different from the application's normal mode of behavior. What this means is that when you pop up a control you want input focused on that control — both the mouse and the keyboard. You also want the control to rise or float above all the other controls. After all, it is pop-up, not a pop-off-to-the-side.

The `PopUpManager` can also create instances of the control for you. This is normally how it is used, although you can create the instance of the control yourself and turn it over to the `PopUpManager`.

The most common pop-up you have already seen is the one from the `ComboBox` and `DateField` controls. Yes — those pick lists that appear from these controls are pop-ups. If you have a control that appears under a `ComboBox`, the `ComboBox`'s list appears above that control. The same goes for the `DateField`'s `DateChooser`. Another common pop-up is a `Menu`. Perhaps your application has a `MenuBar` — those menus are also pop-ups.

There is one catch to using pop-ups: you cannot produce the pop-ups in MXML. You must do this from ActionScript.

Alerts

A common dialog box is the Alert box. For example, suppose that you make a call to a data service and it responds with an error. You can make the user aware of this by using the prebuilt `Alert` control, for example:

```
private function faultHandler( event:FaultEvent ) : void
{
    Alert.show("There was an error on the server. The data could not be retrieved.
        Please try again.", "Server Error");
}
```

This code produces the warning as a pop-up, as shown in Figure 14-5.

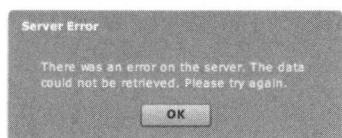

Figure 14-5

The `Alert` is an example of a *modal* pop-up. This is a term given to pop-ups that prevent any action from taking place other than interacting with the pop-up. Flex has a unique way to show the user the pop-up is modal: the application below the pop-up dims a bit and blurs. This really drives home the point that the pop-up is the center of attention.

The `Alert` control can also be used to asked questions and get a response. For example, you might have a place in your code where you need the user to confirm an action before continuing (see Figure 14-6). You can use `Alert` to pose the question and then handle the answer.

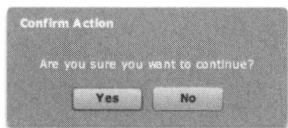

Figure 14-6

This code produces the `Alert`:

```
Alert.show( "Are you sure you want to continue?", "Confirm Action",
    Alert.YES|Alert.NO, null, confirmDecision);
```

The `Alert.show()` function has the following arguments:

```
Alert.show( message:String, title:String, flags:uint=0x4, parent:Sprite,
    closeHandler:Function=null, iconClass:Class=null,
        defaultButtonFlag:uint=0x4) : Alert
```

❑   message — This is the text you want to show in the Alert. In this example it is, "Are you sure you want to continue?"

❑   title — This is the text that appears in the title area of the Alert. In this example it is, "Confirm Action."

❑   flags — This indicates which buttons are to appear on the Alert. The Alert class has several static constants that represent the buttons. By default, the Alert.OK button is used (its hex code is 0x4). In this example, both the YES and NO buttons are required, so Alert.YES | Alert.NO is passed. Other possibilities are: Alert.CANCEL. You can pass as many flags as your question requires by using the logical OR operation (|).

❑   parent — This is the control whose parent owns this Alert. You normally pass null, which means to use the Application itself. The parent determines the position of the Alert, and the position defaults to the center of the parent. You can change this by setting the Alert's x and y properties prior to your function's end:

```
var headsup:Alert = Alert.show("That action is not recommended","Warning");
headsup.x = 10;
headsup.y = 10;
```

❑   closeHandler — This is a function that is called when the user picks one of the buttons. When you are just presenting the Alert with an informational message and it just has the OK button, you do not need to pass a close handler. In this example, you want to know what button the user picked, so you pass the name of a function, which you write in code and which is shown below.

❑   iconClass — This is an icon you want to display in the Alert. Normally, you do not pass anything, but you can embed an icon and pass that, for example:

```
[Embed('/assets/warning_icon.png')]
private var warningIcon:Class;
…
Alert.show("That action is not recommended", "Warning", null, null, warningIcon);
```

❑   defaultButtonFlag — This is the button you want to be the defaultButton so the user can simply press the Enter key and dismiss the dialog. On the default Alert, this is the OK button. If, for example, you want to have the NO button be the default, simply pass Alert.NO for the defaultButtonFlag.

When the user picks one of the buttons on the Alert (or presses the Enter key), the closeHandler function is called. Here is the closeHandler, confirmDecision:

```
private function confirmDecision( event:CloseEvent ) : void
{
    if( event.detail == Alert.YES ) {
        // do whatever is needed
    }
}
```

The CloseEvent has a detail property that is set to the code for whichever button was picked. Depending on the question you asked, you test the detail property against the constant representing the button. In this example, based on the question, you want to check for a positive response and then do whatever is appropriate.

Remember that Flex is an asynchronous system — you cannot post the `Alert` and expect your code to stop at the `Alert.show` and wait until the user has picked a button. Your code continues to execute so you must pass a `closeHandler` function to know what the user has picked.

Using the PopUpManager

When you need to create a pop-up that's more complex that the `Alert` control can handle, you have to create a custom pop-up and use the `PopUpManager` to display it.

Suppose that you have an application that lets the user change some options. You may not have a place on your application to display these options because they are not something that are often changed. This is a good use for a pop-up.

The first step is to design the pop-up. A good base or root control for pop-ups is the `TitleWindow`. A `TitleWindow` is just like a `Panel`, except that it can be moved by the user when the `PopUpManager` displays it, and the `TitleWindow` has a small close button on its upper-right corner.

Figure 14-7 shows the `TitleWindow` with the fields.

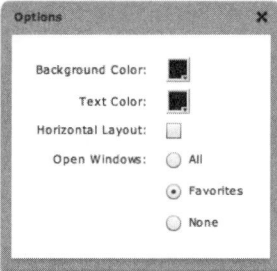

Figure 14-7

Here is the code that displays it:

```xml
<?xml version="1.0" encoding="utf-8"?>
<mx:TitleWindow xmlns:mx="http://www.adobe.com/2006/mxml" title="Options"
     showCloseButton="true" x="80" y="59">

    <mx:Form x="47" y="64">
        <mx:FormItem label="Background Color:">
            <mx:ColorPicker/>
        </mx:FormItem>
        <mx:FormItem label="Text Color:">
            <mx:ColorPicker/>
        </mx:FormItem>
        <mx:FormItem label="Horizontal Layout:">
            <mx:CheckBox/>
        </mx:FormItem>
        <mx:FormItem label="Open Windows:">
            <mx:RadioButton label="All" groupName="sample1"/>
            <mx:RadioButton label="Favorites" selected="true" groupName="sample1"/>
```

```
                    <mx:RadioButton label="None" groupName="sample1"/>
            </mx:FormItem>
        </mx:Form>

    </mx:TitleWindow>
```

This is written in MXML and exists as the file, UserOptions.mxml, making it the class UserOptions.

The next thing to do is pop it up when the user wants to see it:

```
<mx:Script>
    <![CDATA[
            import mx.managers.PopUpManager;

            private function showPopup():void
            {
                var options:UserOptions = PopUpManager.createPopUp
    ( Application.application as DisplayObject, UserOptions, true ) as UserOptions;
            }
    ]]>
    </mx:Script>

    <mx:Button label="click me" click="showPopup()"/>
```

The mx.managers.PopUpManager.createPopUp() function has the following signature:

```
createPopUp( parent:DisplayObject, className:Class, modal:Boolean=false ) :
    IFlexDisplayObject
```

❑   parent — This is the owner of the pop-up. You can pass any Flex control, but normally you want the entire Application to be the owner. This lets the pop-up be centered over the application's entire space. If you want the pop-up to be positioned relative to another control, just pass that control for the parent.

❑   className — This is the class used to create the pop-up. In this example, the UserOptions class contains the TitleWindow and controls so that is passed.

❑   modal — This Boolean indicates if the pop-up will be modal. The default is false, but in this case you do not want the user to interact with the rest of the application until the UserOptions' TitleWindow is dismissed.

The createPopUp function returns the instance of the pop-up, but as an IFlexDisplayObject object. In this example, since it is to be assigned to the options variable, the result is cast to UserOptions.

Once you have created the pop-up, you can set its fields. For example:

```
options.backgroundColor.selectedColor = 0xff0000; // read
options.numPages = 4;
```

Remember that nothing is displayed on the screen until the Flash Player has finished the code it is executing, which is your function. Even though you have created the pop-up, it is still not visible. The user will see a blank form and then see the values appear in it.

If you want the pop-up to appear centered within its parent, then you have to tell the PopUpManager to do this, as follows:

```
PopUpManager.centerPopUp( options );
```

or else the pop-up will be positioned at the parent's (0, 0), or upper-left, corner.

Interacting with Pop-Ups

Now that the pop-up is being shown to the user, you need a way to dismiss the pop-up when they are done, and you need a way to get the information the user changed. There are a number of possibilities for this and no matter what you decide, you should handle all of your pop-ups the same way to be consistent throughout your application.

In this example, the UserOptions pop-up has a Save button as well as the Close button in the upper-right corner.

Once you have instructed the PopUpManager to center the pop-up, you need to know when the user has picked the Close button so that you can remove the pop-up. You can do this by using a CloseEvent handler. You can put that close event handler in one of two places:

```
<mx:TitleWindow … close="handleClose(event)" />
```

or

```
options.addEventListener( CloseEvent.CLOSE, handleClose );
```

The first choice places the CloseEvent handler right in the UserOptions MXML file. This is a good choice because it makes the UserOptions a bit more self-contained. Since you may not care that the user has dismissed the pop-up and does not want to save any changes they may have made, you can have the UserOptions class handle the removal of the pop-up itself.

The second choice places the CloseEvent handler in the class that has popped up the UserOptions. This is a good choice if you care about knowing the user does not want to save the options, or if you want to be consistent with having all of your event handlers for the UserOptions to be in one place.

In both classes, the CloseEvent handler is the same:

```
private function handleClose( event:CloseEvent ) : void
{
    PopUpManager.removePopUp( event.currentTarget );
}
```

The PopUpManager's removePopUp() function takes care of dismissing the pop-up and removing it from the DisplayList.

Of course, you also want to know when the user has picked the Save button. This is bit more complex because you have more choices. These are two most common: you can create a custom event and have the UserOptions class dispatch the custom event and then remove the pop-up, or you can dispatch a simple event, catch it from the class that popped up the UserOptions and then remove the pop-up.

In both cases, you need to add an event listener in the class that popped up the UserOptions. You do this right after you have created the pop-up:

```
options.addEventListener( "save", handleSave );
```

If you are using a custom event, the handleSave function should have all the data in the event:

```
private function handleSave( event:SaveEvent ) : void
{
    // use the contents of the SaveEvent as the data
}
```

If you are using a simple event, you can access the UserOptions pop-up from within the event handler and extract the values to save them:

```
private function handleSave( event:Event ) : void
{
    var options:UserOptions = event.currentTarget as UserOptions;
    // save options.backgroundColor, options.numPages, etc.
}
```

Once you have saved the options you can dismiss the pop-up. Again, you have some choices. If you elected to use a custom event, you can dismiss the pop-up from within the UserOptions class Save button click event handler:

```
<mx:Button label="Save">
    <mx:click>
    <![CDATA[
        var newEvent:SaveEvent = new SaveEvent("save");
        newEvent.backgroundColor = backgroundColor.selectedColor;
        newEvent.numPages = numPages;
        // etc.
        dispatchEvent( newEvent );
        PopUpManager.removePopUp(this);
    ]]>
    </mx:click>
</mx:Button>
```

By handling the removal of the pop-up within the UserOptions class in conjunction with creating the custom SaveEvent, you keep things a bit cleaner.

If you decide to use a simple event, then you can dismiss the pop-up from the handleSave function:

```
private function handleSave( event:Event ) : void
{
    var options:UserOptions = event.currentTarget as UserOptions;
    // save options.backgroundColor, options.numPages, etc.
    PopUpManager.removePopUp( options );
}
```

Using a custom event makes your code simpler to use, since the removal of the pop-up is contained with the pop-up class.

Custom Cursors

You should be familiar with the standard mouse cursors: the arrow, the I-beam, the hand, and some sort of "busy" cursor — usually a watch or a spinning ball. The management of cursors in a Flex application is really the domain of the Flash Player. The Player detects where the mouse is and changes the cursor accordingly. The Player also relies upon the operating system to supply the cursor shapes.

However, you can have your own custom cursors, and Flex provides a simple interface to the Flash Player to do so. This is the `mx.managers.CursorManager` class.

Cursor Management

The `CursorManager` is a class whose job is to present the mouse cursor (or hide it). It does this by managing a set of cursors that are assigned priorities. Normally, you have a single cursor, but you can have a series of cursors, and they can appear whenever you want by simply telling the `CursorManager` which one to show at any given time.

For example, you may have some `Images` on display and, depending on the data associated with the `Images`, have the user click the `Images` to get more detail. Some `Images` however, may not have any detail and for those, you have the cursor change to a red X.

You can use a graphic image for the red X cursor, tell the `CursorManager` to create the cursor, and then show the cursor on those images with no data.

The `CursorManager` has a set of static functions that you call to set up your cursors, make them appear, and remove them.

Busy Cursors

The busy cursor is useful when there is a long operation taking place. A very common "long" operation is retrieving data from a server. Since Flex applications are asynchronous, you have no idea when the server will respond.

To make things simple, the data service calls have a `showBusyCursor` Boolean property. If you set this property to `true`, the `CursorManager.setBusyCursor()` function will automatically be invoked when the request goes to the server, and then it will be removed when the data is returned from the server.

```
<mx:RemoteObject id="finServ" showBusyCursor="true" … />
```

You can show a busy cursor whenever you want to tell the user something is happening by invoking the `CursorManager` yourself:

```
CursorManager.setBusyCursor();
```

When your action has completed, remove the busy cursor:

```
CursorManager.removeBusyCursor();
```

Just be sure you do not forget to remove the busy cursor or your users will be trying to operate your application using a stop watch for a cursor.

Hand Cursors

A common cursor in HTML is the hand cursor, which appears whenever the mouse is over a URL link. Flex does not generally present this cursor over LinkButton or Button, but you can use it if want to. And you can use it with any control. All it takes is a few property settings.

```
<mx:LinkButton buttonMode="true" useHandCursor="true" mouseChildren="false"
    label="Click Me" … />
```

The three properties, buttonMode, useHandCursor, and mouseChildren, are all Boolean properties and all three must be set as shown; otherwise, the hand cursor will not appear.

Custom Cursors

In an example above, a red X cursor is used to indicate that an Image has no detail data. This is a good signal to the user and is easy to do in Flex.

First, create a bitmap asset using a graphics program. Make sure that you choose an image data type that allows for transparency such as GIF or PNG. This lets your cursor appear to be nonrectangular. You should also make your cursor fairly small, between 16×16 and 24×24 pixels is ideal. A large cursor can be distracting and have poor performance (it will appear to move in steps as the user moves the mouse).

Once you have done that, import the cursor as an image asset, using the Embed directive:

```
[Embed('/cursors/redX.png')]
private var redXImage:Class;
```

Use the CursorManager when you are ready to show this cursor:

```
var redXCursor:int = CursorManager.setCursor( redXImage );
```

and use the CursorManager to hide this cursor when it moves off of the Image:

```
CursorManager.removeCursor(redXCursor);
```

Put together, the code might look like this:

```
import mx.managers.CursorManager;

[Embed('/cursors/redX.png')]
private var redXImage:Class;
private var redXCursor:int;

private function handleOverImage( event:MouseEvent ) : void
{
    if( ! data.details ) redXCursor = CursorManager.setCursor(redXImage);
```

```
    }

    private function handleOutImage( event:MouseEvent ) : void
    {
        if( ! data.details ) CursorManager.removeCursor(redXCursor);
    }
    ...
    <mx:Image source="{data.imageName}" rollOver="handleOverImage(event)"
        rollOut="handleOutImage(event)" />
```

Of course, this is Flex and the Flash Player, which means you are not limited to static image graphics. You can make animated cursors, too, if you know how to use Flash CS3. You want to create an SWF that is cursor-sized and that has its (0,0) location in the upper-left corner of the symbol. You set the hot spot for the cursor when you create it in Flex.

Suppose that you want your cursor to be a bee that is flapping its wings and you want the hot spot to be its stinger. First, you import the SWF:

```
[Embed('/cursors/bee.swf')]   or [Embed(source='/cursors/beeCursor.swf',
    symbol='bee')]
private var bee:Class;
```

You can either use the entire SWF or, if you have created a SWF full of Flash symbols, select the symbol by its name.

When you are ready, set the cursor:

```
CursorManager.setCursor( bee, CursorManagerPriority.HIGH, -16, -21 );
```

This indicates that the hot spot for the cursor is in the cursor's lower-right corner (assuming the symbol is 24×24 pixels).

Summary

This chapter covered a hodgepodge of somewhat related concepts in Flex, loosely centered around the notion of providing feedback and limited interactivity with Flex.

The next chapter covers Adobe AIR, which enables you to write web applications that work from the desktop instead of from the browser. AIR applications expand the Flex framework with classes that cover access to the file system, an HTML browser, and more.

Getting Started with AIR

Adobe AIR is a cross-platform runtime that allows applications to be run natively from the desktop of both OS X and Windows without the need for either a web browser or an Internet connection. Developers creating applications with AIR will write their software once and be able to deploy it to Windows, OS X, and Linux without recompiling their code. If developers take care in using the default AIR APIs, their applications will automatically render appropriately in the destination operating environments using native windows, and native operating system functionality, like the Windows Taskbar or OS X's Dock, and allow Flex-based applications to save files to default user documents, folders, and so forth.

While one can develop AIR applications in JavaScript and HTML, or Flash CS3, the focus of this book is on building AIR applications with the Flex framework using Flex Builder 3. It should be noted that like regular Flex applications, Adobe AIR applications can also be built with command-line tools included in the Flex 3 SDK, but the command-line tools are outside the scope of this book.

This chapter will explain what AIR is and how to use it. You'll start by building a simple application. Later in the chapter, advanced AIR configurations will be discussed. And finally, a sample application with a fancy splash screen will be created that highlights some of the modern operating system integration for which Adobe AIR enables development.

What Does AIR Provide?

Adobe AIR includes a set of API programming extensions to the Flex framework that give the developer unified, cross-platform access to the following:

- ❑ SQLite database access for local storage of data
- ❑ Native operating system menus
- ❑ Native operating system windows
- ❑ Native drag and drop that interacts with the operating system and software written by other developers in other toolkits

❑ Access to operating system clipboard data allowing users to copy data to and from other applications

❑ Interaction with the Dock (OS X) or System Tray (Windows) allowing AIR applications to look like they were specifically designed to run on only a given platform

❑ Interaction with local filesystems, including opening, writing, and deleting files, and reading directory structures

❑ An API for updating AIR applications

❑ And much, much more

Why Use AIR?

There are important reasons to use AIR to develop an application as opposed to just creating a Flex application running inside the browser. The number one reason to use AIR is to develop cross-platform native desktop applications. AIR is one of the few cross-platform toolkits that allow a developer to write an application once and deploy it to multiple operating systems, taking advantage of operating-system-specific features and functionality. For example, an AIR application will run on OS X, looking just like a native OS X application with windows that contain the red, yellow, green buttons on the toolbar in the upper left, while the application, from the same code base, will have the Minimize, Maximize, and Close buttons on the toolbar in the upper right on a Windows machine. When the user minimizes the application, it'll minimize to the OS X Dock, or the Windows Taskbar, just as though the application were written using native toolkits. AIR takes care of all this native interaction with the operating system on behalf of the developer.

Another essential reason to use AIR would be when a Flex application needs to be able to run without an Internet connection. For example, the user could be using a word processor developed in Flex. Without AIR, the user would be unable to use the application at the airport without an Internet connection. AIR allows the user to run the application and to save their data locally without the need to proxy through the server. On some types of applications, users might be more confident to use them if their private and personal data remained their own and isn't transferred over the Internet to be stored on a third-party website.

The final reason for using AIR is the more generous security sandbox. Since AIR applications run on the user's machine, under the user's credentials, they have more liberal security policies, allowing for things like bitmap editing without the proper cross-domain security policies normally needed in a traditional web-based Flex application running on a server over the Internet.

Applications That Can Be Built with AIR

Many classes of applications are prime candidates for being built with AIR:

❑ Newfangled word processors

❑ Photo-editing tools that want to take advantage of Flex/Flash's rich graphical APIs

❑ Photobook building software

❑ Instant messaging clients

❑ Email clients

- ❑ Application mashups that take advantage of all the HTTP-based APIs of hosted applications
- ❑ Image uploader tools
- ❑ Scheduling software

Or any other application that needs to potentially go offline and feel familiar to a user like a native application. In the future, there'll be support for AIR applications on embedded devices, so what you write now might be able to easily move to other platforms.

Requirements for AIR

Adobe AIR applications require modern flavors of most operating systems (Windows, Linux, and OS X) for both development and runtime execution.

Developer Requirements

Both the Flex 3 SDK and Flex Builder 3 come with everything you need to start developing Adobe AIR applications. Prior versions of the Flex SDK or Flex Builder are not supported for building AIR application. AIR applications can be developed on Windows, OS X, and Linux platforms using either the Eclipse-based Flex Builder or the plain SDK with your favorite text editor.

The Command-Line Tools

This book is written with the developer using Flex Builder in mind. However, a developer can use their favorite text editor and AIR-specific command-line tools included with the SDK to develop full, working AIR applications. While the use of these tools is beyond the scope of this book, I'll list the command line tools of importance to the AIR developer in the following table, and leave it as an exercise for you to read the documentation on these tools.

Command-Line Tool	Description
Adl.exe	The AIR debug launcher that allows running of the program without packaging and installing it
Amxmlc	The compiler for AIR that invokes regular Flex compiler, except with the AIR-config, which will link to AIR-specific libraries not available to Flex application running in the web browser
Acompc	The compiler for making AIR libraries for reusable components
ADT	Tool for packaging up the application into an .AIR file for distribution, including the digital signing of the application

If your weapon of choice is the command-line tools and your favorite text editor, don't forget to incorporate ANT for managing these AIR SDK tools for simplifying your builds and debugging.

User Runtime Requirements

Users of your application will need Adobe AIR installed. Either they can install this manually or you can add it as extra payload to your application, but you'll learn more about this later. To install it manually, go to the Adobe AIR download website at http://get.adobe.com/air.

The system requirements for the AIR applications (without full-screen support) are as follows:

- **Mac OS X**
    - PowerPC G4 1GHz or faster processor or Intel Core™ Duo 1.83GHz or faster processor
    - Mac OS X v10.4.910 or 10.5.1 (PowerPC); Mac OS X v10.4.9 or later, 10.5.1 (Intel)
    - 512MB of RAM

- **Windows**
    - Intel Pentium 1GHz or faster processor
    - Microsoft Windows 2000 with Service Pack 4; Windows XP with Service Pack 2; or Windows Vista Home Premium, Business, Ultimate, or Enterprise
    - 512MB of RAM

Adding full-screen video playback to your applications increases these minimum system requirements.

Building an AIR Application

Let's build our first Adobe AIR application from inside Flex Builder. We're going to build a simple application to familiarize you with development of an AIR application. Later in the chapter we'll add a splash screen to show off how AIR can use transparent windows native to the operating system for that truly polished look, and to occupy the user's attention while you load other possible resources, just like many traditional desktop applications such as Photoshop or Word.

Let's get started by creating a new Flex project, just as you would when creating a regular Flex application. In Flex Builder, click on File ⇨ New ⇨ Flex Project. This will bring up a window familiar to Flex developers like the one displayed in Figure 15-1. Type in the name of the project, Intro to AIR, and since we're creating an AIR project, select Desktop Application (runs in Adobe AIR) option for creating the new project.

Click on the Next button to bring up the Configure Output selector and leave the Output folder as is, which is `bin-debug`. Click Next again, which will bring up the final input screen for the New Flex Project Wizard. Leave the Main source folder as is, but change the name of the Main application file to `IntroToAIR.mxml`, and change the Application ID to `com.proflex3.IntroToAir`. Your screen should look like the one shown in Figure 15-2. However, you can leave the default values if you like, or change them to have more meaning for your specific project. Click the Finish button to let the wizard generate the boilerplate application code.

Flex Builder will generate two key files:

- `IntroToAir.mxml` — The application entry point where all startup code will reside
- `IntroToAir-app.xml` — The AIR descriptor file for configuring the AIR environment, the installer, the default window, and so forth

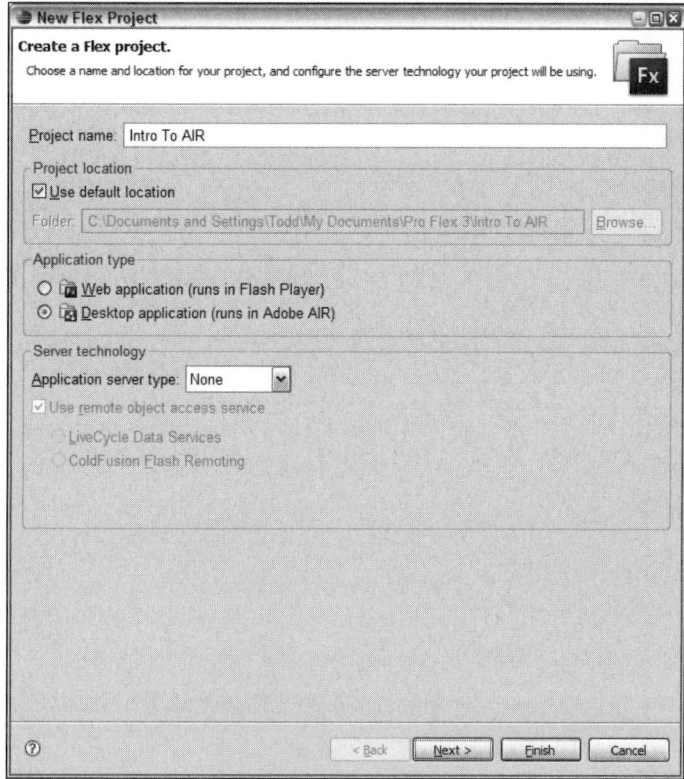

Figure 15-1

Let's take a look at both generated files in a little more detail.

The IntroToAIR.mxml File

The first file, IntroToAir.mxml, is the main application file where all your logic starts. The generated content looks like this:

```
<?xml version="1.0" encoding="utf-8"?>
<mx:WindowedApplication xmlns:mx=http://www.adobe.com/2006/mxml layout="absolute">

</mx:WindowedApplication>
```

The WindowedApplication is the application container MXML component for describing an AIR desktop application. It's very similar to Flex's default <mx:Application> you read about earlier, except this allows for creating an initial window that will run in the user's desktop environment instead of the user's web browser.

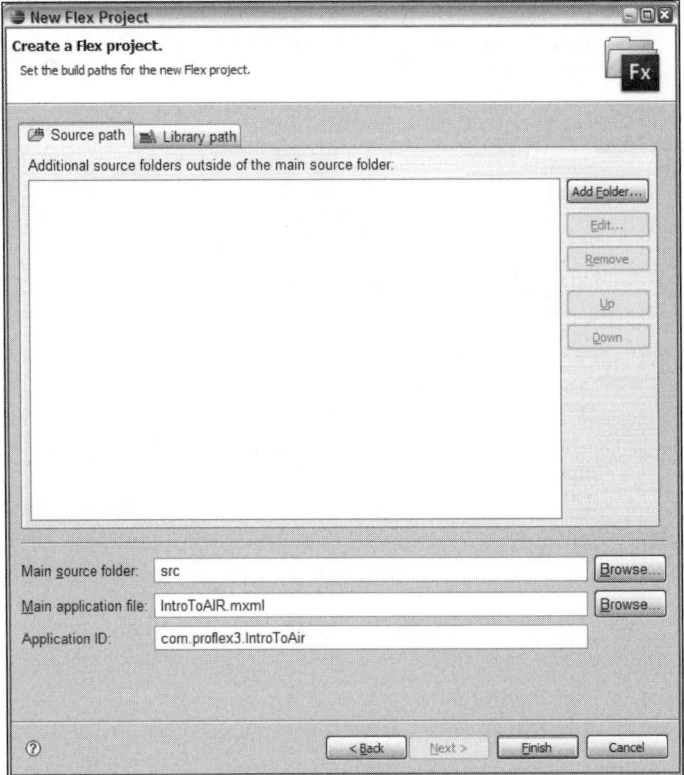

Figure 15-2

Just like when developing a regular web-based Flex application, you'll add child MXML components and ActionScript child tags inside the WindowedApplication tag. Let's add a couple of Label controls between the <mx:WindowedApplication> tags:

```
<mx:Label text="Welcome to Adobe AIR" fontSize="30" />
<mx:Label text="(in lieu of Hello World!)" fontSize="15" />
```

That's it for creating your first application window. Let's take a quick peek at the AIR descriptor file that the compiler will use when assembling your application.

The IntroToAIR-app.xml Descriptor File

The second key file that Flex Builder produces is the IntroToAir-app.xml. This file is the AIR application descriptor file containing all the configurable properties that describe the environment for launching and running you AIR applications. It allows you to configure startup options like the name of the application, unique identifiers, the visual skin to use, version, and so forth. We'll get to all the configuration options later in this chapter, but for now, let's take a look at the default configuration file with all the comments and optional elements removed:

```xml
<?xml version="1.0" encoding="UTF-8"?>
<application xmlns="http://ns.adobe.com/air/application/1.0">
  <id>com.proflex3.IntroToAir</id>
  <filename>IntroToAIR</filename>
  <name>IntroToAIR</name>
  <version>v1</version>
  <initialWindow>
    <content>[This value will be overwritten by Flex Builder in the output
        app.xml]</content>
  </initialWindow>
</application>
```

This is the minimal information needed in a descriptor file to create an AIR application.

The `id` is essential as it gives your application a unique identifier string, and you should use similar namespace package-naming techniques that you would for your Java or Flex development. The wizard we used filled this in with `com.proflex3.IntroToAIR`.

The `filename` defines the name of the file that will be installed to the user's operating system, and is the file that the user calls to start the application. Our filename is `IntroToAIR`. Notice that it doesn't have the file extension; the AIR installer will give it an appropriate one when it installs.

The `name` element defines the name of the application that the AIR installer displays during installation of the application. The wizard set ours to `IntroToAIR`.

The `version` element is a user-generated string identifying version information of the application, not to be confused with version information of AIR. This is the typical version information that you'd display to a user to let them know what build of your application they are running. Ours is set to `v1`, but something more appropriate, like `1.0.0`, might be a more familiar versioning scheme for desktop software.

Finally, the `initialWindow` element defines the default settings and startup information that AIR will use when launching the main application window. Right now, only `content` is defined, and it is set so that Flex Builder will populate it with an appropriate value during compilation. No need to touch this.

Let's run what we've got. In Flex Builder's menu, select Run ➪ Run (or Ctrl+F11) to launch this spectacular application. You should see something very similar to the screen shown in Figure 15-3.

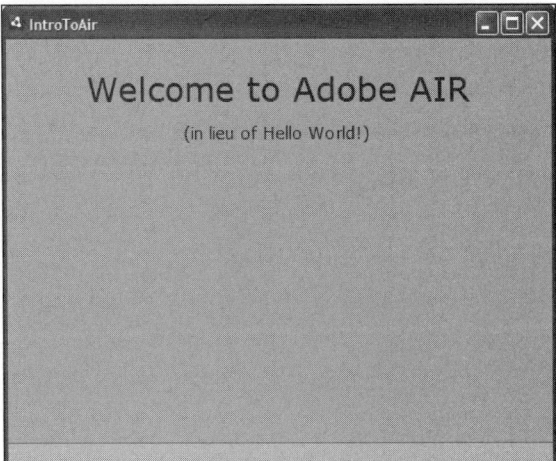

Figure 15-3

That's it! You're running your first AIR application!

The AIR Configuration File

The application descriptor file we created in the previous section was quite simple and uses default properties populated by the Flex Builder New Project Wizard. AIR offers many more options to configure, when you start requiring more advanced runtime support, all of which are listed in the default AIR descriptor file that Flex Builder created for you upon completion of the New Project Wizard. All the elements are well commented in the file, and it will be helpful to read through them when you have questions.

In the meantime, let's introduce all the various AIR descriptor file configuration options here as a detailed reference. And don't worry if you don't understand everything listed in the description. The following is intended to use as a reference and should be revisited when needed after reading the other AIR chapters in this book.

The Application Configuration Tags

The following elements tags configure the AIR application, providing default names, descriptions, and various types of metadata used by the AIR installer. Afterwards, there will be a section on configuring the default window, and finally a section covering the remaining elements thus far unmentioned.

Each of the following subsections detail one of the configurable XML elements that's defined within the AIR descriptor file. If that element doesn't need to be filled in, it's marked Optional. As you saw in the previous sample application, there are only five elements that are required.

Id

This is the unique ID of the application. It should be unique across each company's product names. Using package namespace names is highly recommended. For example, ours is `com.proflex3.introToAir`.

filename

This is the name of the file that the AIR installer uses to install the application into the operating system. There is no file extension here; AIR will manage that for you. On Windows, it'll take a value of "Intro To AIR" and make `Intro To AIR.exe`.

name

Optional. This is the application name string displayed by the AIR application installer during installation.

version

Optional. This is a developer-designated version, which can be any string. Here are some examples: 1.0.123, v1, 1.0 Alpha, BETA. Use a standardized desktop versioning scheme, such as 1.0.10, which designates a major version of the software, followed by a revision number, and finally a unique build number for tracking software.

description

Optional. This is an application description that is displayed by the AIR application installer during installation. This can be any string.

copyright

Optional. This is copyright text to be included and displayed by the AIR installer. Don't forget to include your copyright symbol (see the sidebar about inserting copyright symbols into the text file) although many of you might already know how to do this.

> *How to insert a copyright symbol into a text file varies according to the operating system you're using to develop your AIR application.*
>
> *On Windows, go to Start ⇨ All Programs ⇨ Accessories ⇨ System Tools ⇨ Character Map. A program will start that will allow you to copy special characters onto the clipboard. After you've selected your special character, © in our case, paste it into the document's destination using either the Edit ⇨ Paste or Ctrl-V.*
>
> *In OS X, it's much simpler. Press Option-G to insert the copyright symbol into a text file.*

Initial Window Tags

The following elements configure how the initial window is displayed by AIR when the application starts. A lot of the elements that are configurable in the AIR descriptor file are just properties on the `NativeWindow` object (which is discussed in further detail in Chapter 42, "Native Desktop Support with AIR").

content

This is the URL of the main SWF that is used to launch the application. When using Flex Builder, this is automatically managed for us by Flex Builder, including a reference to the main SWF file created by the Flex Builder project.

title

Optional. This is the text that is displayed in the title bar of the initial window.

systemChrome

Optional. This defines the systemChrome (the skin that provides the look and feel of the window) that is used to skin the application. This can be set to either `standard` or `none`. When it is set to `standard`, the native operating system look and feel will be used. Use standard to make your users believe they're using a native application; otherwise, set it to `none` and use your own custom skins for defining how the windows will look.

transparent

Optional. Set this to true when you want your window to be transparent and to allow the background of the desktop or external applications to be visible through the window. This offers a polished modern effect, which is becoming more and more popular in applications. This will be explained in further detail in the second sample application that follows.

visible

Optional. This property sets the window's initial visible property. In some instances when custom calculations for placing a window are needed, it might be beneficial to keep the window hidden until these calculations are performed. For example, if you're creating an instant messaging client that should always dock to the right side of the screen, the code to size and position the window should be executed before displaying the window; otherwise, the user will see the screen drawn in the default startup location and then moved to the right, which isn't a very polished behavior for an application.

minimizable

Optional. This property determines whether the `minimizable` button in the title bar is enabled, allowing the user to minimize the window to either the OS X Dock or Windows Taskbar.

maximizable

Optional. Like `minimizable`, this element configures whether the Maximize button in the title bar is enabled, allowing the user to maximize the window. On OS X, this should be set to `false`, since OS X doesn't have the concept of maximizing windows.

resizable

Optional. This element configures whether the initial window can be resized by user interaction.

width and height

Optional. This is the initial size of the window, in pixels, of the default window. Usually, a developer will have custom code that determines such values, but setting a width and height is useful for displaying splash screens.

x and y

Optional. These are the x and y coordinates where the upper-left corner of the initial window is rendered on the screen. Just as with width and height, this is probably calculated during the window's initialize event for determining how to center a window.

minSize and maxSize

Optional. These are the minimum and maximum sizes of the initial window. Values are entered as a width/height pair, with "800/600" equating to 800 pixels wide and 600 pixels tall.

The Remaining Configuration Tags

The remaining configurable XML elements in the AIR configuration file allow developers to register operating system file types, determine where to install the application, define application icons, and configure how the AIR application updates itself.

installFolder

Optional. During the installation process, the AIR installer will prompt the user for the installation location of the application with the default value that is set during this element configuration at compile time. End users have an opportunity to override the installation path if they choose to do so. In Windows, the default will be the user's Program Files directory; on OS X, it'll be the Applications directory. For example, if you set the `installFolder` element value to "Programming Flex 3," the AIR installer will place the application into either the `C:\Program files\Programming Flex 3\IntroToAir\` or `/Applications/Programming Flex 3/IntroToAir/` directories on Windows and OS X, respectively. If nothing is filled in, the application will be installed to `C:\Program files\IntroToAir` or `/Applications/IntroToAir`, which are folders based on the value populated in the `name` element of this AIR configuration file.

programMenuFolder

Optional. This is only defined for AIR applications running on the Windows operating systems. This will determine where to install the shortcut for launching the application in the system Start Menu (accessed from Start in the lower-left corner of a Windows system). If this is left blank, an icon will be placed at the top level of the Windows Start Menu.

icon

Optional. This defines the icons AIR uses to establish branding for your application. It registers with the operating system the icon used to launch the application and when it's minimized in either the OS X Dock or Windows Taskbar. It also defines the graphic used in the Windows title bar.

When no icon elements are defined, or if they remain commented out, Adobe AIR will use its own default icon to identify the application. Though it's not required, icons should be created and registered to keep end users from getting confused when they have five applications created with AIR installed on their machine, all using the default icons.

There are four different sizes that AIR can use depending on whether it's rendering the icon in a Start Menu, OS X Dock, window, and so forth. These four sizes — 16, 32, 48, 128 — define the square size of the icon. They can be configured via the `image16x16`, `image32x32`, `image48x48`, and `image128x128` XML elements, respectively. Only PNG image files are supported.

Only one of the icon size elements needs to be filled in, and AIR will scale the icon as needed for all other uses. However, if you create only a 128×128 icon, you have no control how that will look at 16×16, and if you create only a 16×16 icon, when AIR needs to display it larger, (for example, on the OS X Dock), it'll be pixilated and look terrible, so it's best to create all icon sizes listed that are manually tweaked for displaying at each resolution.

> **You won't see your custom icon until you actually build the AIR installer via export-release. While running the application from inside Flex Builder, you'll only see the default AIR icon. Don't be alarmed.**

customUpdateUI

Optional. Setting this to `true` allows the developer to have finer-grained control over how AIR manages updating applications. By default (if set to `false`), the updating mechanism of AIR has its own dialog box for managing the automatic updating of an AIR application. When this is set to `true`, AIR will bypass the default update handler and start the AIR application normally with the assumption that the developer coded the startup sequence with custom code to manage the application update.

allowBrowserInvocation

Optional. This setting has security ramifications, so be sure to read the Adobe AIR documentation for further details. Setting this to `true` will allow a link in the web browser to launch your application. This setting is probably useful behind the firewall for applications pushed out on a corporate intranet.

fileTypes

This section allows the developer to register a specific file type with the operating system that when clicked will launch the AIR application. For example, `.doc` files are usually associated with Microsoft Word, `.psd` files with Adobe Photoshop, and so forth. A custom AIR application can have its own file associations just like the aforementioned commercial applications. In this section, you customize the file types and their associated icon, which will be registered and launched.

The `fileTypes` element can have multiple `fileType` elements, each defining a custom file extension to be registered with the operating system. This could be useful for registering multiple file types with an application (JPEG, JPG, and GIF all open your custom AIR image editor software).

Each `fileType` must define a `name` and `extension`. Optionally, the `description`, `contentType` (which is a MIME type), and `icon` can be defined. Icons follow the same conventions previously discussed.

The following example might be how Adobe Photoshop, if it were written in Adobe AIR , would register its PSD file types:

```
<fileTypes>
  <fileType>
    <name>Photoshop Image</name>
    <extension>psd</extension>
    <description>Adobe Photoshop Image</description>
      <icon>
          <image16x16>icon16.png</image16x16>
          <image32x32>icon32.png</image32x32>
          <image48x48>icon48.png</image48x48>
          <image128x128>icon128.png</image128x128>
          </icon>
  </fileType>
</fileTypes>
```

That's the entire AIR description file in a nutshell. Next, we're going to expand upon our initial Intro to AIR application, tweak the configuration file a bit more, and create a modern-looking AIR application.

Building an AIR Application Part II

It's time to expand upon the initial AIR application built earlier. In this example, we're going expand upon the previous sample by adding a splash screen that shows off some of the modern look and feel of AIR with transparent native window integration. To do this, the AIR descriptor configuration file is going to need to be tweaked, taking advantage of many of the configuration elements previously described, and a new window will be created for the splash screen.

The splash screen to be created is going to look a lot like the one shown in Figure 15-4.

Figure 15-4

The splash screen isn't a conventional box. It's defined in shape by text protruding out of the top, and it's semi-transparent, allowing the desktop or other applications to be slightly visible behind it.

Modifying the IntroToAIR.mxml Window

The first thing we need to do to is modify the initial startup window, which now is going to be the splash screen.

Open the `IntroToAIR.mxml` file, and add the following code, highlighted in gray:

```
<?xml version="1.0" encoding="utf-8"?>
<mx:WindowedApplication xmlns:mx="http://www.adobe.com/2006/mxml"
  layout="absolute"
  showFlexChrome="false"
  creationComplete="onCreationComplete ();"
>
```

The `showFlexChrome` property is a property of the `WindowedApplication` component, setting it to false. This must be `false` to achieve the transparent look of the window. Otherwise, AIR will render the default `FlexChrome` for the window, which would make it look like the screen shown in Figure 15-5.

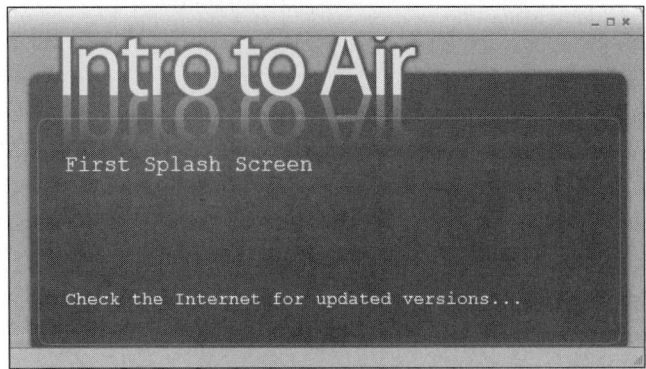

Figure 15-5

The default `FlexChrome` contains a different look and feel from the `systemChrome` setting in the application configuration file.

Next, add a handler for `creationComplete` called `onCreationComplete()` because the custom splash screen window needs to be told how to center itself in the middle of the user's screen. Add an `mx:Script` section to the file and the following code:

```
private const MESSAGE_INTERVAL:int = 900; // in milliseconds
private var loadTimer:Timer;

private function onCreationComplete ():void
{
    // Center the Window on Monitor 1 (if multi-monitor)
    var screenBounds:Rectangle = Screen(Screen.screens[0]).bounds;
    this.nativeWindow.x = (screenBounds.width - this.nativeWindow.width) / 2;
    this.nativeWindow.y = (screenBounds.height - this.nativeWindow.height) / 2;

    // Start the time that will display messages.  In a real application,
    // things will actually initialize, data will be retrieved, etc.
    loadTimer = new Timer(MESSAGE_INTERVAL);
    loadTimer.addEventListener(TimerEvent.TIMER, incrementMessage);
    loadTimer.start();
    displayLoadMessage();
}
```

The important part of this function is the calculation to determine how to center this screen. The `Screen` class is only available in AIR projects and is used to obtain information about the user's system's display (monitor) setup. `Screens.screens` returns an array of available screens (in case the user has a multimonitor setup). Get the `Rectangle`, defining the bounds of their main monitor and perform some simple math to calculate the x and y coordinates on where to position the splash screen so that it's centered on the main monitor.

Most of the remaining code, like the `loadTimer` object and the `incrementMessage` and `displayLoad Message` functions, is used to slow down the loading of the window so that it mimics a real application performing time-intensive initialization that could be anything from querying a website for an application update, to loading saved user preferences from the filesystem, or even loading the last document the user was editing when they closed the application down. It's fully up to the developer to decide what needs to be loaded while displaying the splash screen. In the demo here, they render text messages on the pop-up window, simulating loading external plug-ins. The message is displayed for a few seconds, then the `Timer` is triggered, signaling the next message to be displayed. Eventually, all the messages are displayed, and the window closes.

When the application is done loading, it'll close the splash screen window (which is the `IntroToAir.mxml` application startup), create an instance of the `MainWindow`, which is discussed in the next section, titled `MainWindow.mxml`, and open it. This is all shown here:

```
nativeWindow.close();
mainWindow = new MainWindow();
mainWindow.open();
```

Now add the following MXML markup to declare the layout for the splash screen to the `IntroToAir.mxml` file:

```
<mx:VBox backgroundImage="/assets/splash90.png" backgroundSize="585 319"
  paddingBottom="0" paddingTop="0" width="100%" height="100%" horizontalGap="0"
  verticalGap="0" >
  <mx:VBox width="100%" height="100%"
      paddingBottom="30" paddingTop="100" paddingLeft="50" paddingRight="50">
    <mx:Text text="First Splash Screen" height="100%" selectable="false"
      fontFamily="Courier New" fontSize="20" color="#ffffff"/>
      <mx:Text id="loadStatusMessage" text="Loading the application..."
        fontFamily="Courier New" fontSize="16" color="#ffffff"/>
    </mx:VBox>
    </mx:VBox>
</mx:WindowedApplication>
```

The most important part is the setting of the `backgroundImage` property of the `VBox` component to our transparent PNG, which is really the core of the display of the window. The `splash90.png` image contains all the splash screen's visuals, including the border, shadows, and the graphical text "Intro to AIR" that overlies the top edge of the splash screen.

Finally, end the declaration of our main AIR application with the closing `</mx:WindowedApplication>` component tag, which completes the definition of our newly improved AIR application.

There's more to do, and we'll continue with the building of the `MainWindow.mxml` file.

The MainWindow.mxml File

The `MainWindow.mxml` file is a simple file that contains the main application code. This is where the guts of this application will reside, which will duplicate our original AIR sample's "Welcome to AIR" message functionality!

Let's talk about the following highlighted code:

```
<mx:Window xmlns:mx="http://www.adobe.com/2006/mxml"
  layout="vertical"
  title="Intro to AIR"
```

```
    creationComplete="maximize();"
  >
    <mx:Label text="Welcome to Adobe AIR" fontSize="30" />
    <mx:Label text="(in lieu of Hello World!)" fontSize="15" />
  </mx:Window>
```

The `title` is a property of the `NativeWindow` class that you'll learn more about in Chapter 42, it gives the window a title that is displayed at the top of the window. Also, we have a `creationComplete` event handler that calls a method on the Window class to start the window maximized, filling the user's screen.

That's it for the `MainWindow.mxml`. You've probably noticed that this very similar to the `IntroToAIR.mxml` used in the first sample.

Finally, it's time to tweak the AIR descriptor, which is the last step of creating this sample.

The IntroToAIR-app.xml Descriptor File

There are many tweaks to do now to the AIR descriptor file to support things like modifying the installation folder, configuring the default window, registering a custom file type with the operating system, and so on. This section will review many of the configuration elements that were listed in detail previously, plus provide a few new comments explaining why things were done.

The first few element definitions are the same as in the previous sample application, since they're required by all AIR descriptor files:

```
<?xml version="1.0" encoding="UTF-8"?>
<application xmlns="http://ns.adobe.com/air/application/1.0">
  <id>com.proflex3.IntroToAir</id>
  <filename>Intro To Air</filename>
  <name>Intro To AIR</name>
  <version>1.0.0.100 Extremely Beta</version>
```

Here we're adding a `copyright` and `description` that will be displayed by the AIR installer during the application's installation:

```
  <description>A sample AIR application</description>
  <copyright>©2008 Todd Prekaski</copyright>
  <initialWindow>
    <content>[This value will be overwritten by Flex Builder in the output
      app.xml]</content>
```

The default window being displayed is the transparent splash screen. In order to get the transparent effect, turn off the `systemChrome` and enable transparency on the window.

Notice that you set the `systemChrome` to none, not `false`, as explained by the default comments.

Ignore the `title` element, since there's not going to be any title bar for this window:

```
        <!-- <title></title> -->
        <systemChrome>none</systemChrome>
        <transparent>true</transparent>
```

Set the `visible` element to `false` to avoid any pre-rendering of the window before it's centered:

```
<visible>false</visible>
```

There's no need to set any of the `minimizable`, `maximizable`, or `resizable` elements because there's no title bar for this window since only an image is being displayed on the screen:

```
<!-- <minimizable></minimizable> -->
<!-- <maximizable></maximizable> -->
<!-- <resizable></resizable> -->
```

Set the default width and height to be approximately the same size as the initial image. This will provide enough space on the window so that it doesn't render scrollbars, cut off any of the image, resize itself, or produce any of the other uncontrolled side effects that could occur when a component isn't properly sized.

```
<width>585</width>
<height>319</height>
```

The x and y coordinate positions for the splash screen are calculated in code in the handling of the `creationComplete` event, so there's no need to provide any values here. Also, ignore the `minSize` and `maxSize` for the same reasons that you ignored the other title bar elements:

```
<!-- <x></x> -->
<!-- <y></y> -->
<!-- <minSize></minSize> -->
<!-- <maxSize></maxSize> -->
</initialWindow>
```

Next, we configure the default `installFolder` to be "`Programming Flex 3`" to install the application at `C:\Program Files\Programming Flex 3\Intro to AIR` on Windows or `/Applications/Programming Flex 3/Intro to AIR` on OS X.

```
<installFolder>Programming Flex 3</installFolder>
```

For Windows operating systems, we define a `programMenuFolder` to create the menu in the Start Menu:

```
<programMenuFolder>Programming Flex 3</programMenuFolder>
```

Set up the default application icon to be used by AIR. Here, only the `image128x128` has been defined, but AIR will automatically scale the image to all the appropriate sizes needed:

```
<icon>
  <image128x128>/assets/logo128x128.png</image128x128>
</icon>
```

While developing and debugging the AIR application in the Flex Builder, you won't see the custom icon. A release build must be exported from the project and the AIR application installed in order to preview how the icon looks.

Finally, we define a custom file type (`.tpt`) to register with the operating system. Any files in the operating system filesystem that end with `.tpt` will launch this sample application when clicked upon, just like clicking a `.doc` file launches Microsoft Word. When a file extension is already registered with the filesystem before the AIR application is installed, it *won't* be reassigned to the configuration defined by AIR.

```
<fileTypes>
    <fileType>
        <name>Intro To AIR</name>
        <extension>tpt</extension>
        <description>Intro To AIR File Type</description>
        <icon>
            <image128x128>/assets/logo128x128.png</image128x128>
        </icon>
    </fileType>
</fileTypes>
</application>
```

That's it. The three files have been either modified or created, and the sample application is ready to launch. In the Flex Builder menu, click on Run ⇨ Run (Ctrl-F11) to see the new AIR starter application complete with transparent splash screen.

Summary

This chapter introduced AIR and built two sample applications. All AIR applications have a minimum of two files: a main MXML file that creates a `WindowedApplication` component, the equivalent to Flex's Application component for web-browser-based applications, and an AIR descriptor XML file that defines the startup and installation properties of the application.

Applications built with AIR integrate seamlessly with modern operating systems. In many instances, users of AIR applications will be completely unaware that the software they're interacting with is designed to be run on Windows, OS X, and Linux.

There are other chapters in this book covering the new AIR functionality as follows:

❑ Chapter 35, "Drag and Drop in AIR," discusses drag and drop operations between AIR applications and the user's operating system and other external applications, along with the Clipboard.

❑ Chapter 42, "Native Desktop Support with AIR," covers more Native Desktop Support, including more Toast Windows, Native Menus, Dock/Taskbar interactions, and the System Tray.

❑ Chapter 45, "Local File Management with AIR," tells all about interacting with the local filesystem.

❑ Chapter 52, "Offline Data Access with AIR," explains AIR's offline data management with the SQLite database.

❑ Chapter 69, "Desktop Deployment with AIR," covers all deployment concerns, including code signing the application and installing from a website.

❑ Chapter 70, "Dual Deployment for Flex and AIR," teaches strategies for developing Flex applications for both the web and desktop.

Part IV: Advanced Component Development

16

Custom ActionScript Components

Every Flex application is filled with components. Any time you use an MXML tag, you are using a component. MXML tags are ActionScript classes (although you will see in the next chapter how you can write custom components in MXML, too).

Suppose that you want your company's logo to appear in a number of places within your application. Perhaps the logo appears on every pop-up in the upper-left corner. The easiest way to make that happen is to create a custom component that draws or shows your company's logo and then place that component into every pop-up.

The process of creating custom components follows a formula based on the Flex framework life cycle. Success at writing components comes from understanding how Flex components come into being and how they operate while the application is running.

The following steps, illustrated with a couple of examples, are the blueprint for writing components entirely in ActionScript.

- ❑ **Instantiation** — An instance of a component class (for example, `mx.controls.Button`) is created, using the ActionScript `new` operator.

- ❑ **Setting properties** — The component instance has its properties set. For example, if you have the tag, `<mx:Button label="Submit" />`, the `Button`'s label property is set with the string, "Submit."

- ❑ **Creating child components** — The component instance may have parts that are used to make the component work. The `RichTextEditor` is a good example of this, where the `RichTextEditor`, a subclass of `Panel`, has `Button` children, a `TextArea`, and other components. At this stage, the `RichTextEditor` can create instances of these child components.

The child components then enter their own cycle of the Flex framework life cycle. They go through instantiation, setting properties, and creating child components of their own.

❑ **Committing properties** — At this stage of the life cycle, the properties can be applied to any children created in the previous step. A `Button`'s label, for instance, can be assigned to the `UITextField` child of the `Button`.

❑ **Measuring the size** — Once the properties have been applied to the component and its parts, the component may need to be measured by its parent. For example, you might have this construction:

```
<mx:HBox width="100%">
    <mx:Label text="Hello" />
    <mx:Spacer width="100%" />
    <mx:Label text="World" />
</mx:HBox>
```

❑ The Flex framework does not know how big to make any of these controls until they are measured. The `Label` controls have their text properties set so they can be asked how large they are. Once that is determined, the `HBox` can be assigned the width of its parent and the Spacer's width can be computed by subtracting the width of the two `Label`s from the width of the `HBox`.

Components that have their widths and heights explicitly set to pixel values are not measured, since their sizes are already given. If the Flex framework cannot determine how large a component is, it will ask for its measurements.

❑ **Lay out and draw** — Once all the sizes of the components are determined, they can be placed in the application. The `Button`, for example, can position its label so that it's centered. Your component may have child components; they, and all other subsequent children, can be positioned at this stage.

Company Logo Example

Let's use the company logo idea as a way to illustrate the preceding steps. The idea is that you have a graphic you want to use in a couple of places. This is ideal for a component because any time you want to repeat or duplicate something, a component lets you write it once and then reuse it wherever you need it.

Suppose that your company's logo is a purple doughnut — a purple circle with a white center. You can construct this using the Flash Drawing API by first drawing a purple filled circle and then drawing a white, filled circle over it. Suppose, too, that the logo will be different sizes: on the main application it will be 100 pixels in diameter, but on the pop-ups it will be 40 pixels in diameter.

UIComponent and IUIComponent

All components are ActionScript classes, so you need to make a file called `CompanyLogo.as`. The class must extend the `mx.core.UIComponent` class, the base class for all Flex components. The Flex framework requires components to adhere to a contract whereby each component provides a basic set of properties and functions. You could write all that yourself, but why bother when `UIComponent` is there and it implements all the required properties and functions? All you need to do is replace the properties and functions that you want to change with your own.

`mx.core.IUIComponent` is an interface that defines all the functions necessary for a class to be considered a `UIComponent`. Flex uses `IUIComponent` for variable types whenever possible. This is to avoid compiling the class definition of `UIComponent` into every file. Whenever you see `IUIComponent` used, it means the class (or instance of the class) is behaving as a `UIComponent`.

For the CompanyLogo component, you will want to:

1. **Change the measure step** — Your component will be drawn in two different sizes; one should be the default size as this helps the Flex framework with its layout stage in case someone forgets to specify a size. I recommend that the default be the size used most often.

2. **Change the layout and draw step** — The layout and draw step is the place to render the CompanyLogo component, as it has its own look, a purple doughnut.

CompanyLogo.as

Here is the complete `CompanyLogo` class:

```
package components
{
    import mx.core.UIComponent;

    public class CompanyLogo extends UIComponent
    {
        public function CompanyLogo()
        {
            super();
        }

        override protected function measure() : void
        {
            measuredWidth = 40;
            measuredHeight= 40;
        }

        override protected function updateDisplayList(unscaledWidth:Number,
            unscaledHeight:Number):void
        {
            super.updateDisplayList(unscaledWidth, unscaledHeight);

            graphics.clear();
            graphics.beginFill( 0x663399 ); // purple
            graphics.drawCircle( unscaledWidth/2, unscaledHeight/2,
                unscaledWidth/2 );
            graphics.endFill();

            graphics.beginFill( 0xffffff ); // white
            graphics.drawCircle( unscaledWidth/2, unscaledHeight/2,
                unscaledWidth/4 );
```

```
                    graphics.endFill();
           }


       }
   }
```

Starting from the top, I chose to put the component into a package called "components," but you can you place it anywhere you like.

The component extends UIComponent so it imports the mx.core.UIComponent class definition. The measure() function is an override of the measure() function in the UIComponent class. This is how you hook your component into the Flex framework. When your component is placed into an Application using MXML tags or by using a container component's addChild() function, the Flex framework will call certain functions in your class. Most of the functions will be the ones implemented by the UIComponent class. Key functions, such as measure(), are ones that you override to customize the component and make it unique.

In this class, the measure() function sets two variables, which are members of the UIComponent class: measuredWidth and measuredHeight. These variables are both set to 40 because the default size of the CompanyLogo component should be 40 pixels.

The updateDisplayList() function is also overridden. This is the function used to lay out the component. For the CompanyLogo, it is the place where the logo is rendered or visualized. In case you are not familiar with the Flash Drawing API, the code in updateDisplayList() uses the graphics property, clearing it (erasing any previous drawings); sets the fill color to purple; draws a circle in the center of the component; then draws a white circle on top of that.

The values of unscaledWidth *and* unscaledHeight *are either the explicit width and height given to the component when the component is created, the values determined by the* measure() *method, or values assigned by the component's parent container.*

You can test this component by creating a simple Flex application, as shown here:

```
<?xml version="1.0" encoding="utf-8"?>
<mx:Application xmlns:mx="http://www.adobe.com/2006/mxml"
    layout="absolute" xmlns:ns1="components.*">

    <ns1:CompanyLogo x="170" y="170" />

</mx:Application>
```

An instance of the CompanyLogo component (see Figure 16-1) is placed on the screen with its upper-left corner at (170,170) and a diameter of 40 pixels.

Figure 16-1

Now change the MXML tag to:

```
<ns1:CompanyLogo x="170" y="170" width="100" height="100" />
```

The CompanyLogo now appears at the same location but is 100 pixels in diameter. When you specify the width and height explicitly like this, the `measure()` function is not called — the Flex framework already knows how big it should be. The width and height are passed to the `updateDisplayList()` function in the `unscaledWidth` and `unscaledHeight` parameters.

You now have a component that you can use throughout your program.

Component Structure

The CompanyLogo example shows a very simple, static component that just has a visual aspect. The component is able to plug into the Flex framework because it extends `UIComponent`. This means that the Flex framework can cast this component to `IUIComponent` and use it generically. The framework can manipulate the component (e.g., set its position, resize it), and the component will behave properly.

The customization of a component happens because of the function overrides in the component class. For example, the CompanyLogo component is "custom" because:

❑ **It overrides `measure()`** — This means that the Flex framework can invoke the component's `getExplicitOrMeasuredWidth()` function, and the component either returns 40 (the value `measuredWidth` is set to) or whatever value was explicitly set by the developer using the component (`width="100"`, for example).

❑ **It overrides `updateDisplayList()`** — This means that the component will have a visual aspect. If you want to write a component that does not have a visual aspect, you can leave this step out. You may want to write a class that can appear as an MXML tag but does not have any appearance in the final program. Classes such as a `RemoteObject` and `DateFormatter` fall into this category.

There are other functions that you will wind up overriding as your components become more complex:

❑ **`createChildren()`** — This function is called to give a component an opportunity to create any child components. For example, the `Button` component creates a label by using the `UITextField` class. The `TabNavigator` creates a `TabBar` and a `ViewStack`. The `ColorPicker` creates a pop-up and a small color well.

❑ **`commitProperties()`** — This function is called once all of a components' properties have been set and all of the children have been created. The `commitProperties()` function is where the properties can be applied to the component and its children. For example, a component that scrolls a message would set the message text.

Component Properties and the Flex Framework Life Cycle

When you make your own component, you need to determine what the user of your component can and cannot change. It can be difficult to decide sometimes because you also have to take into account the component's longevity and how it will be maintained and enhanced.

One way to give components more flexibility is with public properties. A *public property* is a member of the component class, which can be set using ActionScript code or from MXML tags. The convention, when writing a component, is to use setter and getter functions for properties. By using functions, instead of simple public variables, you retain a value and may execute other code.

For example, take the Flex HSlider. The HSlider has a property called value. You can change the value at runtime, as follows:

```
<mx:HSlider id="interestRate" minimum="1" maximum="10" />
...
interestRate.value = 6.25;
```

When the value property is set to 6.25 the HSlider's thumb moves to indicate 6.25. That happens because the value property is a setter and getter function, much like this:

```
private var _value:Number;
public function get value() : Number
{
    return _value;
}
public function set value( val:Number ) : void
{
    _value = val;
    invalidateDisplayList();
}
```

Notice the private variable, _value. This is a convention used throughout the Flex framework: any setter and getter property has a *backing variable* of the same name, but prefixed with an underscore (_). The setter functions immediately set the backing variable with the value they are given. The backing variable's sole purpose is to be returned from the property getter function; otherwise, the backing store variable is rarely used and only accessed by using the getter function.

Invalidate Functions

The setter function not only sets the backing store variable, but most often it calls an invalidate function. In this case it is invalidateDisplayList().

The invalidate functions set flags that the Flex framework uses as it runs your application. When invalidateDisplayList() is called, it sets a flag to indicate that the updateDisplayList() function should be called.

An obvious question to ask is, "Why not call the function directly?" There are three reasons why you should not call the Flex framework functions directly in your code:

1. Imagine that for each property you could set on a component you called updateDisplayList() directly. That function takes two parameters, unscaledWidth and unscaledHeight. What would you pass in for those values?

2. Imagine that updateDisplayList() drew something complex and used the values of several properties in its calculations. If updateDisplayList() were called after each property was changed, the user might see the graphics flicker as each property took effect. This not only slows performance but also gives a bad experience to the user.

3. Imagine that a property is being used to set a child component. If the setter function were to attempt to update the child component, there is a good possibility that the child component would not yet exist to be updated. That would happen when a component was being instantiated and the property setter was called before the `createChildren()` function was called to create the child component.

If your component has a number of properties being set and each one calls an invalidate function, all that happens is that some flags are set, nothing more. You can change 10 properties and call `invalidate DisplayList()` 10 times. When the Flex framework deems it appropriate, `updateDisplayList()` will be called and the function can then incorporate those properties' values into a single rendering. The user will only see the final result.

Adding Child Components

More often than not, your component is going to need child components. Adding text is a good example. While the `Button` control looks simple enough, it actually has a child component that is its label. Text is displayed on the screen using the Flash Player's `TextField` class. The Flex `Text` and `Label` controls use an extended version of `TextField` called `UITextField` that contains helpful properties and events to make using text in Flex applications a lot easier. `Button` uses `UITextField` as well.

If your component needs to display text, you can use `UITextField` or even the Flex `Text` and `Label` controls. The difference is performance. The `UITextField` is lighter — it is just a wrapper for `TextField` turning it into a Flex component, and it does not have all the overhead that `Label` and `Text` have. On the other hand, if you want to have a complex layout and sizing constraints, using the Flex `Text` and `Label` components will make your control easier to write. But for simple `Label`s, `UITextField` works just fine.

You create child components by overriding the `createChildren()` function. Here is how you would create a `UITextField` child:

```
private var textField:UITextField;

override protected function createChildren() : void
{
    textField = new UITextField();
    addChild(textField);

    super.createChildren();
}
```

First you create an instance of `UITextField` and then you add it to the display list of your component. You must use `addChild()` to hook the component into the Flex framework. This will trigger the Flex framework life cycle on the child component.

Use `createChildren()` to set up event listeners, too. For example, you might want to know when the mouse has moved over your component or when the mouse has been clicked on your component:

```
override protected function createChildren() : void
{
    textField = new UITextField();
    addChild(textField);
    addEventListener( MouseEvent.MOUSE_OVER, handleMouse );
```

```
        addEventListener.MouseEvent.CLICK, handleMouse );
        textField.addEventListener( TextEvent.LINK, handleLink );

        super.createChildren();
    }
```

When you create your child components, you can set their properties and styles, too. Here is an example of setting up the `textField` child to have a bold, centered, red font and initial text of "Hello There." Calling `setStyle()` before adding children is a good practice, as it is less resource-intensive. Once a component has been made a child, `setStyle()` can add a lot of overhead, since style changes typically require components to be remeasured.

```
override protected function createChildren() : void
{
    textField = new UITextField();
    textField.text = "Hello There";
    textField.setStyle("color", 0xFF0000);
    textField.setStyle("fontWeight", "bold");
    textField.setStyle("textAlign", "center");
    addChild(textField);

    super.createChildren();
}
```

Once your child components are created and properties are set, the Flex framework will invoke `commitProperties()`.

Using invalidateProperties() and Applying Properties to the Component

As previously mentioned, the property set functions on your component will (most likely) be called before `createChildren()` is called and so the property setter functions shouldn't attempt to modify the child components' properties. Instead, a setter property should use the `invalidateProperties()` function to signal the Flex framework to call `commitProperties()` when appropriate.

> *If you have a lot of properties, the Flex framework may not have time to set all of the properties. It is possible that some properties will be set after* `createChildren()` *has been called. Since you do not know the order of the calls to the property setter functions or when they will be called with regard to* `createChildren()`, *you should use* `invalidateProperties()` *and apply them in the* `commitProperties()` *function.*

Suppose that the value of your `textField` is not static as in the previous example but can be set from a property. A very common example is to have a label property on a component:

```
private var _label:String = "Hello There";  // set a default value

public function get label() : String
{
    return _label;
}
```

```
public function set label( value:String ) : void
{
    _label = value;
    invalidateProperties();
}
```

The label property, a setter and getter function pair along with setting the backing variable, _label, invokes invalidateProperties() whenever it is changed.

Later, the Flex framework will invoke commitProperties() where you can apply the label to the textField:

```
override protected function commitProperties() : void
{
    super.commitProperties();
    textField.text = label;
}
```

Measuring Components

Measuring a component may not always happen. If the component has been given an explicit size, there is no need to measure it. Also, the parent container of the component may assign a size when it does its own layout.

However, your components should always override the measure() function and provide, at least, a default size. Sometimes this will be easy, sometimes more complex.

With the CompanyLogo component, setting a default size was easy. You just picked something that looked right or that the copyright department of your company suggested.

If have a component with child components, determining a default size may not be so obvious. Suppose that you have a component that is providing breadcrumbs for navigation purposes. The component would have a varying number of children. For example, in one case there could be a "Home" breadcrumb. Later, there might be a chain of them: "Home," "Forms," "Employee Time Sheets," and the like (see Figure 16-2).

Figure 16-2

Providing an accurate measurement means that your component can be used in containers such as HBox and VBox, which rely on their child components to provide accurate sizes.

The real purpose of the measure() method is not to set a default size, but to set two variables that are members of the base class, UIComponent. The measure() method should set the measuredWidth and measuredHeight variables. The measure() method can also set the measuredMinWidth and measured MinHeight variables, which are used by containers such as an HDividedBox and VDividedBox. A minimum size can also help when the framework is trying to determine if a component should get scrollbars or not.

Suppose that you are writing this breadcrumb navigation component. Here is how the `measure()` method might look:

```
override protected function measure() : void
{
    super.measure();

    var mw:Number = 0; // measured width total
    var mh:Number = 0; // max. measured height
    var n:Number = numChildren; // the number of breadcrumbs

    for(var i:int=0; i < n; i++)
    {
        var child:UIComponent = getChildAt(i) as UIComponent;
        mw += child.getExplicitOrMeasuredWidth();
        mh = Math.max(mh, child.getExplicitOrMeasuredHeight());
    }

    measuredWidth = mw;
    measuredHeight = mh;
}
```

Within the loop you can see that each child has its `getExplicitOrMeasuredWidth()` and `getExplicitOrMeasuredHeight()` function called. These functions returns either the child's explicit width (or height) or the child's `measuredWidth` (or `measuredHeight`) size.

Component Layout

Once a component has been measured, the Flex framework instructs each component to draw itself. Because Flex applications are hierarchical, your component will be called upon to draw itself, which in turn, causes your child components to draw themselves and so forth.

The Flex framework does this by calling your component's `updateDisplayList()` function. The framework may also call this function because your component's `invalidateDisplayList()` function was called (such as from a property setter function).

The job of the `updateDisplayList()` function is to size and position the child components and to draw any graphics. This may seem odd, given that the `measure()` function calls upon the child component's measuring functions, but remember that `measure()` may not be called.

More important, invoking `getExplicitOrMeasuredWidth()` does not set a component's width. Only setting the component's width property explicitly sets the component's width. In most cases, your child components will not have their width and height properties set when `updateDisplayList()` is called.

All that has happened, so far, is to help the framework determine sizes, not set them. Consider a component that has a `Button` and a `Label`:

```
package components
{
    import mx.controls.Button;
```

```
import mx.core.UIComponent;
import mx.core.UITextField;

public class ButtonAndLabel extends UIComponent
{
    public function ButtonAndLabel()
    {
        super();
    }

    private var label:UITextField;
    private var button:Button;

    override protected function createChildren():void
    {
        super.createChildren();

        label = new UITextField();
        label.text = "Select:";
        addChild(label);

        button = new Button();
        button.label = "Press Me";
        addChild(button);
    }

}
```

If you put this component into an `Application` all you will see is the label, "Select:", appearing on the screen but not the `Button`. The reason is that the `UITextField` determines its own size based on the setting of its text property. The `Button`, unfortunately, does not. Some controls you must explicitly size.

Going back to the breadcrumb navigator component example, its version of `updateDisplayList()` would position its children end to end:

```
override protected function updateDisplayList( unscaledWidth:Number,
    unscaledHeight:Number ) : void
{
    super.updateDisplayList( unscaledWidth, unscaledHeight );
    var n:Number = numChildren;
    var xpos:Number = 0;
    var ypos:Number = 0;
    for(var i:int =0; i < n; i++)
    {
        var child:UIComponent = getChildAt(i) as UIComponent;
        child.move( xpos, ypos );
        child.setActualSize( child.getExplicitOrMeasuredWidth(),
                            child.getExplicitOrMeasuredHeight() );
        xpos += child.getExplicitOrMeasuredWidth();
    }
}
```

Here, `updateDisplayList()` loops through the children, moves them into place (the `move()` function is just a handy way to set the x and y properties) and gives them their real sizes (`setActualSize()` is a handy way to set the width and height properties).

Selecting the Base Class for Your Component

So far you have seen `mx.core.UIComponent` being used as the base class of a component. This is a good choice for components that:

❑ Need to have complete control over the positioning of their child components

❑ Do not want any extra properties or layout that another component or container may offer

However, using an existing component as a base class can save you some time. For example, in the breadcrumb navigator example, you may have noticed how similar the component is to an `HBox`: the children are laid out end to end. The differences, are that there is no gap between them and the children were not specified by using MXML tags, but rather are specified using a custom `dataProvider`. Otherwise, the component is just like an `HBox`.

Using an existing Flex component, especially a container component, can make your components smaller and easier to maintain. Using the breadcrumb navigator as an example, suppose that the children of the breadcrumb navigator are `Buttons`. You want to make a navigator that would work like this:

```
<mx:HBox horizontalGap="0">
    <mx:Button label="Home" />
    <mx:Button label="Forms" />
    <mx:Button label="Employee Time Sheets" />
    <mx:Button label="Report Time Off" />
</mx:HBox>
```

The exception is that you cannot specify the `Buttons` in MXML because you need the component to accept a list of places visited, which can change at any time. What you really want is something more like this:

```
<components:BreadcrumbBar dataProvider="{crumbs}" />
```

where the crumbs `dataProvider` might be an `ArrayCollection`. The `BreadcrumbBar` has to create the `Buttons` from the data and lay them out end to end.

Fortunately, the `HBox` can take care of the layout problem. All the component needs to do is create the `Button` children and respond to changes in the `dataProvider`. Here is the `BreadcrumbBar` code:

```
package components
{
    import mx.collections.ArrayCollection;
    import mx.containers.HBox;
    import mx.controls.Button;

    public class BreadcrumbBar extends HBox
```

```
    {
        public function BreadcrumbBar()
        {
            super();

            setStyle("horizontalGap",0);
        }

        private var _dataProvider:ArrayCollection;
        public function get dataProvider() : ArrayCollection
        {
            return _dataProvider;
        }
        public function set dataProvider( value:ArrayCollection ) : void
        {
            _dataProvider = value;
            invalidateProperties();
        }

        override protected function commitProperties():void
        {
            super.commitProperties();

            if( dataProvider )
            {
                for(var i:int = 0; i &lt; dataProvider.length; i++)
                {
                    var item:Object = dataProvider.getItemAt(i);
                    var child:Button = new Button();
                    child.label = item.label;
                    addChild(child);
                }
            }
        }

    }
}
```

Notice that the dataProvider property is a setter and getter function pair, but the setter does not call invalidateDisplayList() — it calls invalidateProperties().

Also notice that the child components are not created in createChildren(). In this case, the children are not known when createChildren() is called and createChildren() is called only once; remember, the properties may not be set when createChildren() is called. It would not be possible to create the Button children in createChildren in this circumstance. The commitProperties() function is a better location.

What you do not see is the measure() and updateDisplayList() functions. That is because the HBox class takes care of measuring the children and positioning them for you. Depending on the layout and other needs of your component, another class besides UIComponent, might be a better class on which to base your component.

Sizing Child Components

Another important consideration when creating your children is their size. How this works depends on what your component's base class is. The `UIComponent` class makes no assumptions and offers no assistance for sizing and placing your child components. If, on the other hand, you were extending `HBox`, then you could have the `HBox` class help size your children.

Suppose that you are creating a component that has a `Label` and a `TextInput` field. You want the `TextInput` field to always take up as much room as possible. If you use `UIComponent`, you can override `updateDisplayList()` and do a little math with the width of the component (the value of the `unscaledWidth` parameter) and the width of the label (using its `getExplicitOrMeasuredWidth()` function) to determine how large to make the `TextInput` control.

Or you could use an `HBox` as the base class and set the `TextInput` control's width to 100 percent. You can do that using the component's `percentWidth` property:

```
override protected function createChildren() : void
{
    super.createChildren();
    label = new Label();
    addChild(label);

    input = new TextInput();
    input.percentWidth = 100;
    addChild(input);
}

override protected function commitProperties() : void
{
    super.commitProperties();
    label.text = labelField;
}
```

By using `HBox` as the base class and by setting the `TextInput` child component's `percentWidth` property to 100, you leave the layout problem to the `HBox` code.

If you decided to use `UIComponent` instead of `HBox`, you would have to determine the size and position of the child components yourself. In other words, the `percentWidth` property does not influence the size or position of the `TextInput` child. You could examine it and use it to determine what to do, but there is nothing automatic that is going to happen if the property is set.

Here is how you might lay out this component if you used `UIComponent` instead of `HBox` as the base class:

```
override protected function updateDisplayList( unscaledWidth:Number,
                                               unscaledHeight:Number ) : void
{
    super.updateDisplayList(unscaledWidth,unscaledHeight);

    label.move(0,0);
    label.setActualSize( label.getExplicitOrMeasuredWidth(),
                         label.getExplicitOrMeasuredHeight() );
```

```
        input.move( label.getExplicitOrMeasuredWidth(), 0 );
        var remainder:Number = unscaledWidth - label.getExplicitOrMeasuredWidth();
        input.setActualSize( remainder, input.getExplicitOrMeasuredHeight());
    }
```

The important thing to remember is that while UIComponent gives you complete freedom with your component, it also means that you are responsible for doing most of the work. Choosing another component class as your base class can save you time.

RockerSwitch Example

This next example is a bit more complex and shows how to make a component react to the mouse. You will see that it follows the same pattern and uses the functions previously discussed.

The component is called RockerSwitch because it looks like a two-sided button (see Figure 16-3). Clicking on the left and right sides dispatch the same event (an mx.events.ItemClickEvent), but with different values. You could imagine using the RockerSwitch as a volume control or scroll between the children of a ViewStack.

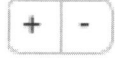

Figure 16-3

The RockerSwitch begins the same way as the CompanyLogo component: by extending UIComponent:

```
package components
{
    import mx.core.UIComponent;

    public class RockerSwitch extends UIComponent
    {
        public function RockerSwitch()
        {
            super();
        }
    }
}
```

Detecting the mouse is pretty easy in Flex, but to make it even easier and to make the control easier to build, the RockerSwitch has two children: leftButton and rightButton:

```
package components
{
    import mx.core.UIComponent;
    import flash.display.Sprite;

    public class RockerSwitch extends UIComponent
    {
        public function RockerSwitch()
```

```
        {
            super();
        }

        private var leftButton:Sprite;
        private var rightButton:Sprite;
    }
}
```

Unless you are familiar with Flash, you may not recognize the Sprite. The Flash Sprite provides a graphics property so that you can draw vector graphics, and it provides for mouse detection. That is, you can set up event listeners on a Sprite to detect when the mouse has been clicked or moved over the Sprite. Remember that Flex is based upon Flash, so you can use Flash classes in Flex. A Sprite is a very lightweight class, which means that your component will not take up much memory and will execute faster. You can use a Flex component such as Canvas or even Button, with some modifications. But using Sprite is really more appropriate here.

You can add an override for createChildren() to the RockerSwitch class, so the leftButton and rightButton children are created:

```
override protected function createChildren() : void
{
    super.createChildren();

    leftButton = new Sprite();
    addChild(leftButton);

    rightButton = new Sprite();
    addChild(rightButton);
}
```

When the Flex framework calls createChildren(), the leftButton and rightButton Sprites are created and added as children to the RockerSwitch component.

The next step is to add in measure() and set a default size for the component. Using a width of 40 pixels and a height of 20 pixels makes the component a comfortable size.

```
override protected function measure() : void
{
    super.measure();

    measuredWidth = 40;
    measuredHeight = 20;
}
```

Remember, someone using this component can explicitly set its size using width and height properties, and the measure() function will not be called at all.

At this point, you can make the RockerSwitch draw itself by overriding updateDisplayList():

```
override protected function updateDisplayList(unscaledWidth:Number,
                                    unscaledHeight:Number):void
{
```

```
            super.updateDisplayList(unscaledWidth,unscaledHeight);

            // Position the leftButton and draw it.
            leftButton.x = 0;
            leftButton.y = 0;
            leftButton.graphics.clear();
            leftButton.graphics.lineStyle(0,0);
            leftButton.graphics.beginFill(0xCCCCCC,1);
            leftButton.graphics.drawRoundRectComplex(0, 0,
                    unscaledWidth/2, unscaledHeight,
                    4,0,4,0);
            leftButton.graphics.endFill();

            // Position the rightButton and draw it.
            rightButton.x = unscaledWidth/2;
            rightButton.y = 0;
            rightButton.graphics.clear();
            rightButton.graphics.lineStyle(0,0);
            rightButton.graphics.beginFill(0xCCCCCC,1);
            rightButton.graphics.drawRoundRectComplex(0, 0,
                    unscaledWidth/2, unscaledHeight,
                    0,4,0,4);
    }
```

As you can see, aside from the complexity of the graphics, the `updateDisplayList()` function is not that much different from the one in CompanyLogo. The exception is that the graphics properties of the `leftButton` and `rightButton` are used instead of the graphics property of the component itself.

You can begin to test this component by placing it into a sample Flex application:

```
<?xml version="1.0" encoding="utf-8"?>
<mx:Application xmlns:mx="http://www.adobe.com/2006/mxml"
                layout="absolute"
                xmlns:ns1="components.*">

    <ns1:RockerSwitch x="170" y="170" />

</mx:Application>
```

At this point, the `RockerSwitch` has its left and right sides but is missing the + and - labels. You could draw these shapes, but using a `UITextField` can give the component diversity and allow someone using it to change the symbols.

To this component a couple more properties are added:

```
/**
 * Label for the leftButton, default to +
 */
private var _leftLabel:String = "+";
public function get leftLabel() : String
{
    return _leftLabel;
}
public function set leftLabel(value:String) : void
```

```
{
    _leftLabel = value;
    invalidateProperties();
}

/**
 * Label for the rightButton, default to -
 */
private var _rightLabel:String = "-";
public function get rightLabel() : String
{
    return _rightLabel;
}
public function set rightLabel(value:String) : void
{
    _rightLabel = value;
    invalidateProperties();
}
```

Notice how these properties simply set their corresponding backing variables and call
`invalidateProperties()`.

The `UITextFields` to display these labels are also added:

```
/**
 * The textField for the leftButton label
 */
private var leftTextField:UITextField;

/**
 * The textField for the rightButton label
 */
private var rightTextField:UITextField;
```

The `createChildren()` function is modified to create these `UITextFields` and add them as children
to the component:

```
override protected function createChildren() : void
{
    super.createChildren();

    leftButton = new Sprite();
    addChild(leftButton);

    leftTextField = new UITextField();
    leftTextField.selectable = false;
    leftTextField.mouseEnabled = false;
    addChild(leftTextField);

    rightButton = new Sprite();
    addChild(rightButton);

    rightTextField = new UITextField();
    rightTextField.selectable = false;
```

```
        rightTextField.mouseEnabled = false;
        addChild(rightTextField);
    }
```

The `commitProperties()` function is now added to apply these labels to the `UITextFields` (see Figure 16-4):

```
override protected function commitProperties():void
{
    super.commitProperties();

    rightTextField.text = rightLabel;
    leftTextField.text = leftLabel;
}
```

<<	>>

Figure 16-4

Once you have this component up and running, you can begin to add the mouse event handling.

Handling events within a component is no different from handling events elsewhere in your program. Once the child components are created, you can assign event listeners to them that will handle the events:

```
private var leftProperties:Object;
private var rightProperties:Object;

override protected function createChildren() : void
{
    super.createChildren();

    leftButton = new Sprite();
    addChild(leftButton);
    leftButton.addEventListener(MouseEvent.MOUSE_OVER, handleMouse);
    leftButton.addEventListener(MouseEvent.MOUSE_OUT,  handleMouse);
    leftButton.addEventListener(MouseEvent.MOUSE_DOWN, handleMouse);
    leftButton.addEventListener(MouseEvent.MOUSE_UP,   handleMouse);
    leftButton.addEventListener(MouseEvent.CLICK,      handleMouse);

    leftTextField = new UITextField();
    leftTextField.selectable = false;
    leftTextField.mouseEnabled = false;
    addChild(leftTextField);

    leftProperties = { borderColor:0xCCCCCC,
        backgroundColor:0xFFFFFF, alpha:0.85 };

    rightButton = new Sprite();
    addChild(rightButton);
    rightButton.addEventListener(MouseEvent.MOUSE_OVER, handleMouse);
    rightButton.addEventListener(MouseEvent.MOUSE_OUT,  handleMouse);
    rightButton.addEventListener(MouseEvent.MOUSE_DOWN, handleMouse);
```

```
    rightButton.addEventListener(MouseEvent.MOUSE_UP,    handleMouse);
    rightButton.addEventListener(MouseEvent.CLICK,       handleMouse);

    rightTextField = new UITextField();
    rightTextField.selectable = false;
    rightTextField.mouseEnabled = false;
    addChild(rightTextField);

    rightProperties = { borderColor:0xCCCCCC,
        backgroundColor:0xFFFFFF, alpha:0.85 };
}
```

Included in the above code are two additional variables: leftProperties and rightProperties. These simple objects, also created in createChildren(), are changed by the mouse event handler, handleMouse(), and are used by updateDisplayList(), shown here:

```
private function handleMouse( event:MouseEvent ) : void
{
    var buttonProperties:Object;
    var buttonIndex:int;

    // Determine which button was selected and set the local variables. This
    // reduces the amount of code below by predetermining which button was
    // picked.

    if( event.currentTarget == leftButton ) {
        buttonProperties = leftProperties;
        buttonIndex = ROCKER_LEFT;
    }
    else {
        buttonProperties = rightProperties;
        buttonIndex = ROCKER_RIGHT;
    }

    // The buttonProperties are changed depending on the event. In the case of a
    // click, an ItemClickEvent is dispatched.

    switch( event.type )
    {
        case MouseEvent.MOUSE_OVER:
        case MouseEvent.MOUSE_UP:
            buttonProperties.backgroundColor =
                ColorUtil.adjustBrightness2(getStyle("themeColor"),80);
            break;
        case MouseEvent.MOUSE_OUT:
            buttonProperties.backgroundColor = 0xFFFFFF;
            break;
        case MouseEvent.MOUSE_DOWN:
            buttonProperties.backgroundColor =
                ColorUtil.adjustBrightness2(getStyle("themeColor"),50);
            break;
        case MouseEvent.CLICK:
            var newEvent:ItemClickEvent =
                new ItemClickEvent(ItemClickEvent.ITEM_CLICK);
```

```
                    newEvent.index = buttonIndex;
                    dispatchEvent( newEvent );
        }

        // Since the button needs to be redrawn with the new colors,
        // signal the Flex framework to call updateDisplayList() by using
        // invalidateDisplayList(). Never call updateDisplayList
        // directly.

        invalidateDisplayList();
    }
```

The `handleMouse()` event listener uses the event's `currentTarget` property to determine which side of the `RockerSwitch` the mouse event occurred on. Knowing this sets the `buttonProperties` local variable to either the `leftProperties` or `rightProperties` object. The local variable, `buttonIndex`, is also set to either `ROCKER_LEFT` or `ROCKER_RIGHT`.

Next, the event's type determines what actions to take. Here, a `MOUSE_OVER` or `MOUSE_UP` sets the `button Properties.backgroundColor` to a light shade of the `themeColor` style. The `MOUSE_OUT` event restores the color to white. The `MOUSE_DOWN` event sets the `buttonProperties.backgroundColor` to a medium shade of the `themeColor`. The `CLICK` event does something different.

When a `CLICK` happens, an event is dispatched by the `RockerSwitcher`. The `mx.events.ItemClick` event is a common Flex event used by navigators to identify which item of the navigator was clicked. Here, the event's index property is set to the value of `buttonIndex`, set at the top of the function.

Once the switch statement completes, a call is made to `invalidateDisplayList()`. As you know now, this triggers a call to `updateDisplayList()`, modified here:

```
override protected function updateDisplayList( unscaledWidth:Number,
                                               unscaledHeight:Number):void
{
    super.updateDisplayList(unscaledWidth,unscaledHeight);

    // Position the leftButton and draw it.
    leftButton.x = 0;
    leftButton.y = 0;
    leftButton.graphics.clear();
    leftButton.graphics.lineStyle(0,leftProperties.borderColor);
    leftButton.graphics.beginFill(leftProperties.backgroundColor,
        leftProperties.alpha);
    leftButton.graphics.drawRoundRectComplex( 0, 0,
            unscaledWidth/2,unscaledHeight,
            4,0,4,0);
    leftButton.graphics.endFill();

    // position the left label
    leftTextField.move((unscaledWidth/2-
                    leftTextField.getExplicitOrMeasuredWidth())/2,
        (unscaledHeight-leftTextField.getExplicitOrMeasuredHeight())/2);

    // Position the rightButton and draw it.
    rightButton.x = unscaledWidth/2;
```

```
        rightButton.y = 0;
        rightButton.graphics.clear();
        rightButton.graphics.lineStyle(0,rightProperties.borderColor);
        rightButton.graphics.beginFill(rightProperties.backgroundColor,
            rightProperties.alpha);
        rightButton.graphics.drawRoundRectComplex( 0 ,0,
            unscaledWidth/2,unscaledHeight,
            0,4,0,4);

        // position the right label
        rightTextField.move(unscaledWidth/2+(unscaledWidth/2-
                        rightTextField.getExplicitOrMeasuredWidth())/2,
            (unscaledHeight-
            rightTextField.getExplicitOrMeasuredHeight())/2);
    }
```

You can see that `updateDisplayList()` is only slightly changed: the `lineStyle` and `fill` properties of the graphics for the `leftButton` and `rightButton` now use the values of `leftProperties` and `rightProperties`.

The entire cycle looks like this:

1. The `RockerSwitch` is created.

2. The `RockerSwitch.createChildren()` is called, creating the `leftButton`, `leftLabel`, `rightButton`, `rightLabel`, `leftProperties`, and `rightProperties`.

3. The `RockerSwitch.commitProperties()` is called to set the `leftLabel` and `rightLabel` text properties.

4. The `RockerSwitch.measure()` method may be called.

5. The `RockerSwitch.updateDisplayList()` is called, drawing the left and right sides using the values contained in the `leftProperties` and `rightProperties` objects. The `leftText Field` and `rightTextField` are also sized and positioned.

6. Some time later, the mouse moves over the `leftButton` Sprite. This triggers the `handle Mouse()` function with the `event.type` set to `MOUSE_OVER`.

7. The `handleMouse()` function sets the `backgroundColor` of `leftProperties`.

8. The `handleMouse()` function calls `invalidateDisplayList()`, telling the Flex framework to call `updateDisplayList()` when it can.

9. Some time later, `updateDisplayList()` is called. The `leftButton` is drawn using the updated values of `leftProperties`, giving the user feedback that the mouse has been detected over the `leftButton` of the `RockerSwitch`.

A similar pattern follows when the mouse leaves or is clicked.

Summary

Although you can say that everything you write in Flex is a custom component, a better definition of custom components is that they are components to be reused, either within a single application or by many applications.

The Flex framework life cycle is an important part of building a successful component. The functions you override in your component classes, such as `updateDisplayList()`, are never called directly; instead, they are called by the framework in response to calls to the invalidate functions from property setter functions. The cyclical nature of the framework makes this all possible.

Further, it is perfectly safe to make multiple calls to the invalidate functions, such as `invalidateProperties()` and `invalidateDisplayList()`. Since these calls set indicators and do not perform any other tasks, calling them multiple times only results in a single action once the framework gets around to servicing them.

The next chapter, "Custom MXML Components," shows how MXML files are nearly identical to ActionScript files when it comes to creating custom components. Using MXML files can speed up your development time and make laying out your custom components much easier.

17

Custom MXML Components

Flex MXML application files are nothing more than a quicker way to create ActionScript classes. The Flex `mxmlc` compiler converts every MXML file into an ActionScript class file. You can see the result of this by adding `-keep-generated-actionscript=true` to your compiler options.

This means that if you have been writing custom components in ActionScript, you can also write custom components in MXML, as you will see in this chapter.

MXML Versus ActionScript Components

You may be under the impression that using MXML files adds overhead — extra code and variables — that your application could do without if you were to write everything in ActionScript. That is technically true, to a degree.

For example, if you take the `CompanyLogo` example from the previous chapter and put the code into a `<mx:Script>` block of an MXML file using `<mx:Canvas>` as the root tag, you would be correct in your assumption. Using `Canvas` as the base class for such a component would add extra code as the `Canvas` has code in it to help manage its children. The `CompanyLogo` component has no children, so using `UIComponent` as its base class makes sense.

However, if you assume that you could write the `CompanyLogo` component in ActionScript and, using a `Canvas` as its base class, it would be more efficient than using an MXML file, you would be wrong. In other words, it is not so much that you are using MXML files versus ActionScript files, it is using `Canvas` versus `UIComponent` as the base class that makes a difference.

Writing custom components using MXML makes sense when you are looking for simplification. For example, if you need your component to extend any container classes, such as `HBox` or `VBox`, using MXML files can make writing your component quicker and easier to maintain.

Here is another example: a ComboBox that lists several types of parts. The first is an ActionScript class:

```
package components
{
    import mx.collections.ArrayCollection;
    import mx.controls.ComboBox;

    public class PartsListSelector extends ComboBox
    {
        public function PartsListSelector()
        {
            super();

            dataProvider = new ArrayCollection(
                        [ {label:"Widget", part:"WDG-1000"},
                          {label:"Gizmo", part:"GZM-2033"},
                          {label:"Cog", part:"COG-900"},
                          {label:"Gadget", part:"GDT-5400"},
                          {label:"Thingy", part:"TGY-3333"} ]
                );
        }

    }
}
```

This is the MXML equivalent:

```
<?xml version="1.0" encoding="utf-8"?>
<mx:ComboBox xmlns:mx="http://www.adobe.com/2006/mxml">
  <mx:dataProvider>
        <mx:Object label="Widget" part="WDG-1000" />
        <mx:Object label="Gizmo" part="GZM-2033" />
        <mx:Object label="Cog" part="COG-900" />
        <mx:Object label="Gadget" part="GDT-5400" />
        <mx:Object label="Thingy" part="TGY-3333" />
  </mx:dataProvider>
</mx:ComboBox>
```

You decide which you want to use and maintain. Both components do the same thing — they can be used as MXML tags or created with ActionScript. Because both components have ComboBox as their base class, there is little difference between the generated code from the MXML file and the ActionScript code above.

At this point you should be thinking of MXML files as just another way to write ActionScript classes. The root tag of an MXML file is the equivalent of using the extends ActionScript keyword when defining a class.

Some things are easier to do with MXML files, for example:

❑ You can declare event listeners on the root tag instead of using the constructor function or an override of the createChildren() function.

❑ You can set up data binding using curly brace syntax in MXML tags as opposed to the BindingUtils ActionScript class.

Customizing the Layout

The default behavior of the Flex containers and components normally does the job you want; however, you can make adjustments. This section shows you how to do that.

Overriding updateDisplayList()

Since MXML files are translated into ActionScript classes, you can also include overrides of the Flex Framework functions if necessary. For example, you may want to fill the background of your component with a gradient of colors. Whenever you want to change the look of a component, you override the updateDisplayList() function, as shown here:

```
<?xml version="1.0" encoding="utf-8"?>
<mx:HBox xmlns:mx="http://www.adobe.com/2006/mxml"
    horizontalAlign="center"
    verticalAlign="middle"
    paddingLeft="5"
    paddingRight="5">

    <mx:Script>
    <![CDATA[

        override protected function updateDisplayList(unscaledWidth:Number,
            unscaledHeight:Number):void
        {
            super.updateDisplayList(unscaledWidth, unscaledHeight);

            var m:Matrix = new Matrix();
            m.createGradientBox( unscaledWidth, unscaledHeight, Math.PI/2 );

            graphics.clear();
            graphics.beginGradientFill( GradientType.LINEAR,
            [0x444444,0xCCCCCC,0xAFAFAF,0xCCCCCC,0x444444],
            [1,1,1,1,1],
            [0,64,100,200,255],
             m);
          graphics.drawRect(0,0,unscaledWidth,unscaledHeight);
          graphics.endFill();
        }
    ]]>
    </mx:Script>

    <mx:Button label="Don't Save" />
    <mx:Spacer width="50%" />
    <mx:Button label="Cancel" />
    <mx:Button label="Save" />
</mx:HBox>
```

Figure 17-1 shows the result.

Figure 17-1

The process of overriding a function in an MXML file is exactly the same as in an ActionScript file, except that you put the function within a <mx:Script> block.

Similarly, when you add properties to an MXML component, you should also call `invalidateDisplay List()`, `invalidateProperties()`, and so on, whenever it's appropriate.

Overriding layoutChrome()

A common use for MXML components is constructing custom containers. For example, you might have a `Panel` that has a special look to it, or specific Flex controls (e.g., `Buttons`, `Labels`, `ComboBoxes`, etc.), that you use throughout your application. Creating custom container classes in MXML is easier than using ActionScript, since you can use Flex Builder's Design View to help layout the contents.

Container components have an additional function, which you can override if you want to give your components a special look. The function, `layoutChrome()`, is called whenever `invalidateDisplayList()` is used or whenever the component is resized.

The "chrome" of a container refers to its border and background. Normally, the border is handled by a skin (see Chapter 23, "Skinning and Theme"), but you can override `layoutChrome()` and do something special.

Suppose that you want a `Panel` to have a brushed metal look. You can do this with a gradient fill and by overriding `layoutChrome()`, replacing the `Panel`'s normal border with your own, as shown in Figure 17-2.

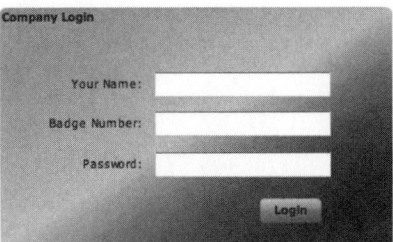

Figure 17-2

The MXML component code, called `GradientPanel.mxml`, is shown here:

```
<?xml version="1.0" encoding="utf-8"?>
<mx:Panel xmlns:mx="http://www.adobe.com/2006/mxml" layout="absolute" >

    <mx:Script>
```

```
    <![CDATA[
    /**
        * Modifies the Panel's normal chrome (border and background) with a
        * gradient fill. Note that in this case, super.layoutChrome() is NOT
        * being called because the look of this component
        * completely replaces the standard chrome and does not add to it.
        * However, part of the Panel's chrome is the ControlBar (if any).
        */
    override protected function layoutChrome(unscaledWidth:Number,
            unscaledHeight:Number):void
    {
        // Size and position the ControlBar, if one is present. The ControlBar
        // will already be created by the Panel base class. It is normally
        // positioned by the super.layoutChrome() method, but that function is
        // not being called, so it has to be done here.

        if( controlBar )
        {
            controlBar.setActualSize(
                unscaledWidth,
                controlBar.getExplicitOrMeasuredHeight());

            controlBar.move(
                0,
                unscaledHeight -
                controlBar.getExplicitOrMeasuredHeight());
        }

        // Color the background with the gradient fill

        var m:Matrix = new Matrix();
        m.createGradientBox( unscaledWidth, unscaledHeight, Math.PI/4 );

        graphics.clear();
        graphics.beginGradientFill( GradientType.LINEAR,
            [0xAFAFAF,0xCCCCCC,0x343434],
            [1,1,1],
            [0,128,255],
            m);
        graphics.drawRoundRect(0,0,unscaledWidth,unscaledHeight,16,10);
        graphics.endFill();
    }
    ]]>
    </mx:Script>
</mx:Panel>
```

Notice that there is no call to super.layoutChrome(). In this case, the Panel's layoutChrome() is not needed because the look is completely custom; no trace of the Panel's normal look is shown here.

Here is a simple Flex application to test it:

```
<mx:Application xmlns:mx="http://www.adobe.com/2006/mxml" >
 <components:GradientPanel width="360" height="211" title="Company Login">
    <mx:Label text="Your Name:" x="55" y="29"/>
```

```
           <mx:Label x="34" y="64" text="Badge Number:"/>
           <mx:Label x="65" y="100" text="Password:"/>
           <mx:TextInput x="134" y="27"/>
           <mx:TextInput x="134" y="62"/>
           <mx:TextInput x="134" y="98"/>
           <mx:Button x="229" y="139" label="Login"/>
   </components:GradientPanel>
   </mx:Application>
```

This produces the Login panel shown in Figure 17-2.

Setting Up Metadata Tags

Your MXML components may need to dispatch events and set up their own styles. Just as with ActionScript files, you use metadata tags to instruct the Flex compiler to allow those attributes when you use the component as an MXML tag.

Here is how to set up meta tags in an MXML file:

```
<mx:Metadata>
    [Event("cancel")]
    [Event(name="submit",type="your.events.SubmitEvent")]
</mx:Metadata>
```

The <mx:Metadata> tag sits at the root level of your MXML file where the Flex compiler will take the entries and place them above the class definition it generates when it compiles the MXML file.

The contents of the <mx:Metadata> tag are exactly the same as those used in an ActionScript component.

Creating Template Components

Flex does not provide the means to create a component and use it as a template for other components. A *template* component would be a component that has some of its layout predetermined and placeholders for other components to be added later.

For example, suppose that in your application's design, every time there is a need for data entry you use a Panel with a ControlBar that has a Submit button, a Cancel button, and a Help button, as shown in Figure 17-3.

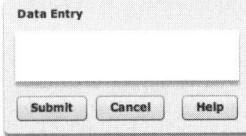

Figure 17-3

The empty space in the `Panel` can now be filled by any controls you wish. Here is an example of using the template component for an Employee Profile form, which appears as shown in Figure 17-4:

```
<templates:DataEntryTemplate title="Employee Profile"
    submit="handleSubmit(event)"
    cancel="handleCancel(event)"
    help="handleHelp(event)">

    <mx:Label x="30" y="0" text="Employee ID:"/>
    <mx:TextInput x="119" y="0"/>
    <mx:Label x="11" y="30" text="Employee Name:"/>
    <mx:TextInput x="119" y="30"/>
    <mx:Label x="53" y="60" text="Manager:"/>
    <mx:TextInput x="119" y="60"/>
    <mx:Label x="35" y="90" text="Department:"/>
    <mx:TextInput x="119" y="90"/>

</templates:DataEntryTemplate>
```

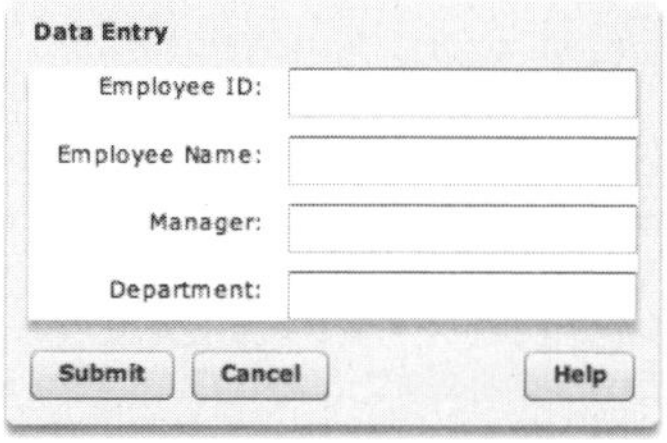

Figure 17-4

If you write an MXML component file and include within it some child components, then use that component in another file with additional child components, you will receive an error when the application is run:

```
Error: Multiple sets of visual children have been specified for this
component (component definition and component instance).
```

The reason for the error is that you are defining two sets of children for the component: one inside the component file and one when the component is used. The Flex framework does not know which set to use and does not know how they should be positioned relative to each other.

This makes writing a component a little difficult, since it would be convenient to supply the children as MXML tags in both cases. Of course, if you are creating the children in ActionScript, this problem would not arise because you have complete control over where and when the child components are created and added.

The preceding `DataEntryTemplate` appears to be used just like any other Flex component. There is the tag for the component instance and MXML tags defining its children. Internally, the `Panel` has been set with a `ControlBar` and three `Button`s. The `ControlBar` and `Button`s could be created with ActionScript code, but they are not. They are defined as MXML tags as well.

The key, or trick if you will, is the use of some Flex compiler meta tags.

DefaultProperty Meta Tag

Within the definition of the `DataEntryTemplate` lies the following code:

```
<mx:Metadata>
    [DefaultProperty("customChildren")]
</mx:Metadata>

[ArrayElementType("mx.core.UIComponent")]
public var customChildren:Array;
```

The `<mx:Metadata>` is naming `customChildren` as the default property of the component. A number of Flex components use this meta tag. For example, the default property of the `<mx:Label>` control is text, which means you can write this in MXML tags:

```
<mx:Label>This is an example of the label control.</mx:Label>
```

which means:

```
<mx:Label><mx:text>This is an example of the label control.</mx:text></mx:Label>
```

For the `DataEntryTemplate`, the `DefaultProperty` means the user of the component does not have to include the `customChildren` property when defining the component:

```
<templates:DataEntryTemplate title="Employee Profile"
    submit="handleSubmit(event)"
    cancel="handleCancel(event)"
    help="handleHelp(event)">

    <templates:customChildren>
        <mx:Label x="30" y="0" text="Employee ID:"/>
        <mx:TextInput x="119" y="0"/>
        <mx:Label x="11" y="30" text="Employee Name:"/>
        <mx:TextInput x="119" y="30"/>
        <mx:Label x="53" y="60" text="Manager:"/>
        <mx:TextInput x="119" y="60"/>
        <mx:Label x="35" y="90" text="Department:"/>
        <mx:TextInput x="119" y="90"/>
    </templates:customChildren>

</templates:DataEntryTemplate>
```

When you remove the `customChildren` property tag from the MXML file, it makes the component easier to use and makes it seem more integrated with the Flex framework.

Creating Custom Children

The `customChildren` property of the `DataEntryTemplate` component is a simple public variable of type `Array`. This makes it possible to pass in a list of Flex components to the template under the `customChildren` property.

An extra step is to use the `ArrayElementType` meta tag to tell the Flex compiler that only objects derived from `UIComponent` are eligible for this property. If you were to include `<mx:String>Hello</mx:String>` in the list, you would get a compiler error.

To actually include the children in the `Array` as members of the component, you must loop through the `Array` and use the component's `addChild()` function on them:

```
private function addCustomChildren() : void
{
    if( customChildren )
    {
        for(var i:int=0; i < customChildren.length; i++)
        {
            var child:UIComponent = UIComponent(customChildren[i]);
            addChild(child);
        }
    }
}
```

You can have this function called as the result handler of the `creationComplete` event on the component, as shown here:

```
<mx:Panel xmlns:mx="http://www.adobe.com/2006/mxml"
    layout="absolute"
    paddingLeft="5"
    paddingRight="5"
    creationComplete="addCustomChildren()">
...
</mx:Panel>
```

Extending MXML Components

Once you have created an MXML component, you can use it as the base class for other components just as easily as you can extend ActionScript classes.

Suppose that you want your `DataEntryTemplate` to use the `GradientPanel` as the base class. All you need to do is change the root tag from:

```
<mx:Panel xmlns:mx="http://www.adobe.com/2006/mxml"
    layout="absolute"
    creationComplete="addCustomChildren()">
```

to:

```
<components:GradientPanel xmlns:mx="http://www.adobe.com/2006/mxml"
    xmlns:components="components.*"
    layout="absolute"
    creationComplete="addCustomChildren()">
```

and the example now looks as shown in Figure 17-5.

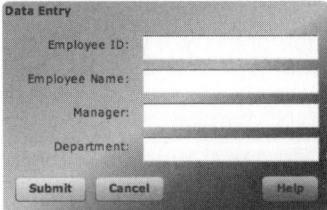

Figure 17-5

You extend an MXML component either by:

❑ Using the `extends` keyword when creating an ActionScript class to extend a component, such as:

```
public class EmployeeProfile extends GradientPanel
```

❑ Using the MXML component as the root tag of another MXML component, such as:

```
<components:GradientPanel xmlns:components="components.*" … >
```

❑ and including the namespace for the package where the component resides.

Simply treat the MXML component as an ActionScript component.

Summary

You can choose to make custom components using purely ActionScript or you can start with an MXML file and add ActionScript code to it. Just remember that MXML files are converted into ActionScript classes by the Flex compiler.

If you keep thinking of MXML files as just a more convenient way to write ActionScript classes, you can save yourself a lot of time by making components out of MXML files. You can always go back and rework the MXML files into ActionScript files if you feel it is necessary.

The next chapter, "Extending Flex Components," shows how to create new components by combining and changing existing components. Topics in the chapter include events and custom containers.

18

Extending Flex Components

The previous chapters provide a taste for how components can be made. This chapter takes a more in-depth look at component development by extending existing Flex components and creating custom container components.

A Look at Composite Components

Perhaps the best example of a composite component is the Flex RichTextEditor control. This control is made up of existing Flex controls — it does not extend UIComponent but rather mx.containers.Panel. The RichTextEditor uses TextArea, ButtonBars, TextInput, and other existing controls to form a new component. This is a composite control.

One of the challenges of a composite control is making it behave seamlessly. For example, the RichTextEditor has both a text and an htmlText property. These properties are not normal for a Panel (the base class for RichTextEditor); they are properties of the TextArea child. You could imagine the designer of the control instructing you to use the RichTextEditor like this:

```
<mx:RichTextEditor id="rte" />
...
rte.textArea.htmlText = "Hello";
```

But this syntax has several drawbacks:

❑   First, you would not be able to access the TextArea child's text property from MXML and use data binding.

❑   Second, the developer of the control might choose to rename the TextArea child from "textArea" to something else; then your code would no longer work.

The way to set the text of a `RichTextEditor` control is to use its `text` or `htmlText` property, for example:

```
<mx:RichTextEditor id="rte" htmlText="{data.description}" … />
```

When you give the `RichTextEditor` control its own `text` and `htmlText` properties, the control feels natural. So much so that you might not even think to look up how to set its text value, since it works just like any other control that uses text.

The `text` property of the `RichTextEditor` is an example of a property that acts as a proxy for a control within the component. In the case of the `RichTextEditor`, the `text` property is a proxy for the `TextArea` control within the `RichTextEditor`. The source code for the `RichTextArea` looks like this:

```
public function get text():String
{
    return textArea ? textArea.text : _text;
}

public function set text(value:String):void
{
    _text = value;
    textChanged = true;
    invalidateProperties();
}
```

The `text` property set function sets an internal property, `_text`. Later in the `commitProperties()` function, `_text` is used to set the `text` property of the inner `TextArea`. You can use this same technique with your own composite controls. This makes your control fit into the Flex framework if you use properties that behave in a way that is similar to what you would expect of a Flex control.

Creating Composite Components

Why create composite components?

When you think about your application and the user interface elements that you'll use, do you see a bunch of unrelated controls or do you see functional groupings? It is often hard to tell at first, and applications can change as you write them.

You should look at your application as functional groups and then develop those groups as composite components. You can drill down into those components and make them out of composite components and so forth.

Consider an application where you want to display a series of `Panels` — perhaps like a wizard or slide show. You could write a monolithic application (a single file) that has a `ViewStack` declared and all of its children within it. If you have done any reasonable amount of software development before, you'll see that this a ridiculous idea and, at best, a short-lived one at that.

Coordinating and changing that single file is difficult. One of the first things that will happen is that you'll turn the children of the `ViewStack` into their own component files. And you will have made a composite component. At least technically, it is a composite component. These types of components are different from components like the `RichTextEditor` control because you do not intend to reuse them. But there are similarities in how you communicate with them.

Creating reusable, composite components involves adding properties, events, and positioning the components to give your new components the look and behavior you want. These techniques are covered next.

Properties

Remember the `text` property issue discussed above? What if your original file had something like this:

```
<mx:ViewStack id="viewStack">
    <mx:Panel label="Reports" title="Reports" >
        <mx:DataGrid width="100%" height="100%" dataProvider="{reportList}">
            ...
        </mx:DataGrid>
    </mx:Panel>
    <!-- more children of the ViewStack here -->
</mx:ViewStack>
```

Notice the `dataProvider` of the `DataGrid` — it is referencing a variable in the file called `reportList`. Once you turn the `Panel` and its `DataGrid` into its own component, how will that `reportList` data be associated with the `DataGrid` in the new component? It is the same problem the developers of `RichTextEditor` faced when they wanted the `RichTextEditor` to behave like any other Flex text control.

To solve this problem, you want your new component to behave similarly, and you might do something like this:

```
<mx:ViewStack id="viewStack">
    <local:ReportPanel label="Reports" dataProvider="{reportList}"/>
    <!-- more children of the ViewStack here -->
</mx:ViewStack>
```

It seems natural to pass data to a component using a property called `dataProvider`. Within the component itself, you can write this several ways.

As an ActionScript variable:

```
<mx:Panel xmlns:mx="http://…" >
    <mx:Script>
    <![CDATA[
        import mx.collections.ArrayCollection;
        [Bindable] public var dataProvider:ArrayCollection;
    ]]>
    <mx:DataGrid width="100%" height="100%" dataProvider="{dataProvider}">
        ...
    </mx:DataGrid>
</mx:Panel>
```

As an MXML tag (which is bindable by default):

```
<mx:Panel xmlns:mx="http://..." >
    <mx:ArrayCollection id="dataProvider" />
    <mx:DataGrid width="100%" height="100%" dataProvider="{dataProvider}">
        ...
    </mx:DataProvider>
</mx:Panel>
```

All you have done is pass the `dataProvider` through to the `DataGrid` child. Your composite component, made up of a `Panel` as its root tag, along with a `DataGrid`, has a `dataProvider` property that acts as a proxy for the inner `DataGrid` child in your new composite component. For the developer, using `dataProvider` as the property seems natural, since that information ultimately appears in the `DataGrid` child of your new component.

Events

Events are handled in a similar way, depending on the event. For example, suppose that in your original file you handle the `MouseEvent.MOUSE_DOWN` event to pop up a menu. You might do it like this:

```
<mx:ViewStack id="viewStack">
    <mx:Panel label="Reports" title="Reports" >
        <mx:DataGrid width="100%" height="100%" dataProvider="{reportList}"
            mouseDown="handleMouse(event)">
            ...
        </mx:DataGrid>
    </mx:Panel>
    <!-- more children of the ViewStack here -->
</mx:ViewStack>
```

You can do the same thing when using a composite component:

```
<mx:ViewStack id="viewStack">
    <local:ReportPanel label="Reports" dataProvider="{reportList}"
        mouseDown="handleMouse(event)"/>
    <!-- more children of the ViewStack here -->
</mx:ViewStack>
```

This works because `MouseEvent` events bubble. If nothing inside of the `ReportPanel` component stops the event, it will automatically bubble up and out of the `ReportPanel`, where it can be handled.

Other events do not normally bubble, and you have to help them along. For example, you might want to intercept the `ListEvent.ITEM_CLICK` event on the `DataGrid` within the `ReportPanel`. Unfortunately, that event does not normally bubble. You will need to intercept the event and redispatch it:

```
<mx:DataGrid itemClick="dispatchEvent(event)" ...>
```

Another event-related issue with composite components has to do with event types. Every Flex component can have listeners set for `MouseEvents`, for example. But only a handful dispatch ListEvent events.

`Panel`, for example, does not. Being the root tag of the `ReportPanel` composite component, you would be tempted to write:

```
<local:ReportPanel itemClick="handleClick(event)" … >
```

That will cause a compilation error since `itemClick` is not an event dispatched by `Panel` or `ReportPanel`. You have two choices in this case:

Add the event listener using ActionScript:

```
reportPanel.addEventListener( ListEvent.ITEM_CLICK, handleClick );
```

Or add `Event` metadata to the `ReportPanel` component:

```
<mx:Panel xmlns:mx="http:…" >
    <mx:Metadata>
        [Event(name="itemClick",type="mx.events.ListEvent")]
    </mx:Metadata>
    <!-- rest of ReportPanel code and tags -->
</mx:Panel>
```

The first case works because you can add an event listener to any component for any event in ActionScript; there is no checking to see if the event is valid for the component. If the component dispatches it, then it will be handled.

The second case is a better approach for several reasons: The Metadata allows you to write the event handler on an MXML tag should you choose to do so, and the metadata acts a documentation tool. Anyone reading your component can tell that it is capable of dispatching a `ListEvent` event. Also this makes the event appear in the Flex Builder IDE's code assist dropdown. While it is true that could be determined from reading the code, the metadata makes it obvious.

Layout

When you make a composite component, you should consider the possibility that the developer using your component (and you yourself, as well) may decide to change its shape. For example, you could write a component that is a form to supply a billing address. You might set the component's size to be 400 pixels wide by 600 pixels high. Later, however, you may have a need to squeeze that into a space that is 300 pixels wide by 500 pixels high.

If your component originally had wide margins, shrinking the component could simply reduce the white space. Or you could see scrollbars. How you lay out the children of the component determines how the component behaves when resized.

The best method is to be as flexible as possible. Use constraint-based layouts whenever possible. For example, you can set the `TextInput` fields to always take up the space by anchoring their left and right sides to the container. Percentage-based layout works well in this case, too. Using absolute pixel positions would be the least flexible.

How to make composite components behave like other Flex components is covered in the next section.

Extending Existing Components

Composite components are not necessarily built by combining two or more existing components. You can start with an existing component and add (or take away) something from it. This section shows the technique using `Button` and `TextInput` components.

Extending Button

Here is a simple `Button` that could be used in an online retail application. The `Button` is called `PriceBuyButton`, and it initially displays the price of an item. When the `Button` is clicked, the label of the `Button` changes to the word, "Buy". Clicking again causes the component to dispatch a `buyClick` event. You would use the component like this:

```
<local:PriceBuyButton price="10.75" buyClick="handleBuy(event)" />
```

Since the `Button` control has all of the behavior you want, it makes more sense to extend `Button` than to write a control by extending `UIComponent`. Here is the code for `PriceBuyButton`:

```
package components
{
    import flash.events.MouseEvent;
    import flash.events.Event;

    import mx.controls.Button;

    [Event(name="buyClick",type="flash.events.Event")]

    public class PriceBuyButton extends Button
    {
        public function PriceBuyButton()
        {
            super();

            addEventListener(MouseEvent.CLICK, handleMouseClick);
        }

        private static const PRICE_MODE:String = "priceMode";
        private static const BUY_MODE:String = "buyMode";

        private var mode:String = PRICE_MODE;

        private var _price:Number;
        public function get price() : Number
        {
            return _price;
        }
        public function set price(value:Number) : void
        {
            _price = value;
            mode = PRICE_MODE;
            invalidateProperties();
```

```
        }

        private function handleMouseClick( event:MouseEvent ) : void
        {
            if( mode == PRICE_MODE ) {
                mode = BUY_MODE;
                invalidateProperties();
            } else {
                dispatchEvent( new Event("buyClick") );
            }

            event.stopPropagation();
        }

        override protected function commitProperties():void
        {
            super.commitProperties();

            if( mode == PRICE_MODE ) label = "$"+Number(price);
            else label = "Buy";
        }

    }
}
```

The logic of the component is simple: On a click event, determine what mode the Button is in: PRICE_MODE or BUY_MODE. If the mode is PRICE_MODE, then switch the label to "Buy" and set the mode to BUY_MODE. If the mode is BUY_MODE, dispatch a buyClick event.

The component is created with its own internal MouseEvent.MOUSE_CLICK handler. The handler examines the mode property and stops the propagation of the click event. This means that adding a click event handler to this component has no effect unless it has been added in the capture phase.

Notice that the label for the Button is changed in commitProperties() and not directly changed in the event handler. This keeps the component's behavior consistent with the Flex framework.

Extending TextInput

Here is an example of extending the TextInput control to display negative values as blank. You might find this useful in cases where certain values are "undefined" or are supposed to represent unset values. For instance, you might have a column in your database for the price of an item. There might be the case that prices haven't been set for some items and you use a value of -1 to represent that. Or at least, the server code receives a value of -1 to indicate an unset price and sends -1 back to the Flex client for unset values.

You do not, however, want the user to see -1 in the price column and you certainly do not want the user to enter -1 to remove a price. You can use an itemRenderer or a labelFunction to display a -1 as blank or, even, "unset," in a List control.

But when it comes time to enter a price, a control that extends TextInput can make it easier for both the user and the developer to deal with unset values.

Using -1 as the unset value, an extended TextInput control can convert a blank to -1 and display -1 as a blank. Here is a simple solution to that, called PositiveInput:

```
package components
{
    import mx.controls.TextInput;

    public class PositiveInput extends TextInput
    {
        public function PositiveInput()
        {
            super();
            restrict = "0-9.";
        }

        public function get number() : Number
        {
            if( text.length == 0 ) return -1;
            else return Number(text);
        }

        public function set number(value:Number) : void
        {
            if( value < 0 ) text = "";
            else text = String(value);
        }

    }
}
```

Rather than using the text property, PositiveInput has a number property. This way, you can set the text property if necessary, but only deal with numeric values through the number property. This means:

```
<local:PositiveInput id="price" />
...
price.number = -1; // displays as blank
price.number = 14.23; // displays as "14.23"
```

Likewise, if the control is blank, price.number returns -1.

Extending UIComponents versus Standard Components

In Chapter 18, you saw how to create custom components. In this chapter, you are seeing how to extend and change existing components and to combine components into composite components. Each time you write an application it is filled with components and you have to ask yourself, "Should I create a component from scratch (extend UIComponent) or extend an existing component?"

The choice isn't always clear. Nor is it clear if you should use purely ActionScript or MXML (with Script blocks, of course).

Some questions to guide your decision are:

❏ Is the component I want unique? If so, then starting from `UIComponent` is probably best. If you use a component that has some overlap with what you need, you may find yourself disabling code and rewriting so much, not to mention working around existing behavior, that starting from `UIComponent` is a better approach.

❏ Is there a component that meets most of my needs? If so, then picking an existing component and enhancing it might be a better choice. For instance, you might like the `RichTextEditor` (RTE) control, but you do not want some of the toolbars. Extending the RTE and removing the toolbars from view would be easier than writing your own RTE. Likewise, the `PositiveInput` control, above, simply added a new property to the `TextInput` control.

❏ Should I used MXML or ActionScript? This question might be best answered by your teammates or colleagues. Some projects are done entirely in ActionScript — so that is your answer. It is often easier to create new composite components in MXML than it is to do this in ActionScript. For example, positioning the children of a `Canvas` is easier to do in Flex Builder's Design View than it would be to override the `createChildren()` and `updateDisplayList()` functions.

Appearance versus Behavior

Suppose that in your project the design calls for all of the `Buttons` to be round and in shades of green. Do you write your own `Button` component to do this? You could, but you should not. Changing the appearance of the `Buttons` does not change how they work — their behavior remains the same.

It is tempting to create new components simply to alter the look of a component. Flex divides the appearance of components from their behavior precisely, so you can change the look of an application without writing code.

To get the round, green `Buttons`, you would create skins and use style sheets. This topic is covered elsewhere in this book. But it is important to know this when deciding how to write a component.

Most often, a component is a combination of appearance and behavior. Using the `PriceBuyButton` as an example, you might want the `Button` to appear white with a green label when it displays the price, then turn to a green background with a black label when it displays "Buy".

In this case, you not only change the behavior of the `Button` into a `PriceBuyButton`, but you also change its styling. This is an example of combining style and behavior changes to make a new component.

Custom Containers

Creating container components is not that much different from creating control components. Some control components have other Flex components as their children, too. In both types of components, you have to size and position the children to get the look you are going for.

The real difference is that with a control component you already know what children you need (or will have) when you build the component. A container component is generic — its children are set by the developer using the container.

Think about HBox — the developer of the HBox container did not know what children it would hold. The developer only knew that its children would be positioned horizontally.

In this section, you will see how to develop a container that is similar to the Flex Tile container, except that there are no fixed width columns or fixed height rows. This container, called Flow, keeps positioning its children one after the other until it runs out of space and then starts a new row. The Flex Tile container will resize its children so that they are all a uniform size; the Flow container will not do that. Figure 18-1 shows the difference between the Tile and Flow container components.

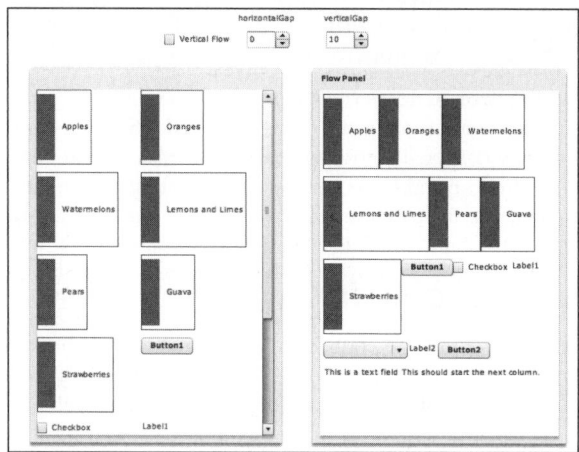

Figure 18-1

The Tile (left) shows two columns of children. While the children are different sizes, the Tile has placed them such that they are all occupying the same size area. The Flow (right) shows a varying number of columns. There are three children in the first two rows, four children in the third row, three children in the fourth row, and two children in the last row. There is no horizontal gap between the children; there is a vertical gap of 10 pixels.

If you run this example and change the horizontal gap, you will see the children of the Flow container between to shuffle to new rows as there is less and less space. But the Flow container's children always occupy the same space as their size.

Applying the Flex Component Life Cycle

The Flow container begins by extending the Flex mx.core.Container class. This is key for container components, since the Container base class provides the code to add and remove children and manage them. This is a case where you are writing a unique Flex component, but since it is a container, starting from scratch means starting from mx.core.Container.

There are two key phases of the Flex component life cycle for this container, as with most containers: measure and layout.

Remember that `measure()` is not called by the Flex framework life cycle if a component has an explicit width and height. If you think about the problem of layout, a problem similar to word-wrapping, you quickly come to the conclusion that you cannot wrap your text or your child components onto a new row without knowing how large a row is. That is, if there is no width set on the container, how do you know when you have reached its edge?

A requirement for the `Flow` container is a width. This width may be explicitly set or it may be determined by the parent, but a width is necessary to know when to wrap the children to new rows.

If `measure()` is called, it determines if the width and height of the container is set or not. If not, measure determines a minimum width. It often happens with containers that the measure phase is run several times until all measurements are known, so it is possible that, in the first pass of `measure()`, the width is not set from the parent, but will be set in a few cycles.

The layout — the sizing and positioning of the children — is a another matter. The `updateDisplayList()` function is critical to the `Flow` container component.

The process works like this: a child's size is examined to see if it fits on the current row. If it does, it is positioned at the end of the row (`horizontalGap` and `verticalGap` values are used in this calculation) and the next child is examined.

If the child does not fit, it is positioned on a new row and the next child is examined. This is a fairly straightforward algorithm.

The key to the `Flow` container is not only the layout — `updateDisplayList` — but also the fact that the component extends `mx.core.Container`. Nowhere in the `Flow` container's own code is there a place where the children are brought into existence and added to the display list. All of the management of the children is done by the base class, `Container`.

Tag Cloud

The `Flow` container can be used with any of the Flex components as its children. This next example extends the `Flow` container to turn it into a specific component: the Tag Cloud. You typically see these components on weblogs. Figure 18-2 shows a sample tag cloud: a swarm of links whose size is determined by their ranking.

Figure 18-2

The `TagCloud` component is simply the `Flow` container whose children are created by renderers. `TagCloudRenderers` to be exact.

The `TagCloud` class begins by extending the `Flow` container and adding two properties: `dataProvider` and `itemRenderer`:

```
public class TagCloud extends Flow
{
    public function TagCloud()
    {
        super();
    }

    /*
     * Properties
     */

    private var _dataProvider:Array;
    public function get dataProvider() : Array
    {
        return _dataProvider;
    }
    public function set dataProvider( value:Array ) : void
    {
        _dataProvider = value;
        invalidateProperties();
    }

    private var _itemRenderer:Class = TagCloudRenderer;
    public function get itemRenderer() : Class
    {
        return _itemRenderer;
    }
    public function set itemRenderer( value:Class ) : void
    {
        _itemRenderer = value;
        invalidateProperties();
    }
```

The `dataProvider` is how the `TagCloud` will give the items to display; the `itemRenderer` is how the items will be displayed.

> The `itemRenderer` is defined in this example as a class. The standard way to define `itemRenderer` is with a `ClassFactory`. Using a class makes the code simpler but may not be as flexible as you might require when your components become complex. The technique of the `ClassFactory` is covered in Chapter 33, "Advanced Data Controls."

Since the `Flow` container's layout algorithm is exactly what the `TagCloud` requires, the only thing the `TagCloud` component needs to do is create the children from the `dataProvider`:

```
override protected function commitProperties():void
{
    super.commitProperties();

    removeAllChildren();
```

```
        for(var i:int=0; i < dataProvider.length; i++)
        {
            var child:IUIComponent = new _itemRenderer();
            (child as IDataRenderer).data = dataProvider[i];
            addChild(child as DisplayObject);
        }
    }
```

Once again, the Flex framework comes into play. Since the data for children are being provided in the `dataProvider` property, they may not be known when `createChildren()` is called. Instead, the children are created in `commitProperties()`. Remember that `TagCloud` extends `Flow`, which extends `Container`. Creating the children is simply a matter of removing any existing children, then looping through the `dataProvider` and creating an `itemRenderer` for each child. The children are added to the component. The Flex framework automatically calls on the `Flow` container's `updateDisplayList()`, which will position the children with the result shown in Figure 18-2.

Customizing Composite Components

The `RichTextEditor` has a number of child components: There is the `TextArea` input control for composing the text, a `ColorPicker` to set the text color, a `ToggleButtonBar` for the text alignment choices, and so forth.

Suppose, however, that you do not want to present all of those controls to the user of your application. How do you remove them?

The secret lies in the use of the `includeInLayout` property of Flex controls. The RTE does make some customization possible with its own API, but when you need to be precise, tinkering with the bits is the only way to go.

This is not against the rules per se, although in a future version of the Flex framework, this specific method on the `RichTextEditor` may no longer work. The point, however, is to show how you can apply this to your own custom components.

If you look at the `RichTextEditor`'s source code, you'll see that each of the children is defined by MXML tags and each has an ID.

Suppose that you want to remove the `ColorPicker`. Create a new component, calling it `ColorlessEditor` and have it extend `mx.controls.RichTextEditor`, for example:

```
package components
{
    import mx.controls.RichTextEditor;

    public class ColorlessEditor extends RichTextEditor
    {
        public function ColorlessEditor()
        {
            super();
        }

        override protected function createChildren():void
```

```
            {
                // critical that super.createChildren() is called to
                // make sure all of the MXML
                // children are instantiated.
                super.createChildren();

                colorPicker.includeInLayout = false;
                colorPicker.visible = false;
            }


    }
}
```

In this example, you override the `createChildren()` function and set the `colorPicker`'s `includeInLayout` property to `false`.

You may wonder why the `colorPicker`'s `visible` property is also being set to `false`. The reason is that `includeInLayout`, when set to false, only removes the child from the layout algorithm — the child's x and y properties still position it as if the child were in a `Canvas`. Or, in other words, the child is still on the display list — `includeInLayout` does not remove the child from the display list. You normally set a child's `visible` property to `false` if you also set its `includeInLayout` property to `false`.

You can apply this technique to your own composite components. For example, if you have a component with three `Buttons`, "Save," "Discard," and "Cancel," you can have a simple property that hides or shows these `Buttons` individually. For example, `showDiscardButton=false`, would make the Discard button disappear as shown in this example:

```
private var _showDiscardButton:Boolean = true;
public function get showDiscardButton() : Boolean { return _showDiscardButton; }
public function set showDiscardButton( value:Boolean ) : void {
    _showDiscardButton = value;
    invalidateProperties();
}
...
override protected function commitProperties() : void
{
    super.commitProperties();
    // ... other properties here ...
    discardButton.includeInLayout = showDiscardButton;
    discardButton.visible = showDiscardButton;
}
```

Notice how the property setter function does not change the child component's `includeInLayout` and `visible` properties explicitly. Rather, as with everything in the Flex framework, the property setter function sets a backing variable (`_showDiscardButton`) and then signals that `commitProperties()` should be called, which will handle the settings.

Summary

Most of your time writing a Flex application is spent extending components. Whether the program is simple and you are extending `Application`, or you have a dozen items in a `TabNavigator`, you are always extending components.

The majority of these components are very specific, such as turning some MXML tags in your main application into a separate file to make things easier to read. Writing reusable components is a slightly different journey.

Components you make from scratch — extending `UIComponent` — allow you to make anything you can imagine. You are responsible for how the component looks, if it uses styles and skins, how it responds to changes in size, and which events it dispatches. Custom components created from scratch take time to write and test as well.

Building components by extending existing components can accelerate your development time. You may get a lot of mileage out of a component by extending it and removing some of its children (or by adding a few more). You can also change a component's behavior by intercepting some of its events, stopping them from propagating, and inserting your own events.

This chapter has shown you how to do all those things. You can use either ActionScript or MXML tags, whichever you prefer. Just remember that changing a component's appearance is different from changing its behavior.

Making components look nice and having the user interfaces you need is only part of making a component. Events make components work. The next chapter shows how events work and how to use events in your custom components.

Summary

19

Advanced Event Programming

Previous chapters have touched upon custom events, and you may have already tried your hand at creating custom events. This chapter goes into detail about how events work and creating your own events, and provides some tips on handling events and guidelines for event usage.

Custom Events versus Standard Events

Since the Flex Framework relies so heavily on events, it is quite natural that your own programs should use events and, further, should use their own custom events.

Remember that the technology underlying Flex is the Flash Player. The Flash Player is an event-driven system. Flex simply makes its own custom events. Most of the events are found in the mx.events package. The ItemClickEvent used with DataGrid and List is a common example.

A "custom" event is a class that extends the flash.events.Event base class. The class includes its own special types.

> *A custom event is useless without its own event type, as event types are how events are distinguished. The* Event *class has a* target *and a* currentTarget *property. The* target *property is set to the object that initially dispatches the event. The* currentTarget *property is the object that has just produced the event. For example, if a button is clicked deep within your application, the* target *property will be the button. If you intercepted the event by placing a* click *event handler on a container that holds the button, the* currentTarget *property will be that container.*

You may be writing a component that receives stock market prices, and it dispatches a "tick" event whenever a new price arrives. The "tick" is the event type (or event name since "type" may be confused with a class, but this is what they are called in Flash, so you have to remember that an event "type" is really the name of the event).

Events, as you may recall from earlier chapters, are sent through the Flex Framework by dispatching them from one component and listening for, or handling, them in other components. The stock "tick" event might be defined by this class:

```
package events
{
  import flash.events.Event;

    public class StockTick extends Event
    {
        public static const TICK:String = "tick";

        public function StockTick(type:String, bubbles:Boolean=false,
            cancelable:Boolean=false)
        {
            super(type, bubbles, cancelable);
        }

        public var symbol:String;
        public var price:Number;
        public var change:Number;

    }
}
```

Notice that the StockTick class extends flash.events.Event, and it defines a static constant, TICK, as the name or type of the event. This is a very common practice, and it simply ensures that anyone using this event gets the name right if they use the constant and not the string itself.

You will find that there are two places where the constant string for the event type does not work: in the event metadata (shown later in this chapter) and in MXML tags.

The constructor function simply calls its super counterpart. What makes this a custom event, then, is:

❑   The fact that you have defined a class extending Event, given the custom event its own class.

❑   It is a unique event type.

❑   Optionally, there is some data to go with the event.

Some events force the event listener to get extra data from the component dispatching the event. In addition, some events include a bit of data to make things easier on the developer, using the Event class. Here, the StockTick event includes a stock symbol, price, and change value since the last tick.

There are several approaches to take when considering custom events. First, you should decide what events your components could dispatch. Here are some examples.

If you have a class that interfaces with a server, that class could dispatch events when data is returned from the server, when a request is made to the server, and when an error is returned from the server. Most of the data service classes already do this, but applications typically massage the data being returned into a form more easily used by the rest of the application. A custom event can either deliver that data along with the event or simply signal that the data is ready.

A pop-up could dispatch a custom event when its Submit button is clicked. The event might contain a copy of the data from all of the fields on the pop-up or the listener function for the event could interrogate the pop-up for the data before removing the pop-up (and losing the data).

Generally speaking, your application is at a higher level than the Flex framework, and application-level custom events tend to be related to higher functions. For instance, when you click on a cell in the DataGrid, the DataGrid dispatches a ItemClickEvent event. The DataGrid doesn't know anything about the purpose for which it is being used. Your application might be using the DataGrid to display financial data, which is being reflected in a sister chart component. A click on the DataGrid isn't simply an ItemClickEvent event, it is a data-selection event that causes the chart to change its display. Your application would intercept the change event and dispatch a FinanceSelect event — something that is related to the broader picture of the application.

Custom events can be as simple as an Event-extending class or as complex as a class that has a payload of extra information. Nonetheless, events are usually pretty simple and only include data relevant to their purpose.

Extending Standard Events

As with custom components that extend existing Flex components, you can also extend existing Flex (and Flash) events.

The FinanceSelect event is one example where you could capitalize on the ItemClickEvent event. The ItemClickEvent event already contains the row index of the item selected. You might want to pass that information along with other finance-related data in the event, so FinanceSelect can extend ItemSelect and include the extra data members.

One versus Many

A good rule to follow when creating events is to create a custom event for every custom component that dispatches events containing extra data.

For instance, if your application has a component with a chart and clicking on the chart is supposed to cause a drill-down, you probably do not want to use a generic ItemClickEvent event. The component listening for this selection on the chart needs to know enough information to get the details for the drill-down from the server.

Instead of using ItemClickEvent, your chart component could dispatch a DrillDownEvent that contains information the server can use to fetch the details. On the other hand, if your chart component is merely displaying data and has no interactivity, there is no point to making an event class for the sake of having an event class to match the component.

It is also tempting to make a single, all-encompassing event class for your application. Your event class could have a number of event types and data associated with it. That can be fine for smaller applications, but as your application grows in complexity, it will be easier to write and maintain if event classes are written for specific components and carry specific messages.

Writing custom events is not just about event flow — it is also about making applications readable, extendable, and maintainable. It is a lot easier to modify the DrillDownEvent for the DrillDownChart component than it is to modify the `FinanceAppEvent` with yet another piece of data that no other component but the `DrillDownChart` and its event listener need.

It is also not a good idea to give multiple meanings to data within an event class. Imagine your `FinanceAppEvent` has a price data member originally intended to be a stock market price. Later, someone adds the ability to sell stocks and decides that the price data member is a good fit. Unfortunately, that same person decides that `price` isn't a useful term and changes it to `sellPrice` and the whole application no longer compiles! It would be a lot better to create a new event, `SellStockEvent`, and apply it just to this new function of the application.

Adding Metadata to AS Class and MXML Files

Metadata is of additions to the ActionScript code that tell the ActionScript compiler about the code and give it additional instructions. It is called "metadata" because the information is not part of the formal definition of ActionScript. A number of other languages have metadata of one sort or another, so this is nothing unusual or suspect about ActionScript.

Event metadata defines the events an ActionScript class may be dispatching. The appearance of the metadata statement allows the user of the component to specify event listeners in MXML tags. It is not necessary to include event metadata with a component for the component to dispatch events and for another component to set up event listeners in ActionScript.

Adding Custom Events to Custom Components

The syntax for adding metadata is either:

```
[Event("eventName")]
```

or

```
[Event(name="eventName",type="ActionScript class")]
```

The first form just gives the event's name while the second associates an ActionScript class (one that extends `flash.events.Event`) with the event. For example:

```
[Event("submit")]

[Event(name="submit",type="components.forms.InsuranceClaimEvent")]
```

As you can see, the second form is more descriptive and is the one preferred. The second form also has another advantage when used with ActionScript tags: type-checking. Here is how you might use this:

```
<components:InsuranceClaimForm submit="handleSubmit(event)" />
```

The event handling function, `handleSubmit`, will be given an event object of the type specified in the event metadata. In the first example, the type is not specified, so you must assume it is `flash.events.Event`. In the second example, you know it will be an `InsuranceClaimEvent`:

```
private function handleSubmit( event:InsuranceClaimEvent ) : void { … }
```

If you use the longer `Event` metadata definition, the compiler can look at the event-handling function and compare the types. If you use the shorter `Event` metadata form, giving just the event name, you will get this compilation error:

```
1118: Implicit coercion of a value with static type flash.events:Event to a
    possibly unrelated type events:InsuranceClaimEvent.
```

In this case, the `handleSubmit()` function was declared with an event parameter of type `InsuranceClaimEvent`, but the event metadata was not. The compiler thinks it will have to cast a generic `Event` to the more specific `InsuranceClaimEvent`. The solution is to declare the event type in the metadata.

Handling Event Runtime Errors

Sometimes things do not go as you have planned. While you can get past the compiler by using `Event` metadata and specifying the event type, sometimes the person who writes the code does not always dispatch the correct event type.

Event Flow

Events make your application work. The engine within the Flex framework dispatches events and intercepts them, directing them to the event handlers. Events are the lifeblood of Flex. This section explains how events work and how you can take advantage of the event flow.

Event Priority

Since the event system has three phases (capture, target, and bubble) you can write event handlers to take advantage of the fact that an event can be handled in the capture phase before it can be targeted to a specific instance. For example, your application may have the ability to drag an object from one container to another, unless the object is marked "read-only." This may be a property your objects get from your server or database. The objects may visually tell the user which is which, but you still need to prevent the user from dragging the "read-only" objects.

If you include a `MouseEvent.MOUSE_DOWN` event handler in the capture phase, you can first determine the object's read-only status. If the object is not read-only, the event can carry on; if the object is read-only, the event can be stopped.

```
addEventListener( MouseEvent.MOUSE_DOWN, checkReadOnly, true );
```

where the `true` parameter indicates this event handler should be called during the capture phase.

The normal target phase of event handling can then proceed normally with the drag and drop operation. If the object in question is marked "read-only," the drag and drop will never take place.

Another way to handle events is to assign them priorities. Using this same example, you can add an event listener for `MouseEvent.MOUSE_DOWN` at a higher priority than the `MouseEvent.MOUSE_EVENT` event handler for the drag and drop operation. The higher-priority event handler can check the object's read-only property and act accordingly:

```
addEventListener( MouseEvent.MOUSE_DOWN, checkReadOnly, false, 10 );
```

The `10` parameter gives this event handler a higher priority.

Preventing or Changing Default Behaviors

Whenever an event handler is called, it has the opportunity of stopping the event flow from going further. Most event handlers do not do this, but it is common practice for event handlers that end things such as `Lists` and `DataGrids`.

In the previous example, the `checkReadOnly()` event handler could stop an event from going further to allow the drag and drop operation to take place. To do this, the event handler can call one of three functions, depending on the desired effect:

❑ `event.preventDefault()` — This function allows the event to continue through the event flow, but tells the event target that it should not carry out its default behavior. This is typical when handling editing events — you check the data and if the value is incorrect, you call `event.preventDefault()` and the new data is not saved. However, the event continues because it is necessary for the control to properly end the editing sequence.

❑ `event.stopPropagation()` — This function prevents the event from continuing its normal path. If the `checkReadOnly()` event handler is assigned to the capture event phase, calling `event.stopPropagation()` will prevent the event from reaching the targeting phase, and the drag and drop operation will not take place.

❑ `event.stopImmediatePropagation()` — This function not only prevents the event from continuing the event flow path, but it also cancels any other event handlers in the current phase. If the `checkReadOnly()` event handler is assigned to the target phase but with a priority of 10, calling `event.stopImmediatePropagation()` will prevent the event from being handled by any other event handlers in the target phase, such as the drag and drop handler.

Forwarding Events

Within the event framework, the capture and bubbling phases only work with user interface objects. Events flow from parent to child (capture phase) and child to parent (bubbling phase) because of the graphical hierarchy of the parent and child relationship. That is, if you have a component in a `VBox` that's contained in a `ViewStack` that's contained in `Form`, which is within a `TabNavigator` in the main `Application`, you can dispatch an event from the component and have it bubble up to an event handler on the `Application`.

If, however, you create objects that are not components, yet still implement the IEventDispatcher interface (or extend EventDispatcher class), the capture and bubbling phases have no meaning. Here is an example.

Suppose that you have created a base class that interfaces with a remote server and call this class BaseServer. The purpose of the class is to handle some of the common and mundane aspects of dealing with remote services. Included in this class is code to receive errors or faults from the server. These error messages should be displayed to the user, so you decide to handle them as events. This means you write the BaseServer class to extend flash.events.EventDispatcher, and you use the dispatchEvent() function. Since you know the BaseServer class may be used anywhere within the application, you make sure the error events bubble by passing true for the bubbles parameter when you create the event.

Now create a new class, LoginServer, which extends BaseServer. The LoginServer class handles the authentication aspect of the connection.

Once LoginServer is created, you create a few more classes, extending BaseServer. Finally, you create a MainServer class, and in this class you have instances of all of the other server classes. MainServer does not need to extend BaseServer; it does extend EventDispatcher, however. The classes might look something like the ones that follow.

The BaseServer.as class:

```
public class BaseServer extends EventDispatcher {
    ....
    protected function handleServerError( error:FaultEvent ) : void {
        var newEvent:ErrorEvent = new ErrorEvent("error", true); // make it bubble
        newEvent.text = error.toString();
        dispatchEvent(newEvent);
    }
}
```

The LoginServer.as class:

```
public class LoginServer extends BaseServer {
    ....
}
```

The MainServer.as class:

```
public class MainServer extends EventDispatch {
    private var loginServer:LoginServer;

    // more server classes here

    public function MainServer() {
        loginServer = new LoginServer();
        // create other server class instances here
```

```
        }

        public function login( userName:String, password:String ) : void {
            loginServer.login( userName, password );
        }
        …
    }
```

When it comes time to log in, your application code calls the `MainServer`'s `login()` function, which in turn calls the `LoginServer`'s login function.

If the incorrect password has been entered, the `BaseServer` code receives a fault from the server and then dispatches an error event.

In your main application you have set up an event listener to handle this:

```
    private function handleServerErrors( event:ErrorEvent ) : void {
        Alert.show( event.text, "Server Error" );
    }
```

which you have established as the event listener on the `MainServer` class instance:

```
    mainServer.addEventListener( "error", handleServerError );
```

With all of that in place, you run the application and give a bad password. And nothing happens — the Alert box does not appear.

While the `BaseServer.handleServerError()` function was called and did dispatch an event with the bubbles flag set to `true`, the event did not bubble to the `MainServer` and onto the `Application` and the event handler function.

The reason is that these classes do not have graphical aspects. That is, they do not hook into the Flash Player's display system. The Event subsystem has no way to know their relationship because the Event subsystem uses the graphical hierarchy to propagate the events.

There is no simple solution to this, but one method is to forward the events. Using the preceding example, you can insert an event handler into the `MainServer` class that listens to all of the events dispatched by its members and redispatch them:

```
    public function MainServer() {
        loginServer = new LoginServer();
        loginServer.addEventListener( "error", forwardEvent );
        // create other server class instances here
    }
    private function forwardEvent( event:Event ) : void {
        dispatchEvent(event);
    }
```

By intercepting the event and dispatching it, the `handleServerErrors` function in the main application will now be called. The event's target and `currentTarget` properties will be changed from the `LoginServer` class to the `MainServer` class. You will lose the identity of the event originator, but you will be able to simulate event bubbling using this technique.

Custom Data Binding

By default, member variables of a class are not bindable. That is, they cannot be used in binding expressions without the compiler issuing a warning. The reason is that when a variable is available for binding, the compiler generates code to handle the watching of the variable for changes and the dispatching of events to notify listeners that the variable has changed. All this is extra code and contributes to the size of the final SWF.

Using the Bindable Metadata Tag

When you do need to use data binding, the [Bindable] metadata tag tells the compiler to generate the code. You simply place the [Bindable] expression before the variable's declaration:

```
[Bindable] private var accountName:String;
```

or

```
[Bindable]
private var accountName:String;
```

Either example is fine; use whichever you prefer. If you want to see what ActionScript code the compiler generates, add -keep-generated-actionscript=true to your compiler options.

Custom Data Binding with the Bindable Metadata Tag

Properties in a component are automatically bindable. For example:

```
private var _accountName:String // not bindable
public function get accountName() : String {
    return _accountName;
}
```

If you include [Bindable] with the getter function:

```
[Bindable]
public function get accountName() : String {
    return _accountName;
}
```

the Flex compiler will give a warning: "Bindable with read-only getter will be ignored." Notice that there is no set property function yet declared. The compiler automatically assumes the read-only properties are not bindable because there is no way to change them since they are read-only.

If, however, you declare a setter function, then you can make the property bindable:

```
public function set accountName( value:String ) : void {
    _accountName = value;
}
```

There is a catch to this. A simple property such as accountName is rarely a problem in data binding. If, however, you are binding to a more complex property, such as a collection, you may run into a snag.

When a property is bindable, the compiler generates code to watch for *changes* in the variable's value. This is important, since it is a change to the variable that triggers the binding. On a complex data type the change may not be detectable. Here is an example using an employee profile.

Assume that the EmployeeProfile class is simple:

```
public class EmployeeProfile {
    public var name:String;
    public var id:String;
    public var department:String;
    public var manager:String;
}
```

and you have a property in your component for an EmployeeProfile, which you declare to be bindable because you are using the values in <mx:Label> components:

```
private var _profile:EmployeeProfile;

[Bindable]
public function get profile() : EmployeeProfile
{
    return _profile;
}
public function set profile( value:EmployeeProfile ) : void
{
    _profile = value;
}

....

<mx:Label text="Employee name: {profile.name}" />
<mx:Label text="Department: {profile.department}" />
<mx:Label text="Manager: {profile.manager}" />
```

As your program runs, the profile property on the component is changed. But nothing is changing in the labels. The first employee's information remains, but subsequent changes are not appearing.

The problem is the way you are changing the profile information. If you change the profile variable with a new EmployeeProfile object, the code the compiler generated will see that the new EmployeeProfile is different from the previous EmployeeProfile and dispatch change events. The Labels will be updated in this case:

```
<components:EmployeeForm id="EmpForm" profile="{empProfile}" />
...

empProfile = new EmployeeProfile();

...
```

```
empProfile = new EmployeeProfile();  // different from previous instance
```

But, if you change just the content of the initial `EmployeeProfile`, the compile does not detect this as a change:

```
empProfile = new EmployeeProfile();

...

empProfile.name = "new name";
empProfile.department = "new department";
empProfile.manager = "new manager";
```

In this case, only the content has changed, so the `Labels` are never updated.

A similar thing happens with `Collections`. Often a `Collection` is created once and then its contents are updated. This usually works well with data binding. But if you have bound the `Collection` itself, then there is no change being detected.

The way to circumvent this is to force an event when these properties change. Give the property a specific event associated with the binding and dispatch an event when the setter function is called:

```
private var _profile:EmployeeProfile;

[Bindable("EmployeeProfileChanged")]
public function get profile() : EmployeeProfile
{
    return _profile;
}
public function set profile( value:EmployeeProfile ) : void
{
    _profile = value;
    dispatchEvent( new Event("EmployeeProfileChanged") );
}
```

You do not need a special event type to do this; `flash.events.Event` works just fine. What you do need to do is force a call to the setter function:

```
empProfile.name = "new name";
empProfile.department = "new department";
empProfile.mananger = "new manager";
empForm.profile = empProfile;
```

This calls the setter function, which then dispatches the event and causes the `Labels` to show the changed values.

If you do find yourself in a situation where data binding appears not to work as you expect, check your properties and set up custom dispatch events for those properties involved in data binding.

Using BindingUtils

The `BindingUtils` class is used to perform data binding in ActionScript. It is used in the code the Flex compiler generates when it encounters binding expressions in MXML tags. One use for `BindingUtils` was covered earlier in this book as a way to create a circular binding — having a UI control bound to a variable such that when either was changed the other was updated.

Custom Data Binding in ActionScript

`BindingUtils` can also be used when creating ActionScript components so that you do not have to write a lot of extra code yourself. For example, you may have a public property that can be changed and a UI control that reflects that property. You might have a `NumericStepper` representing a `quantity` property. The quantity can be changed outside of the component. If you did this in MXML you could write:

```
<mx:NumericStepper value="{quantity}" … />
```

where quantity is declared as a `[Bindable]` public property of the component. If you are creating your component in ActionScript, `BindingUtils` lets you create the same relationship:

```
override protected function createChildren() : void {
    super.createChildren();
    quantityStepper = new NumericStepper();
    addChild(quatityStepper);
    BindingUtils.bindProperty(quantityStepper, "value", this, "quantity");
}
```

The `BindingUtils.bindProperty()` function binds the `value` property of the `quantityStepper` to the quantity property of the component. Reverse these if you also want changes to the `NumericStepper` to be put back into the quantity. Include both if you want binding in both directions:

```
BindingUtils.bindProperty(this,"quantity",quantityStepper,"value");
```

`BindingUtils` has another static function, `bindSetter()`, that enables you to pass in a function that can set the value of a property or do some other action. For example, this is an alternative way to change the quantity property using the `NumericStepper`:

```
BindingUtils.bindSetter(function(b:Number):void{quantity=b}, quantityStepper,
    "value");
```

With `BindingUtils.bindSetter()`, you pass a function that takes a value. The function then "does something" with the value. In this example, the function simply sets the `quantity` property. But you can do other things, such as call other functions and set multiple values or validation.

ChangeWatcher

Both `BindingUtils` functions return an instance of a `ChangeWatcher`. You may not always need the `ChangeWatcher` instance, but it is a way to know when the binding takes place. You can set up an event listener and carry out other actions whenever the values change. For example, when the quantity of an item in your shopping cart changes, you can use a ChangeWatcher to trigger a recalculation of the cart's total. Items that have been set with a zero quantity could be removed as well:

```
var quantityWatcher:ChangeWatcher;

quantityWatcher = BindingUtils.bindProperty(quantityStepper, "value", this,
    "quantity");
quantityWatcher.setHandler( onQuantityChange );

private function onQuantityChange( event:PropertyChangeEvent ) : void
{
    trace(event.type, event.target, event.currentTarget, event.property);
}
```

The quantityWatcher returned by BindingUtils.bindProperty() has an event handler, onQuantityChange, added to it. Whenever the quantity property is changed, onQuantityChange is invoked with a PropertyChangeEvent event. The event tells you the old value, the new value, which property, and so forth. You can use that information to modify other data and controls in your application.

You do not need to use BindingUtils to use ChangeWatcher. If there is a property you want to observe, set up a ChangeWatcher directly, using the ChangeWatcher.watch() function:

```
quantityWatcher = ChangeWatcher.watch(this,"quantity",onQuantityChange);
```

This can be a very powerful mechanism in that first, you do not need to write a setter function for the property, and second, you can observe changes to properties that are not in your component. For instance, you can set up a binding to the NumericStepper's value property. The binding simply sets a variable whenever the NumericStepper's value changes. But suppose that you want to send information to your server whenever the NumericStepper changes? You can set up a ChangeWatcher on that NumericStepper's value property and send the information from there.

Summary

"Advanced" event programming can mean several things:

- ❑ Writing custom events, preferably one per component to make the code easier to understand and change
- ❑ Using ActionScript to supplement the automated data binding (curly-brace notation) of MXML
- ❑ Setting up event listeners when member variables change

Combining these techniques, along with your normal use of data binding and events, can give your application flexibility and make parts of your application reusable.

Sometimes a component has to present alternatives, such as disabling a set of input controls until a check box is selected, or morphing a login form to a registration form. This is when *states* come into play. They are explored in the next chapter, "State Management."

20

State Management

A Flex application can do a lot of things. Managing all of the user interface components can quickly become complex. Sometimes you need components that do nearly the same thing, but are different enough to make you create several components. But what if one component could have two looks? That is exactly what States in Flex do. With States you can condense your application yet still make your project easy to maintain.

This chapter covers States: what they are, how you use them, and how to manipulate them in ActionScript.

What Are States?

Have you ever written a component where a user's action changes the appearance of the component? For example, perhaps you have wanted the ability to expand a component, opening a space to show more details. Or maybe you have wanted to enable some fields and disable others.

Those are the times when using a State can make writing code easier. A State provides changes to a component's own properties and styles, and changes to a component's children's properties and styles, as well as temporarily adding and removing children from the component.

The collection of things to be changed is known as an *override*. Suppose that you have a component called `EmployeeDetails`. The component initially has the employee name and button labeled "Details." When the Details button is clicked, the component expands to show the employee's ID number, department, manager, and so forth.

You could write the component using ActionScript code to add in the additional controls when the Details button is clicked and to remove those controls when the Details button was clicked again. Or the component could be written using States. Writing the component using States is easier and more effective.

In the example, the initial view shown by the component is just the employee's name and the Details button. This is called the *base state*. When the Details button is clicked, the component's state changes and that state does the following:

❑   The physical size of the component increases to accommodate the extra fields. This overrides the component's current height.

❑   The extra fields are added. This overrides the component's collection of child controls.

❑   The label on the Details button changes to "Hide." This overrides a specific control's properties.

The Flex framework applies the overrides in a state to the current state of the component whenever the component's state changes. You do not have to write any code to make this happen; all you need to do is define the States.

When the component's state changes again, the Flex framework undoes the overrides and restores the properties and children to their previous values. Again, you do not have to write any code to achieve this.

The States Property

Every Flex component has a property called `States`. `Buttons` as well as `Panels` have States. This means your components have States as well because your components extend the components in the Flex framework.

The `States` property is an `Array` of `mx.States.State` objects. Each `State` object has a collection of overrides that determine the finished look of the state.

Adding States

There are several ways to add States to your components. The easiest way is with Flex Builder's Design view. You can also add States dynamically using ActionScript. Of course with Flex, you can use both, too.

Creating States Using Flex Builder's Design View

You can use Flex Builder to make States quickly. Start by creating a new MXML component in Flex Builder named `EmployeeDetails.mxml`. (You can find this file with the code samples for this book.) Base the component on `Canvas`. Switch to Design View and add a `Label` component and a `Button` component, making it look something like Figure 20-1. It is not important that it be exact.

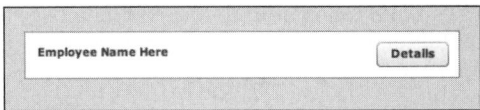

Figure 20-1

Notice that the `Canvas` is just tall enough to enclose the employee name and Details button. The employee name is anchored to the left and top edges of the `Canvas`, while the Details button is anchored to the right and top edges of the Canvas. Doing this allows the Canvas's width to change, while the Details button remains stuck to the right side.

To add the new state, click the Add State button, as shown in Figure 20-2, and give the state a name, such as DetailsState, as shown in Figure 20-3.

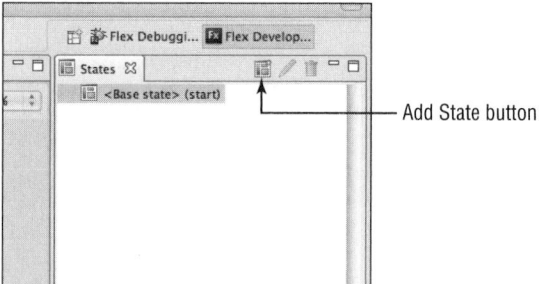

Figure 20-2

Figure 20-3

When you click OK, Flex Builder adds the new state to the States View, as shown in Figure 20-4.

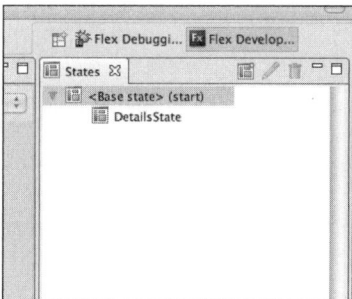

Figure 20-4

At this point, Design View hasn't changed at all. But now, whenever you do anything in Design View, it will be applied to the selected state.

Once you have created States in your components, it is easy to forget which state is selected when you change your component. Therefore, whenever you do make changes in Design View, glance at the States View and make sure the correct state is selected; otherwise, you may find your changes appearing in other States!

Click the Details button and change its label to Hide. Now switch to Source View so that you can see what Flex Builder has done. Scroll to the top of the file, and you will see that Flex Builder has added the following code:

```
<?xml version="1.0" encoding="utf-8"?>
<mx:Canvas xmlns:mx="http://www.adobe.com/2006/mxml" width="400" height="42">
    <mx:States>
        <mx:State name="DetailsState">
            <mx:SetProperty target="{detailsButton}" name="label" value="Hide"/>
        </mx:State>
    </mx:States>
    <mx:Label text="Employee Name Here" fontWeight="bold"
        left="10" top="10" id="employeeName"/>
    <mx:Button label="Details" right="10" top="10" id="detailsButton"/>

</mx:Canvas>
```

Flex Builder added a new element to the component file using the `<mx:States>` tag. Within the `States` property tag are the definitions of the actual States (the `<mx:State>` tags). In this case, there is a single state called `DetailsState`. Notice how changing the name of the button from "Details" to "Hide" maps to the `<mx:SetProperty>` tag:

```
<mx:SetProperty target="{detailsButton}" name="label" value="Hide" />
```

The `SetProperty` tag is an override that identifies the object to change using the `target` attribute (`detailsButton`) and specifies which property of that control to change using the `name` attribute (`label`). The `value` attribute specifies the change to make ("Hide").

Switch back to Design View and make the following changes to the `DetailsState` (make sure `DetailsState` is highlighted in the States View of Flex Builder):

❑   Enlarge the `Canvas`.

❑   Add a `Label` control for Employee ID, Manager, and Department.

The result should look like Figure 20-5.

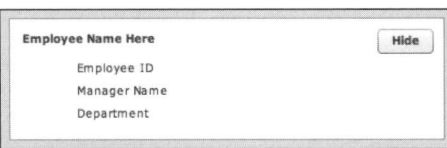

Figure 20-5

In Design View, click the base state and you will see that the component changes to the original view of the Employee Name and the Details button. Click the DetailsState and you will see what's shown in Figure 20-5.

When you switch between States in Design View, Flex Builder applies or removes the overrides defined in the state.

Changing States

Simply adding States to a component will not make those States active. You need some ActionScript to do that. Go back into Source View of the component, and change the Details button to add the following click event handler:

```
<mx:Button label="Details" right="10" top="10" id="detailsButton">
    <mx:click>
        <![CDATA[
            if( currentState == "DetailsState" ) currentState = "";
            else currentState = "DetailsState";
        ]]>
    </mx:click>
</mx:Button>
```

Since a component may have multiple States, the currentState property contains the name of, well, the current state the component is showing. The currentState property is a String, and its value must match exactly to the name of a state defined in the <mx:States> property. A component's base state is simply the empty string (not null).

The click event handler for the Details button checks the currentState property of the component and switches between DetailsState and the base state. That is all that is necessary to switch States: simply change the value of the currentState property. The Flex framework will do the rest by processing the overrides defined in the <mx:State> object.

Testing the Example

Before diving into a more detailed explanation of States, take a moment to run this example: Create a Flex application and add in the EmployeeDetails component:

```
<?xml version="1.0" encoding="utf-8"?>
<mx:Application xmlns:mx= http://www.adobe.com/2006/mxml layout="absolute"
    xmlns:ns1="components.*">

    <ns1:EmployeeDetails x="19" y="10">
    </ns1:EmployeeDetails>

</mx:Application>
```

When you run the application, it initially appears as shown in Figure 20-6.

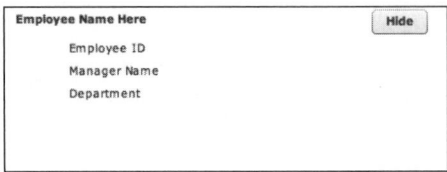

Figure 20-6

If you click the Details button, the application should change to look like Figure 20-7.

Employee Name Here   Hide
    Employee ID
    Manager Name
    Department

Figure 20-7

Understanding the MXML Tags

Flex Builder's Design View does a lot of the work for you when you create or change States. Design View does this by generating MXML tags when you create States and modifying them when you change States. Understanding those tags will make it easier for you to manipulate them as you write more complex applications.

Adding Components

Switch back to Source View in Flex Builder, and take a look at the `<mx:States>` definition:

```
<mx:States>
    <mx:State name="DetailsState">
        <mx:SetProperty target="{detailsButton}" name="label" value="Hide"/>
        <mx:SetProperty name="height" value="108"/>
        <mx:AddChild position="lastChild">
            <mx:Label x="60" y="36" text="Employee ID" id="employeeID"/>
        </mx:AddChild>
        <mx:AddChild position="lastChild">
            <mx:Label x="60" y="56" text="Manager Name" id="managerName"/>
        </mx:AddChild>
        <mx:AddChild position="lastChild">
            <mx:Label x="60" y="76" text="Department" id="department"/>
        </mx:AddChild>
    </mx:State>
</mx:States>
```

In addition to the `<mx:SetProperty>` override tag encountered earlier, Flex Builder added tags to account for the three new fields (the employee ID, manager, and department) using `<mx:AddChild>` override tags.

The <mx:AddChild> tag instructs the Flex framework to add a new control to the component's display list. This overrides the component's child list. The position attribute signals that the control should be added to the end of the display list; this is not an indication of the control's position on the screen.

Within the <mx:AddChild> tag are the normal Flex control tags. In this example, only Labels are being added, but any Flex control — even your custom components — may be added.

The only rule is that only a single child can be added with each <mx:AddChild> tag. This is why there are three <mx:AddChild> tags and not one <mx:AddChild> tag with three <mx:Label> tags in it.

Removing Components

Of course, if there is an <mx:AddChild> tag, there has to be a <mx:RemoveChild> tag, and there is. If a state is created with fewer controls than another state, you would see a <mx:RemoveChild> override tag. For example, if you had wanted to replace the Details button with a Hide button, your DetailsState would look like this instead:

```
<mx:States>
    <mx:State name="DetailsState">
        <mx:SetProperty target="{detailsButton}" name="label" value="Hide"/>
            <mx:RemoveChild target="{detailsButton}"/>
            <mx:AddChild position="lastChild">
                <mx:Button label="Hide" right="10" top="8"/>
            </mx:AddChild>
        <mx:SetProperty name="height" value="108"/>
        <mx:AddChild position="lastChild">
            <mx:Label x="60" y="36" text="Employee ID" id="employeeID"/>
        </mx:AddChild>
        <mx:AddChild position="lastChild">
            <mx:Label x="60" y="56" text="Manager Name" id="managerName"/>
        </mx:AddChild>
        <mx:AddChild position="lastChild">
            <mx:Label x="60" y="76" text="Department" id="department"/>
        </mx:AddChild>
    </mx:State>
</mx:States>
```

The <mx:RemoveChild> tag uses the target attribute to identify the control to removal of the Details button.

Gone, But Not Destroyed

The <mx:RemoveChild> override in the state does not destroy the control. All <mx:RemoveChild> does is remove the control from the component's display list. This is the same as doing the following:

```
detailsButton.includeInLayout = false;
detailsButton.visible = false;
invalidateDisplayList();
```

You can still modify the control. When the state changes, the control is added back to the display list in the same position, and with the same properties, it had before the state change.

`<mx:AddChild>` works in a similar way. The child does not exist until the first time the state is activated. After that, the child is removed from the display list when the state is not active. (This allows you to reference its properties.)

Setting and Changing Properties and Styles

The previous examples showed how controls can be added and removed in States. You can also have overrides that change properties and styles.

In the previous example, the Details button had its `label` property changed using the `<mx:SetProperty>` override. Any property of a control may be overridden. For instance, the following makes a control invisible by changing its `visible` property:

```
<mx:SetProperty target="{control}" name="visible" value="false" />
```

and the following makes the third child of a `ViewStack` the active child:

```
<mx:SetProperty target="{viewstack1}" name="selectedIndex" value="2" />
```

Remember to specify the component or control using the `target` attribute, the property to be changed with the `name` attribute, and specify the new value using the `value` attribute.

Changing styles works the same way, except that you use the `<mx:SetStyle>` override instead.

The following changes a `Label`'s color to yellow:

```
<mx:SetStyle target="{somelabel}" name="color" value="0xFFFF00" />
```

The following changes an `HBox` container's top constraint:

```
<mx:SetStyle target="{someHbox}" name="top" value="134" />
```

Always check the Flex documentation of a control to determine if you have a style or a property so that you know which override to use, `<mx:SetStyle>` or `<mx:SetProperty>`.

Changing Event Handlers

In the preceding example, the Details button's `click` event toggles the `currentState` property. If the `currentState` is `DetailsState` when it is called, the event handler changes the `currentState` to `""` (the base state); if the `currentState` is the base state, the event handler sets the `currentState` to the `DetailsState`. This is a little messy.

Not only can you add and remove children as well as change styles and properties when switching States, you can also change event handlers. To demonstrate this, make the event handler for the Details button a call to a function defined in the `EmployeeDetails` comment, named `onDetailsButton`:

```
<mx:Button label="Details" click="onDetailsButton(event)" />
```

Write this function simply as:

```
private function onDetailsButton ( event:Event ) : void {
    currentState = "DetailsState";
}
```

Now add another function to switch back to the base state:

```
private function onHideButton( event:Event ) : void {
    currentState = "";
}
```

Finally, add a new override tag to the definition of the DetailsState state:

```
<mx:SetEventHandler target="{detailsButton}" name="click"
    handlerFunction="onHideButton" />
```

The `<mx:SetEventHandler>` override tag identifies the component by using the `target` attribute, identifies the event of interest (`click`) by using the `name` attribute, and specifies the alternate function by using the `handlerFunction` attribute.

When the state changes, so does the event handler for the Details button (now the Hide button). Clicking the Hide button runs the `onHideButton()` function, changing the state back to the base state.

As with properties and styles, the `SetEventHandler` override is reset to the previous value when the state is restored.

Data Binding

You can also use data binding in state tags:

```
<mx:SetProperty target="{control2}" name="y" value="{control1.y}" />
[Bindable]
private var currentFontWeight:String = "normal";
...
<mx:SetStyle target="{someLabel}" name="fontWeight" value="{currentFontWeight}" />
```

Keep in mind that when regressing from a state to a previous (or base) state, the previous property or style value of the control is used. Data binding is not used when restoring States.

Creating States in ActionScript

You can create States in ActionScript as well as in MXML. A component's `States` property is an `Array` of `mx.States.State` objects. The strategy follows the MXML example: create a state, create the overrides (`SetProperty`, `SetStyle`, `AddChild`, `RemoveChild`, `SetEventHandler`), add the overrides to the state, and then add the state to the `States` property of the component.

You can create States at any time, but most likely you will create them once, when the component is being initialized. Add an event handler for the component's `initialize` event and mimic the MXML, using ActionScript instead:

```
private function createStates() : void
{
```

Have the initialize event handler call the `createStates()` function:

```
var detailsState:State = new State();
detailsState.name = "DetailsState";
```

Create an instance of `mx.States.State`, and set its `name` property to `DetailsState`:

```
var overrides:Array = new Array();
```

Create an `Array` that will hold all of the overrides for this state:

```
// change the height
overrides.push( new SetProperty(this,"height",108) );
```

The `height` property is changed with a `SetProperty` override. For ActionScript, this means creating a new instance of `SetProperty`. The target for this `SetProperty` override is the component itself, the property being changed is `height`, and the new value is 108. When the `SetProperty` object is created, it is pushed onto the overrides `Array`:

```
// change the label of the Button
overrides.push( new SetProperty(detailsButton,"label","Hide") );
```

The Details button's label is also changed with a `SetProperty` override. In this case, the target is the `detailsButton`, the property being changed is its `label`, and the new value is the String, `"Hide"`:

```
// add the EmployeeID label
employeeID = new Label();
employeeID.text = "EmployeeID";
employeeID.x = 60;
employeeID.y = 36;
overrides.push( new AddChild(this,employeeID) );
```

When it comes time to add a child to a state, you create an instance of the `AddChild` override and give to it an instance of a component. In this example, an `mx.controls.Label` is being added, so the `AddChild` is passed the `Label` instance that corresponds to the Employee ID.

Notice that as with the MXML override tags, the `Label`'s x and y properties are also set. Once the `AddChild` is created, it is also added to the overrides `Array`:

```
// add the manager
managerName = new Label();
managerName.text = "managerName";
managerName.x = 60;
managerName.y = 56;
```

```
        overrides.push( new AddChild(this,managerName) );

        // add the department
        department = new Label();
        department.text = "department";
        department.x = 60;
        department.y = 76;
        overrides.push( new AddChild(this,department) );
```

The manager and department `Label`s are added in the same way the Employee ID is added:

```
        // now add these overrides to the state
        detailsState.overrides = overrides;

        // add the DetailsState to this component's state list - remember that
        // this is an Array of States
        States = [ detailsState ];
    }
```

Once the overrides `Array` is complete, it is set as the `override` property of the state. Once the state is complete, it is added to the `States` property of the component. Notice that the `States` property also takes an `Array`, and in this example, the `Array` is created dynamically using the `[]` `Array` syntax.

Real Estate Management

The amount of space on the computer screen is limited. Sometimes you have to think of clever ways to pack in a lot of information. One technique is to display only the most relevant (or common) data and provide a way to view the rest. The most often used way to display more details is with a pop-up. But pop-ups are distracting and usually lock up the rest of the application until they are dismissed. Further, unless you change some settings, a modal pop-up in Flex blurs the screen a bit, making it difficult to see any related information.

States can help in this situation. The previous example showed how a component can be expanded in place to reveal more information. Once the state has been set up, the code simply changes the `currentState` property and the information is revealed. The application may get a scrollbar, but at least the detail is there along with the rest of the information.

Whenever you are faced with taking the user to different place to see related information, consider using a state to modify the display. Switching contexts on the user is distracting whereas blending content, even if it means hiding something currently visible, is more engaging.

Common Problems

States can be a source of problems if you are not careful. Here are some tips to help you avoid common pitfalls.

States versus ViewStacks

The ViewStack component places a number of components on top of each other but shows only one of them at a time. For example, a Login component might have a ViewStack with three children:

❑ One to get the user's name and password (login form)

❑ One to let them register and get a user name and password (registration form)

❑ One to display error messages (error form)

The Login component could also achieve this using States, one state for each of the above forms. In this example, either States or ViewStacks work well.

Now suppose that you want to do something a little different with the registration form. Since the registration form needs to have user name and password fields, you decide you want to use the same ones from the login form. You envision that picking the Register button on the login form will cause the user name and password fields to slide up and additional fields to fade into view, with the Login button changing its label to "Register."

This change from a simple login form to a registration form is not something that can be done with a ViewStack (which would just replace one child with another). This type of change is what is possible with States. The base state has the login form fields. The RegisterState has those fields moved up and other fields added. The animation of the fields and the fading in of other fields is accomplished with transitions, which are discussed in Part V, "Visual Effects and Multimedia."

Optimization

Suppose that you have created the component shown in Figure 20-8, and then you've created a new state in the component that looks like Figure 20-9.

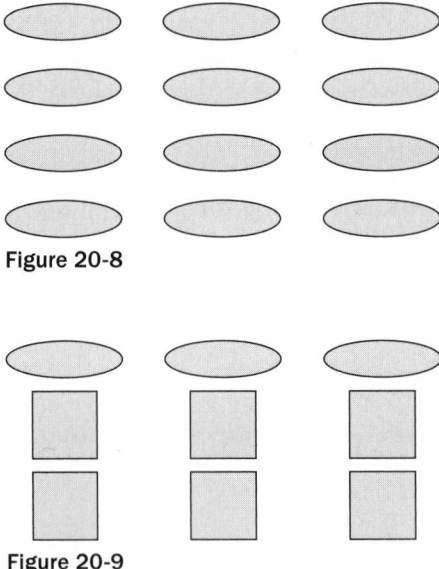

Figure 20-8

Figure 20-9

If you create this new state in Flex Builder's Design View, you'll see many <mx:RemoveChild> and <mx:AddChild> override elements. While this works, you can make things easier on yourself as well as improve the application's performance.

When you have a lot of elements being added and removed, the Flex Framework has to operate on them individually. Not only does this take time, but if you decide to add a new component, you have to remember to add it to the state change.

A better approach is to wrap the common elements of the state change into a container. A Canvas is a good choice because it doesn't add its own layout. If you have positioned all of these components in a Panel, for example, wrapping them with a Canvas is pretty straightforward, as shown in Figure 20-10.

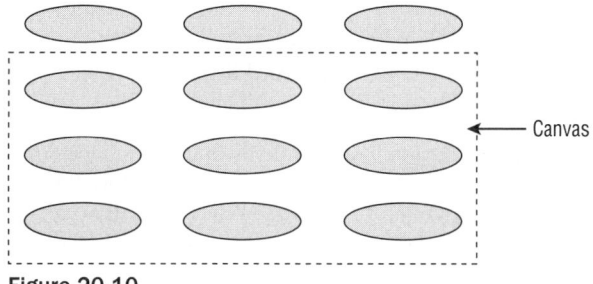

Figure 20-10

The new <mx:State> will consist of a single <mx:RemoveChild> and a single <mx:AddChild>. The Flex framework now removes one element and adds one element, which is a lot faster than operating on the elements individually. Further, if you add a new element, you don't have to do anything to the <mx:State>; the new element will be carried along automatically, as shown in Figure 20-11.

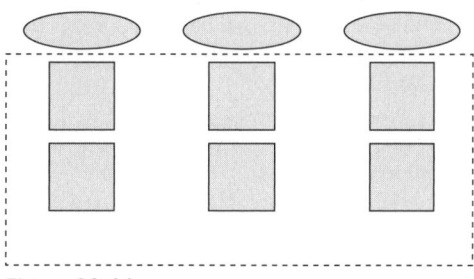

Figure 20-11

Anticipating Transitions

Transitions are special effects applied to the components of States as their values are changed to the next state. Transitions are discussed in detail in Part V, but if you think you want to use transitions, some preparation of your States can make using transitions go smoothly.

Optimizing your States is the biggest improvement you can make. If your transition will involve moving components, moving a dozen components individually will take a lot more effort than moving a `Canvas` with a dozen components. If you can group your state elements into containers, you will find the transitions will work much better.

For every action there is an equal, but opposite, reaction. Whenever you see an `<mx:SetProperty>` or a `<mx:RemoveChild>` state override, there is going to be an `<mx:SetProperty>` to undo the property change when restoring the state. Likewise, there is going to be an `<mx:AddChild>` to undo the `<mx:RemoveChild>` state override. These state overrides aren't always explicitly coded, but these are there nonetheless. Keep this in mind when you set up transitions — it will help you incorporate the transition elements, such as `<mx:SetPropertyAction>` and `<mx:AddChildAction>`.

Suppose that you want to move a `Button` to the top of the screen while resizing a `Canvas`. The effect should be that the `Button` glides to the top of the screen, while the `Canvas` gets taller. When the component goes back to the base state, the `Button` should glide back to its original position and the `Canvas` should shrink to its original height.

The state simply has a `<mx:SetProperty>` override to change the y position of the `Button` and another `<mx:SetProperty>` to change the height of the `Canvas`. To restore the component to the base state, imagine there is a `<mx:SetProperty>` for the `Button` to change its y value back to its original position and a `<mx:SetProperty>` override to change the `Canvas`'s height to its original value.

Your transition effects to the base state may need to incorporate `<mx:SetPropertyAction>` elements for both the `Button` and `Canvas` to get them to move and resize properly.

Summary

Flex States can give your application some added punch by having components change to suit the climate. Think of States as a way to quickly change a bunch of properties, event handlers, and styles, adding new components and removing others, all by setting a single property (`currentState`). Data binding can make the States even more dynamic.

Use Flex Builder's Design View to create the States and fine-tune them in Source view. Just make sure to verify which state you are about to edit when in Design View.

You can also create States in ActionScript, or you can use ActionScript to manipulate the States you create with MXML.

Finally, transitions can apply special effects to the state overrides, giving fluidity to the state change. Read more about transitions in Part V, "Visual Effects and Multimedia."

The next chapter discusses how to prepare your components for delivery to other developers as well as using libraries from other parties.

21

Using Libraries

Code libraries have been around for a long time. The idea is simple: put code into a repository where it can be shared or used by several applications. These days the repository is an archive file — a file of files — in a compressed format, as it tends to hold quite a lot of information. If you are familiar with Java, perhaps you have heard of the JAR file. This is a file that contains compiled Java classes.

Archive files that contain compiled code are known as *libraries*. Libraries are an essential part of software development. Library files make it possible to ship collections of code to many developers. You may find yourself writing components that are needed by another group. If your component is made up of several class files, placing the classes into a single file makes it easier to distribute.

Library files also make it possible to have different versions of the same code. Your component, version 1, might be in use by several groups. Once you finish version 2, you can make a new library file and send that out. Some people might use the newer library, whereas others might wait until their project is done or on a new phase of a project.

This chapter shows you how to make and use libraries, known as SWCs, using Flex Builder and command-line tools.

ActionScript Libraries

ActionScript also has its own archive file. The file contains compiled ActionScript classes and is identified by its .swc file extension.

Flash Player Library

Flex applications run in the Flash Player, which means that Flex applications use some Flash classes. For example, String and Number are classes found in the Flash Player. If you are drawing your own graphics using ActionScript, you will use the Graphics class from the flash.display package. And, of course, all events are based on the Event class, from the flash.events package in the Flash Player.

All the Flash Player classes are left out of the final SWF the Flex compiler creates. There is no need to have the Event class, the Graphics class, and so forth inside of the SWF since those classes are already inside of the Flash Player. The Flex compiler just leaves them out.

Flex Libraries

So where exactly do the Flex Buttons come from? As you know by now, the Flex framework is a set of classes, a lot of classes. Of course, you do not include the source code to those classes when you make a Flex application; you only create your own code.

If you open Flex Builder and look at a project's properties, specifically at the library path, you will see something similar to Figure 21-1.

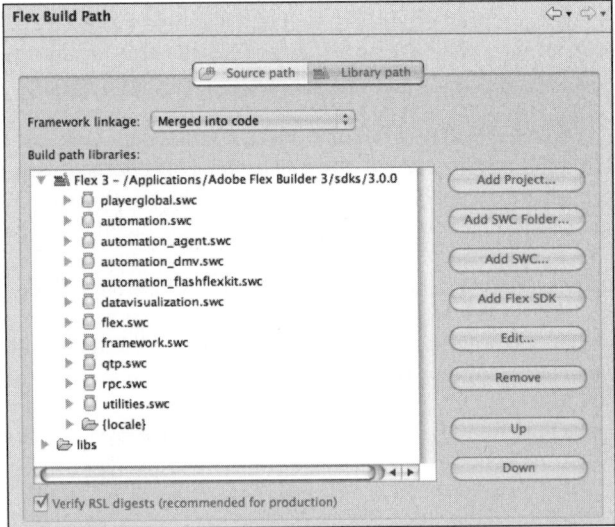

Figure 21-1

The library path of the project's properties lists all the libraries containing ActionScript code that you can use to construct an application. The Flex framework classes largely live in the frameworks.swc file.

The Flash Player classes are defined in the playerglobal.swc file. As mentioned previously, these classes are not linked into the final SWF since the Flash Player already has them. The purpose of the playerglobal.swc is so that the Flex compiler has the definition of those classes and can generate the proper code to make use of them.

SWCs versus SWFs

The Flex compiler creates SWFs, files of byte code instructions that are interpreted by the Flash Player and executed. A SWC, on the other hand, is not an executable file. If given to the Flash Player, it will not execute it because the file is not structured in the same way as a SWF.

A SWC is simply a collection of class definitions, images, fonts, and other resources. These definitions are given to the Flex compiler, along with your source code, so that an executable SWF can be built.

Anatomy of a SWC

You can open a SWC using a file that reads archive files. On Windows, the WinZIP program can do that, as can WinRAR. On Mac OS X, you can open a SWC with the Stuffit utility.

Inside of the SWC you will see a collection of files, which is typical of an archive file. One of the files is `catalog.xml`. If you open `catalog.xml`, you will see an inventory of the contents of the SWC.

Along with the `catalog.xml`, there is a file called `library.swf` — a SWF inside of a SWC. `library.swf` contains the compiled classes listed in `catalog.xml`. When the Flex compiler opens a SWC, it loads the classes in `library.swf` into memory and uses those definitions to build the final application SWF.

There is nothing magical about this. A SWC is simply a convenient way to transport a collection of classes.

Creating a Library with Flex Builder

Suppose that you have found that a set of classes you have created could be used in several programs. Or perhaps you already know you are going to create a set of classes to be used for multiple projects. You can create a Flex Library using Flex Builder. You can also create this library without Flex Builder, as discussed later in the section "Creating Libraries with COMPC."

Creating a Library Project

From Flex Builder, select File ➪ New ➪ Flex Library Project. The New Flex Library Project dialog appears, as shown in Figure 21-2.

Name the project `SampleLibrary` and place it in the `/Flex Examples` folder. Click Finish and Flex Builder creates the project for you.

If you look into the Flex Builder Project Navigator, you will see the project added to the list, as shown in Figure 21-3.

The icon next to the name is a folder with some books, indicating that it is a library project. At the moment, there is only a `bin` directory. (This is where the library will go.)

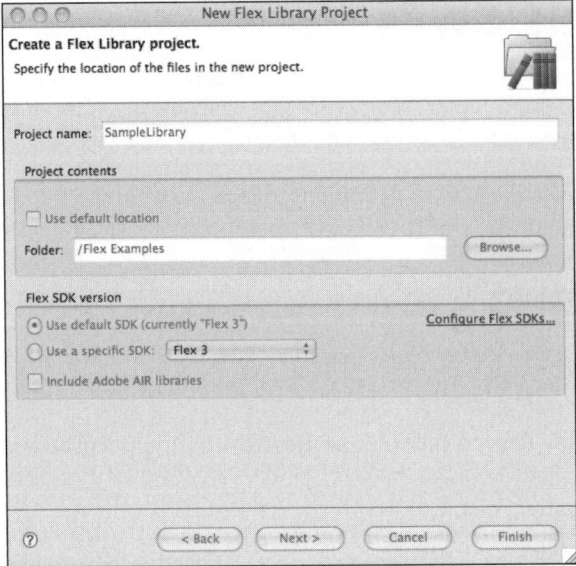

Figure 21-2

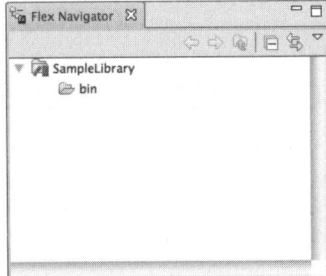

Figure 21-3

Adding Sources

A library needs content. To add content, right-click on the SampleLibrary project and select Import. Into this folder, import any of your existing ActionScript or MXML files that you want to include in this library. You can also create them using the Flex Builder editors. In the end, you should see something like Figure 21-4.

Creating the SWC

Once you have added your source files, you need to include them in the library in order for them to be compiled. To do this, open the library's project properties, select Flex Library Build Path, and then click the Classes tab (see Figure 21-5).

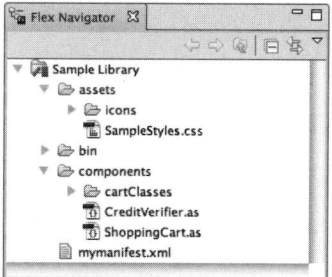

Figure 21-4

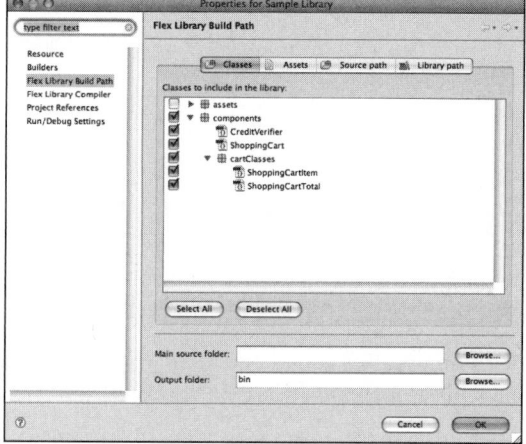

Figure 21-5

Click the check box next to the "components" folder, which automatically selects all its contents.

If you have any asset files, such as images and style sheets, select the Assets tab (see Figure 21-6) and include them. These are assets that you are not embedding in the classes of the library but would embed in the files that use the library.

When you click OK, the classes will be compiled and then included in the SWC. In this case, the SWC is SampleLibrary.swc and is stored in the project's bin directory.

A common mistake is to forget to include any new code in the Library Build Path. For instance, if you create a class, server.shopping.Bag, the class is in the server.* package. So far, only items in the components.* package are being included in the SWC. You must go back to the library build path and include the server.* package in the included classes list. If you create a class somewhere in the components.* package, you do not have to do this, as components.* is already in the list.

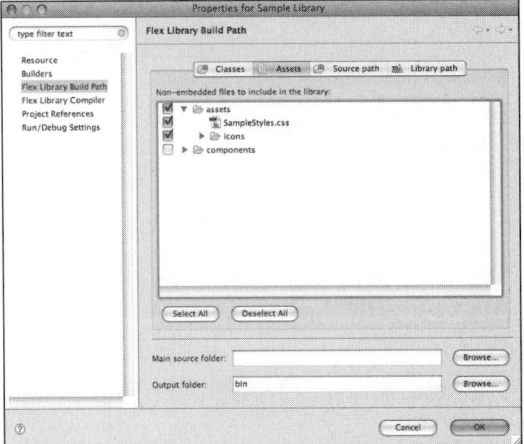

Figure 21-6

Creating Libraries with COMPC

So far this chapter has discussed creating SWC library files using Flex Builder. But what if you do not use Flex Builder? What if you want to have your library files built by an automated process?

The solution is to use the command-line compiler, COMPC. COMPC is an executable command-line tool in the bin directory of the Flex Framework SDK. Its job is to turn MXML files into ActionScript files and then compile all of the ActionScript files into byte code. Additionally, you can use COMPC to assemble a SWC.

For the Flex Framework SDK, COMPC is located in the flex_install/bin directory; for Flex Builder, COMPC is located in the flex_builder_install_dir/sdks/sdk_version/bin directory.

Suppose that you have a directory, src, that contains all the files you want to include in a SWC. The directory structure might look like this:

```
src/
 assets/
     icons/
         company_logo.jpg
         submit_button_up.png
         ...
 com/
     yourcompany/
         yourproject/
             components/
                 LoginWindow.mxml
                 BubbleScroller.as
     ...
```

The following COMPC command will create a library named CompanyCommon.swc from this source directory:

```
compc -source-path=src -output=bin/CompanyCommons.swc -include-classes
  com.yourcompany.yourproject.components.LoginWindow
  com.yourcompany.yourproject.components.BubbleScroller
```

COMPC Options

When you use COMPC to build a library, there are a few command-line options you must give and a few more you will need if you plan on including other assets in the SWC.

❑ -source-path: This option names the directory where the class files are located. If the command is given in the directory where src is a subdirectory, all the class files are assumed to be located somewhere in that directory.

❑ -include-classes: This option names the classes to compile and to include in the library. In this example, there are only two classes, but if you have many classes, you need to include each of them. This is very tedious and it shows how helpful Flex Builder can be.

❑ -output: This option names the resulting SWC file.

Adding Assets

In the previous example, only the class files made it into the CompanyCommons.swc library file. To add the assets, you must include them explicitly:

```
compc -source-path=src -output=bin/CompanyCommons.swc
-include-classes com.yourcompany.yourproject.components.LoginWindow
  com.yourcompany.yourproject.components.BubbleScroller
-include-files company_log.jpg assets/icons/company_logo.jpg submit_button_up.png
  assets/icons/submit_button_up.png
```

The -include-files options expects the values you give it to be in pairs. The pairs are: name path, where name is a unique name for the assets and path is the path to the asset, including its filename. This may be seem redundant because the common practice is to use the filename as the unique name for the asset. But this would work just as well:

```
-include-file logo assets/icons/company_logo.jpg buttonUp
  assets/icons/submit_button_up.png
```

See the upcoming section "Using Assets from Libraries" for more on assets.

Specifying the Manifest File

As you can see from the example COMPC commands, the command line can become long and error-prone very quickly. For that reason, you can place the list of classes in a file and name the file when building your SWC.

The file is called a *manifest*, and it is an XML file that lists all of the classes to be included in the SWC. For example, `sample-manifest.xml` lists the classes from the preceding example:

```
<?xml version="1.0"?>
<componentPackage>
    <component id="ShoppingCart" class="components.ShoppingCart" />
    <component id="CreditVerifier" class="components.CreditVerifier" />
    <component id="CartItem" class="components.cartClasses.ShoppingCartItem" />
    <component id="CartTotal" class="components.cartClasses.ShoppingCartTotal" />
</componentPackage>
```

The `id` of the component gives the name of the MXML tag for the component. For example:

```
<sample:CartItem width="100%" height="100%" id="cart" />
```

The `id` is optional and if left out, you can use the name of the class as the tag.

```
<sample:ShoppingCartItem width="100%" height="100%" id="cart" />
```

Now, instead of listing the classes individually in the COMPC command, you specify the manifest file by using the `-namespace` and `-include-namespaces` options:

```
compc -source-path . -output=bin/test.swc -namespace http://sample
    sample-manifest.xml -include-namespaces http://myspace
```

The `-namespace` option gives both the namespace URI and the manifest file. The `-include-namespaces` option lists just the namespace. Both options must be present.

Best Practices for Component Libraries

Here are some ideas you can use when creating your own libraries.

Sharing Source Directories

Imagine that you are in a development team building several Flex and AIR applications. Perhaps there are several components and object classes that are common to all the projects. Ideally, you want a single copy of the code to be shared among the projects. This keeps things in sync and you always know what version you have. For example, if someone changes component A, you want to make sure you use that update to component A.

Assuming that you are using a source code control system, you probably have a copy of the project where component A is based. But how do you incorporate component A into your project?

One obvious answer is to simply have the project that houses component A be a Flex Library project, which builds a SWC, and include that SWC in your project.

But there is another choice: sharing source code folders. This means your project includes the source folder of component A and compiles the component source directly, rather than getting the component from a SWC.

There are several disadvantages to this technique:

❑ You cannot easily manage revision of component code. That is, if you are happy with how component A is working and someone changes it, you are obligated to pick up the changed code. If component A fails to build, you have to fix it yourself or have someone else do it. If component A were in a SWC, you could get a new SWC when you wanted or use the one you have.

❑ If the project source where component A lives is large, you have to wait for it to compile.

❑ If you are only using a few components from the external project, you may get an extra-large SWF filled with unused code.

However, if you are building several tightly integrated applications (such as an AIR desktop application or a Flex web management application), then sharing code might be a quick solution. You can always convert the project containing the shared code into a SWC library file.

Build to Sell

When you build a Flex component library, picture what it would be like to buy this library from someone. What would you expect to get? Documentation? Installation instructions? Code independence? Of course. This is a good approach to take when building component library SWCs — even if those SWCs will be used internally by your company, group, or even just you.

Code independence is key for component libraries. Suppose that you have a component that relies on a class only your application uses. Someone else could not use that component. Architecting your component library to be independent of your project is a best practice and allows for maximum reuse.

If you find that you do need to hook your project into the component (perhaps you need a reference to your main application), then extend your component, and put the extended component class in your project. For example, you may have a component in a library that scrolls text using some special buttons. As you use it, the scroll action requires a reference to the main Application class, so you can check a global variable. This makes the component's design dependent on your main Application class. If you design the component independently, you can distribute the component to others, but in your application, create a new class that extends the component and overrides the function that will need the reference to the Application object.

Using Libraries

This section describes several ways to use libraries with your Flex projects.

The libs Folder

If you need to add more SWCs to your project, you can make them available simply by dropping them into the libs folder of your project. That folder is on the search path for the Flex compiler.

The `libs` folder is a handy place to keep project-specific libraries with your project. This is especially true if you are using a source code control system. You can check the `libs` folder, along with its contents, into the source code control system. This way, someone else who needs to build the project can get the additional SWCs along with the project right from the source code control system.

The trouble with this solution is that multiple copies of the same SWC will appear throughout the organization, as each project will have its own copy. This is not necessarily a bad thing, however. Consider this: you have built your application with version 1.2 of a component SWC library. Along comes version 2 and your application is not compatible. If you do not have your own version of the library, your application may no longer build. If that application is in production or about to go into production, you will have to scramble to modify your code and have it retested by the quality assurance team. If you have your own copy of the library, you can upgrade during the next development phase for your project.

The Build Path

Although the `libs` folder is part of the build path, it is not always the ideal location for SWCs. This is true when multiple projects are using the same SWCs. In this situation, the SWCs can remain in a central location, known to all developers, and the path to the SWCs can be added to the build path.

While this means that the SWCs needed to build the project are no longer contained within the project's directories, it does mean it is easier to keep track of the copies and versions of SWCs being used.

When you want to add SWCs to the build path, begin by opening the project's properties and then navigate to the Flex Build Path, Library Path tab (see Figure 21-7).

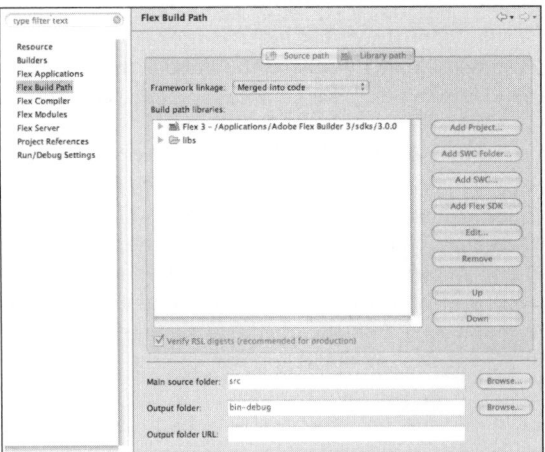

Figure 21-7

On the Library Path tab there are several ways to add SWCs:

❑ **The Add Project button:** Use this button to locate a Flex Project in the workspace that produces a SWC. For example, if your workspace contains the `SampleLibrary` project, you can add this project to the build path by using the Add Project button.

❏ **The Add SWC Folder button:** Use this button if you are adding a number of SWCs that all reside in the same folder. An example of this is the Flex 3 folder already in the build path. Figure 21-1 shows the contents of that folder.

❏ **The Add SWC button:** Use this button if you have a single SWC. Clicking this button allows you to browse to the location of the SWC and select it.

The Up and Down buttons change the order the SWCs are searched. Suppose that there is a class in a SWC that is part of the build path. You may have a class with the same name and want your class to be used instead of this other one. If you move the SWC containing your class above the other SWC, the Flex compiler will find your class first.

The Edit button allows you to change the path of the library, and the Remove button allows you to remove the SWC from the path.

The Add Flex SDK button lets you identify another Flex SDK to use instead of the one already in the build path. This is handy if you want to try your application with a newer version of the Flex SDK.

Using Assets from Libraries

SWC files do not have to contain just code, they can contain assets as well. These are assets to be embedded into the final SWC, not assets to be loaded at runtime. Anything you would normally embed, such as images, sounds, fonts, and XML files, can be placed into SWCs.

Once the SWC is in your build path, there is nothing extra you need to do to embed the assets. You do need to know the path to the assets just as you would if the asset were included in your project. For example, if your asset were normally embedded as:

```
[Embed("/icons/search_icon.png")]
```

and this image were now located in a SWC in the path of `icons/search_icon.png`, then you would use that path in the embed metadata.

The same rule applies for fonts, sounds, and anything else embedded in the final SWF.

Using SWC Files

Using a SWC file is as simple as including it in your build path. You have two choices:

❏ In Flex Builder, open your project's Build Properties ⇨ Build Path page, select the Library Path tab, and include the SWC in the list using the buttons to the right.

❏ If you prefer to use a command-line approach, add `-include-library+=<path to the SWC>/<filename>.swc` and use as many of those as necessary to include all the libraries. For example:

```
mxmlc -library-path+=<path to the SWC>/<filename>.swc YourApp.mxml
```

Summary

SWC files make it simple to share code, whether it is among members of a team or to sell on the open market. Libraries make it possible to package code and assets in a single file that will enable you to have and to maintain multiple versions of your components.

Flex Builder makes it easy to create SWCs and to use them in projects. But if you are not using Flex Builder, simply add the SWC files to your MXMLC and COMPC library path options to include the code in your application.

Part V, "Visual Effects and Multimedia," shows how adding special effects, such as wipes and fades, to movies and sound, can add to the experience of a rich Internet application.

Part V: Visual Effects and Multimedia

22

Styles

"Style" is a generic term. It can be defined as a kind of object, such as a kind of shirt or a kind of application, or it can be defined as how something appears, such as the application of typeface and color. This chapter explores style as it pertains to the Flex framework, in both of these senses. You'll learn how a Flex application's appearance can be styled, how you can reuse styles, and how you can use styles to customize the appearance of your application.

What Are CSS Styles?

Cascading Style Sheets (CSS) styles are a set of rules that define how your application will appear. CSS originated as a language used to control how HTML markup is rendered in the browser. The Flex framework takes advantage of the existing language specification for CSS to define styles as they pertain to Flex components. In Flex, you have a lot of control as to what CSS can dictate. CSS styles control background colors, text colors, font sizes, and layout (among others). In Flex, you are not only limited to specifying colors and sizes, but Flex's CSS supports the ability to control layout, styles applied to child components, shadows, and skins. This chapter focuses on styles and layout. You can expect more on skinning in Chapter 23, "Skinning and Themes."

Inline Styling Versus CSS

Styles on Flex components can be applied in one of two ways. They can either be applied directly on a component instance, or they can be defined in a style declaration that is later applied to a component instance.

Figure 22-1 shows a very simple Flex application. Within this application, there are two text boxes. Both appear the same; each has a red border, a drop shadow, red text, and an off-yellow background color. Although they appear to be visually identical, there is a difference in how the styles are applied to them. The upper text box has styles applied using a CSS declaration, and the lower text box has styles applied directly on the component instance itself.

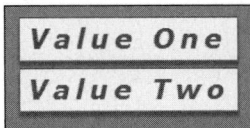

Figure 22-1

The following code was used to create this simple interface:

```
<?xml version="1.0" encoding="utf-8"?>
<mx:Application
    xmlns:mx="http://www.adobe.com/2006/mxml"
    layout="vertical">

    <mx:Style>
        .customTextInput {
            borderStyle: inset;
            borderColor: #ff0000;
            backgroundColor: #ffff99;
            color: #cc0000;
            textAlign: center;
            letterSpacing: 5;
            fontSize: 24;
            fontWeight: bold;
            fontStyle: italic;
            dropShadowEnabled: true;
        }
    </mx:Style>

    <mx:TextInput
        styleName="customTextInput"
        width="200"
        text="Value One" />

    <mx:TextInput
        borderStyle="inset"
        borderColor="#FF0000"
        backgroundColor="#FFFF99"
        color="#CC0000"
        textAlign="center"
        letterSpacing="5"
        fontSize="24"
        fontWeight="bold"
        fontStyle="italic"
        dropShadowEnabled="true"
        width="200"
        text="Value Two"  />

</mx:Application>
```

First, let's examine the `<mx:Style>` attribute of the application. Styles can be declared either directly in the application, as this example shows, or they can be defined in external stylesheets that are linked using the `<mx:Style>` tag (for example, `<mx:Style source="myExternalStyleSheel.css">`).

Now, back to the example. Inside of the `<mx:Style>` declaration, there is the CSS definition that is applied to the first `TextInput` instance. Inside that definition, style values are set for the border style, border color, background color, text color, text alignment, letter spacing, font size, font weight, font style, and drop shadow style. The Flex framework API documentation has a complete list of every CSS style available for each component type.

When using CSS markup, the declaration is defined in the following format:

```
.styleName {
    name: value;
}
```

First, the style name is specified, followed by a set of curly brackets ({ }). Inside of the brackets is a semi-colon-delimited list of key-value pairs. Each key-value pair is the style name, followed by a colon, which is followed by the actual value.

The style is applied to the first `TextInput` instance through the specification of the `styleName` property:

```
styleName="customTextInput"
```

This instructs the Flex framework to apply the styles defined by the `customTextInput` style to the `TextInput` instance.

The second `TextInput` instance has styles applied directly to its specific instance:

```
<mx:TextInput
        borderStyle="inset"
        borderColor="#FF0000"
        backgroundColor="#FFFF99"
        color="#CC0000"
        textAlign="center"
        letterSpacing="5"
        fontSize="24"
        fontWeight="bold"
        fontStyle="italic"
        dropShadowEnabled="true"
        width="200"
        text="Value Two"   />
```

In this case, all the style values are applied directly to this instance and cannot be reused across different component instances. This exemplifies an important attribute of CSS. All style sheets that are defined within CSS can be reused across multiple components. Styles applied directly to component instances cannot.

Component Styles

You may notice that the style was applied manually to the `TextInput` instance in the first example. Through CSS, it is also possible to apply default styles to a component type. Let's take a look at another example, as shown in Figure 22-2. Although there are, once again, two `TextInput` instances, the appearance has changed. The application background color has changed to white, and the text and background colors for each `TextInput` instance have changed.

Figure 22-2

The following code enabled the changes to the appearance:

```xml
<?xml version="1.0" encoding="utf-8"?>
<mx:Application
    xmlns:mx="http://www.adobe.com/2006/mxml"
    layout="vertical"
    xmlns:local="*">

    <mx:Style source="styles.css" />

    <mx:TextInput
        width="200"
        text="Value One" />

    <local:CustomTextInput
        width="200"
        text="Value Two" />

</mx:Application>
```

You can see that no styles were applied to these components. No background colors were specified on the `mx:Application` instance, and no colors were specified on either of the `TextInput` instances. You will also notice that the second `TextInput` is actually a `CustomTextInput` class, which simply extends the existing `TextInput` class. You will also notice that there is a link to an external style sheet `styles.css`.

Inside the file `styles.css`, there are declarations for the display styles for the classes associated with this example:

```css
Application {
    backgroundColor: #ffffff;
}

TextInput {
    borderStyle: inset;
    borderColor: #0000ff;
    backgroundColor: #cccccc;
    color: #0000ff;
    textAlign: center;
```

```
        letterSpacing: 5;
        fontSize: 24;
        fontWeight: bold;
        fontStyle: italic;
        dropShadowEnabled: true;
}

CustomTextInput {
        borderStyle: inset;
        borderColor: #00ff00;
        backgroundColor: #ffffff;
        color: #339900;
        textAlign: center;
        letterSpacing: 5;
        fontSize: 24;
        fontWeight: bold;
        fontStyle: italic;
        dropShadowEnabled: true;
}
```

If you look closely, you will notice that the names of each style declaration match directly with the class names of the visual components used within the applications. These define the default styles for each class instance. Every `TextInput` instance used within the application will use these styles by default, unless another style is specified using the `styleName` attribute. Likewise, every `CustomTextInput` instance will use the default styles defined in this style sheet.

You also may have noticed that none of the CSS styles in this example start with a period (`.`). A period at the beginning of the style name is used only on custom declarations that do not directly map to a class name.

It is also important to understand that CSS styles can be inherited. When changes are made to the `TextInput` style, those styles will be applied to every `TextInput` instance, even if the `TextBox` instance has a custom style applied using the `styleName` property. The custom style may override styles specified in the `TextInput` style declaration, but those that are not overridden will be applied to the component instance.

CSS Constraint-Based Layout

CSS declarations can also determine how component instances are defined within containers that support absolute positioning, such as `mx:Panel` and `mx:Canvas`. These components take advantage of the `top`, `bottom`, `left`, and `right` CSS styles for components, and position the target component relative to the constrains of the parent container's boundaries.

With this approach, you can actually have the layout of your components change depending upon the CSS style, and even have the layout change when changing the styles at runtime (as discussed further in Chapter 23).

Let's take a look at a simple example showing CSS positioning for component layout. Figures 22-3 and 22-4 show two configurations of a simple layout that contains a `TextArea`, and two `Button` instances.

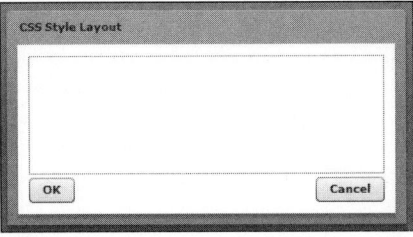

Figure 22-3

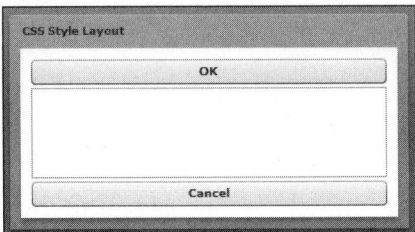

Figure 22-4

These examples are based on the same code; however, they have separate style sheets applied to them. First, let's examine the code used to create these interfaces. The code is actually quite simple:

```
<?xml version="1.0" encoding="utf-8"?>
<mx:Application
    xmlns:mx="http://www.adobe.com/2006/mxml"
    layout="absolute">

    <mx:Style source="styles1.css" />

    <mx:Panel
        title="CSS Style Layout"
        layout="absolute" >

            <mx:TextArea />

            <mx:Button
                label="OK"
                styleName="okButton" />

            <mx:Button
                label="Cancel"
                styleName="cancelButton" />


    </mx:Panel>

</mx:Application>
```

You can see that no positioning information is specified on either the TextArea or Button instances. Now let's examine the CSS that is used to layout Figure 22-3. First, the Panel class is relatively positioned to the boundaries of the parent application. The bottom of the panel will always be 10 pixels from the bottom of the application container; the top will always be 10 pixels from the top of the application container, and so on.

You can also see that the TextArea is positioned to always be 10 pixels from the top, left, and right of the Panel's component area. The bottom of the TextArea will always be 35 pixels from the bottom of the Panel's area. This leaves room for the Button instances, which are constrained to be 10 pixels from the bottom of the Panel's area.

```
Panel {
    top: 10;
    bottom: 10;
    left: 10;
    right: 10;
}

TextArea {
    top: 10;
    bottom: 35;
    left: 10;
    right: 10;
}

.okButton {
    bottom: 10;
    left: 10;
}

.cancelButton {
    bottom: 10;
    right: 10;
}
```

Now, let's review the CSS used to generate the interface shown in Figure 22-4. You can see that the panel layout is exactly the same; it is constrained to 10 pixels on all side. However, in this example, the Button placement and TextArea placement has changed.

```
Panel {
    top: 10;
    bottom: 10;
    left: 10;
    right: 10;
}

TextArea {
    top: 35;
    bottom: 35;
    left: 10;
    right: 10;
}
```

```
.okButton {
    top: 10;
    left: 10;
    right: 10;
}

.cancelButton {
    bottom: 10;
    left: 10;
    right: 10;
}
```

In this case, the `TextArea` is now constrained to 35 pixels on the top and bottom of the `Panel`, and 10 pixels on the left and right of the `Panel`. This leaves room for the buttons, whose styles have been updated to take up the area above and below the `TextArea`, within the `Panel`. The OK button, which uses the `okButton` style is now constrained to 10 pixels on the top, left, and right of the panel's area. This will cause the button to stretch and take up the entire top of the panel. Likewise, the Cancel button, which uses the `cancelButton` style, has been updated to be constrained 10 pixels from the bottom, left, and right of the panel's area. This causes the Cancel button to stretch and take up the entire bottom area of the `Panel` instance.

CSS Styles and Class Inheritance

When working with CSS, it is also important to recognize that default values applied to CSS classes are inherited by child classes. Figure 22-5 shows three `TextInput` classes. Each varies slightly from the next. The first `TextInput` is a standard `TextInput` control. The second one is actually a class that extends from `TextInput`, called `RedTextInput`. It is called `RedTextInput` because in the style declaration for it, the color style is set to red. The third is actually a class called `BoldTextInput`, which extends from `RedTextInput`. In the style declaration, it has a bold attribute applied to its style.

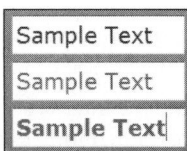

Figure 22-5

Now's let's examine the code used to build this sample. In `main.mxml`, there is just the reference to the style sheet, and the instantiation of the three `TextInput` controls:

```
<?xml version="1.0" encoding="utf-8"?>
<mx:Application
    xmlns:mx="http://www.adobe.com/2006/mxml"
    layout="vertical"
    xmlns:local="*">

    <mx:Style source="styles.css" />

    <mx:TextInput text="Sample Text" />
    <local:RedTextInput text="Sample Text" />
```

```
    <local:BoldTextInput text="Sample Text" />

</mx:Application>
```

The `RedTextInput` class simply extends the `TextInput` class:

```
public class RedTextInput extends TextInput {   }
```

The `BoldTextInput` class simply extends the `RedTextInput` class:

```
public class BoldTextInput extends RedTextInput { }
```

When examining the CSS file used in this example, you can see that the font size is changed to 20 for the `TextInput`, the color red is applied to `RedTextInput`, and the bold font weight is applied to `BoldTextInput`:

```
TextInput {
    fontSize: 20;
}

RedTextInput {
    color: #FF0000;
}

BoldTextInput {
    fontWeight: bold;
}
```

If you go back and review Figure 22-5, you will notice that the font size that was applied to the default `TextInput` class is maintained in both the `RedTextInput` and `BoldTextInput` classes. Likewise, the red color applied to the `RedTextInput` class is maintained in the `BoldTextInput` class.

CSS Styles and Subcomponents

When working with Flex, you may have already noticed that some components have styles that reference other style declarations. For example, a `Panel` has a style called `titleStyleName` that refers to the style used in the title shown at the top of the panel. You can actually create Flex components that exhibit this exact same behavior. This approach enables you to create generic, and highly customizable and reusable components.

This section walks you through creating a basic custom control that has custom referenced styles applied to it. First, let's look at a screenshot of the generated output so that there is a clear understanding of what is being built.

The custom component in this example simply contains two buttons: Button 1 and Button 2. Figure 22-6 shows three instances of this component, each with a different style applied to it, and each is separated by a horizontal rule.

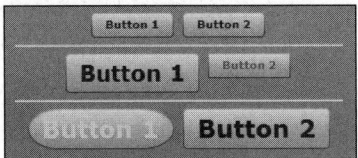

Figure 22-6

The main application code is quite simple. You can see that it is just an application container, which contains three instances of `MyCustomComponent`, separated by `HRule` instances:

```
<?xml version="1.0" encoding="utf-8"?>
<mx:Application
    xmlns:mx="http://www.adobe.com/2006/mxml"
    layout="vertical"
    xmlns:local="*">

    <mx:Style source="styles.css" />

    <local:MyCustomComponent />

    <mx:HRule
        width="300" />

    <local:MyCustomComponent
        styleName="componentStyle1" />

    <mx:HRule
        width="300" />
    <local:MyCustomComponent
        styleName="componentStyle2" />

</mx:Application>
```

Inside of the `MyCustomCompont.mxml` file is where things start to get interesting. You'll notice that the component itself is just an `HBox` that contains two `Button` instances. Inside of the `mx:Script` tag in this component, the `styleChanged` function is overridden to include the custom styles:

```
<?xml version="1.0" encoding="utf-8"?>
<mx:HBox xmlns:mx="http://www.adobe.com/2006/mxml" >

    <mx:Script>
        <![CDATA[

            override public function styleChanged(styleProp:String):void {
                var allStyles : Boolean = (styleProp == null);
                super.styleChanged( styleProp );

                if (allStyles || styleProp == "button1StyleName") {
                    if (button1) {
                        var button1StyleName:String = getStyle("button1StyleName");
                        button1.styleName = button1StyleName;
                    }
                }
```

```
                    if (allStyles || styleProp == "button2StyleName") {
                        if (button2) {
                            var button2StyleName:String = getStyle("button2StyleName");
                            button2.styleName = button2StyleName;
                        }
                    }
                }

        ]]>
    </mx:Script>

    <mx:Button label="Button 1" id="button1" />
    <mx:Button label="Button 2" id="button2" />

</mx:HBox>
```

Inside the overridden `styleChanged` function, you can see that it first calls the parent class' `styleChanged` method. This is done to invoke the default application of styles. If you forget to call this function on the parent (`super`) class, then it's likely that none of your styles will work. After calling the parent class's method, the custom styles specified in the style sheet are applied to the button controls:

```
var button1StyleName:String = getStyle("button1StyleName");
button1.styleName = button1StyleName;
```

The styles specified by `button1StyleName` are applied to the button1 instance, and the styles specified by the `button2StyleName` are applied to the button2 instance.

Now, let's examine the CSS declarations where the styles are applied. You can see that `componentStyle1` has two styles in it, called `button1StyleName` and `button2StyleName`. Each of these actually refers to the name of the class that should be used to apply styles to `button1` and `button2`, respectively.

```
.componentStyle1 {
    button1StyleName: button1Style1;
    button2StyleName: button2Style1;
}

.button1Style1 {
    fontSize: 20;
    fontWeight: bold;
}

.button2Style1 {
    cornerRadius: 0;
    color: #FF0000;
}

.componentStyle2 {
    button1StyleName: button1Style2;
    button2StyleName: button2Style2;
}

.button1Style2 {
```

```
        fontSize: 22;
        cornerRadius: 30;
        color: #00FF00;
    }

    .button2Style2 {
        fontSize: 22;
        fontWeight: bold;
    }
```

Likewise, you can see that componentStyle2 has two styles in it, called button1StyleName and button2StyleName. These also refer to the name of the class that should be used to apply styles to button1 and button2, respectively. You can see that in each case, there are actually three CSS declarations applied to each component instance. The "main" CSS declaration determines the styles applied to its subcomponents.

Summary

CSS provides rules that define how your application will appear. It can be used to manage everything from font references and colors, to how the components of your application are laid out. A thorough understanding of CSS and how the Flex framework applies it will go a long way toward helping you create great-looking applications, with maximal code reuse.

The next chapter takes the styling concepts introduced here and introduces component skinning. Combined, styles and skinning can be used to create themes for your applications, as Chapter 23 will demonstrate.

23

Skinning and Themes

The Flex framework provides for an enormous amount of customization, especially when it comes to the visual displaying of objects. This extreme amount of customization is made possible though skinning capabilities of the Flex component model. This chapter explores various types of skinning techniques and how multiple skins can be applied to your applications as themes.

What Are Skins?

A skin is the visual representation of an object; it controls how the object appears on screen and any visual behavior of that object. In simple objects, such as a `Canvas`, this controls the background appearance and any border styles. With interactive objects, such a `Button` or `ComboBox`, the skin controls how the object appears in its different states; for example, when the mouse is hovering over the object or when the mouse is clicked on that object. All visual components within the Flex framework are designed so that their appearance can be easily changed through modifications to their applied skins.

Visual skins can either be created from embedded images, created from embedded Flash-based content, or programmatically rendered by ActionScript code and the Drawing API. Each method of skinning has its own advantages.

Embedded Assets

Embedded assets can be used as visual skins for your Flex components. This may be achieved through embedding an image file for the skin, embedding a `.swf` file for the skin, or through linkages to `.swc` files that contain Flash assets that can be used as skins.

Image files are generally one of the easiest methods to use for skinning. Any `.jpg`, `.gif`, or `.png` file can be used as a component skin. Files that support transparency, such as PNG or GIF also support transparency when used as a skin. Image-based skins can enable you to create slick and extremely customized interfaces; however, image-based skins are also limited in how they can be displayed.

First, images are static; they cannot be animated when used as a skin. Although you can animate the contents of the component, you cannot animate the image-based skin itself. Additionally, image-based skins become distorted when you resize the component. This is especially true when the size of the component is increased. As the size increases, image-based skins tend to become pixilated.

Flash-based skins come in two forms. You can either embed a .swf file and access movie clip assets that can be used as skins, or you can import .swc files (class libraries) that contain assets to be used as a skin. In either case, you have the power of the Flash Player for your skins. They can be based on vector graphics, so they scale appropriately without distortion or pixilation, or you can have interactive or animated skins. Animated skins will animate inside of your application, without altering the logic of your components. Interactive skins can respond to user input, such as mouse position; however, you should not include logic in the skin class that could alter the behavior of the component itself. Chapter 26, "Flash Integration," is devoted to Flash-based skins and will cover this topic in detail.

Programmatic Skins

Programmatic skins are visual representations of objects that are completely derived from usage of the Flash Player's Drawing API. The Drawing API allows you to draw various shapes, including lines and curves, in a programmatic fashion. Programmatic skins are rendered on-screen at runtime and are completely based on code. They are not based on any embedded bitmap or SWF content. Chapter 25, "Dynamic Skinning and the Drawing API," will cover both programmatic skinning and the Drawing API in greater detail.

Applying Skins

Skins are applied to components as style properties. Therefore, you can set them or access them at runtime as you would any other style property. You can specify skins on object instances directly, or you can create style sheets to define reusable skins on components.

The following sections will walk you through how to apply skins to both Button and Canvas objects. They will show defining skins on specific object instances or defining skins through CSS styles. Each visual component has different styles and skins that can be applied to it; for a complete listing of all styles and skins for a particular object, you should consult the Flex SDK documentation.

Before examining how the skins are applied, let's examine what will be achieved when these skins are applied. In both cases, the generated output is the same. Figure 23-1 shows the skinned canvas containing three buttons that do not have custom skins applied.

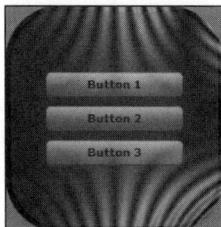

Figure 23-1

You may have noticed that the corners of the canvas shown in Figure 23-1 are rounded. This is because the skin image itself has rounded corners with a transparent background.

In Figure 23-2, you can see a button that has custom skins applied to it. Each of the button states (default/up, mouse over, mouse down, disabled) has a different image skin applied to it. You can see that the button skins are only applied to the graphics area of the button instance, not the label text. Even if you have skins applied to a button, you can customize the label. You could also have stylized text in the button skin itself; in this case, you would not need to specify a label for the button.

Figure 23-2

The series of images shown in Figure 23-3 shows the different states of each button skin. The default skin is a yellow/gold star. This will be shown in the upSkin value of the button and will be the normal state of the button. The overSkin value will contain a green star. The green star will be displayed any time that the mouse is located over the button instance. The downSkin value will contain a red star. Any time that the mouse button is pressed over this button instance, the red star will be displayed.

Figure 23-3

In the disabledSkin style, things are changed up a bit. This value contains a gray star with a red circle and strike through it. Notice that the transparent area of the image is not the same. This is important to remember when working with skins; they do not always need to be the same size, and they can contain different transparency areas.

Now that we have defined what the following examples are going to produce, let's take a look at how the skins are applied to generate that output.

Defining Skins per Object

Skins can be defined either per CSS style declaration or per object instance. Next, we will examine applying skins directly to object instances. Assigning skins to specific object instances allows you to create one-off or exception-case skinned objects.

This example defines an image as the border skin on a single `Canvas` object instance. The image file is embedded in line in the MXML for the `Canvas` object, using the `@Embed` directive. Following, you will find the entire code used to generate the skinned `Canvas`, as shown in Figure 23-1.

```
<mx:Canvas
    width="200" height="200"
    borderSkin="@Embed('assets/canvasSkin.png')" >

    <mx:Button
        label="Button 1"
        width="125"
        horizontalCenter="0"
        verticalCenter="-30" />

    <mx:Button
        label="Button 2"
        width="125"
        horizontalCenter="0"
        verticalCenter="0" />

    <mx:Button
        label="Button 3"
        width="125"
        horizontalCenter="0"
        verticalCenter="30" />

</mx:Canvas>
```

Next, we will examine the application of star-shaped skins to the `Button` instance. You can see that a skin is defined for each button state by embedding an asset, using the `@Embed` directive.

```
<mx:Button
    label="Star Button"
    x="0" y="210"
    upSkin="@Embed('assets/star_up.png')"
    overSkin="@Embed('assets/star_over.png')"
    downSkin="@Embed('assets/star_down.png')"
    disabledSkin="@Embed('assets/star_disabled.png')" />
```

In this case, you need to specify a skin for each button state; otherwise, the default skin will be used for that state. Specifying a skin for the `upSkin` style does not automatically apply skins to any other styles.

Defining Skins in Style Sheets

Skins can also be applied to declarations within CSS. Skins that are defined in style sheets are normally considered best practice for several reasons; first, because all the style definitions are declared in a single location (the .css file); second, because the style definitions are reusable, and finally because they help keep your MXML code clean and free of repeated values and clutter. You can define a style that sets border skins, using it across multiple Canvas, VBox, or HBox instances. A change to the single style declaration will automatically update all object instances that use the particular style.

The next example shows how to create the interface shown in Figure 23-1 — a skinned canvas containing three Button instances — using CSS styles instead of declarations directly on the Canvas object instance.

First, in the mx:Style code segment, a style is created named .skinnedCanvas. In this declaration, an image is specified for the borderSkin style using the Embed directive. Note, there is no @, only the word Embed. @Embed is only used when embedding assets directly on object instance properties inline in MXML.

The Canvas instance that has the style applied references the skinnedCanvas style in the styleName property. The styleName property simply references the CSS declaration that should be used when rendering the object instance:

```
<mx:Style>
    .skinnedCanvas {
        borderSkin: Embed("assets/canvasSkin.png");
    }
</mx:Style>

<mx:Canvas
    styleName="skinnedCanvas"
    width="200" height="200">

    <mx:Button
        label="Button 1"
        width="125"
        horizontalCenter="0"
        verticalCenter="-30" />

    <mx:Button
        label="Button 2"
        width="125"
        horizontalCenter="0"
        verticalCenter="0" />

    <mx:Button
        label="Button 3"
        width="125"
        horizontalCenter="0"
        verticalCenter="30" />

</mx:Canvas>
```

Now, let's reexamine the star button from the previous section. Rather than declaring the skins on the object instance, we will create a style sheet that defines the styles. This approach greatly helps with code reuse and maintaining clean code, repeated values for the upSkin and overSkin and properties can help lead to cluttered code that is more difficult to maintain.

You can see in the following code segment that a CSS declaration is created named .starButton. In this declaration, all the upSkin, overSkin, downSkin, and disabledSkin styles are specified by embedding assets using the Embed directive.

The skins are applied to the specific button instance by specifying the starButton style as the styleName property:

```
<mx:Style>
    .starButton {
        upSkin: Embed('assets/star_up.png');
        overSkin: Embed('assets/star_over.png');
        downSkin: Embed('assets/star_down.png');
        disabledSkin: Embed('assets/star_disabled.png');
    }
</mx:Style>

<mx:Button
    label="Star Button"
    x="210" y="210"
    styleName="starButton" />
```

Although this is a basic example, it is easy to see that if you had multiple buttons, it is much simpler and cleaner to abstract the skin declarations to the style sheet reference. In these examples, all the styles are defined in MXML, within the mx:Style property. You can also define these styles in external style sheets, and they will function in exactly the same way without any performance or compatibility implications.

Scaling and Scale-9 Grids

When you are applying skins to application components, it is important to understand how the skins work and what happens when they are scaled. By default, all skins and images scale with equal distributions to the dimensions in both the x and y directions.

Let's examine what happens when we stretch an image. In Figure 23-4, you will see a square image that is 15×15 pixels. Every 5×5 pixel block of the image is a different color.

Figure 23-4

If this image is scaled to be 100×100 pixels instead of 15×15, you can see in Figure 23-5 that it stretches all the contents of image accordingly. There is even scaling distribution across both the x and y axes.

Figure 23-5

While there is uniform scaling in either direction, this does not necessarily mean that the image scales uniformly. As the aspect ratio changes, images will become stretched or compressed depending how they are scaled.

Figure 23-6 demonstrates uneven scaling in the x and y directions. Even though the dimensions are not the same in each direction, you can see that the contents of the image are scaled with an even distribution across the x and y axes.

Figure 23-6

Flex and the Flash Player support scale-9 grids, which enable greater control of how images scale. A scale-9 grid separates the image into a 3×3 grid that defines how the image scales. Within the 3×3 grid, the corners do not scale, the edges scale only in one direction, and the center cell of the grid scales in both directions.

Figure 23-7 demonstrates the scaling of the 15×15 pixel image shown in Figure 23-4, with a scale-9 grid applied to it. In this example, you can see that none of the corners was scaled in either direction, the top and bottom edges were scaled in the horizontal direction, the left and right edges were scaled in the vertical direction, and the center was scaled to fill all the remaining area.

Figure 23-7

In order to specify a scale-9 grid on an image, you must embed the image. You cannot apply scale-9 grids to dynamically loaded images.

To define a scale-9 grid, you must declare the scale-9 options within the Embed directive. Rather than using the default parameters for the embed instruction, you must specify source (the image), the scaleGridTop, scaleGridBottom, scaleGridLeft, and scaleGridRight properties.

The scaleGridTop, scaleGridBottom, scaleGridLeft, and scaleGridRight properties define the spacing of the 3×3 grid that is used to scale the image. The values of these properties are relative to the top-left corner of the image. The following code snippet demonstrates how the image used in Figure 23-7 was embedded:

```
Embed(source="assets/demo.png",
      scaleGridTop="5", scaleGridBottom="10",
      scaleGridLeft="5", scaleGridRight="10")
```

The image has a scaleGridTop value of 5; therefore, the top row of the 3×3 grid has a height of 5 pixels. The scaleGridBottom value 10 determines that the center row has a height between pixels 5 and

10 (thus, it is also 5 pixels high on the original image), and the bottom row of the 3×3 grid also has a height of 5 pixels on the original source image. The same also applies to `scaleGridLeft` and `scaleGridRight`. These values create a 3×3 grid of 5×5 pixel square cells.

Scale-9 grids do not have to be uniform. In the previous example, all the cell sizes were 5×5 pixel squares. You can vary the width of each column or height of each row to have greater control over how the image scales. This allows you to have complex skins or images that have nonuniform decoration in various areas of your images and skins, and they will still scale in a controlled manner.

The following code segment demonstrates an `Embed` directive that has rows of height 2 pixels, 10 pixels, and 3 pixels from top to bottom, and columns of width 5 pixels, 9 pixels, and 1 pixel from left to right (assuming that this is based on the original 15×15 pixel image shown in Figure 23-4):

```
Embed(source="assets/demo.png",
      scaleGridTop="2", scaleGridBottom="12",
      scaleGridLeft="5", scaleGridRight="14")
```

Scale-9 grids are extremely important to understand when applying image-based skins to your applications.

Changing Styles at Runtime

Although you may typically specify the styles of your components at development/compile time, you might also find it necessary to change styles on objects at runtime. The Flex framework provides you with several mechanisms that allow you to change styles and alter visual component appearances at runtime, with minimal complication.

The Flex framework allows you to alter styles on specific object instances, on style declarations themselves, or even swap the style declarations that a component uses at runtime. The next example will demonstrate each of these techniques:

```
<?xml version="1.0" encoding="utf-8"?>
<mx:Application xmlns:mx="http://www.adobe.com/2006/mxml" layout="vertical">

    <mx:Style>
        Button {
            fontSize: 24;
        }
        .alternate {
            fontSize: 22;
            color: #FF0000;
            textRollOverColor: #00FF00;
        }
    </mx:Style>


    <mx:Script>
        <![CDATA[
            private function changeInstanceStyle() : void
            {
                button1.setStyle( "color", Math.random() * 0xFFFFFF );
```

```
                button1.setStyle( "textRollOverColor", Math.random() * 0xFFFFFF );
            }

            private function changeCSSStyle() : void
            {
                var style : CSSStyleDeclaration = StyleManager.getStyleDeclaration
                    ( "Button" );
                style.setStyle( "color", Math.random() * 0xFFFFFF );
                style.setStyle( "textRollOverColor", Math.random() * 0xFFFFFF );
                StyleManager.setStyleDeclaration( "Button", style, true );
            }

            private function toggleStyleName() : void
            {
                if ( button4.styleName == "" || button4.styleName == null )
                    button4.styleName = "alternate";
                else
                    button4.styleName = "";
            }
        ]]>
    </mx:Script>

    <mx:Button
        id="button1"
        label="Change Individual Style Instance"
        click="changeInstanceStyle()" />

    <mx:Button
        label="Change CSS Style Property"
        click="changeCSSStyle();" />

    <mx:Button
        label="Change CSS Style Property (again)"
        click="changeCSSStyle();" />

    <mx:Button
        id="button4"
        label="Toggle Style Name"
        click="toggleStyleName();" />

</mx:Application>
```

At runtime, this button is a simple Flex application that contains four `Button` instances. These button instances are used to demonstrate each of the aforementioned techniques for changing styles at runtime. One of the first things to notice is that there is a default style declaration created for all `Button` instances. Initially, all the buttons in this example will be displayed using the default style.

Clicking on the first button invokes the `changeInstanceStyle()` method, which demonstrates how to change the styles of a single button instance. This function uses the `setStyle` method to change the style attributes of the singular button instance. In this case, it changes the `color` and `textRollOverColor` styles to be randomly generated colors. When this function is executed, only the first button instance will be affected by these style changes.

```
private function changeInstanceStyle() : void
{
    button1.setStyle( "color", Math.random() * 0xFFFFFF );
    button1.setStyle( "textRollOverColor", Math.random() * 0xFFFFFF );
}
```

You can use setStyle to change any styles of a component instance at runtime. This includes every style attribute of an object, including effects. When invoking setStyle, you simply need to pass into it the style name that you want to change, and the updated value. You can also access styles at runtime from component instances using the getStyle method.

Both the second and third buttons in the previous example perform the same action: they change the properties of the Button style declaration itself, which applies to every button instance that is using the default Button declaration. There are two buttons that perform this action simply to demonstrate that both of the button instances are affected by this change.

When either of the button instances is clicked, it invokes the changeCSSStyle method. This function changes the color and textRollOverColor styles on the Button declaration itself and applies those changes to all Buttons within the application. First, this function gets a reference to the Button style declaration using the StyleManager.getStyleDeclaration function. It then updates the styles of that declaration; however, no changes are actually made to any components within the application until the styles are committed, using the StyleManager.setStyleDeclaration method.

```
private function changeCSSStyle() : void
{
    var style : CSSStyleDeclaration = StyleManager.getStyleDeclaration( "Button" );
    style.setStyle( "color", Math.random() * 0xFFFFFF );
    style.setStyle( "textRollOverColor", Math.random() * 0xFFFFFF );
    StyleManager.setStyleDeclaration( "Button", style, true );
}
```

When invoking changeCSSStyle() method, if you have already invoked the changeInstanceStyle() method from the first example, you will notice that changes to the Button style declaration do not get applied to the button1 button instance. This is because the styles on that button instance have been changed, and it is therefore no longer using the Button style declaration. This is something that should be watched out for when developing your Flex applications, as it has potential to cause problematic scenarios.

The third method of changing component styles at runtime is demonstrated by the toggleStyleName() function. This function demonstrates changing the style declaration on a particular object instance by changing the styleName property of that instance. The styleName property determines which style declaration is used by a particular component instance.

In this example, the style applied to the button4 button instance is swapped between the default style and the alternate style declaration:

```
private function toggleStyleName() : void
{
    if ( button4.styleName == "" || button4.styleName == null )
```

```
            button4.styleName = "alternate";
        else
            button4.styleName = "";
    }
```

You may also notice that any changes made to the default `Button` style declaration from the `changeCSSStyle()` method are applied to the `button4` button instance any time the style is toggled back to the default style declaration. This method of changing styles on an object instance is not subject to the orphaned style risk as opposed to calling `setStyle` on an object directly.

Themes

Skins and styles are simply attributes of objects that control their visual appearance. On the other hand, a theme is the common application of styles and skins to create a uniform appearance, or "look and feel" of an application. Themes don't necessarily have to be complex; they can be as simple as consistent color and font changes to styles, or they can be as complex as fully reskinned interface for a Flex component.

Themes can either be a collection of styles in a single style sheet grouped with their appropriate assets, or they can be packaged as `.swc` component libraries that can be imported into your Flex applications.

Default Flex 3 Themes

The default styles for Flex 3 applications are part of the `Halo` theme. This is the common blue/gray theme, with rounded corners, and so on, which is the default for every Flex application. Flex also has a set of custom themes located in the `{sdk}/frameworks/themes` directory. This includes the `HaloClassic` theme, which will make your Flex applications look as though they are using Flex 1/Flex 1.5 styles, the `Wooden` theme, which makes your application appear to be made out of wood, or the `Smoke` theme, among others.

Applying Themes

When applying a custom theme to your application, you need to update your compiler arguments to reference the theme, and the styles used in the custom theme will be used throughout your application. Whether compiling from the command line, or working within Flex Builder, you must specify the theme to use as a compiler arguments during compilation. From the command line, you simply need to add `-theme`, followed by the theme `css` or `swc` location, as shown in the following code segment:

```
mxmlc -theme themes/MyTheme/MyTheme.css main.mxml
```

If you are working within Flex Builder, you can open the Flex project properties and add the compiler argument within the `Additional compiler arguments` input box, as shown in Figure 23-8.

```
-theme themes/MyTheme/MyTheme.css
```

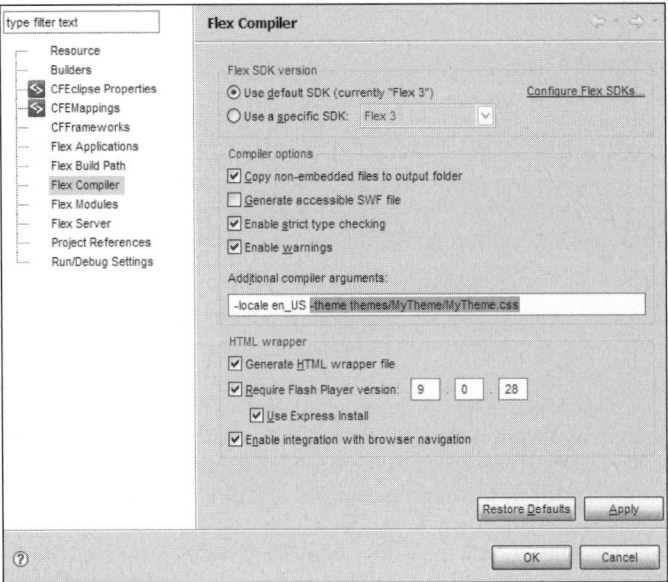

Figure 23-8

When the Flex application is compiled, the output will be generated using the specified themes. Figures 23-9 and 23-10 show a simple Flex interface with a custom theme applied to it. Notice that there are changes to corner radius values, colors, transparencies, gradients, and spacing of components.

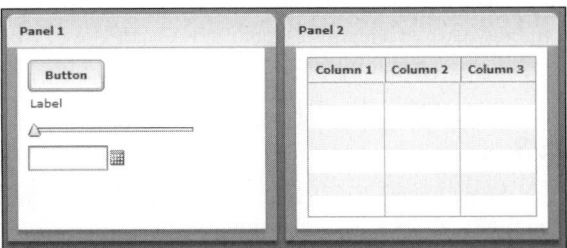

Figure 23-9

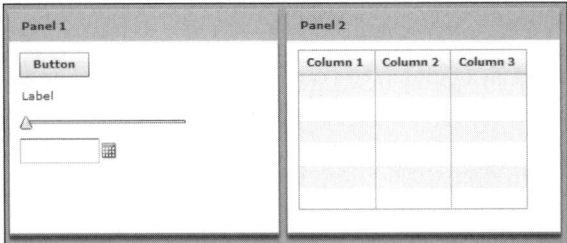

Figure 23-10

Creating Themes

A theme can be as simple as a single CSS or as complex as a folder full of assets, where styles are defined in a style sheet. In either case, the one thing in common is that there is a style sheet that defines all the styles for a theme. When you reference a theme in the compiler arguments, you are instructing the complier to include the specified CSS file.

Separating Themes to Libraries

As mentioned earlier, themes can come in the form of simple CSS or .swc library files that contain the theme CSS and all related assets. Using .swc libraries is typically considered best practice when working with themes as it encapsulates all the theme assets in a single resource that can be easily applied to any Flex project; there are fewer files that can cause error cases.

To create a theme .swc library file, you need to invoke the compc command-line compiler and instruct it to include the appropriate assets necessary for the theme. The following command will compile the MyTheme.css file into the MyTheme.swc file, which can be used as a Flex application theme:

```
compc -source-path c:/dev/flex/themes
    -include-file MyTheme.css themes/MyTheme/MyTheme.css
    -o c:\dev\flex\themes\MyTheme.swc
```

At a minimum, this will include the CSS that defines the styles for the theme. If your theme relies on external assets, such as images or .swf files, you will need to include those using the -include-file argument. If you need to include classes, such as programmatic skins, you can include those in your theme by using the -include-classes compiler argument for the compiling.

Summary

The topics discussed in this chapter are just the tip of the iceberg; the Flex framework provides an enormous amount of customization ability, and it is only limited by your imagination. This extreme amount of customization is made possible by the Flex component model and the advanced styling and skinning capabilities that it supports.

Looking to add some pizzazz to your Flex application? In the next chapter, we will explore adding animation and expressiveness to your applications using Flex visual effects.

24

Visual Effects

This chapter explores visual effects that can be applied to your Flex applications. Fades, glows, resizes, animations, and so on are all examples of visual effects that are available to you within the Flex framework. Visual effects are important components of your development toolbox because they can add additional levels of interactivity, "sex appeal," and "stickiness" to your application's user experience.

What Are Flex Effects?

In the most basic of senses, an "effect" is a perceptible change to an object. This definition doesn't provide much information by itself, so let's look closer at what it means to be an effect. A perceptible change to an object can really be anything; it can be movement, resize, fade, color change, blur, or even an audible sound. Flex effects are classes that allow you to easily control these perceptible changes over time. The controlled changes over time create animations, which in turn allow you to augment your applications with enhanced interactivity.

Effects are often essential to the user experience and can be the differentiator in the style and stickiness of an application. *Stickiness* refers to the ability of your application to keep users engaged. Properly designed effects can help make your application more engaging and fun to work with, even if it doesn't handle a "fun" topic.

All Flex components that extend from `UIComponent` can have effects applied to them through triggers. Triggers allow you to trigger an effect when an action occurs, such as an object being added to the stage, being removed from the stage, or on creation complete. We'll discuss triggers in detail later in this chapter.

In the following example, there is a flex application that contains four buttons. Each button has a `creationCompleteEffect` specified. When the application loads, and these buttons are created, the buttons are shown with an animation determined by the specified effect.

```
<mx:Application
    xmlns:mx="http://www.adobe.com/2006/mxml"
    layout="vertical">

    <mx:Style source="styles.css" />

    <mx:Button
        label="My Button With Basic Effect"
        creationCompleteEffect="Fade" />

    <mx:Button
        label="My Button With Customized Effect" >
        <mx:creationCompleteEffect>
            <mx:Rotate
                angleFrom="45"
                angleTo="0"
                duration="1000" />
        </mx:creationCompleteEffect>
    </mx:Button>

    <mx:Button
        label="My Button With Reused Effect 1"
        creationCompleteEffect="{ wipeDown }" />

    <mx:Button
        label="My Button With Reused Effect 2"
        creationCompleteEffect="{ wipeDown }" />

    <mx:WipeRight
        duration="1000"
        id="wipeDown" />

</mx:Application>
```

There are subtle differences in how each button has the effect applied to it. The first example is the most basic of the three. In this example, you can see that the value of the `creationCompleteEffect` attribute is a text string "Fade". This corresponds to the class `mx.effects.Fade`, with the default settings. This will cause the button to fade in when it is created.

```
<mx:Button
    label="My Button With Basic Effect"
    creationCompleteEffect="Fade" />
```

The next example is slightly more complex. In this case, a `Rotate` effect with customized properties is defined inline within the MXML for the button. Inside of the `mx:Button` component, the `Rotate` instance is created for the `creationCompleteEffect` property. The `Rotate` effect instance has customized properties so that it will start the rotation at 45 degrees and rotate to 0 degrees over a period of 1000 milliseconds (1 second).

```
<mx:Button
    label="My Button With Customized Effect" >
    <mx:creationCompleteEffect>
        <mx:Rotate
            angleFrom="45"
            angleTo="0"
            duration="1000" />
    </mx:creationCompleteEffect>
</mx:Button>
```

One other item worth noting is that this example uses both `Fade` and `Rotate` effects. In order to rotate or fade text, you must be using an embedded font. Text that uses fonts that are not embedded can only have an alpha value 0 or 1, and they cannot be rotated at all. The style sheet used in this example embeds the Arial font and uses it as the default for the entire application.

```
@font-face {
    src: local("Arial");
    fontFamily: arial;
    fontWeight: normal;
}

@font-face {
    src: local("Arial");
    fontFamily: arial;
    fontWeight: bold;
}

Application {
    font-family: arial;
}
```

In the previous example, that effect instance is only applied to a single object. Effects can also be reused across multiple objects. In the third example, there are two buttons, both of which have a `WipeRight` effect applied to them. The `WipeRight` effect instance is created in MXML; however, it is not created as an attribute of any specific object. The two button instances have the effect instance applied to them through the use of bindings on the `creationCompleteEffect` property: `creationCompleteEffect="{ wipeDown }"`.

```
<mx:Button
    label="My Button With Reused Effect 1"
    creationCompleteEffect="{ wipeDown }" />

<mx:Button
    label="My Button With Reused Effect 2"
    creationCompleteEffect="{ wipeDown }" />

<mx:WipeRight
    duration="1000"
    id="wipeDown" />
```

Built-In Flex Effects

In the `mx.effects.*` namespace, you will find a collection of existing effects classes that you can use to add interactivity and animations to your applications. The following sections describe the basics of using default Flex events (in alphabetical order), and after that we will examine some interesting ways that these effects can be applied.

AnimateProperty

The `AnimateProperty` effect is perhaps one of the more complicated effects but also one of the most versatile. It can be used to animate any public numeric property on a component, such as width or height, or any other public property. The following example shows a basic `AnimateProperty` effect instance that is used as the `mouseDownEffect` for an `mx:Button`. In this case, when the mouse is pressed on the button, the button's height will animate to a value of 100 over a 2000-millisecond interval.

```
<mx:Button
    label="Play Effect"
    mouseDownEffect="{ effect }"/>

<mx:AnimateProperty
    id="effect"
    property="height"
    toValue="100"
    duration="2000"/>
```

In the previous example, the `AnimateProperty` effect's target was the button instance, because the effect was applied to the button. That approach keeps the code clean and easy to understand; however, effects can also be set up to have different targets, and they can be triggered by ActionScript functions.

In the following example, the `AnimateProperty` effect's target is actually the component itself, indicated by the `this` keyword. You'll also notice that the property that is being animated is `animationProperty`, which refers to a public getter/setter function pair.

You will notice that as the animation takes place, it not only animates the width of the button but also changes the label of the button to match the value of the width. This technique can be used to perform complex actions, calculations, and animations without complex animation code.

```
<?xml version="1.0" encoding="utf-8"?>
<mx:Canvas
    label="Setter AnimateProperty Example"
    xmlns:mx="http://www.adobe.com/2006/mxml"
    width="100%" height="100%">

    <mx:Script>
        <![CDATA[

            private var _animationProperty : Number;
            public function get animationProperty() : Number
            {
                return _animationProperty;
            }

            public function set animationProperty( value : Number ) : void
```

```
            {
                _animationProperty = value;
                button1.width = _animationProperty;
                button1.label = _animationProperty.toString();
            }

        ]]>
    </mx:Script>

    <mx:Button
        label="Play Effect"
        id="button1"
        click="effect.play();"/>

    <mx:AnimateProperty
        id="effect"
        target="{ this }"
        property="animationProperty"
        fromValue="0"
        toValue="400"
        duration="2000"/>

</mx:Canvas>
```

Blur

The Blur effect applies a visually blurry distortion to the target component. The Blur effect is animated over a period of time, and can blur to a variable size. The default values for the blurXTo and blurXFrom properties of the blur are "0". In the following snippet, the button will have an animated blur from 0 (no blur) to 25 when the button is clicked.

```
<mx:Button
    label="Play Effect"
    mouseDownEffect="{ effect }"/>

<mx:Blur
    id="effect"
    blurXTo="25"
    blurYTo="25" />
```

Behind the scenes, the Blur effect uses the Flash Player's BlurFilter.

Dissolve

The Dissolve effect overlays a colored rectangle over the desired component and modifies the alpha of the overlaid rectangle to create a fade-in/out effect. The alphaFrom and alphaTo parameters are used to determine the visibility of the target component. For a value of 1, the component is completely visible, which equates to an alpha of 0 on the overlay. An alpha value of .25 indicates that your component will be 25% visible, while a .75 alpha is applied to the overlay.

```
<mx:Button
    label="Play Effect"
    mouseDownEffect="{ effect }"/>
```

```
<mx:Dissolve
    id="effect"
    alphaFrom="1"
    alphaTo=".25"
    duration="2000" />
```

By default, the overlay color is the same color as the target component's background color. If no background color is supplied, it will default to white, or you can override it with a custom color.

When using the Dissolve effect, you should be careful that you are only using it over solid-color backgrounds. If you are using transparent or image based backgrounds, visual artifacts from the Dissolve effect will be visible and can detract from the quality of the user interface. However, this is also a useful trick for getting text to fade, without having to embed the font. Using an actual Fade effect on text components requires that the font be embedded in the application; otherwise, the fade will not work.

Fade

The Fade effect animates the alpha of the target component to cause it to fade in and out over time. The following example will cause the button instance to fade from an alpha value of 1 (opaque) to an alpha value of .25 (semitransparent) over a period of 2000 milliseconds:

```
<mx:Button
    label="Play Effect"
    mouseDownEffect="{ effect }" />

<mx:Fade
    id="effect"
    alphaFrom="1"
    alphaTo=".25"
    duration="2000" />
```

As briefly noted in the previous section regarding the Dissolve effect, fading text in a Flex application requires that the font displayed for that text be embedded in the application. If the font is not embedded, the Fade effect will not work; the text will either be visible or invisible, but there will be no partial transparency.

Glow

The Glow effect creates an animated glow around the target component. When using the Glow effect, the visual glow is actually implemented using the GlowFilter. Since it is based on flash filters, the glow outline will follow the shape of any object, and it will follow the contours of transparent or masked areas. When using the GlowFilter, you can specify the glow color and animate the glow outline's blur in both the x and y directions.

The following example will cause an animated red border around the button instance when the button is clicked. The red glow will animate from 0 (tight outline) to 25, where the outline is blurred 25 pixels in both the x and y directions.

```
<mx:Button
    label="Play Effect"
    mouseDownEffect="{ effect }" />
```

```
<mx:Glow
    id="effect"
    blurXTo="25"
    blurYTo="25"
    color="#FF0000"
    duration="2000" />
```

Iris

The Iris effect is a masking effect. The effect animates a rectangle mask inward or outward from the center of the target component to create the effect of showing or hiding the component from the center out.

The following example animates the button when it is clicked. The button will be hidden, and it will animate so that it is visible from the center outward, over a period of 2000 milliseconds.

```
<mx:Button
    label="Play Effect"
    mouseDownEffect="{ effect }" />

<mx:Iris
    id="effect"
    duration="2000" />
```

Move

The Move effect can be used to animate the position of a visual component on any absolutely positioned container. When using the Move effect, you can use either a combination of xFrom/xTo properties or xFrom/xBy properties (as well as yFrom/yTo or yFrom/yBy), where the x* properties animate in the horizontal (x) direction and the y* properties animate in the vertical (y) direction.

The combination of xFrom and xTo will animate the x position of the target component from the xFrom position, to the xTo position, over the specified duration of time. xBy will animate the position from the xFrom (or current position if xFrom is not specified) position to a position that is incremented by the amount specified by xBy.

The following example will animate the button instance's position when it is clicked. The button will animate from the coordinate position 0,0 to 400,300 over a period of 2000 milliseconds.

```
<mx:Button
    label="Play Effect"
    mouseDownEffect="{ effect }" />

<mx:Move
    id="effect"
    xFrom="0"
    xTo="400"
    yFrom="0"
    yTo="300"
    duration="2000" />
```

Pause

The Pause effect actually is not a visual effect. It simply does not do anything for a specified period of time. The Pause effect's only usage is to add a pause for a period of time during a Sequence effect.

```
<mx:Pause duration="500" />
```

This example would be used within a Sequence effect and would cause the running Sequence effect to pause for 500 milliseconds during its execution. Sequence effects are discussed in greater detail later in this chapter.

Resize

The Resize effect is used to animate the size of a component over time. You can animate the width, height, or both. The "from" parameters for the Resize effect are optional. If they are not specified, the effect will use the current size of the target component.

The next example shows you how to create a Resize effect that will alter the button size when it is clicked. When clicked, the button will resize from 100 pixels wide and 30 pixels high to 400 pixels wide and 300 pixels high, over a period of 2000 milliseconds.

```
<mx:Button
    label="Play Effect"
    mouseDownEffect="{ effect }"/>

<mx:Resize
    id="effect"
    widthFrom="100"
    widthTo="400"
    heightFrom="30"
    heightTo="300"
    duration="2000" />
```

Rotate

The Rotate effect can be used to animate the rotation of a component around an x/y point. When using the Rotate effect, you must supply an angleTo value, which determines the degree angle to which you will rotate the object. You can use the angleFrom parameter to determine the starting rotation for the animation, but if this is omitted, the rotation animation will start at the current rotation value of the target component.

Optionally, you can also specify a point of origin to rotate the target component around. By default, the Rotate effect will rotate the target component around its center point. Specifying originX and originY values will change the point of rotation for the effect.

In the following example, the button will do a full 360-degree rotation around the point 90,90 when the button is clicked.

```
<mx:Button
    label="Play Effect"
    mouseDownEffect="{ effect }"/>

<mx:Rotate
```

```
    id="effect"
    angleFrom="0"
    angleTo="360"
    originX="90"
    originY="90"
    duration="2000" />
```

Similarly to fading text in a Flex application, rotating text requires that the font used to display the text is embedded in the application. If the font is not embedded, the Rotate effect will not work. The text will either be visible if the rotation angle is 0 (zero); otherwise, the text will not be displayed on-screen.

SoundEffect

The SoundEffect effect class is another effect that is actually not a visual effect. The SoundEffect class is used to play an audio file when an effect action takes place. When using the SoundEffect effect, you simply need to provide the source of the sound effect. This can either be the fully qualified URL to a MP3 file or an embedded sound file.

The next example will simply play the beep.mp3 audio file when the button is clicked.

```
<mx:Script>
    <![CDATA[
        [Bindable]
    [Embed(source="/assets/beep.mp3")]
    public var beep:Class;
    ]]>
</mx:Script>

<mx:Button
    label="Play Effect"
    mouseDownEffect="{ effect }" />

<mx:SoundEffect
    id="effect"
    source="{ beep }"/>
```

WipeLeft/WipeRight/WipeUp/WipeDown

The WipeLeft, WipeRight, WipeUp, and WipeDown effects are visual masking effects that cause the target component to appear to "wipe" from the specified direction. Wipe effects are traditionally used to show and/or hide visual components from the display. You can optionally specify whether the start or end of the effect is hidden, using the showTarget attribute. Specifying true for showTarget will cause the end state of the effect to be visible, while a false value will cause the end state to be hidden.

The following example uses a check box to control the visibility of a button instance. The animation effects are applied to the button target by using the showEffect and hideEffect properties. When the button is shown, it will wipe from the left to the right, with the effect ending that the button is visible. When the button's visibility is set to false, the hideEffect wipe will play from left to right and will end with the button being hidden.

```
<mx:CheckBox
    left="10"
    id="checkbox"
    label="visible"
```

445

```
        selected="true"/>

    <mx:Button
        top="35" left="10"
        visible="{ checkbox.selected }"
        showEffect="{ showEffect }"
        hideEffect="{ hideEffect }"
        label="Click Checkbox To Play Effect"/>

    <mx:WipeLeft
        id="showEffect"
        showTarget="true" />

    <mx:WipeLeft
        id="hideEffect"
        showTarget="false" />
```

Zoom

The Zoom effect is used to animate the zoom (scale/size) of a component. When setting the zoom from and zoom to options, the values are set as multiple of the current scale of the object. A zoomHeightFrom value of 1 zooms from the normal height of the object. A zoomHeightTo value of 4 zooms the height of the object to four times its normal height.

Unless otherwise specified, the zoom action always zooms into the center of an object. This can be changed to zoom into specific areas of the target visual object by changing the originX and originY properties of the Zoom effect instance.

The following example shows the application of a Zoom effect to a button's mouseDownEffect. When the button is clicked, the button will zoom to four times its normal size.

```
    <mx:Button
        label="Play Effect"
        mouseDownEffect="{ effect }" />

    <mx:Zoom
        id="effect"
        zoomHeightFrom="1"
        zoomHeightTo="4"
        zoomWidthFrom="1"
        zoomWidthTo="4" />
```

Applying Effects

Effects can be applied to components in your Flex applications in various ways. In most of the examples in this chapter, they have been applied as style properties of the visual component instances.

For example, using the mouseDownEffect style property of a button automatically registers the button as the target of the effect. The actual action of pressing the mouse down automatically invokes the effect and animation.

Effects can be applied to visual components by event triggers, as shown with the mouseDownEffect example, or they can be manually invoked through ActionScript.

Event Triggers

A very easy way to associate an effect with a visual component instance is through the use of event triggers. Event triggers actually trigger an effect when the type of event associated with the trigger is dispatched.

Event triggers follow the standard naming convention of event type, followed by the word "Effect". An example of this is the `mouseDownEffect` discussed earlier in this chapter. The effect instance specified by the `mouseDownEffect` style of a component is invoked when the `mouseDown` event is triggered.

Effects can be applied to event triggers on component instances either directly in MXML, through style sheet declarations, or at runtime using the `setStyle()` method on a component instance.

The following example shows how to set an effect directly, inline in an MXML declaration.

```
<mx:Button mouseDownEffect="Fade" />
```

The next example shows how effects can be applied to specific style sheets. This can be used to place common effects on all instances of a particular object, or to create stylized animations for specific class instances.

```
Button {
    mouseDownEffect: ClassReference("mx.effects.Fade");
}
```

The following is an example of how effects can be applied directly to specific object instances through ActionScript, using the `setStyle()` method.

```
button.setStyle( "mouseDownEffect", new Fade() );
```

The following list of event triggers is supported by default for all visual Flex components:

- addedEffect
- creationCompleteEffect
- focusInEffect
- focusOutEffect
- hideEffect
- mouseDownEffect
- mouseUpEffect
- moveEffect
- removedEffect
- resizeEffect
- rollOutEffect
- rollOverEffect
- showEffect

Manual Invocation

Effects do not always need to be invoked by an event trigger. There are countless scenarios where you may want to trigger an event using ActionScript. In ActionScript, you simply need to invoke the play method on the effect instance to start playing the effect.

This approach can be extremely useful when you want to start animating an effect that has a different target, or in composite events that have multiple targets. This approach is also extremely useful if you want to conditionally play targets.

A very common application of this could be playing a specific effect when a user fails to log in to the application.

```
if ( userLoggedIn )
    loginFailedEffect.play();
else
    loginSuccessEffect.play();
```

Using this approach, you can also trigger effects in parent, sibling, or child components. The effects are not locked into specific event handlers.

Data Effects

Flex 3 also provides you with additional tools to add effects to data containers, such as the List and TileList components. Data effects on these components add animations whenever data is added to or removed from the List component.

The following example shows an application containing a TileList component that uses a DefatultTileListEffect to add animation to the tile list whenever data is added to it or removed from it:

```
<?xml version="1.0"?>
<mx:Application
    xmlns:mx="http://www.adobe.com/2006/mxml">

    <mx:Script>
        <![CDATA[
            import mx.effects.DefaultListEffect;
            import mx.collections.ArrayCollection;

            [Bindable]
            private var dataCollection:ArrayCollection =
                        new ArrayCollection();

            private function removeFromList():void {
                if ( !tileList.selectedItem ) return;
                var index : int = dataCollection.getItemIndex(
                                    tileList.selectedItem );
                dataCollection.removeItemAt( index );
```

```
                }

            private function addToList():void {
                var index : int = Math.floor(
                        Math.random() * dataCollection.length );
                dataCollection.addItemAt( Math.random(), index );
            }
        ]]>
    </mx:Script>

    <mx:DefaultTileListEffect
        id="effect"
        moveDuration="250"
        fadeInDuration="250"
        fadeOutDuration="250" />

    <mx:TileList
        id="tileList"
        width="500" height="200"
        dataProvider="{ dataCollection }"
        itemsChangeEffect="{ effect }" />

    <mx:HBox>
        <mx:Button
            label="Add New Item"
            click="addToList();" />
        <mx:Button
            label="Remove Selected Item"
            click="removeFromList();" />
    </mx:HBox>

</mx:Application>
```

Clicking on the Add New Item button will invoke the addToList method, which adds a randomly generated number to a random place within the list's data provider. When the new data is added, the existing data that is shown in the component moves to a new position. The DefaultTileListEffect provides a visual animation of the change of placement of the data.

Clicking on the Remove Selected Item button invokes the removeFromList ActionScript function, which removes the currently selected item from the tile list's data provider. When this item is removed, there is also a visual animation controlled by the DefaultTileListEffect effect.

Easing Functions

By default, all effects are animated in a linear fashion. Each incremental step of the effect is equal in reaching the end result. Easing functions enable you to alter the progression of an animation in a non-linear fashion. They can enable a smooth ease in or ease out progression, a bounce progression, an elastic progression, among others. By using easing functions with timed durations, you can achieve different user experiences and control the overall interactivity and expressiveness of the application.

Each Flex effect has a different set of easing functions. However, all easing functions are applied in the same manner. The following sample shows how to apply an `Exponential.easeOut` easing function to an `mx:Glow` effect instance:

```
<mx:Glow
    easingFunction="{ Exponential.easeOut }"
    color="#FF0000" />
```

The Flex framework provides a collection of predefined easing functions for use within your applications in the `mx.effects.easing` namespace.

Composite Effects

Flex effects also support the creation of composite effects. Composite effects can be made up of `Sequence` or `Parallel` effects, which are made up of other Flex effect instances. Composite effects can significantly add to the interactivity of your application by enabling you to have multiple animations occurring on multiple components, controlled by a single effect instance.

The following sections will cover `Parallel`, `Sequence`, and nested effects in detail. All the effect examples in these sections use the following code to trigger the effects and use these buttons as effect targets:

```
<mx:Button
    id="button1"
    x="10" y="10"
    label="Play Single Target Parallel Effect"
    click="singleTargetParallel.play();" />

<mx:Button
    id="button2"
    x="10" y="40"
    label="Play Multi Target Parallel Effect"
    click="multiTargetParallel.play();" />

<mx:Button
    id="button3"
    x="10" y="70"
    label="Play Single Target Sequence Effect"
    click="singleTargetSequence.play()" />

<mx:Button
    id="button4"
    x="10" y="100"
    label="Play Multi Target Sequence Effect"
    click="multiTargetSequence.play()" />

<mx:Button
    id="button5"
    x="10" y="130"
    label="Play Nested Composite Effect"
    click="nestedComposite.play()" />
```

Parallel Effects

Parallel effects instances are used to execute multiple Flex effects at the same time, in parallel. There is no limit to the number of effects that can be run in parallel; however, you will find that the more effects running at a particular instant, the more the runtime performance of your application will be altered. It is best to experiment with the effects to determine optimal performance.

The follow example shows a Parallel effect that targets a single button instance: button1. When this effect is played, the Zoom and Glow effects will be played on the button1 instance in parallel.

```
<mx:Parallel
    id="singleTargetParallel">

    <mx:Zoom
        target="{ button1 }"
        zoomHeightFrom=".75"
        zoomHeightTo="1" />

    <mx:Glow
        target="{ button1 }"
        color="#FF0000"
        blurXFrom="0"
        blurXTo="25"
        blurYFrom="0"
        blurYTo="25" />

</mx:Parallel>
```

Parallel effects do not necessarily need to always target the same component instance. In many cases, you may find it necessary to perform effects on separate components in parallel. These types of effects can be easily achieved by using a Parallel effect instance and applying different targets to the effects within the Parallel effect instance.

The next example shows usage of a Parallel effect to perform a Glow effect on three separate button instances at the same time. The Parallel effect instance controls the execution of the Glow effects, and each Glow effect controls the application of the glowing border animation on each button instance: button1, button2, and button3.

```
<mx:Parallel
    id="multiTargetParallel">

    <mx:Glow
        target="{ button1 }"
        color="#FF0000"
        blurXFrom="0"
        blurXTo="25"
        blurYFrom="0"
        blurYTo="25" />

    <mx:Glow
        target="{ button2 }"
        color="#0000FF"
        blurXFrom="0"
```

```
          blurXTo="25"
          blurYFrom="0"
          blurYTo="25" />

   <mx:Glow
       target="{ button3 }"
       color="#00FFFF"
       blurXFrom="0"
       blurXTo="25"
       blurYFrom="0"
       blurYTo="25" />

 </mx:Parallel>
```

Sequence Effects

Sequence effects are similar to Parallel effects in that they are composed of multiple Flex event instances, with one major difference. Rather than running at the same time, each of the effect instances is executed in a sequence. One effect does not start executing until the previous effect's execution has completed.

Similarly to Parallel effects, Sequence effects are not limited in how many effect instances that they contain. Also similarly to Parallel effects, when you use Sequence effects, you have the option to choose the targets of the member effect instances. You can have the effects in your sequence all target the same component or multiple components.

The following Sequence effect contains a Zoom effect and a Glow effect that both target the button3 button instance. When this Sequence effect is executed, the Zoom effect will first execute by itself. Once the Zoom effect is complete, the Glow effect instance will be executed automatically.

```
   <mx:Sequence
       id="singleTargetSequence">

    <mx:Zoom
        target="{ button3 }"
        zoomHeightFrom=".75"
        zoomHeightTo="1" />

    <mx:Glow
        target="{ button3 }"
        color="#FF0000"
        blurXFrom="0"
        blurXTo="25"
        blurYFrom="0"
        blurYTo="25" />

 </mx:Sequence>
```

Sequence effects are also extremely helpful and powerful for choreographing effects with multiple targets. For example, you can have a sequential glow on multiple component instances. When the glow on one component is completed, a glow on a separate component is triggered.

The following example demonstrates exactly that scenario; it is a `Sequence` containing three `Glow` instances, where each `Glow` targets a separate button instance. When this example is executed, a red glow initially plays on `button1`. When that is completed, a blue glow executes targeting `button2`, and finally once that is completed, a turquoise glow is executed targeting `button3`. The choreography and synchronization of the three `Glow` effect instances is controlled by the parent `Sequence` effect.

```
<mx:Sequence
    id="multiTargetSequence">

    <mx:Glow
        target="{ button1 }"
        color="#FF0000"
        blurXFrom="0"
        blurXTo="25"
        blurYFrom="0"
        blurYTo="25" />

    <mx:Glow
        target="{ button2 }"
        color="#0000FF"
        blurXFrom="0"
        blurXTo="25"
        blurYFrom="0"
        blurYTo="25" />

    <mx:Glow
        target="{ button3 }"
        color="#00FFFF"
        blurXFrom="0"
        blurXTo="25"
        blurYFrom="0"
        blurYTo="25" />

</mx:Sequence>
```

Nested Effects

Composite effects are not limited to only `Sequence` or `Parallel` effects containing finite effect instances. These effects can be made up of any type of effect, including `Parallel` and `Sequence` effects. This allows you to create parallel execution of multiple sequences, sequences of `Parallel` effects, or a combination of `Sequence` and `Parallel` effects.

Nested `Parallel` and `Sequence` effects provide a framework that is easy to use and easy to understand, which allows for complex synchronization of effects. You can use this technique to choreograph sound effects with visual effects, or multiple complex effects.

The next example shows a sequence of three `Parallel` effects. Each `Parallel` effect instance targets a separate button instance: `button1`, `button2`, and `button3`. When this sequence is executed, the first `Parallel` effect will be played, which will perform a zoom and red glow effect on `button1`. Once this `Parallel` effect is completed, it triggers the second `Parallel` effect, targeting `button2`.

The second `Parallel` effect performs a zoom and causes a red glow on `button2`. Once the effect is completed on `button2`, the third `Parallel` effect is performed, targeting `button3`.

```
<mx:Sequence
    id="nestedComposite">

    <mx:Parallel target="{ button1 }" >
        <mx:Zoom
            zoomHeightFrom=".75"
            zoomHeightTo="1" />
        <mx:Glow
            color="#FF0000"
            blurXFrom="0"
            blurXTo="25"
            blurYFrom="0"
            blurYTo="25" />
    </mx:Parallel>

    <mx:Parallel target="{ button2 }" >
        <mx:Zoom
            zoomHeightFrom=".75"
            zoomHeightTo="1" />
        <mx:Glow
            color="#FF0000"
            blurXFrom="0"
            blurXTo="25"
            blurYFrom="0"
            blurYTo="25" />
    </mx:Parallel>

    <mx:Parallel target="{ button3 }" >
        <mx:Zoom
            zoomHeightFrom=".75"
            zoomHeightTo="1" />
        <mx:Glow
            color="#FF0000"
            blurXFrom="0"
            blurXTo="25"
            blurYFrom="0"
            blurYTo="25" />
    </mx:Parallel>

</mx:Sequence>
```

Nested effects are not limited in how deeply they can be nested. It is up to the designer to use these effects to achieve the desired experience, with optimal execution performance.

Transitions

Transitions are effect instances that are used to provide a visual animation or transition between view states. You should recall from Chapter 20, "State Management," that view states are named layouts of visual components. View states are used to easily toggle between specific named views of a component or set of components.

Without the use of transitions, changes to view states are immediate. Components are added and removed, or repositioned in an abrupt fashion. Transitions use Flex effect instances to create a smooth transition between view states; they can be used to fade in/out components that are added or removed, or they can be used to animate the repositioning of view elements.

The following example shows two separate view states of a component. In the default state, there are three buttons placed vertically above each other, as shown in Figure 24-1.

Figure 24-1

In the alternate state, as shown in Figure 24-2, there are only two buttons, laid out horizontally. (The third button has been hidden.)

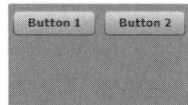

Figure 24-2

The code used to lay out these states is actually fairly simple. The buttons are laid out on the application, and when the state changes, they are moved or hidden accordingly. Here is the code used to lay out this example:

```
<?xml version="1.0" encoding="utf-8"?>
<mx:Application
    xmlns:mx="http://www.adobe.com/2006/mxml"
    layout="absolute">

    <mx:Style source="styles.css" />

    <mx:states>
        <mx:State name="alternate">
            <mx:SetProperty target="{button2}" name="x" value="93"/>
            <mx:SetProperty target="{button2}" name="y" value="10"/>
            <mx:SetProperty target="{button3}" name="visible" value="false"/>
        </mx:State>
    </mx:states>

    <mx:Script>
        <![CDATA[
            private function changeState() : void {
                currentState = (currentState == null) ? "alternate" : null;
            }
        ]]>
    </mx:Script>
```

```
<mx:Button
    x="10" y="10"
    label="Button 1"
    id="button1"
    click="changeState()" />

<mx:Button
    x="10" y="40"
    label="Button 2"
    id="button2" />

<mx:Button
    x="10" y="70"
    label="Button 3"
    id="button3" />

</mx:Application>
```

When the first button is clicked, it simply toggles between the two view states. The change is sudden, abrupt. The use of effects and transitions will enable you to create a smooth change between the two states. Transition instances must be defined within the mx:transitions property of a component that contains view states. Each mx:Transition will contain a standard Flex effect that will control the behavior when changing between states.

The next example shows the addition of transition effects to add a smooth transition between the two view states:

```
<mx:transitions>
    <mx:Transition toState="alternate">
        <mx:Parallel>
            <mx:Fade target="{ button3 }" />
            <mx:Move target="{ button2 }" />
        </mx:Parallel>
    </mx:Transition>
    <mx:Transition toState="">
        <mx:Sequence>
            <mx:Move target="{ button2 }" />
            <mx:Fade target="{ button3 }" alphaTo="1" />
        </mx:Sequence>
    </mx:Transition>
</mx:transitions>
```

You will notice that within the mx:transitions property, there are two transitions defined. The first transition definition defines the transition into the "alternate" state. This transition is defined by a Parallel effect that will smoothly fade out button3 and move button2 to its new position.

```
<mx:Parallel>
    <mx:Fade target="{ button3 }" />
    <mx:Move target="{ button2 }" />
</mx:Parallel>
```

The first transition will only be applied in any view state change going into the "alternate" state. The second transition that is defined determines the behavior when reverting back to the default state.

```
<mx:Sequence>
    <mx:Move target="{ button2 }" />
    <mx:Fade target="{ button3 }" alphaTo="1" />
</mx:Sequence>
```

The second transition that is used to return to the default state is a sequence that will first move `button2` back to its original position. When the `Move` effect is completed, it will fade `button3` back to visible.

These examples show simple transitions, using the default durations and few customized settings on the effects. When you are using effects within transitions, you can use them exactly as you would any other effect; you can alter the duration, change effect properties, and add easing functions to change the effect progression.

Effect Events

When an effect is executed, the Flex event instances dispatch a series of events during their animation process. This allows you to invoke ActionScript functions and trigger other actions based on the execution of an event. In the lifecycle of an effect, there are multiple events that you can use to trigger ActionScript functions.

Effect lifecycle events are dispatched in the following order when an event is played:

1. `activate` — This is dispatched when the effect is activated, before any action takes place.

2. `effectStart` — This is dispatched when the effect is started.

3. `tweenStart` — This is dispatched when the `tween` action of the effect is started, after any pre-processing takes place.

4. `tweenUpdate` — This is dispatched every time a `tween` action of the effect takes place. There will be many `tweenUpdate` events taking place in the lifecycle of an effect. The longer an effect is playing, the more `tweenUpdate` events there will be.

5. `tweenEnd` — This is dispatched when the `tween` action of the effect is completed.

6. `effectEnd` — This is dispatched when the effect is completed, after all effect actions and post-processing logic have been completed.

7. `deactivate` — This is dispatched when the effect is deactivated.

The following example shows the addition of event listeners for all of the events on an `mx:Glow` effect instance. When the button is clicked, the glow effect will play. Any time the effect dispatches an effect event, the `onEvent` handler is invoked, and a statement will be written to the debug trace output.

```
<mx:Script>
    <![CDATA[
        private function onEvent( event : Event ) : void
        {
```

```
                trace( event.type + " event occurred" );
        }
    ]]>
</mx:Script>

<mx:Button
    label="Play Effect" >
    <mx:mouseDownEffect>
        <mx:Glow
            color="#FF0000"
            activate="onEvent( event )"
            deactivate="onEvent( event )"
            effectEnd="onEvent( event )"
            effectStart="onEvent( event )"
            tweenEnd="onEvent( event )"
            tweenStart="onEvent( event )"
            tweenUpdate="onEvent( event )" />
    </mx:mouseDownEffect>
</mx:Button>
```

3D Effects

All default Flex effects in Flex 3 are two-dimensional animations. They involve changing the size, shape, scale, color, or alpha for a particular Flex component. It is worth noting that the open-source community has created Flex effects that give a three-dimensional appearance to Flex applications. These effects enable actions that give the appearance of Flex components rotating around a cube, components spinning through three-dimensional space, or doors opening, and they are based on open-source 3D programming frameworks.

This chapter will not cover these frameworks or effects in detail; however, you may want to look into them for your own applications. You can learn more about these at http://weblogs.macromedia.com/auhlmann/archives/2007/03/distortion_effe.html and www.tink.ws/blog/papervision3d-effects-for-flex-source/.

Flex 4 Effects

Flash player 10 enables powerful 3D graphics effects that you will be able to take advantage of in your Flex applications. In order to take advantage of these effects, you must be using one of the Flex 4 beta builds available from http://opensource.adobe.com. As of this writing, while it is publicly available, Flex 4 is not officially released as a production-ready SDK, so it may change over time.

One interesting feature in Flex 4 and Flash Player 10 is the addition of 3D matrix transformations. These will allow you to rotate your Flex components in a three-dimensional space, without the use of any specialized 3D graphics libraries. Each UIComponent will have properties that enable you to rotate your individual components on the x, y, or z axes.

Another interesting feature available with Flash Player 10 is the inclusion of custom graphics filters using the PixelBender toolkit. PixelBender allows you to write high-performance custom graphics-processing filters. This will allow for custom image manipulation, custom graphics filters, and custom blend modes for visual components.

You can learn more about Flex 4 and Flash Player 10 effects online at
`http://opensource.adobe.com/wiki/display/flexsdk/Flex+SDK`.

You can learn more about the PixelBender toolkit online at
`http://labs.adobe.com/wiki/index.php/Pixel_Bender_Toolkit`.

Summary

Overall, the Flex framework, along with the Flash Player, makes it very easy to add dynamic actions and animations to your applications. The Flash Player is known to have a strong graphics-processing engine, and the Flex framework takes full advantage of that engine. The effects and transitions available to you within Flex and the Flash player provide you with all the tools that you need to create expressive, engaging, and dynamic applications.

The next chapter covers dynamic skinning and the Drawing API. The Drawing API can be used to manipulate bitmap and vector graphics at runtime, and enables the flexibility of nearly every visual object within Flex.

25

Dynamic Skinning and the Drawing API

One of the largest differentiators of Flex and the Flash Player from traditional HTML-based Web development technologies is the Drawing API. The Drawing API allows you to programmatically render vector graphics on the screen within the Flash Player, and it is the foundation for dynamic skinning with the Flex framework. This chapter explores the Drawing API — what it is, and some of the things that you can do with it. The chapter also discusses programmatic component skins using the Drawing API, and additional imaging capabilities that the Drawing API provides.

Understanding the Drawing API

When people refer to the Flex and the Flash Player's Drawing API, they are referring to the set of classes that enable you to render vector graphics at runtime. The Drawing API allows you to draw various shapes, including lines and curves, in a programmatic fashion. This allows you to create polygons, or any other geometric shape. The Drawing API also allows you to render any of these shapes with any type of color, line thickness, fill, bitmap, or alpha transparency value.

While this sounds basic, it actually is the fundamental API that enables some very sophisticated component rendering. Most visual components in the Flex framework use the Drawing API to render themselves; they are typically not based on image assets. A Canvas, for example uses programmatic skins using the Drawing API to draw its borders and background colors. The header and control bars for a Panel control are actually rendered using the Drawing API, as well as the visual display of non-skinned Button instances for all their states (mouse over, mouse down, selected, and so forth).

This is by no means a definitive list. Exploring the Flex framework source code will likely yield a comprehensive and exhausting list. The Drawing API enables everything from the basic components mentioned above, to the runtime charting capabilities of the Flex data visualization libraries, to runtime image manipulation, three-dimensional graphics processing, and so forth.

Basic Programmatic Drawing

Before going any further with programmatic skinning, it is important that you understand the fundamentals of the Drawing API. Every visual object in the Flash Player contains an instance of the flash.display.Graphics class, regardless of whether or not it is a component of the Flex framework. The Graphics class encapsulates everything that is needed to programmatically draw any shape on the screen; it contains all the logic required for drawing shapes, lines, creating fills, and clearing the visual contents of a component.

The most basic visual component that you can have in the Flash Player is a Shape class instance. The Shape class provides the lightest-weight visual component, although it also does not contain the entire API that provides the flexibility of Flex components. Classes that extend the Shape class, such as Sprite, DisplayObject, and UIComponent, extend the capabilities of the Shape class and are often more usable within applications.

The most basic visual Flex component is the UIComponent class. The UIComponent class contains all the information and logic necessary for creating visual objects that are available in ancestor classes (such as Sprite and Shape). All visual Flex components extend from the UIComponent class, and UIComponent should typically be used when creating new custom visual components. This includes Button classes, charting classes, DataGrid classes, Container classes, and so forth — UIComponent is the root of every visual Flex component. This does not mean that all visual classes extend from UIComponent; it just means that all visual components within the Flex framework extend from UIComponent.

In the Flex component life cycle, the updateDisplayList function is responsible for rendering the Flex component on-screen. The updateDisplayList function of a component is responsible for rendering itself and invoking updateDisplayList on any child components.

```
override protected function updateDisplayList(w:Number, h:Number):void
```

In order to take advantage of programmatic drawing inside of Flex components, you should always extend the updateDisplayList function of a component and override the logic used to render the component on-screen.

One very important piece of information to keep in mind whenever you override the updateDisplayList method of a component: if you want to preserve the behavior of this component, and any child components, always call super.updateDisplayList as the first method in your instance of updateDisplayList. If you do not do this, it is very likely that none of your child components will be rendered on-screen, and this can be very confusing to debug.

Another very important and basic piece of information that you will want to remember is that you can always clear the contents of a graphics object by using the clear() method. The clear method removes all data from the graphics object, and your component will appear transparent. This will not affect the graphics contents of sibling, child, or parent components on the display list; it will only affect the graphics object of the target component.

When you are using the Drawing API, it is also extremely important to understand the coordinate plane that you are working with. The top-left corner of any component is always the point of origin (0,0). Values on the horizontal x-axis increase as you move to the right. Values on the vertical y-axis increase as you move down. A point at the coordinate (25, 50) is 25 pixels to the right of the point of origin, and 50 pixels below the point of origin. Negative values on the x axis increase to the left of the point of origin, and negative values on the y axis increase as you move up from the point of origin.

Lines

The most basic operation that you can perform using the Drawing API is drawing a line. Drawing a line is actually a relatively simple task. To draw a line, you simply need to set a line style, set the initial cursor position using moveTo, and then draw the line by using the lineTo method on the Graphics object. The moveTo method is only necessary when you want to move the cursor without drawing a line. If you want to repeatedly draw lines from one point to another, without any breaks in between, then you repeatedly call the lineTo method. Every point that you connect using lineTo will be a vertex on the connected lines.

Using this technique, you can draw squares, triangles, or any other polygon. You simply need to calculate the coordinates of the vertices and "connect the dots."

The following example shows you how to override the updateDisplayList method of a Canvas to draw a line:

```
public class SimpleLinesExample extends Canvas
{
    override protected function updateDisplayList(w:Number, h:Number):void
    {
        super.updateDisplayList(w,h);

        var g:Graphics = this.graphics;
        g.clear();

        g.lineStyle( 2, 0xFF0000 )
        g.moveTo( 0,0 );
        g.lineTo( w, h );

        g.lineStyle( 2, 0x00FF00 )
        g.moveTo( w,0 );
        g.lineTo( 0, h );
    }
}
```

Actually, two lines are drawn. The first thing that this example does after calling the parent class's updateDisplayList method is get a reference to the current object's Graphics class. You can access the Graphics class of a component at any time by referring to the graphics property. It is very common to create a local variable named g as shortcut, and to prevent the redundancy of repeated typing the word "graphics."

After obtaining a reference to the Graphics object g, this function draws two lines. In both cases, it performs the same action to draw the lines. It first sets the line style by using the g.lineStyle method. In the first example, it sets the line style to a thickness of 2 pixels, with the color red (designated by the hexadecimal value for red, 0xFF0000). An optional third parameter to the lineStyle function is the alpha value. Using the alpha value, you can draw transparent or semi-transparent lines on the graphics object.

After setting the line style, the cursor is moved to the point of origin (0, 0), and a line is drawn to (w, h); where w refers to the component width, and h refers to the component height. After drawing the angled red line, the code then repeats the process and renders a green line (designated by the hexadecimal value 0x00FF00) from the point (w, 0) to the point (0, h). The result is an "X" shape created by the two lines, which cross in the center of the component, as shown in Figure 25-1.

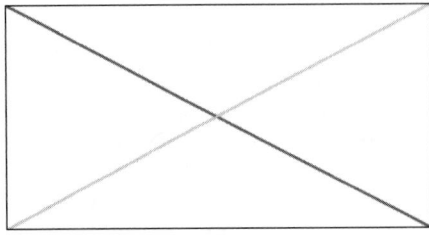

Figure 25-1

While the examples in this chapter reference the functions on the graphics object directly (as g.moveTo, for example), you can also simplify the code using a with block. Both approaches are valid, and which to use is a matter of a preference in coding style. The following example is functionally exactly the same as the previous example, although it is written using a with block:

```
public class SimpleLinesExample extends Canvas
{
    override protected function updateDisplayList(w:Number, h:Number):void
    {
        super.updateDisplayList(w,h);

        with ( this.graphics ) {
            clear();

            lineStyle( 2, 0xFF0000 )
            moveTo( 0,0 );
            lineTo( w, h );

            lineStyle( 2, 0x00FF00 )
            moveTo( w,0 );
            lineTo( 0, h );
        }
    }
}
```

Curves

The next feature of the Drawing API to examine is the ability to draw a curve from one point to another. Using the Graphics class, curves are drawn as quadratic Bezier curves. When drawing curves, it is important to understand the concept of an anchor point. When drawing the curve, you are drawing a curve from one point to another, and the resulting curve bends towards the anchor point. When the curve is drawn, the curve starts by pointing from the first point to the anchor point. It then has a smooth transition to the end point. The concept is tricky, but once you examine what it does, it becomes a bit clearer.

The following example is a variation from the previous example that draws two lines from the corners of a component. The difference is that it is drawing curves instead of straight lines:

```
public class SimpleCurvesExample extends Canvas
{
    override protected function updateDisplayList(w:Number, h:Number):void
    {
        super.updateDisplayList(w,h);

        var g:Graphics = this.graphics;
        g.clear();

        g.lineStyle( 2, 0xFF0000 )
        g.moveTo( 0,0 );
        g.curveTo( 0, h, w, h );

        g.lineStyle( 2, 0x00FF00 )
        g.moveTo( w,0 );
        g.curveTo( w, h, 0, h );
    }
}
```

When drawing the curves, you set the line Style exactly as you would when drawing a line. When actually drawing the curve, the curve starts from the current position of the cursor. The first curve is drawn as a red line that curves from the point of origin to the bottom right corner (w, h). The anchor point of the curve is the point (0, h), or the bottom-left corner. This causes the curve to bend in the direction of the bottom-left corner. When using the curveTo method, the parameters are coordinates of the endpoint, followed by the coordinates of the anchor point.

```
g.curveTo( 0, h, w, h );
```

The second curve is drawn as a green curved line from the top-right corner to the bottom-left corner, which bends towards the bottom-right corner. The result is similar to the "X" from the previous example; however, the lines bend as though they are pulled towards the bottom corners, as shown in Figure 25-2.

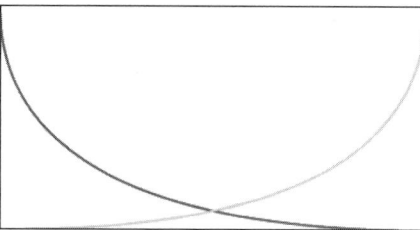

Figure 25-2

Shapes

Shapes can be drawn in the Drawing API by series of moveTo, lineTo, and curveTo methods. Luckily, the Drawing API has some utility functions that make simple shapes much easier to use. The Graphics class contains utility functions that make it easy for you to draw circles, ellipses, rectangles, or rectangles that are stylized with rounded corners.

The next example shows you how to use the shape drawing utility classes to draw a series of shapes in your Flex component. Like the previous two examples, this example extends the `updateDisplayList` method of a Flex component and draws the dynamic vector graphics.

```
public class SimpleShapesExample extends Canvas
{
    override protected function updateDisplayList(w:Number, h:Number):void
    {
        super.updateDisplayList(w,h);

        var g:Graphics = this.graphics;
        g.clear();

        g.lineStyle( 2, 0xFF0000 );
        g.drawCircle( w/2, h/2, 10 );

        g.lineStyle( 2, 0x00FF00 );
        g.drawEllipse( (w/2)-25, (h/2)-15, 50, 30 );

        g.lineStyle( 2, 0x0000FF );
        g.drawRoundRect( 15, 15, w-30, h-30, 15, 15 );

        g.lineStyle( 2, 0xFF00FF );
        g.drawRect( 2,2, w-4, h-4 );
    }
}
```

After calling the parent class's `updateDisplayList` function and getting a reference to the graphics object, this example draws four geometric shapes within the container's bounds, as shown in Figure 25-3.

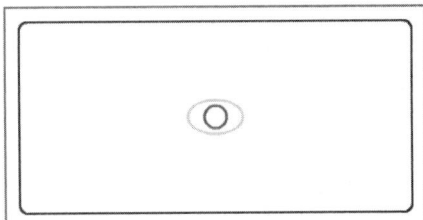

Figure 25-3

The first shape drawn in this example is the red circle shown in the center of Figure 25-3. The `Graphics` class contains the `drawCircle` method, which allows you to specify a centerpoint and a radius, and it takes care of the rest for you. This example shows a circle in the center of the component, with a radius of 10. This results in a circle with a diameter of 20 pixels.

```
g.drawCircle( w/2, h/2, 10 );
```

Next, this example uses the `drawEllipse` method to render a green elipse that stretches. When using the `drawEllipse` method, you specify the top-left corner of the bounding rectangle that would contain the ellipse, and then pass in the width and height. In this example, it draws an ellipse that is 50 pixels wide and 30 pixels tall, positioned so that its centerpoint is the center of the component, thus it surrounds the circle that was just drawn.

```
g.drawEllipse( (w/2)-25, (h/2)-15, 50, 30 );
```

The example then draws a blue rectangle with rounded corners, using the `drawRoundRect` function. When using the `drawRoundRect` method, you specify the x/y coordinate of the top-left corner, a width, a height, and the radius of the corners. In this case, it draws the rectangle at the top left coordinate (15, 15), with a width 30 pixels less than the width of the component, a height 30 pixels less than the height of the component, and a corner radius of 15 pixels.

```
g.drawRoundRect( 15, 15, w-30, h-30, 15, 15 );
```

The last action performed in this example (but certainly not the least) is that it draws a purple rectangle that sits just 2 pixels inside the boundaries of the component. Here, the rectangle is drawn at the top-left coordinate (2, 2), with a width 4 pixels less than the width of the component, and a height 4 pixels less than the height of the component.

```
g.drawRect( 2,2, w-4, h-4 );
```

Fills

Any time that you perform programmatic drawing, you can customize the line style, as shown in the preceding examples. You aren't limited to any thickness, color, or alpha. Additionally, you can also specify fill styles to be used when rendering your components. Fills can be as simple as solid colors, or as complex as semi-transparent gradients or repeating bitmap textures, and they provide the capability to extensively customize the visual appearance of your dynamic vector graphics.

The screen area enclosed by your `lineTo` function invocations will be filled with the dynamic fill. Additionally, the `drawCircle`, `drawRect`, and other helper functions will automatically fill the shape area for you.

Solid Fills

The most basic of all the fill styles is a solid color fill. You can perform solid color fill simply by calling the `beginFill()` method and passing it a hexadecimal color value. Optionally, you can also specify a numeric transparency value between 0 and 1, where 0 is fully transparent, and 1 is fully opaque. Any time that you perform a fill action, you will also want to call the `endFill()` method to ensure that no additional Drawing API logic interferes with your graphics.

The next example shows how to render a filled rectangle that takes up the entire width of the component:

```
public class SimpleFillExample extends Canvas
{
    override protected function updateDisplayList(w:Number, h:Number):void
    {
        super.updateDisplayList(w,h);

        var g:Graphics = this.graphics;
        g.clear();
```

```
        g.beginFill( 0xFF0000 );
        g.drawRect( 0,0,w,h );
        g.endFill();
    }
}
```

It first sets the fill style using the default alpha transparency 1, then draws the rectangle to take up the full area of the component, and finally ends the fill.

Gradient Fills

Gradient fills are slightly more complicated to initially set up than solid color fills; however, once the fill has been defined, the shape-drawing methods are identical. The following example illustrates how to dynamically draw a rectangle that contains a three-color radial gradient:

```
public class GradientFillExample extends Canvas
{
    override protected function updateDisplayList(w:Number, h:Number):void
    {
        super.updateDisplayList(w,h);

        var g:Graphics = this.graphics;
        g.clear();

        g.beginGradientFill( GradientType.RADIAL,
                        [0xFF0000, 0x00FF00, 0x0000FF],
                        [1,1,1],
                        [1,128,255],
                        horizontalGradientMatrix(0,0,w,h) );
        g.drawRect( 0,0,w,h );
        g.endFill();
    }
}
```

You may have noticed that the only difference between this example and the solid color gradient example is the actual specification of the fill type. In the previous example, there was a single `beginFill()` method. In this case, the fill is defined by a slightly more complicated `beginGradientFill()`.

You can see the output of this example in Figure 25-4. It renders a rectangle that has a radial gradient fill. When rendered within the Flash Player, the gradient fill is red in the center, surrounded by a green band, and a blue outer area.

Figure 25-4

When you are specifying a gradient fill, you have a lot of control as to how the gradient is rendered within your component. The first parameter when setting a gradient fill is the fill type. For the gradient type, you can either specify `GradientType.RADIAL` or `GradientType.LINEAR`. A radial gradient renders the gradient from the center of the drawing area (governed by the gradient matrix, which we'll discuss further in this section), where a linear gradient draws a continuous gradient in one direction only.

Next, you will specify the colors used in the gradient. In this case, those colors are red, green and blue, respectively: `[0xFF0000, 0x00FF00, 0x0000FF]`. There is no limit to the number of colors that you can specify for a gradient. It can be as simple as two colors or as complex as 20.

When rendering the gradient, each color can also have its own alpha transparency value. This allows you to create gradients that are transparent in some areas, while fully opaque in other areas. In this case, all the fills of the gradient have a value of 1, which indicates that they are fully opaque: `[1, 1, 1]`. The only rule governing the number of colors used in the gradient is that you must also have the exact same number of alpha values specified, as well as the same number of gradient ratios.

The next parameter of the `beginGradientFill()` method is color distribution ratios. The color distribution ratios determine at which point in the gradient area the color should be at its full value, not blended with any other color. Ratios should be within the values 0 though 255. In this example, 0 is the center of the radial gradient, and 255 is the outermost distance from the center. In a linear gradient, this would represent the leftmost and rightmost sides of the gradient area (depending upon the gradient's rotation in the gradient matrix).

Next in this example, a gradient matrix is supplied by the `horizontalGradientMatrix()` function. There are helper functions within the Flex framework for creating horizontal and vertical matrices. The matrix determines the x/y offset and rotation of the gradient as it is drawn on the screen. Using the helper functions allows you to easily create a gradient that takes up the full area of your component; however you can customize this by creating your own transformation `Matrix`.

Bitmap Fills

Another powerful tool for creating programmatic drawings is the ability to create bitmap fills within your dynamic shapes. When performing a bitmap fill, you can use the `BitmapData` object from any visual component. It is generally obtained from an image file; however, it is not limited to the `BitmapData` from images. You can copy the `BitmapData` from any object, including objects that contain programmatic drawing elements. When using bitmap fills, you can control whether the fill bitmap should be repeated or whether smoothing is applied to its contents.

The next example shows a rectangle that is drawn using a simple bitmap fill:

```
public class BitmapFillExample extends Canvas
{
    [Embed("assets/sunrise.jpg")]
    private var bitmapSource : Class;
    private var bitmapAsset:BitmapAsset = new bitmapSource() as BitmapAsset;

    override protected function updateDisplayList(w:Number, h:Number):void
    {
        super.updateDisplayList(w,h);
```

```
        var g:Graphics = this.graphics;
        g.clear();

        g.beginBitmapFill( bitmapAsset.bitmapData );
        g.drawRect( 0,0,w,h );
        g.endFill();
    }
}
```

In this example, the sunrise.jpg file is embedded as the bitmapSource class. Bitmap fills can be applied from any BitmapData object. In this case, a BitmapAsset object is created from the embedded bitmapSource.

The bitmapData property of the bitmapAsset instance is supplied to the beginBitmapFill() function, and the resulting output can be seen in Figure 25-5. In this case, the bitmap image is used to render the rectangle, and the image is repeated to fill the entire area of the rectangle.

Figure 25-5

Complex Fills

Complex effects can be created by layering simple fills on top of each other. You can layer multiple gradients over solid colors or bitmap fills, or you can layer multiple semi-transparent gradients to achieve smooth effects. Classes within the flex framework itself actually use this technique. For example, the shiny gradients of a standard mx:Button are actually created through layers of multiple semi-transparent gradients.

The next example will show you the complex results of simple actions. In this case, it simply layers the gradient fill from earlier examples as a semi-transparent fill over the top of the bitmap fill from the previous example.

```
public class ComplexFillExample extends Canvas
{
    [Embed("assets/sunrise.jpg")]
    private var bitmapSource : Class;
    private var bitmapAsset:BitmapAsset = new bitmapSource() as BitmapAsset;

    override protected function updateDisplayList(w:Number, h:Number):void
    {
        super.updateDisplayList(w,h);

        var g:Graphics = this.graphics;
```

```
        g.clear();

        g.beginBitmapFill( bitmapAsset.bitmapData );
        g.drawRect( 0,0,w,h );
        g.endFill();

        g.beginGradientFill( GradientType.RADIAL,
                    [0xFF0000, 0x00FF00, 0x0000FF],
                    [.25,.5,.25],
                    [1,128,255],
                    horizontalGradientMatrix(0,0,w,h) );
        g.drawRect( 0,0,w,h );
        g.endFill();
    }
}
```

As you can see, no new techniques were used in this example; it was just layering of techniques that have already been discussed. The result is a composite fill that is a semi-transparent radial gradient rectangle layered over the top of the repeating bitmap, as shown in Figure 25-6.

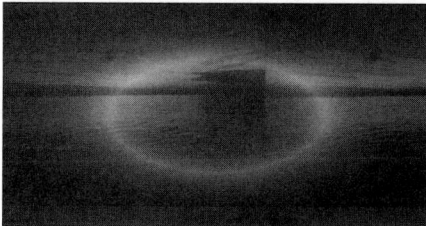

Figure 25-6

Programmatic Skins

You may recall from Chapter 23, "Skinning and Themes," that a skin is the visual representation of an object and that Flex components are designed so that their appearance can be easily changed through modifications to the skin classes.

Programmatic skins are visual representations of objects that are completely derived from usage of the Drawing API. They are not based on any embedded bitmap or SWF content. Programmatic skins typically derive from the mx.skins.ProgrammaticSkin class. When creating your own programmatic skins, all you need to do is extend the ProgrammaticSkin class, and override the updateDisplayList() method to render the skin as you would like.

Using programmatic skins allows you to separate the logic used to render your component from the logic of the component action itself; this also enables you to reuse the skin rendering logic across multiple (potentially unrelated) classes.

A great place to get started with programmatic skinning is by reviewing the source of the mx.skins.halo.* namespace. All the classes contained within the mx.skins.halo.* namespace are the skins that are used to render all the default Flex components; all of which extend from `mx.skins.ProgrammaticSkin` at some point. Extensions from the `ProgrammaticSkin` class encapsulate the logic necessary to render various Flex components.

Creating and Applying Programmatic Skins

Now, let's take a look at creating programmatic skins and applying them to Flex components. Before getting started in the logic used to render the skin itself, we will examine how a skin is applied to a Flex component.

Skins can be applied to Flex components in two different ways; they can either be applied using CSS style sheets, or they can be specified directly on component instances. Application of skins through CSS style sheets allows for further abstraction of the code used to render the component from the logic of the component itself, and allows for reuse of styles. This way, you can have multiple components that use the same skin, and keep your code clean.

When declaring a skin in CSS, you simply need to use the `ClassReference` instruction to define the reference to the programmatic skin class. The following snippet shows the application of a programmatic skin as a border skin for the `Canvas` style, which is the default style for all `Canvas` objects in the Flex framework.

```
Canvas {
    borderSkin: ClassReference("examples.ExampleProgrammaticSkin");
}
```

With this technique, the `examples.ExampleProgrammaticSkin` class will be used to render the skin for every `Canvas` object, unless a different style is explicitly applied to that canvas instance.

Programmatic skins can also be specified directly on a component instance, rather than in the style declaration. It is typically assumed best practice to abstract the skin logic to a CSS class so that it is separated from the rest of the application logic, and so that all skinning is maintained in a single class. However, this is not realistic in every case. For those cases, you can define a skin on a component simply by specifying the fully qualified name of the programmatic skin class on the appropriate skin attribute.

The following shows a button instance that has a custom programmatic skin specified for it. The skin attribute references the `examples.ExampleButtonSkin` class, which will be used to render the actual graphical display of the button instance.

```
<mx:Button
    x="10" y="10"
    label="Sample Button 1"
    skin="examples.ExampleButtonSkin" />
```

Now that you know how skins can be applied, let's take a look at them in practice. Consider the following code that is used to lay out a Flex application. Within the application, there is a `Canvas` that contains three `Button` instances.

```
<?xml version="1.0" encoding="utf-8"?>
<mx:Application xmlns:mx="http://www.adobe.com/2006/mxml" layout="absolute">
```

```
<mx:Style>
   Canvas {
      border-skin: ClassReference("examples.ExampleProgrammaticSkin");
   }
</mx:Style>

<mx:Canvas
   width="100%"
   height="100%">

   <mx:Button
      x="10" y="10"
      label="Sample Button 1"
      skin="examples.ExampleButtonSkin" />

   <mx:Button
      x="10" y="40"
      label="Sample Button 2" />

   <mx:Button
      x="10" y="70"
      label="Sample Button 3" />

</mx:Canvas>

</mx:Application>
```

You may have noticed that both of the approaches for applying programmatic skins, which were described earlier, were used in this example. The Canvas instance will actually be rendered by using the examples.ExampleProgrammaticSkin class.

Only one of the Button instances acutally has a skin applied to it. The two buttons that do not have a custom skin specified will be displayed using the default Flex button skin. The Button instance that has the custom skin applied will be rendered using the examples.ExampleButtonSkin class.

You can view the sample output of this example shown in Figure 25-7.

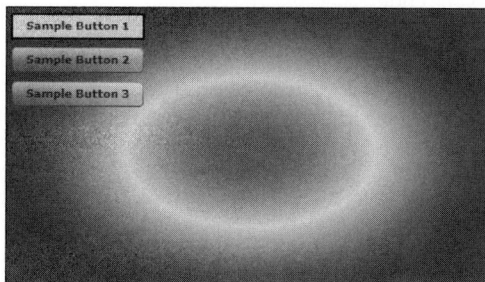

Figure 25-7

The background of the canvas is rendered with a radial gradient, similar to the radial gradient fill example shown in Figure 25-4. The class that is used to render the radial gradient background is an extension of the `ProgrammaticSkin` class, which contains all the base information necessary to create a Flex skin. The only specialized logic in this class is the overridden `updateDisplayList()` method. In this method, a gradient fill is created and a rectangle is drawn to fill the entire area of the component.

You will also notice that in this case the `super.updateDisplayList()` method was not invoked. This does not call the super's method because any logic in that method is not needed to render the gradient background. Calling the parent class's `updateDisplayList()` method would add additional overhead to the rendering, which is unnecessary. Keep in mind; this only applies to skins, not component instances themselves.

```
public class ExampleProgrammaticSkin extends ProgrammaticSkin
{
    override protected function updateDisplayList(w:Number, h:Number):void
    {
        var g:Graphics = this.graphics;
        g.clear();

        g.beginFill( 0xFFFFFF, 1 );
        g.drawRect( 0,0,w,h );
        g.beginGradientFill( GradientType.RADIAL,
                    [0xFF0000, 0x00FF00, 0x0000FF],
                    [.75,.75,.75],
                    [1,128,255],
                    horizontalGradientMatrix(0,0,w,h) );
        g.drawRect( 0,0,w,h );
        g.endFill();
    }
}
```

You may have noticed that of the three buttons, two are displayed as normal Flex buttons, and one appears as a solid filled rectangle. The following `ExampleButtonSkin` class shows how you can programmatically create your own button class. The `ExampleButtonSkin` class extends the `ButtonSkin` class, which contains all the logic necessary to render a Flex `Button` control on-screen. You will also notice in this example that it does not invoke the parent class's `updateDisplayList()` method. If this method had been invoked in the parent class, the logic used to display a default Flex button would have been executed, only to be cleared out by the `g.clear()` method invocation; which would have resulted in unnecessary CPU cycles to render.

In this class, the line style is set as a 2-pixel thick black line, and the fill style is determined by the `name` property. The `name` property dictates which state of the button skin should be rendered. Different states (`upSkin`, `overSkin`, etc.) are filled with a different color. Once the line style and fill color are selected, the area of the button is rendered using a simple `drawRect()` function invocation.

```
public class ExampleButtonSkin extends ButtonSkin
{
    override protected function updateDisplayList(w:Number, h:Number):void
    {
        var g:Graphics = this.graphics;
        g.clear();

        g.lineStyle( 2, 0x000000 );
```

```
switch (name)
{
    case "selectedUpSkin":
    case "selectedOverSkin":
    {
        g.beginFill(0xFF0000);
        break;
    }

    case "upSkin":
    {
        g.beginFill(0x00FF00);
        break;
    }

    case "overSkin":
    {
        g.beginFill(0xFFFF00);
        break;
    }

    case "downSkin":
    case "selectedDownSkin":
    {
        g.beginFill(0x0000FF);
        break;
    }

    case "disabledSkin":
    case "selectedDisabledSkin":
    {
        g.beginFill(0x333333);
        break;
    }
    }
    g.drawRect( 0,0,w,h );
    g.endFill();
    }
}
```

Although this example is very simplistic in what it renders, the process of using a programmatic skin on a component is really this easy. Layers of dynamic shapes with different fill styles, or with semi-transparent fills, can result in some wildly unique and sophisticated visual controls and interfaces.

Additional Drawing API Capabilities

The Flash Player's Drawing API does not only refer to the programmatic drawing aspects of the runtime, but also the additional image manipulation features that are enabled by the Flash Player itself. The Flash Player exposes powerful runtime imaging capabilities, and all these capabilities are available for use within the Flex framework.

Masks

Masks are an extremely useful tool when working with dynamic graphics. Essentially, a mask is a shape that defines where the graphics content of the masked object will be visible. The mask does not actually render anything visual; it just controls where the visual portion of an object is actually visible. You can think of it as negative space or a window. The area that is filled by the mask is shown. Any area that is not filled by the mask will not be visible.

To get a better idea of what a mask is, and what it does, consider the following scenario. You have an image that is masked by a canvas, and the canvas has a fill color. This is extremely important; if the canvas did not have a fill color, it would not allow anything to be shown through the mask, and the image would not appear. Also, notice that the canvas has a corner radius of 30 pixels.

The mask is actually applied to the image simply by specifying the mask canvas in the image's `mask` property:

```
<mx:Application
    xmlns:mx="http://www.adobe.com/2006/mxml"
    xmlns:filters="flash.filters.*"
    layout="absolute">

    <mx:Image
        source="http://media.wiley.com/assets/253/59/wrox_logo.gif"
        x="10" y="10"
        width="338" height="79"
        mask="{ mask }"
        cacheAsBitmap="true"
        id="targetImage" />

    <mx:Canvas
        id="mask"
        x="10" y="10"
        width="{ targetImage.width }"
        height="{ targetImage.height }"
        backgroundColor="#FF0000"
        borderStyle="solid"
        cornerRadius="30"
        cacheAsBitmap="true" />

</mx:Application>
```

Now, let's take a look at the image both before and after the mask has been applied. Figure 25-8 shows the image without a mask applied. You can see that the image has square corners.

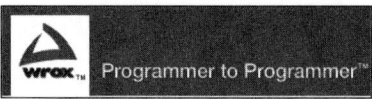

Figure 25-8

Figure 25-9 shows the exact same image with the mask applied to it. Notice that the corners are rounded, exactly as the corners of the mask canvas are. This is because the area of the mask canvas controls the visible area of the image instance. The dark-colored corners in this example area actually the default blue-gray background color for a Flex application.

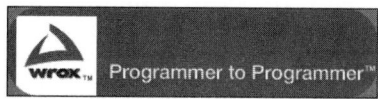

Figure 25-9

Any `DisplayObject` can be used as a mask on another `DisplayObject`. The graphics of the object that is masked will only be displayed in areas of the mask that are not transparent. Masks support static images, static images with transparency, and dynamically rendered images. Masks can even be animated so that the mask changes over time. This is what enables the visual transitions within the Flex framework, such as the `Iris` effect or the `WipeDown` effect.

Filters

Graphics filters are mechanisms that allow you to perform bitmap-level effects on any visual object within the Flash Player runtime. Filters within the Flash Player can enable everything from simple blurs, glows, and drop shadows; all the way to color shifting, black-and-white rendering, image sharpening, and even edge detection.

Every component within the Flex framework can have filters applied to it, and you can have multiple filters per component. In the following code segment, you will see an image that has three filters applied to it: a blur, a glow, and a drop shadow.

```
<mx:Application xmlns:mx="http://www.adobe.com/2006/mxml" layout="absolute">

    <mx:Image
        source="http://media.wiley.com/assets/253/59/wrox_logo.gif"
        x="10" y="10" >

        <mx:filters>
            <mx:BlurFilter />
            <mx:GlowFilter />
            <mx:DropShadowFilter />
        </mx:filters>

    </mx:Image>

</mx:Application>
```

The filters are applied in the order that they are specified. First, the image's original graphics are blurred, then a glow is applied to them. A drop shadow is then applied to the blurred and glowed image. You can see the sample output of this in Figure 25-10.

Figure 25-10

In this case, no custom parameters were specified for each filter, but each filter does in fact have many customization parameters. You can change the intensity of the blur, change the color and intensity of the glow, or change the color, distance, and alpha of the drop shadow. Graphics filters enable you to have greater control over the graphical appearance of your components, and also enable complex animations and effects.

The filters described thus far are not the complete list of filters. For a complete description of the existing filters, consult the Flash Player documentation at http://livedocs.adobe.com/flex/3/html/help.html?content=Filtering_Visual_Objects_15.html.

Blend Modes

In addition to being able to control how your component is rendered (or distorted) with bitmap filters, you can also control how the graphical content is rendered and layered on top of each other using blend modes.

Every visual object within the Flash Player can have a blend mode applied to it. The blend mode dictates how the graphics of the target object will be layered or blended within the graphics of any other object that sits behind it on the display list. Using blend modes, you can invert colors, have additive layering, soft or hard light effects, and so forth.

The following code snippet shows the same image from Figure 25-8, however, the value `BlendMode` `.DIFFERENCE` has been selected as the blend mode. This instructs the image to be rendered as the difference of how it would be typically rendered, which causes the colors to be inverted based on the background color.

```
<mx:Image
    source="http://media.wiley.com/assets/253/59/wrox_logo.gif"
    x="10" y="10"
    blendMode="{ BlendMode.DIFFERENCE }" />
```

The image shown in Figure 25-11 shows the outcome of the application of a blend mode to the image from Figure 25-8. In this case, you can see that light colors are now darker, and dark colors are now lighter.

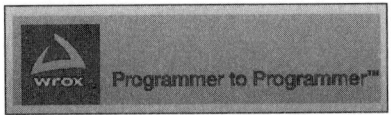

Figure 25-11

There are currently 13 different blend modes supported by Flex and the Flash Player. For more detail regarding each blend mode, consult the Flash Player API documentation.

Degrafa

One thing that you may have noticed with programmatic drawing is that it can get very complicated very quickly. It is based on a series of instructions that dictate how graphics and shapes can be drawn. There is an open-source initiative, known as Degrafa, (short for "Declarative Graphics Framework"), that enables programmatic rendering of dynamic shapes through a declarative XML markup language that is an extension of MXML. In many cases, Degrafa allows for easier-to-understand graphics rendering.

In fact, Degrafa is being integrated into the upcoming Flex 4 codebase as part of the Flex framework itself.

You can learn more about Degrafa at `www.degrafa.org`.

Summary

The dynamic graphics capabilities of Flex and the Flash Player that allow you to programmatically render vector graphics on the screen are the foundation for dynamic skinning with the Flex framework, and they are one of the features of the Flash Player that truly differentiate it from its competitors. Programmatic skinning relies entirely on the Drawing API, which provides the ability to dynamically render graphics based on code instructions rather than on static bitmap images.

The next chapter covers integration topics for using Flash IDE-authored content within Flex applications. The integration with Flash-based content opens the door to animated skins and helps to bridge the designer-developer workflow gap.

26

Flash Integration

Prior to the release of Flex 2 and Flash Player 9, ActionScript developers used mostly the Flash IDE for coding Flash platform rich Internet applications (RIAs). The release of Flash Player 9 with ActionScript 3.0, combined with Flex 2 (and now Flex 3) allows for a much more robust RIA development workflow. Flex Builder has, in large part, assumed the role of ActionScript 3.0 development for the Flash Platform. Despite this, Adobe Flash CS3 can still play an integral part in the development of any Flex application.

In this chapter, you will learn how Flash and its associated workflow can be integrated into the development of any Flex project.

The Flash IDE

IDE is short for "integrated development environment," which refers to an authoring application. In cases such as the Flash IDE, this can also be taken to mean "integrated design environment." When we speak of just "Flash" by itself in this chapter, we are referring to the Flash IDE, currently in version CS3 as of this writing. When we use the term "SWF application" we are referring to a compilation-agnostic process, applicable to any Flash Platform application (or .swf file) that may be authored and compiled by Flash, by Flex Builder, or by a third-party authoring application.

Flash Platform Development Workflows

Development workflows are mostly about tools: the ends requiring you to use them, the ease at which you can integrate them, and the manner in which you achieve those ends. Some of the possible use cases for the different kinds of Flash Platform development can be categorized as follows:

Use Cases	Description	Runtime	Development Type
Banner ads, animations, embedded video	High-impact visuals with limited interactivity	Flash Player, Flash Lite	Rich Content Creation
Websites, microsites, media players, eLearning applications, desktop widgets, mobile applications	Heavily branded interactive experiences, small-scale component-based UI, nonstandard UI	Flash Player, Flash Lite, AIR	Rich Application Development
Games, microsites, interactive creation tools, 3D environments, web/desktop RIAs	Very dynamic visuals, highly engaging experience, data-enabled interactivity	Flash Player, AIR	Dynamic Application Development
Business applications, content management systems, dashboards, videoconferencing solutions, web/desktop RIAs	Data-intensive applications, robust interactivity, standard UI elements, large-scale deployment	Flash Player, AIR	Agile Application Development

If we match up the types of development with specific, client-side development requirements, we might get the following:

Development Type	Client-Side Requirements	Compiler	IDE
Rich Content Creation	Timeline animations Embedded media	Flash CS3	Flash CS3
Rich Application Development	Timeline animations Timeline-based ActionScript Flash CS3 components	Flash CS3	Flash CS3
Dynamic Application Development	Generative/dynamic animation Tween/3D/physics engines Dynamic layout Advanced OOP	Flash CS3/MXMLC	Flash CS3 + ActionScript Editor or Flex Builder - ActionScript Project

Continued

Continued

Development Type	Client-Side Requirements	Compiler	IDE
Agile Application Development	Scripted (MXML-based) animation		
	Dynamic animation	MXMLC	Flex Builder - Flex Project
	Scripted layout		
	Component-based UI		
	Flex framework(s)		
	AIR APIs		
	Agile development (design patterns)		

The preceding two tables represent by no means an exhaustive list of use case scenarios or the final authority on which use case matches which development methodology, but they can serve as a useful guide in our understanding of typical client-side Flash Platform development workflows.

However, there are still a few use case scenarios that do not fit into any of the four development types in the preceding table. What if, as a developer, you need to employ Agile Application Development, but with styling and/or animation from the Rich Content Creation or Rich Application Development workflows? For instance, what if you need to add some Flash timeline animations to some Flex assets?

As covered in Chapter 12, you could load Flash-compiled SWF content into the Flex application with a SWFLoader component. When you load a SWF at runtime, you do not have the run of the external application, as it were, as you did in ActionScript 2 (which is actually a good thing). In other words, you must be careful to account for the security restrictions inherent in the application domain (see Chapter 65), which can require some ActionScripting acrobatics to get access to the class structures inside a loaded SWF. This can tend to complicate matters, which can limit your range of integration options. Since Flash-compiled SWF assets in this scenario are included as a part of the Flex application at runtime, the Flash and the Flex workflows can be completely separate. What you need in this case is a more unified workflow between Flash and Flex, which we call the *Flash-Flex workflow*.

The Flash-Flex Workflow

Figure 26-1 illustrates some situations in which you might want to port functionality native to one workflow to another, whether it be Flash-to-Flex or Flex-to-Flash.

Figure 26-1 represents three common tools used for Flash Platform development:

❑ Flash IDE

❑ ActionScript Editor

❑ Flex Builder

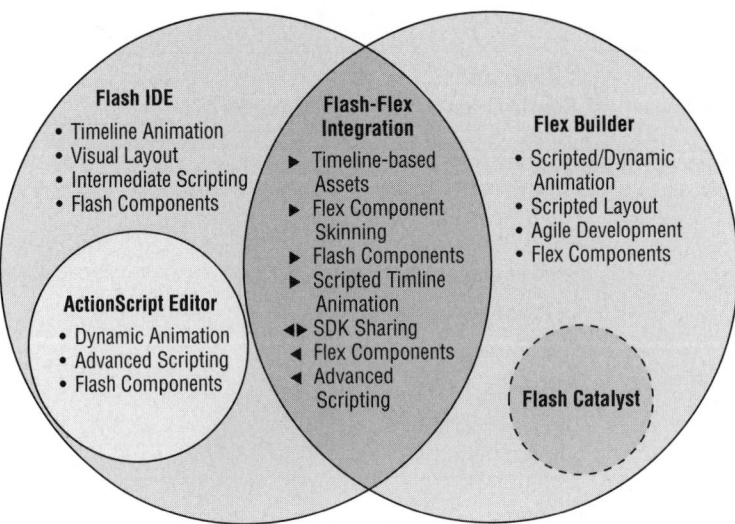

Figure 26-1

By their positions on the diagram, you can also see how these tools integrate into different workflows: the ActionScript Editor is used only in conjunction with the Flash IDE, and although the Flash IDE and Flex Builder represent separate workflows, a middle ground exists where these workflows may overlap.

The following table summarizes the Flash-Flex integration options illustrated in Figure 26-1.

Workflow	Integration	Technique
Flash-to-Flex	1. Timeline-based assets	Embedded SWF/SWC assets (Import Skin Artwork)
Flash-to-Flex	2. Flex component skinning	Flex Skin Design Extension for Flash CS3, Import Skin Artwork
Flash-to-Flex	3. Timeline-based components (not shown)	Flex Component Kit for Flash CS3
Flex-to-Flash	4. Advanced scripting	Editing Flash-compiled ActionScript files in Flex Builder
Flash-to-Flex	5. Flash components	Flex Component Kit for Flash CS3
Flash-to-Flex	6. Scripted timeline animation	Export Motion as XML (`fl.motion` classes)
Flash-to-Flex	7. SDK sharing, Flash components	`fl.*` classes in Flash SWC
Flex-to-Flash	8. SDK sharing, Flex components	`mx.*` classes in Flex SWC

This chapter covers the first two integration categories mentioned in the preceding table.

In the Flash-Flex workflow, the assets from a Flash-compiled SWF or SWC are embedded into the Flex application as a compiletime shared library (CSL), allowing the Flex compiler access to the Flash-compiled classes and class assets.

The Future of the Flash-Flex Workflow

You may notice inside the Flex Builder circle in Figure 26-1 that there is a smaller circle with a dotted line named "Flash Catalyst." At the time of this writing, Flash Catalyst is an upcoming Adobe application that will facilitate a much greater integration between visual assets and the Flex development process, allowing designers and developers to work much more seamlessly in a unified component development workflow. See www.adobe.com/go/flashcatalyst for more details.

The release of Flash CS4 adds several new features that bring a greater range of possibilities to this workflow, such as being able to add parts of the Flex framework into your Flash-compiled application. Another feature is the upcoming FLA document format named *XFL*, which adds FLA capability to the existing XFL format currently used by both Adobe InDesign and Adobe AfterEffects. Because XFL is an XML-based document format, it is anticipated that it could be read and parsed by a SWF application at runtime. This opens up a whole new range of possibilities for the integration of Flash and Flex.

Creating Flex Component Skins in Flash

This first example of Flash-Flex integration follows this possible scenario: as a developer, you need to add some stylish designs to a Flex component. But let's face it: as flexible as styling components is in Flex, the task can be extremely time-consuming for both designer and developer on large projects with a lot of UI elements. I am sure that many of you are familiar with this scenario: the designer creates a static comprehensive layout (comp) of the interface; the developer opens file in image editor, uses the eyedropper to extract color values, maybe uses the Adobe Flex 3 Style Explorer (http://examples.adobe.com/flex3/consulting/styleexplorer/Flex3StyleExplorer.html) or the new Tour de Flex application (www.adobe.com/devnet/flex/tourdeflex), slices and saves bitmap assets, and creates a CSS file importing colors and bitmap assets. The designer does not think the final interface matches the comp, and after a discussion, the designer, the developer, or both adjust the styling ... and on the cycle goes. Fortunately, there is a better way.

You could go into the Flex SDK source and give the designer on the team the default Aeon Graphical theme Flash source file, but what if you don't want to monkey around with the default Flex theme? (See http://livedocs.adobe.com/flex/3/html/styles_12.html for more information). What if you want to change the skin for just one Flex component, or just a few? Wouldn't it be great if you could pass the designer one FLA source file, let them work their magic, feed a single reference to a Flex component, and have the entire Flash-designed skin magically "appear" with all component states?

Adobe has created a Flex 3 integration tool for Flash CS3 that enables you to compile a Flex component skin as class library and then embed that class as the skin of a Flex component. This tool is called the *Flex Skin Design Extension for Flash CS3* and is available on the Adobe website at www.adobe.com/go/flex3_cs3_swfkit. You'll need your Adobe ID to get this free extension.

Using the Flex Skin Design Extension

In this example, you'll learn to skin a Flex `Button` component using the Flex Skin Design Extension for Flash CS3.

1. Go to `www.adobe.com/go/flex3_cs3_swfkit` in your browser, and download the `.mxp` file from the Flex Skin Design Extension for Flash link.

2. Install the Flex_Skins_12_05.mxp file. In the Adobe Extension Manager, under the Flash CS3 category, you should see an entry that says "Flex Skinning Templates."

   More detailed information on installing this extension can be found at `http://blog.flexexamples.com/` `2007/12/06/installing-the-flex-skin-design-extensions-for-cs3-from-adobe-labs`.

3. Create a new Flex project named `Chapter_26_Flash_Integration`. This project will contain the final source files for you to follow along in the creation of this example. Unzip the Chapter 26 project files into this workspace folder.

   If you have Subclipse installed, you can also download the source files from the Professional Flex 3 Chapter 26 Subversion directory into your Flex project. Look for the folder in the repository with the name `Chapter_26_Flash_Integration`. *See Chapter 9 for details on using Subclipse and the Professional Flex 3 Subversion repository.*

4. Create a second Flex project named `Chapter_26_Flash_Integration_working`. This is the project that will contain the files you will build in this chapter.

5. In Flash CS3, create a new document, and click on the Templates tab. You should see a new Category called Flex Templates.

6. Select Flex Templates to see a list of Flex component templates, as shown in Figure 26-2.

Figure 26-2

If you scroll down the Templates list on the right, you'll notice that there is a flex_skins template. If you select this template, you will be able to edit every single UI component skin in the Flex framework. This is a much safer way to edit the default Aeon Graphical theme and doesn't modify the original Flex SDK source. It also makes it extremely easy for a designer to customize an entire user interface from just one file.

7. Select the Button template and click OK.

The assets you see on the stage should look exactly as seen in the Preview part of the New from Template window, as shown in Figure 26-2.

8. Save this file in `/flash` as `CustomButtonSkin.fla`.

In this file you will see four layers:

- ❑ Information
- ❑ Symbols
- ❑ Labels
- ❑ Background

Notice that all layers are locked except the symbols layer. You can edit the content on these layers, but it's really only for show to lend instruction and show a background for the actual skin in the design. It's the content on the symbols layer that is important.

Since specific instructions on creating certain aspects of a Flash document are outside the scope of this book, this example may require you to follow along with the final source file `Chapter_26_Flash_Integration/flash/CustomButtonSkin.fla` in order to complete the creation of this example.

9. Open `CustomButtonSkin.fla` from the final source files in your `Chapter_26_Flash_Integration` project. You'll be copying some assets from this file into the current FLA for this example.

You should now have two files open in Flash, both called `CustomButtonSkin.fla`. Don't lose track of which is the final source file and which is your current working file, or you may end up editing the wrong file later in this exercise. If you need to, resave your working file as `CustomButtonSkin_working.fla`, and then change the filename back when you've completed the Flash part of this exercise.

10. In your working file, double-click on the button graphic on the stage to edit the symbol.

11. Delete the art layer.

If this were a Flash tutorial, we could take the long route and show you just how the default graphics from the template were modified into those of the final example, but a cut-and-paste from the final source must suffice.

12. In the library of final source file, `Chapter_26_Flash_Integration/../CustomButton Skin.fla`, right-click and copy the `Graphics` folder, and paste it into the library for your working file `Chapter_26_Flash_Integration_working/../CustomButtonSkin.fla`.

13. Select all the frames on the border layer of the final source file, and copy them.

14. Create a new layer in your working file below the transitions layer, and paste those frames. In this example, the border graphics have been reworked so that they no longer turn blue on rollover.

One important caveat to using the Flex Skin Design templates is that certain programmatic style coloring may no longer work, such as the themeColor *property and others. For most teams, this is more of an annoyance than a show-stopper, since the Skin Design templates are intended for a mixed designer-developer workflow rather than a strictly style-driven or programmatic approach.*

15. Do the same for the animation and background layers of the final source file.

In this exercise, the border and background layer graphics are simply reworked from the original template. If this were all you were contributing to the design, this would constitute a poor reason for using the Skin Design template. So let's add a little pizzazz to the button, which only Flash can provide.

You can certainly use the Skin Design templates for simple recoloring of the existing theme if it aids in your workflow, but that would be a use better suited to CSS styling than skinning. Where the design skin really shines is the realm in which Flash excels: vector design and illustration, which is exemplified on the animation layer.

If you position the Flash playhead between Frames 10 and 21 and select the graphic on the animation layer, in the Properties panel you'll notice that an instance of the sunburst_animated symbol is on the stage. The timeline is also divided into the different button states with frame labels up, over, down, and disabled. When the button switches to the over state, the sunburst animation will appear. On Frames 22 to 33, the sunburst_static symbol has been placed on the stage. Thus, when the button switches to the down state, the sunburst animation will "pause."

16. Right-click and choose Properties on the Button_skin library symbol, and then change the Name and Class to CustomButtonSkin. This will create the class reference for the skin asset.

Notice that the base class for the symbol is mx.flash.UIMovieClip. *We will go into this and other integration class details in the next exercise later in this chapter.*

If you added _working *to the FLA filename, change it back before going on to the next step.*

17. Go to the Publish Settings (Ctrl+Shift+F12 in Windows; Cmd+Shift+F12 in Mac OS X), and in the Flash tab, check Export SWC.

18. In the Formats tab, check only type: Flash (.swf), and enter a file location of ..\libs\Custom ButtonSkin.swf.

This will compile CustomButtonSkin.swc in the /libs directory of your Flex project, so that it is automatically recognized as an embedded library by the Flex compiler.

19. Select Control ➪ Test Movie (Ctrl+Enter in Windows; Cmd+Enter in Mac OS X) to compile CustomButtonSkin.swc.

20. Create a new folder under /src, named assets, and then copy the orange_parchment.jpg file from the same folder in the source file project so that the file location in your working project reads /src/assets/orange_parchment.jpg.

21. In Flex Builder, add the following code to CustomButtonExample.mxml:

```
<?xml version="1.0" encoding="utf-8"?>
<mx:Application xmlns:mx="http://www.adobe.com/2006/mxml" layout="absolute"
    backgroundImage="assets/orange_parchment.jpg" backgroundSize="100%">
```

```
        <mx:Button label="Button with Custom Skin Class"
            width="300" height="200" horizontalCenter="0" verticalCenter="0"
            skin="@Embed(skinClass='CustomButtonSkin')"/>
    </mx:Application>
```

22. Run `CustomButtonExample.mxml`. When you mouse over the button, what happens? Disaster!

You'll find that when you mouse over the button, its size either oscillates between the two extremes illustrated in Figure 26-3 or the button seems to "pulse" between two smaller sizes when you mouse over the button text. Clearly, this isn't the expected behavior for a Flex button. It would be neat if this were done by design, but obviously this is a glitch. So what caused it?

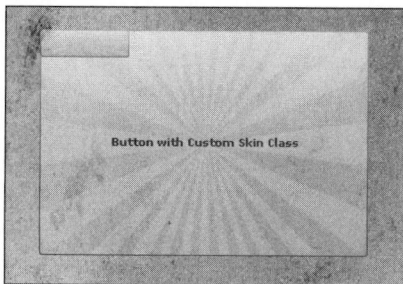

Figure 26-3

23. Go back to Flash CS3, and in the Library panel `Graphics` folder, double-click on the `sunburst_animated` symbol to enter into symbol editing mode.

24. Drag the red playhead indicator at the top of the timeline to scrub the animation back and forth.

You will notice a sunburst graphic rotating on the stage, with a mask graphic on top. This is the problem with our button. The `getBounds` method of the `Button` class is picking up the bounds (that is, the dimensions) of the total graphic, because it doesn't understand masking. This leads to some pretty erratic behavior, because the component class does not know how to intelligently measure the correct bounds for the skin. The skin bounds vary according to whether the animation is present, which in turn leads to the size oscillation you observed. The rotating sunburst graphic results in the "pulsing" behavior. To fix this, you need to tell the component specifically what the bounds of that skin should be. Fortunately, there is a relatively simple fix.

25. Navigate to the `CustomButtonSkin` symbol timeline, and copy and paste the `boundingBox` layer from the source file into your working file.

26. Hide all the other layers and then select the `bounds` symbol on the stage.

If you look at the Properties panel, you'll notice that the symbol has an instance name of `boundingBox`. This is a special, reserved keyword that tells the skin class "use this object to measure the correct bounds for the component skin."

27. In Flash CS3, select Control ➪ Test Movie (Ctrl+Enter in Windows; Cmd+Enter in Mac OS X).

28. In Flex Builder, run `CustomButtonExample.mxml`.

You will probably get a runtime error, something like:

```
ReferenceError: Error #1056: Cannot create property boundingBox on
CustomButtonExample__embed_mxml__426050441.
```

489

This runtime error is caused by a "bug" in the integration kit. To work around this bug, add the missing property declaration (see the following sidebar for details).

29. Create a new layer in your working file below the transitions layer, named *actions*.

30. Select the first frame of the actions layer, and add the following code in the Actions panel:

```
var boundingBox:MovieClip;
```

This will force the Flash compiler to add the `boundingBox` property declaration, thereby prompting it to add the import statement to the bytecode of the SWC (again, see The Flex Integration Kit Bug later in this chapter for details).

31. In Flash CS3, select Control ➪ Test Movie (Ctrl+Enter in Windows; Cmd+Enter in Mac OS X).

32. In Flex Builder, run `CustomButtonExample.mxml`.

Now your button skin should work with the Flex application without errors or unpredictable behavior.

Skinning a Custom Flex Component

Suppose that you want to skin a custom component in a Flex application made up of subcomponents, but having many custom components, each with its own skinning assets, is making the design-to-development workflow a little unwieldy. The designer gives you (the developer) a comp of the final design, and you extract the elements from the design, be it a Photoshop, Fireworks, or Illustrator file. After individual image assets are created, either by the designer or by you, they must be placed in a specific folder inside your assets folder inside the Flex project so that skinning elements for one component or subsystem of the application can be distinguished from those of others. Then you match up the individual component skinning elements in the CSS file with the design comp for the application interface. This can get rather tedious. Fortunately, there is a better way.

Wouldn't it be great if all the skinning assets for your custom component were located in one file, and the designer could lay out the design of the component in Flash and simply pass you an FLA file with all the assets in it? You could have all your design assets laid out in an Illustrator of Fireworks file, but Flash skinning CSLs are much more flexible.

In this example, you'll learn how to skin a custom Flex component using Flash-compiled assets.

Planning Your Custom Flex Component

The Flex application to which you will apply the custom skin in this example will be a custom draggable "panel," named `DragPanelComponent`, based on a `Canvas` component containing two controls, both `Button` components — one serving as a drag control and the other as a resize control.

The mockup of the component layout might look like Figure 26-4.

Since the background and drag button skin will need to be resized with the component, these elements need to have a skin with 9-slice scaling, so the corners do not deform when the component is resized.

For more information on the 9-slice scaling capability (also called scale-9 or scale9grid), see Chapter 23, "Skinning & Themes," or search for "9-slice" in the Flex 3 documentation, which is also listed in the scale9grid *property for the* DisplayObject *class.*

Note that the terms 9-slice scaling, scale-9, and scale9grid are often used synonymously, and all refer to the same capability.

The Flex Integration Kit Bug

When you declare the base class for a MovieClip symbol in the Flash library as UIMovieClip, you are declaring that the symbol is not a MovieClip; rather, it is a UIMovieClip, such that "CustomButtonSkin extends UIMovieClip." If there is a class name indicated for that symbol (which as a best practice should be the same name as the library symbol), such as "CustomButtonSkin," the Flash compiler looks for an .as file with a CustomButtonSkin class definition to associate with that asset. If it finds a CustomButtonSkin.as file, it will use that class definition. If the Flash compiler does not find such a file (as is the case with the preceding example), it creates an empty class definition by default.

But it seems that when using MovieClip assets on the timeline of a symbol with a base class of UIMovieClip (instead of MoviecClip), the Flash compiler doesn't declare stage instances of that class object when it should (i.e., when there is no external class file), and it declares stage instances when it's not supposed to (i.e., when there is an external class file), and then forgets the accompanying import statement. In other words, the compiler behavior is somewhat the reverse of what's expected, which is why most Flash developers come across compiler or runtime errors. Turning off "Automatically declare stage instances" in the Flash compiler (Publish) settings does not yield the expected behavior either.

This bug appears whenever you use a MovieClip instance on the timeline of a UIMovieClip, without declaring those instance properties in the correct (albeit counterintuitive) fashion, as described later in this chapter. This bug is also documented at https://bugs.adobe.com/jira/browse/SDK-15225.

Both the Flex Skin Design Extension and the Flex Component Kit use the UIMovieClip class to enable Flash assets to be used in a Flex application, so this bug applies to both integration extensions.

There are two workarounds for this bug: keep "Automatically declare stage instances" checked in the Flash publish settings per the default, and do one of the following:

❑ If you are *not* linking the UIMovieClip symbol to an external class file, add var boundingBox:MovieClip; to the symbol timeline. If you have any other MovieClip assets on the stage, declare them as well.

❑ If you *are* linking the UIMovieClip symbol to an external class file, add import flash.display.MovieClip; to the package body of the class file. Do not declare the MovieClip property instances.

This will enable you to use the Flex Skin Design or Flex Component Kit extensions without compiler or runtime errors.

More information on the UIMovieClip class can be found in Chapter 29, "Advanced Flash Integration."

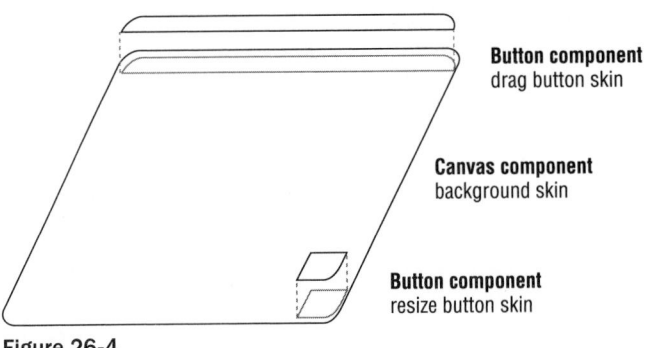

Button component
drag button skin

Canvas component
background skin

Button component
resize button skin

Figure 26-4

Building the Flex Component

For this example, you will first create the custom Flex component. Next, you will create the component skin in a Flash document (.fla), which will serve as a template for the designer to modify later on. This Flash document will lay out the graphics on the Flash stage as they will look in the Flex application, making it easy for the designer to communicate the component layout. You will then apply the skin to the Flex application in Flex Builder 3.

1. If you have not already done so, repeat steps 1–3 from the previous exercise to create the Flex projects you will need to complete this example. The main MXML file in your working project should be named DragPanelExample.mxml.

2. Create a new MXML component in your Chapter_26_Flash_Integration_working project, and name it DragPanelComponent.mxml.

3. Add the following code:

```
<?xml version="1.0" encoding="utf-8"?>
<mx:Canvas xmlns:mx=http://www.adobe.com/2006/mxml
    backgroundSize="100%">
    <mx:Script>
        <![CDATA[
            private const RESIZE_RIGHT_PADDING:uint = 5;
            private const RESIZE_BOTTOM_PADDING:uint = 5;
        ]]>
    </mx:Script>
    <mx:HBox id="footerContent"
        left="15" bottom="5" height="25">
        <mx:Button id="testBtn" label="Test Scale-9" height="20" />
        <mx:CheckBox id="dragSelectCB"
            label="Dragging" selected="true"
            change="dragBtn.enabled = dragSelectCB.selected" />
        <mx:CheckBox id="resizeSelectCB"
            label="Resizing" selected="true"
            change="resizeBtn.enabled = resizeSelectCB.selected" />
    </mx:HBox>
    <mx:Button id="dragBtn"
        styleName="dragBtnStyle"
        top="5" left="5" right="5" />
```

```
<mx:Button id="resizeBtn"
    styleName="resizeBtnStyle"
    right="{RESIZE_RIGHT_PADDING}"
    bottom="{RESIZE_BOTTOM_PADDING}" />
</mx:Canvas>
```

As you can see in the preceding code, the custom DragPanelComponent is a Canvas containing a drag button, resize button, and check boxes for activating these controls.

4. Add the following code to DragPanelExample.mxml:

```
<?xml version="1.0" encoding="utf-8"?>
<mx:Application xmlns:mx="http://www.adobe.com/2006/mxml" layout="absolute"
    xmlns:local="*">
    <local:DragPanelComponent
        x="50" y="50"
        width="400" height="300"
        borderColor="green" borderStyle="solid" />
</mx:Application>
```

5. Run DragPanelExample.mxml.

You should see just a plain green box outline with a few controls. This is what your component looks like without skinning.

But how do you know, once this component has been skinned, whether the 9-slice scaling is working? You could manually resize the DragPanelComponent object a bunch of times, but there is an easier, automated way.

6. In DragPanelComponent.mxml, add the code creationComplete="init()" to the Canvas tag.

7. Add the following lines to the Script block after the property declarations:

```
// -------- scale-9 test --------
[Bindable] private var defaultWidth:uint;
[Bindable] private var defaultHeight:uint;

private function init():void
{
    defaultWidth = this.width;
    defaultHeight = this.height;
}
```

8. Add the code mouseDownEffect="{resizeEffect}" to the testBtn button instance tag.

9. Now add the following Sequence after the end of the Script tag and before the HBox tag:

```
<mx:Sequence id="resizeEffect">
    <mx:Resize heightBy="400" widthBy="600"
        duration="500" target="{this}"
        effectStart="testBtn.enabled = false; testBtn.mouseEnabled = false;"/>
    <mx:Resize heightTo="{defaultHeight}" widthTo="{defaultWidth}"
        duration="500" startDelay="5000" target="{this}"
        effectEnd="testBtn.enabled = true; testBtn.mouseEnabled = true;"/>
</mx:Sequence>
```

This creates an animation sequence that will stretch the component, thereby testing the scale-9 property of the skin. While the animation sequence is running, testBtn is disabled.

10. Run DragPanelExample.mxml.

When you click the Test Scale-9 button, the component is resized to 600×400 pixels and then returns to its original size after a 5-second pause. If done correctly, when you skin this component and click the Test Scale-9 button, you should see the corners of the component background and the sides of the drag button retain their shape and relative position.

Building the Flash Skin

Now that you have a working test application in Flex, you can proceed to creating the Flash skin for that component.

11. In your Chapter_26_Flash_Integration_working project, if you have not already done so, create a new folder in the root of your Flex project folder, named flash.

Since specific instructions on creating certain aspects of a Flash document are outside the scope of this book, this example may require you to follow along with the final source file, Chapter_26_Flash_Integration/flash/DragPanelSkin.fla, in order to complete the creation of this example.

Flash-Flex Workflow Best Practices

Placing all your Flash-compiled files in a /flash directory on the root of the Flex project folder can be considered a best practice for Flash-Flex workflows. Your /flash directory should be considered the root for all Flash files, whether they be FLA, SWF, SWC, or AS files, so start any Flash-compiled package structure from this location (such as /flash/com/domain/foo). All your Flex-compiled files will reside in your Flex source /src directory as usual. This ensures that all Flash-compiled files are separated from the Flex source files, avoiding possible Flex (or Flash) compiler errors when creating the application.

---

12. Copy and paste /flash/DragPanelSkin_start.fla from the Chapter_26_Flash_Integration project source files into the same location in your new Chapter_26_Flash_Integration_working project. Rename the file as DragPanelSkin.fla. You can create your own graphics for the exercise, or you can use the ones provided in this Flash document, which will be the starting point for this exercise.

13. Open DragPanelSkin.fla in Flash CS3.

Since all the skinning assets you'll be using are located in the SWC library, anything that does not get compiled as a class object has no bearing whatsoever on its use in the Flex application, so you can disregard such things as size of the stage, certain timeline objects, and non-linked library symbols.

To prevent nonessential objects from being compiled into the SWF/SWC library (thus conserving filesize), place them on guide layers.

14. Select the graphic on the Canvas background layer, and convert the graphic to a Movie Clip symbol, with a name of `DragPanelComponent_backgroundImage`, and with "Enable guides for 9-slice scaling" checked. Check "Export for ActionScript" to fill in the Class and Base class fields, as in Figure 26-5.

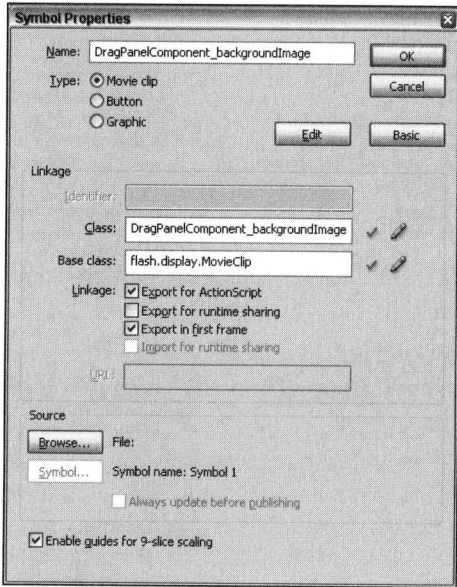

Figure 26-5

15. Convert each button state graphic into a movie clip symbol, and name them according to the names in the final source file library, as shown in Figure 26-6. Make sure that Export for ActionScript is checked for each symbol (refer to Figure 26-5) and that "Enable guides for 9-slice scaling" is checked for all `dragBtnStyle` objects. The library assets you're converting are:

- ❏ `DragPanelComponent_backgoundImage`
- ❏ `DragPanelComponent_dragBtnStyle_disabledSkin`
- ❏ `DragPanelComponent_dragBtnStyle_downSkin`
- ❏ `DragPanelComponent_dragBtnStyle_overSkin`
- ❏ `DragPanelComponent_dragBtnStyle_upSkin`
- ❏ `DragPanelComponent_resizeBtnStyle_disabledSkin`
- ❏ `DragPanelComponent_resizeBtnStyle_downSkin`
- ❏ `DragPanelComponent_resizeBtnStyle_overSkin`
- ❏ `DragPanelComponent_resizeBtnStyle_upSkin`

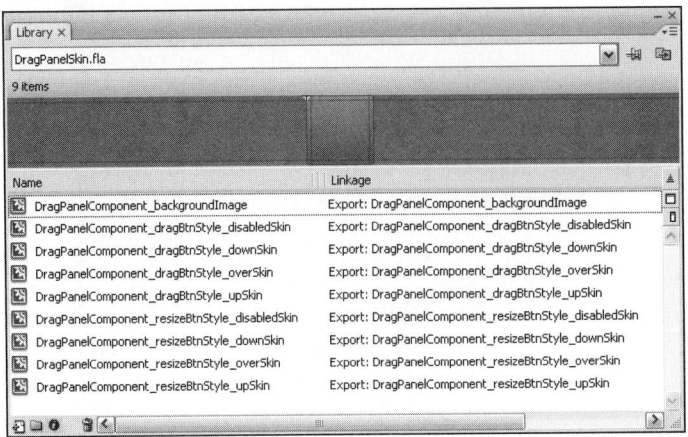

Figure 26-6

These symbol names will be very important later on when you connect the skin to the Flex component.

16. Edit `DragPanelComponent_backgroundImage` by double-clicking the movie clip symbol in the library.

17. Double-click the black line stroke with the selection tool, and select Modify ➪ Shape ➪ Convert Line to Fills.

18. Magnify the stage to 1000% or more. With the Subselection tool, select both inside and outside paths for the border line. Move the scale-9 guides over the anchor points, as shown in Figure 26-7. You may have to select the object paths a few times to line up the guides.

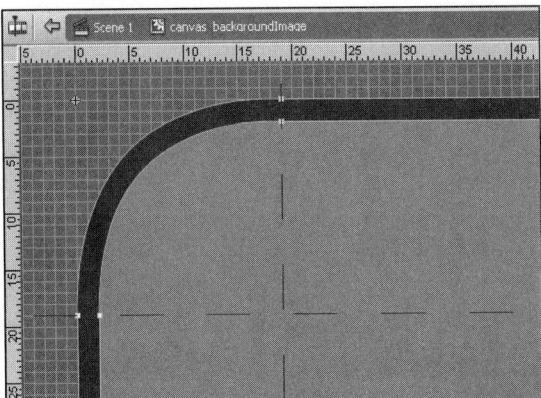

Figure 26-7

Placing the 9-slice guides over the anchor points dividing a graphic ensures that the object will observe proper 9-slice scaling rules.

Scale-9 Tips

❑ 9-slice scaling does not always "take" for line stroke vectors. To avoid this possible gotcha, it is suggested that you convert all lines to fills in a 9-slice graphic.

❑ For 9-slice scaling to work, the graphic symbol with 9-slice scaling turned on must only contain drawing objects or graphic symbols, and those graphic symbols must contain only drawing objects. Any movie clips or other objects within the 9-slice symbol will not have the scale-9 grid applied.

❑ For the scale-9 grid to be applied to the object successfully, each object path must have at least two anchor points inside each corner of the grid. When dealing with simple objects without many anchor points, you can "cheat" by positioning the grid lines on the anchor, as we have done in our example.

---

19. Go back to the main timeline.

20. Go into symbol edit mode for the DragPanelComponent_dragBtnStyle_downSkin symbol, select the entire graphic, and position it at x:1.0, y:1.0. This ensures that when you click the button, the graphic shifts slightly. If you want a more dramatic shifting, move it slightly more.

21. Do the same for the DragPanelComponent_resizeBtnStyle_downSkin symbol.

22. Go to symbol editing mode for the DragPanelComponent_dragBtnStyle_disabledSkin symbol.

Since you don't want the drag button to scale vertically when the DragPanel is resized, position the top and bottom horizontal 9-slice guides outside above and below the graphic. Position the vertical 9-slice guides inside of the graphic's rounded corners. If your graphic lacks anchor points (remember the tip on anchor points above), as is the case of the graphic used in this example, you can create new anchor points for raw drawing objects simply by grouping the outer part along the scale-9 guide, as shown in Figure 26-8.

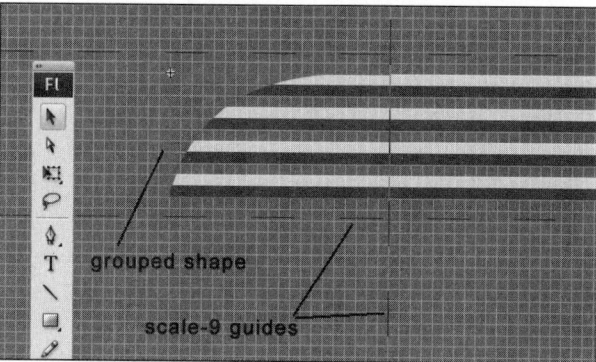

Figure 26-8

23. Go to Publish Settings (Ctrl+Shift+F12 in Windows; Cmd+Shift+F12 in Mac OS X), and in the Flash tab, check Export SWC.

24. In the Formats tab, check only type: Flash (.swf), and enter a file location of `..\libs\Custom ButtonSkin.swf`.

This will compile `CustomButtonSkin.swc` in the `/libs` directory of your Flex project to be automatically recognized as an embedded library by the Flex compiler.

25. Select Control ⇨ Test Movie (Ctrl+Enter in Windows; Cmd+Enter in Mac OS X) to compile `DragPanelSkin.swc`. The `.swf` file is compiled as a preview and will not be used in the Flex application.

You should see something like Figure 26-9.

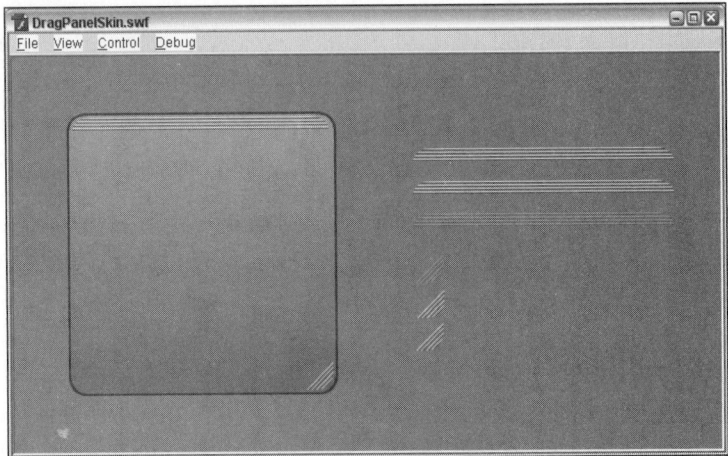

Figure 26-9

Now you're all set to use the 9-slice-enabled skin in the Flex application. The skin assets representing button states for three buttons plus a background skin for the `Canvas` container is neatly encapsulated in the `DragPanelSkin.swf` compiletime shared library, ready for embedding.

Skinning the Flex Component

Skinning Flex components in Flex 2 was somewhat of a chore. You had to manually "wire up" each library symbol/class name from the Flash document to a style selector in a CSS file and apply that stylesheet to your Flex component. If you had multiple Flex components to skin, that task might become quite tedious.

Fortunately, Flex 3 provides two new features that make the task of Flash-Flex skinning integration much easier. The first is an addition to the Flex 3 framework known as subcomponent styling and skinning (see Chapter 22, "Styles"). The second is the Skin Artwork Import Wizard in Flex Builder 3. In the final part of this exercise, you will use both techniques to apply the skin to the Flex component — without writing a single line of CSS.

26. In Flex Builder 3, open `DragPanelExample.mxml` and remove the `borderColor` and `border-Style` properties from the `DragPanelComponent` tag. This border was just for testing; now that you'll be using a skin, you don't need it.

Using the Import Skin Artwork Wizard

Now you're going to use the Import Skin Artwork Wizard to import the skins.

27.   Select File ➪ Import ➪ Skin Artwork.

28.   In the Import Skin Artwork Wizard window, select SWC or SWF file, and browse to `/flash/`
`DragPanelSkin.swc`, as illustrated in Figure 26-10.

> *Your wizard will differ slightly from the one in Figure 26-10 in that your source folder should begin*
> *with* `Chapter_26_Flash_Integration_working`.

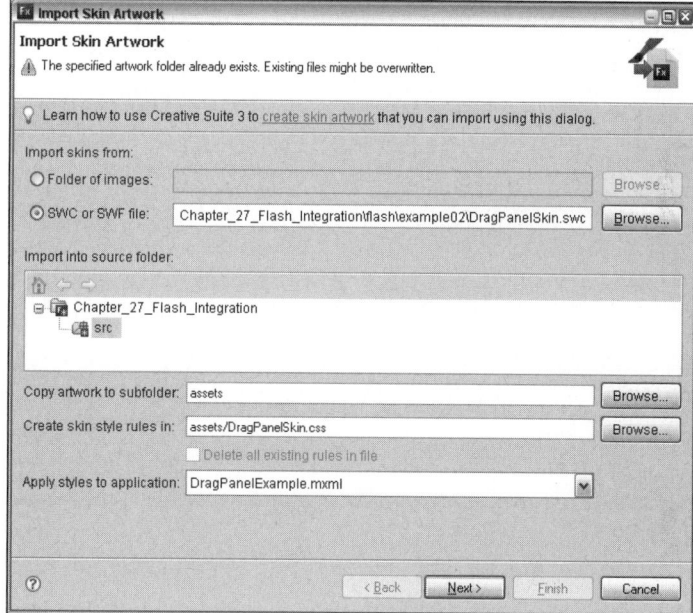

Figure 26-10

29.   In the Copy artwork field, browse to or type **assets**. This will ensure that the SWC file is compiled into this folder so that you don't clutter up the root `/src` folder with embedded assets.

30.   Notice that, in the Create skin style field, the wizard has already filled in `DragPanelSkin.css`, based on the SWC name you selected. Prefix this with `assets/` so that the entry reads `assets/`
`DragPanelSkin.css`. This will ensure that the CSS file is created in the `assets` folder.

> *As a best practice, always place your embedded assets in folders different from the main* `src` *folder,*
> *with names that indicate their function, such as* `/src/assets` *or* `/src/skins`.

31.   Select `DragPanelExample.mxml` in the Apply styles dropdown menu, as indicated in Figure 26-10.

> *Always apply styling to the main* `Application` *class file. Styles defined in a component MXML file*
> *may not be rendered correctly at runtime.*

Mapping Symbols to Subcomponent Styles

Now you're going to associate the Flash library symbols to their respective subcomponent styles in Flex.

32.   Click Next.

Now you can see why you named the symbols in the Flash library with all those impossibly long names. This naming convention maps directly to the following CSS format, as illustrated in Figure 26-11:

```
[component class]_[subcomponent style]_[style selector]
```

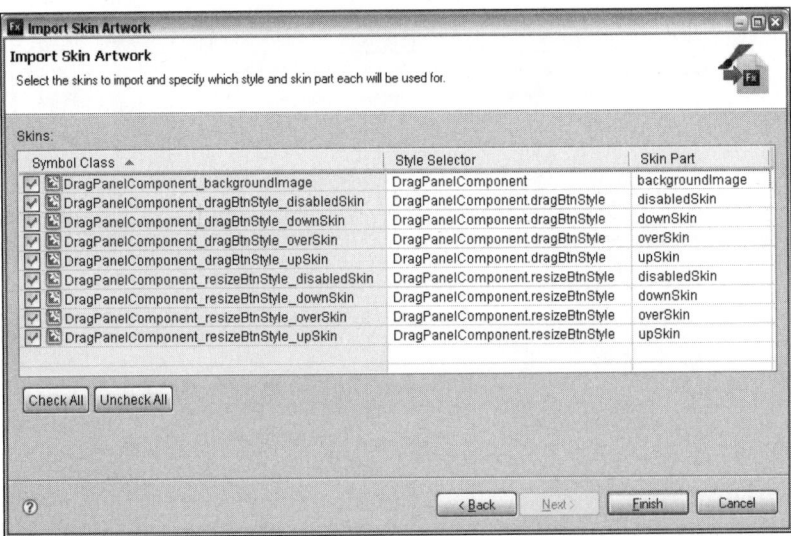

Figure 26-11

33.   Open /src/assets/DragPanelSkin.css in the editor. You should see the following code:

```
DragPanelComponent
{
    backgroundImage: Embed(skinClass="DragPanelComponent_backgroundImage");
}
DragPanelComponent.dragBtnStyle
{
    disabledSkin: Embed(skinClass="DragPanelComponent_dragBtnStyle_disabledSkin");
    downSkin: Embed(skinClass="DragPanelComponent_dragBtnStyle_downSkin");
    overSkin: Embed(skinClass="DragPanelComponent_dragBtnStyle_overSkin");
    upSkin: Embed(skinClass="DragPanelComponent_dragBtnStyle_upSkin");
}
DragPanelComponent.resizeBtnStyle
{
    disabledSkin: Embed(skinClass="DragPanelComponent_resizeBtnStyle_
disabledSkin");
    downSkin: Embed(skinClass="DragPanelComponent_resizeBtnStyle_downSkin");
    overSkin: Embed(skinClass="DragPanelComponent_resizeBtnStyle_overSkin");
    upSkin: Embed(skinClass="DragPanelComponent_resizeBtnStyle_upSkin");
}
```

As you can see, the `DragPanelComponent_dragBtnStyle_disabledSkin` asset name maps directly to the `DragPanelComponent` component class type selector, followed by the `dragBtnStyle` subcomponent style, followed by the `disabledSkin` style property.

Testing the Skin

Now you're going to test the skin by compiling the application and trying it out for yourself.

34. Run `DragPanelExample.mxml`.

You should now see the component with the Flash skin applied. As you can see, a well-designed skin makes all the difference to a custom component, as illustrated in Figure 26-12.

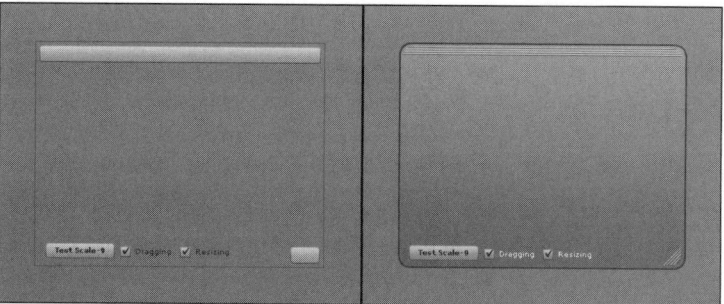

Figure 26-12

You can test the disabled skin states by clicking on the Dragging and Resizing check boxes.

35. Click on the Test Scale-9 button. You should see the component resize and then return to its original dimensions. Now you know that the scale-9 property works!

And that's all there is to it. As you can see, creating a unified skin repository with properly named assets, compiled in the form of an embedded SWC library, combined with the Import Skin Artwork Wizard, is an incredibly powerful tool for skinning custom Flex components.

> **Experiencing the Full DragPanel Application**
>
> A demonstration of a completed, user-draggable/resizable component using this technique is outside the scope of this book. However, if you download the examples for this chapter and run `DragPanelExampleFinal.mxml`, which uses the `DragPanelComponentFinal` component, you will find a working demo of this skin used in a fully functional Flex application. Enjoy!

Summary

In this chapter, you learned about the different options available through an expanded workflow that integrates Flash CS3 and Flex Builder 3 in the same workflow, and the reasons that this would be helpful in developing applications.

In the first example, you learned how to use the Flex Design Extension for Flash CS3 to create a skin in Flash for use in a Flex component. The Flex Integration Kit Bug was also discussed, and some insight into working around this Flash-Flex integration quirk was offered.

In the second example, you learned how to design a skin asset in Flash using a compiletime shared library or SWC file, for a complex custom Flex component. Along the way, some Flash-Flex workflow best practices and scale-9 tips were covered. You learned how to use the Import Skin Artwork Wizard in Flex Builder to map Flash symbol names to Flex subcomponent styles, an important shortcut tool in the Flash-Flex workflow. And you built a Flex application that enables you to test the scale-9-enabled component skin.

In the next chapter, you'll learn about loading assets into a Flex application, and in Chapter 28 you will learn about using sound and video in Flex. These two chapters help set up the conversation for a more advanced look at Flash integration in Chapter 29.

27

Loading External Assets

While building your Flex applications, you will undoubtedly run into scenarios where you will need to load external assets into your application. Luckily, the Flex framework makes this task extremely easy for you. Flex has built-in classes that make the act of loading an external image or Flash file painless and easy, and if those classes don't suit your needs, you can use the lightweight `Loader` class and take on some of the logic yourself. The focus of this chapter will be methods of loading assets into your application.

Depending on the type of application that you are building, loading external assets can be an extremely important feature. You may not want to include all the visual assets embedded into your application for a variety of reasons; assets could make the file size too large, or assets may be loaded dynamically based on application data. Another case is that you do not have control over assets; they are served from a server/domain that you do not administer.

When we talk about loading assets at runtime, it is also important to understand what we mean by assets. Assets are multimedia elements that can be loaded into your application. They can be images, Flash files, audio, or video content.

In this chapter, we will only focus on the basics — images and SWF files. Chapter 28, "Video and Sound," will discuss audio and video in greater detail.

Loading Images

Working with images is a task made easy by Flex. You can load images, monitor loading progress events, or resize images very easily. The `mx:Image` class encapsulates everything that you need to load image assets at runtime. All that you need to do is specify a source for the image. The source can be either a full URL to an asset or a relative URL to the current application, and it can refer to a `.jpg`, `.gif`, or `.png` image.

The next example shows how easy it is to load an image in a Flex application. It consists of an image that is loaded from a remote server, with a progress bar bound to the image. Since the Image instance is bound to the source of the progress bar, the progress bar will automatically be updated as progress events are dispatched from the image as it downloads.

```
<?xml version="1.0" encoding="utf-8"?>
<mx:Application
    xmlns:mx="http://www.adobe.com/2006/mxml"
    layout="absolute">

    <mx:Image
        id="image"
        source="http://flex.org/files/garland_logo.gif"
        complete="progress.visible = false;"
        horizontalCenter="0"
        verticalCenter="0" />

    <mx:ProgressBar
        id="progress"
        mode="event"
        source="{ image }"
        horizontalCenter="0"
        verticalCenter="0" />

</mx:Application>
```

No part of the image is visible while it is downloading to the Flex client. Once it has been downloaded, the image is displayed, and the progress bar is hidden, based on the complete event for the image.

You may have noticed that the image is being downloaded from a remote server that is not relative to the current Flex application instance. It is important to understand the security policy regarding remote images. You can load any image from any location on the Internet; however, you can only access the underlying bitmap data of the image, and perform transformations and effects on that image if you have permission to its content/bitmap data. Permission can be granted to modify remote images using cross domain policies. You can read more about in Chapter 65, "The Security Model."

The previous example was as basic as you can get for working with images; it is an image displayed within an application. You may have noticed that the image was declared in MXML and the image source was specified; the image was not dynamically created and added to the application display list.

In the next example, almost an identical scenario occurs: a remote image is loaded and displayed in the Flex interface. The difference here is that the image instance is created completely in ActionScript. There are no predefined image containers in the MXML markup.

```
<?xml version="1.0" encoding="utf-8"?>
<mx:Application xmlns:mx="http://www.adobe.com/2006/mxml" layout="absolute">

    <mx:Script>
        <![CDATA[
```

```
        import mx.controls.Image;

        private var image : Image;

        private function loadImage() : void
        {
            image = new Image();
            image.source = "http://flex.org/files/garland_logo.gif ";

            image.addEventListener( ProgressEvent.PROGRESS, onProgress );
            image.addEventListener( Event.COMPLETE, onComplete );

            progress.visible = true;
            progress.setProgress( 0, 0 );

            imageContainer.addChild( image );
            loadButton.enabled = false;
        }

        private function onProgress( event : ProgressEvent ) : void
        {
            progress.setProgress( event.bytesLoaded, event.bytesTotal );
        }

        private function onComplete( event : Event ) : void
        {
            image.removeEventListener( ProgressEvent.PROGRESS, onProgress );
            image.removeEventListener( Event.COMPLETE, onComplete );
            progress.visible = false;
        }

    ]]>
</mx:Script>

<mx:Button
    id="loadButton"
    label="Load Image"
    top="10" left="10"
    click="loadImage()" />

<mx:ProgressBar
    id="progress"
    mode="manual"
    visible="false"
    right="10" top="10"/>

<mx:Canvas
    id="imageContainer"
    bottom="10"
    top="40"
    left="10"
    right="10" />

</mx:Application>
```

When the user clicks on the Load Image button, the loadImage() function is invoked. The loadImage() function creates a new Image instance, sets the source to the remote image's URL, adds the event listeners necessary to update the progress bar, and adds the Image instance to the imageContainer canvas.

One other slight, but important difference in this example is that the progress bar's mode is set to manual. Specifying manual mode allows you to use the progress bar's setProgress() function manually, which is performed in the onProgress() event handler. When the image is completely loaded, the progress bar is hidden, and the image is displayed on-screen.

If you want to have your application load a series of images based on data loaded within some XML, this second method is the approach that you want to take. Once your data was loaded, you would loop over data collection, create multiple Image instances for each data point, and specify the URL for each image based on the data content.

The SWFLoader Class

Loading SWF files is another task made easy by the Flex framework. Like the Image class, which enables you to easily load remote images into your application, the mx:SWFLoader class encapsulates everything that you need to load into SWF assets at runtime. The SWFLoader component allows you to load either AVM1 (Flash 8 and earlier), or AVM2 (Flash 9) based Flash content inside of your Flex applications.

The next example shows how easy it is to load SWF-based content inside of a Flex application. This is a simple example showing a SWF file that is loaded from a remote server, with a progress bar bound to the SWFLoader instance to show download progress. When the application loads, it will automatically start downloading the SWF file.

```
<?xml version="1.0" encoding="utf-8"?>
<mx:Application
    xmlns:mx="http://www.adobe.com/2006/mxml"
    layout="absolute">

    <mx:SWFLoader
        id="swf"
        source="http://www.tricedesigns.com/proflex/testswf.swf "
        complete="progress.visible = false;"
        horizontalCenter="0"
        verticalCenter="0" />

    <mx:ProgressBar
        id="progress"
        mode="event"
        source="{ swf }"
        horizontalCenter="0"
        verticalCenter="0" />

</mx:Application>
```

You can also create SWFLoader objects purely in ActionScript and add them to your components, using exactly the same technique that was shown earlier in this chapter for adding images based on ActionScript functions.

You can even have the Flash content communicate directly with the Flex application for seamless operation between the two; however there are a few tricks involved with this, depending on the Flash version of the SWF file and how methods are exposed. Chapters 26, "Flash Integration," and 29, "Advanced Flash Integration," focus on Flash integration in much greater detail.

The Loader Class

If, for some reason you do not want the additional capabilities provided by either the mx:Image or mx:SWFLoader objects, you can also use the Loader class directly to load external content. Both Image and SWFLoader classes actually use a Loader class behind the scenes to dynamically load the remote content.

The flash.display.Loader class is a low-level class that is part of the Flash Player's API. You cannot access the source of it, as you can all Flex components. The Loader class actually takes care of the loading of assets for you. You simply need to specify a URL for the remote asset, and call the load function to load the external content into your application.

The next example shows you how to create a Loader class instance, and load an image into it. It is essentially very similar to the previous example showing how to load an Image class completely using ActionScript, although there are some definite differences.

The first of those differences is that you don't just pass a URL string into the loader. You must first create a URLRequest object, with the URL, and instruct the Loader to load the content by using the load method. You can see in this example that the loadContent() method creates the URLRequest and loads the image content appropriately.

The next difference you will see is that the Loader does not dispatch progress events. The event listeners for progress and complete are actually on the Loader's contentLoaderInfo property. The contentLoaderInfo property is an instance of a LoaderInfo class, which contains information about the Loader's content, loading progress, and location.

```
<?xml version="1.0" encoding="utf-8"?>
<mx:Application xmlns:mx="http://www.adobe.com/2006/mxml" layout="absolute">

    <mx:Script>
      <![CDATA[

         private var loader : Loader;

         private function loadContent() : void
         {
            var requst : URLRequest = new URLRequest(
               "http://flex.org/files/garland_logo.gif" );

            loader = new Loader();
            loader.load( requst );

            progress.visible = true;
            progress.setProgress( 0, 0 );

            loader.contentLoaderInfo.addEventListener( ProgressEvent.PROGRESS,
```

```
            onProgress );
        loader.contentLoaderInfo.addEventListener( Event.COMPLETE,
            onComplete );

        loaderContainer.addChild( loader );
        loadButton.enabled = false;
    }

    private function onProgress( event : ProgressEvent ) : void
    {
        progress.setProgress( event.bytesLoaded, event.bytesTotal );
    }

    private function onComplete( event : Event ) : void
    {
        loader.contentLoaderInfo.removeEventListener( ProgressEvent.PROGRESS,
            onProgress );
        loader.contentLoaderInfo.removeEventListener( Event.COMPLETE,
            onComplete );
        progress.visible = false;
    }
    ]]>
</mx:Script>

<mx:Button
    id="loadButton"
    label="Load Content"
    click="loadContent()"
    x="10"
    y="10" />

<mx:ProgressBar
    id="progress"
    mode="manual"
    visible="false"
    left="10" top="40" />

<mx:UIComponent
    id="loaderContainer"
    left="10" top="40" />

</mx:Application>
```

The last difference between using a Loader class and using an Image class is that you cannot add a Loader instance directly to a mx:Container (Canvas, HBox, etc.). This is because Container instances expect their child components to extend from the Flex UIComponent class. Since the Loader class does not inherit from the UIComponent class, it cannot be added to a Container. To get around this, you need to create a UIComponent instance and add the loader as a child of the UIComponent. In the previous example, you can see that the Loader instance is actually added to the loaderContainer instance, which is an instance of a UIComponent class.

Another interesting feature of the Loader class is that you can use it to load content from a ByteArray in local memory, using the loadBytes() method. This feature enables you to generate or transform content before loading it as a graphic on-screen. Using the `loadBytes()` method, you could completely generate content "from scratch." As long as it contains valid encoded content, it can be loaded.

This approach can be useful for a number of scenarios. First, let's consider that you are using a file format that is unknown to the Flash Player. You could perform a conversion of the file format to a JPG-encoded byte array and load that into a `Loader` object. Another potential scenario is that you could have an XML file that contains lots multiple images, each in a Base-64-encoded string. This would allow you to load all the images based on a single XML file.

The next example shows how to load graphical content into a loader by using the `loadBytes()` method. This example is actually very simple; when the application loads, there is only a single button on the screen. When the user clicks on the Load Content button, the Base-64-encoded string is converted to a `ByteArray`, using the `Base64Decoder` class. The `ByteArray` is then loaded into the `Loader` class instance, and the encoded image is displayed on the screen.

```xml
<?xml version="1.0" encoding="utf-8"?>
<mx:Application xmlns:mx="http://www.adobe.com/2006/mxml" layout="absolute">

    <mx:Script>
        <![CDATA[
            import mx.utils.Base64Encoder;
            import mx.utils.Base64Decoder;

            private var loader : Loader;

            private function loadContent() : void
            {
                var decoder : Base64Decoder = new Base64Decoder();
                decoder.decode( base64EncodedData );

                var byteArray : ByteArray = decoder.flush();

                loader = new Loader();
                loader.loadBytes( byteArray );

                loaderContainer.addChild( loader );
            }

        ]]>
    </mx:Script>

    <mx:Button
        label="Load Content"
        click="loadContent()"
        x="10"
        y="10" />

    <mx:UIComponent id="loaderContainer"  x="10" y="45"/>

    <mx:String id="base64EncodedData">
iVBORw0KGgoAAAANSUhEUgAAAVIAAABPCAYAAAC56k0eAAAL8ElEQVR42u2dz48UxxmG98g1CvAAH
gCLBDeIjuSThBJJ1lg3MfAfDJJBBc4xLElODkQCSRQrEBAsS9g55+QlJ9gL61yAQxYYReRHRBrCJFoyd
sNjA2vGusR219y37G39T2z3TM93307371PRqzZqpqqqqu7v3v3rmq189I9dG7nkkQQgjj1rxEuAkAkIIVKVE
    </mx:String>
```

EAKkCCEESBFCCJAihBACpAghBEgRQmiJgpTQPWBICAFSQApIEUKAFJAihAApIEUIAVJAihACpIAU
kCKElhZIv/r4CSBFCAHSIuGDll5L7vzileTza1OAFCEESPsJgqjVYfpXh5O5f94BpAghQNpLmP7l
oUV1kZf61cPHgBQhBEhzgXTBC02rz+QPf5Z8/OYYIEUIAdJ+QWp6f9tvk/mb04AUIQRI+wWpqQ7e
KYaEECCtJUi/vP8gufP8y7lOQtAd5nIpDAkhQFrrBfkfvfp6rhOZ+vGuoc3sY0gIAdLa72x6MnYl
9wl9+s4EIEUILV+Qfv3402T24t9T0+Rtasa+juOmGBJCgLQWINUM/PvPvZQJUhs3ndq4M9eJ/ff4
XwApQmj5gPSzy+8Gb1ML7rvuwX/4OLm56cVcJ/fR794ApAihpQ/SR+f+Fo5z40fP9fRAk9wwffV1
QIoQWrog1Vhmv5NEX344E2bq85zkzKlRQIoQWnog1RimHUMPKOknfPHvD5PJlT8f+gQUhoQQIK0c
pB6i0vytu32X9fk//pX7ZDUWC0gRQo0HqbrZ8a6kouGTt8ZynawmtOTFAlKEUGNB6sdEW95oSQ8e
ybs3X5NU///fHCBFCDUPpGm7k/Isd+ol5F1j+sFv/gBIEULNAqm8zrRJobL3xmsMNO+Ja9kVIEUI
NQKkWvOZ5imWMTZapIsvsJc1XoohIQRIBwpS/99LVcygC455T77fZVeAFCFUGUhn/vR25oTPIEO8
MqCTNHYLSBFCtQRpp/Wdve400vCA1prKi300+k6Y/VcZ2kuvLaAtuc95L4CWRBV9KDSGhBAgLR2k
WeOiBi5t70wLWpak/7EXKMP/2j//cihH45l5H6HXj4quHsCQEAKkpYNUnmFWeX6SScCdHZ8I+fUI
vUHCspuKrGfFkBACpKWCVEuaOpWn7aGCpyZ6hgnOMieeMCSEAGmpIH1vy76uy47qejE0rABIEUJD
BWkv/61UR/XrlWJICAHS0kCa9/mgdVY/u60wJIQAaSkgTXXsgSRPVzww+hoQQIC0FpHn/+mOQCsuk
FqQlU/KOJdUrTa08etUSq+8mvvp51B6GhBAgLQzSQY6NCmwCnSaxNIYpj1Ez/3oGqf6eRIv01R0X
/LScSmtR+5G+qzI04dTrY/YwJIQAaWGQZu2n7wWWN3+yuwVKDRMIklrbqX8NrXvAkBACpIVA2m3d
6CLvcqE7LWBqG6eAqa2kRbdoAlKEUKNBmvVgEkldcm3zFDTV/Rd0y346fRNB+p8jZ8KmhDTdf+WP
ydQzL2Ccy0DYQX01/evft90P3Qu93t68t3XvpFJAKk/SL7AXOLUFNHia16Yy99Qvd5DqhnQLakgY
dH1k98waUpllYgf11O617pG9V3j4578m7/7gp+G9pRUGqcYwtUdeT2KSt9n0LnrVII0biW6Q4izc
WPMsBr0MQIodNAOkev/FnfvBW3309nh5IFV4+vRpstxDWQ0o3qpq6bqJ1s3Tq+J9g1ZD07izxash
djIO5VN+5dN3FWeNVeVb2YpTXhmOb+S+jLj7aekWb3l9fZXH6ht/345vdVM+Hd/DxK6B4rPO1V+T
tC5yt2san4+/J3G++JrkBV+d7cA+K03Stfb1HLQd+Pr4Y/l8SrN6ZV3zInaQBlJ5pF8/mm11/Qey
s+n8+fPJmTNnkrNnz4bXu3e///7/6ycynJJEBfHX716tZVfr9r9PT08n8/Hz4fPHixW+9gnNu3k2k3k8PY2jgVd
uHAhmzZ2dDfEq59yc5nx48eTQ4Oh/X4cGHNX5ijeNjo4mT5586GrfF9Xpc8iNzNzdUGpgHG6dSN0
8+Iun88Zp44fmjb0AObjbs+FkCyqdfVl+eHVtGpXTfhVGZFueD0q3q3qRWhdIx1q+qPp89pyPZcg443NX3K3KX/kfn0O
eONziBtI12jXxxdex2TeOG1umeZ10TP37WRDswj1gQ8+vmrsgM7vuoV57PxyTT7KNMOOkBqg180nlQ7S
gwcPJiMmjIy3t37/1bZ2p06bU+A0bnNrR9R8A9efJkeK/vCJQrVqxoyzM+Ph4U+5k+bU7IL5PDqu
ICzo+vz79u1rQXBbyIPN5N134Zw1/O9GzsMCZ+bhySY5bsbOT8r1+Lq7
197ymxH7+tuxlM/q75fL+bzmUVh5OpbzVv33dzdzd+mpVjjz2qAls9fJ2/Xade0F4/U6u+BFedtqhlY
mTqeytFnqSo78Pcfcg63110IL5dgPqpK/roOyg2oeWLMBozzo1bUBT3OXXL9l9uAtmrVquAxyhv18Vu3
bg1xGzdubH0/hqTAe+nSpWWT79u1t8SozziuQCsr+GPqe/7x79+4ZAZMxmxYVYNUN9DPDppfbfb9v9r9l+Xl
mEHH3Rr7dZVhWJclNrSs7qPVzRtbVjffG2s7PGxs7+Hnj++GW//cIONr4M//VHjLjr5WuiRR3a61c
a7y9eI5ZY6QG8riuqqMBtq12YPdLZftyq7KDrHxp9mGTP74tDsoOKnuMXuztTCWS7duIaBDnlk4cY
51X3PM4rz1QSWJUU+FmawKly9F2BM4avIOnze8gbRItw4o2XP2tvSl7j7j7ETCUaxQx8LxhWUOOjbxT
A8gCWewt2bhT7J1YA/IA6FSHGFBZkzppp1zo+lgeFeVCmtG5yLxM5afWyc08bizQwdFrCVGc7yAJZ
VXaQN1+afQzSDioDqTw77x16sK1bty5Zu3ZteC+v0HuGaAqw8OdjT1GeNZO5MTAToqRsep+uYGvdU
iKEpwNpQQQxSjcHa9+oO2ZR1DzpBpNN3+gFp2oSK7wKq4epzPLY2TJD6rnbW+kz7gej13q4XVq1MZ
eWb562wHHWXmrsoMiiIB2kHVQGUoXDhw+njl0qPivtwIkqVp8ntLlkQqgI8ioF
2vXr1y8Caez5egg3FaTWfUzrpsVp1sVL8y6yJptiQ/UeiveSsrp0wwCpnXead5bnmuYK0hhtbS/Nm
OqGU1wQ6y7ldVdlAEpIO0g0pBqvHPuItwGlsU7/PyNgbqqYag0QW3Lli1taZVb9u9SOjeXbnbW+kz7gej13q4XVq1MZ
PFt5wfHkk6As8Nq4rbze+NiCqe/a37L7ly5UpLoLoTHcuPF9F8C9HyZIfWPtBD1vWHFX07pAeUCa
FW/eSR1A6q9J3KXOGhsrAtL43N6pcpGtKXKbX8jKtoMiiIB2kHK0rSxUnmFqgqhCPA6q7rh1z2OQ
yqOMg2b2BcmsWXxVFK11jpuahCqZa7qRVADa8YNIxbbJJPwIC6J49e1ogXblyZYID2tNhYsmPHjtqA
1CZbbFZVxmUGHU8S2FIQxdvyEb3PmmyKDdW+b0tXdGzfxbPZO0WGD1F8Tq6d5W/FsbS/3zpfhZ6tt
bFDXwmbQLa7bw3zqbAdZ96sqOygK0khZQeUgFgEyG3Q3btiU7d+d4+4MazWtG6G600gVXXeoCaiBDhLE+gs
XtLntCAoy1vVMZRf4BQQ9dnWm6pcDRmoHIH9+vXr4btK88ewcVgfjhw50nq/d//eANFTp061xQ8b
pGYwfkfmJGW/aJIdYf4goq84cZ18j+u3nbAqYWi/8Maz1WZ50JwDtYTQ78pU2wwUJa02QOieHqqn
j+OBefTo0fZ69mDZ+n15gpy8jNt+OIqr4wM72l2TQW0p7LSbCDtYYCbUuAAU+qZBfj8gs
T580XmldQdpN1t2Mt9hlrUFES1PYASBdMnvth/VYMN/1890znjC0vB4Phx0AUkBasOvpn4Gp91V2
fRF2AEgJjQcpQgiQAlKEECCAFpAghQEoApAghQApIEUKAFJAihAApIEUIAVICIEUIAVJAihACpIAU
IQRIASlCCJJASAClCKOgbEa1Rksk6NqIAAAAASUVORK5CYII=
    </mx:String>

    </mx:Application>

When you execute this example, you will see that the encoded string shown in the preceding code is actually converted to image data and rendered. Figure 27-1 shows the sample output. If you run this example, you will see the Wrox logo, loaded using the `loadBytes()` method.

Figure 27-1

Runtime Shared Libraries

Although not necessarily something that developers interact with directly, runtime shared libraries (RSLs) are external assets that get loaded into the Flash Player as a part of your compiled application.

Essentially, RSLs are precompiled code libraries that can be downloaded and used within multiple Flex applications. These can contain image or media assets, code libraries, or runtime frameworks (including the Flex framework itself). They do not get compiled directly into your Flex application. However, if you are using them, RSLs get loaded when your application is loaded. They are an integral component, as your application will not work without them.

RSLs are often used as common libraries of media or classes that get shared across multiple projects. This way, those assets or code libraries have to be compiled only once, downloaded to the client machine only once, and are loaded only once, although they may be shared across multiple Flex applications. Additionally, RSLs can be cached, thus greatly reducing the compiled Flex application overall's size and downloading time. When they are cached, RSLs are downloaded only once, regardless of how many Flex applications link to them. Because the RSLs are cached in the browser, multiple Flex applications that reuse these cached libraries will each have smaller file sizes and load faster.

You can read more about RSLs and how to use them within your own projects in the Adobe Livedocs at `http://livedocs.adobe.com/flex/3/html/help.html?content=rsl_01.html`.

Summary

Whether you are building a simple photo slideshow, an informational dashboard, a complex image manipulation application, or anything in between, you will run into scenarios where you will need to load external assets into your Flex application. The default `Image` and `SWFLoader` classes built into the Flex framework should provide you with everything you need for most scenarios; however, in those fringe cases, you can still load data using the `Loader` class.

The next chapter explores using video and sound in your Flex applications to enhance the online experience.

Video and Sound

This chapter discusses the audio and video capabilities of the current Flash Player (10) and what power Flex has to offer for creating enhanced user experiences consuming rich media. The Flash Player is the most commonly installed application on any platform in the world. When it comes to delivering rich media experiences with audio and video via the Internet, there is no other solution with the same ubiquity or creative freedom as the Flash Player. Pair that with the advanced application development capabilities of the Flex framework and the myriad tools and libraries available for the platform, and there seems hardly a reason not to use the Flash Player for delivery of audio and video on the Web. That is why more than 70% of all video streamed over the Internet leverage the Flash Player for their delivery platform.

This chapter covers the types and formats of audio and video content supported by Flex and the Flash Player, as well as some specifics to new content types more recently supported by the Flash Player MovieStar update. In addition, this chapter spends time explaining the basics and practical how-to's when it comes to implementing these rich media elements into your applications. Focusing first on the sound capabilities and classes, this chapter takes a hands-on approach to the various methodologies for implementing and controlling audio in Flex. Then it's onto the details of video streaming and a deeper dive into the classes, components, and options, including the basics parts needed for custom video player components and exploring the Flex `VideoDisplay` component.

Methods for Bringing in Media

A host of different formats are used for delivering media content on the Internet. Flash now handles many different types and formats of media and allows developers and designers to combine this content with the rich interfaces made possible by Flash. This section covers the different media Flash can bring in and how to bring this content into rich applications.

Usable File Formats

Flash Player has supported audio and video for many releases. Both the original release (Flash Player 9) and the current release for Flex 3 (Flash Player 10) support external media content of type and extension of MP3 and FLV. However, since the initial release of Flash Player 9, there have been a few dot releases. One of the specific ones named MovieStar (Flash Player 9.0.115), which will be discussed further later in this chapter, enabled additional media types of H.264 MPEG-4 video, AAC, and AAC+/HE-AAC.

MP3 is a well-known file format, so we will not discuss much of the internals. However, FLV warrants some deeper explanation. FLV is really just an extension and does not directly dictate only one video type. Generally, FLV files actually contain a video track encoded with either Sorenson Spark or On2 VP6, an audio track (usually Nelly Moser or MP3), and an optional AMF-based data track for metadata or cue points. We will be discussing the data track later, so for now let's discuss the two video options. Sorenson Spark and On2 VP6 are the video CODEC (*compression de*compression) options. It defines how the video is compressed and how it is decompressed. What this really means for you is how the quality and bandwidth will be affected as well as any other options the particular CODEC may offer. On2 VP6 offers superior quality at a lower bandwidth in comparison to the Sorenson Spark CODEC; however, it requires greater CPU consumption during playback. The general recommendation is to use On2 VP6 unless heavy performance limitations are already in play, which appropriate application testing will usually make clear.

With the release of the Flash Player MovieStar update, Flex now has the capability of working with high-definition (HD) AAC, AAC+/HE-ACC audio content, and H.264 MPEG-4 video content. MPEG-4 is a container format, which means that as long as the content is encoded to the proper specs (H.264 and AAC/AAC+), the extension really doesn't matter. That being said, some of the most common file types include .AAC, .MP4, .M4a for audio, and .MP4, .M4V, .3GP, .3g2, and even .MOV. Once again, though, just because a file has an aforementioned extension does not mean that it is encoded to the proper spec and, therefore, does not guarantee that it will be compatible. For more details and hands-on exercises using H.264 and AAC/AAC+ content, see the article I wrote for Adobe Devnet at www.adobe.com/devnet/flashplayer/articles/hd_video_flash_player.html. In addition to the preceding file types, Adobe has recently started a new file type standard for the MPEG-4 content now supported. The extensions Adobe are now using are .F4a, .F4b for audio and .F4v, and .F4P for video. More details can be found about this new initiative at www.kaourantin.net/2007/10/new-file-extensions-and-mime-types.html.

A few caveats are worth mentioning. iTunes and many other providers use H.264 and AAC/AAC+ for the content types but sometimes have rights management integrated as well. If there are rights management features within the files, they will not be able to be played via Flex and the Flash Player unless the rights are managed specifically via the Adobe Media Rights Management Server. Rights management controls when and how media content can be viewed, even after it has been downloaded. Also, since the MovieStar update came out after the initial release of the Flex 3 framework, there are some initial minor hurdles when it comes to playing the new HD file content. When using the original built-in components, you will run into an issue playing any content with an extension other than .FLV. The solution to this is to either change the extension of your content to .FLV (it will work, although it can be messy) or not use the prebuilt VideoDisplay component and play the content via a custom NetStream implementation. (See "Video Classes and Components" later in this chapter for more about NetStream.) There is also a new version of the FLVPlayback component (version 2.5) that can be used in Flash or Flex that handles different file extensions. It is available from the Adobe Flash Media Server Tools page (www.adobe.com/go/fms_tools).

Integrating the Media Content

Generally, you can integrate external media files for both audio and video either by embedding the media directly into a compiled SWF, thereby increasing the weight of the application, or by loading/streaming the content in at runtime. In Flex there is the option to embed audio into an application but not directly embed video content. Flex can play embedded video content within a Flash 9 SWF compiled from the Flash CS3 IDE, although it's generally not recommended except for visual requirement edge cases. With audio, in general, it is only recommended for very short audio clips that need precision timing, such as sound effects, or it could impact the load time and performance of the application.

You have a few options when embedding audio into a Flex application. Either embed sound assets via the `Embed` meta tag and the generic `Class` class, and then use an instance on the generic class cast as a `mx.core.SoundAsset` instance, or embed the asset into a style sheet or MXML component, using the embed directive (`@Embed`).

Example:

```
[Embed(source="assets/bang.mp3")]
private var bangClass:Class;
```

The `SoundAsset` class is a subclass of the `flash.media.Sound` class and, therefore, inherits all the properties and methods of the `Sound` class. After generating the instance of the `SoundAsset` to play the sound, at any point all you have to do is call the `play()` method on the instance.

Example:

```
var bangSound:SoundAsset = SoundAsset( new bangClass() );
bangSound.play();
```

Embedding a sound in MXML can be done directly in an attribute of an MXML tag. For instance, the source attribute of a SoundEffect tag allows embedded sounds that use the embed directive.

Example:

```
<mx:SoundEffect id="mySound" source="@Embed(source='mySoundEffect.mp3')"/>
```

Exercise 1: Embedding Sound in ActionScript

In this exercise, you will embed an audio file inline:

1. Open the `EmbeddingSound_wt1.mxml` file in the `{tutorial_directory}/VideoAndSound/src/` directory.

   This file already includes the simple UI that you will use to play the sound. There is a `Button` and a `MouseEvent.CLICK` event handler method `_onPlay()` to handle the click event of the button. You will add code to embed and play an MP3 file.

2. In the File Navigator, right-click `EmbeddingSound_wt1.mxml` and select Set as Default Application.

3. Under the comment `// Embed the sound`, add the metadata to embed the MP3 file `bang.mp3` in the `assets` directory:

   ```
   [Embed( source="assets/bang.mp3" ) ]
   ```

4. Under the `Embed` statement, create a private variable named `_bangClass` of the type `Class`:

```
private var _bangClass:Class
```

5. Under the comment `// SoundAsset`, create a private variable `_bangSound` of the type `SoundAsset`:

```
private var _bangSound:SoundAsset;
```

The code up to this point should resemble the following:

```
// Embed the sound
[Embed( source="assets/bang.mp3" ) ]
private var _bangClass:Class;

// SoundAsset
private var _bangSound:SoundAsset;
```

6. Inside the `_onPlay()` event handler method, under the comment `// Using the sound via SoundAsset`, set the `_bangSound` variable equal to a new instance of the `_bangClass`, making sure to type the new instance as a `SoundAsset`:

```
_bangSound = SoundAsset( new _bangClass );
```

7. Call the `play()` method on the `_bangSound` `SoundAsset` object:

```
_bangSound = SoundAsset( new _bangClass );
_bangSound.play();
```

The completed code should look like the following:

```
<mx:Application xmlns:mx="http://www.adobe.com/2006/mxml" layout="absolute">

    <mx:Script>
        <![CDATA[
            import mx.core.SoundAsset;

            // Embed the sound
            [Embed( source="assets/bang.mp3" )]
            private var _bangClass:Class;

            // SoundAsset
            private var _bangSound:SoundAsset;

            private function _onPlay( p_event:MouseEvent ):void
            {
                // Using the sound via SoundAsset
                _bangSound = SoundAsset( new _bangClass );
                _bangSound.play();
            }

        ]]>
    </mx:Script>

    <mx:Button id="play_btn"
        label="PLAY"
```

```
            click="_onPlay( event );" />

    </mx:Application>
```

8. Save the file and run the application. Click the Play button. The sound should play.

The other option is to embed the MP3 file via MXML into a `mx:SoundEffect` component's source property. The `SoundEffect` class extends the Flex `mx.effects.Effect` class and thus can be triggered from UI Components just as a visual effect would be, such as a fade or blur. The next example covers how to do this. The `SoundEffect` component supports loading MP3's at runtime or using embedded audio content, both of the options use the source property and either pass the path to a MP3 file to load at runtime, embed an audio inline, or reference a audio clip embedded in a class with a generic `Class` reference, as was done before, as long as that instance is bindable.

```
Example:

<!--Embedding in-line -->
<mx:SoundEffect id="soundEffect" source="@Embed(source='assets/bang.mp3')" />
<!

<!--Using previously embedded bindable asset -->
<mx:SoundEffect id="soundEffect" source="{ _BANGCLASS }" />
```

Exercise 2: Embedding Sound in MXML

In this exercise, you will:

❑ Embed an audio file in the MXML code using the `SoundEffect` class

❑ Play the sound on the `mouseDownEffect` event of a `Button`

❑ Use the `useDuration` and `duration` properties of the `SoundEffect` class

❑ Use the `volumeFrom`, `volumeTo`, and `volumeEasingFunction` properties of the `SoundEffect` class

1. Open the file `EmbeddingSound_wt2.mxml` in the `{tutorial_directory}/VideoAndSound/src/` directory.

2. In the File Navigator, right-click `EmbeddingSound_wt2.mxml` and select Set as Default Application.

3. Under the comment `<!-- Inline SoundEffect Embed -->`, add the MXML tag `<mx:SoundEffect />`, with the id attribute of `"bangSoundEffect"` and a source attribute that embeds the `drone.mp3` audio file from the `assets` directory:

```
<mx:SoundEffect id="bangSoundEffect"
        source="@Embed( 'assets/drone.mp3' )" />
```

4. Under the comment `<!-- Button to play the sound -->`, add a MXML `Button` tag with the following properties:

❑ id: play_btn

❑ label: PLAY

❑ mouseDownEffect: bangSoundEffect

```
<!-- Button to play the sound -->
<mx:Button id="play_btn"
        label="PLAY"
        mouseDownEffect="bangSoundEffect" />
```

The completed code should look like the following:

```
<mx:Application xmlns:mx="http://www.adobe.com/2006/mxml" layout="absolute">
    <mx:Script>
        <![CDATA[
            import mx.effects.easing.Elastic;
        ]]>
    </mx:Script>

    <!-- Inline SoundEffect Embed -->
    <mx:SoundEffect id="bangSoundEffect"
        source="@Embed( 'assets/drone.mp3' )"  />

    <!-- Button to play the sound -->
    <mx:Button id="play_btn"
        label="PLAY"
        mouseDownEffect="bangSoundEffect" />

</mx:Application>
```

5. Save the file and run the application. Click the Play button. The sound should play, but only briefly. Next, we will use the duration to extend the length of the SoundEffect play time.

6. Return to the MXML file EmbeddingSound_wt2.mxml.

7. Add the following properties and values to the SoundEffect MXML tag:

❑ useDuration: true

❑ duration: 4000

The adjusted SoundEffect MXML tag should look like the following:

```
<!-- Inline SoundEffect Embed -->
<mx:SoundEffect id="bangSoundEffect"
        source="@Embed( 'assets/drone.mp3' )"
        useDuration="true"
        duration="4000" />
```

8. Save the file and run the application. Click the Play button. The sound should now play for 4 seconds.

9. Return to the MXML file EmbeddingSound_wt2.mxml.

10. Add the following properties and values to the SoundEffect MXML tag, making sure that the mx.effects.easing.Elastic class is imported:

❑ volumeFrom: 1

❑ volumeTo: 0

❑ volumeFunction: { Elastic.easeInOut }

The updated code should look like the following:

```
<mx:Application xmlns:mx="http://www.adobe.com/2006/mxml" layout="absolute">
    <mx:Script>
        <![CDATA[
            import mx.effects.easing.Elastic;
        ]]>
    </mx:Script>

    <!-- Inline SoundEffect Embed -->
    <mx:SoundEffect id="bangSoundEffect"
        source="@Embed( 'assets/drone.mp3' )"
        useDuration="true"
        duration="4000"
        volumeFrom="1" volumeTo="0"
        volumeEasingFunction="{ Elastic.easeInOut }" />

    <!-- Button to play the sound -->
    <mx:Button id="play_btn"
        label="PLAY"
        mouseDownEffect="bangSoundEffect" />

</mx:Application>
```

11. Save the file and run the application. Now the audio will play, and you should be able to hear the easing function affect the audio's volume.

Understanding Progressive Loading and Streaming

There are two primary options of streaming in audio and video at runtime within the Flex framework and the Flash Player: progressive loading and true streaming. Progressive loading is a linear loading of the contents specified to be loaded or played. Because the content is loaded linearly, audio and video content cannot be played or accessed with the seek function past the current position that has been loaded. That means if you have a 30-minute video and the user is interested only in the last 3 minutes, they will have to wait and load the previous 27 minutes of video before they can see the last 3 minutes. If the user has enough buffer to load the contents faster than real-time playback (which can be likely with non-high-definition video), he or she can seek or wait the amount of time the bandwidth requires, which is not necessarily the same as the rate of the linear playback. Also a key difference of progressive loading is that the audio or video content will be cached on the user's local machine. This can be a content security concern but is rather common. In addition, there is no need for any additional server technologies such as the Flash Media Server, since progressive streaming works similarly to just loading in an image or textual content. The following sections and chapters discuss in greater detail the technical and coding requirements for progressive loading and true streaming using the Flash Media Server.

The Sound Class

This section explores the sound capabilities and related classes in Flex for playing and controlling audio. The flash.media.Sound class is the main launching point for sound control in Flash. Its primary purpose is to load and play external MP3 files at runtime. In addition, the Sound class provides important information about your sound file, including the number of bytes loaded (bytesLoaded), the total number of bytes in the files (bytesTotal), and ID3 metadata within the file, as well as information such as artist, album, or other custom data. The Sound class itself does not do much more than load and or play a file as well as provide data; however, once you start playing a file via the Sound class, a flash.media.SoundChannel instance is created for you and provides more information and control of the currently playing data.

A key point to understand with the Sound class is the difference in loading versus playing, as this somewhat differs from the previous methodologies for working with sound in the Flash Player and Flex. The concept is simple. Before any sound can be played and heard, it must be directed to load. There are primarily two options for loading an audio file into a Sound instance. The first is to pass a URLRequest into the constructor when you generate a Sound instance. This will automatically call the load() method for you.

```
EXAMPLE:
var request:URLRequest = new URLRequest( "theFile.mp3" );
var soundManager:Sound = new Sound( request );
```

The second option is to use the load() method of the Sound class and pass in a URLRequest.

```
EXAMPLE:
var request:URLRequest = new URLRequest( "theFile.mp3" );
var soundManager:Sound = new Sound();
soundManager.load( request );
```

A very important thing to note about the Sound class is that once you have loaded an MP3 file with a Sound class instance, you cannot load any other sound file with that instance. You need to create a completely new instance of the Sound class for each MP3 file you want to load.

The SoundLoaderContext Class

Optionally, you can also pass a flash.media.SoundLoaderContext instance as the second parameter of the load() method to provide security checks, as well as set your bufferTime for the audio stream to something other than the default of 1000 milliseconds. The SoundLoaderContext has two properties that can optionally be sent to the constructor or set after. The first is bufferTime, which, as mentioned, sets the initial amount of time of the file to be loaded before playback will begin after a play() method has been invoked on the Sound instance. While the audio file is loading into the specified buffer, the playback will be halted and the isBuffering property of the Sound instance will be true. The second parameter, checkPolicyFile, is a Boolean indicating whether the Flash Player should check for a cross-domain policy file to be loaded and verified from the sound assets server before loading the asset itself. The following are some key points from Adobe on the Flash Player security model:

❑ Loading and playing a sound is not allowed if the calling SWF file is in a network sandbox and the sound file to be loaded is local.

❑ By default, loading and playing a sound is not allowed if the calling SWF is local and tries to load and play a remote sound. A user must grant explicit permission to allow this.

❑ Certain operations dealing with sound are restricted. The data in a loaded sound cannot be accessed by a SWF file in a different domain unless you implement a cross-domain policy file.

Sound-related APIs that fall under this restriction are the `Sound.id3` and `SoundMixer.bufferTime` properties and the `SoundMixer.computeSpectrum()` and `SoundTransform()` methods.

```
EXAMPLE:
var sRequest:URLRequest = new URLRequest( "mySound.mp3" );
var soundContext:SoundLoaderContext = new SoundLoaderContext( 5000, true );
var soundManager:Sound = new Sound();
soundManager.load( sRequest, soundContext );
```

Playing and Controlling Sound

Once a `load()` method has been invoked, either automatically by passing in the `URLRequest` to the constructor or by explicitly calling the `load()` method, you can call the `play()` method of the `Sound` instance. As soon as the buffer has been filled per the default or the specified value in the `SoundLoader Context` after the `play()` method has been called, the sound will start. The `play()` method, however, does have a few optional parameters to control the playback. You can optionally pass a start-time offset in milliseconds as the first parameter (default is 0), the number of times you want your audio file to loop as an `int` (default is 0) as the second parameter, or you can pass a `flash.media.SoundTransform` instance to control features such as volume and panning.

The `SoundTransform` class provides the ability to have fairly fine-tuned control over the panning and volume. The constructor takes two optional parameters to initialize with. The first being the volume, which ranges from 0 (muted) to 1 (full blast) — default is 1, and the second parameter of panning, which accepts a range between -1 (full left pan) to 1 (full right pan) — default is 0 (balanced). In addition to being able to set volume and pan easily from the constructor, they can also be set via their public properties of `volume` and `pan`. There are also properties for shifting and adjusting the input levels from either channel to the other or itself. These properties enable you to shift the input levels of one channel to the other, or simply control the input level per channel. The `leftToLeft` and `rightToRight` properties enable you to control how much of the input is played in their respective channels by specifying a value between 0 (none) and 1 (all). The `leftToRight` and `rightToLeft` properties allow you to shift or remap the input to the other channel by specifying a value between 0 and 1 as well.

Whenever the `play()` method is called, it returns a `flash.media.SoundChannel` instance for the current stream. The `SoundChannel` class provides information on the current position of the playhead for a stream currently being played. It also provides an API for monitoring the amplitude (volume) of the channel, a `stop()` method for stopping the sound in the channel, dispatches a generic event with the type of `soundComplete`, which indicates the sound has finished playing, and a property for getting/setting the `SoundTransform` instance for the channel.

Exercise 3: Controlling Sound

In this exercise, you will create a class to handle:

❑ Loading audio

❑ Playing, stopping, pausing, and resuming audio

❑ Setting volume and pan SoundTransforms

Loading Audio

1. Open the `ControllingSound_wt1.mxml` file in the `{tutorial_directory}/VideoAndSound/src/` directory.

    Much of this file has been provided. You will add code to provide the actual functionality to control audio. Please review the file's components and structure.

2. In the File Navigator, right-click `ControllingSound_wt2.mxml` and select Set as Default Application.

3. Open `ProfxSound.as` in `{tutorial_directory}/VideoAndSound/src/com/wrox/profx3/sound`.

4. `ProfxSound.as` is a class file that has been provided with most of the structure and methods predefined. This is so that you can concentrate on the key concepts of controlling audio through the rest of this exercise. `ProfxSound` is an extension of the `flash.media.Sound` class. You will step through adding to this class the functionality to load and control audio. The following is a list of properties of the class and their intended functions:

    ❑ `_source` — The path to the sound file

    ❑ `_sndLoaderContext` — Provides security checks for loading sound

    ❑ `_currentPosition` — The value to track the current position when the audio is paused

    ❑ `_soundChannel` — The `SoundChannel` object that will be used to control the audio

    ❑ `autoPlay` — A Boolean value to determine if the audio is played automatically when the file is loaded

5. In the `_loadSource()` method in the CONTROL METHODS section of the class, under the comment `// Load the audio file`, call the `load()` method and pass it a `URLRequest` with the `source` property as the only parameter and the `_sndLoaderContext` as the `load()` method's second parameter:

    ```
    load( new URLRequest( source ), _sndLoaderContext );
    ```

6. In the `_initListeners()` method, under the comment that begins `// Listen for the Event.COMPLETE...`, add an event listener for the `Event.COMPLETE` event. Assign the `_onComplete()` method as the handler for this event:

    ```
    addEventListener( Event.COMPLETE, _onComplete );
    ```

7. In the `_onComplete()` event handler method, under the comment `// Play the audio file`, call the `play()` method.

Controlling Sound

1. Locate the `play()` method.

2. Under the comment `// Play the audio file`, set the `__soundChannel` property equal to the result of calling the `super.play()` method and passing it the `startTime`, `loops`, and `sndTransform` parameters:

    ```
    _soundChannel = super.play( startTime, loops, sndTransform );
    ```

3. Locate the set source setter method, under the comment `// Set the value of source`, and set the _source property equal to the `p_value` parameter:

```
_source = p_value;
```

4. Next, add a conditional statement that evaluates if `source` is null. If `source` is not null, call the `_loadSource()` method:

```
if( source )
{

    _loadSource();
}
```

The `source` setter method should look like the following:

```
public function set source( p_value:String ):void
{
    // Set the value of source
    _source = p_value

    // If source is not null, call _loadSource()
    if( source )
    {
        _loadSource();
    }
}
```

5. Save the file, then run the application. The sound should play. If you review the `ControllingSound_wt1.mxml` file, you will see that `autoPlay` is set to `false` on the `ProfxSound` component. Next we will fix this.

6. Return to the `ProfxSound.as` class, and locate the `_onComplete()` event handler method.

7. Under the comment "`//Check the autoPlay flag`", add a conditional statement to check the value of `autoPlay`. If `autoPlay` is `false`, call the `stop()` method:

```
if( !autoPlay )
{
        stop();
}
```

The completed `_onComplete()` method should look like the following:

```
private function _onComplete( p_event:Event ):void
{
    // Play the audio file
    play();

    // Check the autoPlay flag
    if( !autoPlay )
    {
        stop();
    }
}
```

8. Locate the `stop` method.

9. Inside the `stop` method, call the `stop()` method of the `_soundChannel` property:

```
_soundChannel.stop();
```

The completed `stop` method should look like the following:

```
public function stop():void
{
    // Stop the audio
    _soundChannel.stop();
}
```

10. Save the file and run the application. Now when the application starts, the audio doesn't automatically play. You can click the Play button, the audio should start. You can click the Stop button, and the audio should stop.

11. Return to `ProfxSound.as`.

12. Locate the `pause()` method. Under the comment that begins "`// Set the _currentPosition`", set the `_currentPosition` property equal to the `position` property of the `_soundChannel` object:

```
// Set the _currentPosition so we can resume at the same place
_currentPosition = _soundChannel.position;
```

13. Next, stop the audio by calling the `stop()` method.

```
// Set the _currentPosition so we can resume at the same place
_currentPosition = _soundChannel.position;

// Stop the audio
stop();
```

The completed `pause()` method should resemble the following:

```
public function pause():void
{
    // Set the _currentPosition so we can resume at the same place
    _currentPosition = _soundChannel.position;

    // Stop the audio
    stop();
}
```

14. Locate the `resume()` method.

15. Inside the `resume()` method, call the `play()` method, passing it the `_currentPosition` property:

```
public function resume():void
{
    // Play the audio from the last recorded position
    play( _currentPosition );
}
```

16. Save the file and run the application. Now you should be able to use the Play, Stop, Pause, and Resume buttons to control the audio.

Setting SoundTransforms

1. Locate the setter method for the `volume` property.

2. Create a local variable transform typed as a `SoundTransform` object, and set it equal to the `soundTransform` property of the `_soundChannel` object:

```
var transform:SoundTransform = _soundChannel.soundTransform;
```

3. Set the `volume` property of the `transform` variable equal to the `p_value` parameter:

```
transform.volume = p_value;
```

4. Set the `soundTransform` property of the `_soundTransform` object equal to the `transform` variable:

```
_soundChannel.soundTransform = transform;
```

The completed setter method should look like the following:

```
public function set volume( p_value:Number ):void
{
    // Set the volume value on the sound
    var transform:SoundTransform = _soundChannel.soundTransform;
    transform.volume = p_value;
    _soundChannel.soundTransform = transform;
}
```

5. Locate the setter method for the `pan` property. Add similar code as you did for the `volume` setter, but set the `pan` property instead of `volume`. The setter for `pan` should look like the following:

```
public function set pan( p_value:Number ):void
{
    // Set the pan value on the sound
    var transform:SoundTransform = _soundChannel.soundTransform;
    transform.pan = p_value;
    _soundChannel.soundTransform = transform;
}
```

6. Save the file and run the application. The Volume slider on the left side of the application will now control the volume, and the pan slider on the right will control the panning of the audio.

Accessing ID3 Information

The `Sound` class instance provides access to any ID3-based metadata supported. Flash Player 9 and later supports ID3 2.0 tags (specifically 2.3 and 2.4); however, only ID3 tags that use the UTF-8 character set are supported. To access the ID3 information, you use the `id3` property of the `Sound` instance.

```
EXAMPLE: Retrieves the artist ID3 information
soundManager.id3.artist
```

However, a key step that must be taken before accessing the ID3 information from a MP3 file is waiting until the information is available to the Sound instance. The Sound instance broadcasts a generic event with the type of id3 to notify that the ID3 information is loaded and available to be accessed. You should always listen for this event if you want to retrieve the ID3 data and only do so after the handler has fired.

The primary set of ID3 tags have mapped ActionScript property accessors. The following table shows the ID3 to ActionScript mappings.

ID3 2.0 Tag	ActionScript Property
COMM	Sound.id3.comment
TALB	Sound.id3.album
TCON	Sound.id3.genre
TIT2	Sound.id3.songName
TPE1	Sound.id3.artist
TRCK	Sound.id3.track
TYER	Sound.id3.year

There is a decent sized list of supported ID3 tags that do not have direct ActionScript property but can be accessed via the ID3 tag key off of the Sound instance's id3 property. Refer to the ActionScript documents for the supported list.

Exercise 4: Accessing Sound Metadata

In this exercise, you will access and display the ID3 data from an MP3 audio file:

1. Open the ControllingSound_wt2.mxml file in the {tutorial_directory}/ VideoAndSound/src/ directory.

    This file adds onto what was created in the preceding sample. It has the same user interface and uses the ProfxSound class that you built in the last sample to play and control the audio.

2. In the File Navigator, right-click ControllingSound_wt2.mxml and select Set as Default Application.

3. Under the comment <!-- Add Script Block -->, add an MXML script block:

    ```
    <!-- Add Script Block -->
    <mx:Script>
        <![CDATA[

        ]]>
    </mx:Script>
    ```

4. Add a private method named _onPreInitialize() with a return type of void to the script block:

    ```
    <mx:Script>
    ```

```
<![CDATA[
    private function _onPreInitialize():void
    {

    }
]]>
</mx:Script>
```

5. Inside the _onPreInitialize() method, add an event listener for the Event.ID3 event on the sound object and assign the handler of the event to an _onID3 method, which you will create shortly:

```
private function _onPreInitialize():void
{
    sound.addEventListener( Event.ID3, _onID3 );
}
```

6. Under the _onPreInitialize() method, create a private method named _onID3 with the return type of void:

```
private function _onID3( p_event:Event ):void
{

}
```

7. Inside the _onID3() event handler method, call the trace() method and pass it the id3 property of the sound object. Use the ObjectUtil.toString() utility to trace a string of the object:

```
private function _onID3( p_event:Event ):void
{
    trace( ObjectUtil.toString( sound.id3 ) );
}
```

8. Under the trace method, set the text property of the songName_lbl Label component to the value of songName on the sound.id3 object:

```
private function _onID3( p_event:Event ):void
{
    trace( ObjectUtil.toString( sound.id3 ) );
    songName_lbl.text = sound.id3.songName;
}
```

9. Save the file and run the application. You should now see the name displayed above the Play controls. If you run the application in Debug mode, you will also see all of the ID3 information displayed in the debug output.

    If you get an error when you run the application about "cannot access local resource," you may need to add an argument to your Flex compiler string. To add the argument, choose the Project ➤ Properties menu option. In the dialog that appears, select the Flex Compiler option. Then enter **-use-network=false** in the Additional Compiler Arguments field after any existing text in the field. Make sure that there is a space between this new argument and any text already in the field. Click OK to save this new setting. You should now be able to run the application without the local resource error.

When playing MP4 or other forms of AAC/AAC+ audio-only files, you cannot use the Sound *class. You have to stream the audio in as if it were a video file through a* NetConnection *and* NetStream *instance. We will be going in depth on how to use these classes for steaming both audio and video content later in this chapter.*

The SoundMixer Class

The flash.media.SoundMixer class provides static properties and methods for global sound control for embedded audio within a SWF. This class does not have any control over instances created directly by Sound class and ActionScript. The SoundMixer class has a property to set the bufferTime for embedded sounds and a soundTransform getter/setter to set a custom SoundTransform instance for volume and pan control. The SoundMixer class also has two other methods worth noting. The stopAll() method stops all currently playing sounds. This method can be very valuable since all sounds must be stopped before a SWF — if loaded externally — can properly be removed and garbage collected. The other method is the computeSpectrum() method that requires at least one parameter, which is the reference to a ByteArray to store the snapshot of the sound wave. You can also optionally pass in two additional parameters. The first parameter after the ByteArray reference is a Boolean for the FFTMode to indicate if a Fourier transformation should be applied first to the sound data. A Fourier transformation is a process that converts a complex type of data into another data type. For our purposes here, this means setting the FFTMode parameter to true will cause the returned value to be a frequency spectrum instead of a raw sound wave. The second parameter after the required ByteArray reference is an int for the stretchFactor, which indicates the sample rate to use. The default of 0 should be used for 44.1KHz, a value of 1 for 22.05KHz, and a value of 2 for 11.025KHz.

The Microphone Class

The flash.media.Microphone class lets users access the audio from a microphone connected to their machine and stream it through the SWF. Normally, the use case for the Microphone class involves the Flash Media Server or some other streaming server and live broadcasting of audio and or audio and video. There are some edge cases to use the Microphone class for standalone applications not utilizing a media server such as user sound input reactive applications. For more information on using the Microphone class, see Chapter 48, "Flex and Flash Media Server."

Video

As fun as it is to play with sound, incorporating video into Flex applications really packs a punch by providing visual and audio content together. The next section covers what is available in Flex for working with video and some techniques for bringing rich video content into Flex applications.

Video Classes and Components

The flash.net.NetConnection class is one of the foundation parts for streaming in video through the Flash Player. It enables you either to establish a connection for standard external file progressive streaming from a server or to establish a true streaming connection to a media server like the Flash Media Server. After you instantiate a NetConnection object and set up any event listeners needed, the key step is to call the connect() method to establish an outside connection. When using NetConnection without the use of a special streaming media server to load in video content that is progressively streamed over HTTP, you connect the NetConnection to simply null.

```
EXAMPLE: Establish a NetConnection for HTTP progressive streaming
var nc:NetConnection = new NetConnection();
nc.connect( null );
```

Chapter 48 explores connecting a NetConnection to a streaming server. The other foundation class for streaming video content is flash.net.NetStream. The NetStream class communicates through a NetConnection and provides the streaming content to the Flash Player and Flex and then can be shown or heard by the end user by attaching to a Video display object. A NetConnection can have many NetStream instances streaming through it like multiple channels, but each NetStream instance can only handle one stream at a time. NetStream is a powerful class with a number of methods and properties, some of which are only meant for working with the Flash Media Server. To link a NetStream instance with a required NetConnection instance, you pass a reference to the NetConnection into the constructor of the NetStream instance. Be sure that the NetConnection is already connected before instantiating the NetStream instance.

```
EXAMPLE: Establish a NetConnection lor HTTP progressive streaming
var nc:NetConnection = new NetConnection();
nc.connect( null );
var ns:NetStream = new NetStream( nc );
```

After the NetStream has been instantiated and appropriately associated with an active NetConnection instance, you can load a stream via the play() method of the NetStream instance. The play() method accepts a HTTP path to the audio/video content you want to stream.

```
EXAMPLE: Establish a NetConnection lor HTTP progressive streaming
var nc:NetConnection = new NetConnection();
nc.connect( null );
var ns:NetStream = new NetStream( nc );
ns.play( "video/myVid.flv" );
```

Starting to play a stream using the NetStream does not mean that the users will be able to see the content. For them to be able to see it, the content must be displayed through a flash.media.Video instance that is in the display list. The Video class is a simple class that extends DisplayObject and provides a window through which to view video content, either played progressively, streamed in from a media server, or directly hooked in through a camera (see Chapter 48). To display the streaming video content through a Video instance, you call the attachNetStream() method on the Video instance and pass it a reference to the NetStream, being sure to add the Video instance to the display list.

```
EXAMPLE: Establish a NetConnection lor HTTP progressive streaming
var nc:NetConnection = new NetConnection();
nc.connect( null );
var ns:NetStream = new NetStream( nc );
ns.play( "video/myVid.flv" );
var vid:Video = new Video();
vid.attachNetStream( ns );
addChild( vid );
```

Let's explore some of the key features to look out for with the NetStream class. One of the most important events the NetStream dispatches is the flash.events.NetStatusEvent with a type of onStatus.

This `onStatus` event reports on the status of the stream and any errors if they exist. This is the main way that you will know if there are any issues with playing back your content.

Another key bit of functionality that the `NetStream` has to offer, which is new in ActionScript 3, is the ability to set a client object instance to handle callback methods from the `NetStream`. The default value of the client property on the `NetStream` class is `this`, indicating the `NetStream` instance itself. One of the main reasons to use a client object is to handle the metadata within the video files, which often contains very important data such as the duration and dimensions of the video stream. A standard recommended approach for handling the client object is to create a custom class with appropriate handlers. To handle the metadata, the class should have a `onMetaData()` method that receives one parameter of generic `Object` type. If you also have cue points in your video, you would add a `onCuePoint()` method to your client as well. We will be discussing cue points further later in this section.

The `NetStream` class also has a `soundTransform` property for setting a `SoundTransform` instance on to control the volume and panning of the audio within the stream. An important note is that you have to set a whole `SoundTransform` instance when you want to adjust the volume or pan, you cannot just set a single property.

Exercise 5: Displaying Video

In this exercise, you will create a class to:

- ❏ Load video
- ❏ Handle metadata
- ❏ Pause and restart a video

Loading Video

1. Open the `VideoDisplay_wt1.mxml` file in the `{tutorial_directory}/VideoAndSound/src/` directory.

2. In the File Navigator, right-click `VideoDisplay_wt1.mxml` and select Set as Default Application.

3. Open `ProfxVideo.as` in the `{tutorial_directory}/VideoAndSound/src/com/wrox/profx3/video/` directory.

4. `ProfxVideo` is a class that you will build to load and control video. Much of the structure has been provided, so you can concentrate on the fundamentals of loading and controlling video. Please review the following in the `ProfxVideo` class:

- ❏ `ProfxVideo` extends `UIComponent`, so you can easily add it to the display list
- ❏ Properties
    - ❏ `_source` — The path to the video
    - ❏ `_netConnection` — The `NetConnection` object
    - ❏ `_netStream` — The `NetStream` object
    - ❏ `_video` — The `Video` object used to display the video
    - ❏ `_onSecurityError()` method — Handles `SecurityErrorEvents`, just in case
    - ❏ `CustomClient` class — A simple class used to communicate with the `_netStream`

5. Locate the setter method for the `source` property.

6. Under the `// Set the source` comment, set the value of the _source property equal to the p_value parameter:

```
// Set the source value
_source = p_value;
```

7. Add a conditional statement to evaluate if _source is defined. If _source is defined, then call the _connectStream() method (you will build this method later).

```
// Set the source value
_source = p_value;

// If we have a value for source, try to play the video
if( _source )
{
    _connectStream();
}
```

The completed setter function should look like the following:

```
public function get source():String
{
    return _source;
}
public function set source( p_value:String ):void
{
    // Set the source value
    _source = p_value;

    // If we have a value for source, try to play the video
    if( _source )
    {
        _connectStream();
    }
}
```

8. Locate the constructor for the class.

9. Under the `// Create the NetConnection` comment, set the _netConnection property equal to a new NetConnection object:

```
// Create the netconnection
_netConnection = new NetConnection();
```

10. Add an event listener on the _netConnection object for the NetStatusEvent.NET_STATUS, and assign the _onNetStatus method as the handler method:

```
// Create the netconnection
_netConnection = new NetConnection();

// Listen for NetStatusEvent.NET_STATUS
_netConnection.addEventListener( NetStatusEvent.NET_STATUS, _onNetStatus );
```

11. Under the `// Listen for SecurityErrorEvent.SECURTY_ERROR` comment, add an event listener on the _netConnection object for the `SecurityErrorEvent.SECURITY_ERROR` and assign the _onSecurityError method as the event handler method:

```
// Listen for SecurityErrorEvent.SECURITY_ERROR
_netConnection.addEventListener( SecurityErrorEvent.SECURITY_ERROR,
    _onSecurityError );
```

12. Call the `connect()` method on the _netConnection object, passing it null as the only parameter:

```
// Call connect()
_netConnection.connect( null );
```

The completed constructor should look like the following:

```
public function ProfxVideo()
{

    // Create the netconnection
    _netConnection = new NetConnection();
    // Listen for NetStatusEvent.NET_STATUS
    _netConnection.addEventListener( NetStatusEvent.NET_STATUS, _onNetStatus );
    // Listen for SecurityErrorEvent.SECURITY_ERROR
    _netConnection.addEventListener( SecurityErrorEvent.SECURITY_ERROR,
        _onSecurityError );
    // Call connect()
    _netConnection.connect( null );
}
```

13. Locate the `_onNetStatus()` method.

14. Under the `// Evaluate the event.info.code` comment, add a conditional statement to evaluate if the value of `event.info.code` is equal to the string `NetConnection.Connect.Success`. If this condition is true, call the `_connectStream()` method (we will build the method later):

```
if( event.info.code == "NetConnection.Connect.Success" )
{
    _connectStream();
}
```

15. Next, add an `else..if` statement that evaluates if the value of `event.info.code` equals `NetStream.Play.StreamNotFound`. If this is true, trace the string `Stream not found:` and the `source` property:

```
trace( "Stream not found: " + source );
```

The completed _onNetStatus() event handler method should resemble the following:

```
private function _onNetStatus( event:NetStatusEvent ):void
{
    // Evaluate the event.info.code
    if( event.info.code == "NetConnection.Connect.Success" )
    {
```

```
            _connectStream();
        }
        else if( event.info.code == "NetStream.Play.StreamNotFound" )
        {
            trace( "Stream not found: " + source );
        }
    }
```

16. Locate the `_connectStream()` method.

17. Under the `// Create the NetStream` comment, set the `_netStream` property equal to a new `NetStream` object:

```
// Create the NetStream
_netStream = new NetStream( _netConnection );
```

18. Add an event listener on the `_netStream` object for the `NetStatusEvent.NET_STATUS`, and assign `_onNetStatus()` as the event handler method:

```
// Listen for the NetStatsEvent.NET_STATUS
_netStream.addEventListener( NetStatusEvent.NET_STATUS, _onNetStatus );
```

19. Under the `// Set the client` comment, set the `client` property of the `_netStream` object equal to a new instance of the `CustomClient` class:

```
// Set the client
_netStream.client = new CustomClient();
```

20. Create the video display by setting the `_video` property equal to a new `Video` object. Then call the `attachNetStream()` method on the `_video` object and pass it the `_netStream` property as its only parameter:

```
// Create the video component
_video = new Video();
_video.attachNetStream( _netStream );
```

21. Under the `// Play the video` comment, call the `play()` method on the `_netStream` object:

```
// Play the video
_netStream.play( source );
```

22. Add the `_video` object to the display list by calling `addChild()` and pass it the `_video` property as its only parameter:

```
// Add the video display to the stage
addChild( _video );
```

The completed `_connectStream()` method should look like the following:

```
private function _connectStream():void
{
    // Create the NetStream
    _netStream = new NetStream( _netConnection );

    // Listen for the NetStatsEvent.NET_STATUS
```

```
_netStream.addEventListener( NetStatusEvent.NET_STATUS, _onNetStatus );

// Set the client
_netStream.client = new CustomClient();

// Create the video component
_video = new Video();
_video.attachNetStream( _netStream );

// Play the video
_netStream.play( source );

// Add the video display to the stage
addChild( _video );
}
```

Handling Metadata

1. Locate the onMetaData() method in the CustomClient class.

2. Under the // Dispatch a MetadataEvent with the info object comment, dispatch a new MetadataEvent with a type of MetadataEvent.METADATA_RECEIVED, the bubbles parameter as false, the cancelable parameter as false, and p_info as the value for the fourth parameter, which is info:

```
// Dispatch a MetadataEvent with the info object
dispatchEvent( new MetadataEvent( MetadataEvent.METADATA_RECEIVED, false, false,
    p_info ) );
```

3. In the _connectStream() method, under the code that set the client property of the _netStream object, add an event listener on the _netStream.client object for the MetadataEvent.METADATA_RECEIVED event, and assign the _onMetaDataReceived() method as the event handler method:

```
// Set the client
_netStream.client = new CustomClient();
_netStream.client.addEventListener( MetadataEvent.METADATA_RECEIVED,
    _onMetaDataReceived );
```

4. Locate the _onMetaDataReceived() method.

5. Under the // Update the display's width and height comment, set the width property of the _video object equal to the value returned from p_event.info.width:

```
// Update the display's width and height
_video.width = p_event.info.width;
```

6. Set the height property of the _video object equal to the value returned from p_event.info.height:

```
// Update the display's width and height
_video.width = p_event.info.width;
_video.height = p_event.info.height;
```

7. Redispatch the `MetadataEvent`:

```
// Update the display's width and height
_video.width = p_event.info.width;
_video.height = p_event.info.height;

// Pass on the event
dispatchEvent( p_event );
```

8. Save the file and run the application. The video should play at its full size.

Controlling Video

1. In the `ProfxVideo.as` file, locate the `pauseStream()` method.

2. In the `pauseStream()` method, call the `pause()` method on the `_netStream` object:

```
public function pauseStream():void
{
    // Pause the stream
    _netStream.pause();
}
```

3. In the `playStream()` method, call the `resume()` method on the `_netStream` object:

```
public function playStream():void
{
    // Call resume on the stream
    _netStream.resume();
}
```

4. Open `VideoDisplay_wt1.mxml`, if it isn't open already.

5. Just above the `ProfxVideo` component, add a `Button` component with an id of `pause_btn` and a label of `PAUSE`, and set the `toggle` attribute to `true`:

```
<mx:Button id="pause_btn"
    label="PAUSE"
    toggle="true" />

<video:ProfxVideo id="videoDisplay"
    source="assets/sample_HD_H264.mp4" />
```

6. Add a click event to the `pause_btn` component. Assign `_onClickPause()` as the event handler and pass it the `event` object:

```
<mx:Button id="pause_btn"
           label="PAUSE"
           toggle="true"
           click="_onClickPause( event )" />
```

7. Locate the `_onClickPause()` event handler method in the script block.

8. Create a conditional statement to evaluate whether the p_event.target typed as a Button is selected. If the Button is selected, call the pauseStream() method on the videoDisplay component; otherwise, call the playStream() method on the videoDisplay component:

```
private function _onClickPause( p_event:MouseEvent ):void
{
    if( Button( p_event.target ).selected )
    {
        videoDisplay.pauseStream();
    }
    else
    {
        videoDisplay.playStream();
    }
}
```

9. Save the file and run the application. You should be able to pause and resume the video.

The VideoDisplay Component

The mx.controls.VideoDisplay component is a Flex-specific component that allows progressive playback and streaming from the Flash Media Server. It can be used in ActionScript or with MXML as a display object, as it extends the UIComponent. This component has quite a few methods and properties to control playback, work with cue points, adjust audio volume, and load external FLV content:

```
EXAMPLE: Create a VideoDisplay in MXML and set it to autoplay the content in the
    source attribute
<mx:VideoDisplay id="myVidDisp" height="320" width="240" source="video/theVid.flv"
    autoPlay="true"/>
```

One important note about the VideoDisplay is that it does not have any UI elements for playback control. There is no Play, Pause, Stop, or Visual Progress indicator of any kind prebuilt into the VideoDisplay. Instead, it offers the properties and methods to enable you to build your own if you desire, but regardless provides a somewhat robust display component to solely load, play, and display the video itself.

Exercise 6: Using the VideoDisplay Component

In this exercise, you will

- ❏ Use the VideoDisplay object to load and play a video
- ❏ Create an interface to control playback of the video

Loading Video

1. Open the VideoDisplay_wt3.mxml file in the {tutorial_directory}/VideoAndSound/src/ directory.

2. In the File Navigator, right-click VideoDisplay_wt3.mxml and select Set as Default Application.

3. Under the `<!-- VideoDisplay -->` comment, add a `VideoDisplay` MXML tag with the `id` of `videoDisplay`. Set the `horizontalCenter` and `verticalCenter` to 0.

```
<!-- VideoDisplay -->
<mx:VideoDisplay id="videoDisplay"
    horizontalCenter="0" verticalCenter="0" />
```

4. Set the `source` attribute of the `VideoDisplay` component to `assets/sample.mp4`.

```
<mx:VideoDisplay id="videoDisplay"
    horizontalCenter="0" verticalCenter="0"
    source="assets/sample.mp4" />
```

5. Save the file and run the application. The video should successfully play.

Controlling the Video

1. Add a click event handler to the `Button` with the `id` of `play_btn`. In the click handler, call the `play()` method on the `VideoDisplay` component:

```
<mx:Button id="play_btn"
    label="PLAY"
    click="videoDisplay.play();" />
```

2. Add a click event handler to the `Button` with the `id` of `stop_btn`. In the click handler, call the `stop()` method on the `VideoDisplay` component:

```
<mx:Button id="stop_btn"
    label="STOP"
    click="videoDisplay.stop();" />
```

3. Add a click event handler to the `Button` with the `id` of `pause_btn`. In the click handler, assign the `_onClickPause()` method as the event handler:

```
<mx:Button id="pause_btn"
    label="PAUSE"
    toggle="true"
    click="_onClickPause( event );" />
```

4. Locate the `_onClickPause()` method in the script block.

5. In the `_onClickPause()` method, add a conditional statement to evaluate if the `pause_btn` `Button` component is selected or not.

```
if( Button( p_event.target ).selected )
{

}
else
{

}
```

6.   If the `pause_btn` is selected, call the `pause()` method on the `VideoDisplay` component; otherwise, call the `play()` method on the `VideoDisplay` component:

```
if( Button( p_event.target ).selected )
{
        videoDisplay.pause();
}
else
{
        videoDisplay.play();
}
```

7.   Save the file and run the application. You will now be able to stop, pause, and resume the video.

Cue Points

Cue points are timed triggers during playback of a video file that are generally inserted to indicate a certain action within the application should take place at that time. Cue points can be directly encoded into your video files (other than MPEG-4 H.264 video) or added at runtime via ActionScript, generally via the API of a `mx.controls.videoClasses.CuePointManager` instance, especially when used with the `VideoDisplay` component. The `VideoDisplay` component also has support for encoded or runtime cue points via the property `cuePointManager`, which is the read-only instance of the `cuePointManagerClass` property. That property lets you set your own custom class that could extend the default `CuePointManager` or use the `CuePointManager` directly. To handle cue points as they fire, the `mx.events.CuePointEvent` is dispatched with the type of `cuePoint`, which provides all the appropriate information when a cue point is triggered during playback. An array of all the cue points associated with the `VideoDisplay` component is stored on the `VideoDisplay` instance within the `cuePoints` property.

The Camera Class

The `flash.media.Camera` class is used to access video cameras or devices hooked into a user's machine and display the content in the Flash Player and Flex or stream it to a media server for live broadcasting or recording. Although the majority of use of the `Camera` class is with a media server, it can have some uses in client applications where users can visually interact or insert themselves or their bitmap-based motion data into your application. The `Camera` class has a number of compression settings that can be controlled and seen in use even without a streaming server if the `setLoopback()` method is invoked and a parameter of a Boolean `true` is passed in. To access a camera or video device that is hooked into a your machine, you call the static method `Camera.getCamera()`. By default, it will return a `Camera` instance hooked in with the first supported or default device it finds. Then attach the `Camera` instance to a `Video` display object to see the output of the camera.

```
EXAMPLE:
var myVid:Video = new Video();
mvVideo.attachCamera( Camera.getCamera() );
addChild( myVid );
```

For normal use, do not pass in a parameter to `Camera.getCamera()`; however, if you have multiple devices attached that are supported, you can pass a string indicating the name of the camera/device you want to connect to as a parameter to the `Camera.getCamera()`. The names of the supported cameras/devices attached to a machine will be strings of numbers starting at "0". To retrieve a list of available cameras/devices currently attached to a user's machine, you can read the `Camera.names` static property, which will return the list as an `Array`.

Undocumented Video Classes

Advanced users wanting a good building block to enhance an existing video display solution, rather than building one from scratch, should look at the `mx.controls.videoClasses` package — specifically, the `VideoPlayer` class. This class is undocumented and, therefore may not be around in the next release of Flex, so use at your own risk; however, it offers access to many internal video display and management controls that the `VideoDisplay` uses but does not expose.

Another very powerful class that can be of use is the `NCManager` class in the same package. It manages connections for the `VideoPlayer` component and is primarily intended for use with the Flash Media Server to enable fallback connection management.

Flash Player MovieStar Update

The Flash Player MovieStar update (Flash Player 9.0.115) added the ability to stream and display full 1080p video with the support of MPEG-4 H.264 video and AAC/AAC+ audio. When using the new H.264 content, you need to make sure the moov atom is at the beginning of your file if you want your video to progressively stream appropriately. The moov atom is some of the byte data that has the metadata and keyframe information about the video. Many encoding applications, including the Adobe CS3 product line, add the moov atom at the end of the file when they generate H.264 content. There are two commonly used solutions to moving the moov atom on H.264 content:

❑ **QTIndexSwapper (AIR)** — http://renaun.com/blog/2007/08/22/234

❑ **Qt-faststart (C)** — http://svn.mplayerhq.hu/ffmpeg/trunk/tools/qt-faststart.c?revision=9634&view=markup

A feature of MPEG-4 content for both audio and video is more in-depth metadata. This includes the ability to include cover art or multiple images within the audio or video file metadata.

The MovieStar update also added some great new power to the Flash Player along the lines of hardware acceleration and multi-core CPU support. Hardware acceleration is now used when your application goes into full-screen rectangle mode if the user's machine supports it and it is not deactivated from the Flash Player settings panel. Multi-core support now enables up to 4 CPU cores for visual rendering. One of the most useful is video rendering. The MovieStar player will now divide the rendering load among the cores by effectively dividing the video display into quadrants, matching the number of cores on the machine. If the user has a dual-core CPU, the video display rendering would be divided in 2, and so forth. As a side note, vector art and bitmap filters also can take advantage of the new multi-core rendering support, but the new multi-core support is not used for ActionScript code execution. For more detailed information about the latest internal working of the Flash Player media capabilities, check out Tinic Uro's blog, at www.kaourantin.net.

Exercise 7: Full-Screen Video Display

In this exercise, you will

❑   Make the video display full-screen

❑   Load image data from the metadata of the video

Making the Video Display Full-Screen

1.   Open the `VideoDisplay_wt2.mxml` file in the `{tutorial_directory}/VideoAndSound/src/` directory.

2.   In the File Navigator, right-click `VideoDisplay_wt2.mxml` and select Set as Default Application.

3.   Locate the `_onClickFullScreen()` event handler. This event is fired when the user clicks on the toggle button with the id of `fullScreen_btn`.

4.   Add a conditional statement to determine if the toggle button is selected. If it is, set the `fullScreen` property of the `videoDisplay` object equal to `true`:

```
// Determine if we are full screen or not
if( Button( p_event.target ).selected )
{
    videoDisplay.fullScreen = true;
}
```

5.   Next, if the `fullScreen_btn` Button is not selected, set the `fullScreen` property of the `videoDisplay` object equal to `false`:

```
if( Button( p_event.target ).selected )
{
    videoDisplay.fullScreen = true;
}
else
{
    videoDisplay.fullScreen = false;
}
```

6.   Open `ProfxVideo.as` in the `{tutorial_directory}/VideoAndSound/src/com/wrox/profx3/video/` directory.

7.   Locate the setter method for the `fullScreen` property.

8.   Under the `// Set the fullscreen rect` comment, create a conditional statement to evaluate if the value of `_fullScreen` is `true` and the `displayState` of the stage is equal to `StageDisplayState.NORMAL`:

```
// Set the fullscreen rect
if( _fullScreen == true && stage.displayState == StageDisplayState.NORMAL )
{

}
```

9. In the `if` condition, create a local variable named `scalingRect` with a type of `Rectangle` and set it equal to a new `Rectangle` object. Pass the new `Rectangle` object the x, y, width and height properties of the _video object:

```
if( _fullScreen == true && stage.displayState == StageDisplayState.NORMAL )
{
    var scalingRect:Rectangle = new Rectangle( _video.x, _video.y, _video.width,
        _video.height );
}
```

10. In the `if` condition, set the `fullScreenSourceRect` property of the stage using bracket (`[]`) notation equal to the `scalingRect` variable:

```
var scalingRect:Rectangle = new Rectangle( _video.x, _video.y, _video.width,
    _video.height );
stage["fullScreenSourceRect"] = scalingRect;
```

11. In the `if` condition, set the `displayState` property of the stage equal to `StageDisplayState.FULL_SCREEN`:

```
stage["fullScreenSourceRect"] = scalingRect;
stage.displayState = StageDisplayState.FULL_SCREEN;
```

12. Create an `else` condition and in the `else` block set the `displayState` of the stage equal to `StageDisplayState.NORMAL`:

```
else
{
    stage.displayState = StageDisplayState.NORMAL;
}
```

13. The completed setter method for the `fullScreen` property should look like the following:

```
public function set fullScreen( p_value:Boolean ):void
{
    _fullScreen = p_value;
    // Set the fullscreen rect
    if( _fullScreen == true && stage.displayState == StageDisplayState.NORMAL )
    {
        var scalingRect:Rectangle = new Rectangle( _video.x, _video.y,
            _video.width, _video.height );
        stage["fullScreenSourceRect"] = scalingRect;
        stage.displayState = StageDisplayState.FULL_SCREEN;
    }
    else
    {
        stage.displayState = StageDisplayState.NORMAL;
    }
}
```

14. Open the `index.template.html` file in the `{tutorial_directory}/VideoAndSound/html-template` directory.

15. Locate the AC_FL_RunContent() JavaScript methods (there are two). Add allowFullScreen, true to the one that contains "swf", "${swf}":

```
AC_FL_RunContent(
    "allowFullScreen","true",
    "src", "playerProductInstall",
```

16. Save the file and close it.

17. Save the files and run the application. Now when you click the Full Screen button, the Video will be blown up. Click the button again, and the video will go back to its normal state.

Loading Image Data from Metadata

1. Locate the _onPreinInitialize() event handler method.

2. Under the // Listen for MetadataEvent.METADATA_RECEIVED comment, add an event listener on the videoDisplay object for the Metadata.METADATA_RECEIVED event and assign _onMetaDataReceived() as the event handler:

```
private function _onPreInitialize():void
{
    // Listen for MetadataEvent.METADATA_RECEIVED
    videoDisplay.addEventListener( MetadataEvent.METADATA_RECEIVED,
        _onMetaDataReceived );
}
```

3. Locate the _onMetaDataReceived() event handler method.

4. Create a local variable named metaData typed as an Object and set it equal to p_event.info.

```
var metaData:Object = p_event.info;
```

5. Create a conditional statement to evaluate if metaData.tags.covr contains a value:

```
alue.
var metaData:Object = p_event.info;
if( metaData.tags.covr )
{

}
```

6. Inside the conditional block, create a local variable named coverData typed as a ByteArray and set it equal to the first index of the covr Array. Make sure that you cast the object as a ByteArray:

```
var metaData:Object = p_event.info;
if( metaData.tags.covr )
{
    var coverData:ByteArray = metaData.tags.covr[0] as ByteArray;
}
```

7. Call the `load()` method on the `coverImage` component and pass it the `coverData` variable and set the `visible` property of the `coverImage` component to `true`:

```
var metaData:Object = p_event.info;
if( metaData.tags.covr )
{
    var coverData:ByteArray = metaData.tags.covr[0] as ByteArray;
    coverImage.load( coverData );
    coverImage.visible = true;
}
```

8. Save the file and run the application. Now when the application runs a large image will be placed on top of the video. You can drag the image around to move it out of the way.

Summary

The Flash Player is a great way to deploy rich media content because of its platform agnosticism and its wide adoption across the world. Whether the content is embedded or loaded from an outside source, bringing media into a Flex application is easy to do with the methods covered in this chapter. The MovieStar update has opened the door to higher-quality content for Flash Player applications and useful metadata associated with it.

Video and audio are not the only rich content that can be brought into Flex applications. The next chapter will look at bringing content from Flash into Flex applications, as well as taking content from Flex and bringing it into Flash.

29

Advanced Flash Integration

This chapter covers the more advanced methods of integrating Flex and Flash together. This means bringing components and classes from one IDE to another, which allows you to reuse code and components, making for quicker development and more consistent applications.

This chapter will cover:

- ❑ Bringing Flex classes into Flash
- ❑ Using the Flex Component Kit to create Flex components in Flash
- ❑ Porting Flash UI components to Flex
- ❑ Creating custom states and transitions for Flex components

Bringing Flex Classes into Flash

After spending a lot of time developing classes in Flex, it would be nice to be able to use those classes directly in Flash. Reusing code is a good way to save time and effort, and using the exact same classes between your Flex and Flash applications without having to maintain multiple copies saves even more time and effort.

There are some techniques to use to bring in those functional Flex classes into Flash to create a powerful framework that crosses boundaries. It was possible in Flex 2 to create a SWC file to bring programmatic classes from Flex to Flash. Unfortunately, Flex 3 uses a different SWC version than Flash CS3, so Flash does not easily recognize SWCs generated by Flex. There are some techniques that involve hacking the Flex-generated SWCs, but these techniques are difficult and do not always work.

One way to circumvent this issue is to generate a runtime shared library (RSL) from the SWC created by a Flex library project. The downside of this is that it provides no compile-time checking in a Flash application, and there is no means to do strict data typing inside your Flash code. Data typing is allowed in your Flex code, but in Flash the imported Flex classes are referred to with the generic `Class` data type. This method also requires load in a separate SWF file containing the classes at runtime. Unfortunately this method is unable to bring in visual classes into Flash from Flex.

Importing Custom Flex Classes through RSLs

To create an RSL to bring programmatic classes into Flash from Flex, start with a library project in Flex. This will take the classes in it and compile them into a SWC. SWC files are essentially fancy ZIP files, so to access the contents of a SWC, a change to the file extension is all that is required. Change the `.swc` extension to `.zip` and then use your preferred zipping utility to extract the contents from that ZIP file.

Inside the unzipped directory is a SWF file called `library.swf` and an XML file called `content.xml`. If any UI components made it into the SWC, there may be some other files in the directory, but the library SWF is what will be useful as an RSL. The content XML file holds metadata about the classes included in the SWC. The library SWF holds the code itself, and that's what is useful in this situation.

Using a `flash.display.Loader` class in Flash, you can load in the library SWF file and then retrieve the classes inside it by using the `getDefinition()` method of the `ApplicationDomain` class. That method returns a `Class` object. You can then use that `Class` object to create instances of that class.

```
var Echo:Class;
var myEcho:Object;

context = new LoaderContext();
context.applicationDomain = ApplicationDomain.currentDomain;
loader = new Loader();
urlRequest = new URLRequest( 'rsls/library.swf' );

loader.contentLoaderInfo.addEventListener( Event.COMPLETE, _onLoadComplete, false,
    0, true );

loader.load( urlRequest, context );

function _onLoadComplete( p_event:Event ):void
{
    var domain:ApplicationDomain = loader.contentLoaderInfo.applicationDomain;
    Echo = domain.getDefinition( 'com.wrox.profx3.utils.Echo' ) as Class;

    myEcho = new Echo();
    myEcho.echo( 'From Flex With Love' );
}
```

Unfortunately, because the classes are not available at runtime, those instances must remain generic objects and can't be data-typed to their true class. This setup also means that any static methods on these classes will cause problems. When you try to access a static method, `Echo.staticEcho()` for instance, it will throw a compile error, because `Echo` is actually an instance of the `Class` object, not the actual class itself.

Again, it is not possible to bring in visual components from Flex to Flash. Flash can import the classes and access their properties and methods, but when a visual class is added to the stage, it is not rendered.

Importing Native Flex Classes

Native Flex classes can be brought in a bit more easily. Flex has some exceptionally useful classes, such as `mx.utils.ObjectUtil` and `mx.collections.ArrayCollection`, that are absent from the standard Flash framework. It is possible to create proxy classes that access the methods of these Flex classes and then bring them into Flash through an RSL or some other method, but it is considerably easier to just access these classes directly. By pointing the class path for a Flash application to the `src` directory that contains the Flex framework, the Flex framework becomes available for import just like any custom Flash classes.

```
import mx.utils.ObjectUtil;
```

To set the class path for a Flash application, choose File ⇨ Publish Settings. In the dialog box that appears, switch to the Flash tab. Click the Settings button next to the ActionScript version combo box. In the new dialog box that appears, click the Browse to Path button (which has a crosshairs icon on it). Then browse to the `/src` directory in the Flex installation directory that contains the Flex framework. Select OK on the dialog boxes and the Flex framework has now become available for use in Flash.

Of course, there is a rather large exception to this rule. As mentioned earlier, only nonvisual classes can be used in Flash, and only those that don't use the `mx_internal` namespace. If a Flash movie tries to instantiate a visual class, it will throw a compile-time error because it can't resolve the `mx_internal` namespace.

Bringing Flash into Flex

The more easily traveled route is to bring code and components from Flash into Flex. Some developers prefer developing their components in Flash rather than in Flex. Some components are just easier to develop in Flash, especially those that don't fit in with the traditional application interface. We'll cover some of the different ways you can bring Flash components and code into Flex, including the Flex Component Kit.

The Flex Component Kit for Flash CS3

When developing completely custom components, sometimes it is easier to make those components in Flash. Flash allows for high control over the design and the appearance of the component directly using drawing tools and lays the graphical elements out however you wish. Components made in Flash can then be turned into Flex components using the Flex Component Kit for Flash.

The Flex Component Kit is a command for Flash CS3 that turns movie clips in your library into components usable in Flex. It does this by making `UIMovieClip` the base class for the movie clip and packaging it up as a SWC for use in Flex when you publish your movie.

You can download the Flex Component Kit for Flash CS3 at `www.adobe.com/go/flex3_cs3_swfkit`.

In the Flex 3 beta, the Flex Component Kit was available in the SDK, but since the official release of Flex 3, the Flex Component Kit is no longer located in either the standalone Flex 3 SDK or the Flex 3 SDK bundled with Flex Builder 3. To get the most recent version of the Flex Component Kit, you can download it from the preceding download page or from the Adobe Open Source Repository mentioned next.

Do not use the version of the Flex Component Kit available through the Adobe Exchange (www.adobe.com/cfusion/exchange), since it is an early beta version intended for use with Flex 2.01 and is not fully featured. The version of the Flex Component Kit in your Extension Manager should be 1.1.2 or higher. If it is not, you are using an older out-of-date version of the extension that may not function as described in this chapter .

You can also download the Flex Component Kit for Flash CS3 from the Adobe Flex SDK Subversion repository at http://opensource.adobe.com/svn/opensource/flex/sdk. The extension itself can be found in /tags/3.x/frameworks/flash-integration, and the source classes for the mx.flash package can be found in /tags/3.x/frameworks/projects/flash-integration.

To use the Flex Component Kit, download and install the `FlexComponentKit.mxp` extension file. If you have the Adobe Extension Manager installed, the Flex Component Kit is easy to install. Here is the quick run through on installing the Kit:

1. Double-click on the MXP file. The Extension Manager will handle installing the Kit and placing all the files where they need to be.

2. Open Flash CS3.

3. Open the Command menu in Flash CS3 and verify the Convert Symbol to Flex Component and the Convert Symbol to Flex Container options are there.

Now that the Flex Component Kit is installed, the process of creating a Flex component in Flash is as easy as creating a component as a movie clip in Flash, selecting it in the Library Panel, and then selecting the Convert Symbol to Flex Component option from under the Command menu. We'll run through this whole process in the next exercise. Now when the FLA file is published, it will generate a SWC. The process is generally the same for creating a Flex container. However, after the Convert Symbol to Flex Container command is executed, Flex Component Kit will add a symbol to the library called `FlexContentHolder`. This is a movie clip that tells Flex where in your container child components should be placed. In the container clip, drag in an instance of the `FlexContentHolder` and position and size it to your satisfaction. Remember to set the scale-nine grid to make your container component flexible and resizable.

With the Flex Component Kit, it is also possible to create a bounding box for your component. The bounding box tells Flex where the bounds of the component are, rather than having it based on the actual dimensions of the asset. This is particularly useful for masked components, since Flex will automatically use the actual size of the component for bounds, not just the visible area of the component. With the bounding box in place, if the component animates outside of its designated bounds, it won't change the position of the component. To specify the bounding box for a component, create a rectangular movie clip and drag an instance onto the stage. After resizing and positioning it to form the bounds for the component, give it the instance name `boundingBox`. The Flex Component Kit will automatically use this clip to set the width and height of the component.

Remember that the Flex Component Kit needs components to be at 24 frames per second, as that is Flex's native frame rate. If your Flash movie is not already at 24 fps, the Flex Component Kit commands will prompt you to change the frame rate.

After making a SWC containing custom components, place that SWC in the /libs folder of a Flex project. By default, Flex looks in the /libs folder of Flex projects for compiled libraries of code in the format of SWC files. Flex analyzes the SWCs in the /libs folder to get information about those classes and their methods and properties. Through that, Flex provides code insight and hinting for those components. One caution here is that with the default settings, the Flex Component Kit will create the class for a custom component in the same directory as the parent FLA file, with the UIMovieClip listed as the base class. A component whose class file is at the same level will be created in the local namespace in MXML. This can create some interesting problems when your custom component is nested inside components from other namespaces, and on top of that, it is bad practice to have a component in the local package.

When creating custom components with the Flex Component Kit, make the class for the component adhere to a logical class package and don't just leave it in the local package. However, changing the class path from the local package means Flash will no longer allow specifying UIMovieClip (or ContainerMovieClip) as the base class for the component. The solution is to have the class for the custom component extend the class listed as the base class (located in the mx.flash package), change the class path for the component to the new class path, then switch the base class for the component to flash.display.MovieClip. Flash will allow this setup and the Component Kit will still create the SWC correctly with the component class in a proper class package. Everybody wins.

Taking a closer look at the mx.flash package, it contains the UIMovieClip, ContainerMovieClip, and FlexContentHolder classes. The UIMovieClip class is the main attraction here. It is a class that was specifically designed for bringing Flash components into Flex. It extends MovieClip, but it can be put on the Flex stage just like a UIComponent. However, it does not extend UIComponent itself.

The same is true for the ContainerMovieClip class, which extends the UIMovieClip class. It also contains all the code to allow the custom container to be put on the stage, just like a standard Flex container. However, one caveat is that a custom container component cannot contain more than one Flex component as an immediate child. The easy workaround for this is that you can make that one Flex component a native Flex container such as a Canvas or HBox and then you can fill that with other Flex components.

The FlexContentHolder class is for internal use only. Although it is in this package with these other classes, you should generally ignore it and only use it as the symbol placed in the Library panel when creating a Flex Container using the Flex Component Kit.

Exercise 1: Using the Flex Component Kit For Flash CS3

In this exercise, you will:

- ❑ Create a custom component using the Flex Component Kit for Flash
- ❑ Use the component in a Flex application
- ❑ Use a bounding box to set the size of the component

Creating a Custom Flex Component Using the Flex Component Kit

1. Make sure that you have the Flex Component Kit installed. As mentioned previously, you can download the Kit from www.adobe.com/go/flex3_cs3_swfkit.

2. Open the BoxIcon_wt1.fla from the /Chapter_29_Advanced_Flash_Integration/ AdvancedFlashIntegrationStart /flash directory.

3. The FLA contains a MovieClip named 'BoxIcon'. BoxIcon is a box with three states — open, closed, and expanded. We will turn this MovieClip into a Flex component in the following steps.

4. Open the library panel (Window ⇨ Library).

5. Select the BoxIcon in the Library.

6. From Flash's main menu, select Commands ⇨ Convert Symbol to Flex Component. Flash will prompt you about the frame rate if it is not set to 24. Click the OK button. You should see the following output to confirm that you now have a Flex component:

```
Command made the following changes to the FLA:
  Imported FlexComponentBase component to library
Symbol "BoxIcon" can be used as a Flex component.
Select File > Publish to create the SWC file for use in Flex.
```

If your library now contains the UIMovieClip *component instead of the* FlexComponentBase *component, this means you're using an older version of the Flex Integration Kit released for use with Flex 2, when the* mx.flash *package contained only the* UIMovieClip *class. Download the latest Flex Integration Kit* .mxp *file from the preceding URL, and make sure the version number in your Extension Manager reads 1.1.2 or higher.*

7. Open the Publish settings (File ⇨ Publish Settings).

Notice that the files are being published to the ../libs/ directory. This will place the necessary files in the Flex Project's /libs directory. The Flex compiler automatically compiles any SWC libraries found in the /libs directory into the Flex project.

8. Select the Flash tab.

In the SWF Settings, notice that Export SWC is now checked.

9. Publish the project by clicking the Publish button at the bottom of the settings panel.

10. Open the /libs directory. There should now be a BoxIcon.swc file present.

Using the Custom Component in a Flex Application

1. Open the file FlashIntegration_wt1.mxml in the /Chapter_29_Advanced_Flash_Integration/AdvancedFlashIntegration/src directory.

2. In the Navigator view, right-click FlashIntegration_wt1.mxml and select "Set as Default Application."

3. Under the comment add the BoxIcon component with an id of box. You should get code hinting for the namespace and component properties.

```
<!-- BoxIcon Component -->
<local:BoxIcon id="box" />
```

4. Save the file and run the Flex application. The BoxIcon should appear with four labels around it. You should also notice that the animation plays and the labels surrounding the box jump around as the shape of the box changes.

Setting Up the Component Bounding Box

1. Return to the `BoxIcon_wt1.fla`.

2. Open the `BoxIcon` MovieClip by double-clicking `BoxIcon` in the library.

3. Select the `BoundingBox` layer in the timeline.

4. Using the Rectangle tool, draw a box around the `BoxIcon` graphics, making sure to keep all items in each "state" inside the box.

5. Make the rectangle a `MovieClip` by selecting the item on the stage, then selecting Modify ⇨ Convert to Symbol. Give the new MovieClip the name `BoundingBox`.

6. With the `BoundingBox` MovieClip still selected on the stage, open the properties panel and give it an instance name of `boundingBox`.

7. Publish the file.

8. Return to `FlashIntegration_wt1.mxml`. Run the application. You should now see that the labels surrounding the `BoxIcon` no longer move as the animation plays.

If you are using FlexBuilder, you might need to refresh the project by selecting the project in the File Navigator, and then selecting File ⇨ Refresh in the main view for the new SWC to be used when the project compiles.

If for some reason you get a runtime error related to `boundingBox`, see the solutions for the Flex Integration Kit Bug in Chapter 26, "Flash Integration."

Porting Flash Native Components into Flex

The Flex Component Kit allows you to incorporate components from Flash into Flex, but it also provides a way to move native Flash components into Flex. Of course, the question arises: why would you want to do such a thing? After all, the Flex framework is built to be an exhaustively thorough collection of every component you could wish to have in an application. Well, unfortunately there are still a few components that are not full featured. For instance, the video components in the Flex framework are a bit lacking in features. Flash, on the other hand, has the robust `FLVPlayback` component, complete with its complementary `FLVCaptioning` component. There are plans for bringing a more robust video player into Flex, but currently the `VideoDisplay` is all that is available in the Flex framework out of box.

A person could spend a whole lot of time using the basic `VideoDisplay` class and building in the functionality and cobbling together other components to control the video. Alternatively, bringing in the `FLVPlayback` component from Flash to use in Flex can save a good deal of time.

FLVPlayback versus VideoDisplay

The `FLVPlayback` component differs in several ways from the `VideoDisplay` component provided in Flex. One difference is obviously the variety of control bars included with the `FLVPlayback` component. A subtler difference is that both classes are built upon different packages. The `VideoDisplay` component in Flex is built from the `VideoPlayer` class and other classes in the largely undocumented mx.controls.videoClasses package mentioned in the previous chapter. Other than the CueManager class, this package has little that the FLVPlayback component does not.

The FLVPlayback component is also built on the VideoPlayer class, but this one is in the fl.video package rather than mx.controls.videoClasses. Like the Flex version, it has its own NCManager class in this package. However, in this case, it is possible to substitute the NCManagerNative class from the fl.video package in place of the NCManager. The NCManagerNative class supports bandwidth detection without the use of a main.asc file on your Flash Media Server. The substitution of the NCManagerNative class for the NCManager class is done by accessing a static property of the VideoPlayer class:

```
VideoPlayer.iNCManagerClass = fl.video.NCManagerNative;
```

Porting the FLVPlayback

Before the actual port of the FLVPlayback to Flex, there are some necessary tasks. First, the Flex Component Kit commands target MovieClips rather than components, so the component we want to transfer needs to be in a movie clip and put in the Library panel. While wrapping the component in a movie clip, we should also give it an instance name. The MovieClip wrapping the component could be its own proxy class, exposing the properties of its child FLVPlayback instance, but for the sake of brevity, this exercise will use it as nothing more than a wrapper to allow the Flex Component Kit to package it up. Giving the component itself an instance name will let us access it through the wrapper.

Another thing to consider is the skin that is used for your player will also need to be brought into the Flex application. Unfortunately, the Flex Component Kit is not smart enough to incorporate this into the SWC as well. When you publish your source FLA containing the FLVPlayback component, it will generate a SWF file that holds the skin and interface for the component. Transfer this over as well into the project, and place it in the /src folder of your project.

One benefit about porting over the component is that its methods and properties are still available to use in Flex. This means you can create external custom controls for the FLVPlayback that allow for programmatic control and resizing of the playback component. In the following exercise, you will actually do the porting of the FLVPlayback component into Flex.

Exercise 2: Using the FLVPlayback Component in Flex

In this exercise, you will port the FLVPlayback Flash component to be used as a Flex component:

1. Open the FXFLVPlayback.fla in the /Chapter_29_Advanced_Flash_Integration/ AdvancedFlashIntegrationStart/flash directory.

2. In the main menu, select Insert ➪ New Symbol.

3. Create a new MovieClip and name it FXFLVPlayback and then click the OK button.

4. Double-click the MovieClip in the Library (Window ➪ Library) to edit it.

5. From the components panel (Window ➪ Components), drag an FLVPlayback component onto the stage and position it at x:0, y:0.

6. Give the FLVPlayback component an id of pb.

7. Select the FXFLVPlayback MovieClip in the Library.

8. From the main menu, select Commands ➪ Convert Symbol to Flex Component.

9. Publish the project. The FLA is set to publish to the Flex project /libs directory. You should see that an FLVPlayback.swc and a SkinOverPlaySeekMute.swf file have been created in the /libs directory. You may have to refresh the folder to see the new files.

10. Copy the SkinOverPlaySeekMute.swf to the projects /src directory. This filename may have changed if you changed the default settings for the FLVPlayback component in the FLA.

11. Open the FlashIntegration_wt2.mxml file in the /Chapter_29_Advanced_Flash_ Integration/AdvancedFlashIntegrationStart/src directory.

12. Under the comment <!-- FXFLVPlayback -->, add an FXFLVPlayback MXML tag with an id of player. The local namespace should be created for you.

    ```
    <!-- FXFLVPlayback -->
    <local:FXFLVPlayback id="player" />
    ```

13. In the _init() event handler, set the source of the pb property of the FXFLVPlayback component to 'media/sample.flv':

    ```
    player.pb.source = 'media/sample.flv';
    ```

14. In the Application MXML tag, add an event handler for the creationComplete event and assign the _init() method as the event handler method.

15. Save the file and run the application. The video should successfully play. But there are a few issues about the component you just built.

    The first issue is the horizontal scrollbar that appears when the application runs. This is because the FLVPLayback component skin contains masked elements that give an erroneous bounds reading for the UIMovieClip.

    We could fix the bounds issue by adding a boundingBox MovieClip in the FLA, but in this exercise you'll set the bounds of the component "manually."

    The second issue is that because the FXFLVPlayback class contains the FLVPlayback component (composition), as opposed to extending FLVPlayback (inheritance), you need to set the source in an event handler, not a property of the MXML tag.

    There is a third issue, one of the FLVPlayback skin stretching versus sizing when FXFLVPlayback is sized, but this technique is beyond the scope of this chapter. For the curious, it involves overriding the width and height methods in FXFLVPlayback, which will manually call the FLVPlayback's setSize method. More on this technique can be found in the following Flash-Flex Integration series tutorial at Community MX: www.communitymx.com/abstract.cfm?cid=74D62.

16. Open the FXFLVPlayback.as file in the /Chapter_29_Advanced_Flash_Integration/ AdvancedFlashIntegration/flash/com/wrox/profx3/fxvideo directory.

17. This class extends the UIMovieClip class, and you'll assign it to the FXFLVPlayback component.

18. Override the protected getter function for the bounds property. The getter returns a Rectangle object.

    ```
    // Manually set the bounds
    override protected function get bounds():Rectangle
    {

    }
    ```

19. Inside the bounds getter, return a new `Rectangle` with the `width` and `height` of the pb `FLVPlayback` component:

```
override protected function get bounds():Rectangle
{
    var rect:Rectangle = new Rectangle( 0, 0, pb.width, pb.height );
    return rect;
}
20.        Now create source property setter function.
// Source property setter
public function set source( value:String ):void
{

}
```

20. Inside the source setter, set the `source` property of the pb object equal to the value passed into the setter:

```
public function set source( value:String ):void
{
    pb.source = value;
}
```

21. Save the file.

22. Return to the `FXFLVPlayback.fla` and open the Library (Window ⇨ Library).

23. You need to specify `com.wrox.profx3.fxvideo.FXFLVPlayback` as the class for your component. Right-click the `MovieClip` in the library and select Properties.

24. If the advanced options are not showing, click the Advanced button.

25. Change the entry for class from `FXFLVPlayback` to `com.wrox.profx3.fxvideo.FXFLVPlayback.` and remove the entry for base class.

26. Click the OK button, then Publish your project.

27. Return to `FlashIntegration_wt2.mxml`.

28. Remove the `creationComplete` event from the `Applicaiton` MXML tag.

29. Remove the `Script` MXML tag and its contents.

30. Remove the `FXFLVPlayback` MXML component. Because we assigned a class within a package, the namespace for the component has changed.

31. Create a new `FXFLVPlayback` MXML tag with an `id` of `player`. The new namespace should be `fxvideo`. Set the `source` to `media/sample.flv`:

```
<fxvideo:FXFLVPlayback id="player"
    source="media/sample.flv" />
```

If you are having trouble with getting the `fl.video` *namespace, refresh your FlexBuilder project.*

32. Save the file and run the application. Now, when the video plays, the horizontal scrollBar is gone, which means that the `FXFLVPlayback` component is registering the correct bounds.

If you are using the FLVPlayback component fullscreen control, in order for this feature to work, you need to set the allowFullScreen *property to* true *in the* index.template.html *file, which will have the Flex compiler create the correct support parameters in the HTML file. Since the* index.template.html *file gets rewritten by Flex Builder when you create the project, it is a good idea to store your modified file in another location as a backup.*

Examining the FXFLVPlayback Compilation Process

To get a clear idea of the steps you have taken to author and compile the FXFLVPlayback in the preceding exercise, it helps to visualize the flow of this Flash-Flex integration process (see Figure 29-1).

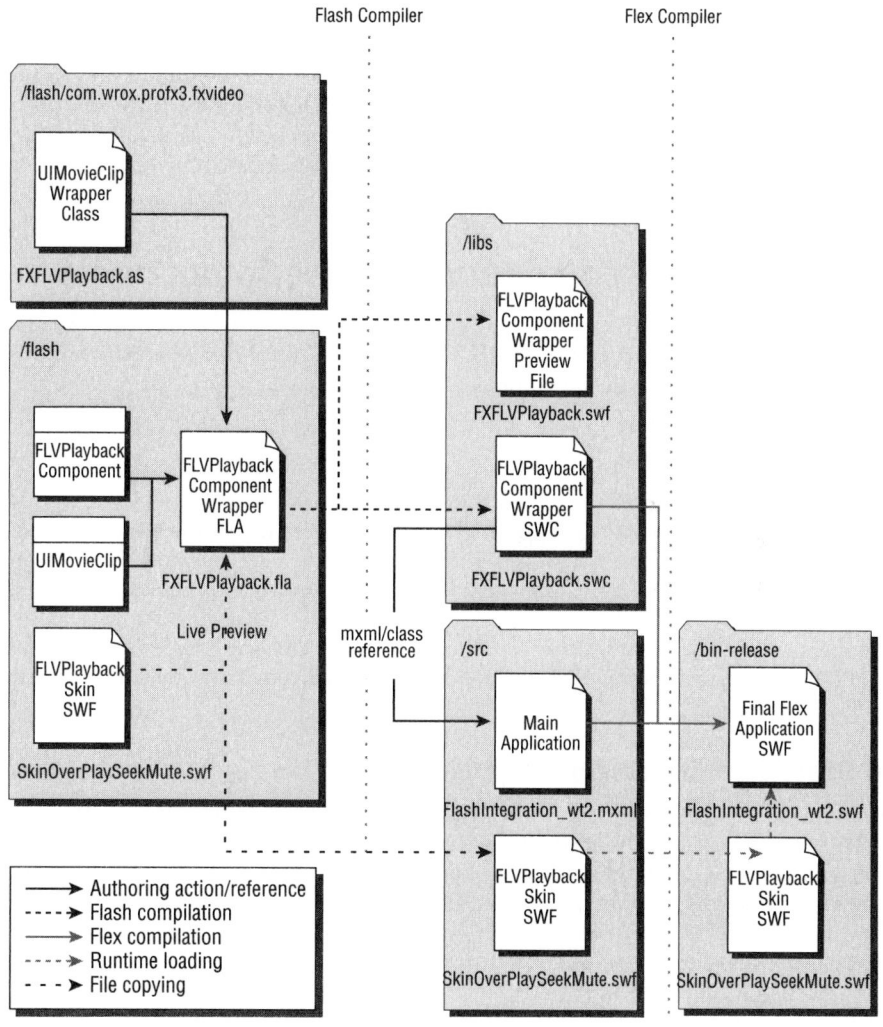

Figure 29-1

As you can see, the Flash and Flex compiler lines indicate a division between authoring and compilation, and the legend at the bottom indicates to which process the lines belong.

First, you create the `FXFLVPlayback.fla` file in Flash CS3, and save it to the `/flash` directory for the Flex project. Then you position the `FLVPlayback` component and select the `SkinOverPlaySeekMute.swf` skin file via live preview mode. The `UIMovieClip` class is then set as the base of the `FXFLVPlayback` symbol using the Flex Component Kit, and the `FXFLVPlayback.as` class file is created in the designated `com.wrox.profx3.fxvideo` package location. When that is done, the `FXFLVPlayback.fla` file is compiled to the Flex `/libs` folder, which creates the `FXFLVPlayback.swf` preview application and the `FXFLVPlayback.swc` files. To ensure that the `FLVPlayback` skin file `FXFLVPlayback.swf` is accessible for later compilation, we copy the file from the Flash CS3 installation directory to either the `/flash` or the `/libs` folder, and place another copy in the `/src` folder for Flex compilation.

The `FXFLVPlayback` class compiled into `FXFLVPlayback.swc` is referenced when you create the `FlashIntegration_wt2.mxml` application. Then both the SWC and the MXML files are compiled into the `FlashIntegration_wt2.swf` Flex application. The `SkinOverPlaySeekMute.swf` skin file is copied by into the `/bin` directory upon compilation, where it is loaded into the `FLVPlayback` component inside the Flex application SWF at runtime.

Custom States and Transitions in Flex Components

The Flash Component Kit allows you to bring custom components and native Flash components from Flash into Flex. While that is all well and good, that does not tap the full potential of the Flex Component Kit. The Kit allows for even more integration of Flash components with Flex by providing a means to create custom states and transitions in your custom components that can take advantage of Flex's state management.

The benefits of creating components with custom states in Flash are pretty evident. First, doing so allows for easy state creation. Each state in a custom Flash component for Flex is merely a frame label in the timeline. The same goes for the transitions in and out of these custom states. By using the right frame label names, Flex will automatically manage transitions between the states of the component.

Making transitions in Flash can greatly ease the difficulty in creating complex transitions. Animations that would require many lines of MXML and ActionScript can be easily created and tweaked on the timeline.

Custom State and Transition Techniques

The technique for creating stateful custom components for Flex is fairly similar to the method for creating stateful skins for existing Flex components. As you saw in Chapter 26, "Flash Integration," the Flex Skin Design Extension for Flash is a great tool for creating custom skins for Flex components. Some of the principles for making custom component states are very similar to those for creating stateful skins.

To make custom states for an application, make sure that the Flex Component Kit for Flash is already installed. Adding a custom state to a custom component is as easy as opening the symbol from the Library panel to edit it and adding in frame labels for the individual states. These frame labels should reside on their own layer in the timeline called `states`. Each frame label represents an individual state of the component.

After using the Flex Component Kit to turn the component into a Flex component and bringing the component into Flex, the state of the component is changeable through the `currentState` property. Setting the value of `currentState` to a frame label in the component makes the component switch to that frame label and display that state of the component.

Transitions in custom components work similarly but are slightly more involved, since the process allows for the creation of transitions between multiple states. Flex makes the process slightly easier by managing these transitions effectively. For instance, if a component has open and closed states, it is not necessary to create two transitions. If there is a transition for going from the open state to the closed state, Flex will reverse that transition when going from the closed state to the open state. It is possible to have different transitions for both open to closed and closed to open, but by default, Flex will cleverly use the one transition for both directions.

To enable this sort of transition management, it is necessary to follow some naming conventions. Like states, transitions are indicated by frame labels in the timeline of the custom component. They should reside on their own layer in the timeline named `transitions`. Each transition should also have two frame labels; one to mark the start and one to mark the end of the transition. The frame label at the start of the transition should be named in this format: `fromState-toState:start`. In the example of a component with open and close states, the start of the transition would have the label `open-closed:start`. The end label would be along the same lines, except that `start` is replaced by `end`: `open-closed:end`. To create a transition going the opposite direction, you would close the beginning state and open the end state: `closed-open:start` and `closed-open:end`.

In between the start and end labels of the transition is where the animation for the transition goes. The start and end frame labels on the transition layer need to line up with the start and end keyframes of the transition on the layer containing your animation. Obviously, there need to be enough frames in the space marked by the frame labels for the animation to complete.

Exercise 3: Adding Custom States and Transitions

This exercise continues where you left off in Exercise 1. You will:

❑   Add custom states to the `BoxIcon` component

❑   Add a custom transition to the `BoxIcon` component

Adding Custom States

1.   Open the file `BoxIcon_wt3.fla` in Flash CS3 located in the `/Chapter_29_Advanced_Flash_Integration/AdvancedFlashIntegrationStart/flash` directory.

2.   Publish the project.

3.   Open the file `FlashIntegration_wt3.mxml` in Flex Builder 3 located in the `/Chapter_29_Advanced_Flash_Integration /src` directory.

4.   In the File Navigator, right-click `FlashIntegration_wt3.mxml` and select Set as Default Application.

5.   Run the application. You should see the `BoxIcon` and its three views: opened, closed, and expanded. You'll assign some view states so that you can control your icon based on user interaction.

6. Return to `BoxIcon_wt3.fla`.

7. Double-click the `BoxIcon` MovieClip in the library.

8. In the timeline, select the first frame of the ~LABELS layer.

9. Add the frame label "closed."

10. Select frame 10 of the ~LABELS layer, and add the frame label "open."

11. Select frame 31 of the ~LABELS layer, and add the frame label "expanded."

12. Publish the project.

13. Return to `FlashIntegration_wt3.mxml`, and add the `currentState` attribute to the `BoxIcon` MXML tag with the value of `closed`.

14. Add the `mouseOver` handler. Inside the mouse handler, set the `currentState` property of the `event.target` object equal to `open`.

15. Add the `mouseDown` handler. Inside the handler, set the `currentState` property of the `event.target` object equal to `expanded`.

16. Add the `mouseOut` handler. Inside the handler, set the `currentState` property of the `event.target` object equal to `closed`.

17. Add the `mouseUp` handler. Inside the handler, set the `currentState` property of the `event.target` object to `open`.

Your `BoxIcon` MXML tag should now look like this:

```
<local:BoxIcon id="box"
    currentState="closed"
    mouseOver="event.target.currentState = 'open'"
    mouseDown="event.target.currentState = 'expanded'"
    mouseOut="event.target.currentState = 'closed'"
    mouseUp="event.target.currentState = 'open'" />
```

18. Save the file and run the application. Now the `BoxIcon` no longer cycles through its views, and it will respond to the following user interactions: rollover, rollout, mouse down, and mouse up.

Adding Transitions

1. Return to the `BoxIcon` MovieClip timeline in `BoxIcon.fla`.

2. Select frame 20 of the ~LABELS layer, and add the label `open-expanded:start`.

3. Select frame 30 of the ~LABELS layer, and add the label `open-expanded:end`.

4. Publish the Flash application, and return to the `FlashIntegration_wt3.mxml` file in Flex Builder.

5. Save and run the Flex application. Now when you click on the `BoxIcon`, the inner box will animate, move up, and when you release your mouse button, the inner box will move down.

Exercise 4: Punkhead and Ticklehead — A Case Study

This exercise examines a real-world scenario, where you have engaging character animation, built in Flash, which must be faithfully and accurately built into a custom Flex component, while maintaining Flex-controllable states. Our thanks go to Tim Saguinsin at www.ricecookerstudios.com for providing the Flash animations for this example. This example, shown in Figure 29-2, will show you how an engaging Flash experience can be ported to a Flex application through the construction of a custom Flex component with its own unique animations and transitions. In fact, in this exercise, you're going to build two animations into Flex components.

Figure 29-2

Creating The Punkhead and Ticklehead Animations

1. Download Punkhead.fla and Ticklehead.fla from the book code repository located in the /Chapter_29_Advanced_Flash_Integration/AdvancedFlashIntegrationStart/flash directory into your Flex project for this exercise.

   You'll also need to follow along with the final FLA source files located in the /Chapter_29_ Advanced_Flash_Integration/AdvancedFlashIntegration/flash book code repository directory, so you might want to create separate _source and _working Flex projects to keep your working file and the final source files separate.

2. Open the starting file Punkhead.fla in Flash CS3. Double-click on the Punkhead movie clip to edit its timeline.

3. Scrub the timeline back and forth, and you will observe the kind of animation that will be present in the final component.

4. Open the starting file Ticklehead.fla in Flash CS3. Double-click on the Ticklehead movie clip to edit its timeline.

5. Scrub the timeline back and forth, and you will observe the kind of animation that will be present in the final component.

   You will notice that in both files, the timeline layers and the animations have been created for you, to save time with this exercise.

   Also notice that in both FLA files, the boundingBox clip has already been created in anticipation of converting the main animation movie clip into a UIMovieClip using the Flex Component Kit for Flash CS3.

Launching Flash Documents from Flex Builder

To launch a Flash file from Flex Builder, configure the file association in Flex Builder:

1. Select Window ⇨ Preferences ⇨ General ⇨ Editors ⇨ File Associations.

2. Select File types: Add ⇨ Define A New File Type: *.fla.

   Finding "Flash Document" in the "Associated Editors" list does not always successfully launch Flash documents, so you must manually point Flex to the launching application.

3. Click Browse, and find `Flash.exe` in your Flash CS3 installation directory.

Now when you double-click on an FLA file in Flex Builder, it will launch the file in Flash CS3. You may have to restart Flex Builder for this change to take effect. Using this technique, other file types can be launched in their native applications directly from Flex Builder as well, such as Photoshop or Fireworks files.

Adding The Animation States

1. Open the source file `Punkhead.fla` from the `/AdvancedFlashIntegration/flash` book code repository directory.

2. Copy the frames on the state labels layer in the `Punkhead` movie clip from the source `Punkhead.fla` file to your working file.

   You should see the following state frame labels in the timeline:

   - ❑ NormalState
   - ❑ SneeringState
   - ❑ PunchState
   - ❑ KnockoutState

   If you're having trouble seeing the frame labels in the timeline, you can make the individual frames wider by selecting the properties button at the top right of the Timeline panel and selecting the Medium or Large size from the menu.

   So now you have a cartoon animation where the character has four main behavioral states: he's either relaxed, sneering, being punched in the face (for sneering, I guess), or knocked out cold.

3. Open the source file `Ticklehead.fla` from the `/AdvancedFlashIntegration/flash` book code repository directory.

4. Copy the frames on the state labels layer in the `Ticklehead` movie clip from the source `Ticklehead.fla` file to your working file.

   You should see the following state frame labels in the timeline:

   - ❑ NormalState
   - ❑ SmileState

❑   LaughState

❑   SnoozeState

These state frame labels will allow the Flex application to track and set the "state" of the component, which is to say the position of the Flash playhead in the animation timeline.

Again you have a cartoon animation where the character has four main behavioral states: he's either relaxed, smiling, laughing or giggling, or sleeping off all that joviality.

Later in this exercise, you're going to build a Flex application that makes these custom components act very much like a custom button, where the character reacts in response to the user's interaction.

Adding The Transition States

1.   Copy all the frames on all layers in the transition labels timeline folder in the `Punkhead` movie clip from the source `Punkhead.fla` file to your working file.

State Labels Layer Order Gotcha

Notice that the *state labels* layer is below the *transition labels* layers. There is an important reason for this order. If you check out the *Publish Settings* for the Flash application, you will notice that the *Load order* is set to *Bottom up*, which is the default. This means that all assets and all frame labels are loaded (i.e., declared) from the bottom layer to the top layer at runtime.

Since the Flex application must parse the component state information in order to properly interpret the transition information in the frame labels, it is important that *state frame labels be declared before any transition frame labels*. If they aren't, the Flex application may misinterpret label information, resulting in irregular component responsiveness. This means that your state labels layer must be *below* any transition labels layers if the *Load order* is set to *Bottom up*, or the state labels layer must be *above* any transition labels layers if the *Load order* is set to *Top down*.

You should see the following transition frame labels in the transition labels layers on the timeline:

❑   `*-NormalState:start , *-NormalState:end`

❑   `*-SneeringState:start , *-SneeringState:end`

❑   `SneeringState-NormalState:start , SneeringState-NormalState:end`

❑   `*-PunchState:start , *-PunchState:end`

❑   `*-KnockoutState:start , *-KnockoutState:end`

The `*-[somestate]:start/end` transition labels tell the Flex application to play the timeline between those frames when switching from *any state* to `somestate`. By replacing the asterisk in the transition label with a specific state name, as in `SneeringState-NormalState`, you can declare a specific animation to occur if the component is told to switch from a specific state to another specific state. In the case of the Punkhead animation, by defining a specific transition from the `SneeringState` to the `NormalState`, (note that we can declare this transition playback "backward" in the timeline), so that the animation from "normal" to "sneering" and "sneering" to "normal," has the Flash playhead go from one state to the other in forward and reverse in a smooth animation flow. Without this specific transition, the animation would seem to animate the character's sneer, but "jump" back to its normal facial expression when called back.

Figure 29-3 illustrates the main animation states defined at four different places on the Punkhead timeline.

2. In both the Punkhead.fla and Ticklehead.fla working files, on Frame 1 of the Actions layer, place this single line of code in the Actions panel:

    ```
    stop();
    ```

    This will stop the timeline from playing until the Flex application tells it to switch to another frame, or play from one transition state to another.

Figure 29-3

3. Copy all the frames on all layers in the transition labels timeline folder in the Ticklehead movie clip from the source Ticklehead.fla file to your working file.

    You should see the following transition frame labels in the transition labels layers on the timeline:

    ❑ *-NormalState:start , *-NormalState:end

    ❑ NormalState-SmileState:start , NormalState-SmileState:end

    ❑ SmileState-NormalState:start , SmileState-NormalState:end

    ❑ *-LaughState:start , *-LaughState:end

    ❑ *-SnoozeState:start , *-SnoozeState:end

    ❑ SmileState-SnoozeState:start , SmileState-SnoozeState:end

By combining generic transitions using wildcards (*) and specifically defined state transitions, you can very tightly control how the animation will perform under nearly any circumstance, as is the case with the Ticklehead animation. Here the animation between any state to the "snooze" state is left open, but transitions to the "smile" state are more tightly controlled.

Figure 29-4 illustrates the main animation states defined at four different places on the Ticklehead timeline.

When defining transition states, it may not be necessary to declare every possible combination ahead of time. Try out a few basic state transitions, compile the component SWC in Flash, try it out in your Flex application, and if you find the need to tweak the transition states, you can go back into Flash, tweak the frame labels, recompile the SWC, and recompile the Flex application.

Unfortunately, it is not possible to dynamically declare frame labels in ActionScript, so you'll need to define all your component states and transitions using timeline frame labels. If you require program-matic control of frame state/label declaration, a UIMovieClip component may not be the solution for you. As an alternative, you might consider using a series of canned Flash SWF animations embedded into the Flex application as independent assets, controlled by Flex State and Transition classes, in which case you would not use the Flex Component Kit.

Now you're ready to convert the MovieClip symbols in the two files into UIMovieClip symbols using the Flex Component Kit.

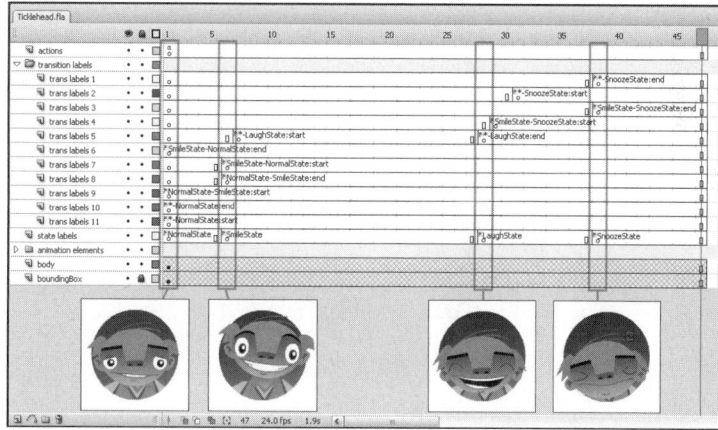

Figure 29-4

Creating Integrated Components

1. In your Punkhead.fla working file, select the Punkhead library symbol in the Library panel, and select Commands ⇨ Convert Symbol to Flex Component to convert it into a UIMovieClip. You will not need an associated Punkhead.as class file for this exercise, since you are not adding any coding functionality to the component, as you did in Exercise 2.

2. In your Ticklehead.fla working file, select the Ticklehead library symbol in the Library panel, and select Commands ⇨ Convert Symbol to Flex Component to convert it into a UIMovieClip. You will not need an associated Ticklehead.as class file for this exercise, since you are not adding any coding functionality to the component as you did in Exercise 2.

3. In both Punkhead.fla and Ticklehead.fla working files, check to be sure that the compile path for the Publish Settings (File ⇨ Publish Settings ⇨ Format ⇨ Flash) reads ..\libs\Punkhead.swf and ..\libs\Ticklehead.swf, respectively.

4. Compile each Flash component SWC by selecting Ctrl/Option-Enter. You should now see the files Punkhead.swf, Punkhead.swc, Ticklehead.swf, and Ticklehead.swc show up in the libs folder of the Flex project.

Building the Punkhead Flex Application

1. In Flex Builder, create a new Flex application named `PunkheadExample.mxml`.

2. In `PunkheadExample.mxml`, add the following code:

```
<?xml version="1.0" encoding="utf-8"?>
<mx:Application xmlns:mx="http://www.adobe.com/2006/mxml"
    xmlns:ff="*" layout="vertical"
    creationComplete="initApp()">

    <mx:Script>
        <![CDATA[
            private function initApp():void {
            }
        ]]>
    </mx:Script>

    <ff:Punkhead id="punk" boundingBoxName="boundingBox"
        mouseEnabled="true" mouseChildren="false" doubleClickEnabled="true" />

    <mx:HBox>
        <mx:VBox horizontalAlign="center">
            <mx:Button label="Normal"
                click="punk.currentState='NormalState';"/>
            <mx:Label text="rollOut"/>
        </mx:VBox>
        <mx:VBox horizontalAlign="center">
            <mx:Button label="Sneering"
                click="punk.currentState='SneeringState';"/>
            <mx:Label text="rollOver"/>
        </mx:VBox>
        <mx:VBox horizontalAlign="center">
            <mx:Button label="Punch"
                click="punk.currentState='PunchState';"/>
            <mx:Label text="click"/>
        </mx:VBox>
        <mx:VBox horizontalAlign="center">
            <mx:Button label="Knockout"
                click="punk.currentState='KnockoutState';"/>
            <mx:Label text="double-click"/>
        </mx:VBox>
    </mx:HBox>
</mx:Application>
```

This Flex application instantiates the `Punkhead` custom component and the buttons below the animation manually control its states.

3. Run the `PunkheadExample` application.

These buttons could be considered to be a means of manually testing the animation states, but they don't display the precisely correct behavior a "live and interactive" situation would provide to the animation. To give users the impression that they are interacting directly with the character, we'll add some mouse listeners, which will set the animation states and more accurately model the character behavior. As you can see from the labels below each button, next you'll match those mouse events to the appropriate animation state.

4. Add the following code to the `Script` part of the MXML application:

```
<mx:Script>
    <![CDATA[
        private function initApp():void {
            punk.addEventListener(MouseEvent.ROLL_OUT,punkMouseEventListener);
            punk.addEventListener(MouseEvent.ROLL_OVER,punkMouseEventListener);
            punk.addEventListener(MouseEvent.CLICK,punkMouseEventListener);
            punk.addEventListener(MouseEvent.DOUBLE_CLICK,punkMouseEventListener);
            trace("punk.currentState = "+punk.currentState);
        }
        private function punkMouseEventListener(event:MouseEvent):void {
            var pnk:Punkhead = event.target as Punkhead;
            // get 'goto' state based on event type
            var gotoState:String;
            switch(event.type){
                case MouseEvent.ROLL_OUT:
                    gotoState = "NormalState";
                    break;
                case MouseEvent.ROLL_OVER:
                    gotoState = "SneeringState";
                    break;
                case MouseEvent.CLICK:
                    gotoState = "PunchState";
                    break;
                case MouseEvent.DOUBLE_CLICK:
                    gotoState = "KnockoutState";
                    break;
            }
            // if target is not in the 'KnockoutState' (disabled), set new state
            if(punk.currentState!="KnockoutState"){
                punk.currentState = gotoState;
                trace("punk.currentState = "+punk.currentState);
            }
        }
    ]]>
</mx:Script>
```

In the preceding code addition, you have set the same listener method to four different mouse events. Reusing the same listener method saves code. In the listener method, a `switch` statement is used to determine the response based on the dispatched event type. After determining what the new state should be, we then check to see if the `currentState` for the component is not `KnockoutState`, in which case the character would be "knocked out" and be unable to respond, similar to the "disabled" state of a button. If it is not, then the new state is set, and the component responds according to the behavior defined by the transition labels on the animation timeline.

5. Run the `PunkheadExample` application.

As shown in Figure 29-5, now you can see the way the character responds directly to your input: mouse over Punkhead, and he snarls at you; click on Punkhead, and he gets a punch in the face (serves him right for snarling at you, right?). If you really want to get even, double-click on him and deliver a KO that will "lay him out" until he's manually "awakened" by clicking on one of the state buttons below.

Figure 29-5

Compiling in Flex Builder Using a Flash Shortcut

If you're like me and you find yourself doing a lot of compiling in both Flash and Flex when designing an interface, it is easier to use the same shortcut for both Flash and your Flex Builder. If you're more used to reaching for the Flash shortcut Ctrl/Option+Enter to compile your application, you can set this shortcut to the Run option in Flex Builder. To do this, you need to reconfigure the Flex Builder Run command to have the same shortcut as Flash.

1. Select Window ⇨ Preferences ⇨ General ⇨ Keys.

2. Find the Run Last Launched entry.

3. Click Remove Binding to clear the shortcut.

4. Select the Binding field, and type Ctrl+Enter for Windows or Option+Enter for OS X.

5. Click Apply and OK.

This means that the default Ctrl/Option-F11 will no longer work, as it has been replaced with the new shortcut. You may have to restart Flex Builder for this change to take effect.

Mr. Ticklehead, on the other hand, is a much nicer fellow. He'd rather laugh and giggle than snarl, which makes people react differently to him. Let's make him come alive by building the TickleheadExample application.

Building the Ticklehead Flex Application

1. In Flex Builder, create a new Flex application named TickleheadExample.mxml.

2. Copy all the code from PunkheadExample.mxml to TickleheadExample.mxml.

3. Make the following changes to the TickleheadExample code:

❑ In both the MXML and ActionScript, change references for the `Punkhead` component class to `Ticklehead`.

❑ In both the MXML and ActionScript, change references for the `punk` variable to `tickle`.

❑ In ActionScript, change the name of the mouse event listener from `punkMouseEvent Listener` to `tickleMouseEventListener`.

❑ In ActionScript, change references for the `pnk` variable to `tkl`.

❑ Change the button labels from `Sneering`, `Punch`, `Knockout` to `Smile`, `Laugh`, and `Snooze`.

❑ Change references for `SneeringState` to `SmileState`.

❑ Change references to `PunchState` to `LaughState`.

❑ Change references to `KnockoutState` to `SnoozeState`.

When you're finished, your code should look like the `TicklerheadExample.mxml` file in the final source files for this example.

4. Run the `TicklerheadExample` application.

As shown in Figure 29-6, now you can see the way the character responds directly to your input: mouse over Ticklehead, and he gives you a warm smile; click on Ticklehead, and he gets a tickle that makes him laugh. Eventually, he'll get tired of all that good humor, in which case you can put him calmly to sleep by double-clicking on him, until he's manually "awakened" by one of the state buttons below.

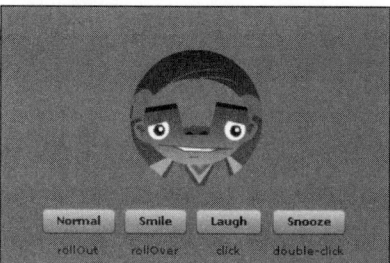

Figure 29-6

Summary

Advanced techniques in integrating Flash and Flex can make it easier to reuse code between your Flex and Flash projects, which means less time spent writing code and more consistent code between projects. This chapter looked at the ways of bringing Flex code into Flash and creating powerful custom components in Flash and bringing them into Flex. The Flex Component Kit enables you to easily bring many components in from Flash, making it easier to develop visually rich and animated components for Flex.

You've also seen the potential for bringing native Flash components into Flex using the Flex Component Kit for Flash. This allows you to fill in some of the holes in the Flex framework, such as a lack of robust video components.

By integrating Flash and Flex, you can make our Flex applications more visually rich and a bit easier to code. By using detailed Flash animation states and transitions, the Flex Component Kit also enables you to use Flash's impressive animation capabilities in a Flex application. Flex and Flash are great on their own, but combined they can be an even more powerful tool for creating compelling experiences.

Part VI: Data Management

Chapter 30: Working with Data

Chapter 31: Formatters and Validators

Chapter 32: Using the List Components

Chapter 33: Advanced Data Controls

Chapter 34: Drag and Drop in Flex

Chapter 35: Drag and Drop in AIR

Chapter 36: Using the Charting Components

Chapter 37: Resource Bundles and Data Localization

30

Working with Data

This chapter starts the discussion on ActionScript 3.0 language features and Flex framework elements that are available to the modern Flex 3 developer for working with data. The items that will be covered are:

- ❏ XML
- ❏ The Collections API
- ❏ Associative arrays/the `Dictionary` class
- ❏ Repeaters

XML

The Extensible Markup Language (XML) is a very prevalent means of describing, transferring, and storing data. If you create a Flex application via an MXML editor, you are using a custom declarative language that is based on XML. If you create an application that consumes a SOAP-based Web Service, you receive XML. If you create a configuration file to be distributed with your Flex application, there is a good chance that you will use XML.

Quick XML Primer

For those of you new to XML, let's talk about how XML is constructed before proceeding. If you need to use XML, you have to keep in mind that it needs to be well formed. If the XML you are using is not well formed, the XML parser will choke, and either your application will not compile or it will throw runtime exceptions.

XML is composed of nodes in a hierarchical tree structure. This structure consists of exactly one root node and zero to many child nodes, or more specifically, zero to many XML elements. In the following example, the root node `<players/>` has two immediate children, each an XML element of type `<player/>`:

```
<?xml version="1.0" encoding="UTF-8"?>
<players>
    <player>
        <category>battery</category>
        <position>pitcher</position>
        <name>Roger Doger</name>
        <battingaverage>.295</battingaverage>
        <earnedrunaverage>2.50</earnedrunaverage>
        <runbattedin>323</runbattedin>
    </player>
    <player>
        ...        <!-- // SNIPPED to save space -->
    </player>
</players>
```

XML nodes cannot only have XML element children or text content, but can have XML attributes. These XML attributes are defined inside each node, versus being nested as a child of each node.

```
<?xml version="1.0" encoding="UTF-8"?>
<players>
    <player
        category="battery"
        position="pitcher"
        name="Roger Doger"
        runbattedin="323" />
    <player
        category="infield"
        position="first base"
        name="Mandy Randis"
        runbattedin="754" />
</players>
```

Note that this last example is the same player data as the first. However, instead of defining the details of the `<player/>` nodes as XML elements, we're using XML attributes.

As you work with XML in real-world applications, you may have no choice of the format used — for instance, when consuming a third-party Web Service. However, if you are the one creating the XML structure, and find yourself defining many of an XML node's "adjectives" as child nodes, you may want to refactor them as attributes. There are at least a couple reasons for doing this refactoring:

❑ When dealing with object-oriented languages, if you think of an XML node as an object with properties, using attributes makes much more sense than using child nodes.

❑ When you use attributes as opposed to child nodes, you actually condense your XML. This is handy both for reducing the local XML file size and in decreasing network traffic.

> *There will be a time when attribute contents are either very large or contain special characters that will break the XML parser. In those cases, you should look into nesting that content in XML elements that make use of* CDATA *tags, similarly to how MXML files nest complex ActionScript content within their* <mx:Script/> *tags.*

The last item to mention before talking about working with XML using ActionScript is the namespace. A namespace is used when you would like to reuse an identifier in different contexts. For instance, on a baseball team, everyone is a player, but there are different categories of players. Using a namespace allows you to reuse node names and not worry about ambiguity when changing the meaning of that node. Here is the XML sample using XML namespaces:

```
<?xml version="1.0" encoding="UTF-8"?>
<players
    xmlns:battery="http://www.junheider.data/xml/players/battery"
    xmlns:infield="http://www.junheider.data/xml/players/infield">
    <battery:player
        position="pitcher"
        name="Roger Doger"
        runbattedin="323" />
    <infield:player
        position="first base"
        name="Mandy Randis"
        runbattedin="754" />
</players>
```

If you notice, the `battery`, `infield`, and `outfield` namespaces allow us to reuse the "player" identifier in different contexts. This concludes the Quick XML primer that covered the very basics of XML to allow you to start utilizing it within your Flex applications. There is so much more you can learn about XML and so much more you can do with it. To learn more about XML, check out `www.w3schools.com/xml/default.asp`.

XML and ActionScript: Before E4X

If you're only reading this to learn current application development techniques, skip to the next section, "XML and ActionScript 3.0: Using E4X." If you're curious about how things were done before ActionScript 3.0, read on.

ActionScript developers have had the ability to work with XML since before the days of ActionScript 3.0. The interaction with XML in these earlier days consisted of a Document Object Model (DOM)-based interaction. In other words, how you got around the XML was based on the structure of the XML document itself:

```
<?xml version="1.0" encoding="UTF-8"?>
<players>
    <player>
        <category>battery</category>
        <position>pitcher</position>
        <name>Roger Doger</name>
```

```
            <runbattedin>323</runbattedin>
        </player>
        …          <!-- // SNIPPED to save space -->
</players>
```

Before getting started, we'd like to mention that this section will not show you ActionScript 2.0 code. Instead, it will discuss and show you examples of this DOM-based XML interaction using the ActionScript 3.0 classes flash.xml.XMLDocument and flash.xml.XMLNode. These two classes were implemented in ActionScript 3.0 to allow for legacy support and compatibility when coding XML interactions.

```
private var _myXMLRequest:URLRequest;
private var _myURLLoader:URLLoader;
private var _myLegacyXML:XMLDocument;

private function _onCreationComplete( p_evt:Event ):void
{
    // Set up our path to the XML
    _myXMLRequest =
        new URLRequest( "assets/data/players_nodes_example.xml" );

    // Instantiate our URLLoader
    _myURLLoader = new URLLoader();

    // Let's listen for when the data is loaded
    _myURLLoader.addEventListener( Event.COMPLETE, _onXMLLoad );

    _myURLLoader.load( _myXMLRequest ); // Start the load
}

private function _onXMLLoad( p_evt:Event ):void
{
    _myLegacyXML = new XMLDocument(); // Instantiate our XMLDocument
    _myLegacyXML.ignoreWhite = true; // Let's ignore whitespace

    // Load the XML string data into the XMLDocument
    _myLegacyXML.parseXML( URLLoader( p_evt.target ).data );

    // Let's examine our XMLDocument using various XMLDocument/XMLNode API.
    _traceXML();
}
```

The preceding snippet gives you an idea of how to load an XML source file and populate the XMLDocument by using parseXML(). Also, text nodes that contain only whitespace are parsed by default. To turn this off, explicitly set the XMLDocument ignoreWhitespace instance property to true, as shown above.

When working with XML in this DOM-based approach, you access child elements via XMLNode properties such as childNodes, firstChild, lastChild, and nextSibling. Accessing attributes is done via the XMLNode attributes property. If you want to get to a parent, you use the XMLNode parentNode property.

```
private function _traceXML():void
{
    // displays the root <players/> node
```

```
    trace( _myLegacyXML.childNodes[0] );

    // displays the root <players/> node
    trace( _myLegacyXML.firstChild );

    // This will display null since there is only one childNode
    trace( _myLegacyXML.childNodes[0].nextSibling );

    // displays the root <players/> node
    trace( _myLegacyXML.lastChild.firstChild.parentNode );

    // This will display the <player> node for "Roddy Godder"
    trace( _myLegacyXML.lastChild.firstChild.nextSibling );
}
```

In the preceding example, notice how the XML document's structure is very important when working with the XML. If the structure of the XML document changes, there is a very good chance that code would have to be refactored to account for the change. Accessing nodes in a highly nested XML hierarchy becomes very cumbersome, as myLegacyXML.lastChild.firstChild.nextSibling illustrates.

One way of getting around the drawbacks of structure-based XML access is to use the idMap property of the XMLDocument class. Basically, when using idMap you are given an Object containing any XML nodes that have an id attribute, as shown here:

```
<?xml version="1.0" encoding="UTF-8"?>
<players>
    <player id="godder">
        <category>battery</category>
        <position id="catcher">catcher</position>
        <name>Roddy Godder</name>
        <battingaverage>.275</battingaverage>
        <earnedrunaverage>3.50</earnedrunaverage>
        <runbattedin>243</runbattedin>
    </player>
    <player id="handis">
        ...      <!-- // SNIPPED to save space -->
    </player>
</players>
```

The benefit of using id attributes, as shown in this example, is that you can now access the nodes directly through the idMap via their id attributes, as illustrated in the following snippet:

```
// This will display the <player> node for "Roddy Godder"
trace( _myLegacyXML.idMap["godder"] );

// This will display the <player> node for "Roddy Godder"
trace( _myLegacyXML.idMap["catcher"].parentNode );

// Since there is a typo in "players_nodes_example_idMap.xml" this will
// display the "third base" node
trace( _myLegacyXML.idMap["secondBase"] );
```

This example shows that you should work to ensure that the data you provide for your `id` attributes is unique. If the `id` values are not unique, the application will still run, but you will get unexpected results.

Although using `idMap` helps, it requires you to have complete control of your XML, which of course isn't the case when you're consuming Web Services and working with other people's XML. This is where E4X comes into play.

XML and ActionScript 3.0: Using E4X

ECMAScript for XML, aka E4X, is a powerful and robust tool in the ActionScript 3.0 arsenal. As we discuss E4X and the newly revamped `XML` class, you will see that it is easier to work with and more intuitive than the legacy XML APIs. If you build an ActionScript 3.0 application and need to work with XML, E4X is the way to go.

Classes of Interest

As you work with ActionScript 3.0, XML, and E4X, there are several top-level classes that you'll need to know, including `XML`, `XMLList`, `Namespace`, and `QName`.

The XML Class

The `XML` class is most important when working with XML in ActionScript 3.0. Not only is it the class that represents your XML document in ActionScript 3.0, but it is also the class that defines the method and properties you use to work with XML. The `XML` class also contains the methods necessary to access your XML elements, such as `attributes()` and `children()`, and properties used to configure the behavior of XML parsing such as `ignoreComments`, `ignoreWhitespace`, and `prettyPrinting`.

There are two ways to create your XML object. The first way is to use a literal definition, and the second is to use the `XML()` constructor. Here is an XML instance created via a literal definition:

```
private var _myXML:XML = <players><player>
                <category>battery</category>
                <position>pitcher</position>
                <name>Roger Doger</name>
                <runbattedin>323</runbattedin>
            </player></players>;
```

Here is some XML content created using the `XML()` constructor:

```
private var _myXML:XML =
    new XML( '<players><player>' +
                '<category>battery</category>' +
                '<position>pitcher</position>' +
                '<name>Roger Doger</name>' +
                '<runbattedin>323</runbattedin>' +
            '</player></players>' );
```

The example was geared toward brevity and book formatting. The XML constructor method of instantiating an instance of XML is usually used when you're loading in XML from an external source such as `HTTPService`.

The XMLList Class

The `XMLList` class is used to represent an array of `XML` or `XMLList` instances and contains a number of methods used to work with its children. The main difference between `XML` and `XMLList` is that whereas `XML` objects must have one and only one root node, an `XMLList` can exist without a root node. `XMLList` is a very important class to know since `XMLList` is the data type returned by E4X expressions. Here is an example of an `XMLList`:

```
private var _myXMLList:XMLList =
    new XMLList( '<player name="Roger Doger"/>' +
            '<player name="Mandy Randis"/>' +
            '<player name="Jose Regas"/>' );
```

In an `XMLList` *with one* `XML` *child, you can access that child in the same manner that you would if it were being accessed directly as an XML instance. In other words, any method call on the* `XMLList` *will be automatically passed on and executed on the single* `XML` *child. Although this helps with saving some keystrokes, it can often be an area of confusion for someone who is new to the* `XMLList` *class.*

The Namespace Class

As you learned in the previous section, XML documents may contain multiple namespaces to help them reuse identifiers in different contexts without worrying about name conflicts. Working with these namespaces in ActionScript requires the use of the `Namespace` class:

```
private var _myXML:XML =
    <players
        xmlns:battery="http://junh.data/battery">
        <battery:player
            position="pitcher"
            name="Roger Doger"
            runbattedin="323" />
    </players>;

private var batteryNamespace:Namespace =
    new Namespace( "http://junh.data/battery" );

private function _onCreationComplete( p_evt:Event ):void
{
    trace( _myXML.batteryNamespace::player.toXMLString() );
}
```

As you can see, to make use of XML namespaces, you define the namespace as an ActionScript `Namespace` by providing it the namespace URI (Uniform Resource Identifier) during instantiation. Once you have the ActionScript `Namespace` object, you can access elements at that namespace using a {namespace}::{element} syntax.

The QName Class

When working with XML namespaces, the QName class is used to help you work with fully qualified names of XML elements and attributes. Here is an example of how to work with QName:

```
private var _myXML:XML = <players xmlns:battery="http://junh.data/battery">
        <battery:player
            position="pitcher"
            name="Roger Doger"
            runbattedin="323" />
    </players>;

private var batteryPlayerQName:QName =
    new QName( "http://junh.data/battery", "player" );

private function _onCreationComplete( p_evt:Event ):void
{
    trace( _myXML.child( batteryPlayerQName ).toXMLString() );
}
```

Accessing XML

Thanks to E4X, accessing XML objects in ActionScript has never been easier. In general, there are usually two ways to access a particular XML element. The first way to access XML elements is via the methods of the XML class. The second way is to utilize E4X operators and expressions. Although there is simply not enough room in this book to go through all the methods and E4X expressions, let's get a general feel for how to access elements of an XML object in ActionScript 3.0.

Using XML Class Methods

The XML class is chock full of useful access methods. Some of the main methods are: attributes(), attribute(), child(), children(), descendants(), and parent().

Let's take a look at how these methods are used:

```
//  displays values of all attributes of all "player" child nodes
trace( _myXML.player.attributes().toXMLString() );

//  displays value of all "category" attributes of all "player" child nodes
trace( _myXML.player.attribute('category').toXMLString() );

//  displays "player" child nodes
trace( _myXML.child( "player" ) );

//  displays all the descendants of the root <players/> node
trace( _myXML.descendants() );

//  displays the root <players/> node and all of it's contents
//  (since it's the parent node)
trace( _myXML.*[0].parent() );
```

Although the first four trace statements are pretty easily explained in the code comments, the last statement `trace( _myXML.*[0].parent() );` is a little bit more complex. Let's break it down:

1. First use `.*` to grab the descendents of `_myXML`.

2. Then use array access notation `[0]` to get the first descendent.

3. Finally, access the parent of this descendent via the `parent()` method.

With this trace statement, the full XML data from `players_attributes_example.xml` is output to the debug console.

Using E4X Operators and Expressions

The nice thing about E4X is that, in general, you have the ability to access elements of your XML through expressions versus using the `XML` instance methods. When using E4X expressions, you need to familiarize yourself with the standard operators:

❑   To access a direct child you will use the "`.`" dot operator. In other words, the general syntax is `Node.childNode;`

❑   If you need to access any descendent of a particular node, you will use the "`..`" descendents operator. In other words the general syntax is `Node..descendent;`

❑   If you're trying to access an attribute as opposed to a child node, you use the "`@`" attribute operator in combination with the dot operator. Accessing an attribute follows this general syntax: `Node.@attribute;`

❑   If you are trying to grab any child, descendent, or attribute, you use the "`*`" wildcard operator in combination with any of the other operators. Here are a couple examples of the wildcard syntax: `Node.*;` `Node..*;` `Node.@*;`

❑   If you need to return a subset of child elements based on attribute criteria, you can use a predicate filter. For example: `Node.( @attribute == "someValue");`

The sample below utilizes E4X expression syntax to access XML data:

```
// displays the stats for the first player
trace( _myXML.player[0].stats.toXMLString() );

// displays any descendant nodes named "stats"
trace( _myXML..stats.toXMLString() );

// displays the value of the name attribute for the first player
trace( _myXML.player[0].@name );

// displays the value of any attribute of the first player
trace( _myXML.player[0].@*.toXMLString() );

// displays the value of the name attribute
// of any player with a batting average over .350
trace( _myXML.player.(stats.battingaverage > .350).@name.toXMLString() );
```

Modifying XML

Sometimes you find yourself needing to modify an XML instance. For example, you need to add another node to the XML data before sending it back to a server for processing. ActionScript 3.0 has methods to add, edit, and delete elements in your XML objects.

Adding Elements to Your XML Object

Adding elements to your XML object is relatively easy with ActionScript 3.0. There are several methods built into the XML class with the sole purpose of making the job of adding elements easy. These methods include: appendChild(), insertChildAfter(), insertChildBefore(), and prependChild().

```
_myXML.appendChild( "<child>I was appended to the XML!</child>" );

_myXML.insertChildAfter( _myXML.player[0],
    "<child>I was inserted after the first player node!</child>" );

_myXML.insertChildBefore( _myXML.player[0],
    "<child>I was inserted before the first player node!</child>" );

_myXML.prependChild( "<child>I was prepended to the XML!</child>" );
```

Modifying Elements in Your XML Object

When you need to modify the existing elements in your XML object, you can use both methods and E4X expressions. Among the XML instance methods available are: replace(), setChildren(), and setName().

```
//remove Roger Dodger's batting average
_myXML.player[0].replace( "stats",
    new XML( "<stats><earnedrunaverage>2.50</earnedrunaverage>" +
    "<runbattedin>323</runbattedin></stats>" ) );

//change Roger Dodger's ERA to 5.50
//and re-add batting average if it's gone
_myXML.player[0].stats.setChildren(
    new XMLList( "<battingaverage>.295</battingaverage>" +
    "<earnedrunaverage>5.50</earnedrunaverage>" +
    "<runbattedin>323</runbattedin>" ) );

//change Roger Dodger 'category' attribute to 'group'
_myXML.player[0].@category.setName( "group" );
```

Deleting Elements in Your XML Object

For those of you that come from an ActionScript 2.0 background, you're probably missing the opportunities to use the delete keyword. This is due to sealed classes in ActionScript 3.0. That being said, we're happy to say that you can use the delete keyword to delete elements in your XML object.

```
delete _myXML.player[0];
```

The nice thing is that, if there's no remaining player[0], the application won't throw an exception.

Miscellaneous Debris

Before moving on to Collections API, here are a couple things that might come up when working with XML in ActionScript 3.0.

By default, if there are comments and processing instructions in your XML document, they are ignored. To parse them, you need to modify the corresponding static properties of the XML class before you work with the XML. Once they're parsed, you can access them with the XML comments() and processing Instructions() instance methods:

```
// Set parsing behavior
XML.ignoreComments = false;
XML.ignoreProcessingInstructions = false;

// Instantiate our XML and load the XML string data
_myXML = new XML( URLLoader( p_evt.target ).data );

// Show the comments
xmlMonitor_ta.text += "\n\n" + _myXML.comments();

// Show the processing instructions
xmlMonitor_ta.text += "\n\n" + _myXML.processingInstructions();
```

If you are either reading, creating, or modifying XML that makes use of namespaces, and the main namespace of the XML is qualified, you can change the default namespace. When you do this, ActionScript will utilize the namespace you set as the default whenever fully qualified namespaces are not provided in your code:

```
// Set the default XML namespace to
// "http://www.junheider.data/xml/players/battery"
_batteryNS = new Namespace( "http://www.junh.data/xml/players/battery" );
default xml namespace = _batteryNS;

// Instantiate our XML and load the XML string data
_myXML = new XML( URLLoader( p_evt.target ).data );

// Load the first "<battery:player/>" node into the text area
xmlMonitor_ta.text = _myXML.player[0].toXMLString();
```

Bug ASC-2800 with Flash Player 9 prevents you from defining the Namespace *variable as function local. You need to create instance variables with which to set the default namespace, at least until this bug has been resolved.*

Working with XML has come a long way since the days of ActionScript 2.0. With the new APIs based on the E4X standard, XML processing in ActionScript 3.0 has never been easier.

Collections API

As you work with data in your Flex applications, you will soon realize that you need some standard method to store and update your client-side data. Once you've figured out the issues with storage, you will realize that there are several operations that you need to perform on that data on a fairly frequent basis.

One operation that you usually see in an application is sorting data based on some criteria. For instance, email programs usually have the ability to sort message based on date, sender, and subject. This sorting capability will usually work in both an ascending or descending manner.

Another operation that you might notice in an application is filtering data based on some criteria. In the email program example from above, you can usually filter based on the same criteria that you can sort on.

As the data set in an application grows, the ability to find particular pieces of it in a relatively quick timeframe becomes increasingly important. For instance, some of the more robust email applications have some type of indexing service to allow a user to find messages matching specific criteria quickly.

If any of the mentioned scenarios sound like they'll occur in your applications, you'll be glad that the Flex framework has implemented a Collections API.

IList

No talk about Flex Collections API would be complete without discussing the `mx.collections.IList` interface. `IList` is where methods such as `addItem()`, `getItemIndex()`, and `removeAll()` come from. In Chapter 32, "Using the List Components," and Chapter 33, "Advanced Data Controls," you'll become familiar with these methods and the classes that implement this interface. In the meantime, you just need to know that `IList` is part of the Collections API and provides methods to be used with ordinal data.

> *"Ordinal data" simply means data that is stored in an indexed and sequential fashion. For instance, data stored in an ActionScript `Array` is ordinal, since you can access that data based on an index value from 0 to (`Array.length - 1`).*

ICollectionView

The next interface important in fulfilling the requirements of a Collections API is `mx.collections.ICollectionView`. This interface is responsible for sorting, filtering, and providing view cursor access to data in the collection.

One thing to note about this interface is that it represents a view of the data. When you sort or filter, you're not actually sorting or filtering the source data, but instead you are sorting and filtering the view. This comes in handy since you can sort and filter all you want and the ordinal state of the original source data will remain the same until you really need it to change for good.

Sorting

The ability to sort data based on criteria is one requirement of an implementer of the `ICollectionView`. Based on the interface, the implementer will need to provide a public `sort` property and a `refresh()` method to activate the `sort`.

The value assigned to the sort property must be of type mx.collections.Sort. The Sort class provides various properties and methods that are useful in determining fields to sort by, finding particular items, reversing the direction of the sort, and sorting data. Also, there is mx.collections.SortField that is used to describe each of the sort field values passed to the Sort class.

The general course of action when sorting data is to assign a Sort object to the sort property of an ICollectionView implementer and then call that implementer's refresh() method:

```
private function _onSortNames( p_evt:MouseEvent ):void
{
    // only create and assign the sort once.
    if( !_sortInited )
    {
        // create the sort
        var nameSort:Sort = new Sort();
            // add a sort field
            nameSort.fields = [ new SortField( "@name", true ) ];
        // assign the sort to the XMLListCollection
        _myXMLListCollection.sort = nameSort;
        // let's remember that we've created and assigned the sort
        _sortInited = true;
    }
    else
    {
        // the sort already exists. let's reverse the direction
        _myXMLListCollection.sort.reverse();
    }
    // we need to call refresh to get the view to update
    _myXMLListCollection.refresh();
}
```

Filtering

When you have a large amount of data displayed in your user interface, being empowered to filter this data into smaller, more manageable chunks is very beneficial. Thanks to the ICollectionView interface, you have the blueprint for filtering your collection data.

Filtering data is very similar to sorting your data: First, you apply something, then you call the refresh() method on the ICollectionView implementer. The thing you apply is called a filter function, a function reference that is assigned to the filterFunction property of ICollectionView:

```
private function _onFilterNames( p_evt:MouseEvent ):void
{
    // turn on the filter
    if( !_filterOn )
    {
        _myXMLListCollection.filterFunction = _filterNames;
        _filterOn = true;
    }
    // turn off the filter by setting it to null
    else
    {
```

```
            _myXMLListCollection.filterFunction = null;
            _filterOn = false;
        }
        // we need to call refresh to get the view to update
        _myXMLListCollection.refresh();
    }


    // our filter function
    private function _filterNames( p_item:Object ):Boolean
    {
        // only return true if the name starts with an R
        if( String( p_item.@name ).charAt( 0 ).toUpperCase() == 'R' )
        {
            return true;
        }
        else
        {
            return false;
        }
    }
}
```

IViewCursor

The `ICollectionView` interface defines the ability to create a view cursor, for example:

```
private var _myCursor:IViewCursor;

private function _onXMLLoad( p_evt:Event ):void
{
    // Instantiate our XML and load the XML string data
    _myXML = new XML( URLLoader( p_evt.target ).data );

    // Instantiate the XMLListCollection to facilitate
    // data binding and view cursors
    _myXMLListCollection = new XMLListCollection( _myXML.player );

    // create a reference to the view cursor
    _myCursor = _myXMLListCollection.createCursor();
}
```

This view cursor must be of type `mx.collections.IViewCursor`. Using a view cursor, you can traverse and seek through a collection, as shown in the following code. Also, notice in the code that you can access the collection item data at each stop using the `current` property of the `IViewCursor`:

```
private function _onSeek( p_evt:MouseEvent ):void
{
    // start at the beginning
    _myCursor.seek( CursorBookmark.FIRST );

    // display the items in the collection until we reach the end
    while( !_myCursor.afterLast )
    {
```

```
            // spit out the item data we want to display
            output_ta.text += XML( _myCursor.current.@position ) + "\n";
            // move on to the next item in the collection
            _myCursor.moveNext();
        }


        // let's move to the last item (since we're one past)
        _myCursor.seek( CursorBookmark.LAST );
    }
```

Another thing you can do with a view cursor is use its instance methods such as findFirst() when a user selects something in a list control. The instance method will find the selected item in the collection, which you can then use the CursorBookmark class to take a note of. For instance, in case you might want to remove it later:

```
private function _onBookmark( p_evt:ListEvent ):void
{
    // seek to the selected item using the cursor
    _myCursor.findFirst( p_evt.target.selectedItem );

    // create a bookmark at the current location
    _myBookmark = _myCursor.bookmark;
}
```

Then, during removal, the item can be tracked so that the IViewCursor can be used to re-add the item to the collection at a later time:

```
private function _onRemove( p_evt:MouseEvent ):void
{
    // use the bookMark to seek to the item we'd like to remove
    _myCursor.seek( _myBookmark );

    // if the cursor is before the first item
    // or after the last it would throw an error
    if( _myCursor.beforeFirst && _myCursor.afterLast )
    {
        Alert.show( "Invalid selection, aborted" );
    }
    else
    {
        // make a note of the item
        _deletedItem = XML( _myCursor.current );

        // remove the item
        _myCursor.remove();
    }
}
```

One thing to note about IViewCursor is that it enables you to access items in a collection without having to worry about indexes and array notation.

ListCollectionView

You may have realized that during the discussion of `IList` and `ICollectionView` we were talking about interfaces. Interfaces are blueprints used to ensure that their implementing class fulfills certain needs. In the case of the `IList` and `ICollectionView` interfaces, the feature requirements of the implementing classes are sorting, filtering, and view cursors. Within the Flex framework there is a base class that makes use of the aforementioned interfaces: `mx.collections.ListCollectionView`. This base class is then extended by the `mx.collections.ArrayCollection` and `mx.collections.XMLListCollection` classes, which are heavily used in Flex applications. Let's move on and take a look at these two classes.

ArrayCollection

The class `mx.collections.ArrayCollection` implements the collections API, and as the name implies, was meant to wrap an `Array` source. In other words, you use your `Array` to store data and the `ArrayCollection` to provide the useful collections functionality, as shown here:

```
import mx.collections.ArrayCollection;

// The array of players used to populate the ArrayCollection
private var _myArray:Array = [
    { category:"battery", position:"pitcher"
        ,name:"Roger Doger", stats:{ battingaverage:".295"
        , earnedrunaverage:"2.50", runbattedin:"323" } }
    ,{ category:"battery", position:"catcher"
        , name:"Roddy Godder", stats:{ battingaverage:".275"
            , earnedrunaverage:"3.50", runbattedin:"243" } }

    ...
];


[Bindable]
private var _myArrayCollection:ArrayCollection;

private function _onCreationComplete( p_evt:Event ):void
{
    // initializing the ArrayCollection with the array of players.
    _myArrayCollection = new ArrayCollection( _myArray );
}
```

XMLListCollection

The class `mx.collections.XMLListCollection` is to `XMLList` as `ArrayCollection` is to `Array`. In other words, specify an `XMLList` as the source of `XMLListCollection` and you've just added collections API functionality to your `XMLList`.

```
private var _myXML:XML;
private var _myXMLList:XMLList;

[Bindable]
private var _myXMLListCollection:XMLListCollection;
```

```
private function _onXMLLoad( p_evt:Event ):void
{
    // Instantiate our XML and load the XML string data
    _myXML = new XML( URLLoader( p_evt.target ).data );

    // grab the players and dump them in an XMLList
    _myXMLList = new XMLList( _myXML.player );

    // Create our XMLListCollection
    _myXMLListCollection = new XMLListCollection( _myXMLList );
}
```

A Source for Binding — dataProvider

There are many UI controls in the Flex framework that implement a dataProvider property: ComboBox, List, DataGrid, and TileList just to name a few. The dataProvider is an object representing the underlying data required by the control to generate its UI display. For instance, if a ComboBox has a dataProvider that is an ArrayCollection of countries, with the right labelField configuration, you can then use that ComboBox as a country drop-down in a form.

When you specify the dataProvider property of a control, you generate a binding between that data and the display state of that control. In other words, if the data changes, the display state should update to reflect those changes. Based on this requirement, classes that implement the collections API such as ArrayCollection and XMLListCollection are perfectly suited as dataProvider sources.

For example, take a situation where an Array is used as a dataProvider source for a control. Although an Array is a perfect object to store data in, it does not implement the collections API. In this scenario, the binding will work on initialization, but if items in the Array change, the binding would no longer work. This is due to the control not receiving any data change notifications, resulting in a stale view of the data in the UI.

Now, take that same Array and use it as the source for an ArrayCollection. If an item in the Array changes, the ArrayCollection will dispatch an event notifying any interested parties that the state of the data has changed. If you then use the ArrayCollection as the dataProvider for the control mentioned in the previous scenario, the binding will continue to work no matter how many times the underlying Array data is changed.

> We have known Flex developers in the past who use Array objects as dataProvider sources rather than ArrayCollection objects. The reason behind this decision is an erroneous assumption that by utilizing the much smaller Array object, they are cutting down on instance size. The problem is that when an Array is specified as a dataProvider, it is automatically converted into a ListCollectionView object. This ends up not saving much on instance size and the side effect is not having the collection API features available when using ArrayCollection as the dataProvider.

Working with CollectionEvent

Classes that implement the IList or ICollectionView interface must dispatch events of type mx.events.CollectionEvent whenever they've been updated. This requirement is why classes that implement the collections API are good dataProvider sources.

Although the `CollectionEvent` has only one event type, `CollectionEvent.COLLECTION_CHANGE`, it includes a `kind` property that represents a collection `constants` of type `mx.events.Collection EventKind`. The `CollectionEventKind` class contains `constants`; these describe the various types of changes that can occur in the collection, such as ADD, REMOVE, and UPDATE, which you can then act upon, as the next example shows:

```
private function _onCreationComplete( p_evt:Event ):void
{
    // Instantiate our XMLListCollection
    _myXMLListCollection = new XMLListCollection();
    // Add a CollectionEvent Listener
    _myXMLListCollection.addEventListener(
        CollectionEvent.COLLECTION_CHANGE, _onCollectionChange );
}

private function _onCollectionChange( p_evt:CollectionEvent ):void
{
    // We're going to update the TextArea with information
    // on the kind of collection change event that occurred
    switch( p_evt.kind )
    {
        case CollectionEventKind.ADD:
        {
            collectionEventInfo_ta.text += "Item(s) Added\n";
            break;
        }
        case CollectionEventKind.UPDATE:
        {
            collectionEventInfo_ta.text += "Item(s) Updated\n";
            break;
        }
        case CollectionEventKind.RESET:
        {
            collectionEventInfo_ta.text += "Collection Reset\n";
            break;
        }
        default:
        {
            collectionEventInfo_ta.text += "\nCollection Event" +
                " - Move, Refresh, Remove, Replace - " +
                "Kind Occurred";
        }
    }
}
```

Now that we've taken a look at hierarchical and ordinal data through XML and the Collections API, let's move on and discuss how to store and manipulate associative data.

Associative Arrays/Dictionary

Associative arrays have many aliases throughout the programming world. Some call them *maps*, some refer to them as a *hash*, and others may call them *lookup tables*. No matter what a programmer refers to an associative array as, the general concept is the same. An associative array is a container that stores values accessible via a key. For instance, in a states lookup table you would provide the key "CO" and get back the value "Colorado."

In ActionScript 3.0, there are two different ways to implement an associative array. The first is by using a dynamic class, such as `Object`. The second is to make use of the class `flash.utils.Dictionary`. Often, the way you decide between the two is based on the type of key you would like to use.

Using Strings as Keys

In the states lookup table example given earlier, the key that was provided to the associative array was the string "CO." In many associative array scenarios, using strings for keys works just fine. If you need to use a string as your key, you can make use of the `Object` class or the `Dictionary` class.

Dynamic Classes

In ActionScript 3.0, classes are usually sealed. This means that if you need to add or modify properties and methods of a class at runtime, you will not be able to. To override this, use the `dynamic` keyword in your class declaration, as follows:

```
public dynamic class MyDynamicClass
```

Object

The good thing is that the top-level `Object` class is dynamic. This makes it perfect to use as an associate array with string-based keys. Here is an example:

```
// Instantiate the object
_myAssociativeArray = new Object();

// Create a couple dynamic properties
_myAssociativeArray.CO = "Colorado";
_myAssociativeArray.WA = "Washington";
```

Dictionary

The `flash.utils.Dictionary` class is new to ActionScript as of version 3. It is a class that was developed with the associative array concept in mind.

```
// Instantiate the Dictionary
_myAssociativeArray = new Dictionary();

// Create a couple dynamic properties
_myAssociativeArray.CO = "Colorado";
_myAssociativeArray.WA = "Washington";
```

Using Objects as Keys

There are often times when you need to relate an object to some additional data that the object itself does not support. The `Dictionary` class provides the ability for you to use objects as keys.

```
// Instantiate our points
_point1 = new Point( 100, 100 );
_point2 = new Point( 100, 200 );

// Instantiate the Dictionary
_myAssociativeArray = new Dictionary( );

// Create a couple dynamic properties using object keys
_myAssociativeArray[ _point1 ] = "firstbase";
_myAssociativeArray[ _point2 ] = "secondbase";
```

Not All Equality Is Equal

When working with object keys, it's good to know the difference between equality (==) and strict equality (===). In general, they operate in the same manner, but there are a couple differences that come into play when you're using an object as a key.

One difference is when you compare an object that represents a string value to a literal string with the same value. With the equality operator, this comparison results in `true` and with the strict equality operator it results in `false`. This is due to the fact that the equality operator will attempt an automatic data conversion of the object to a string using it's `toString()` method, whereas the strict equality operator will compare them without running the conversion. If you examine the following sample, you will see that strict equality will prevent you from using a string to access a `Dictionary` key even though the string is equal to the object.

```
// Instantiate our keys
_key1 = { value:"one" };
_key2 = new Object();
_key2.toString = function() { return "two" };

// Instantiate the Dictionary
_myAssociativeArray = new Dictionary();
// Create a couple dynamic properties using object keys
_myAssociativeArray[ _key1 ] = "first base";
_myAssociativeArray[ _key2 ] = "second base";

// equality vs. strict equality
trace( "_key2 == 'two'? " + ( _key2 == "two" ) ); // returns true
trace( "_key2 === 'two'? " + ( _key2 === "two" ) ); // returns false

// access the value
trace( "_myAssociativeArray[ _key2 ]: " + _myAssociativeArray[ _key2 ] );
// since the Dictionary uses strict equality this returns undefined
trace( "_myAssociativeArray[ 'two' ]: " + _myAssociativeArray[ 'two' ] );
```

Another thing to note is that the strict equality operator distinguishes the difference between the values `null` and `undefined`.

Iteration

The next two samples are looping through the `Dictionary` instance that was defined in the previous code sample. There are a couple of different ways to iterate through a `Dictionary`.

Using a `for-in` loop:

```
// for-in loop
for( var key:Object in _myAssociativeArray )
{
    // This will display the keys.
    // For instance:
    //      (flash.geom::Point)#0
    //          length = 141.4213562373095
    //          x = 100
    //          y = 100
    trace( ObjectUtil.toString( key ) );
}
```

Using a `for-each-in` loop:

```
// for-each-in loop
for each( var value:Object in _myAssociativeArray )
{
    // This will display the values
    // For instance:
    //      "first base"
    trace( ObjectUtil.toString( value ) );
}
```

The difference is that the `for-in` loop focuses on keys and the `for-each-in` loop focuses on the values.

Using Weak Keys

The Flash Player and Adobe AIR use a garbage collection system to manage memory. Although a full discussion of garbage collection is outside the scope of this chapter, it's worth mentioning that in the Flash Player and Adobe AIR garbage collection system, if an object has a references to it, it will not be eligible for garbage collection until references have been removed.

When you use an object as a key in a `Dictionary`, the key is considered a reference to that object, and therefore the object will not become eligible for garbage collection as long as that `Dictionary` key is referencing it. There are two ways to handle this situation.

The first is to remove object keys whenever you no longer need them; this requires due diligence on your behalf:

```
// delete the keys
delete _myAssociativeArray[ _point1 ];
delete _myAssociativeArray[ _point2 ];
```

The second way is much easier. Weak references are not counted in the garbage collection scenario mentioned, so when you create the `Dictionary`, you set the `weakKeys` constructor parameter to `true`.

```
// Instantiate the Dictionary (When you set the first parameter to "true"
// the dictionary will make all keys weak)
_myAssociativeArray = new Dictionary( true );
```

Repeaters

The `mx.core.Repeater` class is a non-display class that you declare in your MXML files. `Repeater` is used to generate user interface controls at runtime. The power of the `Repeater` is that it has a `dataProvider` that can be set to a collection of items. When the `dataProvider` is set, the `Repeater` will run through MXML code nested within it, once for each item in its `dataProvider`.

A good example of what you can do with `Repeater` is generating check boxes or radio buttons based on an array of choices. For example, the buttons shown Figure 30-1 use a `Repeater`.

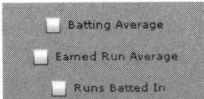

Figure 30-1

During Execution

If you look at the `mx.core.Repeater` class in the Flex 3 Language Reference, you will notice that `Repeater` has a `currentIndex` and a `currentItem` property. If you notice, the `currentItem` property is used in the following sample to generate the `CheckBox` labels.

```
<?xml version="1.0" encoding="utf-8"?>
<mx:Application xmlns:mx="http://www.adobe.com/2006/mxml" layout="vertical">
    <mx:Script>
        <![CDATA[
            import mx.collections.ArrayCollection;

            private var _myCheckBoxValues:Array =
                [   { label:"Batting Average", data:"battingaverage" },
                    { label:"Earned Run Average", data:"earnedrunaverage" },
                    { label:"Run Batted In", data:"runbattedin" } ];

            [Bindable]
            private var _myRepeaterDP:ArrayCollection
                = new ArrayCollection( _myCheckBoxValues );
        ]]>
    </mx:Script>

    <mx:Repeater id="comboBox_rpt"
        dataProvider="{ _myRepeaterDP }">
        <mx:CheckBox id="filterSetting_chk"
```

```
                label="{ comboBox_rpt.currentItem.label }" />
        </mx:Repeater>
    </mx:Application>
```

The main thing to note is that these two properties are only available during execution. In other words, after the `Repeater` has finished generating its display, children based on a change in its `dataProvider` data, `currentIndex` and `currentItem` will no longer be accessible.

After Execution

If you need to access `Repeater` children from outside the `Repeater`, you reference them using array notation, as the following sample illustrates, while accessing the `CheckBox` instances:

```
<mx:Script>
    <![CDATA[
        private function _onDisplayValues( p_evt:MouseEvent ):void
        {
            // loop through the CheckBoxes that were created in the Repeater
            // and display their labels.
            for( var i:int=0; i < filterSetting_chk.length; i++ )
            {
                output_ta.text += "CheckBox filterSetting_chk[" + i
                                  + "].label: "
                                  + filterSetting_chk[ i ].label + "\n";
            }
        }
    ]]>
</mx:Script>

<!-- The Repeater is not a UIComponent but
        its children can be -->
<mx:Repeater id="comboBox_rpt"
    dataProvider="{ _myRepeaterDP }">
    <!-- There will be a checkbox generated for each
            item in the ArrayCollection -->
    <mx:CheckBox id="filterSetting_chk"
        label="{ comboBox_rpt.currentItem.label }" />
</mx:Repeater>
```

Handling Interaction

Since a `Repeater` is used to generate display controls, there is a very good chance that you'll want to handle user interaction. For instance, suppose that a `Repeater` is used to generate three `CheckBox` controls and you would like to know when the user clicks on a particular `CheckBox`. Handling this interaction requires setting an event handler, and in that handler you can access the `getRepeater Item()` instance method of `event.currentTarget`. Please note that this method is inherited from `mx.core.UIComponent`. Here is an example:

```
<mx:Script>
    <![CDATA[
        private function _onCheckBoxClick( p_evt:MouseEvent ):void
        {
            Alert.show( "You clicked on " +
```

```
                        p_evt.currentTarget.getRepeaterItem().label );
            }
        ]]>
    </mx:Script>

    <!-- The Repeater is not a UIComponent but
            its children can be -->
    <mx:Repeater id="comboBox_rpt"
        dataProvider="{ _myRepeaterDP }">
        <!-- There will be a checkbox generated for each
                item in the ArrayCollection -->
        <mx:CheckBox id="filterSetting_chk"
            label="{ comboBox_rpt.currentItem.label }"
            click="_onCheckBoxClick( event )" />
    </mx:Repeater>
```

When Not to Use Repeater

As you start working with the `Repeater` class, you need to keep in mind that all children created in a `Repeater` are instantiated in memory, regardless of whether they're showing. Imagine an `ArrayCollection` that contains a hundred items. Now imagine a `Repeater` using this `ArrayCollection` as its `dataProvider`. In the display the `Repeater` creates a `Tile` for each item, and in this UI display you only ever see 10 tiles.

In the preceding situation, the `Repeater` unnecessarily instantiates 100 tiles in memory when it only needs 10. Although the application will work, it is an example of ineffective use of framework components. There is another component that you'll learn about in Chapter 32, called the `TileList`. Functionality-wise, the `TileList` is similar to the `Repeater`/`Tile` combination as described previously, however, `TileList` will only ever instantiate tiles that show in the display. In other words, by using the more appropriate `TileList` component, you save yourself the system memory that would have been allocated to the 90 invisible tiles in the `Repeater`/`Tile` combination that the user may never choose to see. You would also save on the initial time it takes to instantiate and display the UI in the Flash Player.

To sum up, `Repeater` is great when you have a small amount of items to iterate through, but if you need to iterate through a larger number of items, look for alternative components that make better use of system memory and startup time.

Summary

From hierarchical, to ordinal, to associative data, you know you can count on XML and E4X, collection API classes, `Object`, and `Dictionary` to store and manipulate your data. On top of that, you can also take your data and use it to create dynamically generated UI controls at runtime using the `Repeater`. Between ActionScript 3.0 and Flex 3.0, Adobe has provided a great number of API features to facilitate your interactions with data.

Although this chapter touched on some of the most important aspects of working with data in your Flex applications, there's no way that we could cover everything in the number of pages we had at our disposal. We highly recommend taking a look at the Flex 3 documentation and language reference after you've had a chance to absorb this information.

Now that you have a feeling on how to work with data in your Flex 3 applications, the next chapter discusses how to format your data and validate new data provided by the users of your application.

31

Formatters and Validators

This chapter examines the support built into the Flex framework for working with data input and output. In addition, we will touch on regular expression support in Flex. The items that will be covered are:

- ❑ Formatters
- ❑ Validators
- ❑ Regular expressions

Overview

In a data-driven application, data can come from various places. Existing data might come from a backend database or XML file. It may even come from an external source such as an RSS feed. The fact that the source of data can come from so many places sheds light on the need to ensure that this data is presented to the end user in a consistent fashion.

In addition, when new data is provided to the application, it is often provided by end users through forms. When you provide the ability for an end user to enter data into your system, you are going to want to make sure that the new data adheres to certain formats and/or business rules. Otherwise, you will end up with a very inconsistent and dirty database, which can be much harder to deal with than doing the verification up front at the time of data collection.

This chapter examines formatters, validators, and regular expressions, and introduces you to the ways to use these constructs to control the presentation and format of your data in and data out. Let's first take a look at how to control data displayed in your user interface by utilizing formatters.

Formatters

The Flex framework provides the `Formatter` classes to assist you with manipulating data for purposes of displaying it within the UI. For instance, you may have a product catalog and you would like to output the prices of each item in the UI. If you display the data directly from the data source, you might output 1.3 when you'd rather be displaying $1.30. This is where the formatters come into play.

The base class for the built-in formatters of the Flex framework is `mx.formatters.Formatter`. The class provides the following functionality to its subclasses:

❑   The `format()` method, which is invoked whenever you need to perform the format operation.

❑   Its `error` property is populated and an empty string is returned whenever an error occurs during a `format()` operation.

❑   The static string properties `defaultInvalidFormatError` and `defaultInvalidValueError` are used to override the error message issued when the formatter is given an invalid format string or format value.

❑   The read-only protected property `resourceManager` and protected method `resourcesChanged` are used with localized applications that interact with the `ResourceManager`.

If you'd like to learn about localization in Flex, refer to Chapter 37, "Resource Bundles and Data Localization."

The `Formatter` class provides a good skeleton, but doesn't offer very specific formatting options. Being very specific is the job of a custom formatter, which we'll cover later in this chapter. However, your formatting can be relatively specific when using the standard formatters, which we will cover next.

Using Standard Formatters

The Flex framework uses the `mx.formatters.Formatter` class to implement a number of standard formatters. The standard formatters are located in the `mx.formatters` package and consist of:

❑   `CurrencyFormatter`

❑   `DateFormatter`

❑   `NumberFormatter`

❑   `PhoneFormatter`

❑   `ZipCodeFormatter`

The benefit of using these formatters over the base formatter is that they bring the formatting operation into context. For instance, if you need to make sure the UI display shows prices with dollar sign and two decimal places, you use the `CurrencyFormatter`. In the same respect, you use a `ZipCodeFormatter` if you want UI display output to resemble the standard format of a U.S. Zip + 4 formatted zip code.

Looking at an excerpt from `chapter31_example1.mxml` in the source code, here is the standard way you would utilize a `Formatter`:

```
<mx:Application xmlns:mx="http://www.adobe.com/2006/mxml">
    <mx:Script>
        <![CDATA[
            // US zip codes
            [Bindable]
            private var _nineDigitZipCode:String="801202121";
        ]]>
    </mx:Script>

    <mx:ZipCodeFormatter id="usFiveDigit_zcf"
        formatString="#####"/>

    <mx:Label id="usFiveDigit_lbl"
        text="{ 'My zipcode is: '
                + usFiveDigit_zcf.format( _nineDigitZipCode ) }"/>
</mx:Application>
```

Basically:

1. Make sure that you have a value to pass into the `format()` method of the instance of the `Formatter` subclass you decided to use. In the case of the preceding example, we set up the string variable `_nineDigitZipCode` with the value `"801202121"`. This is the value that will be passed into the `format()` method of the `ZipCodeFormatter` instance `usFiveDigit_zcf`.

2. Define a formatter and set its properties. The preceding example defines a `ZipCodeFormatter` and sets its `formatString` property to `"#####"`.

3. Utilize the `format()` method of your `Formatter` subclass instance wherever you need your formatted display value. You can see that the example uses the formatted value in the `usFiveDigit_lbl` label.

Now that you know how to use standard formatters, let's take a look at the standard formatters available in the framework.

ZipCodeFormatter

As you saw in the previous code sample, `ZipCodeFormatter` is used to format zip codes. It was written to handle five- and nine-digit numeric US zip codes and six-character alphanumeric Canadian zip codes. In addition to the properties and methods it inherits from `mx.formatters.Formatter`, it provides a `formatString` property.

The `formatString` property is a mask that is used by the formatter to determine how to format the input value. For instance, if `formatString` was set to #####-####, you would receive a U.S. nine-digit zip code format with a dash. If it were ### ###, you would receive a six-character Canadian zip code.

Although you can reference the last code sample to see how the `ZipCodeFormatter` is used, more examples of using `ZipCodeFormatter` can be found in `chapter31_example2.mxml` in the source code.

PhoneFormatter

When you need to format phone number data, you can use the `PhoneFormatter`. Like the `ZipCodeFormatter`, the `PhoneFormatter` has the `formatString` property. However, the `PhoneFormatter` also has an `areaCode`, `areaCodeFormat`, and `validPatternChars` properties to assist you in formatting your data in the context of a phone number. Here are two examples of `PhoneFormatter` code taken from `chapter31_example3.mxml` in the Chapter 31 source code.

```
<mx:PhoneFormatter id="sevenDigitNumber_zcf"
    areaCode="303"
    areaCodeFormat="###."
    formatString="###.####"/>
```

```
<mx:PhoneFormatter id="tenDigitNumber_zcf"
    formatString="1+###.###.####"
    validPatternChars="+()#- .1"/>
```

In the first example, `sevenDigitNumber_zcf` we take in seven-digit values, add an area code to them, and then apply a format using a combination of the `areaCodeFormat` and `formatString` values. In the second example, `tenDigitNumber_zcf`, we take in a 10-digit phone number and format it with a "1+" at the beginning. Notice how you have to use the `validPatternChars` property of `tenDigitNumber_zcf`. This is because the "1" you use in the `formatString` is not a standard pattern character.

DateFormatter

The `DateFormatter` is used when you need to display date information in your user interface. The `DateFormatter` will take a `String` or `Date` object as input. Like the `ZipCodeFormatter` and `PhoneFormatter` classes, the `DateFormatter` class has a `formatString` property, which allows you to provide a format mask.

Whereas the nonliteral mask replacement characters for the `ZipCodeFormatter` and `PhoneFormatter` are limited to "#", the `formatString` in `DateFormatter` accepts many different nonliteral mask characters, including:

- ❑   Y — Year. For instance, YY=09 whereas YYYY=2009
- ❑   M — Month. As in M=1, MMM=Jan, and MMMM=January
- ❑   D — Day in the month. D=3 and DD=03
- ❑   E — Day of the week. As in E=7, EEE=Sun, EEEE=Sunday
- ❑   A — AM/PM
- ❑   J — The hour in a 24-hour format starting with 0. (0-23)
- ❑   H — The hour in a 24-hour format starting with 1. (1-24)
- ❑   K — The hour in AM/PM. Starts with 0. (0-11)

❑   L — The hour in AM/PM. Starts with 1. (1-12)

❑   N — Minutes. N=1 and NN=01

❑   S — Seconds. SS=09

In addition to the preceding patterns, you can add other text into your formatString. The recommendation on this is to use punctuation, numbers, and lowercase letters. Although you can use uppercase letters, as you can tell from the preceding mask characters, many uppercase letters have special meaning and would be replaced by the formatter.

Here is a code snippet of a DateFormatter taken from chapter31_example4.mxml.

```
<mx:DateFormatter id="currentDateTime_zcf"
    formatString="YYYY-MM-DD || LL:NN:SS A"/>
```

NumberFormatter

The NumberFormatter does not contain the formatString property that we have discussed so far. However, the NumberFormatter has a wealth of properties that can be used to make your numeric data display exactly as you need it to:

❑   decimalSeparatorFrom: The decimal separator character that is used, while parsing an input string.

❑   decimalSeparatorTo: The decimal separator character that is used, while outputting the formatted numeric values.

The difference to notice between decimalSeparatorFrom *and* decimalSeparatorTo *is that* decimalSeparatorFrom *refers to the decimal separator being used with the input value of the* NumberFormatter, *whereas* decimalSeparatorTo *refers to the decimal separator being used for the output value of the* NumberFormatter.

❑   precision: Determines how many decimal places will show up in the formatted value. You can disable precision by setting it to –1 which is the NumberFormatter default.

❑   rounding: Indicates how a number will be rounded. The valid values are "none," "down," "nearest," "up," which are all defined as static constants of the NumberBaseRoundType class. The NumberFormatter default is "none," or NumberBaseRoundType.NONE.

❑   thousandsSeparatorFrom: When parsing the input string, this defines the character you want to use as the thousands separator.

❑   thousandsSeparatorTo: Used to define the character you'd like to use as the thousands separator in the formatted output string.

❑   useNegativeSign: A Boolean value to determine whether you use a minus sign or parenthesis around a number to signify negative numeric values. The default true indicates that a minus sign will be used.

❑   useThousandsSeparator: If set to true, the default, thousands separators will be used.

Here's an example of using the `NumberFormatter` taken from `chapter31_example5.mxml`:

```
<mx:NumberFormatter id="number_zcf"
    precision="2"
    useNegativeSign="false"
    useThousandsSeparator="true"/>
```

CurrencyFormatter

Take the `NumberFormatter`, and add some properties specific to money, and you have the `CurrencyFormatter`. The `CurrencyFormatter` supports all the properties we listed about the `NumberFormatter` and adds the following two:

❏   `alignSymbol`: Determines whether the currency symbol will be to the left or right of the currency value. The default is "`left`".

❏   `currencySymbol`: Indicates the symbol to use for the currency unit. This can be any number of characters and spaces, although the default is "`$`". The other thing to note is that the `currencySymbol` will appear between the negative indicator and the numeric value.

Based on the preceding explanation, you would think that the `CurrencyFormatter` *is a subclass of* `NumberFormatter`. *However, even though the* `CurrencyFormatter` *contains all the properties that the* `NumberFormatter` *does, it does not subclass* `NumberFormatter`. *Instead,* `CurrencyFormatter` *subclasses* `Formatter` *directly.*

The following is an excerpt from `chapter31_example6.mxml` to illustrate `CurrencyFormatter`:

```
<mx:CurrencyFormatter id="money_zcf"
    currencySymbol="BIG MONEY! $ "
    alignSymbol="left"/>
```

Handling Input Data Errors

As previously mentioned, by default `Formatter` will return an empty string when you pass it an invalid value or configure one of its attributes incorrectly. There will be times when you will want to handle this so that you can return something more meaningful. To do this, you wrap `format()` calls in your own custom method then call your custom method when you need to perform format operations.

Here is an excerpt from the `chapter31_example7.mxml` source file:

```
private function myMoneyFormatter( value:Object ):String
{
    var moneyFormatted:String = money_zcf.format( value );

    if( moneyFormatted == '' )
    {
        if( money_zcf.error == 'Invalid value' )
        {
            moneyFormatted = 'the data you pass into myMoneyFormatter() ' +
                'needs to be numeric';
```

```
        }
        else if( money_zcf.error == 'Invalid format' )
        {
            moneyFormatted = 'please check the attributes of money_zcf ' +
                'and make sure they are set to valid values';
        }
    }

    return moneyFormatted;
}
```

If both the value being passed into the formatter and the formatter's configuration is invalid, the error issued will be "Invalid value."

To utilize this custom method, you would just call it in place of the `format()` method, as shown here:

```
<mx:Label id="myMoney_lbl"
    text="{ myMoneyFormatter( 'one dollar' ) }"/>
```

So, to handle input data errors:

1. Create a method to wrap the `format()` call to your formatter. Make sure to catch the return value so that you can check to see if it's an empty string.

2. If the return value of the call to `format()` is an empty string, you can check to see if it's an invalid input data value or an issue with the way that the formatter was configured.

3. Set the return value to a `String` that matches your need and pass it back to the method that invoked the call to your wrapper. In the case of the preceding examples, it would be the binding on the `text` property of `myMoney_lbl`.

Validators

As discussed earlier in this chapter, formatters are used to parse existing data and massage it into a very human-readable format. Validators in the Flex framework are very similar to formatters; however, the purpose of a validator is to parse new data provided by users to ensure that it meets certain data criteria.

The class `mx.formatters.Formatter` is to formatting as `mx.validators.Validator` is to validation. `Validator` is the core validation class in the Flex framework and provides a good amount of core functionality. Although the entire API can be referenced in the Flex 3 language reference, here are some highlights:

❑   The `source` property points to the object containing the field that needs to be validated.

❑   The `trigger` property points to the component firing an event that will cause the validation to run.

❑   The `triggerEvent` property describes the event type that will trigger the validation.

❑   The `required` property, which defaults to `true`, will cause the `Validator` to issue a validation error when the value being validated is empty.

❑ The requiredFieldError property enables you to specify a custom display error when a field is required and not provided. The key thing to note about this property is that every validation type comes with a corresponding property to override default error messages.

❑ The validate() method is what needs to be invoked when you want the validator to run. As you will see shortly, this may not necessarily be directly invoked in code.

❑ The event mx.events.ValidationResultEvent is both returned and dispatched by a call to validate(). By default, the call to validate() will dispatch the event, but you can turn the dispatch off with an optional second parameter suppressEvents to the call to validate().

❑ The results property of mx.events.ValidationResultEvent contains an Array of mx.validators.ValidationResult objects. When validating a form, there is a ValidationResult object for each field that had been validated.

Let's now take a look at the standard framework validators and how to use them.

Using Standard Validators

There are 10 standard framework validators based on mx.validators.Validator:

❑ mx.validators.CreditCardValidator

❑ mx.validators.CurrencyValidator

❑ mx.validators.DateValidator

❑ mx.validators.EmailValidator

❑ mx.validators.NumberValidator

❑ mx.validators.PhoneNumberValidator

❑ mx.validators.RegExpValidator

❑ mx.validators.SocialSecurityValidator

❑ mx.validators.StringValidator

❑ mx.validators.ZipCodeValidator

To illustrate the use of the standard framework validators, we've mocked up a member registration form. This form makes use of all the standard validators, and the source can be examined in full by opening chapter31_example8.mxml in the Chapter 31 code. Figure 31-1 shows the form after validation.

In Figure 31-1, standard validators are being used to ensure that required fields are populated. If a required field is not filled out when validation is triggered, the field will display a red border. In addition, mousing over the field is what causes the red error tip to appear as can be seen above on the SSN field.

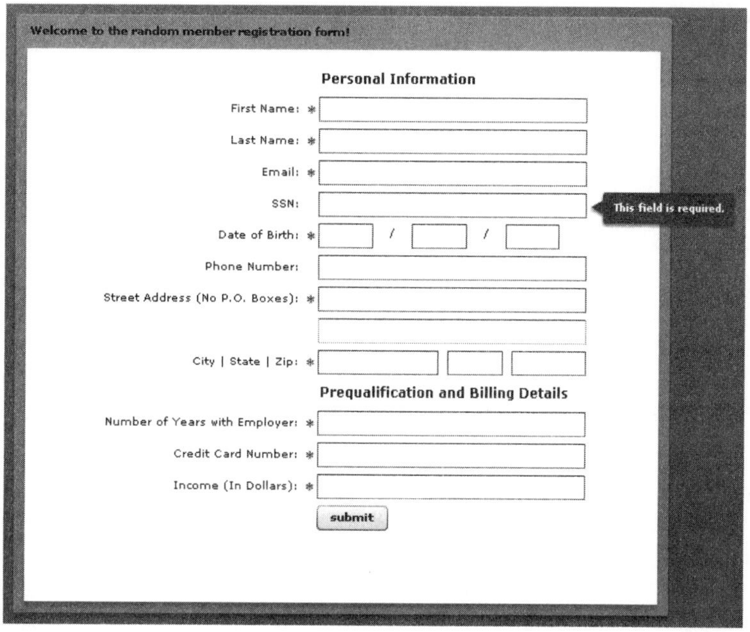

Figure 31-1

Here is a code snippet on how to hook up a standard validator taken from `chapter31_example8.mxml`:

```
<mx:StringValidator id="fname_vld"
    minLength="1"
    maxLength="100"
    required="true"
    requiredFieldError="First name is required"
    source="{ fname_ti }"
    property="text"
    trigger="{ submit_btn }"
    triggerEvent="click"/>

<mx:Panel width="600" height="100%"
    title="Welcome to the random member registration form!"
    horizontalAlign="center">
    <mx:Form>
        <mx:FormHeading label="Personal Information"/>
        <mx:FormItem label="First Name: " width="444"
            required="true">
            <mx:TextInput id="fname_ti"
                width="100%"/>
        </mx:FormItem>
```

When you set up validation in a form, as you can from the sample, the validators are separate from the form controls. In other words, there's an `<mx:TextInput/>` in the form, and to validate it we put an `<mx:StringValidator/>` on the page.

Binding Controls to Validators

The way to bind a form control to a validator, at least in the case of `StringValidator`, is to bind the `source` property of the `StringValidator` to the `id` of the `TextInput`. The `property` attribute of the `StringValidator`, a `String` value, is set to the property of the `source` component that contains the value to be validated, which in this case is the `text` property of the `TextInput` with an `id` of `fname_ti`, as you can see in the following abbreviated version of the preceding code:

```
<mx:StringValidator id="fname_vld"
    source="{ fname_ti }"
    property="text" />
```

Some of the standard validators have additional source/property options in addition to the standard `source` and `property` properties. For instance, `DateValidator` has `daySource`, `dayProperty`, `monthSource`, `monthProperty`, `yearSource`, and `yearProperty`. With the `DateValidator`, the additional `source` and `property` options can come in handy when you might want to use different form controls for each piece of data, as shown in this snippet:

```
<mx:DateValidator id="dateOfBirth_vld"
    daySource="{ day_ti }"
    dayProperty="text"
    monthSource="{ month_ti }"
    monthProperty="text"
    yearSource="{ year_ti }"
    yearProperty="text"/>
```

Setting Validation Parameters

The standard framework validators inherit the generic `required` property from `Validator` and then add their own validation criteria properties. For instance, `ZipCodeValidator` has a `domain` property used to configure whether the `ZipCodeValidator` will validate both U.S. and Canadian zip codes or just U.S. zip codes. In the same regard, `StringValidator` has `maxLength` and `minLength` properties to indicate the maximum and minimum allowed length for the value being validated.

Here's an example, taken from `chapter31_example8.mxml`, of using the `StringValidator` with `maxLength` and `minLength`:

```
<mx:StringValidator id="fname_vld"
    minLength="1"
    maxLength="100"/>
```

There are many other properties that you can set when tweaking the validation parameters. Unfortunately, there isn't enough space in this book to list them all. If you'd like to learn more about them, you can look in the Flex 3 Language Reference.

Now that you know how to set up validation, let's talk about controlling the error messages that are generated and when the validation is triggered.

Changing the Default Error Messages

Various validation types will have a default error message that is displayed when you mouse over the control being validated. For instance, in Figure 31-1 you can see that the default error message for required validation is "This field is required." If you would like to be more specific, you can change the default error message by finding the correct property and setting it to the error message you would like to display.

Here is an example based on the code from `chapter31_example8.mxml`. Notice how the property to change the error message for `required` validation is `requiredFieldError`:

```
<mx:StringValidator id="fname_vld"
    minLength="1"
    maxLength="100"
    required="true"
    requiredFieldError="First name is required"
    source="{ fname_ti }"
    property="text"/>
```

Notice in the preceding example that there's also `minLength` and `maxLength` validation. Note the default error message when the `minLength` validation rule kicks in, as shown in Figure 31-2.

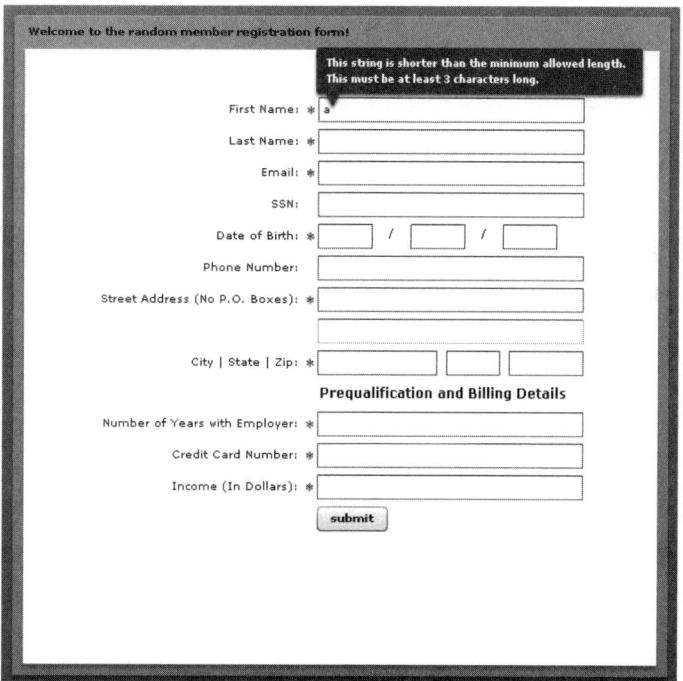

Figure 31-2

If this error message is too verbose for your taste, you customize it by setting the `tooShortError` property. Also, while you're in there, you can customize the error message for `maxLength` validation by setting the `tooLongError` property, as follows:

```
<mx:StringValidator id="fname_vld"
    minLength="3"
    tooShortError="You must enter at least 3 characters."
    maxLength="100"
    tooLongError="You must enter less than 100 characters."/>
```

Triggering Validation

By default, a validator will validate when you focus out of the form control that's bound to it. Although this may be what you want, it means that if you create a Submit button on your form, validation will not be triggered when the user clicks on the Submit button. Having a form validated when the Submit button is clicked is a very standard use case, so let's discuss a couple different ways to trigger validation.

Setting Trigger/TriggerEvent

The easiest way to override default behavior and trigger validation in a custom manner is to make use of the `Trigger` and `TriggerEvent` properties of the `Validator`. Let's trigger the `StringValidator` on the click of the form's Submit button, as shown in the following snippet derived from `chapter31_example8.mxml`:

```
<mx:StringValidator id="fname_vld"
    required="true"
    source="{ fname_ti }"
    property="text"
    trigger="{ submit_btn }"
    triggerEvent="click"/>
```

As you can see, you set the `trigger` to the control that will dispatch the event. In this case, it's the Submit button with an id of `submit_btn`. Then you specify the type of event that will be dispatched using the `triggerEvent` property, which in this case is set to the "click" event.

Utilizing Validator.validateAll() to Trigger Multiple Validators

The good thing about specifying `trigger` and `triggerEvent` is that it's easy. The downside is that if you have many controls in your form, you will need to specify the `trigger` and `triggerEvent` on each one individually. To get around this, you can utilize a little ActionScript to invoke the static method `Validator.validateAll()` to trigger multiple validators.

The following code is based on the code in `chapter31_example8.mxml`:

```
private function _onSubmit( event:MouseEvent ):void
{
    var results:Array = Validator.validateAll( [ fname_vld,
                                                  lname_vld,
                                                  email_vld ] );
}
```

In the preceding code, the _onSubmit() event handler is run when the Submit button is clicked. Then an Array of validators is passed into the static Validator.validateAll() method. This will result in all these validators being triggered. Once they've run, the validateAll() method will return an Array of ValidationResultEvent objects, one for each validator.

As you can see, this is a more efficient way to trigger multiple validators on a form submission and is the method used in chapter31_example8.mxml.

Talking about chapter31_example8.mxml, you may have noticed that one of the validators being used in the form is of type mx.validators.RegExpValidator. Regular expression-based validators are very powerful, and we'll be fleshing out the one used in our form in the next example. But first we need to cover a little bit about regular expressions.

Regular Expressions in ActionScript 3

In a nutshell, regular expressions are a very powerful pattern-matching feature in programming languages. Regular expressions allow you to search strings using very concise string-matching patterns. They are also a good vehicle for performing bulk replacements and modifications. Although regular expression support has been around in programming languages for a long time, ActionScript has just now received native support for regular expressions as of version 3.0.

Common Regular Expression Use Cases

Before diving into the specifics on how to utilize regular expressions in your Flex application, you must first understand the types of scenarios that regular expressions are suited for:

❑ Testing an email address to make sure it has an @ followed by ".com"

❑ Taking a big block of text and stripping HTML tags out of it

❑ Examining a street address to make sure that it contains numbers followed by a space followed by anything else

As you can see, regular expressions can allow you to do some pretty advanced string searches. They enable you to find things that simply cannot be found by a simple keyword/wildcard search.

A Regular Expression Primer

The key behind using regular expressions is to understand how to create the search patterns. Once you've figured that out, you will unleash the potential of regular expressions. When building a search pattern, you use the escape character, flags, metacharacters, quantifiers, and literals.

Here is a search pattern created for the address example mentioned above. The regular expression checks that the address starts with numbers followed by a space and then any other characters.

```
/^\d+[ ].+/
```

Here's a breakdown of what the pattern means:

1. ActionScript regular expressions are bounded on the left and right by the '/' character.

2. The first character '^' is a metacharacter. Metacharacters are not taken literally. In the case of the caret, it means start of the string.

3. The next two characters are first an escape character '\'. The escape character is used to tell the regular expression parser that what follows should not be taken literally. In this case, the character that follows is a 'd' and it represents any decimal digit. The two characters '\d' can also be referred to as a metasequence.

4. After the metasequence, is a '+'. The '+' is another metacharacter, and it represents a pattern of the previous character repeated one or more times.

5. Next is '[ ]'. When you see the brackets, it means that a range of characters is being defined. In the case of the pattern above, the range is a space character. A range will match a single character in the string being parsed.

6. The '.' is another metacharacter and it matches any character. In the case of the previous example, it's followed by a '+', which indicates to search for one or more of any character at the end of the string.

Now that you have a regular expression pattern, plug it into your form using the RegExpValidator.

RegExpValidator: A Validator's Validator

Once you've harnessed the power of regular expressions, you'll be able to make use of mx.validators.RegExpValidator. In your form, use regular expression pattern to make sure address line 1 is a street address number followed by a space and then any characters.

To utilize the search pattern in the RegExpValidator, you must first strip off the leading and trailing forward '/' slashes. After that you can assign the regular expression pattern to the expression property of the RegExpValidator as shown in the following chapter31_example8.mxml excerpt:

```
<mx:RegExpValidator id="address1_vld"
    required="true"
    requiredFieldError="Address Line 1 is required"
    expression="^\d+[ ].+"
    source="{ address1_ti }"
    property="text"/>
```

The nice thing about the RegExpValidator is that once you have your regular expression pattern defined, setting up the validator is as simple as setting the expression property.

Customizing and Centralizing Formatters and Validators

Although using formatters and validators is very convenient and relatively straightforward, there is a lot of redundancy when it comes to the standard one-to-one relationship between a Formatter and its parent component, and a Validator and its associated form control. It would be nice to have a centralized utility class to handle the validation and/or formatting for you so that you wouldn't have to define a multitude of similar formatters and validators in a multitude of components and forms throughout your application.

One good use case for centralization is when you have strict corporate formatting and validation requirements. When you have validators and formatters spread throughout your application, it makes it more cumbersome to update and maintain the application as corporate policies change. Centralizing formatters and validators is a way to ensure that you'll only need to make the change in one place.

Centralizing Formatters

Centralizing your formatters is a much easier task than centralizing your validators. Basically, you create a utility class and invoke the formatters from that centralized class. You can reference the full class by taking a look at src\com\wrox\util\CorporateFormatters.as in the Chapter 31 source code, but here's the meat of how you would initialize and wrap your formatters:

```
private var _corpDateFormatter:DateFormatter;

private function initFormatters():void
{
    _corpDateFormatter = new DateFormatter();
}

public function formatDate( value:String ):String
{
    _corpDateFormatter.formatString = 'MM/DD/YYYY';
    return _corpDateFormatter.format( value );
}

public function formatTime( value:String ):String
{
    _corpDateFormatter.formatString = 'L:NN A';
    return _corpDateFormatter.format( value );
}
```

From looking at the preceding code, no matter where you are in the application, by utilizing utility classes, you can ensure that the formatString of the DateFormatter is always configured correctly. Also note that by dynamically setting the formatString, you can reuse the same formatter instance for different scenarios. The code above utilizes the DateFormatter for both date formatting via the formatDate() method and time formatting via the formatTime() method.

Now that you have your utility class, you can make use of it throughout the application, as illustrated in this snippet from `chapter31_example9.mxml`:

```
private function _onCreationComplete( p_evt:Event ):void
{
    _corpFormatter = CorporateFormatters.getInstance();

    currentDate_lbl.text = _corpFormatter.formatDate( new Date().toDateString() );
    currentTime_lbl.text = _corpFormatter.formatTime( new Date().toString() );
}
```

Centralizing Validators

As you can see, centralizing formatters is a pretty easy process. However, centralizing validators is a little trickier. The reason being that formatters only need to know about their input data, whereas validators need to know about both their input data and the control where the data had originated from.

The good news is, with a little extra work, you can centralize your validators, too. Although there are many ways this can be implemented, there is an example of validator centralization in `chapter31_example10.mxml`. Here are the steps that were taken:

1. A validation utility class was created: `src\com\wrox\util\CorporateValidators.as` in the Chapter 31 source code.

2. In the utility class, a `RegExpValidator` was declared and the various corporate validation types were defined, as shown in this snippet from `CorporateValidators.as`:

```
private var _corpRegExpValidator:RegExpValidator;

// Bad Word Validator
static public var VALIDATE_NAME:String = "validateName";
private var _validateNamePattern:String = "^[A-Za-z]*$";
private var _validateNameError:String = "A person's name can only contain letters";

// Address 1 Validator
static public var VALIDATE_ADDRESS1:String = "validateAddress1";
private var _validateAddress1Pattern:String = "^[0-9]+[ ].+";
private var _validateAddress1Error:String = "Addess Line 1 is Invalid";

private function _initValidators( ):void
{
    _corpRegExpValidator = new RegExpValidator();
}
```

3. A transfer object was created to shuttle data between the various forms in the application and `CorporateValidators.as`. This transfer object is `src\com\wrox\util\Corporate ValidationItem.as` in the Chapter 31 source code.

4. The transfer object is used to implement specific validation routines and return results to the invoking form in the `CorporateValidators`' `validate()` method, as shown in the following snippet:

```
public function validate( value:CorporateValidationItem ):CorporateValidationItem
{
    _corpRegExpValidator.expression = this[ "_" + value.validationType +
        "Pattern" ];
    _corpRegExpValidator.noMatchError = this[ "_" + value.validationType +
        "Error" ];
    value.validationResultEvent = _corpRegExpValidator.validate
        ( value.dataToValidate, true );

    return value;
}
```

5. Transfer objects are set up for form fields in the UI component containing the form. This is how they're set up in chapter31_example10.mxml:

```
private function _onCreationComplete( event:FlexEvent ):void
{
    _corpValidators = CorporateValidators.getInstance();

    _lname_cvi = new CorporateValidationItem();
    _lname_cvi.validationType = CorporateValidators.VALIDATE_NAME;
    _lname_cvi.formFieldId = lname_ti.id;

    _address1_cvi = new CorporateValidationItem();
    _address1_cvi.validationType = CorporateValidators.VALIDATE_ADDRESS1;
    _address1_cvi.formFieldId = address1_ti.id;

    _validators =  [ _lname_cvi, _address1_cvi ];
}
```

6. When the Submit button is clicked, the form's _onSubmit() handler is run, causing the validation to occur and stopping the submission of the form when the data is invalid. This is illustrated in the following excerpt from chapter31_example10.mxml:

```
private function _onSubmit( event:MouseEvent ):void
{
    var len:int = _validators.length;
    var i:int;
    var validationItem:CorporateValidationItem;

    _lname_cvi.dataToValidate = lname_ti.text;
    _lname_cvi = _corpValidators.validate( _lname_cvi );

    _address1_cvi.dataToValidate = address1_ti.text;
    _address1_cvi = _corpValidators.validate( _address1_cvi );

    for( i=0; i < len; i++ )
    {
        validationItem = _validators[ i ] as CorporateValidationItem;

        if( validationItem.validationResultEvent.results.length )
        {
            this[ validationItem.formFieldId ].errorString = ValidationResult
                ( validationItem.validationResultEvent.results[ 0 ] ).errorMessage;
```

```
        }
        if( validationItem.validationResultEvent.type ==
            ValidationResultEvent.INVALID )
        {
            _formValid = false;
        }
    }

    if( _formValid )
    {
        Alert.show( "yay, successful form submit!" );
    }
}
```

Summary

Formatters and validators are useful mechanisms for ensuring proper data interaction with your end user and regular expressions are very powerful constructs for manipulating data.

Although the most important aspects of these Flex framework features were covered throughout this chapter, there is always more to learn in the Adobe LiveDocs. Information on formatters, validators, and regular expressions can be found at the following links:

❑ **Formatting data** — `http://livedocs.adobe.com/flex/3/html/help.html?content=formatters_1.html`

❑ **Validating data** — `http://livedocs.adobe.com/flex/3/html/help.html?content=validators_1.html`

❑ **Using regular expressions** — `http://livedocs.adobe.com/flex/3/html/help.html?content=12_Using_Regular_Expressions_01.html`

The next chapter dives into list components, expanding the breadth of your knowledge on how to work with data in your Flex applications.

32

Using the List Components

This chapter starts the discussion on Flex 3's various list-based components. The topics covered include:

- ❑ ListBase
- ❑ List
- ❑ Menu
- ❑ TileBase
- ❑ HorizontalList
- ❑ TileList

ListBase Is Everywhere

You had a chance to learn about Collections API and the `dataProvider` property in Chapter 30. Having knowledge of the Collections API and `dataProvider` is very important to taking the next step in the discussion: `mx.controls.listClasses.ListBase`.

`ListBase` is an important class because it lays down the foundation necessary for managing how the user sees and interacts with the `dataProvider` data in your Flex applications. As an added benefit, `ListBase` inherits from `mx.core.ScrollControlBase`, providing `ListBase` objects data scrolling capabilities for situations in which there isn't enough display area allocated to the control to show all items at once.

The functionality derived from using the `ListBase` class as a base class is extensive. `ListBase` encompasses a user's interaction with the data displayed to that user within the controls that extend the `ListBase` class. Here is a list of controls that extend `ListBase`:

❑   mx.controls.List

❑   mx.controls.Menu

❑   mx.controls.Tree

❑   mx.controls.FileSystemList (Adobe AIR only)

❑   mx.controls.FileSystemTree (Adobe AIR only)

❑   mx.controls.HorizontalList

❑   mx.controls.TileList

❑   mx.controls.DataGrid

As you can see, Flex applications interact with the ListBase class indirectly through some of the UI controls most commonly used by Flex developers.

> *Those of you who are familiar with the* AdvancedDataGrid *will see that it was not mentioned in the preceding list. That is because* AdvancedDataGrid *inherits from* AdvancedListBase *instead.*

ListBase APIs

ListBase is not normally a class that developers choose to implement in their UI. That said, the code examples will make use of mx.controls.List to demonstrate the ListBase APIs.

Selection and Update API

The ListBase manages user selection and modification of its dataProvider data. To start the dialog, a List control is defined below. The control mx.controls.List is a direct descendent of ListBase, and in this particular sample the dataProvider being used is the XMLListCollection that we started to discuss in Chapter 30:

```
<!-- List control with XMLListCollection dataProvider -->
<mx:List id="players_ls"
    height="100%" width="100%"
    labelField="@name"
    dataProvider="{ _myXMLListCollection }" />
```

In this example, the ListBase class is responsible for providing the functionality to the List control used to determine how a user can interact with the underlying XMLListCollection dataProvider. For instance, through ListBase properties you can decide on whether a user can select multiple items, one item, or no items in the dataProvider at all. This is done through Boolean properties of the ListBase class such as allowMultipleSelection and selectable:

```
<!-- List control with XMLListCollection dataProvider -->
<mx:List id="players_ls"
    height="100%" width="100%"
    labelField="@name"
    dataProvider="{ _myXMLListCollection }"
    allowMultipleSelection="false"
    selectable="true" />
```

Another function the `ListBase` provides is dispatching events whenever a user interacts with the items in the list. For example, when a user clicks an item an `mx.events.ListEvent` object of type `ListEvent.ITEM_CLICK` is dispatched. In another example, when a user rolls over a list item, a `ListEvent` object of type `ListEvent.ITEM_ROLL_OVER` is dispatched. Here's some code to illustrate:

```
<mx:Script>
    <![CDATA[
        private function _onItemRollOver( p_evt:ListEvent ):void
        {
            // ListEvent has a rowIndex property that we can display
            trace( "Row " + p_evt.rowIndex + " was rolled over" );
        }

        private function _onItemClick( p_evt:ListEvent ):void
        {
            // If you notice, we're accessing an XML attribute from the
            // dataProvider item
            trace( "The player '"
                    + p_evt.target.selectedItem.@name + "' was selected" );
        }
    ]]>
</mx:Script>

<!-- List control with XMLListCollection dataProvider -->
<mx:List id="players_ls"
    height="100%" width="100%"
    labelField="@name"
    dataProvider="{ _myXMLListCollection }"
    allowMultipleSelection="false"
    selectable="true"
    itemClick="_onItemClick( event )"
    itemRollOver="_onItemRollOver( event )"/>
```

The `ListBase` is also responsible for keeping tabs on which items are currently selected. For a `ListBase` that is in single-selection mode, there's `selectedIndex` and `selectedItem`. For a `ListBase` that is in multi-selection mode, there's `selectedIndices` and `selectedItems`.

```
// create a temporary array for selected item(s)
var items:Array;

// initialize the temporary array based whether the list
// allows multiple selection or not
if( players_ls.allowMultipleSelection )
{
    items = players_ls.selectedItems;
}
else
{
    // only single selection so only a single item
    items = [ players_ls.selectedItem ];
}
```

In this last example, the `allowMultipleSelection` Boolean is used to determine which selection mode the `ListBase` control is in. Once that decision has been made, the developer can access the selected item(s) through the corresponding selected item property. Also notice, that `selectedItems` is an `Array` whereas `selectedItem` is an `Object`.

Drag and Drop API

Drag and drop is discussed in both Chapter 34 and Chapter 35, but it's worth mentioning here that `ListBase` implements APIs to manage the drag and drop capabilities of a particular `ListBase` instance. This is managed through `Boolean` properties, such as `dragEnabled`, `dragMoveEnabled`, `dropEnabled`, and public methods such as `calculateDropIndex()`, `hideDropFeedback()`, and `showDropFeedback()`. If you would like more detailed information on drag and drop, skip to Chapters 34 and 35.

Additional Features

In addition to providing features for handling user interaction with list data, the `ListBase` contains a healthy, display-centric set of features geared toward providing the user feedback and improved user experience during their use of the `ListBase` controls.

Data Tips

The `ListBase` class provides mouse-over data tips. By default, they're meant to show text that is too wide to display in the row of a `ListBase` object, but you can set them to whatever you'd like.

Data tips are turned off by default. To turn them on, set the `showDataTips` property to `true`. When the data tips are turned on, the Flex framework will look for a property named "label" in each item in the list. If you have a property in the list item you'd like to use, you can set it by using the `dataTipField` property. However, if the list items don't contain an appropriate property or if you'd like to customize the data tip, you can use the `dataTipFunction` property, as shown in the following code:

```
<mx:Script>
    <![CDATA[
        private function _dataTipFunc( p_obj:Object ):String
        {
            // let's show the player's position as the data tip
            return p_obj.@position;
        }
    ]]>
</mx:Script>

<mx:List id="players_ls"
    height="100%" width="100%"
    labelField="@name"
    dataProvider="{ _myXMLListCollection }"
    showDataTips="true"
    dataTipFunction="_dataTipFunc"/>
```

Icons

The `ListBase` class supports icons through the `iconField` or `iconFunction` property. To display an icon in your `ListBase` instance, set the value of `iconField` to an object property in the `dataProvider` data. As an alternative, you can specify a custom function as the value of the `iconFunction` property of your `ListBase` instance. In either case, the name value must specify a class that can be typed to `IFlexDisplayObject`. Note that the `DataGrid` class ignores these properties.

Labels

The `ListBase` class supports custom text labels via the `labelField` or `labelFunction` property. Setting the field or the function is similar to how you would set them for data tips or icons. As you can see, in our instance of `List` we're setting `labelField` to the `"@name"` attribute of the baseball players in the `XMLList`-based `dataProvider` data:

```
<mx:List id="players_ls"
    labelField="@name"
    dataProvider="{ _myXMLListCollection }"/>
```

If you wanted to show the player names along with their position, you would use `labelFunction` instead, as illustrated in the following code snippet:

```
<mx:Script>
    <![CDATA[
        private function _labelFunc( p_obj:Object ):String
        {
            // player name : position
            return p_obj.@name + " : " + p_obj.@position;
        }
    ]]>
</mx:Script>

<mx:List id="players_ls"
    labelFunction="_labelFunc"
    dataProvider="{ _myXMLListCollection }"/>
```

Item Renderers

The `ListBase` class supports using custom item renderers via the `itemRenderer` property. The significance of item renderers is that they allow a developer to customize how the items in each row appear. Rather than the default item renderer, one row of text for each item in a list, if you use a custom item renderer, you can do things like add subcomponents and other assets.

For instance, in the baseball player list, rather than just showing their names on each row, you could assign a custom baseball card-style item renderer to the list using the `itemRenderer` property. Custom item renderers are a significant topic and are discussed in the next chapter, after we've had a chance to cover the rest of the data components. If you can't wait, feel free to skip to that section and come back when you're done.

Working with the List Class

If a one-dimensional, scrollable, vertical list of items works for you, then you're going to want to use `mx.controls.List`. Out of the `ListBase` subclasses, `List` would probably be considered the one with the least amount of deviation from the `ListBase` blueprint. Since Flex developers normally don't instantiate `ListBase` directly, if you haven't already noticed, we've been illustrating features of `ListBase` by using the `List` control. To build on what's already been discussed, the most significant feature that the `List` class adds to its parent class `ListBase` is an API to handle editing items.

Item-Editing Functionality in List

A `List` control provides the ability to edit its `dataProvider` elements. To do this, you must first turn the `List` on for editing. This can be accomplished by setting the `editable` property to `true`. Once `editable` is set to `true`, you can start managing the edit interaction that the user has with the `List`. In general, this is handled by listening for the dispatch of `ListEvent` objects such as the types `ListEvent.ITEM_EDIT_BEGINNING`, `ListEvent.ITEM_EDIT_BEGIN`, and `ListEvent.ITEM_EDIT_END`.

> *Notice that two of the `ListEvent` types look very similar:* ITEM_EDIT_BEGIN *and* ITEM_EDIT_BEGINNING. *The* ITEM_EDIT_BEGINNING *event is dispatched when users have indicated that they would like to edit an item, whereas* ITEM_EDIT_BEGIN *is dispatched after an item editor has been set up and the item is actually ready to be edited.*

The following code example illustrates how to handle `ListEvent` dispatched by `List` instances:

```
<mx:Script>
    <![CDATA[
        import mx.controls.Alert;
        import mx.controls.TextInput;
        import mx.events.ListEvent;
        import mx.controls.listClasses.ListItemRenderer;

        private var _alertShown:Boolean;

        private function _onItemEditBeginning( p_evt:ListEvent ):void
        {
            // reset the alert tracker for new edit session
            _alertShown = false;
        }

        private function _onItemEditEnd( p_evt:ListEvent ):void
        {
            // If the user tries to type new data let's prevent it
            if( TextInput( List( p_evt.target).itemEditorInstance ).text
                != ListItemRenderer( p_evt.itemRenderer ).listData.label )
            {
                // stop the event from doing what it normally does
                p_evt.preventDefault();

                // ListEvent.ITEM_EDIT_END will fire twice
                // - hit the enter key: fires reasons "newRow" and "other"
                // - click different list item fires reasons "other" x2
                // We only want to show the alert once
                if( !_alertShown )
                {
                    _alertShown = true;
                    // Notify the user that they've been veto'd
                    Alert.show( "New data? We will not allow it." );
                }
            }
```

```
                }
            }
        ]]>
    </mx:Script>

    <mx:List id="players_ls"
        height="100%" width="100%"
        labelField="@name"
        dataProvider="{ _myXMLListCollection }"
        editable="true"
        itemEditBeginning="_onItemEditBeginning( event )"
        itemEditEnd="_onItemEditEnd( event )"/>
```

List Descendents

Interestingly enough, there are two classes that inherit from List that you wouldn't expect. The first is the Tree control, which will be discussed in the next chapter. The second is the Menu control, discussed next.

The Menu Class

If you've ever used a Windows OS and invoked File ⇨ Exit, you have an idea of what mx.controls .Menu is all about. For those of you on a Mac, think of Application ⇨ Quit. Not only does the Menu control emulate standard operating system functionality, when not in use Menu controls take up very little of the display real estate. And when invoked, they pop up and can be very large, nesting deeply to the nth degree.

Creating Menu Objects

The Menu class was designed to work well with an XML structured dataProvider. Feeding the Menu usually requires some XML and a little hint on what to use as the display text via the labelField property. Also, there are various types of Menu items you can create: normal, check, radio, and separator. These types can be specified in the dataProvider data by using XML attributes named type. Similarly, Menu items can have some indicative states right off the bat, such as enabled or toggled. Here's a sample that shows how to create Menu objects:

```
<?xml version="1.0" encoding="utf-8"?>
<mx:Application xmlns:mx="http://www.adobe.com/2006/mxml"
    creationComplete="_onCreationComplete( event )" layout="absolute">
    <mx:Script>
        <![CDATA[
            import mx.controls.Menu;

            private var _menuXML:XML = <baseball>
                    <league name="West Coast League">
                        <team name="San Jose Noisers"
                            type="radio" toggled="true" />
                        <team name="Seattle Slicksters"
                            type="radio" />
```

```
                            <team name="Portland Pridepins (Eliminated)"
                                  enabled="false" type="radio" />
                        </league>
                        <menuitem type="separator" />
                        <league name="East Coast League">
                            <team name="Boston Redcars (Eliminated)"
                                  enabled="false" type="radio" />
                            <team name="DC Denriders"
                                  type="radio" toggled="true" />
                            <team name="Atlanta Arisenmen"
                                  type="radio" />
                        </league>
                    </baseball>;

            private var _baseballMenu:Menu;

            private function _onCreationComplete( p_evt:Event ):void
            {
                // create the menu (false means don't show XML root node)
                _baseballMenu = Menu.createMenu( null, _menuXML, false );
                // specify the data that will serve as the label
                _baseballMenu.labelField = "@name";
            }

            private function _onMenuLabelClick( p_evt:MouseEvent ):void
            {
                // show the menu under the label (x,y is 0,0 by default)
                _baseballMenu.show( 0, p_evt.currentTarget.height );
            }
        ]]>
    </mx:Script>
    <mx:Label id="menu_lbl"
        text="Baseball Menu (Click to Access)"
        click="_onMenuLabelClick( event )" />
</mx:Application>
```

Working with the Menu Class

Working with the Menu class is relatively straightforward: the user interacts with the Menu. The Menu dispatches an event. You set up an event handler and get the information you need to process the interaction using the event data. When working with Menu, all of the events you need to concern yourself with are of type mx.events.MenuEvent.

Take a look at the following code snippet and notice how you can handle both interaction with the Menu items and also events that are dispatched when the Menu is opened or closed:

```
// menu event listeners
_baseballMenu.addEventListener( MenuEvent.CHANGE, _onMenuEvent );
_baseballMenu.addEventListener( MenuEvent.ITEM_CLICK, _onMenuEvent );
_baseballMenu.addEventListener( MenuEvent.ITEM_ROLL_OUT, _onMenuEvent );
_baseballMenu.addEventListener( MenuEvent.ITEM_ROLL_OVER, _onMenuEvent );
_baseballMenu.addEventListener( MenuEvent.MENU_HIDE, _onMenuEvent );
_baseballMenu.addEventListener( MenuEvent.MENU_SHOW, _onMenuEvent );
```

The TileBase Class

When creating a page in HTML that requires rows and columns, you would use HTML tables. When attempting to do the same in Flex, one of your options is to use `mx.controls.listClasses.TileBase`. The `TileBase` class is a direct descendent of `ListBase`, and like `ListBase`, the `TileBase` class is never really instantiated directly.

After inheriting `ListBase` functionality, `TileBase` adds three properties (`direction`, `maxColumns`, and `maxRows`) and a number of methods primarily dealing with drawing tiles, scrolling, and managing the positioning of the on-screen contents correctly. As you may be thinking, `TileBase` was designed to handle rows and columns of data items efficiently. `TileBase` can generally be seen in Flex applications through the subclasses `HorizontalList` and `TileList`.

HorizontalList

A `HorizontalList` creates one horizontal row of tiles. It is a direct descendent of `TileBase`, and amazingly `HorizontalList` does not define any custom properties or methods.

A couple of things to note are that, by default, a `HorizontalList` is four columns and it receives its size based on the dimensions of its cells. Here is an example of using the `HorizontalList` class:

```
<mx:HorizontalList id="players_hl"
    height="50" width="300"
    labelField="@name"
    dataProvider="{ _myXMLListCollection }"
    columnWidth="150"/>
```

The `columnWidth` *was set explicitly in this example. If the* `columnWidth` *was not explicitly set, the text would have been truncated.*

The nice thing is, when you decide to set the `width` and `height` of the `HorizontalList` too small to view all data items, a scrollbar will appear automatically to allow the user to view all the data.

TileList

If you are looking to create a grid of tiled items, you will want to use the `TileList`. Like `HorizontalList`, `TileList` does not define any custom properties or methods and is a direct descendent of `TileBase`. Here is some code representing a `TileList`:

```
<mx:TileList id="players_hl"
    height="300" width="400"
    labelField="@name"
    dataProvider="{ _myXMLListCollection }"
    columnWidth="150"
    direction="horizontal"
    maxColumns="2"/>
```

Looking at this sample, `direction="horizontal"` `maxColumns="2"` *means start at the top left, create two columns of data, and move to the next row.*

Although a `maxRows` *property could have been added with no ill effect, it would be ignored unless the direction was changed to vertical. In other words,* `direction="vertical" maxRows="2"` *means start at the top left, make two rows, and move on to the next column.*

Using `TileList` can require some tweaking on the `TileList` dimensions to get optimal tiling. For example, by default, if there's enough display area and data items, the `TileList` will be four columns by four rows with tiles that are 50 × 50 pixels each. Also, you can play with `columnWidth` and `rowHeight` properties to help make sure that your display data doesn't get truncated. In the next chapter, we'll be discussing custom item renderers, which are by far the best way to pretty up your `HorizontalList` and `TileList` display presentation.

List, HorizontalList, and TileList — Optimized Memory Consumption

On a closing note, we mentioned `TileList` when we discussed `Repeater` in Chapter 30. The reason we mentioned `TileList` is that it can look identical to `Repeater` with a nested `Tile` control. Also, there will be times when you might be tempted to create something with a `Repeater` that can be done with `List`, `HorizontalList`, or `TileList`.

`List`, `HorizontalList`, and `TileList` only instantiate children that can be seen in the display, and these controls continue to instantiate children in a just-in-time manner as the user scrolls them into view. This differs from a `Repeater`-based solution in which all children are immediately instantiated, including the invisible children.

`List`, `HorizontalList`, and `TileList` are designed with optimal memory consumption in mind, and you will increasingly reap the benefits of using them rather than `Repeater`-based solutions as the number of items in the `dataProvider` grows.

A good rule of thumb to live by is, if there are too many items in the `dataProvider` to display all at once, you shouldn't use a `Repeater`; instead, look to `List`, `HorizontalList`, and `TileList`.

Summary

`ListBase` and its subclasses are a powerful set of components to present data to the users of your Flex applications. `List` is great at representing a vertical, scrollable, one-dimensional view of your data. Through `TileBase` you get `HorizontalList` and `TileList`, which are used to generate customizable tiles for each of their data items, and are smart enough to handle memory in an efficient manner. Thanks to `Menu`, you can have compact hierarchical controls that fly open only when you decide that you need them.

Although you had a chance to get started, there's simply no way to cover everything about `List` components in one brief chapter. If you are interested in furthering your studies of the preceding topics, make sure to check out the Flex 3 Livedocs.

That being said, move on to the next chapter if you are curious about the other fancy controls that are based on `ListBase`, want to learn how to work with custom item renderers, or are interested in some of the more advanced data visualization components that have been introduced with Flex 3.

33

Advanced Data Controls

This chapter will cover the advanced data controls built into the Flex framework. It will also touch on how to interact with them and examine some of the main ways to customize their display. The following controls will be discussed:

- ❏ `mx.controls.Tree`
- ❏ `mx.controls.DataGrid`
- ❏ `mx.controls.AdvancedDataGrid`
- ❏ `mx.controls.OLAPDataGrid`

> Both the `AdvancedDataGrid` and the `OLAPDataGrid` are only available via the Flex Visualization Components bundled with Flex Builder 3 Professional.

Overview

As framework developers, we're always on the search for elements that can be integrated into our applications to provide large amounts of functionality with a minimal investment of writing new code. The Flex framework provides many controls that meet this criteria, and the advanced data controls are no exception.

The advanced data controls were designed with displaying large amounts in mind. Coupled with an adequately robust data provider, the advanced data controls and their core data provider classes offer an extensive API to allow the developer to perform data filtering, sorting, manipulation, and data display customizations.

Chapter 30 and Chapter 32 have set the stage and supporting infrastructure to allow us to take advantage of these robust controls. Now that we've built the foundation, let's examine what we can build on top of it.

Tree

Chapter 30 discussed XML, a modern-day standard for descriptively marking up data. Coupling XML with the Collections API that we also discussed in that chapter, we are provided with the `XMLListCollection`, a class that provides robust sorting and filtering mechanisms to its underlying XML-based data source. The `Tree` control, `mx.controls.Tree`, was built to work with XML and is a display component that represents its data in a hierarchical structure, similar to the way that XML is structured.

Because of its hierarchical nature, the `Tree` control consists of leaves and branches. A branch is a node that can have one to many leaf or branch children, and a leaf is terminal node within the `Tree` control that does not have any children. Figure 33-1 illustrates `mx.controls.Tree`.

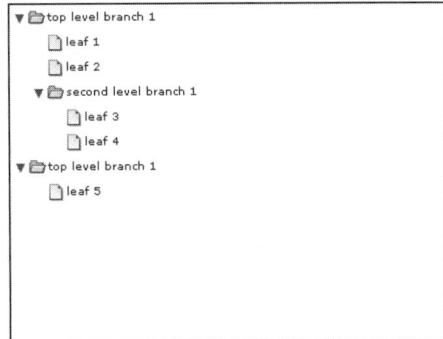

Figure 33-1

Feeding the Tree

The `Tree` control was designed to use `XML`, `XMLList`, and `XMLListCollection` as its `dataProvider`. In the Figure 33-1 example, we just assigned some static `XML` to the `Tree`.

1. First we defined our `XML` object:

```
[Bindable]
private var _myTreeXML:XML =
    <root label="root node">
        <branch label="top level branch 1">
            <leaf label="leaf 1"/>
            <leaf label="leaf 2"/>
            <branch label="second level branch 1">
                <leaf label="leaf 3"/>
                <leaf label="leaf 4"/>
            </branch>
        </branch>
        <branch label="top level branch 1">
            <leaf label="leaf 5"/>
        </branch>
    </root>;
```

2. Then we bound the XML object to our Tree control:

```
<mx:Tree id="example1_tr"
  labelField="@label"
  showRoot="false"
  dataProvider="{ _myTreeXML }"
  width="400" height="300"/>
```

A couple of notes:

❏ If you have a root node that you don't want to display, you need to set the showRoot property to false.

❏ If you don't specify the labelField, the Tree will not know what to display and just spit out the XML string for the node at that branch or leaf.

Although we're using a static XML object as the dataProvider for the Tree shown in Figure 33-1 and the preceding code, we can interchangeably use XML, XMLList, and XMLListCollection. You can view how to bind all three of these data types to a Tree in chapter33_example1_tree.mxml within the Chapter 33 source code.

Although you can set the Tree *dataProvider to* XML, XMLList, *or* XMLListCollection, *when all is said and done,* XML *or* XMLList *is converted to an* XMLListCollection *when it is assigned as the* dataProvider. *As an added bonus, you can also set the* dataProvider *to an* Array *or* ArrayCollection, *keeping in mind that an* Array *will be converted to an* ArrayCollection.

Changing the Look of the Tree

Listing all the ways you could change the look of a Tree would be a chapter in and of itself. That being said, let's take a look at one of the most common stylizing requests, changing the icon for the branches and nodes of the Tree control. Feel free to follow along with chapter33_example2_treeCustomize.mxml.

1. The first thing to do is to create your dataProvider data and instantiate a Tree bound to that data. Take a look at the last section for a refresher.

2. Now that you have a working and populated Tree, you will need some icon images. You can get your images from anywhere. You could even create your own in an image-editing program such as Adobe Fireworks. We've provided some images for you in the src\assets\images folder of the Chapter 33 source code.

3. The easiest way to get the icon images into your application for use in MXML and ActionScript code is to embed the images into your SWF. The following code block embeds two folder images and one leaf image, using the Embed metadata tag.

```
// Embedding the custom icons for the tree
[Bindable]
[Embed(source="assets/images/folderIsClosed.png")]
private var folderIsClosed:Class;

[Bindable]
```

```
[Embed(source="assets/images/folderIsOpen.png")]
private var folderIsOpen:Class;

[Bindable]
[Embed(source="assets/images/leaf.png")]
private var leaf:Class;
```

Because embedded images are compiled into your SWF, you will want to keep embed statements to a minimum; otherwise, you could end up with a very large SWF that takes a long time to download and initialize.

4.   Now that the images have been embedded, bind to the `folderOpenIcon` and `folderClosedIcon` properties of the `Tree` to change the look and feel of the branch open and close icons.

```
<mx:Tree id="xml_tr"
    labelField="@label"
    showRoot="false"
    dataProvider="{ _myTreeXML }"
    folderOpenIcon="{ folderIsOpen }"
    folderClosedIcon="{ folderIsClosed }"
    width="400" height="300"/>
```

5.   Finally, let's set the leaf icons programmatically via ActionScript. During the initialize handler of the application, loop through the `XMLList` within the `dataProvider`, find the nodes named `"leaf"`, and then set the icon programmatically using `{tree_instance}.setItemIcon()`:

```
private function _onInitialize( event:FlexEvent ):void
{
    // grab a local reference to the XMLList
    var itemList:XMLList = xml_tr.dataProvider.source as XMLList;

    // loop through the "leaf" descendents to set the icons
    for each( var item:XML in itemList.descendants( "leaf" ) )
    {
        xml_tr.setItemIcon( item, leaf, leaf );
    }
}
```

Although we used `setItemIcon()`, the property it modifies is the `itemIcons` property. The `itemIcons` property can be used if we want to set the icons once and already have a ready-made object reference to the node that we're setting the icon for.

Working with the Tree Control

There are many ways to interact with a `Tree` control. A couple common use cases would be auto-expanding and collapsing branches and examining the node contents when events are dispatched from the `Tree`.

Expanding and Collapsing Branches

The `Tree` control contains the `expandChildrenOf()` and `expandItem()` methods for working with expanding and collapsing branches. The `expandChildrenOf()` will expand or collapse multiple child items whereas the `expandItem()` will expand or collapse one item. Let's walk through some of the code from `chapter33_example3_treeWorkWith.mxml` to see how `expandChildrenOf()` can be implemented.

1. Start with a `Tree` control populated with data. Take a look at some of the previous sections for more information on this.

2. It is suggested in the Flex documentation not to expand items right after data has been set on a `Tree` control. So, we create some listeners to expand the tree nodes the next time the component has finished updating:

```
private function _onInitialize( event:FlexEvent ):void
{
  // creating an XMLList and XMLListCollection for comparison
  _myTreeXMLList = new XMLList( _myTreeXML );
  _myTreeXMLListCollection = new XMLListCollection( _myTreeXMLList );

  // initialize happens early on, let's catch the next update cycle so that we
  // can expand the trees.
  xml_tr.addEventListener( FlexEvent.UPDATE_COMPLETE, _expandItems );
  xmlList_tr.addEventListener( FlexEvent.UPDATE_COMPLETE, _expandItems );
  xmlListCollection_tr.addEventListener( FlexEvent.UPDATE_COMPLETE, _
expandItems );
}

private function _expandItems( event:FlexEvent ):void
{
  // We're only expanding the first time around so after the first call let's
  // remove the listener
  event.target.removeEventListener( FlexEvent.UPDATE_COMPLETE, _expandItems );

  // let's verify that the expand target is valid
  if( event.target.dataProvider && event.target.dataProvider.length )
  {
    // time to expand the tree
    event.target.expandChildrenOf( event.target.dataProvider[0], true );
  }
}
```

Handling Common Tree Events

When you click on an item in a `Tree` control, it will dispatch a `ListEvent.ITEM_CLICK`. In addition, there are several `TreeEvents` that the `Tree` control will dispatch:

❑ `mx.events.TreeEvent.ITEM_CLOSE`: Dispatched when a `Tree` node has been closed

❑ `mx.events.TreeEvent.ITEM_OPEN`: Dispatched when a `Tree` node has been opened

❑ `mx.events.TreeEvent.ITEM_OPENING`: Dispatched when a `Tree` node is being opened or closed

Here's how you would listen to these events when instantiating your `Tree` via MXML:

```
<mx:Tree id="xml_tr"
  labelField="@label"
```

```
            showRoot="false"
            dataProvider="{ _myTreeXML }"
            itemClick="_onListEvent( event )"
            itemOpening="_onTreeEvent( event )"
            itemOpen="_onTreeEvent( event )"
            itemClose="_onTreeEvent( event )"
            width="400" height="300"/>
```

Here's an example of the handler used for these events from `chapter33_example3_treeWorkWith.mxml`:

```
    private function _onTreeEvent( event:TreeEvent ):void
    {
        output_ta.text += "node with a label of '" + XML( event.item ).@label
                        + "' is '" + event.type + "'\n";
    }
```

As you can see, when working with `TreeEvent` you will access the branch or leaf in question via the `event.item` property.

DataGrid

Whereas the `Tree` control was designed to work with hierarchical data, `mx.controls.DataGrid` was designed to work with tabular data. The easiest way to think about the `DataGrid` control is to imagine a spreadsheet in your Flex application. If you've seen a Flex application, there's a good chance that you've seen a `DataGrid` before, but if not, Figure 33-2 illustrates the `DataGrid`.

favoriteMusic	fname	lname
Green Day	Hiromi	Heider
J. Iglesias	Heide	Heider
Rolling Stones	Kathryn	Heider
Mary J. Blige	Lisa	Heider
Björk	Mayumi	Heider
Beatles	Robert	Heider

Figure 33-2

Populating the DataGrid

The process of populating the `DataGrid` shown in Figure 33-2 involves coming up with an `Array` of data, setting it as the source of an `ArrayCollection`, and finally binding the `ArrayCollection` to the `dataProvider` property of the `DataGrid`.

> *Like the `Tree` control, the `DataGrid` can also use `XMLListCollection` or `ArrayCollection` data as its `dataProvider` source data.*

Here is what this looks like in code. Feel free to open `chapter33_example4_dataGrid.mxml` to view the code in full.

1. Make sure that you have a data provider ready. Although the data provider data is hard-coded in this sample, the data can come from anywhere: an XML file or a service call or be hard-coded or user-provided.

```
_myArrayCollection = new ArrayCollection();
_myArrayCollection.addItem( { lname:'Heider', fname:'Hiromi',
    favoriteMusic:'Green Day' } );
_myArrayCollection.addItem( { lname:'Heider', fname:'Heide',
    favoriteMusic:'J. Iglesias' } );
_myArrayCollection.addItem( { lname:'Heider', fname:'Kathryn',
    favoriteMusic:'Rolling Stones' } );
_myArrayCollection.addItem( { lname:'Heider', fname:'Lisa',
    favoriteMusic:'Mary J. Blige' } );
_myArrayCollection.addItem( { lname:'Heider', fname:'Mayumi',
    favoriteMusic:'Björk' } );
_myArrayCollection.addItem( { lname:'Heider', fname:'Robert',
    favoriteMusic:'Beatles' } );
```

2. Now you can instantiate your `DataGrid` and assign the `dataProvider`. The following code shows about the bare minimum code you need to instantiate your `DataGrid` via MXML:

```
<mx:DataGrid id="musicInterests_dg"
    dataProvider="{ _myArrayCollection }" />
```

Working with Columns

One of the main reasons to use a `DataGrid` over a `List` control is because a `DataGrid` offers multiple columns, one for each `dataProvider` object property by default. As a matter of fact, when you look at your `dataProvider` data, you can actually think of each object in the `ArrayCollection` as a row of data and each object's properties as a column.

The Flex `DataGrid` has a fair amount of functionality built in to allow the user to interact with its columns. For instance, by default a user can reorder the columns, sort the columns, and even resize the columns. In addition, through several Boolean properties, the user can turn various features on and off such as whether columns are visible or not, editable or not, even if they're resizable.

Introducing <mx:DataGridColumn/>

When you start working with columns, you will need to know that the `DataGrid` has a columns property that you can set to an array of `<mx:DataGridColumn/>` components. Take a look at this code from `chapter33_example5_dataGridWorkColumns.mxml`:

```
<mx:DataGrid id="musicInterests_dg"
    dataProvider="{ _myArrayCollection }"
    editable="true">
    <mx:columns>
```

```
        <mx:DataGridColumn dataField="fname" headerText="First Name"
            editable="false" visible="false" />
        <mx:DataGridColumn dataField="lname" headerText="Last Name"
            editable="false" visible="true" />
        <mx:DataGridColumn dataField="favoriteMusic" headerText="Favorite Music"
            editable="true" visible="true" />
    </mx:columns>
</mx:DataGrid>
```

Here are some things to notice about the preceding code:

❑ You can make the DataGrid editable by setting the editable property to "true".

❑ Inside the columns array of the DataGrid, we have defined an <mx:DataGridColumn/> instance for each property in the dataProvider object: "fname", "lname", and "favoriteMusic". You can see which <mx:DataGridColumn/> corresponds to which property in the dataProvider object by looking at what the dataField property is set to.

❑ You can set a customized header text display string for each column by taking advantage of the headerText property of the <mx:DataGridColumn/>.

❑ You can choose columns within the dataProvider object to hide from view by setting the <mx:DataGridColumn/> visible property to "false".

An alternative and more commonly used means of choosing which columns in the dataProvider object to show is to only instantiate an <mx:DataGridColumn/> for the columns you want to show.

❑ You can choose which <mx:DataGridColumns/> are editable via the editable property.

For the editable property to work in each <mx:DataGridColumns/>, you need to first make sure that <mx:DataGrid/> is set to editable.

Interacting with <mx:DataGridColumn/>

The previous code sample defined one <mx:DataGridColumn/> for each property within the dataProvider object. By knowing how to interact with the <mx:DataGridColumn/> from the outside, you can do things such as allowing the user to decide which columns to display by clicking on external check boxes.

Let's take a look at some of the code from chapter33_example6_dataGridColumnsCheckboxes.mxml to see how it's done.

1. The first thing to do is to create one CheckBox for each column. In the sample application, all CheckBox controls will start off checked and all DataGridColumns will start off visible.

2. Next, assign an id to the DataGridColumn so that it can be accessed externally.

3. Once you've assigned the id to the DataGridColumn, you can use a change handler on the CheckBox to sync up the value of the CheckBox selected property to the value of the DataGridColumn visible property.

Here is what the resulting code looks like. We're just showing one pair to keep the snippet concise:

```
<mx:CheckBox id="fname_chk"
    label="Show First Name"
    selected="true"
    change="fname_dgc.visible = fname_chk.selected"/>

<mx:DataGridColumn id="fname_dgc"
    dataField="fname" headerText="First Name" editable="false" />
```

As you can see, when you assign an `id` to a `DataGridColumn`, it can be worked with just like any other framework component.

Handling Events

An `event` is what you use to work with the underlying data within a `DataGrid`. You handle them just like any other events in the Flex framework. For instance, the previous `DataGrid` examples set `editable` to `"true"`, allowing the end user to modify the value of the "favorite music" column. As the user updates the data, the changes are saved in the `ArrayCollection` being used as the `dataProvider` for the `DataGrid`.

Unfortunately for the user, the `ArrayCollection` is not persistent and will be deleted once the Flex application is closed. The next time the user opens the application, the data changes they had made in the previous session will be gone. This scenario is a perfect example of something that can be handled with events.

The process of handling `DataGrid` events is the same as handling events in any other framework component. Half of the battle is just getting to know the custom event types that the `DataGrid` will dispatch. Here's a list:

- ❏ `mx.events.DataGridEvent.COLUMN_STRETCH`
- ❏ `mx.events.DataGridEvent.HEADER_RELEASE`
- ❏ `mx.events.IndexChangedEvent.HEADER_SHIFT`
- ❏ `mx.events.DataGridEvent.ITEM_EDIT_BEGIN`
- ❏ `mx.events.DataGridEvent.ITEM_EDIT_BEGINNING`
- ❏ `mx.events.DataGridEvent.ITEM_EDIT_END`
- ❏ `mx.events.DataGridEvent.ITEM_FOCUS_IN`
- ❏ `mx.events.DataGridEvent.ITEM_FOCUS_OUT`

Thinking back to the earlier `DataGrid` example that allows the user to edit the "favorite music" column, any of the `"ITEM_EDIT"` events such as `mx.events.DataGridEvent.ITEM_EDIT_END` would have been worthwhile if you were trying to handle the user edit interaction. If you look at the types of the other events in the list, this should give you an idea of the types of `DataGrid` events you can handle by default.

Now that we're talking about editing, let's shift our thoughts for a moment to `DataGrid` customizations using `itemRenderer` and `itemEditor`.

Customizing Renderers

When you implement any of the advanced data controls, by default, users of your application will see unformatted string labels being used to represent your data. It would be nice to customize the way that data is presented to the user. One example of adding a little spice to the UI would be to show check boxes for Boolean values. Another would be to show images within your control rather than a string representing their path on disk. Customizing renderers requires a knowledge of how to customize the cells and headers within your controls.

Customizing Cells

Cells within advanced data controls represent the data you are presenting to the user. Each of the controls has a default class used to render the data contents of the cells and one to render the cell while it's being edited. For instance, the default item renderer for a `DataGrid` is `mx.controls.dataGrid-Classes.DataGridItemRenderer`, which just outputs the text associated with the item in the cell being rendered. The default renderer for a `DataGrid` cell while the value is being edited is `new ClassFactory(mx.controls.TextInput)`, which is essentially `mx.controls.TextInput`. Let's take a look at how to customize item renderers and item editors.

Item Renderers

An item renderer is the display class for a cell within an advanced data control. We're going to use the `DataGrid` as our use case since it is a pretty widely used component that often requires customized item renderers. There are three ways to assign a custom item renderer: drop-in, inline, and custom component.

Drop-In Item Renderers

Using drop-in renderers is the simplest method of customizing your renders. In a nutshell, you pick a class such as `mx.controls.CheckBox` and you assign it to the `itemRenderer` property of the component. In the case of a `DataGrid`, you will actually assign the renderer to the `<mx:DataGridColumn/>` `itemRender` property of the `DataGridColumn` you need to customize. Here is an example from chapter33_example7_dataGridRenderers.mxml:

1. Make sure that the `dataProvider` column has data that will work with your renderer choice. For instance, since the `likesIceCream` property is Boolean, you can configure its data grid column to use a Checkbox as the item renderer.

```
_myArrayCollection.addItem( { lname:'Heider', fname:'Robert',
        favoriteMusic:'Beatles',
    likesIceCream:true } );
```

2. Assign the `itemRenderer` class to the `DataGridColumn`. Use a fully qualified class name.

```
<mx:DataGridColumn headerText="Likes Ice Cream?"
    editable="true" visible="true"
    dataField="likesIceCream" itemRenderer="mx.controls.CheckBox" />
```

Figure 33-3 shows the `DataGrid` with the newly customized renderer.

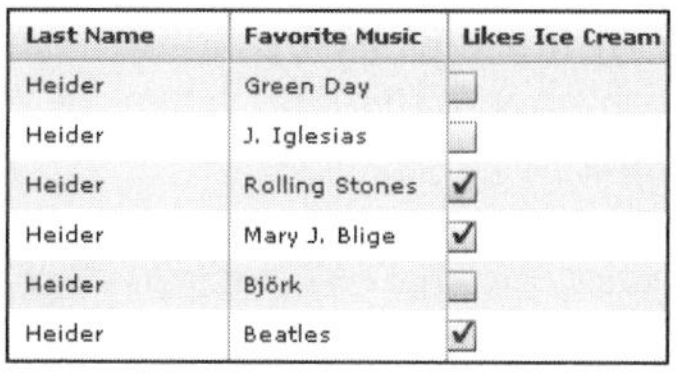

Last Name	Favorite Music	Likes Ice Cream
Heider	Green Day	☐
Heider	J. Iglesias	☐
Heider	Rolling Stones	☑
Heider	Mary J. Blige	☑
Heider	Björk	☐
Heider	Beatles	☑

Figure 33-3

As you can see, using drop-in renderers is a very quick and simple process. However, the trade-off is that you cannot customize any properties of the drop-in renderer. If you want to do this, you'll need to move on and read about inline item renderers.

Inline Item Renderers

With inline item renderers, you actually nest the controls inside the `itemRenderer` property of an `<mx:DataGridColumn/>` via MXML. You have to use a special compile time MXML tag for this, called `<mx:Component/>`. Here's the snippet from `chapter33_example7_dataGridRenderers.mxml`:

```
<mx:DataGridColumn dataField="likesIceCream" headerText="Likes Ice Cream?"
    editable="true" visible="true">
    <mx:itemRenderer>
        <mx:Component>
            <mx:CheckBox
                toolTip="true"
                fillColors="[0xFF0000,0x00FF00]"/>
        </mx:Component>
    </mx:itemRenderer>
</mx:DataGridColumn>
```

Notice that using the inline item renderer rather than the drop-in renderer enables you to turn on the tooltip and customize the fill colors of the `CheckBox`. Figure 33-4 is the result of these inline `itemRender` efforts.

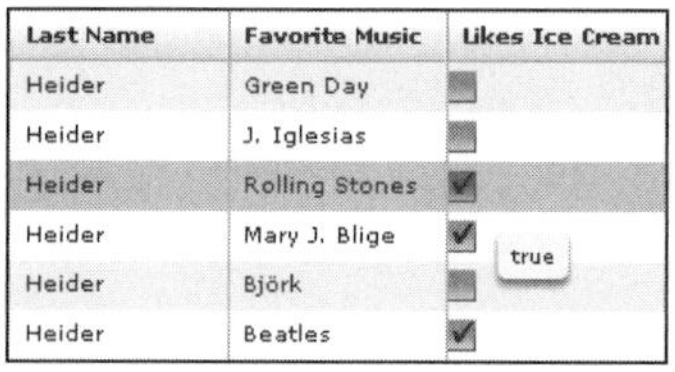

Last Name	Favorite Music	Likes Ice Cream
Heider	Green Day	▣
Heider	J. Iglesias	▣
Heider	Rolling Stones	☑
Heider	Mary J. Blige	☑ true
Heider	Björk	▣
Heider	Beatles	☑

Figure 33-4

When using `<mx:Component/>`, you are actually externalizing its contents into a separate scope. The first thing to note is that you cannot assign an `id` to the first-level tag within the `<mx:Component/>`. The second thing to note is since the scopes are separated, you need to prepend `outerDocument` to anything you want to access within the parent MXML document, such as `outerDocument.someVar`.

Custom Component Item Renderers

The third method of utilizing customized renderers is to create a custom component and use that as your renderer. You can use either the drop-in style or inline style of renderer assignment with your custom renderer. You use a custom component renderer when the built-in framework controls don't provide the functionality you're looking for.

In the case of our example application chapter33_example7_dataGridRenderers.mxml, we decide to use a custom component item renderer, since we want to place an image next to our CheckBox. Here's a code snippet of how to add the custom component as a renderer:

```
<mx:DataGridColumn dataField="likesIceCream" headerText="Likes Ice Cream?"
    editable="true" visible="true"
    itemRenderer="com.wrox.view.itemrenderers.FrownySmileyRenderer" />
```

Here are the contents of the actual custom component being used as an item renderer.

```
<?xml version="1.0" encoding="utf-8"?>
<mx:Canvas xmlns:mx="http://www.adobe.com/2006/mxml">
    <mx:Script>
        <![CDATA[
            override public function set data( value:Object ):void
            {
                if( value.likesIceCream )
                {
                    smiley_img.visible = true;
                    internal_chk.selected = true;
                }
                else
                {
                    frowny_img.visible = true;
                    smiley_img.visible = false;
                    internal_chk.selected = false;
                }
            }
        ]>
    </mx:Script>
    <mx:Image id="frowny_img"
        width="20" height="20"
        visible="false"
        source="assets/images/frowny.png"/>
    <mx:Image id="smiley_img"
        width="20" height="20"
        visible="false"
        source="assets/images/smiley.png"/>
    <mx:CheckBox id="internal_chk"
        x="21"/>
</mx:Canvas>
```

The main thing to keep in mind when implementing components as item renderers is to make sure to override the data setter function as we did in the code above. When the component is activated as an item renderer, the DataGridColumn will pass in the object at the current row of the dataProvider.

That fact is why we have access to the `likesIceCream` property in the preceding code and can use it to determine which images to show and whether or not to check the `CheckBox`.

Although many people try to come up with really creative ways to hack their components in as item renderers, since the `DataGrid` and many other controls recycle their renderers to help with performance and memory management, the only consistent way to get an accurate representation of the current data in the display of the renderer is to configure the display based on values passed in with the `data` setter.

If you're not properly using the `data` setter, it will become very obvious that the renderers are being recycled when you scroll up and down within your control. An example of the type of issue that might occur is that as you scroll up and down in the `DataGrid` and renderers are being recycled, the checked `CheckBox` controls start to get out of sync with the rows of data, erroneously showing the wrong `CheckBox` controls being checked.

Use the override data setter method with your custom item renderers. It may work for you not to do so in a certain instance, but don't say we didn't warn you.

Figure 33-5 illustrates how beneficial it can be to use custom components as renderers.

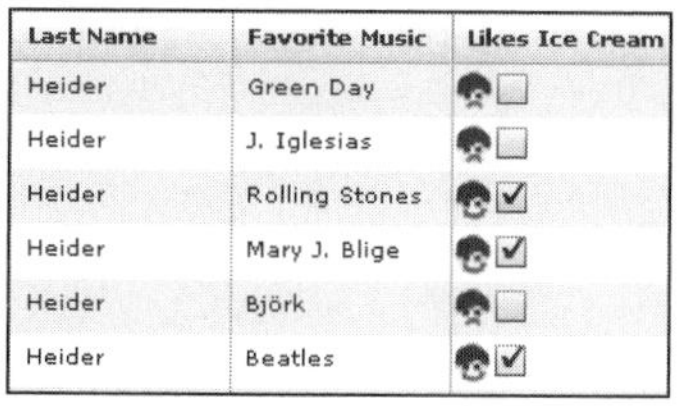

Figure 33-5

Item Editors

Item editors are used within advanced data controls when a user initiates a data-editing session within a cell. Just as with item renderers, you can use them to customize your data control in a drop-in, inline, or custom-component-style implementation. The key difference between an item editor and an item renderer is that an item editor is only displayed while the user is modifying the information in the cell.

For instance, if you had a numeric value in a column, you could specify an `mx.controls.NumericStepper` as the `itemEditor`. Once you've done that, the cell data will show up as text when being displayed and will turn into a `NumericStepper` while being edited. Here is some sample code using the inline style of item editor. The full source is in `chapter33_example8_dataGridEditors.mxml`.

```
<mx:DataGridColumn dataField="age" headerText="Age" editable="true" visible="true"
    editorDataField="value">
  <mx:itemEditor>
    <mx:Component>
      <mx:NumericStepper maximum="150" />
    </mx:Component>
  </mx:itemEditor>
</mx:DataGridColumn>
```

There's a couple things to note about using `itemEditor`. The `DataGridColumn.editorDataField` property is set to `"text"` by default. The reason we set it to `"value"` is because the `NumericStepper` uses a property called `"value"` to store the data field data in rather than a property called `"text"`. If we had let it use the default, we would have received a runtime exception.

Also, although you can use drop-in item editors, we don't recommend it, since it doesn't allow you to specify property values. The default for the `NumericStepper.maximum` property is 10, and if we had not implemented it at least as an inline item editor, we would have not been able to set the `maximum` property to 150.

Ever-Present Item Editors

Since the `itemEditor` goes away after the user is done editing the contents of a cell you're probably wondering how to have a custom editor that is always showing. To do this, you would actually use an `itemRenderer` and set the `rendererIsEditor` property to `true`. Here's a snippet, also from `chapter33_example8_dataGridEditors.mxml`:

```
<mx:DataGridColumn dataField="age" headerText="Age"
    editable="true" visible="true"
    editorDataField="value"
    rendererIsEditor="true">
    <mx:itemRenderer>
        <mx:Component>
            <mx:NumericStepper maximum="150" />
        </mx:Component>
    </mx:itemRenderer>
</mx:DataGridColumn>
```

Even if you use an `itemRenderer` *as an editor, you still need to specify the* `editorDataField` *if the field to set on the renderer is not* `"text"`.

Headers

Advanced data controls usually have headers to summarize what their data contents consist of. As with their cells, you can customize the headers of the advanced data controls. Here's a snippet from `chapter33_example9_dataGridHeaderRenderer.mxml`:

```
<mx:DataGridColumn dataField="likesIceCream"
    editable="true" visible="true"
    itemRenderer="com.wrox.view.itemrenderers.FrownySmileyRenderer">
    <mx:headerRenderer>
        <mx:Component>
            <mx:Image source="assets/images/iceCream.png"
                height="20" width="20"/>
        </mx:Component>
    </mx:headerRenderer>
</mx:DataGridColumn>
```

Figure 33-6 illustrates a custom header renderer.

Now that we've discussed the `Tree` and the `DataGrid`, it's time to take a look at their offspring, the `AdvancedDataGrid`.

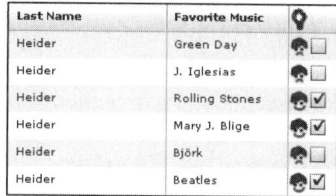

Figure 33-6

AdvancedDataGrid

During the days of Flex 2, custom components were built and feature requests were made around the concept of the DataGrid or the Tree control. Developers wanted to extend their features or even merge them into one component. It was components like the TreeGrid in the FlexLib project (http://code.google.com/p/flexlib) and requests such as having the ability to group rows or columns together that spawned mx.controls.AdvancedDataGrid.

> The AdvancedDataGrid is available only through the Flex Visualization Components bundled with Flex Builder 3 Professional.

Implementing the AdvancedDataGrid

Implementing a simple AdvancedDataGrid is just like implementing a DataGrid:

```
<mx:AdvancedDataGrid id="musicCatalogSimple_adg"
    width="400" height="300"
    dataProvider="{ _myArrayCollection }"/>
```

The full code is in chapter33_example10_advancedDataGrid.mxml and Figure 33-7 illustrates the default AdvancedDataGrid.

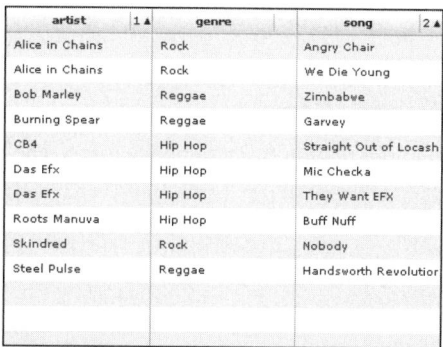

Figure 33-7

> Without needing to enable properties or code anything, you can sort with multiple columns in an AdvancedDataGrid. In Figure 33-7, the data is being sorted by artist first and then song.

Grouping Data in the AdvancedDataGrid

Another very useful feature in the `AdvancedDataGrid` is the ability to group your data. There are a couple different ways to do this, depending on the intended functionality.

Grouping Columns under a Common Header

If you want to group columns under a common header, you can utilize `<mx:AdvancedDataGrid ColumnGroup/>` to nest the `<mx:AdvancedDataGridColumn/>`. Here is the code from `chapter33_ example10_advancedDataGrid.mxml` required to group columns under a common header:

```
<mx:AdvancedDataGrid id="musicCatalogGroupedColumns_adg"
    dataProvider="{ _myArrayCollection }">
    <!-- We're going to group columns -->
    <mx:groupedColumns>
        <!-- Standard Columns -->
        <mx:AdvancedDataGridColumn dataField="genre" />
        <!-- Columns to group on -->
        <mx:AdvancedDataGridColumnGroup headerText="Catalog Items">
            <mx:AdvancedDataGridColumn dataField="artist"/>
            <mx:AdvancedDataGridColumn dataField="song"/>
        </mx:AdvancedDataGridColumnGroup>
    </mx:groupedColumns>
</mx:AdvancedDataGrid>
```

Also notice that, when grouping columns under a common header, you use the `<mx:groupedColumns/>` array instead of the standard `<mx:columns/>` array. Figure 33-8 illustrates the end result of the "artist" and "song" columns being grouped under a "Catalog Items" column group.

Figure 33-8

Grouping Data Logically into Groups

This example groups data together based on a common column. The end result resembles a `DataGrid` with a `Tree` control in one of its columns. Here's the snippet from `chapter33_example10_advanced DataGrid.mxml`:

```
<mx:AdvancedDataGrid id="musicCatalogGroupedCollection_adg"
    width="400" height="300">
    <!-- Our grouped dataProvider -->
    <mx:dataProvider>
        <mx:GroupingCollection source="{ _myArrayCollection }">
            <mx:Grouping>
                <mx:GroupingField name="genre"/>
```

```
            </mx:Grouping>
          </mx:GroupingCollection>
        </mx:dataProvider>
        <!-- Our Columns -->
        <mx:columns>
            <mx:AdvancedDataGridColumn dataField="genre" />
            <mx:AdvancedDataGridColumn dataField="artist"/>
            <mx:AdvancedDataGridColumn dataField="song"/>
        </mx:columns>
    </mx:AdvancedDataGrid>
```

Notice that, when grouping data, you create an <mx:GroupingCollection/> based on the original
ArrayCollection data. Once you have your GroupingCollection, you choose one or more columns to
group with by specifying them as the name of an <mx:GroupingField/> nested in the <mx:Grouping/>
block within the GroupingCollection.

Also, you then populate the standard <mx:columns/> property of the AdvancedDataGrid with the
columns you want to display. Figure 33-9 shows the end result of using a GroupingCollection as the
dataProvider of your AdvancedDataGrid.

Figure 33-9

Hierarchical Data in the AdvancedDataGrid

When working with the AdvancedDataGrid, you're not just limited to using ArrayCollection.
AdvancedDataGrid works perfectly well with XML and even ArrayCollections with objects that
have nested Array objects.

In addition to being able to set an AdvancedDataGrid dataProvider with an ArrayCollection and
a GroupingCollection, there is also the mx.collections.HierarchicalData class that can be used
as an AdvancedDataGrid dataProvider. As a matter of fact, HierarchicalData is the parent class
of GroupingCollection.

For more information on HierarchicalData and the AdvancedDataGrid in general, follow the link to
the Adobe LiveDocs provided at the end of this chapter.

OLAPDataGrid

OLAPDataGrid is another new data control added to the Flex 3 feature set. Before we discuss the actual component, it would be wise to briefly cover what OLAP is. If you already know OLAP feel free to skip past the primer.

> *The OLAPDataGrid is only available through the Flex Visualization Components bundled with Flex Builder 3 Professional.*

An OLAP Primer

Many of the databases these days implement an online transaction processing (OLTP) style of transaction-oriented architecture. These types of database systems were designed to handle processing transactions and run standard information queries. OLTP systems were not designed or optimized to handle multi-dimensional analysis.

As the amounts of collected data increases, businesses are starting to utilize their sheer volumes of data to perform various data analysis tasks. Tasks can include planning budgets around the general state of a company or even forecasting where to build new stores based on market trends in various regions of the country. The ability to perform "what-if" style queries that rely on multidimensional data quickly and efficiently is where online analytical processing (OLAP) really shines.

If you think of your typical database query, data comes back in a two-dimensional tabular format. You think of data in terms of rows and columns. With multidimensional data, the type of data you would receive when running OLAP queries, you think of your data in terms of cubes.

For instance, with a standard OLTP query you might run a query to gather sales per store. If you want to add another dimension, time for example, you can, but the data returned will still be in a very tabular format not conducive to efficient analysis. To get the data to the point where it becomes more efficient would require subqueries, potentially multiple queries, and would involve either high amounts of client-side processing or high amounts of server-side database processing.

In the example query above where sales data is the first dimension, stores are the second, and time is the third, using OLAP is a much better route to take than to use OLTP. OLAP systems were designed to query and present data in a multidimensional format. OLAP systems are also optimized to allow analysts to run many multidimensional queries to look at data from multiple viewpoints. Moving forward, as you learn more about how analysts make use of OLAP systems you will hear terms such as: pivot, slice, dice, drill-down, and roll up.

Working with the OLAPDataGrid

The Flex Data Visualization Components package available with Flex Builder 3 Professional comes with a subclass of AdvancedDataGrid called mx.controls.OLAPDataGrid, which is the Flex answer to presenting a control geared toward working with data in an OLAP fashion.

Some of the things you can do with an OLAPDataGrid include:

❑ Taking large amounts of data and massaging it into a more analysis-friendly format

❑ Writing queries to create OLAP cubes

❑ Support a multidimensional axis using a hierarchical display

The general process to bring up a useful OLAPDataGrid in your application:

1. Start with some data.

2. Define an OLAP schema.

3. Write OLAP queries.

4. Display the results of your OLAP queries also known as aggregations in your OLAPDataGrid.

Although we wish there were, there is simply not enough room in this chapter to discuss OLAPDataGrid in full. We highly recommend following this primer up with the Adobe LiveDocs that can be found at the link provided at the end of this chapter.

This section walks you through a very simple example of an application that demonstrates the general workflow of OLAPDataGrid. Here is the OLAPDataGrid instance we'll be working with in the sample application:

```
<mx:OLAPDataGrid id="musicCatalogOlap_adg" width="400" height="300"/>
```

Figure 33-10 shows what the sample application looks like, and you can view the source in chapter33_example11_olapDataGrid.mxml within the Chapter 33 source code.

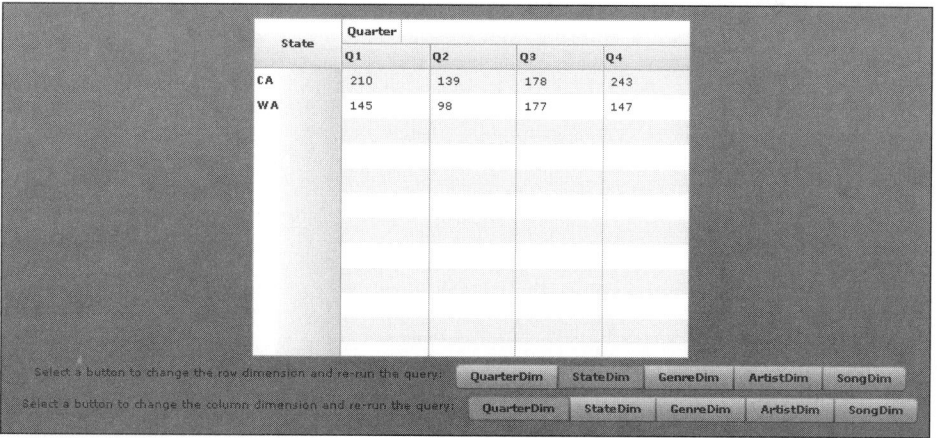

Figure 33-10

Creating an OLAP Schema for Your Data

Before you start thinking about creating your OLAP schema, you need to make sure that you have a data set of objects all with the same structure. This example uses the following structure within the source data:

```
{ artist:'CB4', song:'Straight Out of Locash', genre:'Hip Hop',
    state:'CA', units:'23', quarter:'Q1' }
```

Now that you have the data structure, you need to examine it to figure out the items that can be considered dimensions. A way to think about what to consider a dimension is to think about what an analysis would want to run a report on. For instance:

❑ Units sold by sales quarter and state

❑ Units sold by genre and state

❑ Units sold by state and artist

Looking at the potential reports that might be run, you can consider several potential dimensions: quarter, state, genre, and artist. In actuality, you could probably even consider song as a dimension. The ability to have more than two dimensions is what supports the ability to create our schema, ultimately resulting in an OLAP cube.

In addition to having the dimensions, you need at least one numerical measure to gauge; otherwise, your reporting wouldn't mean anything. Here is the code used to build our OLAP schema:

```
<mx:OLAPSchema>
  <mx:OLAPCube id="musicSales_cube"
      name="FlatSchemaCube"
      dataProvider="{ _myArrayCollection }"
      complete="_onOLAPCubeReady( event )">
    <!-- First Dimension -->
      <mx:OLAPDimension name="QuarterDim">
          <mx:OLAPAttribute name="Quarter" dataField="quarter"/>
          <mx:OLAPHierarchy name="QuarterHeir" hasAll="false">
              <mx:OLAPLevel attributeName="Quarter"/>
          </mx:OLAPHierarchy>
      </mx:OLAPDimension>
    <!-- Second Dimension -->
      <mx:OLAPDimension name="StateDim">
          <mx:OLAPAttribute name="State" dataField="state"/>
          <mx:OLAPHierarchy name="StateHeir" hasAll="false">
              <mx:OLAPLevel attributeName="State"/>
          </mx:OLAPHierarchy>
      </mx:OLAPDimension>
      <!-- Third Dimension -->
    <mx:OLAPDimension name="GenreDim">
        <mx:OLAPAttribute name="Genre" dataField="genre"/>
        <mx:OLAPHierarchy name="GenreHier" hasAll="false">
            <mx:OLAPLevel attributeName="Genre"/>
        </mx:OLAPHierarchy>
    </mx:OLAPDimension>
    <!-- Forth Dimension -->
```

```
        <mx:OLAPDimension name="ArtistDim">
            <mx:OLAPAttribute name="Artist" dataField="artist"/>
            <mx:OLAPHierarchy name="ArtistHier" hasAll="false">
                <mx:OLAPLevel attributeName="Artist"/>
            </mx:OLAPHierarchy>
        </mx:OLAPDimension>
          <!-- Fifth Dimension -->
          <mx:OLAPDimension name="SongDim">
            <mx:OLAPAttribute name="Song" dataField="song"/>
            <mx:OLAPHierarchy name="SongHier" hasAll="false">
                <mx:OLAPLevel attributeName="Song"/>
            </mx:OLAPHierarchy>
          </mx:OLAPDimension>
        <mx:OLAPMeasure name="Units"
            dataField="units"
            aggregator="SUM"/>
    </mx:OLAPCube>
  </mx:OLAPSchema>
```

Note that you define all the `<mx:OLAPDimension/>`, and then the `<mx:OLAPMeasure/>`. Also, within the `OLAPDimensions`, you define an `<mx:OLAPAttribute/>` and an `<mx:OLAPHierarchy/>` of at least one level.

The next thing to do is to `refresh()` the cube. So, in the application `initialize` handler or something to that extent, fire the `refresh()` method of your `OLAPCube` instance. Once the `refresh()` is completed, the `OLAPCube` will fire a `complete` event, which you can use as the distinguishing factor on whether the `OLAPCube` is ready for queries.

> *Running* `refresh()` *and waiting for the cube to dispatch the* `complete` *event before generating and running OLAP queries is absolutely necessary. If you don't wait, you'll receive a runtime exception.*

Creating an OLAP Query for Your Data

Now that the `OLAPCube` instance is ready for queries, you can think about creating your OLAP query. You use `OLAPQuery`, `IOLAPQueryAxis`, and `OLAPSet` objects as your query building blocks. Here is the method to generate and execute the query:

```
private function _generateOLAPQuery( ):void
{
   // create our query
   _olapQuery = new OLAPQuery();

   // deal with our ROW dimension
   _olapRow = _olapQuery.getAxis( OLAPQuery.ROW_AXIS );
   _olapRowSet = new OLAPSet();
   _olapRowSet.addElements( musicSales_cube.
     findDimension( row_tbb.dataProvider[ row_tbb.selectedIndex ].dim ).
     findAttribute( row_tbb.dataProvider[ row_tbb.selectedIndex ].attrib )
     .children );

   // deal with our COLUMN dimension
   _olapColumn = _olapQuery.getAxis( OLAPQuery.COLUMN_AXIS );
   _olapColumnSet = new OLAPSet();
```

```
_olapColumnSet.addElements( musicSales_cube.
    findDimension( column_tbb.dataProvider[ column_tbb.selectedIndex ].dim ).
    findAttribute( column_tbb.dataProvider[ column_tbb.selectedIndex ]
                .attrib ).children  );

// add our sets to their axes
_olapRow.addSet( _olapRowSet );
_olapColumn.addSet( _olapColumnSet );

// run the query
_token = musicSales_cube.execute( _olapQuery );
_token.addResponder( new AsyncResponder( _onSuccess, _onFault ) );
}
```

There are a few things to note from the preceding code. First, during our `addElements()` calls to add dimensions to our row sets, we're using dynamic data. That way the user can regenerate and re-run this query with different dimension combinations in true OLAP style during runtime. Second, the `OLAPCube execute()` method is asynchronous. It's being handled via an `AsyncToken` object and responder methods.

Applying Aggregations to Your OLAPDataGrid

If the OLAP Query was successful in producing an aggregation, then you can assign it as your `OLAPDataGrid dataProvider`. You'll know if the query was successful if the success responder is fired and the `result` object is populated. Here is the code:

```
private function _onSuccess( result:Object, token:Object ):void
{
    // this is a query…sometimes no results might be returned.
    if( result )
    {
        musicCatalogOlap_adg.dataProvider = result as OLAPResult;
    }
}
```

Once the `OLAPDataGrid dataProvider` is set, you will see your new result set and the row and column headers will update accordingly.

Summary

This chapter discussed the advanced data controls that are provided by the Flex framework: `Tree`, `DataGrid`, `AdvancedDataGrid`, and `OLAPDataGrid`. We also discussed item renderers and other customization areas within these controls.

If you would like to do additional reading on any of the advanced data controls discussed, here are the links to them in the Adobe LiveDocs:

- ❑   Tree: http://livedocs.adobe.com/flex/3/html/dpcontrols_8.html
- ❑   DataGrid: http://livedocs.adobe.com/flex/3/html/dpcontrols_6.html

❑ AdvancedDataGrid: `http://livedocs.adobe.com/flex/3/html/advdatagrid_01.html`

❑ OLAPDataGrid: `http://livedocs.adobe.com/flex/3/html/olapdatagrid_1.html`

❑ Item renderer/item editor: `http://livedocs.adobe.com/flex/3/html/cellrenderer_1.html`

Also, here's a link to OLAP for those of you new to the concept: `http://en.wikipedia.org/wiki/OLAP`

The next chapter moves away from data-driven controls and starts looking into how to manage dragging and dropping data within your Flex applications.

34

Drag and Drop in Flex

This chapter examines the capabilities in the Flex framework for dragging and dropping entities from one area of an application to another. The items covered are as follows:

- ❑ Working with the drag and drop-enabled components
- ❑ Working with drag and drop events
- ❑ Adding drag and drop to nonenabled components
- ❑ Additional drag and drop tips

Overview

Dragging and dropping is a very natural way for a user to interact with a modern graphical user interface. Drag and drop support is built into modern operating systems such as Windows and Mac OS. Some of the use cases that come to mind when talking about drag and drop in a modern operating system include:

- ❑ Dragging an item such as an audio file, image, or video file onto a player or viewer.
- ❑ Relocating an item between two different item groups. For instance, you might use classroom management software to drag and drop a student record from one classroom roster to another.
- ❑ Deleting an item by dragging it onto a trash can icon.
- ❑ Rearranging your UI preferences by dragging and dropping around the various display components.

As you can see, dragging and dropping is something that is used very extensively these days, and luckily, drag and drop was factored into the Flex framework. Let's start by taking a look at the components that natively support drag and drop.

Working with Drag and Drop-Enabled Components

Fortunately for you as a Flex developer, there are a number of components that support drag and drop right out of the box. Turning on drag and drop within these components is a very quick and simple thing to do, as long as you know which properties to enable.

One thing to note is that the components that support drag and drop in the Flex framework are list-style components that were designed to represent a set of items. It makes very good sense that you would need to drag and drop from one set to another, for instance, moving a student record from one class roster to another.

Here is a list of these components:

- ❑ `mx.controls.DataGrid`
- ❑ `mx.controls.HorizontalList`
- ❑ `mx.controls.List`
- ❑ `mx.printing.PrintDataGrid`
- ❑ `mx.controls.TileList`
- ❑ `mx.controls.Tree`

So, if you are using any of these components in your applications, their built-in drag and drop capabilities can be turned on by using one of these two properties:

- ❑ `dragEnabled`: A Boolean property; set it to `true` if you would like to be able to drag an object out of the component. When this property is set, the component is known as a *drag initiator*.
- ❑ `dropEnabled`: Another Boolean property. Set this one to `true` if you would like the component to accept items being dropped into it. When this property is set, the component is known as a *drop target*.

The following code examples are excerpts from a classroom roster application. If you'd like to follow along with the complete code, open `DandD_BuiltIn_Example1.mxml` in the Chapter 34 project.

The first thing you do is create two list controls. You can tell from the last property in each of these `List` components that the first one is enabled for dragging and the second one is enabled for dropping, as shown in the code here:

```
<!-- Enabled for Dragging -->
<mx:List id="src_lst"
    width="100%" height="100%"
    dataProvider="{ _classA_AC }"
    dragEnabled="true"/>

<!-- Enabled for Dropping -->
<mx:List id="dest_lst"
    width="100%" height="100%"
    dataProvider="{ _classB_AC }"
    dropEnabled="true"/>
```

Once you build and run your application, you'll see the screen shown in Figure 34-1.

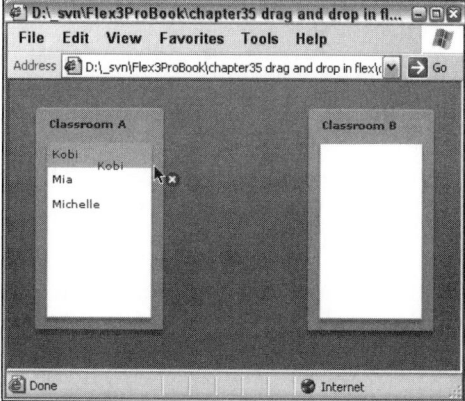

Figure 34-1

Note that in Figure 34-1, when you start dragging the student record out of the first List, you get a red circle with an "X" in it. It is an indicator that informs the user that the data item being dragged cannot be dropped into the display object occupying the current position. Once again, you don't have to do too much work because this indicator is built into the Flex framework drag and drop system.

When you drag the item over the second List inside the Classroom B panel, you'll see the indicator turn into a green circle with a "+" in it. This indicates that you can drop the item into the display object occupying the current position. You can see this in Figure 34-2.

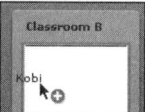

Figure 34-2

Once you let go of the mouse button, you will see the item drop into the dropEnabled List. Feel free to play around with the application some more. Figure 34-3 is a screenshot of what you might see after testing the application for a little while.

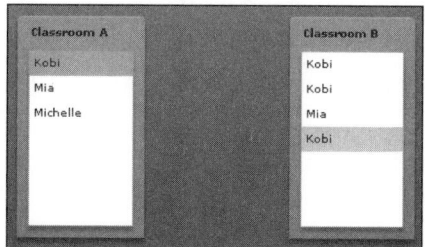

Figure 34-3

A couple things you'll notice at this point:

❑ There's no way to drag an item back into the first List from the second List. In a class roster application, it would be bad if there were no way to move a student back to the first List.

❑ When you drop an item into the second List, it remains in the first List. This is okay in a situation when you can have multiple occurrences of an item, but not when you're dealing with objects that represent named students.

❑ If you try to drag the same item out of the first List into the second List, it will allow you to do so, and the end result is multiple occurrences of that item in the second List. Once again, when building a class roster application this doesn't make sense.

You will work through fixing these issues during the next several sections. Refer to DandD_BuiltIn_ Example2.mxml for the complete source code.

Enabling a List for Drag and Drop

Enabling a List for both drag and drop is a very straightforward procedure. All you need to do is set dragEnabled and dropEnabled to true. Here is the first List, now with support for both drag and drop.

```
<!-- Enabled for Dragging & Dropping -->
<mx:List id="src_lst"
    width="100%" height="100%"
    dataProvider="{ _classA_AC }"
    dragEnabled="true"
    dropEnabled="true"/>
```

One thing you may notice as you're playing around with this application is if a component has these two properties set to true, you can actually reorder items in your component. For instance, if there's an item at the top and you want it to be second from the bottom, setting these two properties to true, will allow this to work.

The downside to this implementation is that you're still copying items. In other words, you'll now see two of the same item in the list after the drag and drop operation. To learn how to move instead of copy, read on.

Moving an Item

As you can tell, by default, when you turn on drag and drop, items are copied. However, there will be plenty of scenarios in which you need to move an item instead. To do this, you need to set an additional property to true. This property is dragMoveEnabled. This property has been set to true in the second list:

```
<!-- Enabled for Dropping & Dragging (Move) -->
<mx:List id="dest_lst"
    width="100%" height="100%"
    dataProvider="{ _classB_AC }"
    dropEnabled="true"
    dragEnabled="true"
    dragMoveEnabled="true"/>
```

The Tree *component is different from all the other components with built-in drag and drop support in that its* dragMoveEnabled *property is set to* true *by default.*

Preventing Duplicates

Now that you've enabled the second list to prevent duplicates, you'll need to do the same for the first list. When all your drag and drop-capable components have their dragMoveEnabled properties set, for the most part, you will prevent duplicates. This means if a user decides to be smart and hold down the Ctrl key while dragging an item, the item will be copied as if you had never set the dragMoveEnabled property. Feel free to run DandD_BuiltIn_Example3.mxml to test this out.

In the case of the application, you simply cannot have a student on the roster for two classes at the same time, so you'll need to figure out how to prevent this Ctrl key feature from copying instead of moving. Unfortunately, there's no dragDisableControlKey property at your disposal. For this reason, you're going to need to learn about the drag and drop events and how to manually handle them.

Working with Drag and Drop Events

Although there is pretty good support for drag and drop built into the Flex framework, there will be times when you need to extend the preexisting capabilities to roll your own functionality. For instance, in the student roster example from the previous section, you found out that even though you turned off the capability to create a copy of a student, the end user could override this by holding down the Ctrl key when moving a student.

When a user is dragging and dropping in a Flex application, DragEvents are dispatched at various points throughout the drag and drop operation. Although there are several more DragEvent types, these are some of the key ones:

- ❑ The user grabs the item to start the drag, and DragEvent.DRAG_START is dispatched.
- ❑ The user moves the item into a drop target, and DragEvent.DRAG_ENTER is dispatched.
- ❑ The user drops the item onto the drop target and DragEvent.DRAG_DROP is dispatched.
- ❑ The user either drops the item on the drop target or cancels the drag operations and the DragEvent.DRAG_COMPLETE is dispatched.

Examining the DragEvent in the language reference, you'll see some very useful properties:

- ❑ The dragInitiator property represents the component from where the data had been dragged.
- ❑ The dragSource property represents the actual data being dragged.

Now that you know which event to handle and the data that's available, you can start thinking about how to prevent the copy operation in your student roster application. The first step is to figure out how to tell the difference between a copy operation and a move operation.

Taking a step back to the beginning of the chapter, you'll notice that all the controls that have built-in drag and drop support are list-style components of some form or fashion. As you will recall from Chapter 32,

"Using the List Components," the list-style components all inherit from ListBase. Keeping that in mind, let's assume for a second that the Flex framework engineers were doing their jobs and implementing things in the right classes.

In other words, you should see this drag and drop support built into ListBase. Thinking about copying versus moving, if you take a look at the event handler named dragDropHandler in the ListBase class for DragEvent.DRAG_DROP, you will see a reference to DragManager.MOVE. Specifically, you will see a line of code comparing DragManager.MOVE to event.action.

Thinking about what you've learned, you might predict that you should try to override something so that the event.action is always set to DragManager.MOVE no matter what, even if the user is holding down the Ctrl key. Taking a look at the events above, the last event to be dispatched is the DragEvent. DRAG_COMPLETE. Assuming that it's at that point that the item is removed from the drag initiator, you should look for the ListBase method that is set as a listener for DragEvent.DRAG_COMPLETE. The listener is the dragCompleteHandler method.

Looking in the Chapter 34 code, you will see the full source code for the new student roster application. It is the DandD_BuiltIn_Example4.mxml application. Feel free to run the application to verify that you can't copy items from one List to the next and within the same List via drag and drop.

To enable the prevent copy functionality, you had to have knowledge of the events mentioned in this section so that you could subclass List and override the dragCompleteHandler method inherited from the ListBase class. Here is the override:

```
override protected function dragCompleteHandler(event:DragEvent):void
{
    // will prevent the ability to copy from one component
    // to another when the CTRL key is held down
    event.action = DragManager.MOVE;

    // will prevent the ability to copy within the
    // same instance when the CTRL key is held down
    event.relatedObject = null;

    super.dragCompleteHandler( event );
}
```

Now that you know how to deal with components that have built-in drag and drop support, let's talk about what is needed to know to build drag and drop support into nonenabled components.

Adding Drag and Drop Support to Nonenabled Components

In the previous section, you learned about the events that are dispatched during drag and drop operations. In addition, DragManager.MOVE was mentioned when discussing move versus copy operations. The DragManager class is something that you're going to want to acquaint yourself with if you want to enable nonenabled components for drag and drop.

When you enable your components for drag and drop, the most important things to know about the DragManager class are:

❑ The method DragManager.doDrag(), which should be called when you'd like to start a drag and drop operation. This method should be called by a drag initiator component on a mouse down event.

❑ The method DragManager.acceptDragDrop(), if you would like your drop target component to accept the data being dragged. If the data is something that the drop target will accept, this method should be called on a DragEvent.DRAG_ENTER event.

The other thing you'll need to know about to enable your components for drag and drop is the DragSource class. This is a class that is used to contain the data that is being dragged and dropped. To access the data you need to know the data type format to retrieve, specified by a string. Here are the three most important DragSource methods:

❑ The DragSource method addData() is used to add data to the DragSource instance that will be used in the DragManager.doDrag() call. By default, the DragDropMoveOnlyList components in the application provide it an Array of objects of type "items" format.

❑ The DragSource method hasFormat() is used to determine if the data is available in a particular format. The format that the DragDropMoveOnlyList objects in the application use is "items".

❑ The DragSource method dataForFormat() is used to retrieve data from the DragSource instance that matches the format you specify. For instance, if you wanted to get data of "items" format, you would call dataForFormat("items").

Setting Up Your Component as a Drag Initiator

Going back to the class roster application, pretend that some of the students can be potentially home-schooled. To meet this feature requirement, you will need a custom component that can handle drag and drop events. The key points will be discussed here; however, you can view the full code in DandD_BuiltIn_Example5.mxml, specifically the custom component DragDropToHomeSchool.mxml.

1. The first thing you do to the DragDropToHomeSchool.mxml component is enable it to start a drag operation by making it a drag initiator. Create an event handler for MouseEvent.MOUSE_DOWN, and in it set up the DragSource data and call DragManager.doDrag(), passing it the component as the dragInitiator, currentSource as the dragSource, and the mouseDown event as the mouse event. Notice how the currentSource.addData() call emulates the passing of data in Array format, using the default "items" format like the DragDropMoveOnlyList objects in your application.

```
private function _onMouseDown( p_evt:MouseEvent ):void
{
    if( _homeSchooledStudents.length )
    {
        var currentSource:DragSource = new DragSource();
        currentSource.addData( [ _homeSchooledStudents.pop() ], "items" );

        DragManager.doDrag( this, currentSource, p_evt );
    }
}
```

2. As a drag initiator, the only other thing important to deal with is the `DragEvent.DRAG_COMPLETE` event. When you deal with this event, you can decrement the count if the student record has been dropped somewhere, or take the data back if the operation has been canceled. Notice in the following handler code that the `DragManager` constant `NONE` is used to represent a type of drag action for use with some conditional logic. (The others are `MOVE`, `COPY`, and `LINK`.) The application code is also making use of some of the `DragEvent` properties. The first one is `action`, which represents what drag action has been requested, and the second one is `dragSource`, which contains the data that has been dragged.

```
private function _onDragComplete( p_evt:DragEvent ):void
{
    if( p_evt.action != DragManager.NONE )
    {
        _totalStudents--;
    }
    else
    {
        _getDropData( p_evt.dragSource );
    }
}
```

Setting Up Your Component as a Drop Target

1. The first event to handle as a drop target is the `DragEvent.DRAG_ENTER` event. Within this handler, `DragManager.acceptDragDrop()` is invoked when the drag and drop data is accepted by the drop target component. Indicate the drop target component by passing in the `this` reference as a parameter to the `acceptDragDrop()` call. Notice also that the `DragEvent` property `drag Initiator` is being used to make sure that the data didn't come from the drop target component before it is accepted.

```
private function _onDragEnter( p_evt:DragEvent ):void
{
    if( p_evt.dragInitiator != this )
    {
        DragManager.acceptDragDrop( this );
    }
}
```

2. The next event that is handled is the `DragEvent.DRAG_DROP` event. This event is dispatched when the user releases the mouse button over a component, indicating that he or she would like the data to be placed in the component. Once again, you can see the use of the event's `dragInitiator` property to disallow dragging within the same drag and drop-enabled component. The format of the data is also being double-checked using `hasFormat()`. Notice, however, that the data is not being retrieved directly as an instance property of `p_evt.dragSource`, but instead is being retrieved via a helper method, `_getDropData()`. This helper method is discussed in the next step.

```
private function _onDragDrop( p_evt:DragEvent ):void
{
    var numberOfStudents:int;

    if( p_evt.dragInitiator != this && p_evt.dragSource.hasFormat( "items" ) )
    {
```

```
numberOfStudents = _getDropData( p_evt.dragSource );
_totalStudents = _totalStudents + numberOfStudents;
        }
    }
```

3. Shown here is the helper method _getDropData(). The reason the logic within this method is not implemented directly in the _onDragDrop() handler is because similar logic is needed in the _onDragComplete() method. The most important line of this helper method is highlighted in the code example below. During this line of code, the actual data is retrieved from p_drag Source by using the dataForFormat() method with a string argument "items" describing the format of the data needed.

```
private function _getDropData( p_dragSource:DragSource ):int
{
    var itemCount:int;
    var dropData:Object = p_dragSource.dataForFormat( "items" );

    for each( var item:Object in dropData )
    {
        _homeSchooledStudents.push( item );
        itemCount++;
    }

    return itemCount;
}
```

Although there's more to DragEvent, the preceding section should have given you a good idea on how to add drag and drop capabilities to any component.

Additional Drag and Drop Tips

Here are a couple other things that will help you further with customizing drag and drop in your applications.

Custom DragSource Formats

In the student roster application, if both a "publicSchoolStudent" and a "homeSchoolStudent" format are needed, add the data by using a custom format string, as follows:

```
currentSource.addData( [ _homeSchooledStudents.pop() ], "homeSchoolStudent" )
```

Custom Drag Proxy

If you run the final example application DandD_BuiltIn_Example5.mxml, you'll notice that when you drag from the DragDropToHomeSchool.mxml component, the image that is dragged along with your mouse is just a translucent canvas. You'll also notice that the image that is dragged along with your mouse when you drag from one of the DragDropMoveOnlyList.as components is a snapshot of the text you dragged out of that List-based component.

The image that gets dragged along with your mouse is called the drag proxy. To customize the drag proxy, you specify an object of type IFlexDisplayObject as the fourth parameter of your DragManager.doDrag() call, as shown here:

```
DragManager.doDrag( this,
                    currentSource,
                    p_evt,
                    iFlexDisplayObjectAsDragImage );
```

If you do decide to use a custom drag proxy, you must make sure to explicitly set a height and width for the image to actually appear.

Maintaining Type Information

When dragging and dropping custom data types, you may lose type information after a drag and drop operation. To maintain your type information, you need to put the [RemoteClass] metadata tag right above the class declaration. Here is an example:

```
package com.wrox
{
    [RemoteClass]
    public class CustomDragDropDataType
    {
        public function CustomDragDropDataType()
        {
        }

    }
}
```

Summary

Drag and drop is a very powerful mechanism that can be utilized in the modern graphical user interface. It's a very natural way for a user to interact with the system. The Flex framework not only supports drag and drop but goes far enough to build in support into some of the standard components. In addition, you can add drag and drop support to your own components relatively easily, along with building in support to selectively allow certain items to be accepted by your components.

Hopefully, you walk away from this chapter armed with the knowledge to build some robust drag and drop functionality into your Flex applications. If you're still thirsty for more, take a look at the Adobe LiveDocs. They can be found at the following link: http://livedocs.adobe.com/flex/3/html/dragdrop_1.html

Up next is a chapter on what AIR has to add to the drag and drop feature set.

35

Drag and Drop in AIR

In the previous chapter, you learned all about drag and drop within a Flex application running inside a web browser. This chapter introduces you to the drag and drop functionality offered within Adobe AIR running on the desktop. In addition to the functionality offered in a traditional Flex-based application, like dragging data between Flex components, AIR offers the ability to drag to and from the operating system or external applications, including other AIR applications.

A developer, with AIR, could drag data from an AIR application into Microsoft Excel, drag photos from the user's desktop into an AIR application, drag links to a web browser, and so forth. Developers are limited by their imagination and by the native clipboard support of their chosen operating system and destination application.

In this chapter, you're going to learn about the `Clipboard` class and types of data it supports, which is essential for understanding what can be done with drag and drop. Then we'll cover everything you need to know about the `NativeDragManager` and its events. Finally, we'll finish off with a sample application for dragging images of various formats to and from an AIR application.

Overview of AIR Drag and Drop

To get data to and from AIR applications, AIR uses a `Clipboard` object found in `flash.desktop.Clipboard` package to transport the data. This is because the operating system's native clipboard is used to make the actual transfer of data to and from AIR. Another way to look at drag and drop as implemented by AIR is that mouse gestures are being used to make cut/copy and paste operations. Think of drag and drop like that, and you'll be well on your way to understanding the innards of how AIR operates with the operating system.

The `NativeDragManager`, located in the same `flash.desktop` package as the `Clipboard` class, coordinates dragging data to and from the application.

Let's look at the `Clipboard` class, since it's the foundation for implementing both drag-in and drag-out operations within an AIR application.

The Clipboard

Before getting into the specifics of the Drag and Drop API, it's necessary to look at the `flash.desktop` `.Clipboard` class, which is only available to AIR. The `Clipboard` is used to transport data into an out of an AIR application. The clipboard facilitates this by being passed from the AIR application through the AIR runtime, eventually communicating with the native operating system's clipboard, making the movement of data from an AIR application to another AIR application, the native OS's file manager, or any external application, like Photoshop, possible.

AIR's `Clipboard` object supports transporting various types of data. The class `flash.desktop.Clipboard` `.ClipboardFormats` defines the constants used to describe the type of data that can be copied to and from the clipboard, as shown in the following table.

Data Type	Clipboard Formats	Data
Bitmap/Image	BITMAP_FORMAT	The raw pixels of an image. Usually the `Bitmap.bitmap Data` associated with a loaded `Image` object.
File(s)	FILE_LIST_FORMAT	A `flash.filesystem.File` that references a physical file on the operating system's filesystem. The file will be covered in more detail in Chapter 45.
Text	TEXT_FORMAT	Any text exposed as a string in ActionScript.
URL	URL_FORMAT	Exposed as raw strings in ActionScript, but that native applications might be able to better interpret the plain text.
HTML	HTML_FORMAT	HTML-formatted string.
Custom String		Custom ActionScript objects that support serialization. Useful only for dragging to external applications developed in AIR or current AIR applications.

Adding Data to the Clipboard

Copying data onto the clipboard first requires accessing a `Clipboard` object, which can be accomplished in one of two ways:

1. Through the `flash.desktop.Clipboard.generalClipboard`, which is a static method on the `Clipboard` singleton that returns access to the operating system's clipboard (as exposed by AIR).

2. Or by creating a new `Clipboard` object that will be passed into the `NativeDragManager`.

Let's stick with the first option for now, and get to the latter when we begin working with the `NativeDragManager`. First, access the static `generalCliboard` method to get at an instance of a `Clipboard`: in this case, AIR exposes it through a `Clipboard` singleton. Next, make a call to `setData`, like so:

```
Clipboard.generalClipboard.setData(ClipboardFormats.BITMAP_FORMAT,
                    Bitmap(image.content).bitmapData, false);
```

The first parameter of `setData` is the type of data being placed on the clipboard. Here, the built-in type `BITMAP_FORMAT` is telling the AIR runtime to expose the data to the operating system's native clipboard in a format that it might know how to deal with like this generic bitmap data. An external program like Microsoft Word will be able to use this data to embed an image in a document. The type can be any of the `ClipboardFormats` from the preceding table.

> *Not all external programs will be able to use bitmap data. Most of the time, one of the other types will work best, such as a URL/File that resolves to an image on the Internet or an image file on the local filesystem.*

The second parameter of `setData` is the actual data to put on the system clipboard, whether it's a `string` of text, a URL, an array of files (or a single file), an `Image` component's `bitmapData`, or a custom entity or value object containing custom properties defining a unique ActionScript data type to your AIR application, like a `CustomerVO` (a value object that holds typed data about a domain entity; see Part X for more information on value objects).

The third parameter is useful for customized objects placed on the clipboard (like `CustomerVO`). When a customized object is placed on the clipboard, it can either be passed around by reference or serialized. When copying a custom object to an external AIR application, the serializable parameter must be set to `true`. Otherwise, the custom object is being passed by reference, and that reference is only available inside the current application.

> *The serializable parameter is ignored when copying all the default clipboard formats to the operating system or external applications. AIR will copy raw data into the native operating system's clipboard.*

Reading Data from the Clipboard

Reading data from the system clipboard requires only a call to `getData`, but it's best to check whether the `Clipboard` class even has data in the right format first with a call to `hasFormat`.

The following code demonstrates reading raw bitmap data off the clipboard and setting a Flex Image component's source property to this image data. (This sample is reading from an event raised by the `NativeDragManager`, which you'll read more about in the next section.)

```
if (Clipboard.generalClipboard.hasFormat(ClipboardFormats.BITMAP_FORMAT )){
  var bmd:BitmapData = BitmapData(event.clipboard.getData(
                            ClipboardFormats.BITMAP_FORMAT));
  image.source= new Bitmap(bmd);
}
```

The call to `hasFormat` is straightforward, passing in one of the default `ClipboardFormat` types to check whether data exists of that type. Here, just check to see if the clipboard has any bitmap data on it. If it does, then let's read that data into the application.

To read the data, call `getData`, telling it what type of data to copy from the clipboard (here it's bitmap). The `bitmapData` now has it's own copy of the data and the easiest thing to do with it is to display it in an image component, but feel free to apply any image filters or any other Flex bitmap manipulation operations at this stage, since it's now just a regular bitmap internal to Flex.

There's an additional parameter in `getData`, specifying the `TransferMode`. It's ignored for all the built-in types and is only valid when copying custom data between AIR applications, which is covered next.

Reading and Writing Custom Data from the Clipboard

You're not limited to using just the built-in types of the `ClipboardFormats`, though. Alternatively, any string could be passed in, creating a custom type that will be available to only AIR applications. For example, an AIR customer relationship management application could enable dragging a custom `CustomerVO` object to an AIR invoicing application or to a Flex component of the current application. If this is the case, your call to `setData` might look like this:

```
Clipboard.generalClipboard.clear();
Clipboard.generalClipboard.setData("customer", CustomerVO, true);
```

First, clear off any potential data that's sitting on the clipboard. This will put the clipboard with a known state and not mix any new data with old. Next, to read custom data from the `Clipboard`, just make a call to `getData`, passing in the string of the name given when placing data on the clipboard. In this case, it's `"customer"`.

```
var customer:CustomerVO = CustomerVO(
                          Clipboard.generalClipboard.getData("customer"),
                          ClipboardTransferModes.CLONE_PREFFERED);
```

In the case of custom data and the clipboard, it'll only be available to the current AIR application. Outside applications most likely won't know how to deal with an ActionScript defined object. However, copying the data to the clipboard could be useful for other AIR applications.

The additional parameter `ClipboardTransferModes.CLONE_PREFFERED` retrieves an actual copy of the data off the clipboard, if available. If it's not available, a reference to the object will be placed on the clipboard. There are a few other `ClipboardTransferMode` parameters available to define preferences for how to copy the custom data off the clipboard: `CLONE_ONLY`, which forces a copy of the data; `ORIGINAL_ONLY`, which returns the object reference; and `ORIGINAL_PREFERRED`, which will return the object reference if it exists (otherwise, it will return copied data).

Make sure to clear the clipboard before writing new data to it, ensuring that all old data is released.

Knowing how the clipboard works and the types of data that can be placed on it will make it easier to understand the next section, where you'll learn to actually drag files from an AIR application.

The NativeDragManager

Now that you've learned about moving data to and from AIR applications with the clipboard, it's time to learn about drag and drop. Drag and drop operations in AIR use the clipboard to transfer data. Usually, a `mouseDown` event will start a drag operation and copy data onto the system clipboard to be made available when the drop action is raised.

The `NativeDragManager` is a static class that oversees all drag and drop operations in an AIR application. It communicates via events to registered targets that wish to have data dropped on them. It also coordinates with source data while it's being dragged around looking for a drop target. The `NativeDragManager` dispatches different events, depending on whether or not the user is dragging data to or from an AIR application.

The Phases of Drag and Drop

All drag and drop operations have three main phases:

❑ **Initiation** — The user initiates the drag operation, usually by holding down the mouse button on a selected Flex component. This initiation could occur from either inside an AIR application, or from an external source.

❑ **Dragging** — The user drags the selected object around the screen, looking for a place to drop it. The `NativeDragManager` will monitor all dragging and communicate with potential targets.

❑ **Dropping** — The user releases the dragged object's data onto a target that is enabled to consume the data.

All drag operations will be initiated from within an AIR application from a call to `NativeDragManager.doDrag()`. This begins all the drag and drop magic in Adobe AIR.

Depending on whether the user is dragging data into or out of an AIR application, the `NativeDragManager` will dispatch various events of type `flash.events.NativeDragEvent` that the developer needs to implement. Let's have a look at these events.

Events Used in Drag-Out Operations

The most common events the developer must implement to support drag-out operations in an AIR application are:

❑ `nativeDragStart`

❑ `nativeDragUpdate`

❑ `nativeDragComplete`

`nativeDragStart` is dispatched when the drag operation starts from a call to `NativeDragManager.doDrag()`, which usually occurs from a `mouseDown` event triggering the beginning of the drag operation. This event isn't dispatched when the drag begins externally, for example from the operating system desktop or an external application like Adobe Photoshop.

`nativeDragUpdate` is continually dispatched while the drag is ongoing. While the user is dragging the selected item around the screen, this event will be fired, notifying the event listener with the mouse's location. Again, this event is only raised from the `NativeDragManager` if the drag is initiated from within the AIR application.

`nativeDragComplete` is dispatched when the selected object is dropped onto a target. This event is only fired if the drag operation begins inside an AIR application. This event isn't dispatched if the drag was initiated externally, just as with the `nativeDragStart` event above.

By implementing these three events, you can provide support to drag data from an AIR application to an external, non-AIR program or operating system.

Events Used in Drag-In Operations

The following events are common events that must be implemented to support dragging data from an external program into an Adobe AIR application.

- ❏ `nativeDragEnter` and `nativeDragOver`
- ❏ `nativeDragExit`
- ❏ `nativeDragDrop`

`nativeDragEnter` and `nativeDragOver` events are dispatched when a Flex component has registered with the `NativeDragManager` to receive drop notifications. For example, you register an `Image` component to listen for `nativeDragEnter` and `nativeDragOver` events when you want that component to be drop-enabled.

`nativeDragExit` is dispatched when a drag operation leaves a potential drop target. Most of the time, the user can ignore this, but this could be handy for implementing different effects to let the user know when they can no longer drop data onto a given component.

`nativeDragDrop` occurs when the mouse button is released and the data being dragged is dropped on the target component. It is in this handler where data would be copied from the clipboard into the target Flex object. For example, bitmap data copied from the clipboard that is dropped onto an image control to display in the AIR application.

This has been a quick introduction to the events that you need to know about when supporting drag and drop, but it's not expected that you understand them fully yet. Let's look at some samples to fully understand how this works.

Dragging Data from an AIR Application

In the first sample shown in Figure 35-1, we're going to show you how to drag an image out of AIR to another application or the desktop.

The application is set up to be a test bed useful for exploring how an AIR application interacts with the operating system when dragging data from it, since drag and drop behavior will vary on each operating system, as well as with each target application.

The Clipboard Data behind an Image

When a user selects an image to drag in an AIR application, there are many ways in which this image can be interpreted by the destination drag target. The image could be thought of as a bitmap (the raw pixels, the 1's and 0's). Alternatively, an image could be a file on the filesystem, such as `image1.png` or `c:\image2.jpg` for PNG and JPEG image files. Images could also be URLs, such as `http://yourwebsite.com/image1.jpg`. How you support what data you make available for dragging data out of an application is up to you, and what data an external application supports is totally out of your control. It's up to you to place the data onto the clipboard in the appropriate format. Some external applications will mange better with bitmap data, some with references to files.

When dragging image data out of AIR, you should treat it as a file reference. Most applications, such as Microsoft Word, an operating system's desktop, or a web browser, all know how to act when a file is dragged into them. And they usually have internal default handlers for those specific file types. In Microsoft Word, when dragging an image file into it, it'll open it and embed the image. Dragging an image file onto the desktop will create a copy of that image file there, and dragging the image into a web browser, such as Firefox, will open and display the image. Fewer programs can deal with actual bitmap data, but Microsoft Word accepts it if you want to experiment with dragging raw bitmap data there.

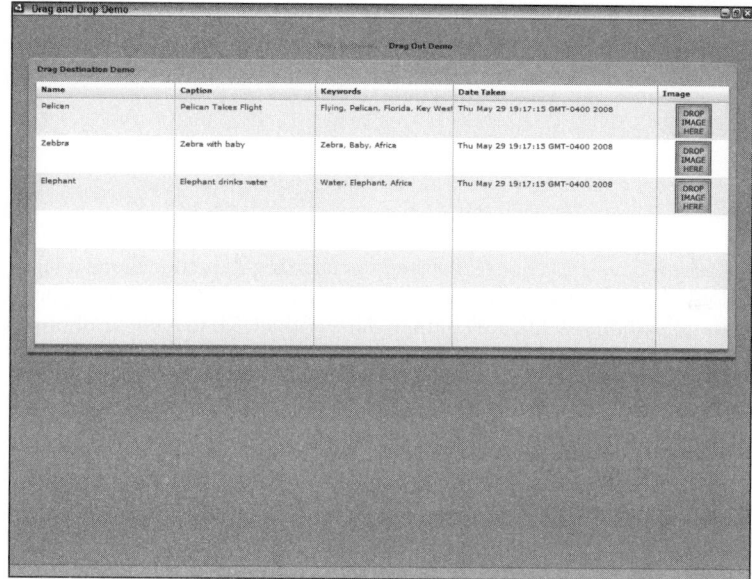

Figure 35-1

The drag-out sample actually shows dragging an image out as three different types: bitmap, file, and URL. This will allow you to experiment with applications you're thinking about supporting with your AIR application. But don't worry. You don't need to decide whether a given drag operation supports only bitmap or file; you can support all of them.

Let's take a look at the code of the drag-out functionality of the Demo drag and drop application, which is in the DragOut.mxml file (only the code for one of the drag sources supporting all clipboard types will be shown for the sake of brevity and clarity).

Dragging data from AIR requires the developer to implement the same basic steps:

1. The developer registers with a Flex component that will be treated as the drag source to listen for all the necessary events that the NativeDragManager will eventually call throughout the process. In the onCompletionComplete event, register for an Image to be the source providing handlers for the following NativeDragManagerEvents: NATIVE_DRAG_____, and NATIVE_DRAG_START.

```
private function onCreationComplete():void
{
    //Register for essential events for drag out operations
```

```
    image.addEventListener(NativeDragEvent.NATIVE_DRAG_START,
                            onDragStart);

    image.addEventListener(NativeDragEvent.NATIVE_DRAG_COMPLETE,
                            onDragComplete);

    image.addEventListener(NativeDragEvent.NATIVE_DRAG_UPDATE,
                            onDragUpdate);
}
```

2. When a user initiates a DRAG, usually by holding the mouse button down, create a Clipboard object, add data for the supported formats, like bitmap, file, URL, text, or all of these.

```
    private function onMouseDown(event:MouseEvent):void
    {
      // Create the clipboard data transfer object
      var clipboardData:Clipboard = new Clipboard();
```

Now that you have a Clipboard object, start adding data to it. Since images can be represented by various clipboard formats, you're going to make available to the clipboard all the formats for maximum flexibility. A file, raw bitmap data, and a URL to a Flickr photo are all placed on the clipboard.

```
      // Adding file data to Clipboard transfer object
      var file:File =
              File.applicationDirectory.resolvePath(PATH_TO_LOCAL_IMAGE);

      clipboardData.setData(ClipboardFormats.FILE_LIST_FORMAT,
                            new Array(file), false);

      // Adding bitmap data to Clipboard transfer object
      clipboardData.setData(ClipboardFormats.BITMAP_FORMAT,
                            Bitmap(image.content).bitmapData, false);

      // Add URL data to Clipboard transfer object
      clipboardData.setData(ClipboardFormats.URL_FORMAT, FLICKR_PHOTO,
                            false);

      // a bitmapPreview for the drag manager.
      var bitmapPreview:Bitmap = new Bitmap(
              Bitmap(image.content).bitmapData.clone());
```

3. Call NativeDragManager.doDrag() to start the notification of data being dragged. (Usually called from a mouseDown event.) Pass in the source (an Image component), the created clipboard data, and a preview for the drag manager. Calling doDrag() will inform the NativeDragManager that a drag operation has begun.

```
      // Start the dragManager
      NativeDragManager.doDrag(image,
                               clipboardData,
                               bitmapPreview.bitmapData);
    }
```

4. NativeDragManger will raise the NATIVE_DRAG_START event, signifying that a drag has begun. Optionally, you could modify the UI during the drag operation here, but supporting this event isn't necessary. Here you're just tracing it, to show that it's raised early on.

```
private function onDragStart(event:NativeDragEvent):void
{
  trace("onDragStart");
}
```

5. While the user continues to drag the data around, the NativeDragManager will continually raise the NATIVE_DRAG_UPDATE event that provides metadata on the current location of the mouse, and the actions allowed, such as copying, linking, or moving the source data.

```
private function onDragUpdate(event:NativeDragEvent):void
{
    trace("onDragUpdate");
}
```

6. Eventually, the user releases the mouse button, raising the nativeDragComplete event. The destination either supports the data or ignores it. When the destination is an external application, it's up to that application to manage the data that was copied onto the native operating system's clipboard in step 1. There's nothing for the AIR developer to do. However, if the drag and drop is inside an AIR application, the NATIVE_DRAG_COMPLETE of the source could potentially need action; for example, if the user were dragging one image from one list box to another, and it should be removed from the first box. See Chapter 34 on intra-Flex drag and drop for more information on this.

```
private function onDragComplete(event:NativeDragEvent):void
{
  if (event.dropAction == NativeDragActions.NONE)
    trace("onDragComplete, drag has been aborted");
  else
    trace("onDragComplete, target is using source as:" +
          event.dropAction);
}
```

There was nothing done in the onDragComplete, but some trace messages have been included so you can use the drag and drop sample application to monitor dragging and dropping information with your specific operating system and application, as each one will behave differently.

That's all there is to it. Give the application a test drive and drag images onto your desktop, web browser, Microsoft Word, Adobe Photoshop, and so forth. Also use different source data types as some external programs will have preferences to different source formats.

When dragging data out of an AIR application, you're at the mercy of the operating system or external application to what data they expect and handle.

Deferred Data

Dragging data out of AIR could potentially be expensive, for example when copying an entire Flex TileList of images into a new directory on the filesystem. You don't want to make available all the data to the clipboard before you know that the user's actually going to drop the data somewhere.

Luckily, instead of placing data on the clipboard by calling `setData`, all you have to do is call `setDataHandler`, passing in a callback function that will be called when the drop target asks for the data. At that point in time, the callback function will copy the data onto the system clipboard.

```
private function onMouseDownDeferred(event:MouseEvent):void
{
    //  This uses a deferred callback that doesn't move the data to the
    //  clipboard until the destination application asks for it.
    var clipboardData:Clipboard = new Clipboard();
    clipboardData.setDataHandler(ClipboardFormats.BITMAP_FORMAT,
                                 deferredBitmapHandler );

    //  Start the dragManager
    NativeDragManager.doDrag(bitmapSourceDeferred ,
                             clipboardData);
}
```

The callback bitmap handler returns the data to be copied from the application:

```
private function deferredBitmapHandler():BitmapData
{
    //  Perform Bitmap transformations or expensive pixel operations here.
    return Bitmap(bitmapSourceDeferred.content).bitmapData;
}
```

Dragging Files to an AIR Application

Developers have more control over the data being dragged into an AIR application than when dragging data to someone else's application. You can inspect the type of data, or the file type that's about to be brought in, and then perform your own parsing of that data. Maybe it's an XML snippet containing data about an image file (including the location), a Microsoft Outlook vCard (which is just a text file with certain tags and the `.vcf` file extension) that you want to support, a link, or a link to a specific site that you want to parse out. You get the idea. When bringing data in, you have total control as to whether you accept it, parse it, manipulate it, and then use it.

The sample application has a tab demonstrating the ability to drag files to an AIR application (shown in Figure 35-2). It supports dropping image files, image URLs, and raw bitmap data onto the labeled targets, so play around with the application on your preferred operating system.

Dragging data into AIR requires the developer to implement the same basic steps:

1. The developer registers a Flex component that will be treated as the drag target (a Flex `HBox` component in this case) to listen for all the necessary events that the `NativeDragManager` will eventually call throughout the process. In the `onCompletionComplete` register for a custom component to be the drag destination, you provide handlers for the following `NativeDragManagerEvents`: `NATIVE_DRAG_EXIT`, `NATIVE_DRAG_OVER`, `NATIVE_DRAG_DROP`, and `NATIVE_DRAG_ENTER`.

```
public function onCreationComplete(evt:Event):void
{
```

```
// Register for Drag and Drop Events
addEventListener(NativeDragEvent.NATIVE_DRAG_ENTER, onDragEnter);
addEventListener(NativeDragEvent.NATIVE_DRAG_DROP, onDragDrop);
addEventListener(NativeDragEvent.NATIVE_DRAG_OVER, onDragOver);
addEventListener(NativeDragEvent.NATIVE_DRAG_EXIT, onDragExit);
}
```

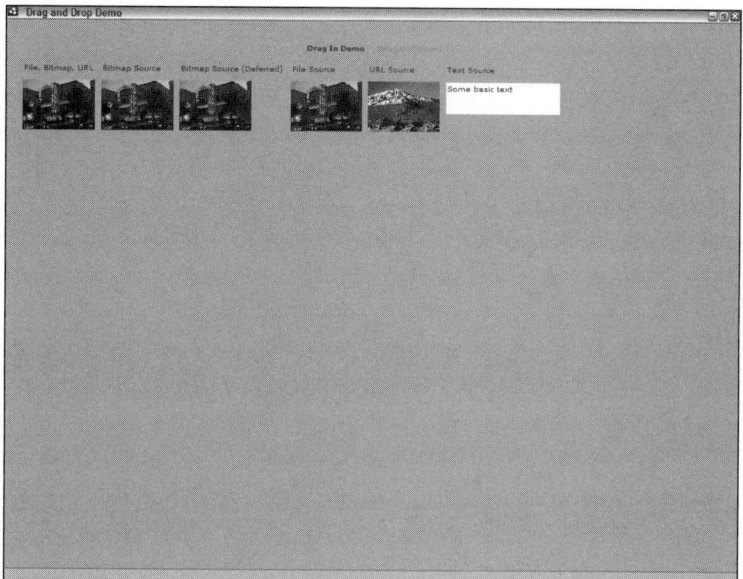

Figure 35-2

2. When the user drags data over the AIR application, the NativeDragManager will be watching it. Once the user drags over the target that has been registered with the NativeDragManager in step 1, the NativeDragManager will raise the NATIVE_DRAG_ENTER event, calling the drop target's onDragEnter handler. The drag handler allows the developer to notify the NativeDragManager whether it can accept the data on the clipboard.

The target drag component we've created here can read data off the system clipboard in Bitmap, File, and URL formats. This is so the end user can drag an image into the application from a variety of external sources: an image file on the filesystem, an image URL from the Web (like Flickr), or even raw bitmap data. Call Clipboard.hasFormat to determine the type of data that's waiting on the clipboard and to provide alternative handlers:

```
private function onDragEnter(e:NativeDragEvent):void
{
    // Allow either BITMAP data or IMAGE File DATA
    if (e.clipboard.hasFormat(ClipboardFormats.BITMAP_FORMAT )){
        // Working with BITMAP Data
        trace("Bitmap Data was dragged in");
```

If the data on the clipboard is valid for our component and we want to accept it, we make a call to `NativeDragManager.acceptDragDrop()`. In this snippet, we're going to accept any bitmap data.

```
            NativeDragManager.acceptDragDrop(this);
    }else if
```

When files are dragged onto the target, make sure they're of a supported image type. Here, we're accepting JPEG and PNG image files, since Flex can render these pretty easily. We don't want to try to render a `.doc` or `.mxml` file as an image!

```
        (e.clipboard.hasFormat(ClipboardFormats.FILE_LIST_FORMAT)){
    var files:Array =
    e.clipboard.getData(ClipboardFormats.FILE_LIST_FORMAT) as Array;
        //e.dropAction
        if(files.length == 1 )
        {
            //  Grab that first File
            var f:File = File(files[0]);

            //  Only Accept Known Image Types:  JPEG, PNG, BITMAP
            if (f.extension == null) return;

            if (f.extension.toUpperCase() == "JPG" ||
                f.extension.toUpperCase() == "PNG" ) {
                trace("A JPEG or PNG file was dragged in");
                //accept the drag action
                NativeDragManager.acceptDragDrop(this);
            }
        }
    }else if (e.clipboard.hasFormat(ClipboardFormats.URL_FORMAT )){
```

Finally, our drop target can also accept URLs. Here, we're blindly accepting any URL, but a more careful developer would probably check the URL for a proper PNG or JPEG file type.

```
        // A URL was dragged in.  This should accept URLS of common
        // image form
          var url:Object =
                    e.clipboard.getData(ClipboardFormats.URL_FORMAT);
        // Should validate URLS of supported image Types:  JPEG, PNG,
          NativeDragManager.acceptDragDrop(this);
        }
    }
}
```

3. When the `NativeDragManager` receives notification of the `acceptDragDrop` from the drop target, it will change the icon being displayed.

4. While the user's mouse is positioned over a registered target, the `NativeDragManager` will continue to dispatch `NATIVE_DRAG_OVER` events to the target until either the user releases the mouse button, or the mouse leaves the drop target area and the `NativeDragManager` dispatches the `NATIVE_DRAG_EXIT` event. The next time the user drags the source data over the drop target, `onDragEnter` will be called again.

5. When the user releases the mouse button over the drop target, the `NativeDragManager.NATIVE _DRAG_DROP` is dispatched, calling the drop target's `onDragDrop` handler, giving the drop target access to the data on the clipboard.

And just as you learned in the previous discussion of the clipboard, a simple call to `getData` retrieves the data from the clipboard. In this implementation, since we can accept either file, URL, or bitmap data, we must manipulate the data into a common format to display in the `Image` component. For bitmap data, just copy it to the `Image`'s source; file and URL data will need to be loaded into the `Image`.

```
private function onDragDrop(e:NativeDragEvent):void
{
  // Perform the Drop Action.
  if (e.clipboard.hasFormat(ClipboardFormats.BITMAP_FORMAT )){
    var bmd:BitmapData =
    BitmapData(e.clipboard.getData(ClipboardFormats.BITMAP_FORMAT));
    imageDrop.source= new Bitmap(bmd);
  }else if
     (e.clipboard.hasFormat(ClipboardFormats.FILE_LIST_FORMAT)){
    // Read the File name off the Clipboard
    var files:Array =
    e.clipboard.getData(ClipboardFormats.FILE_LIST_FORMAT) as Array;
    var f:File = File(files[0]);
    imageDrop.load(f.url);
  }else if (e.clipboard.hasFormat(ClipboardFormats.URL_FORMAT)){
    // Read the URL off the clipboard
    var url:Object =
             e.clipboard.getData(ClipboardFormats.URL_FORMAT);
    imageDrop.load(url);
  }
}
```

Voilà, the image data that you dragged into the AIR application either from a file, a bitmap, or a URL is now rendered in the destination image component.

Summary

In this chapter, you learned about the clipboard, which is the transport used to move data to and from an AIR application with drag and drop. The clipboard supports various types of data. Each has a degree of flexibility in how it can be handled within the confines of different native operating systems and applications.

The `NativeDragManager` controls all drag and drop operations to and from an AIR application, and combined with the clipboard, offers a developer a clean bridge to the desktop from within their AIR application.

The next chapter takes a look at Flex's charting components for building rich, interactive data visualizations.

36

Using the Charting Components

Most of us have heard the saying "a picture is worth a thousand words." Expressing complex data stories can be difficult, verbose, or even ineffective. The goal of data visualization is to negate that difficulty by describing the data story with graphics rather than words. Data visualization in the Flex framework is handled by the Flex charting components.

Although you can practice using the Flex charting components with the watermarked components available in Flex Builder Standard, you will need Flex Builder Professional if you want access to nonwatermarked charting components.

Understanding Charting

Before you can start using the charting components effectively, you need to understand the building blocks that make up the Flex charting components. Let's start by taking a look at how you can assign data to a chart.

Assigning Data to a Chart

Flex charting components work like many of the other Flex framework components when it comes to assigning data. The Flex charting components have a standard `dataProvider` property, which is meant to be bound to an `ArrayCollection`. We'll be discussing chart types in the next portion of this chapter, but long story short, there are different types of charts and they may require different data structures for the objects within the `ArrayCollection`.

The first chart type that we'll be discussing is an area chart. This type of chart uses a data structure similar to the majority of the chart types. Here is an example of a data provider that will work with most of the charts. You can see it in the first example, `chapter36_example1_areaChart.mxml`, in the Chapter 36 source code.

```
// set up our chart data
_chartDP = new ArrayCollection();
_chartDP.addItem( { quarter:1, shooter:1000, racing:400, rpg:550 } );
_chartDP.addItem( { quarter:2, shooter:875, racing:230, rpg:600 } );
_chartDP.addItem( { quarter:3, shooter:920, racing:310, rpg:512 } );
_chartDP.addItem( { quarter:4, shooter:750, racing:130, rpg:489 } );
```

Once you have populated your data, it can be bound to the chart in a standard manner, as this snippet illustrates:

```
<mx:AreaChart id="gameSales_chrt" type="stacked"
    dataProvider="{ _chartDP }">
```

For the most part, you can stick to this data structure, but we'll call out when the structure needs to be different as we move through and discuss the various chart types.

Chart Types

Before you put a chart into your Flex application, you will need to take a second to determine the type of chart that will most effectively describe the data in the manner that you need. In other words, the type of chart that's effective at showing product sales would be a different kind of chart than the type of chart that shows the history of a stock's selling price on the stock exchange. Fortunately, the Flex charting components come in nine different flavors.

Area Charts

An area chart can be used when you want to compare multiple sets of data. In an area chart, the contrast between the data sets is emphasized by the differences in the area fills for each set. There are three types of area charts:

❑ **Stacked** — This type of area chart stacks the series on top of each other. As shown in Figure 36-1, this shows how each series makes up the total.

❑ **100%** — This type is similar to stacked, but instead of representing a total, it shows how each series makes up a percentage of the total.

❑ **Overlaid** — In an overlaid area chart, each series is started at a baseline point. You don't use this type to see how they make up the whole; instead, you use it to compare the data series values side by side.

The `chapter36_example1_areaChart.mxml` example application used to produce the screenshot for Figure 36-1 can be found in the Chapter 36 source code. Here is a snippet of the actual charting code portion of the example:

```
<!-- defining the chart -->
<mx:AreaChart id="gameSales_chrt"
    type="stacked"
    dataProvider="{ _chartDP }">

    <!-- Setting our Axis/Axes -->
    <mx:horizontalAxis>
```

```
        <mx:CategoryAxis categoryField="quarter" title="Sales Quarter" />
    </mx:horizontalAxis>

    <!-- Set up our data series -->
    <mx:series>
            <mx:AreaSeries yField="shooter"
                displayName="First Person Shooter" form="segment" />
            <mx:AreaSeries yField="racing"
                displayName="Racing Simulation" form="segment" />
            <mx:AreaSeries yField="rpg"
                displayName="Role Playing Game" form="segment" />
    </mx:series>
</mx:AreaChart>

<!-- Set up the legend for the chart -->
<mx:Legend dataProvider="{ gameSales_chrt }" direction="horizontal" />
```

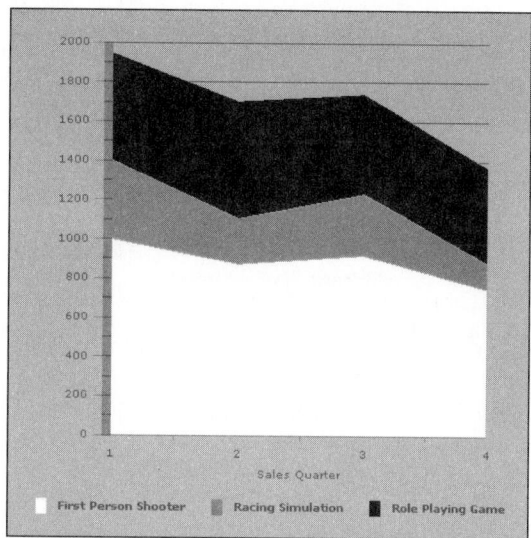

Figure 36-1

We'll discuss the <mx:series/> block in the next section, but it's worth pointing out that the children of <mx:series/> are rendered from top down. In other words, in the preceding code, the shooter <mx:AreaSeries/> will be rendered, followed by the racing simulation <mx:AreaSeries/> and then the RPG <mx:AreaSeries/>.

Based on this behavior, be aware that if you set up your area chart to be type "overlaid", if one of the series children defined earlier in the <mx:series/> block, such as the shooter <mx:AreaSeries/> in the preceding example, has values that are consistently less than a series child defined lower in the <mx:series/> block, such as the RPG <mx:AreaSeries/>, the series child that is rendered first may be completely covered up by the lower series child.

If you want to show all series children at all times, you can set the alpha property of the <mx:AreaSeries/> children to something less than one (such as .5).

Bar Charts

The bar chart is used to compare multiple sets of data, but unlike an area chart, a bar cart uses the width of the horizontal lines representing each data set as a way of comparing the values. Like the area chart, the bar chart has stacked, 100%, and overlaid types, but the bar chart also has the clustered type. Figure 36-2 shows a clustered bar chart representing the same video game sales data as the area chart in the previous figure.

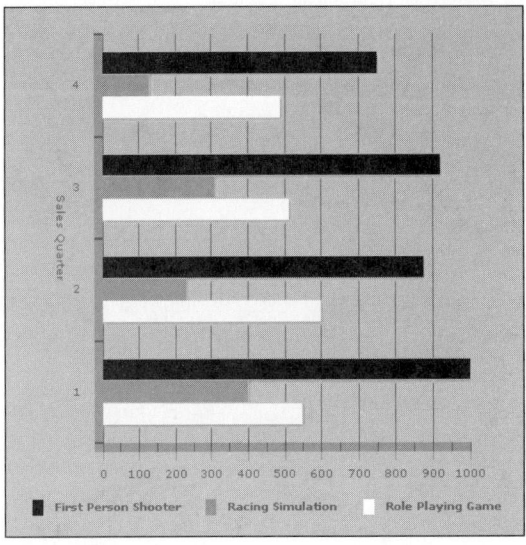

Figure 36-2

Here is the accompanying code for the chart shown in Figure 36-2. The full source code can be referenced in `chapter36_example2_barChart.mxml`.

```
<!-- defining the chart -->
<mx:BarChart id="gameSales_chrt"
    type="clustered"
    dataProvider="{ _chartDP }">

    <!-- Setting our Axis/Axes -->
    <mx:verticalAxis>
        <mx:CategoryAxis categoryField="quarter" title="Sales Quarter" />
    </mx:verticalAxis>

    <!-- Set up our data series -->
    <mx:series>
        <mx:BarSeries yField="quarter" xField="shooter"
            displayName="First Person Shooter" />
        <mx:BarSeries yField="quarter" xField="racing"
            displayName="Racing Simulation" />
        <mx:BarSeries yField="quarter" xField="rpg"
            displayName="Role Playing Game" />
    </mx:series>
```

```
    </mx:BarChart>

    <!-- Set up the legend for the chart -->
    <mx:Legend dataProvider="{ gameSales_chrt }" direction="horizontal" />
```

In the preceding example, you can see that a difference between the area chart example and this one is that we're now using the "clustered" type. Also, we moved from an <mx:horizontalAxis/> to an <mx:verticalAxis/>. Finally, we've changed the series types from <mx:AreaSeries/> to <mx:BarSeries/>. Although each type of chart supports its own types, axes, and series, for the most part the MXML format of hooking up a Flex charting component to your application follows a pretty standard procedure, making them pretty easy to swap out.

Bubble Charts

The bubble chart uses different-sized bubbles to describe its data. It is a great chart for showing how net profits are affected by varied amounts of gross profits and expenses (see Figure 36-3).

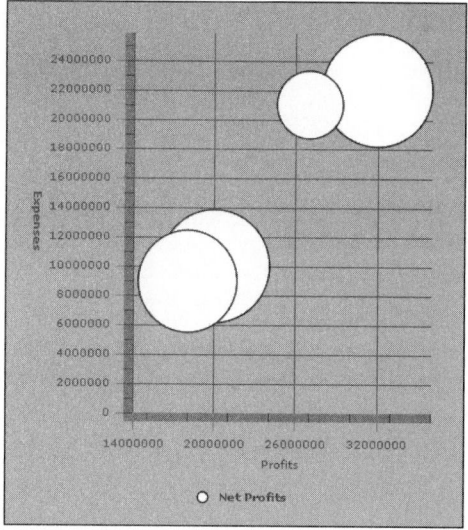

Figure 36-3

Bubble charts require a different type of object structure in their dataProvider data than other charts such as the area chart or bar chart. Here's what data geared toward a bubble chart might look like:

```
    // set up our chart data
    _chartDP = new ArrayCollection();
    _chartDP.addItem( { quarter:1, profits:20000000, expenses:10000000,
        netprofit:10000000 } );
    _chartDP.addItem( { quarter:2, profits:18000000, expenses:9000000,
        netprofit:9000000 } );
    _chartDP.addItem( { quarter:3, profits:32000000, expenses:22000000,
        netprofit:10000000 } );
    _chartDP.addItem( { quarter:4, profits:27000000, expenses:21000000,
        netprofit:6000000 } );
```

The code to generate the chart shown in Figure 36-3 can be found in `chapter36_example3_bubble Chart.mxml`.

Candlestick Charts

The candlestick chart is a very good choice for describing stocks and trading. It was designed to show you a stock's open, close, high, and low values in a very concise manner. Figure 36-4 illustrates a candlestick chart that simulates the value of a stock over a five-day period.

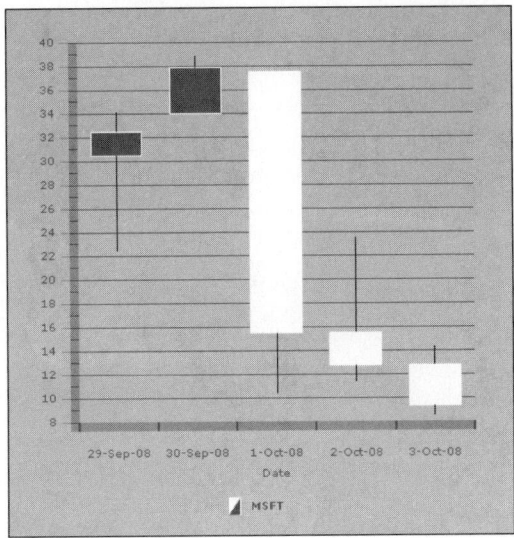

Figure 36-4

The code for the chart show in Figure 36-4 is in `chapter36_example4_candlestickChart.mxml` of the Chapter 36 source code. Once again, the data provider structure deviates from the structure described in the "Assigning Data to a Chart" section. Here is the structure you would use for a candlestick chart data provider:

```
// set up our chart data
_chartDP = new ArrayCollection();
_chartDP.addItem( { date:"29-Sep-08", high:34.10, low:22.39, open:30.45,
        close:32.43 } );
_chartDP.addItem( { date:"30-Sep-08", high:38.87, low:34.00, open:32.43,
        close:37.50 } );
_chartDP.addItem( { date:"1-Oct-08", high:37.52, low:10.32, open:37.50,
        close:15.47 } );
_chartDP.addItem( { date:"2-Oct-08", high:23.54, low:11.32, open:15.47,
        close:12.74 } );
_chartDP.addItem( { date:"3-Oct-08", high:14.32, low:8.43, open:12.74,
        close:9.32 } );
```

Column Charts

The column chart is very similar to the bar chart; the difference is that the lines that represent the sets of data are vertical columns rather than horizontal bars. The column chart is illustrated in Figure 36-5.

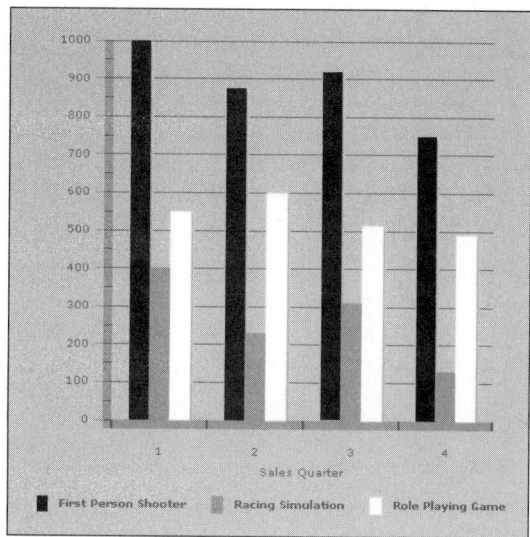

Figure 36-5

You can view the source code for the column chart in `chapter36_example5_columnChart.mxml`.

HighLowOpenClose (HLOC) Charts

Like the candlestick chart, the HighLowOpenClose chart can be used to show the history of a security's value on the market. Also, the data provider structure is not the typical structure, but it is the same as the candlestick chart's data structure. The sample data structure and code for the HLOC chart can be found in `chapter36_example6_HLOCChart.mxml`. Figure 36-6 shows what a HLOC chart looks like.

Line Charts

The line chart is similar to the area chart; the difference is that fills are not used to visualize the differences between the sets of data as in the area chart. Instead, differences are indicated by how high or low the lines are that represent each set of data in the chart. Figure 36-7 illustrates a line chart.

The source code for the chart shown in Figure 36-7 is in `chapter36_example7_lineChart.mxml`. If you take a look at the `<mx:series/>` code block, you will see that the form of the `<mx:LineSeries/>` children is set to `"segment"`.

```
<mx:LineSeries yField="shooter" displayName="First Person Shooter"
    form="segment" />
```

The `LineSeries` has many different types of forms: `curve`, `horizontal`, `reverseStep`, `segment`, `step`, and `vertical`. You might want to play around with them to see the different ways that the renderer for the `<mx:LineSeries/>` can draw them.

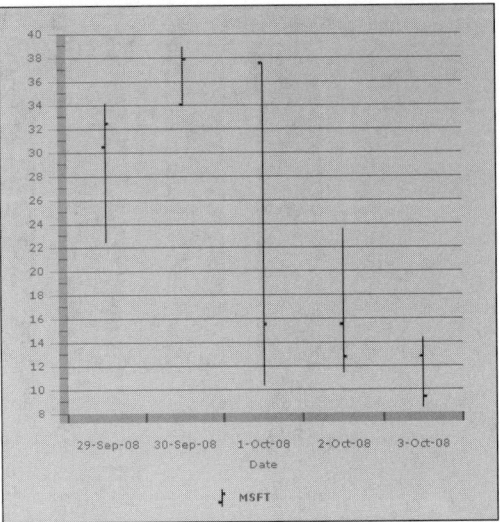

Figure 36-6

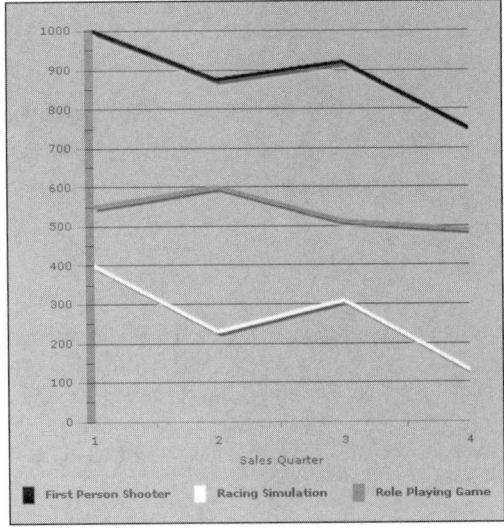

Figure 36-7

Pie Charts

A pie chart, shown in Figure 36-8, is very good at describing what part of a whole each set of data takes up. It is a perfect graph for showing percentages and is often used in conjunction with some of the other chart types to show how the data set is distributed at a single point in time.

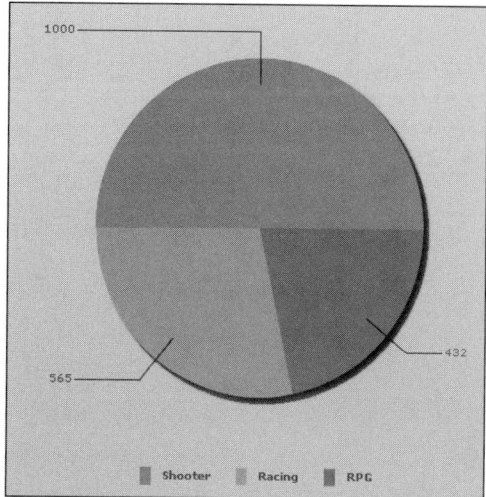

Figure 36-8

As you can see, a pie chart provides a much different style of visualization than most of the other charts. Producing a pie chart requires implementing code in a different manner than for most other charts. You can find the code in `chapter36_example8_pieChart.mxml`. Here is the portion used to instantiate and configure the pie chart:

```
<!-- defining the chart -->
<mx:PieChart id="gameSales_chrt"
    dataProvider="{ _chartDP }"
    showDataTips="true">

    <!-- Set up our data series -->
    <mx:series>
            <mx:PieSeries
                    nameField="genre"
                    field="quarter1"
                    labelPosition="callout" />
    </mx:series>
</mx:PieChart>
```

Also, notice the structure of the `dataProvider` data required by a pie chart is different from the structure that was illustrated in the "Assigning Data to a Chart" section earlier. Here is the structure that works well with the pie chart. It is also the one you will see in the `chapter36_example8_pieChart.mxml` sample application.

```
// set up our chart data
_chartDP = new ArrayCollection();
_chartDP.addItem( { genre:"shooter", quarter1:1000, quarter2:932,
        quarter3:845, quarter4:663 } );
_chartDP.addItem( { genre:"racing",  quarter1:565,  quarter2:875,
        quarter3:732, quarter4:432 } );
_chartDP.addItem( { genre:"rpg",     quarter1:432,  quarter2:743,
        quarter3:531, quarter4:289 } );
```

Plot Charts

Plot charts are used to visualize data based on a distribution of plot points. In a way, you can think of a plot chart as similar to the way that you would place a component on the stage using x and y coordinates. Plot charts are good for visualizing two pieces of data and how they correlate (for instance, number of movie-goers based on ticket price). Figure 36-9 illustrates a plot chart.

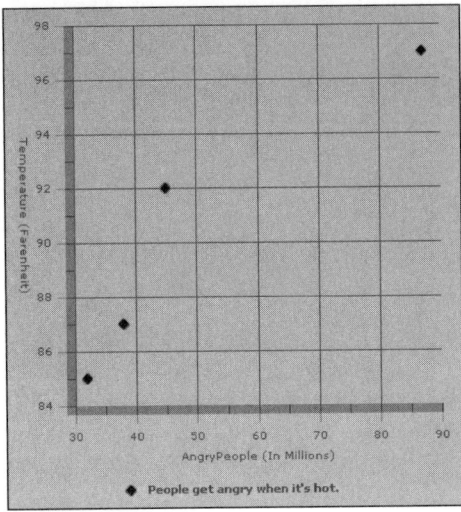

Figure 36-9

Since a plot chart is used to map two pieces of data, the `dataProvider` structure that's best suited for use with a plot chart is unique. Here is an example of an object structure geared toward use with the plot chart:

```
// set up our chart data
_chartDP = new ArrayCollection();
_chartDP.addItem( { temperature:85, angryPeople:32 } );
_chartDP.addItem( { temperature:87, angryPeople:38 } );
_chartDP.addItem( { temperature:92, angryPeople:45 } );
_chartDP.addItem( { temperature:97, angryPeople:87 } );
```

You can view the code for the Figure 36-9 plot chart in the `chapter36_example9_plotChart.mxml` file.

Chart Axes

Most of the chart types have vertical and horizontal axes to describe the vectors being used for data visualization. For instance, some of the most common vectors you see in charts are: time, quantity, temperature, cost, and date. The type of data you are describing will tell you which style of axis to use.

Pie charts don't use chart axes.

Axis Types

When defining chart axes in your code, you will need to take the type of data you want to represent on a particular axis into account. Based on the type of data you want to represent, you can choose from the following axis types:

❑   CategoryAxis — Used when the type of data you would like to describe is textual in nature. For instance, an axis with the values: "Quarter 1," "Quarter 2," "Quarter 3," and "Quarter 4."

❑   LinearAxis — Used when you want to plot out standard numerical data. For instance, if you want to describe an axis that spans a range of 1000–10,000.

❑   LogAxis — Like the LinearAxis, the LogAxis plots numerical data on the axis. The difference is the range is incremented logarithmically.

❑   DateTimeAxis — Used when you would like to plot a date or time range on your axis.

Customizing Your Axis Label

All the axis classes described previously have a labelFunction property that you can take advantage of to override their display label. Take, for instance, the CategoryAxis. When running chapter36_example10.mxml, notice that the labels for the sales quarter show up as "1," "2," "3," and "4." You would prefer they be labeled "Q1," "Q2," "Q3," and "Q4." Making this change will require a labelFunction:

1.   First, define labelFunction:

```
private function _axisLabelFunc( categoryValue:Object
                               ,previousCategoryValue:Object
                               , axis:CategoryAxis
                               , categoryItem:Object ):String
{
   return 'Q' + String( categoryValue );
}
```

When applied, this labelFunction will run for each item in the dataProvider. The categoryValue parameter represents the data field that the CategoryAxis is using from the dataProvider.

2.   Next, apply labelFunction using the labelFunction property of the CategoryAxis:

```
<mx:CategoryAxis id="quarter_ca"
  categoryField="quarter"
  title="Sales Quarter"
  labelFunction="_axisLabelFunc" />
```

Now when you run chapter36_example10.mxml, you will see that the labels on the horizontal axis display the corrected values.

Chart Series

Without a chart series, chart visualizations are useless. The series represents the data that is being visualized on the chart. For instance, a series could represent the number of video game sales over the course of a year. Charts can have one to many series defined. For instance, if you were plotting video game sales over the course of a year in three different states, you would have three chart series defined.

Series Types

There are many different chart series classes in the Flex Charting API. For the most part, you can be safe in assuming that a specific chart type will have a corresponding series type. As an example, if you were using an `<mx:BarChart />`, you could add your data via a `<mx:BarSeries />`. Although we're not going to go into explicit detail on every series available, here is a list of them, each with a quick example:

❑ AreaSeries

```
<mx:AreaSeries yField="shooter" displayName="FP Shooter" form="segment" />
```

❑ BarSeries

```
<mx:BarSeries yField="quarter" xField="shooter" displayName="FP Shooter" />
```

❑ BubbleSeries

```
<mx:BubbleSeries xField="profits" yField="expenses" radiusField="netprofit"
    displayName="Net Profits"/>
```

❑ CandlestickSeries

```
<mx:CandlestickSeries highField="high" lowField="low" openField="open"
    closeField="close" displayName="MSFT" />
```

❑ ColumnSeries

```
<mx:ColumnSeries xField="quarter" yField="shooter" displayName="FP Shooter" />
```

❑ HLOCSeries

```
<mx:HLOCSeries highField="high" lowField="low" openField="open" closeField="close"
    displayName="MSFT" />
```

❑ LineSeries

```
<mx:LineSeries yField="shooter" displayName="FP Shooter" form="segment" />
```

❑ PieSeries

```
<mx:PieSeries nameField="genre" field="quarter1" labelPosition="callout" />
```

❑ PlotSeries

```
<mx:PlotSeries xField="angryPeople" yField="temperature"
    displayName="People get angry when it's hot."/>
```

You can see the various series classes in action when looking at the charting code in the chart types section earlier in this chapter or when viewing examples 1–9 in the Chapter 36 source code.

Chart Data Tips

If the feature is enabled, when a user interacts with a Flex chart, as they hover over the data points, they will see a little mouse tooltip describing the data at the point they are hovering over. This tooltip is called a data tip. An example of a data tip is shown here in Figure 36-10, highlighting that the racing game genre accounts for 28.3% of sales.

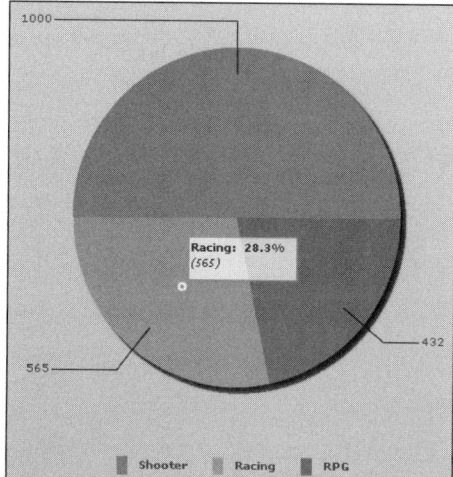

Figure 36-10

Data tips are disabled by default with Flex charting components, To enable data tips in a chart, you set the charts showDataTips property to true. Here is a snippet illustrating this taken from chapter36_example8_pieChart.mxml:

```
<mx:PieChart id="gameSales_chrt"
    dataProvider="{ _chartDP }"
    showDataTips="true">
```

If you find yourself needing to customize the information displayed in the chart data tip, you can make use of the dataTipFunction property in your Flex charting component. See the Flex language reference for more information.

Chart Legends

In many cases, it may not be immediately obvious what each data series within a chart represents. The Flex charting components support adding a legend to your chart to help describe each series. A chart legend is similar to the one you might see on a road map. You add the legend to your chart by specifying <mx:Legend/> and binding its dataProvider property to the chart.

Looking at Figure 36-10 from the last section, you can see the legend at the bottom, mapping the colors in the pie chart to their corresponding data series: "shooter," "racing," or "RPG." This legend was added to the application via the following line of code:

```
<mx:Legend dataProvider="{ gameSales_chrt }" direction="horizontal" />
```

In this snippet, the chart that the legend was associated with goes by the id of gameSales_chrt. You can see this code in action through chapter36_example8_pieChart.mxml in the Chapter 36 source code.

Runtime Chart Interaction

One of the most powerful features of charts in the Flex framework is the ability to interact with them as the application is running. For instance, when we mentioned data tips earlier, those are data summaries that display in context when a user mouses over points of interest within a chart. There are other ways to handle user interaction and programmatic interaction.

Handling User Interaction

Thanks to the ancestor of all Flex chart types, the `mx.charts.chartClasses.ChartBase` class, Flex charts inherit the ability to handle the user mouse click and distinguish whether or not the user clicked on a valid data point or just on an empty region of the chart.

When the user clicks on an empty region of the chart, the chart will dispatch one of these two events in the `mx.charts.events` package:

- ❏ `ChartEvent.CHART_CLICK`
- ❏ `ChartEvent.CHART_DOUBLE_CLICK`

If a valid data point exists where the user clicked or interacted with the mouse, then the chart will dispatch an `mx.charts.events.ChartItemEvent`. The specific event type will be one of the following:

- ❏ `MOUSE_CLICK_DATA`
- ❏ `ITEM_DOUBLE_CLICK`
- ❏ `ITEM_MOUSE_DOWN`
- ❏ `ITEM_MOUSE_MOVE`
- ❏ `ITEM_MOUSE_UP`
- ❏ `ITEM_ROLL_OUT`
- ❏ `ITEM_ROLL_OVER`

After you configure a listener for one of these event types, you can handle the chart specific event like any other event you handle in your Flex application.

Programmatic Interaction

Anything you can do in MXML can be done in ActionScript. This still holds true when working with Flex charting components. Interacting with an instance of one of the Flex charting components can be done using the component's API via ActionScript. For instance, if you wanted to swap the data view driving a pie chart programmatically at runtime, you could do it with ease using the following steps.

1. Since you're swapping the data view driving a pie chart, you'll need to make sure that the `PieSeries` in the `PieChart` has an `id`:

   ```
   <mx:PieSeries id="salesQuarters_ps"
       nameField="genre" field="quarter1" labelPosition="callout"
       showDataEffect="{ zoomChartData }">
   ```

2. Now that you've verified that you can access the `PieSeries` programmatically, you will choose a way to initiate the programmatic interaction. In this case, you're going to use an `<mx:Button/>` click handler to change the `field` in the `dataProvider` object that the `PieSeries` is using to generate the pie chart view.

```
<mx:Button label="Q2 Sales Data"
  click="salesQuarters_ps.field = 'quarter2'"/>
```

As you can see, when the user clicks the button, you'll programmatically reset the `PieSeries` field to `"quarter2"`, causing the `PieChart` to refresh and display the wedges that represent the 2nd quarter sales data. Feel free to view the full source code in the `chapter36_example11.mxml` file.

Customizing a Chart's Look and Feel

There are many different ways that you can customize the look and feel of a Flex charting component. The options range from setting stroke widths to modifying renderers on up to using effects during data transitions. Although there are simply too many customizations to discuss in the span of this chapter, here are a few.

Custom Renderers

You can tweak some of the renderers in the charting API. For instance, if you want to tweak the strokes of one of the axes, you customize the renderers for that axis. The following example customizes some strokes of a horizontal axis. The full source is in `chapter36_example10.mxml`.

1. Give your axis an `id`. In this case, use `<mx:CategoryAxis/>` and name it `"quarter_ca"`.

```
<mx:CategoryAxis id="quarter_ca"
  categoryField="quarter"
  title="Sales Quarter"
  labelFunction="_axisLabelFunc" />
```

2. Define the axis renders block. In this case, you're styling a horizontal axis, so use `<mx:horizontalAxisRenderers/>`.

3. Populate the `<mx:horizontalAxisRenderers/>` block with the renders you would like to customize — here, it's an `<mx:AxisRender/>`.

4. When you specify the `<mx:AxisRender/>`, make sure to bind its axis property to the `id` of the axis you want to customize. In this case, you're customizing `"quarter_ca"` from step one.

5. Populate the `<mx:AxisRender/>` with any stroke customizations you would like. In this case, you're making the `tickStroke` a little thicker with a red color. You're also making the `axisStroke` really thick, partially transparent with a grayish color.

Here is the completed code for steps 2–5:

```
<mx:horizontalAxisRenderers>
 <mx:AxisRenderer
        axis="{ quarter_ca }">
        <mx:tickStroke>
```

```
                  <mx:Stroke weight="3" alpha="1" color="0xFF0000"/>
            </mx:tickStroke>
            <mx:axisStroke>
                  <mx:Stroke weight="5" alpha=".75" color="0xCCCCCC"/>
            </mx:axisStroke>
      </mx:AxisRenderer>
    </mx:horizontalAxisRenderers>
```

Styling

Sometimes the only way to get the chart to look the way you want it to is by styling it. The following example customizes the colors for each of the wedges of the pie chart. The full source code can be found in chapter36_example11.mxml.

1.   First, add an array of <mx:SolidColor /> instances to the fills property of the PieSeries:

```
<mx:PieSeries id="salesQuarters_ps"
nameField="genre" field="quarter1" labelPosition="callout"
showDataEffect="{ zoomChartData }">
<!-- Customize the colors -->
<mx:fills>
    <!-- This goes top-down just like in the data provider -->
        <mx:SolidColor color="0xFF0000" /> <!-- "shooter" color -->
        <mx:SolidColor color="0x00FF00" /> <!-- "racing" color -->
        <mx:SolidColor color="0x0000FF" /> <!-- "rpg" color -->
</mx:fills>
</mx:PieSeries>
```

As you can see, we specify one <mx:SolidColor/> instance for each wedge of the pie chart. The top-down order of these instances will match the order of the items in the dataProvider of the pie chart.

Effects

When you load new data into a chart, you may notice that transitions within the chart seem very abrupt. If you would like to smooth out those transitions and improve the user experience, you can make use of one of the three built-in effects available for Flex charts:

❑   SeriesInterpolate — An effect used to morph the old data set into the new data set.

❑   SeriesSlide — The SeriesSlide effect is used to slide the old data out as the new data is slid in.

❑   SeriesZoom — This effect uses zooming mechanisms to transition the data.

Here is an example that makes use of the SeriesZoom effect, taken from chapter36_example11.mxml:

1.   First, define the effect instance:

```
<mx:SeriesZoom id="zoomChartData" duration="1000"/>
```

2. Next, assign the chart effect to the appropriate event. In this case, you want this effect to run when new data is shown within the `<mx:PieSeries/>`. To do this, use the property `showDataEffect`:

```
<mx:PieSeries id="salesQuarters_ps"
  nameField="genre" field="quarter1" labelPosition="callout"
  showDataEffect="{ zoomChartData }" />
```

Now when you run `chapter36_example11.mxml`, you will see the `SeriesZoom` effect whenever you click a button to show the sales data of a particular quarter.

Summary

This chapter discussed the Flex charting components available in Flex Builder Professional. The Flex charting components are a perfect solution to the problem of visualizing your data quickly and efficiently. In addition to making many different types of charts available, the Flex Charting API was built with extensibility and customization in mind. This makes it very easy for a developer to build highly customized visualization applications on top of the built-in Charting API.

If you would like to do additional reading on the Flex Charting Components, here is the link to the Adobe LiveDocs: `http://livedocs.adobe.com/flex/3/html/Part1_charting_1.html`

The next chapter examines how the Flex 3 platform supports globalized applications for use in a worldwide context.

37

Resource Bundles and Data Localization

This chapter describes how Flex 3 supports properties files and resource bundles. The core focus will be on the benefits that these two features provide for internationalizing and localizing your Flex applications. The topics that will be covered include:

❑ Globalizing Flex applications (internationalization and localization)

❑ Loading resources at runtime

❑ Globalizing AIR applications

Overview

In this increasingly connected global Internet community, it is becoming very important to think about supporting multiple languages in your Flex and AIR applications. Even if you're not thinking about supporting multiple languages during the initial release of your application, it's worth considering building in the support up front so that you will not have to retrofit multilanguage support in during subsequent releases. As an added incentive, it's worth noting that building in multilingual support in your application can help with separating your copy from your code.

The process of separating your application code from the copy and supporting assets for each language is known as *internationalization*, or *i18n* for short. By building i18n support into your application, you are enabling it to add support in for new languages without having to change your application code. A proper i18n-enabled application will not have any locale-specific information hard-coded into it.

The process of adding in support for specific locales is called *localization* , or *L10n* for short. You can think of a locale as a combination of a language and a country — for instance, English in the

United States, and English in Britain are two different locales. There are many aspects that allow you to distinguish one locale from another. Here is a quick list of some of the most common ones:

❑ When the language is the same, differences in the way words are spelled and used

❑ Character encoding

❑ Differences in language

❑ Differences in currency symbols

❑ Differences in the way numbers and dates are formatted

❑ Cultural differences in what is deemed appropriate

When your application supports both i18n (internationalization) and L10n (localization), it implicitly supports (g11n) globalization. A properly globalized application will allow you to kick back when bringing on new languages and leave the work to the lawyers, copyeditors, and translators.

L10n Using Properties Files

Creating new locale resources in your application to support L10n involves more than just writing code. You need to have people that speak the locale's dialect to translate copy, subject matter experts to make sure that the localized content of your application is appropriate, and possibly some lawyers to make sure that when you launch your application it won't be in violation of local laws.

Once you have your content in order, the standard way to implement L10n in Flex applications is via resource properties files, or properties files for short.

Understanding Properties Files

The first step in creating a g11n application is to understand the properties file. The properties file is a simple text file that stores key-value pairs. Each locale that your application supports will have its own copy of a properties file. For instance, the Flex framework supports multiple locales by default and has a couple versions of properties files for its framework components.

If you look for the root directory of your 3.x framework, you should be able to drill down to the `{SDK_ROOT}\frameworks\projects\framework\bundles\` directory, where you will see `en_US` and `ja_JP`, indicating that the 3.x version of the Flex framework supports the English (US) locale and the Japanese (Japan) locale.

> *If you're using a Mac, the path to the* `bundles` *directory is the same as the one above; you would just replace \ with /.*

Go ahead and drill into the `{SDK_ROOT}\frameworks\projects\framework\bundles\en_US\` directory. You'll see a `src` directory containing a bunch of properties files. Open up `controls.properties` and you should see the following, snipped to save space:

```
# Alert

okLabel=OK
```

```
yesLabel=Yes
noLabel=No
cancelLabel=Cancel
```

As you can see, a properties file separates its keys (listed on the left) from its values (listed on the right) using an equal sign. You can comment a properties file by prepending the comment with a pound sign. Also, properties files allow for multi-line values using a backslash (\) to indicate that the string continues on the next line. In addition, properties files support HTML data in their values.

Going back to how properties files are used to support multiple locales, open the `controls.properties` file in the `{SDK_ROOT}\frameworks\projects\framework\bundles\ja_JP\` directory. You should see the following data when you look for that same `# Alert` block:

```
# Alert

okLabel=OK
yesLabel=はい
noLabel=いいえ
cancelLabel=キャンセル
```

Now, you may have lucked out and opened the `controls.properties` file in an application that supported a Japanese character set. However, you may have not, and you're now looking at garbled characters on the right-hand side of the equal sign. This is due to character encoding, which is a very important topic to discuss when creating properties files.

Dealing with Character Encoding

Various locales use different character encoding types. This is because of the need to support different types of characters in different languages. For instance, ISO-8859-1 might be used in Western Europe and the United States, whereas in Japan the encoding type EUC-JP might be used.

If you're building the properties files for your applications, it can become very cumbersome to continually remember to verify encoding types when working with the files. If you make a mistake and save something in an incompatible type, you risk losing your character representations and might have to start all over. The best practice here is to use a universal format when creating your files and an editor that supports that format. For now, the character encoding format UTF-8 is the way to go.

Eclipse and Character Encoding

If you create a properties file with a default configuration of Eclipse, the character encoding will be determined by content. If you're curious to see what the encoding type is set to, right-click your file in the Navigator and go to Properties. For the preceding example, the encoding for the properties file was ISO-8859-1, as shown in Figure 37-1.

To change the file to UTF-8, just select the Other radio button, choose UTF-8 and then Apply. However, to have to remember to do this on every file would be a real bummer. The next section will describe how to ensure that the encoding type is set to UTF-8 when creating your properties files.

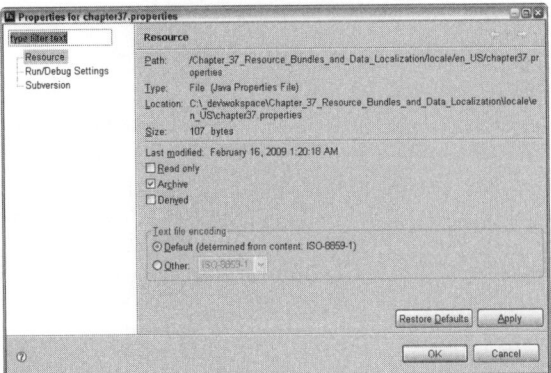

Figure 37-1

Changing the Default Encoding Type for Properties Files in Eclipse

Eclipse determines how to encode your properties file through its `*.properties` file extension. In other words, if you modify the default encoding for the `*.properties` extension, you will be able to ensure that all your `*.properties` files are set to UTF-8 when you create them:

1. In Eclipse, choose Window ➤ Preferences on a Windows machine, or the Eclipse menu ➤ Preferences… on a Mac.

2. In the Preferences dialog, navigate to General ➤ Content Types.

3. In the Content Types pane to the right, expand Text and find and select Java Properties File. You'll see that the default encoding will be set to ISO-8859-1. Go ahead and type **UTF-8** instead, click the Update button, and then exit the Preferences dialog.

Now when you create your `*.properties` files, they'll be set to UTF-8 by default.

Setting Up Locales in Your Flex Project

In this section, you will learn about the Flex project settings and compiler arguments involved when adding support for multiple locales within your Flex applications. You will also learn about the command-line tool used to create new locale resources.

Project Settings

The "Understanding Properties Files" section mentioned two different locales, en_US and ja_JP, and the location where the Flex framework stores its properties files, `{SDK_ROOT}\frameworks\projects\framework\bundles\`. Any properties files you create should be created elsewhere.

If you want to add L10n into your application, add a `locale` folder to your Flex or AIR project structure. Then, you create a folder named after each locale as a subdirectory of the `locale` folder. What you end up with is a directory structure similar to the one you see in Figure 37-2.

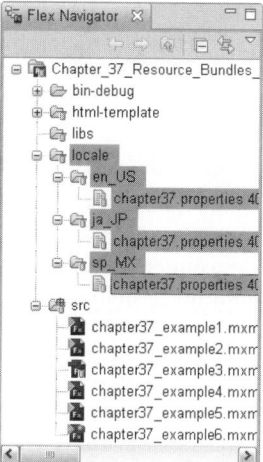

Figure 37-2

Now that you have your `locale` folder structure created, you will need to make sure to let your Flex or AIR project know that you want to include the new `locale` folders. You do this by completing the following steps:

1. Right-click your project, select Properties, and go to the Flex Build Path settings page in the project properties dialog. Add the `locale\{locale}` to your source path settings. When the application is compiled, the `{locale}` variable will cause the compiler to compile the locale subfolders based on what is specified in step 2.

2. Go to the Flex Compiler settings page and modify the Additional Compiler Arguments. You will want to add the `locale` argument and assign either a single locale value or a comma-separated list of locale values, such as `-locale=en_US, ja_JP`. Note that since these are the values the compiler will replace the `{locale}` variable specified in step 1 with, the locale strings must match the name of the `locale` subfolders.

Locale Chains

Notice that step 2 of the preceding section specified `-locale=en_US, ja_JP`. A comma-separated list of locales is also known as a *locale chain*. When the Flex application is compiled, the locale chain will be used to determine the actual locale resources that should be compiled into the application. In addition, the locale chain will be used to determine the order of precedence when searching these locale-specific resources for data while the application is running.

Given the preceding locale chain, the en_US and ja_JP locale folders will be compiled into the application. Then the compiler and the Flex application would first look for and apply the values in properties files from the en_US locale folder. If the Flex application runs across a key it couldn't find in the en_US resources, it would continue to work its way from left to right until it found the key.

For example, if no data was found in the properties files from the en_US locale, the Flex application would then look through ja_JP. The good news is that, if the application finishes searching the locale chain with no luck, it would just simply return a blank string, preventing your application from throwing an exception.

Using the copylocale.exe Command-Line Tool

If you need to support a locale other than en_US or ja_JP in your Flex and AIR applications, you will need to create the Flex framework locale resources for this new locale; otherwise, you will receive a compiler error stating that the compiler cannot open the framework's locale folder. To resolve this issue, the Flex SDK includes a command-line tool in its bin directory called copylocale.exe.

For example, to add the Mexican Spanish locale sp_MX, you need to set it as one of the "locale" compiler argument values. However, if you try to compile the project after populating the locale\sp_MX directory with properties files and assets, you will receive a compiler error stating that the compiler was unable to open {SDK_ROOT}\frameworks\locale\sp_MX. To resolve the compiler error, you will need to use copylocale.exe to create the sp_MX locale resources for the Flex framework:

1. Open a command prompt or terminal window and change directory to the {SDK_ROOT}\bin directory.

2. The syntax for the copylocale.exe tool is copylocale "original locale" "destination locale". So, type **copylocale en_US sp_MX** on a Mac you would type **./copylocale en_USB sp_MX**. If you're on a Mac you will need to make sure that the copylocale tool is set as an executable file.

    This will cause locale-specific files for the framework to be created, so you should now be able to compile the application with the sp_MX locale.

Now that your Flex/AIR project is configured to use your locale folders, you will need to finish the g11n puzzle with the i18n features in Flex 3.

Implementing i18n in Flex 3

If you want to support i18n (internationalization) in your Flex applications, you will need to know the mechanisms and API capabilities that you have at your disposal. This section begins by discussing the ways that you can utilize the resources you have defined in your locale packages.

Utilizing Your Resources

In Flex 3, there are several ways that you can utilize your resources:

❑   Using @Resource

❑   Using the ResourceBundle metadata tag and the corresponding ActionScript 3 class

❑   Using the Flex 3 ResourceManager class

Using @Resource

If you just need a quick MXML-based way to access your resources, you can use `@Resource`. The general syntax is

```
@Resource( key='someKey',bundle='someBundle' )
```

The following is a snippet from `chapter37_example1.mxml` in the Chapter 37 source code:

```
<mx:Label htmlText="@Resource( key='WELCOME_MESSAGE', bundle='chapter37' )"/>
```

If you open the Chapter 37 source, navigate to `locale\en_US\chapter37.properties`, and open that properties file, you will see the following:

```
WELCOME_MESSAGE=This application is an example of g11n, i18n, and L10n.
```

Putting the two together, you can assess the following about `@Resource`:

❑   The `key` argument points to the key in the properties file that you would like to look up and use the value for.

❑   The `bundle` argument points to the name of the properties file minus the `.properties` file extension.

As you can see, using `@Resource` is very simple, but it does have it drawbacks. `@Resource` is a compile-time directive, so if you would like runtime locale changes, you cannot use `@Resource`. In addition, `@Resource` will only return strings. Also, the `@Resource` directive can only be used in an MXML file, so if you need to access locale data within your ActionScript code, you're out of luck. That being said, an option that supports ActionScript is discussed next.

> *Locale chains were discussed earlier in this chapter. One odd thing to note about locale chains when using @Resource is when you specify locales in your chain other than en_US the compiler will search all locales from left to right during the compile.*

> *However, once you throw en_US into your locale chain, all key values will come from the en_US properties files unless they're missing. In other words, en_US will take precedence over the left to right search order and data from one of the other locales in the chain will only be used if the data from the en_US locale is missing.*

Using ResourceBundle

When your Flex application is compiled, each resource properties file is compiled into a subclass instance of `mx.resources.ResourceBundle`. You can access these instances via ActionScript as an alternative to using the `@Resource` directive.

Take a look at the following snippet from `chapter37_example3.mxml` in the Chapter 37 source to see how to use `ResourceBundle` to access your resources:

```
<mx:Script>
  <![CDATA[
```

```
        import mx.resources.ResourceBundle;

        [Bindable]
        [ResourceBundle('chapter37')]
        private static var _chapter37Bundle:ResourceBundle;
    ]]>
 </mx:Script>
 <mx:Label htmlText="{ _chapter37Bundle.getString( 'WELCOME_MESSAGE' ) }"/>
```

As you can see, you can now access your resources via ActionScript. Although there is a static
`ResourceBundle` member method `getResourceBundle()` to access your "chapter37" bundle, you can
also use the `[ResourceBundle]` metadata tag to do the same thing. Once the `ResourceBundle` exists,
you access your data by calling its method and passing in your keys as the argument.

Other than being able to work with resources in ActionScript, the `ResourceBundle` class is not limited to string data like its `@Resource` counterpart. The `ResourceBundle` class contains useful methods such as `getBoolean()`, `getNumber()`, and `getObject()`. However, if you compiled
`chapter37_example3.mxml` in the Chapter 37 source code, you will notice that you get warnings.
These warnings indicate that in Flex 3 working with the `ResourceBundle` class directly has been
deprecated in favor of using the Flex 3 `ResourceManager` class.

Using the Flex 3 ResourceManager

New to Flex 3 is `mx.resources.ResourceManager`, and it is the preferred way to work with your
resource bundles. The data access API of `ResourceManager` has some access methods named similarly
to `ResourceBundle`, but other than that it's a completely different beast. With `ResourceManager`, you're
now working with a singleton that is aware of all the resource bundles available to the application and
the locales that are currently available.

Accessing Data Using ResourceManager

Here is the example from the "Using ResourceBundle" section reworked to use `ResourceManager`. To
view the full code for this snippet, refer to `chapter37_example4.mxml` in the Chapter 37 source code:

```
<mx:Metadata>
   [ResourceBundle('chapter37')]
</mx:Metadata>
<mx:Script>
  <![CDATA[
        import mx.resources.IResourceManager;
        import mx.resources.ResourceManager;

        [Bindable]
        private var _resources:IResourceManager = ResourceManager.getInstance();
    ]]>
</mx:Script>
<mx:Label htmlText="{ _resources.getString( 'chapter37','WELCOME_MESSAGE' ) }"/>
```

When working with the `ResourceManager` singleton, the methods are implemented from
`mx.resources.IResourceManager` which is the return type that you receive when you make a call
against `ResourceManager.getInstance()`. In addition, when invoking the various accessor methods,
such as `getString()`, you now have to specify the resource bundle name as the first argument before

you specify the key as the second argument. The final thing to note is that you are required to have an <mx:Metadata/> block with a [ResourceBundle] metadata tag declaring the resource bundle you're using.

> *When compiling the preceding code in the* chapter37_example4.mxml *file, if you remove the* <mx:Metadata/> *block, you will not receive an error, but any calls to the resource bundles declared within it will return nothing. In other words, if you removed the metadata declaring the* 'chapter37' *resource bundle, the* 'WELCOME_MESSAGE' *call in the code above will result in a blank* <mx:Label/>.

Although the preceding code is valid, if you are using your resource data with classes that extend mx.core.UIComponent, creating your own reference to the ResourceManager singleton is unnecessary. Instead, you can make use of the protected resourceManager property defined by UIComponent. In other words, your code can look like the following snippet from chapter37_example5.mxml:

```
<mx:Metadata>
  [ResourceBundle('chapter37')]
</mx:Metadata>
<mx:Label
htmlText="{this.resourceManager.getString('chapter37','WELCOME_MESSAGE')}"/>
```

The next thing that will be discussed is runtime locale switching. However, to learn some more specifics on the ResourceManager you should take a look at the Flex 3 language reference to see the other data accessor methods that IResourceManager has to offer, such as getClass() for retrieving data as a class, getObject() for retrieving data as an object, and getUint() for retrieving data as unsigned integers.

Switching Locales at Runtime

ResourceManager is aware of the locales that are available. This is through a method called getLocales() and a property defined by IResourceManager called localeChain. The getLocales() method returns an unordered Array of locales that currently have resource bundles defined. The localeChain property is an ordered Array of the locales that the application will search when requests are made.

Although getLocales() can be useful, the localeChain property is the key component in switching your locale at runtime in Flex 3. Here is the code from chapter37_example6.mxml:

```
<?xml version="1.0" encoding="utf-8"?>
<mx:Application xmlns:mx="http://www.adobe.com/2006/mxml">
  <mx:Metadata>
      [ResourceBundle('chapter37')]
  </mx:Metadata>
  <mx:Label
    htmlText="{ resourceManager.getString( 'chapter37', 'WELCOME_MESSAGE' ) }"/>
  <mx:Label
    htmlText="{ resourceManager.getString( 'chapter37', 'FRIENDLY_NAME' ) }"/>
  <mx:HBox>
      <mx:Button label="view in Spanish (Mexico)"
              click="resourceManager.localeChain = ['sp_MX','en_US']"/>
      <mx:Button label="view in English (US)"
              click="resourceManager.localeChain = ['en_US']"/>
      <mx:Button label="view in Japanese (Japan)"
              click="resourceManager.localeChain = ['ja_JP','en_US']"/>
```

```
            <mx:Button label="view: ja_JP, sp_MX, en_US"
                    click="resourceManager.localeChain =
                                        ['ja_JP','sp_MX','en_US']"/>
    </mx:HBox>
</mx:Application>
```

As you can see from the preceding code, the first three buttons give the end user the ability to switch between three different locales at runtime: sp_MX, en_US, and ja_JP. In addition, the last button, which sets a locale chain that includes all three locales, will display locale-specific data from ja_JP as the preference followed by sp_MX, and en_US as a last resort.

The code above brings up some interesting points about the localeChain property. The localeChain property enables you to work with locales in an override fashion. It also allows you to bring the application online more quickly, even if all of a locale's specific resources haven't been completed. In the preceding example, en_US is always used as a default. This works out well for sp_MX since the key FRIENDLY_NAME has not yet been defined in the sp_MX chapter37.properties file. In other words, if en_US was not specified as a fallback, the second label would be blank when the user clicked the button to "view in Spanish (Mexico)."

Loading Resources at Runtime

When working with a multilingual application, the file size of the SWF can get very large very quickly when supporting many locales or if you're embedding a large amount of assets into your resource bundles. Several methods are available to you as a developer to handle this situation. Although there is simply not enough room to go into detail on these items, a quick overview will be given on each one.

Resource Modules

A resource module is a SWF file that contains the resource bundles for a single locale. This SWF file is generated via the mxmlc command-line tool. Here's an example of what you would type on the command line if you want to create a resource module for the ja_JP locale from the chapter37 project:

```
mxmlc -locale=ja_JP -source-path=locale/{locale} -include-resource-bundles=chapter37 ↵
    -output ja_JP_ResourceModule.swf
```

Once the SWF is available, you can use the loadResourceModule() method of ResourceManager, passing in a string representing a path to the SWF to dynamically load the resource module. The thing to keep in mind is that this is an asynchronous operation. The loadResourceModule() call returns an IEventDispatcher that will dispatch a ResourceEvent.COMPLETE or ResourceEvent.ERROR based on whether the loading of the resource module is successful. So, create a reference to this IEventDispatcher and listen for the events. Once they've been fired, you can do what you need to do.

For more information on using resource modules, refer to the Adobe LiveDocs at http://livedocs.adobe.com/flex/3/html/help.html?content=l10n_5.html.

Programmatically Generating ResourceBundle

The ResourceBundle class has a content property of type Object that you can use to add key-value pairs in dynamically. Just create a new ResourceBundle instance, add in the key-value pairs that you need as dynamic properties of the content object, add the ResourceBundle to the ResourceManager using addResourceBundle(), and then call update() on the ResourceManager.

If you're thinking about pulling locale-specific data from a remote data source, this method would be worth looking in to. For more information, visit http://livedocs.adobe.com/flex/3/html/help .html?content=l10n_6.html.

Pairing Resources with Modules

If your application makes use of modules, you might want to look into compiling ResourceBundles in with their associated modules. When taking this route you don't incur the overhead of the locale data until the module that needs it is loaded into your application. You also derive the benefit of keeping locale data paired with the module that makes use of it, which can be especially useful if you share your modules among several applications. For more information on modules, check out Chapter 66, "Modular Application Development."

Globalizing AIR Applications

The components of globalizing your applications, i18n and L10n, are supported in AIR as of version 1.1. The easiest way to set up your AIR project to work with i18n and L10n is to make sure to update your Flex Builder installation to the 3.0.1 update.

Although there is an AIR HTML Localization Framework built into AIR 1.1 to allow developers to build HTML-based AIR applications, a discussion of localizing HTML-based AIR applications is outside the scope of this book. If you're curious about that, you should reference the Adobe LiveDocs at http://help .adobe.com/en_US/AIR/1.1/devappsflex/WS7097DF4C-EFCF-4d55-ADE1-682F0FDA26AC.html.

ActionScript-based AIR applications primarily use the same mechanisms as a Flex application, with the addition of a couple of really cool features:

- ❑ Language rendering support in the HTML content being rendered in your AIR applications
- ❑ Localization support in the AIR runtime and AIR application installers
- ❑ The Capabilities.languages API call

Rendering and installer localization are automatic and don't require any work on your part. However, you will need to implement any interaction with Capabilities.languages in your code. Luckily, working with Capabilities.languages is very simple, as shown in this snippet from chapter37_ example7.mxml in the Chapter_37_Resource_Bundles_and_Data_Localization_AIR_1_1 project source code:

```
trace( 'Capabilities.languages: ' + Capabilities.languages );
```

When you run the application, this call will return an `Array` of the user's preferred languages. When running this call you will receive something similar to `"Capabilities.languages: en-US"` in your console output.

The API property `Capabilities.languages` *(plural) provided by AIR 1.1 should not be confused with the* `Capabilites.language` *(singular) property available in the standard Flash Player API. Unlike the* `languages` *property available in the AIR 1.1 API, the* `language` *property returns a string representing the language code being used on the system that the player is running on.*

Summary

This chapter discussed the main points you need to know when adding i18n and L10n support to your Flex applications. From properties files, to `ResourceBundle`, to `ResourceManager`, to `ResourceModule`, Flex 3 provides a very robust and complete API to allow you to globalize your Flex and AIR applications.

If you're interesting in gathering more details on localizing your Flex 3 applications, take a look at the Adobe LiveDocs at `http://livedocs.adobe.com/flex/3/html/help.html?content=l10n_1.html`.

If you're interested in gathering more details on localizing your AIR 1.1 applications, take a look at the Adobe DevNet article at `www.adobe.com/devnet/air/flex/articles/localizing_flex_air_apps.html`.

This chapter concludes Part VI, "Data Management." Part VII, "Client Communications," begins with a discussion on how your Flex applications can communicate with the browser.

Part VII: Client Communications

Browser Communication in Flex

In the vast majority of cases, Adobe Flex applications are presented to the user through a web browser. This chapter explores the methods that you can use to exchange data between your Flex application and the HTML page that contains your Flex application.

The following sections will walk you through scenarios that show you how to pass data into Flex applications using `flashVars`, how to exchange information back and forth from Flex to your containing HTML page using JavaScript, and seamless JavaScript/Flex integration using the Flex Ajax Bridge (FABridge).

Understanding the Web Context

Most commonly, Flex applications are presented to the user as compiled SWF files that are embedded within HTML content that is delivered over the Internet. The other option is that the Flex application is accessed directly as a SWF file. The end user does not necessarily need to know this, but from the developer's perspective, you must be aware of how the application is presented. The following sections will focus on the first scenario: interactions with Flex applications that are embedded within HTML content.

Flex applications are often delivered as *full-page* content within web pages. In this scenario, the Flex application takes up the entire available space within the web page. The application is designed to be a standalone application, with no user interface elements coming from outside of the Flex application itself.

Another common scenario is that Flex applications are used as *widgets,* or smaller embedded applications within HTML web pages. In this case, there could be one, or many, Flex applications within a single web page.

In both cases, it will often be necessary to communicate with the browser for a variety of reasons, including (but not limited to):

❑   Passing initialization data to the Flex application

❑   Communication with external APIs

❑   Communication with separate application components

❑   Opening other URLs

Using flashVars to Pass Data into Flex

The easiest way to pass simple data values into a Flex application is through the use of the flashVars property. There are really two ways that you can specify flashVars for a Flex application. The way that the flashVars values are passed into the application depends on how the application is accessed.

Regardless of how the flashVars values are passed into the Flex application, they are accessed within the application in the exact same manner. This section explores using flashVars to pass a string value (Hello Professional Flex 3) and a numeric value (12345) into a Flex application.

If you are accessing the Flex application through a HTML wrapper, the flashVars property is specified when embedding the Flex application into the HTML application. In this manner, flashVars can only be specified when the application is embedded in the HTML container; modifying these values at run-time will not alter their values within the Flex application.

With this approach, the first thing you need to do is to specify the flashVars values in the HTML that will contain your Flex application. In this case, the index.template.html file will be modified to contain the flashVars values. Flex Builder uses this file to generate the actual HTML that is used to embed your Flex application.

When embedding the flashVars values, all values will be concatenated to a single string value that is used to specify the flashVars data. Multiple flashVars values will be passed as name/value pairs delineated by an ampersand (&). This is basically the same format in which query string parameters would be passed into the browser (and should also be URL-encoded for special characters):

```
myString=Hello Professional Flex 3&myNumber=12345
```

The index.template.html file uses the JavaScript function AC_FL_RunContent to embed the Flex application within the HTML content. You can add flashVars values to the Flex application by adding them to the parameters of the AC_FL_RunContent JavaScript function:

```
AC_FL_RunContent(
    "src", "${swf}",
    "width", "${width}",
    "height", "${height}",
    "align", "middle",
    "id", "${application}",
    "quality", "high",
```

```
        "bgcolor", "${bgcolor}",
        "name", "${application}",
        "allowScriptAccess","sameDomain",
        "type", "application/x-shockwave-flash",
        "pluginspage", "http://www.adobe.com/go/getflashplayer",
        "flashVars", "myString=Hello Professional Flex 3&myNumber=12345"
);
```

The `index.template.html` file also contains a `<NOSCRIPT>` tag block that is used to embed the Flex application if JavaScript is unavailable to the browser. The `flashVars` value must also be specified on both the `object` and `embed` tags within the HTML so that the data values are still accessible within the Flex application if JavaScript is not available:

```
<object classid="clsid:D27CDB6E-AE6D-11cf-96B8-444553540000"
    id="${application}" width="${width}" height="${height}"
    codebase="http://fpdownload.macromedia.com/get/flashplayer/current/swflash.cab">
    <param name="flashVars" value="myString=Hello Professional
        Flex 3&myNumber=12345" />
  <param name="movie" value="${swf}.swf" />
    <param name="quality" value="high" />
    <param name="bgcolor" value="${bgcolor}" />
    <param name="allowScriptAccess" value="sameDomain" />
  <embed
src="${swf}.swf" quality="high" bgcolor="${bgcolor}"
flashVars="myString=Hello Professional Flex 3&myNumber=12345"
width="${width}" height="${height}" name="${application}" align="middle"
        play="true"
        loop="false"
        quality="high"
        allowScriptAccess="sameDomain"
        type="application/x-shockwave-flash"
        pluginspage="http://www.adobe.com/go/getflashplayer"
        >
    </embed>
</object>
```

If you are directly accessing the Flex application's SWF file, without an HTML wrapper, then you can simply append the `flashVars` to the URL as query parameters. This is an interesting approach, as it does not require the HTML container, and can be used to pass values into a SWF loaded via a `SWFLoader` component, or if you are loading a SWF file in a non-web context — for example, inside of a .NET win-Forms application. If you are accessing the SWF file directly, you can append the preceding parameters directly through the query string, as follows:

```
http://myserver/main.swf?myString=Hello Professional Flex 3&myNumber=12345
```

As noted previously, regardless of which approach you use to pass in the `flashVars` values, you access them internally with the exact same approach. Within the Flex application, you can access the `flashVars` values through the `Application.application.parameters` static variable. The following ActionScript code segment shows how to access the `myString` value as a string and how to access `myNumber` as a number (specifically integer) value.

The `readFlashVars()` function will read the `flashVars` values that were passed into the application and will display the values in standard `Alert` windows:

```
private function readFlashVars() : void
{
    var flashVars : Object = Application.application.parameters;

    var myString : String = flashVars.myString;
    var myNumber : Number = parseInt( flashVars.myNumber );

    Alert.show( myString, "myString Value:" );
    Alert.show( myNumber.toString(), "myNumber Value:" );
}
```

If you wanted to access `myNumber` as a floating point number, instead of an integer, you should use the `parseFloat` function instead of the `parseInt` function:

```
var myNumber : Number = parseFloat( flashVars.myNumber );
```

The `flashVars` property can only contain simple values; it cannot contain complex objects.

Linking to an External Page URL

Perhaps the most common interaction between Flex applications and the browser is to open a new URL. You can use the `navigateToURL` ActionScript function to load new URLs. The following `openLink()` function demonstrates this task:

```
private function openLink() : void
{
    var request : URLRequest = new URLRequest( "http://www.wrox.com" );
    navigateToURL( request, "_blank" );
}
```

The `navigateToURL` function accepts two parameters: a `URLRequest` object that contains the URL that you want to view, and the target window for the new URL. In this scenario, the target is `_blank`, which tells the browser to open the URL in a new window. By default, the target value is null, which would open the specified URL in the current window. The target can contain any named window in the browser and is functionally equivalent to the `target` attribute in an HTML anchor tag (`<A href="http://www.wrox.com" target="_blank" />`).

Interacting with JavaScript

Another common way of communicating with the browser is through the use of JavaScript, using the `ExternalInterface` class. The `ExternalInterface` class manages all communication between the Flex application and its parent container.

The `ExternalInterface` class enables bidirectional communication between your Flex application and its container, meaning both that ActionScript inside of your Flex application can invoke JavaScript, and that JavaScript can invoke ActionScript functions inside of your application.

Invoking JavaScript from Flex

Invoking JavaScript functions from Flex is actually very straightforward. You use the `ExternalInterface.call` static method to invoke a JavaScript function in the HTML page that contains the Flex application.

The following code snippet is a very basic JavaScript function. This function must be accessible in the page that contains the Flex application.

```
<script>
function myBasicFunction()
{
    alert( "'myBasicFunction' was called" );
}
</script>
```

This function will simply display a JavaScript alert message when it is invoked, and it can be invoked from within Flex using the following ActionScript function:

```
private function callJavaScriptFunction() : void
{
    if ( ExternalInterface.available )
    {
        ExternalInterface.call( "myBasicFunction" );
    }
    else
    {
        Alert.show( "ExternalInterface Unavailable" );
    }
}
```

The first thing that this function does is check if `ExternalInterface` is available. JavaScript external access can be disabled for Flex applications, and the `ExternalInterface.available` static variable will provide you with information as to whether you can invoke JavaScript from within your Flex application.

If the `ExternalInterface` class is available, the JavaScript function is called using the `ExternalInterface.call` static method.

```
ExternalInterface.call( "myBasicFunction" );
```

`ExternalInterface.call` accepts multiple parameters. The first parameter is a string value that contains the name of the JavaScript function to invoke. In this case, it is the string value `myBasicFunction`. All additional parameters used in `ExternalInterface.call` will be passed as parameters to the JavaScript function, which will be discussed later in this chapter.

Invoking ActionScript from JavaScript

Invoking ActionScript functions from JavaScript is also very straightforward. However, it requires an additional step that is not necessary to invoke JavaScript from ActionScript. ActionScript functions within the Flex application must first have callbacks registered within the ExternalInterface class. The callback maps a string value to the ActionScript function that will be invoked. The string value used in the callback will be used as the publicly available name for the ActionScript function.

The following Flex code example shows an example of registering a JavaScript function to an ActionScript function:

```
<?xml version="1.0" encoding="utf-8"?>
<mx:Application
    xmlns:mx="http://www.adobe.com/2006/mxml"
    layout="absolute"
    initialize="onInitialize()">

    <mx:Script>
    <![CDATA[
      import mx.controls.Alert;

        private function onInitialize() : void
        {
            ExternalInterface.addCallback( "myActionScriptFunction", onJSCallback )
        }

        private function onJSCallback() : void
        {
            Alert.show( "'onJSCallback' ActionScript function invoked by JavaScript" );
        }

    ]]>
    </mx:Script>
</mx:Application>
```

On the initialize event of the application, the onInitialize function is invoked, which registers the onJSCallback ActionScript function with the ExternalInterface class using the mapping myActionScriptFunction.

External to the Flex application, this method will be publicly exposed as myActionScriptFunction and can be invoked by calling the myActionScriptFunction() function on the embedded Flex SWF instance.

In this example, the HTML page that contains the Flex application also contains the following HTML and JavaScript code:

```
<script>
function onJSButtonClick()
{
    main.myActionScriptFunction();
}
</script>
```

```
<input
   type="button"
   value="Click to Invoke ActionScript"
   onclick="onJSButtonClick()" />
```

When the HTML button is clicked, it invokes the `onJSButtonClick()` JavaScript function, which in turn calls the `main.myActionScriptFunction()` function. The `myActionScriptFunction()` function invokes the callback on `ExternalInterface`, which invokes the `onJSCallback` ActionScript function.

In the `onJSButtonClick()` JavaScript function, `main` refers to the Flex application that is embedded with the name "main". This example is very simple because the Flex application is embedded directly as a child on the root of the HTML document. If the page contains a complex DOM (Document Object Model), then you may need some more complex JavaScript to get a reference to the Flex application. You may need to use the `getElementById` function, as follows:

```
document.getElementById( "main" ).myActionScriptFunction();
```

Depending on the complexity of your HTML structure, you may also need to use JavaScript to conditionally handle references to your embedded Flex application, depending on the browser and operating system. Once you have a reference to your Flex application in JavaScript, invoking an ActionScript function through `ExternalInterface` does not change based on the browser or operating system.

Passing Data Between ActionScript and JavaScript

Communication between Flex and JavaScript is not limited to method invocation only. You have full capability to pass parameters and return values in both directions between Flex and JavaScript. You can pass both simple and complex objects in parameter sets and return values.

Parameters

You can very easily pass parameters to JavaScript functions from Flex. When you create your JavaScript function, you add parameter values as you normally would. The following is a basic JavaScript function that accepts one parameter and displays it within an alert message:

```
<script>
function myParameterFunction( param )
{
   alert( "'myParameterFunction' was called with parameter: " + param );
}
</script>
```

You can pass parameters from Flex into this JavaScript function by adding additional parameter values when you invoke the `ExternalInterface.call` method:

```
<mx:Application xmlns:mx="http://www.adobe.com/2006/mxml" layout="absolute">
  <mx:Script>
    <![CDATA[
      import mx.controls.Alert;
      private function callFunction() : void
      {
```

```
              if ( ExternalInterface.available )
              {
                  ExternalInterface.call( "myParameterFunction", myParam.text );
              }
              else
              {
                  Alert.show( "ExternalInterface Unavailable" );
              }
          }
      ]]>
  </mx:Script>

  <mx:Label x="10" y="10" text="parameter value:"/>
  <mx:TextInput x="120" y="8" id="myParam" text="abc123" />
  <mx:Button x="120" y="38" label="Call JavaScript Function"
        click="callFunction()" />

</mx:Application>
```

There is no limit to the number of parameters that you can pass between JavaScript and Flex using the
ExternalInterface class; however, good coding practice dictates that they should be kept to a minimum for easy-to-maintain code.

Just as you can pass values into JavaScript from Flex, you can pass values into Flex from JavaScript. As
in earlier examples, you still need to register ExternalInterface callbacks to your ActionScript functions. To pass parameters, there is no change to how you register the callbacks. The only changes are on
the ActionScript function itself, and how the function is invoked.

```
<mx:Application
 xmlns:mx="http://www.adobe.com/2006/mxml"
 layout="absolute"
 initialize="onInitialize()">

 <mx:Script>
   <![CDATA[
       import mx.utils.ObjectUtil;
       import mx.controls.Alert;

       private function onInitialize() : void
       {
           ExternalInterface.addCallback( "myActionScriptFunction", onJSCallback )
       }

       private function onJSCallback( param : * ) : void
       {
           Alert.show( "'onJSCallback' parameter: " + ObjectUtil.toString( param ) );
       }
   ]]>
 </mx:Script>
</mx:Application>
```

As you can see, the `onJSCallback` ActionScript function has been modified to accept a parameter, and to display that parameter value in an Alert message. When the function is invoked in JavaScript, a parameter is specified.

```
<script>
function onJSButtonClick()
{
    main.myActionScriptFunction( Math.random() );
}
</script>

<input
    type="button"
    value="Click to Invoke ActionScript"
    onclick="onJSButtonClick()" />
```

In this case, a randomly generated number is passed from JavaScript into the ActionScript function.

Return Values

Just as you can pass values into functions from both JavaScript and Flex, you can pass return values from functions, and use the return values in your applications.

The following scenario shows the previous example modified to display the return value from a JavaScript method in an ActionScript Alert message:

```
<mx:Application xmlns:mx="http://www.adobe.com/2006/mxml" layout="absolute">

    <mx:Script>
        <![CDATA[
            import mx.controls.Alert;
            private function callFunction() : void
            {
                if ( ExternalInterface.available )
                {
                    Alert.show( ExternalInterface.call( "myReturnFunction" ), "Value" );
                }
                else
                {
                    Alert.show( "ExternalInterface Unavailable" );
                }
            }
        ]]>
    </mx:Script>

    <mx:Button x="10" y="10"
            label="Call JavaScript Function"
            click="callFunction()" />

</mx:Application>
```

The JavaScript function that returns the value to the Flex application simply returns a randomly generated number value:

```
<script>
function myReturnFunction()
{
    return Math.random();
}
</script>
```

The following example shows how to return value from Flex into JavaScript. As in the previous examples, you still need to register your JavaScript callbacks in the Flex application by using the ExternalInterface.addCallback method. The only difference in this case is that the callback method has been modified to return a value.

```
<mx:Application
    xmlns:mx="http://www.adobe.com/2006/mxml"
    layout="absolute"
    initialize="onInitialize()">

    <mx:Script>
        <![CDATA[
            import mx.utils.ObjectUtil;
            import mx.controls.Alert;
            private function onInitialize() : void
            {
                ExternalInterface.addCallback( "myActionScriptFunction", onJSCallback )
            }

            private function onJSCallback() : Number
            {
                return Math.random();
            }
        ]]>
    </mx:Script>

</mx:Application>
```

In JavaScript, the method has been changed so that it will use the return value from myActionScript Function in a simple JavaScript alert message:

```
<script>
function onJSButtonClick()
{
    alert( main.myActionScriptFunction() );
}
</script>
```

All return values are processed synchronously, inline with the code execution.

Complex Objects

Complex objects can be used in both function parameters and return values between Flex and JavaScript functions. However, this is limited to value objects only. Only the concrete values of an object are accessible between the two languages. Any functions associated with either the ActionScript or JavaScript object instance are no longer available once they are passed through the `ExternalInterface` class.

The following example shows how you can pass a complex object from an ActionScript function into a JavaScript function that was invoked using `ExternalInterface`:

```
<mx:Application xmlns:mx="http://www.adobe.com/2006/mxml" layout="absolute">

    <mx:Script>
        <![CDATA[
            import mx.controls.Alert;
            private function callFunction() : void
            {
                if ( ExternalInterface.available )
                {
                    var param : Object = new Object();
                    param.myString = "Hello Professional Flex";
                    param.myNumber = Math.random();
                    ExternalInterface.call( "myComplexFunction", param );
                }
                else
                {
                    Alert.show( "ExternalInterface Unavailable" );
                }
            }
        ]]>
    </mx:Script>

    <mx:Button x="10" y="10" label="Call JavaScript Function"
        click="callFunction()" />

</mx:Application>
```

You can see that you create a new object instance as you would normally in ActionScript. You can assign practically any simple or complex value object to the properties of that object, although you cannot pass function values.

The parameter is passed into the JavaScript function using the second argument of the `ExternalInterface.call` method:

```
<script>
function myComplexFunction( param )
{
    alert( "'myComplexFunction' was called with param.myString='" +
        param.myString + "' and param.myNumber='" + param.myNumber + "'");
}
</script>
```

In the JavaScript function that is having the complex object value passed into it, you access the object exactly as you would any other object instance. You can access the properties of that object using traditional object syntax:

```
param.myString
```

As is with simple value objects, this type of communication is bidirectional. You can also pass complex objects from JavaScript into an ActionScript callback function. The following example demonstrates how to pass a complex object from JavaScript into an ActionScript callback:

```
<mx:Application
    xmlns:mx="http://www.adobe.com/2006/mxml"
    layout="absolute"
    initialize="onInitialize()">

    <mx:Script>
        <![CDATA[
            import mx.utils.ObjectUtil;
            import mx.controls.Alert;
            private function onInitialize() : void
            {
                ExternalInterface.addCallback( "myActionScriptFunction", onJSCallback )
            }

            private function onJSCallback( param : * ) : void
            {
                Alert.show("'onJSCallback' parameter: " + ObjectUtil.toString(param));
            }
        ]]>
    </mx:Script>

</mx:Application>
```

In this example, the ActionScript function will simply display an Alert message that contains the object structure that is returned from the `ObjectUtil.toString()` method. You may notice that this code is identical to the code that was previously used to display a simple result.

```
<script>
function onJSButtonClick()
{
    var param = {
            myString : "Hello Professional Flex, from JavaScript",
            myNumber : Math.random()
        };
    main.myActionScriptFunction( param );
}
</script>

<input
    type="button"
    value="Click to Invoke ActionScript"
    onclick="onJSButtonClick()" />
```

The difference in this example is that simple values are not passed as parameters into the ActionScript callback function. The onJSButtonClick() JavaScript function creates an object instance param and assigns a string value to myString and a numeric value to myNumber.

When this code is executed, you can see that the complex object is resolved in ActionScript, and it has the properties myString and myNumber, with the same values that were passed in from JavaScript. You can also access these values using standard object syntax in ActionScript:

```
param.myString
```

Exchanging complex objects between JavaScript and ActionScript is not limited only to function parameters. You can also use function return values to pass complex objects between the function invocations by using ExternalInterface.

The next example shows how to use a complex object returned from JavaScript into ActionScript. In this example, clicking on the button invokes the callFunction ActionScript method, which invokes the myReturnFunction JavaScript method and displays the result in an Alert message.

```
<mx:Application xmlns:mx="http://www.adobe.com/2006/mxml" layout="absolute">

    <mx:Script>
        <![CDATA[
            import mx.utils.ObjectUtil;
            import mx.controls.Alert;
            private function callFunction() : void
            {
                if ( ExternalInterface.available )
                {
                    Alert.show(
                        ObjectUtil.toString(
                            ExternalInterface.call( "myReturnFunction" )
                        ), "JavaScript Return" );
                }
                else
                {
                    Alert.show( "ExternalInterface Unavailable" );
                }
            }
        ]]>
    </mx:Script>

    <mx:Button x="10" y="10" label="Call JavaScript Function"
        click="callFunction()" />

</mx:Application>
```

The myReturnFunction JavaScript function returns a complex object with a string and a number parameter, as follows:

```
<script>
function myReturnFunction( param )
{
```

```
        return {
                myString : "Hello Professional Flex, returned from JavaScript",
                myNumber : Math.random()
        };
    }
</script>
```

Of course, you can also return complex objects from ActionScript functions to JavaScript functions, as the next example demonstrates. In this case, you would register the callback function with the ExternalInterface class as you normally would.

```
<mx:Application
    xmlns:mx="http://www.adobe.com/2006/mxml"
    layout="absolute"
    initialize="onInitialize()">

    <mx:Script>
        <![CDATA[
            import mx.utils.ObjectUtil;
            import mx.controls.Alert;
            private function onInitialize() : void
            {
                ExternalInterface.addCallback( "myActionScriptFunction", onJSCallback )
            }

            private function onJSCallback() : Object
            {
                var obj : Object = new Object();
                    obj.myString = "Hello Professional Flex";
                    obj.myNumber = Math.random();
                return obj;
            }
        ]]>
    </mx:Script>

</mx:Application>
```

The difference between this example and the previous examples is that the onJSCallback ActionScript function returns an object to the JavaScript caller. In JavaScript, the invocation of the function returns an object that contains the exact values that were specified by the ActionScript function.

```
<script>
function onJSButtonClick()
{
    var obj = main.myActionScriptFunction();
    alert( "'myActionScriptFunction' was called with return: obj.myString='" +
        obj.myString + "' and obj.myNumber='" + obj.myNumber + "'");
}
</script>
```

You can also access the properties of the returned object by using standard object syntax in JavaScript:

```
obj.myString
```

Using the Flex-Ajax Bridge

Another option for integration with the browser and JavaScript is through the Flex-Ajax Bridge (FABridge). The FABridge is a code library that enables direct access between JavaScript and Flex components. The FABridge can be used to have JavaScript event listeners on Flex events, or it can be used to invoke functions directly on Flex components.

Within Flex Builder, you can enable the FABridge for your MXML components by right-clicking on the target MXML file in the project file hierarchy and selecting the Create Ajax Bridge option. You will then be walked through a wizard that will allow you to select the components that you want to expose to JavaScript using the FABridge. The wizard will generate the necessary JavaScript classes necessary to use the FABridge within your application, and it will include the FABridge libraries in your Flex project to enable the interaction. You may notice that the FABridge component has been added to your Flex application.

```
<mx:Application
    xmlns:mx="http://www.adobe.com/2006/mxml"
    layout="absolute"
    xmlns:fab="bridge.*">

    <fab:FABridge/>
```

Now you will be able to use the FABridge to communicate directly with your Flex application through JavaScript. Any time that you want to access values from your Flex application using the FABridge, you will need to get access to the FABridge instance by using the following JavaScript snippet:

```
FABridge.flash.root();
```

Whenever you want to retrieve the value of a Flex component from JavaScript, you will have to access it as a getter function on the FABridge instance. Consider the following TextInput control:

```
<mx:TextInput id="myTextInput" />
```

Using the FABridge, you would access as follows:

```
function getTextInputValue()
{
 var flexApp = FABridge.flash.root();
 var textValue = flexApp.getMyTextInput().getValue();
}
```

This function syntax applies to any public property of the Flex component, so you could also access the width of the TextInput control using the following JavaScript code:

```
function getTextInputHeight()
{
 var flexApp = FABridge.flash.root();
 var textHeight = flexApp.getMyTextInput().getHeight();
}
```

If you wanted to set the value of a Flex component using the FABridge, you could do so using setter functions. For example, you could execute the following JavaScript code to set the value of the `TextInput` component:

```
function setTextInputValue ()
{
 var flexApp = FABridge.flash.root();
 flexApp.getMyTextInput().setValue( "Hello Professional Flex 3" );}
```

The FABridge also enables you to add JavaScript event listeners to Flex components. The next scenario shows you how to add an event listener to the `change` event on the same `TextInput` object.

```
function listenForChangeEvent()
{
 var flexApp = FABridge.flash.root();
 var callback = function(event)
 {
    alert( "text input value changed." );
 }
 flexApp.getMyTextInput().addEventListener("change", callback);
}
```

The `callback` variable actually contains a JavaScript function that will be invoked any time a "change" event occurs on the Flex `TextInput` control. This approach could be very helpful in handling data synchronization between Flex and JavaScript components, or could be used to trigger animations in the HTML/JavaScript from an action that occurs within the Flex application.

Disabling Browser Integration

One thing to keep in mind when using `ExternalInterface` is that browser integration can be disabled for Flex applications. If browser integration has been disabled, `ExternalInterface.available` will always return `false`, and your application should handle it accordingly.

When the Flex application is embedded in the HTML container, the `allowScriptAccess` parameter determines the accessibility of the `ExternalInterface` JavaScript interaction.

```
<noscript>
    <object classid="clsid:D27CDB6E-AE6D-11cf-96B8-444553540000"
        id="${application}" width="${width}" height="${height}"
        codebase="http://fpdownload.macromedia.com/get/flashplayer/current/
            swflash.cab">
        <param name="movie" value="${swf}.swf" />
        <param name="quality" value="high" />
        <param name="bgcolor" value="${bgcolor}" />
        <param name="allowScriptAccess" value="sameDomain" />
        <embed src="${swf}.swf" quality="high" bgcolor="${bgcolor}"
            width="${width}" height="${height}" name="${application}"
                align="middle"
            play="true"
            loop="false"
```

```
                    quality="high"
                    allowScriptAccess="sameDomain"
                    type="application/x-shockwave-flash"
                    pluginspage="http://www.adobe.com/go/getflashplayer">
            </embed>
        </object>
    </noscript>
```

The `allowScriptAccess` parameter can be set to `always`, `sameDomain`, or `never`. The "always" value means that `ExternalInterface` will be able to invoke JavaScript regardless of whether the Flex application and the HTML are served from the same domain. The `sameDomain` value will only allow the `ExternalInterface` call to succeed if the Flex application and the HTML container are served from the same domain. If the `never` option is specified, then no Interaction between JavaScript and ActionScript using `ExternalInterface` will ever be successful; thus it is disabled.

Summary

There are many ways that you can have your Flex application interact with the browser, or you can disable it completely! Flex allows you to open new URLs by using the `navigateToURL` function. You can pass information directly into the Flex application by using `flashVars`, or you can take advantage of the `ExternalInterface` class to synchronously execute ActionScript from JavaScript, or execute JavaScript from ActionScript. `ExternalInterface` enables you to share data across the languages by using both simple and complex values as either function parameters or return values between the browser and the Flex application.

The next chapter examines some approaches for consuming data, interacting with HTML, and creating mashup applications using Adobe AIR.

39

HTML Mashups with AIR

Adobe AIR includes functionality to render HTML content in a native application. Unlike traditional Flex applications running in the web browser that require IFrame HTML hacks to overlay rendered HTML in an application, Adobe AIR leverages its WebKit web browser engine for rendering any HTML content, including CSS and JavaScript, inside an AIR application.

Using the Flex mx:HTML tag, both remote and local HTML content can be rendered in an AIR application. Additionally, bidirectional interaction between ActionScript and JavaScript, including HTML DOM manipulation, is available to the developer.

Why Embed HTML in an AIR Application?

With traditional Flex applications running inside a web browser, the developer is limited to rendering HTML to a small subset of HTML tags supported by Flex's Label component through the htmlText property (<a>, <b>, <br>, <font>, <image>, and a few others). There are also workarounds in Flex applications for overlaying an HTML IFrame (provided by the host web browser) over a portion of the visible Flex application, which is crude, but often necessary for displaying complex HTML in an application. With Adobe AIR, these techniques are no longer necessary, as AIR provides a complete implementation of the WebKit web browser (complete with Squirrelfish JavaScript VM) in which any HTML and JavaScript can be rendered and executed (as long as security sandbox constraints are met — more later).

While complete AIR applications can be written solely in HTML and JavaScript, with total access to the AIR-specific APIs, our focus here will be only in using the Flex AIR APIs. You might be wondering what some of the uses to the Flex developer are?

1. Using third-party APIs that are only provided for in HTML/JavaScript
2. Building Web mashups that integrate between third-party data and local user data
3. Creating a custom report engine based on CSS/HTML, with Flex providing string-substitutions logic

4. Embedding the Adobe PDF reader for displaying PDF documents from inside an AIR application

5. Reusing existing Flash SWF content embedded on existing HTML pages

In this chapter, we're going to be interacting with embedded HTML content using the Google's YouTube Chromeless Player for displaying YouTube videos. This will demonstrate rendering an HTML page inside AIR, sending data from JavaScript into ActionScript methods, and sending data from ActionScript to JavaScript.

While you could figure out how to access YouTube's video streams directly (Flash FLV files), it's against their terms, and they want you to use their embedded player API, which is made available so that the developer can customize the look and feel. The only catch is, that it's all HTML/JavaScript based, which is why using AIR's HTML APIs are going to be very handy.

YouTube Sample

This chapter's AIR application takes advantage of the YouTube Chromeless Player API offered by Google/YouTube. The YouTube documentation can be found at `http://code.google.com/apis/youtube/chromeless_player_reference.html`.

The YouTube Chromeless Player API gives developers access to customizing the YouTube player with their own controls and player skins. From JavaScript, developers can choose which videos are loaded, and control whether to play, pause, stop videos, and so on.

The demo AIR application in this chapter will use the YouTube Chromeless Player, embedded in an HTML page that's loaded into an AIR application for displaying videos. Furthermore, in MXML and Flex components, we'll create buttons for controlling the state of a video stream, whether it's to play, pause, or stop a video. In addition, in order to choose which videos to play, we'll use the YouTube Data APIs for discovering videos to play based on basic search criteria. And finally, to demonstrate the transfer of data from JavaScript into ActionScript, we'll send statistics and metrics about the currently streaming video back up to our AIR application for display.

> *The chapter's sample isn't a lesson on the most efficient ways to access YouTube content from an AIR application, but merely to use the existing YouTube APIs to demonstrate working with HTML content in AIR. There are probably better APIs that are more fully flushed out if you want to directly work with YouTube content from your Flex/AIR applications, like the* `as3youtubelib`, *found at* `http://code.google.com/p/as3youtubelib`.

Displaying HTML in AIR

HTML content displayed in an AIR application can be created in memory, loaded from local files, or loaded from remote websites. To display HTML content in your Flex-based AIR application, you'll use the `mx:HTML` component, a Flex-friendly wrapper around the raw Adobe AIR `flash.html.HTMLLoader` class. The Flex version inherits from `UIComponent`, allowing it to render in Flex-based display hierarchy. From the `mx:HTML` component, the actual `HTMLLoader` class is made available through the `htmlLoader` property.

Loading Remote Content

The simplest way to look at HTML content in an AIR application is to load remote content with the following MXML:

```
<mx:HTML
  id="htmlContainer"
  width="100%" height="100%"
  complete="onHtmlLoadComplete(event)"
  location="http://www.wrox.com"
  >
</mx:HTML>
```

Using the Flex mx:HTML component, set the location property to a remote URL, http://www.wrox.com, to load and display the web page. Upon completing the loading of the remote content, the onHTMLLoad Complete event is called, signaling the HTML content has completed. From this point on, custom code can access the HTML content's DOM or JavaScript for manipulation (see the sections "Controlling the HTML DOM from ActionScript" and "Interacting with JavaScript," respectively).

Working with Security Sandboxes

Adobe AIR partitions executable code into sandboxes, depending on where the HTML content originates. In most cases, loading local HTML content directly from the AIR application's install directory will pace the content in the *Application* sandbox, and full access to the Adobe AIR APIs, as well as bidirectional JavaScript/ActionScript communication, will be supported. When HTML data is loaded from the local filesystem (outside the application install directory), it will be placed in the *local* sandbox. Finally, all remote HTML content, as is the case above with our sample code, will be placed in its own security sandbox based on the domain of content origination and will have limited access to resources outside of the sandbox created for it.

The main Application sandbox allows full access to the Adobe AIR APIs, as well as access to the ActionScript code from JavaScript and vice versa. This is the security sandbox we'll be working with for the rest of this chapter since all our HTML will be loaded from the AIR application's local directory.

> *Just because HTML content is loaded into the Application security sandbox doesn't mean the JavaScript will have a free-for-all access. There are quite a few limitations as to what JavaScript can be executed while running in the Application sandbox:* eval() *expressions are limited; loading remote JavaScript libraries is forbidden;* XMLHttpRequest *responses are limited to JSON objects only — no executable JavaScript, no cookies, and so on. For a complete listing, see "Section 7: HTML Content" in the Adobe documentation titled* Developing Adobe Air Applications With Adobe Flex 3, *which can be found at* www.adobe.com/support/documentation/en/air/#flex.

Interacting between Different Sandboxes

Content loaded into the application sandbox can't directly communicate with HTML content loaded into any other sandbox. A lot of bad things could happen (think in terms of cross-site scripting attacks, but throw in local files that the user's AIR application has access to, and you can begin to see the potential disaster).

However, because it would be too limiting not to have any interaction between content in different sandboxes, Adobe AIR provides a couple of ways to explicitly enable content in different sandboxes to communicate with each other.

❑ **Sandbox bridging**, in which you explicitly create a JavaScript interface explicitly declaring the data that can flow back and forth.

❑ **Cross-scripting**, in which you place HTML content in AIR-specific `iframe` tags in embedded HTML content and then set a couple of AIR-specific properties, `sandboxRoot`, and `documentRoot`.

The details of working with and communicating between different security sandboxes within AIR is beyond the scope of this book. Be sure to read the section titled "HTML Content" in the Adobe documentation referenced earlier. It's being mentioned here in passing so that when you experience security errors in your applications, or broken JavaScript code in embedded HTML pages, you'll know to go read the Adobe documentation in detail as to what limitations are in place.

Loading In-Memory Content

You might want to generate your own HTML on the fly from inside your AIR application. Instead of accessing a remote location, you'd just supply the `mx:HTML.htmlLoader` with your own HTML string:

```
private function loadInMemoryHTML():void
{
  var html:XML =
    <html>
      <head>
        <title>Test Title</title>
      </head>
      <body>
        This is in-memory html
      </body>
    </html>;

  htmlContainer.htmlLoader.loadString(html.toString());
}
```

Here, `htmlContainer` is the same `mx:Flex` component as defined earlier, except that, instead of setting the `location` property, the content is loaded at runtime by setting the `loadString` property of the contained `htmlLoader`. This code sample also uses Flex's XML native XML for declaring XML in code without the need of messy string concatenation.

The HTML in this case is loaded into the AIR application's domain, allowing any JavaScript to access the complete AIR APIs directly, and any ActionScript to access the HTML content's DOM, JavaScript.

Loading Local File Content

Finally, since Adobe AIR can access local files directly, you can read HTML content into the `mx:HTML` component. This is how you create the custom code for the embedded YouTube control that you want the sample application to have:

```
private function loadCustomEmbeddedPlayerHTML():String
{
```

```
    var file:File = File.applicationDirectory.resolvePath("embeddedPlayer.html");

    var fs:FileStream = new FileStream();
    fs.open( file, FileMode.READ );

    //  Read the entire contents of the HTML file
    var html:String = fs.readUTFBytes( fs.bytesAvailable )

    fs.close();

    youTubeEmbeddedPlayer.htmlLoader.loadString(html);
}
```

This function uses the AIR `File` class to resolve a reference to a file called `embeddedPlayer.html` from the filesystem path where the AIR application was installed. The `embeddedPlayer.html` declares all the HTML, including code to embed the YouTube embedded Flash video player in the HTML. This code includes referencing external JavaScript as well as remote SWF files.

After the file reference is obtained and assigned to the `file` variable, a `FileStream` is created and opened in read-only mode to read the contents of the HTML file into a variable. Don't forget to close all your open file references when you're done.

And then, just as when working with in-memory HTML earlier, we load the HTML string into the `youTubeEmbeddedPlayer`, which is an `mx:HTML` control for rendering in the AIR application and is defined in MXML as:

```
<mx:HTML
    id="youTubeEmbeddedPlayer" width="600" height="400"
    complete="onHtmlLoadComplete(event)"
    verticalScrollPolicy="off"
    horizontalScrollPolicy="off"
/>
```

Examining EmbeddedPlayer.html Content

The YouTube `embeddedPlayer.html` file contains a lot of JavaScript code, which uses the public YouTube Embedded Player API that has documented for controlling their embedded player.

Additionally, the `embeddedPlayer.html` page has an embedded SWF object, which contains the actual player for displaying the videos. To embed the player, the HTML code uses the `swfobject.js` code library, as declared on the following line of HTML:

```
<script src="swfobject.js" type="text/javascript"></script>
```

This loads the `swfobject.js` from the local application directory, the same directory as the parent `embeddedPlayer.html`, as HTML content loaded into the `mx:HTML` component will continue to use the relative paths for child content.

YouTube's original embedded sample HTML page referenced the loading of the `swfobject.js` JavaScript code to one of their servers in a `script src` HTML that looked like:

```
<script
  src="http://swfobject.googlecode.com/svn/tags/rc3/swfobject/src/swfobject.js"
```

```
      type="text/javascript">
    </script>
```

Google stores the `swfobject.js` on their servers so that, when you're using their API, you don't have to worry about hosting any of their specific files. However, this doesn't help us out when we're trying to load local HTML content that accesses these APIS because of AIR sandbox constraints.

Loading the `swfobject.js` from the Google servers into our AIR application that loaded content locally won't work because of sandbox violations as discussed previously. Since the `embeddedPlayer.html` content was loaded from the AIR application's directory, it's placed into the regular AIR application sandbox. When the AIR application loads the `swfobject.js` from the remote `http://swfobject.googlecode.com` domain, all the JavaScript code and references are then placed in the `swfobject.js`'s own sandbox, and it can only access code limited to its own sandbox, which excludes the default AIR application sandbox.

The easiest thing to do to make this work was to just download the `swfobject.js` and load it from the local directory, which is what we've done in the sample. However, it would be possible to load up the JavaScript files from the different domains into the AIR application and create a script bridge. But for this example, and probably many of yours, it won't be worth the hassle of setting up script bridging when you have total control of the HTML files you distribute with your AIR application.

Interacting with JavaScript

HTML content loaded into the `HTMLLoader`, whether with the `mx:HTML` control or directly by creating an `HTMLLoader`, has bidirectional access between the JavaScript and ActionScript environments. JavaScript can call ActionScript methods, create ActionScript objects, and even raise events into ActionScript handlers. Conversely, ActionScript can call into JavaScript methods, handle unhandled JavaScript exceptions, manipulate HTML DOM, and raise ActionScript events with JavaScript end points. There's quite a bit that can be done, and we're only going to touch the basics here.

Calling Embedded JavaScript from ActionScript

The YouTube Chromeless Player that's embedded on the `embeddedPlayer.html` page has several JavaScript functions for controlling the video player, such as play, pause, mute, and the like (see Listing 39-1). Any publicly defined JavaScript function will be available to be called from ActionScript.

We'll be defining our own UI for listing out potential videos to play in MXML. When the user presses screen elements defined in an MXML `List`, the ActionScript will call into the JavaScript `loadNewVideo()` function, which will then have the embedded YouTube player begin playing a video. The same will hold true for our custom buttons that will control when the video can be played, paused, or stopped. And even the volume slider, defined completely in Flex, will call into the JavaScript API.

Listing 39-1: A Partial Listing of JavaScript Functions Available to ActionScript

```
function loadNewVideo(id, startSeconds) {
  if (ytplayer) {
    ytplayer.loadVideoById(id, parseInt(startSeconds));
  }
```

```
    }

    function play() {
      if (ytplayer) {
        ytplayer.playVideo();
      }
    }

    function pause() {
      if (ytplayer) {
        ytplayer.pauseVideo();
      }
    }

    function stop() {
      if (ytplayer) {
        ytplayer.stopVideo();
      }
    }

    function mute() {
      if (ytplayer) {
        ytplayer.mute();
      }
    }

    function unMute() {
      if (ytplayer) {
        ytplayer.unMute();
      }
    }

    function setVolume(newVolume) {
      if (ytplayer) {
        ytplayer.setVolume(newVolume);
      }
    }

    function getVolume() {
      if (ytplayer) {
        return ytplayer.getVolume();
      }
    }
```

In order for AIR to call JavaScript code, you wait for the HTML content to be loaded (via the HTMLLoader), and then you use the reference to the htmlLoader to call the method.

The following ActionScript code demonstrates calling the JavaScript method loadNewVideo():

```
public function loadVideoAndPlay(videoId:String):void
{
  youTubeEmbeddedPlayer.domWindow.loadNewVideo(videoId ,0);
}
```

The youTubeEmbeddedPlayer is the same mx:HTML component defined above with the embedded Player.html loaded. Access the domWindow, which is the root of the HTML DOM contained within this instance of mx:HTML. All the public JavaScript functions listed in Listing 39-1 are accessible from the domWindow property; the calls to playing, stopping, and muting videos would look very similar.

It's that easy to call JavaScript functions from ActionScript code. The code in the Chapter_39_Demo.mxml file shows similar execution of JavaScript code from ActionScript methods.

Calling ActionScript from JavaScript

Accessing the ActionScript code from JavaScript is almost as easy. However, you need to create a reference to the main ActionScript code so that the JavaScript can access it. This is done by dynamically creating a variable in the JavaScript context that references the actual AIR application. This is performed upon completion of the HTML content loading.

Remember, the mx:HTML component defined had a complete event handler:

```
<html:HTMLLoader id="youTubeEmbeddedPlayer" width="600" height="400"
        complete="onHtmlLoadComplete(event)"
/>
```

Upon completion of the HTML content loading, the complete handler is executed, calling into the onHtmlLoadComplete handler, which is responsible for setting of the reference to the AIR application in the JavaScript context:

```
private function onHtmlLoadComplete(event:Event):void
{
  trace("onHtmlLoadComplete");
  youTubeEmbeddedPlayer.domWindow.airAppRef = this;
}
```

Again, use the domWindow, and create the airAppRef variable, which is dynamically added into the JavaScript context with a reference to this AIR application. It's that easy to bridge between AIR and JavaScript.

Now, let's call some ActionScript methods from the JavaScript that was loaded with the embedded Player.html. When a new video is loaded into the embedded YouTube player, a bunch of metrics are made available: video length, size in bytes, number of bytes loaded, and so on. The goal is to pass this data back into the ActionScript context so that the AIR application can present the data.

When the embedded JavaScript loads, it sets up an interval to call the updateytplayerInfo() every 250 milliseconds, or about 4 times/second. This function then calls the appropriate AIR ActionScript through the airAppRef that we established upon successful loading of the HTML content in the AIR application:

```
function updateytplayerInfo() {
  airAppRef.setBytesLoaded( getBytesLoaded());
  airAppRef.setBytesTotal( getBytesTotal());
  airAppRef.setLengthOfVideo( getDuration());
```

```
    airAppRef.setCurrentTime( getCurrentTime());
    airAppRef.setStartBytes( getStartBytes());
    airAppRef.setVolume( getVolume());
}
```

This JavaScript function relies on many helper functions (getBytesLoaded(), getBytesTotal(), getDuration(), etc.) that inspect properties on the embedded YouTube video player for reading metadata about the loaded video. The most important thing here is to make the connection that the airAppRef is the same reference that we created in the onHtmlLoadComplete event earlier, and it's the lifeline between the JavaScript and ActionScript worlds.

Now, on the ActionScript side, there's a function implementation for each of the metrics set by updateytplayerInfo(), setBytesLoaded, setBytesTotal, setLengthOfVideo, and so on. They all follow a similar convention as the example for setBytesLoaded, as follows:

```
public var setBytesLoaded:Function = function( value:String ) : void
{
  currentBytesLoaded = value;
  bytes.text = currentBytesLoaded + "/" + currenttotalBytes ;
}
```

This might be a bit confusing, as we have a variable called setBytesLoaded that is set to a generic function that takes a string value. In this sense, setBytesLoaded isn't really a method but a pointer to a method, even though the JavaScript side of things thinks it is and treats it accordingly.

With all these methods implemented, the JavaScript has no trouble passing data back into ActionScript for the AIR application to consume.

Controlling the HTML DOM from ActionScript

Another desire might be to manipulate the loaded HTML's DOM from the ActionScript code. In the embeddedPlayer.html, there's an h2 HTML tag that will render the title of the currently playing video. This h2 tag can be manipulated directly from ActionScript:

```
<h2 id="videoTitle"></h2>
```

The HTML markup will render the title of the video in a header font, and from ActionScript, when a video is played as a result of a user pressing the Play button, you can load up the title in the HTML page by accessing the videoTitle DOM element and modifying the innerHTML property.

```
public function setVideoTitleinHtml(title:String):void
{
 youTubeEmbeddedPlayer.domWindow.document.getElementById("videoTitle").innerHTML =
     title;
}
```

Using the standard JavaScript getElementById, search the DOM for the appropriate object, and then set the property. This pattern can be used just as you would from within JavaScript.

Summary

We've only begun to discuss the possible integration between HTML content and ActionScript in AIR. AIR offers a complete API for integrating JavaScript/HTML, whether from an external website or generated internally at runtime. Bidirectional events, method invocation, objects, HTML DOM manipulation all provide for complex possibilities. Be sure to read the Adobe documentation, which delves deeper into the intricacies.

Another great use case for embedding HTML in your AIR application is to render an existing HTML/JavaScript UI-based component based on one of the many popular JavaScript frameworks — such as Dojo, script.aculo.us, JQuery, and so on — in your desktop application without re-creating existing functionality. Or, maybe you'll just take an existing web application, load it locally, and then use the AIR API to facilitate persisting data to the local user's file system (sandbox restrictions apply). Adobe AIR is a powerful technology to facilitate both the online and offline world of application development.

The next chapter takes a look at Flex's support for deep linking, which makes it easier for your applications to share their content with the Internet as URLs.

Deep Linking

This chapter describes techniques for deep linking in Flex applications, in which the browser URL and the state of the application are tightly coupled.

We begin with a definition of the term and a simple example of the idea. An initial example demonstrates the fundamental Flex API for deep linking. We also explore the underpinnings of the technology and then present two increasingly complex and realistic examples of applications. The chapter concludes with a note about some important related technologies.

Deep Linking on the Web

The term "deep linking" was first applied to HTML websites, well before before the advent of Flash and Flex. A deep link is any hyperlink that points to a location within the site, as opposed to the home page or some other main page. For example, a deep link into a news site might take the form `http://news.example.com/2005/boston/man-bites-dog.html`. Following it would take one straight to the story about that ill-fated encounter, rather than to the `news.example.com` home page. The link is "deep" because it bypasses all the manual navigation a user would otherwise have to go through. Instead of the user accessing the site's home page, choosing to view stories from 2005, further clicking through to a page showing 2005 stories from Boston, and finally clicking through the "Man Bites Dog" story headline, this deep link takes the user directly to their destination.

Deep links in HTML are very useful, for many reasons familiar to Internet users. Users can use the Back and Forward buttons to access recently viewed pages in their browser's history. They can also bookmark these URLs to record the locations of interesting content, email or IM them to other people, and use them as hyperlinks in other web pages.

Deep Linking with Flex

Many Flex applications also have a similar notion of "location." A Flex application often has multiple *navigational states*, which reflect the navigational actions that the user has taken within the application. Just as with an HTML site, users often would like to be able to work with these states using their browser's history, their bookmarks, email/IM, and external hyperlinks.

For example, imagine a Flex application that — like the website mentioned previously — shows a large collection of news stories, allowing the viewer to browse stories from those feeds by specifying the date and location. Suppose that this Flex application is embedded in a web page at URL `http://flexworldnews.com`. A user of this application visits that URL and narrows her focus to the year 2005, using an `mx:ComboBox` component in the application. She then clicks on a map of the world in an `mx:Image` control to look at stories in Boston, and finally selects "Man Bites Dog" from an `mx:List` control to view the selected story.

Our user expects to be able to do the following:

❑ Bookmark the URL so she can look at the story again later, using the same Flex application.

❑ Email or IM the URL to a friend who is interested in this kind of story. The friend should be able to click the link and see the same story in the same application.

❑ Click the Back button to go back to the last state of the application, in which she was viewing all 2005 stories from Boston. This should not cause the page and the application to be reloaded (which could be a lengthy process and also might result in the loss of important UI state). Instead, it should merely cause the currently loaded application to change its appearance.

❑ At all times, see a window title on her web browser that makes sense given the content that she's looking at.

Without special support for deep linking in Flex, none of these things can work. A Flex application's state isn't automatically known to the browser; the browser has no way to know that a user interacted with a `ComboBox`, `Image`, or `List` component inside the application. Nor, if it knew, could the browser understand how those actions should affect the URL. Without deep linking, the URL just stays stuck on `http://flexworldnews.com`.

> *To give users what they expect, it seems that a Flex application has to put extra information into the browser URL, and must also make use of this information when present in the URL.*

We can express this more rigorously. For deep linking to work in a Flex application (or any browser-based application, for that matter), the following things must happen:

1. The application must update the browser URL to reflect navigation by the user. Whenever the user navigates using the Flex application's user interface, the browser's URL must be updated to match the navigational state at all times. This means that the URL will always work as expected when it is used as a bookmark, hyperlink, or browser history item. In our example, navigating to the "Man Bites Dog" story must automatically change the URL from `http://flexworldnews.com` to something like `http://flexworldnews.com#2005/Boston/ManBitesDog`.

2. The application must update its navigational state to reflect the browser URL. Visiting a bookmark, a hyperlink, or a history URL that was generated from the application must always take the

application to the correct state. So in our imaginary example, visiting `http://flexworldnews.com#2005/Boston/ManBitesDog` should start the application and immediately show the story in question. Subsequently changing the URL to `http://flexworldnews.com#2005/Chicago` causes the application to update so that 2005 Chicago stories are viewed instead.

3. The window title should be updated in both of the preceding cases to reflect the navigational state.

Fragment Identifiers in URLs

The URLs in the preceding scenario look somewhat different from most HTML links. All of our example URLs include a hash mark (#) followed by some string. It looks as though the changed portion of the URL — the part that expresses the notation of "where" the application is — always follows that pound sign.

This part of a URL is called a *fragment identifier* or *fragment ID*. In HTML documents, the string after the hash mark is interpreted as a pointer to some chunk of the document, and usually causes the browser to automatically scroll so as to place this chunk in view. However, fragment identifiers can be used in many different ways. The part of the URL before the hash mark tells the *server* what data to return to the client for rendering. The part after the hash, the fragment ID, instructs the *client* what to do with that data once it arrives, in a way that in large part is up to the client:

> . . . for any new data type one can be creative about using the fragment ID in a relevant way. For example, for a 3D object the fragment ID could give a viewport. For a music object, the fragment ID could give a section in time, or a set of parts, or it could include a suggested tempo.

— Tim Berners-Lee

This flexibility is exactly what allows Flex applications to make use of the fragment for deep linking. The fragment identifier is what encodes the application's navigational state.

Web browsers are clever about fragments in another really important way. When the fragment is the only part of the URL that changes from one URL to another, the browser understands that there is no need to reload the page. This is another vital ingredient in deep linking, because navigation between different states in a Flex application should not reload or reinitialize the program.

Flex 3 Support for Deep Linking

In Flex 3, Adobe introduced a new ActionScript API called the `BrowserManager`, which makes deep linking much easier than before by isolating the programmer from the messy, browser-dependent details. Applications can use this API to change the browser URL, and also be notified via an event whenever the URL changes. The API can also be used to change the browser window title.

Deep-linking support is not just an ActionScript API, however: it requires integration with the browser. Part of Flex 3's deep-linking implementation is a set of JavaScript, HTML, and CSS files that live in a special folder named `history`. This folder must accompany every application that uses the `BrowserManager` API. It is automatically included in the `html-templates` directory of any Flex project created with Flex Builder 3 that has browser navigation enabled. Templates containing this same folder are also available in the Flex 3 standalone SDK's `templates` directory.

Using the BrowserManager API

The `BrowserManager` class is very simple. It provides access to a singleton object that implements the `IBrowserManager` interface. You can obtain the object by calling the static function `BrowserManager.getInstance()`. All API usage involves the `IBrowserManager` interface; `BrowserManager` is simply a way to get at an object implementing that interface.

To make use of deep linking, at application startup, you must initialize the `IBrowserManager` interface by calling its `init()` method:

```
// common initialization sequence for BrowserManager API
var browserManager:IBrowserManager = BrowserManager.getInstance();
browserManager.addEventListener(BrowserChangeEvent.BROWSER_URL_CHANGE,
                                handleBrowserUrlChange);
browserManager.init();
```

An event listener is usually added just before the call to `init()`, to handle notification of changes to the browser URL. It has to go before the `init()` call, because `init()` dispatches this event as part of doing its job.

Examining the Browser URL

After initializing the API, you can examine the browser URL's initial fragment ID string at application startup. You can also look at the entire URL:

```
// show the current fragment ID and URL
trace("fragment identifier is:", BrowserManager.getInstance().fragment);
trace("browser URL is:", BrowserManager.getInstance().url);
```

You can also tell the `BrowserManager` to set the fragment ID to a new value, changing the URL in the browser:

```
// change the current fragment ID
BrowserManager.getInstance().setFragment("newFragmentValue");
```

You can respond to changes in the fragment ID initiated by browser, by adding a listener for events of the type `BrowserChangeEvent.BROWSER_URL_CHANGE`, which are dispatched when the browser URL changes:

```
// respond to changes in the browser URL's fragment ID
private function handleBrowserUrlChange(e:BrowserChangeEvent):void
{
    trace("fragment changed to:", BrowserManager.getInstance().fragment);
}
```

You can also set the title of the browser window:

```
// change the window title
BrowserManager.getInstance().setTitle("The Title Of My Window");
```

That's almost the whole API! (There are two other events that can be dispatched, having to do with sensing whether the application itself has changed the URL.) The BrowserManager is very simple and has few built-in complexities. Using it effectively, however, requires some careful design and attention to details, as we'll see.

Example #1: The BrowserManager API in Action

Our first example explores the aspects of BrowserManager API that were mentioned above, in a very simple setting.

> *If you are using Internet Explorer, a number of aspects of deep linking do not work properly when a Flex application is accessed directly from your computer's file system. Instead, you must copy the Flex application to an actual HTTP web server (typically, one that runs locally on your computer) and access it from a URL that points to that server. For convenience, therefore, the Firefox browser is recommended for experimenting with deep-linking applications, since it doesn't have this problem.*
>
> *If you still would like to use another browser, you will need to set up a local web server on your computer and arrange for your deep-linking examples and applications to be accessed from that server over HTTP.*

Compile and run the example application example01/src/example01.mxml and read the code. This example sets up a very simple two-way connection between a text input field and the URL fragment, allowing you to play with the API and see how it works. It also shows how the browser window title can be manipulated with the API.

Upon starting this application, you'll see the display shown in Figure 40-1.

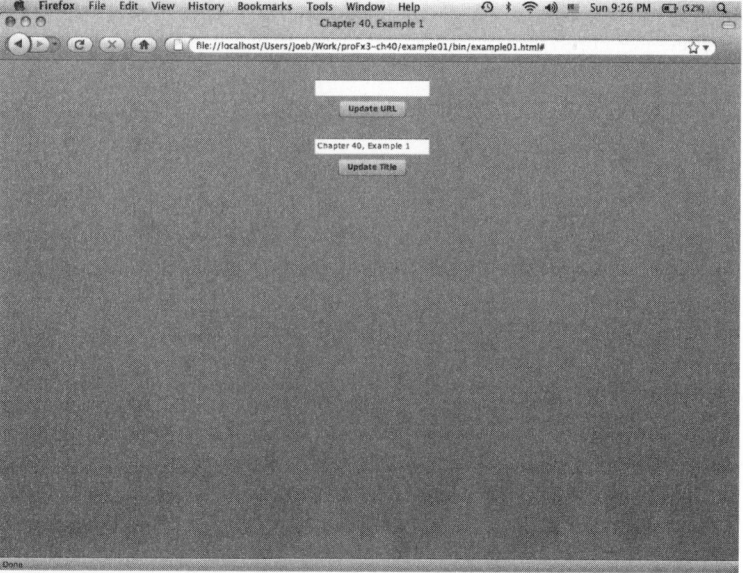

Figure 40-1

Next, change the contents of the first text field to **xxx** and click Update URL. Also change the second text field to **Some Other Title** and click Update Title. You see an updated display similar to Figure 40-2.

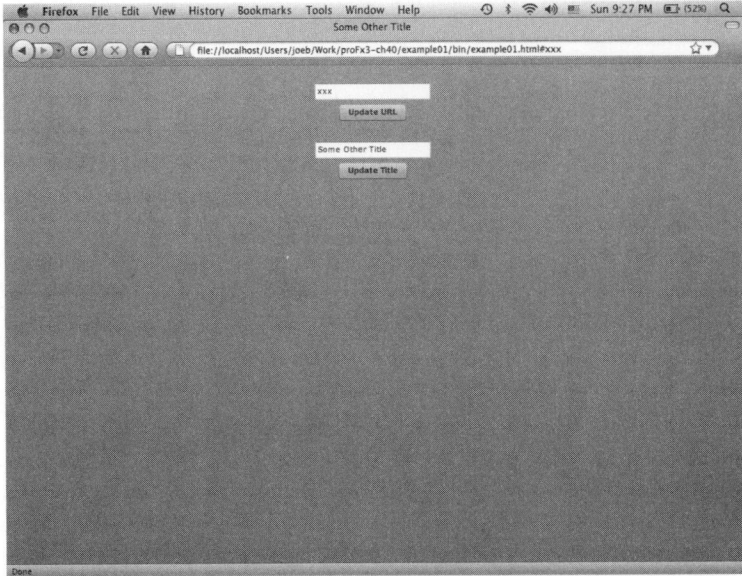

Figure 40-2

Update the text field again to **yyy**, and then click Update URL. You'll see the display change again to reflect the new state (see Figure 40-3):

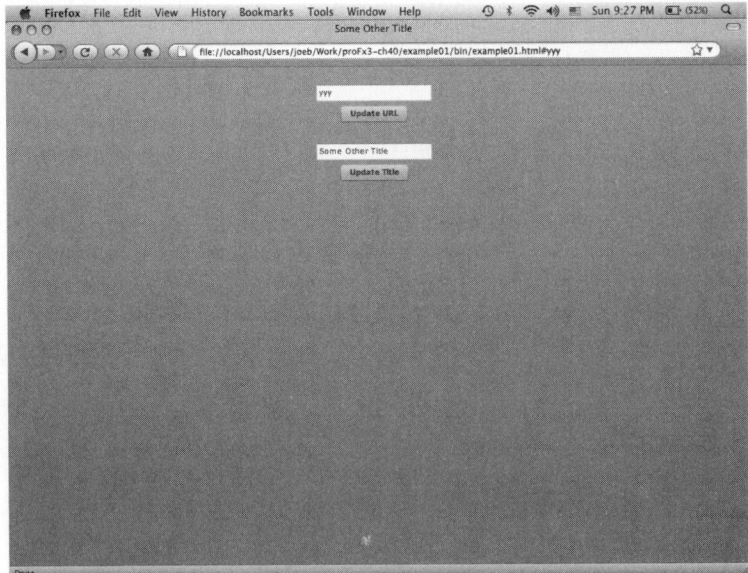

Figure 40-3

Now hit the browser's Back button. Not only will xxx reappear in the browser URL, but it will also appear instantly appear in the application's text field without reloading. The application is aware of the URL contents and is dynamically adjusting its state to match that URL, without a page refresh taking place!

Page refreshes only take place when the browser history reaches a URL whose portion exclusive of the fragment is different. You can experiment with this behavior by visiting a different site altogether and then clicking the Back button to step back into the preceding sequence of URLs in the example application. Switching between adjacent history URLs that were recorded from the same Flex application does not cause a refresh, but switching to a URL for a different site does (as indeed it must).

Finally, copy the current browser URL into the clipboard. Open a new browser window, paste the URL into its location bar, and then go to that location. The application will reappear, but not only that; the value xxx will also appear in the Flex application's text field. We have effectively bookmarked the state of one application instance and communicated it to another, separate instance by merely copying a URL around.

These behaviors are simple and do not in themselves suffice to add deep linking to a complex rich Internet application. However, they provide a core on which you can build a powerful set of deep-linking capabilities.

Encoding and Decoding URI Components

This is a good moment to highlight an important aspect of deep linking: the escaping of data that is placed into the URL. Such escaping is not done by the BrowserManager for you; your application must do it. The example shows how to do this, using the top-level Flash functions encodeURIComponent() and decodeURIComponent().

Data encoded in any part of a URL may require escaping, because the Internet standards for URLs impose restrictions on the set of characters that may be used in different parts of a URL. Certain characters called *metacharacters* may only be used in the correct places, where they delimit parts of the URL. Also, characters outside the basic ASCII character range (hexadecimal 20–7E) may not occur at all. These characters must be escaped by replacing them with the syntax %xx, where xx is the hex encoding of the character. Unicode characters are encoded with multiple such escape sequences, using their UTF-8 encoding.

What this means in practice is that you cannot set the URL fragment to any string value you want; you must escape any parts of it that could contain characters such as the ones just mentioned. For this reason, the example code to move data between the application and the browser URL looks like this:

```
private function updateApplicationUrl():void
{
    var value:String = BrowserManager.getInstance().fragment;
    value = decodeURIComponent(value);   // decode escaped characters
    fragmentInput.text = value;
}

private function updateBrowserUrl():void
{
    var value:String = fragmentInput.text;
    value = encodeURIComponent(value);   // escape any special characters
    BrowserManager.getInstance().setFragment(value);
}
```

So, using this technique (as you can verify with the example), a string such as "étude #5" must be represented by using the URL fragment `%C3%A9tude%235` in order to avoid generating an illegal URL or losing data.

As you will see in later examples, there are further subtleties to escaping such characters; in practice we won't want to escape the entire URL fragment all of the time!

Under the Hood: How Flex Deep Linking Works

In this section, we'll take a very brief detour to examine how deep linking works in Flex. It's worth understanding the basic mechanism, because it affects the way in which your applications will be built and how they can break.

The Flex Deep-Linking Architecture

Figure 40-4 illustrates the essential components in the Flex deep-linking architecture:

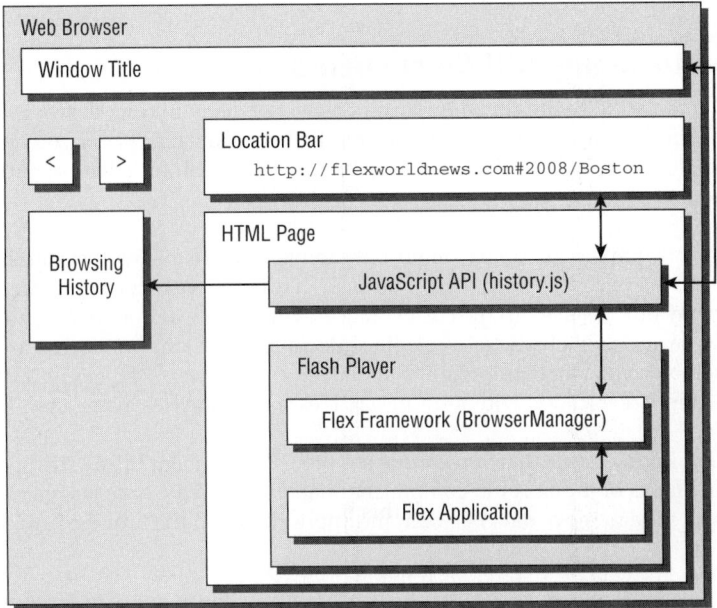

Figure 40-4

There are a number of elements in play here. All these elements cooperate to support deep linking and play a distinct role:

❏   The web browser, which is the container for the entire user experience.

❏   The window title, location bar, and browsing history controls are not part of the page but are controlled directly by the web browser.

- ❑ The Flex SDK's `history.js` JavaScript API library. This library communicates with the web browser using JavaScript to change the current location bar URL, make entries in the browser, and change the window title. It hides these details from the `BrowserManager` API, since they vary considerably from one browser to another, and exposes a uniform set of JavaScript functions and callbacks.

- ❑ The Flash Player, running an application that includes the Flex Framework.

- ❑ Within the Flex Framework, the `BrowserManager` API. which hides the JavaScript API from your application code, in its place exposing a simpler, strongly typed ActionScript API. It uses the Flash Player's `ExternalInterface` class to talk to the JavaScript layer.

- ❑ Your own Flex application, which communicates with the `BrowserManager`.

Handling Changes in Navigational State

When the navigational state changes, the application will ask the `BrowserManager` to set the URL fragment and title to the appropriate strings. The `BrowserManager` then makes `ExternalInterface` calls to functions in `history.js` that take care of doing these things in the correct way for the user's web browser. Ultimately the browser's location bar, internal browsing history, and window title are updated to reflect the change.

Handling Changes in the Browser's URL

When the browser URL changes, a callback is made to a `history.js` function, notifying it that the page was loaded or that the URL changed. The exact mechanism for this notification is extremely browser-dependent. The `history.js` function then uses an `ExternalInterface` callback to notify the `BrowserManager` inside the Flex framework of the new or changed URL. Finally, the `BrowserManager` dispatches a Flex event to the application code, notifying it of this fact.

Why history.js Is So Important

Although the need for deep linking was foreseen very early in the development of the Web, the ugly reality is that today's browsers do not support it in a uniform way. The DOM properties, methods, and events that serve as the interface to the location bar and browsing history are anything but standard. Some browsers require very tricky approaches or complex bug workarounds.

The `history.js` JavaScript library hides all this browser-dependent logic, exposing a uniform API to Flex applications via `ExternalInterface`. In fact, it is more complex than the ActionScript portion of the `BrowserManager` API and will probably continue to grow in complexity as browsers evolve. According to one way of thinking, `history.js` might be the most valuable asset in the `BrowserManager` — and it's not really even part of the Flex framework!

Real-World Deep Linking: the Space Image Browser

The remainder of this chapter provides a couple of examples that show how to build a real-world example that successfully employs deep linking. A concrete application makes it easier to discuss the principles with which we will be working, so we'll wave in discussions of relevant concepts as we go.

Our example is that of an *image browser*: a Flex application that allows the user to search and browse through a small database of images. (Our example images are photographs taken with the Hubble Space Telescope.) There are different ways of browsing and searching these images, so this small application has a distinct notion of navigation. Many states of the application (such as looking at a particular image) can be represented as a deep link of some kind.

Example #2: Working with Navigational States

This first version of our image viewer employs deep linking to couple the browser URL to the choice of an image being viewed from a single, flat list of images.

This example introduces some key architectural notions:

❑   Defining your application's navigational states

❑   Deciding how to encode navigational states in the URL

❑   Encapsulating "browser knowledge" inside just a few classes (in this case, only one!)

Figure 40-5 illustrates `example02.mxml` doing its thing.

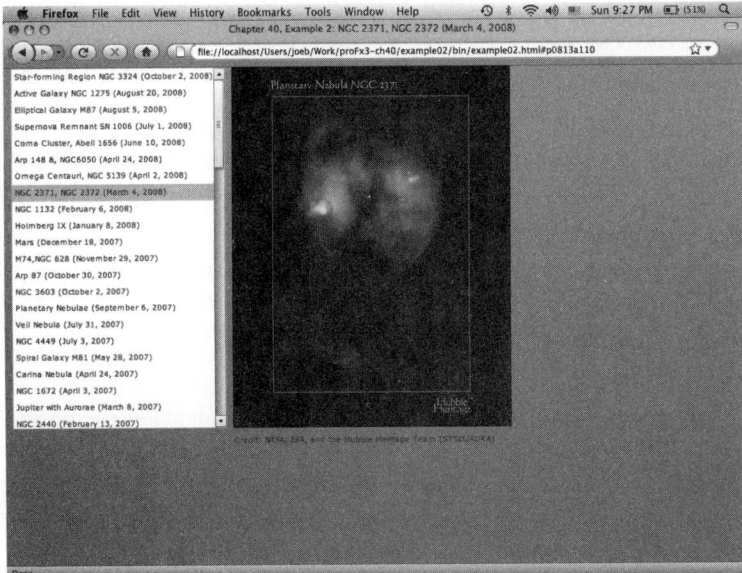

Figure 40-5

On the left is a list of image descriptions; on the right, a display of the currently selected image with its photography credits below. There is a check box that allows the user to decide whether the image should be stretched to fit the available display space. Altogether, this is a pretty simple application.

What Is Navigational State?

Most applications can be in different states, depending on the user's interaction with them. But the word "state" can mean many different things. At a very general level, it could cover the value of every property in the program, as well as the call trees of all active threads. What kind of state are we talking about here?

Navigational state represents the user's main focus of attention.

We've been using the term *navigational state* for a while in this chapter, to talk about an important subset of the application's overall state. Navigational state is not the whole state of the program: it's just the part of it that has to do with *the main focus of the user's attention*, and nothing else.

Doesn't this raise even more fuzzy questions about what "main focus of attention" means? Yes, and those are reasonable questions, and ones that are worth answering if you are building a real-world application.

This example defines "main focus of attention" as something really simple: it's the photograph that the user is looking at. That is our navigational state, and it's a pretty obvious choice for this program.

There are other states of our example application that are *not* navigational state. For example, the check box that controls image scaling isn't part of the user's "attentional focus." Why? Because we decided it was more of a local viewing option, sort of like the current window size. Someone else might have made a different call. All in all, the definition of navigational state is subjective, but it tends to have an obvious component of "where the user is."

Encoding Navigational State

If you asked someone at a computer what they were busy doing, their answer would probably be a natural-language representation of their navigational state: "I'm looking at the Whirlpool Galaxy!" In an application with deep linking, not surprisingly, a central question is deciding how to represent the navigational state in the fragment identifier of a URL: a simple string.

Our navigational state is simple, and so is the encoding solution. Each image in our catalog has a unique ID. So, we will represent the choice of an image by using its ID as the URL fragment. If they're looking at the Whirlpool Galaxy picture with ID p0512a110, then the URL fragment will be #p0512a110. The entire URL will look something like this:

```
http://your.site.here.com/ch40/example02/example02.html#p0512a110
```

Here is an important principle for encoding your navigational state: encode thoughtfully the first time, because you will be stuck with your decisions for a long time.

Deep links in your Flex application are just like URLs; once they're out there on the Web in people's emails and bookmark lists, they're potentially there to stay. You don't want all those deep links out there to stop working if you change your mind. If you do change your mind, you will have to consider supporting "legacy" deep link formats. So, it's best not to change your mind!

A Basic Deep-Linking Architecture

Our application has to do three things: change the browser URL to reflect the choice of image, change the choice of image to reflect the browser URL, and change the window title to make sense in both of those cases.

The code that does this could be scattered around the application. But if it were, we'd be seeing calls and event handlers for the `BrowserManager` API all over the place, and it would be really hard to change the program if we ever wanted to change the definition of navigational state or the way that state was represented in the URL. Debugging interaction with the browser would be a nightmare, too.

This example puts all the `BrowserManager`-related code in a single class, `CatalogNavigationManager`. This class hides all `BrowserManager` interaction from the rest of the app.

In fact, this class holds the entire navigational state of the application! The rest of the application doesn't have to worry about navigation much: it just sets the `image` property of the `CatalogNavigation Manager` to reflect changes in the image being viewed. It also uses a data listen for changes in the `CatalogNavigationManager`'s `image` property, and adjusts its view accordingly.

This might feel like overengineering for such a simple example, but it results in a clean design. And in our final example, this approach pays off with a larger dividend.

Adjusting the View State

It's sometimes a bit tricky to adjust the state of a view to correspond to the navigational state, because Flex commonly performs many actions asynchronously, particularly the setting of properties on complex components. Even in this example, this issue comes up: the application needs to not only show the correct image when the application navigates to a URL, but it also needs to scroll the image list to a position where that image's description is visible.

Consider the following function from `example02.mxml`:

```
public function set image(img:CatalogImage):void
{
    // Update the UI state to select the indicated image and force its visibility.
    catalogList.selectedItem = img;
    catalogList.validateProperties();
    if (catalogList.selectedIndex >= 0)
    {
        catalogList.scrollToIndex(catalogList.selectedIndex);
    }
}
```

It would be nice if you could just set the `selectedItem` property of a list and then call `scrollToIndex(selectedIndex)`. That doesn't actually work, though, because changes to a list's selected item are not reflected until after a short time interval goes by. Instead, you must make a call to `validateProperties()` to force the list to make the selection change before consulting its `selectedIndex` property.

This issue is not unique to deep linking, but it comes up very frequently when building a deep link–aware application. In some cases, the view itself is constructed asynchronously, and there is not even a view to adjust at the time that a URL change is detected!

Example #3: A More Sophisticated Image Browser

The final version of the image viewer employs a more sophisticated navigational state: a user can browse images by year or search for images whose description matches a substring.

This example introduces some new ideas:

❑ Defining complex navigational states affecting multiple, alternative views

❑ Generating and parsing URLs for complex navigational states

❑ Creating a set of `Route` subclasses to represent each URL syntax used by the application

❑ Generalizing the `NavigationManager` to become truly application-independent

There are many ways to address the issues raised by complex navigational state, and the approach shown in this example is only one such way. Whether it's the approach you end up using or not, it concretely illustrates some of the challenges involved in building a real-world deep-linking solution.

Figure 40-6 shows `example03.mxml` in browse-by-year mode. And Figure 40-7 shows its Search mode.

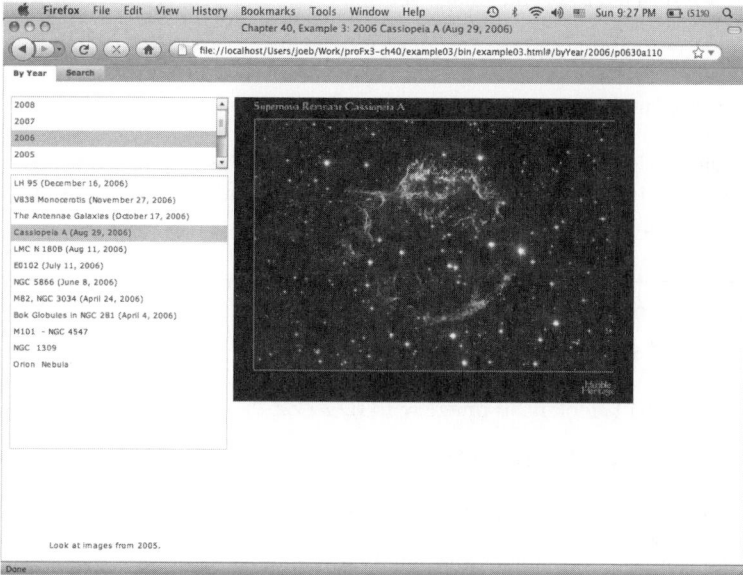

Figure 40-6

Figure 40-7

In both cases, the user may or may not be looking at a specific browse/search result list, and if they are, they may not have selected a specific image yet.

A Richer Notion of Navigational State . . .

What represents the "main focus of attention" for this more complex example?

As before, this is a design decision, not a cut-and-dried fact. This example was designed with the idea that each of the following cases represents a distinct focus of attention, with its own URL syntax:

State	URL syntax
By Year tab viewed, no year selected	/byYear/
Browsing by year *YYYY*, no image selected	/byYear/YYYY
Browsing by year *YYYY*, looking at image with ID *ZZZZ*	/byYear/YYYY/ZZZZ
Search tab viewed, no search performed	/search/
Searching for string *SSSS*, no image selected	/search/SSSS
Searching for string *SSSS*, looking at image with ID *ZZZZ*	/search/SSSS/ZZZZ

There are a lot of other ways this decision could have been made — this is just the way this application happens to have been built.

Notice that the URL /byYear/ can be thought of as the same as /byYear/*YYYY*, but with a blank year. The same argument applies to /search/, which can be thought of as /search/*SSSS* with a blank search string.

And a Larger Number of Views ...

This example has several views, and its view components are decomposed more carefully. The MainView component is always visible, and shows the top-level tab navigator. When browsing by year, the YearImageBrowseView component is shown. When searching for a substring match, the ImageSearchView is shown.

One of the more complex aspects of this example is the number of views. Each one of these views interacts with a different aspect of the URL syntax as shown in the following table.

View	Relevant aspect of URL fragment
MainView	whether /byYear/... or /search/...
YearImageBrowseView	Year and imageID portions of URL
ImageSearchView	Search string and imageID portions of URL

Require a Richer Deep-Linking Architecture

The approach taken in this richer example is to decompose the earlier CatalogNavigationManager into two different kinds of objects with separate responsibilities. One family is a set of Route objects. Each Route object represents a particular kind of navigational state and its translation to and from fragment strings. A YearRoute object represents the state when browsing by year, while a SearchRoute represents navigational state for searching by string match. Routes also know how to generate a meaningful window title from their own state. Each flavor of route object thus insulates all the interested views from knowledge of how this state is encoded. View can also examine the current route and decide if it is a route that affects them or if it's one they don't care about. For example, a YearRoute is not of interest to an ImageSearchView.

The other kind of object is the NavigationManager, which continues to mediate between the entire application and the BrowserManager API. Unlike the previous example, however, this manager is generic; it does not know anything about application state or about URL syntax. The Route objects take care of those responsibilities, and the NavigationManager holds onto a current route at all times.

The NavigationManager's route property thus holds the current navigational state for the application. The manager dispatches a CHANGE event whenever this property changes; all interested views listen for these changes and adjust themselves to the new Route accordingly. In the other direction, the views also request that the manager update its route when the user undertakes some action.

To further simplify the programming, the views in this example extend a RouteView superclass. This class extends Canvas to update the view when the NavigationManager's route changes, and update the manager's route when the view changes. Each view need override only two methods: getRoute(), which returns the Route representing the current view and its descendants, and updateViewState(), which examines the current route and adjusts the view.

To illustrate the flavor of this approach, here are those two functions as overridden in `ImageSearchView.mxml`:

```
override public function getRoute():Route
{
    return new SearchRoute(catalog, searchInput.text,
                            catalogList.selectedItem as CatalogImage);
}

override public function updateViewState():void
{
    var sr:SearchRoute = route as SearchRoute;
    if (sr != null)  // test to see if the current route is of interest
    {
        searchInput.text = sr.keyword;
        if (sr.keyword != "")  // test to see if a search string is in the route
        {
            catalogList.dataProvider =
                catalog.getImagesByDescriptionMatch(searchInput.text);
            catalogList.selectedItem = sr.image;
        }
        else    // no search string, show empty search result list
        {
            catalogList.dataProvider = new ArrayCollection();
        }
    }
}
```

Adjusting the View State, Version 2

When the application is started or its URL fragment changes, the `NavigationManager` must create the correct `Route` object to represent the URL syntax. It does so by making use of an implementation of the `IRouteFactory` interface to get a set of new `Route` objects. Each `Route` gets a chance to parse the URL fragment; if it succeeds, the resulting `Route` is taken to be the new navigational state of the application.

Given the variety of URL syntaxes, it's not a surprise that `Routes` should turn to ActionScript's `RegExp` class to help with the parsing! Here's the parsing function from `SearchRoute`:

```
override public function parseFragment(fragment:String):Boolean
{
    var matchExpression:RegExp = /\/search\/([^\/]*)(\/(.+))?/;
    var match:Array = matchExpression.exec(fragment);
    if (match)
    {
        keyword = decodeURIComponent(match[1]);
        if (match[3])
        {
            image = _catalog.getImageById(decodeURIComponent(match[3]));
        }
        return true;
    }

    return false;
}
```

Note how the URL is taken apart into exactly the right pieces by the `matchExpression` regular expression. The `RegExp` looks messy, but it's a lot easier than calling `indexOf()` and `substring()` a whole bunch of times!

Using HTML Navigation to Change States

The whole technique of using URL fragments suggests a neat trick: one can use ordinary HTML linkage techniques in the page containing a deep-linked Flex app to force the app into different states. And, indeed, this is the case! It can be a very handy trick for integrating HTML presentations with Flex. The example we've been discussing contains some hyperlinked HTML text at the start of the page's body:

```
<!-- Example of using HTML fragment navigation to jump to a state. -->
<p>Look at <a href="#/byYear/2005">images from 2005</a>.</p>
```

Clicking on the link "images from 2005" causes the application to navigate to show the browsing results for the year 2005, regardless of its current state. Naturally enough, this navigational change is treated properly by the browser and becomes part of the browsing history.

You might think that inside your Flex application, you could call `navigateToURL()` to pull the same trick, but unfortunately this appears to cause a page reload in Internet Explorer and Safari.

Search Engine Indexing and Optimization

One obvious benefit to building a deep-linked Flex application would seem to be the ability to have its locations indexed by search engines. With search indexing, people could look for Flex-hosted content using the most familiar search techniques on the Web. Having found a result, the link could take them straight to the application state that shows this content. Couldn't it?

Sadly, we'll all have to keep on wishing.

There are a couple of missing and/or faulty pieces to this puzzle, and this technique is still mostly out of reach as of press time. Everyone is looking for a solution and hoping for something better than the patchwork quilt of semi-solutions that exists today.

Here are the big problems:

❑ Deep-linked locations can't be found by crawling other HTML pages. The fragment portion of a URL after the "#" character is simply ignored by crawlers, because all links with the same non-fragment portion are presumed to refer to the same content. And, in any case, even if this weren't true, it isn't other HTML pages that need crawling to discover the structure of a deep-linked Flex app; it is the navigational states of the app that require crawling. Adobe and search engine companies say that they are grappling with the problem (which is difficult and which may require modifications to the Flash Player) but no reliable solution has emerged yet.

❑ If a deep-linked Flex application state could be found, there would be no way to figure out the searchable content in that state. Adobe and search engine companies continue to try to define a standardized way to expose searchable content to web crawlers, along with some "route-like" string that identifies this content. As of press time, there is a brand-new approach to doing so; it is not well documented by Adobe or the search engine firms and is reported to work either unreliably or not at all by some who have tried it.

❑ It is technically against the search engine companies' use guidelines to expose "fake HTML pages" that redirect users to the corresponding deep-linked state. It is tempting to think that one might expose ordinary, crawlable HTML pages that expose the correct content to search engine crawlers, which when accessed by a browser automatically replace the HTML content with the appropriate deep-linked state of your Flex application. Technically, this is a bit painful to pull off — those HTML pages have to be generated by something — but it does work perfectly. There is one big catch, though: providing one kind of content for search indexing and another type of content for actual viewing is frowned upon by the search engine providers, since it can lead to very real types of abuse. They have a nasty name for it: "cloaking," and if they catch you doing it, they can blacklist your site and refuse to index it. Some companies are using this approach in spite of these objections. Is it safe? Different people will give you different answers.

In short, there is no good advice right now for those who would like to see their deep-linked application search indexed. The one technique that actually works is officially out of bounds. There is hope, at least, in that the companies that can make a difference are making slow progress on the problem.

Related Technologies and Tools

In this final section, we take a very brief look at some other related techniques and tools.

SWFAddress

The SWFAddress open-source project has been around for several years. It is available from `www.asual.com/swfaddress`. SWFAddress predates the `BrowserManager` API and has no dependencies on Flex and requires only the Flash Player. This makes it an ideal choice for use with ActionScript applications that do not employ the Flex framework. It serves a very similar purpose to the `BrowserManager` in that it provides access to fragment and window title changes, isolating the application from knowledge of the ugly, browser-dependent matters taking place at the JavaScript level.

Some useful things about SWFAddress include:

❑ SWFAddress can work with multiple Flash clients in the same page

❑ SWFAddress is a bit more flexible in some ways; for example, you can disable the interaction with the browsing history if all you want to do is generate a permalink to a deep-linked state in the browser's location bar

UrlKit

UrlKit is available at `http://code.google.com/p/urlkit`. It works in conjunction with the `BrowserManager`, not as a replacement for it: it adds a notion of declarative URL syntax rules on top of the basic functionality provided by the `BrowserManager`. Using UrlKit, one can hook up MXML `UrlRule` components into a structure that both parses and generates URL fragments. Parts of these rule components correspond to variables embedded in the fragment syntax and can be bound to properties of other objects in the same component.

Overall, the approach of UrlKit's rules somewhat resembles the `Route` notion seen in the final example of this chapter, although rules are nested in a grammatical tree structure, whereas routes are simple alternatives in a flat list. While little or no coding is required to make use of UrlKit to couple URL syntax to your application, the rules are less flexible than the route approach, and it's sometimes not so obvious how to persuade the rule objects to do what one wants. If you want to try a declarative approach, in any case, UrlKit has that.

The UrlKit project was coauthored by Joe Berkovitz and Todd Rein, and was first created for Flex 2. The JavaScript portion of UrlKit was later refashioned into the `history.js` library used by the `BrowserManager` API and was considerably enhanced in the process. Some of the ActionScript portion migrated into the `BrowserManager`, but the majority of the rest is largely unchanged.

History Manager

Flex 2 had an API known as the `HistoryManager`. It was a simple system, requiring almost no programming effort, that automatically generated and parsed a URL fragment syntax representing the state of all "navigational components" in the application. The definition of a "navigational component" was hardwired into the Flex framework although the application had some control over how components participated.

There were a number of deficits in this API. The URL syntax it generated was opaque, in the sense that it consisted of automatically generated codes that were not intelligible to the reader. Furthermore, these codes can change unpredictably between versions of the same application, making it difficult to impossible to maintain forward compatibility with deep links. In truth, the `HistoryManager` exactly lives up to its name: it supports a limited notion of browsing history but does not support durable deep links.

This API is still available in Flex 3 but is deprecated and generally not recommended for use.

Summary

Deep linking is fascinating and powerful, in that it lives at the boundary between a Flex application and the HTML-based web ecosystem that supports and houses it. It enables many kinds of connections between the Flex and HTML worlds that are not obvious at first sight, and that carry with them a great deal of promise for new invention. The URL fragment syntax is an idea whose power has been mostly untapped by the creators of rich Internet applications.

In this chapter, we've explored the concept of deep linking through a number of examples, ranging from an initial exploration of the API to a full-blown deep-linked application with the beginnings of a general framework. The `BrowserManager` is among the simplest APIs in the Flex framework, and yet exploiting it with a clean and simple architecture presents some interesting and challenging problems. The `NavigationManager`/`Route` approach outlined here is one of many possible attempts to generalize some of the solutions.

Finally, deep linking's relationship to search indexing remains frustrating in the lack of a clean, officially approved approach. One hopes that this part of the picture will clear up soon.

41

System Interactions in Flex

The Flex/Flash platform provides an extremely rich and capable runtime for use in building your applications. When building those applications, you aren't just limited to the traditional scope of a HTML-based web application. You can play audio, display the application in full screen, add system menus, and so on.

When building your rich Flex applications, there a few things to keep in mind. First, not all machines that will be loading your application will be the same. Fortunately, the Flash Player allows you to detect what capabilities are available for you to use on the client machine. Second, you can build your application to take advantage of a cross-platform full-screen layout. This could be helpful in a variety of circumstances, such as kiosk-style applications or media players. Third, you are not just limited to a simple left-click. You can build your application to have custom context menus for any visual object displayed within your Flex application.

This chapter discusses approaches you can use to tailor your applications to the capabilities of the client runtime. We will examine how to detect system capabilities, launch the Flash Player in full-screen, and extend your applications' interactivity using custom context menus.

Detecting Client System Capabilities

Because of the distributed nature of the Internet, your application potentially could be accessed by quite a few machines. An important thing to keep in mind is that not all machines are created equal. The machines running your application may have different operating systems and/or different screen resolutions, some may or may not have the capability to playback audio, some may or may not be able to play video, and so on. Or you may need to tailor the user experience depending on the operating system or screen capabilities. Luckily, Flex and the Flash Player have classes that will enable you to customize your application based on the capabilities of the client environment.

Detecting the capabilities of a machine is actually very simple. All the logic that you will need is encapsulated into the `flash.system.Capabilities` class. The `flash.system.Capabilities` class exposes a collection of read-only public values to make your system capability detection easier. You can basically just use an `if` statement to check if the capability exists (or check for the appropriate string or numeric value, depending on the capability property). If it does not exist or is an invalid value, then handle it accordingly. For example:

```
if ( Capabilities.hasAudio )
{
  //play an audio file
}
else
{
  //handle the negative case gracefully
}
```

This approach allows you to control the overall experience on a granular level, regardless of the capabilities of the system. As in the preceding example, if audio playback is enabled, then go ahead and use it. If the system is not capable of audio playback, show an Alert message, provide some kind of visual feedback, or just ignore it. It is really up to the designer/developer to decide what works best for their own application.

The following is a simple example of a Flex application that reads all the system capabilities from the `flash.system.Capabilities` class and displays the result as a formatted text string in an `mx:TextArea` control. When the application's `creationComplete` event is dispatched, the `showCapabilites()` method gets invoked.

```
<?xml version="1.0" encoding="utf-8"?>
<mx:Application
    xmlns:mx="http://www.adobe.com/2006/mxml"
    layout="absolute"
    creationComplete="showCapabilities()">

    <mx:Script>
        <![CDATA[

            private function showCapabilities() : void
            {
                var str : String = "";

                str += "Capabilities.avHardwareDisable = <b>"
                    + Capabilities.avHardwareDisable + "</b>\n";

                str += "Capabilities.hasAccessibility = <b>"
                    + Capabilities.hasAccessibility + "</b>\n";

                str += "Capabilities.hasAudio = <b>"
                    + Capabilities.hasAudio + "</b>\n";

                str += "Capabilities.hasAudioEncoder = <b>"
                    + Capabilities.hasAudioEncoder + "</b>\n";

                str += "Capabilities.hasEmbeddedVideo = <b>"
                    + Capabilities.hasEmbeddedVideo + "</b>\n";

                str += "Capabilities.hasIME = <b>"
```

```
                        + Capabilities.hasIME + "</b>\n";

    str += "Capabilities.hasMP3 = <b>"
        + Capabilities.hasMP3 + "</b>\n";

    str += "Capabilities.hasPrinting = <b>"
        + Capabilities.hasPrinting + "</b>\n";

    str += "Capabilities.hasScreenBroadcast = <b>"
        + Capabilities.hasScreenBroadcast + "</b>\n";

    str += "Capabilities.hasScreenPlayback = <b>"
        + Capabilities.hasScreenPlayback + "</b>\n";

    str += "Capabilities.hasStreamingAudio = <b>"
        + Capabilities.hasStreamingAudio + "</b>\n";

    str += "Capabilities.hasStreamingVideo = <b>"
        + Capabilities.hasStreamingVideo + "</b>\n";

    str += "Capabilities.hasTLS = <b>"
        + Capabilities.hasTLS + "</b>\n";

    str += "Capabilities.hasVideoEncoder = <b>"
        + Capabilities.hasVideoEncoder + "</b>\n";

    str += "Capabilities.isDebugger = <b>"
        + Capabilities.isDebugger + "</b>\n";

    str += "Capabilities.language = <b>"
        + Capabilities.language + "</b>\n";

    str += "Capabilities.localFileReadDisable = <b>"
        + Capabilities.localFileReadDisable + "</b>\n";

    str += "Capabilities.manufacturer = <b>"
        + Capabilities.manufacturer + "</b>\n";

    str += "Capabilities.os = <b>"
        + Capabilities.os + "</b>\n";

    str += "Capabilities.pixelAspectRatio = <b>"
        + Capabilities.pixelAspectRatio + "</b>\n";

    str += "Capabilities.playerType = <b>"
        + Capabilities.playerType + "</b>\n";

    str += "Capabilities.screenColor = <b>"
        + Capabilities.screenColor + "</b>\n";

    str += "Capabilities.screenDPI = <b>"
        + Capabilities.screenDPI + "</b>\n";

    str += "Capabilities.screenResolutionX = <b>"
```

```
                            + Capabilities.screenResolutionX + "</b>\n";

                str += "Capabilities.screenResolutionY = <b>"
                    + Capabilities.screenResolutionY + "</b>\n";

                str += "Capabilities.serverString = <b>"
                    + Capabilities.serverString + "</b>\n";

                str += "Capabilities.version = <b>"
                    + Capabilities.version + "</b>\n";

                output.htmlText = str;
            }

        ]]>
    </mx:Script>

    <mx:TextArea
        id="output"
        editable="false"
        top="10"
        left="10"
        right="10"
        bottom="10" />

</mx:Application>
```

As you can see, the `showCapabilites()` method is just reading all the system capabilities and adding them to a text string, marked up with HTML tags. The text string is then displayed in an `mx:TextArea` using the `htmlText` property.

The following is the sample output from running the code on my local machine. In reality, the chances are very high that a significant number of machines connected to the Internet will have a very different output.

```
Capabilities.avHardwareDisable = false
Capabilities.hasAccessibility = true
Capabilities.hasAudio = true
Capabilities.hasAudioEncoder = true
Capabilities.hasEmbeddedVideo = true
Capabilities.hasIME = true
Capabilities.hasMP3 = true
Capabilities.hasPrinting = true
Capabilities.hasScreenBroadcast = false
Capabilities.hasScreenPlayback = true
Capabilities.hasStreamingAudio = true
Capabilities.hasStreamingVideo = true
Capabilities.hasTLS = true
Capabilities.hasVideoEncoder = true
Capabilities.isDebugger = true
Capabilities.language = en
Capabilities.localFileReadDisable = false
Capabilities.manufacturer = Adobe Windows
Capabilities.os = Windows XP
```

```
Capabilities.pixelAspectRatio = 1
Capabilities.playerType = PlugIn
Capabilities.screenColor = color
Capabilities.screenDPI = 72
Capabilities.screenResolutionX = 1680
Capabilities.screenResolutionY = 1050
Capabilities.serverString = A=t&SA=t&SV=t&EV=t&MP3=t&AE=t&VE=t&ACC=t&PR=t&SP=t&SB
    %209%2C0%2C124%2C0&M=Adobe%20Windows&R=1680x1050&DP=72&COL=color&AR=1.0&OS
    E=t&PT=PlugIn&AVD=f&LFD=f&WD=f&TLS=t
Capabilities.version = WIN 9,0,124,0
```

Some of these properties might make sense, but others might leave you scratching your head. The following table describes what each value actually means. You can access more detail from the Adobe documentation at `http://livedocs.adobe.com/flex/3/langref/flash/system/Capabilities.html`.

Property	Description
avHardwareDisable	A Boolean value that can be used to determine if access to the client machine's microphone or camera has been restricted. A `true` value indicates that access has been restricted. A `false` value indicates that access has not been restricted.
hasAccessibility	A Boolean value that can be used to determine if the client machine provides accessibility support, such as a screen reader application. A `true` value indicates that this capability is available. A `false` value indicates that there is no accessibility support.
hasAudio	A Boolean value that can be used to determine if the client machine is capable of playing audio. A `true` value indicates that audio capabilities are available.
hasAudioEncoder	A Boolean value that can be used to determine if the client machine is capable of encoding audio (for example, from the microphone or any other audio input device). A `true` value indicates that the system is capable of encoding audio. This could be very helpful when using a streaming server, such as Flash Media Server.
hasEmbeddedVideo	The `hasEmbeddedVideo` property is a Boolean value that determines whether the client machine supports embedded video playback. A `true` value indicates that embedded video is supported.
hasIME	A Boolean value that determines if the client machine has an IME (Input Method Editor) installed. An IME is computer program that will allow a user to input characters that are not actually on the keyboard or other input device. An IME would be used to input characters in languages that have more characters than the number of keys on the keyboard. For Example, Chinese or Japanese.
hasMP3	A Boolean value that can be used to determine if the system has a MP3 decoder and is capable of playing MP3 audio. A `true` value indicates that a MP3 decoder is present on the client machine.

Property	Description
hasPrinting	A Boolean value that can be used to determine if the system supports printing. A `true` value indicates that the client machine does support printing. This could be useful in cases where you may want to disable any printing options if printing is not available.
hasScreenBroadcast	A Boolean value that can be used to determine if the system supports broadcasting streaming media to Flash Media Server. A `true` value indicates that the client machine is in fact capable of sending streaming media.
hasScreenPlayback	A Boolean value that can be used to determine if the system supports playback of streaming media from Flash Media Server. A `true` value indicates that the client machine is in fact capable of receiving and playing streaming media.
hasStreamingAudio	A Boolean value that can be used to determine if the system supports streaming audio. A `true` value indicates that the client machine can play streaming audio.
hasStreamingVideo	A Boolean value that can be used to determine if the system supports streaming video. A `true` value indicates that the client machine can play streaming video.
hasTLS	A Boolean value that can be used to determine if the system supports SSL (Secure Socket Layer) using NetConnection. A `true` value indicates that SSL using NetConnection is supported.
hasVideoEncoder	A Boolean value that can be used to determine if the client machine is capable of encoding video (from any video input device such as a web-cam or video camera). A `true` value indicates that the system is capable of encoding video.
isDebugger	A Boolean value that can be used to determine if the client machine's Flash Player is a debug version. A `true` value indicates that the Flash Player is a debug version.
language	A string value that can be used to detect the language specified on the client machine.
localFileReadDisable	A Boolean value that can be used to determine if the client machine has disabled read access to the local hard drive. A `true` value indicates that access to the local disk has been restricted.
manufacturer	A string value that identifies the manufacturer of the Flash Player.
os	A string value that identifies the operating system of the client machine.
pixelAspectRatio	A numeric value that identifies the aspect ratio of the screen on the client machine.

Property	Description
playerType	A string value that identifies the type of player currently running on the client machine. Valid values for this are StandAlone, External, PlugIn, and ActiveX.
screenColor	A string value that identifies the capabilities of the screen. Valid values for this are "color", "gray", and "bw".
screenDPI	A numeric value that identifies the DPI of the screen on the client machine. DPI indicates pixel density, or the number of pixels (dots) per linear inch of the screen display.
screenResolutionX	A numeric value that identifies the width of the screen on the client machine. This is measured in the number of pixels.
screenResolutionY	A numeric value that identifies the height of the screen on the client machine. This is measured in the number of pixels.
serverString	A string value that contains all of the properties of the flash.system.Capabilities class in an encoded string format.
version	A string value that identifies the version of the Flash Player currently running on the client machine.

Going Full Screen

An interesting feature of the Flash Player is that it also supports full-screen rendering of the content within the current instance of the Flash Player. When you run in full-screen mode, the content of your application will take up the entire screen of the active monitor on your system. In single-monitor systems, this will be your entire display. In multi-monitor systems, the full-screen content will be displayed in the monitor that actively contains the Flash/Flex content when the full-screen instruction is invoked.

Full-screen capability opens the doors to a number of scenarios for your applications. You could use this capability for full-screen video playback, full-screen gaming, Kiosk mode applications, or data visualizations, among others. However, one thing to keep in mind when using the Flash Player's full-screen capability is that keyboard input is blocked for security reasons when users are in full-screen mode (discussed in more detail in the upcoming section, "Limitations of Full-Screen Mode").

Full-screen capability is controlled by the Stage class, the root visual component of any Flex/Flash application. You can control full-screen mode by changing the displayState property on the Stage instance. When users are running an application in full-screen mode, the available width and height for the application is the number of pixels in the screen. If the screen is currently set to display 1024×768, then your full-screen mode application will have a width of 1024 pixels and a height of 768 pixels.

In order to provide full-screen capability in your Flex/Flash application, you must embed the application with the allowFullScreen option enabled. If this is not specified, your application's users will not be able to use full-screen capability. The following object/embed statement shows how to properly specify the allowFullScreen option:

```
<object classid="clsid:D27CDB6E-AE6D-11cf-96B8-444553540000"
    id="main" width="100%" height="100%"
    codebase="http://fpdownload.macromedia.com/get/flashplayer/current/swflash.cab">
    <param name="movie" value="main.swf" />
    <param name="quality" value="high" />
    <param name="bgcolor" value="#869ca7" />
    <param name="allowScriptAccess" value="sameDomain" />
    <param name="allowFullScreen" value="true" />
    <embed src="main.swf" quality="high" bgcolor="#869ca7"
        width="100%" height="100%" name="main" align="middle"
        play="true"
        loop="false"
        quality="high"
        allowScriptAccess="sameDomain"
        allowFullScreen="true"
        type="application/x-shockwave-flash"
        pluginspage="http://www.adobe.com/go/getflashplayer">
    </embed>
</object>
```

The following is a simple example of a Flex application that illustrates how to control the display state of your Flex application:

```
<?xml version="1.0" encoding="utf-8"?>
<mx:Application xmlns:mx="http://www.adobe.com/2006/mxml" layout="absolute">

    <mx:Script>
        <![CDATA[
            import mx.controls.Alert;
            import flash.display.StageDisplayState;

            public function isFullScreen() : Boolean
            {
                return (this.stage.displayState == StageDisplayState.FULL_SCREEN);
            }

            public function goFullScreen() : void
            {
                try {
                    this.stage.displayState = StageDisplayState.FULL_SCREEN;
                }
                catch ( e : Error )
                {
                    Alert.show( "Fullscreen Capability Unavailable", "Error" );
                }
            }

            public function exitFullScreen() : void
            {
                this.stage.displayState = StageDisplayState.NORMAL;
            }

            public function toggleFullScreen() : void
            {
```

```
                if ( !isFullScreen() )
                   goFullScreen();
                else
                   exitFullScreen();
            }
        ]]>
    </mx:Script>

    <mx:Button
        label="Toggle FullScreen"
        click="toggleFullScreen()" />

</mx:Application>
```

As you can see, managing full-screen capability is actually quite easy. First, let's take a look at getting into full-screen mode. As shown in the following code snippet, all you need to do to enter full-screen mode is to set the displayState property to StageDisplayState.FULL_SCREEN:

```
public function goFullScreen() : void
{
    try {
        this.stage.displayState = StageDisplayState.FULL_SCREEN;
    }
    catch ( e : Error )
    {
        Alert.show( "Fullscreen Capability Unavailable", "Error" );
    }
}
```

It is very important to add the try-catch block in this scenario because it will catch any errors that may occur when trying to enter full-screen display mode. If you do not specify the allowFullScreen option when the Flex application is embedded in the HTML container, this action will fail and the code in the catch block will be executed.

Next, let's examine how to exit full-screen mode. Exiting full-screen mode is very easy. You only need to change the displayState property back to the "normal" setting (StageDisplayState.NORMAL).

```
public function exitFullScreen() : void
{
    this.stage.displayState = StageDisplayState.NORMAL;
}
```

In many scenarios, you may find it necessary to determine whether the application is currently running in full-screen mode. You can easily detect if the application is running in full-screen mode by comparing the current stage display state to the full-screen option. The following isFullScreen function will return true if you are actively in full-screen mode.

```
public function isFullScreen() : Boolean
{
    return (this.stage.displayState == StageDisplayState.FULL_SCREEN);
}
```

The `toggleFullScreen()` function puts these together and makes toggling back and forth between full-screen and normal easy. You can toggle back and forth between modes simply by using the preceding `isFullScreen` function to determine whether you want to switch into or out of full-screen mode.

```
public function toggleFullScreen() : void
{
   if ( !isFullScreen() )
      goFullScreen();
   else
      exitFullScreen();
}
```

Enabling Right-Click Context Menus

Every visual object in your Flex application can have a custom context menu. For example, you could have grids that have one menu and trees that use another menu, and so on. This option can enable sophisticated and specific actions per user interface item, and, when used correctly, can aid in overall application usability.

Adding and Removing Context Menu Options

You can add and remove context menu items simply by changing the `contextMenu` options for a given visual object (`Sprite`, `DisplayObject`, `UIComponent`, etc.).

By default, the context menu for the Flash Player has options to control the Flash movie (Zoom In, Zoom Out, Show All, Quality, Play, Loop, Rewind, Forward, Back, and Print). Flex normally hides these options from you in a right-click scenario, although sometimes they do actually show up. You can hide these options simply by creating a new `ContextMenu` instance and calling the `hideBuiltInItems()` method.

```
private var cm : ContextMenu;

private function setUpContextMenus() : void
{
   cm = new ContextMenu();
   cm.hideBuiltInItems();
   this.contextMenu = cm;
}
```

Note that this will not get rid of all context menu items. You can never get rid of the context menu options Settings or About Adobe Flash Player. The Settings option allows you to configure system settings for the Flash Player. The About Adobe Flash Player option will take you to Adobe's website to provide specific information about your installed version of the Flash Player.

If you are running the debug version of the Flash Player, you can also never get rid of the context menu options Show Redraw Regions and Debugger. The Show Redraw Regions option shows a red border around the areas of the screen that are actively being redrawn. This can be helpful in identifying graphics-intensive areas of your application. The Debugger option allows you to connect to a debugging IDE. These options are only displayed in Debug versions of the Flash Player; they do not appear in the non-debug version, which the vast majority of end users will be using. When you add your custom menu options, they will always be displayed above the menu options that you cannot get rid of.

When you add an item to the context menu, you can specify several options: The caption for the menu item as it will be displayed (string), whether to show a separator line before your menu option (Boolean), whether the menu item is enabled (Boolean), and whether the menu item is visible (Boolean). The following snippet continues with the context menu created in the previous code block, and adds a custom menu item to the menu:

```
var menuItem : ContextMenuItem =
    new ContextMenuItem(
        "My Custom Menu Item",
        showSeparatorBefore,
        enabled,
        visible );

cm.customItems.push( menuItem );
```

At any time, you can add or remove items to and from the menu, or change whether those items are visible or enabled. To remove items from the menu, you simply need to remove them from the context menu's customItems array, as demonstrated by the following removeContextMenuItem() function:

```
private function removeContextMenuItem() : void
{
    if ( cm.customItems.length > 0 )
    {
        cm.customItems.pop();
        Alert.show( "Last menu item removed" );
    }
    else
    {
        Alert.show( "No items to remove" );
    }
}
```

The following application is a simple lab that will allow you to add and remove custom menu items on the fly. You can enter caption text and use check boxes to determine whether the context menu item is enabled or visible.

```
<?xml version="1.0" encoding="utf-8"?>
<mx:Application
    xmlns:mx="http://www.adobe.com/2006/mxml"
    layout="absolute"
    creationComplete="setUpContextMenus()">

    <mx:Script>
        <![CDATA[
            import mx.controls.Alert;

            private var cm : ContextMenu;

            private function setUpContextMenus() : void
            {
                cm = new ContextMenu();
                cm.hideBuiltInItems();
                this.contextMenu = cm;
```

```
        }

        private function addContextMenuItem() : void
        {
            var menuItem : ContextMenuItem =
                new ContextMenuItem( caption.text,
                                     separator.selected,
                                     menuEnabled.selected,
                                     menuVisible.selected );

            cm.customItems.push( menuItem );
            Alert.show( "New menu item added.  Right-click to see it" );
        }

        private function removeContextMenuItem() : void
        {
            if ( cm.customItems.length > 0 )
            {
                cm.customItems.pop();
                Alert.show( "Last menu item removed" );
            }
            else
            {
                Alert.show( "No items to remove" );
            }
        }

    ]]>
</mx:Script>

<mx:Form x="10" y="10">

    <mx:FormItem label="Caption">
        <mx:TextInput id="caption" />
    </mx:FormItem>

    <mx:FormItem label="Separator Before">
        <mx:CheckBox id="separator" />
    </mx:FormItem>

    <mx:FormItem label="Enabled">
        <mx:CheckBox id="menuEnabled" />
    </mx:FormItem>

    <mx:FormItem label="Visible">
        <mx:CheckBox id="menuVisible" selected="true" />
    </mx:FormItem>

    <mx:FormItem >

        <mx:Button
            label="Add Context Menu Item"
            click="addContextMenuItem()" />

        <mx:Button
```

```
          label="Remove Last Context Menu Item"
          click="removeContextMenuItem()" />

     </mx:FormItem>

  </mx:Form>

</mx:Application>
```

When the application's `creationComplete` event is dispatched, the `setUpContextMenus` function is invoked to initialize the context menus for the application. Whenever `addContextMenuItem` or `removeContextMenuItem` are invoked, they just update the context menu that was initialized by the `setContextMenus` function. This example shows how to change the context menus for the entire application; however, this same technique could be used to customize the context menu for any child visual object in the application.

Invoking Actions from Context Menus

When context menus are displayed, or clicked, they dispatch events through an `EventDispatcher` instance, just like any other events in a Flex application. When a context menu is shown, it dispatches a `ContextMenuEvent.MENU_SELECT` event, and when a context menu item is clicked, the specific context menu item dispatches a `ContextMenuEvent.MENU_ITEM_SELECT` event. Using these events, you can have your application respond accordingly to the menu options, whether they are being displayed or clicked upon.

The following code shows a simple application that responds to context menu events. When the context menu is shown (just by a right-click), the application background color is set to white. When a context menu option is selected, the application's background color is set to either red, green, or blue, depending on which menu option was selected.

```
<?xml version="1.0" encoding="utf-8"?>
<mx:Application
   xmlns:mx="http://www.adobe.com/2006/mxml"
   layout="absolute"
   creationComplete="setUpContextMenus()"
   backgroundColor="#FFFFFF">


   <mx:Script>
     <![CDATA[
        private var cm : ContextMenu;
        private var menuItemR : ContextMenuItem;
        private var menuItemG : ContextMenuItem;
        private var menuItemB : ContextMenuItem;

        private function setUpContextMenus() : void
        {
           cm = new ContextMenu();
           cm.hideBuiltInItems();
           cm.hideBuiltInItems();

           menuItemR = new ContextMenuItem( "Make Me Red" );
```

```
            menuItemG = new ContextMenuItem( "Make Me Green" );
            menuItemB = new ContextMenuItem( "Make Me Blue" );

            cm.customItems = [menuItemR, menuItemG, menuItemB];

            cm.addEventListener(ContextMenuEvent.MENU_SELECT, onMenuSelect);

            menuItemR.addEventListener(
                ContextMenuEvent.MENU_ITEM_SELECT, onMenuItemSelect );
            menuItemG.addEventListener(
                ContextMenuEvent.MENU_ITEM_SELECT, onMenuItemSelect );
            menuItemB.addEventListener(
                ContextMenuEvent.MENU_ITEM_SELECT, onMenuItemSelect );

            this.contextMenu = cm;
        }

        private function onMenuSelect( event : ContextMenuEvent ) : void
        {
            this.setStyle( "backgroundColor", 0xFFFFFF );
        }

        private function onMenuItemSelect( event : ContextMenuEvent ) : void
        {
            switch ( event.currentTarget )
            {
                case menuItemR:
                    this.setStyle( "backgroundColor", 0xFF0000 );
                    break;
                case menuItemG:
                    this.setStyle( "backgroundColor", 0x00FF00 );
                    break;
                case menuItemB:
                    this.setStyle( "backgroundColor", 0x0000FF );
                    break;
            }
        }

    ]]>
    </mx:Script>

</mx:Application>
```

When the application's `creationComplete` is dispatched, the `setUpContextMenus` function is invoked to initialize the context menus. You can see that it first hides the built-in menu options and then adds the menu options for changing the background color to red, green, and blue.

```
private function setUpContextMenus() : void
{
    cm = new ContextMenu();
    cm.hideBuiltInItems();

    menuItemR = new ContextMenuItem( "Make Me Red" );
    menuItemG = new ContextMenuItem( "Make Me Green" );
```

```
      menuItemB = new ContextMenuItem( "Make Me Blue" );

      cm.customItems = [menuItemR, menuItemG, menuItemB];

      cm.addEventListener(ContextMenuEvent.MENU_SELECT, onMenuSelect);

      menuItemR.addEventListener( ContextMenuEvent.MENU_ITEM_SELECT, onMenuItemSelect );
      menuItemG.addEventListener( ContextMenuEvent.MENU_ITEM_SELECT, onMenuItemSelect );
      menuItemB.addEventListener( ContextMenuEvent.MENU_ITEM_SELECT, onMenuItemSelect );

      this.contextMenu = cm;
   }
```

Once the menu options are created, the `customItems` property of the context menu is updated to an array containing the new menu options, and the appropriate event listeners are set up to handle the context menu events. First, the `onMenuSelect` function is added as an event listener to the context menu's `ContextMenuEvent.MENU_SELECT` event. This will be dispatched any time that the context menu is shown.

```
      cm.addEventListener(ContextMenuEvent.MENU_SELECT, onMenuSelect);
```

Next, the `onMenuItemSelect` function is added as an event listener to each of the custom menu options:

```
      menuItemR.addEventListener(
         ContextMenuEvent.MENU_ITEM_SELECT, onMenuItemSelect );
      menuItemG.addEventListener(
         ContextMenuEvent.MENU_ITEM_SELECT, onMenuItemSelect );
      menuItemB.addEventListener(
         ContextMenuEvent.MENU_ITEM_SELECT, onMenuItemSelect );
```

When the `onMenuItemSelect` function is invoked, it will update the application background color according to whichever menu item was selected.

Limitations of System Interactions

Obviously, there are some limitations to the system interactions that are available to the Flex framework and the Flash Player. Some are obvious, some aren't nearly as obvious.

Limitations of Full-Screen Mode

As mentioned earlier in this chapter, there are a few limitations to full-screen mode. The following are known limitations of full-screen mode:

❑　Full-screen mode is governed by how the Flex application is embedded within the HTML page. If the `allowFullScreen` option is not specified, your application cannot enter full-screen mode.

❑　An application cannot automatically go into full-screen mode. Full-screen mode must be invoked by a user action (click or keypress).

❑ Keyboard input is limited when in full-screen mode. When you are in full-screen mode, you can only use the Tab, Space, and arrow keys. Note that this applies to Flex and Flash applications only. You can have keyboard input in AIR applications by using `StageDisplayState.FULL_SCREEN_INERACTIVE`.

All these limitations are to prevent applications from taking over the experience of the HTML container or to prevent malicious applications from misleading you in an attempt to invade your privacy. The `allowFullScreen` option prevents a Flex application from taking over the experience of the HTML container (perhaps if the Flex application was embedded as a blog widget or social networking site). Those sites may not want the integrity or experience of their sites to be compromised and, thus, can limit the full-screen experience by disallowing the `allowFullScreen` option.

The limitation on keyboard input and automatically launching into full-screen mode prevents malicious applications from tricking the user into giving up sensitive information. If these restrictions were not in place, there would be very little to stop a malicious user from creating a full-screen application that mimics the desktop and requires a username and password to proceed. This would have potentially created a very problematic scenario for the Flash platform.

Limitations of Custom Context Menus

As mentioned before, you cannot get rid of all context menus. The system-level menus for the Flash Player are used to specify security settings or hardware configuration settings. They have to be available to the user, and you cannot get rid of them.

Another limitation of custom context menus is that they are not hierarchical. Custom context menus only allow a flat menu that is limited to 15 custom menu items. Any additional menu items will not be displayed in the menu.

Custom menu items must have distinct caption text. If you have multiple menu options with the same caption text, only the first will be displayed in the context menu. Additionally (and potentially more confusing), if one of those has the visible value set to `false`, then neither will be displayed. This also applies to the default Flash Player menu options. If you call the `hideBuiltInItems()` function, which contains a menu option called "Play," and then create a new custom menu option with the caption "Play," that new option will never be displayed.

Custom context menus block mouse input to the underlying Flex application. Mouse rollover events and mouse focus will be ignored. If you would like your application to maintain a "selected" state of an object when you right-click, you have to build that capability into your application.

Summary

System interactions in Flex can be very useful to create a rich experience and custom interaction. You are not limited to the standard browser paradigm. The Flex framework and Flash platform enable you to easily create cross-platform, full-screen interactive applications, with custom menus, where the experience is tailored to the capabilities of the client system.

One of the benefits of development with Flex is that you can target applications for the Web or for the desktop, using the AIR runtime. The next chapter examines the AIR runtime and techniques for developing applications with desktop support.

42

Native Desktop Support with AIR

In this chapter, we'll be looking more at Adobe AIR's support for interacting with native operating system functionality. We'll cover working with native windows and native menus, both of which will be rendered by the operating system. For those users of your software running on OS X, you'll be able to provide support for the Dock and application menus. Windows users will get support for the System Tray. Both can be supported from the same AIR application and allow your users to work with your software with the native look and feel of the operating system they've chosen.

Plus, we'll look at a couple of techniques, network detection, and user presence, useful for writing chat or instant messaging software.

Working with Windows

When creating applications with Adobe AIR, your applications will be able to take advantage of the native operating system's windows for displaying data. This is nice because users of your application will feel right at home with their chosen operating system while using your application. `NativeWindows` are also useful because you don't have to rely on only rendering windows inside the Flash Player's main stage of your AIR application (as you would if you used Flex's `TitleWindow`). With AIR, you can display pop-up message notification windows from the Windows Status Bar or OS X Dock or transparent window with animation floating over the desktop of your preferred operating system.

When creating cross-platform applications with AIR, the operating system is given the responsibility of creating the native windows. AIR acts as a mediator, setting properties on these operating system windows for displaying, and then translating events from the native operating system back into Flex-based events, like `flash.events.NativeWindowDisplayStateEvent` and `flash.events.NativeWindowBoundsEvent`. Both operating systems will communicate back into AIR with events notifying you when things like the minimize button, or close button are pressed. The developer doesn't have direct access to any of the functionality offered by the operating system, only to the events that the OS raises through AIR.

Creating a Native Window

There are a couple of different ways to create a native window from an AIR application:

1. With the `flash.display.NativeWindow` class, which is created and accessed only through ActionScript.

2. With the Flex MXML components `mx:Window` or `mx:WindowedApplication`. These are wrappers around the `NativeWindow` class that are simpler to use than the `NativeWindow` class.

However, no matter which API you choose to create windows, you'll need to know a bit about some of the properties that define windows and which ones must be set before the window is created. You'll learn about these first, and then we'll move on to creating windows.

Important Properties for Rendering Windows

When creating a `NativeWindow` whether through ActionScript using Flex's Window or the `NativeWindow` class, you must declare the following window properties before the window is created: `type`, `systemChrome`, `maximizable`, `minimizable`, `resizable`, and `transparent`. These properties cannot be changed at runtime. Once the window has been created, its defining characteristics cannot be changed.

The systemChrome Property

The `systemChrome` defines controls on a window, which include the title bar, buttons (minimize, maximize, close, etc.), the border, and resizing grippers (see Figure 42-1). Setting `systemChrome` to `none` hides all the default chrome controls (see Figure 42-2).

Figure 42-1

Figure 42-2

The operating system controls the system chrome rendered on a window. This includes the minimize/maximize/close buttons. Adobe AIR acts as a mediator and forwards all operating system events onto your custom AIR application as events (events are discussed later in this chapter).

The following table provides a list of possible systemChrome property values, as defined by the NativeWindowSystemChrome class.

Value	Description
NativeWindowSystemChrome.NONE	No system chrome. No buttons, title bars, and so on will appear in the window.
NativeWindowSystemChrome.STANDARD	The operating system will display the default system chrome, including the appropriate buttons for minimizing and closing windows, title bar, and so on.
NativeWindowSystemChrome.ALTERNATIVE	The operating system will display the alternate system chrome, if supported.

The transparent *property can be set to* true *only when the* systemChrome *property is set to* none. *The* transparent *property must be set before the window is created.*

The type Property

Type controls what kind of window is rendered, whether it contains the full toolbar, whether it registers itself in the system, and so on. The possible values for this property are defined in flash.display.NativeWindowType class and are shown in the following table.

Value	Description
NativeWindowType.Normal	A regular window that displays the full system chrome found in either OS X or Windows
NativeWindowType.Utility	A window with a minimal title and only the option for a close button
NativeWindowType.Lightweight	A window that doesn't register in taskbar or OS X menubar; no specific chrome

Play around with the sample Native Window Explorer application to view the options available and how they work and look on the target operating system. See Figure 42-3 for what a default utility window looks like on Windows — notice there's no resize, maximize, or status bars.

When creating a very customized notification window (which is discussed later in this chapter), use a lightweight window that is transparent.

Figure 42-3

When the type property is NativeWindowType.Lightweight, the systemChrome property must be set to none. This is because lightweight windows don't display operating specific chrome, or any of the Minimize, Maximize, Close buttons and the AIR API requires you to be explicit with this setting.

The transparency Property

Creating transparent windows is useful when you want to create windows with irregular boarders (like the sample splash screen back in Chapter 15, "Getting Started with AIR," that used text as a window border) or maybe a window with rounded corners.

As a gentle reminder, as stated previously, for the systemChrome property, the transparent property can only be set to true when the systemChrome is set to none.

The maximizable, minimizable, resizable Properties

These are the last of the properties that cannot be changed after the window is created. As you probably expect, the properties control whether the window can be maximized, minimized, and resized.

Now that the properties have been discussed, let's start creating some windows! Our first example is going to use the NativeWindow class.

Using the NativeWindow Class

Using the flash.display.NativeWindow class, Listing 42-1 shows how you'd create a simple window.

Listing 42-1 *Opening a Native Operating System Window*

```
private function openNativeWindow():void
{
  var windowOptions:NativeWindowInitOptions = new NativeWindowInitOptions();
  windowOptions.systemChrome = NativeWindowSystemChrome.STANDARD;
  windowOptions.transparent = false;

  // Now create the window
  var window:NativeWindow = new NativeWindow(windowOptions);
  window.width = 400;
  window.height = 500;
  window.title = "A Simple Window";

  // Show the window
  window.visible = true;
}
```

To create a window, you'll first set the NativeWindowInitOptions that'll be used for creating the window. Here, we're setting the systemChrome to standard and transparent property to false. Standard system chrome will show you the default window chrome as shown back in Figure 42-1. As you can see, the NativeWindowInitOptions are all set before the window is even created. This explains why, when using the Window class, certain properties must be set before the window is created.

After you set the default NativeWindowInitOptions, pass them into the constructor of NativeWindow, then set the rest of the window properties. These additional window properties (width, height, and title) can all be adjusted after the window is created.

Finally, although the window is created, it's not shown until you set the visibility to true. This will show the window through the operating system.

Using the NativeWindow method, the window won't be displayed until the visible property is set to true. This differs from using the MXML Window component, which is shown in the next section, where the method open is used instead.

Now let's look at the Window class for creating a window.

Using the Window Class

The `mx.core.Window` class provides a wrapper for the `NativeWindow` class. It's a bit simpler to use and allows the developer to lay out children components defined in MXML. Any time we're discussing `mx.core.Window`, we're also talking about the `mx.core.WindowedApplication` class, which we discussed in Chapter 15, "Getting Started with AIR"). The only difference is that the `WindowedApplication` class is the entry point to the entire application.

With `mx:Window` or `mx:WindowedApplication`, you have the option of creating it with ActionScript code or defined in MXML. Listing 42-2 shows an example of how to create a simple Flex window from within ActionScript.

Listing 42-2 *Opening a Window without Chrome*

```
private function openMXWindowWithoutChrome():void
{
  var mxWindow:Window = new Window();
  mxWindow.systemChrome = NativeWindowSystemChrome.STANDARD;
  mxWindow.transparent = false;
  mxWindow.title = "A sample window";
  mxWindow.width = 400
  mxWindow.height = 500;
  mxWindow.open(true);
}
```

This code does the exact same thing that our code for `openNativeWindow` did previously (see Listing 42-1). You'll notice a couple differences, though, in Listing 42-2. First, there's no separate declaration of a `NativeWindowInitOptions` object to set the properties on the `NativeWindow`. Instead, these properties are all set on a `Window` class. Second, instead of setting the visible property to `true` on the `NativeWindow` class (as we did in Listing 42-1), you call `mxWindow.open` to both create and display the new window.

Now, let's look at the final basic window code sample by declaring a window in MXML complete with some child components and launch it from code.

And here's a similar window defined with MXML. This window has a few child components (`Text` and `DataGrid`) already added so that you can see how Flex components, by default, will be rendered inside a `NativeWindow`.

```
<mx:Window xmlns:mx="http://www.adobe.com/2006/mxml" layout="vertical"
  width="400" height="500"
  title="A sample window"
  systemChrome="standard"
  transparent="false" >
  <mx:Text text="Here is a popup window with some children controls" />
  <mx:DataGrid width="100%">
      <mx:columns>
          <mx:DataGridColumn dataField="Column 1"/>
          <mx:DataGridColumn dataField="Column 2"/>
          <mx:DataGridColumn dataField="Column 3"/>
      </mx:columns>
  </mx:DataGrid>
</mx:Window>
```

This code is declared in an MXML component called `MXWindowComponent` contained in the `MXWindowComponent.mxml` file. The `mx:Window` class is a Flex container and must be declared the top-level component in the MSML definition (just like the `WindowedApplication`). The rest of the code should be pretty self-explanatory at this point, as we're declaring the title, the `systemChrome`, size, and transparent properties just as we did previously.

However, nothing happens yet; no window is displayed. To do that we need the following code, which declares and creates an `MXWindowComponent` and then opens it:

```
private function openMxWindowComponent():void
{
  var window:MXWindowComponent  = new MXWindowComponent();
  window.open();
}
```

The big difference between using `Window` and `NativeWindow` is that with `Window` you'll usually add components in the defined MXML. With `NativeWindow`, you'll be accessing the Flash stage directly and adding components directly to the display list or an existing object on the display list.

That's it for simple windows. Let's have a quick look at the sample Native Window Explorer AIR application included in the code.

The Native Window Explorer

Enclosed with the code base is a sample application called Native Windows Explorer that's part of the sample code for this chapter. It's included so that you can play with the various `NativeWindow` properties to see how they render on your operating system with the various properties set.

Included in the Native Window Explorer (see Figure 42-4) are other properties that we haven't really talked about, such as the `showTitleBar`, `showStatusBar`, and `showGripper`.

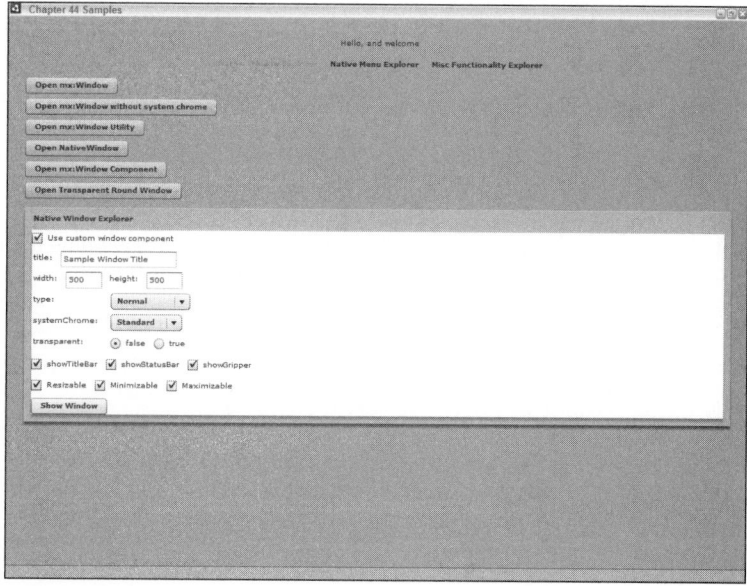

Figure 42-4

The Native Window Explorer will throw errors when you try to set properties on a window that are incongruent with each other, such as creating a transparent window with system chrome at the same time it's transparent, or creating a lightweight window with system chrome.

Using the Native Windows Explorer, experiment with the other window properties. Notice the showTitleBar *only has an effect when the* systemChrome *is set to* none. *In other words, you can't hide the title bar at the same time you've set the* systemChrome *to* NativeWindowSystemChrome .standard *because* systemChrome *trumps other properties.*

Native Menus

Adobe AIR gives the developer access to support menus rendered by the native operating system through the flash.display.NativeMenu and flash.ui.contextMenu classes. Native menus come in many flavors: they pop up when a user right-clicks (Windows) or option-clicks (OS X) an interactive Flex object, they are displayed when a user right-clicks (or option-clicks) icons in the System Tray (Windows) or Dock (OS X), or they can appear at the application developer's whim anywhere inside an application. Additionally, and this is the big one, they can render natively at the top of a window as is the case for most applications written for Microsoft Windows as a menu bar, or they can appear natively in the OS X application bar at the top of Apple's OS X inside the menu bar shared by all applications.

Flash.display.NativeMenu is designed similarly to how NativeWindow works in the earlier example. First, AIR again acts as a mediator between the user's application and the native operating system, by asking the operating system to render the menu and by forwarding events raised from the operating system onto the appropriate Flex ActionScript event handlers. Second, the NativeMenu APIs are only available through ActionScript. There is no coding done with MXML markup for NativeMenu. Because of this, a developer looking to use MXML to define menu hierarchies will need to use the mx.controls .FlexNativeMenu, which is a wrapper around NativeMenu that provides a dataProvider property and the ability to define menus within MXML. Since we're covering programming AIR from Flex, we're going to focus on the FlexNativeMenu class here.

Context Menus

Context menus are the simplest form of menus to create and can be attached to any Flex interactive object, like buttons, items in a list, and so on. However, note that all menus will work the same way, with the same APIs; only how and where they're displayed will change, with the exception of application-level menus on OS X and window menus on Windows.

Let's jump right in to some code for creating a context menu. First, since we'll be using the FlexNativeMenu component, let's define the menu layout within MXML:

```
<mx:XML format="e4x" id="contextMenuXMLDeclaration">
    <root>
        <menuitem label="Menu Item 1" toggled="true" />
        <menuitem type="separator"/>
        <menuitem label="Menu Item 2" />
        <menuitem label="Menu Item 3" />
        <menuitem label="Menu Item 4" enabled="false"/>
        <menuitem label="Menu Item 5" data="this is some test data" />
        <menuitem label="Menu Item 6">
```

```
                    <menuitem label="Sub Item 1"/>
                    <menuitem label="Sub Item 2"/>
                    <menuitem label="Sub Item 3"/>
            </menuitem>
        </root>
    </mx:XML>
```

Inside the MXML file, this creates an XML object with an `id` of `contextMenuXMLDeclaration`. This XML is laying out a hierarchy of menu items. Most of it is straightforward, like assigning the menu name to the `label` property. Notice that nested `menuitem` XML nodes will render a submenu. I'm not sure how many submenus you can nest, but I've tested it with five levels of submenus, which is probably way more than should be needed, and more than enough to sound alarm bells of your UI design team.

The `toggled="true"` attribute places the menu item in a selected mode, and you can see what that looks like on Windows by looking at Figure 42-5. There's also an enabled property that can be set (also visible in Figure 42-5) that allows the user to select the menu item or not.

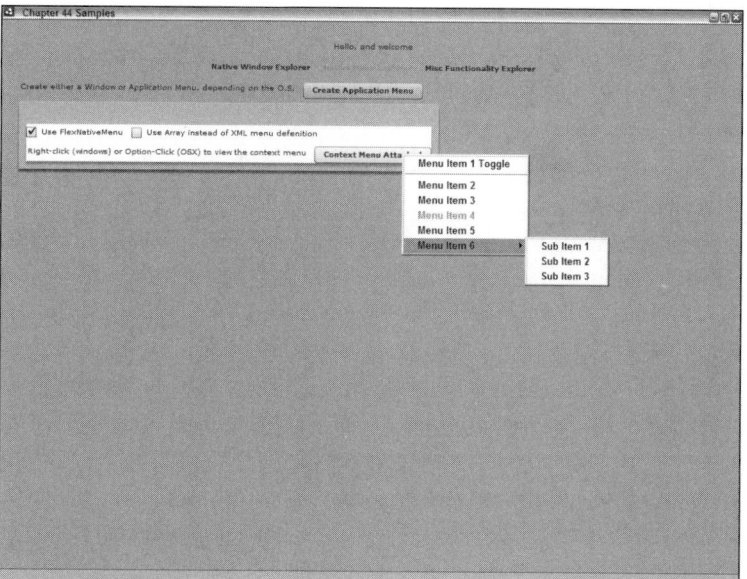

Figure 42-5

A menu line separator is also defined. Set the `menuitem` type to `"separator"` and a separator line will be rendered in the menu (displayed in Figure 42-5).

To display this menu that was defined by the XML, we need to create a `FlexNativeMenu` and bind it to a Flex component in the display list. This can be most any type of component, though we're using a button here. Let's look at the code that creates the menu:

```
var flexUserContextMenu:FlexNativeMenu = new FlexNativeMenu();
flexUserContextMenu.dataProvider = contextMenuXMLDeclaration;
flexUserContextMenu.labelField = "@label";
flexUserContextMenu.showRoot = false;
```

```
flexUserContextMenu.addEventListener(FlexNativeMenuEvent.ITEM_CLICK
                          , onFlexNativeMenuItemSelected);
flexUserContextMenu.setContextMenu(btnDisplayContextMenu);
```

First, create a new `FlexNativeMenu` component that is a Flex class that wraps the `flash.display`
`.NativeMenu` AIR class, then set the `dataProvider` property to the XML we declared that defines the
menu structure. Alternatively, instead of an XML declaration, this could be an `Array`, which you'll see
in an example that follows. Next, we set the `labelField` property to the XML attribute that we want to
have displayed for the menu item. In this case, it's straightforward because it's called `label` (don't forget the @ for reading the label name from the attribute of the XML element), but it could be called anything. Next, set `showRoot` to `false`; otherwise, the entire XML document, including the root node, would
be displayed as a menu item as a gigantic hierarchical mess of text, and we're really only interested in
the subitems, so most likely `showRoot` will always be set to `false`.

Next, an event listener is bound for the entire menu item, so that when a menu item is clicked, a handler
is raised. In this case, the handler is `onFlexNativeMenuItemSelected` (see Listing 42-3 for
implementation).

Finally, bind the menu to the appropriate `UIComponent` with a call to `setContextMenu`. Now, when the
user right-clicks on the button (which is a `UIComponent`) when using Windows, or option-clicks on the
button when using OS X, the native pop-up menu will appear, as shown in Figure 42-5.

Native Menu Events

When the user selects an item in a menu, the `mx.events.FlexNativeMenuEvent.ITEM_CLICK` event
is raised. `FlexNativeMenuEvent`, just like `FlexNativeMenu`, is a wrapper around the pure AIR
`NativeMenuItem` event.

In the preceding example, the `FlextNativeMenuEvent.ITEM_CLICK` event is bound to the
`onFlexNativeMenutItemSelected` handler. The handler is called when the user clicks an item in
the menu, and the code for the example is shown in Listing 42-3.

Listing 42-3 *Handling a FlexNativeMenuEvent*

```
/**
 * Handler use when FlexNativeMenu is used
 */
private function onFlexNativeMenuItemSelected(e:FlexNativeMenuEvent):void
{
  switch (e.label)
  {
    case "Menu Item 1 Toggle":
      // Toggle the menu item.
      e.nativeMenuItem.checked = !e.nativeMenuItem.checked;
      Alert.show("Menu Item 1's checked state: " +
                        e.nativeMenuItem.checked.toString());
      // enable or disable a menu item
      NativeMenuItem(e.nativeMenu.items[2]).enabled =
                        e.nativeMenuItem.checked;
      break;
    case "Menu Item 5":
```

```
          Alert.show("Menu Item 5 has data:\n " + e.nativeMenuItem.data.@data);
          break;
      default:
          Alert.show("Menu Item Selected: " + e.label);
          break;
      }
  }
```

The handler code is one gigantic `switch` statement that, based on the label name of the menu item that was selected, will support various operations. In the sample application, we toggle one of the menu items with a checkmark, and then enable/disable another of the menu items on this given context menu.

Inspect the `FlexNativeMenuEvent` for the `nativeMenuItem` for the checked and toggle properties.

The other major event is the `FlexNativeMenuEvent.MENU_SHOW`, which is fired when either a menu or submenu is opened.

NativeFlexMenuEvent Properties

The following table shows properties on `NativeFlexMenuEvent` that might be useful for getting at the information in the menu you've defined.

Property	Description
Index	The index value of an item in a menu
Item	The data provider item correlated to the index of the event
Label	The label of the menu item
nativeMenu	The raw `NativeMenu` that the event item is related with
nativeMenuItem	The raw `NativeMenuItem` that was clicked, raising the event

Alternative Ways of Defining Menus

At the beginning of this section, we defined the menu using MXML and bound it to the `dataProvider` of the `FlexNativeMenu` control. An alternative way of defining menu options is by either defining an `Array` or using ActionScript to declare `NativeMenuItems` directly and build up the menu via a hierarchy of code elements.

First, let's look at defining a menu with an `Array`:

```
[Bindable]
public var contextMenuArrayDeclaration:Array = [
  {label: "Menu Item 1 Toggle", toggled: true, type: "check" },
  {type: "separator"},
  {label: "Menu Item 2"},
  {label: "Menu Item 3"},
  {label: "Menu Item 4", enabled: false},
  {label: "Menu Item 5 with Data", data: "Here's some data, this could be a bitmap,
        file, or any object"},
```

```
    {label: "Menu Item 6", children: [
      {label: "Sub Item 1"},
      {label: "Sub Item 2"},
      {label: "Sub Item 3"},
      ]}
  ];
```

This code declares the exact same menu we declared previously, except that we're using an `Array` object declared in ActionScript. To bind this to a `FlexNativeMenu`, just set the `dataProvider` property in the same way as you did for the MXML defined menu:

```
flexUserContextMenu.dataProvider = contextMenuArrayDeclaration;
```

That's all there is to defining a menu with an ActionScript `Array`.

Now, let's look at dynamically creating a menu definition at runtime with ActionScript:

```
private function generateActionScriptMenu():NativeMenu
{
  // Create top-level menu
  var menu:NativeMenu = new NativeMenu();

  // Create a sample toggle menu item
  var menuItem1:NativeMenuItem = new NativeMenuItem("Menu Item 1
                                        Toggle");
  menuItem1.checked = true;
  menu.addItem( menuItem1);

  // Create a sample seperator
  menu.addItem( new NativeMenuItem("Seperator", true));

  // Create other menu items.
  menu.addItem( new NativeMenuItem("Menu Item 2"));
  menu.addItem( new NativeMenuItem("Menu Item 3"));

  // Here's a menu item that's disabled
  var menuItem4:NativeMenuItem = new NativeMenuItem("Menu Item 4");
  menuItem4.enabled = false;
  menu.addItem( menuItem4 );
  // Menu item with data
  var menuItem5:NativeMenuItem = new NativeMenuItem("Menu Item 5
                                        with data");
  menuItem5.data = "Here's some data, this could be a bitmap, file,
                                        or any object";
  menuItem5.addEventListener(Event.SELECT, onMenuItem5Selected);
  menu.addItem( menuItem5 );

  // Create sub-menu
  var subMenu:NativeMenu = new NativeMenu();
  subMenu.addItem( new NativeMenuItem("Sub Item 1"));
  subMenu.addItem( new NativeMenuItem("SubItem 2"));
  subMenu.addItem( new NativeMenuItem("Sub Item 3"));
```

```
    // Add sub-menu to top-level menu
    menu.addSubmenu( subMenu, "Menu Item 6");

    // Add an event listener to the menu
    menu.addEventListener(Event.SELECT, onNativeMenuItemSelected);

    return menu;
}
```

The preceding code creates essentially the same menu as the earlier MXML- and `Array`-based samples. However, this is quite a bit more verbose, which is probably overkill for creating simple menus, but essential if you need to conditionally add menu items, wire up specific event listeners, or set nontextual data.

The first thing you'll notice is that the `FlexNativeMenu` wrapper isn't being used. Instead, AIR's `NativeMenu` and `NativeMenuItem` are being used. They behave the same way as the `FlexNativeMenu`, except that they have slightly different names, raising events that also vary by type but share most of the same properties.

> `NativeMenu` *doesn't have a* `dataProvider` *property and, therefore, doesn't support Flex's native data object-binding API.*

In the preceding code snippet, notice how the special event handler `onMenuItem5Selected` has been attached only to `menuItem5`. Whenever a user clicks on `menuItem5`, the custom handler specific to that menu item will be called. This could be useful for partitioning code into smaller chunks so that you don't have to try and maintain one gigantic `switch` statement.

The custom handler for `menuItem5`:

```
private function onMenuItem5Selected(event:Event):void
{
    Alert.show("Custom event handler for Menu Item 5");
    event.stopPropagation();
}
```

The important thing here is the call to `stopPropagation()`, which will stop the event from bubbling up to the `onNativeMenuItemSelected` handler that was attached as a handler the top-level menu.

> *An alternative way of displaying a* `FlexNativeMenu` *or* `NativeMenu` *is by calling the* `display` *method on any created menu. This creates a pop-up menu that can appear anywhere on a given stage. For example, calling* `menu.display(this.stage, 20, 20);` *will display the pop-up menu on the main stage.*

The advantages of using an Array or ActionScript to define a menu is that you can add complex data objects, like bitmaps or custom value objects to the event. Also, there may be times in your code that you just need to define the menu in ActionScript as the MXML equivalent might not be convenient: simpler access to localization or to dynamically generated menu items based on certain application state.

Windows- and Application-Level Menus

Applications render differently on OS X and Windows. In OS X, users are accustomed to having a singular menu bar for the entire application that is rendered at the top of their screen. Window's users are used to their main application window having a menu perched at the top. Adobe AIR allows you to provide the menu in the appropriate manner for the operating system running the application so that all your users will feel at home when using your application on their preferred operating system. AIR manages the visual differences for you, and you'll create your menus with the AIR APIs, and let AIR mediate with the native operating system to render the application- or window-level menus.

Determining AIR System Capabilities

AIR includes the classes `flash.display.NativeApplicatoin` and `flash.display.NativeWindow` for inspecting the runtime environment of the operating system to determine the capabilities for supporting certain features. The important feature for this section is determining the types of menus to display. Using these classes, you can determine whether you should be displaying the main menu at either the application level (for OS X) or the top of a window (Windows). You can also determine whether your AIR application is running in an environment that supports the OS X Dock or Windows System Tray.

The `NativeWindow` class supports checking the capabilities of the AIR environment, as shown in the following table.

Property	Description
supportsMenu	Returns `true` when AIR application is running in the Windows operating system or `false` in when running in OS X.
supportsNotification	On Windows, returns `true`. The window minimized to the Taskbar will flash when a call to `NativeWindow.notifyUser()` is made. Alternatively, on OS X, a call to `notifyUser` will bounce the Dock icon.

The `NativeApplication` supports checking the operating system capabilities, as shown in the following table.

Property	Description
supportsMenu	Returns `true` when it supports application menus, as in OS X. Returns `false` in Windows.
supportsDockIcon	Returns `true` for OS X, `false` for Windows.
supportsSystemTrayIcon	Returns `true` for Windows, `false` for OS X.

Now how does all this relate to window- and application-level menus? When designing your cross-platform AIR application, you'll want to target each operating system's native look and feel as much as possible. You don't want to render application menus at the top of each window when your application is running on OS X, and conversely, you won't even be able to create an application menu bar at the top of your Windows Desktop. To render native operating system-friendly application menus, the following code will help:

```
private function createApplicationMenu():void
{
  // Create a menu
  var appMenu:NativeMenu = createWebBrowserMenu();

  if (NativeApplication.supportsMenu) {
    NativeApplication.nativeApplication.menu = appMenu;
  } else {

    if (NativeWindow.supportsMenu ) {
        // Attach a menu to a window
      stage.nativeWindow.menu = appMenu;
    }
  }
}
```

First things first; create the menu. Not shown here is the implementation for `createWebBrowserMenu()`. It's a long method that creates an application menu similar to Firefox's web browser menu. The source code included for the chapter has the full details.

Next, check to see if the AIR application is running in an environment that supports application menu bars (like OS X) by inspecting the `NativeApplication.supportsMenu` property. If it does, that means to render the menu as an application menu. Do that by setting the `NativeApplication.nativeApplication.menu` to the dynamically generated web browser menu created via code. Take note that the `nativeApplication` is a static reference to the main application, in much the same way that most Flex web-based applications have access to the application via `Application.application`. The main menu for your AIR application should now be rendered naturally in OS X.

When `NativeApplication.supportsMenu` returns false, a check is made to `NativeWindows.supportsMenu` to see if the menu rendering is supported in the current window. When it is, attach the menu to the `NativeWindow` by setting the `stage.nativeWindow.menu` to the dynamically created menu.

In AIR, when creating a menu for a Windows application, it must attach to a `FlexNativeWindow` (or `NativeWindow`) that's using standard chrome (transparent windows, need not apply).

That's all there is to it. Your AIR application is looking more and more native to the user's operating system with each section we go through.

When working with window- or application-level menus, developers have full access to keyboard-level shortcuts via key accelerators and mnemonics. It's beyond the scope here, but it's essential for building native applications your user will feel comfortable with. After all, most OS X users expect an Option-Q shortcut for closing the application, and most Windows users expect Ctrl+S to save their current work. Adobe has some great API documentation on how to add these features to your menus.

Interacting with the System Tray/Dock

AIR provides full support for interacting with the Windows' System Tray or OS X's Dock. Interacting with the System Tray or Dock is all done via the `NativeApplication.nativeApplication.icon` property, which is of type `InteractiveIcon`, but will be set to either type of `DockIcon` (OS X) or `SystemTrayIcon` (Windows), depending on the operating system the AIR application is running on. The `icon` property is set automatically by AIR when the application starts. Yes, `icon` is an odd name for a property, but if you think of it as an interactive application icon that has extra functionality, like the ability to display menus, render itself in operating system specific locations, and so on, then it makes sense.

When working with `NativeApplication.nativeApplication.icon`, be very cognizant of whether you're working with a `SystemTrayIcon` or `DockIcon`. Use either `supportsDockIcon` or `supportsTrayIcon` (found in the `NativeApplication` class discussed above) to determine what operating system the application is running in, and plan accordingly. Better yet, any code you write should support both `DockIcon` and `SystemTrayIcon`.

Be aware of differences in the supported features of `DockIcon` and `TrayIcon`. `DockIcon` supports the `bounce()` method discussed below, and the `TrayIcon` supports the `tooltip` property. When calling a property or method on the `NativeApplication.nativeApplication.icon` that doesn't exist, a run-time error results.

Let's look at some sample code that interacts with the System Tray or Dock:

```
private function minimizeToSystemTrayOrDock():void
{
  var icon:Loader = new Loader();
  icon.contentLoaderInfo.addEventListener(Event.COMPLETE, iconLoaded);
  icon.load(new URLRequest("assets/logo128x128.png"));
```

The first thing is that we need is an icon we can display in either the System Tray or Dock. Load that up through a Loader. When the Loader has finished loading the image, the `iconLoaded` callback is called, which looks like this:

```
private function iconLoaded(event:Event):void
{
  NativeApplication.nativeApplication.icon.bitmaps =
                            [event.target.content.bitmapData];

}
```

After the icon is loaded, it's added to the `InteractiveIcon`'s bitmaps array. Remember, an `InteractiveIcon` will always be a concrete class of `DockIcon` or `SystemTrayIcon`.

Let's continue looking at the rest of the code for `minimizeToSystemTrayOrDock()`:

```
var menu:FlexNativeMenu = createTrayDockMenu();

if (NativeApplication.supportsSystemTrayIcon) {
  NativeApplication.nativeApplication.autoExit = false;
  var trayIcon:SystemTrayIcon = NativeApplication.nativeApplication.icon
                                     as SystemTrayIcon;
```

```
       trayIcon.tooltip = "Demo AIR application";

   }else if (NativeApplication.supportsDockIcon){
     var dockIcon:DockIcon = NativeApplication.nativeApplication.icon as
                                                        DockIcon;

     dockIcon.menu = menu.nativeMenu;
   }

   if (stage.nativeWindow.minimizable) stage.nativeWindow.minimize();
}
```

The next thing we do is create a `FlexNativeMenu` using one of the techniques discussed earlier in the chapter, whether the menu is created via ActionScript or MXML. The call to `createTrayDockMenu()` creates a menu and binds to the proper `ITEM_SELECT` event listener. Later, it'll be bound to the proper `InteractiveIcon` menu property.

Now the fun starts. Using the `NativeApplication` static method `supportsSystemTrayIcon`, determine whether the current AIR environment is in Windows or OS X and take the appropriate path. For Windows, `supportsSystemTrayIcon` returns `true`. Retrieve the actual instance of the `SystemTrayIcon` from the `nativeApplication.icon` property. Cast the icon from the abstract class of `InteractiveIcon` to the concrete class of `SystemTrayIcon` so that you can work with it. Set the very Windows-specific `tooltip` property. Note that `tooltip` isn't supported by the `DockIcon` class.

When `NativeApplication.supportsDockIcon` returns `true`, then we know the AIR application is running on OS X. And the `NativeApplication.nativeApplication.icon` will be of concrete type `DockIcon`.

Time to add the menus. Just like a `NativeMenu` can be attached to any `UIComponent` with a call to `set-ContextMenu`, we can attach a menu to an `InteractiveIcon` via the `menu` property. Just attach the created menu to either the `SystemTrayIcon` (Windows) or the `DockIcon` (OS X). Take special interest in the call to `menu.nativeMenu`, remembering that `FlexNativeMenu` is just a wrapper for `NativeMenu`, and that both `DockIcon` and `SystemTrayIcon` expect a `NativeMenu`.

Finally, hide the window. This isn't necessary for the example, but it shows you how, for most user gestures in AIR, there's a way to conditionally determine whether it should be permitted. Explore the AIR APIs for other possible techniques.

This code sample creates either a Dock or System Tray icon that, when the user either right-clicks or option-clicks, will display a menu of options. This could be useful when creating windowless applications that are only notification proxies to some online social networking site, or if you want to provide a minimized state to the application where it hides on the Dock or System Tray until further user interaction is required.

There are some subtle differences in `DockIcon` and `SystemTrayIcon`, even though they both derive from the `InteractiveIcon` abstract class. On Windows, you can set a tooltip that will appear when the application icon in the System Tray is moused over. OS X's `DockIcon` doesn't support tooltips, but does support the `bounce()` method, which you'll learn about later in this chapter. Always, when developing cross-platform, notice the subtle differences in the AIR APIs.

Sending Notifications

In modern operating systems, users use multiple applications at the same time. When an application window is minimized, or hidden behind other application windows, a developer may need to grab the attention of the user. This is useful for instant messaging programs where the user gets a subtle clue that there are new messages waiting. Naturally, AIR provides ways to implement this. In OS X, we can bounce the Dock icon of the AIR application; Windows can flash the window on the Taskbar, for example:

```
private function crossPlatformNotifyUser(event:TimerEvent):void
{
  if (NativeWindow.supportsNotification) {
    // For Windows
    stage.nativeWindow.notifyUser(NotificationType.CRITICAL);
  }else {
    // For OSX, bounce the Dock icon.
    var di:DockIcon = NativeApplication.nativeApplication.icon as DockIcon;
    di.bounce(NotificationType.CRITICAL);
  }
}
```

In the method of crossPlatformNotifyUser, we again use the flash.display.NativeWindow class to determine operating system capabilities. Only when the AIR application is running on Windows will a call to supportsNotification return true. On Windows, to notify the user, call NativeWindow .notifyUser(). This is accessed from the nativeWindow property of the stage. On OS X, call the bounce() method, which is a member of the DockIcon object that can be accessed from a call through NativeApplication.nativeApplication.icon.

NotificationTypes are either CRITICAL or INFORMATIONAL. When sending INFORMATIONAL messages, the window will flash once, or the dock icon with bounce once. When sending CRITICAL notifications, the Dock icon will continually bounce or the Windows Taskbar icon will continually flash until the user interacts with the window.

Detecting User Presence

AIR provides the ability to detect and track when a user has been using their computer. This is important for developing instant messaging applications that should change a user's online status if they've walked away from their computer and aren't immediately available to chat.

To have an AIR application detect whether the user is using the keyboard and mouse, you must register some events and set a timeout. Set the value of the NativeApplication.idleThreshold property to a timeout (in seconds). Then listen for two events: Event.USER_IDLE, and Event.USER_PRESENT. Here's the code to get you started:

```
NativeApplication.nativeApplication.idleThreshold = 30;
NativeApplication.nativeApplication.addEventListener(Event.USER_IDLE,
                                              onIdle);
NativeApplication.nativeApplication.addEventListener(Event.USER_PRESENT,
                                              onUserPresent);
```

After 30 seconds of no user activity, the AIR application will raise the `Event.USER_IDLE` event. When the user returns to their machine and presses a key on the keyboard, or wiggles the mouse, the AIR application will raise the `Event.USER_PRESENT`.

Our simple event handlers only toggle a variable that is used to change the message on the screen:

```
[Bindable]
private var isUserPresent:Boolean = true;

private function onIdle(event:Event):void
{
   isUserPresent = false;
}

private function onUserPresent(event:Event):void
{
   isUserPresent = true;
}
```

User presence detection is simple to add to an application and can be quite powerful for most types of real-time software clients like chat, instant messaging, or stock quotes. With presence detecting, you can have your application stop calling back to a server to save on server resources if there's no one actually using the computer.

Monitoring Network Connection

AIR provides a simple API for monitoring the network connections, so you can determine whether the application is connected to the Internet or not. Furthermore, it can monitor these connections for network status changes so that you can notify the user when they're no longer online.

Use either the `URLMonitor` or `SocketMonitor` classes to detect changes in network activity. These classes can be set up to poll at specific intervals. For simplicity, we'll ping a URL somewhere on the Web.

Let's look at one way of using the `URLMonitor`:

```
private var urlMonitor:URLMonitor;

private function onApplicationComplete():void
{
   NativeApplication.nativeApplication.addEventListener(Event.NETWORK_CHANGE,
                                           onNetworkChanged);
   urlMonitor = new URLMonitor(new URLRequest('http://www.wrox.com'));
   urlMonitor.addEventListener(StatusEvent.STATUS, onStatusChanged);
}

private function onNetworkChanged(event:Event):void
{
   urlMonitor.start();
}
```

```
private function onStatusChanged(event:StatusEvent):void {
    Alert.show("Network status: " + URLMonitor(event.target).available);
    urlMonitor.stop();
}
```

When the application loads up, add a listener for Event.NETWORK_CHANGE event called onNetworkChanged. Since NETWORK_CHANGE doesn't return any status as to the actual availability of a network resource, only that a connection has changed, the URLMonitor is needed to actually reach out to a network resource (alternatively, the SocketMonitor could be used to ping any other TCP/IP service, like a mail server, chat server, etc.). A URLMonitor is created and set to make a specific URLRequest to http://www.wrox.com. And then an event listener is added to urlMonitor to listen for the StatusEvent.STATUS to call the onStatusChanged handler.

How this all works is that, when a NETWORK_CHANGE event is raised by the application, a call to URLMonitor.start() makes the request to the network resource. And then we wait for the StatusEvent to be raised, giving the status.

The implementation of onStatusChanged will display an Alert box containing a message of network service availability and then stop monitoring the URL. After all, we don't want to continually ping the network while the application is constantly running. Instead, we wait for the application to tell us that the Network status has changed, and then we repeat the cycle.

> *Make sure to include the* servicemonitor.swc *in your build process to use the* ServiceMonitor *classes. They aren't included in AIR by default and reside in the separate class library.*

AIR Capabilities and the Flash Runtime

Code that's been written and compiled into a SWF can inspect to see what the runtime environment is that it's running in. Typically, in Flex applications this is to check to see if the Flash player is running as a plug-in, in a web browser, inside an Active-X control, the standalone Flash Player, and so on. With AIR, there's an additional possible value.

To check whether the SWF is running as part of an AIR application, a simple call to Capabilities .playerType will return the value of "Desktop" as shown here:

```
if (Capabilities.playerType == "Desktop" )
{
    //Do something here that's specific to an AIR application.
}
```

An alternative way to check whether the SWF is running in AIR is by looking at the Security.sandboxType. When it's set to Security.APPLICATION, the SWF file is running in Adobe AIR.

The following is a quick example:

```
if (Security.sandboxType == Security.APPLICAION) {
    // The code is running in the AIR runtime.
}
```

This is quite a simple call but very powerful if you plan on making libraries that need to support running both in the browser and on the desktop.

Enabling Full-Screen Mode

Having applications using the full screen can be essential for a lot of multimedia applications, whether they're playing a video, showing a slideshow, or editing a photo. Regular Flash and Flex applications running in the web browser allow a full-screen mode. It's almost as simple as setting the `stage.displayState` property to `flash.display.StageDisplayState.FULL_SCREEN`. However, with Adobe AIR, there's a new state that's only supported by AIR: `FULL_SCREEN_INTERACTIVE`. This differs from `FULL_SCREEN` in that keyboard input is still allowed in AIR supplications, as opposed to Flash's (or Flex's) normal `FULL_SCREEN` that allows for any keyboard input except to cancel the full-screen mode.

Without further adieu, here's how to enable full-screen mode in Adobe AIR:

```
private function setFullScreenDisplayState():void
{
  Alert.show("Press ESC to exit full screen mode");
  stage.displayState = StageDisplayState.FULL_SCREEN_INTERACTIVE;
}
```

It's as simple as setting the stage's `displayState` property to `StageDisplayState.FULL_SCREEN_INTERACTIVE`. Don't forget to inform your users how they can exit full-screen mode! They can press the Escape key, which is enabled by default, or you can provide functionality via a button that restores the `stage.displayState` to `StageDisplayState.NORMAL`.

While AIR applications are being displayed in full-screen mode, the screen saver and power-saving options are disabled.

Summary

There's a lot to digest in this chapter. Hopefully, you've gotten an idea of the types of functionality that AIR supports with tight operating system integration. Use the enclosed source code and sample applications to explore how AIR will render the native functionality, whether it's windows, menus, or interacting with the Dock or System Tray on your targeted operating systems.

Coming up in the next chapter, you'll learn about persisting data with shared objects. You'll also learn about intra-application communication with the Flash Player's `LocalConnection` class.

43

LocalConnection and Shared Objects

This chapter will cover features in the Flash Player that enable you to implement local inter-SWF communication and persist local data. The following concepts are covered in this chapter:

❑   The `LocalConnection` class

❑   Local shared objects (LSOs)

Overview

There are times when you would need to allow your Flex and AIR applications to communicate with other applications that are running on the local system. For example, you might want to use an AIR debug tool that receives debug messages from Flex applications that you are debugging. Or you might need to communicate from an ActionScript 3-based application running in the AVM2 to an ActionScript 2-based application running in the AVM1.

It would also be nice if you could persist data locally. In one application, you might want to automatically log a user into your Flex application. In another, you might want to save user preferences such as background colors, layout style, or default search orders. The following sections take a look at two technologies built into the Flash Player to enable you to handle these scenarios.

The LocalConnection Class

Chapters 38 and 39 discussed features such as `ExternalInterface` and the Flex-AJAX bridge. Although you can use those features to allow inter-SWF communication, you can communicate without having to rely on cross-scripting. The `flash.net.LocalConnection` class is used to leverage the built-in capabilities of Flash Player and the AIR runtime for local inter-SWF communication.

SWF-to-SWF Communication

The communication flow when using `LocalConnection` is a one-to-many scenario. With `LocalConnection`, one connection can have one receiver receive messages sent by many senders. In other words, if you have two SWF movies, and you would like them both to receive messages, you will need to configure two connections, one for each SWF, and each of those connections would have exactly one receiver. After you have configured a `LocalConnection` receiver, you can then connect your `LocalConnection` senders to the connection to send messages to it.

Working with a LocalConnection Receiver

In general, setting up a `LocalConnection` receiver is a four-step process:

1. Instantiate your `LocalConnection` instance.

2. Specify the `LocalConnection` `client` property, which indicates the class containing the methods to be run on receive.

3. Create the receive method.

4. Connect to the `LocalConnection` while passing in a unique connection name.

The preceding steps can be seen in the following snippet from `chapter43_example1_receiver.mxml` in the Chapter 43 source code. Just follow along and you can see from the comments in the code where each of the four steps is handled.

```
private var _myLocalConnection:LocalConnection;

private function _onInitialize( event:FlexEvent ):void
{
    // Step 1: Instantiate your LocalConnection Instance
    _myLocalConnection = new LocalConnection();

    // Step 2: Specify the client containing the methods
    // to be run on receive
    _myLocalConnection.client = this;

    // Step 4: Connect to the LocalConnection
    // passing in a unique connection name
    _myLocalConnection.connect( "receiver" );
}

// Step 3: Create your receive method
public function receiveData( param1:Object ):void
{
    trace( ObjectUtil.toString( param1 ) );
}
```

Looking at the preceding code, you can see that the connection that senders will need to connect to is called "`receiver`," and they have access to the `receiveData()` method. Also, by specifying the client as `this`, you're telling the `LocalConnection` class that the methods to invoke when data is received exist in the class implementing the `LocalConnection` instance.

The following are some things to note about setting up LocalConnection receivers:

❑   If you do not set the client property as shown in step 2, the default is for the LocalConnection class to try to invoke the methods that senders are requesting to run on itself.

❑   In step 3 make the receive method public. You must ensure that the receive method is public for LocalConnection communications to be successful.

❑   You could have created more than one receive method. You just need to make sure they're all defined in the LocalConnection client and that they're all set as public methods.

❑   Since a LocalConnection connection can only ever have one receiver, in step 4 you must ensure that the connection name specified as the input parameter is unique.

Working with a LocalConnection Sender

Now that you know how to set up a LocalConnection receiver, here is how to set up a LocalConnection sender. Setting up a LocalConnection sender is much easier than setting up a LocalConnection receiver, since it only requires you to perform two steps:

1.   Instantiate your LocalConnection instance.

2.   Invoke send() on your LocalConnection instance when you're ready to send data over the LocalConnection.

Here's an example of the steps above taken from chapter43_example2_sender.mxml:

```
private var _myLocalConnection:LocalConnection;

private function _onInitialize( event:FlexEvent ):void
{
    // Step 1: Instantiate your LocalConnection
    _myLocalConnection = new LocalConnection();

    // Step 2: Invoke send on your LocalConnection instance
    _myLocalConnection.send( "receiver", "receiveData"
                        , { prop1:'hello', prop2:'world' } );
}
```

As you can see, when you're on the sending end of a LocalConnection conversation, the magic really only happens during the invocation of the LocalConnection send() method. Here's an explanation of the parameters you can pass into the send() method:

❑   The first parameter is required. It is a string that represents the LocalConnection connection that you would like to connect to. Since the receiver was set up to listen on the connection receiver, the string "receiver" will be passed in as the first parameter.

❑   The second parameter is also a required string. It represents the method on the receiver that you would like to invoke. In the case of the receiver created earlier, the method name was receiveData, so that's what you invoke.

❑ After the second parameter is a nonrequired ... (rest) parameter. The ... (rest) parameter is an array of additional parameters. The best way to think of this is that you would create one parameter in the array for each parameter the receiving method would need. In the case of `receiveData`, it requires one `Object` to be passed in. So, the preceding code populates ... (rest) with `{ prop1:'hello', prop2:'world' }`.

For more information on the ... (rest) parameter, see the Adobe LiveDocs entry at `http://livedocs.adobe.com/flex/3/langref/statements.html#..._(rest)_parameter`.

Crossing Domain Boundaries

By default `LocalConnection` communication can only occur between SWF files in the same domain. If you would like to get around this restriction, you will need to pay attention to the connection name that you choose for your receiving SWF. Also, you will need to specify security policies allowing SWF files from specific domains to connect.

Specifying the Connection Name

Sometimes you need to implement a `LocalConnection` receiver that might receive messages from SWF in varying domains, for instance a debugging tool. When you invoke `connect()`, you will need to prepend an underscore (_) to the connection name, as shown here in the snippet from `chapter43_example3_receiver.mxml`:

```
// passing in a unique connection name (prepending with an underscore)
_myLocalConnection.connect( "_receiver" );
```

Now that you've taken care of setting up the receiving connection, you'll need to make sure you use the underscore in the sender. Here's a snippet from `chapter43_example4_sender.mxml` showing the use of underscore in the sender:

```
// Invoke send on your LocalConnection instance
// using a receiving connection prepended by an underscore
_myLocalConnection.send( "_receiver", "receiveData"
                       , { prop1:'hello', prop2:'world' } );
```

You don't have to add the underscore, but without it you're required to specify the domain name in your `send()` *invocations like* `_myLocalConnection.send("{domainname}:receiver"`, `"receiveData"`, ... *rest). Since there may be many cases when you don't know the domain name up front, it's just best to use an underscore.*

Allowing Domains

Using an underscore in the connection name will allow you to connect to a connection name regardless of the domain that the connection name was connected from. However, you will not be able to connect unless the domain of your sender is an allowed domain. By default, only the same domain is allowed, and there are two methods for you to use to change this: `allowDomain()` and `allowInsecureDomain()`.

Both of these methods are members of the `LocalConnection` class. They both take a single domain name string, an array of multiple domain names, or even a wildcard (`"*"`), meaning any domain. The difference between the two methods is that the `allowInsecureDomain()` method is meant to be used when you're serving your receiving SWF over a secure HTTPS connection. If that's not the case, then just use the standard allowDomain().

Here are several examples of how to use these methods taken from chapter43_example3_receiver.mxml:

```
// allow domains (if served over HTTPS, only other HTTPS domains will work)
// any domain
_myLocalConnection.allowDomain( "*" );

// local domain and one other
_myLocalConnection.allowDomain( "one.domain.com" );

// local domain and two others
_myLocalConnection.allowDomain( "one.domain.com", "two.domain.com" );


// allow insecure domains (if we're being served over HTTPS)
// any domain
_myLocalConnection.allowInsecureDomain( "*" );
```

A couple best practices to keep in mind:

❑ Limit the number of domains that you expose your SWF movie to a minimum. In other words, only use "*" when necessary.

❑ Connecting a SWF being served from a nonsecure domain to a secure domain using allowInsecureDomain() can be a potential attack vector. If security is important to you, keep this in mind.

Working with Data

By default, you can send primitives and certain built-in types such as Object, Array, and XML over a LocalConnection, but you cannot send custom data types. Reason being, LocalConnection uses Action Message Format (AMF) version 0 to communicate. AMF 0 is used because it's backward compatible with ActionScript 1– and ActionScript 2–based SWF movies, making LocalConnection a perfect vehicle for communicating between AVM1 and AVM2.

There are ways to get around the inability to pass complex user-defined objects, but these methods are also applicable to LSOs. Since LSOs will be discussed during the second half of this chapter, discussion on these methods will be deferred until after the LSO section. If you'd like to read about these methods now, feel free to skip to the section titled "Serializing Custom Classes."

Working around the 40KB Limit

Messages sent over the Flash Player and AIR local connection are limited to 40KB. In many cases this limit is more than adequate, such as when sending a short debugging message. In other cases, however, such as sending a large complex object containing detailed information and a large ByteArray, you could find yourself hitting that 40KB limit way too quickly. By borrowing an approach used in many networking architectures, chunking the data up into smaller packets, you can work around the 40KB limit.

If you do decide to go down this route, you will need to spend more time building your `LocalConnection` architecture. Here are some of the things that you will need to take into account:

❑ A data disassembler in the sender and a reassembler in the receiver to handle data broken into packets.

❑ A queue container to save the packets in the sender until the receiver has timed out or has received them all, and a container in the receiver to hold the packets until they're ready for reassembly.

❑ Packet header information for the sender to set and the receiver to read. Some of the information you may want to save into this header includes the sequence number, the number of packets, and the size of the current packet.

❑ Acknowledge and retry messages so that the receiver can acknowledge the packets it has received and re-request the missing packets.

❑ Timeout mechanisms in case either the sender or receiver is terminated before the communication is completed.

Although there is not enough room in this book to build and discuss a robust communication architecture for `LocalConnection`, the preceding points should assist you with implementing your own.

Standard LocalConnection Errors

Before moving on to the LSO discussion, here are some of the standard runtime errors you may encounter when you're working with `LocalConnection`:

❑ When your sending SWF tries to connect to a connection name that has not been connected to `LocalConnection`, the sender will issue `Error#2044: Unhandled StatusEvent`.

❑ If a receiving SWF is requested to run a method that either does not exist in the client class or is not marked public, the receiving SWF will issue `Error #2044: Unhandled AsyncErrorEvent`.

❑ When the domain that the sending SWF is being served from has not been allowed by the receiving SWF, and the sending SWF attempts to send a message, the receiver will issue `Error #2044: Unhandled SecurityErrorEvent`.

Working with Local Shared Objects

Many applications persist user login status between sessions. Other applications may persist user interface settings, such as application theme and color choices. Using the `flash.net.SharedObject` class is a way to persist data between those sessions. Although the `SharedObject` class was designed to work with both remote shared objects implemented by Adobe Flash Media Server and the standard LSOs, only LSOs will be discussed in this chapter.

To work with LSOs, you must know how to create or retrieve them, store data in them, retrieve data from them, and destroy them.

Creating or Retrieving Local Shared Objects

To create or retrieve an LSO requires the same method call. In other words, if you try to retrieve an LSO that doesn't exist, it will be created. Here is a simple excerpt from `chapter43_example5_lso.mxml`:

```
private var _myLSO:SharedObject;

private function _onInitialize( event:FlexEvent ):void
{
    // Either retrieve or create the local shared object "example5"
    _myLSO = SharedObject.getLocal( "example5" );
```

Storing Data in Local Shared Objects

Once you have a reference to your shared object, you can start storing data in your shared object. The `SharedObject` class has a `data` property for use with storing data in the LSO. Here is an example of how to save data from `chapter43_example5_lso.mxml`:

```
// set the lsoString property on the shared object
_myLSO.data.lsoString = thingToRemember_ti.text;
```

This saves the data to a property called `lsoString`. However, the `data` property of the `SharedObject` class is an `Object`, so you can dynamically create any property on it to suit your needs.

Retrieving Data from Local Shared Objects

Now that you've created a reference to your LSO and added data to it, the way to retrieve it is just like retrieving data from a standard object. Here is an example of how to retrieve data from `chapter43_example5_lso.mxml`:

```
// get the lsoString property from the shared object
_lsoString = _myLSO.data.lsoString;
```

If you're wondering what will happen if you try to retrieve a property of the `data` object that does not yet exist, you'll receive the value `null`.

Explicitly Saving Local Shared Objects

By default, an LSO will be saved when the application is closed or the reference to the `SharedObject` instance goes out of scope and is garbage collected. If you need to make sure that your LSO is saved, it's probably not best to rely on the Flash Player since various circumstances may arise to prevent the LSO from being saved.

To immediately save the LSO by writing the in-memory state of the `SharedObject` to disk, you use the `flush()` method of the `SharedObject` class, as used in `chapter43_example5_lso.mxml`:

```
// immediate write the LSO to disk
var flushStatus:String = _myLSO.flush( );
```

Notice that the return value of `flush()` is being captured in a local variable. This is because a call to `flush()` will return that the flush was successful or that the flush is pending. A pending flush indicates that the flush request exceeds the current LSO storage maximum allowed by the Flash Player and the user is prompted by a Flash Player dialog, as illustrated in Figure 43-1.

Figure 43-1

This dialog will dispatch a `NetStatusEvent` when the user has finished clicking on either the Allow or Deny button. The `NetStatusEvent` that is dispatched has an `info` property, and in the `info` property there will be a `code` property. If the user clicked the Allow button, the `code` property will be set to the string "`SharedObject.Flush.Success`", and if the user clicked on the Deny button, it will be set to "`SharedObject.Flush.Failed`". In this excerpt from `chapter43_example5_lso.mxml`, you can see how to handle the various cases of the `flush()` call:

```
private function _onFlush( event:MouseEvent ):void
{
  // immediate write the LSO to disk
  var flushStatus:String = _myLSO.flush( );

    if( flushStatus == SharedObjectFlushStatus.FLUSHED )
    {
        // the LSO was written to disk successfully
        _showFlushResult( FLUSH_SUCCESS );
    }
    else if( SharedObjectFlushStatus.PENDING )
    {
        // We'll need to listen for a netStatus event
        // in case the size of the LSO exceeds the Flash Player
        // allowable disk size
        _myLSO.addEventListener( NetStatusEvent.NET_STATUS, _onNetStatus );
    }
}
// handle the result of the settings manager dialog
private function _onNetStatus( event:NetStatusEvent ):void
{
  // allow button was clicked
  if( event.info.code == "SharedObject.Flush.Success" )
  {
        _showFlushResult( FLUSH_SUCCESS );
  }
  // deny button was clicked
  else if( event.info.code == "SharedObject.Flush.Failed" )
  {
        _showFlushResult( FLUSH_FAILURE );
  }
}
```

Deleting Properties and Destroying Local Shared Objects

The `data` property of the `SharedObject` class is an `Object`. Since `Object` is a dynamic class, you can use the `delete` keyword to delete the properties that you have created in your LSO. Here is an example from `chapter43_example5_lso.mxml`:

```
// Let's delete the property from the LSO
delete _myLSO.data.lsoString;
```

If you want to destroy the LSO, you will need to run the `clear()` method of the `SharedObject` class, as shown in this `chapter43_example5_lso.mxml` excerpt:

```
// Let's delete the LSO
_myLSO.clear();
```

Additional Information

When you work with `SharedObject`, there's some environment specifics that you'll need to take into account. The first is how much local storage the user is going to allow you to use, and the second is where the LSO files will be written to and stored.

Flash Player Settings Manager

You can use the Flash Player Settings Manager to predetermine the amount of disk storage that you would like to allocate to LSOs. The default setting is 100KB per website.

If you would like to change the setting for all SWF movies run in the Flash Player, you will need to view the Global Storage Settings panel on the Adobe site (see Figure 43-2). The Global Storage Settings panel will allow you to set the storage preferences for all SWF movies run in the Flash Player. To get to the manager, visit `www.macromedia.com/support/documentation/en/flashplayer/help/settings_manager03.html`.

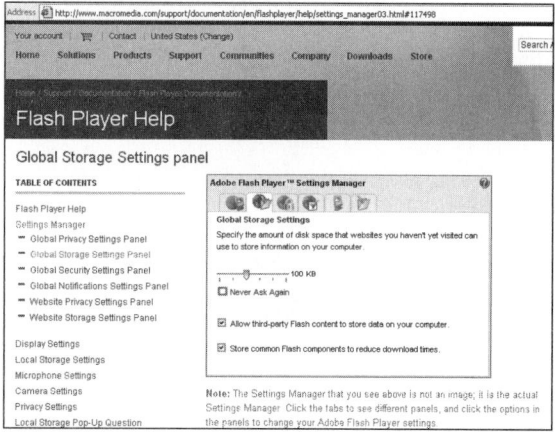

Figure 43-2

Directory Locations

When working with LSOs, you need to keep in mind where they're being written to disk. This becomes important when you need to delete the LSO file from the system. It is also important when you would like to have multiple applications share a LSO file.

Operating System Defaults

If you find yourself needing to delete LSO files, here are the defaults for getting to the shared object root storage directory:

❑　**Windows XP**: `C:\Documents and Settings\{username}\Application Data\Macromedia\Flash Player\#SharedObjects\{random directory name}`

❑　**Windows Vista**: `C:\Users\{username}\AppData\Roaming\Macromedia\Flash Player\#SharedObjects\{random directory name}`

❑　**Mac OS X**: `/Users/{username}/Library/Preferences/Macromedia/Flash Player/#SharedObjects/{random directory name}`

❑　**Linux/Unix**: `/home/{username}/.macromedia/Flash_Player/#SharedObjects/{random directory name}`

In each case, the folder just under the shared object root storage folder "`#SharedObjects`*" is a folder named with a random directory name. This random directory name was implemented to help with LSO security. Otherwise, it might be pretty easy for a rogue SWF to guess the location of an LSO.*

Custom Locations

By default, a shared object is stored in a subdirectory of the main shared object folder. Although you can reference the last section for more details on where to find the main "`#SharedObjects`" folder, the remainder of the path to the LSO follows the following path by default:

```
{shared object root storage}\{random directory name}\{domain name}
\{domain subdirectory(s)}\{application name}\{shared object name}.sol
```

For instance, if you're developing a new application and the application is launched from:

```
D:\_svn\Flex3ProBook\chapter43 LocalConnection and Shared Objects\chapter43\
bin-debug\chapter43_example5_lso.html
```

the path to the `.sol` file will be:

```
C:\Documents and Settings\{username}\Application Data\Macromedia\Flash Player\
#SharedObjects\{random directory name}\localhost\_svn\Flex3ProBook\chapter43
LocalConnection and Shared Objects\chapter43\bin-debug\chapter43_example5_lso.swf\
example5.sol
```

Based on this path to the `.sol` file, the problem with using the default location is that the LSO is available only to the `chapter43_example5_lso.swf` application. That is, Flash Player applications can only access LSOs stored in the path to the application. So, from the `C:\Documents and Settings\ {username}\Application Data\Macromedia\Flash Player\#SharedObjects\{random directory name}\localhost` directory, `chapter43_example5_lso.swf` can access `.sol` files stored in any of the following directories:

- ❏ `{path to localhost LSO}\`
- ❏ `{path to localhost LSO}\_svn\`
- ❏ `{path to localhost LSO}\_svn\Flex3ProBook\`
- ❏ `{path to localhost LSO}\_svn\Flex3ProBook\chapter43 LocalConnection and Shared Objects\`
- ❏ `{path to localhost LSO}\_svn\Flex3ProBook\chapter43 LocalConnection and Shared Objects\chapter43\`
- ❏ `{path to localhost LSO}\_svn\Flex3ProBook\chapter43 LocalConnection and Shared Objects\chapter43\bin-debug\`
- ❏ `{path to localhost LSO}\_svn\Flex3ProBook\chapter43 LocalConnection and Shared Objects\chapter43\bin-debug\chapter43_example5_lso.swf\`

By taking a note of this and an additional parameter during your `SharedObject.getLocal()` call, you can start sharing LSOs between multiple applications served from the same domain. The additional parameter is the second parameter of the `getLocal()` call, which is a string that represents a path relative to the domain directory for storing the LSO.

If you have two applications being served from your "localhost" domain, and they both have the `\_ svn\Flex3ProBook` part of the path in common, you could issue the following line of code taken from `chapter43_example5_lso.mxml`:

```
_myLSO = SharedObject.getLocal( "example5", "/_svn/Flex3ProBook" );
```

The preceding code will allow any SWF being served from the "localhost" domain with `\_svn\ Flex3ProBook` in its path to use the same `"example5"` LSO.

Similarly, if you have an LSO that you would like to share among all SWF applications in a domain, you can just specify `"/"` as your path parameter.

Serializing Custom Classes

The downside to working with both `LocalConnection` and `SharedObject` out of the box is that their support for custom data types is lacking. The good news is that with a little extra work, you can build support for custom data types into your `LocalConnection` or `SharedObject` implementation.

Using registerClassAlias()

The first method you can use is to register a class alias for your custom class in every application that will need to use it. This is done by using the `flash.net.registerClassAlias()` method, which requires a string parameter representing the fully qualified class name.

Using registerClassAlias() with LocalConnection

When using `registerClassAlias()` with `LocalConnection`, you need to perform the registration for all custom classes that will be sent in both the sender application and receiver application. Here is an example of this that can be found in both `chapter43_example6_cdt_receiver.mxml` and `chapter43_example7_cdt_sender.mxml`:

```
// we need to register the Student alias
registerClassAlias( "com.wiley.customdatatypes.Student", Student );

// we need to register the Teacher alias
registerClassAlias( "com.wiley.customdatatypes.Teacher", Teacher );

// we need to register the Classroom class alias
registerClassAlias( "com.wiley.customdatatypes.Classroom", Classroom );
```

In the `LocalConnection` sender, `chapter43_example7_cdt_sender.mxml`, you can then send your custom data type:

```
private function _onSendClassroom( event:MouseEvent ):void
{
    var classroom:Classroom = new Classroom();
        classroom.teacher = new Teacher( 'michelle', 'heider' );
        classroom.students.push( new Student( 'kobi','heider' ) );
        classroom.students.push( new Student( 'mia','heider' ) );

    _myLocalConnection.send( "receiver", "receiveData", classroom );
}
```

In the receiving SWF, if you perform an `ObjectUtil.toString()` on the received object, you will see the following output:

```
(com.wiley.customdatatypes::Classroom)#0
  students = (Array)#1
    [0] (com.wiley.customdatatypes::Student)#2
      fname = "kobi"
      lname = "heider"
    [1] (com.wiley.customdatatypes::Student)#3
      fname = "mia"
      lname = "heider"
  teacher = (com.wiley.customdatatypes::Teacher)#4
    fname = "michelle"
    lname = "heider"
```

Using registerClassAlias() with SharedObject

When working with `SharedObject`, you will register class aliases for the classes you need to serialize, just as you did in the preceding `LocalConnection` example. Then you can save and load that object as a property of the shared object instance `data` property, just like any other object.

If you would like to see the code behind utilizing `registerClassAlias()` with LSO, take a look at `chapter43_example8_cdt_lso.mxml` in the chapter 43 source code. One last thing to keep in mind regarding LSO and `registerClassAlias()` is that any application that will be using that shared object will need to perform the same `registerClassAlias()` code block.

Cons of Using registerClassAlias() with LocalConnection

A downside to using `registerClassAlias()` is that when you are using it with `LocalConnection`, it does not support custom data type classes that have required arguments in their class constructors. If you try to use a class with a required argument, the translation of this class will throw an argument mismatch runtime error. `SharedObject` doesn't have this problem.

Summary

This chapter discussed some very powerful features in Flash Player. The first item covered was the `LocalConnection` class and how it can be used to effectively communicate from one local running SWF to another. The second item covered was the `SharedObject` class and how it can be used to persist data in LSOs between sessions. The third thing that was covered was serialization of custom classes using `registerClassAlias()`.

If you would like to do additional reading on `LocalConnection`, `SharedObject`, or `registerClassAlias()` feel free to take a look at the following Adobe LiveDocs:

- ❑ `http://livedocs.adobe.com/flex/3/html/security2_13.html`

- ❑ `http://livedocs.adobe.com/flex/3/html/lsos_1.html`

- ❑ `http://livedocs.adobe.com/flex/3/langref/flash/net/`
  `package.html#registerClassAlias()`

The next chapter looks at the limited ways that Flex applications can interact with local files that are not LSOs. The chapter after that will discuss how AIR brings robust support for local file interaction to your applications.

File Management with Flex

This chapter will examine the local file management capabilities built into the Flex framework. Specifically, the following topics are discussed:

❑ The `FileReference`, `FileReferenceList`, and `FileFilter` classes

❑ Server-side considerations

Overview

Flex applications have the capability to work with local shared objects, a very specific type of local file, which was covered in Chapter 43, "LocalConnection and Shared Objects." In addition, if a Flex application SWF is local, its security sandbox settings can be set to either "local-with-filesystem" or "local-trusted" to allow reading from local files via classes such as `flash.net.URLLoader`. Security sandboxes are covered in Chapter 65, "The Security Model."

The majority of files are not local shared objects, and the majority of Flex application SWF files are served from remote servers. Therefore, the above-mentioned use cases will not be discussed in this chapter. Instead, this chapter will concentrate on the `FileReference` and `FileReferenceList` classes. We will discuss how to upload and download files to and from a remote server. We will also discuss some things to keep in mind when implementing the server-side code used to support file uploads.

Prerequisites

This chapter assumes that the user has a default installation of ColdFusion 8 Developer Edition. ColdFusion or any other application server technology is required to provide the server-side functionality necessary for a file upload.

The source code for Chapter 44 is meant to be set up as a Flex Project in Flex Builder with ColdFusion set as its application server type. Also, you don't need to check the "Use remote object access service" check box on the first step of the wizard. Here are some of the settings that you'll want to mimic:

- **Project location** — Uncheck "Use default location" and use `C:\ColdFusion8\wwwroot\wiley` if you're running a default installation of ColdFusion on Windows, and "`/Applications/ColdFusion8/wwwroot/wiley`" if you're using Mac OS X.

- **Output folder** — `bin-debug`

- **Output folder URL** — `http://localhost:8500/wiley/chapter44/bin-debug`

If you need further information on setting up Flex Projects in Flex Builder refer to Chapter 6, "Using Flex Builder 3."

Using the FileReference Class

Access to local files from a Flex application is accomplished via `flash.net.FileReference`. The key thing to note when working with the `FileReference` class in a Flex application is that it does not give you direct access to a file's content; instead, you get information on the file itself such as path, size, and file type. The other thing to note is that a `FileReference` is populated via interaction, through either its `browse()` or `download()` method.

To kick things off, here is the `FileReference` used in `chapter44_example1.mxml`. In addition, we declare a `URLRequest` object that represents the server-side ColdFusion page that we will be uploading our files to:

```
private var _myUploadURL:URLRequest;
private var _myFileRef:FileReference;

private function _onCreationComplete( event:FlexEvent ):void
{
    _myUploadURL = new URLRequest( './upload.cfm' );

    _myFileRef = new FileReference();
    _myFileRef.addEventListener( Event.SELECT, _onFileSelect );
}
```

Handling FileReference Events

Using `FileReference` to upload and download files requires knowledge of the various events that it dispatches. When handling the actual uploading process you will want to be familiar with the following:

- `Event.CANCEL` — Dispatched when a file upload or download operation is canceled by the user via the file-browsing dialog window.

- `Event.SELECT` — Dispatched when a user selects the files they would like to upload. This event will let you decide when to start uploading files.

❑   `Event.OPEN` — Dispatched when the upload starts. If you want to use a progress indicator, the handler for this event will be a good time to display your progress indicator.

❑   `ProgressEvent.PROGRESS` — Dispatched periodically during the upload process. If you'd like to provide a progress indicator to the user of your application, updating the percentage complete value in the progress indicator will be performed in a handler for this event.

❑   `Event.COMPLETE` — Dispatched when the file upload has completed successfully. The handler for this event would be the place to remove your progress indicator and do anything else you need to do on a successful file upload.

Now, the preceding events are nice to know about when everything works out fine; however, there will be times when problems arise. If you want to gracefully handle issues that arise during uploading operations, you will need to know the events that occur when your uploading process is unexpectedly terminated:

❑   `SecurityErrorEvent.SECURITY_ERROR` — Dispatch due to a security violation during a file upload attempt.

❑   `HTTPStatusEvent.HTTP_STATUS` — Dispatched when an HTTP error occurs.

❑   `IOErrorEvent.IO_ERROR` — There are several reasons why this error will occur. The first reason is a file I/O error. The second reason would be that the server required authentication. The third would be that the URL requested is not using the HTTP or HTTPS.

Although there are three different error types for you to be concerned with, you may not necessarily need to handle them all in a different manner. That being said, if you just want to make sure that the faults are caught, you can just reuse one handler for all three error situations, as shown in this snippet from `chapter44_example1.mxml`:

```
        // Error Listeners
        _myFileRef.addEventListener( SecurityErrorEvent.SECURITY_ERROR,
            _onUploadFault );
        _myFileRef.addEventListener( HTTPStatusEvent.HTTP_STATUS, _onUploadFault );
        _myFileRef.addEventListener( IOErrorEvent.IO_ERROR, _onUploadFault );
    }

    private function _onUploadFault( event:Event ):void
    {
        trace( "there was an issue with the upload" );
    }
```

If a download fails because of an `HTTPStatusEvent` *error, then an* `IOErrorEvent` *is also dispatched. In other words, if you use one handler to catch both types of errors, that handler will be executed twice for each download failure.*

Uploading Files

Writing the code to support file upload in your Flex application is a two-step process. In step 1, you need to write the client-side Flex code that is responsible for uploading the file to the server. In step 2, you need to make sure that you have some server-side code written to accept the file being uploaded by the client-side Flex application. The two steps are described in more detail within this section.

Client-Side Code

If you have a server-side page to post your uploads to, setting up file uploads in your Flex application is a pretty quick and easy thing to implement. Here are the steps on how to set up file uploads:

1. As discussed earlier in this chapter, as a bare minimum you will need to create a URLRequest and FileReference object. The FileReference object will be used to access the file, upload it, and monitor progress. The URLRequest is used to define the location of the upload page:

   ```
   _myUploadURL = new URLRequest( './upload.cfm' );
   _myFileRef = new FileReference();
   ```

2. You will most likely have some UI component such as a button for the user to initiate the upload. In the handler for the user interaction used to start the process, you will need to invoke the browse() method of the FileReference class. Here is an excerpt from chapter44_example1.mxml:

   ```
           private function _onUploadRequest( event:MouseEvent ):void
           {
               _myFileRef.browse();
           }
       ]]>
   </mx:Script>
   <mx:Label
       text="File Upload Form"
       fontSize="24" />

   <mx:Button id="requestUpload_btn"
       label="select file to upload"
       click="_onUploadRequest( event )" />
   ```

When the browse() method is invoked, it will cause an operating system file chooser window to open. Figure 44-1 shows a screenshot of the file chooser window that is displayed when you click requestUpload_btn on a Windows XP system.

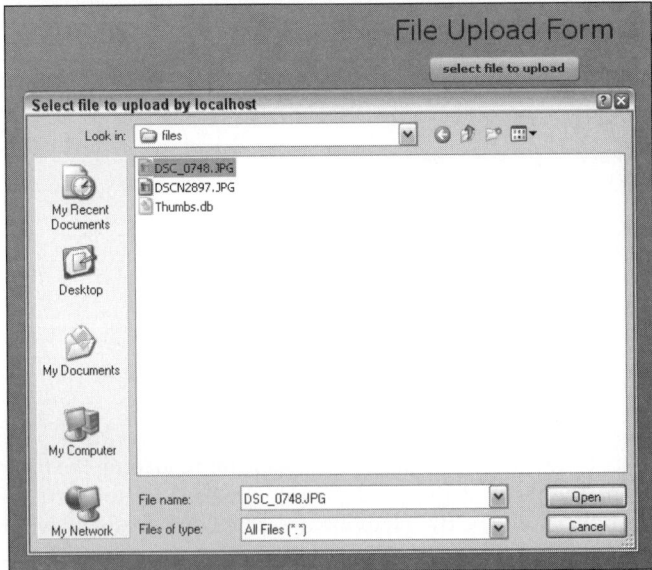

Figure 44-1

3. After the `FileReference` object's `browse()` method is invoked and the user has selected a file, the `FileReference` object will dispatch an `Event.SELECT`. So, if you listen for this event, you will know when the `FileReference` is populated with the information of the file that the user would like to upload.

```
_myFileRef.addEventListener( Event.SELECT, _onFileSelect );
```

4. Although you can perform other tasks if you'd like, once the file has been selected it is ready for uploading. So in the `Event.SELECT` handler, you can invoke the `upload()` method of your `FileReference` object to upload the file, as shown in this snippet from `chapter44_example1.mxml`:

```
private function _onFileSelect( event:Event ):void
{
    _myFileRef.upload( _myUploadURL );
}
```

Notice that in the `FileReference` object's `upload()` method is where you use the `URLRequest` object that you created.

5. At this point, you are welcome to monitor the progress of your file upload and inform the user on their upload. The events you want to keep in mind for this, `Event.OPEN`, `ProgressEvent.PROGRESS`, and `Event.COMPLETE`, were discussed earlier in this chapter in the section on handling `FileReference` events.

6. The file upload will either end successfully with the dispatching of `Event.COMPLETE` or, if it failed, it will result in at least one of the following errors: `SecurityErrorEvent.SECURITY_ERROR`, `HTTPStatusEvent.HTTP_STATUS`, or `IOErrorEvent.IO_ERROR`. These errors were discussed earlier.

Server-Side Code

Detailing all the aspects of server-side uploading code is outside the scope of this book. However, if you meet the ColdFusion prerequisites detailed earlier in this chapter, you should take a look at the `upload.cfm` file in the Chapter 44 source code. This file contains a pretty basic uploading implementation. In a nutshell, the file does the following:

❑ Double-checks to make sure that the directory that the files will be saved in exists on the server.

❑ Once any directory-specific concerns have been resolved, the server-side ColdFusion code saves the uploaded file, using `<cffile>`.

Here is the code from `upload.cfm`:

```
<cfif NOT #DirectoryExists( ExpandPath('files/') )#>
    <cfdirectory action = "create" directory = "#ExpandPath('files/')#" >
</cfif>

<cffile
    action="upload"
    filefield="Filedata"
    destination="#ExpandPath('files/')#"
    nameconflict="OVERWRITE" />
```

Downloading Files with FileReference

In addition to uploading files, `FileReference` can be used to download files. You can accomplish this by utilizing the `download()` method of the `FileReference` class. The `download()` method has one required argument, `request`, and one optional argument, `defaultFileName`.

The `request` argument is a `URLRequest` pointing to the file that will be downloaded. The `defaultFileName` argument is a string that can be used to customize the default filename that shows up in the file save dialog window. If you don't specify `defaultFileName`, the filename of the file specified in the `request` argument will be shown as the default filename in the file save dialog. Seeing the name of the file from the request argument might not be what you prefer, for instance when the `URLRequest` is pointing at a server-side application script such as a CFM page.

Here is an excerpt from `chapter44_example2.mxml` in the Chapter 44 source code:

```
        _myDownloadURL = new URLRequest( './files/randomText.txt' );
    }

    private function _onDownloadRequest( event:MouseEvent ):void
    {
        _myFileRef.download( _myDownloadURL, "myDownloadedTextFile.txt" );
    }
```

Notice how we're preventing the filename `randomText.txt` from showing up as the default filename in the file save dialog. Instead, you'll see `myDownloadedTextFile.txt` when you click to download the file.

Canceling a File Upload or Download

If you want to enable your users to cancel a file upload or download, for instance, if they decide they really don't want to upload a 90MB movie file, you can make use of the `cancel()` method available in the `FileReference` class. The `cancel()` method requires no arguments and returns nothing. The `cancel()` method does exactly what you would think; it cancels any ongoing upload or download operation.

Working with Multiple Files

So far we've taken you through the steps required to upload a single file. To take your application to the next level and enable support for uploading multiple files, you will need to use `flash.net.FileReferenceList`. The `FileReferenceList` class was created to work with an `Array` of `FileReference` objects.

Like `FileReference`, `FileReferenceList` has a `browse()` method to invoke a file-selection dialog window. It also dispatches `Event.CANCEL` or `Event.SELECT` when the user cancels the process or selects files via the file-selection dialog. The difference is that after an `Event.SELECT` is dispatched, the `FileReferenceList` will have its `fileList` property populated with an `Array` of `FileReference` objects.

In other words, you use `FileReferenceList` to make a multi-file upload selection, then you perform and monitor the actual uploading process individually for each `FileReference` object. Let's step through the key points of the multiple file upload example `chapter44_example3.mxml` in the Chapter 44 source code.

1. Along with the `URLRequest` pointing to the server-side script, we create a `FileReferenceList` object and configure a listener for the `Event.SELECT` event that is dispatched when a user has selected a file or files:

    ```
    private var _myFileList:FileReferenceList;

    private function _onCreationComplete( event:FlexEvent ):void
    {
        _myUploadURL = new URLRequest( './upload.cfm' );

        _myFileList = new FileReferenceList();

        // Standard Listeners
        _myFileList.addEventListener( Event.SELECT, _onFilesSelect );
    }
    ```

2. In a button click handler, we invoke the `browse()` method of the `FileReferenceList` to bring up the file-selection dialog window:

    ```
    private function _onUploadRequest( event:MouseEvent ):void
    {
        _myFileList.browse();
    }
    ```

3. Thanks to the event listener we pointed out in step 1, when the `Event.SELECT` is dispatched the `_onFileSelect()` handler will run. This handler is where the `FileReferenceList fileList` property is evaluated. If the `fileList` Array is populated, then we can loop through the `Array` and invoke upload operations on each of the `FileReference` objects stored in the `Array`:

    ```
    private function _onFilesSelect( event:Event ):void
    {
        var currentFileReference:FileReference;
        var len:int = _myFileList.fileList.length;
        var i:int;

        if( len )
        {
          for( i=0; i < len; i++ )
          {
            currentFileReference = _myFileList.fileList[ i ] as FileReference;

            // complete listener
            currentFileReference.addEventListener( Event.COMPLETE,
             _onSuccessfulUpload );
            // error listeners
            currentFileReference.addEventListener( SecurityErrorEvent.SECURITY_ERROR,
             _onUploadFault );
    ```

```
                          currentFileReference.addEventListener( HTTPStatusEvent.HTTP_STATUS,
                          _onUploadFault );
                          currentFileReference.addEventListener( IOErrorEvent.IO_ERROR,
                          _onUploadFault );

                          // upload the file
                          currentFileReference.upload( _myUploadURL );
                      }
                  }
              }
```

Server-Side Considerations

Before concluding this chapter, we need to bring up a couple points regarding server interaction, especially with file uploads. The first thing to consider is server disk space. The second is to consider assisting server-side administrators by filtering out unwanted file types.

As a courteous and proactive developer, the last thing you want to do is cause your application server to run out of disk space. There are many ways to handle disk space on the server ranging from disk quotas to scheduled processes on the application server that monitor disk space utilization to custom code implemented in the server-side upload script to check disk space before uploading your files. As a client-side developer, keep in mind that the FileReference class has a size property that reports the size of the file on disk in bytes and can be used to filter out uploads that are larger than the allowed upload limit.

> *Although you can upload and download much larger files, officially the Flash Player only supports file uploads and downloads up to 100MB. For more information, see* http://livedocs.adobe.com/flex/3/langref/flash/net/FileReference.html#download().

Also, there may be times when server-side administrators or the application requirements will need to enforce that only specific file types are uploaded to the server. The FileReference class has a type property that will return the file extension for you to check against. In addition, when you invoke the browse() method of the FileReference or FileReferenceList class, you can pass it an optional typeFilter argument of type flash.net.FileFilter to specify the file types you'll accept. Here's a snippet taken from chapter44_example4.mxml to detail how to use FileFilter:

```
private function _onUploadRequest( event:MouseEvent ):void
{
    // Let's use an MP3 only fileFilter
    var onlyMP3:FileFilter = new FileFilter( "Only MP3", "*.mp3" );
    // Display the file-selector dialog with a limited selection of only mp3
    _myFileRef.browse( [ onlyMP3 ] );
}
```

Summary

The FileReference, File ReferenceList, and FileFilter classes are relatively painless classes to work with. Although their feature sets are limited, they provide a Flex developer with what they need to allow their users to upload and download files from a server. In addition, a good thing about the FileReference and FileReferenceList classes is that they piggyback on the operating system file browse dialogs, providing the user with a familiar way to select and save files with your application.

If you would like additional API and usage information on the FileReference, FileReferenceList, and the FileFilter classes, you can view the Adobe LiveDoc at http://livedocs.adobe.com/flex/3/html/help.html?content=17_Networking_and_communications_7.html.

The next chapter examines the additional file management capabilities that are provided by the AIR-specific framework elements that are available for you to utilize in your AIR applications.

Local File Management with AIR

The AIR extensions to Flex include the ability to work with files and directories. AIR applications can access the user's filesystem to create, delete, read, and write files, as well as perform a variety of directory operations such as create, delete, move, list files, and so forth.

In addition, AIR will interact with operating system-specific dialog boxes for picking files, saving files, and browsing directories, giving your AIR application an authentic feel in the user's operating system of choice.

This chapter covers working with files and directories, the native dialog boxes, specific Flex components designed to work with filesystems, and a specific method for encrypting data saved on the user's hard drive.

File Operations

Most of the `File` operations available to AIR are accessed through the `flash.filesystem.File` class — everything from listing, copying, moving, and deleting files and directories to working with special operating system directories like the user application. The `File` class is a pointer used to represent either a path to a directory or a specific file. Once you're pointing at either a file or directory, you then pass the reference into the rest of the APIs, such as `FileStream` for reading a file or `File.getDirectoryListing` for listing all the files in a given directory.

Referencing Directories

As an example, here is a `File` object that represents a directory:

```
var file:File = File.documentsDirectory.resolvePath("My Pictures");
trace(file.nativePath.toString());
```

This creates a file object that starts at the `userDirectory` and then navigates down to My Pictures. The call to `nativePath` on my Windows machine returns the `C:\Documents and Settings\USER\My Documents\My Pictures` directory.

On OS X, to get at the default Pictures directory, you'd use the following snippet:

```
file = File.userDirectory.resolvePath("Pictures");
```

Notice that on OS X you're navigating down to the pictures directory via the user's home directory, compared to the Windows version that begins in the My Document's directory. The call to native `Path` on the OS X version returns `/Users/USER/Pictures`. When the file is pointing at a directory, you can call any of the expected directory operations against the created file pointer, such as reading directories.

Referencing Files

Now to reference an actual file, use the same syntax described previously, but instead feeding a filename into `resolvePath`, create a `File` pointer to a `File`:

```
var file:File = File.applicationDirectory.resolvePath("test_data_file.txt");
Alert.show(file.nativePath.toString());
```

First, create the file pointer object that's pointing to the default `applicationDirectory`, which is where the AIR application has been installed. Then by calling `resolvePath`, passing in a filename, the file is now pointed at a file.

With a file pointer pointed at a file, you can now open it with the `FileStream` object for reading or writing, but we'll get to this later in the chapter.

Navigating Paths

Using `File.resolvePath` and `File.nativePath` are preferred methods for manipulating valid path or file pointers. The easiest way to understand the `File` class is to just start navigating the filesystem with it.

You can create a file pointer that starts in the user's My Pictures folder (on Windows):

```
var file:File = File.documentsDirectory.resolvePath("My Pictures");
```

Then using `resolvePath`, navigate up a directory using the relative path notation found:

```
file = file.resolvePath("..");
```

The file object is now pointing at the documents directory, which on Windows would be: `C:\Documents and Settings\USER\My Documents` or on OS X, `/Users/USER/Documents`.

Now let's navigate back into the My Pictures directory; this time, instead of using `resolvePath`, let's just set the `nativePath` directly:

```
file.nativePath += "/My Pictures";
```

This now moves the file pointer back up to the My Pictures directory. Notice here that we're using a forward slash. AIR automatically translates forward slashes into backslashes in Windows.

Alternatively, we could have expressed the previous with:

```
file.nativePath += "\\My Pictures";
```

This returns the exact same thing. Notice that we had to escape the backslash. If we didn't, and instead called `file.nativePath += "\My Pictures"`, the results wouldn't have been what we expected. They would have pointed the file at an invalid path of C:\Documents and Settings\Todd\My DocumentsMy Pictures. And when we went to actually use the file pointer, it would have thrown an error.

As you can see, navigating down directories on different operating systems from the same code isn't always going to be fun, so you could write the following, and have AIR manage your operating-specific path separators:

```
file = File.applicationDirectory.resolvePath("dir1").resolvePath("dir2");
```

This will return the appropriate paths on both Windows and OS X without us having to think about whether we're in forward-slash or backslash land.

Another way to return the appropriate path is to always use the forward slash. A side benefit of never thinking in Windows backslashes when writing cross-platform software is that you also don't need to worry about escaping the backslash in a path with the extra backslash (\).

The previous use of resolve path could have also been written alternatively as:

```
file = File.applicationDirectory.resolvePath("dir1/dir2");
```

Be careful though, when using slashes in the strings to define paths. The following won't append the directory to the `applicationDirectory` as the previous example will; it'll resolve to a literal path:

```
file = File.applicationDirectory.resolvePath("/dir1/dir2");
```

In this case, `file` will resolve to `/dir1/dir2` instead of `C:\Documents and Settings\User\My Documents\Pro Flex 3\45 File Management\bin-debug\dir1\dir2`, as you'd expect. The leading slash before `dir1` caused the file to interpret the path as a full path, instead of a relative path.

OS X and Windows use specific different directory separators when defining paths. OS X uses the forward slash (/) and Windows uses the backslash (\). When defining native paths in AIR, it's important to always use the operating system-specific delineator when searching for files. However, there's a trick so that you can define a path for both operating systems at the same time: always use the forward slash. On Windows, AIR translates the forward slash into an appropriate Windows backslash.

It's best to use `resolvePath` as much as possible when defining paths, both relative and literal. This way, you don't have to worry about any operating system-specific formatting, and don't need to worry about whether you should or shouldn't place leading slashes on your path definitions.

You've seen the uses of `applicationDirectory` and `userDirectory` above. The following table shows a complete listing of all the default folder path shortcuts available on the `flash.filesystem.File` object.

Property	Description
`applicationDirectory`	The directory where the AIR application is installed
`applicationStorageDirectory`	Special AIR directory
`desktopDirectory`	The user's desktop on both OS X and Windows
`documentsDirectory`	OS X: points to the user's documents directory. Windows: points to the user's My Documents
`userDirectory`	On OS X it points to the `/Users/user`; on Windows points at `C:\Documents and Settings\user`

Synchronous versus Asynchronous API

When working with files and directories, AIR includes many file operations with both synchronous and asynchronous versions. There's synchronous and asynchronous APIs for copying files, deleting files, deleting directories, displaying directory listings, and so on. The asynchronous version of the APIs append `Async` to the name of the synchronous call. For example, `File.copyTo()` is the synchronous API, and its asynchronous counterpart is `File.copyToAsync()`.

The synchronous and asynchronous versions accomplish the exact same action, although the asynchronous versions raise events to notify you when they're complete so that the Flash Player doesn't lock up the UI while the user is waiting for a directory of files to be deleted.

There is no one or right way as to when to use which version of the API. Always error on the asynchronous, although, since this will have minimal impact in locking up the UI while file operations are being called. The synchronous are included, though, because there might be multiple operations to a file that you might need to perform in a synchronous fashion, like opening it up, looking for specific data, then moving to a target destination based on the data. Doing this with the asynchronous API, the file would be read and moved all at the same time causing all sorts of problems and errors.

There aren't asynchronous versions of some of the file APIs that have short durations, like `File.createDirectory`, which takes no significant amount of time to perform.

The synchronous operations are for file operations that could take longer than a moment.

When would you use the asynchronous versions? Well, when you want to do the following:

- ❑ **Copy a large file:** Instead of `File.copyTo`, use `copyToAsync`.
- ❑ **Delete a directory with many files:** Instead of `File.deleteDirectory`, use `File.deleteDirectoryAsync`.
- ❑ **Delete a large file:** Instead of `File.deleteFile`, use `File.deleteFileAsync`.

- ❏ **Get a listing of files in a directory:** Instead of `File.getDirectoryListing`, use `File.getDirectoryListingAsync`.

- ❏ **Move a large file, especially to another drive:** Instead of `File.moveTo`, use `File.moveToAsync`.

- ❏ **Move a file or directory to the trash:** Use `File.moveToTrashAsync` instead of `File.moveToTrash`.

When using the asynchronous versions of the APIs, make sure that you add an `IOError` event listener in case the file or directory you're working with doesn't exist, or if there's a specific error in either reading or writing the data.

Copying a File Synchronously

The following code will copy a test file from the application source directory into the application storage directory:

```
var fileSource:File =
  File.applicationDirectory.resolvePath("dir1/test_file.txt");

var fileDest:File = File.applicationStorageDirectory.resolvePath
    ("dest/test_file_copied.txt");

if (fileDest.exists) {
  trace("overwriting file at destination");
}

fileSource.copyTo(fileDest, true);
```

First, create the `fileSource` File pointer for the source of the copy. This is the file from the application directory that is going to be copied. Note that we use `resolvePath` and forward slashes for maximum cross-platform compatibility. Next, create `fileDest`, which is the target location and filename. A quick call to `File.exists` is made to see if the file already exists in the destination. This is done here only to show off the `File.exists` method, which is quite useful for determining whether files will be overwritten, or whether target directories exist. Finally, call `File.copyTo` to perform the file copy. Any folders in the `fileDest` path that don't exist will be created, and the file will be copied to this target directory.

Note that with the synchronous `copyTo`, *you need to provide inline error handling, most likely inside a* `try/catch` *block.*

The Adobe AIR security sandbox doesn't allow files inside the `applicationDirectory` *to be modified. Therefore, use the* `applicationStorageDirectory` *for storing application-specific configuration files that might need to be modified through the AIR application's user interface. You can, however, read any file from the* `applicationDirectory`.

Copying a File Asynchronously

This is just like the synchronous file copy described earlier, except that this time it uses the asynchronous API with both `EVENT.COMPLETE` and `IOErrorEvent.IO_ERROR` events attached to the source file:

```
private function copyAsyncronous():void
{
```

```
var fileSource:File =
        File.applicationDirectory.resolvePath("dir1/test_file.txt");

// Bind the COMPLETE and IOErrorEvent Handlers
fileSource.addEventListener(Event.COMPLETE, onFileCopyComplete);
fileSource.addEventListener(IOErrorEvent.IO_ERROR, onIOError);

var fileDest:File =
File.applicationStorageDirectory.resolvePath("dest/test_file_copied.txt");

// Copy asynchronously, overwriting if file exists.
fileSource.copyToAsync(fileDest, true);
trace("after call to copyAsync");
}
```

First, create both the source file (`fileSource`) and the destination file (`fileDest`), just as in the previous synchronous example. Additionally, attach event listeners to the source file, listening for the events `Event.COMPLETE` and `IOErrorEvent.IO_ERROR`. These events will be raised either when the copy is completed or, in case of a copy error, a call to `file.copyToAsync` begins the file copying process. The asynchronous version of the API is quite useful if you are copying large files across disk partitions or the network, as it will keep the application UI from locking up.

The `Event.COMPLETE` handler is called when the file copy has been completed, in this case an alert box displays to show that the copy has been successful:

```
private function onFileCopyComplete(event:Event):void
{
  trace("inside onFileCopyComplete ");
  Alert.show("File copy successful");
}
```

However, if there's an error in the copy, such as the destination file exists and is write protected, or if we modify the preceding call to `file.copyToAsync`, passing in `false` for the overwriting destination file passing in false for the overwrite-destination-file-if-exists parameter, like so:

```
file.copyToAsync(fileDest, false);
```

then the following error handler will be executed (see the code for `copyAsyncronousWithError` in the source code included for this chapter to trigger an error condition):

```
private function onIOError(event:IOErrorEvent):void
{
  Alert.show("IOError: " + event.text);
}
```

This `IOError` handler will display the reason that the copy failed. In this case, the error is raised because the destination file already exists, and it's not being deleted before trying to copy a file with the same name into the destination directory.

That's the quick overview of asynchronous versus synchronous file operations. Remember, there are both synchronous and asynchronous operations for listing contents of directories, moving files, and deleting files.

Other File and Directory Operations

Now that you know how to get a proper `File` pointer to either a directory or a file, and you are familiar with the asynchronous/synchronous API, let's perform some of the remaining file and directory manipulations.

Checking for Existence

Both files and directories can be checked for existence to make sure that the `File` pointer you created references an existing file or directory.

Here, let's see if the user has a document titled `ProFlex3.doc` using *File.exists*:

```
File.documentsDirectory.resolvePath("ProFlex3.doc").exists
```

Calling `exists` returns either `true` or `false`, depending on whether the file exists. Checking for directory existence is very similar, except that the `File` pointer references a directory instead of a file:

```
File.documentsDirectory.exists
```

Hopefully, this returns `true`, as everyone should have a default documents directory.

Deleting Files and Directories

To delete a file, call `File.deleteFile` (or `File.deleteFileAsync`) on an existing file reference. The following code ensures that the file `ProFlex3.doc` exists before attempting to delete it to eliminate possible runtime errors:

```
var fileExists:File = File.documentsDirectory.resolvePath("ProFlex3.doc");
if (fileExists.exists) fileExists.deleteFile();
```

Here we've created a file pointer (`fileExists`) referencing a file in the user's documents directory. Then we check for existence. If there is such a file, it's deleted by the call to `fileExists.deleteFile()`.

To delete a directory, use `File.deleteDirectory` (or `File.deleteDirectoryAsync`):

```
var dirExists:File = File.documentsDirectory.resolvePath("Directory ABCD Demo");
if (dirExists.exists) dirExists.deleteDirectory(true);
```

This creates the file reference to the directory `Directory ABCD Demo`. Then, if it exists, the directory and all its files are deleted. If you don't want to delete directories that have files, set the `deleteDirectoryContents` parameter to `false` on the call to `deleteDirectory`.

Moving Files and Directories

Moving files and directories works very similarly to copying files as shown previously in the asynchronous section. To move files and directories, create both a source and a destination that point to either a file or a directory.

To move a directory and all its files:

```
var dirABCD:File = File.applicationDirectory.resolvePath("Directory ABCD Demo");
var destDir:File = File.documentsDirectory.resolvePath("Directory ABCD Demo");
dirABCD.moveTo(destDir, true);
```

Here we've created `dirABCD`, which is referencing the directory `Directory ABCD Demo`. Next, create the destination directory that references the user's documents directory. It's important to notice that `resolvePath` was called to create a destination pointer that includes the destination directory name. You could name the destination directory anything you want. Finally, call the `dirABCD.moveTo` to move the files, passing in `true` to overwrite any files that already exist with the same name.

The code to move a file would look exactly the same, with the exception that both `dirABCD` and `destDir` file pointers would reference files instead of directories — and you'd probably name the variables more intelligently, like `fileABCD` and `destFile`.

You can also move directories and files to the Trash Can by using the `File.moveToTrash` (or `File.moveToTrashAsync`).

Enumerating a Directory

To enumerate a directory's files, use `File.getDirectoryListing` (or `File.getDirectoryListingAsync`):

```
var userDocuments:Array= File.documentsDirectory.getDirectoryListing();
for each (var file:File in userDocuments)
{
  trace(file.name);
}
```

First, using a valid `File` pointer to a directory (here just use the default user's documents directory), call `getDirectoryListing`, which will return an array of `File` references. Next, iterate through each object of the array, which happens to be a `File`. Then print out the filename, or one of the other `File` properties like, `creationDate` or `modificationDate`.

Creating Temporary Directories and Files

To create temporary directories and files, use `File.createTempDirectory` and `File.createTempFile`, which will create directories and files in the System folder:

```
var tempDir:File = File.createTempDirectory();

var tempFile:File = File.createTempFile();
```

This code creates one temporary directory and one temporary file. On Widows, these files and directories are created in the `C:\Documents and Settings\USER\Local Settings\` directory. These file and directory names are guaranteed to be unique each time one is created. Make sure to delete temporary files and directories when you're done working with them; otherwise, they'll be left to clutter the filesystem when the AIR application closes.

There are many other properties and methods on the `File` object worth exploring, but we've run out of room here. Check the *Adobe Flex 3 Language Reference* for the complete functionality of the `flash.filesystem.File` class.

Working with Native File Dialogs

When working with files and directories, there are four different methods on the `flash.filesystem.File` class used to display native operating system dialog boxes. The four methods are:

1. `File.browseForDirectory`, which is used to choose a working directory
2. `File.browseForOpen` is used to select a file to open in your AIR application
3. `File.browseForOpenMultiple` is used to open multiple files, maybe for use in FTP or file uploading software
4. `File.browseForSave`, which is used to choose a destination filename and path to save a file on the user's filesystem

In the enclosed source code for Chapter 45, there's a demo tab titled "Working with Native File Dialogs" that will demonstrate these different dialog boxes. It is useful to see what they exactly render on your operating system of choice.

Native Directory Browser

The function `browseForDirectory` will bring up a native operating system directory browser dialog box so the user can choose a directory. This is useful for setting a default save directory or choosing a directory of images to import into the application.

Let's look at some code for browsing for a directory:

```
private function browseForImageDirectory():void
{
  var userDir:File = File.userDirectory;
  userDir.addEventListener(Event.SELECT, onDirectorySelected);
  userDir.addEventListener(Event.CANCEL, onCancelDialog);
  userDir.browseForDirectory("Select an image folder");
}
```

This creates a File pointer to the user directory. Attach a couple of event listeners, one for `Event.SELECT` for when the user selects a directory, and one for `Event.CANCEL` for when the user cancels the dialog. Most likely, you won't actually need the handler for `CANCEL`, but it's demonstrated here to show that the event will be raised from the native dialog.

Then call `browseForDirectory` with an appropriate title; in our case, we want the user to choose a directory that contains images. The call to `browseForDirectory` will open a native operating system window prompting the user to select a directory.

The user then navigates down the appropriate path until they choose the directory that they want to open. When they do this, the onDirectorySelected event is called. It has the following implementation, which loops through all the files in the selected directory and compiles a list of all the JPEGs:

```
private function onDirectorySelected(event:Event):void
{
  var selectedDirectory:File = event.target as File;

  var imageFiles:String = "";
  var directoryFiles:Array = selectedDirectory.getDirectoryListing();
  for each( var currentFile:File in directoryFiles)
  {
    if (currentFile.isDirectory == true) continue;  // Ignore the directories

    if (currentFile.extension.toUpperCase() == "JPG" ||
      currentFile.extension.toUpperCase() == "JPEG")
      {
        imageFiles += currentFile.name + "\n";
      }
  }

  Alert.show("You selected the directory: " + selectedDirectory.name + "\n" + "
    ...with the following JPEGS:\n" + imageFiles);

}
```

First, the selected directory is passed into the event handler through the target parameter. The target needs to be cast as a File. Don't be confused though; we're working with a directory, it's accessed via the File class. Remember the File class is just a pointer to either a directory or a file. In the case here, it's going to be a directory, which we assign to selectedDirectory.

With the selectedDirectory, we then call getDirectoryListing, which is a synchronous call to get a listing of all the files and directories in the selectedDirectory. It's important to understand that both files and directories are being returned and assigned to the directoryFiles array, because we're going to have to weed out the directories when we start compiling a list of JPEGs in the user-selected directory.

Start looping through each file in the selectedDirectory. Check to see if the currentFile is a pointer to a directory; the File.isDirectory property returns true when it's indeed a directory. Since directories aren't files, and don't have file extensions, skip to the next file pointer in the array of directoryFiles. However, if it is a file, then inspect the extension, looking for valid JPEG extensions and add all JPEG files to the master imageFiles string for displaying.

Finally, after all the files and directory pointers in the directory have been inspected, show the user a list of JPEG image files.

Native Browse for Open Dialog

When opening files on the user's operating system for use inside your AIR application, use the File.browseForOpen to prompt the user to select a file. The browseForOpen allows file filters to be set, so only specific file types are allowed to be opened. After all, you don't want the user to open a document that your application can't properly handle. This is really useful for when you have a file type declared that works with your application, the way that .PSD files work with Adobe Photoshop.

Pretend for a second that we have an image editing program, such as Photoshop, and we want to prompt the user to open a file for editing. We'd use code that looks similar to this:

```
private function browseForImage():void
{
  //    Create a filter for Image file types
  var pictureFilter:FileFilter = new FileFilter
    ("Image Files", "*.jpeg; *.jpg; *.png;*.gif");

  var browseDir:File = picturesDirectory()
  browseDir.addEventListener(Event.SELECT, onFileSelected);
  browseDir.addEventListener(Event.CANCEL, onCancelDialog);
  browseDir.browseForOpen("Pick a Picture file to open" , [pictureFilter]);
}
```

First, create a `FileFilter` that will allow the user to only open JPEG, PNG, or GIF images. You can create multiple filters if you want, including one for each file type. But in this example, we're using one filter, separating the file extensions with semicolons, and giving the filter a title that will be displayed by the native dialog box.

Second, start at the default picture path on the user's operating system. We have a helper function called `picturesDirectory` that will return either the user's Pictures folder (on OS X) or the user's My Pictures folder (on Windows). The explanation of this follows.

Next, listen for the exact same events as the previous `browseForDirectory` example. Listen for `Event.SELECT` and `Event.CANCEL`, and implement the appropriate handlers, which are `onFileSelected` and `onCancelDialog`. Again, `Event.CANCEL` is most likely optional.

Finally, call `browseDir.browseForOpen`, passing in a title for the dialog box, and the array of file filters. Here, the array contains only one item, the `pictureFilter`, but you could break down each image type into its own filter if you wanted.

The user selects an image and then the event to handle the selection of files, `onFileSelected`, is called, which looks like this:

```
private function onFileSelected(event:Event):void
{
  var selectedFile:File = event.target as File;
  Alert.show("You selected the file: \n" + selectedFile.name);
}
```

Again, cast the `event.target` as a `File` to get the selected file. Here the only thing we're doing with it is displaying the `Name`. But in reality, you'd probably create a `FileStream` object to open the file and read its contents into the application for editing.

OS X and Windows have slightly different paths where default user images are stored. With the `flash.filesystem.File` class, there's a method to get the default documents directory (`File.documentsDirectory`), but there's no method called `picturesDirectory`. We implemented our own cross-platform version, called `picturesDirectory`. It looks like this:

```
private function picturesDirectory():File
{
```

```
        var file:File;
        if (Capabilities.os.indexOf("Windows") > -1 ){
          // The default Windows directory for pictures
          file = File.documentsDirectory.resolvePath("My Pictures");
        } else if(Capabilities.os.indexOf("MacOS") > -1 ){
          // The default OSX directory for pictures
          file = File.userDirectory.resolvePath("Pictures");
        }
        return file;
      }
```

This method determines which operating system the AIR application is running in and whether it's Windows or OS X, and then builds the appropriate file pointer.

OS X's default picture directory is at USER/Pictures. On Windows, the default pictures directory is located at \USER\My Documents\My Pictures. Notice that, for the OS X version, we start our path at the File.userDirectory, whereas in Windows, we start at the File.documentsDirectory. There are many subtle differences that you, the developer, will need to be aware of when developing cross-platform applications. The default folder structure is one of them.

Native Browse for Open Multiple Dialogs

The method File.browseForOpenMultiple works pretty much like File.browseForOpen with one major difference. Instead of adding a handler for Event.SELECT (as you did for browserForOpen), add a listener for FileListEvent.SELECT_MULTIPLE. The FileListEvent has a files property on it that is used to store multiple file pointers, as opposed to Event.SELECT, which had a target property that pointed at only a single file.

To use the browseForOpenMuliple, use the following code:

```
    private function browseForImages():void
    {
      var pictureFilter:FileFilter = new FileFilter("Picture Files", "*.jpeg;
    *.jpg; *.png;*.gif");

      var browseDir:File = picturesDirectory();
      browseDir.addEventListener(FileListEvent.SELECT_MULTIPLE,
                                              onFilesSelected);
      browseDir.addEventListener(Event.CANCEL, onCancelDialog);
      browseDir.browseForOpenMultiple("Pick a Picture file to open" ,
                                [pictureFilter]);
    }
```

As you can see, the code is exactly the same as in the example of browseForOpen, except that we're listening for FileListEvent.SELECT_MULTIPLE, and we're calling browseForOpenMultiple. The call to browseForOpenMultiple opens the exact same dialog as browseForOpen, which is shown in Figure 45-1. However, the dialog allows the user to select multiple files.

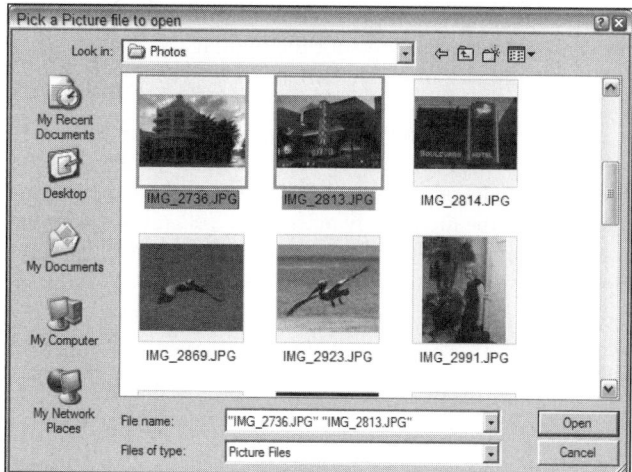

Figure 45-1

When the user approves the file selections, the `onFileSelected` event handler is called, which looks like this:

```
private function onFilesSelected(event:FileListEvent):void
{
  var selectedFiles:String = "";

  for each (var selectedFile:File  in event.files) {
    selectedFiles += selectedFile.name + "\n";
  }
  Alert.show("You selected the files:\n" + selectedFiles);
}
```

Here, there's no need to cast anything; the `FileListEvent` has a `files` property that contains an array of `Flash.filesystem.File` pointers. Iterate through each file performing whatever action is needed to open the file. We're just listing the selected files out here.

Native File Save Dialog

The native File Save dialog is used when prompting users to save a file to the native filesystem. It works in exactly the same way as `browseForOpen`, with the following code prompting the user to save the file in their chosen operating system:

```
private function browseForSave():void
{
  var userDocsDir:File = File.documentsDirectory;
  userDocsDir.addEventListener(Event.SELECT, onSave);
  userDocsDir.addEventListener(Event.CANCEL, onCancelDialog);
  userDocsDir.browseForSave("Save the image file");
}
```

This method prompts the user to save a file in their documents directory (Documents in OS X, My Documents in Windows). Add event listeners for the regular `Event.SELECT` and `Event.CANCEL` events, this time creating an `onSave` implementation.

The call to `browseForSave`, with the appropriate title, will bring up the native save dialog box, allowing the user to browse and type in a filename to save the file. The user then types in the name of the file. Notice, that when the native dialog is open, and the user enters the name of an existing file, the native dialog box warns the user that the file already exists, and asks if they want to overwrite it. Nothing needs to be done in AIR to manage this. After the user is happy with the name they've chosen, they close the native dialog box and the `onSave` event handler is raised with the user's filename:

```
private function onSave(event:Event):void
{
  var fileToSave:File = event.target as File;

  saveBitmapDataFile(fileToSave);
}
```

First, cast the `event.target` to a `File` type. This is a pointer to the file. Next, you'll need to open the file and start writing data to it. In this case, we're going to write JPEG image data to a file, and `saveBitmapDataFile` will handle opening of a `FileStream`, writing the data, and closing the `FileStream`. But the specifics are covered in the next section.

Unfortunately, the `browseForSave` API doesn't have the same concept of `FileFilters` that `browseForOpen` does. Therefore, you'll have minimal control in the native dialog box to require proper file extensions. However, in the `Event.SELECT` event handler, there is access to the file extension property that can be used to ensure proper filename/extension settings.

Reading and Writing File Data

We've discussed at length how the `flash.filesystem.File` pointer object works for directories and files. But when it comes down to reading and writing the actual data from a file, `flash.filesystem.FileStream` is where the action is.

When working with a `FileStream`, always perform the following actions:

1. Acquire a `File` pointer either using native dialogs or through ActionScript code.

2. Open the `FileStream` using either `open` or `openAsync` either for `Read`, `Write`, `Append`, or `Update`. These open modes are defined in the `flash.filesystem.FileMode` class.

3. Either read or write data using appropriate methods of the `FileStream` class. Use `readUTF`, `readByte`, `readBoolean`, `readDouble`, `readMultiByte`, `readObject`, and so forth for reading from a `FileStream`; or `writeUTF`, `writeBytes`, `writeByte`, `writeBoolean`, `writeDouble`, and so on for writing to a `FileStream`.

4. Close the `FileStream`.

All uses of `FileStream` follow a similar pattern.

Saving Bitmap Data as a JPEG File

In a previous section, we talked about saving files to the filesystem with native dialog boxes. There was a reference to saving `BitmapData` as a JPEG, which we're going to implement here. Assume that we have acquired a `File` pointer (either via a native dialog or through saving to some default directory declared in code) to a file where we want to save the `BitmapData` and pass it into the following method as the `fileToSave` parameter:

```
private function saveBitmapDataFile(fileToSave:File):void
{
```

First, we need some `BitmapData` to save off into the file. Let's use the UI of the sample application for this chapter. Here, we capture the current Flex component's bitmap data by initializing a new `BitmapData` object, passing in the width and height of the Flex component that will be saved as a JPEG, along with some default transparency and background image color. Then call `bitmapData.draw`, which actually writes the image data into the `bitmapData` object:

```
var bitmapData:BitmapData = new BitmapData( this.width, this.height, true,
    0x000000);
bitmapData.draw(this);
```

Next, we need to take the `bitmapData` and convert it into JPEG data. Fortunately, Flex now comes with a `JPEGEncoder`, which we instantiate with a default image quality of 50. (It can be up to 100 if you want the least amount of image quality lost in the conversion.)

```
var jpegEncoder:JPEGEncoder = new JPEGEncoder(50);
```

With the `jpegEncoder`, encode the bitmap data into a `ByteArray`:

```
var byteArray:ByteArray = jpegEncoder.encode(bitmapData);
```

Now the fun happens with the `FileStream`. First, create a new `FileStream` object:

```
var fileStream:FileStream = new FileStream();
```

Open the `filestream` with the `File` pointer where the JPEG is being saved. Pass in the mode `FileMode.WRITE`, since data is being written to the file:

```
fileStream.open(fileToSave, FileMode.WRITE);
```

Next, write the actual bytes of the converted image data out to the file:

```
fileStream.writeBytes(byteArray);
```

Finally, as with all `FileStream` operations, close the stream:

```
fileStream.close();
```

And here we'll just inform the user that the image file was saved:

```
Alert.show("Saved the image file: " + fileToSave.nativePath);
}
```

In this example, we used `writeBytes` to write data to a file, but you could use any of the many `write*` methods, depending on the data, for writing to the `FileStream`.

Reading XML Data from a File

Reading data from files using `FileStream` involves the basic steps outlined previously. Here's a quick sample of reading an XML file containing a list of people's names and binding it to a `List` component:

```
private function loadXMLConfig():void
{
```

First, acquire the file pointer. Here, we're just setting it to a known `people.xml` file in the AIR application directory. The file very easily could have been acquired with one of the native dialog calls, such as `browseForOpen`:

```
var file:File = File.applicationDirectory.resolvePath("people.xml");
```

Second, create the file stream, and open it with the appropriate mode. In this case, we want to read the `people.xml` file into the application. It probably wouldn't hurt to put some error checks in here to make sure that indeed the file `people.xml` exists so that we don't accidently try to open a nonexistent file:

```
var fileStream:FileStream = new FileStream();
fileStream.open(file, FileMode.READ);
```

Next, read from the `FileStream` with a call to `readUTFBytes`, passing in the number of bytes to read, which is the length of the `FileStream`:

```
var people:XML = XML(fileStream.readUTFBytes(fileStream.bytesAvailable));
```

Close the `FileStream`. Always close the `FileStream`:

```
fileStream.close()
```

View the data of the XML file by setting the data provider to a proper e4x expression:

```
peopleList.dataProvider = people.person.name;
}
```

That's all there is to reading and writing data with the `FileStream`.

Filesystem Controls

Included with the Flex SDK for AIR are some additional controls that encapsulate working with the filesystem. These additional controls are rendered purely by Flex using basic Flex controls for navigating the operating system's filesystem. They are mostly inherited from other components of the Flex component framework such as `ComboBox`, `DataGrid`, `List`, and `Tree`.

The source code for this chapter has a section title "Flex FileSystem Component Explorer" that has instances of the following Flex classes:

1. `FileSystemComboBox` — A combo box used to display a currently selected folder from a hierarchy path of folders.

2. `FileSystemTree` — A tree control that displays folders in a collapsible and explorable folder tree, very similar to Window's Explorer.

3. `FileSystemDatagrid` — A data grid used to display the names of a current folder hierarchy, including both folders and files. Also extra file information like size, created, modified, and so on is displayed in this view.

4. `FileSystemList` — A list control that's similar to the `FileSystemDatagrid`, except without the extra file information.

5. `FileSystemNavigationHistory`. A pop-up menu button that displays the history of navigation, both forward and backward.

The Flex FileSystem Component Explorer is shown in Figure 45-2.

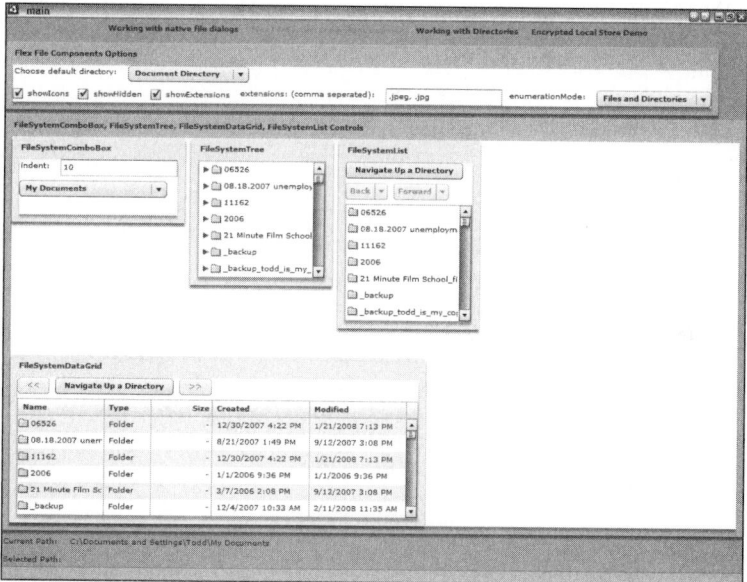

Figure 45-2

The top panel of the Flex FileSystem Component Explorer lets you choose the default directory, whether it's the user's desktop, documents, user, and so on. You can play with the properties to see how each of the components reacts.

When browsing through a filesystem, you'll also notice that the Current Path and Selected Path change as you navigate the filesystem with any one of the controls.

Let's look at the sample code for the `FileSystemDataGrid`, since this uses most of the unique properties for all the `FileSystem` components:

```
<mx:FileSystemDataGrid id="fileSystemDataGrid"  width="100%"
    directory="{File.desktopDirectory}"
    showIcons="true"
    showHidden="true"
    showExtensions="true"
    extensions="{['.jpg', '.JPG', '.jpeg']}"
    enumerationMode="{FileSystemEnumerationMode.FILES_AND_DIRECTORIES}"
    directoryChange="onDirectoryChange(event)"
    fileChoose="onFileChoosen(event)"
/>
```

Declare a `FileSystemDataGrid` in MXML (it could be any of the other Flex FileSystem components, since they all work the same way). Set the starting directory to the desktop directory, as defined by `File.desktopDirectory`, or use any file path created with the `File` class.

Then set the following properties, `showIcons`, `showHidden`, and `showExtensions`. The property `showIcons` determines whether the control will display a little folder or file icons in the control. These icons are absolutely skinnable, so feel free to use your own. The `showHidden` property shows files hidden by the operating system. And `showExtensions` property will show the file extensions (`.jpg` for example) in the file listing.

Next, apply a filter to the extensions property. The `FileSystemDataGrid` in this case is being set up to show only JPEG file types. The `extensions` property takes an array of strings and is case sensitive.

Set the `enumerationMode` to `FileSystemEnumerationMode.FILES_AND_DIRECTORIES`. This tells the component to display both directories and files. All the available settings for `enumerationMode` are as shown in the following table.

FileSystemEnumerationMode	Description
FILES_AND_DIRECTORIES	Displays both files and directories in the `FileSystem` component.
DIRECTORIES_FIRST	Displays both files and directories, with all directories displayed before the file listings.
DIRECTORIES_ONLY	Displays only directories.
FILES_ONLY	Displays only files. There needs to be an alternative way to navigate the hierarchy when displaying only files.
FILES_FIRST	Displays both files and directories, with all the files displayed before the directories.

Finally, implement some event handlers for the `directoryChange` and `fileChoose` events. The `directoryChange` event is called every time the directory is changed, whether through code or through user navigation in the grid (a double-click navigates into that folder). The `fileChoose` event is thrown every time the user double-clicks a file (or selects it and presses Enter).

All the Flex FileSystem components use the same structure and API, so check out the sample code and experiment with the functionality provided.

Encrypted Local Data

Along with the ability to write data to files on the filesystem, Adobe AIR provides support for encrypting data to the user's local hard drive, in the class `flash.data.EncryptedLocalStore`. Adobe AIR uses AES-CBC 128-bit encryption when writing data to the local data store, so you can be sure that malicious software scanning a hard drive storing AIR applications data won't be able to find saved passwords, bank card numbers, and so forth.

AIR keeps an encrypted local store for each user of every AIR application on the user's machine. This data is kept in the user's filesystem located in his or her application data directory, followed by the subdirectories `Adobe/AIR/ELS/`, and then finally a subdirectory with a unique application ID. For example, on Windows, the encrypted data can be found at `C:\Documents and Settings\USER\ Application Data\Adobe\AIR\ELS\applicationID`.

Writing Data

It's very easy to encrypt some data to the local hard drive for future use:

```
private function writeEncryptedData(key:String, value:String):void
{
  var byteArray:ByteArray = new ByteArray();
  byteArray.writeUTFBytes(value);
  EncryptedLocalStore.setItem(key, value);
}
```

Start by creating a `ByteArray` for the data that you want to store. Next, take a `String` (or `Number`, or any data) that you want to save; it's passed into this helper function as `value` in this code, and write it to the `byteArray` using `writeUTFBytes` (or any of the `ByteArray`'s `write*` methods). Finally, and this is a one-liner for writing all data to the application's encrypted local data store, call `EncryptedLocalStore .setItem`, passing in the key name that you want to save the data under and the value to stash.

To use the little helper function `writeEncryptedData` to save a user's password, write:

```
writeEncryptedData("password", passwordText.text);
```

This saves the password that the user entered into a `TextArea` called `passwordText` to the encrypted local store.

Reading Data

Reading data back into the application requires minimal code as well:

```
private function readEncryptedData(key:String):String
{
  var byteArray:ByteArray = EncryptedLocalStore.getItem(key);
```

```
         return byteArray.readUTFBytes(byteArray.length);
     }
```

First, create a `byteArray` to store the decrypted bytes. Next, retrieve the data by calling the static `EncryptedLocalStore.getItem` method. Finally, convert the bytes back into a string by calling `readUTFBytes`.

To use this helper function to read a saved password from the encrypted store, write:

```
     unencryptedText.text = readEncryptedData("password");
```

Deleting Data

To delete data from the encrypted local store, use `EncryptedLocalStore.removeItem`. To remove the password created above, call:

```
     EncryptedLocalStore.removeItem("password");
```

Furthermore, if you want to delete all the data stored in an application's local store, a call to `EncryptedLocalStore.reset` is all that's needed:

```
     EncryptedLocalStore.reset();
```

This removes all encrypted data for the AIR application.

> When uninstalling AIR applications, the encrypted local storage file is left intact on the user's filesystem in `Application Data Directory/Adobe/AIR/ELS`. On a Windows machine, this is `C:\Documents and Settings\USER\Application Data\Adobe\AIR\ELS\`.

Managing data in the encrypted local store is very simple. And since it's so easy to use, there's no excuse not to protect sensitive user data in your AIR applications.

Summary

This chapter covered most of the classes of the `flash.filesystem` package that enable an Adobe AIR cross-platform desktop application to access the user's local filesystem. Using these APIs, a developer has the power to build Internet applications that can work offline, with cached data and better performance, along with total access to the user's data without needing to proxy it through a server as is the traditional method of a Flex application.

In the next section, "Part VIII, Server Integration," you'll learn how to access remote data from your Flex application. We'll show .NET, Java, and PHP developers how Flex works with their server-side data. And we'll introduce you to the Flash Media Server.

Part VIII: Server Integration

46

Introduction to RPC Services

Flex comes with a rich set of libraries for interacting with data from remote servers. Whether you need to connect to existing SOAP-based Web Services being delivered by .NET or Java EE platforms, or XML/JSON-based Web Services via HTTP on any web server, or even AMF (Active Message Format) messages from LiveCycle, BlazeDS, or any of the many open-source AMF implementations out there, there's an API in Flex to meet your needs.

While Part IX will cover all Adobe's LiveCycle Data Services and ColdFusion in great detail, this part's chapters will cover working with data being delivered from other server implementations. First, we'll introduce you to how the RPC (remote procedure call) libraries work, and then in future chapters we'll discuss connecting them to a .NET backend via SOAP, a PHP sample working with RESTful HTTP, and, finally, a Java EE-based SOAP solution.

We'll be assuming that you're already familiar with your server platform of choice, whether it's JAVA EE, .NET, or one of the LAMP-based scripting languages.

Overview

The `mx.rpc` package is where all the action is for connecting to any of the types of remote services that Flex supports. The `mx.rpc` package supports asynchronous calls to backend services such as Web Services, HTTP-based services, and Adobe's open-source protocol, AMF. In MXML, these services are available as components: `<mx:HTTPService>` for HTTP-based Web Services, `<mx:WebService>` for SOAP-based Web Services, and `<mx:RemoteObject>` for remote AMF object-based services. These same services classes are also available for use in ActionScript.

Regardless of the services you use to connect to remote data, the process will be the same:

1. Create the Flex RPC object (`HTTPService`, `WebService`, `RemoteObject`) to manage the server communication. Create the object either as an MXML component or as an ActionScript object.

2. Point the object to a service endpoint (`WebService`, `RemoteObject`), or URL (`HTTPService`).

3. Establish a result and fault handler to deal with the returned data or errors.

4. Make a call on a service operation (`RemoteObject`, `WebService`) or make a URL request using `GET`/`POST` (`HTTPService`).

5. Work with the data returned from the server (Result) or handle the service error (Fault).

Figure 46-1 shows how the `mx.rpc.*` components and objects communicate with remote servers.

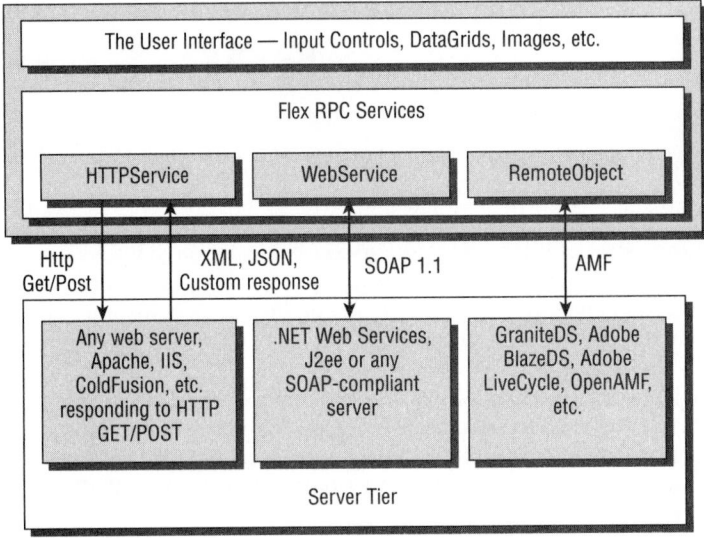

Figure 46-1

Figure 46-1 is broken into two sections: the Flex client (which includes everything distributed in the SWF file), and the server layer. From the Flex client, you use either `HTTPService`, `WebService`, or `RemoteObject` to make asynchronous calls against the server tier.

For example, using `HTTPService`, you can make HTTP `POST`s or `GET`s against a remote URL on the Internet, passing in parameters when required. The web server will then respond by sending back custom XML, JSON, or other valid text responses. The Flex client will then parse the data for consumption. Any RESTful-based web service would also be accessed with the `HTTPService` component. The upcoming section "Working the HTTPService Component" uses `HTTPService` for a quick demo.

Using `WebService`, you can connect to a remote SOAP 1.1 compliant Web Service and make calls to SOAP operations. The remote Web Service will respond, and the Flex client will either parse the response using the `SOAPDecoder` class, translating the XML response into an ActionScript value object or consume it as regular EMCAScript for XML (E4X), or utilize the raw XML data in the application. The Amazon.com search example in the section "Working with the WebService Component" will show you how to use the `WebService` RPC class.

Finally, there's the option of `RemoteObject`. Part IX of this book deals with everything related to `RemoteObject`, so we'll defer you to those chapters for more information on `RemoteObject`. We just wanted to introduce them to you here so that you can see the relationship to the other remote services available.

The mx.rpc Libraries

The `mx.rpc` libraries are distributed in their own SWC file called `rpc.swc` that's contained in the Flex SDK directory. But don't worry, when you install Flex Builder, it's included as part of the Flex SDK in your project by default.

As mentioned previously, using the RPC services follows a similar convention. This is because both the `WebService` and `RemoteObject` call their remote services as operations, which perform the actual call to the backend, and all this logic is defined in `mx.rpcAbstractService`. And the `HTTPService` follows a similar convention, but on its own code path, since it's only making HTTP requests via `POST` or `GET`.

As illustrated in Figure 46-2, there are a couple of different versions of each `HTTPService` and S. There are the components used when defining either in an MXML file, and then there are the classes used when creating service requests inside an ActionScript code block using the `new()` operator. The reason this is being pointed out is that with the same names, but different namespaces, things can get a little confusing, especially since the MXML wrappers add some functionality and expose some inherited functionality differently.

Mx.RPC Object Hierarchy

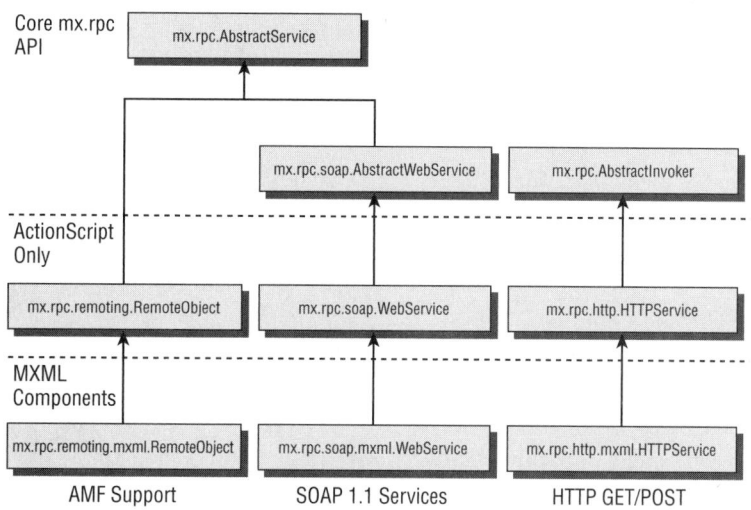

Figure 46-2

Differences between MXML and ActionScript Classes

You can see in Figure 46-2 that the MXML components inherit from an ActionScript class of the same name. The MXML versions, `mx.rpc.http.mxml.HTTPService` and `mx.rpc.soap.mxml.WebService`, inherit from `mx.rpc.http.HTTPService` and `mx.rpc.http.WebService`, respectively, adding some user interface-specific properties that are useful when declaring services directly in MXML, such as `showBusyCursor` and `concurrency`.

The showBusyCursor Property

To have the Flex UI automatically show a waiting cursor, set the property `showBusyCursor` to `true`. When the service request begins, the mouse pointer will change the default Flex waiting icon. Upon completion, either result or fault, the mouse pointer will return to normal.

The concurrency Property

The `concurrency` property has a few different settings: `multiple`, `single`, and `last`. With `multiple`, multiple requests can be made through the service, and it's up to you to keep track of which response is returned for each request. The `single` setting limits the service to making only one request at a time; making a second request will raise an error. And finally, `last` will cancel any existing request when a new one is made.

Parameter Binding versus Explicit Parameter Passing

Another difference between the MXML component and its ActionScript parent is in how parameter values are passed to the remote service. In Flex, there are two ways of passing in values on remote services:

1. With parameter binding, which is available only if you declare the service using the MXML component version, you can bind from user interface components or ActionScript value objects directly into the call. This allows you to tap in the default component binding infrastructure of Flex, including the use of `Validation` controls in your defined MXML.

    Setting the nested `<mx:request>` property on either an `HTTPService` or a `WebService`'s defined `operation` declaration allows you to bind its nested name-value pairs to actual values in input controls using Flex's binding mechanisms.

    The first of the two upcoming `WebService` examples will demonstrate this technique, although it's also available for `HTTPService`.

2. Explicit parameter passing is available to RPC components declared both in MXML and ActionScript. Again, it doesn't matter whether you're using the `WebService` or `HTTPService` component.

    Using parameter passing involves passing the values around, just like a traditional method call. There's no access to MXML's default data binding. The value you pass from ActionScript code into the service is the value at the time it's set; you treat this like a traditional function call.

    The second of the upcoming `WebService` examples will demonstrate explicit parameter passing. The important thing to note is that in the actual ActionScript function that's making the call, you build up the exact object's name-value pairs that are passed as a parameter into the remote service method call.

It's fine that you might not understand these two concepts yet. We just wanted to introduce you to them so that you'll recognize them in the examples to come.

Working with the HTTPService Component

The easiest form of remote service invocation is calling an HTTP Web Service. To do this, use the HTTPService MXML component. Since Flickr has a comprehensive API available, we'll start with a sample to query their HTTP Web Service for their latest posted news. Keep in mind that the examples in this chapter don't do anything mind blowing with the results received; they output only the raw textual representation, usually XML, of the server response. In Chapter 49, we'll get into more details about using the HTTPService and actually process some results.

To create an HTTPService component, open an MXML file and add the following declaration:

```
<mx:HTTPService id="httpServiceSuccess"
  url="http://api.flickr.com/services/feeds/news.gne"
  resultFormat="e4x"
  result="onFlickrNewsFeedResult(event)"
  fault="onHttpFault(event)"
  showBusyCursor="true" />
```

This MXML declaration creates a new HTTPService component with the id of httpServiceSuccess (there's also a service defined in the chapter's sample application that will return a failure). The first, and most important, parameter is setting the url to be the destination URL, which is an RSS feed from Flickr listing their latest news using their publically available API.

Next, set the resultFormat to e4x, meaning that when the result is returned from the server, the Flex framework deserializes the HTTP response into a Flex E4X XML object, ready to use in the result handler with E4X expressions. Other options for resultFormat to deserialize data off the wire into native ActionScript types are object, xml, array, and so on. A resultFormat of object would return an untyped generic ActionScript object with properties that would be accessed via normal object .property notation, including nesting objects (if the results contain nested XML). A resultFormat of array will create an ActionScript Array to make it easy to loop through results.

Next, set up the result and fault handlers. Every service call will always have a result and fault handler. Handlers are set by the developer at this level. Here, the result handler is onFlickrNewsFeed Result(event), which will be the event handler managing a successful Flickr response. The fault handler is set to onHttpFault(event). This is a generic fault handler that we wrote that displays the error in an Alert box. Feel free to reuse the onHttpFault fault handler because usually you'll want to inform the user that an error occurred and log it in a consistent way across all remote service calls.

Next, you'll want to invoke the service. Create a button and add a click event handler that calls the MXML service httpServiceSuccess with the send() method:

```
<mx:Button click="httpServiceSuccess.send()" label="HTTPService Result" />
```

When the user presses the `HttpService Result` button, the `url` request defined in `httpServiceSuccess` will be requested. And when the remote Flickr service responds, either with a valid result or an error, the appropriate event handler will be called.

Let's look at the result handler, `onFlickrNewsFeedResult`, for when the server returns a valid successful response:

```
private function onFlickrNewsFeedResult(data:ResultEvent):void
{
  rawOutput.text = data.result.toString();
}
```

This is the most basic of handlers meant only to demonstrate receiving a valid server response. First, this handles the `ResultEvent` that's passed back. Second, all you're doing here is writing the output to a `TextArea` called rawOutput. The `data.result` is the ActionScript object returned by the `HTTPService` deserialization process, which depends on the setting of `resultFormat` declared in the `HTTPService` component. Because you chose e4x, `data.result` is an XML object.

But the `data.result` property could be other types, too, depending on the HTTP `resultFormat` preference configured in `HTTPService.resultFormat`. The following table shows the different values you can set for the `HTTPService.resultFormat` property, and the corresponding ActionScript return type as decoded by the `HTTPService`.

HttpService.resultFormat	ResultEvent.return Type
Object	mx.utils.ObjectProxy
xml	flash.XML.XMLNode
e4x	XML
text	String
Array	Array or ArrayCollection, depending on the setting for HTTPService's makeObjectsBindable property. When makeObjectsBindable is true, an ArrayCollection; otherwise, just a regular Array.
flashVars	Object

Here's the `FaultEvent` handler:

```
private function onHttpFault(faultEvent:FaultEvent):void
{
  Alert.show(faultEvent.fault.faultCode + ": " + faultEvent.fault.faultString);
}
```

This fault handler is pretty basic and very generic. All it's doing is displaying the `faultCode` and `faultString` to the end user in an Alert window. A more robust fault handler would add some form of logging, probably to a remote server, as well as a more informational message for the user on what actions he or she should take.

Working with the WebService Component

Another option for calling remote services is using SOAP-based Web Services. Web Services are commonly used in an enterprise environment, as they provide a lot of functionality beyond that which basic HTTP services support. Web Services are commonly delivered by Java EE and .NET services, so chances are if you're on a project in the financial world, you'll probably be connecting your Flex application to an existing Web Service. However, our sample in this section is going to use an Amazon-based Web Service to search their online catalog for books. This will allow us to work with Flex without worrying about the server implementation, which we'll get to in future chapters.

Using the `WebService` component in Flex follows a similar workflow to that of `HTTPService`, with a few changes and additions:

1. Instead of setting the `url` property on `HTTPService`, set the `wsdl` property on `WebService` to an appropriate remote URL that references a published WSDL file. Unlike HTTP-based services, SOAP-based Web Services are tightly coupled to a predefined contract, called a *schema*. When you set the `wsdl` property in the `WebService` component, Flex will go retrieve it from the remote server. Upon doing this, Flex parses and learns a little about the preestablished contract to help you work with the remote operations.

2. Instead of calling `send()`, as you do with `HTTPService`, you'll call the Web Service operation name as a method, or `send()` on the name of the operation. For example (pseudo-code):

   ```
   //[WebService Object].[WebService Operation Name]
   AmazonService.ItemSearch();
   ```

3. Define the WSDL operations in MXML (if using parameter binding) based on the contents of the remote WSDL file.

Following are two examples of working with `WebService`. The first example uses the `WebService` MXML component and parameter binding to make a remote service call. The second example uses explicit parameter passing with a `WebService` created in ActionScript.

Using a WebService in MXML

Let's look at the definition of a `WebService` component in MXML. Note that the `wsdl` value of Amazon's WSDL URL has been truncated for the sake of space. (See the chapter's sample code for a complete listing.)

```
<!--  You must get an AWS Security ID to run this code, visit
      http://aws.amazon.com/ to sign up.  -->
<mx:WebService id="aws"
  wsdl="http://webservices.amazon.com/[truncated]/AWSECommerceService.wsdl"
  showBusyCursor="true"
  fault="onWebServiceFault(event)"
>
```

The `WebService` component declaration establishes the remote WSDL file and the default `fault` handler. And since this example uses the `WebService` MXML component, you can set `showBusyCursor` to `true`.

Then you define the name of the remote operation, which is `ItemSearch`. (You learned about `ItemSearch` from scanning through Amazon's WSDL file.) We'll explain in a moment how to understand the WSDL file. Set the `result` handler and `resultFormat` properties just like you did for the `HTTPService`. Notice that the fault is declared at the service level, because you want the service to handle all errors in a consistent manner across operations; however, the fault handler could be declared at the operation level:

```
<mx:operation name="ItemSearch"
  result="onAmazonSearchResult(event)"
  resultFormat="xml"
>
```

Next, map values to the parameters that the operation requires using the parameter-binding technique discussed previously. This allows you to bind values from MXML user interface components directly into the request:

```
<mx:request>
    <AWSAccessKeyId>YOUR_ACCESS_KEY_HERE</AWSAccessKeyId>
    <Shared>
      <Keywords>{bookTitle.text}</Keywords>
      <SearchIndex>Books</SearchIndex>
      <Count>25</Count>
    </Shared>
  </mx:request>
 </mx:operation>
</mx:WebService>
```

The preceding code passes into the operation a request consisting of `AWSAccessKeyId` and `Shared` property objects, the latter of which have a few nested properties. The `Keywords` property binds to a `TextInput` called `bookTitle`, in which the user will type in the name of a book, author, or other metadata. Next, populate the `SearchIndex` and `Count`, which identify which catalog to search and how many results to return.

And that's it! That's how the `WebService` component is created and configured. We'll actually call it in the section "Using a WebService in ActionScript," but first, let's look a little more at how we came to define the `<mx:request>` for the `ItemSearch` operation.

Converting WSDL Operations to MXML Requests

Downloading Amazon's WSDL from the Web will give you about 200KB of information defining their Web Service. You can look at the WSDL in the web browser by viewing the page source of the WSDL URL. To figure out what the `ItemSearch` operation call needs, though, you'll only need to look at a bit of it. The following WSDL definition has been truncated to save 20 pages of space.

First, the WSDL operation name that you're calling in this example is `ItemSearch`. (We learned this little tidbit from reading some of Amazon's published documentation.) So, start your exploration of the WSDL file by searching for the `ItemSearch` operation. You'll find the following definition:

```
<operation name="ItemSearch">
  <input message="tns:ItemSearchRequestMsg" />
  <output message="tns:ItemSearchResponseMsg" />
</operation>
```

This tells you that the operation `ItemSearch` is defined as having an input message of type `ItemSearchRequestMsg`. But what does `ItemSearchRequestMsg` look like? Continue searching the WSDL to find a message definition:

```
<message name="ItemSearchRequestMsg">
  <part name="body" element="tns:ItemSearch" />
</message>
```

This tells you the `ItemSearchRequestMsg` is made up of an `ItemSearch` type. So, again, you need to search the WSDL file to find the type:

```
<xs:element name="ItemSearch">
  <xs:complexType>
    <xs:sequence>
      <xs:element name="MarketplaceDomain" type="xs:string" minOccurs="0" />
      <xs:element name="AWSAccessKeyId" type="xs:string" minOccurs="0" />
      <xs:element name="SubscriptionId" type="xs:string" minOccurs="0" />
      <xs:element name="AssociateTag" type="xs:string" minOccurs="0" />
      <xs:element name="XMLEscaping" type="xs:string" minOccurs="0" />
      <xs:element name="Validate" type="xs:string" minOccurs="0" />
      <xs:element name="Shared" type="tns:ItemSearchRequest" minOccurs="0" />
      <xs:element name="Request" type="tns:ItemSearchRequest" minOccurs="0"
                  maxOccurs="unbounded" />
    </xs:sequence>
  </xs:complexType>
</xs:element>
```

And, voilà, you find the core of what you're looking to pass into the `ItemSearch` operation. We're not going to get into all the details of defining WSDL (there are entire books written on the topic), but let's quickly examine the necessities. All the elements of `ItemSearch` have the attribute `minOccurs` set to `0`, implying that the property is optional. However, by executing the `ItemSearch` operation against the Amazon Web Service without passing in any parameters, you quickly learn that the `AWSAccessKeyId` is indeed required, so you include it when you define the operation in preceding MXML.

The `ItemSearch` type also has an `Shared` element that is of type `ItemSearchRequest`. Again, search the WSDL, and find the following definition for `ItemSearchRequest`, keeping in mind that what is listed here has been severely truncated because the actual `ItemSearchRequest` has many elements not shown:

```
<xs:complexType name="ItemSearchRequest">
  <xs:sequence>
    <!-- See the Amazon WSDL file for complete listing -->
    <xs:element name="Count" type="xs:positiveInteger" minOccurs="0" />
    <xs:element name="Keywords" type="xs:string" minOccurs="0"/>
    <xs:element name="SearchIndex" type="xs:string" minOccurs="0"/>
  </xs:sequence>
</xs:complexType>
```

The elements `Count`, `Keywords`, and `SearchIndex` are all used in the binding of the operation in the preceding MXML. Remember that the `ItemSearchRequest` was the type as defined by the `Shared` property above it.

It's a bit of a goose chase to explore everything inside a WSDL file, but it's the price to pay for explicitly establishing a contract for your services. Now that you understand where the MXML operation definition came from, let's get back to executing the remote Web Service.

```
<mx:Button click="aws.ItemSearch()" label="Amazon WebService Result" />
```

Pressing the `Amazon WebService Result` button will call `aws.ItemSearch()`, invoking the remote request. Wait a few moments. The remote service will respond, Flex will receive the response and, using the `SOAPDecoder`, decode the response into the appropriate ActionScript type as defined by the `resultFormat` property. In this case, the TextArea will fill up with an XML string.

And that's how you call a `WebService` component using parameter binding.

Calling a WebService in ActionScript

Now suppose that you've created a complex application that's going be calling multiple services, and you'll be reusing these services on multiple screens. Or, suppose you want to establish service endpoints at runtime because you have dev, qa, and production environments. It'll probably be best to define your `WebService` using `ActionScript` in a reusable class that'll be globally accessible.

There are a couple differences between using the WebService MXML component and the ActionScript version. With the ActionScript version:

❑ Parameter binding isn't supported. You won't be able to bind to values in MXML components using Flex's default binding infrastructure. You must use explicit parameter passing, which involves making sure that your parameters are passed as function arguments.

❑ When using the `WebService` class from ActionScript, you must explicitly call `loadWSDL()` to initialize the service; otherwise, calls to operations will queue up until the WSDL is loaded. If the WSDL is never loaded, the remote calls will never actually be made across the wire. When using the `WebService` MXML component automatically loads the WSDL from the remote server for you during initialization.

The following example makes the same call to `ItemSearch` as described earlier, except that, instead of using the `WebService` MXML component, it uses its ActionScript ancestor and explicit parameter passing.

First, declare a variable to hold a reference to your loaded `WebService`. This allows you to call it multiple times, with multiple operations:

```
private var ws:mx.rpc.soap.WebService;
```

Notice that it's explicitly being declared with the full namespace path. This is to keep the compiler from getting confused, thinking it's the MXML derivative.

Next, create the function `createWebServiceFromActionscript()` that will be called from a `Button`'s click handler. This function first checks to see if a `WebService` has been created; if not, it creates one:

```
private function createWebServiceFromActionscript():void
{
```

```
    if (ws == null) {
      ws = new mx.rpc.soap.WebService();
      ws.addEventListener(FaultEvent.FAULT, onWebServiceFault);
      ws.ItemSearch.addEventListener(ResultEvent.RESULT, onAmazonSearchResult);
      ws.ItemSearch.resultFormat="xml";
      ws.loadWSDL("http://webservices.amazon.com/AWSECommerceService.wsdl");
    }
```

Bind the `fault` and `result` event handlers to the `onWebServiceFault` and `onAmazonSearchResult` handler used in the preceding example. Set the `resultFormat`, which unlike the `HTTPService`, can only have the values `xml`, `e4x`, or `object`.

Next, using explicit parameter passing, create the object hierarchy representing the proper WSDL definition for `ItemSearchResult` that was shown above. When the `WebService` is called, Flex will encode the object into a proper SOAP request, intelligently mapping the ActionScript objects defined here into a valid schema SOAP envelope for delivery to the remote server:

```
    /Use explicit parameter passing in Actionscript
    var shared:Object = {SearchIndex: "Books",
                         Keywords: "Professional Adobe Flex 3",
                         Count: 25 };
    var request:Object = new Object();
    request.AWSAccessKeyId = "YOUR_ACCESS_KEY_HERE";
    request.Shared = shared;
```

Finally, set the arguments on the operation and then make the service call by calling `ws.ItemSearch()`:

```
    // Set the arguments on the WebService
    ws.ItemSearch.arguments = request;
    ws.ItemSearch();
  }
```

Flex will work its magic, create a proper SOAP request, encoding the preceding ActionScript with the `SOAPEncoder`, and then send the request off to the server. When the server has finished processing, the event bound to either result or fault will execute.

Debugging Remote Service Calls

There are a couple of essential techniques that aid in debugging the calls to remote services. The first is using some form of network packet sniffing to watch the raw data being transferred across the wire, completely removing Flex from the debugging process. With an external tool, you'll be able to watch both the HTTP requests and the encoded SOAP envelopes cross back and forth across the wire.

The second technique involves turning on trace logging in Flex to watch all the `mx.rpc` debug messages generated during the lifespan of a remote call.

Network Packet Sniffing

For network packet sniffing, we've been successful using the WireShark software, which is available for both OS X and Windows. Others have been successful using the FireBug plug-in for the Firefox web browser, located at `https://addons.mozilla.org/en-US/firefox/addon/1843`.

Explaining how to use these tools is beyond the scope of this book, but any developer developing applications dependent upon remote services will quickly learn how to watch the raw data leaving the computer in a request, and the response returned from the server. Also, be aware that there are many tools that perform the same task. Find the one you're most comfortable with.

Debug Tracing in mx.rpc

Another essential tool to help with debugging remote services is debug tracing for the Flex framework. Note, you'll need the debug Flash player installed to see the trace messages. Luckily, turning it on is as simple as adding the following to your main MXML file:

```
<mx:TraceTarget includeDate="true" includeTime="true"
    includeCategory="true" includeLevel="true"
    level="0" />
```

The only thing required is setting `TraceTarget level="0"`, which tells the default Flex logging mechanism to output debug messages, including info, error, and fatal messages. See Chapter 75, "The Logging Framework," for more information on how logging works. I prefer to include the date, time, category, and level information with appropriate `includeDate`, `includeTime`, `includeCategory`, and `includeLevel` properties, respectively.

Logging an HTTPService Request

When you turn on logging, you might be wondering what you might see. For an HTTP Request, looking at the debug output console in Flex, you might see something similar to the following for the preceding Flickr `HTTPService` example. Note that we've cleaned up the log output here, removing unreadable CLSIDs and replacing them with more readable strings, such as THE_PRODUCER, REQUEST_MESSAGE, and RESPONSE_MESSAGE, to make the log more readable:

```
[INFO] mx.messaging.Producer 'THE_PRODUCER' producer set destination to
    'DefaultHTTP'.
[INFO] mx.messaging.Channel 'direct_http_channel' channel endpoint set to http:
[INFO] mx.messaging.Producer 'THE_PRODUCER' producer connected.
[INFO] mx.messaging.Producer 'THE_PRODUCER' producer sending message
    'REQUEST_MESSAGE'
[DEBUG] mx.messaging.Channel 'direct_http_channel' channel sending message:
(mx.messaging.messages::HTTPRequestMessage)#0
  body = (Object)#1
  clientId = (null)
  contentType = "application/x-www-form-urlencoded"
  destination = "DefaultHTTP"
  headers = (Object)#2
  httpHeaders = (Object)#3
  messageId = "REQUEST_MESSAGE"
  method = "GET"
```

```
      recordHeaders = false
      timestamp = 0
      timeToLive = 0
      url = "http://api.flickr.com/services/feeds/news.gne"
[INFO] mx.messaging.Producer 'THE_PRODUCER' producer acknowledge of
    'REQUEST_MESSAGE'.
[INFO] mx.rpc.http.HTTPService Decoding HTTPService response
[DEBUG] mx.rpc.http.HTTPService Processing HTTPService response message:
(mx.messaging.messages::AcknowledgeMessage)#0
    body = "  …the payload of the server response here … "
    clientId = "DirectHTTPChannel0"
    correlationId = "047C275F-CF10-55B4-38E3-E7FF2789EEAC"
    destination = ""
    headers = (Object)#1
    messageId = "RESPONSE_MESSAGE"
    timestamp = 0
    timeToLive = 0
[ResultEvent messageId="RESPONSE_MESSAGE" type="result" bubbles=false
    cancelable=true eventPhase=2]
```

The flow is similar for all HTTP requests. It starts with initializing the Producer, setting it up for HTTP transport, and then creating the REQUEST_MESSAGE and sending it over the direct_ http _connect channel. The interesting part is HTTPRequestMessage, which has all the information of the HTTP request that Flex is sending out over the web, including header information, body payload, and the type of request, whether HTTP POST or GET, and the destination URL.

Then you can see debug information of the response coming back from the server. The HTTPService emits a Decoding HTTPService Response, then displays the raw message in AcknowledgeMessage, and finally raises the ResultEvent, which brings the message data into the code you control. All this information can aid in debugging.

Sometimes, when your Flex UI isn't working as expected, you'll see some of these mx.rpc output [Debug] and [Info] messages, but they'll stop at specific steps along the line. Poof, no more output, but no exception thrown, either. And then you know there's something wrong with your message. This becomes even more important when working with the SOAP-based WebService, which has a lot of rules and structure that the messages inbound and outbound must adhere to, which we'll look at next.

Logging a WebService Initialization

Let's look at a sample SOAP WebService request. This first part is the WebService requesting the WSDL file from the remote server, using standard HTTPService request to retrieve the WSDL service. Note that I've cleaned up the log output here, as I did earlier:

```
[INFO] mx.messaging.Producer 'A_PRODUCER' producer set
        destination to 'DefaultHTTP'.
[INFO] mx.messaging.Producer producer sending message REQUEST_MESSAGE
[DEBUG] mx.messaging.Channel 'direct_http_channel' channel sending message:
(mx.messaging.messages::HTTPRequestMessage)#0
  body = (Object)#1
  clientId = (null)
  contentType = "application/x-www-form-urlencoded"
  destination = "DefaultHTTP"
```

```
    headers = (Object)#2
    httpHeaders = (Object)#3
    messageId = "REQUEST_MESSAGE"
    method = "GET"
    recordHeaders = falsetimestamp = 0
    timeToLive = 0
    url =
        "http://webservices.amazon.com/AWSECommerceService/AWSECommerceService.wsdl"
[INFO] mx.messaging.Producer 'A_PRODUCER' producer connected.
```

Here you start seeing where the response is returned from the server:

```
[INFO] mx.messaging.Producer 'A_PRODUCER' producer acknowledge of
       'REQUEST_MESSAGE'.
```

Then it's decoded, using the standard HTTPService since it just performed a regular HTTP GET to retrieve the WSDL document:

```
[INFO] mx.rpc.http.HTTPService Decoding HTTPService response
```

The following will log the entire raw WSDL file that was returned from the server:

```
[DEBUG] mx.rpc.http.HTTPService Processing HTTPService response message:
(mx.messaging.messages::AcknowledgeMessage)#0
  body = "
Amazon RAW WSDL Returned here  Truncated for the sake of brevity.
  "
  clientId = "DirectHTTPChannel0"
  correlationId = "E7257A71-EFBA-2ABD-809F-E7E575547E10"
  destination = ""
  headers = (Object)#1
  messageId = "RESPONSE_MESSAGE"
  timestamp = 0
  timeToLive = 0
```

And, finally, you're notified that the WSDL file has been loaded and that the WebService is ready to call operations on the remote service:

```
10/10/2008 13:54:48.412 [DEBUG] mx.rpc.soap.WebService WSDL loaded
```

Logging a Call to a Web Service Operation

With the WSDL loaded, it's time to follow what happens when an actual remote operation is called. First, invoke the SOAP operation ItemSearch. Encoding will transform the parameters from the ActionScript they were defined in, into a proper SOAP envelope (shown next):

```
[DEBUG] mx.rpc.soap.Operation Invoking SOAP operation ItemSearch
[DEBUG] mx.rpc.soap.SOAPEncoder Encoding SOAP request envelope
[DEBUG] mx.rpc.soap.SOAPEncoder Encoding SOAP request body
[INFO] mx.messaging.Producer 'A_PRODUCER' producer sending message
       'OPERATION_MESSAGE'
[DEBUG] mx.messaging.Channel 'direct_http_channel' channel sending message:
(mx.messaging.messages::SOAPMessage)#0
```

Here's the core of a raw SOAP envelope, complete with XML hierarchical formatting:

```
body = "<SOAP-ENV:Envelope xmlns:SOAP-ENV="http://schemas.xmlsoap.org/soap/
    envelope/" xmlns:xs="http://www.w3.org/2001/XMLSchema"xmlns:xsi=
        "http://www.w3.org/2001/XMLSchema-instance">
<SOAP-ENV:Body>
    <tns:ItemSearch xmlns:tns="http://webservices.amazon.com/AWSECommerceService/
        2008-10-06">
      <tns:AWSAccessKeyId>YOUR_ACCES_ID_HERE</tns:AWSAccessKeyId>
      <tns:Shared>
        <tns:Count>25</tns:Count>
        <tns:Keywords>Programming Flex 3</tns:Keywords>
        <tns:SearchIndex>Books</tns:SearchIndex>
      </tns:Shared>
    </tns:ItemSearch>
  </SOAP-ENV:Body>
</SOAP-ENV:Envelope>"
```

The following is metadata on the actual request. Notice that with SOAP, this is posting to a URL, like a regular HTTP request:

```
clientId = "DirectHTTPChannel0"
contentType = "text/xml; charset=utf-8"
destination = "DefaultHTTP"
headers = (Object)#1
httpHeaders = (Object)#2
SOAPAction = ""http://soap.amazon.com""
messageId = "OPERATION_MESSAGE"
method = "POST"
recordHeaders = false
timestamp = 0
timeToLive = 0
url = "http://soap.amazon.com/onca/soap?Service=AWSECommerceService"
[INFO] mx.messaging.Producer 'A_PRODUCER' producer acknowledge of
    ' OPERATION_MESSAGE '.
```

From this point on is a good place to look for problems when debugging Web Services. Random acts of strangeness have been known to occur inside the SOAPDecoder, depending on how the remote Web Service was defined in the WSDL:

```
[INFO] mx.rpc.soap.SOAPDecoder Decoding SOAP response
```

Luckily, you can see the raw response from the server here (since SOAP responses can be huge, we've removed it from the text):

```
[DEBUG] mx.rpc.soap.SOAPDecoder Encoded SOAP response <?xml version="1.0" -
            RESPONSE TRUNCATED.
```

Then, the SOAPDecoder will convert the XML from the server into the appropriate ActionScript type that you defined for the resultFormat when setting up the operation:

```
[DEBUG] mx.rpc.soap.SOAPDecoder Decoding SOAP response envelope
```

Finally, when the message was decoded successfully, you'll find the following debugging message:

```
[INFO] mx.rpc.soap.SOAPDecoder Decoded SOAP response into result [115 millis]
```

And then, your result handler for the operation is called where you're back in control of the code. It's important to note that if any of these steps fails, a message won't be logged. After you gain experience with what the message flow is supposed to look like, you'll get comfortable debugging Web Services.

Choosing a Protocol and Server Implementation

Given the three different methods of accessing remote services, which one should you use? It all depends on your needs, existing infrastructure (including existing server platforms), and existing services that you want your application to connect to.

The following are some general rules of thumb:

1. An `HTTPService` connecting to regular RESTful web services will have the most flexibility, as they're just HTTP requests and responses. A number of server-side third-party libraries and frameworks exist to promote service creation on any platform. These are also the easiest to create, debug, and extend to any client platform.

2. `RemoteObject` and the AMF protocol will most likely be faster over the wire because they are binary and compact. There are a lot of options for server platforms to support this now, especially since Adobe has open-sourced the AMF protocol.

3. Web Services are more difficult to write; however, they provide type safety in that response and request messages are required to conform to the definitions contained in the WSDL file that defines the schema of the SOAP-based Web Service. `WebService` will be more of a necessity when implementing bigger enterprise software that integrates with third parties who already expose a lot of functionality through Web Services. Using `WebService` will probably be more dictated by existing infrastructure and interoperability requirements than either `HTTPService` or `RemoteObject`.

Alternative Server Implementations for AMF

Since Flex has been open-sourced from Adobe, and they've open sourced their AMF protocol, several open-source and third-party implementations are available for server-side development. It's up to you to choose your server-side language of choice, whether it's PHP, Java, .NET, Python, or another one.

Here's a list of some third-party solutions that work with Flex RPC services:

❑ **Red 5** (`http://osflash.org/red5`): An open-source Flash server supporting AMF remoting (and a plethora of FLV streaming)

❑ **Zend Framework** (`http://framework.zend.com`): A PHP framework Adobe is aiding with support of the AMF protocol

- ❑ **Granite Data Services** (`http://www.graniteds.org`): An open-source JAVA EE alternative to Adobe LiveCycle ES services that provides a framework for Flex/EJB3/Seam/Spring/Pojo application development, supporting full AMF3 via Flex's `RemoteObject`.

- ❑ **WebOrb by Midnight Coders** (`http://www.themidnightcoders.com`): A commercially supported services layer that supports working with AMF and `RemoteObject` in .NET, PHP, Ruby on Rails, and Java

- ❑ **PyAMF** (`http://pyamf.org`): An open-source AMF implementation written in Python and supported by many popular Python web frameworks, including Django, Pylons, Twisted, TuboGears, and so forth

- ❑ **AMFPhp** (`http://www.amfphp.org`): An open-source project hosted at SourceForge with a very active community and production-ready stability

Summary

This chapter introduced you to Flex's RPC services working with `HTTPService` and `WebService` in both MXML and ActionScript. We've only touched the basics, though. Most likely your applications will be calling multiple methods on multiple services, in which case, the following chapters will explain more details.

Chapter 51 will delve into an `HTTPService` with a PHP backend exposing HTTP-based Web Services. Chapters 52 and 53 will go in depth into `WebService`, using both Java and .NET as backend platforms, and will introduce some of Flex Builder's newer data tools. Part IX, Chapters 53 to 59, will explain everything about `RemoteObject` and the AMF protocol.

Error Handling

This chapter will introduce error handling. We'll cover both handling error events raised by various Flex APIs, such as the RPC services, as well as synchronous inline errors with the ActionScript's runtime exception handling. Compiler errors won't be discussed in this chapter.

Handling errors in Flex is a bit of a tricky proposition because of the asynchronous nature of everything. There is no one main function to place a global error trap catching all unhandled exceptions. Furthermore, many error conditions are triggered by specific events that the developer must implement event handlers in order to be notified of, such as various RPC, file uploading, and drag and drop operations. Failure to implement the handler can sometimes result in silent failures.

Let's get started by looking at working with synchronous error handling with ActionScript's exception-handling functionality.

Exception Handling with Synchronous Code

With Flex, you get the same exception handling provided by ActionScript with the `try/catch/finally` statements. With this, you'll be able to handle runtime errors in a given method, or bubble errors up the call stack until an appropriate `try/catch` error handler is found. This will be your tool of choice for managing error conditions and exceptions in synchronous code. However, since Flex is based on an asynchronous timeline event model, there are also plenty of error events raised when failures to open files, call out to services, and so on occur. We'll cover asynchronous event error handling later in the chapter.

Flash Debug Player versus Release Player

When an application running in the Flash Debug Player (installed with Flex Builder) throws an unhandled exception, there will be a pop-up informing the user of an unhandled runtime exception, complete with a stack trace (see Figure 47-1). This will alert you early on in your development cycle that your code has bugs. With this knowledge, you can fix the errors in your code before releasing the application for public consumption.

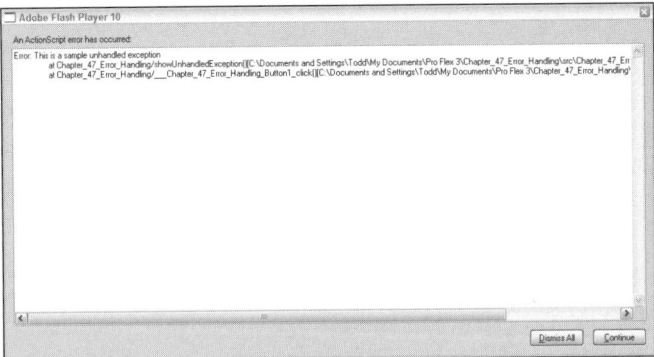

Figure 47-1

However, when running this same code in the Release version of the Flash Player, these unhandled runtime exceptions won't be shown to the end user. They will be swallowed, and all code remaining on the stack will be aborted and then execution will continue. Hopefully, an exception doesn't occur during a critical path of state changing code, such as navigating to a new screen that could leave your application in an inconsistent state.

Having Flash swallow unhandled exceptions is both a good and bad thing. First, it keeps end users from seeing ugly errors. Second, for the most part, it keeps the Player from crashing. Third, and this one is a bit controversial, is that there are plenty of times when just continuing execution is a proper thing to do, although it's not controlled by the developer. We'd like to see more control for how the developer manages unhandled exceptions; read the following sidebar for further information.

Global Exception Handling and the Flash Player

Adobe has a public issue management portal for existing bugs and feature requests for the Flash Player (there's also a website dedicated to the open-source Flex framework). One of the features the issue management portal for Flash has is voting for your favorite features that Adobe should implement in the future.

There's an outstanding issue (as of this writing) in how the Flash Player should deal with unhandled exceptions. As stated above, the Debug version of the Player will show you a stack trace and notify you that an error has occurred, whereas the Release version will just stop execution of everything on the stack and then continue on as though nothing had happened. If you're an enterprise developer, usually the first thing you implement in an application is a global exception handler because you want to be notified that your application is doing things you didn't expect. You can vote over at Adobe on JIRA issue FP-444 at http://bugs.adobe.com/jira/browse/FP-444 if you feel that you'd like to have a global hook for unexpected exceptions that would allow you to report errors (log them to a server or send them via email) and present the user with a friendly message. After all, it's an unexpected exception; if you expected it, you'd have already built proper handling around it.

Try/Catch/Finally

Using a try/catch/finally statement in code is the simplest way to control errors happening in code blocks. The following shows a simple try/catch/finally error handler, which operates in a manner similar to that of other object-oriented languages such as Java and C#:

```
private function basicExceptionDemo():void
{
  try
  {
    trace("Before error condition");

    if (checkboxRaiseError.selected){
      throw new Error("This is a custom error message because the checkbox
                       was selected");
    }

    trace("After error condition");

  }catch(e:Error)
  {
    trace("Error: " + e.message);
  }
  finally
  {
    trace("The finally section.");
  }
}
```

This code demonstrates code flow through the most basic of exception handlers. First, the code you want to protect is placed inside a try code block. In the sample here, there's the option to select a checkbox to throw an error. A catch statement code block will capture any errors thrown above or in nested function calls.

When executing this sample code without an error being thrown (the checkbox unchecked), the following output will occur:

```
Before error condition
After error condition
The finally section
```

As you can see, the trace statements within the try block are executed, and then the finally block is executed. The finally block will always be executed, even when there are errors in the try block. The finally handler is an excellent location to clean up code.

Now, looking at the code with the checkbox selected, an error is going to be "raised" or "thrown." This simulates an error that could occur anywhere in the Flex framework, or even your own code. The throw statement is very powerful when you start building your own components and want to validate state and data and need to communicate error state and messages without building a function that returns error codes.

When executing the preceding code, with the check selected, the following output will occur:

```
Before error condition
Error: This is a custom error message because the checkbox was selected
The finally section
```

This is the most basic of error/exception handling; it writes text messages only out to the Flex Builder console window. However, it shows the important logic flow when an error occurs.

First, the code executes into the `try` block. Then a `throw` statement is reached, which is how an error exception is created. In this sample, we're throwing an exception of type `Error`, which is the root `Error` exception class type found in the Flash Player. Next, the code flow jumps to the appropriate `catch` condition for the error. In this case, only one `catch` statement is available to handle the most generic of error types, the `Error`. There are many types of `Error` classes defined in the Flex library (`RangeError`, `IllegalOperationError`, `StackOverflowError`, etc.), and we'll teach you to roll your own in the section "Custom Error Types."

Next, the `catch` handler processes the error that it caught. In this case, it's an `Error` with the message we set up previously. In reality, however, this is where you'd either have the code correct itself, notify the user, or log the error somewhere.

After the `catch` block, the `finally` block executes. Just as it did previously when the code executed without an error; the `finally` block executes here, too. Implement all your state management and code cleanup in the `finally` block that you expect to be handled.

> `Try/catch/finally` code blocks can also be nested within each other for finer-grained exception management.

Exception Bubbling

When an exception is raised in Flex, it'll bubble up the call stack until a developer-implemented `try/catch` handler is found, the Flash Player handles it by displaying the error box in Figure 47-1 when in the Debug player, or ignores it and clears the call stack in the Release player.

The chapter's sample code includes a bubble exception demo application that operates in four modes, demonstrating a few different concepts:

1. In the first mode, when Throw Sub Error is selected, an exception will be thrown in a subfunction and handled by the parent. This is the most basic form of exception bubbling.

2. Second, when Throw VeryBadException Custom Error is selected, a custom exception type created by the developer will be thrown in a nested function and handled with a designated `catch` statement for handling exceptions of the `VeryBadException` type.

3. When Test subFunction Error Handler is selected, an error will be thrown deep into a nested function, but instead of bubbling up to the topmost exception handler, it'll be handled by the function where it occurs.

4. The last mode, Run Without Errors, will operate without any exceptions being thrown.

The following code implements an error handler in the parent function. This example demonstrates how a parent exception handler manages a nested function's exceptions by providing a single exception handler to deal with any errors that occur higher up on the call stack.

Listing 47-1: The Main bubbleExceptionDemo Exception Handling Code

```
private function bubbleExceptionDemo():void
{
  try
  {
    trace("Running in main bubbleExeptionDemo()");
    subFunction();
    trace("After call to subFunction()");
  }
  catch (e:UserAccountError){
    trace("UserAccountError: " + e.message + " for user: " + e.user.userId);
    Alert.show(e.message + " " + e.user.userId);
  }catch (e:Error){
    trace("Error: " + e.message);
  } finally {
    trace("The finally section.");
  }
}
```

Just as in the previous demo, running bubbleExeptionDemo with the Run Without Errors option selected will result in the following code execution flow:

```
running in main bubbleExeptionDemo()
executing inside subFunction()
executing inside subSubFunction()
after call to subSubFunction()
after call to subFunction()
the finally section
```

What's not shown here is the implementation of subFunction or the functions that subFunction calls (see the next code snippet below). It nests a couple of levels deep, with subFunction calling subSubFunction.

Now, in the demo, select the Throw Sub Error option and let's look at what happens when an error occurs in the call to subFunction, which looks like this:

```
private function subFunction():void
{
  trace("executing inside subFunction()");

  if (radioButtonSubError.selected)
  {
    throw new Error("this is an error inside subFunction()");
  }

  subSubFunction();

  trace("after call to subSubFunction()");
}
```

This code continues a basic path of trace statements, except that this time with the appropriate option selected, an error is thrown showing how it propagates back up the call stack until a proper handler is found. When the error is thrown, an appropriate handler is looked for in the current function. If it's not found, the code searches the call stack in reverse until it finds one. Luckily in the case of this demo, the bubbleExceptionDemo function has an exception handler that gracefully prints out the error. The important thing to notice is that subSubFunction is never executed.

With the error being raised inside a nested function call, notice the flow of the code that's executed:

```
running in main bubbleExeptionDemo()
executing inside subFunction()
Error: this is an error inside subFunction()
The finally section
```

When the error is thrown in subFunction, and no exception handler is found, the next executable line of code will be the first exception handler that is encountered, as long as one is present somewhere along the call stack. The next line of code in this case is the catch statement in bubbleExceptionDemo for the Error type of exception.

The exception handler in bubbleExceptionDemo actually handles different exceptions in potentially different ways. There are two different catch statements: one for an exception of type Error and the other for an exception of type UserAccountError, which is a custom error type and will be explained more in the next section. While both the catch handlers trace the error message, it's quite possible to have different code that displays business logic errors, like "invalid login" or "user offline," as opposed to an unplanned generic error coming from deep in the code.

Next, let's add to the sample application a custom error class.

Custom Error Types

Custom error types enable you to distinguish between error types in an exception handler. You could just use the regular Error class and do string comparison on the message or numeric errorId; however, you may want to pass some other custom data along with the error, such as user login information in case there's a login error or the user's session times out.

The UserAccountError custom error type is:

```
public class UserAccountError extends Error
{
  static public const SESSION_TIMEOUT_ERROR:String="The user session timed out";
  static public const INVALID_LOGIN:String = "Invalid login.";
  static public const INVALID_USERNAME:String = "Invalid user name.";

  public var user:LoginVO;

  public function UserAccountError(message:String, user:LoginVO = null)
  {
    this.user = user;
    super(message);
  }
}
```

All custom error classes will inherit from Flex's base `Error` type. The `Error` class is the root of all errors in Flex, keeping track of the error `message` text and the `errorId`, and providing a method to return the call stack trace (via the function `getStackTrace`), which is useful when trying to assess where the error originated — in the case where only an outer exception handler is in place.

There's also some `static consts` that define the different errors, such as `SESSION_TIMEOUT_ERROR`, `INVALID_LOGIN`, and `INVALID_PASSWORD`. These were only added to demonstrate the types of errors this class might work with. Having these constants here could also prove useful for providing a way to inspect errors of a given subtype.

The custom `UserAccountError` error constructor requires that an error message be passed in. Additionally, there's also an optional `LoginVO` object being passed in that holds the information about the current login data, such as the username, password, session data, and so on, which could be useful information to have about the error. All the constructor does is store the optionally passed in `LoginVO` to a local variable called `user`, and then calls the constructor on the base class, passing in the `message` string.

That's how you create a custom error type. Next we'll look at how to raise a custom error.

Throw

We've mentioned throwing an error before when throwing a generic error with a custom error message. Now let's look at it in practice with a custom error by returning to the `bubbleExceptionDemo` sample code. This time, in the chapter's sample application, select the Throw UserAccountError Custom error option.

The code will execute down a path, eventually executing the new `subSubFunction`, which is shown here:

```
private function subSubFunction():void
{
  trace("executing inside subSubFunction()");
  if (radioButtonSubError2.selected)
  {
    var loginVO:LoginVO = new LoginVO();
    loginVO.userId = "test_user";

    throw new UserAccountError(UserAccountError.INVALID_USERNAME, loginVO);
  }

  if (radioButtonSubError3.selected) {
    subFunctionWithHandler();
    trace("after call to subFunctionWithHandler()");
  }
}
```

When this code executes, the custom `UserAccountError` type is going to be created, along with a `LoginVO` that contains potentially useful information that the `UserAccountError` catch handler in the function `bubbleExceptionDemo` will eventually use. Now in a real-world scenario, this exception isn't going to be raised by inspecting whether a radio button is selected or not, but more likely it will be raised when a given `LoginVO` object doesn't meet certain requirements regarding its state. Nonetheless, this code demonstrates using the `throw` statement to raise a custom error type with custom messages and parameters that will eventually be handled by a `try/catch` handler somewhere on the call stack.

When the exception handler (shown in Listing 47-1) catches a `UserAccountError`, logs the error, and displays information about the error to the end user, it informs them of the error condition that they control, such as logging back in or inputting a different password.

To see the actual flow of the code, let's look at the debug trace output:

```
running in main bubbleExeptionDemo()
executing inside subFunction()
executing inside subSubFunction()
UserAccountError: Invalid user name. for user: test_user
The finally section
```

The code starts out running `bubbleExceptionDemo`, and then enters `subFunction`, which in turn calls `subSubFunction`, where the exception occurs. Since there are no handlers in either `subSubFunction` or `subFunction`, the exception travels back up the call stack until the exception handler in `bubble ExceptionDemo` handles the error.

It's also important to note the order in which multiple `catch` conditions are handled. They need to be listed from the specific (`UserAccountError`) to the generic (`Error`) because all error types are of type `Error`, and if it's listed first, then it'll always handle any error type thrown.

Handling Errors in Functions

The final part of the demo will demonstrate handling an error deep in a program. Selecting Test sub-Function Error Handler will trigger a function to be called that both raises an exception and handles it gracefully.

Continuing with the flow of execution introduced previously, the `subSubFunction` calls another function, `subFunctionWithHandler`, which throws an error during execution. The difference with the implementation of this deep function is that the exception is handled, and no exception bubbling occurs. The sample code and application for the chapter show how a function implements its own `try/catch` handler.

Asynchronous Error Handling with Events

The ActionScript exception handling explained previously works very well for inline code occurring in a continuous fashion, all being processed in a given frame. Things are a bit different when using many of the built-in Flex APIs that are asynchronous in nature, like almost anything that has to do with network communications or file access. Because of this, Flex and Flash provide a lot of events that the developer must implement in order to properly deal with errors.

The previous chapter introduced `mx.rpc.events.FaultEvent` when working with `HTTPService` and `WebService` RPC services. When an error occurs while calling a service operation, an event handler executes such that the developer could handle the error. We'll get into more details of the `FaultEvent` in the next three chapters as we build deeper RPC examples, but for now, let's have a look at a very basic request to a remote server.

Important Error Events

Flex uses a lot of low-level functionality found in the Flash API. Flex will often provide a wrapper, like `HTTPService`, which eventually calls the basic Flash `URLoader` class to make remote server requests. As a developer, you can either use the `HTTPService` or the `URLLoader` to make a simple HTTP request to a remote server. Here, we're going to work with the `URLLoader` for a minute because it exposes all the raw error events involved with asynchronous communication.

All asynchronous error events inherit from the base `ErrorEvent`, a lot like all the synchronous errors inherit from `Error`. There are a few important error events to always keep watch for and to make sure you provide event handlers for. For example, when you start working with, say, the `FileReference` or the `URLoader` classes, both defined in the Flash API that's exposed to Flex, you'll need to add implementations to the following three events for complete error-handling coverage:

❑ `flash.events.HTTPStatusEvent`

❑ `flash.events.SecurityErrorEvent`

❑ `flash.events.IOErrorEvent`

Included in the chapters sample application is a quick demo that can be run by pressing the URLLoader Demo button. The following code makes a raw URL request using the `URLLoader`:

```
private function urlLoaderDemo():void
{
 var urlLoader:URLLoader = new URLLoader();
 urlLoader.addEventListener(HTTPStatusEvent.HTTP_STATUS, onHttpStatusReceived);
 urlLoader.addEventListener(SecurityErrorEvent.SECURITY_ERROR, onSecurityError);
 urlLoader.addEventListener(IOErrorEvent.IO_ERROR, onIOError);

 // Non-error events
 urlLoaderr.addEventListener(Event.COMPLETE, onUrlLoaderComplete);

 var request:URLRequest;
 if (checkboxHttpError.selected == true) {
   // Create a request that will result in an IOError
   request = new URLRequest("http://www.adobe.com/bad_file_request.html");
 }else {
   // Create a request that will result in an HTTP Status 200
   request = new URLRequest("http://www.adobe.com/");
 }
   urlLoader.load(request);
}
```

First, you create a new `URLLoader`, which is declared in the Flash APIs. Next, you need to bind to several events that the `URLLoader` class can emit. We're only focusing on the error events here for the sake of brevity, as there are other events one should implement for complete use of `URLLoader`.

The first event to add a listener for is the `HTTPStatusEvent`. The `event.status` will contain the status code being returned from the server, whether 200 for everything being okay, or HTTP error code 404 when a requested resource wasn't found. Sometimes the status will be 0, when it's unknown whether it's because of a quirk in certain web browsers not passing it onto the Flash player, or whether server communication couldn't take place. The `HTTPStatusEvent.HTTP_STATUS` handler looks like the following:

```
private function onHttpStatusReceived(event:HTTPStatusEvent):void
{
  if (event.status == 200) trace("Http success ");

  if ( event.status == 404) trace("Resource not found");

  trace(event.toString());
}
```

All this method is doing is tracing output based on various responses from the server, but your application should probably display an intelligent error to the user, like letting them know that the requested URL couldn't be found.

The next event to listen for is the `SecurityErrorEvent.SECURITY_ERROR`, which will be raised when there are security issues, like cross-domain policy violations occurring when the Flash Player connects to a web server that didn't originate the SWF file and no `crossdomain.xml` file has been set up. This is another type of communication error, even though it's enforced by the Flash Player's security sandbox. While it's not very important for your users, when this error is being raised, it's usually a clue for the developer to tweak something in the deployment environment. As such, the error should be caught early on before the application is deployed into production. (Note the `SecurityErrorEvent` handler isn't shown here, as it's only logging that it occurred; see the source code for the chapter.)

Finally, the third error event to listen for is the `IOErrorEvent.IO_ERROR`, which will occur when there's an error during transmission of the file from the server, or the requested file couldn't be downloaded.

Then the code adds another event listener for the `Event.Complete`, which will let you know as soon as all the content is done downloading. Then the code either requests a valid document from a Web server, or an invalid one to raise an `IOError`.

This code here just demonstrates what you need to be looking for when using any of the asynchronous APIs in Flex and Flash.

Asynchronous Events in the Debug Player

Just like with synchronous events, the Flash Player will display a message box with an error for all unhandled error events. When running the Release version of the Flash Player, these events will be swallowed up, and execution will continue on the next frame. This will be problematic when security errors are being thrown and your UI will look like nothing is happening. Make sure you implement the basic events for proper error handling.

Summary

The reason we reviewed the basic ActionScript exception handling along with the asynchronous event error handling nature of Flex APIs is that in order to get a total error handling strategy in your own code, you're going to need to implement both. Sometimes you'll be calling a generic logging helper function within a `try/catch` handler, and sometimes you'll be calling that same code from within an RPC fault event. And remember most importantly how the Flash Player handles runtime errors differently when running code in either the Debug or Release version. Your boss will be telling you that nothing is happening when he clicks a button, but when you run the application in the Debug version of the Flash Player on your development machine, you'll be seeing an exception debug dialog window.

The next chapter delves into Flash Media Services to describe real-time streaming of video and data.

Flex and Flash Media Server

The Flash Media Server (FMS) family of products from Adobe enables you to create rich social media services and stream high-quality audio and video through a protected and scalable server solution. This chapter will focus on the media streaming capabilities of the Flash Media Server and how it can be utilized with Flex.

There are three versions of the Flash Media Server: Flash Media Interactive Server (FMIS), Flash Media Streaming Server (FMSS), and the Flash Media Development Server. The FMIS is the flagship of the product and has no limitations in bandwidth, connections, or functionality. It supports server-side shared objects, scalable server deployment with origin and edge configurations, and the ability to record video to the server from a client. The FMSS is a solution paired for video streaming but without the more advanced data and server features. It has all the power for streaming audio and video as the FMIS without the ability to record your content to the server. The Flash Media Development Server has all the same functionality of the FMIS but is limited to 10 concurrent connections. The Development server is free and can be used for production or local development. For a more concise comparison, see www.adobe.com/products/flashmediaserver/compare.

Benefits of Streaming Video with the FMS

There are a few key benefits that should definitely be called out concerning streaming content with the FMS. First is its ability to stream live video from a camera source on a client to the server and from there out to any connected clients. This live video broadcasting can become 2-way or multi-way video conferencing or social networking.

The second feature worth noting is the overall enhanced playback for prerecorded content. This includes the ability to have rapid-start playback with concise dynamic buffering control and enhanced seeking capability, which is not possible with progressive display. Seeking can take place to anywhere within the video, and is not limited by linear loading or existing keyframes. In addition, when streaming MPEG-4 H.264 content with the FMS there is no issue with the moov atom position, as there is with progressive loaded content.

> ## MOOV Atom Note:
>
> The moov atom is a chunk of byte data that contains the key metadata necessary to be able to appropriately play back the H.264 content. With progressive playback, no video will be able to be viewed until the moov atom is read, which is why it is very important for such cases that it is at the beginning of the file instead of at the end, as it is by default very often. As previously mentioned, this is not an issue for streaming when using the Flash Media Server; it is meant only as reference and to note that no action is needed to adjust the default position of the moov atom.

Another area of great benefit that the FMS offers is security. The FMS will stream over multiple secure protocols, including the RTMPE for enhanced encrypted content over the wire, as well as HTTPS as a less recommended alternative. In addition, when streaming content with the FMS, the content itself is never cached, and it is therefore much more secure by nature. The new FMS 3 line also has a new excellent feature for SWF verification. When enabled, it enforces that only SWF files defined on the FMS server are allowed to connect to the media server. This effectively keeps outside unwanted sources from using your Flash Media servers for their own unapproved purposes. An important note with this feature is that the SWF does not need to be served up from the media server, just defined there for verification. In addition, it is worth noting the verification is very specific, and if the binary SWF file is changed even in the slightest — such as only moving the position of one element — the server will see it as an unauthorized SWF and deny the connection.

Last, a great new feature of FMS 3 is the addition of the video-on-demand (VOD) folder. This enables quick setup and distribution for recorded video content streaming. It is a predefined application folder within your FMS installation for easily managing basic streaming of audio/video content with no need for server-side scripting.

Exercise 1: Playing Video On Demand

In this exercise, you will use the VOD service on the Flash Media Server with a VideoDisplay component to play FLV, MP4, and MP3 files.

Playing an FLV File

1. Copy the `sample.flv` file from `{tutorial_directory}`/MediaServerStart/media/ to `{fms_install}`/applications/vod/media.

2. Open the file `VOD_wt1.mxml` in the `{tutorial_directory}`/MediaServer/src/ directory.

3. In the File Navigator, right-click on `VOD_wt1.mxml` and select Set as Default Application.

4. Add a VideoDisplay component with a `source` attribute set as follows:

   ```
   <mx:VideoDisplay source="rtmp://{fms_url}/vod/sample.flv" />
   ```

5. Save the file and run the application. The sample video should automatically play.

Playing an MP4 File

1. Copy the file `sample.mp4` from `{tutorial_directory}`/MediaServerStart/media/ to `{fms_install}`/applicaitons/vod/media.

2. Open the file `VOD_wt1.mxml` in the `{tutorial_directory}/MediaServer/src/` directory.

3. In the File Navigator, right-click on `VOD_wt1.mxml` and select Set as Default Application.

4. Add a VideoDisplay component with a `source` attribute set as follows:

   ```
   <mx:VideoDisplay source="rtmp:/{fms_url}/vod/mp4:sample.mp4" />
   ```

5. Save the file and run the application. The MP4 video file should play.

Playing a MP3 File

1. Copy the `sample.mp3` file from `{tutorial_directory}/MediaServerStart/media/` to `{fms_install}/applicaitons/vod/media`.

2. Open the file `VOD_wt1.mxml` in the `{tutorial_directory}/MediaServer/src/` directory.

3. In the File Navigator, right-click on `VOD_wt1.mxml` and select Set as Default Application.

4. Add a VideoDisplay component with a `source` attribute set as follows:

   ```
   <mx:VideoDisplay source="rtmp://{fms_url}/vod/mp4:sample.mp3" />
   ```

5. Save the file and run the application. The MP3 video file should play.

Setting Up Applications and Understanding Instances

If you do not already have a Flash Media Server installed, you can go to `www.adobe.com/go/tryflash mediaserver` and use your Adobe login to download the free Developer version of the server.

Once your FMS is installed and actively running, the next step is to set up an application instance. Application instances are stored in the `applications` directory of the installation folder by default. Each folder represents an application that utilizes the media server. Each application can also be configured and controlled in various ways. When using the FMIS, you can also utilize server-side ActionScript to have fine-tuned control over the server-side application and client-to-server interactions.

When connecting to an FMS, you need to connect to an application. Thus, if an application existed with the name `sampleApp` and you wanted to connect to it from your local dev installation with the default port (which is 1935) and the preferred RTMP (Real Time Messaging Protocol), the connection string would be `rtmp://localhost:1935/sampleApp`.

Application instances are one of the very powerful features of the FMS and its application management capabilities. When you connect directly to an application, you are connecting to the default instance (`_definst_`). All users connecting to the same application instance will be grouped together. The powerful part of this is the ability to specify which instance to connect to within an application. This can often be seen as "rooms" in the similar chat or social media paradigm. To connect to a specific instance other than the default instance, specify a name for that instance as part of your connection stream after the application ID — for example, `rtmp://localhost:1935/sampleApp/mySpecialInstance`.

Audio and video content that is going to be streamed to connected users of an application also will need to be organized by application instances. By default, any audio/video files should be stored within a `streams` directory and then within a directory matching the instance name within the application directory. This path shows an example of where to put a FLV called `myVideo.flv` within the local file system of the server:

```
[INSTALLATION DIR]\applications\sampleApp\streams\_definst_\myVideo.flv.
```

Developing for the Flash Media Server in Flex

To create a custom connection to an FMS, use the `NetConnection` class. Use this class just as it was used for progressive playback, except don't connect to null; connect to the URI for your FMS and the specific application and instance if you desire. If the FMS application requires additional parameters that the server-side ActionScript would receive, you would pass those after the URI to the `connect()` method of the `NetConnection` instance. When using a `NetConnection` instance with the FMS, it is much more important to handle and react to your `NetConnection` netStatus events. The `info` property of the `flash.events.NetStatusEvent` will provide critical information to let clients know if the connection to the media server was successful, has been terminated and a number of other important status information keys. A very good strongly recommended practice is always wait until you have received the `NetConnection.Connect.Success` (which indicates the connection was successful) before proceeding with any actions — including streaming — between the client application and the FMS. A standard approach for handling the `netStatus` events for the `NetConnection` instance is to have a single handler with a switch ... case statement to handle the different `info` code properties to handle such items as stream initialization and sequencing, reconnections, and alerting users of issues.

Another good practice to get into is always setting the `objectEncoding` property for the NetConnection instances. The `objectEncoding` defines which AMF encoding to use with the server you are working with. FMS 3 and above supports AMF 3, whereas anything below FMS 3 only will support AMF 0. There are two supported values for the `objectEncoding` property recommended for use from the static properties of the `flash.net.ObjectEncoding`: `ObjectEncoding.AMF0` and `ObjectEncoding.AMF3`.

A very powerful and often very useful feature new to FMS 3 is native bandwidth detection without the need of any server-side code. The end result is an accurate measure of the round-trip bandwidth in Kbps between the connected client and the server. This method can be called on demand at any point in your application after the `NetConnection` has successfully connected (identified by receiving the `NetConnection.Connect.Success` info as detailed before). To initiate the bandwidth detection cycle, you must invoke the `call()` method on the `NetConnection` instance and pass the first parameter of the reserved command `checkBandwidth` as a string. The second parameter you should pass should be null. To receive and process the bandwidth check, you must specify a client object for your `NetConnection` that has two methods. The first method it requires must be called `onBWCheck()` and should receive a ... `rest` parameter set. It should be defined to return a value of type `Number` and coded to return a fixed value of `0`. This method is used for data packet handling and is time checked for calculations and does not directly provide any information client side.

```
Example:

    public function onBWCheck(... rest):Number
    {
```

```
            return 0;
    }
```

The second method is `onBWDone()` and should as well receive a ... `rest` parameter set, although it will have no returned value and thus be typed as `void`. The actually available bandwidth is retrieved from the ... `rest` parameter set and will be the first parameter, and therefore accessed as `rest[0]`.

```
Example:

    public function onBWDone(… rest):void
    {
        trace("bandwidth = " + rest[0] + " Kbps.");
    }
```

Exercise 2: Using the Bandwidth Check System of the Flash Media Server

In this exercise, you will check the client's bandwidth.

1. Open the file `Bandwidth_wt1.mxml` in the `{tutorial_directory}/MediaServerStart/src/` directory.

2. In the File Navigator, right-click on `Bandwidth_wt1s.mxml` and select Set as Default Application.

3. Under the comment `<!-- Check Bandwidth Button -->`, add a `Button` component with an id attribute of `check_btn` and a `label` attribute of `Check Bandwidth`:

    ```
    <!-- Check Bandwidth Button -->
    <mx:Button id="check_btn"
        label="Check Bandwidth"
        click="_checkBandWidth();" />
    ```

4. Under the comment `<!-- Bandwidth Label -->`, add a `Label` component with an id of `bw_lbl`, a `fontSize` of 16, and a `fontWeight` of `bold`:

    ```
    <!-- Bandwidth Label -->
    <mx:Label id="bw_lbl"
        fontSize="16" fontWeight="bold" />
    ```

5. Add a `Script` block to the MXML file:

    ```
    <mx:Script>
        <![CDATA[

        ]]>
    </mx:Script>
    ```

6. Create a private variable named `_netConnection`, typed as a `NetConnection`:

    ```
    <mx:Script>
        <![CDATA[

        private var _netConnection:NetConnection;
    ```

7. Create an event handler method named _init() with a return type of void:

```
private var _netConnection:NetConnection;

private function _init():void
{

}
```

8. Inside the _init() method, set _netConnection equal to a new NetConnection object:

```
private function _init():void
{
    _newConnection = new NetConnection();
}
```

9. Add an event listener for the NetStatusEvent.NET_STATUS event to the _netConnection object, and assign the method _onNetStatus (we will create this later) as the event handler method:

```
_newConnection = new NetConnection();

_netConnection.addEventListener( NetStatusEvent.NET_STATUS, _onNetStatus );
```

10. Set the client property of the _netConnection object equal to the this. Setting the client to this allows you to handle the bandwidth check more easily for purposes of this exercise. Usually you would create a custom client class, as in Exercise 1.

```
_netConnection.addEventListener( NetStatusEvent.NET_STATUS, _onNetStatus );
_netConnection.client = this;
```

11. Now call the connect() method on the _netConnection object, passing it the path of your vod application on your FMS server as the first parameter, and true as the second parameter:

```
_netConnection.client = this;

_netConnection.connect( "rtmp://{fms_url}/vod", true );
```

12. In the Application MXML tag, set _init as the event handler method for the creationComplete event:

```
<mx:Application
    xmlns:mx="http://www.adobe.com/2006/mxml"
    width="400" height="300"
    creationComplete="_init();" >
```

13. Create a new private method named _onNetStatus that receives a parameter named event and is typed as a NetStatusEvent. The method should have a return type of void.

```
private function _onNetStatus( event:NetStatusEvent ):void
{

}
```

14. In the _onNetStatus method, create an if conditional statement to check if the value of event.info.code equals NetConnection.Connect.Success. If it does, set the enabled property of the check_btn to false and then call a _checkBandwidth() method (we will create this method in a moment); otherwise, trace the value of event.info.code.

```
private function _onNetStatus( event:NetStatusEvent ):void
{
    if( event.info.code == "NetConnection.Connect.Success" )
    {
        check_btn.enabled = false;
        _checkBandwidth();
    }
    else
    {
        trace( event.info.code );
    }
}
```

15. Create a new public method named onMetaData with a return type of void. Leave the method empty. This is to avoid an error when the NetConnection object tries to call onMetaData on the client.

```
public function onMetaData():void
{
    // to handle the client call to onMetaData
}
```

16. Create a new private method named _checkBandwidth() with a return type of void:

```
private function _checkBandwidth():void
{

}
```

17. Inside of the _checkBandwidth() method, set the text property of the bw_lbl equal to Checking bandwidth..., and then call the setBusyCursor() method on the cursorManager object:

```
private function _checkBandwidth():void
{
    bw_lbl.text = "Checking bandwidth..."
    cursorManager.setBusyCursor();

}
```

18. To finish the _checkBandwidth() method, call the call() method on the _netConnection object. Pass the String checkBandWidth as the first parameter and null as the second parameter.

```
private function _checkBandwidth():void
{
    bw_lbl.text = "Checking bandwidth..."
    cursorManager.setBusyCursor();
    _netConnection.call( "checkBandWidth", null );
}
```

19. Create a new public method named onBWCheck() with a return type of Number. The method should receive a ... rest parameter and the body of the function should return 0.

```
public function onBWCheck( ...rest ):Number
{
    return 0;
}
```

20. Create another new public method named onBWDone() with a return type of void. The method receives a ... rest parameter.

```
public function onBWDone( ...rest ):void
{

}
```

21. Inside the onBWDone() method, set the enabled property of the check_btn equal to true, and then call the removeBusyCursor() method on the cursorManager object:

```
public function onBWDone( ...rest ):void
{
    check_btn.enabled = true;
    cursorManager.removeBusyCursor();
}
```

22. To finish the onBWDone method, set the text property of the bw_lbl component equal to the first index of the rest parameter, and then add the string Kbps:

```
public function onBWDone( ...rest ):void
{
    check_btn.enabled = true;
    cursorManager.removeBusyCursor();
    bw_lbl.text = rest[ 0 ] + " Kpbs.";
}
```

23. Save the file and run the application. When the NetConnection object connects, it should automatically check the bandwidth and update the label with the calculated bandwidth. You can also click the Check Bandwidth button to run the check again.

Understanding the Netstream with FMS

The NetStream class is used for the same purposes with the Flash Media Server as it is without and basic progressive display. When using a NetStream instance with the FMS, there is the option to use some additional properties and methods, as well as using some of the same ones slightly different. Once the NetStream instance is generated and has been associated with the NetConnection instance, the first big change that must be addressed when using the FMS and a NetStream is the play() method. The end result of calling the play() method is the same, but the parameters that should be passed in are different.

The first parameter is the name of a file on the media server within the connected application instance's streams directory. Do *not* specify a file extension. When using the FMS to stream MP3 files of MPEG-4 H.264/AAC files, you have to use a prefix when passing the stream name. For streaming MP3 files, add the string of mp3: before your stream name; for MPEG-4 content, use mp4:.

The second parameter is the position of the file, in seconds, from where the streaming will begin. This is a very powerful attribute not only because it allows you to specify to start streaming at any point of a file, including the beginning (0), but also because it gives you the ability to specify priority for playing recorded or live streams if they exist. The supported values are -2, -1, 0, or any positive number that is less than the total duration. -2 is the default and will look first for a live stream to play with the specified ID — which was the first parameter of the stream name. If it cannot find a live stream with that name, it will look for a recorded stream on the server with the same name and play that. If it can find neither, it opens a new live stream. -1 will check only if there is a live stream, and if it finds one will play it. It is a very good practice to always specify a value, especially when playing a recorded file that you want to play from the beginning, and pass a value of 0.

The third optional parameter is the duration of the playback for the specified stream in seconds. The allowed values are -1, which indicates the whole file and is the default; 0, which indicates to play one frame from the beginning, and any other positive value in seconds to play a portion of the stream whether it is live or recorded.

The fourth and final parameter provides the ability to create or clear playlists with multiple streams. The default value is 1, or true, which clears any previous play() calls and immediately plays the stream specified in that call. The other accepted values are 0, or false, which adds the current stream to any existing streams and continues playback as it was; the value of 2, which keeps any existing playlist and immediately returns any stream messages; and finally the value of 3, which does the same thing as 2 but also clears the playlist.

Buffer Control

Controlling the media buffer is a powerful ability that can enhance the user experience through the streaming and decrease the initial wait time to start display. The buffer is the amount of audio/video loaded into the Flash Player memory. The initial NetStream instances bufferTime value in seconds is how much media will be loaded into memory before the media begins to play and display. The bufferLength is a read-only property that reports on how much data in seconds is currently loaded into the buffer. The bufferLength property will generally fluctuate regularly as the media content plays, and its bandwidth requirements fluctuate as does network latency. The default value for bufferTime is 0.1, thus allowing the video to start playing quickly once it is requested, although this does not give much room for latency fluctuation. A powerful technique to get a quick initial playback with sustained playback for the duration is to set the initial buffer to a minimal value (less than 1), and once the buffer is full — as indicated through the NetStream's netStatus event with a info property value of NetStream.Buffer.Full — to increase the buffer to a more sustainable value, usually 5 seconds or more. An important note on the NetStatus event that is dispatched with the info value of NetStream.Buffer.Full is that this will only ever be dispatched once unless the buffer has been completely cleared again or the video has been stopped. When not using the FMS, it is not recommended to ever set the bufferTime to 0, as this may have some adverse affects. When using the FMS, when you set the bufferTime to 0, this is actually interpreted as something close to 10 milliseconds.

When publishing a live stream, bufferTime works quite differently for the publisher. It specifies how much time in seconds to allow to fill in a buffer on the publisher's machine while broadcasting before frames are dropped. Generally, on a high-bandwidth connection, this is not needed very much, as the content is sent to the server almost immediately as it hits the buffer.

New with FMS 3 and the MovieStar Flash Player update is something referred to as *smart pause functionality*. With the new FMS and Flash Player, the media content will now be buffered when paused.

This provides the ability to start the stream immediately and pause the content to allow the buffer to fill before the end user starts playing. In addition, this is very powerful now when a user pauses a stream and does not need to rebuffer to resume. The general rule for how much will be buffered is whichever is larger of either twice the size of the set buffer or 60 seconds. For more detailed information on the smart pause capabilities, see www.adobe.com/go/learn_fms_smartpause_en.

Publishing Video

One of the greatest features of the Flash Media Server is the ability to publish live video. This opens up a whole new level of communication and collaboration possibilities within your Flex applications. Both the FMIS and FMSS support live publishing but only the FMIS allows recording of the live publishing stream directly to the server. However, if you use the Adobe Flash Media Encoder (FME or now called the Flash Media Live Encoder) 2.5 or above, you can publish a live stream to your server and save a flat file version locally on the publisher's machine, then manually move it to your media server later for recorded playback. The Flash Media Encoder is a great application that is free and can be found as a download from Adobe's site. One of the major benefits of publishing video from the FME is the ability to stream MPEG-4 H.264– or On2 VP6–encoded media live to the media server. When publishing to the media server from a Flex application via the Flash Player, the encoding is limited to the Sorenson Spark CODEC, since that is the only CODEC included in the Flash Player for publishing. What that means is that if you are publishing directly from your applications, it will require more bandwidth and generally be of lesser quality than if you use an external tool like the Flash Media Encoder.

To publish from your application use a NetStream instance just like playing, but instead of calling the play() method, call the publish() method. You will pass two parameters to the publish() method. The first parameter is the stream name. This is the same value that needs to be passed by any consumers to play the stream to the play() method. The second parameter is the identifier string for the type publish for this stream. The supported strings include "record," which will record and save a file with the same name inside of the applications streams directory in the _definst_ directory if no specific instance was specified. These folders in the streams directory for an application instance do not need to be manually created; the FMS will do so on its own if they do not exist. The string of "append" for the publish type parameter will append the live video to a file with the specified stream name if it exists or will create one like the "record" type does if it cannot find a matching stream for the application instance. The last supported value for the publish type is "live," which is also the default value and indicates that the stream should not be saved but simply published and available to any live consumers.

One property worth noting on the NetStream instance when working with live video on the subscribing consumer feed is the liveDelay property. The liveDelay property reports the lag time between the broadcaster and the consumer and is such generally only used with the FMS.

A key step to make sure is addressed before calling the publish() method is to associate a video feed with the NetStream instance. This is done by using the Camera class and passing a reference to the specified Camera instance to the attachCamera() method of the NetStream instance. There is also an attachAudio() method that accepts a Microphone instance. For basic use you can call the static getCamera() method of the Camera class to retrieve the default camera connected and return a Camera instance, which you can pass directly to the attachCamera() call. However, if you want to have explicit control over the bandwidth, quality, and frame rate, you can retrieve a Camera instance in the same way, then use the methods of the Camera class, such as setMode(), setKeyFrameInterval(), and `setQuality()`, to specify settings for the quality of the video being published. You can also use the `setLoopback()` method and pass a Boolean value of `true` to see the encoding parameters in affect on the publishing stream if you then attach the `NetStream` to a `Video` instance, or you can spawn another `NetStream` and play the live stream back in a true round-trip fashion though that can impact your bandwidth greatly.

Exercise 3: Using the Flash Media Server for Live and Recorded Streams

In this exercise, you will:

- ❑ Set up the FMS application
- ❑ Stream a preexisting video
- ❑ Publish and record a live stream

Setting Up the FMS Application

1. To create the FMS application, copy the `fx3pro` directory from `{tutorial_directory}/MediaServer/` to your FMS server's application directory, `{fms_install}/applications`.

2. The `profx3` application contains a sample video, `sample.flv`, that you will use to test the `profx3` application.

Streaming a Preexisting Video

1. Open the file `NetStream_wt1.mxml` in the `{tutorial_directory}/MediaServer/src/` directory.

2. In the File Navigator, right-click `NetStream_wt1.mxml` and select Set as Default Application.

   You will see that this file is made up of a `Viewer` component nested in an `HBox`. You will build out the main functionality of the `Viewer` components and add in a `Recorder` component in this exercise.

3. Open the `Viewer.mxml` file in the `{tutorial_directory}MediaServer/src/com/wrox/profx3/netstream/` directory.

   Much of this file has been created for you, so we can concentrate on how to connect to the Flash Media Server to record and play video streams. This component makes use of a slightly modified version of the `ProfxVideo` component we built in the Video and Sound walkthroughs to display our video. The addition of the source setter function allows us to connect to the FMS server and the server's video streams. Please feel free to review the `ProfxVideo` file in the `{tutorial_directory}/MediaServer/com/wrox/fx3pro/video/` directory.

4. On the `ProfxVideo` component, add a `server` attribute pointing to the `profx3` application on your FMS server:

   ```
   <video:ProfxVideo id="videoDisplay"
       top="40" left="10"
       width="320" height="240"
       server="rtmp://{fms_url}/profx3"/>
   ```

875

5. On the `Button` component, add a click event handler. In the event handler, set the source property of the `videoDisplay` `ProfxVideo` component equal to the `text` property of the `stream-Name_ti` `TextInput` component:

```
<mx:Button id="connect_btn"
    left="178" top="10"
    label="Connect As Viewer"
    click="videoDisplay.source = streamName_ti.text;"/>
```

6. Save the file and run the application. Type the string **sample** (the name of the `sample.flv` file that was in the profx3 FMS application) into the `TextInput`, and click the Connect As Viewer Button. The sample video should begin to play.

Publishing and Recording a Live Stream

1. Open `NetStream_wt1.mxml` in the HBox MXML tag, add a `Broadcaster` component from the `com.wrox.profx3.netstream` package. Give the component an id of `videoBroadcaster`:

```
<mx:HBox top="0" left="0" right="0" bottom="0">
    <netstream:Broadcaster id="videoBroadcaster" />
    <netstream:Viewer id="videoViewer" />
</mx:HBox>
```

2. Open the `Broadcaster.mxml` file in the `{tutorial_install}/MediaServer/src/com/wrox/profx3/netstream/` directory.

3. In the `_onClickConnect()` event handler method, under the comment `// Connect to the FMS server`, call the `connect()` method on the `_netConnection` object. Pass the URL to your FMS server with the profx3 application name as a single string.

```
// Connect to the FMS server
_netConnection.connect( "rtmp://office.realeyesmedia.com/profx3" );
```

4. In the `_createNetStream()` method, under the comment `// Get the camera`, call the static method `getCamera()` on the `Camera` class and assign its result to the `_camera` property:

```
// Get the camera
_camera = Camera.getCamera();
```

5. Next, call the `attachCamera()` method on the `_video` object and pass the `_camera` property as the only parameter:

```
// Get the camera
_camera = Camera.getCamera();

// Attach the camera to the video object
_video.attachCamera( _camera );
```

6. Now, under the comment `// Attach the microphone and video to the NetStream`, call the `attachCamera()` on the `_netStream` object, passing the `_camera` property as the only parameter. Also, call the `attachAudio()` on the `_netStream` object, and pass the result of calling the static `getMicrophone()` method on the `Microphone` class.

```
// Attach the microphone and video to the NetStream
_netStream.attachCamera( _camera );
_netStream.attachAudio( Microphone.getMicrophone() );
```

7. Finally under the comment `// Publish the stream`, call the `publish()` method on the `_netStream` object. Pass the `text` property of the `streamName_ti` TextInput component as the first parameter and the string `record` as the second parameter.

```
// Publish the stream
_netStream.publish( streamName_ti.text, "record" );
```

8. Save the file and run the application. You will now see two `TextInputs` and two `Buttons`. Click the Connect As Presenter Button; you will see a live video being recorded from your web camera. The stream that is being recorded is named whatever was in the `TextInput` (`streamName`, if you didn't change it).

9. Now click the Connect As Viewer Button, making sure that the value in the second `TextInput` is the same as the first. You should now see the stream that is being broadcast from your web camera.

10. Refresh the application. This time set the `TextInput` for the Connect As Viewer to the name of the stream that you just recorded, click the Connect As Viewer Button. You should now be viewing the recorded video from the stream you just broadcast.

Data with the Stream

A very powerful feature of streaming media with the FMS is the ability not only to stream audio and video but also to incorporate data into your stream. This is very valuable when you want to send commands or data for custom-built features such as "add overlay/insertion" or even closed captioning to name a couple. One of the most powerful aspects of this capability is that you can send messages on a live broadcast, and if the stream is being recorded, then the messages will be recorded in the media file on the server and reexecuted when played back in prerecorded mode.

To send data synched with a stream, you use the `NetStream` instance's `send()` method. The send method requires one parameter — the string name of the handler to call on the connected users `NetStream` client instance when the message is received — and can have any number of additional parameters you wish to send as parameters to the handler.

When recoding a stream the FMS also allows you to set data that is received up front when the stream starts, such as metadata, instead of synching with the content. Data keyframes will be triggered when a client subscribes to a stream to make sure that users get metadata (or other info) when they subscribe. To set keyframe data use the `send()` method, but for the first parameter of the handler, pass the string value of `@setDataFrame`; the second parameter will be the handler to execute on the `NetStream` client instance. Any further parameters will be sent to your custom handler. Data keyframes must have unique handler names and require no server-side scripting. To set custom metadata to be used just as if it were normal encoded metadata, call the `send()` method and set a data keyframe with the handler of `onMetaData` and pass it a third parameter of the metadata you want to use. To remove a previously set data keyframe, call the `send` method and instead of using `@sendDataFrame` as the first parameter, pass `@clearDataFrame` as the first parameter, and also pass the same handler as the second parameter, although no additional parameters are needed to clear the data keyframe.

Exercise 4: Flash Media Server

In this exercise, you will:

❑ Add data to the FMS stream

❑ Use the data as it arrives in the FMS stream

Adding Data to the FMS Stream

1. Open the file `NetStream_wt2.mxml` in the `{tutorial_directory}/MediaServer/src/` directory.

2. In the File Navigator, right-click `NetStream_wt2.mxml` and select Set as Default Application.

3. Change the `Broadcaster` component to the `Broadcaster_wt2` component and the `Viewer` component to the `Viewer_wt2` component:

```
<mx:HBox top="0" left="0" right="0" bottom="0">
    <netstream:Broadcaster_wt2 id="videoBroadcaster" />
    <netstream:Viewer_wt2 id="videoViewer" />
</mx:HBox>
```

4. Open the `Broadcaster_w2` component in the `{tutorial_directory}/MediaServer/src/com/wrox/profx3/netstream` directory. You'll see that a `List` component with the ID `imageChoice_list` has been added.

5. Add a change event handler to the `List` MXML tag, and assign the `_onSelectImage()` method as the event handler:

```
<mx:List id="imageChoice_list"
    left="10" bottom="10"
    change="_onSelectImage( event );">
```

6. Inside the `onSelectImage()` method, in the script block, call the `send()` method on the `_netStream` object. Pass the String `onNSMessage` as the first parameter and `imageChoice_list.selectedItem` as the second parameter.

```
private function _onSelectImage( event:ListEvent ):void
{
    // Add info to the stream
    _netStream.send( "onNSMessage", imageChoice_list.selectedItem );
}
```

Using the Data as It Arrives in the FMS Stream

1. Open the `Viewer_w2` component in the `{tutorial_directory}/MediaServer/src/com/wrox/profx3/netstream` directory. You'll see that an `Image` component and a Script block have been added.

2. In the Script block, add a private method to handle a `NetStreamMessageEvent`. The parameter name should be `event`, and the method should have a return type of `void`. The `NetStream`

MessaageEvent is a custom event that has been provided and is located in the {tutorial_directory}/MediaServer/src/com/wrox/profx3/video/events directory.

```
private function _onMessageReceived( event:NetStreamMessageEvent ):void
{

}
```

3. In the _onMessageReceived() method, set the source property of the Image component equal to the String images/ plus the event.message plus the String .png:

```
private function _onMessageReceived( event:NetStreamMessageEvent ):void
{
    img.source = "images/" + event.message + ".png";
}
```

4. Open ProfxVideo.as in the {tutorial_directory}/MediaServer/src/com/wrox/profx3/video directory.

5. At the bottom of the file, locate the onNSMessage() client method in the CustomClient internal class.

6. Inside the onNSMessage(), dispatch a new NetStreamMessageEvent. The type parameter should be NetStreamMessageEvent.MESSAGE_RECEIVED. The second parameter should be the variable message.

```
public function onNSMessage( message:* ):void
{
    // Dispatch a NetStreamMessageEvent
    dispatchEvent( new NetStreamMessageEvent(
        NetStreamMessageEvent.MESSAGE_RECEIVED, message ) );
}
```

7. Now, locate the _connectStream() method in the ProfxVideo class.

8. Under the comment // Listener for the NetStreamMessageEvent.MESSAGE_RECEIVED event, add an event listener to the _netStream.client object for the NetStreamMessageEvent.MESSAGE_RECEIVED event. Assign the _onNetStreamMessage() method as the event handler method.

```
// Listener for the NetStreamMessageEvent.MESSAGE_RECEIVED event
_netStream.client.addEventListener(
        NetStreamMessageEvent.MESSAGE_RECEIVED,
        _onNetStreamMessage );
```

9. The _onNetStreamMessage redispatches the NetStreamMessageEvent so that components can listen on the ProfxVideo component.

10. Save the files and run the application. Click the Connect As Presenter button to begin recording a new stream. Click the Connect As Viewer button to view the live stream. Click an item in the list. You should see an image displayed in the Viewer component.

11. Refresh the browser. Click the Connect As Viewer button. When you watch the recorded stream, the images should appear at the same points in the view.

Summary

The Flash Media Server family of products offers an excellent blend of functionality and performance to enhance media delivery, enable multi-user interaction, and offer live video capabilities, all within the Flash Player. This chapter has only scratched the surface as to what the Flash Media Server can do, but it has provided a good starting point for enhancing the user experience with streaming media of both live and prerecorded content to Flex applications.

The next chapter discusses using Flex's `HTTPService` class to connect to a RESTful Web Service written in PHP and the Zend framework.

RESTful Web Services with Flex and the Zend Framework

This chapter digs deeper into Flex RPC services, focusing on using Flex's `HTTPService` class to connect to a RESTful Web Service written with PHP and the Zend framework. The Zend framework is a full-featured web framework for the PHP developer that offers a variety of APIs, from MVC support to database API wrappers to HTML templating and caching support. The main design philosophy around Zend is that it allows you to use as much or as little of it as you want. You can use the MVC libraries independently of the view templating language or database access layers.

While we're using PHP on a Linux, Apache, MySql, PHP (LAMP)-based service stack, the exact same techniques will work with your favorite open-source web framework, whether Ruby on Rails, Python's Turbo Gears (or Django), or another one. The techniques in this chapter for building a RESTful interface and interacting with Adobe Flex are even available if your platform preference is Java EE or .NET using Windows Communication Foundation Services, although these last two we'll cover in more detail in the next couple of chapters focusing on SOAP-based Web Services.

We've chosen to use the Zend framework to aid PHP development because recently Adobe has partnered with Zend Technologies to provide Action Message Format (AMF) support in the Zend framework. (You'll read more about AMF in Part IX, "Data Services.") What this means is that besides supporting RESTful, XML-RPC, and so on, communications from the shared Zend libraries, you'll also soon be able to use Adobe's optimized AMF protocol for pushing data down to your Flex or Flash applications.

What Is a RESTful Web Service?

RESTful Web Services use Uniform Resource Locators (URLs) to locate unique resources on the Internet that can potentially provide services, and these services are controlled using HTTP verbs to execute essentially database Create, Retrieve, Update, Delete (CRUD) data operations on these resources. This is a very loose definition that's pretty specific for manipulating data mapped to database tables. Most official definitions for a RESTful service will map the HTTP verbs with the CRUD operations as shown in the following table.

HTTP VERB	Sample URI	Action
DELETE	http://service/api/customer/1	Deletes customer 1 from the backend storage system
PUT	http://service/api/customer/1	Updates customer 1 with the posted data included in the HTTP request
POST	http://service/api/customer	Creates a new customer with data included in the HTTP request
GET	http://service/api/customer/1	Retrieves data on customer 1 from the Web Service

However, most RESTful implementations on the Web aren't pure implementations according to the definition that uses the full array of HTTP verbs. (Some developers get bent out of shape about this.) Sites like Flickr and Yahoo! call their HTTP RPC-style Web Services RESTful, and popular frameworks like Ruby on Rails use the terminology loosely. Since this has become the norm, we'll continue to call what we're about to build RESTful as well.

The reason for the looseness in the RESTful implementation is that most browsers only support the HTTP verbs GET and POST. The common workaround is to include an attribute with the posted data, like what Ruby on Rails does with the _method form element, or some other parameter value defining the HTTP verb along with an HTTP POST. Working in the Flash Player, and consequently, Flex, is no exception, as both are dependent upon Flash communicating through the web browser it's running in. And if the web browser doesn't support PUT or DELETE, the Flash Player can't either. Hopefully, in the future we'll see browser support for both PUT and DELETE improved and, subsequently, the Flash Player's integration. For now, we'll just work with the limitations we have and pass in URL parameters to our RESTful Web Service.

The Flex HTTPService class does support all the HTTP verbs, including PUT and DELETE when used with a LiveCycle Data Services (LCDS) server. The HTTPService.useProxy property must be set to true and the HTTPService.method property set to either PUT or DELETE. When the remote call is made using the proxy service (which is an LCDS), the proxy will convert the method into an HTTP request with the proper verb set before calling out to the remote service.

The Routes Sample RESTful API

This section builds an HTTP-based Web Service that will manage route information that would be useful in an application that tracked your running, biking, hiking, and similar routes used as part of an exercise program.

The URL for this service is http://your_server/api/. When retrieving this URL, there should be a page defining how to use the API, including the proper use of HTTP verb and query parameter requirements.

The service supports the following RESTful API for managing route data:

Action	HTTP Verb	URL parameter	Sample URI
Retrieve all routes	GET	(None)	`http://server/api/route/`
Create a route	POST	(None)	`http://server/api/route/`
Retrieve a route	GET	(None)	`http://server/api/route/5`
Update a route	POST	(None)	`http://server/api/route/5`
Delete a route	POST	`;DELETE`	`http://server/api/route/5;DELETE`

For our RESTful client calls, we'll be passing a parameter up the URL defining additional HTTP verb information as needed for the HTTP DELETE. As you can see, to delete a route, make an HTTP POST to the following URL: `http://server/api/route/5;DELETE`. Also notice that for the UPDATE, instead of using the traditional RESTful HTTP verb PUT, just POST to the URL with a route `id` appended to the URL.

We'll be building out a Flex application (`Chapter_49_Fit_Tracker.mxml` in the chapter's sample code) that will use this HTTP-based Web Service to display a list of routes, as well as performing all the traditional CRUD operations. But first we need to set up the server environment.

Setting Up the Server and Development Environment

Since entire books exist for configuring Apache and MySQL, and programming with the Zend framework, we're only going to give the high-level directions to set up the server. It's assumed that if you're reading this chapter, you're a PHP developer familiar with a LAMP-based development stack.

Server Software Requirements

The server stack is going to be implemented on open source technologies. Flex works really well with both Adobe's proprietary LCDS, as well as open source technologies. So you can start with the free stuff when your company is small, and move up to some of the supported server products as needed.

Configuring Apache and MySQL

First, get Apache and MySQL running on your development server. On Windows, this is really easy to do. Download WAMP, which is an excellent preconfigured LAMP stack complete with PHP. All you have to do is install it, and then perform some minor tweaks to be fully operational with the Zend framework. To get started and download WAMP, visit: www.wampserver.com.

On OS X, the quickest way to a LAMP development stack is with MAMP, found at www.mamp.info.

Both these will quickly get you up and coding in PHP, Apache, and MySQL. However, don't feel limited to the two offerings mentioned here. Feel free to use your existing LAMP best practices for your organization, including using Linux as a development environment.

Configuring the Zend Framework

Download the Zend framework from `http://framework.zend.com`. The sample code for this chapter was written using version 1.6, but the framework is constantly evolving, and 1.7 is now available with complete support for AMF.

At the end of summer 2008, Adobe announced they're going to work with Zend in supporting the AMF protocol in the Zend framework. Look for some AMF packages soon for your Zend-based PHP packages to use a supported AMF server package. The Zend_AMF package has finally been released in the 1.7 version of the Zend Core framework.

Changes to Apache to Support the Zend Framework

To install Zend, you first need a public document root directory. Our sample project and WAMP stack use `c:/wamp/www` as the root directory (the default). Depending on your LAMP stack, you'll need to adjust the following according to your document root directory.

1. Install the sample Fit Tracker RESTful application. In your root document directory, copy the `application`, `library`, and the `public` directories from the `/server/www_root` folder of this chapter's sample code and paste them into the `c:\wamp\www` directory, or wherever your wwwroot directory is. From now on, we'll refer to your root document directory as wwwroot.

2. Decompress the Zend framework (either the ZIP file for windows or the TAR file for OS X) that you downloaded into the `wwwroot/library` directory so that there's a `wwwroot/library/Zend` directory and a whole slew of subdirectories that contain all the Zend framework PHP classes.

3. Modify your Apache `httpd.conf` configuration file to enable `mod_rewrite`. This is an Apache module that will allow for rewriting URLs. If you're using WAMP, or one of the preconfigured Apache implementations, you'll just need to make sure that the `mod_rewrite` module is loading, usually by uncommenting (comments are prefaced by the # symbol) the following line:

   ```
   LoadModule rewrite_module modules/mod_rewrite.so
   ```

4. Create/configure the Apache `.htaccess` file for the public directory.

   a. Windows only. Since Windows doesn't like filenames to begin with a period (.), and Apache needs to have a file called .htaccess created, you need to change Apache's configuration to use an `.htaccess` file called `htaccess.txt`. Near the end of `httpd.conf`, or in the already existing section called `rewrite_module`, add the following Access FileName line:

      ```
      <IfModule rewrite_module>
      AccessFileName htaccess.txt
      </IfModule>
      ```

      This tells the Apache `mod_rewrite` module (which allows Apache to rewrite URLs on the fly) to use a file called `htaccess.txt` (Windows only, remember) for the Apache rewrite rules.

   b. OS X or Linux only. Rename the `wwwroot/public/htaccess.txt` file as `wwwroot/public/.htaccess`. This will create a standard `.htaccess` file as normally required by Apache. This `.htaccess` file has been preconfigured to route all URL requests on the public document directory through the `index.php` file, as required by the Zend framework.

If you have a custom Apache configuration, just make sure to add the following rewrite rules in the .htaccess file for the wwwroot/public folder:

```
RewriteEngine On
RewriteCond %{REQUEST_FILENAME} -s [OR]
RewriteCond %{REQUEST_FILENAME} -l [OR]
RewriteCond %{REQUEST_FILENAME} -d
RewriteRule ^.*$ - [NC,L]
RewriteRule ^.*$ /index.php [NC,L]
```

5. In httpd.config, either change the Apache document root or add a virtual root to point at the wwwroot/public folder. In our sample, running on Windows, we made the following change:

```
DocumentRoot "c:/wamp/www/public"
```

You should make the change appropriate to your configuration, of course.

These tweaks are all discussed in the Zend framework documentation. Configuring Apache this way is only making one document public to the outside world, the wwwroot/public/index.php. With the rewrite rules, the URL requests to the web server, such as http://yourserver.com/foo/foo/foo, will all be rerouted to the index.php file, which will then pass the requests on to the Zend framework's MVC configuration.

Configuring MySQL

On your MySQL installation, create a database called fittracker. Managing and working with databases is beyond the scope here, so your ability to create a database is assumed.

Enclosed in the chapter's sample code, at /server/mysql_sql, are two scripts: schema.sql and data.sql. The first, schema.sql, should be run against the MySQL fittracker database that you'll have connected to using your favorite MySQL client, or use the default command-line tools. Next, run the data.sql to populate some test data into the fittracker database.

If you're using an alternative database (Oracle, MS SQL Server, Postgress, etc.) or you have a customized environment, you may need to tweak the database settings that the Fit Tracker web application uses to connect to the database. In the wwwroot/application/bootstrap.php file, there's a section for tweaking database connection settings (adjust accordingly):

```
$dbConfig = array(
    'host'        => 'localhost',
    'username'    => 'root',
    'password'    => '',
    'dbname'      => 'fittracker'
);
```

Any other tweaks that are required will most likely be made in the bootstrap.php file. But they should all be covered here. Because of the brevity of this setup guide, and the complexity of what's been configured, along with the multiple platforms this all works on and with, there still may need to be other tweaks.

For now, however, the RESTful Zend Route API should be up and running. Point your web browser to http://localhost/, and you should see a page confirming that you've connected to the RESTful service.

Client Software You Might Need

When working with PHP, you may want a fancier code editor. Zend offers one based on Eclipse (in much the same way that Adobe has built Flex Builder on Eclipse), but other PHP-editing tools, like Aptana (http://aptana.com) or Komodo (www.activestate.com) can work wonders when you are developing and debugging PHP scripts.

When debugging PHP scripts, it might be useful to use the Firefox Firebug plug-in in conjunction with the FirePHP plug-in. Our sample Zend project will actually output some debug messages for FirePHP to intercept on the browser client. Visit https://addons.mozilla.org/en-US/firefox/addon/6149 along with the optional PHP Library found at www.firephp.org/HQ/Use.html.

Finally, curl, a command-line tool for creating HTTP requests, is available at http://curl.haxx.se and is quite useful for debugging your RESTful Web Services without bringing Flex into the equation during development. In the chapter's sample code, in the /server/test_scripts directory, there are a few Windows batch files that make appropriate RESTful calls to the sample Routes Web Service. These scripts rely on curl to be installed to the development operating system and can be easily modified to run on OS X.

How Zend Works

Zend is a full-featured, open-source, web application framework. The Zend website has great documentation, plus other books exist to solely explain how the Zend framework works. But we'll offer a quick overview so that you can understand the minimal amount the code to make sense of the Routes Web Service.

Here's what the Zend application does when a user makes a RESTful request to retrieve information on a specific route available in the Fit Tracker sample application.

1. An application URL HTTP GET request is made to the Apache server hosting PHP and the Zend framework — for example, http://localhost/api/route. This URL is defined in our RESTful interface as returning a list of all the routes available. A fancier implementation would page the data. But we're keeping things simple.

2. Apache receives the request for http://localhost/api/route/1, and because of the rewrite rules we set up in Apache's .htaccess file, will redirect the request to the /public/index.php file. Index.php is the only public document available. Index.php includes a file called bootstrap.php, which is where the Zend framework configures itself, including database access, how URL routing will work, logging, and all the MVC routing magic that happens.

3. After the bootstrap.php code is executed, the front controller is called, and the request is dispatched to the Zend framework. This magic all happens with the code in the index.php file:

   ```
   Zend_Controller_Front::getInstance()->dispatch();
   ```

4. Zend now works its framework magic, parsing the request URL into the name of the controller and the action that should occur. In our sample, with the URL /api/route/1, the controller is api and the action is route. The number 1 is the route ID parameter. The front controller then passes the workload on to wwwroot/application/controllers/ApiController.php to finish handling the request.

5. Inside ApiController.php, there's a routeAction function that handles the specific action that Zend parsed from the URL. The routeAction looks at the request, determines which HTTP verb was used, whether any URL parameters were passed in (1 for the route ID), and then calls the appropriate method on the Zend_Rest_Server, which had wwwroot/services/FitTracker ServiceProvider.php injected as its handler. The code for the routeAction function follows. (This is the only PHP code we'll show here; for the rest, you'll have to look at the sample code):

```php
public function routeAction() {
    // Turn off the view Renderer for this Action.
    $this->_helper->viewRenderer->setNoRender();

    $routeId = $this->getRequest()->getParam('routeId');

    // Strip parameter decorating from the routeId if appropriate.
    $routeId = str_replace(";DELETE", "" ,$routeId);

    $rawRequest = $this->getRequest()->getRawBody();

    // Determine which Service Provider function to call based on
    // HTTP Verbs and parameter values
    if ( $this->isDelete() ) {
        $request = array('method' => 'deleteRoute',
                         'id' => $routeId);
    }elseif($this->getRequest()->isGet()) {
        if ($routeId == null){
            //  When no specific route id is passed in, just return all the routes
            $request = array('method' => 'getAllRoutes');
        }else{
            // Define mapping to service method in service provider class
            $request = array('method' => 'getRoute',
                             'id' => $routeId);
        }
    }elseif($this->getRequest()->isPost() ) {
        if ($routeId == null){
            //  When no specific route id is passed in, this is a new route
            $request = array('method' => 'createRoute',
                             'routeXml' => $rawRequest);
        }else{
            // Update an Existing Route
            $request = array('method' => 'updateRoute',
                             'routeXml' => $rawRequest);
        }
    }

    // Now that we have a request to pass onto the RESTFUL server
    $server = $this->getRestServer();

    // Pass in our newly formed request for the Zend restful service
    $xmlResponse = $server->handle($request);

    // send the response back to the client
    $this->getResponse()->setHeader('Content-Type', 'text/xml')
                        ->setBody($xmlResponse);

}
```

As you can see, depending on the HTTP verb and the URL parameters, an appropriate call will be made on the `FitTrackerServiceProvider`: updateRoute, deleteRoute, getAllRoutes, getRoute, or createRoute.

6. The `FitTrackerServiceProvider` is injected into the Zend_Rest_Server as a custom handler for all the various methods that the route action can manage, as explained above. This service provider will then use other Zend components, like a custom `Model_DbTable_Route` based on the `Zend_Db_Table_Abstract` for working with data stored in the database.

7. Finally, at the end of `routeAction` function, a response will be written back to the client in the form of XML. The client will need to be aware of the format, the elements, and so forth of the XML in order to use it. In most cases, there's a predetermined format for both business errors that occur on the server, as well as returning specific data for the given call.

For example, a business error condition for requesting information on a specific route with an HTTP GET to the URL `http://localhost/api/route/266` will result in a response that looks like the following:

```
<?xml version="1.0" encoding="UTF-8"?>
<FittrackerServiceProvider generator="zend" version="1.0">
  <getRoute>
    <msg>Route doesn't exist</msg>
    <status>failed </status>
  </getRoute>
</FittrackerServiceProvider>
```

Notice the format of `msg` and `status`. This convention is used consistently in the Fit Tracker sample Web Service. In fact, a successful request will have the status node in it, too, in order to make it easy for the Flex client to know whether a request was successful.

A successful call to requesting a route with an HTTP GET the URL `http://localhost/api/route/1` will yield the following XML response:

```
<?xml version="1.0" encoding="UTF-8"?>
<FittrackerServiceProvider generator="zend" version="1.0">
  <getRoute>
    <route>
      <id>1</id>
      <name>Run #1</name>
      <description>Make 20 laps around the block</description>
      <distance>4.60</distance>
      <created_by>1</created_by>
      <created>2008-11-07 16:11:18</created>
      <modified>2008-11-07 16:11:18</modified>
    </route>
    <status>success</status>
  </getRoute>
</FittrackerServiceProvider>
```

Notice that the `status` is set to `success` this time. And, of course, there's a bunch of route data included with this response.

Pure RESTful services would have the web server return a standard HTTP status of 404, file not found. Since we've already mentioned that we're using more of a hybrid RESTful service, we'll let this slide. Plus, it's a little more useful to have the server return an error message that the client can actually understand, especially since there are probably other error messages, such as access control errors, that the server could be returning.

That's it. That's the abbreviated version of how our RESTful Routes Web Service works using the Zend framework. Now it's time to build a simple client with Flex to work with this Web Service.

The Flex Sample Application

This chapter's sample code includes a Flex project that runs a sample application used to manage routes via the Routes Web Service that we set up earlier. The main MXML file, `Chapter_49_Fit_Tracker.mxml`, contains all the code needed to call the route services. The application performs all the operations that the Routes Web Service supports: getting a list of routes and all the CRUD operations for a given route.

Retrieving Data from a RESTful Service

The first thing to do when operating the Flex application is to load some route data from the Web Service. Do this by clicking on the Retrieve Routes button on the `Chapter_49_Fit_Tracker.mxml` screen, and then the data grid will be populated with a list of routes retrieved from the MySQL database. Let's look at all the moving parts to make this happen.

The HTTPService Declaration

In MXML, declare the following `HTTPService` (review Chapter 46, "Introduction to RPC Services," if this is the first time you're seeing the `HttpService` class being used):

```
<mx:HTTPService id="httpService"
  fault="onServiceFault(event)"
  result="onServiceResult(event)"
  resultFormat="e4x"
  showBusyCursor="true"
  concurrency="single"
/>
```

This simply established a `fault` and `result` handler to manage messages coming back from the server, whether successful or not. Bind the `fault` event to the `onServiceFault` event listener, and bind the result to the `onServiceResult` listener. Then set the `resultFormat` to e4x, because the RESTful Web Service will be returning XML, and working with XML with e4x is very natural. Set the `showBusyCursor` to `true`, which will make the mouse pointer turn into a waiting icon while the request is being made.

Notice that you haven't declared a `url` that this `HTTPService` is bound to but only set the very generic properties, as all the action functions will set the `url`, `data`, and HTTP verbs to send to the service.

Requesting All Routes

To request the routes from the service, make an HTTP GET request to the route service with a URL that look like `http://server/api/route/`. The Flex code that actually makes the call is called from a Button click handler, and looks like this:

```
private function retrieveRoutes():void
{  startWaiting("Retrieving Routes...");
    httpService.url = StringUtil.substitute("{0}/route/" ,
```

```
                                                            baseUrl);

        httpService.contentType = "text/html";
        httpService.method = "GET" ;  var token:AsyncToken = httpService.send();
        token.typeOfRequest = "list";
    }
```

First thing is that a fancier method of displaying a wait state in the application has been created, complete with a custom message. You have already set `showBusyCursor` on the `HTTPService` definition, so the mouse cursor will show busy during service invocation. In addition, call a helper function, `startWaiting()`, that triggers a richer user experience, with the application displaying "Retrieving Routes ... " in a contrasting orange that will fade away once a response has been received from the server.

Next, create the `url`, complete with query string parameters of the RESTful service, if needed. Then set the `contentType` to text/html. This is important because the `HTTPService` definition is reused among several types of calls, some of them posting raw XML data, which uses a different `contentType`.

As defined by the RESTful service in the table in the section "The Routes Sample RESTful API," the retrieve action uses the HTTP `GET` method, which is set here.

Working with AsyncToken

Finally, `send` the request to the server. When calling `httpService.send`, you can optionally get a handle of the `AsyncToken`, which tracks the asynchronous request. An `AsyncToken` is created and associated with individual calls to the remote server, and can be used to maintain state information about a particular call.

When an `HTTPService` supports making multiple requests (when the `HttpService.concurrency` property is set to `multiple`), you keep track of all the individual `AsyncTokens` and later match the calls with the expected results in the result handler. However, here in this sample, the `httpService.concurrency` is set up to make only `single` requests, so only a single handle of the `AsyncToken` is needed in order to set a custom `typeOfRequest` property to any value that we want, in order to inspect it later when the results come back from the server to the Flex HTTP result handler. In this sample, set the `typeOfRequest` to `list` in order to be able to match with the appropriate Flex-side behavior when the list is actually returned to the Flex client.

Managing Client State during Server Requests

The `startWaiting` function controls the UI state, by setting a message that appears while the application is communicating with the server. The sample application calls this at the beginning of all the server requests in order to inform the user that a remote server invocation is occurring and that they shouldn't (or can't) do anything with the application while this is processing:

```
    private function startWaiting(message:String = null):void
    {
      if (msg){
        waitMessage = msg;
      } else {
        waitMessage = "Please hold while I chat with the server...";
      }
      customWait = true;
    }
```

The user can optionally pass in a `message` to display during the server operation. This function sets the bindable properties `waitMessage` and `customWait` so that listeners will react and change their state. In this case, the Flex application will display an orange notification box with the custom message in it, and the box will then slowly fade away after a couple of seconds.

Processing the Results

The request has been made to the server, the user has been informed that the route data is being retrieved, and then the Zend-based PHP Web Service has processed the request. When the service is done processing, it sends an XML response back to the client that looks like the following:

```
<FittrackerServiceProvider generator="zend" version="1.0">
  <getAllRoutes>
    <route_count>
      6
    </route_count>
    <routes>
      <itemRows>
        <id>
          2
        </id>
        <name>
          Ironman bike ride around Boston
        </name>
        <description>
          This is a 110ish mile ride that will work you.
        </description>
        <distance>
          100.10
        </distance>
        <created_by>
          1
        </created_by>
        <created>
          2008-11-07 16:11:19
        </created>
        <modified>
          2008-11-07 19:41:24
        </modified>
      </itemRows>
      <itemRows>
        <id>
          3
        </id>
        <name>
          Boston Marathon Running Route
        </name>

  [More returned route data removed from here for the sake of brevity]

    <status>
      success
    </status>
  </getAllRoutes>
</FittrackerServiceProvider>
```

This response is generated by the Zend framework, and therefore it's in charge of formatting the XML output. Inside the server implementation, we could have created a more customized XML response format but chose to use the default for the sake of server programming simplicity. As you can see, there's a route_count giving the number of routes being returned from the backend. Then there's a node tree, called itemRows, for each of the routes returned. (For your own Web Services, it's worth the effort to make itemRows more meaningful for the data; for example, by calling it routeItem.) Finally, we have a status element, which we've set up to be common to all our server responses for the sake of consistency. After all, we could get a valid response from the server that didn't do as the client expected, as is the case when business errors occur, but we'll get to that in a moment.

First, Listing 49-1 shows the HTTPService result handler to process all successful results from the server called onServiceResult.

Listing 49-1: The HTTPService Result Handler

```
private function onServiceResult(event:ResultEvent):void
{
  //  Turn off custom wait, if it was on.
  customWait = false;

  //  Check for server-side business errors
  //  We can get valid results from the server, but where something went wrong.
  if(String(event.result..status).toUpperCase() == "FAILED") {
    Alert.show(event.result..msg);
    return;
  }else {
    //  There could be an id returned from the backend service.
    var id:Number = event.result..id
  }

  switch(event.token.typeOfRequest)
  {
    case "delete":
      retrieveRoutes();
      Alert.show("Route Deleted: " + id)
      break;
    case "list":
      var results:XML = event.result as XML;
      routeData = results..itemRows;
      break;
    case "update":
      retrieveRoutes();
      Alert.show("Route Updated: " + id)
      clearForm();
      break;
    case "create":
      retrieveRoutes();
      Alert.show("Route Created: " + id)
      clearForm();
      break;
    case "getSingle":
      Alert.show(event.result.toString());
```

```
      break;
    }
  }
```

This is the `result` handler that handles a successful call for all the remote Routes Web Service calls. Each of the different service calls is routed through this one handler. First, whenever the Flex client receives a message back from the server, turn off the waiting notification by setting `customWait = false`; it is bound via Flex data binding to the application's notification area's `visible` property. When `customWait` is `false`, the notification will disappear.

Next, inspect the XML response's `status` node for whether there were any server-side errors. Just because an HTTP request was successful and calls the `HTTPService` result handler, this doesn't mean that the requested route exists, or could be deleted and created, or even failed some business-specific backend rule. All it means is that at the basic HTTP communication level, the request was a success. This will be more important later when you are requesting to delete, update, or retrieve particular routes from the Web Service. Using an e4x expression, `event.result..status == "FAILED"`, match the status result to SUCCESS or FAILED in order to know how to continue processing the result. We'll look at the FAILED case in the next section.

When the result is a SUCCESS, continue processing the function and inspect the `AsycnToken` to see what kind of request this response was for. The token is found on the event passed into the handler, `event.token.typeOfRequest`. Using conditional logic, process the result accordingly; in this case, the `typeOfRequest` is "list." And then, again using e4X data binding, display the XML results in the DataGrid for all the results by setting the `routeData` property to the results of the e4X expression.

Voilà, the route data will appear in the DataGrid.

Managing Errors

Two types of errors need to be managed. First, there's the `HTTPService` `fault` handler that is raised when any error occurs on the communication transport with the remote server. Second, there's the server-side business errors that can occur when data isn't valid in the backend (for example, when a requests route couldn't be found in order to be deleted.)

The Fault Handler

The following is the default fault handler:

```
private function onServiceFault(event:FaultEvent):void
{
  customWait = false;

  if (event.fault.faultCode == "Server.Error.Request") {
    Alert.show("Error connecting to server, try again later.");
  } else {
    Alert.show("Unplanned Service Error: " + event.fault.faultString);
  }
}
```

First, turn off the `customWait` message. Since requests to a remote service always end in either a result or fault handler, the code to clean up the request must be handled in both event handlers.

Next, inspect the event's `faultCode`. When a `Server.ErrorRequest` is sent back, it basically means the server couldn't be reached and there was some form of connectivity issue between the client and the server. Handle the error appropriately.

Alternatively, you should provide some form of default error-logging service in your application for all unexpected and unhandled errors, as you learned in Chapter 47, "Error Handling." A default handler should exist for all error conditions. Here, an `Alert` pop-up window informs the user something bad happened, but it should probably also log specific details somewhere to facilitate debugging the user reported error.

Server-Side Business Errors

The next errors that need to be handled are the server-side business logic errors. These are errors spawned from the backend when you try to delete data that doesn't exist or to create data that doesn't meet validation requirements. For these errors, you need to define your own message format. Here's what our error message format looks like. Notice that it shares the same status elements as a successful message earlier. This is because the same successful result handler manages all successful communications with the server, whether good or bad.

The following sample error message is returned from the server when the user requests a route that doesn't exist:

```
<FittrackerServiceProvider generator="zend" version="1.0">
  <getRoute>
    <msg>
      Route doesn't exist
    </msg>
    <status>
      failed
    </status>
  </getRoute>
</FittrackerServiceProvider>
```

This XML is quite simple and is generated by the PHP backend. It consists of a `status` and `msg` nodes that the Flex application can use in a universal manner. When developing the backend, all business errors will conform to this format, so the Flex application can manage them in a consistent manner.

Looking back at code listing 49-1, you can see that the `HTTPService result` handler inspects the returned XML. When the status is `FAILED`, it then uses an `Alert` pop-up window to display the error message to the user.

Creating and Updating Data with a RESTful Service

Creating and updating data on the RESTful Web Service uses the same approach as retrieving route data from the service. A server request will be generated by defining the `url`, `contentType`, and `method` and then passing in some preformatted XML that meets the service specification. Since updating and creating the data are so similar, we'll only look at the data creation code here. The update code is available in the chapter's sample code.

For creating new routes in our sample application, the XML message looks like this:

```
<request>
  <name>The new route name</name>
  <description>The description of the route for searchability</description>
  <distance>15.3</distance>
  <created_by>4</created_by>
</request>
```

This is simple XML defining the data. This block of XML is completely defined by you. The top-level node doesn't need to be named "request," and the hierarchy of elements can be nested as deeply as you want. With HTTP Web Services, the format of the message is left up to the developer.

The code in Flex to create a new route request looks very similar to that for retrieving data from the Web Service:

```
public function createRoute():void
{
  startWaiting("Creating Route..." );

  // POST with no id, if there was an id, it'd be an update
  httpService.url = StringUtil.substitute("{0}/route/{1}" ,
                      baseUrl,
                      debugServer.selected ? DEBUG_PHP : "");

  httpService.method = "POST" ;
  httpService.contentType = "application/xml";
  var params:XML =
    <request>
      <name>{txtName.text}</name>
      <description>{txtDescription.text}</description>
      <distance>{txtDistance.text}</distance>
      <created_by>2</created_by>
    </request>

  // Or Post via XML Message
  var token:AsyncToken = httpService.send(params);
  token.typeOfRequest = "create";
}
```

This code uses the same message notification helper function (startWaiting) and uses the same instance of the HTTPService. In addition to setting the url to the appropriate RESTful URL, there's also embedded XML that uses Flex data-binding expressions to bind to the appropriate input controls for the user to create data.

Additionally, the httpService.method is set to POST. Remember, use the table in the section "The Routes Sample RESTful API" to determine how to use the RESTful service, whether you need to use GET or POST and what the URL should be. Set the contentType to application/xml, which is very important as this tells the server that the XML data we're sending to it is contained in the body of the HTTP POST. Finally, call send, and then set the typeOfRequest to "create" so that the HttpService result handler knows what to do when the service call succeeds.

The result handler is very similar to the other CRUD-based service operations, in terms of all the other service operations, with the addition of reading the `id` of the newly created route. The code that manages uses simple `e4x` to find an `id` element nested somewhere in the XML:

```
// There will be an id returned from the backend service.
var id:Number = event.result..id
```

Other route services, such as `updateRoute` and `deleteRoute` will also return the id in the server response, which will be useful for manually removing specific items from `ArrayCollection`, and for informing the user what item was updated or removed.

Updating a route (see the sample code `updateRoute`) is very similar to creating a route, except that the XML being sent to the server in the request will contain an `id` element used by the service to understand which item to update.

We've used custom XML for sending data to the server. Sending valid query string or HTML form name/value pairs is also a perfectly reasonable way to manage this data. XML is being used here because real-world APIs will probably have hierarchical data and be more complex than just name/value pairs. Also, if you are sending name/value pairs, you'll have to decide whether you're sending them in HTML form data or as part of the query string, and modify the `HTTPService.contentType` accordingly.

Deleting Data from a RESTful Service

Deleting data from the Routes Web Service follows the same pattern described previously for retrieving and updating routes. Pressing the Delete button in the sample Flex application will call the `deleteRoute()` function and a server request will be made. An id will be passed on the URI in the form of `http://server/api/route/[routeId];DELETE`. Substitute any existing (or even nonexisting, as we handle this error condition) route ID in the URL for `[routeId]`. You'll notice that the `routeId` is part of the unique URI resource and not a traditional query string parameter, which would look like `http://server/api/route?routeId=5`.

The Flash Player plug-in isn't able to send HTTP `DELETE` up through the web browser to the service, so `;DELETE` is appended to the URL. The Web Service knows how to interpret this as a request to `DELETE`, and is a viable workaround for not having access to the HTTP `DELETE` method from within Flash or most web browsers.

That's it for creating a RESTful service. See the chapter's sample code for the complete code listings, as a lot has been truncated for the sake of brevity in this text.

Summary

This chapter used XML to communicate with a PHP-based Web Service using custom XML messages to perform CRUD operations in a remote database. With the Zend framework supporting native Adobe AMF messaging, most of the sample code in this chapter can be written using `mx:RemoteObject` instead of `mx:HTTPService` to take advantage of the performance gains provided by AMF. Using AMF, the time required to transport data over the wire is decreased, as is time spent decoding the payload, since AMF is decoded by the Flash Player using native C libraries. Read more about AMF in Part IX, "Data Services."

Most Web Services you work with will require similar strategies in the Flex application: waiting for service responses, handling server-side business errors, handling the results and binding data, and dealing with unknown and unexpected service communication errors.

Coming up next in Chapter 50, we'll create a similar Fit Tracker application that connects to a backend written in Java, using Web Services for its **Remote Procedure Call (RPC)** strategy.

50

Integrating Flex and Java

This chapter explores more deeply into Flex RPC services, focusing on using Flex's `WebService` class to connect to a SOAP-based Web Service written with Java using the Grails framework. The Grails framework is an agile web development platform very similar to Ruby on Rails, except that it runs on the Java VM, which many enterprises already support in their data centers. Grails is based on the Groovy Java language extensions, which bring a lot of dynamic language syntactical sugar to the Java runtime, increasing developer productivity. With Grails, Groovy, and an XFire plug-in, which exposes Java objects at Web Services, you can create Web Services that are easily accessed from Flex applications in no time.

Building on the previous chapter's `HTTPService` sample, we're going to build this chapter's RPC communication with typed Web Services. While developing custom server messaging formats in pure XML is simple, it offers no runtime type-checking. The more complex the messages are that go back and forth, the more useful it becomes to have Web Services defined using WSDL (Web Services Description Language). In addition, this chapter's sample code will advance the Flex client design by breaking all the service layer calls into their own class, separating the view functionality out — a practice that you'll want to employ as the services you call increase in number and complexity. Plus, it's a stepping stone to using a full-blown Flex framework, like Cairngorm, which is discussed in Part X, "Using Cairngorm."

Also, just because we're exposing SOAP-based services and using the `mx.rpc.soap.WebService` class to access the remote data, it doesn't mean that you couldn't implement a RESTful service in much the same way using Grails and Java, or whatever your preferred backend development platform. Any platform these days can offer up data to Flex using any of your preferred RPC libraries, whether that's `HTTPService`, `WebService`, or `RemoteObject`. Chapter 51 looks at Web Services with .NET.

Introduction to the Routes Web Service

Web Services written to the WSDL 1.1 specification are supported by Flex's `mx.rpc.soap` `.WebService` library. With a WSDL-based service, methods (operations) and types (defined by XML Schema 1.0) are defined so that clients consuming the service will know the explicit contract for how to invoke the service, including the appropriate parameters to pass to the methods, and what the methods will return in a type-safe manner. The more complex the operations, their parameters, and the hierarchy of returned data, the more beneficial it is use to WSDL-based Web Services, which provide the foundation of enterprise service-oriented architecture (SOA).

The developer either designs the WSDL interface first (known as *contract first development*) and then fills in the implementation to meet the contract, or they develop Java code first and then, using some tools, have a WSDL generated based on mapping files and domain object hierarchies (known as *code-first*). This chapter's sample takes the code-first approach to exposing Web Services.

When you want to call the remote operation defined in the WSDL, you create an XML message supporting the SOAP format, which is the XML protocol used to exchange the messages defined in the WSDL over HTTP. The Flex `WebService` library is designed to communicate with remote Web Services and provides serialization support for translating objects from ActionScript into XML for transferring across the wire to the Web Service, and then vice versa for the responses coming back from the server.

Chapter 49 introduced you to working with Web Services from within Flex, as well as providing a very basic introduction to WSDL. If you haven't read that chapter, it's suggested you do so now. After you've set up the server-side code for this chapter, you'll be able to view the complete WSDL of the Routes Web Service.

Setting Up the Server and Development Environment

Let's get started with setting up the developer and server tools you need to run the demo application.

Server Software Requirements

The server stack for the Routes Web Service is implemented on open-source technologies. We're going to be using MySQL for the database, Jetty for the application server (because that's what Grails uses by default for a development environment, but feel free to use Tomcat, JBoss, WebSphere, or whatever else as determined by your Java infrastructure, especially if you're looking to release into a production environment), the Grails application framework, and the Groovy dynamic language extensions for the Java language.

Configuring Java, Grails, Groovy, and MySQL

It's assumed that you have experience working with Java, as this isn't intended as an introduction to the many concepts we'll be glancing at in passing, and that you understand these basic setup directions, since many Java environments follow similar conventions.

1. Download Grails from `http://grails.org`. As of this writing, 1.03 was used for the sample applications. Make sure that you have version 1.4 or newer of the Java SDK, and that `JAVA_HOME` has been set in your environment.

2. Extract Grails into a local directory, henceforth referred to as `grails_home`, and set up an environment variable called `GRAILS_HOME` that points to your `grails_home` directory. On our

Windows machine, we installed Grails at `c:/grails` and opened up the Windows System Control Panel ⇨ System ⇨ Advanced ⇨ Environment Variables ⇨ System Variables to set the `GRAILS_HOME` variable.

3. Modify your `PATH` so that `grails_home/bin` is set in it. This is so all the Grails scripts can be easily found for execution. You can set the `PATH` in Windows by going to Control Panel ⇨ Advanced ⇨ Environmental Variables ⇨ System Variables.

4. Verify that Grails is properly installed by opening a command window and typing **grails**.

   The following should be displayed if you've set up Grails properly:

   ```
   Welcome to Grails 1.0.3 - http://grails.org/
   Licensed under Apache Standard License 2.0
   Grails home is set to: c:\grails

   No script name specified. Use 'grails help' for more info or 'grails interactive
   ' to enter interactive mode
   ```

5. Next, get the source code for this chapter's `GrailsServer` project down to your machine (it's found in the Subversion repository). This will become the project folder, henceforth referred to as `project_home`.

6. Next, install the XFire Grails plug-in, which will give our Grails application WSDL Web Service support. Open a command prompt in `project_home` directory. This is very important, as Grails requires you to be in a Grails application directory in order to install the plug-in. Then at the command prompt, type **grails install-plugin xfire**.

   The XFire plug-in and all its dependencies (a long list of JAR files) will be installed into the demo application. (Newer versions of the XFire plugin might require upgrading the Grails framework.)

7. Install the appropriate JDBC driver for MySQL to the `project_home/lib` directory. The `mysql-connector-java-5.1.7-bin.jar` can be found at http://dev.mysql.com/downloads/connector/j/5.1.html.

8. Start MySQL and create a new database called `fittracker`. (As mentioned, this example uses MySQL by default). When the Grails server application starts, it will build the necessary database table to persist routes, but the `fittracker` database needs to exist first. Additionally, after you've started the Grails application for the first time, you can run the `data.sql` script to populate the database with some default data.

   You can support alternative database configurations, however. If you've installed the `fittracker` database to a different server or with different default login or even a different database system (like Oracle, SQL Server, etc.), you can modify the `project_home/grails-app/conf/DataSource.groovy` file to match your own database configuration. Those of you familiar with JDBC will be able to figure out the different settings. By default, the `DataSource.groovy` file that was downloaded is already configured to connect to the database `fittracker` with the default root user. Modify the JDBC driver section and database login to meet your specific deployment settings.

That should be it. Grails automatically installs Groovy, so your environment should be all set there. The XFire plug-in should be setup, as well.

Running the Server

To run the server environment, make sure that your MySQL service has been started. Then, at a command prompt, navigate to the `project_home` directory where you installed the code of the `fittracker` application and type **grails run-app**.

The Grails application should start and eventually in the output window, if all goes as planned, you should see something similar to the following:

```
2008-11-28 20:22:05.536::INFO:  Started SelectChannelConnector@0.0.0.0:8080
Server running. Browse to http://localhost:8080/fittracker_demo
```

Now, in a web browser, to see the generated WSDL from the application, navigate to `http://localhost:8080/fittracker_demo/services/route?wsdl`. If you can see WSDL, you're ready to continue.

Advanced Eclipse users (see the next section, "Client Software You Might Need") can run the Grails project (and enable debugging) by importing the project into an existing Eclipse workspace. However, programming the server code is beyond the scope of this chapter.

Client Software You Might Need

When working with Web Services, you may want some additional tools:

❑ **Eclipse with the Java development tools** (`www.eclipse.org/jdt`) — If you're running stand-alone Flex Builder or Flex Builder as a plug-in, you are already running Eclipse. However, to run and edit server-side Java code, you'll need to install the Java development tools, as well.

❑ **soapUI** (`www.soapui.org`) — This tool helps you test and consume the Web Services you build. It's quite handy for making sure that your Web Services work first outside the Flex platform, before trying to call them from inside the Flex platform. This is available as either a stand-alone program or an Eclipse plug-in.

❑ **Web Services tools** (`www.eclipse.org/webtools/ws`) — This is an Eclipse plug-in with support for creating and designing your WSDL contracts for contract-first development.

❑ **Groovy Plugin for Eclipse** (`http://groovy.codehaus.org/Eclipse+Plugin`) — This is an Eclipse plug-in that provides syntax highlighting, code completions, refactoring, and source code formatting for the Groovy language extensions.

The Grails Routes Web Service

If you've been hearing about Ruby on Rails and are a bit jealous of how simple it is to get up and running to develop your applications, but you're limited to supporting an existing Java infrastructure, Grails and Groovy are worth looking at. Grails is an MVC web development framework that emphasizes convention over configuration. By following certain conventions, you can provide automatic domain model classes to access data in relational database tables, or provide implied MVC coding conventions to your application.

Grails works with existing Java technologies like Spring and Hibernate, so if you're an existing Java developer experienced in these technologies, Grails provides wrapper APIs to quickly get you coding applications and enables you to configure your custom Java EE stack for the more complex needs of your enterprise.

Our sample `fittracker` Web Services application doesn't use any of the specific Grails MVC infrastructure necessary for typical web applications; however, it does take advantage of Grails Object Relational Mapping (GORM), which makes reading and writing domain objects to a database a breeze, as you'll see below in Listing 50-1. Plus, as you saw in step 6 above, it made installing XFire Web Service support a one-line, 10-second operation. Also, Grails comes with Groovy, so that's configured for you as well.

Grails Code Supporting the Web Service

Our sample application is going to be performing the same CRUD-based operations on route information as in the previous chapter: `createRoute`, `updateRoute`, `retrieveRoute`, `retrieveRoutes`, and `deleteRoute`. These operations will be available to any application that supports calling Web Services, including our sample Flex application, discussed later in this chapter.

With Grails, you start with a simple domain object written in Groovy and then define a service class and let Grails and XFire work their magic.

The Route.groovy Domain Class

The domain object for the route can be found in `Route.groovy`, and it doesn't look like your everyday Java class:

```
class Route   String name  String description  Float distance   Integer created_by
Date created  ate modified   static optionals = [ "created", "modified" ] }
```

The `Route` class defines some basic properties, including `name`, `description`, `distance`, and so forth, as well as an `optionals` static property, which is used when the `Route` is persisted to the database, informing GORM of the properties that don't require values. The `Route` class is also used to facilitate WSDL generation, where XFire automatically translates (with the help of AEGIS) the POGO (Plain Old Grails Object) into an appropriate WSDL definition that describes how the object will fly across the wire.

The following is the WSDL that's generated to describe the `Route` and that will be referenced in many of the different Web Service operations:

```
<xsd:complexType name="Route">
  <xsd:sequence>
    <xsd:element minOccurs="0" name="created" type="xsd:dateTime"/>
    <xsd:element minOccurs="0" name="created_by" nillable="true" type="xsd:int"/>
    <xsd:element minOccurs="0" name="description" nillable="true" type="xsd:string"/>
    <xsd:element minOccurs="0" name="distance" nillable="true" type="xsd:float"/>
    <xsd:element minOccurs="0" name="id" nillable="true" type="xsd:long"/>
    <xsd:element minOccurs="0" name="modified" type="xsd:dateTime"/>
    <xsd:element minOccurs="0" name="name" nillable="true" type="xsd:string"/>
  </xsd:sequence>
</xsd:complexType>
```

This basic schema definition will eventually be used by Flex's low-level `SOAPDecoder` class to translate the XML into ActionScript objects based on these properties (we'll talk about this later.)

RouteService.Groovy

The actual service methods are implemented in `RouteService.groovy`. There's one method for each SOAP operation that is being supported by the service. Using Java annotations (more specifically, annotations defined in JSR 181), you can configure a plain class to operate as a Web Service.

To define the `RouteService`, annotate a class with the `@WebService` annotations, passing in both the name and namespace of the Web Service:

```
@WebService(name = "RouteService", targetNamespace =
   "http://www.acme.com/2008/11/RouteService")
class RouteService {
 static expose=['xfire']
```

Next, in the `RouteService`, you need to start defining the actual operation that the service will expose. Listing 50-1 shows the `createRoute` function, which you will eventually expose as a SOAP operation to your Flex client.

Listing 50-1: The createRoute function Web Service Implementation

```
def Route createRoute(@WebParam(name="route")Route route) throws
  BusinessException {
   if (route.id != null && Route.exists(route.id)){
      throwBusinessExeption "It appears this route is already exists."
   }

   def r = new Route()
   r.name = route.name
   r.description = route.description
   r.distance = route.distance
   r.created_by = route.created_by
   r.created = new Date()
   r.modified = new Date()
   r.save()

   if (r.id == null){
      throwBusinessExeption("Route $route.name wasn't saved, try again.")
   }
   return r;
}
```

As you can see, this method takes in a parameter named `route`, which is an instance of the `Route.groovy` domain object defined previously. This `route` was passed into the `RouteService` as XML off the wire, and decoded into a Java object. Using some basic GORM (the `r.save` method), a new object is created and saved into the database.

There's more code for the rest of the `RouteService` implementation code that's included with the sample code for the chapter in the `/GrailsServer` directory.

Web Service Fault Handling

In the previous chapter, you used custom XML to define server-side business error conditions that you passed back to the client. With SOAP-based Web Services, there's already the concept of SOAP faults that both Flex and WSDL are aware of. SOAP faults are optional elements included with SOAP messages that can communicate to clients when something has gone wrong. And naturally our server-side platform supports sending errors back to the Flex client.

In listing 50-1, the method `createRoute` is defined as potentially throwing a `BusinessException`. And exceptions are raised if either a route is passed in that already has been persisted to the database, in which case the `createRoute` function should have been called, or when the new route failed to persist to the database.

When a `BusinessException` is raised from the server, it will be translated into a SOAP fault, passed across the wire using standard SOAP XML infrastructure, and decoded in the Flex client application as an `mx.rpc.SoapFault`. A custom fault in WSDL is defined as follows:

```
<wsdl:fault name="BusinessException" message="tns:BusinessException" />
```

Enabling Flex to Receive SOAP Faults

By default, Flex Web Services won't be able to receive SOAP faults because of existing limitations with current web browser technology and the Flash Player plug-in. The response's details with an HTTP status other than 200 aren't passed into the Flash Payer, and consequently the Flex applications. Traditionally, SOAP faults are sent from the server with an HTTP status of 500.

> *When connecting a Flex application to a remote Web Service, you might see some mysterious faults being raised in the fault handler of the Web Service. Upon inspecting the fault details of the* faultEvent, *if you're seeing values similar to the following, chances are that Flex isn't properly receiving the SOAP fault from the Web browser. In this case, you should modify the server to return Web Service responses with a status code of 200.*
>
> ```
> fault.code = 'Server.Error.Request'
> faultDetail = 'Error: [IOErrorEvent type = 'ioError…truncated for brevity
> fault.rootCause = "Error #2032: Stream Error…"type="warning"
> ```

To enable Flex applications to properly receive SOAP faults, do one of the following:

- ❏ Set useProxy to true on the WebService class, which will use an intermediary server that will translate the HTTP status of 500 into an HTTP status code of 200. Adobe's BlazeDS supports proxying Web Service requests.

- ❏ Change the SOAP responses on the server to return with an HTTP status of 200. This is what we do with the chapter sample application by creating a Servlet filter. See the enclosed ExceptionFilter.groovy and ExceptionHttpServletRepsonseWrapper.groovy for implementation details. Note that we've modified the web.xml deployment descriptor to assign the ExceptionFilter to the XFireServlet, which is responsible for the Web Service calls.

For additional details about the Java implementation of the RouteService Web Service implementation, browse through the sample code in the GrailsServer subdirectory for this chapter's sample code.

The Flex Sample Application

This chapter's sample code includes a Flex project that runs a sample application used to manage routes via the Routes Web Service that was created earlier. It's the same application as the previous chapter on HTTPService, except that the architecture has changed slightly on the client, separating out the service calls into their own file to help the application design. Also, we're using mx.rpc.soap.WebService instead of the HTTPService. The sample application performs all five of the operations that the Routes Web Service supports: getting a list of routes, and all CRUD operations for a given route.

The Flex application consists of three files:

❑ Chapter_50_Web_Services_with_Java.mxml — The main MXML file containing the main user interface of the application called

❑ RouteService.as — An ActionsScript file that manages all the conversation with the remote Routes Web Service implemented in Grails earlier

❑ RouteVO.as — The domain object used to communicate back and forth with the Web Service by taking advantage of Flex's SOAP-specific serialization between ActionScript and SOAP-based Web Services

The RouteService.as Service Class

As opposed to defining all the code in one MXML file, as was done in the previous chapter, here the RouteService.as class was created to manage all aspects of communicating with the remote server. In the future, if you want to change the Web Services that you communicate with, or even switch the protocol of communication, you need to modify only the RouteService class. Also, in Part X you'll learn about how Cairngorm manages the separation of services from the view code in a Flex application, so consider this a steppingstone to full-blown Cairngorm application.

As described in the following sections, the RouteService class consolidates all the remote service access using a lot of specific APIs, including SchemaTypeRegistry, IResponder, and AsyncToken.

Using IResponder

The mx.rpc.IResponder interface is used as a contract for communicating success or failure on asynchronous calls. Usually when you create a WebService component, you set the fault and result event handlers to your custom functions. However, you can implement the IResponder interface in your MXML component and then pass a reference to the interface around different layers of the Flex application and have the appropriate methods called when your service calls complete.

To do this, you first must implement the IResponder interface in MXML. Do this in the main Application tag, as follows:

```
<mx:Application xmlns:mx="http://www.adobe.com/2006/mxml" layout="vertical"
  paddingBottom="0" paddingLeft="0" paddingRight="0" paddingTop="0"
  pageTitle="WebService Route Demo"
  implements="mx.rpc.IResponder">
```

Next, implement the interface by creating `fault` and `result` methods as defined by the `IResponder` interface. After adding the `implements` directive to the `Application` class, you must implement the `fault` and `result` methods of the interface; otherwise, the compiler will complain.

The following `result` implementation handles all the successful calls to the Web Service:

```
public function result(data:Object):void
{
  var event:ResultEvent = data as ResultEvent;

  // Turn off custom wait, if it was on.
  customWait = false;

  switch(event.token.typeOfRequest)
  {
    case RouteService.DELETE_ROUTE_REQUEST:
      // event.result is of type Route
      retrieveRoutes();
      Alert.show("Route Deleted: " + event.result.id)
      break;
    case RouteService.RETRIEVE_ROUTES_REQUEST:
      routeData = event.result as ArrayCollection;
      break;
    case RouteService.UPDATE_ROUTE_REQUEST:
      retrieveRoutes();
      Alert.show("Route Updated: " + event.result.name)
      clearForm();
      break;
    case RouteService.CREATE_ROUTE_REQUEST:
      retrieveRoutes();
      Alert.show("Route Created: " + event.result.name)
      clearForm();
      break;
    case RouteService.RETRIEVE_ROUTE_REQUEST:
      var route:RouteVO = event.result as RouteVO;
      Alert.show("Retrieved route: " + route.name);
      currentRouteId = route.id;
      txtName.text = route.name;
      txtDescription.text = route.description;
      txtDistance.text = route.distance.toString();
      break;
  }
}
```

The following fault handler handles all the failures of the service layer, including the specialized SOAP faults thrown from the Web Service, as well as standard HTTP communication errors, such as those produced when the remote service can't be reached:

```
public function fault(info:Object):void
{
  var event:FaultEvent = info as FaultEvent;

  customWait = false;

  // event.fault can be a SOAPFault
```

```
    if (event.fault.faultCode == "Server.Error.Request") {
      Alert.show("Error connecting to server, try again later.");
    } else if (event.fault.faultString == "BusinessException"){
      var bf:XML = new XML(event.fault.faultDetail);
      Alert.show(bf.text(), "Oops, an error occurred....");
    } else {
      Alert.show(event.fault.faultString, "Unplanned Service Error..." );
    }
  }
```

The client will make a request to the service layer (`RouteService.as`), passing in a reference to its implemented `IResponder` interface, which in this case is the main MXML file. The service layer will then use the reference to communicate success or fail back to the UI layer.

For example, the call to get a route looks like this:

```
private function retrieveRoute(routeId:Number):void
{
  startWaiting(StringUtil.substitute("Retrieving Route {0}...", routeId) );
  var rs:RouteService = new RouteService(this);
  rs.retrieveRoute(routeId);
}
```

The `startWaiting` method displays a custom wait message while the remote service is being called. The important thing to notice here is how `this` is being passed into the constructor of `RouteService`. Since `RouteService` is expecting the interface `IResponder`, it's casting the entire MXML component so that it'll have access to only the `IResponder` implementation, which it'll use when making the actual service call.

The service call to retrieve a route is implemented in the `RouteService.as` class, as follows:

```
public function retrieveRoute(routeId:Number):void{
  var ws:WebService = getWebService();
  var token:AsyncToken = ws.retrieveRoute(routeId);
  token.addResponder(_responder);
  token.typeOfRequest = RouteService.GET_ROUTE_REQUEST;
}
```

First, an instance of `WebService` is created. There's a helper function called `getWebService` that returns a cached instance of a `WebService` or a created one if this is the first time the `WebService` is being called. Next, you call the Web Service operation, `getRoute` (which was defined on the Java service layer and communicated to the client through WSDL).

Optionally, when calling `WebService` operations, a handle to an `AsyncToken` is returned. An `AsyncToken` is created and associated with individual calls to the remote server, and can be used to maintain state information about a particular Web Service call. `AsyncToken` also has a very handy `addResponder` method that takes an `IResponder` as a parameter. And guess what? That reference to `IResponder` that you passed into the constructor of the `RouteService` object is now passed into the `AsyncToken` where, upon completion of the service call, the appropriate `fault` or `result` `method` of the `IResponder` will be called, which in this case is implemented on the main view of the application.

Finally, to the token, you set the `typeOfRequest` to a static variable on the `RouteService`. This way, when the result handler is called, the `typeOfRequest` can be inspected and the appropriate action in the view of the application can take place, whether it's populating a `DataGrid` with a list of routes or displaying an Alert box when a route has been deleted.

This completes how the `IResponder` interface facilitates separation and communication between the layers of a Flex application.

Working with Custom Server-Side Errors

Unlike working with custom `HTTPService`, where it's up to the server-side developer to define how errors in business logic are returned to the client (usually via custom XML), `WebService` depends on SOAP faults. On the server Grails application, a Java-based, custom `BusinessException` fault will be raised and propagated down to the client as a Flex `SOAPFault`.

Whenever a Groovy/Java exception is raised from the server, using a regular Java exception syntax:

```
throw new BusinessException("BusinessException", "This is an error!")
```

it will be translated into a Web Service fault response:

```
<soap:Envelope xmlns:soap="http://schemas.xmlsoap.org/soap/envelope/"
  xmlns:xsd="http://www.w3.org/2001/XMLSchema"
  xmlns:xsi="http://www.w3.org/2001/XMLSchema-instance">
  <soap:Body>
    <soap:Fault>
      <faultcode>soap:Server</faultcode>
      <faultstring>BusinessException</faultstring>
      <detail>
        <BusinessException>This is an error.</BusinessException>
      </detail>
    </soap:Fault>
  </soap:Body>
</soap:Envelope>
```

which will then call into the fault handler of the Flex application and be handled according to the appropriate condition:

```
// Truncated code from the fault handler
else if (event.fault.faultString == "BusinessException"){
    var faultDeail:XML = new XML(event.fault.faultDetail);
    Alert.show(faultDeail.text(), "Oops, an error occurred....");
```

The fault handler of the main application tests to see if a custom `faultString` returned from the server is equal to a `BusinessException`. When it is, extract the specific error message from the `faultDetail` using e4X XML processing, and then display the error with an Alert box to the user of the application.

Serialization with SchemaTypeManager

When working with SOAP-based Web Services, Flex supports automatically deserializing XML off the wire into actual ActionScript objects. Objects can be translated into either generic objects or specific

ActionScript objects that you define. This example uses the `Route.VO` object for both inbound and outbound communication with the Web Service.

When calling an operation on a remote service, pass in an instantiated `RouteVO` object, just as the `createRoute` function does:

```
public function createRoute(route:RouteVO):void
{
    var ws:WebService = getWebService();
    Operation(ws.createRoute).encoder.strictNillability = true;
    var token:AsyncToken = ws.createRoute(route);
    token.addResponder(_responder);
    token.typeOfRequest = RouteService.CREATE_ROUTE_REQUEST;
}
```

A route that was created in the UI and set to values of `TextInput` controls is passed into `createRoute`. The `WebService` is created, and the `SoapEncoder`'s `strictNillability` is set to `true` (more about this in a minute), and then the call to the Web Service operation `createRoute` is made, passing in the ActionScript `RouteVO`.

The `RouteVO` is translated into the XML schema type, Route, which is defined in the Routes Web Service WSDL. Flex manages this with the help of the `SchemaTypeRegistry`, which maps ActionScript object to definitions in the WSDL. For example, in the `RouteService.as` file, this mapping is done every time a `RouteService` is created for an operation to be called:

```
SchemaTypeRegistry.getInstance().registerClass(new QName("http://DefaultNamespace",
"Route"), RouteVO);
```

The `SchemaTypeRegistry` is a singleton that you configure for the application, and it is used by Flex's `SoapEncoder` and `SoapDecoder` when calling operations and when receiving responses from the server. In this case, you have to map the schema type (`Route`) to the ActionScript type, `RouteVO`. Pay special attention to the `QName`; since the Routes Web Service WSDL defines a `targetNamespace` of `http://DefaultNamespace`, you must respect that here; otherwise, the `SchemaTypeRegistry` will neither find the definition of `Route`, nor be able to translate it. (This target namespace — `http://DefaultNamespace` — is a poor choice. Never do this in a production application. All the WSDL operations, however, are declared with an appropriate namespace.)

When results are returned from the Web Service and processed in the `result` handler, you can access them as ActionScript objects, for example, when a route is retrieved from the server from a call to `getRoute`:

```
var route:RouteVO = event.result as RouteVO;
```

Now, if you didn't tell the `SchemaTypeRegistry` about the mapping between `RouteVO` and the XML schema Route, don't worry, you'd still get results. The route would just be returned from the server and deserialized into Flex as a generic `ObjectProxy`, making it available to your ActionScript code in a manner similar to that of a regular ActionScript `object`:

```
var route:RouteVO = event.result as ObjectProxy;
```

Mapping ActionScript types to XML Schema types

`SoapEncoder` and `SoapDecoder` facilitate conversion between ActionScript and XML schema types. Although you might not need to know how things are mapped for basic services, the more complex the service, the more familiar you might want to be with how ActionScript objects are converted to and from SOAP messages. The Adobe documentation outlines all the supported mappings between ActionScript and WSDL, but the following table lists a few of the more commonly used mappings.

XML Schema Type	Decoding XML to ActionScript	Encoding Actionscript to XML
xsd:anyType or xsd:anySimpleType	String/Boolean/Number	Object
xsd:Boolean	Boolean	Boolean/Number/Object
xsd:byte		Number/String
xsd:date or xsd:dateTime	Date	Date/Number/String
xsd:decimal, xsd:double, xsd:float, xsd:int, xsd:integer, xsd:long, xsd:unsignedLong, xsd:short	Number	Number/String
xsd:string	String	Object

Notice than when encoding ActionScript into XML, most values can be converted into `Strings`. However, the inverse isn't necessarily true when decoding from XML into ActionScript, as is the case with most numeric values.

Although WSDL 1.1 is supported, not every attribute is — for example, `simpleType::restrictions`. Be sure to read the Adobe Flex 3 documentation on Web Services, which you can find by searching for "Web Services" at: http://livedocs.adobe.com/flex/3/html/index.html. There's a comprehensive list of what isn't supported, as well as a complete table of ActionScript to WSDL serialization mapping.

Strict Nillability

In the preceding Web Service operation, the `strictNillability` property is to `true`. With this property set, the `SOAPEncoder` will not include XML elements for properties that aren't set on the `RouteVO`. For example, in the WSDL both `created` and `modified` aren't defined as nillable, meaning that they are expected in the SOAP request:

```
<xsd:element minOccurs="0" name="created" type="xsd:dateTime"/>
<xsd:element minOccurs="0" name="created_by" nillable="true" type="xsd:int"/>
<xsd:element minOccurs="0" name="modified" type="xsd:dateTime"/>
… more properties are defined
```

Because the `RouteVO` is defined as having these properties (mostly for the sake when reading values passed back from the Web Service), these properties will be added when the `SOAPEncoder` persists the `RouteVO` into the SOAP format for transport over the wire. The trouble is that the values in this particular instance of RouteVO are null, because the server-side implementation is going to create a modified value, and the created value isn't being passed back up because it's not changed. Since the SOAPEncoder is using the WSDL definition received from the server as a template on how it should encode the object, it's going to complain when trying to encode the RouteVO into XML for passing up passing null values for required fields.

To get around this, set the strictNillability property to true for the operation:

```
Operation(ws.createRoute).encoder.strictNillability = true;
```

Now when encoding the RouteVO, the null properties will be left off the SOAP request (no modified or created elements will be created based on the RouteVO's values), and since the WSDL defines the minOccurs as 0, it's perfectly valid. Here's what the Web Service requests for updateRoute looks like when passing over the network:

```
<SOAP-ENV:Envelope xmlns:SOAP-ENV="http://schemas.xmlsoap.org/soap/envelope/"
  xmlns:xsd="http://www.w3.org/2001/XMLSchema"
  xmlns:xsi="http://www.w3.org/2001/XMLSchema-instance">
  <SOAP-ENV:Body>
    <tns:updateRoute xmlns:tns="http://www.acme.com/2008/11/RouteService">
      <tns:route>
        <tns:created_by>2</tns:created_by>
        <tns:description>44444</tns:description>
        <tns:distance>25</tns:distance>
        <tns:id>2</tns:id>
        <tns:name>Updated Route Name</tns:name>
      </tns:route>
    </tns:updateRoute>
  </SOAP-ENV:Body>
</SOAP-ENV:Envelope>
```

With the encoder.strictNillability property, you can control how your objects are encoded and passed up to the Web Service.

Calling Web Services from Other Servers

The Flash Player has built-in security protection that will keep you from directly calling Web Services from domains other than the domain that served up the Flex application. To get around this, either you create a crossdomain.xml file and place it in the root of the remote server or you use a proxy server, as explained previously when working with HTTP status codes.

The easiest thing, although it's not very controlled, is to create a crossdomain.xml file at the root of the domain that allows total access to any remote Flash/Flex application:

```
<?xml version="1.0"?>
<!DOCTYPE cross-domain-policy SYSTEM "http://www.macromedia.com/xml/dtds/
  cross-domain-policy.dtd">
<cross-domain-policy>
    <allow-access-from domain="*" />
</cross-domain-policy>
```

However, if you want a little more control, you can open only Web Services to be delivered to specific domains by limiting which HTTP headers have access through a `crossdomain.xml` file:

```
<?xml version="1.0"?>
<!DOCTYPE cross-domain-policy SYSTEM "http://www.macromedia.com/xml/dtds/
    cross-domain-policy.dtd">
<cross-domain-policy>
    <allow-access-from domain="*" />
    <allow-http-request-headers-from domain="*" headers="SOAPAction"/>
</cross-domain-policy>
```

Notice that the preceding filters allowed requests based on headers containing `SOAPAction`. Both of the preceding sample `crossdomain.xml` files are allowing any domain access, but you can just as easily limit which domains delivering your Flex applications are allowed access by setting the `allow-access-from` element's `domain` attribute:

```
<allow-access-from domain="www.alloweddomain.com" />
```

Or, if you want to allow any subdomain for a domain, such as `www.alloweddomain.com` and `blog.alloweddomain.com`, then use a wildcard:

```
<allow-access-from domain="*.alloweddomain.com" />
```

Summary

This chapter built on the basics of RPC communication, working with SOAP-based Web Services delivered via the Java platform. Be sure to explore the sample code, as there's a lot of code to help facilitate creating your own CRUD-based Web Service consumption for your own Flex applications.

The key to working with Web Services in Flex is to develop and test the server-side independently with tools like soapUI, and then integrate the Web Service into your Flex application.

Feel free to mix and match your favorite RPC APIs with the ways you develop your server applications. The sample code from this chapter isn't limited to being used only as a `WebService`. A simple conversion would make it work with an `HTTPService` or `RemoteObject`, too.

Coming up in Chapter 51, "Web Services with .NET and Flex," we'll create a similar Fit Tracker application that connects to a backend written in .NET, using Web Services for its RPC strategy.

Web Services with .NET and Flex

This chapter explores working with Flex RPC services, focusing on using Flex's `WebService` class to connect to a SOAP-based Web Service written with the .NET Framework. Many existing enterprises with existing .NET infrastructure can still benefit from integrating a Flex UI with their existing Web Services.

Building on the previous chapter's Java Web Service sample, we're going to continue focusing on typed Web Services, using Flex's built-in Import Web Service (WSDL) tool that will generate all the code assets necessary to communicate with a properly exposed third-party Web Service. The Import Web Service (WSDL) tool takes only moments to fetch the WSDL and parse it into classes, making accessing typed data a breeze. It even generates typed value objects so that you get the full benefit of Flex Builder's code completion.

Additionally, any of the techniques of accessing remote data using `HTTPService` or hand coded using `WebService` are still valid for .NET. With the new .NET 3.5 platform and ADO.NET Data Services or WCF (Windows Communication Foundation), it's just as easy to build a RESTful Web Service accessible from Flex via the `HTTPService` as it is to formally build Web Services. Flex gives you a way to get at your existing Web Services, no matter how they were architected, using your preferred RPC library: `HTTPService`, `WebService`, or `RemoteObject`.

Introduction to the Routes Web Service

Flex supports Web Services written to the WSDL 1.1 (Web Services Description Language) through the `mx.rpc.soap.WebService` library — the same as in the previous chapter on Web Services. Microsoft's newer Web Services support more recent versions of the spec, so be careful when working with such Web Services. Additionally, when working with Microsoft Web Services, you can choose to expose the service as a 1.1-compatible or newer flavor.

You can design Web Services either by creating the WSDL interface first (known as *contract-first development*) and then filling in the implementation to meet the contract or by developing .NET code first, and then applying the appropriate method attributes (such as [WebMethod]) to expose your objects as services — this is known as code-first development. For the best platform-independent WSDL definitions, it's best to perform the contract-first development. That way Microsoft's own tools don't build the WSDL for you, optimized for the .NET environment.

This chapter's sample takes the code-first approach to exposing Web Services. We've taken the WSDL from the previous Java Web Service chapter and, using Microsoft's wsdl.exe tool, generated the appropriate service definitions in code. The command line is:

```
Wsdl.exe /serviceInterface /:oIRouteService.cs routeService.wsdl
```

This generated a C# code service interface asset that we then implemented in our traditional ASP.NET Web Service that uses an ASMX file. If you want to use the new WCF method of creating and exposing Web Services, use the svcutil.exe (which comes with Visual Studio) to generate the appropriate service stub files from an existing WSDL file.

Chapter 46, "Introduction to RPC Services," taught the basics of working with Web Services and Flex, as well a very basic introduction to WSDL. If you haven't read that chapter, it's suggested that you do so now. After you've set up the server-side code for this chapter, you'll be able to view the complete WSDL of the RouteService Web Service and begin managing routes.

Setting Up the Server and Development Environment

Let's get started by installing the required software for working with a .NET implementation. Caution, this is geared mostly toward Window's programmers, but those of you using OS X can try installing these tools into a virtualized runtime environment like Parallels or Boot Camp.

Server Software Requirements

The server stack for the Routes Web Service is implemented on Microsoft's .NET 3.5 platform to take advantage of the newer ORM (Object Relational Mapping) services called ADO.NET Entity Framework. This example uses the same MySQL database as the prior two chapters' samples, and then runs the project from within Visual Studio 2008 using the built-in web server; thus, there's no need for IIS to be installed on your machine. The server code was written in C# with the older-style ASMX ASP.NET Web Service infrastructure.

Configuring Visual Studio and MySQL

It's assumed that you have experience working with .NET, as this isn't intended as an introduction to the many concepts we'll be glancing at in passing, and that you'll understand these basic setup instructions.

1. Download and install Visual Studio 2008 with Service Pack 1 from www.microsoft.com, if you don't already own a copy. We've used the Professional version here, but the code samples should work with the Visual Studio Express Edition. By installing Visual Studio 2008, you'll get the

required .NET 3.5 Framework on which this sample depends. Also, if you're hardcore, you can probably get the samples to work from the command line with just the SDK.

2. Install a MySQL Database adapter so that .NET can communicate with the MySQL database. Download a demo of the MySQL Database Connector 5.2.5, or newer from `www.devart.com/dotconnect/mysql/download.html`. While there's a database adapter available from MySQL directly, it neither supports some of the new .NET conventions nor the new ADO.NET Entity Framework, which makes object persistence a breeze in this sample.

3. Configure the MySQL database, if you haven't already in one of the prior chapters. Install MySQL and create a new database called `fittracker`. Then run the `schema.sql` and `data.sql` scripts to create the database table and some sample data.

   If you only have SQL Server, you can probably run the MySQL scripts there to avoid setting up an additional database, which would keep you from having to download an additional data provider listed in step 2. Our scripts were written for MySQL, though, and haven't been tested on SQL Server.

4. Install a Subversion client for Visual Studio 2008, or just use your favorite client to get the code for this project, which is in the `/DotNetServer` subfolder for this chapter's sample code. It includes a Visual Studio solution file to make it really easy to work on the server code. We suggest using the AnkhSVN plug-in with Visual Studio 2008, found at `http://ankhsvn.open.collab.net`.

That should be it. Visual Studio 2008 Professional comes with all the appropriate dependencies and technologies to run the service with the exception of the MySQL database adapter. You're now ready to run the server and start looking at the Flex client. Run the sample application and then make sure the WSDL is available at `http://localhost:1221/RouteService.asmx?WSDL`. (Note that the port number could be different on your machine.) When the service starts, you should see the following `RouteService` landing page in a web browser, as shown in Figure 51-1.

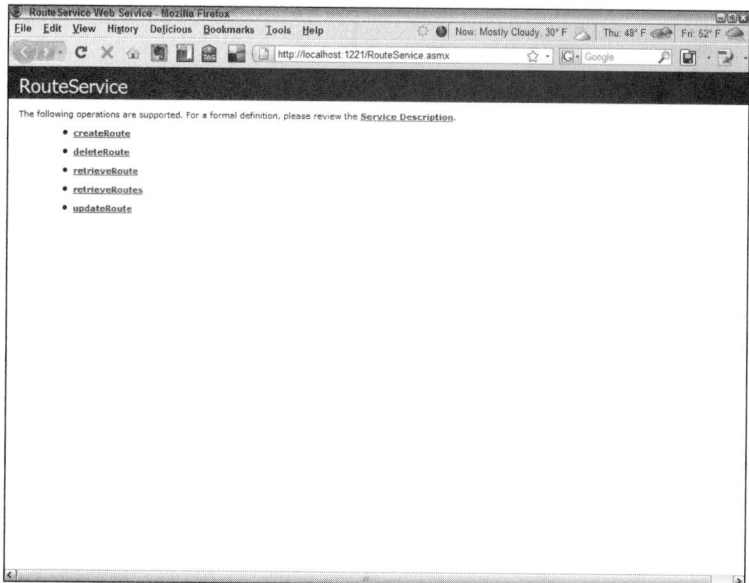

Figure 51-1

Client Software You Might Need

Even programming in the .NET work, we've found soapUI to be indispensable for diagnosing platform-independent Web Service issues, as well as for providing great support for testing them. And no matter which platform was used to develop the service, soapUI facilitates watching the messages to and from the server. It is available from `www.soapui.org` as either a standalone program or an Eclipse plug-in.

The .NET Routes Web Service

The.NET implementation of the Routes Web Service uses ASP.NET Web Services (the old style, using ASMX files) and the new ADO.NET Entity Framework (available as of .NET 3.5 SP1) to facilitate in persisting data to the database.

.NET Code Supporting the Web Service

Our sample application is going to be performing the same CRUD-based operations on route information as the previous chapter: `createRoute`, `updateRoute`, `retrieveRoute`, `retrieveRoutes`, and `deleteRoute`. These operations will be available to any application that supports calling Web Services, including the sample Flex application discussed next.

The IRouteService Interface

The `IRouteService` interface defines the service contract. It's an interface littered with attributes on how the defined methods should be exposed as a Web Service. For example, the beginning of the interface definition uses the `WebServiceBindingAttribute` to define the name and namespace of the Web Service:

```
[WebServiceBindingAttribute(Name = "routeHttpBinding",
             Namespace = "http://www.acme.com/2008/11/RouteService")]
public interface IRouteService
{
```

And then the first service, `retrieveRoutes`, has the following `WebMethodAttribute` and `SoapDocumentMethodAttributes` defined:

```
[WebMethodAttribute()]
[SoapDocumentMethodAttribute("retrieveRoutes",
   RequestNamespace = "http://www.acme.com/2008/11/RouteService",
   ResponseNamespace = "http://www.acme.com/2008/11/RouteService",
   Use = System.Web.Services.Description.SoapBindingUse.Literal,
   ParameterStyle =
       System.Web.Services.Protocols.SoapParameterStyle.Wrapped)]
   [return: System.Xml.Serialization.XmlArrayAttribute("out", IsNullable = true)]
   Route[] retrieveRoutes();
```

Keep in mind that the IRouteService *was automatically generated by the* wsdl.exe tool *based on the WSDL created in the previous chapter.*

These attributes define data that is used when .NET generates the WSDL file for the Routes Web Service. They define the request and response namespaces, the type of SOAP binding to use, and the name of the return parameters that the service will respond with, which is out here, but could probably be named something more informational, like routesFound or allRoutes — but that's a WSDL design issue to be fixed.

Route DTO versus Route persistence

Also defined in the IRouteService interface file is an actual Route class that should be thought of solely as a Data Transfer Object (DTO). It's only purpose is to move data across the wire through the Web Service. Also in the project is a DataLayer.Route, which has been created to facilitate writing data to the database as a form of ORM. ADO.NET Entity Framework built for us the DataLayer.Route automatically, based on existing database schema.

The DataLayer.Route inherits from an EntityObject, and as such, if you let .NET create an schema type based on it, there'd be extra layers of nodes in the schema, polluting a clean object design, and putting the mark of the .NET Framework on your service contract — which should be written independent of the platform that's exposing it.

The regular Route class is just a POCO (plain old CLR object) that has attributes defined on it for how it should be serialized to XML.

These two Route objects aren't compatible with each other. One Route couldn't be used with .NET attributes to facilitate both passing over the wire , as well as saving into the database. For example, an ID might be required on the DataLayer.Route but might be optional when crossing the wire from the Web Service. Both Route objects were auto-generated for us, so it's not really a big deal to manage.

We have to convert between the two types of routes in the service layer when writing the responses from the Web Service. When building production-quality Web Services, you might want to use some other forms of object persistence, such as NHibernate, for managing all this. But for now, we're keeping the contracts of the Web Services (including how objects are sent across the wire) separate from how data is being written to the database).

Now, let's look at the actual service implementation.

RouteService.asmx

The actual service methods are implemented in RouteService.asmx.cs. There's one for each of the SOAP operations that are being supported by the service (createRoute, updateRoute, deleteRoute, etc.). RouteService implements the IRouteService interface, filling in the implementation for how all the service definitions should work. Let's look at the implementation of createRoute, which is as follows:

```
Route IRouteService.createRoute(Route route)
{
    fittrackerEntities fit = new fittrackerEntities();
```

```
            DataLayer.Route newRoute = new DataLayer.Route();
            newRoute.name = route.name;
            newRoute.description = route.description;

            if(route.distanceSpecified)
                newRoute.distance = (float)route.distance;
            else
                newRoute.distance = 0;

            newRoute.modified = DateTime.Now;
            newRoute.created = DateTime.Now;
            newRoute.created_by = 2; // Just hard-code for demo

            fit.AddToRouteSet(newRoute);
            fit.SaveChanges();
            return toRouteDto(newRoute);
    }
```

The `createRoute` implementation takes a `Route` DTO object that was passed in off the wire. A new `DataLayer.Route` is then created, which facilitates writing data to the database. Then we bind values that were passed in onto the `DataLayer` route, optionally checking to see if values were set, as is the case with the `distance` property.

Once the `DataLayer.Route` has been populated, we add it to the `RouteSet` of the `fittrackerEntities` object, which is the core of the ADO.NET Entity Framework, and manages the persistence with the database. A call to `fit.SaveChanges()` writes the changes back into the database.

Finally, we convert the `newRoute` object, which now has an `id` set after being saved to the database, into a `Route` DTO for transferring to the client via a Web Service response.

Web Service Fault Handling

To support server-side validation, the Web Services communicate back to the client errors that the client can and should handle. This communication is handled with SOAP faults.

A helper function in our service layer called `BuildSoapException` will modify the default `SoapException` that .NET passes down to the client. You call it whenever you want to communicate an error to the client that should be recoverable, such as when attempting to update or delete a route that doesn't exist, from the service:

```
    throw BuildSoapException("Route doesn't exist for updating");
```

`BuildSoapException` creates a new `SoapException` and modifies the `details` element of it that you'll specifically read on the Flex client side to display an error condition.

Enabling Flex to Receive ASP.NET SoapExceptions

By default, Flex Web Services won't be able to receive SOAP faults because of existing limitations with current web browser technology and the Flash Player plug-in, the response details with an HTTP status other than 200 isn't passed into the Flash Player, or consequently the Flex applications. Traditionally, SOAP faults are sent from the server with an HTTP status of 500.

When connecting a Flex application to a remote Web Service, you might see some mysterious faults being raised in the fault handler of the Web Service. If, upon inspecting the details of the `faultEvent`, *you see values similar to:*

```
fault.code = 'Server.Error.Request'
faultDetail = 'Error: [IOErrorEvent type = 'ioError...truncated for brevity
```

and

```
fault.rootCause = "Error #2032: Stream Error...
```

then chances are that Flex isn't properly receiving the SOAP fault from the web browser. Modify the server to return Web Service responses with a status code of 200.

To enable Flex applications to properly receive a `SOAPFault`, do one of the following:

❏ Set `useProxy` to true on the `WebService` class, which will use an intermediary server that will translate the HTTP status of 500 into the HTTP status code 200. Adobe's BlazeDS supports proxying Web Service requests.

❏ Change the SOAP responses on the server to return with an HTTP status of 200. This is what we do with the chapter sample application by creating a modifying the SOAP response as it leaves the server.

Changing the HTTP status as the response leaves the server is really easy in ASP.NET Web Services. Just create a `global.asax` file and implement the `Application_EndRequest` event, as follows:

```
protected void Application_EndRequest(object sender, EventArgs e)
{
    if (this.Context.Response.StatusCode == 500)
    {
        this.Context.Response.StatusCode = 200;
    }
}
```

Now when your ASP.NET Web Service throws a `SoapException`, the Flex application will be able to read the details as a `SOAPFault`.

The Flex Sample Application

The chapter sample code includes a Flex project that runs a sample application used to manage routes via the Routes Web Service that was created earlier. It's the same application as in the previous two chapters, except that we're using Flex's Import Web Service (WSDL) tool to create the service-level code. The sample application performs all five of the operations that the Routes Web Service supports: getting a list of routes, and all CRUD operations for a given route.

The Flex application consists of two parts: the main MXML file (`Chapter_51_Flex_Client.mxml`), which contains the main user interface of the application, and a group of auto-generated files created by the Import Web Service tool, which you'll learn about in the following section.

The Import Web Service (WSDL) Tool

Flex Builder's Import Web Service tool makes it ridiculously easy to access the remote Web Service. By pointing the Import Web Service tool at a remote service that has been properly set up with a crossdomain.xml file (see Chapter 50 on setting up the crossdomain.xml file), client-side ActionScript code will be automatically generated, creating a proxy to access the remote operations, including typed objects. The ActionScript code generated will include specific events, typed objects, and a service object that can be accessed via MXML or pure ActionScript that manages the whole show.

Begin by starting MySQL and the Visual Studio 2008 server project (Chapter_51_RouteService.sln) included in the chapter's source code in the /DotNetServer subdirectory. It's important that the server is running or that the remote WSDL file is available while Flex's Import Web Service Wizard is running because it needs the WSDL contract in order to know how to generate the ActionScript code.

1. Open Flex Builder, create a new project, and then navigate to the Data menu and choose the Import Web Service (WSDL) option. This will bring the screen shown in Figure 51-2.

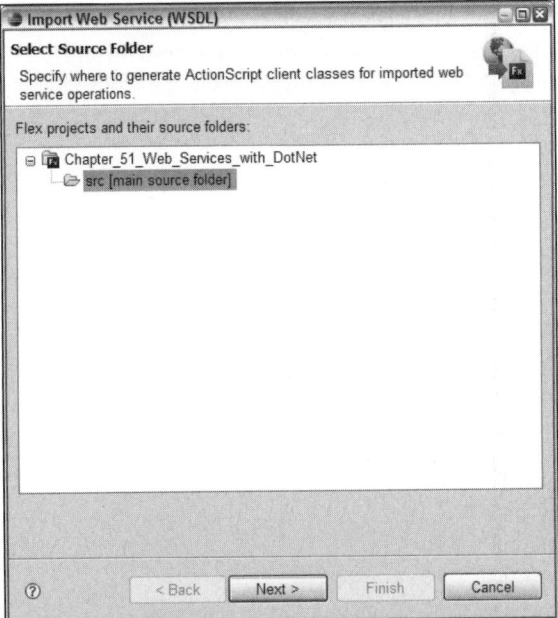

Figure 51-2

2. Select the root folder to generate code in. Step 1 of the wizard establishes the base folder that will hold all the generated ActionScript code. Select the main default src folder of your Flex application; most of the time this will be the only option. Note that the files won't actually be created at this level. In a future step, you'll choose a package name, and the appropriate folders will be created using this root folder as the base. Click Next to continue the wizard.

3. Select the remote WSDL file to use as the template for the service. Step 2 of the wizard requests the URL of the WSDL file. This can be a local or remote machine. Additionally, you can select the option to use a proxy service or to acquire the WSDL directly from the source.

Accessing a Web Service on a remote server that doesn't have a `crossdomain.xml` file (more about this below) set up can only be done through a proxy service. Additionally, if the service doesn't output SOAP faults with an HTTP status of 200, a proxy service will be needed. Otherwise, stay with the option to access the WSDL directly from the client.

4. Click Next to go to the final step (see Figure 51-3).

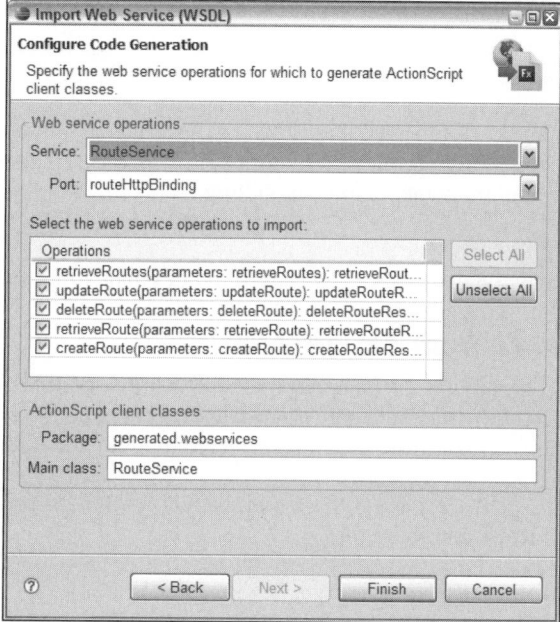

Figure 51-3

5. The final step allows you to choose the service, the port, and which operations you want to import from it. Chances are, you'll want them all, but there might be instances where you only need a couple of the operations, and want to keep your compiled Flex application as small as possible. In this case, only use what you need.

6. Next, fill in the package name. In Figure 51-3, we've added `com.acme.webservices`. When the wizard runs and generates the code, it'll put the ActionScript in the proper directory. In the case of this project, all the code will be generated in the `src/com/acme/webservices` folder.

7. Fill in the class name as `RouteService`. This will be the main Web Service class that is created and all operations are called through.

8. Click Next. Wait a minute, and if all goes well, ActionScript files representing each operation, the schema objects, and the Web Service will be created and ready to be accessed with only a few lines of code.

> Warning, the WSDL Import tool is sometimes difficult to work with. There are some services that it can't digest into a usable service for you. Others, it generates the code for just fine, but then errors occur during runtime. Also, depending how your Flex application architecture is set up (for example, if you're using a framework like Cairngorm) it might be difficult to integrate the generated code. For many projects, however, the WSDL Import tool will make your life easy.

Accessing the Web Service

The WSDL Import tool created a bunch of ActionScript code in the `src/com/acme/webservices` directory that can now be used by both MXML or ActionScript code. Open the main `RouteService.as` file to read how to use the service.

To use the generation Web Service proxy class, `RouteService.mxml`, instantiate an object of it, bind the result events for the particular operation you'll be calling, optionally bind the fault event, and then finally call the operation.

And now let's look at how the `RouteService` is used in our client application.

Using the Web Service from ActionScript

Calling the Web Service from your ActionScript methods is fairly straightforward, especially since you have typed events to bind to, instead of contextual string tags attached to the `AsyncToken`, as you did in both previous chapters to determine which Web Service operation had been called.

In the `Chapter_51_Flex_Client.mxml file`, add the following `retrieveRoutes()` function to use the generated Web Service ActionScript files:

```
private function retrieveRoutes():void
{
   startWaiting("Fetching Routes…");
   var myService:RouteService= new RouteService();
   myService.addretrieveRoutesEventListener(retrieveRoutesResult);
   myService.addRouteServiceFaultEventListener(fault);
   myService.retrieveRoutes();
}
```

The sample code starts with setting the state in the client in a waiting mode, so that the user can't click on other operations while the `retrieveRoutes()` operation is running. Next, create the `RouteService` class, which was generated by the Web Service Import tool.

Then, taking advantage that the wizard-created typed events, bind to the `addretrieveRoutesEvent Listener` a local function that will be called upon completion of the service call. For every operation that you selected to have code generated from, there will be an `addXYZEventListener` function (replace *XYZ* with the appropriate Web Service method name) created that you use to bind to your local implementation.

Don't forget to bind to your default fault handler, just as in the previous two chapters. Although each of our operations will have its own `result` handler, they can easily all share the `fault`, since it'll mostly display unexpected server messages.

All the Web Service operations will have a similar client helper function for calling the service.

Using the Web Service from MXML

Now suppose that you want to be really quick and dirty and just work the auto-generated Web Service classes directly in MXML markup. Declare the `RouteService` and set up the `retrieveRoute` operation by entering the following MXML:

```
<srv:RouteService id="wsRouteService"  fault="fault(event)"
    RetrieveRoute_result="retrieveRouteResult(event)">
  <srv:retrieveRoute_request_var>
    <srv:RetrieveRoute_request>
      <srv:routeId>{parseInt(textRouteId.text)}</srv:routeId>
    </srv:RetrieveRoute_request>
  </srv:retrieveRoute_request_var>
</srv:RouteService>
```

Using MXML markup, you create a `RouteService` object with an `id` of `wsRouteService`. Then you bind both the `fault` and `RetrieveRoute_result` event to local handlers. Then you bind the actual operation, binding the actual values that need to be passed into the operation. In this case, you're setting the `routeId` to the `textRouteId.text` input field via regular Flex data binding.

Finally, to call the `retrieveRoute` operation, call the `retrieveRoute_send()` method on the service:

```
<mx:Button label="Fetch Route" click="wsRouteService.retrieveRoute_send()" />
```

That's how you use the generated Web Service stub from MXML. You'll notice a couple things, though. Typing the MXML didn't really save much typing of code from the ActionScript way. Also, the fancy wait message isn't being displayed. To achieve that, you'd have to implement more data binding for the message string, and the code that you put in the click event would be more complicated. The ActionScript style will be cleaner and simpler to maintain in the long run, so you'll probably want to stick with that.

Working with Custom Server-Side Errors

Just as in the previous chapter on Java Web Services, the .NET version also uses SOAP faults to communicate client-side validation errors caught on the server back into the client. The .NET version will send SOAP faults when attempting to update routes, or delete nonexistent routes.

To see this in action, in the sample Flex application, click the button labeled Update nonexistent route to send a request to the server to update a route with ID of 500. The server will receive the route, figure out that it doesn't exist for updating, and then throw a `SoapException` (.NET class for base SOAP faults), sending a `SOAPFault` back to the Flex client.

The Flex client will then raise the `fault` handler to handle the `SOAPFault`, as follows:

```
//  Truncated code from the fault handler
..else if (event.fault is SOAPFault){
    var sf:SOAPFault = event.fault as SOAPFault;

    if (sf.faultactor == "BusinessException") {
      Alert.show(XML(sf.detail).@value, "Oops, a BusinessException
                                        occurred....");
    }else {
      Alert.show(sf.faultstring, "Oops, an unplanned SOAPFault
                    occurred....");
    }
  }
}
```

The `handler` is a little different for the .NET fault than for the Java handler, mostly because to control the exact `SoapException` in an ASP.NET Web Service takes some kung fu. Additionally, the .NET `SoapException` creates a `faultactor` node that is easy to set to a string to trigger a custom `SOAPFault` code path. Not every fault that can be raised is necessarily a `SOAPFault`, so test for that condition first since the `faultactor` won't be on a regular `FaultEvent`.

The server raises a `SoapException` with the `faultactor` set to `BusinessException` and attaches the appropriate message to display to the client. When the fault handler matches this condition, it displays the message returned from the server. The message is stored in the custom detail node of the `SOAPFault`, so you need to extract the error with some e4X XML (`XML(sf.detail).@value`) processing before displaying the error with an Alert box to the user of the application.

Calling Web Services from Other Servers

Flash has built-in security protection that will keep you from directly calling Web Services from domains other than the domain that served up the Flex application. To get around this, either create a `crossdomain.xml` file and place it in the root of the remote server, or use a proxy server, as explained previously when working with HTTP status codes.

The easiest thing, though not very controlled, is to create a `crossdomain.xml` tile, placed at the root of the domain, that allows total access to any remote Flash/Flex application:

```
<?xml version="1.0"?>
<!DOCTYPE cross-domain-policy
    SYSTEM "http://www.macromedia.com/xml/dtds/cross-domain-policy.dtd">
<cross-domain-policy>
    <allow-access-from domain="*" />
</cross-domain-policy>
```

However, if you want a little more control, you can open only Web Services to be delivered to specific domains by limiting which HTTP headers have access, through a `crossdomain.xml` file:

```
<?xml version="1.0"?>
<!DOCTYPE cross-domain-policy
    SYSTEM "http://www.macromedia.com/xml/dtds/cross-domain-policy.dtd">
<cross-domain-policy>
    <allow-access-from domain="*" />
```

```
      <allow-http-request-headers-from domain="*" headers="SOAPAction"/>
   </cross-domain-policy>
```

Notice here that we're filtering allowed requests based on headers containing `SOAPAction`.

All the preceding sample `crossdomain.xml` files allow any domain access, but you can just as easily limit which domains that are delivering your Flex applications are allowed access by setting the `allow-access-from` element's domain attribute:

```
      <allow-access-from domain="www.alloweddomain.com" />
```

Or, if you want to allow any subdomain for a domain, such as `www.alloweddomain.com` and `blog.alloweddomain.com`, then use a wildcard:

```
      <allow-access-from domain="*.alloweddomain.com" />
```

Summary

This chapter demonstrated how simple it is to access SOAP-based Web Services delivered from the .NET platform. But this technique isn't limited to .NET Web Services. Backend Web Services written with Java, PHP, Python, and so forth are all perfectly capable of providing Web Service contracts that the Flex WSDL Import tool can digest.

Also, .NET isn't limited in only offering WSDL-based Web Services. With the newer ADO.NET Data Services, it's just as easy to create a RESTful service that's accessible from Flex with the `HTTPService` API. Match your favorite Flex RPC API to that of your backend server development platform of choice.

Coming up next in Chapter 52, "Offline Data Access with AIR," you'll learn about using SQLite for managing local data with AIR applications.

52

Offline Data Access with AIR

The `flash.data` libraries are available as part of Adobe AIR runtime to provide local relational database support. Developers can store data in an embedded database local to the user's machine. Storing data locally is useful for providing offline services to the AIR application, whether it's stored email, music preferences, tabular stock quotes, image metadata, or another service.

Storing this data offline in a relational database that supports most of the ANSI SQL-92 standard provides the ability to access this data using a language most developers are already familiar with whether coming from a desktop or web programming background.

Introduction to SQLite

SQLite is a lightweight (225 KB on OS X, 231KB on Windows), embedded database available on many platforms, from OS X, Windows, and Linux on the desktop to Symbian and iPhone-based mobile devices. And now, it'll be used in your applications that you write with Adobe AIR. It's fully capable of transactions, supporting full ACID (atomic, consistent, isolated, and durable) and ensuring that all changes inside a single transaction either occur completely or not at all. And, of course, SQLite supports most of the ANSI SQL-92 standard, so those familiar with writing SELECT, CREATE, DELETE, UPDATE SQL statements will feel right at home working with the SQLite database.

Adobe already uses SQLite in the Lightroom product line to store and maintain users' image libraries. Another popular use is with Mozilla Firefox, which uses SQLite databases to store cookies, preferences, history, form data, and so forth.

SQLite databases are amazingly simple. They are just a file stored anywhere in the user's filesystem that is opened and used by the platform-specific implementation of SQLite. Therefore, SQLite databases are easy to move around and provide an excellent way of managing application data for desktop applications.

SQLite isn't a server technology. It's not designed for use in an environment that supports multiple connections from multiple users. Think of SQLite as providing relational database access to flat files. For more information on SQLite, visit www.sqlite.org.

SQLite versus XML

You might be asking yourself, why not just store my local data in an XML file? In some cases, this will be perfectly valid and the appropriate thing to do. After all, with Flex's simple XML-handling API and e4X, it's easy to get data directly from an XML file.

Use XML to store local data:

❏   When the data set is small

❏   When the data set is simple

❏   When users should have the ability to edit data simply inside a text editor.

❏   For ease of transfer between applications or different Web-based services.

Use SQLite to store local data:

❏   When the data set is large

❏   When the data set is complex

❏   When performing complex manipulations of set-based data that benefit from using ANSI-92 SQL's aggregate functions (AVG, COUNT, MAX, MIN, etc.) for set-based calculations

❏   When you want to store lots of heterogeneous data in one file

❏   When there's a lot of updating of existing data or inserting of new data

❏   When it's best to use transactions to maintain the consistency of the data store

Synchronous versus Asynchronous

Just like the `flash.filesystem` APIs for file management, the `flash.data` package supports both synchronous and asynchronous APIs while working with SQLite databases. There are synchronous and asynchronous APIs for opening databases and executing SQL statements. The asynchronous version of the APIs append *Async* to the name of the synchronous call. For example, `SQLConnection.open()` is the synchronous API, and `SQLConnection.openAsync()` is its asynchronous counterpart.

How you open your database will determine which API functions you can use. Opening a database in synchronous mode will give you access to only the synchronous API. And opening a database with `openAsync` will allow only use of the asynchronous API. Once the connection is made to the database, you can't change the execution mode until it's closed and reopened.

Use the synchronous APIs when you're performing operations in a mandated sequential order, such as when importing data into a database that depends on parent data to be present before importing the child data. Synchronous operations will be easier to work with when chaining together a complex database import operation.

Use asynchronous APIs when you're performing long-running tasks and don't want the user's screen to freeze — for example, for complex queries, filtering, or opening a large database. Using asynchronous operations can make code more complex, as you'll have to chain together event listeners, responding to either error or success events of prior SQL operations.

Creating a Database

In this section, you'll create a sample database schema that will enables users to track their fitness progress. Users can enter their favorite running, biking, hiking routes, and then record when they perform them. The goal is to capture enough fitness data like heart rate and average speed (probably captured from a sports watch or GPS device) that will allow them to eventually track their fitness progress over time. The sample application here only manages working with CRUD-bases route data and doesn't go further than that. Figure 52-1 shows the database schema for this example.

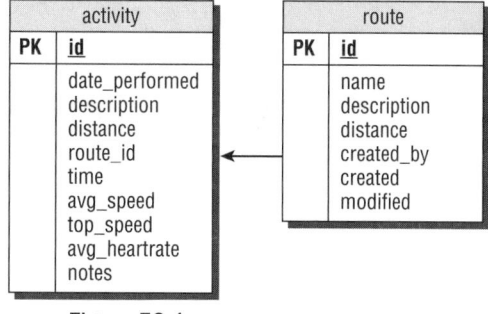

Figure 52-1

As you can see, there are only two tables: an activity table, which will track a single use of user activity, like going for a run, and a routes table, where users will enter their favorite routes, such as a weekly 15-mile jog around the lake. (We're assuming that they're very fit.) The routes table will hold the frequently used metadata and enable a feature where multiple users will share their favorite routes.

Let's get started by creating our first database, opening it, and creating the layout of tables. Using the SQLConnection.open or SQLConnection.openAsync APIs on the filename will either open the database, if it exists, or create a new one.

Opening a Database Asynchronously

When working with SQLite databases and AIR, the first step is getting a connection to the local database. This chapter's sample code demonstrates many of the AIR SQLite APIs, so let's look at connecting to a SQLite database. The first example uses openAsync, which is demonstrated in the createDatabase Asynchronously function (see Listing 52-1).

Listing 52-1: Opening a Database Asynchronously

```
private function createDatabaseAsynchronously(event:MouseEvent):void
{
    var newDB:File =
        File.applicationStorageDirectory.resolvePath(txtDatabaseName.text + ".db");

    if (newDB.exists){
      Alert.show("Database already exists. Try a different name.");
      return;
    }

    var dbConn:SQLConnection = new SQLConnection();
    dbConn.addEventListener(SQLEvent.OPEN, onSqlOpen);
    dbConn.addEventListener(SQLErrorEvent.ERROR, onSqlError);

    // Create the DB asynchronously.
    dbConn.openAsync(newDB);
}

private function onSqlOpen(event:SQLEvent):void
{
    Alert.show("Database " + txtDatabaseName.text + " was successfully created.");
}

private function onSqlError(event:SQLErrorEvent):void
{
    Alert.show(StringUtil.substitute("SQLError #{0} occurred.\rmessage: {1}\rdetails: {2}",
                event.error.errorID,
                event.error.message,
                event.error.details));
}
```

The code to open the database first declares the newDB variable to be of type File, as a SQLite database is just a file stored on the local file system. Next, check to see if the database file exists. If it does, tell the user that the file exists and to choose a different name for the database.

Using SQLConnection, create the connection to the database that all subsequent database operations will rely on. On this new SQLConnection, since you're going to be using the asynchronous operations in the code sample, you'll need to listen for a couple of events. To be notified when the database has completed opening, listen for SQLEvent.OPEN. To handle unexpected errors, listen for the event SQLErrorEvent.ERROR.

Finally, you call openAsync on the file pointer. This will either open the existing SQLite file or create a new database file. After calling openAsync, the AIR UI will continue to process other events, user actions, and the like, until the asynchronous event onSqlOpen is fired, informing the user that the database was open/created and is ready for action.

Opening a Database Synchronously

For comparison, let's open the same database in synchronous mode, as shown in Listing 52-2. Remember that how the database is opened (asynchronously versus synchronously) determines whether the database will perform all operations asynchronously or synchronously.

Listing 52-2: Opening a Database Synchronously

```
private function createDatabaseSynchronously(event:MouseEvent):void
{
  var newDB:File =
        File.applicationStorageDirectory.resolvePath(txtDatabaseName.text + ".db");

  try
  {
    var dbConn:SQLConnection = new SQLConnection();
    dbConn.open(newDB);
  }
  catch(error:SQLError)
  {
    Alert.show(StringUtil.substitute("SQLError #{0} occurred.\rmessage:
                              {1}\rdetails: {2}",
                              error.errorID,
                              error.message,
                              error.details));
  }

  Alert.show("Database " + txtDatabaseName.text + " was successfully created.");
}
```

The synchronous method of opening a database is simpler than the asynchronous method, requiring less code. The first thing you'll notice is that we've enclosed the call to open the database in a `try/catch` statement. Just as with the asynchronous code version's `SQLErrorEvent.ERROR` handler, this will capture any unforeseen `SQLError`; except that, because the code is run synchronously, you don't have to listen for error events.

Notice that instead of `openAsync`, you call the synchronous version, `open`. Remember that, after opening a database with the `open` function, all future database calls against the database will have to use the synchronous versions of the API — methods like `execute()`, which we'll cover for the first time in the next section.

> *When using the synchronous version of the* `flash.data` *APIs, you should catch the* `SQLError` *inside a* `try/catch` *statement.*

Working with Data Definition Language

Adobe AIR and SQLite provide support for Data Definition Language (DDL), part of the SQL language. This enables you to edit the database schema by creating, deleting, and altering tables.

The scope of DDL and SQL-92 in general is beyond the scope of this book, as entire books exist on SQLite. However, to get you started, let's create a simple table. In Listing 52-3, the createTrainingDatabase Schema function demonstrates the code required to create the two tables in a sample application: activity and routes.

Listing 52-3: Creating Tables with DDL

```
private function createTrainingDatabaseSchema(event:MouseEvent):void
{
  //  Create and open the database
  openTrainingDatabase(txtDatabaseName.text);

  if (trainingDB.connected ) {
    var sqlStatement:SQLStatement = new SQLStatement();
    sqlStatement.sqlConnection = trainingDB;

    var createActivityTableSQL:String = "CREATE TABLE IF NOT EXISTS " +
      " [activity] ( " +
      "[id] INTEGER  PRIMARY KEY AUTOINCREMENT NOT NULL, " +
      "[date_performed] DATE  NULL, " +
      "[description] TEXT  NULL, " +
      "[distance] FLOAT  NULL, " +
      "[time] TIME  NULL, " +
      "[avg_speed] FLOAT  NULL, " +
      "[top_speed] FLOAT  NULL, " +
      "[avg_heartrate] FLOAT  NULL, " +
      "[notes] TEXT  NULL), " +
      "[created] DATE DEFAULT CURRENT_TIMESTAMP NULL, " +
      "[modified] DATE DEFAULT CURRENT_TIMESTAMP NULL)"

    // See the sample code for the DDL defining the route table
    // it has been truncated here for the sake of brevity.

    try
    {
      //  Create the Activity Table
      sqlStatement.text = createActivityTableSQL;
      sqlStatement.execute();

      //  Create the Route Table
      sqlStatement.text = createRouteTableSQL;
      sqlStatement.execute();

      Alert.show("Training database created.") ;
    }
    catch (error:SQLError)
    {
      displayErrorData(error);
    }

  }else {
    Alert.show("The database isn\'t opened.");
  }

}
```

First, the `createTrainingDatabaseSchema` function opens a database by calling a helper function called `openTrainingDatabase`, which creates a database connection using techniques similar to those in Listings 52-1 and 52-2. Next, check to make sure there's a valid connection to a database file by calling `trainingDB.connected`. Now, the good stuff starts to happen: defining the DDL that will create the first table, the activity table. In the code it's formatted with ActionScript strings, but in reality, you could run the following statement directly against any SQLite database from almost any external tool:

```
CREATE TABLE [activity] (
    [id] INTEGER  PRIMARY KEY AUTOINCREMENT NOT NULL,
    [date_performed] DATE  NULL,
    [description] TEXT  NULL,
    [length] FLOAT  NULL,
    [time] TIME  NULL,
    [avg_speed] FLOAT  NULL,
    [top_speed] FLOAT  NULL,
    [avg_heartrate] FLOAT  NULL,
    [notes] TEXT  NULL,
    [created] DATE DEFAULT CURRENT_TIMESTAMP NULL,
    [modified] DATE DEFAULT CURRENT_TIMESTAMP NULL)
```

This definition tells the SQLite engine to create a table called activity, with several columns. The columns are defined with the following metadata: column name, column type, default value. The `id` is its own beast because it's defining the primary key of the table, with an auto-incrementing `Integer` that will render a default value every time data is entered into the table. In addition, two `DATE` fields, `created` and `modified`, are used to keep track of when records were created and last updated, respectively. By setting the `DEFAULT CURRENT_TIMESTAMP`, these fields will automatically be created and updated when a new record is created by the database engine.

> *Note the use of square brackets surrounding the column identifier. Although this isn't required here, it causes SQLite to always interpret the name as an identifier instead of considering it as a reserved word or data type.*

Back to the code in listing 52-3; finally, call `execute()` to execute the SQL text against the database engine. Note here that if the database was opened with `openAsync()`, you'd have to call `executeAsync()` and have the appropriate event listeners wired up for asynchronous operations. The code then executes the DDL (the definition truncated from code sample for sake of brevity) to create the route table.

That's it. You've created a database and defined it in your application. Next, you'll start to add and manipulate data.

Working with Data

With the training database created, you can start adding data from an AIR application. The data can be created from a user input form, or the application could be coded to support a data format where the user could import data from a file.

Creating Data

Start by creating some route data in the application for your favorite running route. In the sample application, there's a Create Routes panel where the user enters the name of the route, its description, and the distance. After opening the database and creating the schema, start filling out the form to create routes by pressing the Create Route button in the sample application. The `createRoute` function (see Listing 52-4) is then executed.

Listing 52-4: Creating a Route Record

```
private function createRoute(name:String, desc:String, distance:String):void
{
  if (trainingDB == null || trainingDB.connected == false){
    Alert.show("Connect to database first");
    return;
  }

  // The SQL for inserting the route name.
  var createRouteSQL:String =
      "INSERT INTO route ( route_name, description, distance ) " +
      " VALUES (  @name, @desc, @distance) ";

  var sqlStatement:SQLStatement = new SQLStatement();
  sqlStatement.sqlConnection = trainingDB;

  try
  {
    // Create the new Route
    sqlStatement.text = createRouteSQL;
    sqlStatement.parameters["@name"] = name;
    sqlStatement.parameters["@desc"] = desc;
    sqlStatement.parameters["@distance"] = distance;

    sqlStatement.execute();

  }
  catch (error:SQLError)
  {
    displayErrorData(error);
  }
}
```

First, verify that the database has been created and that it's connected with the code `trainingDB != null && trainingDB.connected()`. The global `trainingDB` variable has already been created and contains a reference to an open database, so that multiple calls can be made against the database without incurring the penalty of opening the database each time. You verify that it's connected solely for a sanity check.

Create the SQL string, using named parameter notation. Here the `createRouteSQL` is an INSERT SQL statement with the parameterized values @name, @desc, and @distance. These parameters will be substituted by the SQL statement. The advantages of using parameterized queries is that they prevent SQL injection attacks, provide strong typing (dates will get mapped properly as dates, and not dates represented as strings), and are optimized by the SQL engine once and potentially reused. You should get in the habit of doing things this way.

An alternative to naming parameters with the at sign (@) is to use the colon (:) character. For example, instead of @name, the parameter could be named :name.

After the SQL string is created, create a SQLStatement object and set the sqlConnection property to the global trainindDB connection object. Now it's time to assign all the parameters of the SQL statement to the actual values being passed in. In this case, we're adding to the SQLStatement's parameters collection three values (name, desc, distance) and assigning them the appropriate parameter name that the SQL engine will substitute the values for.

Finally, call execute() to perform the INSERT. Any errors from the SQLite database engine will be thrown as exceptions that you're waiting for here. No errors, no exceptions, and all is well with the INSERT. A new row will exist in the SQLite database containing the new data that was inserted.

Let's look at how you can retrieve the primary key that the database generated for the record that was inserted. This is a useful technique for inserting parent records that a child belongs to. With our database schema for this sample, the routes need to exist before you can start assigning users to them.

Retrieving the Primary Key Field ID

The previous INSERT code sample created a new database record. Although you passed in three items of critical data (the name, description, and mileage), there's actually other data that the database created for you. An id is generated by the database engine that is the unique identifier of the newly created row, as well as a couple of timestamp columns marking when the record was created and last updated.

After calling execute() in the previous code example, retrieve the generated ID with the following code:

```
// Retrieve the Primary Key created by the database.
var sqlResult:SQLResult = sqlStatement.getResult();
var id:Number = sqlResult.lastInsertRowID;

Alert.show("Route " + name + " created with id:" + id ) ;
```

This code creates a new SQLResult instance called sqlResult that you assign to the SQLStatements' getResult() method. A SQLResult object holds the response information from any call made to the database. With a valid SQLResult instance, the lastInsertRowID property stores the value of the primary key of the newly created row. In the sample application here, the primary key is an automatic incrementing integer, as defined when the routes table was created.

Finally, display the id of the newly created route. This id value could be assigned to a global variable for future use, to update the activity table by logging the routes the user ran on any given date. To add this data to the training database, the activity ID (when the user did something) and the route ID (what they did) would also need to be known.

Why Use Parameters?

As demonstrated in Listing 52-4, the createRoute function used SQL parameters to pass data to the database engine. This was done because of the advantages of using parameterized queries (preventing

SQL injection attacks, providing strong typing, and SQL engine optimization). However, the preceding `createRoute` function could have implemented the entire `INSERT` statement using string concatenation, creating one simple string containing a raw SQL statement to be run on the database, as follows:

```
var createRouteSQL:String = StringUtil.substitute(
        "INSERT INTO [route] (name, description, distance) " +
        " VALUES ('{0}', '{1}', {2} )",
          name,
          desc,
          distance);
```

This would render to the following perfectly valid SQL statement string, which will happily run without errors against the SQLite database:

```
INSERT INTO [route] (name, description, distance)
```

VALUES ('A Favorite Boston Run', 'Winding route along river', 6.2)

The problem is that this isn't secure. It would be a possible haven for SQL injection attacks, although with a localized database like SQLite, it's probably not as much of an issue as a database sharing multiple user's data on a remote machine. But let's keep our database access hygiene consistent.

Another pitfall of this code sample is that when a user inputs data containing a single quote (as in "Todd's favorite run"), the developer will have to write helper routines to help escape the single quotation marks, avoiding an error with the SQL parser.

And finally, using parameterized queries, the SQL engine can optimize the query, retaining it for future use, as would be the case if you created an import routes routing that called `createRoute` hundreds of times.

Retrieving Data

To read data from the database, start with the standard code for opening and connecting to an existing database file, as shown in Listing 52-1 or 52-2. After the database connection has been established, you can read data, as demonstrated by the `retrieveRoutes` function in Listing 52-5, which will create a SQL `SELECT` statement to retrieve data from the database.

Listing 52-5: Reading Records from a SQLite Database

```
private function retrieveRoutes():void
{
  if (trainingDB == null || trainingDB.connected == false){
    Alert.show("Connect to database first");
    return;
  }

  var sqlStatement:SQLStatement = new SQLStatement();
  sqlStatement.sqlConnection = trainingDB;
  sqlStatement.text = "SELECT id, route_name, description, distance, created," +
                      " modified FROM route";
```

```
        sqlStatement.execute();

        var result:SQLResult = sqlStatement.getResult();

        results = new ArrayCollection(result.data as Array);
    }
```

With data created in the database and a valid connection, create a new SQLStatement, and set the text to any valid SELECT statement. Call execute() to run the query. Then read the results by creating a SQLResult and assigning it to the SQLStatment's getResult() method.

This call will return all the routes contained in the routes table. The results variable is bound to a DataGrid via Flex data binding, so when you create a new ArrayCollection, passing in the result.data (which is just an Array), all the new data is automatically displayed in a DataGrid for easy viewing.

> *When binding a returned data set with a DataGrid, the DataGrid will alphabetize the result fields and ignore the requested SQL order. To get around this, explicitly declare the columns in your grid.*

Updating Data

To update data with the training application, open an existing database that contains data, press the Load Routes button to display all the current routes, and then select a route to load into the Edit Route's panel.

To update an existing record, you need to know the unique primary key to perform the update against. This is the key difference between creating a record and updating it. The updateRoute function in Listing 52-6 shows the code required to update an existing record in the database.

Listing 52-6: Updating Records of a SQLite Database

```
    private function updateRoute(id:Number, name:String, desc:String,
                                               distance:String):void
    {
      if (trainingDB == null || trainingDB.connected == false){
        Alert.show("Connect to database first");
        return;
      }

      // The SQL for updating the route data.
      var updateRouteSQL:String =
        "UPDATE route  set route_name = @name, description = @desc, distance =" +
        " @distance, modified = @modified " +
        " WHERE id = @id ";

      var sqlStatement:SQLStatement = new SQLStatement();
      sqlStatement.sqlConnection = trainingDB;

      try
      {
```

Continued

Listing 52-6: Updating Records of a SQLite Database *(continued)*

```
            //  Update the Route
            sqlStatement.text = updateRouteSQL;
            sqlStatement.parameters["@name"] = name;
            sqlStatement.parameters["@desc"] = desc;
            sqlStatement.parameters["@distance"] = distance;
            sqlStatement.parameters["@id"] = id;
            sqlStatement.parameters["@modified"] = new Date();

            sqlStatement.execute();

            // Optional code demonstrating the rowsAffected property.
            var sqlResult:SQLResult = sqlStatement.getResult();
            trace("Rows affected: " +  sqlResult.rowsAffected);

            Alert.show("Route " + id + " updated.") ;

            retrieveRoutes();  //Load the routes into the grid.
            clearRouteForm(); // Clear the route form
        }
    }
```

Again, start by ensuring that there's a valid database and that it's connected. Next, compose the UPDATE statement. The syntax is a little different from the INSERT statement that was composed earlier. This syntax has absolutely nothing to do with AIR and everything to do with ANSI-92 SQL syntax, so keep a reference handy for composing your SQL text.

Next, bind all the parameters that you want to update, including the @id, which is the unique qualifier of the record that will be updated. Bind the @modified date, passing in a new Date object containing the current date and time. This will record in the database the last time the record was modified, something that could be useful for detecting dirty data in the future. Notice that the raw ActionScript Date object is automatically typed into the appropriate SQLite database type. All the heavy lifting is done behind the scenes for you with no need to convert the Date object into a database-specific string.

Next, call execute() to run the query, updating the appropriate record in the SQLite database.

Finally, retrieve the SQLResult of the last executed query for no other purpose than to demonstrate the rowsAffected property. Since this query is only updating a specific record, the value returned is 1. However, you could write an UPDATE statement that updates each record that has the word "AIR" in the description column. In this case, rowsAffected could be a lot more useful, as it would report the number of rows that changed in the database when the query was executed.

Deleting Data

As you've probably figured out by now, there's a familiar pattern emerging for working with data and executing SQL commands against SQLite databases: create the SQL text, bind parameters, execute the code, and then optionally review the SQLResult. Deleting data is as simple as running a query with a bound id parameter, just as when updating the data. The deleteRoute function in Listing 52-7 shows the code for a simple delete.

Listing 52-7: Deleting Data from SQLite

```
public  function deleteRoute(id:Number):void
{
  //  The SQL for Updated the route data.
  var deleteRouteSQL:String = "DELETE FROM route WHERE id = @id ";

  var sqlStatement:SQLStatement = new SQLStatement();
  sqlStatement.sqlConnection = trainingDB;

  try
  {
    //  Delete  the Route
    sqlStatement.text = deleteRouteSQL;
    sqlStatement.parameters["@id"] = id;
    sqlStatement.execute();

    Alert.show("Route " + id + " deleted.") ;
    retrieveRoutes();  //Load the routes into the grid.
  }
  catch (error:SQLError)
  {
    displayErrorData(error);
  }
}
```

To delete the data, ensure that there's a valid database connection, create the SQLStatement with the appropriate DELETE text, bind the parameters, and then execute the code. And, optionally (not shown in this code sample), view the affectedRows property of the SQLResult, as DELETE queries can affect multiple rows.

Using Transactions to Import Data

Transactions are a common database feature used to ensure that all database operations in a given batch are successful. If one INSERT, UPDATE, or DELETE statement in a batch of statements changing multiple tables and rows in a database fails, the entire transaction isn't committed to the database.

This is very useful when importing data into a database of a hierarchy of data, such as importing all the sales data of a company into a SQLite database for offline viewing. To import sales data properly, for example, you'd first need to import all the salespeople's personal data, then their accounts, their customers, their customer purchase orders, the purchase order line items, and so forth. As you can see, there's a long train of dependencies to ensure that all salespeople are loaded into the database properly, assigned a proper primary key, and that key is then used to align them to customers, purchase orders, and so on.

In this sample, you'll start with something much simpler: you'll import default routes that are described in an XML file. This technique will be useful because there's a lot of data available through Web Services to AIR applications via XML. This code will even use some of what you learned in Chapter 45, "Local File Management with AIR," about reading XML from local files.

First, using the enclosed sample application for the chapter, open an existing database that you've created the database schema on, as you did earlier. Then press the Create Default Routes button to have all the routes defined in the `defaultRoutes.xml` imported into the routes table. To test a transaction failing, press the Create Default Routes with Fail button, and an error will be thrown when the code attempts to create the last record in the database, rolling back the transaction, and leaving the database in the state it was prior to attempting the import.

Listing 52-8 shows the code for the `createDefaultRoutes` function, which implements transactions for a data import.

Listing 52-8: Importing Data Using Transactions

```
private function createDefaultRoutes(failTransaction:Boolean = false):void
{
  // Validate and Assert a that traininDB is connected here. See enclosed code.

  var createRouteSQL:String =
      "INSERT INTO route ( route_name, description, distance ) " +
      " VALUES (  @name, @desc, @distance) ";

  var sqlStatement:SQLStatement = new SQLStatement();
  sqlStatement.sqlConnection = trainingDB;

  try
  {
    trainingDB.begin(); // Begins a transaction on the connection
    sqlStatement.text = createRouteSQL;

    var defaultRoutes:XML = loadDefaultRoutesXML();

    // Create all the sample records found in the defaultRoutes.xml
    for each (var route:XML in defaultRoutes.route)
    {
      sqlStatement.parameters["@name"] = route.@name ;
      sqlStatement.parameters["@desc"] = route.@description;
      sqlStatement.parameters["@distance"] = route.@distance;
      sqlStatement.execute();
    }

    trainingDB.commit(); // No errors, commit all the changes to the database

    Alert.show("Number of routes created: " + trainingDB.totalChanges);
    retrieveRoutes();   //Load the routes into the grid.
  }
  catch (error:SQLError)
  {
    trainingDB.rollback();  // Roll back all the changes if there's one error
    displayErrorData(error);
  }
}
```

Start by ensuring that the database file is open and connected. Next, call `trainingDB.begin()` to start the transaction on the connection. Every call to execute from now on will occur inside this transaction until either `commit()` or `rollback()` is called. Then load the XML from the `defaultRoutes.xml` file by calling `loadDefaultRoutesXML()`. (Again, the technique here was explained back in Chapter 45 on how to read XML from a local file.)

With an ActionScript XML instance containing a list of all the routes, loop through each of the routes, binding the values from each of the XML route elements to that of the current `SQLParameter`. For example, using e4X, assign a value from the expression `route.@name` to the parameter `sqlStatement.parameters["@name"]`. Do this for every property of each route and for every route in the XML file, calling `execute()` each time.

When no errors occur, the code will naturally continue on to the call to `trainingDB.commit()`. Up until this point, none of the successful calls to execute have actually been persisted into the database. Calling `commit()` will make all the changes stick in the database.

However, if an error occurred, the `catch` clause would take over. The first thing `catch` does is call `trainingDB.rollback()`. This removes any pending changes of heretofore successful executes, and no changes occur in the database.

To test the transaction to verify that none of the data that was inserted into the database was bad, force it to fail by creating bad data and inserting it into the database with the following code:

```
if ( failTransaction) {

    sqlStatement.parameters["@name"] = "Bad Record";
    sqlStatement.parameters["@desc"] = "This will roll back entire transaction";
    sqlStatement.parameters["@distance"] = "bad_data_should_be_a_number";
    sqlStatement.execute();
}
```

When this code is executed, an error will occur while trying to insert the record that has the string `bad_data_should_be_a_number`, where a numeric value should be. This error will trigger the `catch` handler and a subsequent call to `rollback()`. When `rollback` is called, none of the data that was inserted since the transaction started (with the call to `begin()`) won't be added to the database, even if previous successful calls to creating data were made .

Making Online Data Available for Offline Access

At this stage of the game, it's time to start discussing extending AIR's SQLite functionality to host an offline data cache of data. An offline cache will hold data that was read from the server but saved locally, so the user doesn't have to be connected to the Internet while working with the data. With our implementation, we'll develop structure in saving simple XML into a local SQLite database. This data cache will persist records declared in XML into the SQLite database in a generic fashion, mapping XML nodes to column names, and the parent XML node as a record. This could be useful for storing data such as customer contacts, sales reports, documents, and so forth or to persist any textual data for a time when an Internet connection isn't readily available. The XML could come from other applications in the form of exported data, or from a Web Service. (See Part VIII, "Server Integration," for a discussion of accessing data on remote servers).

Although the techniques in this section used to make data available offline could also be performed by storing plain XML files in the local filesystem, having the ability to work with SQL has its advantages over having to work with XML. With SQL you can take advantage of transactions for maintaining data integrity or use SQL's query syntax for complex manipulation of data. Also, when working with large data sets, using set-based relational SQL makes more sense than manipulating raw XML stored in a file. It's really up to the developer how to set it up.

It's important to note that the technique presented here is only for read-only data from the remote service. Additional work needs to be done if you want to edit the data and send it back up to the server.

Importing XML into a SQLite Database

You can see the samples in this section by clicking on the Persist XML to local database sample link on top of this chapter's sample application. There's a couple of different data import buttons that, when clicked, will take a generic XML file and convert it into a SQLite database table, with each XML node parsed into a database row and each XML attributes on the given node parsed into column data.

Presently, this tool is only reading XML files to import from the local hard drive in order to eliminate the need to set up the code to retrieve from the server. Listing 52-9 shows the main worker function, `importData()`.

Listing 52-9: The Main importData Routine

```
private function importData(xml:XML):void
{
  try
  {
    // Step 1: Create/Open the SQLite Database file
    var sqlConnection:SQLConnection = createDatabaseSynchronously("test_import");
    //Start the transaction
    sqlConnection.begin();

    // Step 2: Create the new table schema for the current import
    createGenericSchema(sqlConnection, xml);

    // Step 3: Create and insert each of the rows of data
    insertData(sqlConnection, xml);

    // Commit the data
    sqlConnection.commit();

    // Step 4: Retreive data for display, passing in the name of the XML node.
    retrieveGenericData(sqlConnection, xml.name());
```

```
    // Reset the column mapping cache.
    columnMapping = null;

  }
  catch(error:SQLError)
  {
    sqlConnection.rollback(); // Roll back if any errors occur.
    columnMapping = null;  // Reset the column mapping cache.
    displayErrorData("Import Data Failed." , error);

  }
}
```

Pass a valid XML object into this routine, whether it's read from a local file (as is the case of this sample application) or returned from a server via HTTPService. The routine then creates a SQL connection based on a hard-coded "test_import" filename. Once the connection is established to the local database, begin a transaction by calling sqlConnection.begin(). After all, if there are any errors, whether with creating the table or inserting the data, there shouldn't be any leftover scraps of partial created data of an unknown state. This is a nice advantage that working with a SQL engine has over raw XML.

Next, dynamically create the generic table to hold the data stored in the XML file by calling the method createGenericSchema(), which will be discussed in more detail in the following section. After the generic table has been created, it's time to absorb the data into it by calling insertData(), which will do all the heavy lifting of creating an appropriate INSERT statement and binding each of the elements of the XML to the SQLStatments via parameters, and then executing the INSERT. Commit the changes to the database, as long as there hasn't been any unforeseen errors, by calling sqlConnection.commit().

Finally, perform some cleanup, such as clearing out the columnMapping ArrayCollection so that it can be reused in the future with possible other imports.

Creating a Table Based on XML Data

The createGenericSchema's main function is to build the table for the given XML file that all the data will be imported into. It does this by executing the SQL statement created by buildGenericCreate TableSchema(). Listing 52-10 shows how the dynamic SQL is generated from the XML.

Listing 52-10: Building a CREATE TABLE SQL Statement Based on XML Attributes

```
private function buildGenericCreateTableSchema(tableName:String,
                                               xml:XML):String
{
  var columnMapping:ArrayCollection = buildAttributeColumnMapping(xml);

  var sql:String = "CREATE TABLE IF NOT EXISTS [" + tableName + "] (";

  for each( var columnName:String in columnMapping){
    sql += "[" + columnName + "] TEXT  NULL";

    if (columnMapping[columnMapping.length - 1] != columnName ){
      //  Not the last column to map, insert a comma
```

Continued

Listing 52-11: Source code for the buildAttributeColumnMapping Method *(continued)*

```
        sql += ",";
    }
}

sql += ")";

trace("Generated SQL Create Statement: " + sql);
return sql;
}
```

First and foremost, the importer needs to know the names of the columns that the database table should hold. The idea here is that for every attribute in the XML, there will be a corresponding column in the database. However, there is a catch: with each XML node, it is never known if it contains every possible attribute because XML usually doesn't explicitly have null attribute fields included in the output. The method buildAttributeColumnMapping helps out here (see Listing 52-11).

After calling buildAttributeColumnMappings, all column names will be known and generated from the XML attribute names. Loop through the columnMapping Array, adding the columnName to the CREATE TABLE statement that will be executed by a SQLStatement. All the columns are going to be of type TEXT with nullable fields. Watch out for appending extra commas after the last column is defined.

Let's look at more details on how and why we built up the columnMapping Array, which is done in the buildAttributeColumnMapping method.

Listing 52-11: Source code for the buildAttributeColumnMapping Method

```
private function buildAttributeColumnMapping(xml:XML):ArrayCollection
{
  // Return cached version of column mappings
  if (columnMapping != null) return columnMapping;

  columnMapping = new ArrayCollection();

  for each (var row:XML in xml.children())
  {
    for each (var attr:* in row.attributes()) {

      var attributeName:String = attr.name();
      if (columnMapping.contains(attributeName) ){
        // Ignore, it already exists
      }else {
        //  The attribute doesn't exist yet, add to the columnMapping
        columnMapping.addItem(attributeName);
      }
    }
  }
  return columnMapping;
}
```

The `buildAttributeColumnMapping` function scans the entire XML file, parsing every node, and adding all unique attributes that it finds into a common `columnMapping ArrayCollection` that will be used for both creating the table schema and mapping the data to parameters in the `INSERT` statement.

After `buildAttributeColumnMapping` and `buildGenericCreateTableSchema` have finished creating the new database table schema in the SQLite database, it's time to start inserting data into it.

Inserting XML Data into the Database

Performing the actual `INSERT`s consists of mapping the XML attributes to columns of the newly created table, as shown in Listing 52-12. The `insertData` function is where all data in the XML file/message is transformed into a SQL INSERT in order to save it into the database.

Listing 52-12: The insertData Workhorse Function

```
private function insertData(connection:SQLConnection, xml:XML):void
{
  var sqlStatement:SQLStatement = new SQLStatement();
  sqlStatement.sqlConnection = connection;

  try
  {
    var sql:String = buildGenericInsertStatement(xml.name(), xml);
    sqlStatement.text = sql;

    var columnMapping:ArrayCollection = buildAttributeColumnMapping(xml);

    var rowCount:int = 0;
    for each (var row:XML in xml.children())
    {
      for each (var columnName:String in columnMapping){
        var cnp:String = "@" + columnName;
        //trace("Reading paramter " + cnp);
        sqlStatement.parameters[cnp] = e2n(row.attribute(columnName));
      }
      sqlStatement.execute()
      rowCount += 1;
    }
    trace(rowCount + " inserted into the generic table .");
  }
  catch (error:SQLError)
  {
    displayErrorData("Error inserting data into generic table: " , error);
    throw error; // re-toss the error so that the master method knows it failed
  }
}
```

The `insertData()` method receives the current connection hosting the transaction that everything has been executed against thus far, and a reference to the XML that is being introduced into the database. First, the `buildGenericInsertStatement` is called. Just like the `buildGenericCreateTableSchema()`

method, `buildGenericInsertStatement()` creates a `String` holding the `INSERT` statement that each row of the XML will use to update the database. This SQL statement only needs to be generated once, and when combined with parameter binding, it will only be parsed once by the database engine, ensuring the fastest possible way to insert data.

The generated `INSERT` statement (truncated for the sake of brevity) will look a lot like the following:

```
INSERT INTO [userData] ( title, first_name, middle_name, last_name, suffix,
    company, department, job_title, business_street, business_street_2, …)
VALUES (@title, @first_name, @middle_name, @last_name, @suffix,
    @company,@department,@job_title,@business_street,@business_street_2,…)
```

Next, it's time to start looping through the XML that was passed in and bind all the possible parameters with attribute values on the XML:

```
var cnp:String = "@" + columnName;
sqlStatement.parameters[cnp] = emptyToNull(row.attribute(columnName));
```

Basically, resolve a `String` with the at sign (@) concatenated to the column name. This is the name of the parameter in the parameters collection. Then get the value of the XML node for the particular attribute that's being mapped to the parameter. The `emptyToNull` function is a helper that converts all empty strings to `null`, if needed. The e4x expression, `row.attribute(columnName)`, grabs the actual value from the XML.

With every parameter bound, execute the `SQLStatement`, inserting the new row into the database. Repeat this process for every node in the XML file. After all the nodes in the XML file have been added to the database, call `commit()` to make all the changes to the database permanent.

That's all the important working code for persisting generic XML to a local SQLite database. Be sure to check out the chapter's sample code listing in `PersistXMLToDatabase.mxml` for the complete code.

Improving the XML to SQLite Importer

The previous code in this section is just a starting point for creating an offline data cache. There are several more features requiring additional work for more complex systems:

❑   Detecting types of data to import (`Date`, `Number`, `Boolean`) and creating specific typed columns in the create table database schema.

❑   Detecting duplicate data and performing an update of an existing record instead of always adding the record as a new row. Each additional time the import runs, it should be able to detect duplicate records based on some form of unique ID *and* using a modified timestamp to know when to update the records.

❑   Making nested XML nodes become new tables and providing appropriate linking between parent/child tables with the use of foreign keys.

❑   Adding unique primary keys locally.

These things, implemented in their entirety, would probably make a great third-party library. But since everyone's offline access to a data cache will vary, whether it's read-only or fully interactive and updatable, this section's code is here to inspire ideas. Also, remember that offline data doesn't refer to only persisting in SQLite. Feel free to use plain old XML or your own custom text formats.

Using Third-Party SQLite Database Management Applications

Although you can work with SQLite from within ActionScript code, sometimes it's easier to use a tool for defining a database schema and to test complex queries for debugging purposes. This is especially true once your database has several tables with thousands of records.

To facilitate working with AIR's SQLite implementation, any third-party SQLite administration tool will work, whether it's open source or a commercially supported tool. The SQLite website, `www.sqlite.org/cvstrac/wiki?p=ManagementTools`, has an extensive list of administration tools.

Windows users should check out the free SQLiteMan, available at `http://sqliteman.com`. OS X users should check out MesaMySQL, available at `www.mesamysql.com`.

Summary

SQLite is a powerful, yet lightweight database engine embedded into AIR applications. It enables you to store a lot of data locally, with a solid implementation of the ANSI-92 SQL specification. For keeping track of a lot of local data, the performance for getting data in and out will top any e4x XML parsing that a developer will want to do. Combined with SQL's set-based calculations, it's a welcome tool for any desktop developer's arsenal.

Coming up next in Part IX, "Data Services," you'll learn all about Adobe's commercial product LiveCycle Data Services (LCDS) for simplifying your server development for Flex applications. You'll also learn how to work with Adobe's open source BlazeDS, another technology for pushing data from the backend into your Flex/AIR application.

Part IX: Data Services

53

Introduction to LCDS

LiveCycle Data Services (LCDS) is a client- and server-side technology for integrating Flex and AIR client applications with different kinds of data resources and simplifying otherwise complex data management problems, such as data synchronization, conflict resolution, and paging of large data sets.

Overview of LCDS

LCDS is an enterprise framework that makes it easy to develop any manner of data-intensive applications — from a Flex trading application that consumes live price feeds at a rate of many updates-per-second, to a collaborative experience built in AIR that allows multiple users to edit and interact with the same document concurrently. To achieve all this, LCDS provides an assortment of Flex and Java components that encapsulate the complexities of remote data access and management, while integrating with existing backend systems.

Figure 53-1 shows a screen grab from the AMGEN Tour of California application built by Adobe in four weeks, using LCDS and Flash Media Server. The application featured live GPS tracking of riders, route maps, geo-positioned photos, video clips, and live chat. It demonstrates the kind of application that can be created with LCDS in a relatively short amount of time and how the technology can be integrated with other parts of the Flex ecosystem.

Figure 53-1

Part IX, "Data Services," devotes six chapters to LCDS and one chapter to its open-source relation, BlazeDS. The number of chapters devoted to LCDS gives an idea of the breadth of its features. There's publish-subscribe messaging, relational database integration, and offline data caching. There's paging of large data sets, quality-of-service guarantees, and an open architecture for integrating with proprietary systems. There's PDF generation and invocation of LiveCycle Enterprise Suite (LCES) service operations. In reality, the feature set justifies a whole book of its own, but the chapters in Part IX seek to provide a useful cross-section:

- **Chapter 53, "Introduction to LCDS"** — Provides an overview of the LCDS features, the architecture and the four main services, as well as instructions for creating a new LCDS project in Flex Builder.

- **Chapter 54, "LCDS and ColdFusion"** — Discusses the close integration between LCDS and ColdFusion.

- **Chapter 55, "Message Service"** — Covers publish-subscribe messaging with the Message Service, including integration with Java Message Service (JMS) and a simple PDF-generation scenario.

- **Chapter 56, "Data Management Service"** — Introduces the Data Management Service (DMS), which provides automatic synchronization of data across clients and many other features.

- **Chapter 57, "Advanced Data Management Services"** — Provides further guidance for making best use of the DMS in real-world scenarios.

❑ **Chapter 58, "Using the Flex Stress Testing Framework"** — Introduces the free stress-testing framework provided by Adobe for testing LCDS applications.

❑ **Chapter 59, "Using BlazeDS"** — Covers the open-source technology that lies at the heart of LCDS, including the Remoting Service and the Proxy Service for invoking Java methods from Flex and calling HTTP Services and SOAP Web Services.

The purpose of these chapters is to provide enough detail for a developer to begin building their own "data-intensive" application. There is inevitably some overlap with the official Adobe *LCDS Developer Guide*, but the text here focuses on self-contained examples rather than providing comprehensive documentation for the whole product.

LCDS Resources

In addition to this book and its accompanying source code, there are many other resources for learning LCDS. The LCDS distribution includes a broad range of sample applications that can be studied, and the following official documentation should be kept close at hand:

❑ *LCDS Developer Guide* — Hundreds of pages of comprehensive documentation, explaining the architecture and covering all of the service types in detail from client and server perspectives.

❑ **LCDS ActionScript classes** — API documentation for the ActionScript classes provided by LCDS and LCES. An essential reference for building Flex and AIR clients.

❑ **LCDS Javadoc** — API documentation for the LCDS Java classes, required for integrating LCDS with other systems through the various extensibility points and interfaces.

These are available from the LCDS documentation page, at `www.adobe.com/support/documentation/en/livecycledataservices`.

In addition, there are many blogs that cover LCDS and BlazeDS. Of particular note is the blog of Christophe Coenraets, (`http://coenraets.org`), who has created and shared many example applications that demonstrate the simplicity and power of LCDS for collaboration, data synchronization, offline caching, and so on.

Understanding LCDS

LCDS is essentially a Java web application suitable for deploying into a compatible application server, such as JBoss, BEA WebLogic, IBM WebSphere and Apache Tomcat. This web application offers various services to Flex or AIR clients, for accessing, updating, and otherwise interacting with data. The services fall into two broad categories: call-and-response and data-push. In the former, the client requests data from some kind of resource, while in the latter data can be pushed out by the server to multiple clients. Clients communicate with these services via a message broker servlet in the application server or by connecting to a separate, high-performance socket server, both of which are included with LCDS. The latter approach provides greater performance and scalability, since it is not confined by rules of the Java Servlet specification. This high-level architecture is shown in Figure 53-2.

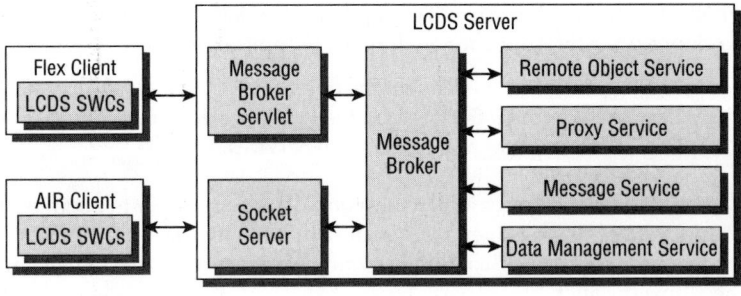

Figure 53-2

Data Service Solutions

Adobe provides the following three data service solutions:

❑ **LiveCycle Data Services ES** — The complete LCDS solution, including the full range of services, the high-performance socket server, and components for integrating with Adobe LiveCycle Enterprise Suite (LC ES).

❑ **LiveCycle Data Services, Community Edition** — A subscription offering that includes access to certified builds of BlazeDS (the open-source subset of LCDS) and developer and enterprise support resources. This doesn't include the data management features, the high-performance socket server or the high-scalability features.

❑ **BlazeDS** — The free open-source Java remoting and web messaging framework that lies at the heart of LCDS ES. Like the LCDS Community Edition, this doesn't include the full range of services. The data management features and high-performance and scalability features are not included, but services for invoking remote Java methods and proxying calls to Web or HTTP services are included.

This book focuses on LCDS ES, and the examples have been tested with release 2.6. Most of the examples can also be run with BlazeDS or LCDS Community Edition, with the exception of those requiring the Data Management Service (DMS).

Client Architecture

The purpose of the LCDS client libraries is to make it simple to integrate a Flex or AIR application with the LCDS services. Each service type has one or two corresponding Flex components that can be instantiated in ActionScript or declared in MXML. These components hide the complexities of sending messages between the client and server, so a developer just invokes higher-level methods and handles various events. In some cases, LCDS takes care of more, by encapsulating data translation between ActionScript and Java objects and performing data management duties, such as synchronizing a strongly typed object model with a persistent data store on the server. Figure 53-3 shows the main components of a Flex or AIR LCDS client.

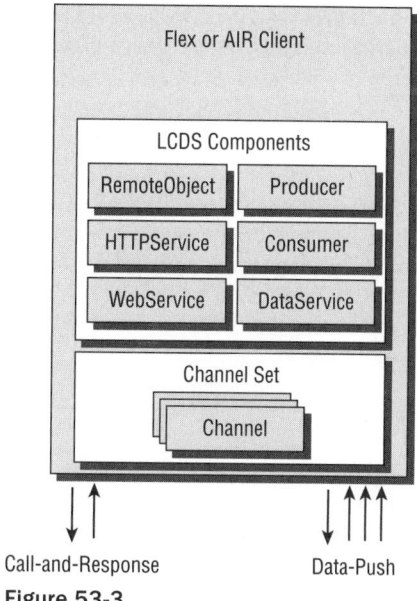

Figure 53-3

The three service components to the left — RemoteObject, HTTPService, and WebService — are for call-and-response style interactions with LCDS services, while those to the right — Producer, Consumer, and DataService — are for use with the data-push services provided by LCDS. All these components use a Channel object to actually communicate with the LCDS server. Various channels are available, as detailed later, to communicate in different ways. Multiple channels can be contained inside a ChannelSet to provide failover, so that any client that is unable to establish a connection over one channel will automatically attempt the next channel in the set. This allows an LCDS client to degrade gracefully when it is run in a more restrictive environment that may prevent certain kinds of connections.

The LCDS client libraries are contained in various SWC files, included with the LCDS distribution, as follows:

- ❑   fds.swc and fds_rb.swc — The LCDS components and their associated resource bundle.

- ❑   datavisualization.swc and datavisualization_rb.swc — The Flex data visualization components and an accompanying resource bundle are included with LCDS. These are not directly related to the LCDS services, but are covered in Chapter 36 of this book.

- ❑   playerfds.swc — Contains classes needed to build LCDS applications for Flash Player.

- ❑   airfds.swc — Contains classes needed to build LCDS applications for AIR.

These libraries need to be on the build path in order to compile Flex applications. In addition, the path to an XML configuration file describing the services and channels can optionally be provided to the compiler. The details from this file are then compiled into the resultant SWF, so the correct channels are used for communication without needing to initialize them manually.

The example later in this chapter shows how to configure and build a new LCDS project in Flex Builder. To do the same with the command-line tools, please refer to the *Building your client-side application* section of the *LCDS Developer Guide*.

Server Architecture

Figure 53-4 shows the server-side architecture for LCDS. At a high level, a Flex client communicates with an LCDS service by sending and receiving messages over a channel. The channel is connected to an end point on the server, which directs messages to and from the message broker. When the message broker receives a message, it is routed to the correct destination, within one of the LCDS services. The destination uses an adapter to process the message, and in some cases this is delegated to an assembler responsible for querying and updating data.

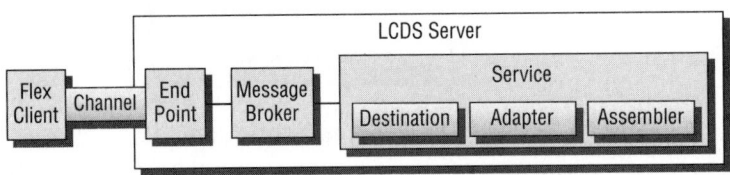

Figure 53-4

The following describes the components in more detail:

❑   **Channel** — A client-side object encapsulating the connection behavior between a Flex client and an LCDS server. There a various channels provided for different transport protocols and message formats. Channels can be grouped into sets to support failover, so Flex clients can degrade gracefully from one type of channel to another, depending on restrictions in their environment.

❑   **End point** — A URL and corresponding Java class for processing the messages sent over a channel between a Flex client and LCDS server. Each type of channel has a corresponding end point. When messages are received at an end point, they are directed to the message broker.

❑   **Message broker** — Routes message to a destination for one of the LCDS service types. A Flex client addresses messages to particular destinations and LCDS is responsible for delivering them, through the channel, end point and message broker. There is just one instance of the message broker within an LCDS server, so it provides centralized routing.

❑   **Service** — LCDS provides the following four main service types for different purposes:

    ❑   The Remoting Service, for integrating with Java objects

    ❑   The Proxy Service, for proxying SOAP and HTTP requests

    ❑   The Message Service, for publish-subscribe messaging

    ❑   The Data Management Service, for integrating with data resources and synchronizing data across multiple clients.

❑   **Destination** — An address on the server for a Flex client to send or receive messages to or from. A destination corresponds to a particular service type and is reached through a channel, an end point and the message broker. A destination has an adapter responsible for processing the messages that are received.

❑ **Adapter** — Processes messages sent to destinations. LCDS provides several adapters for different service-types and purposes. For instance, the Message Service has two adapters, one for transient publish-subscribe messaging and another for integrating with JMS. The adapter is an open extensibility point, so custom adapters can be developed for special purposes.

❑ **Assembler** — An assembler applies only to the DMS and is responsible for querying and updating a data store. It is used in conjunction with the Java object adapter, which delegates these responsibilities to an assembler. There are two assemblers provided out of the box: one for integrating with Hibernate, the other for integrating with a relational database directly, using SQL and JDBC. It is straightforward to write a custom assembler for integrating with different kinds of resources.

The Service Types

LCDS provides four main service types, each of which has the same general architecture, involving Flex components, channels, end points, the message broker, destinations, and adapters. These services are introduced here and then covered in detail in the chapters that follow. Each chapter features various example applications describing them from the Flex client and LCDS server perspectives.

The Remoting Service

The Remoting Service allows Flex clients to invoke methods of Java objects on the server and receive the results. It handles the conversion between ActionScript and Java objects transparently and provides an exceptionally simple programming model for Flex developers.

Figure 53-5 illustrates the Remoting Service and its corresponding Flex client component, the RemoteObject class. Chapter 59 covers the Remoting Service in detail within the context of BlazeDS. This service is included with BlazeDS and LCDS.

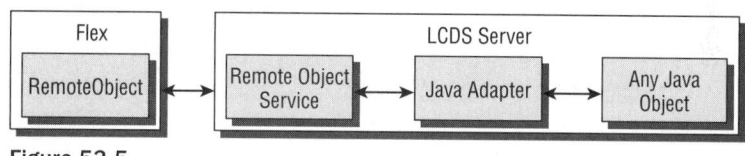

Figure 53-5

The Proxy Service

The Proxy Service proxies requests from Flex clients to remote HTTP Services and SOAP Web Services. In contrast to connecting directly, the Proxy Service offers several advantages, including authorization and authentication, centralized management of the services that the Flex client connects to, and logging of service requests. It also supports more HTTP operations than direct connections, provides access to response error codes, and bypasses the cross-domain.xml policy file that can otherwise prevent a Flex client from connecting to a remote service.

Figure 53-6 shows the Proxy Service and the pair of Flex components that can be used for interacting with it: WebService and HTTPService. The same components may also be used for making direct connections to the remote services, subject to the limitations described earlier. The Proxy Service is included with BlazeDS and LiveCycle Data Services. It is covered in more detail in Chapter 59.

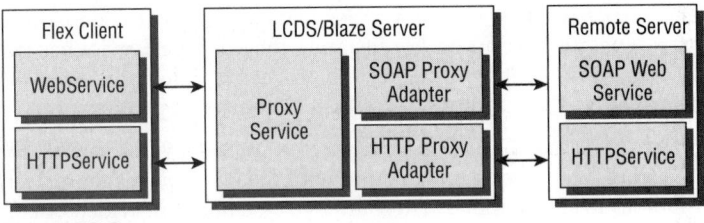

Figure 53-6

The Message Service

The Message Service provides publish-subscribe messaging, so the producer of a message is decoupled from the consumers. A Flex client may publish (or produce) a message by sending it to a Message Service destination. The message is then delivered to any subscribers (or consumers) of the same destination, so it may be delivered to zero or many other Flex clients. Messages can also be produced on the server side and pushed out to individuals or groups of clients. The Message Service also integrated with JMS queues and topics.

Figure 53-7 shows the Message Service and the Flex components for producing and consuming messages: the `Producer` and `Consumer`. Behind the Message Service are two adapters — the ActionScript adapter and the JMS adapter — the first for simple messaging between producers and consumers, the second for integrating with JMS message queues and topics on a JMS server. The Message Service is included with BlazeDS and LCDS, and is covered in Chapter 55.

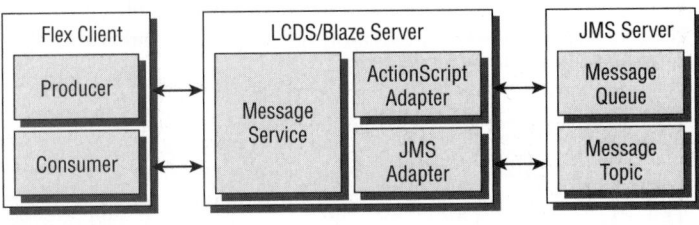

Figure 53-7

The Data Management Service

The DMS is the highest-level LCDS service, providing the richest set of features for simplifying the development of data-intensive applications. It deals with synchronization of data across multiple clients, conflict resolution when multiple clients alter the same data concurrently, automatic paging of large data sets for building more responsive applications, integration with relational databases through Hibernate or SQL, and tracking and reverting changes. Like the Remoting Service, it performs Java-to-ActionScript object mapping transparently, and like the Message Service it distributes data to multiple clients, pushing out changes in real time.

Figure 53-8 shows the DMS and its Flex counterpart, the `DataService` component.

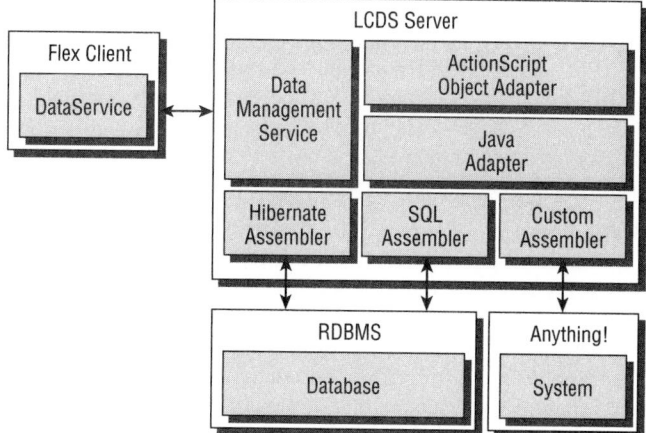

Figure 53-8

There are two standard adapters for the DMS: the ActionScript object adapter and the Java object adapter. The first manages a collection of transient data sent from Flex clients, tracking changes and distributing them to other clients. The second integrates with various assemblers to provide persistence and integration with other backend systems. Two assemblers are provided for integrating with relational databases through Hibernate and SQL, but custom assemblers can be written in Java to integrate with practically any kind of backend system. The DMS is covered in detail in Chapters 56 and 57.

PDF Generation

As well as the four main service types, LCDS provides some additional server-side features. In particular it includes a Java library for generating PDF documents by importing XML data into template files. This can be used in conjunction with one of the services, such as a Remoting Service or Message Service, to allow Flex clients to spawn PDF generation jobs and download the results. There is a simple example of this in Chapter 55, "The Message Service."

Communication Channels

There are various channels available for sending messages between Flex or AIR clients and an LCDS server. They each offer different behavior and are suited to different environments, so it's important to choose the correct channel types for a particular application.

Communication channels vary from one another in four ways:

❑ **Message format** — There are two formats available: AMF and AMFX. AMF (Action Message Format) is a compact binary data format, while AMFX is a more verbose XML representation of the same data, suitable for environments where binary messaging is disallowed.

❑ **Transfer protocol** — Four transport protocols are available: HTTP, HTTPS, RTMP, and RTMPS. The first two are standard HTTP and its secure (SSL) variation, HTTPS. The second two are proprietary protocols based on TCP for real-time streaming of binary data. Real Time Message Format (RTMP) and its secure variation, RTMPS, can be used with LCDS for sending AMF messages but not AMFX. The RTMP/S protocols are also used by other Adobe products, such as Flash Media Server (see Chapter 48) and Connect Professional for sending audio, video, and data between the client and server.

❑ **Communication model** — There are two basic communication models: call-and-response and streaming. Call-and-response is all that is needed for performing remote procedure calls on Java objects or proxying requests to HTTP Services or SOAP Web Services. For streaming or pushing data from the server, there are more possibilities and trade-offs to be considered. LCDS supports real duplex connections with the proprietary RTMP protocol; HTTP long-polling, which parks requests on the server until there is data to delivery to a client or a duration elapses; HTTP streaming, which establishes a "permanent" connection for receiving data from LCDS and sends upstream requests over a separate transient connection; and finally simple client-side polling, where the client polls the server periodically.

❑ **Endpoint type** — These can be servlet-based or new I/O (NIO)-based. The former relies on the J2EE servlet container to manage input and output, networking and sessions, whereas the latter takes advantage of the custom socket server provided with LCDS that runs outside of servlet container. The socket server uses the Java NIO APIs to improve performance and scalability, by sharing server threads among multiple requests instead of blocking in the manner of a servlet.

Channel sets can be defined for LCDS applications, containing multiple channels in order of preference. A client will first attempt to connect with the first channel, but if this is unsuccessful, it will fail over to the next channel in the set. This allows an LCDS application to support clients running in very different environments, offering the best experience to those able to use a streaming connection but degrading gracefully to a scenario where the clients a polling the server periodically.

Choosing the Best Channels

One of the engineers on the LCDS team, Seth Hodgson, has compiled general guidelines that make it easy to select the best channels for a particular application. This can be found in the Adobe LiveCycle archive of Damon Cooper's blog: www.dcooper.org.

The example applications that are featured in the subsequent chapters make use of different channels for different purposes. Call-and-response channels are used for remote object calls and Proxy Service interactions, whereas data-push channels are used with the Message Service and the DMS. However, all the applications use only a single connection between the client and server, which is shared by each of the destinations.

> It is almost always best to use a single connection between the client and server for all destinations that the client interacts with. Otherwise, there may be problems with failover, if the client cannot connect on one channel within a channel set.

Action Message Format (AMF)

LCDS applications make extensive use of the Action Message Format (AMF) for sending data between client and server because of its efficiency when compared with XML-based message formats. Strongly typed ActionScript and Java objects can be serialized quickly into AMF messages and sent over the wire, then deserialized again, back into strongly typed objects on the other side. AMFX, the XML variation, does not offer the same performance benefits as AMF, but satisfies the needs of enterprises that forbid binary message formats.

For those interested in the finer detail, Adobe has published the full specification for AMF at `http://download.macromedia.com/pub/labs/amf/amf3_spec_121207.pdf`.

Creating an LCDS Project in Flex Builder

Flex Builder supports LCDS and provides a wizard for creating new LCDS projects. This section explains how to create a new LCDS project in Flex Builder, with the server-side components deployed to an Apache Tomcat application server. The sample applications provided with this book are ready to be dropped into such a project. Each example contains a README.txt file with further details.

The following assumptions are made:

❑ The Flex Builder 3 or later plug-in has been installed on top of the Eclipse IDE for Java EE Developers. This version of Eclipse is recommended because it includes the Web Tools Platform, which simplifies the deployment of LCDS applications and creation of projects containing Java and Flex.

❑ The LiveCycle Data Services ES distribution has been downloaded and installed. A free trial version of this is available from the Adobe website, which also includes installation instructions and information about supported application servers:

    www.adobe.com/go/trylivecycle_dataservices

❑ An Apache Tomcat 5.5 or later application server has been installed locally and is configured to run on the default port, 8080. Apache Tomcat can be downloaded from:

    http://tomcat.apache.org/download-55.cgi

❑ The Java Open Transaction Manager (JOTM) 2.0.10 binary distribution has been downloaded and unpacked. This is needed for using the DMS in Apache Tomcat because its operations are transactional and Apache Tomcat does not include a transaction manager by default. JOTM can be downloaded from:

    http://jotm.objectweb.org

There are, of course, many ways to configure and deploy an LCDS application. The instructions that follow apply to the above, but with minor changes a different application server could be used.

The New Flex Project Wizard

To begin, launch the New Flex Project wizard by selecting File ⇨ New ⇨ Flex Project.

Stage 1: Name and Server Technology

1. In the first step of the wizard, specify the following settings:

❏   Project name: LCDSExample (or whatever you like)

❏   Application type: Web application (runs in Flash Player)

❏   Application server type: J2EE

❏   Use remote object access service: checked

❏   LiveCycle Data Services: selected

❏   Create combined Java/Flex project using WTP: checked

Figure 53-9 shows the state of the wizard with these settings.

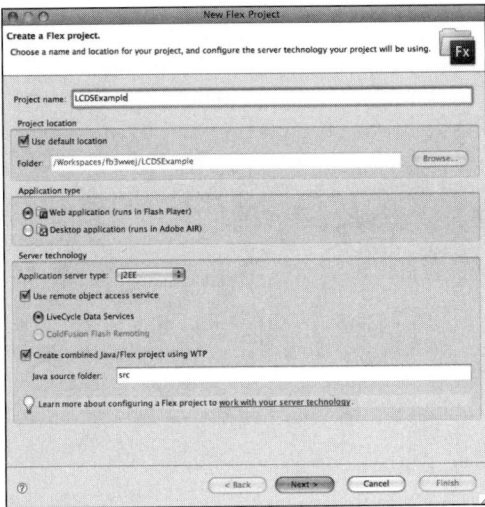

Figure 53-9

2.   Click the Next button to proceed to the J2EE settings stage.

Stage 2: J2EE Settings

If the Target runtime combo box does not already include Apache Tomcat 5.5 or later, do the following:

1.   Click New.

2.   Select Apache ⇨ Tomcat v5.5 Server (or your later version).

3.   Click Finish.

4.   Make the following settings:

❏   Target runtime: Apache Tomcat v5.5 (or later).

❏   Flex WAR file: LCDS/lcds.war, where LCDS is the path to your LCDS installation

The other settings can be left with their default values. The wizard should look close to Figure 53-10, with the correct path for your system.

5. Click the Next button again to proceed to the build path stage.

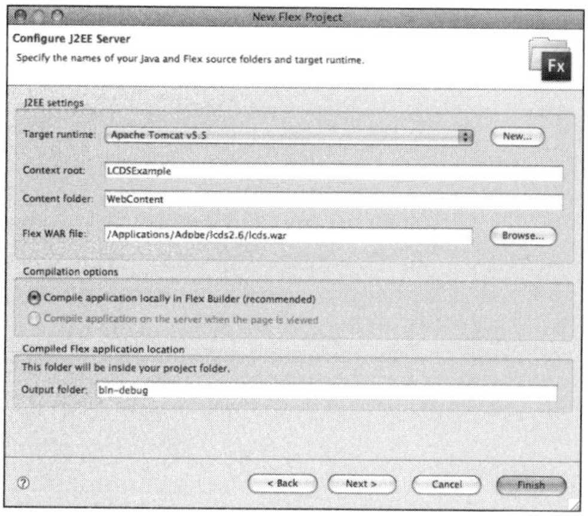

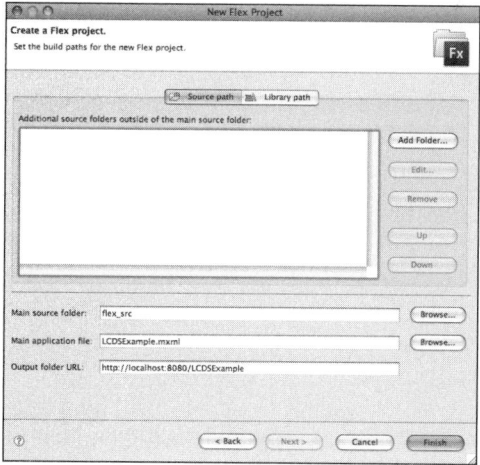

Figure 53-10

Stage 3: The Build Path

This stage of the wizard is the same as for a normal Flex project. In most cases, the default settings are fine, but additional source folders or build libraries can be added at this point. These can always be added later via the Project Properties dialog. Note that the output URL is shown; this is the address that the LCDS application will be accessible from when it has been deployed to Apache Tomcat. Figure 53-11 shows the wizard with default settings.

Figure 53-11

Click Finish to complete the creation of an empty, combined Java-and-Flex LCDS project. The following table describes the structure of the project.

Folder	Description
bin-debug	The compiled SWF client and HTML template.
flex-libs	The Flex build path libraries. This is initially empty, but any SWCs required for building the application can be added here. For instance, the Cairngorm.swc may be added if the client is based on the Cairngorm micro-architecture.
flex-src	The Flex client source code. This is where the source code for the LCDS client application should be placed.
src	The Java server-side source code. This is where any custom assemblers, adapters, or other server-side classes written in Java should be placed.
WebContent	The root folder of the LCDS web application. The contents of this folder will be deployed into the application server.
WebContent/WEB-INF	Contains the web application deployment descriptor, web.xml. This defines the message broker servlet used as the entry point to LCDS services when the servlet-based channels are used.
WebContent/WEB-INF/classes	The compiled Java classes produced from the source code in the src folder.
WebContent/WEB-INF/flex	The LCDS XML configuration files, including services-config.xml, data-management-config.xml, messaging-config.xml, proxy-config.xml, and remoting-config.xml. These are used to configure channels, end points, destinations, adapters, and assemblers.
WebContent/WEB-INF/lib	The LCDS Java libraries and other dependencies.

Configuring the Application Server

The Web Tools Platform (WTP) makes it simple to deploy an LCDS application to an application server from within the Eclipse IDE. This is achieved using the Servers view: Window ⇨ Show ⇨ Other ⇨ Servers.

If the Apache Tomcat 5.5 server that was configured during the New Flex Project Wizard is not shown, then register it with the Servers view by following these instructions:

1. Right-click in the Servers view and choose New ⇨ Server.

2. Specify the following settings:

   ❑ Server's host name: localhost

   ❑ Select server type: Apache ➪ Tomcat v5.5 Server (or your later version)

   ❑ Server name: Tomcat 5.5 for LCDS Example (or any other descriptive name)

3. Click Next.

4. Select LCDSExample from the available projects.

5. Click Add, and then Finish.

The Servers view should now show the "Tomcat 5.5 for LCDS Example" entry. If this is expanded, the LCDSExample project should be visible, as shown in Figure 53-12.

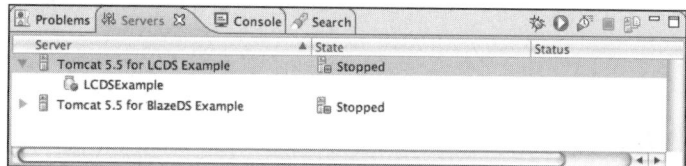

Figure 53-12

From this view, the server can be started and stopped in normal or debug mode, using the controls at the top of the view or the right-click context menu. Whenever the server is started, the LCDS application will be deployed. When changes are made, these are detected and the application is redeployed, but it is sometimes safest to stop and start the server manually to be sure the latest version of the application is running.

Installing the Transaction Manager

Apache Tomcat is a servlet container rather than a full-blown J2EE application server, so it doesn't include a transaction manager. The DMS is transactional, so it is necessary to manually configure a transaction manager. Luckily, the Java Open Transaction Manager (JOTM) is freely available from `http://jotm.objectweb.org`.

After unpacking the distribution, copy the following JOTM files into the Apache Tomcat application server, as described in the following table:

JOTM Files	Tomcat Location
jotm/conf/carol.properties	tomcat/common/classes/
jotm/conf/log4j.properties	tomcat/common/classes/
jotm/lib/*.jar	tomcat/common/lib/

Now create a `context.xml` file inside the `LCDSExample` web application:

```
WebContent/META-INF/context.xml.
```

Type the following XML into the file to associate the LCDS application with the JOTM transaction manager:

```
<Context privileged="true" antiResourceLocking="false" antiJARLocking="false">
    <Transaction factory="org.objectweb.jotm.UserTransactionFactory"
        jotm.timeout="60"/>
</Context>
```

And that is that. A new LCDS project ready for deployment into Tomcat. In the chapters that follow, various sample applications are described, making use of each of the service types and many of the features of LCDS. These projects are each built on top of an empty project, created according to these instructions.

Troubleshooting

It's fair to say that there are more things to go wrong in an LCDS application than a basic Flex client. There's the server side as well as the client side, and networks in between. The Java and Flex libraries need to be used correctly, and the application needs to be configured to suit the environment in which it is deployed, so that firewalls or proxy servers don't interrupt communications. This section describes some measures to help troubleshoot when LCDS is not behaving as expected.

Logging

Both LCDS and BlazeDS produce extensive client- and server-side logs. These can be switched on and off, and filtered in various ways to help developers diagnose problems or simply better understand the behavior of LCDS. All the messages that are sent back and forth can be viewed, and detailed stack traces are recorded whenever something goes awry.

Client-Side Logging

Client-side log statements are issued through the Flex logging framework, which is covered in detail in Chapter 74, "The Logging Framework." To enable client-side logging, add the following trace target to the MXML application file:

```
<mx:TraceTarget loglevel="{ LogEventLevel.DEBUG }"/>
```

When the application is run in debug mode from Flex Builder, a quantity of log messages will appear in the Flex console. These can be filtered and targeted differently by configuring the Flex logging framework, as described in Chapter 74, "The Logging Framework."

Server-Side Logging

Server-side logging is configured in the `services-config.xml` file. Towards the bottom of this file is a `logging` element that specifies the level of logging and filters to apply.

```
<logging>
    <target class="flex.messaging.log.ConsoleTarget" level="Debug">
        <properties>
            <prefix>[LCDS] </prefix>
            <includeDate>false</includeDate>
            <includeTime>false</includeTime>
            <includeLevel>false</includeLevel>
            <includeCategory>false</includeCategory>
        </properties>
        <filters>
            <pattern>Endpoint.*</pattern>
            <pattern>Service.*</pattern>
            <pattern>Configuration</pattern>
            <pattern>SocketServer.*</pattern>
        </filters>
    </target>
</logging>
```

Here the log level is `Debug`, so a lot of messages will be generated. To show only error messages, change the `level` attribute value to `Error`. The data, time, level, and category are not shown alongside log statements, but they can be enabled by changing the `false` values to `true`. The filter patterns ensure that logs generated by the most important LCDS classes are captured.

Server-Side Debugging

LCDS projects often involve writing server-side classes in Java, such as custom assemblers for the DMS or classes for use by the Remoting Service. This code can be debugged with the Eclipse debug perspective, by placing breakpoints and starting the application server in debug mode. When the server code executes and the breakpoint is reached, processing will be suspended, state can be examined, and processing can be resumed in a step-by-step manner. More information about server-side debugging is provided in Chapter 71, "Debugging Flex Applications."

Summary

This chapter set the scene for those that follow, where the features of each of the LCDS and BlazeDS service types are explored in detail. Each chapter includes one or more sample applications to demonstrate these features: there's a stock price ticker, a chat room, and PDF generation in the Message Service chapter; there's a synchronized vehicle tracking application built with the DMS; and there's weather forecasting via the Remoting Service and Proxy Service. These cover LCDS from the client and server perspectives, including the LCDS Flex components, the configuration files, the Java APIs, and integration with other systems such as JMS and remote SOAP Web Services.

LCDS and ColdFusion

The release of ColdFusion 8 has brought with it some major breakthroughs in building robust solutions that take advantage of both ColdFusion's data access capabilities and the capabilities of LiveCycle Data Services (LCDS) ES for managing data and build real-time push-enabled multi-client applications.

This chapter details some of the advances in ColdFusion and LCDS integration since the release of ColdFusion 8. Although this chapter focuses more on ColdFusion and LCDS concepts, it is worthwhile information for a Flex developer, since ColdFusion and LCDS are the Adobe-provided back-end solutions for Flex applications. The following topics are covered in this chapter:

- ❏ ColdFusion and LCDS integration
- ❏ LCDS-specific event gateways
- ❏ LCDS data management with ColdFusion

ColdFusion 8 and Integrated LCDS

As of ColdFusion 8, Adobe has provided some features to further the interaction capabilities of ColdFusion and an external LCDS server. To take it even further, Adobe has given the user the ability to install an integrated copy of LCDS during the ColdFusion installation.

LCDS-Specific ColdFusion Installation Screens

Although the entire ColdFusion installation process will not be covered, the section of the installation specific to the integrated installation of Adobe LCDS will be covered.

Subcomponent Selection Screen

During the ColdFusion 8 installation, you are prompted to select the integrated technologies you would like to install. Here is where you can specify to install the integrated LCDS server, as shown in Figure 54-1.

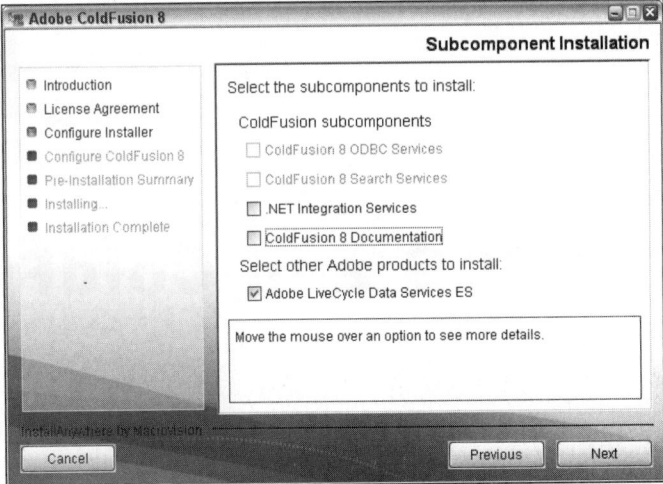

Figure 54-1

LCDS ES License Acceptance Screen

Further on in the installation you will be prompted to accept the license agreement for your integrated LCDS installation, as shown in Figure 54-2.

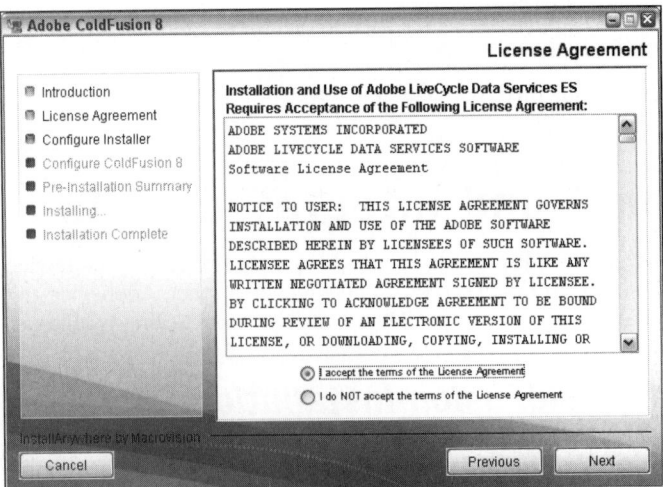

Figure 54-2

LCDS ES Serial Number Screen

The next screen you will need to take into account is the serial number screen for LCDS ES, as illustrated in Figure 54-3.

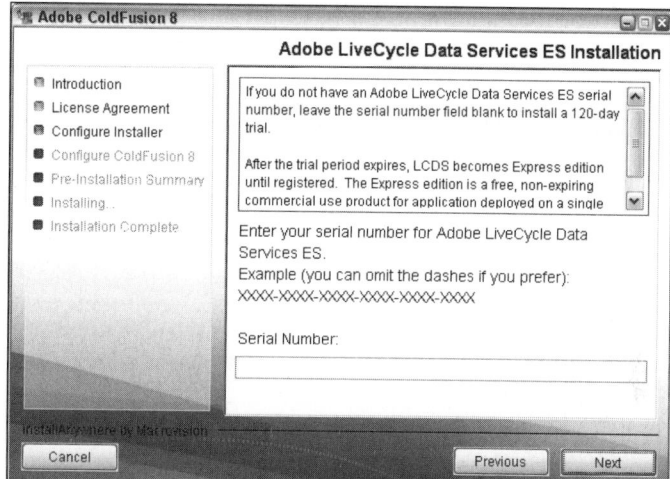

Figure 54-3

Note that you don't have to enter a serial number at this point, since the installation of the integrated LCDS will default to a 120-day trial. As a matter of fact, if you prefer not to purchase LCDS, at the end of the 120-day period, the installation will scale down to a nonexpiring express edition.

Complete the Installation

The preceding three screens are the only LCDS-specific screens that you need to be concerned about during the ColdFusion 8 installation. Other than that, complete the remainder of the installation as you normally would for your ColdFusion installations.

LCDS-Specific ColdFusion Administrator Screens

For the most part, ColdFusion servers are managed via the ColdFusion Administrator web application. Within the ColdFusion Administrator, there are a couple screens that could affect the interaction between LCDS instances and the ColdFusion server.

Data & Services ⇨ Flex Integration

The Flex Integration screen within the ColdFusion Administrator serves a dual purpose. First, it is used to turn Flash Remoting on and off. If you are having issues with a Flex or AIR application that communicates directly with the ColdFusion server by using `RemoteObject`, you'll want to make sure that Flash Remoting is enabled.

As mentioned previously, ColdFusion works with both an integrated version of LCDS and an external version. If you installed LCDS as a subcomponent of your ColdFusion installation, everything was pre-configured for you and there's no reason to access this screen. However, if you have an external LCDS installation and need to connect to ColdFusion using remote method invocation (RMI), you'll need to make configuration changes to this screen. You'll also need to make changes if you have an external LCDS installation and need to take advantage of some of the data management capabilities built into ColdFusion. Figure 54-4 shows the Data & Services ⇨ Flex Integration screen.

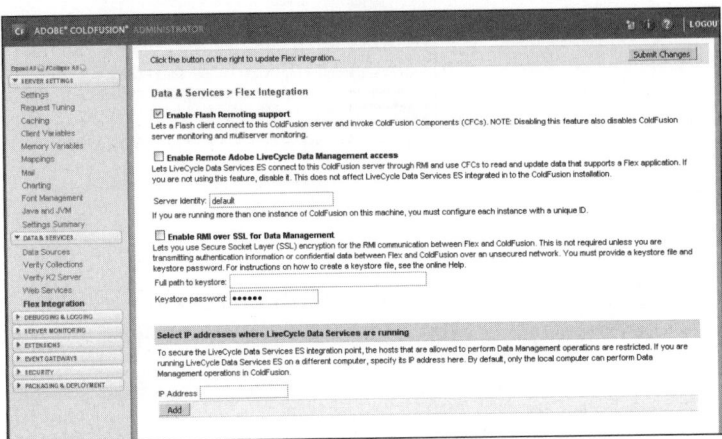

Figure 54-4

Event Gateway Configuration

This section discusses event gateways and notification. This is the core means of communicating between ColdFusion and LCDS. There are a couple screens in the ColdFusion Administrator that you'll need to be familiar with if you are planning to start working with event gateways.

Event Gateways ⇨ Gateway Types

Gateway types are Java classes that you instantiate into gateway instances on your ColdFusion server. ColdFusion offers a couple predefined gateway types for use with LCDS integration:

❑ `DataManagement` points to the Java class `coldfusion.eventgateway.flex` `.FlexDataManagementGateway`.

❑ `DataServicesMessaging` points to the Java class `coldfusion.eventgateway.flex` `.FlexMessagingGateway`.

If you need to view, update, or delete their configuration, use the Event Gateways ⇨ Gateway Types screen, as shown in Figure 54-5.

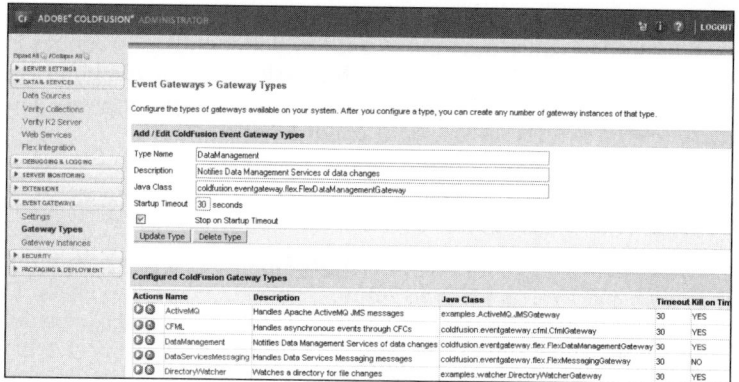

Figure 54-5

Event Gateways ⇨ Gateway Instances

Before you can use the `DataManagement` or `DataServicesMessaging` gateway types, you need to configure gateway instances, which you can do via the Event Gateways ⇨ Gateway Instance screen (see Figure 54-6).

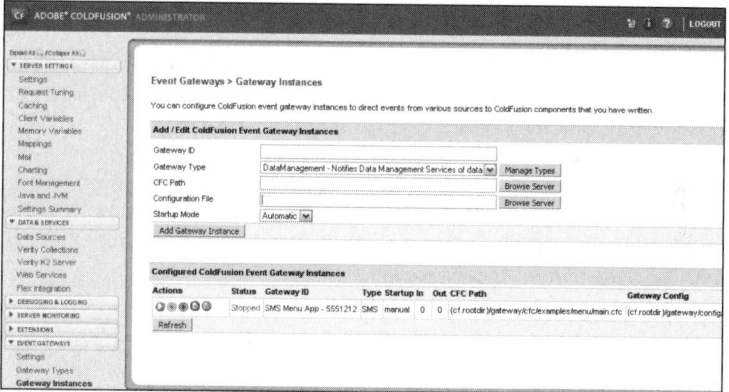

Figure 54-6

Notice that the Gateway Instance configuration screen is also where you can start, stop, edit, delete, and monitor your event gateway instances.

Event Gateways

Event gateways are a powerful and extensible protocol-agnostic communication architecture in ColdFusion. Using event gateways, ColdFusion can send and receive messages asynchronously with many different types of external services, including Short Message Service (SMS), Extensible Messaging and Presence Protocol (XMPP), sockets, Flash Media Server, and, most importantly, LCDS.

Event gateway types are Java classes that can be instantiated by the ColdFusion server to create an event gateway instance at runtime, which can then be used by both ColdFusion applications and applications built with other technologies, such as Flex applications. Although you can build your own event gateway, when you install LDCS with ColdFusion, you get two LCDS-specific event gateway types that are prebuilt and ready for you to implement in your applications.

DataServicesMessaging

`DataServicesMessaging` is an event gateway type that allows two-way communication between a ColdFusion application and Flex applications running on an LCDS server. The LCDS feature that this gateway type utilizes is the Flex Message Service. One of the things that can be done with this service is sending messages from your ColdFusion application to Flex clients connected to an LCDS Message Service channel.

If you need to build a ColdFusion application to utilize this event gateway, there is a link at the end of this chapter to the ColdFusion LiveDocs. If you would like to learn how to build Flex applications that work with the LCDS Message Service, see Chapter 55, which discusses the Message Service in detail.

DataManagement

Unlike the `DataServicesMessaging` gateway type, the `DataManagement` gateway type is a one-way communication gateway to allow ColdFusion to communicate data-related messages to the LCDS Data Management Service. For instance, if a ColdFusion application updates some backend data that Flex clients are viewing through the Flex Data Management Service, the `DataManagement` event gateway can be used by the ColdFusion application to have the LCDS Data Management Service synchronize the Flex applications with the changed data.

Once again, if you need assistance with building the ColdFusion application to utilize this gateway type, a link has been provided to the ColdFusion LiveDoc on Data Management Event Gateways at the end of this chapter. For information on how to implement Flex applications that utilize the LCDS Data Management Service, take a look at Chapters 56 and 57.

Data Management

The ColdFusion server platform is an exceptional solution for accessing data from various sources, such as backend database systems, LDAP directories, and even Exchange Server. However, there aren't really any multi-client data management facilities built into the ColdFusion architecture. LCDS does not have any native data access capabilities but does offer these extended data management capabilities that ColdFusion lacks through its Data Management Service. This makes pairing ColdFusion and LCDS a very capable data management solution.

In a nutshell, working with LCDS data management in ColdFusion is very similar to working with LCDS data management while using Java as the data-access technology. The main differences between using Java and ColdFusion with data management are:

❑ Rather than using Java classes to build your data management assemblers, Data Access Objects (DAO), and Value Objects (VO), you use ColdFusion components (CFCs).

- ❏ A ColdFusion assembler's `fill()` method can not only return an array of VOs but also return ColdFusion query objects and ColdFusion structures.

- ❏ When you create your `services-config.xml` channels, you need to make sure that any channel to be used with ColdFusion has the `<instantiate-types/>` property set to `false`.

- ❏ ActionScript and Java are both case-sensitive languages, whereas ColdFusion is not.

Case sensitivity is a major tripping point when developers migrate from ColdFusion to ActionScript and vice versa. When you start using ColdFusion as your LCDS data access layer, you will need to keep this in mind. Here are a couple tips to help you out:

- ❏ When you create your LCDS destinations in your `data-management-config.xml` file, you have access to certain elements used to force ColdFusion identifiers to lowercase:

  - ❏ `<force-cfc-lowercase/>`

  - ❏ `<force-query-lowercase/>`

  - ❏ `<force-struct-lowercase/>`

- ❏ When you work with structures in ColdFusion, you can use a dot notation, `structure.property`, or an array access notation, `structure["property"]`. When you use dot notation, all characters in the property name will be capitalized, whereas when you use array notation, the characters will be preserved. Needless to say, use array notation when you can.

Some of the terms and concepts discussed about data management might be foreign to you. Although no more detail about the integration of ColdFusion with the LCDS Data Management Service will be covered at the moment, some useful links to the Adobe LiveDocs have been provided at the end of this chapter. In addition, LCDS data management will be covered in greater detail during Chapters 56 and 57. If you're enticed and can't wait to get started with LCDS Data Management, feel free to jump ahead.

Summary

This chapter discussed some very powerful LCDS and ColdFusion integration features. It is apparent when looking at the ColdFusion installation and administration screens that this tight integration was intentionally architected into ColdFusion 8. Having this integration is very useful for allowing ColdFusion-based applications to communicate with Flex applications through event gateways and LCDS. You can also leverage the sheer power of ColdFusion as a data access solution to be used as the backend for the LCDS Data Management Service thanks to the LCDS and ColdFusion 8 integration.

If you would like to do additional reading on LCDS and ColdFusion integration, here are Adobe LiveDocs of particular interest:

- ❏ **ColdFusion 8 Help Documentation Start Page:** www.adobe.com/support/documentation/en/coldfusion

- ❏ **LCDS ES Assembler/Data Management:** http://livedocs.adobe.com/coldfusion/8/htmldocs/UseFlexDataService_01.html

- ❏ **Data Type Translation between ActionScript and ColdFusion:** http://livedocs.adobe.com/coldfusion/8/htmldocs/UseFlexDataService_10.html

❑ **Event Gateways:** `http://livedocs.adobe.com/coldfusion/8/htmldocs/UseGateways_1.html`

❑ **Data Services Messaging Event Gateway:** `http://livedocs.adobe.com/coldfusion/8/htmldocs/UseFlex2Gateway_1.html`

❑ **Data Management Event Gateway:** `http://livedocs.adobe.com/coldfusion/8/htmldocs/UseLiveCycleGateway_1.html`

In the next chapter, you will look at the Message Services available in LCDS. This will build upon the knowledge you have acquired over the last two chapters and enable you to start building some really powerful real-time collaboration and communication applications.

The Message Service

The Message Service component of LiveCycle Data Services makes it easy to build Flex applications that consume or produce messages. These messages are simply packets of data containing anything of interest to an application. For example, a stock market prices application might consume messages containing the latest stock prices, while a chat feature built into an application could produce and consume chat messages while users converse with one another.

Message Service Overview

This chapter covers the Message Service in detail. It begins by explaining the basic workings of the technology, and then explains how to use the main client and server-side features before diving into three sample applications. The first of these is a chat client that consumes and produces messages, and supports multiple chat rooms; the second is a live stock prices client that uses the LCDS Java APIs to push pricing messages out from the server; the third demonstrates Java Message Service (JMS) integration and the PDF document generation capabilities of LCDS.

Message Service Technology Explained

This section explains the basic workings of the Message Service in preparation for learning how to use the client- and server-side features to build real messaging applications. Figure 55-1 shows the main components of such an application.

Publish and Subscribe

Flex and AIR clients can both interact with the Flex Message Service, first by publishing (or sending) messages to a Message Service destination and second by subscribing to one or more destinations, in order to receive the messages that are sent to them. This is an implementation of the *publish-subscribe paradigm*, which is an asynchronous method of communication that decouples the senders from the receivers of messages, so one can know nothing of the other. A sender can publish a message without knowledge of whether it will be consumed by any client, and similarly, a receiver can subscribe and consume messages with no knowledge of where they originated.

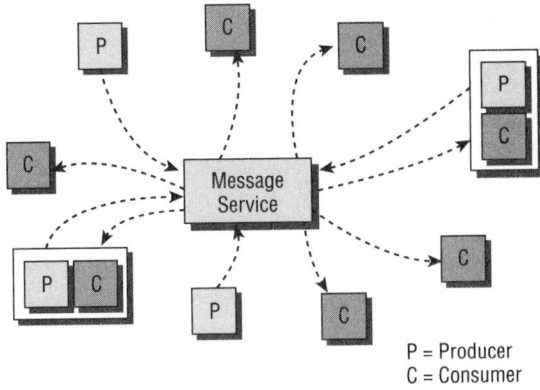

P = Producer
C = Consumer

Figure 55-1

Producers and Consumers

The senders or publishers or messages are known as *producers*, while the receivers or subscribers are known as *consumers*. A Flex or AIR client can be both a producer and consumer of messages, or may be just one or the other, depending on the application. For example, the chat application that features later in the chapter acts as producer and consumer of chat messages, while the stock price application only consumes messages pushed out from the server side.

The LCDS Flex APIs make it easy to produce and consume messages to and from different Message Service destinations. To do so, instances of the Producer and Consumer class are used and these provide methods and properties for establishing subscriptions and controlling message filtering, as well as dispatching various events, including the MessageEvent whenever a messages is received. These classes and events are covered in detail in the "Using the Message Service" section and the example applications that follow.

Messages Travel through a Channel

In the same manner as the Remote Object Services and Data Management Service, the messages sent between the client and server travel through a channel. The particular type of channel depends on the LCDS configuration and the client environment, as described in Chapter 53, "Introduction to LCDS." In any case, it is possible to build fast and responsive messaging applications, but the best performance is achieved when a real-time streaming channel, such as RTMP, is available rather than a polling channel. If a client is connected to multiple destinations of an LCDS application concurrently, the messages that are sent backward and forward will share the same channel.

Pushing Messages from the Server

A Java server-side component can also act as a client to the Message Service by routing messages to a destination or pushing them to specific subscribers. The LCDS Java APIs allow a Java programmer to interact directly with the Message Service. Various extensibility points are provided so that the Message Service can be integrated with other backend systems. These APIs are used by the JMSAdapter, provided for integration with Java Message Services, and also the ColdFusion Event Gateway Adapter, described in the ColdFusion documentation.

Using the Message Service

Building a Flex or AIR application that makes use of the Message Service usually involves client-side coding together with some server-side configuration. This section explains how to perform the most common tasks, beginning with configuring a Message Service destination then covering different aspects of client-side programming, including connecting to destinations, sending and receiving messages, filtering in different ways, and recovering from errors.

Configuring a Destination on the Server

When a client sends a message, the message must be directed to a Message Service destination. The same is true in the other direction: a client must be subscribed to a destination in order to receive messages from it. Message Service destinations are configured in the messaging-config.xml file within the WEB-INF/flex folder of an LCDS web application, for example:

```
<service id="message-service" class="flex.messaging.services.MessageService">
    <adapters>
        <adapter-definition id="jms"
            class="flex.messaging.services.messaging.adapters.JMSAdapter"/>
        <adapter-definition id="actionscript"
            class="flex.messaging.services.messaging.adapters.ActionScriptAdapter"
            default="true"/>
    </adapters>
    <destination id="myDestination"/>
</service>
```

The adapters element is automatically generated when a new LCDS project is created in Flex Builder. It defines two adapters for the Message Service, the first being the JMSAdapter, for integrating with Java Message Services, and the second being the ActionScriptAdapter for standard Flex messaging without further integration. The adapters are given unique identities with the id property, and the actionscript adapter is made the default by specifying default="true".

Below the adapters element, zero or more Message Service destinations can be specified using destination elements. The default settings for a Message Service destination are sensible and appropriate for many cases, so defining a new destination can be as simple as adding a single line to the configuration file, as shown here:

```
<destination id="myNewDestination"/>
```

All destinations must have unique identities specified with the id property. These will be needed on the client side in order to publish and subscribe to the destination.

Enabling Subtopics

The default settings that apply to a Message Service destination mean that subtopics are disabled. If subtopics are required, the allow-subtopics server configuration property must be specified and the optional `subtopic-separator` property may be used to change the separator from the default . (period) character.

```
<destination id="myDestinationWithSubtopics">
    <properties>
        <server>
            <allow-subtopics>true</allow-subtopics>
            <subtopic-separator>#</subtopic-separator>
        </server>
    </properties>
</destination>
```

In this case, subtopics have been enabled and the # character will be used to separate parts of the subtopic, so `room#flex` and `room#lcds` would both be valid subtopic names.

Expiring Messages

By default messages that are received by a destination do not expire and are only cleaned up after they have been delivered to all subscribers. However, in some cases it is perfectly acceptable for messages to expire and be discarded by the Message Service before they have been delivered. When this is true, the message stream is considered *lossy* and expected to expire some portion of messages before delivery, thus reducing network bandwidth and client load.

For example, consider a Flex client hooked up to a GPS system that displays the current locations of a fleet of vehicles. The tracking system is publishing messages every few seconds, but the Flex clients are only polling every 30 seconds in order to reduce network bandwidth. In this case, messages may become obsolete before they have been delivered and so can safely be expired. This can be achieved by setting the `message-time-to-live` server property of the destination, as shown here:

```
<destination id="myDestinationWithSubtopics">
    <properties>
        <server>
            <message-time-to-live>5000</message-time-to-live>
        </server>
    </properties>
</destination>
```

In this example, the value of 5000ms is specified, so undelivered messages will expire after 5 seconds, and Flex clients will only receive messages that are newer than that. Note that this setting is redundant when a streaming channel is used instead of a polling channel since messages are pushed out as soon as they are received with streaming channels.

Message Queue Processing

The Message Service maintains a queue of outbound messages for each subscribed client. A queue processor is used for managing these queues, which may involve prioritizing and filtering messages, throttling (restricting) the message flow, conflating (merging) multiple messages into one, and deciding when to flush the message queue by passing the messages to the network layer for delivery. The default implementation flushes the message queue whenever a poll is received for a polling channel, allowing the queue to grow in between polls, or flushes immediately when a message is received for RTMP push channels.

A custom message queue processor can be implemented to prioritize, filter, throttle, conflate, and flush messages in the best way for a particular application. Special-purpose prioritization rules can be applied to allow certain messages to jump to the front of the queue, while others are relegated to the back. For a trading application, a trade message is usually more important than a stock price tick. Throttling can be used to restrict the outward flow of messages and apply a chosen policy when the limit is exceeded. This policy may be to merge or *conflate* two or more messages into one, to replace older messages with newer ones, or to discard lower-priority messages. There is no "one size fits all" for message queue processing and the most suitable behavior depends on the specific requirements of the application.

The official *LCDS Developer Guide* includes a good chapter about custom queue processors, but unfortunately this topic is beyond the scope of this book.

Creating Messages on the Client

A Flex client can create messages and send them to a destination, as well as receive messages that were created externally. These messages implement the IMessage interface, which defines a number of read-write properties for setting and getting the details of a message. These are shown in the following table.

Property	Description
headers	An associative array of header information, where the key is the header name. This can be used for specifying additional information relating to a message that may be used for routing, filtering, identification, or other purposes specific to your application.
body	An object containing the main content of the message. For example, a message describing a stock price may have a body object with three properties—name, price and change—to identify the stock, its current price, and the change since the last published price.
clientId	The unique identity of the client that produced the message.
messageId	The unique identity of the message. This can be used to correlate a message with its acknowledgment.
destination	The Message Service destination that the message was sent to or received from.
timestamp	The date and time that a message was sent.
timeToLive	The number of milliseconds, from the timestamp, during which the message is considered valid and deliverable.

The most important properties are the headers and body, which contain the application-specific message data. This data may be simple dynamic objects, strings or number, but can also be XML or strongly typed objects with remote class mappings. The message body is normally used for the main message data, while headers are used for supplementary data or metadata.

To create a message in Flex, an instance of the AsyncMessage class is constructed and initialized. In the simplest case, this requires one line of code, with the message body being passed into the constructor:

```
var message:AsyncMessage = new AsyncMessage("hello world");
```

More complex messages can be assembled by setting elements of the headers array and specifying a body object with nested properties:

```
var message:AsyncMessage = new AsyncMessage();
message.headers.priority = priorityCombo.selectedItem;
message.headers.nickname = nicknameInput.text;
message.body = {
    text: messageTextArea.text,
    emotion: emotionCombo.selectedItem };
```

XML data can also be used for the message body, but not for the header values, which must be strings or numbers:

```
var xmlData:XML = <parent><child>Hello World!</child></parent>;
var message:AsyncMessage = new AsyncMessage( xmlData );
```

Instead of loosely typed objects and XML, a strongly typed object with a remote class mapping can be used. This offers the advantage of type safety when the message is parsed by a consuming client.

```
var person:Person = new Person();
person.firstName = "Joe";
person.lastName = "Blogs";
var message:AsyncMessage = new AsyncMessage(person);
```

Whether to store data in a header element or as part of the message body depends on how the data will be used. The Message Service supports filtering of messages based on the contents of the headers, so when this is required, the data to filter on should be stored in the headers. More information about filtering by subtopic and selector expression follows.

Sending Messages

To send a message to a destination, an instance of a `Producer` must first be created. The `destination` property is set to the ID of one of the destinations configured on the server side. Messages can then be sent using the `send()` function.

```
var producer:Producer = new Producer();
producer.destination = "myDestination";
var message:AsyncMessage = new AsyncMessage("Hello World!");
producer.send(message);
```

Although a `connect()` function is defined for the `Producer` class, there is no need to explicitly connect to a destination. The connection will be established automatically the first time a message is sent.

Acknowledgment and Fault Events

After a message has been sent, the producer will dispatch an acknowledgment or fault event. The acknowledgment event indicates that the message has been processed successfully by the Message Service on the server, while the fault event indicates that a has problem occurred, preventing the message from being processed correctly.

```
producer.addEventListener(MessageAckEvent.ACKNOWLEDGE,messageAcknowledgeHandler);
producer.addEventListener(MessageFaultEvent.FAULT,messageFaultHandler);
```

The `MessageAckEvent` contains a `correlation` property that references the original message which the acknowledgment correlates to. This can be used to confirm that an acknowledgment message relates to a particular outgoing message.

```
private function messageAcknowledgeHandler(event:MessageAckEvent):void
{
    if (event.correlation == originalMessage)
    {
        trace("The acknowledgment correlates to the original message");
    }
}
```

The `MessageFaultEvent` is used to propagate error messages from the messaging system. These may have originated on the server side or be due to problems on the client while attempting to connect to the Message Service destination and send the message.

```
private function messageFaultHandler(event:MessageFaultEvent):void
{
    trace("Simple error description:", event.faultString);
    trade("More details of the error:", event.faultDetail);
    trade("Route cause of error, if one exists", event.rootCause);
}
```

In most cases, a Flex client would display its own friendlier message to the client when a fault occurs, rather than passing on the fault message or details from the `MessageFaultEvent`. These properties are more useful for logging purposes to help developers understand why message sending has failed.

Receiving Messages

To receive messages from a destination, an instance of `Consumer` must first be created and initialized. In a manner similar to that of the `Producer`, the destination is set to the ID of a destination configured on the server:

```
var consumer:Consumer = new Consumer();
consumer.destination = "myDestination";
```

The consumer is subscribed using the `subscribe()` function to begin receiving message. An acknowledgment or fault event will be dispatched to indicate whether the subscription was successfully or not.

```
consumer.addEventListener(MessageAckEvent.ACKNOWLEDGE,subscribeAcknowledgeHandler);
consumer.addEventListener(MessageFaultEvent.FAULT,subscribeFaultHandler);
consumer.subscribe();
```

Handling Message Events

With the subscription in place, a consumer will begin to dispatch message events whenever it receives a message from the server. These message events have a `message` property of type `IMessage`, which contains the actual message.

```
consumer.addEventListener(MessageEvent.MESSAGE,messageEventHandler);
...
private function messageEventHandler(event:MessageEvent):void
```

```
    {
        var message:IMessage = event.message;
        textArea.text += message.body;
    }
```

In this example, the body of each message is simply appended to the text contained in a `TextArea`. Messages are handled in many different ways by different applications. In simple cases, the message body may be left unchanged and rendered immediately, while in other cases it may first be converted into a strongly typed object and passed through various layers of application code.

Extracting Message Data

Recall that application-specific message data is stored in the `headers` and `body` properties of a message. It is good practice to extract this data and store it in properties of a strongly typed object.

```
    private function messageHandler(event:MessageEvent):void
    {
        var price:Price = createPrice(event.message);
        ...
    }

    private function createPrice(message:IMessage):Price
    {
        var price:Price = new Price();
        price.name = message.headers.stockName;
        price.change = message.headers.percentageChange;
        price.price = message.body as Number;
        return price;
    }
```

In this example, the `createPrice()` method is used to create a `Price` object from the headers and body of a message. It is, of course, necessary to know something of the format of the message in order to extract data correctly. A message body may also be XML, in which case `e4x` can be used to extract the data and initialize strongly typed objects. Furthermore, strongly typed objects can be used as message bodies, in which case all that is required is a cast or coercion.

```
    var message:IMessage = event.message;
    var price:Price = Price(event.body);
```

In order for this to work, the `Price` class must define `[RemoteClass]` metadata so that it is properly serialized and deserialized by LCDS. Remote class mapping is described in more detail in Chapter 59, "Using BlazeDS."

Declaring Producers and Consumers in MXML

As well as instantiating producers and consumers in ActionScript, they can also be declared in MXML. This can be especially convenient for hooking up events handlers.

```
    <mx:Producer id="myProducer"
        destination="myDestination"
        acknowledge="producerAcknowledgeHandler(event)"
```

```
            fault="producerFaultHandler(event)"/>

    <mx:Consumer id="myConsumer"
        destination="myDestination"
        acknowledge="consumerAcknowledgeHandler(event)"
        fault="consumerFaultHandler(event)"
        message="consumerMessageHandler(event)"/>
```

Filtering Messages

There are two ways to filter the messages received by a consumer. The first is by message selector and the second by subtopic. Message selectors are expressions that are evaluated on the server to determine whether a message should be pushed out to a subscribed client, while subtopics are really categories of messages at a destination; a producer can send a message to a specific subtopic, and similarly, a consumer can subscribe to a specific subtopic (or multiple subtopics in advanced scenarios).

Filtering by Message Selector

A message selector is a string containing an SQL conditional expression. This is evaluated against the headers of any messages reaching a destination. Only when the expression evaluates to true will the message be pushed out to a subscribed client. A message selector might be used to ensure that a client only receives price-update messages when the price change is greater than 1.

```
    consumer.selector = "priceChange > 1";
```

The message selector syntax is based on the SQL92 specification.

Filtering by Subtopic

A subtopic is a named category at a destination that messages can be produced to and consumed from. For example, a user chat destination may use subtopics to represent different chat rooms, such as the room.flex and room.lcds subtopics. Subtopics are hierarchical and must be enabled for a destination in the server-side configuration file, as described earlier.

When sending a message to a subtopic, the subtopic is specified on the Producer instance:

```
    var producer = new Producer();
    producer.destination = "chatRoomsDestination";
    producer.subtopic = "room.flex";
    producer.send(new AsyncMessage("Hello World!"));
```

A MultiTopicProducer can be used instead of a conventional Producer in order to publish messages to multiple subtopics simultaneously. Please refer to the *LCDS Language Reference* for more details about multi-topic producers.

To receive messages from a subtopic, the subtopic property of the Consumer is specified:

```
    var consumer = new Consumer();
    consumer.destination = "chatRoomsDestination";
    consumer.subtopic = "room.flex";
    consumer.addEventListener(MessageEvent.MESSAGE, flexChatRoomMessageHandler);
    consumer.subscribe();
```

The wildcard character * can be used at the end of a subtopic name to subscribe to all subtopics under the parent subtopic. For example, room.* would subscribe to all messages sent to any subtopic with a name beginning in room.

Detecting Connectivity

The connected property of a consumer can be used to determine whether the consumer is subscribed to a destination. This property is bindable, so it can be used within a view to display the connectivity.

```
<mx:Consumer id="consumer" destination="chatRoomsDestination"/>
<mx:Label text="{ consumer.connected ? 'connected' : 'unconnected' }"/>
```

Here a binding expression is used to display "connected" or "unconnected," depending on the value of the consumer's connected property.

A consumer also dispatches events whenever the channel connecting it to a destination is disconnected or suffers a fault. A client can listen for these error events and handle them appropriately. From LCDS version 2.6.1, automatic recovery will be attempted on a specified interval, so your LCDS application can recover seamlessly from service or network problems. Please refer to the LCDS Language Reference for more details.

Publishing from the Server

Messages can be published directly from the server side using the LCDS Java APIs. This allows Java classes to act as message producers and provides an important means of integration with other backend systems. For instance, a Java class could be written to periodically poll a relational database and push out messages summarizing the latest data, or a class could be written to integrate with a mail server and push email messages to a Flex client.

Constructing Messages

On the server side, messages are constructed in much the same way as on the client side. There is an AsyncMessage class in the Java APIs that echoes the AsyncMessage class of the Flex APIs. An instance is created with the default constructor, the body and header properties are specified through setter methods.

```
AsyncMessage message = new AsyncMessage();
message.setHeader("myHeader","myHeaderValue");
message.setHeader("myOtherHeader","myOtherHeaderValue");
message.setBody("Hello World!");
```

There are various other properties that can be set on the message, including the destination, client ID, message ID, and timestamp. The message will be addressed to the given destination, which corresponds to a destination declared in the messaging-config.xml configuration file. The client ID is a unique identifier for the Java client that is sending the message. The message ID is unique identifier for this particular message, and the timestamp just an indication of when in time the message was created.

```
message.setDestination("myDestinationpdfNotificationDestination");
message.setClientId(javaClientID);
```

```
message.setMessageId(UUIDUtils.createUUID(false));
message.setTimestamp(System.currentTimeMillis());
```

Please refer to the *LCDS Java Language Reference* for more details about the `AsyncMessage` class.

Routing Messages to a Destination

The `MessageBroker` class can be used to route messages to specific destinations. An LCDS application normally has a single message broker instance that acts as the hub for all its messages. This can be accessed by using the static `getMessageBroker()` method:

```
MessageBroker broker = MessageBroker.getMessageBroker(null);
```

The parameter passed to `getMessageBroker()` can be used to identify a specific message broker instance; however, in most cases on a single instance exists for an LCDS application, so a null value can be passed. Please see the LCDS Javadoc for more information about message broker instances.

Once retrieved, a message can be routed to a Message Service destination by using the `routeMessageToService()` method. This method first locates the correct service, based on the type of the message parameter, then locates the destination that matches the `destination` property of the message object.

```
AsyncMessage message = new AsyncMessage();
message.setBody("Hello World!");
message.setDestination("myDestination");

MessageBroker broker = MessageBroker.getMessageBroker(null);
broker.routeMessageToService(message,null);
```

The second parameter of the `routeMessageToService()` method is not currently used, so a `null` value should be specified.

Pushing Messages to Specific Clients

The previous example showed how to push a message to a destination, from which it will be received by all subscribers, subject to the rules of subtopic and message selector filtering. It is also possible to direct messages to specific clients by using the `pushMessageToClients()` method of the `MessageService` class. First, the `MessageService` is located by the `MessageBroker`:

```
MessageBroker broker = MessageBroker.getMessageBroker(null);
MessageService service = (MessageService) broker.getService("message-service");
```

The `MessageBroker` instance is accessed through the same static method as before. The `getService()` method can then be used to retrieve any of the LCDS services. The parameter is the service ID as specified in the LCDS configuration files for each service type. In this case, we use `message-service` to identify the `MessageService` instance declared in the `messaging-config.xml` configuration file.

Once the `MessageService` have been retrieved, a message can be pushed out to a collection of clients. Every LCDS client has a universally unique identifier (UUID) or client ID that can be used for addressing purposes. These IDs are generated on the client side though, so it is normally necessary for a client to first tell the server its identity, so the server knows which client to push a message to.

In the PDF Generation example, covered in the next section, the client ID is first sent to the server side using a header property of a message. The Java Message Service (JMS) adapter is used and the client ID is extracted from the message by a JMS Listener. It is then stored and used to push out a message later, when the PDF document generation is complete.

```
AsyncMessage message = new AsyncMessage();
message.setDestination("pdfNotificationDestination");
message.setClientId(javaClientID);
message.setMessageId(UUIDUtils.createUUID(false));
message.setTimestamp(System.currentTimeMillis());
message.setBody("Hello World!");

Set<String> clients = new HashSet<String>();
clients.add(flexClientId);

service.pushMessageToClients(clients, message, false);
```

This excerpt from the PDF Generation example shows how a notification message is assembled and then routed back to a specific Flex client. The identity of the Flex client was stored earlier, after being retrieved from an incoming message. Note also that the outgoing message is given a UUID and a client ID. This client ID is the identifier of this Java object, which is acting as a client to the Message Service.

Message Service Applications

Having covered the main features of the Message Service, from the client and server perspectives, this section attempts to stitch the pieces together to from three coherent example applications. The source code for each should be referred to, since there is only enough space here for code excerpts.

The first example is a simple chat client that makes use of subtopics to allow users to converse in different chat rooms. The second example consumes stock price messages pushed out from the server with the LCDS Java APIs. The third example uses the PDF generation capabilities of LCDS in conjunction with the Java Message Service (JMS) adapter to integrate with a JMS Queue.

Example 1: Chat Rooms

The full source code for this example is contained in the `ChatRooms` project. This example demonstrates a simple, multi-room chat application built using the Message Service. Figure 55-2 shows a screenshot of the finished application.

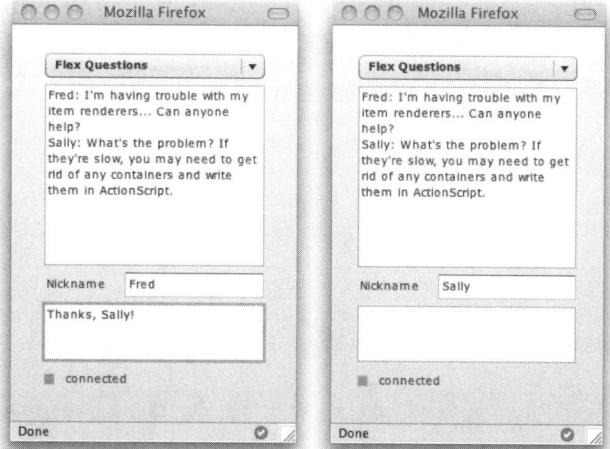

Figure 55-2

On the client side, the `Producer` and `Consumer` components are used for sending and receiving chat room messages, and different topic subscriptions are used for each chat room. On the server side, the ActionScript message adapter is used to process message and route them to subscribed clients.

The Chat Destination

First of all, a destination is configured to use the ActionScript adapter. This is the simplest adapter but is sufficient for our needs. It receives ActionScript messages and broadcasts them back to subscribed clients, applying subtopic and selector filtering.

The `destination` element of the `messaging-service.xml` configuration file is shown here:

```
<destination id="chatDestination">
    <properties>
        <server>
            <allow-subtopics>true</allow-subtopics>
        </server>
    </properties>
</destination>
```

The destination has the identity `chatDestination` and uses the default connection channels defined at the root level in `services-config.xml`. The default channel set contains the RTMP and polling AMF channels, so a client will first attempt to connect by RTMP before falling back to polling AMF if necessary. As discussed in Chapter 53, an LCDS application is best served by a single connection between the client and server, shared by all the destinations.

The `allow-subtopics` server property is set to true to enable subtopics, since a different subtopic will be used for each chat rooms. The default `subtopic-separator` of `.` will apply, so the following would be valid subtopic names: `room.flex` and `room.lcds`. No additional configuration settings are needed, since the Message Service defaults are suitable for most simple cases.

The ChatRoom Class

The `ChatRoom` class is defined to model chat rooms. It has three public properties: `label`, `subtopic`, and `conversation`. The first two are used when declaring chat rooms in MXML.

```
<mx:Array id="rooms">
    <model:ChatRoom label="Flex Questions" subtopic="room.flex"/>
    <model:ChatRoom label="LiveCycle Data Services" subtopic="room.lcds"/>
</mx:Array>
```

The `label` is rendered in a combo box used to select a chat room, while the `subtopic` is used for subscribing to the correct topic of the `chatRooms` destination. The `conversation` property is a bindable string. It is for storing the conversation that takes place in the chat room. When a new chat message is received it is appended to this string. The view binds to the `conversation` property.

The Chat Rooms Application

The view for this chat application is declared in a single MXML application file that contains a `Producer` and `Consumer` for the `chatRooms` destination:

```
<mx:Producer id="producer" destination="chatRooms"/>
<mx:Consumer id="consumer" destination="chatRooms"
    message="messageHandler(event)"/>
```

The consumer message event is hooked up to the `messageHandler()` function. This function extracts the nickname and message text from the `MessageEvent` and appends the message details to the `conversation` string for the active `ChatRoom` object.

```
private function messageHandler(event:MessageEvent):void
{
    var nickname:String = event.message.headers.nickname;
    var message:String = event.message.body.toString();
    var room:ChatRoom = ChatRoom(rooms.selectedItem);
    room.conversation += nickname + ": " + message;
}
```

A combo box is declared to allow users to select the current chat room. This is bound to the `rooms` array. When the chat room changes, the `roomChangeHandler()` is called.

```
<mx:ComboBox id="rooms" dataProvider="{rooms}" change="roomChangeHandler()"/>
```

The `roomChangeHandler()` sets the correct subtopic for the producer and consumer and resubscribes the consumer, so that messages posted to the selected chat room will be received:

```
private function roomChangeHandler():void
{
    subscribeToSubtopic(ChatRoom(rooms.selectedItem).subtopic);
```

```
    }

    private function subscribeToSubtopic():void
    {
        var subtopic:String = ChatRoom(rooms.selectedItem).subtopic;
        producer.subtopic = subtopic;
        consumer.subtopic = subtopic;
        consumer.subscribe();
    }
```

The actual conversation is rendered in a read-only `TextArea` that binds to the `conversation` string for the selected `ChatRoom` object:

```
<mx:TextArea id="conversation" editable="false"
    text="{ChatRoom(rooms.selectedItem).conversation}"/>
```

A chat message can be typed into the text area and when the user hits the enter key the message will be sent. The `keyUp` event is handled by the `keyUpHandler()` function, which constructs a new `AsyncMessage` object and sends it to the `chatRoom` destination using the `producer`. The text area is then cleared, ready for the next message.

```
    private function keyUpHandler(event:KeyboardEvent):void
    {
        if (event.keyCode == Keyboard.ENTER)
        {
            var message : AsyncMessage = new AsyncMessage();
            message.headers.nickname = nickname.text;
            message.body = input.text;
            producer.send(message);
            input.text = "";
        }
    }
```

Chat Rooms Summary

This example demonstrated a simple Message Service application that used a producer and consumer to send and receive messages to different subtopics of a single destination. On the server side, the destination used the default ActionScript adapter to route messages to connected clients over RTMP or polling AMF channels. On the client side, the `subtopic` property of the `Consumer` and `Producer` class was used, `AsyncMessage` objects were constructed, and `message` events were handled.

There are several ways in which this example may be extended or implemented differently to provide more features, such as integration with enterprise communication servers and persistence of chat messages. The JMS message adapter can be used to integrate with Java Message Services, and customized adapters can be plugged in to integrate with other enterprise systems. Alternatively, the Data Management Service, which is covered in subsequent chapters, can be used to persist chat messages to a database, provide access to chat history, and enable searching of chat messages.

Example 2: Stock Price Ticker

The requirement to push data efficiently from the server to distributed clients is a common one. In this example, the implementation of a simple stock price ticker is examined. On the server side, a Java thread is started to generate random prices simulating the market. This thread uses the LCDS Java APIs to route messages and broadcast them to users. On the client side, a consumer is used to receive price messages and update a model containing a dictionary of `Price` objects. These objects are rendered in a data grid that plays an effect to highlight price changes and indicates whether the prices have risen or fallen. Figure 55-3 shows a client that consumes stock price messages.

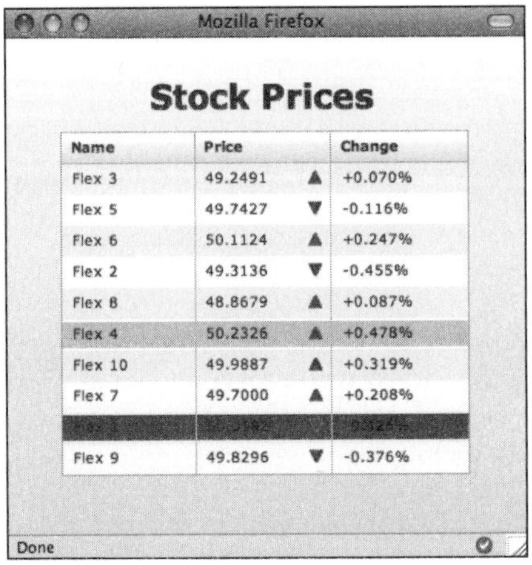

Figure 55-3

Please refer to the `StockPriceTicker` project, which includes the full source code for this example, as well as instructions for building and deploying it.

The Java Stock Feed

The stock feed is created by a Java thread spawned in the `service.StockFeeds` class. This class is registered in the `web.xml` deployment descriptor and implements the `javax.servlet.ServletContextListener` interface, so it receives events when the web application starts and stops. The feed thread is started when the web application starts and interrupted when it ends.

However, the most interesting part is the `sendPriceMessage()` method, which utilizes the LCDS Java APIs to assemble a price message, access the `MessageBroker` component, and then route the message to connected clients. The first part of the method simply gets the stock name, price change, and new price, then calculates the percentage change and updates the current price member variable.

```
String stockName = getStockName();
double change = getPriceChange();
double percentageChange = getPercentageChange( change );
double newPrice = getNewPrice( change );
currentPrice = newPrice;
```

The second part constructs an `AsyncMessage` object, which is the server-side counterpart to a Flex `AsyncMessage` object. The destination for the message is set to `stockFeed`, which is the name of a Message Service destination configured in the `messaging-config.xml` file. The client and message identifiers are also set. The `clientId` is an identifier for the `StockFeed` itself, since it is acting as a client to the Message Service. It is the same for all messages sent by this instance of the stock feed. The `messageId` is a unique identifier for each message that is sent and is generated using the static

`UUIDUtils.createUUID()` method provided by LCDS. The message is then timestamped before the header and body properties are set to contain the stock name, new stock price, and percentage change.

```
AsyncMessage message = new AsyncMessage();
message.setDestination("stockFeed");
message.setClientId(clientID);
message.setMessageId(UUIDUtils.createUUID(false));
message.setTimestamp(System.currentTimeMillis());
message.setHeader("stockName", stockName);
message.setHeader("percentageChange", new Double(percentageChange));
message.setBody(new Double(currentPrice));
```

The third part accesses the `MessageBroker` object through the static `getMessageBroker()` function of the same class. A `null` parameter is passed in, since the message broker has not been given an identity in the configuration files for this LCDS project. With the `MessageBroker` accessed, the message can be routed to all connected clients by using the `routeMessageToService()` function. The second parameter is currently unused by LCDS, so it is set to `null`. In the future, it may be used for identifying the end point through which the message will be sent. See the LCDS Javadoc for more information about the functions available on the `MessageBroker` class.

```
MessageBroker broker = MessageBroker.getMessageBroker(null);
if ( broker != null )
{
    broker.routeMessageToService(message, null);
}
```

The Stock Feed Destination

The stock feed sends messages to the `stockFeed` destination, which is configured in the `messaging-config.xml` configuration file:

```
<destination id="stockFeed"/>
```

The destination uses the default ActionScript Adapter, defined at the top of the `messaging-config.xml` file:

```
<adapters>
    <adapter-definition
        id="actionscript"
        class="flex.messaging.services.messaging.adapters.ActionScriptAdapter"
        default="true"
        />
</adapters>
```

And the destination uses the default channel set, specified at the root level in the `services-config.xml` file:

```
<default-channels>
    <channel ref="my-rtmp" />
    <channel ref="my-polling-amf"/>
</default-channels>
```

A client-to-server connection will be established over RTMP if possible, falling back to polling AMF if necessary.

The Flex Prices Model

An ActionScript class called `StockPrices` is used to receive messages from a `Consumer` and update both a `Dictionary` and an `ArrayCollection` of stock prices. The dictionary is used for looking up the current price while the collection is public and bindable for use by the view components.

The following excerpt shows the `initialize()` function, which sets the destination for the consumer, adds an event listener to handler message events, and subscribes to the destination:

```
private var consumer:Consumer = new Consumer();
...
public function initialize() : void
{
    consumer.destination = "stockFeed";
    consumer.addEventListener(MessageEvent.MESSAGE, messageEventHandler);
    consumer.subscribe();
}
```

Whenever a message event is received, the `messageEventHandler()` is invoked:

```
private var lookup:Dictionary = new Dictionary();
[Bindable]
public var prices:ListCollectionView = new ArrayCollection();
...
private function messageEventHandler(event:MessageEvent):void
{
    var newPrice:Price = createPrice(event);
    var oldPrice:Price = Price(lookup[newPrice.name]);

    if (oldPrice)
    {
        var index:Number = prices.getItemIndex(oldPrice);
        prices.removeItemAt(index);
        prices.addItemAt(newPrice, index);
    }
    else
    {
        prices.addItem(newPrice);
    }

    lookup[newPrice.name] = newPrice;
}
```

This function creates a `Price` object from the message then looks up the old price in the `lookup` dictionary. If an old price exists, it is replaced with the new price in the `prices` collection; otherwise, the new price is added straight into the collection. Finally, the `lookup` dictionary is updated with the new price, overriding the older entry.

The source code for the `createPrice()` function follows. It simply pulls data out of the message event and constructs a `Price` object to model the stock price.

```
private function createPrice(event:MessageEvent):Price
{
    var price:Price = new Price();
    price.name = event.message.headers.stockName;
    price.percentageChange = event.message.headers.percentageChange;
    price.price = Number(event.message.body);
    price.increased = price.percentageChange > 0;
    return price;
}
```

The stock name and percentage change values are pulled out of the message header. These header values were originally set in the Java `StockFeed` class. The actual price was contained in the message body, so it is retrieved from the `body` property and cast to a `Number`. The `increased` property is a `Boolean` and is set by determining whether the percentage increase was positive.

The Stock Price Ticker Application

In the main application file, an instance of the `StockPrices` class is declared in MXML. This is initialized on `creationComplete` and its `prices` collection is bound to the data provider for a data grid.

```
<mx:Application … creationComplete="stockPrices.initialise()">…
    <model:StockPrices id="stockPrices"/>…
    <mx:DataGrid … dataProvider="{stockPrices.prices}">…
```

The item renderers each contain a special child component for playing the increase and decrease effects. When the price increases, a green background appears and fades back to transparent, and in the same way, when a red background shows when the price decreases. Note, however, that effects like these can be CPU-intensive, so this approach should be avoided when implementing a large price grid that changes frequently. Instead, more efficient item renderers should be written that derive directly from `DataGridItemRenderer` or `UIComponent`.

Stock Prices Summary

This simple example has demonstrated several important aspects of a Message Service application. On the server side, the Java APIs for assembling and routing messages to destinations were shown, along with some of the configuration properties for throttling, caching, and subtopic control. On the client side, a `Consumer` subscription was made and `MessageEvent` objects were converted into strongly typed `Price` objects for storing in a dictionary and rendering in a data grid.

The pricing data for a real-life stock prices client would be produced by an enterprise system. This could be integrated with the Message Service by writing a Java class to receive price changes from the enterprise system, translating them into `AsyncMessage` objects, and routing them through the Message Service in a similar way to the `StockFeed` class.

Example 3: Generating a PDF

This final example demonstrates one way to perform server-side generation of PDF documents from a Flex client via the Message Service. PDF document generation is well suited to an asynchronous solution, since it may not be instantaneous, depending on the size and content of the document. The Message Service can be used to initiate a document generation job and then send a notification when it is complete. Figure 55-4 shows a simple Flex client for generating a customized PDF document.

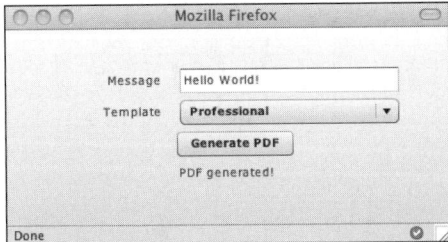

Figure 55-4

In this example, the Flex client sends a message to instruct the generation of a PDF. This is placed onto a Java Message Service (JMS) queue by the JMS Adapter for sequential processing by a JMS Listener. The JMS Listener performs the PDF document generation by importing data into a pre-prepared XFA template created earlier using LiveCycle Designer. When the PDF document generation is complete, a notification message is pushed out from the server to the client containing the URL from which it can be downloaded. A JBoss application server is used for hosting the LCDS web app and JMS queue.

Please refer to the `PdfGeneration` project for the full source code for this example. Note that in this case, PDF document generation is achieved by using the `XFAHelper` class, included as part of the LCDS server-side libraries. There are many more sophisticated options for the server-side generation and processing of PDF documents, several of which are packaged as solution components of Adobe LiveCycle Enterprise Suite.

PDF Generation Overview

The steps involved in this example are:

1. Prepare the Project.
2. Configure the JMS queue in JBoss.
3. Configure the Message Service destination.
4. Define the Resource References
5. Create the Java class for generating PDF documents.
6. Create the Java class for dequeuing messages and publishing notifications.
7. Create the Flex client to submit jobs, consume notifications, and download PDF documents.

Each step will now be explained, and the full source code is included in the `PdfGeneration` project.

Preparing the Project

Use the Flex Builder New Project Wizard to create a new Flex project using LCDS as the remote object access service, as described in Chapter 53. Specify the content folder as `web.war` and the output folder as `web.war/bin`. This means that the compiled SWF will be deposited inside the WAR for the LCDS web application, and deployment to JBoss will be simplified.

Configuring the JMS Queue

For the purposes of this example, the JBoss test queue is used. This is a preconfigured JMS queue included with JBoss 4 distributions. The specifics of JMS configuration depend on the application server and are beyond the scope of this book. For curious readers, the test queue is configured in the `jboss/server/default/deploy/jms/jbossmq-destinations-service.xml` file. The name of the test queue is, unsurprisingly, `testQueue`.

Configuring the Message Service Destination

Next, a Message Service destination must be configured. This will receive messages from the client to initiate PDF generation and publish messages to notify the client when generation is complete. As usual, the destination should be added to `messaging-config.xml`. In this case, the JMS adapter is defined at the top of the file in order to integrate the Message Service with a JMS queue:

```
<adapters>
    ...
    <adapter-definition
        id="jms"
        class="flex.messaging.services.messaging.adapters.JMSAdapter"
        />
</adapters>
```

The destination contains an assortment of JMS-related properties necessary for the Message Service to connect to the JMS queue:

```
<destination id="pdfGeneratorDestination">
    <properties>
        <jms>
            <destination-type>Queue</destination-type>
            <message-type>javax.jms.ObjectMessage</message-type>
            <connection-factory>
                java:comp/env/jms/connectionFactory
            </connection-factory>
            <destination-jndi-name>
                java:comp/env/jms/testQueue
            </destination-jndi-name>
            <destination-name>PdfQueue</destination-name>
            <delivery-mode>NON_PERSISTENT</delivery-mode>
            <message-priority>DEFAULT_PRIORITY</message-priority>
            <acknowledge-mode>AUTO_ACKNOWLEDGE</acknowledge-mode>
            <transacted-sessions>false</transacted-sessions>
        </jms>
    </properties>
    <adapter ref="jms"/>
</destination>
```

Note that the JMS connection factory has the name `java:comp/env/jms/connectionFactory`, and the JMS destination has the name, `java:comp/env/jms/generatePdfQueue`. These names are references to the JMS connection factory and queue, which are configured elsewhere. The adapter element references the JMS adapter declared previously. The default RTMP and polling AMF channels will be available for connecting from the client to the server.

Defining the Resource References

Resource references must be defined for the JMS connection factory and queue. These are used by the JMS adapter to locate and connect to the JMS message queue. They are defined in two places, the first of which is the `web.war/WEB-INF/web.xml` deployment descriptor. This maps the resource names to their Java class types and specifies the authorization and scope of the resources. The `resource-ref` elements should be declared beneath the existing `tag-lib` element.

```
<resource-ref>
    <res-ref-name>jms/connectionFactory</res-ref-name>
    <res-type>javax.jms.ConnectionFactory</res-type>
    <res-auth>Container</res-auth>
    <res-sharing-scope>Shareable</res-sharing-scope>
</resource-ref>
<resource-ref>
    <res-ref-name>jms/generatePdfQueue</res-ref-name>
    <res-type>javax.jms.Queue</res-type>
    <res-auth>Container</res-auth>
    <res-sharing-scope>Shareable</res-sharing-scope>
</resource-ref>
```

These tags correspond to a further pair of resource references declared in the `jboss-web.xml` file. This is the JBoss specific part of the web application deployment descriptor. Here a mapping is made from the resource references to the JNDI names that will be used for looking up and connecting to the JMS queue from Java classes.

```
<jboss-web>
    <class-loading java2ClassLoadingCompliance="false">
        <loader-repository>
            ROOT:loader=ROOT.war
            <loader-repository-config>
                java2ParentDelegation=false
            </loader-repository-config>
        </loader-repository>
    </class-loading>
    <context-root>PdfGenerator</context-root>
    <resource-ref>
        <res-ref-name>jms/connectionFactory</res-ref-name>
        <jndi-name>ConnectionFactory</jndi-name>
    </resource-ref>
    <resource-ref>
        <res-ref-name>jms/generatePdfQueue</res-ref-name>
        <jndi-name>queue/testQueue</jndi-name>
    </resource-ref>
</jboss-web>
```

Note that the `context-root` element specifies the same context root value that is contained with the Flex Builder web project settings. By default this is the name of the Flex project. The JNDI name for the queue is the name of the JBoss test queue mentioned earlier.

Creating the PDF Generator

The LCDS distribution includes the `XFAHelper` class, which is a utility class for generating PDF documents by importing data sets into XFA templates. These templates can be created using tools such as LiveCycle Designer. A template might be created for a bank statement or investment portfolio, then different data sets for different customers can be imported to create high-quality, personalized documents for printing, archiving, distribution, or processing.

A Java class called `PdfGenerator` is used to generate PDF documents. The code that performs the generation is shown here:

```
final String templatePath = templates.get(templateName);
final Document dataSet = createDataSet(text);
final XFAHelper helper = new XFAHelper();

try
{
    System.out.println("Opening PDF template: " + templatePath);
    helper.open(templatePath);

    System.out.println("Importing data-set into template…");
    helper.importDataset(dataSet);
    final byte[] pdfData = helper.saveToByteArray();
    helper.close();

    System.out.println("Writing PDF to the following path: " + path);
    final FileOutputStream file = new FileOutputStream(path);
    file.write(pdfData);
    file.close();
}
catch (IOException e)
{
    throw new PdfGenerationException(e.getMessage());
}
```

First, the filesystem path to the PDF template is pulled out of the `templates` map into a `templatePath` variable, and a `dataSetDocument` is created containing the text that will be pumped into the PDF template. Next, the `XFAHelper` class is constructed. This is the workhorse for performing PDF generation; it opens templates, imports data sets, and produces complete PDF documents. In this example, the `templatePath` is passed into the `open()` method to open the template, then the `dataSet` document is imported through the `import()` method, and the resulting PDF is saved to a byte array with the `saveToByteArray()` method. Afterward, the `close()` method is called to allow the `XFAHelper` to clean up after itself. Any errors that occur during the process are wrapped in a `PdfGenerationException`.

Creating the JMS Queue Listener

The JMS Queue Listener is a Java class that implements the `MessageListener` interface and listens to the preconfigured `testQueue` JMS queue. Each time a message is received, the `onMessage()` method is called. The main part of the implementation of this method is:

```
String client = message.getStringProperty("client");
String template = message.getStringProperty("template");
String text = ((ObjectMessage) message).getObject().toString();

String pdfName = UUIDUtils.createUUID(false) + ".pdf";
String path = basePath + "/" + pdfName;
String url = baseUrl + "/" + pdfName;

generator.generatePdf(path, template, text);
pushMessageContainingUrl(client, url);
```

The first part of the method extracts the useful data from the JMS message. This is the data sent from the Flex client in an `AsyncMessage` object. The `client` property contains the unique identifier of the Flex client and will be used later for routing the notification message when the PDF generation is complete. The `template` property contains an identifier for selecting the correct PDF template with which to perform generation. The message body contains the data to actually import into the PDF template. In this case, it is a simple string.

Next, a unique name is generated for the PDF using the `UUIDUtils` class that ships with LCDS. From this, the path to write the generated PDF to is constructed and the URL from which the client will be able to download the results. Everything is now in place to begin the PDF generation. The `path`, `template`, and `text` variables are passed into the `generatePdf()` method of the `PDFGenerator` class. Afterward, assuming no error has occurred, a message containing the URL for the PDF is pushed out to the client, using the `pushMessageContainingUrl()` method, shown here:

```
private void pushMessageContainingUrl(String flexClientId, String url)
{
    AsyncMessage message = new AsyncMessage();
    message.setDestination("pdfNotificationDestination");
    message.setClientId(javaClientId);
    message.setMessageId(UUIDUtils.createUUID(false));
    message.setTimestamp(System.currentTimeMillis());
    message.setHeader("status", "complete");
    message.setBody(url);

    MessageBroker broker = MessageBroker.getMessageBroker(null);
    MessageService service = (MessageService) broker.getService("message-service");

    Set<String> clients = new HashSet<String>();
    clients.add(flexClientId);
    service.pushMessageToClients(clients, message, false);
}
```

Here, the notification message is first constructed. A `status` header property is set to complete, and the message body contains the URL from which the PDF can be downloaded. The `MessageService` instance is located through the `MessageBroker`, and the message is then pushed out to the client. Recall that the client ID was retrieved from the original request message and is now used to address to notification.

Create the Flex PDF Generation Client

On the client side, the application file is very simple, containing only `TextInput` for typing the message that will end up inside the PDF, a `ComboBox` for selecting a PDF template name, a `Button` to initiate the PDF generation, and a `Label` to display the current status. Most of the work is actually performed by the `PdfGenerator` class, which is written in ActionScript and declared in MXML at the top of the application file.

The `PdfGenerator` initializes a producer and consumer. The producer is used for sending messages to initiate PDF generation jobs, while the consumer is used to receive notification messages when PDF generation is complete.

```
private function initializeServices() : void
{
    producer = new Producer();
    producer.destination = GENERATOR_DESTINATION;
```

```
    producer.addEventListener(MessageAckEvent.ACKNOWLEDGE, onGeneratorAcknowledge);
    producer.addEventListener(MessageFaultEvent.FAULT, onFault);
    producer.connect();

    consumer = new Consumer();
    consumer.destination = NOTIFICATION_DESTINATION;
    consumer.addEventListener(MessageEvent.MESSAGE, onNotificationMessage);
    consumer.addEventListener(MessageFaultEvent.FAULT, onFault);
    consumer.subscribe();
}
```

Event listeners are attached to the services to hear `acknowledge` events when PDF generation requests have been received, `message` events when PDF generation is complete, and `fault` events if an error occurs while communicating with either of the destinations.

When a PDF generation job is initiated, a message is sent by the producer. The message contains in its body the text to import into the PDF. Its headers are used for storing the unique identifier of the client and the selected template for the PDF. The client ID is used on the server side for addressing the notification message back to the client, while the template name is used for identifying the PDF template into which the text will be imported.

```
public function startPdfGeneration(text:String, templateId:String):void
{
    var message : AsyncMessage = new AsyncMessage();
    message.headers.template = templateId;
    message.headers.client = consumer.clientId;
    message.body = text;

    generateMessage = message; // keep for correlation purposes

    producer.send(message);
}
```

Note that a copy of the message is stored for correlation purposes. This is checked against any `acknowledge` events received from the producer, to determine that the request message has been reached its destination.

```
private function onGeneratorAcknowledge(event:MessageAckEvent):void
{
    if (event.correlation == generateMessage)
    {
        status = "Generating PDF…";
    }
}
```

When the PDF generation is completed on the server, a notification message is sent back to the client. This is handled by checking the status header to ensure that the PDF completed successfully. For long-running processes, multiple notification messages could be sent to indicate the state of progress or to describe error conditions. The URL is then extracted from the message body, and the `navigateToUrl()` method is used to download the PDF to the user's computer.

```
private function onNotificationMessage(event:MessageEvent):void
{
    if (event.message.headers.status=="complete")
    {
```

```
            var url:String = String(event.message.body);
            status = "PDF generated!";
            navigateToURL(new URLRequest(url), "_root");
        }
    }
```

PDF Generation Summary

This example was the most involved of the three, involving several server-side components, producers and consumers, client identification, and acknowledgment correlation. There are server-side products, such as the PDF Generator component of Adobe LiveCycle Enterprise Suite, that are designed specifically for large-scale, centrally controlled PDF generation. In many cases, these products will be preferable to rolling your own solution. However, the XFAHelper class included with LCDS, can be used for simple PDF generation, as demonstrated by this example.

Summary

Through the introduction to using the Message Service and three detailed examples, this chapter has touched on many of the service's features. On the client side, this included publishing and subscribing, handling acknowledgment and message events, and filtering by subtopic and selector expression; while on the server side, the Java library has been used for pushing out messages, integration with JMS, and generating PDF documents asynchronously.

There are, however, many further topics that are deserving of attention but could not be covered here. For instance, a custom Message Service adapter can be developed to integrate with a proprietary back-end messaging system, and the multi-topic variations of the Consumer and Producer classes could be used to send and receive messages to and from multiple topics simultaneously. The rate of message flow and the rules that govern prioritization, expiration, and conflation (merging of messages) can even be tailored to suit the specific requirements of an application. The official *LCDS Developer Guide* covers all these topics, and further information can be found in Flex and Java API documentation.

In the next chapter, the dark horse of LCDS is introduced: the Data Management Service. This service operates at a higher level than the other service types and provides more functionality for developers. Its purpose is to manage all the data required by an application, and it does so by tracking changes, synchronizing automatically across connected clients, handling all synchronization and desynchronization duties, managing transactions, persisting data into remote data stores, and ensuring that clients remain fast and responsive by loading large data sets incrementally. Read on to discover more about the remarkable Data Management Service and how to take advantage of its rich feature set.

56

The Data Management Service

The Data Management Service (DMS) operates at a higher level than the other LCDS types, providing more functionality to help develop data-intensive applications in Flex. As well as basic create, read, update, and delete (CRUD) operations, the DMS can automatically detect changes made by one user and synchronize them with all other users. This chapter introduces the DMS and describes an example application.

Overview of the DMS

If you're developing a Flex application that creates, reads, updates, and deletes data, the DMS is designed to help you. If you're dealing with multiple users and need to synchronize data between them, the DMS can do more, ensuring that a change made by one user is quickly reflected to the other users. Furthermore, if your application needs to stay fast and responsive, even when handling large quantities of data, the DMS has that covered, too.

The DMS provides higher-level, more broad-ranging functionality than the other LCDS types. It reaches farther into the client- and server-side code base of a rich Internet application, so developers can concentrate on the distinct parts of their application, instead of expending effort on the infrastructure for managing data. The DMS is composed of both client- and server-side libraries that work together to simplify the task of building data-intensive applications, which integrate Flex clients with practically any kind of server-side data store.

The DMS is covered in two chapters. This chapter introduces the technology, covering the main features from client and server perspectives. Chapter 57 deals with some more advanced topics and contains advice for those working on larger-scale DMS projects.

Why Use the DMS?

Before diving into example code, it is worth considering the motivation for the DMS, in contrast to building a Flex application that accesses lower-level services, such as HTTP services, Web services, or consumers and producers of the Message Service.

All about Domain Modeling

At the heart of most applications lies a domain model, describing the entities and relationships of interest to the business and relevance to the software. For example, a banking application may model account holders, overdraft limits, and monthly statements, whilst a video library would be more concerned with viewing preferences, genres, and video ratings. The DMS enables developers to focus on this important domain modeling, without worrying about the mechanics of data access, updates, and synchronization. Figure 56-1 shows a simple domain model for a video library.

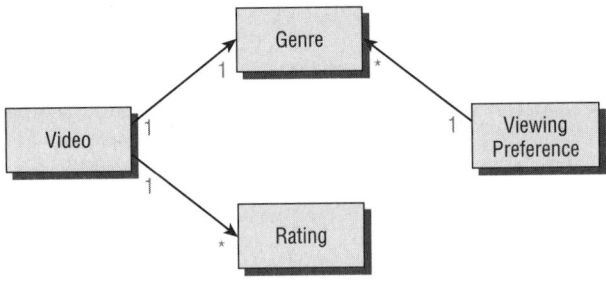

Figure 56-1

Create, Read, Update, Delete

The so-called CRUD operations — create, read, update, delete — are the elementary functions of many Internet applications, yet they're implemented and reimplemented time and time again. DMS provides a consistent, high-level API for these operations, encapsulating the complexities of client-server communication and concurrent updates.

Sharing Data Among Users

Consider a scenario where two users of a word processor are collaborating to create a new document. If the first user types a new paragraph, it should be immediately visible to the second user. If the second user spots a mistake, they should be able to correct it quickly, and the correction should be reflected back to the first user.

The DMS performs this kind of data synchronization automatically and supports more complex scenarios. When a change is made to a property of a data model that is being synchronized — or managed — through the DMS, this change can be transported to the server, updated in a persistent data store, and pushed back out to collaborating users with a minimal amount of effort. Figure 56-2 shows a change made by one user being applied on the server and synchronized for another user.

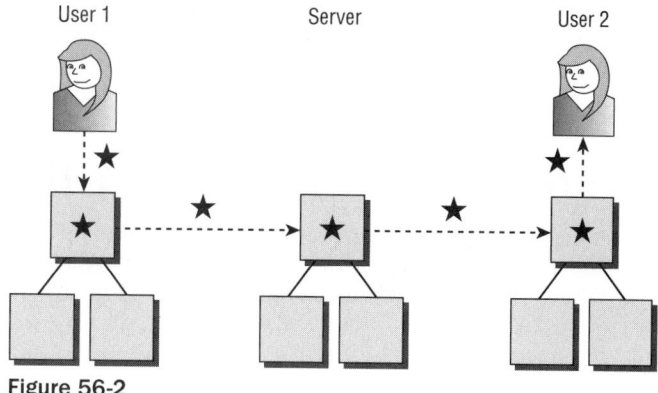

Figure 56-2

Paging Large Data Sets

Paging is the process of moving portions of a large data set from the server to the client as required. For example, the results of a Google search query are sent to the user in pages, rather than sending all three million hits in one go. It takes less time to move less data, so paging enables a user interface to remain fast and responsive. When an over-large data set is sent in one go, a user interface may stop responding while that data is processed, particularly in a single-threaded environment like Flex.

DMS integrates with the Flex collections API to provide automatic paging and pre-fetching of data from the server. This allows the user interface to remain fast and responsive while displaying large quantities of data in list controls, such as data grids or tile lists. DMS fetches the data that is needed for immediate rendering, pre-fetches the data that is likely to be needed soon, and leaves the rest of the data in place on the server until it is required, as illustrated in Figure 56-3.

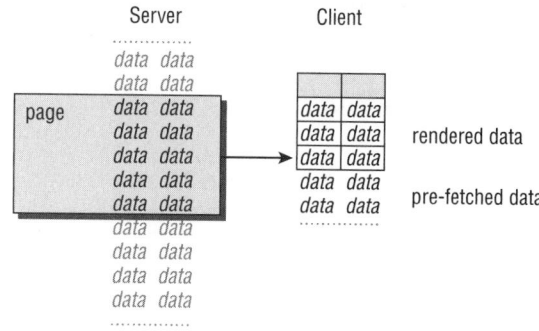

Figure 56-3

Occasional Connectivity

A DMS client is able to detect whether a connection is available for talking to the server and adjust its behavior accordingly. It can continue to operate in unconnected situations, by tracking changes that occur on the client and providing a simple mechanism for synchronizing them when connectivity returns. In offline situations, data can also be persisted on the client side.

Seeing Is Believing: The Six-Line Demo

Many of the features of the DMS can be demonstrated with just six lines of code! This is what makes it so compelling for Flex developers, enabling them to build data-intensive applications with remarkable speed. Achieving the same level of functionality using lower-level services would require more code and more time.

The example that follows is adapted from a demo given by Marc Meewis, an Adobe systems engineer. Marc builds a simple employee management system in a matter of minutes. He opens multiple browser windows and shows that data changed in one window is instantaneously applied to the others. The audience is already impressed, but Marc proceeds to demonstrate features such as failover, conflict detection, and reverting of changes, with just a few lines more. Anyone who has tried to implement these features themselves will appreciate the assistance of the DMS.

Source code for the "Six-Line Demo" can be found in the accompanying project, SixLineDemo, and is shown below. The shaded lines highlight the six lines of LCDS code within a simple Flex application.

```
<mx:Application
    xmlns:mx="http://www.adobe.com/2006/mxml"
    width="100%" height="100%">

    <!-- 1. Declare data service for accessing and updating employees. -->
    <mx:DataService id="service" destination="employeeService" autoCommit="false"/>

    <!-- 2. Declare collection for storing employees. -->
    <mx:ArrayCollection id="employeeData"/>

    <!-- 3. Bind employees collection to data provider of a data grid. -->
    <mx:DataGrid width="100%" height="100%" editable="true"
        dataProvider="{employeeData}">
        <mx:columns>
            <mx:DataGridColumn dataField="id" editable= "false"/>
            <mx:DataGridColumn dataField="firstName"/>
            <mx:DataGridColumn dataField="lastName"/>
            <mx:DataGridColumn dataField="department"/>
        </mx:columns>
    </mx:DataGrid>

    <mx:HBox>
        <!-- 4. Click to fill the collection with employees. -->
        <mx:Button label="Get Employees"
```

```
                    click="service.fill(employeeData)"/>

        <!-- 5. Click to commit changes and synchronize clients.-->
        <mx:Button label="Save"
                enabled="{service.commitRequired}" click="service.commit()"/>

        <!-- 6. Click to revert any uncommitted changes. -->
        <mx:Button label="Undo"
                enabled="{service.commitRequired}" click="service.revertChanges()"/>
    </mx:HBox>
</mx:Application>
```

Line 1: Declaring a Data Service

First, a `DataService` is declared for the destination `employeeService`. This is the client-side class for interacting with a DMS destination on the server. Configuring a DMS destination is similar to other kinds of LCDS destinations and more details are provided later in the chapter. The `autoCommit` property is set to `false`, which means that any changes made to employee data must be explicitly committed back to the server data store, rather than being applied automatically. This gives the client control over when changes are sent to the server, allowing multiple changes to be batched.

Line 2: Declaring a Collection for the Managed Data

A `DataService` can be used to fill a collection with managed data. This data will be retrieved from the `employeeService` destination on the server side and then observed on the client side to detect any changes. In this case, the collection is declared in MXML and given the `id` `employeeData`.

Line 3: Providing Managed Data to a Data Grid

An editable `DataGrid` is declared, and the `employeeData` collection is bound to its `dataProvider` property. As soon as some data is available, it will be rendered to the screen, and the user can make changes by editing the fields (except for the `id` field). Furthermore, when the user scrolls down through the items, the subsequent pages of data will be pre-fetched. This behavior allows the application to remain responsive even when handling large quantities of data.

Line 4: Filling the Collection

It is the row of buttons at the bottom that perform the real magic. When the Get Employees button is clicked, the `fill()` function is called on the `DataService`. This causes the first page of employee data to be fetched from the server and filled into the `employeeData` collection. In response to this, the binding on the `DataGrid` will fire and the employee details will be shown.

When a collection is filled it becomes a *managed collection*. This means that any changes to the collection or the data inside it will be tracked, paging will be performed when data that has not yet been fetched is required, and changes made by other users will be detected and applied automatically. Any data that is managed in this way by LCDS is known as *managed data*.

Line 5: Committing Changes and Synchronizing Clients

The Save button is enabled through a binding to the `commitRequired` property of the `DataService`. This means that it can only be clicked when a change has been made to the managed data by editing one of the cells of the `DataGrid`. This bindable property of the `DataService` is convenient for preventing users from performing pointless tasks, such as saving unchanged data.

When the button is clicked the `commit()` function is called on the `DataService`. This pushes all tracked changes from the client to the server and automatically synchronizes them with other users. Depending on the server-side configuration, the changes may also be persisted to a data store.

Line 6: Reverting Changes

The Undo button is also disabled until a change has been made, by binding to the `commitRequired` property. When it is clicked the `revertChanges()` function is called on the `DataService`. This discards any changes made by the user, reverting the data to its earlier state. This can be very useful for cancelling changes made to a form.

Behind the Scenes

There is of course more to this six-line demo than meets the eye. Behind the scenes, a DMS destination has been configured to synchronize changes with connected users. This might be storing these changes transiently in memory or persisting them to a data store, such as a relational database, depending on its configuration.

As the chapter continues, the workings of the DMS are explained in more detail. Configuration details for the server side are provided and an example application for tracking a fleet of vehicles is provided.

DMS Technology Explained

The Six-Line Demo showed the DMS in action; now this section reveals some of its mysteries. The close relationship between the client and server components is explained, including a discussion of the ways that different kinds of data properties are managed, and the extensibility points available for integrating the DMS with backend data stores. This theory is then reinforced with the Fleet Tracker example application.

Client and Server Components

On the client-side, a `DataService` object is used to fill collections with managed data and access individual items of managed data. It is also responsible for tracking changes made to managed data and applying changes made elsewhere, by another user or server-side process.

On the server side, the DMS handles the fetching and persistence of data to and from data stores, and the synchronization of data among connected clients. Within the DMS, an adapter is used to integrate with a backend data store, such as a relational database. This relationship between the client and server components is shown in Figure 56-4.

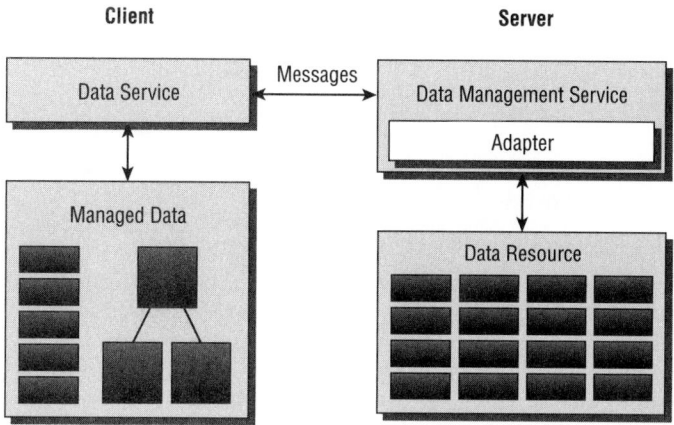

Figure 56-4

Managed Data

As the name suggests, the DMS manages data, but what does this "management" actually entail? In the context of DMS, data management means creating, reading, updating, and deleting items of data, as well as synchronizing them among users, detecting changes, handling conflicts, and persisting to back-end data stores.

Managed data consists of collections of strongly typed objects and object compositions that are observed and sometimes altered by the DataService. For client developers, managed objects look and behave in most ways like normal objects; new instances can be created, properties can be set, items can be added and removed from collections. However, managed objects are not quite so ordinary. They are in fact proxies that represent items of data on the server. All managed data items have a unique identity that ensures there is only one instance on the server and one instance on each client. This makes efficient use of memory and enables the DataService to track changes in specific items and synchronize them across the server and other clients.

LCDS applies the Highlander Principle ("There can be only one!") to ensure there can be only one instance of any managed object in memory on a client. If two collections contain the same item, they will both reference the same object in memory.

Managed Relationships

In addition to managing objects with simple properties, the DMS can manage the relationships between objects. For example, an Employee may have several Projects, an Address, and a Department. Multiple Employees may belong to the same Department. This model is shown in Figure 56-5.

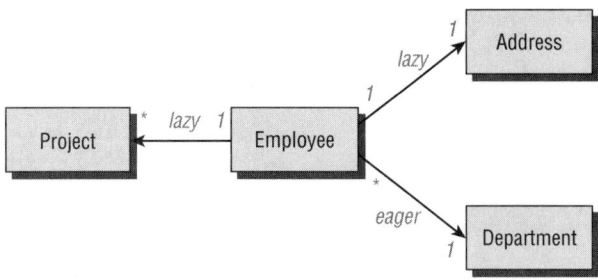

Figure 56-5

The DMS can manage the relationships between Employee, Project, Address, and Department objects, so that changes are detected when, for example, an Employee changes his or her Address or a Department expands by recruiting more Employees. Four types of relationships are supported:

- **One-to-one** — One Parent object is associated with one Child object, that is, one Employee has one Address.

- **One-to-many** — One Parent object is associated with many Child objects, that is, one Employee has many Projects.

- **Many-to-one** — Many Parent objects are associated with one Child object, that is, Many Employees belong to the same Department.

- **Many-to-many** — Many Parent objects are associated with many Child objects, that is, an Employee has many Roles and a Role applies to many Employees.

These relationships can take two forms:

- **Eager** — When the Parent data is sent from the server, the Child data is also sent. For example, if a collection was filled with Employees, their corresponding Department would also be retrieved.

- **Lazy** — When the Parent data is sent from the server, the Child data is not sent. Instead the Child data is fetched the first time an attempt is made to access it. For example, if a collection was filled with Employees, their corresponding Addresses would not be retrieved. They would instead be fetched independently, at some later point, if they are required.

Lazy relationships reduce the amount of unnecessary data sent between the server and client, but they can introduce complexity on the client. The first time the child property of a lazy relationship is accessed, an `ItemPendingError` is thrown and must be handled. This triggers the process of fetching the child data and realizing the relationship. These errors are handled effortlessly by the Flex binding mechanism, but must be dealt with manually in ActionScript code. The relative merits of eager and lazy relationships are discussed in more detail in Chapter 57, "Advanced Data Management Service," along with strategies for overcoming item pending errors.

Client Programming

As demonstrated in the Six-Line Demo, the `DataService` class is the main player on the client side. It defines methods for filling collections with managed data, accessing and updating items, committing changes to the server, and so on. The following table describes the most commonly used methods.

Method	Description
commit()	Commits any pending changes for all collections managed by this service. For example, commit the updated Employee details now that Department A and B have been merged. This method only needs to be called when the auto-synchronization feature is disabled.
count()	Calls a count() method on the server to determine how many items satisfy some condition. For example, count the number of Employees in the IT Department.
createItem()	Requests that a specified item be created on the server side, in the remote data store. For example, when a new Employee is added to an Employee Management System.
deleteItem()	Requests that a specified item be deleted from the remote store on the server side. For example, an Employee has left the company and their entry should be removed.
fill()	Fills a specified collection with managed data that satisfies some condition. For example, fill a collection with all the Employees that have second names beginning with A. When a collection is filled it becomes a managed collection.
getItem()	Gets an item with a specified identity from the remote store on the server. For example, get the Employee with the ID 1034.
revertChanges()	Reverts any uncommitted changes to a specified item or reverts all uncommitted changes. This restores the managed objects to their state before the modifications began. For example, Revert the change to Employee 1034's salary.

Also defined on the DataService class are a number of bindable properties, the most useful of which are summarized in the following table. These can be used for establishing connectivity and determining whether a commit is required, and whether local changes need to be merged with changes made by other users.

Property	Description
autoCommit	Determines whether local changes are automatically committed to the server. When autoCommit is true, there is no need to explicitly call the commit() method, but changes are not batched.
autoConnect	Determines whether the client should attempt to connect to the server automatically whenever required. For example, in order to fill a collection with data or commit some changes.
commitRequired	Shows whether there are uncommitted changes. This property is particularly useful for disabling and enabling user interface controls through bindings.
mergeRequired	Shows whether there are uncommitted changes that need to be merged with changes made concurrently by other users or server-side processes. When this is true, conflicts may need to be resolved.

As well as using these methods and properties, the `DataService` class also raises exceptions when conflicting changes are detected and provides access to various conflict resolution strategies. Many of these features of the `DataService` class are demonstrated in the Fleet Tracker sample application and further examples can be found in the samples distributed with LCDS.

In addition to the `DataService` class, there are several other client-side classes that play a part in data management. These include the `Channel` class used for communicating with the server and the `DataStore` that batches transactions and detects conflicts. More details are provided in the LCDS Language Reference.

Server Integration

On the server side, the DMS handles caching of managed data, detecting changes, and synchronizing them with connected clients, but it delegates other responsibilities to the `Adapter` and `Assembler` interfaces, as shown in Figure 56-6.

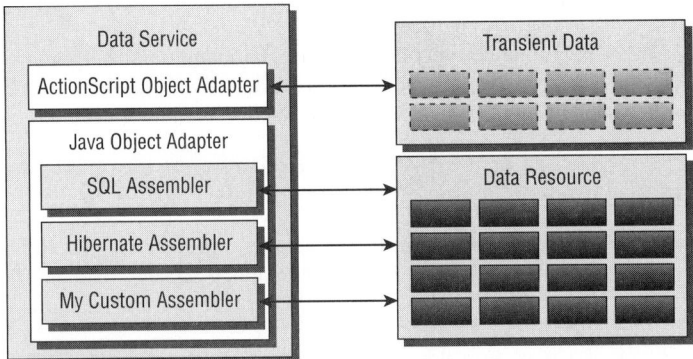

Figure 56-6

These interfaces are configured in the `data-management.xml` configuration file. They are used for performing `count()` and `fill()` methods, and for creating, reading, updating, and deleting items of managed data. Several implementations are provided out of the box, but these are also public extensibility points to facilitate integration with various backend systems.

DMS Adapters

A DMS adapter handles the messages sent to the DMS from a client application. The LCDS distribution includes two standard implementations:

❏ **ActionScript object adapter** — Used only for simple use cases involving transient data that is not persisted and so is lost when the server restarts.

❏ **Java object adapter** — Handles messages and calls down onto an `Assembler` interface to perform `count()` and `fill()` methods and to create, read, update, and delete items of managed data.

Most DMS applications require data persistence, so it is recommended that you make use of the Java object adapter. For instance, this adapter is used to integrate with a relational database or Hibernate system, and also for integration with other backend systems, such as internal Web Services or file systems.

DMS Assemblers

The Java object adapter delegates its data operations to the `Assembler` interface. This interface can be implemented in many different ways to integrate with different backend systems; however, the LCDS distribution includes two standard implementations for common use cases:

❏ **SQL Assembler** — For integrating with a relational database. This is achieved by specifying the database details and relevant SQL statements in a DMS configuration file.

❏ **Hibernate Assembler** — For integrating with Hibernate entities using the Hibernate `get` operation, HQL queries and named queries. This assembler is also configurable through a DMS configuration file.

In many real projects, neither of these assemblers are used and a custom assembler is implemented instead. This is a straightforward task, since an `AbstractAssembler` base class is provided, leaving only a few methods of the `Assembler` interface to be implemented. Implementing a custom assembler has several benefits, including full control over the behavior for accessing and updating data, enabling integration with other backend systems, and stubbing of the backend when a persistence layer is not yet available.

An example of a custom assembler is contained in the Fleet Tracker sample application, covered later in the chapter. The SQL and Hibernate assemblers are described in detail in the official LCDS Developer Guide.

Client and Server Collaboration

It's the collaboration between the client- and server-side components of the DMS that enables the data synchronization, persistence, paging, and other capabilities of the technology. While the client APIs make it easy to program data-intensive Flex applications, the server-side components enable integration with relational databases and other kinds of data stores. This collaboration is demonstrated in the Fleet Tracker sample application that follows.

Example Application: DMS Fleet Tracker

With the theory out of the way, this section contains a detailed walkthrough of a sample application. The sample is more complex than the Six-Line Demo and looks at the DMS from both the client and server perspectives. The full source code is contained in the `DMSFleetTracker` project, except for the commercial LCDS libraries. Figure 56-7 shows the DMS Fleet Tracker application.

The DMS Fleet Tracker project has been started by Parcel Flex, an imaginary international transit company. Their fleet of vehicles is outfitted with GPS tracking systems, and they need a system to monitor the locations of their fleet and determine the status of particular parcels inside those vehicles. Naturally, they have chosen to deliver the project with Flex, making use of the DMS to save them from implementing their own data access and synchronization framework.

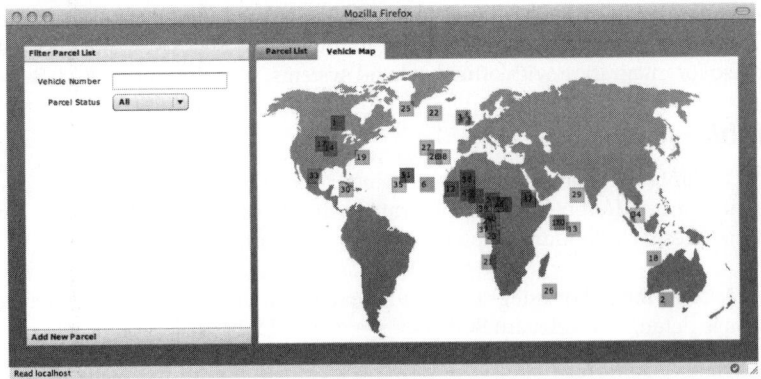

Figure 56-7

Developing the DMS Fleet Tracker involves the following steps, described in more detail in the following sections:

1. **Domain modeling** — Developing the client- and server-side model for describing the vehicles and parcels.

2. **DMS configuration** — Configuring the DMS destinations for managing the vehicle and parcel data.

3. **Custom assemblers** — Developing two custom assemblers for accessing and updating vehicle and parcel data.

4. **Client coding** — Coding the Flex client to access, visualize, and update the managed data.

Domain Modeling

Parcel Flex needs to track their fleet of vehicles and the parcels they contain. For identification purposes, these vehicles and parcels all have unique identifiers. The company has a GPS tracking system that provides the longitude and latitude readings for its vehicles at frequent intervals. In addition to this, each parcel has a status that indicates whether it is being processed, is in transit, or has been delivered. The following domain model should meet the needs of the DMS Fleet Tracker. Figure 56-8 shows the simple domain model for DMS Fleet Tracker.

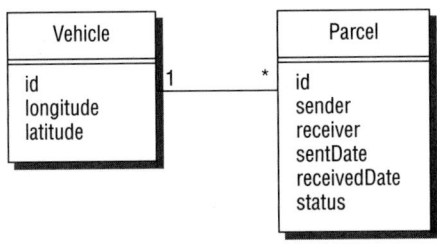

Figure 56-8

The Parcel Flex GPS tracking system needs to be integrated with the DMS. This can be achieved by using the Java object adapter in conjunction with a custom assembler. When using the Java object adapter, it is normal to create both Java and ActionScript implementations of the domain model classes. The adapter will deal with converting from one to the other by serializing the ActionScript objects on the client side and deserializing into the Java objects on the server side, and vice versa. This process is similar to that employed by the Remote Object Service, except that these strongly typed objects are managed.

The Vehicle Class

Managed objects must have public setters and getters for all their managed properties. The Java implementation for a `Vehicle` class is shown here:

```
package com.proflex.model;

public class Vehicle
{
    private long id;
    private long longitude;
    private long latitude;

    public long getId() { return id; }
    public void setId(long id) { this.id = id; }

    public long getLongitude() { return longitude; }
    public void setLongitude(long longitude) { this.longitude = longitude; }

    public long getLatitude() { return latitude; }
    public void setLatitude(long latitude) { this.latitude = latitude; }
}
```

Three properties are defined to identify a `Vehicle` instance and record its current location in longitude and latitude. As is the convention in Java, the member variables are declared private with public getter and setter methods.

The corresponding `Vehicle` class in ActionScript has a similar implementation but includes two metadata tags, `[Managed]` and `[RemoteClass]`. The first informs the Flex compiler that the class is to be managed, which has the knock-on effect of ensuring the class is bindable without the need for the `[Bindable]` metadata. The second identifies the corresponding Java class to use for serialization and deserialization purposes.

```
package com.proflex.model
{
    [Managed]
    [RemoteClass(alias="com.proflex.model.Vehicle")]
    public class Vehicle
    {
        public var id:Number;
        public var longitude:Number;
        public var latitude:Number;
    }
}
```

For consistency, it is good practice to package both implementations of a managed class in the same way. In this case, they are both defined in the com.proflex.model package. The properties in the ActionScript class are simply defined as public member variables, since this is the convention. They could just as easily be defined with public getters and setters.

> Do not *initialize the properties of a managed ActionScript class. The LCDS code relies on the existence of a no-argument constructor and expects any properties with lazy relationships to other objects to be uninitialized after construction.*

The Parcel Class

The Java and ActionScript implementations of the Parcel class are defined in a similar way.

```
package com.proflex.model;

public class Parcel
{
    private long id;
    private String sender;
    private String receiver;
    private Date sentDate;
    private Date receivedDate;
    private Vehicle vehicle;
    private String status;

    public long getId() { return id; }
    public void setId(long id) { this.id = id; }
    ...etc...
}
```

Once again, an identity property is first defined. This will be used on the client and server sides to distinguish managed objects and preserve the Highlander Principle. The other properties are simple types, except for the vehicle property, which references a Vehicle object. A Parcel has a Vehicle and many parcels may have the same Vehicle, so there exists a many-to-one relationship between Parcel and Vehicle. The DMS will later be configured so that it understands how to manage this relationship correctly.

The corresponding ActionScript class defines properties with the same name and again includes the [Managed] and [RemoteClass] class-level metadata.

```
package com.proflex.model
{
    [Managed]
    [RemoteClass(alias="com.proflex.model.Parcel")]
    public class Parcel
    {
        public var id:Number;
        public var status:String;
        public var sender:String;
        public var received:String;
        public var sentDate:Date;
        public var receivedDate:Date;
        public var vehicle:Vehicle;
    }
}
```

Take care to ensure the property names match on the Java and ActionScript classes. An ActionScript property named myProperty *must correspond to a Java setter/getter pair called* getMyProperty() *and* setMyProperty().

The rules for converting between simple types in ActionScript and Java are the same as those that apply to the Remote Object Service. These are not repeated here but can be found in the "Converting data from Java to ActionScript" section of the *LCDS Developer Guide*.

DMS Configuration

With the domain model in place, the DMS destinations for managing Vehicle and Parcel classes can be configured. A single DMS destination is normally responsible for managing a single type of object, so the Fleet Tracker application requires two destinations, the vehicleService and parcelService.

There is an exception to the one-destination-to-one-class-type rule: a single destination can be used for managing objects of types within the same class hierarchy, as long as each type shares the same relationships and has both a Java and ActionScript implementation.

DMS destinations can be specified in the data-management-service.xml configuration file, but that file can become cluttered when several destinations are involved. Instead, it is good practice to define each destination in its own file and then reference these from the main configuration file, using <destination-include> elements. The data-management-service.xml for the Fleet Tracker application is given below. This file can be found in the usual place, within the WebContent/WEB-INF/flex folder.

```
<service id="data-service" class="flex.data.DataService">
    <adapters>
        <adapter-definition id="java-dao" class="flex.data.adapters.JavaAdapter"/>
    </adapters>
    <destination-include file-path="destinations/vehicleService.xml"/>
    <destination-include file-path="destinations/parcelService.xml"/>
</service>
```

Use the <destination-include> *element to include destinations specified in separate files, rather than specifying all the destinations in a single file.*

The Vehicle Destination

A DMS destination specifies the object adapter to use and a number of additional settings, including the identity property, any relationships with other destinations, page size, synchronization policy, and security constraints. When the Java object adapter is used, the Assembler class must also be specified.

The configuration for the destination that manages Vehicles is given here.

```
<destination id="vehicleService">
    <adapter ref="java-dao"/>
    <properties>
        <source>com.proflex.service.VehicleAssembler</source>
        <scope>application</scope>
        <use-transactions>true</use-transactions>
        <auto-sync-enabled>true</auto-sync-enabled>
        <metadata>
```

```
            <identity property="id" />
        </metadata>
        <network>
            <paging enabled="false"/>
        </network>
        <server/>
    </properties>
</destination>
```

Each of the elements is described in the following table.

Element	Description
destination	Specifies the unique ID for the destination and contains the other configuration elements. The ID of `vehicleService` will be needed on the Flex client to connect to the destination.
adapter	References the object adapter to use for the DMS destination. When the Java object adapter is used, an `Assembler` class must also be specified using the `source` element.
source	Specifies an `Assembler` implementation class. The Java object adapter will delegate data operation to an instance of this class. Here, the `com.proflex.service.VehicleAssembler` is used.
scope	Specifies the scope of the assembler. When this is set to `application` a single instance of the assembler is created at initialization time and reused for all requests.
use-transactions	Indicates whether updates should be transactional. When set to `true`, LCDS encapsulates a batch of updates inside a J2EE distributed transaction to ensure that all the updates are applied or none at all.
auto-sync-enabled	Specifies the default behavior for clients that connect to this destination. By default, when `true` those clients will synchronize changes to managed data automatically.
metadata	Contains identity and relationship definitions that determine how managed objects are distinguished and the associations between properties and other destinations.
identity	Specifies the identity property of the type of object managed by the destination. Here, the `id` property of the `Vehicle` class is the identity. Composite identities of more than one property are also supported.
network	Contains paging settings and can contain various other settings, some of which are deprecated.
paging	Indicates whether paging should be performed for this destination. In this case, paging is disabled since the number of Vehicles is not large, so they can all be fetched in one go.
server	Contains definitions for custom `count()` and `fill()` methods. The `parcelService` does not use any, so this element is empty.

When the DMS initializes, it processes each destination file and constructs the `Assembler` objects.

The Parcel Destination

The destination for managing `Parcel` objects is configured in a similar way in the `parcelService.xml` file. However, in this case, a relationship and two fill methods are also defined.

```xml
<destination id="parcelService">
    <adapter ref="java-dao" />
    <properties>
        <source>com.proflex.service.ParcelAssembler</source>
        <scope>application</scope>
        <cache-items>true</cache-items>
        <use-transactions>true</use-transactions>
        <auto-sync-enabled>true</auto-sync-enabled>
        <metadata>
            <identity property="id" />
            <many-to-one property="vehicle"
                destination="vehicleService" lazy="false"/>
        </metadata>
        <network>
            <session-timeout>20</session-timeout>
            <paging enabled="true" pageSize="100"/>
        </network>
        <server>
            <fill-method>
                <name>filterParcels</name>
                <params>java.lang.Integer, java.lang.String</params>
            </fill-method>
            <fill-method>
                <name>filterParcels</name>
                <params>java.lang.Double, java.lang.String</params>
            </fill-method>
        </server>
    </properties>
</destination>
```

Like before, the destination specifies the Java object adapter and provides an `Assembler` implementation class, this time `com.proflex.service.ParcelAssembler`.

This time the `cache-items` element is specified to tell the DMS to cache the results of a fill method on the server. These can then be used for paging results to the clients, if paging is enabled. In this case, paging is enabled with a page size of 100, so parcel data will be sent to clients in batches of 100.

A `many-to-one` relationship is defined to associate the `vehicle` property of a `Parcel` object with the `vehicleService` destination. This informs the DMS that the `Vehicle` objects references by parcels are the same objects that are managed by the `vehicleService` destination. The relationship is `eager`, which means that the vehicle data for a parcel will be sent to the client along with the parcel data. Since the vehicle data is small compared with the parcel data, and many parcels share the same vehicle, this makes good sense.

Inside the `server` element, a pair of fill methods is defined. These map to methods of the `Assembler` implementation and can be thought of as named queries analogous to stored procedures that run against the data managed by the assembler. Recall that on the client side, a fill method is invoked to fill a collection with managed data. So in this case, the `filterParcels` fill method can be called to fill a collection with parcels that pass through a given filter.

Both fill methods are named `filterParcels` but take slightly different parameters. Strictly speaking, only the first method is required for this example. However, both are defined because `Number` values in ActionScript can be converted into both `Integer` and `Double` values on the Java side. So it is safest to overload fill methods and handle both cases, connecting the two implementations in the `Assembler` class, as shown in the next section.

ActionScript `Number` values convert into both `Integer` and `Double` values in Java, depending on their contents. For this reason, it is safest to overload fill methods that are parameterized with numeric values, handling both cases.

Custom Assemblers

In the previous step, two destinations were configured with custom `Assembler` classes: `VehicleAssembler` and `ParcelAssembler`. The implementations for these can be found in the `src` folder of the accompanying project. At the least, an assembler is responsible for implementing a fill method, while at the most, it may implement multiple custom count and fill methods as well as create, read, update, delete methods, and special functions to page efficiently.

The Vehicle Assembler

LCDS provides the `AbstractAssembler` base class to simplify the development of a custom assembler. Since the `vehicleService` does not define any custom count or fill methods, its implementation is very simple. To begin with, the abstract `fill()` method is implemented.

```
public class VehicleAssembler
    extends AbstractAssembler
    implements VehicleMovementListener
{
    private final FleetTrackingSystem tracker = FleetTrackingSystem.getInstance();

    public VehicleAssembler()
    {
        tracker.addEventListener(this);
    }

    public Collection fill(List fillParameters)
    {
        return tracker.getVehicles().values();
    }
    ...
```

The `fill()` method simply retrieves the current `Vehicle` data from the `FleetTrackingSystem`, which represents the Parcel Flex backend GPS tracking system. Please see the accompanying source code for details of this class, but basically it holds two data structures containing the parcel and vehicle data and spawns a thread to update the vehicle positions every two seconds.

The assembler also listens to the `FleetTrackingSystem` for vehicle movement events that are dispatched whenever new locations are available for the vehicles. This event causes the `vehicleMoved()` function to be called.

```
public void vehiclesMoved(Collection<Vehicle> vehicles)
{
    final DataServiceTransaction transaction = DataServiceTransaction.begin(true);

    for (Vehicle vehicle:vehicles)
    {
        transaction.updateItem(
            "vehicleService", vehicle, vehicle,
            new String[] { "longitude", "latitude" } );
    }

    transaction.commit();
}
```

This function uses the LCDS Java APIs to begin a transaction, update the `longitude` and `latitude` properties of a collection of managed `Vehicle` objects, then commit the transaction. When the transaction is committed, the new positions will be pushed out to the connected Flex clients.

The Parcel Assembler

The implementation of the `ParcelAssembler` class is slightly larger because two custom fill methods are implemented.

```
public Collection filterParcels(Integer vehicleId, String status)
{
    return filterParcels(new Double(vehicleId.doubleValue()), status);
}

public Collection filterParcels(Double vehicleId, String status)
{
    Collection<Parcel> results = new ArrayList<Parcel>();
    for (Parcel parcel:tracker.getParcels().values())
    {
        if (filterByVehicleId(parcel, vehicleId.longValue())
            && filterByStatus(parcel, status))
        {
            results.add(parcel);
        }
    }
    return results;
}
```

These two methods match the fill methods defined in the `parcelService.xml` configuration file. The implementation of the first method simply calls the second. When a client invokes a fill method, a message will be sent to the DMS destination and the matching fill method on the assembler is called. The role of the fill method is simply to return a collection of objects, which will be distributed to the client or multiple clients, in pages or a single large delivery, depending on configuration.

The `filterParcels()` method just iterates over all the parcels known to the `FleetTrackingSystem` and checks whether they are contained in the specified `Vehicle` and what their status is. Any matching parcels are added to the `results` collection and returned at the end of the method. Two simple private methods are used for performing the vehicle and status filtering.

```
private boolean filterByStatus(Parcel parcel, String status)
{
    return status.equals("All") || parcel.getStatus().equals(status);
}

private boolean filterByVehicleId(Parcel parcel, long vehicleId)
{
    return vehicleId == 0 || parcel.getVehicle().getId() == vehicleId;
}
```

The `ParcelAssembler` also defines a `createItem()` method for creating new `Parcel` objects. This method is called when a client has created a new `Parcel` object and committed it. The code for this will be demonstrated in the next section. On the server side, an assembler's only responsibility is making sure that the new item is persisted along with the existing data.

```
public void createItem(Object item)
{
    final Parcel parcel = (Parcel) item;
    tracker.addParcel(parcel);
}
```

The new object created by the client is passed into the `createItem()` method by the DMS. The new item is downcast to a `Parcel` and added to the Fleet Tracking System data store. LCDS is clever enough to realize that when a new item is created, managed collections on the clients need to be refreshed. This causes fill methods to reexecute and the new item to appear automatically for connected clients.

When a new item is created, existing fill methods are reexecuted and changes are pushed out to clients. Chapter 57 discusses various ways to fine-tune this behavior.

Client Coding

All that is left is the Flex client. This time the client is a little more complicated than the Six-Line Demo, since custom fill methods are used, new items are created, and the user interface is richer. However, the client code is still remarkably simple with much of the complexity handled automatically by the DMS.

Filling Collections with Vehicles and Parcels

In the top-level application file, two `DataService` objects are declared for the `vehicleService` and `parcelService` destinations. A pair of `ArrayCollection` objects are also declared, to store the managed `Vehicle` and `Parcel` objects.

```
<mx:DataService id="vehicleService" destination="vehicleService"
    autoCommit="false" autoSyncEnabled="true"/>
<mx:DataService id="parcelService" destination="parcelService"
    autoCommit="false" autoSyncEnabled="true"/>
<mx:ArrayCollection id="vehicles"/>
<mx:ArrayCollection id="parcels"/>
```

Auto-commit is disabled so that local changes have to be explicitly committed to the server rather than being sent automatically. In most cases, this is appropriate, since changes can be batched and reverted if necessary. Auto-sync is enabled, so that the client receives changes made by other users once they have been committed to the server without having to manually refresh.

On the `creationComplete` event for the main application, the two collections are filled using the default fill methods. Since the `vehicleService` destination is not configured to use paging, the vehicles collection will be filled with all the `Vehicle` objects. The `parcelService`, on the other hand, uses paging with a page size of 100, so it will initially be filled with the first 100 `Parcel` objects.

```
private function creationCompleteHandler():void
{
    vehicleService.fill(vehicles);
    parcelService.fill(parcels);
}
```

Visualizing the Vehicle Movements

The positions and movements of all the vehicles are rendered on a map of the world. This is achieved by using a simple custom control that extends `Canvas`. The managed collection of `Vehicle` objects is used as the data provider and an item renderer is created for each `Vehicle` object. The item renderers are all added as children of the canvas and take care of their own positioning through bindings.

The `VehicleView.mxml` class is used as the item renderer.

```
<mx:Box xmlns:mx="http://www.adobe.com/2006/mxml" …
    x="{vehicle.longitude * (UIComponent(parent).width / 120) + 10}"
    y="{vehicle.latitude * (UIComponent(parent).height / 120) + 10}">
    <mx:Script>
        <![CDATA[
            [Bindable]
            private var vehicle:Vehicle;

            override public function set data(value:Object):void
            {
                super.data = value;
                vehicle = Vehicle(value);
            }
        ]]>
    </mx:Script>
    …
    <mx:Label text="{vehicle.id}"/>
</mx:Box>
```

The item renderer's `data` setter is overridden in the normal way, and a bindable reference is stored to the `Vehicle` object being rendered. The x and y coordinates, relative to the enclosing canvas, are set by binding to the vehicle's `longitude` and `latitude` and performing a small calculation. This means that every time the vehicle's position is updated, the x and y coordinates of the item renderer will automatically reflect the change. Note that the client developer does not need to do anything more. It is all achieved by the magic of the Data Service and Flex binding mechanism.

Item renderers are a common source of performance problems in Flex applications, particularly when derived from container classes, which are expensive to create and add to the display list. A Box *is used in the preceding example for the sake of simplicity, but in production the item renderer would perform better if it was written in ActionScript, extending a lighter-weight class such as* UIComponent.

Filtering the Parcel List

A data grid is used for rendering all the parcels known to the system. Since paging is employed, only the first 100 parcels are loaded initially and the remaining parcels will be fetched as required, if the user scrolls down through the data grid. In the Filter Parcel List view in the accordion at the side, the user can specify a vehicle ID or select a parcel status to filter the list by.

```
<mx:TextInput id="vehicleId" restrict="0-9" change="filterChangeHandler()"/>
...
<mx:ComboBox id="parcelStatus" change="filterChangeHandler()">
    <mx:dataProvider>
        <mx:ArrayCollection id="statuses">
            <mx:String>All</mx:String>
            <mx:String>Processing</mx:String>
            <mx:String>In Transit</mx:String>
            <mx:String>Customs</mx:String>
            <mx:String>Delivered</mx:String>
        </mx:ArrayCollection>
    </mx:dataProvider>
</mx:ComboBox>
```

When a vehicle ID is specified or the parcel status is changed, the filterChangeHandler() is called:

```
public var parcelService:DataService;
public var parcels:ArrayCollection;

private function filterChangeHandler():void
{
    var vehicleId:Number = vehicleId.text == null ?
        0 : Number(vehicleId.text);
    var status:String = parcelStatus.selectedItem == null ?
        'All' : String(parcelStatus.selectedItem);
    parcelService.fill(parcels, vehicleId, status);
}
```

This function pulls the vehicle ID and parcel status out of the input controls and uses them to parameterize the fill method of the parcelService. On the server side, these parameters will be matched with the fill method configured for the parcelService destination. In response to this, the filterParcels() method of the ParcelAssembler will be invoked and the first page of results will be sent back to the client. So in the end, the parcels collection will contain the filtered Parcel objects matching the specified vehicle ID and status.

Creating a New Parcel

The accordion at the side of the DMS Fleet Tracker application contains an Add New Parcel view. This can be used for creating a new Parcel object and committing it to the server. The DMS will pass the new object to the ParcelAssembler for persistence and automatically refresh the fills for the clients, which may push the new item out depending on the fill criteria.

A simple form is defined containing two inputs for gathering the sender and received details.

```
<mx:Form>
<mx:FormItem label="Address of Sender">
<mx:TextInput id="sender"/>
</mx:FormItem>
<mx:FormItem label="Address of Receiver">
<mx:TextInput id="receiver"/>
</mx:FormItem>
<mx:FormItem>
<mx:Button id="addButton" label="Add new parcel"
    click="addButtonClickHandler()"/>
</mx:FormItem>
</mx:Form>
```

When the add button is clicked, the addButtonClickHandler() is called.

```
private function addButtonClickHandler() : void
{
    var parcel:Parcel = new Parcel();
    parcel.receiver = receiver.text;
    parcel.sender = sender.text;
    parcelService.createItem(parcel);
    parcelService.commit();
}
```

This creates a new Parcel object in the normal way, then passes it to the createItem() function of the DataService. The new Parcel is added to the change list and committed to the server on the next line, when the commit() function is called. A message is sent to the destination containing the new Parcel data, and on the server side this is converted into a new Java Parcel object. The new object is passed into the createItem() method of the ParcelAssembler, which is responsible for persisting it.

Further Considerations

The first release of the Fleet Tracker is delivered and Parcel Flex is suitably impressed with the DMS. The application demonstrated many features, including custom fill methods, custom assemblers, the Java API for pushing changes out from the server side, and the createItem() method.

There are, of course, more features that were not covered and might be incorporated into a second release of Fleet Tracker. For instance, the getItem() method could be used for a customer-facing version of the application that allowed recipients to locate a specific parcel that they're expecting. A custom count() method could be used for counting all the parcels with a certain status, and these counts could be charted on a dashboard screen. The domain model could be expanded to include Depots, where vehicles congregate to load and unload parcels.

Summary

The DMS is a novel technology with many features to simplify the development of data-intensive applications. By handling these common requirements, developers can focus their efforts elsewhere, on the distinct challenges of their application. The LCDS client and server libraries perform the heavy lifting, accessing data, tracking changes, synchronizing clients, and integrating with different backend systems.

Getting the most out of the DMS requires knowledge of its more advanced features. The best way to gain this knowledge is to begin developing a DMS project and read more about the technology. The *LCDS Developer Guide* provides comprehensive documentation of the entire feature set, complemented by the Java and ActionScript language references. The distribution includes a number of sample applications, and further examples are available publicly, such as Christophe Coenraet's Salesbuilder (http://coenraets.org/blog).

The next chapter is targeted mostly at readers with some prior experience of the DMS. It covers more advanced topics and contains advice to help with developing larger-scale DMS applications.

57

Advanced Data Management Services

This chapter supplements the previous chapter on the Data Management Service (DMS) by providing a collection of tips for working with lazy associations, overcoming item-pending errors, and managing user-specific data.

Overview of DMS

There are a great many ways to use the DMS, and these possibilities can sometimes be overwhelming. From evaluating the relative merits of lazy and eager associations to choosing from the multitude of channels and end points available for communication, and making best use of the client and server-side libraries, there are some pitfalls to be avoided along the way.

This chapter covers three topics relevant for many DMS projects. These are lessons learned in the field that may not be covered in the official documentation.

- ❑ **Summary-to-Details Modeling** — It is common to provide users with a lists of summary information before allowing them to view the full details of one item at a time. There are various ways to achieve this using LCDS, but there are some subtle yet important differences in the outcome.

- ❑ **Overcoming Item-Pending Errors** — The null object errors of LCDS are handled transparently in MXML bindings but require special attention in ActionScript code. There's a simple technique for enclosing a function that may raise item-pending errors and calling it repeatedly until all the pending items have been fetched.

- ❑ **Managing Shared and User-Specific Data** — LCDS makes it easy to synchronize data among users, but sometimes the opposite is required so that certain parts of a data model belong exclusively to a single user.

At the end of the chapter are some pointers to the official documentation for important topics that have not been covered in detail in this book.

Summary-to-Details Modeling

Many rich Internet applications present lists of summary information to users before allowing them to "zoom in" to a selected item and view its full details. For example, email clients often display summary lists containing the titles, sender, and date of the messages in a user's inbox. When the user selects a message, they may then be presented with the message body or perhaps the whole conversation to which it belongs.

This patterns makes good sense from a performance and memory point of view, because only the summary information needs to be fetched up front. There's no point in fetching the full details of every conversation if the user is only interested in viewing one or two of them. Instead, they can be fetched on demand. This behavior may lead an LCDS developer to take advantage of lazy relationships for populating the message details, using a managed object model similar to that shown in Figure 57-1.

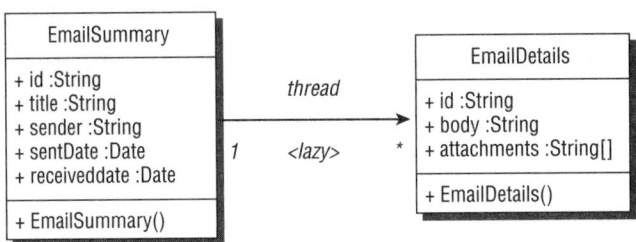

Figure 57-1

However, this decision should not be made lightly, because it may lead to poor performance, higher memory consumption, and unnecessary service requests — exactly the opposite of what was intended! It depends on the quantity of data involved, how bindings are used, and the way in which a user can interact with the data.

Imagine that the user interface is divided in two; on the left is the summary list of email messages, while on the right, the details of the selected message are shown. If the user selects the top message, then quickly scrolls down through the list with the cursor keys, every message will be selected briefly. If bindings are used to render the message details via the lazy relationship, then each time a message is selected, its details will automatically be fetched from the server. This causes many unnecessary service requests and an increase in the size of the managed object model, since these detail objects are not automatically cleaned up when they are no longer being rendered.

Replace Lazy Relationship with Get Item

In scenarios such as this, it is generally better to use a `getItem()` or `fill()` method instead of a lazy relationship to establish the link between summary and details information. This makes it easier to control when the details for a message are actually fetched, and easier to clean up afterwards. If a details object is no longer needed, it can be nullified and made eligible for garbage collection. The implementation of the email client may choose to keep the full details of just one email conversation in memory, rather than collecting more and more data each time a new message is viewed. Figure 57-2 shows an approach to the Summary-to-Details pattern based on a custom fill method.

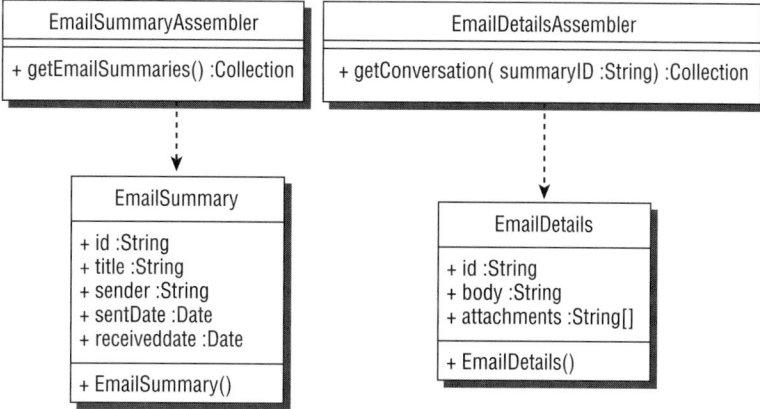

Figure 57-2

The `EmailSummaryAssembler` defines a fill method, `getEmailSummaries()` that fills a managed collection with `EmailSummary` objects. The `id` property of an `EmailSummary` can then be used to parameterize a second fill method, `getConversation()`, on the `EmailDetailsAssember` that fills a managed collection with the `EmailDetails` objects that apply to a single conversation. The coordination takes place on the client side to call the `getConversation()` fill method appropriately when an `EmailSummary` is selected from the list view.

Overcoming Item-Pending Errors

Item-pending errors are to LCDS what null object errors (`ErrorID 1009`) are to Flex. They occur frequently and unexpectedly, often because of small programming mistakes or the side effects of changes to other parts of a system. A suite of unit tests can easily defend against null object errors, but it is more difficult to protect against item-pending errors, since they can appear or disappear depending on configuration changes on the server.

Item-pending errors are most elegantly handled by binding expressions. When binding to a chain of properties, some of which are lazy associations, the item-pending errors that occur are swallowed by the binding mechanism. Each time a property has been fetched, the binding fires again, until the associations have all been loaded. For example, if the person-to-address association is lazy, the following MXML will hide the item-pending error and fetch the address data, then render the street.

```
<mx:Label text="{ person.address.street }"/>
```

However, there are occasions when item-pending errors need to be handled programmatically inside ActionScript classes. The conventional technique for this is to attach a responder to the item-pending error, so a result handler is invoked when the property has been fetched. The result handler would then call the function again that required the lazy association.

```
try
{
    processAddress(person.address); // do something involving a lazy association
}
catch (ipe:ItemPendingError)
{
    ipe.addResponder(new ItemResponder(
        fetchAddressResult, fetchAddressFault, person));
}
...
private function fetchAddressResult(data:Object, person:Object):void
{
    processAddress(Person(person).address);
}
```

This technique has some limitations. If the property chain in question had more than one lazy association, then the `fetchAddressResult()` method may itself throw an item-pending error. It is cumbersome to handle each level of item-pending error individually, so a better solution is needed.

Repeated Attacks

Repeated attack is a simple technique to overcome these kinds of errors in ActionScript. It involves repeatedly calling (or attacking) the piece of code that raises the item-pending errors until it no longer raises such an error. The error-handling code is confined to a single place. This is achieved with recursion by hooking the responder up to the original function, as shown here:

```
private function processPersonalDetailsLazily(
    unused:Object, person:Object=null):void
{
    try
    {
        // call the function that may raise multiple IPEs
        processPersonalDetails(Person(person));
    }
    catch (ipe:ItemPendingError)
    {
        ipe.addResponder(new ItemResponder(
            processPersonalDetailsLazily, // recursion!
            processPersonalDetailsFault,
            person));
    }
}
```

This technique allows the code inside the `processPersonalDetails()` function to be kept simple, without concern for the item-pending errors. The function can be coded as if the associations were eager and not lazy, creating code that is easier for other developers to read and understand.

It is important to note that this technique is only suitable when the function call enclosed in the `try-catch` block has no side effects when called repeatedly. This technique is a trade-off in favor of simplicity over efficiency, since the target function is kept simple but logic may be reprocessed a number of times. In some cases it may be better to revise the managed data model to reduce lazy relationships.

Managing Shared and User-Specific Data

The DMS makes it easy to synchronize data amongst users, but there are times when data needs to be kept specific to a single user and not shared. In fact, collaborative applications often require both forms of data, so the shared part of a managed data model can be accessed and updated by multiple users concurrently, while other parts belong only to individual users. A managed data model such as this needs to be designed carefully, so that private information is not shared and synchronized incorrectly.

A Simple Instant Messaging System

Consider the case of an instant messaging system built into a Flex application. A user can send a message to one or more recipients, after which it appears in their inboxes as a new, unread message. When they open the message, it will be recorded as read. For modeling this, the main message details — subject, body and sender — are shared between the recipients, but the flag that indicates whether or not the message has been read is user-specific. A simple managed data model for an instant messaging system is shown in Figure 57-3.

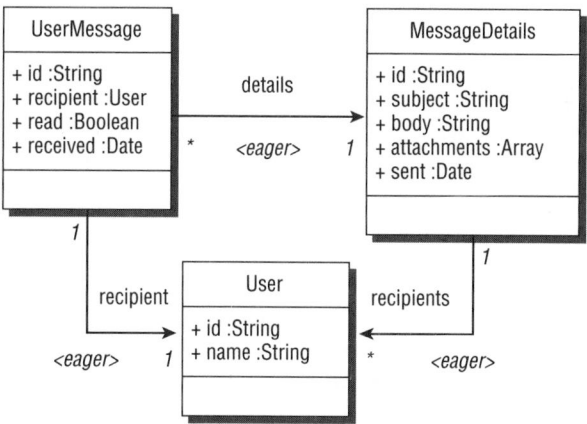

Figure 57-3

The `MessageDetails` class contains the general message information, while the `UserMessage` class has the user-specific properties. There's an eager, many-to-one association from the `UserMessage` to the `MessageDetails` class. The `MessageDetails` has an eager, one-to-many association with the `User` class for modeling the recipients for a message. Each `UserMessage` belongs to a single `User` model through an eager, one-to-one association.

The source code for this simple instant messaging system can be found in the InstantMessaging project that accompanies this book. It provides an example of a managed data model that is partly shared among users and partly user-specific. In addition, it demonstrates a streaming AMF connection to the high-performance NIO-server and the addItemToFill() feature of the Java LCDS library for pushing changes efficiently from the server to specific users.

Creating a New MessageDetails Item

With LCDS, there are various ways to create new managed data items. They can be created on the client using the createItem() method or by addition to an already managed collection, or they can be created directly on the server and pushed out to clients. In the case of the instant messaging system, the client first creates a new instance of the MessageDetails class when the send button is clicked, as shown here:

```
private function sendMessage():void
{
    var message:MessageDetails = new MessageDetails();

    message.recipients = new ArrayCollection(recipients.selectedItems.slice());
    message.subject = subject.text;
    message.body = body.text;
    message.sent = new Date();

    messageDetailsService.createItem(message);
    messageDetailsService.commit();
}
```

The message object is constructed, then its properties are set to the values of the various input controls. The recipients property is set to an ArrayCollection of managed User objects to whom the message is addressed. The new message is then passed into the createItem() method of the data service before being committed to the server explicitly, since the auto-commit feature is disabled. This causes the new object to be transported to the corresponding createItem() method on the server.

Creating and Delivering the User Messages

On the server side, the MessageDetailsService destination uses the Java object adapter and a custom assembler, MessageDetailsAssembler. The implementation of the createItem() method persists the new MessageDetail object using the InstantMessageData class, but also creates and persists a new UserMessage object for each recipient of the messages. These objects are then pushed out to the correct users with addItemToFill() method of the DataServiceTransaction class as shown here:

```
public void createItem(Object item)
{
    MessageDetails message = (MessageDetails) item;

    // persist message details
    data.addMessageDetails(message); // persist message

    DataServiceTransaction transaction =
```

```
        DataServiceTransaction.getCurrentDataServiceTransaction();

    // create, persist and deliver user messages
    for (Iterator i = message.getRecipients().iterator(); i.hasNext();)
    {
        User recipient = (User) i.next();

        // create and persist user message
        UserMessage userMessage = data.createUserMessage(message, recipient);

        // create fill parameters for user specific fill
        List fillParameters = Arrays.asList( new Object[] { recipient.getId() } );

        // deliver user message by adding it to the user's fill
        transaction.addItemToFill(
            "UserMessageService", fillParameters, 0, message);
    }
}
```

The creation and persistence of data is handled by the `InstantMessageData` class through the `data` member variable. In the sample project, the class does not really persist the data to a backend data store, but simply maintains a few simple data structures in memory.

The important part of the method is the use of the `DataServiceTransaction` class. The current transaction is first grabbed with the static `getCurrentDataServiceTransaction()` method. During each iteration of the loop that follows, a new `UserMessage` object is created for the next message recipient, then it is delivered to that user with the `addItemToFill()` method of the transaction. This simple process works because the `UserMessageService` fill method is parameterized by user ID, so each user has his or her own fill method.

Back on the client, the new `UserMessage` will be received by a data service for the `UserMessageService` destination and added to the `messages` managed collection. Since the `UserMessageService` has an eager association with the `MessageDetails` service, the corresponding `MessageDetails` object will be sent to the client together with the `UserMessage`. The message is then rendered in a list control, and when the user clicks on a message, its `read` property is set to `true`. Since this `UserMessage` belongs to the specific user, the change is not synchronized with other users, which is correct for this situation.

```
private function markSelectedMessageAsRead():void
{
    if (messageList.selectedItem == null) return;

    var message:UserMessage = UserMessage(messageList.selectedItem);

    if (message.read == false)
    {
        message.read = true;
        userMessageService.commit();
    }
}
```

Streaming AMF to an NIO End Point

The instant message example also demonstrates a streaming AMF connection to the high-performance NIO server provided with LCDS 2.6. This combination provides a great experience for users, because a permanently streaming connection is maintained from each client to the server, so LCDS can push new messages out immediately. The use of the NIO-server means that multiple users can be served by the same Java threads, providing scalability many times greater than the servlet-based end points that are confined by the thread-blocking rules of the Servlet specification.

The channel and end point are configured in the `services-config.xml` file:

```
<channels>
    <channel-definition
        id="my-streaming-amf"
        class="mx.messaging.channels.StreamingAMFChannel">
        <endpoint
            url="http://localhost:2080/nioamfstream"
            class="flex.messaging.endpoints.StreamingNIOAMFEndpoint"/>
        <server ref="my-nio-server"/>
        <properties>
            <server-to-client-heartbeat-millis>
                10000
            </server-to-client-heartbeat-millis>
            <user-agent-settings>
                <user-agent match-on="MSIE"
                    kickstart-bytes="2048"
                    max-streaming-connections-per-session="1"/>
                <user-agent match-on="Firefox"
                    kickstart-bytes="0"
                    max-streaming-connections-per-session="1"/>
            </user-agent-settings>
        </properties>
    </channel-definition>
<channels>
```

In this channel definition, the `StreamingAMFChannel` is paired with the `StreamingNIOAMFEndpoint`. The configuration properties specify that the server will send a heartbeat message to each connected client every 10 seconds to maintain the streaming connection. The `user-agent` elements are used to configure browser-specific settings that ensure that a streaming connection can be properly established and limit the number of concurrent connections per session.

More comprehensive details about configuring streaming channels is provided in the "Streaming AMF and HTTP Channels" section of the *LCDS Developer Guide*.

Learning More

There are a number of important topics that haven't been covered in this book but are detailed in the official *LCDS Developer Guide*. Before embarking on a serious LCDS project, developers are encouraged to read the *Developer Guide* thoroughly, since it covers the full range of features in fine detail over several hundred pages.

The following three features of the DMS deserve special attention, since they were either omitted or only touched upon in this book.

❑ **Hierarchical data** — Each of the sample applications provided with this book used a single DMS destination to manage a single type of class. A DMS destination can in fact be used to manage a type hierarchy, although some restrictions apply. The classes in the type hierarchies must share the same identity and association properties.

❑ **Data paging** — Although server-to-client paging was explained and used in the sample applications, the DMS also supports paging between a backend database (or other system) and the assembler layer on the server. This can be important for scaling DMS applications to very large data sets. Furthermore, since LCDS 2.6, paging is supported for associations between DMS destinations.

❑ **Conflict resolution** — When building a collaborative application with the DMS it is often necessary to handle data conflicts. These can occur when multiple users change the same managed data properties concurrently. The LCDS libraries provide features for detecting and resolving conflicts.

The topics that follow are not specific to the DMS but apply to LCDD in general. They are all important for developing and deploying enterprise LCDS applications.

❑ **Adaptive polling** — This is an advanced server-side extensibility point that allows developers to customize the message queuing and delivery behavior of an LCDS server. It can be used for reasons of efficiency and quality of service, to throttle delivery rates, conflate multiple messages into one, or discard older messages replacing them with newer items.

❑ **Security** — LCDS can be integrated with the security framework of the underlying J2EE application server into which it is deployed, but it can also support custom authentication and authorization processes. Secure variations of each of the communication channels are provided and credentials can be passed from a client through the Proxy Service to a remote HTTP service of SOAP Web Service. The NIO end points can be protected using white-list and black-list filtering, so only certain IP addresses are allowed to access an end point (white list), or certain IP addresses are forbidden from accessing an end point (black list).

❑ **Clustering** — Clustering is necessary to deploy a scalable and robust LCDS application that can withstand a degree of software and hardware failure on the server side. LCDS includes a software clustering feature which provides failover and message-state replication, as well as supporting load-balancing when used in conjunction with an external load balancer.

❑ **Profiling** — LCDS includes some features for measuring message processing performance which can be useful for identifying bottlenecks and improving the efficiency of an LCDS application before it goes into production. Message-processing metrics can be enabled in the channel configuration properties and accessed through the client API.

Summary

There's no denying the versatility of the DMS, with its rich feature set, for accessing, updating, integrating, paging, and synchronizing data. However, some care must be taken when deciding the best way to use these features to solve a particular problem. Lazy relationships are an elegant way to model relationships between objects, but they're not suited to every situation. Likewise, automatic data synchronization is miraculous when compared with doing the same job by hand, as long as the data being synchronized to 1000 users in real time is not private and confidential, intended for only one recipient!

For large applications, it can be simpler to create several distinct managed data models, rather than attempting to create a single model for the entire application's data requirements. The different functional areas of an application can be separated from one another, with each one accessing and updating data using its own distinct services. There are other challenges that present themselves as an LCDS application or the number of concurrent users grows. For instance, the performance of the LCDS server-side implementation may need to be tuned. The Data Services Stress Testing Framework is a tool provided by Adobe for this purpose. It is the subject of the next chapter.

58

The Data Services Stress Testing Framework

The Data Services Stress Testing Framework is a free tool provided by Adobe for stress testing the server-side implementation of LiveCycle Data Service (LCDS) applications. This chapter explains how to configure and run stress tests using the tool.

Overview

LCDS supports the rapid development of data-intensive applications, where Flex or AIR clients exchange large quantities of data with server-side components in real time. The quality of user experience provided by these clients depends both on the design of the user interface and its responsiveness. If the server-side implementation is slow or unstable under load, the client application will feel unresponsive and may become unusable.

The Data Services Stress Testing Framework is a simple tool provided by Adobe to help developers test their server-side implementations and ensure adequate performance under high loads. This chapter explains first how the Stress Testing Framework operates, then provides instructions for installing and configuring the tool, writing a test application, running the tests, and interpreting the results. The results of stress testing can be used to identify server-side performance bottlenecks and help determine the hardware requirements for an LCDS application before it goes into production.

The Stress Testing Framework consists of Java, Flex, and LCDS components that communicate with one another to launch multiple browser instances on multiple machines, and then to start and stop tests that interact with the server-side of an LCDS application. Figure 58-1 shows the topology of a stress test built using the Stress Testing Framework, with the Java, Flex and LCDS server-side components distinguished from one another.

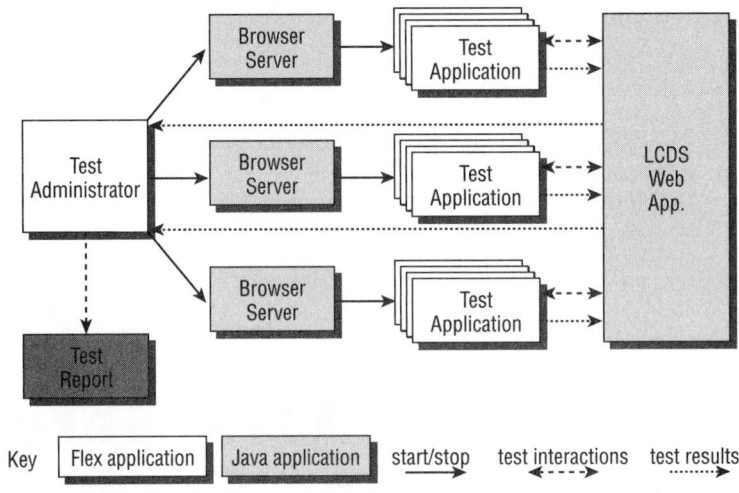

Key ☐ Flex application ☐ Java application start/stop test interactions test results

Figure 58-1

The *DSS Test Administrator* is a Flex client application that runs in a browser on one machine and is responsible for coordinating the stress test and ultimately producing a report containing the test results. It is configured to communicate with a number of Browser Servers, usually running on different machines.

A *Browser Server* is a Java server that launches browser instances on a particular machine. It loads a Flex test application into each instance and starts and stops some test code within these applications upon instruction from the Test Administrator. So when a stress test is started through the Test Administrator client, each Browser Server is instructed to launch a certain number of browsers containing the test application, and then to start the test processing.

A *test application* is a Flex client written by a developer specifically for testing the server-side implementation of an LCDS project. It makes use of the Flex library provided with the Stress Testing Framework to receive start and stop signals from a Browser Server and generate test results, which are sent back to the Browser Server, and then on to the Test Administrator.

When a test application receives a start signal from a Browser Server it begins interacting with the server-side of the LCDS application under test. The specifics of these interactions depend on the requirements of the application. It may invoke fill methods on a Data Service, call methods on a Remote Object, or perform any other kind of interaction that is important to the application being tested.

When a stress test is stopped through the Test Administrator client, a stop message is sent to each of the Browser Servers, causing them to send a stop signal to each test application instance. At this point, a test application will stop its test interactions, assemble some result data, and send it back to the Browser Server using the Flex Library provided with the Stress Testing Framework. The Browser Server will send any test results it received back to the Test Administrator, which collates them and outputs a test report.

The test report can then be analyzed to determine the performance of the server-side implementation when under load. If necessary, improvements can be made to the implementation to achieve better performance and scalability, before subsequent stress tests are run.

Stress Testing a Data Management Service Application

The remainder of this chapter consists of a worked example that shows how to stress test a Data Management Service (DMS) application. Three Browser Servers will be used, each spawning five browser instances, so a total of fifteen instances of the test application will be running.

The following steps are involved:

1. Writing the test application
2. Configuring the server
3. Configuring and starting the Browser Servers
4. Compiling the Test Administrator
5. Running the stress test

Prerequisites

Before starting, download the Data Services Stress Testing Framework from Adobe Labs: http://labs.adobe.com/wiki/index.php/Flex_Stress_Testing_Framework.

View the license and unzip the ZIP file. The Adobe Labs page also contains comprehensive documentation for the tool. This chapter covers much of the same ground but is based on a working example involving the DMS and includes figures to aid understanding.

The source code and configuration files for this example are contained in the StressTesting project that accompanies this book. There is a README.txt file inside the project that explains how to incorporate the source and configuration files into a new LCDS project.

Writing the Test Application

The test application is the Flex client that performs the test by accessing and interacting with LCDS services and recording success or failure counts. It normally consists of a simple Flex application that uses the Stress Testing Framework library classes to listen for start and stop messages from the Browser Server and to send back test results. When a start message is heard, the application begins its interactions with the LCDS service under test, and these continue until a stop message is received. Figure 58-2 shows the main classes and interfaces.

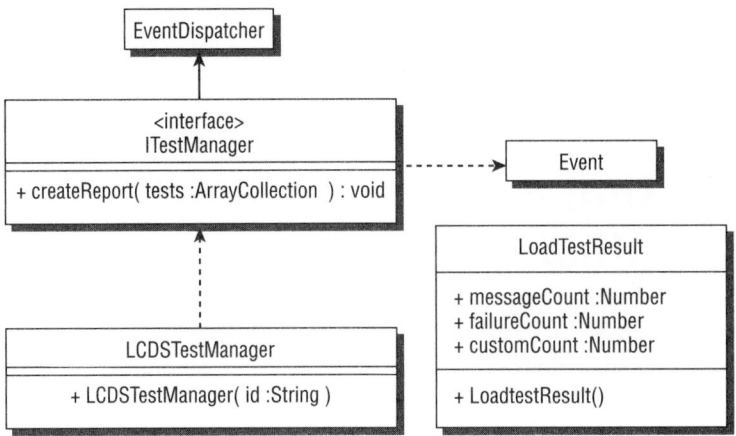

Figure 58-2

The test application must create an instance of the `LCDSTestManager` and listen for the `startTest` and `stopTest` events. This class is contained in the `dsstress.swc` library contained in the `resources/frameworks/libs` folder of the Stress Testing Framework distribution. This library must be added to the Flex Builder path in order to compile a test application.

The constructor of the `LCDSTestManager` class takes an ID that uniquely identifies the test application instance. This ID should be retrieved from the application parameters, where it is passed in by the Browser Server.

```
private var manager:ITestManager;

private function creationCompleteHandler() : void
{
    var id:String = Application.application.parameters.id;

    manager = new LCDSTestManager(id);
    manager.addEventListener("startTest", startTestHandler);
    manager.addEventListener("stopTest", stopTestHandler);
}
```

The manager object will dispatch a `startTest` event when the load test is started through the Test Administrator client, and a `stopTest` event when it is stopped.

Starting the Test Scenario

The `startTestHandler()` function should begin the test scenario. What the test scenario actually consists of depends on what needs to be tested for the particular application in question. If the stress test is focusing on a Message Service implementation, the test scenario may involve subscribing to a destination and consuming messages, or connecting to a destination and producing messages, or a combination of both. Whatever the scenario, the outcome is recorded on a `LoadTestResult` object by incrementing one of the count properties — `messageCount` or `failureCount` — depending on success or failure. A third count property — `customCount` — is provided for recording another metric, if required, such as the number of repetitions of the test scenario. The test scenario is then repeated again and again until the load test is stopped by the Test Administrator.

The example provided in the StressTesting project involves a Data Service fill operation. When the test is started, a fill method is executed on the data service under test, as shown here:

```
private function startTestHandler(event:Event) : void
{
    status.text = "Starting Test";
    performFill();
}

private function performFill():void
{
    var token:AsyncToken = myDataService.fill(myCollection);
    token.addResponder(new AsyncResponder(resultHandler, faultHandler));
    testCount++;
}
```

Counting Success and Failure

A testCount variable is incremented to keep track of the number of fill method calls. A responder is attached to the asynchronous token. Each time the collection is successfully filled, the successCount variable is incremented, and each time a failure occurs, the failureCount is incremented.

```
private function resultHandler(data:Object, token:Object=null):void
{
    status.text = "Test success";
    successCount++;
    performFill();
}

private function faultHandler(error:Object, token:Object=null):void
{
    status.text = "Test failure";
    failureCount++;
    performFill();
}
```

Stopping the Test

When the Test Administrator stops the test, the stopTest event is dispatched by the Test Manager in each instance of the test application. The handler for this event constructs a LoadTestResult object and sets the messageCount, failureCount, and customCount properties to record the successful, failed, and total number of test runs. The results are then passed in to the addResults() method of the test manager, which sends them back to the Test Administrator.

```
private function stopTestHandler(event:Event) : void
{
    myDataService.disconnect();

    status.text = "Test stopped, sending results";

    var result : LoadTestResult = new LoadTestResult();
```

```
        result.messageCount = successCount;
        result.failureCount = failureCount;
        result.customCount = testCount;

        manager.addResults(result);
    }
```

Configuring the Server

The Stress Testing Framework uses services to coordinate a stress test and gather the results. The following services need to be deployed inside the LCDS application that is going to be tested:

❏   A DMS destination is used for receiving results from the test applications and making them available to the Test Administrator.

❏   A Remoting Service destination is used for logging debug messages from the test applications to `System.out` on the server.

❏   The default Proxy Service destination is used to allow the Test Administrator to communicate with the Browser Servers.

The Stress Testing Framework uses a separate RTMP endpoint to communicate with the DMS and Remoting Service destinations, so as not to interfere with server interactions that are part of the test. Configuration fragments for this endpoint and each of the service destinations are contained in the `resources/config` folder of the Stress Testing Framework distribution. These need to be inserted into the appropriate LCDS configuration files, as described in the next section.

The `dsstress.jar` JAR contains the server-side libraries for the Stress Testing Framework and needs to be added to the libs folder of any LCDS Web application that is going to be stress tested. In a Flex Builder Flex/LCDS project, this folder is normally to be found at `WebContent/WEB-INF/lib`.

Adding the Separate End Point

Add the channel definition from the `resources/config/services-config.xml` file into the `<channels>` element of the `services-config.xml` file for the LCDS application that is going to be tested. This channel is used for sending test result messages between the test application instances, the LCDS Web application, and the Data Services Stress Test Administrator.

```
...
<channels>

    <channel-definition id="perf-rtmp-internal"
        class="mx.messaging.channels.RTMPChannel">
        <endpoint class="flex.messaging.endpoints.RTMPEndpoint"
            url="rtmp://{server.name}:2152"/>
        <properties>
            <idle-timeout-minutes>0</idle-timeout-minutes>
            <serialization>
                <enable-small-messages>true</enable-small-messages>
            </serialization>
            <!-- for deployment on WebSphere, must be mapped to a WorkManager
```

```
                    available in the web application's jndi context.
                <websphere-workmanager-jndi-name>
                    java:comp/env/wm/MessagingWorkManager
                </websphere-workmanager-jndi-name>
                -->
            </properties>
        </channel-definition>
        ...
    </channels>
    ...
```

The channel has the ID `perf-rtmp-internal`, which will be referenced from the DMS and Remoting Service configuration files.

Adding the DMS Destination for Result Data

Add the destination from the `resources/config/data-management-config.xml` file into the `data-management-config.xml` file for the LCDS application that is going to be tested. Place the destination after the `</adapters>` element closure.

```
<destination
    adapter="java-dao"
    channels="perf-rtmp-internal"
    id="Perf.Participants">
    <properties>
        <source>adobe.dsstress.controller.lcds.ParticipantAssembler</source>
        <scope>application</scope>
        <use-transactions>false</use-transactions>
        <metadata>
            <identity property="id"></identity>
        </metadata>
        <network>
            <session-timeout>0</session-timeout>
            <paging enabled="false"></paging>
        </network>
        <server>
            <fill-method>
                <name>fill</name>
            </fill-method>
            <sync-method>
                <name>sync</name>
            </sync-method>
        </server>
    </properties>
</destination>
```

This DMS destination references the `perf-rtmp-internal` channel and uses a custom Java assembler to receive results from the test application and provide them to the Test Administrator. The implementation for this assembler is contained in the `dsstress.jar` provided with the Stress Testing Framework distribution. For more information about custom assemblers, refer to Chapter 56, "The Data Management Service," or to the *LCDS Developer Guide.*

Adding the Remote Object for Logging

Add the destination from the `resources/config/remoting-config.xml` file into the `remoting-config.xml` file for the LCDS application that is going to be tested. Place the destination after the `<adapters>` and `<default-channels>` elements, alongside any other destinations.

```
<destination id="dsstress.Logger">
    <channels>
        <channel ref="perf-rtmp-internal"/>
    </channels>
    <properties>
        <source>adobe.dsstress.Logger</source>
        <scope>request</scope>
    </properties>
</destination>
```

This destination is used for logging debug messages to the server from the test applications. It references the Java object, `adobe.dsstress.Logger`, which is included in the Stress Testing Framework distribution.

Configuring the Default Proxy Service

Copy the destination from the `resources/config/proxy-config.xml` file on top of the destination with the same name in the `proxy-config.xml` file of the LCDS application. Place the destination after the `<adapters>` and `<default-channels>` elements, alongside any other destinations.

```
...
<destination id="DefaultHTTP">
    <properties>
        <dynamic-url>*</dynamic-url>
    </properties>
</destination>
...
```

This destination allows the Proxy Service to connect to any URL. This is not recommended for production environments for security reasons but is fine for running a stress test behind a firewall. A more restrictive URL pattern could be specified, as described in the *LCDS Developer Guide*.

Configuring and Starting the Browser Servers

Before a stress test can be started the Browser Servers need to be up and running. These are simple Java processes that receive communications from the Test Administrator on a specified port. In response to these communications, the Browser Servers launch and then terminate browser instances.

The Browser Server application needs to be copied to each machine involved in the stress test. The application is contained in the `resources/browserServer` directory of the Stress Testing Framework distribution. It consists of a JAR and a properties file. The properties file should be configured before starting the server. Its contents are as follows:

```
ie="C:\\Program Files\\Internet Explorer\\iexplore.exe"
firefox="C:\\Program Files\\Mozilla Firefox\\firefox.exe"
```

```
default=ie
serverPort=7777
```

The first two properties give the paths to launch the Internet Explorer and Firefox browsers for the current system. If the Browser Server is being launched on a system with different browsers or different filesystem paths, these need to be changed. For instance, to launch the Safari browser on Mac OS X the following property can be added:

```
safari=Open -a Safari
```

The third property identifies the default browser type for a stress test, while the fourth property identifies the port on which communication with the Browser Server will take place. The default port is 7777. When a Browser Server has been properly configured, it can be started with the following command:

```
java -jar browserServer.jar
```

The following output, or similar output, should be produced if the server has started properly:

```
Sat Aug 30 20:33:38 BST 2008  : browserServer version 0.95
Sat Aug 30 20:33:38 BST 2008  : starting server on port 7777
Sat Aug 30 20:33:38 BST 2008  : server ready
```

Compiling the Test Administrator

The Test Administrator is the Flex application provided with the Stress Testing Framework for coordinating stress tests. It needs to be compiled into the same Web application containing the test application, since it makes use of the services configured in Step 2. These are used for communicating start and stop messages with the Browser Manager and receiving test results produced by the test applications.

The source for the Test Administrator can be found in the `resources/src` folder of the Stress Testing Framework distribution. The `TestAdmin.mxml` application file and the accompanying `images` folder should be copied into the source folder of the LCDS project under test. At the time of this writing, version 0.80 of the Stress Testing Framework contains a small bug in the `TestAdmin.mxml` application file. This can be fixed by commenting out line 434.

```
//currentTest = null;
```

With the Test Administrator and the test application both compiled, and the LCDS Web application containing the pair of them deployed to an application server, the stress testing can begin.

Running the Stress Test

With the test application written, the server-side configured, the Test Administrator compiled, and the Browser Servers running, the stress test can finally begin. To get things going, launch the Test Administrator application, as shown in Figure 58-3.

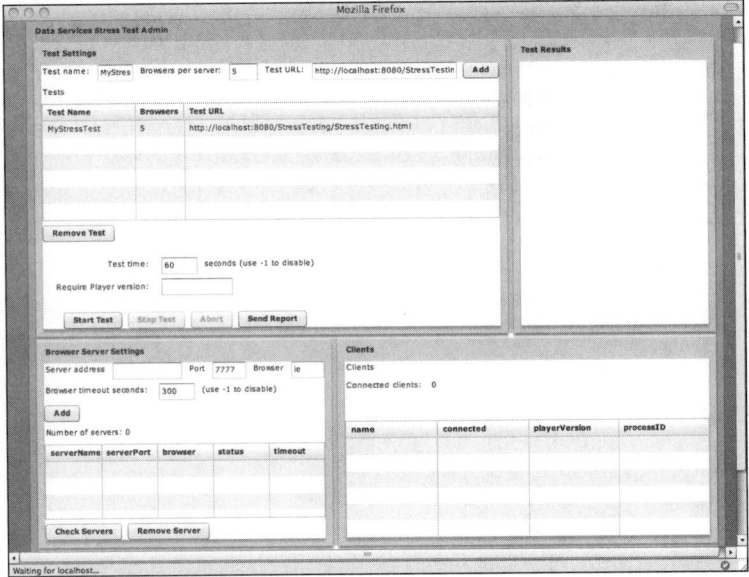

Figure 58-3

The Test Administrator application is divided into four main areas. At the top left is the Test Settings panel. The following settings can be made in this panel:

- ❏ The name of a stress test
- ❏ The number browsers to spawn with each Browser Server for a stress test
- ❏ The URL for the test application that will be started on each browser instance
- ❏ The time in seconds to allow the test to run if it is not stopped manually (-1 to disable)
- ❏ The required version of Flash Player for running the test application

When the first three settings have been made, the Add button can be clicked to register the stress test. It will be displayed in the Tests data grid. Afterward, another stress test run can be specified and added. In this manner, multiple stress tests can be configured to run concurrently.

At the lower left is the Browser Server Settings panel. In this panel, each of the Browser Server instances can be registered. The server address, port number and browser name need to be specified for the first Browser Server, then the Add button pressed. The Browser Server details should appear in the data grid below along with a status message indicating that the Browser Server is connected. Ensure that the Browser Server is running at the specified address. This process should be repeated for each of the Browser Servers.

Now the stress test can be started by clicking the Start Test button at the bottom of the Test Settings panel. Each Browser Server should spawn the correct number of browser instances and launch the test application. Meanwhile, the Clients panel at the bottom right should list each of the clients running the test application. The individual test scenarios should begin for each test application and the server-side implementation should start to take a pounding, as request after request is made from multiple places simultaneously.

When the test has been running for long enough, the Stop Test button can be clicked, or else the test can be left to stop automatically when the test time is reached. This should cause each test application to transmit its results data to the server, where the Test Administrator will read it and render the counts in the Test Results panel at the top right. The Send Report button can be clicked to trace the test results to the Flex Builder console or Flash log file.

Further Topics

This section covers a few further topics. It explains how parameters can be passed into test application instances, the Test Administrator can be preconfigured from an XML file, and customized test reports can be generated by implementing a simple interface.

Parameterizing Test Applications

It can be useful to pass parameters into the test application instances that are launched by the Browser Servers during a stress test. For example, a channel parameter may be used to tell the test application which channel to use for communicating with the server-side implementation during the test. This would allow the same test application to be used for comparing the performance over different channels. Perhaps some users are able to use an application over RTMP, while others sit behind a firewall and proxy server that restricts them to polling-AMF.

The Stress Testing Framework allows two parameters to be passed into test applications: `channel` and `dataSize`. These can both be specified by adding them to the Test URL setting in the Test Administrator. The standard URL query string notation is used, for example:

```
http://localhost:8080/StressTesting/StressTesting.html?channel=my-rtmp&dataSize=5
```

These parameters can then be extracted from the Application parameters inside the test application and used accordingly. The `dataSize` parameter might be used to determine the amount of data to request from or send to the server in each test scenario. A series of stress tests could then be performed with ever-increasing data sizes to determine the scalability of the server-side implementation.

```
var dataSize:Number = Number( Application.application.parameters.dataSize );
```

The Stress Testing Framework distribution includes a sample application that reads these parameters. It can be found in the `samples/simpleLoadTestWithParams` directory. The official documentation also contains two examples, one for creating a channel at runtime based on the `channel` parameter, the other for adding a number of items to a managed collection based on the `dataSize` parameter.

Preconfiguring the Test Administrator

In the preceding example, the Test Administrator was configured manually through the user interface, typing into input boxes and hitting the various Add buttons. This is fine for a one-off test run but tedious when the same stress tests need to be repeated. Luckily, a feature has been added to the Stress Testing Framework to allow the stress test configuration to be loaded from an XML file.

The Test Administrator can be configured with a file named `config.xml`, which is loaded from the same location as the `TestAdmin` SWF. The structure of the file is shown here:

```
<config>
    <serverAddress value="192.168.x"/>
    <testDelaySeconds value="5"/>
    <servers>
        <server ip="localhost" port="7777" browser="ie" timeout="-1"/>
    </servers>
    <tests>
        <test testName="SimpleMessagingTest"
            browsersPerServer="5"
            testURL=http://localhost:8400/lcds/simpleLoadTest/simpleLoadTest.swf
            />
    </tests>
    <reports>
        <report reportClass="adobe.dsstress.admin.reports.FlashlogCSVReport"/>
    </reports>
</config>
```

The elements are described as follows:

❑   `serverAddress` — Used to specify the default server address for the Browser Servers. This value is placed into the Server Address field of the Browser Server Setting panel.

❑   `testDelaySeconds` — The number of seconds to delay after completing a stress test run before starting the next. This is only applicable if more than one stress test has been registered in the Test Settings panel. The delay is to allow enough time for the clients from the previous test to be cleaned up before the next test begins.

❑   `tests` — Contains one or more `test` elements describing stress tests. The settings for each stress test name, the number of browsers per server, and the URL for the test application can be specified. When the `.config` file is loaded by the Test Administrator, these tests will appear in the Tests data grid of the Test Settings panel.

❑   `reports` — Contains one or more `report` elements each specifying a class name. These classes are used for generating reports at the end of a stress test when the Send Report button is clicked. They must implement the `IReport` interface as described in the next section.

Creating Customized Test Reports

The Stress Testing Framework includes a public interface for creating test reports. This can be implemented in different ways to produce different kinds of reports. As discussed previously, the default implementation simply writes the test results using the global trace function, so they end up in the Flex Builder console or the Flash log file. A more sophisticated implementation could be written to generate HTML result reports or to persist the results in a database. Figure 58-4 shows the `IReport` interface through which test reports are generated and the `LoadTestResult` class.

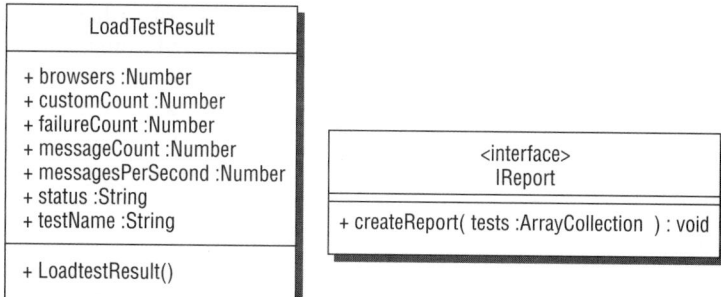

Figure 58-4

The `createReport()` method is passed an `ArrayCollection` of `LoadTestResult` classes representing the results of a stress test. Note that this `LoadTestResult` class is, in fact, different from the `LoadTestResult` class discussed earlier! They both have the same name but different packages: `adobe.dsstress.client.LoadTestResult` is the class used for sending results from a test application, while `adobe.dsstress.admin.LoadTestResult` is the class used by the Test Administrator for reporting test results.

An implementation of the `IReport` interface can choose to do whatever it likes with the `LoadTestResult` objects it receives. When a custom implementation has been written, it needs to be compiled into the same SWF as the Test Administrator, then specified in the `report` element of a Test Administrator `config.xml` file, as described in the previous section.

```
<config>
    ...
    <reports>
        <report reportClass="adobe.dsstress.admin.reports.FlashlogCSVReport"/>
    </reports>
</config>
```

Summary

When developing an LCDS application, it is always wise to test the server-side implementation to ensure that it performs well under load. Stress testing may reveal performance and scalability problems that need to be addressed, and these are best dealt with before an application has moved into production, so that real users are not frustrated or otherwise deterred.

This chapter has shown how a simple form of stress testing can be conducted using the Data Services Stress Testing Framework, provided for free by Adobe on their Adobe Labs site. There are also commercial tools available for stress testing, which should be evaluated before deciding on the best approach for a particular project.

59

Using BlazeDS

Blaze Data Services (BlazeDS) is an open-source data-exchange technology that connects Flex clients to server-side resources, such as remote Java objects, HTTP services, and SOAP-based Web Services. It also supports publish-subscribe messaging so that live data can be streamed efficiently between the server and multiple clients.

This chapter introduces you to the Remoting Service and Proxy Service components of BlazeDS that have not been covered elsewhere. It begins with an introduction to the technology and then continues with a detailed example project that uses the Remoting Service and touches upon the Proxy Service. After reading this chapter, you should be able to create your own simple BlazeDS project, before learning more about the more advanced features in the official documentation.

Overview

While Flex provides a framework for rapidly developing applications with rich user interfaces, BlazeDS provides the same for connecting these applications to server-side resources. With BlazeDS, it's simple to connect a Flex or AIR client to a remote Java object deployed on the server, or to some other resource, such as a SOAP-based Web Service or RESTful-style HTTP service. BlazeDS provides a straightforward programming model and an efficient binary transport protocol to help you build rich and responsive Internet applications quickly.

BlazeDS is free and open source but is closely related to the commercial LiveCycle Data Services (LCDS) product, covered in detail in the preceding chapters. In fact, BlazeDS is the technology that sits at the heart of LCDS, providing the data-exchange framework on which the Data Management Service and other features of LCDS are built. For this reason, some of the content from previous chapters applies, including the description of channels, end points, destinations, and the Message Service. The Data Management Service is not included with BlazeDS and neither is the PDF generation feature, nor the LCDS NIO server that provides greater scalability and improved performance.

BlazeDS Features

BlazeDS provides a broad range of features to enable Flex clients to integrate with different kinds of server-side resources. These features are shown in Figure 59-1 and summarized in the following sections.

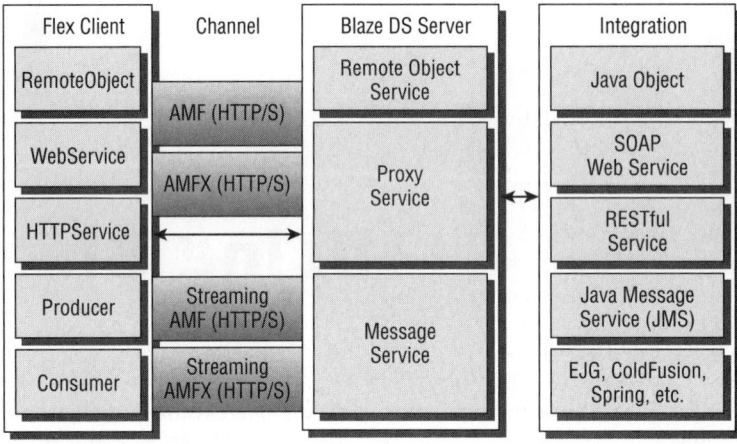

Figure 59-1

Services and Client Components

BlazeDS provides three kinds of service, which are accessed using five different client components.

❑   **Remoting Service:** This integrates Flex applications with remote Java objects residing on the server so that a method called in Flex results in a remote method call on the server, and the translation of data between strongly typed ActionScript objects and strongly typed Java objects is handled automatically. The Flex RemoteObject component is used for invoking remote Java objects via the BlazeDS Remoting Service on the server.

❑   **Proxy Service:** Proxy requests and responses pass to and from HTTP services and SOAP-based Web Services through BlazeDS, where they can be centrally managed, authenticated, authorized, logged, and localized. The Proxy Service also enables Flex clients to access the response code and response body for HTTP errors that are otherwise inaccessible to Flex clients. The Flex HTTPService and WebService components are used to interact with the Proxy Service.

❑   **Message Service:** This provides public-subscribe messaging, enabling the server to push live data out to multiple connected clients in real time. This can be used for building collaborative features, such as online chat, shared document editing, and assisted form filling. The Producer and Consumer components are used in Flex to integrate with the Message Service.

The Remoting Service is covered in the most detail in this chapter, with some attention also being given to the Proxy Service. Since the Message Service was the subject of Chapter 55, albeit in the context of LCDS, it is not covered again here. The Message Service included with BlazeDS does not differ from the LCDS Message Service, except that LCDS supports additional channels of communication, including the non-blocking I/O channels, which provide better performance and scalability.

Channels of Communication

BlazeDS provides various channels for communicating between Flex clients and a BlazeDS web application. These differ from one another in three ways:

- ❏ **Message format:** A compact binary data format known as Action Message Format (AMF) and its more verbose XML representation, AMFX, are both supported.

- ❏ **Transfer protocol:** Both HTTP and HTTPS transfer protocols are supported.

- ❏ **Communication model:** BlazeDS supports call and response style communication, ideal for remote procedure calls (RPC), as well as streaming connections, more suited to pushing live data out from the server to clients in real time.

AMF provides a compact binary data format for sending data back and forth between Flex clients and a BlazeDS web application on the server. Strongly typed ActionScript and remote Java objects can be quickly serialized into AMF messages for transportation over the wire, then quickly deserialized quickly back into strongly typed ActionScript and remote Java objects on the other side. The use of AMF is significantly increases performance when compared to working with XML data.

The XML variation of AMF, known as AMFX, does not offer the same performance benefits as AMF but does satisfy the requirements of more restrictive enterprises, where binary message formats are disallowed. Like AMF, AMFX also offers the benefit of automatic serialization and deserialization between strongly typed ActionScript and remote Java objects.

Integration Points

BlazeDS is middleware that enables communication with different kinds of server-side resources. It uses an open-adapter architecture, so new adapters can be implemented to integrate with different backend technologies. A number of adapters are provided out of the box, including:

- ❏ **JavaAdapter:** Calls methods on remote Java objects

- ❏ **HTTPProxyAdapter:** Proxies requests to RESTful HTTP services

- ❏ **SOAPProxyAdapter:** Proxies SOAP requests to Web Services

- ❏ **ActionScriptAdapter:** Provides transient publish-subscribe messaging without requiring any backend data store

- ❏ **JMSAdapter:** Provides publish-subscribe messaging that integrates with the Java Message Service (JMS)

In addition to these, BlazeDS also provides server-side APIs for runtime configuration of a BlazeDS web application, and an Administration Console application.

Developing a BlazeDS Project

This chapter describes the `BlazeExample` Flex Builder project that accompanies this book. The project is a simple Flex client for displaying five-day weather forecasts, as shown in Figure 59-2. On the server side, the forecasts are initially provided by a remote Java object, and then the implementation is adjusted to use an HTTP service and a SOAP-based Web Service instead. The instructions include the preparation steps of downloading BlazeDS and configuring a new Flex Builder BlazeDS project.

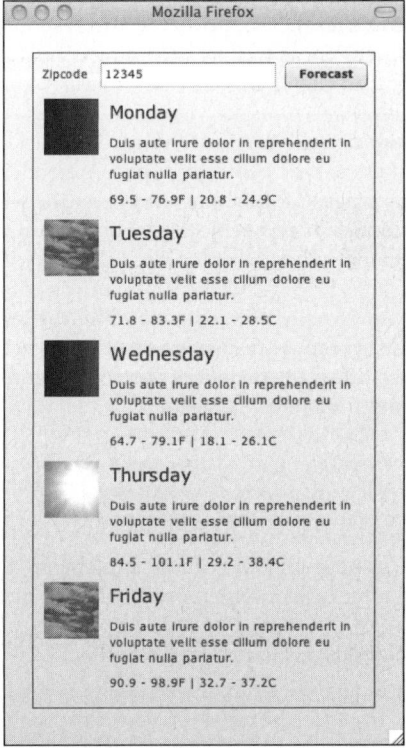

Figure 59-2

Installing the BlazeDS Turnkey

BlazeDS release builds are available from the Adobe Open Source website, at `http://opensource.adobe.com/wiki/display/blazeds/Release+Builds`. There are source and binary distributions, but the turnkey distribution is most convenient for learning purposes, since it includes a preconfigured Tomcat server and various sample applications. The remainder of this example assumes the turnkey distribution has been installed, as described here:

1. Unzip the turnkey distribution to a folder named `blazeds`.

2. Start the preconfigured Tomcat application server.

    On Windows, navigate to `blazeds/tomcat/bin`, where `blazeds` is the installation directory, then double-click on `catalina.bat`.

For Unix-based systems (Mac, Linux, or Solaris), open a terminal and navigate to `blazeds/tomcat/bin` then enter the `./startup.sh` command.

3. Start the embedded HSQLDB database that is used by the sample applications. Open a command prompt or terminal and navigate to `blazeds/sampledb`, then run `startdb.bat` (Windows) or `startdb.sh` (Unix-based systems).

4. Open a browser, and access the Test Drive sample applications at `http://localhost:8400/samples`.

The samples include a 30-minute test drive that demonstrates most of the features of BlazeDS, including remote procedure calls with each service type (remote object, HTTP, and SOAP-based) and data push using the Message Service. Figure 59-3 shows the Collaborative Dashboard, one of the additional sample applications provided with BlazeDS to demonstrate how collaborative features can be implemented with publish-subscribe messaging.

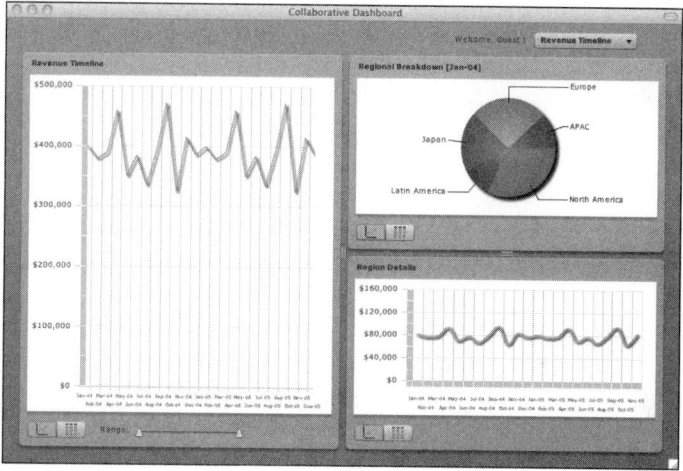

Figure 59-3

Creating a Combined Flex/Java Project

The simplest way to develop a BlazeDS project is to create a combined Java and Flex project in Flex Builder and to make use of the Web Tools Platform (WTP) for quickly deploying the compiled web application to an application server such as Apache Tomcat. Detailed instructions for setting up such a project are contained in Chapter 53, "Introduction to LiveCycle Data Services (LCDS)." The following are condensed instructions with the changes necessary for using BlazeDS instead of LCDS.

It is assumed that the Flex Builder plug-in has been installed on top of Eclipse for Java EE distribution, because this includes the Java development features and the Web Tools Platform. It is also assumed that an Apache Tomcat application server has been installed.

1. Add the Flex SDK included with BlazeDS to the Installed Flex SDKs pane of the Flex Builder Preferences. The SDK is located at `blazeds/resources/flex_sdk/flex_sdk_3`.

2. Create a new Flex project with the following settings:

- ❏ Project name: BlazeExample
- ❏ Application type: Web application (runs in Flash Player)
- ❏ Application server type: J2EE
- ❏ Use remote object access service: checked
- ❏ LiveCycle Data Services selected
- ❏ Create combined Java/Flex project using WTP: checked

3. Click Next.

4. Configure the J2EE Server with the following settings:

- ❏ Target runtime: Apache Tomcat 5.5 (or newer)
- ❏ Context root: `BlazeExample`
- ❏ Content folder: `WebContent`
- ❏ Flex WAR file: `blazeds/blazeds.war` (use the correct path to your BlazeDS installation)
- ❏ Compile applications locally in Flex Builder

5. Click Next, and then Finish to create the new project.

6. Now right-click on the new project and select Properties, then make the following change:

- ❏ Flex Server ➪ Context root: /BlazeExample

This should create a new combined Java/Flex project with the following important folders.

Folder	Description
`bin-debug`	The compiled SWF client and HTML template
`flex-libs`	The Flex build path libraries
`flex-src`	The Flex client source code
`src`	The Java server-side source code
`WebContent`	The root folder of the complete BlazeDS web application
`WebContent/WEB-INF/classes`	The compiled Java classes produced from the source code in the `src` folder
`WebContent/WEB-INF/flex`	The BlazeDS XML configuration files, including `services-config.xml`, `messaging-config.xml`, `proxy-config.xml`, and `remoting-config.xml`
`WebContent/WEB-INF/lib`	The BlazeDS Java libraries and other necessary Java libraries

Deploying the Project to Tomcat

Now deploy the project to an Apache Tomcat 5.5 (or newer) using the Server view provided with the Web Tools Platform (WTP) extension to Eclipse/Flex Builder, as follows:

1. Select Window ➪ Show View ➪ Others ➪ Servers.

2. Select New ➪ Server ➪ Apache Tomcat 5.5 ➪ Next.

3. Select BlazeExample ➪ Add ➪ Finish.

You can stop and start the server in normal or debugging mode using the controls at the top of the Servers view. Whenever you make changes to Java server-side code or BlazeDS configuration files, it is a good idea to restart the application server. When the server is running, you can launch the BlazeDS example application by selecting `BlazeExample.mxml` and choosing Run As ➪ Flex Application.

Enabling Client- and Server-Side Logging

It is useful to enable debug-level logging before going any further. BlazeDS includes detailed client- and server-side logging that can be useful for diagnosing problems and learning more about the workings of the technology.

To enable client-side debug-level logging, declare a `TraceTarget` in the `BlazeExample.mxml` application, as follows:

```
<mx:Script>
    <![CDATA[
        import mx.logging.LogEventLevel;
    ]]>
</mx:Script>

<mx:TraceTarget level="{ LogEventLevel.DEBUG }"/>
```

You can enable server-side debug-level logging using the `target` XML element, beneath the `logging` element in the `services-config.xml` file:

```
<logging>
    <target class="flex.messaging.log.ConsoleTarget" level="Debug">
        <properties>
            <prefix>[BlazeDS] </prefix>
            <includeDate>false</includeDate>
            <includeTime>false</includeTime>
            <includeLevel>true</includeLevel>
            <includeCategory>false</includeCategory>
        </properties>
        <filters>
            <pattern>Endpoint.*</pattern>
            <pattern>Service.*</pattern>
            <pattern>Configuration</pattern>
        </filters>
    </target>
</logging>
```

You can adjust the properties to suit your needs, of course. When logging is enabled, detailed messages about all service interactions will be outputted to the server and Flex consoles. The Flex client needs to be running in debug mode in order for log messages to appear in the Flex console, unless a different logging target is configured.

See Chapter 74 for more information on the Flex logging framework.

Using a Remote Object

The Remoting Service provides the simplest way to connect a Flex client to a Java server-side object. The beauty of the Remoting Service is that all communication and data translation is handled automatically. So, all you need to do on the Flex side is create a `RemoteObject` instance, invoke a method, and handle the result asynchronously.

Creating a RemoteObject Instance

The `BlazeExample` project uses a `RemoteObject` to fetch a five-day weather forecast. The `RemoteObject` is declared in MXML toward the top of the application file. MXML declaration provides a concise way to hook up event handlers for result data and fault information, although `RemoteObject`s can also be created in ActionScript.

```
<mx:RemoteObject
    id="weatherService"
    destination="weatherService"
    />
```

The `RemoteObject` has been given the ID `weatherService`. It is mapped to a destination named `weatherService` on the server side. More information about this will be given in the "Configuring the Remoting Service" section, but essentially the destination represents a remote Java object on the server side.

Invoking a Remote Method

This is the easy part: just call the method! Use the same method name and parameters as a method on the remote Java object. In the `BlazeExample` project, the `getFiveDayForecast()` method is called when the Forecast button is pressed.

```
<mx:Button
    label="Forecast"
    enabled="{ zipcode.text.length &gt;= 5 }"
    click="weatherService.getFiveDayForecast(zipcode.text)"
    />
```

Behind the scenes, Flex sends the ZIP code string over the wire to the server side, converts it into a Java String, and invokes the `getFiveDayForecast()` method of a remote Java object.

Handling the Results of a Remote Method Call

All remote method calls are asynchronous. The results generated by the remote Java object are sent back to the Flex client, translated by Flash Player into ActionScript objects, and surfaced in `result` events. There are two common ways to handle the results of remote method calls:

❏ Listen for the `result` event from the `RemoteObject` and extract the results from the `event.result` property. This is particularly convenient when the `RemoteObject` is declared in MXML and has only one method on it, such as the `weatherService` used in the `BlazeExample`.

❏ Attach a responder to the asynchronous token returned by the remote method call. All remote method calls in Flex return an `AsyncToken` object that represents the asynchronous process and makes it easy to attach functions for processing result data or handling faults. This is the more flexible approach, since it makes it easy to distinguish the results of one method call from another.

The `BlazeExample` makes use of the first approach by declaring an inline `result` event handler in MXML. There is only one remote method — `getFiveDayForecast()` — and the results are always handled in the same way, so this is the most concise solution.

```
<mx:RemoteObject
    id="weatherService"
    destination="weatherService"
    result="fiveDayForecast = event.result as Array"
    />
```

When the `getFiveDataForecast()` remote method call successfully returns, a `fiveDayForecast` member variable is set to an `Array` of result data, extracted from the `event`. Each element of the `Array` is in fact a strongly typed `Forecast` object, because Flash Player and BlazeDS have performed automatic data translation between remote Java objects, AMF messages, and ActionScript objects. More on this later.

Instead of using an MXML inline event handler, you could have handled the result of the remote method call in ActionScript via the asynchronous token design pattern. For example, the following `onForecastButtonClick()` method could be invoked when the Forecast button is clicked:

```
private function onForecastButtonClick():void
{
    var token:AsyncToken = weatherService.getFiveDayForecast(zipcode.text);
    token.addResponder(new Responder(onForecastResult, onForecastFault));
}

private function onForecastResult(data:Object, token:Object = null):void
{
    fiveDayForecast = ResultEvent(data).result as Array;
}

private function onForecastFault(info:Object, token:Object = null):void
{
    Alert.show(FaultEvent(info).fault.faultString);
}
```

The remote method call returns an AsyncToken object to which a Responder is attached. In the preceding example, the onForecastResult and onForecastFault function references are passed into the Responder constructor. These functions will be called when the remote method call returns, depending on whether or not it has been successful.

Note that in the case of a remote method call, the data and info parameters passed to the result and fault-handling methods are of type ResultEvent and FaultEvent, so they can safely be downcast, as shown in the preceding onForecaseResult() and onForecastFault() methods. A token of data can optionally be passed through, from the constructor of the AsyncToken to the result and fault methods.

In both cases, whether using MXML inline event handlers or an ActionScript AsyncToken, a fiveDayForecast array has been initialized with the results data. This array is then bound to the dataProvider of a List, declared in MXML.

```
<mx:List
    dataProvider="{ fiveDayForecast }"
    itemRenderer="com.wrox.view.ForecastRenderer"
    />
```

Handling a Fault Generated by a Remote Method Call

Faults can be handled in much the same way as results, using either the events dispatched by the RemoteObject itself or the asynchronous responder mechanism. In the BlazeExample project, an inline MXML event handler is used to show an Alert box if a fault occurs, as follows:

```
<mx:RemoteObject
    id="weatherService"
    destination="weatherService"
    result="fiveDayForecast = event.result as Array"
    fault="Alert.show(event.fault.faultString)"
    />
```

The BlazeExample.mxml application file also shows how to handle a fault via an AsyncToken in ActionScript, as shown earlier and repeated here:

```
private function onForecastButtonClick():void
{
    var token:AsyncToken = weatherService.getFiveDayForecast(zipcode.text);
    token.addResponder(new AsyncResponder(onForecastResult, onForecastFault));
}

private function onForecastFault(info:Object, token:Object = null):void
{
    Alert.show(FaultEvent(info).fault.faultString);
}
```

A FaultEvent contains various properties detailing the cause of the fault. In this case, a summary string is displayed from the fault.faultString property. See the language reference for full details of this class.

A robust Flex application should handle errors elegantly and attempt to recover from them automatically. For example, instead of just alerting the user to an error, the service could be retried a number of times, and nonoperational parts of the user interface could be temporarily disabled until the service recovers. With a little forethought, the inconvenience of errors can be minimized.

Configuring the Remoting Service

You need to configure the Remoting Service by registering the remote Java object before it can be invoked by a Flex client. This is achieved by defining a destination in the `remoting-config.xml` file. The `BlazeExample` project registers a destination with the ID `weatherService`, as follows:

```
<service id="remoting-service" class="flex.messaging.services.RemotingService">

    <adapters>
        <adapter-definition id="java-object"
            class="flex.messaging.services.remoting.adapters.JavaAdapter"
                default="true"/>
    </adapters>

    <default-channels>
        <channel ref="my-amf"/>
    </default-channels>

    <destination id="weatherService">
        <properties>
            <source>com.wrox.service.WeatherService</source>
            <scope>request</scope>
        </properties>
    </destination>

</service>
```

The `id` of the destination is used on the Flex client to identify the remote object. In Flex, it must be specified as the destination property of a `RemoteObject` instance. The `source` element contains the qualified class name of the remote Java object. This class must exist in the web application class-path, but Eclipse and the Web Tools Platform will take care of that for the `BlazeExample` project. Any classes specified in the Java `src` folder are compiled into the `WebContent/WEB-INF/classes` folder.

The `scope` element is used to configure the lifetime of the remote object. It can take three values:

❑ `application`: The remote object is instantiated only once by BlazeDS and used for servicing all requests to the application. This results in the least remote object instances on the server, but it means that concurrency needs to be managed by the remote object so that requests do not block one another.

❑ `request`: A new instance of the remote object is created for servicing each request. This creates the highest number of instances, but it allows the application server to manage concurrency. This scoping is suitable when the remote object is stateless, as a new instance is used for each request and the old instances normally become eligible for garbage collection.

❑ session: A new instance of the remote object will be created for each session on the server. This means that requests originating from the same user are serviced by the same remote object instance. The remote object can potentially store state about that user and use it to alter the behaviour of subsequent requests in some way. Multiple tabs within the same web browser also share the same session.

The BlazeExample project uses the request scope.

Coding the Remote Java Object

The remote Java object specified in the remoting-config.xml can be any Java class available to the web application, as long as it has an empty constructor. This makes it very easy to connect Flex clients to existing Java code — easier than setting up a Web Service and easier than using a Java servlet.

The BlazeExample project uses simple Java class, WeatherService, to generate random weather forecasts. The following is an excerpt from the source code:

```
public class WeatherService
{
    private final Random random = new Random();

    public Forecast[] getFiveDayForecast(String zipcode)
    {
        final Forecast[] forecast = new Forecast[5];

        for (int i = 0; i < 5; i++)
        {
            float minTempF = random.nextFloat() * 20 + 60;
            float maxTempF = minTempF + random.nextFloat() * 20;

            Forecast day = new Forecast();

            day.setDay(getDay(i));
            day.setMinTempF(minTempF);
            day.setMaxTempF(maxTempF);
            day.setMinTempC(convertToCelsius(minTempF));
            day.setMaxTempC(convertToCelsius(maxTempF));
            day.setSummary("Duis aute irure dolor … nulla pariatur.");
            day.setImageUrl(getImageUrl(maxTempF));

            forecast[i] = day;
        }

        return forecast;
    }
    …
}
```

There's nothing much to it. An array of five Forecast objects is filled with random data. A couple of helper methods are used for converting units and another two for generating day strings and image URLs. The array is returned and BlazeDS will take care of serializing the data to AMF, sending it over the wire back to the Flex client.

Object Mapping

The Flash Player provides native support for mapping between AMF messages and ActionScript objects. This means it's fast! Performance tests show that this native mapping between AMF messages and ActionScript objects is many times faster than manually parsing XML data and constructing objects. In addition to the performance benefit of fast translation and the reduced network load of a condensed binary message format, using AMF simplifies client code, since there's no need to develop data translation infrastructure or take the risk of working with loosely typed data.

The Remoting Service uses the same object mapping process as the Data Management Service, described in detail in Chapter 56. The following table shows the default mappings between ActionScript and Java, although the mapping rules are more versatile than this. You can find a complete table of conversions in the "Converting Data from ActionScript" to Java section of the *BlazeDS Developer Guide*.

ActionScript Type	Java Type
Array (dense)	List
Array (sparse)	Map
Boolean or "true" and "false" strings	Boolean
ByteArray	byte[]
Date	Date
int/uint	Integer
Number	Double
Object	Map
String	String
Undefined	Null
XML or XMLDocument	Document

For complex types (i.e., custom classes), the `[RemoteClass]` metadata should be specified on the ActionScript class to map it to a corresponding Java class. The ActionScript class must have public getters and setters for all of its mapped properties, and similarly the Java class must define public `getX()` and `setX()` methods, where *X* is the property name. There is no special language support for property setters and getters in Java at the time of writing.

The `BlazeExample` project maps `Forecast` objects from Java to ActionScript. The ActionScript instances are created automatically by Flash Player when it receives the AMF results of a remote call to the `getFiveDayForecast()` method. The implementation is:

```
package com.wrox.vo
{
    [Bindable]
    [RemoteClass(alias="com.wrox.vo.Forecast")]
```

```
        public class Forecast
        {
            public var day:String;
            public var summary:String;
            public var imageUrl:String;
            public var maxTempF:Number;
            public var minTempF:Number;
            public var maxTempC:Number;
            public var minTempC:Number;
        }
    }
```

Note the [RemoteClass] metadata, which maps the ActionScript class to its Java partner. This information is used by Flash Player to deserialize AMF messages received from the server side into strongly typed Forecast objects in ActionScript. The [Bindable] metadata is also applied at the class level, so the ForecastRenderer view can bind onto it.

On the server side, the Java class echoes the ActionScript class, except that getter and setter functions are defined according to the conventions of the Java language, with getX() and setX() methods, as follows:

```
package com.wrox.vo;

public class Forecast
{
    private String day;
    private String summary;
    private String imageUrl;
    private float maxTempF;
    private float minTempF;
    private float maxTempC;
    private float minTempC;

    public String getDay() {
        return day;
    }
    public void setDay(String day) {
        this.day = day;
    }
    public String getSummary() {
        return summary;
    }
    public void setSummary(String summary) {
        this.summary = summary;
    }
    ...
}
```

To summarize, the Remoting Service is the simplest way to connect a Flex client to Java server-side code because there's no need to deal with serializing and deserializing request and response data. However, there are times when a remote object is not feasible, since a Flex client may be expected to interact with existing HTTP or SOAP-based Web Services. At some enterprises there are strict rules about what kind of services are allowed and disallowed.

The example now continues by replacing the WeatherService remote object with an HTTP service and then a SOAP-based Web Service. Less detail is given that for this section, but the general pattern is the same: define a destination, create a service object, invoke the service, handle the results, and so forth.

HTTP and Web Services

Flex provides two further components for Remote Procedure Calls (RPCs): the HTTPService and WebService classes. You can use these to interact with basic HTTP services and SOAP-based Web Services, respectively, in two different ways:

❑ **Directly:** Flex components connect directly to remote HTTP Services and SOAP-based Web Services without involving BlazeDS. However, Flash Player only permits connection to services that reside on the same host that was used to load the application, unless those hosts provide a cross-domain.xml policy file granting permission. In other words, a service host must explicitly grant permission for Flex applications from different hosts to connect. Furthermore, only the HTTP GET and POST methods are supported and data from the body of HTTP responses with error codes cannot be retrieved.

❑ **Proxied:** Flex components connect to the BlazeDS Proxy Service, which proxies requests onwards to remote HTTP services and SOAP-based Web Services, without the need for cross-domain.xml policy files. The Proxy Service can perform client authentication, white-list URL filtering, security checks, logging, and localization before it proxies a request. It also provides a centralized place for management of the RPC services that a Flex application connects to. When connecting to an HTTP service via the Proxy Service, HTTP GET, POST, HEAD, OPTIONS, PUT, TRACE, and DELETE requests are supported, and data can be extracted from HTTP responses with error codes.

When these service components are used directly, as shown in Figure 59-4, BlazeDS is not required, although certain limitations apply. When using the BlazeDS Proxy Service, as shown in Figure 59-5, you have greater control over how a Flex client connects to remote services.

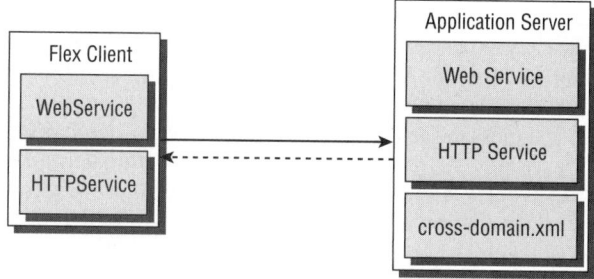

Figure 59-4

This section now explains how to modify the BlazeExample application to use the HTTPService and WebService components for connecting to services via the Proxy Service. The process is similar to that of the Remoting Service. Destinations will be defined in the BlazeDS configuration file and referenced in the Flex application to establish a connection. Methods are invoked on the service components resulting in asynchronous service calls and the dispatch of result or fault events.

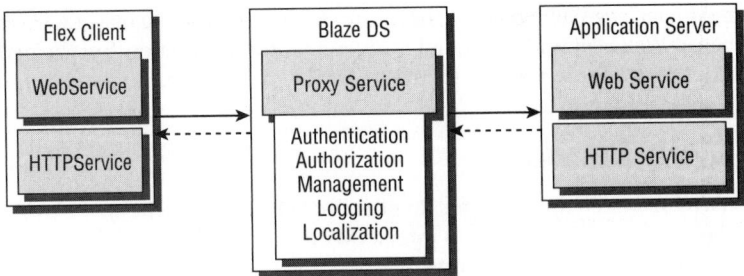

Figure 59-5

Configuring a Proxy Service Destination

Proxy Service destinations are configured in the `proxy-config.xml` file within the `WEB-INF/flex` folder of a BlazeDS web application. A unique `id` is given to a destination for later use by the Flex application to address requests. A destination then defines a URL for the actual service that a client's requests will be proxied to. It can also define dynamic URL patterns that include wildcards to allow the Flex client to connect to any URL that matches a certain pattern, via the proxy.

The `proxy-config.xml` file for the `BlazeExample` project defines two destinations. These offer the same weather-forecasting service as the remote Java object from earlier, but from an HTTP service and a Web Service instead. The first destination is:

```
<destination id="weatherHttpService">
    <properties>
        <url>http://www.wrox.com/weatherService</url>
    </properties>
    <adapter ref="http-proxy"/>
</destination>
```

The `weatherHttpService` is defined to proxy requests and responses to and from an HTTP service. The URL for this service is specified, and the `http-proxy` adapter is referenced. This adapter is provided with BlazeDS and contains the logic to proxy HTTP requests and responses.

When a Flex client sends a message to the `weatherHttpService` destination, it is received by BlazeDS, where it can be authorized, authenticated, logged, and so on, before being forwarded to the remote service at `http://www.wrox.com/weatherService`. When a response is received by the Proxy Service, it is forwarded back to the Flex client.

The second destination is very similar, except that the `soap-proxy` adapter is used instead to enable BlazeDS to proxy requests and responses to a remote SOAP-based Web Service.

```
<destination id="weatherWebService">
    <properties>
        <wsdl>http://www.wrox.com/services/WeatherWebService?wsdl</wsdl>
        <soap>*</soap>
    </properties>
    <adapter ref="soap-proxy"/>
</destination>
```

Note that the URL for the Web Service Definition Language (WSDL) descriptor is referenced. This provides a description of the operations and message formats available to clients of the Web Service, using the open WSDL 1.1 standard. A wildcard is specified in the soap element to allow Flex clients to invoke any of the operations described in the WSDL descriptor for the service.

The adapters and default communication channels for the BlazeDS Proxy Service are specified above the destinations in the proxy-config.xml file. Note that the default=true attribute is specified for the http-proxy adapter, so it was not strictly necessary to reference it in the weatherHttpService destination.

```
<adapters>
    <adapter-definition id="http-proxy"
        class="flex.messaging.services.http.HTTPProxyAdapter"
        default="true"/>
    <adapter-definition id="soap-proxy"
        class="flex.messaging.services.http.SOAPProxyAdapter"/>
</adapters>

<default-channels>
    <channel ref="my-amf"/>
</default-channels>
```

At the very top of the proxy-config.xml file, a number of additional properties are specified. These configure the general behavior of the Proxy Service and include the total number of simultaneous connections that can be made, as well as the default connection limit per client. When proxying service requests, multiple Flex clients will be sending their communications through the same Proxy Service instance on the server, so these properties need to be used to ensure the server is not overloaded. You can set the allow-lax-ssl element to true when using SSL during development to allow self-signed certificates, but you should set it to false in production.

```
<properties>
    <connection-manager>
        <max-total-connections>100</max-total-connections>
        <default-max-connections-per-host>2</default-max-connections-per-host>
    </connection-manager>
    <allow-lax-ssl>true</allow-lax-ssl>
</properties>
```

These configuration properties and more are described in further detail in the Configuring the Proxy Service section of the BlazeDS Developer Guide.

Connecting a Flex Client via the Proxy Service

A Flex client can communicate with HTTP services and SOAP-based Web Services in a similar manner to remote object services. The HTTPService and WebService components are used, and these can be declared in MXML or created in ActionScript code. An example of each kind of service is included in the BlazeExample project, although server-side implementations are provided only for the Remoting Service. The following is the declaration for the HTTPService:

```
<mx:HTTPService
    id="weatherHttpService"
    destination="weatherHttpService"
    useProxy="true"
```

```
method="GET"
resultFormat="e4x"
result="weatherHttpServiceResult(event)"
fault="weatherHttpServiceFault(event)"
/>
```

An `HTTPService` is declared in MXML. The service references the `weatherHttpService` destination configured on the server. The `useProxy` property is set to `true` to indicate that the client connects to an HTTP Service through the BlazeDS Proxy Service rather than a direct connection. This property is not strictly necessary, since a destination has been specified instead of a URL, so it is already clear that the Proxy Service is being used.

The `method` property is specified to GET and the `resultFormat` to e4x. Recall that only the GET and POST methods are supported for direct HTTP service connections, but a wider range of methods are available through the Proxy Service (GET, POST, HEAD, OPTIONS, PUT, TRACE, and DELETE). The `resultFormat` of e4x means that the HTTP service is expected to return XML data, which will be parsed into an XML literal that can be accessed using ECMAScript for XML (E4X) expressions. There are various other `resultFormats` available, as described in the following table.

resultFormat	Description
object (default)	The response from the service is XML, and this is converted into an ActionScript object tree.
Array	The response from the service is XML, and this is converted into an `Array` of ActionScript object trees. If the response does not contain multiple top-level elements, then the entire result tree will end up in the first element of the `Array`. An `ArrayCollection` is used to wrap the Array when the `makeObjectsBindable` property is set to `true`.
Xml	The response from the service is XML, and this is converted into an ActionScript `XMLNode` object.
e4x	The response from the service is XML, and this is converted into an ActionScript XML literal that can be accessed with E4X expressions.
Flashvars	The response from the service is plain text, containing name-value pairs separated by ampersands, and this is converted into an ActionScript object.
Text	The response from the service is plain text, and this is left raw, so it can be cast to a string or other simple types, depending on its value.

Like the `RemoteObject` component, the `HTTPService` component dispatches `result` and `fault` events when the response to a remote method call is received from BlazeDS. However, unlike the `RemoteObject`, the result data is typically untyped XML or ActionScript `Object` trees, perhaps contained in an `Array` or `ArrayCollection`. This means that some translation is required to produce strongly typed objects, unless you are prepared to accept the risks of programming with loosely typed objects. An example can be seen in the `weatherHttpServiceResultHandler()` method of the main application file in the `BlazeExample` project.

It is good practice to convert loosely typed XML and object instances into strongly typed objects as soon as possible. This allows the compiler to detect any programming mistakes involving property names, makes the code more descriptive, and enables the virtual machine to perform more quickly.

Please refer to the `BlazeExample` project for an example of a declaration of a `WebService` component. The general approach is the same: reference the destination configured in the `proxy-config.xml` and attach event handlers for `result` and `fault` events.

Requesting Data

An `HTTPService` is invoked by using the `send()` method that optionally takes a parameter's object containing name-value pairs, as follows:

```
// send an HTTP request
var params:Object = { zipcode : zipcode.text };
var token:AsyncToken = weatherHttpService.send(params);
```

A `WebService`, on the other hand, is invoked by calling a method that matches the name of an operation in the WSDL definition. You can pass parameters directly into the method, as long as they also match the WSDL definition. For example:

```
// send a WebService request
var token:AsyncToken = weatherWebService.getFiveDayForecast(zipcode.text);
```

There are various other ways to pass parameters to `HTTPService` and `WebService` components. For example, the `contentType` property of an `HTTPService` can be set to `application/xml` to send requests as XML. Sometimes URL parameters are appended directly to the `url` property of an `HTTPService` instead of being passed into the `send()` method. MXML can also be used to declare parameter names and then bind values into them. The full capabilities are described in the *BlazeDS Developer Guide* and *Flex Language Reference*.

Summary

This chapter has only touched on the capabilities of BlazeDS. The purpose was to give you the confidence to set up a simple BlazeDS project and start performing RPC calls with a remote object, before perhaps experimenting with the Proxy Service and learning more through the *BlazeDS Developer Guide* and other official documentation.

The Message Service was not covered here, since it was the subject of Chapter 55, and many more advanced topics were omitted due to space limitations. For instance, BlazeDS can be integrated with the basic authentication and authorization mechanisms provided by various application servers; BlazeDS can be deployed to a cluster of servers using JGroups for node-to-node communications; and the `SchemaTypeRegistry` can be used to automatically translate the results of Web Service calls into strongly typed ActionScript objects.

BlazeDS makes it really easy to integrate Flex clients with various kinds of data sources and even to push live data from the server to distributed clients. You are encouraged to find out more by reading the *Developer Guide* from cover-to-cover, studying the sample applications provided with the turnkey distribution, and making use of the online discussion forums at Adobe Open Source (`http://opensource.adobe.com/wiki/display/blazeds/BlazeDS`).

Coming up next, Part X covers Cairngorm, a popular framework for building Flex applications. Cairngorm guides developers to organize their code in a particular way, so that data modeling, business logic, service interactions, and view layout code is well separated.

Part X: Using Cairngorm

60

MVC Frameworks

When building Adobe Flex applications, you'll often find it necessary to organize your application components into consistent architecture. The architecture dictates how each component will interact with the other components and data, and how information is exchanged between the application and the server.

This chapter examines Model-View-Controller (MVC) frameworks at a high level. The following sections examine the MVC paradigm, what a framework is, and why you would want to use an MVC framework. These sections will also go in depth into what each component that creates an MVC architecture should do.

This chapter will not cover any Flex frameworks or code in detail. Later in this book, you will find several chapters devoted to Cairngorm, the Adobe-sponsored MVC framework.

What Is MVC?

MVC is an architecture, or paradigm, that divides your application into separate logical components: the data model, the user interface (view), and the controller. We'll dive into greater detail on MVC components later in this chapter, but this should be enough to get you ready.

In the simplest of terms, a framework is a structure used to solve a complex problem. When applied strictly to computer software, a framework is the set of core logic, classes, and design patterns that create the structure of your application. All components of the application rely on the framework structure to function correctly. Frameworks typically consist of a common set of libraries and design patterns to use when building your application components. Design patterns are commonly used patterns in coding; they are templates that you can follow to enable your software to solve commonly occurring problems.

When examining the "MVC framework," you can see that it is a software structure that divides the logical components of the application into the data model and the view, and provides a controller for the view to interact with the data. The MVC framework provides the application core. It provides a consistent architecture for building the separate components of your application, handles controlling the application flow, enables communication between separate views, and provides the entire infrastructure necessary to build the application.

It is also important to understand that not all frameworks are MVC, although all MVC architectures require a core framework.

MVC Components

As mentioned above, applications built with MVC frameworks are composed of three main components: the data model, the user interface/data view, and the controller. Each is an integral component of the application. If any of those pieces is missing, you either don't have a true MVC, or your application is incomplete.

Understanding the Data Model

The data model is the component of your application that logically represents data. The data model maintains the state of the application because it contains all of the data that your application is using. This includes all data loaded from the server, and all data generated inside the application.

There is no restriction as to what format the data is within your data model. It can be XML-based or it can use collections of value objects. The distinction factor for an MVC data model is that all of the data is maintained within logical components, and that the data is separated from the view and the controller.

This does not mean that there will only be only one component that contains all of the data for your application. In larger applications, this would have the potential to be a massive class. Let's think about a simple media player application to exemplify this.

If the media player application required a user to log in first, you would have a "user" model. The user model would contain all the information about that user. You would also have a "playlists" model, which would be the collection of all the playlists for that user. Each playlist would be an object with a name, and a collection of media assets. Each media asset would have identifying information about the media asset (name, artist, etc.). Your application could also have an "artists" model that contains collections of information about the artist information used within your application.

There is no right or wrong way to organize the data model. In many cases (and also in Cairngorm), there is a ModelLocator class, which is a singleton class that contains all your application data. Inside of this "main" model, you would have a user model, a playlist model, and an artists model.

```
package model
{
    [Bindable]
    public class ModelLocator
    {
        /* singleton getInstance() would be here too */
        public var userModel : UserModel;
        public var artistsModel : ArtistsModel;
```

```
            public var playlistsModel : PlaylistsModel;
    }
}
```

Another option would be that you have multiple singleton models, such that there is a singleton user model, a singleton playlists model, and a singleton artists model. The singleton design pattern is very common in MVC data models because there can only be one instance of that class within the application. Any invocation of the getInstance() method on the singleton will always return the same class.

Understanding the View

The "view" within an MVC architecture refers to the view of data model as it is presented to the user. In other words, the view is simply the user interface. The view itself does not contain any application data, and does not control how data is handled throughout the application. In an MVC application, the view is strictly used for presenting the data or gathering data to be used within the application. The user may read data contained within a table, or view a chart of data, or may input values into a form, but the persistence of that data is controlled by the model and controller. The model would contain the in-memory reference to the data, and the controller would handle persisting data to the server and loading data into the application.

The view is responsible for rendering any data and providing a mechanism for the user to interact with the controller and model. This interaction mechanism covers everything from responding to keyboard and mouse events, to common user interface controls such as text boxes, buttons, grids, trees, and the like.

Just as the data model is modularized to logically organize the data, the view is typically broken into components based on their logical functionality. Different modules of the application are typically composed of multiple views, and it is not uncommon to have finer-grained views reused across multiple modules.

Once again, this sounds confusing, but it really isn't. Let's stop and think about a medical practice management application. There is a lot of information that can be presented to the user — everything from appointment history to billing to prescriptions and insurance. No matter which module you are viewing, you will always want to see patient information. This is a case where you would create a fine-grained patient information view, and you would reuse that view throughout the billing, prescriptions, and insurance modules. Each module would have its own data model associated with it, and the view would display the appropriate data.

Understanding the Controller

Now that we have discussed the model and the view, it is time to examine the controller. The controller does exactly as its name describes; it dictates what the application does. In many senses, the controller is the actual backbone of the application. If the user clicks on a button in the view, it would dispatch a message to the controller, which would determine what type of action should be done. The controller would determine whether the application should show a different view, save or load data, or update the current view based on the user input.

The controller typically involves a central event dispatching or communication mechanism for communication between application components. In Flex applications, this can either be a custom class based on the EventDispatcher class or it can use the built-in event propagation mechanism within the Flex framework itself.

The controller is in charge of all data serialization to and from the server, and all updates to the data model. All data that is loaded into the application would be loaded into the data model through the controller. Any data that comes from a user input form would go through the controller to be verified before updating the model or saving any data to the server.

Not only does the controller dictate how to respond to user input, but it also handles any business logic within the application. The controller handles business rules that determine workflow and data validation.

Putting the Pieces Together

Now that you understand the logical structure and components of an MVC architecture, the next step is to understand how it all works together. Figure 60-1 shows the general flow of events and interaction within a Flex application using an MVC architecture.

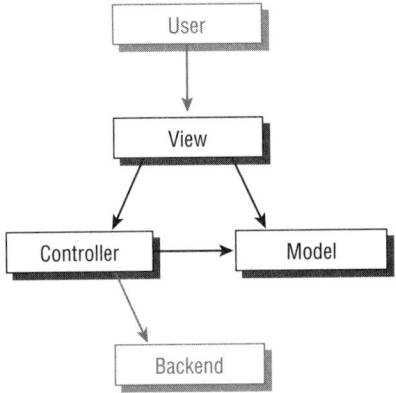

Figure 60-1

The user interacts directly with the view (user interface). The view displays data and information from the model. Any user action, whether it is keyboard input or a mouse event, is sent to the controller, which determines the appropriate action.

The controller can then update the model, change the view, or make calls to the backend data services to store, retrieve, or delete data. All responses from the server would be handled within the controller, which would then either update the model or instruct the view to change.

Why MVC?

You may also be wondering, "Why would I want to use MVC?" Not all Flex applications require an MVC architecture. MVC architectures provide an infrastructure for you to build complex applications. Simple applications that do not have a complex user interface or do not require modular development do not necessarily need them. You may want to consider the use of an MVC architecture based on the information in the following few paragraphs.

Abstraction

MVC architectures typically involve abstraction of logic and data within the application into distinct components. Each component is typically designed to only perform one action. The view components only define the interface that the user interacts with, the model classes only define the data model structure, and the controller only defines how the view, model, and backend services interact.

Each of these separate components is typically made up of smaller logical components and results in finite application components that typically only perform one task. When put together, the small, finite components make up the larger application modules, which in turn make up the entire application. This might sound confusing, but simply put, it means that complex components and actions are actually made up of very small, simple components and actions.

Breaking things down to simple, finite components provides a number of advantages for larger applications. Applications that properly use an MVC framework typically result in cleaner, more reusable code.

Component Reuse

One component of the view may be made up of other view components, which are also used in different view components. For example, let's reexamine the media player application. That application could have several components in the "main" user interface view. You have the playback controls, the playlist, and perhaps some audio waveform visualization. Each one of these controls could be embedded within another view; thus, they are modular and reusable.

While views are made up of view components, there is also reuse within the data model and controller. Let's keep the media player example in mind. In your data model, you could have a playlist object, which is made up of media asset objects. Media asset objects and playlists could be used in any of the views, and are also used throughout the controller. Updating a playlist object in the data model to contain more data would result in the playlist objects used throughout the application being updated, thus making those changes available to the entire application.

Additionally, the logic in the controller that is used to load a playlist or play a media asset can be reused anywhere within the application. You could have the application load the default playlist when the application initializes, or you can load another playlist from a different part of the application, using the exact same controller logic.

Distributed Development

Because of the abstraction and inherent modular nature of MVC applications, MVC architectures make distributed development easier. With an MVC architecture, your application is already divided into separate modules for the view, model, and controller. Each of those is likely broken into its own modules based on the size and complexity of the application.

Because the application is already modularized with this approach, it is much easier to delegate development of specific components to different teams. You can have your team of designers in New York working on the user interface, while your development team in San Jose works on the model and controller interaction in parallel. On larger projects, you can even have development divided by module, not just by the model/view/controller layers. Your team in New York could be working on the inventory module, while your team in San Diego is working on the payments and billing module (both covering development of every layer).

Although the separate teams may be working on the same application, chances are there are only a few common files between the separate modules. With proper source code versioning control, "stepping on other developer's toes" is minimized and distributed, and concurrent development is enabled.

Maintenance

While MVC-based applications may have numerous components between the model, the view, and the controller, they are all based on a common set of design patterns, are all organized in the same way, and follow the same conventions. This generally equates to cleaner and more readable code.

It is also typically easier to maintain an application built on top of a common MVC framework because the application structure is known. The developer who is maintaining the code may not have been involved with the initial development, however if that person already knows the structure of the MVC architecture, he or she will get "up to speed" more easily. The developer will already be familiar with how the application components interact with each other and will just need to focus on the maintenance tasks. He or she will not need to learn a new architecture.

Another feature for MVC architectures is that updating them is typically fairly easy because of the modularity of the application. Changing the view of a module does not alter the view, any of the business logic, or how it interacts with the server. Additionally, changing the business logic in the controller would change it throughout the entire application.

As another example, consider the medical practice management application mentioned earlier. If you wanted the patient details view to be updated everywhere in the application, you would only need to update the patient details view, not every module within the application.

Is There a Definitive MVC?

That is a definitive, no. Every technology has its own MVC framework. There are multiple MVC frameworks for building Adobe Flex applications. MVC frameworks in Flex are like ice cream — everyone has their favorite, and everyone's favorite is not the same thing. However, the Cairngorm framework supported by Adobe is the most widely used Flex MVC framework.

The following is a list of common Flex MVC frameworks. Each has the goal of making complex applications easier, and each provides the backbone infrastructure to build applications with a separate data model, view classes, and controller.

- **Cairngorm** — `http://opensource.adobe.com/wiki/display/cairngorm/Cairngorm`
- **Model – Glue Flex** — `www.model-glue.com/flex.cfm`
- **PureMVC** — `http://puremvc.org`
- **Swiz** — `http://code.google.com/p/swizframework`
- **Mate** — `http://mate.asfusion.com`

An MVC Approach to Component Architecture

It is also worth noting that coming soon in Flex 4, Flex will also support MVC architectures per component. This means that normal components (scrollbars, buttons, sliders, etc.) each will have their own internal MVC architecture. To be clear, this is not exactly MVC architecture per application, as we have discussed in this chapter. What this will provide is a component structure that is easily customizable and extendable.

Flex 4 (Gumbo) will feature component skins that can change or be customized depending on the state of the component, without altering the underlying functionality of the component — for example, a button whose skin changes based on the mouse position or on the toggled state of the button. However the underlying code for the button will remain unchanged. In essence, it allows you to override the view of the component without the need to subclass the Button control and manually override its behavior.

This feature is already available for downloading at http://opensource.adobe.com/wiki/display/flexsdk/Flex+SDK.

Summary

Model-View-Controller frameworks are not necessary for every Flex application. However they are an integral component when building medium to large-scale applications. MVC frameworks provide the infrastructure necessary to separate the data model, the user interface, and business logic.

MVC frameworks enable you to build very large applications made up of loosely coupled components that are easier to maintain and provide more code reuse than applications that do not take advantage of the MVC architecture styles.

The remaining three chapters of Part X are devoted to Cairngorm, the Adobe-sponsored MVC framework.

Introduction to Cairngorm

This chapter is the first of three covering Cairngorm, the most established architectural framework for building Flex and AIR applications. It provides a brief introduction for those new to Cairngorm, while the later chapters examine the underlying patterns in more detail, covering best practices, common pitfalls, and customizations to get the most out of Cairngorm on larger projects.

Overview

Cairngorm dates from the early days of Flex but has been updated several times as the Flex framework has evolved. Its unusual name comes from a mountain range in the Scottish Highlands, while its substance is derived mostly from well-known patterns of the Enterprise Java world. The main objective of Cairngorm is to provide a consistent structure for building Flex and AIR applications that helps developers to separate concerns and focus on implementing new features.

This chapter uses a single end-to-end interaction to introduce the main concepts of Cairngorm and demonstrate how it is traditionally applied. More detailed information about the patterns that comprise the framework and their subtleties when applied in real project situations is postponed until Chapter 62, "Applied Cairngorm." Chapter 63, "Advanced Cairngorm," is aimed at those already familiar with Cairngorm and covers alternative approaches to using Cairngorm, customizations, and anti-patterns.

The Steps of a Cairngorm Interaction

Most of this chapter covers a single Cairngorm interaction, beginning with a user's click of a button and ending with the outcome, reflected back to the user through a change in the user interface. Cairngorm occupies the space between this click and the user interface update, encapsulating logic in commands, performing business operations, locating and interacting with services, and updating an application model.

Figure 61-1 illustrates the stages of a traditional Cairngorm interaction. This is not the only way to use Cairngorm, and some interesting alternatives are discussed in later chapters, but this is the way that Cairngorm was originally intended to be used.

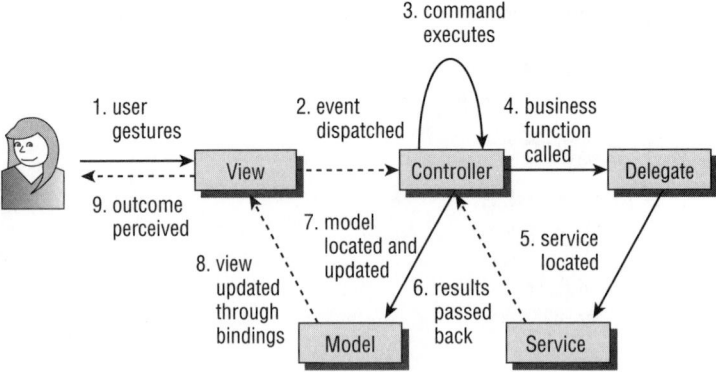

Figure 61-1

Those of you familiar with the Model-View-Controller pattern will see in the center a variation of this. With Cairngorm, developers are encouraged to separate *view* classes, which structure and style the user interface, from *model* classes, which represent the state and behavior of the application, and *control* classes that coordinate changes to the model in response to user interactions and system events. Cairngorm also assists with locating services and calling them through delegates, which hide their complexity.

The Cairngorm library consists of a mixture of coordinating classes, base classes, interfaces, and some prescriptive guidelines for using them. The following sections examine each stage of a Cairngorm interaction in more detail.

The User Gestures

Most Cairngorm interactions begin with a *user gesture*. Perhaps the user clicks on something on the screen, types into an input box, or drags and drops between two locations. A user gesture is simply an action performed with the user interface for a purpose. This stage of the Cairngorm interaction is highlighted in Figure 61-2.

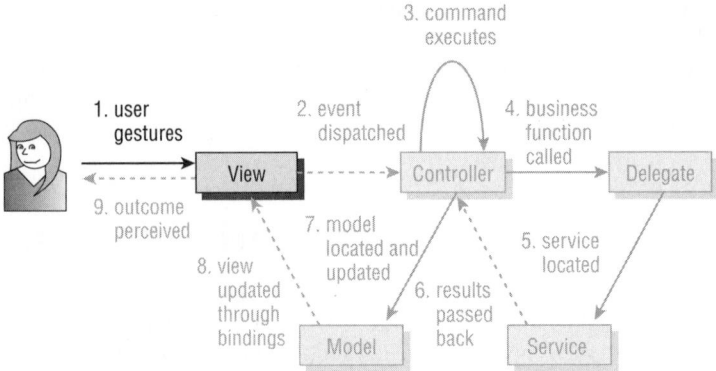

Figure 61-2

The following example shows a button that a user can click on to send a message to customer services:

```
<mx:Button label="Send Message" click="sendMessageClickHandler()" />
```

An Event Is Dispatched

A user gesture results in the dispatching of an event, but not just any event. In Cairngorm, a user gesture results in the dispatching of a special *Cairngorm event*. These events differ from normal Flash events in that they are self-dispatching. In other words, a Cairngorm event dispatches itself when its `dispatch()` function is called, instead of the conventional approach of passing an event to the `dispatchEvent()` function of a `flash.events.EventDispatcher`. This stage of the Cairngorm interaction is highlighted in Figure 61-3.

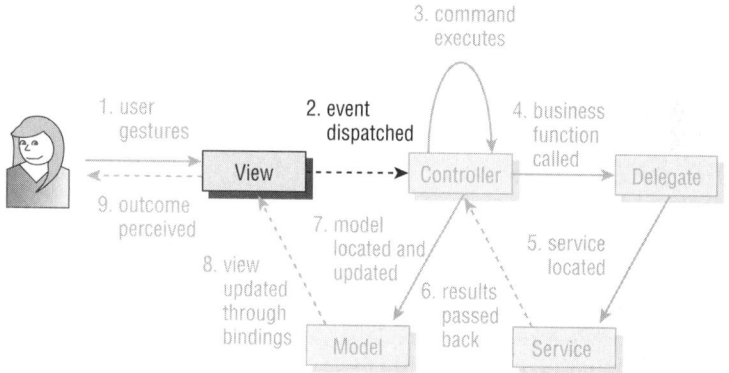

Figure 61-3

A Cairngorm event usually represents a distinct piece of functionality. For example, the sending of an email message, the saving of a document, or the check-out process for an online store. A Cairngorm event is dispatched to start the execution of that functionality. The following example shows the event handler function that is called when the user clicks on the previously described button. A `SendMessageEvent` is constructed and initialized, and then dispatched by calling the `dispatch()` function:

```
private function sendMessageClickHandler():void
{
    var event:SendMessageEvent = new SendMessageEvent();
    event.subject = subject.text;
    event.body = body.text;
    event.dispatch();
}
```

The following is the implementation for a `SendMessageEvent`. It is a Cairngorm event, so it must extend the `CairngormEvent` base class, which defines the `dispatch()` function. A number of properties are also defined to parameterize the operation represented by the event. You will see how these properties are used in the next section, "A Command Executes."

```
public class SendMessageEvent extends CairngormEvent
{
```

```
public static const SEND_MESSAGE:String = "sendMessage";

public var subject:String;

public var body:String;

public function SendMessageEvent()
{
    super(EVENT_NAME);
}

override public function clone() : Event
{
    var event:SendMessageEvent = new SendMessageEvent();
    event.subject = subject;
    event.body = body;
    return event;
}
}
```

A Command Executes

When a Cairngorm event is dispatched, it is heard by an internal component of Cairngorm known as a front controller. A front controller associates Cairngorm events with `Command` classes. These commands contain the logic to actually perform the operations instructed by the events. A front controller will instantiate, then execute, the commands associated with any events that it hears. A command will typically interact with a remote service and update the application model in some way. This stage of the Cairngorm interaction is highlighted in Figure 61-4.

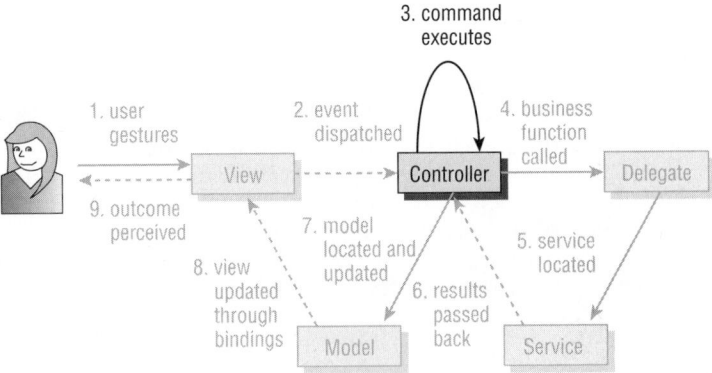

Figure 61-4

A Cairngorm project must include a front controller to register the events and commands used by the application. Larger projects may contain multiple front controllers for different aspects of the application.

The following example shows a simple front controller that registers just one event and command pair: the SendMessageEvent used earlier and its corresponding command.

```
public class MessengerController extends FrontController
{
    public function MessengerController
    {
        addCommands();
    }

    private function addCommands():void
    {
        addCommand(SendMessageEvent.SEND_MESSAGE, SendMessageCommand);
        // add more commands here
    }
}
```

When the front controller hears a Cairngorm event, it will execute the associated command. A Command class encapsulates some kind of operation and must implement the ICommand interface, which defines an execute() function. This is where the operation is performed, or at least started, if the operation is asynchronous. The associated Cairngorm event is passed in to the execute() function, where it can be downcast to access the properties of the event in a type-safe manner.

The following is a skeleton implementation of the SendMessageCommand:

```
public class SendMessageCommand implements ICommand
{
    public function execute(event:CairngormEvent):void
    {
        var sendMessageEvent:SendMessageEvent = SendMessageEvent(event);
        sendMessage(sendMessageEvent.subject, sendMessageEvent.body);
    }

    private function sendMessage(subject:String, body:String):void
    {
        // to be completed
    }
}
```

Note that the command name echoes the event name. A SendMessageEvent results in a SendMessageCommand, just as a DeleteMessageEvent would result in a DeleteMessageCommand. This is the naming convention for Cairngorm events and commands and there is usually a 1:1 mapping, although there is no need for this always to be the case.

A Business Function Is Delegated

When a command relies on a remote object, Web Service, or some other kind of server-side service to execute, this dependency is delegated. Delegation allows the infrastructure code that interacts with the service to be hidden from the command behind a more descriptive, higher-level interface. It separates concerns and increases readability. This stage of the Cairngorm interaction is highlighted in Figure 61-5.

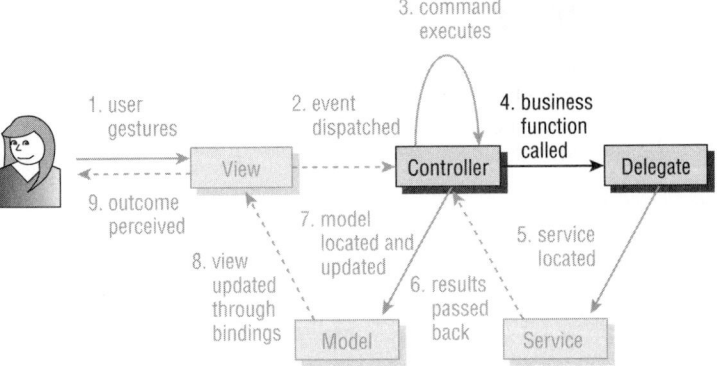

Figure 61-5

The following shows a further developed command. The `sendMessage()` function has been fleshed out with a call to the `MessengerDelegate`, which encapsulates the service interactions involved in actually sending the message:

```
public class SendMessageCommand implements ICommand, IResponder
{
    public function execute(event:CairngormEvent):void
    {
        var sendMessageEvent:SendMessageEvent = SendMessageEvent(event);
        sendMessage( sendMessageEvent.subject, sendMessageEvent.body );
    }

    private function sendMessage(subject:String, body:String):void
    {
        var delegate:MessengerDelegate = new MessengerDelegate();
        delegate.sendMessage(subject, body, this); // this command is passed in
    }

    public function result(data:Object):void
    {
        // to be completed
    }

    public function fault(info:Object):void
    {
        // to be completed
    }
}
```

Delegates are lightweight classes that are disposable, so the command simply creates a new instance when it needs one, without preserving a reference.

Delegated operations are often asynchronous, since the service interactions inside them are asynchronous. For this reason, it is common for a command to implement the Flex `IResponder` interface and pass itself into the delegated function. The delegate will then call back onto the command upon success or failure, as shown in the later stage, "The Model Is Located and Updated."

A Service Is Located and Invoked

Inside the delegate, the service must be located so that it can be invoked. Cairngorm provides a `Service Locator` class that makes it easy to declare services in MXML and later locate them. The `ServiceLocator` class is a *singleton*, meaning only one instance can exist in an application. This instance can be accessed from anywhere using the static `getInstance()` function. This stage of the Cairngorm interaction is highlighted in Figure 61-6.

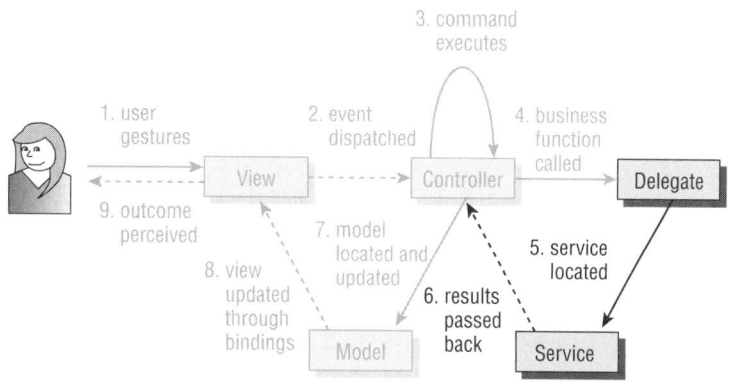

Figure 61-6

The following example shows a `ServiceLocator` containing a single `RemoteObject` service for the sample application. The service is given a unique `id`, which will be used later for locating it, and a `destination`, which corresponds to the destination ID in the data service configuration files. The optional `showBusyCursor` property is also set so that the user can easily see when a service request is underway:

```
<cairngorm:ServiceLocator
    xmlns:mx="http://www.adobe.com/2006/mxml"
    xmlns:cairngorm="http://www.adobe.com/2006/cairngorm">

    <mx:RemoteObject
        id="messengerService"
        destination="messengerService"
        showBusyCursor="true" />

    <!-- further services could be declared below -->

</cairngorm:ServiceLocator>
```

Back in the delegate, the `messengerService` can now be located using the `getRemoteObject()` function provided by the `ServiceLocator`. Afterward, the remote function call can be made. The returned `AsyncToken` is then hooked up to the responder. This process is shown in the following code for the `MessengerDelegate`:

```
public class MessengerDelegate
{
```

```
    private varlocator:ServiceLocator = ServiceLocator.getInstance();

    public function sendMessage(
        subject:String,
        body:String,
        responder:IResponder):void
    {
        var messenger:RemoteObject = locator.getRemoteObject("messengerService");
        var token:AsyncToken = messenger.sendMessage(subject, body);
        token.addResponder(responder);
    }
}
```

Recall that the responder is in fact the Cairngorm command (which implements IResponder) that was passed into the sendMessage() function. When a result or fault is produced by the RemoteObject service, the corresponding IResponder function will be called on the SendMessageCommand object, as shown in the next stage.

The Model Is Located and Updated

A successful or failed service invocation results in a callback to the command. The next step for the command is usually to modify the model in some way. The model is an object structure representing the state of the application. It typically consists of multiple objects of different types that model both the business domain and the state of the user interface. This stage of the Cairngorm interaction is highlighted in Figure 61-7.

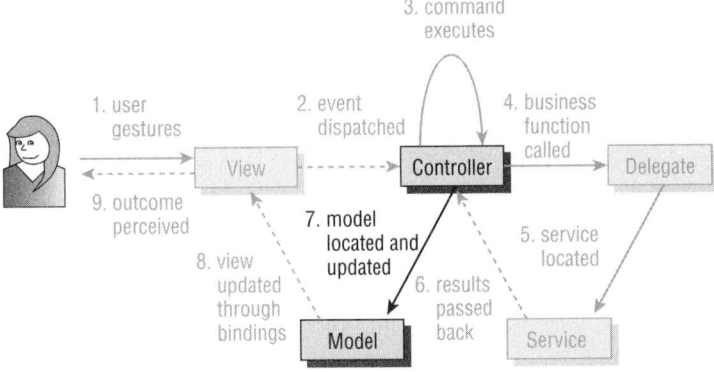

Figure 61-7

Cairngorm does not provide guidance for how the model should be designed, only for how it can be located. Developers must rely on their own object-oriented design skills to build a model that is a good representation of the business domain and user application state. The standard best practices apply: use interfaces to minimize dependencies, refactor mercilessly to prevent code duplication and redundancy, name classes, functions and properties descriptively, and so on.

In a similar manner to that of the ServiceLocator class, Cairngorm provides a means of locating the model from anywhere in the code base, using a ModelLocator singleton. In addition to being a convenient point of access, the singleton pattern ensures that there is only one instance of the model. A `ModelLocator` is used most often within commands and view classes. There are some special considerations to be made when using a `ModelLocator` in view classes. These are discussed in the next chapter.

The following is the revised source for the `SendMessageCommand` class. A private member variable has been defined for the `MessengerModel`, which is accessed via the `MessengerModelLocator`. The `result()` and `fault()` callbacks have also been implemented to update the model accordingly. You will see the effect this has on the user interface later. When the message has been sent successfully, you set a `sentSuccessfully` flag, reset the message `subject` and `body` properties, clear the `errorMessage`, and increment the `numberOfMessages` counter. If a fault occurs, you instead update the model to reflect that the message was not sent successfully.

```
public class SendMessageCommand implements ICommand, IResponder
{
    private var messenger:MessengerModel =
        MessengerModelLocator.getInstance().messenger;

    public function execute(event:CairngormEvent):void
    {
        var sendMessageEvent:SendMessageEvent = SendMessageEvent(event);
        sendMessage( sendMessageEvent.subject, sendMessageEvent.body );
    }

    private function sendMessage(subject:String, body:String):void
    {
        var delegate:MessengerDelegate = new MessengerDelegate();
        delegate.sendMessage(subject, body, this); // this command is passed in
    }

    public function result(data:Object):void
    {
        messenger.sentSuccesfully = true;
        messenger.errorMessage = null;
        messenger.subject = null;
        messenger.body = null;
        messenger.numberOfMessages++;
    }

    public function fault( info : Object ) : void
    {
        messenger.sentSuccesfully = false;
        messenger.errorMessage = FaultEvent( info ).message;
    }
}
```

The following is the implementation for the `MessengerModelLocator`. A `ModelLocator` is just a singleton with properties that are parts of the application model. Cairngorm only provides a marker interface for a `ModelLocator`, `IModelLocator`. In other words, there are no functions on the interface, but its use marks the class as a "model locator." The `MessengerModelLocator` defines a singleton accessor using a static private `_instance` member and a public static `instance` getter. Since ActionScript does not support private constructors, the singleton is enforced at runtime by throwing an error if the constructor is used more than once. There are various other ways to implement the Singleton design pattern in ActionScript.

```
public class MessengerModelLocator implements IModelLocator
{
    private static var _instance:MessengerModelLocator;

    public static function get instance():MessengerModelLocator
    {
        if (_instance == null)
        {
            _instance = new MessengerModelLocator();
        }
        return _instance;
    }

    public function MessengerModelLocator()
    {
        if (_instance)
        {
            throw new Error("Singleton constructed more than once!");
        }
    }

    /** The actual model for the messenger application. */
    public var messenger:MessengerModel = new MessengerModel();
}
```

The View Reflects the Changes

This brings us full circle, back to the view that contained the button that initiated the Cairngorm process. When the command has updated the model, the view reacts automatically through bindings. If a message has been sent successfully, the message subject and body inputs will be cleared and the counter display increased. On the other hand, if a failure occurs while trying to send the message, an error message will be displayed in red. This final stage of the Cairngorm interaction is highlighted in Figure 61-8.

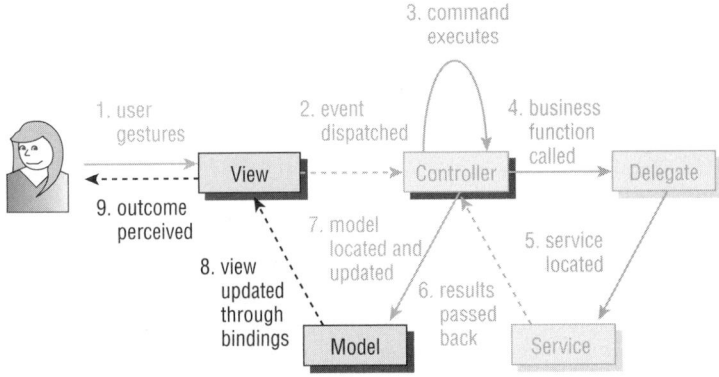

Figure 61-8

The following is the MXML source for the application view:

```
<mx:Application
    xmlns:mx="http://www.adobe.com/2006/mxml"
    xmlns:control="proflex.control.*"
    xmlns:service="proflex.service.*">

    <mx:Script>
        <![CDATA[
            import proflex.model.MessengerModel;
            import proflex.model.MessengerModelLocator;
            import proflex.control.event.SendMessageEvent;

            [Bindable]
            private var messenger:MessengerModel =
                MessengerModelLocator.instance.messenger;

            private function sendMessageClickHandler() : void
            {
                var event:SendMessageEvent = new SendMessageEvent();
                event.subject = subject.text;
                event.body = body.text;
                event.dispatch();
            }
        ]]>
    </mx:Script>

    <service:MessengerServiceLocator />

    <control:MessengerController />

    <mx:TextInput id="subject" width="400" text="{ messenger.subject }" />

    <mx:TextArea id="body" width="400" height="200" text="{ messenger.body }"/>

    <mx:Button label="Send Message" click="sendMessageClickHandler()" />

    <mx:Label
        includeInLayout="{ ! messenger.sentSuccesfully }"
        color="#FF0000"
        text="{ messenger.errorMessage }"
        />

    <mx:Label text="Messages sent: { messenger.numberOfMessages }" />

</mx:Application>
```

The script block defines a private `messenger` variable to hold the `MessengerModel` object, accessed via the `MessengerModelLocator`, and a handler function that is called when the button clicks. This function was shown earlier, and it simply constructs and dispatches the `SendMessageEvent`, which is a Cairngorm event.

Below the script block, the `MessengerServiceLocator` and `MessengerController` are declared. The former allows the delegates to locate the services, whereas the latter ties Cairngorm events to their corresponding commands. The remainder of the view consists of user interface controls that bind directly to the `MessengerModel` so that they will be updated automatically whenever the model changes.

Summary

That's all for this simple example. It's something like the "Hello World!" of Cairngorm applications: a small demonstration of an entire Cairngorm interaction, from a user gesture to an updated view. Some of the details and many of the deeper considerations were skated over, but these will be examined in the two chapters that follow. For now, just take note of the way that concerns have been separated in a clearly defined way.

A user gesture causes a Cairngorm event to be dispatched, which prompts the front controller to execute a command. The command invokes a business delegate, which encapsulates a service interaction. The `ServiceLocator` retrieves the service, which is then invoked by a business delegate. The result or fault of the service call is handed back to the command for processing. The command locates and updates the model, via the `ModelLocator`, which causes the view to react automatically through bindings. Phew!

For this simple example, the path through Cairngorm may seem to twist and turn as if through a forest, but along the way were several well marked clearings, ready for development. As a Cairngorm project grows, more functionality can be placed in these clearings, allowing the application to grow incrementally and maintain a consistent structure. Additional Cairngorm events and commands will be created, more business delegates will be needed to integrate with new services, and the model will grow and evolve over time. If these clearings hadn't been made, it's more likely that trees would be felled haphazardly, blocking off the pathways to consistency, extensibility, and maintainability.

The next chapter looks in more detail at the workings of Cairngorm, discussing the motivation for the design patterns it is composed of, and considering some of the subtleties and trade-offs to be made when developing a real-life Cairngorm project.

62

Applied Cairngorm

Flex applications built using Cairngorm usually contain a number of regular parts, including a front controller, model locator, service locator, and a collection of business delegates, Cairngorm events and commands. This chapter examines each of these parts in more detail, explaining their purpose with reference to a sample application, the Cairngorm Store.

The last chapter provided a whistle-stop tour of Cairngorm, racing from user gesture to view update, with no time for deeper considerations. This chapter aims to address those shortcomings by examining each part of Cairngorm in detail, explaining its purpose and recommending the best way to make use of it while avoiding common pitfalls.

The largest section is concerned with the model locator and the model itself. This is because much of the complexity of large Cairngorm applications resides within the model, yet neither Cairngorm nor any of the other popular Flex frameworks provides much guidance for object modeling. After this, the other aspects of Cairngorm, including Cairngorm events, commands, business delegates, service location, and value objects are all covered.

Throughout the chapter, reference is made to the Cairngorm Store application. The source code for this simple Cairngorm application accompanies this book.

Getting Started

Most of the sections that follow make reference to classes within the Cairngorm Store application. Therefore, you should compile and run the Cairngorm Store project prior to continuing. The project is a client/server application; the client side is a Flex frontend to an online store, while the server side contains a couple of Java remote objects for providing catalog information and validating credit cards. The Flex frontend is shown in Figure 62-1.

Figure 62-1

To install the Cairngorm Store, import the project into Flex Builder, and then build the project. Deploy the resulting WAR to an application server such as Tomcat or JBoss. More details are provided in the README.txt file within the CairngormStore project.

The Main Players

This section discusses the main components of a Cairngorm application with reference to their implementation in the Cairngorm Store. Each section explains the purpose of the component, illustrates its design with a Unified Modeling Language (UML) class diagram and provides some advice for avoiding pitfalls and making the best use of the framework.

Model Locator

The Model Locator pattern provides a convenient, single point of access for application state. This is used by view components to locate the model they want to render, and by commands to locate the model they want to update. For example, a view of a shopping cart would access a model describing the items in the shopping cart, whereas a check-out command would access and update a model to indicate whether the check-out process completed successfully.

The Model Locator pattern is a prescriptive part of a Cairngorm. In other words, its existence and design is not enforced by the framework. However, it is normal for a Cairngorm application to have a model locator for storing state. Furthermore, it is suggested that the model locator should be a singleton so that it can be accessed wherever it is needed. Figure 62-2 shows the ShopModelLocator class from the Cairngorm Store application.

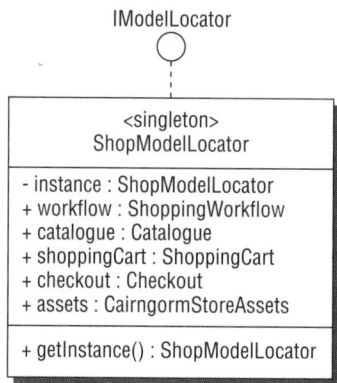

Figure 62-2

Single Point of Access

The ShopModelLocator class is a singleton, which means that only one instance can exist and this instance is accessed through the static getInstance() method. The singleton code is:

```
private static var instance:ShopModelLocator;

public static function getInstance():ShopModelLocator
{
    if (instance == null)
    {
        instance = new ShopModelLocator();
    }
    return instance;
}

public function ShopModelLocator()
{
    if (instance != null)
    {
        throw new Error( "Cannot create more than one instance" );
    }
}
```

When creating a new model locator, the singleton accessing code needs to be added by hand. This is because it relies on a static member variable and method, so it can't be inherited from a base class. Note that instead of the static getInstance() method, a more concise alternative is to use a static getter named instance, as follows. However, the Cairngorm ServiceLocator and CairngormEventDispatcher library classes both use the getInstance() approach, so that is used here for consistency. Either approach is fine.

```
private static var _instance:ShopModelLocator;

public static function get instance():ShopModelLocator
```

```
{
    if (_instance == null)
    {
        _instance = new ShopModelLocator();
    }
    return _instance;
}
```

If any view or command class needs access to the application model, the singleton access method can be used. In many cases, a view or command class interacts multiple times with the application model, so it makes sense to define a private member variable, as shown in the top-level `CairngormStore.mxml` application file, instead of accessing the singleton repeatedly.

```
[Bindable]
private var model:ShopModelLocator = ShopModelLocator.getInstance();
```

Child components of the view can then bind to properties of the model, as follows:

```
<details:ProductDetails
    width="100%" height="325"
    selectedItem="{ model.catalogue.selectedItem }"/>
```

Self-Documenting Code

The `ShopModelLocator` implements the `IModelLocator` interface provided by Cairngorm, as follows:

```
public class ShopModelLocator implements IModelLocator
```

This is an empty "marker" interface that serves no functional purpose except to mark the class as a model locator. One of the aims of Cairngorm is to promote "self-documenting code"; that is, code that describes its own purpose without the need for detailed comments. The `IModelLocator` marker interface exists for this reason alone.

Modeling the Application

Although Cairngorm prescribes the use of a singleton model locator for "locating" the model, it does not provide any guidance on modeling itself. Yet the way in which the business and presentation concerns of an application are modeled is extremely important. Much of the complexity of an enterprise application exists within the realm of the model classes, so it is crucial that they are well designed.

More than anything, a fluency in the principles of object-oriented design is needed for successfully modeling large-scale Flex applications. This means making best use of abstraction, encapsulation, polymorphism, aggregation, composition, and extension to produce a model that balances simplicity, testability, extensibility, and reusability. Easier said than done, of course, but there are many books and online resources to help. Of particular note are the articles by Robert Martin, available at `www.objectmentor.com`, and the following three books: *Design Patterns: Elements of Reusable Object-Oriented Software* by the "Gang of Four," *Refactoring: Improving the Design of Existing Code* by Martin Fowler, and *Domain-Driven Design: Tackling Complexity in the Heart of Software* by Eric Evans.

The subject of object-oriented modeling lies outside the scope of this book. However, the important point to remember when building a Cairngorm application is that the model locator only locates the model, rather than being the model itself. The ideal object model for an application can be elusive and depends on many factors, including the structure of the user interface and the business domain. The resources referenced in preceding the paragraph are essential reading for enterprise software developers working in any object-oriented programming language.

Binding the View to the Model

One of the aims of Cairngorm is to minimize the amount of ActionScript code contained in view components. This separation improves readability and is also desirable because view components are difficult to unit test, because of their asynchronous life cycle and relationship with the display list. In a Cairngorm application, most state and logic is moved out of the view and into model and command classes, which can be unit tested more easily. Binding expressions and Cairngorm events are then used to render state and perform logic.

A simple example can be seen in the `ProductsAndCheckoutControlBar` view component of the Cairngorm Store:

```
[Bindable]
public var workflow:ShoppingWorkflow;

private function startCheckout():void
{
    new ValidateOrderEvent().dispatch(); // a Cairngorm event; you can tell by
}                                        // the way it's dispatched
...
<mx:ViewStack id="controlStack" selectedIndex="{ workflow.workflowState }">
...
<mx:Button label="Complete Purchase" click="startCheckout()"/>
```

Here a `ViewStack` and various other child components are bound directly to properties of the `ShoppingWorkflow` model. When the Complete Purchase button is clicked, a Cairngorm event is dispatched to validate the order. Cairngorm events are dispatched using the `dispatch()` function of the `CairngormEvent` base class. They are said to be self-dispatching and more details are given in the Cairngorm Events section later in the chapter. Note that the script block contains minimal code; only one member variable and a single-line function to dispatch the Cairngorm event.

Controlling View Navigation

The previous example demonstrated a common technique for controlling view navigation in a Cairngorm application. The `workflowState` property of the `ShoppingWorkflow` model class was bound to the `selectedIndex` property of a `ViewStack` container.

```
<mx:ViewStack id="controlStack" selectedIndex="{ workflow.workflowState }">
```

This means that whenever the `workflowState` is updated, the `ViewStack` will automatically navigate to the associated child. The `ShoppingWorkflow` model contains a number of static constants for each of the stages of the workflow.

```
public class ShoppingWorkflow
{
    public static const VIEWING_PRODUCTS_IN_THUMBNAILS : Number = 0;
    public static const VIEWING_PRODUCTS_IN_GRID : Number = 1;
```

```
        public static const VIEWING_CHECKOUT : Number = 2;

        [Bindable]
        public var workflowState:Number = VIEWING_PRODUCTS_IN_THUMBNAILS;
    }
```

These constants have numeric values corresponding to the children of the `ViewStask`. This results in a concise view without logic but does create a dependency between the order to the container's children and the constant values in the model. It may be desirable to remove this dependency by creating a small function in the view to translate between the constants and the container's children, as follows:

```
public function getSelectedChild(workflowState:Number):Container
{
    switch (workflowState)
    {
        case ShoppingWorkflow.VIEWING_PRODUCTS_IN_THUMBNAILS : return filterCtrl;
        case ShoppingWorkflow.VIEWING_CHECKOUT               : return checkoutCtrl;
        case ShoppingWorkflow.VIEWING_PRODUCTS_IN_GRID       : return gridCtrl;
    }
    throw new Error("Invalid workflow state");
}
```

Minimizing Dependencies

One of the most important principles of software engineering is to minimize dependencies between components so that one can be changed with little consequence on others. However, the Model Locator pattern provides the freedom to access the model from anywhere and to navigate downwards through a hierarchy of child objects. This freedom is convenient in the short term but can lead to chains of dependency between otherwise unrelated objects that make software more difficult to maintain. You need to take care to minimize dependencies so that view and model components have the least possible knowledge about the application model.

Favor Dependency Injection over Singleton Access

When a view component only needs access to a specific part of the application model, then inject that part from the parent, instead of navigating to it through the model locator singleton. For example, in the Cairngorm Store application, the `ProductDetails` panel, which renders the image and description of a single product, only needs to know about a `ProductVO` object. Instead of accessing this object inside the `ProductDetails` component, using the model locator, the property is injected from the parent into a `selectedItem` property.

```
<details:ProductDetails
    width="100%" height="325"
    selectedItem="{ model.catalogue.selectedItem }"/>
```

This means that the `ProductDetails` panel has no dependency on the `ShopModelLocator` or even the `Catalogue` model. The structure and design of these parts of the model can change without impacting the `ProductDetails` panel. In addition to this, the `ProductDetails` panel can be more easily reused elsewhere.

The preceding code shows a manual approach to dependency injection — also known as *inversion of control* (IoC) — where the dependent property is set by the parent object. However, there are now a number of IoC frameworks for Flex that provide more sophisticated ways to manage the dependencies in a Flex project. These are outside the scope of the current chapter, but an example is given in Chapter 63, "Advanced Cairngorm," of integrating an IoC framework with Cairngorm. Dependencies should also be minimized in Cairngorm commands. These are several ways to achieve this:

- ❑ Pass the model that the command needs into the associated Cairngorm event, and then retrieve and update it within the command.

- ❑ Extend the Cairngorm `FrontController` class to inject models into commands before execution, as described in Chapter 63.

- ❑ Define a private member variable in the command for the model, and then access it through the model locator, and thus confine the dependency to one place in the class. Furthermore, if there are several commands that update the same piece of the model, define a base class containing the look-up for that part of the model.

The first approach can be applied only when the necessary model is available in the place where the Cairngorm event is dispatched. In practice, this is often, but not always, the case.

The second approach is the most flexible solution and is described in the next chapter. It requires customizing Cairngorm by extending the `FrontController` class and overriding the method that creates and executes commands. This approach can be used to inject models manually into commands before they are executed, or to integrate with an IoC framework and allow it to automatically inject the dependencies of the command.

The third approach is used in the Cairngorm Store for commands that interact with the `ShoppingCart` model. Instead of each command looking up the shopping cart, a base class, `ShoppingCartCommand` is defined with a protected getter for retrieving the shopping cart.

```
private var _shoppingCart:ShoppingCart =
    ShopModelLocator.getInstance().shoppingCart;

protected function get shoppingCart():ShoppingCart
{
    return _shoppingCart;
}
```

The `AddProductToShoppingCartCommand` and `DeleteProductFromShoppingCart-command` classes both extend `ShoppingCartCommand` and use the protected getter. So they have no direct dependence on the `ShopModelLocator`, only on the `ShoppingCart` model with which they interact directly.

For unit-testing purposes, the `ShoppingCartCommand` could also provide a means of setting the `shoppingCart` property to a simple, mock implementation. This would allow the logic inside the command to be tested in isolation, instead of relying on the current state of the singleton model locator, which may have been altered by an earlier unit test. More details about this approach to testing using mock objects is provided in Chapter 73, "Unit Testing and Test-Driven Development with FlexUnit."

When code is duplicated in multiple commands, refactor this into a common base class or else move it into another class that the commands can aggregate with.

In the case of the Cairngorm Store, it is arguable that the view component could just update the model directly instead of going through the Cairngorm front controller at all. However, in a real online store, the Cairngorm commands would be likely to encapsulate more complex logic, including persistence to ensure that a user's shopping cart is preserved on the server between visits.

Front Controller

A user interacts with a Flex application by making gestures, such as clicking on a button, dragging and dropping items from one place to another, or typing into a text input. These user gestures result in the dispatch of Cairngorm events, which instruct actions, such as sending a message to a recipient, adding items to a shopping basket, or updating a document.

The Cairngorm `FrontController` listens for the Cairngorm events that are dispatched when the user makes gestures. Whenever such an event is heard, the `FrontController` looks up a corresponding command class, which is responsible for executing the action. A mapping of Cairngorm event names to command classes is maintained in a dictionary within the `FrontController`. These mappings are registered by a subclass of `FrontController` that is specific to the application. So the `FrontController` provides a centralized point for listening to user gestures and executing commands that perform actions.

Inside the Front Controller

Figure 62-3 shows the Cairngorm `FrontController` class and its dependent classes. Cairngorm events are dispatched through an internal class known as the `CairngormEventDispatcher`. The `FrontController` listens to the `CairngormEventDispatcher` to hear these events. It also maintains a dictionary of command classes in its `commands` property. Each of these classes must implement the `ICommand` interface, which defines an `execute()` method for performing the action. When a Cairngorm event is heard, the `FrontController` looks up the command class and creates a new instance, and then executes it through the `ICommand` interface, as follows:

```
protected function executeCommand(event:CairngormEvent):void
{
    var commandClass:Class = getCommandClass(event.type);
    var commandToExecute:ICommand = new commandClass();
    commandToExecute.execute(event);
}
```

The `getCommandClass()` method looks up the command class in the commands dictionary or raises an exception if a mapping doesn't exist. Assuming that a command class is found, a new instance is created and executed as described previously.

The ShopController

A Cairngorm application subclasses the `FrontController` to create an application-specific front controller. In the case of the Cairngorm Store, this class is called the `ShopController`. It is the centralized point through which all the mappings between Cairngorm events and commands are registered.

Figure 62-4 shows that the `ShopController` extends the `FrontController` class and defines a private `initializeCommands()` method. This registers three groups of commands with the `addCatalogueCommands()`, `addShoppingCommands()`, and `addCheckoutCommands()` functions.

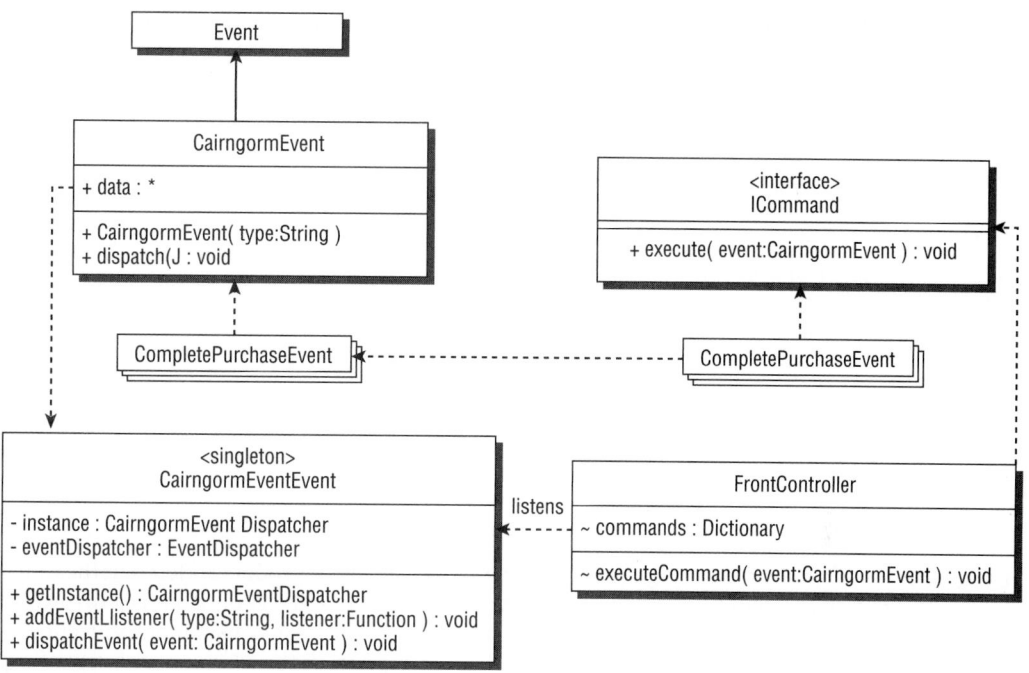

Figure 62-3

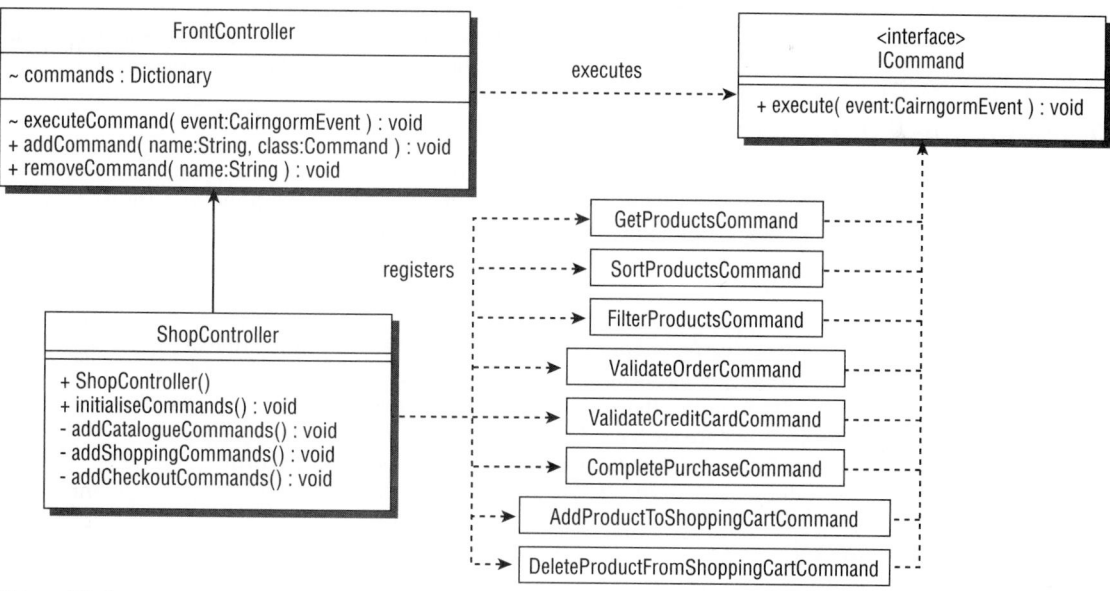

Figure 62-4

To increase the readability of a FrontController *class, group the commands into categories and register them in a separate function for each category.*

The implementation of addCatalogueCommands() is as follows:

```
private function addCatalogueCommands():void
{
    addCommand(
        GetProductsEvent.GET_PRODUCTS,
        GetProductsCommand);

    addCommand(
        SortProductsEvent.SORT_PRODUCTS,
        SortProductsCommand );

    addCommand(
        FilterProductsEvent.FILTER_PRODUCTS,
        FilterProductsCommand );
}
```

Here, three commands are registered, each relating to the catalog of products offered in the Cairngorm Store. Registration is achieved using the addCommand() function of the FrontController, which takes two parameters: the first is the event name, which is normally a string constant of the event class; the second is the corresponding command class, which must implement the ICommand interface. So in this case, commands for getting, sorting, and filtering products are registered.

Note that a removeCommand() function is also defined on the FrontController, so it is possible to add and remove commands dynamically at runtime, although this is not required in the Cairngorm Store application. There are also some protected functions that can be overridden to customize the behaviour of the FrontController. More information on this is provided in the Advanced Cairngorm chapter.

Declaring the Front Controller

An instance of the front controller of a Cairngorm application must be declared and initialized so that the commands are properly registered. This declaration normally takes place in the root application MXML file, below the script block, but before any visual components.

```
<control:ShopController id="controller" />
```

In the CairngormStore.mxml file, the ShopController is declared in a single line of MXML and given the ID controller. For larger applications, it is better to create separate front controllers for the different parts of the application, rather than centralizing all the events and commands. This is particularly true for modular projects, where each module encapsulated a functional area with its own set of events and commands. This topic is covered in Chapter 63, "Advanced Cairngorm."

Cairngorm Events

When a Cairngorm event is dispatched to the front controller, a corresponding command is executed. In most cases, the event corresponds to a user gesture to perform some action, although it may also indicate a system event, such as a periodic backup of data to the server, in case of failure.

Event Classes

A Cairngorm application contains a collection of Cairngorm events that are used to initiate actions upon user gestures. Cairngorm provides a base class that is extended to create a new Cairngorm event. The base class is shown in Figure 62-5.

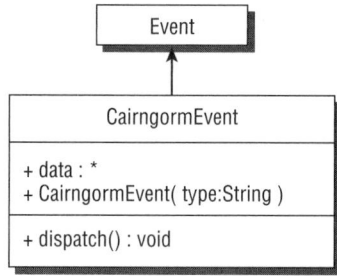

Figure 62-5

Cairngorm events (and their corresponding commands) are given class names that describe the action they perform. Several of these can be seen in the Cairngorm Store: `GetProductsEvent`, `AddProductToShoppingCartEvent`, `ValidateCreditCardEvent`, and so on. This is a form of self-documenting code, so an overview of the feature set of a Cairngorm application can be seen by reading the event and command class names.

> *The name of a Cairngorm event class should describe the action that will be performed when the event is dispatched.*

Event Types

In a manner similar to that of Flash events, Cairngorm events must have a `type` property. This is used by the front controller for mapping to a command class. The event type should be declared as a constant of the event class. Its value must be unique within the scope of the application.

```
public class GetProductsEvent extends CairngormEvent
{
    public static var GET_PRODUCTS:String = "getProducts";
    ...
}
```

In most cases, there is a one-to-one mapping between a Cairngorm Event class and its `type` property. It is conventional for the event name constant and its value to match the class name, as shown previously. A `GetProductsEvent` has a `GET_PRODUCTS` constant with the value `getProducts`.

There are two common ways to set the `type` property of a Cairngorm event:

❑ **Internally:** Within the constructor, the `type` property is set to the constant value. This approach is the most concise, minimizing the code required to create and dispatch a Cairngorm event. Because most Cairngorm Event classes have only one possible type, this approach is generally preferable.

❑ **Externally:** The event name is passed into the constructor through the type parameter, in the same manner as most Flash and Flex events. This is more consistent with the Flex framework but requires more code to create and dispatch the event. When a Cairngorm event has several possible event names, this approach is appropriate. Alternatively, several static factory methods can be defined on the event class for creating the different types of events.

In the Cairngorm Store, the internal approach is favored and all of the type properties are initialized within event constructors. The simplest example is the `GetProductsEvent`, which has no constructor arguments:

```
public function GetProductsEvent()
{
    super(GET_PRODUCTS);
}
```

This means that the event can be created and dispatched in a very concise fashion within the view. A `GetProductsEvent` is dispatched when the application creation completes. This takes places in the `CairngormStore.mxml` application file.

```
private function onCreationComplete():void
{
    new GetProductsEvent().dispatch();
}
```

Cairngorm event type strings must be unique within the scope of a Flex application. In other words, if there are two modules, each containing Cairngorm front controllers, the event type strings must be unique in both controllers; otherwise, an event dispatch may cause multiple commands to be executed (which is not usually the desired behavior).

Events as Parameter Objects

A Cairngorm event is used to parameterize its associated command. The execute method of the `ICommand` interface takes a single event parameter, as follows:

```
public interface ICommand
{
function execute(event:CairngormEvent):void;
}
```

It is usual to define a number of properties on a concrete event, for storing the data needed to execute the command. In the Cairngorm Store, the `FilterProductsEvent` has three properties for parameterizing the filter operation:

```
public var filterOn:String; // field to filter on
public var min:uint;        // minimum value of field
public var max:uint;        // maximum value of field
```

The first, `filterOn`, specifies the name of a product field to filter on, while `min` and `max` define a range of values for that field. These properties are initialized through the constructor of the event:

```
public function FilterProductsEvent(filterOn:String, min:uint, max:uint)
{
    super(FILTER_PRODUCTS);
```

```
        this.filterOn = filterOn;
        this.min = min;
        this.max = max;
    }
```

In some cases, it may be more convenient to set the properties directly, but passing them in through the constructor is often the most concise approach. This allows an event to be constructed, initialized, and dispatched in a line or two of code.

Self-Dispatching Events

The `FilterProductsEvent` is created and dispatched when the user adjusts a price slider in the `FilterControls.mxml` view.

```
public function onSliderChange():void
{
    new FilterProductsEvent(
        "price", priceSlider.values[0], priceSlider.values[1]).dispatch();
}

<mx:HSlider id="priceSlider" … change="onSliderChange()" />
```

Cairngorm events are "self-dispatching," which means that they're dispatched using their own `dispatch()` method. This is in contrast to normal Flash events, which are dispatched through the `dispatchEvent()` method of the `EventDispatcher` class. This design decision was made by the Cairngorm engineers to provide the simplest means of routing the event to the centralized `FrontController`. A single short function call does the trick.

Behind the scenes, the `CairngormEventDispatcher` singleton is used to dispatch the event and pass it to a handler function on the `FrontController`. This can be seen in the following implementation of the `CairngormEvent` class:

```
public class CairngormEvent extends Event
{
    …
    public function dispatch():Boolean
    {
        return CairngormEventDispatcher.getInstance().dispatchEvent(this);
    }
}
```

And similarly, inside the `FrontController`, an event listener is added for each command that is registered:

```
public function addCommand(
    commandName:String,
    commandRef:Class,
    useWeakReference:Boolean=true):void
{
    …
    CairngormEventDispatcher.getInstance().addEventListener(
        commandName, executeCommand, false, 0, useWeakReference);
}
```

Cairngorm Commands

Cairngorm commands perform actions in response to user gestures. As explained earlier, the `FrontController` class is responsible for creating a new command instance and executing it when a Cairngorm event is heard. A command instance is used only once, so another new instance is created the next time the same event is heard. Figure 62-6 shows the `ICommand` interface provided by Cairngorm. All commands must implement this interface.

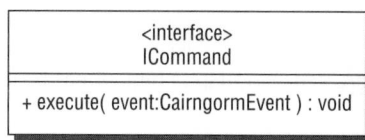

Figure 62-6

Command Execution

When the front controller executes a command, the corresponding Cairngorm event is passed in as the parameter of the `execute()` function. The command can then extract any information needed to perform its work from the Cairngorm event. In fact, the Cairngorm event is what's known as a *parameter object* — an object that holds a group of properties that naturally go together — that exists to parameterize the command.

In general, commands can be classified as synchronous or asynchronous:

❑ **Synchronous:** Simple commands that update the application model directly or perform other sequential actions. These tend to be quick operations, during which time the user cannot make further gestures.

❑ **Asynchronous:** Commands that perform asynchronous operations, such as calling a Web Service or invoking a method of a remote object. These can have varying response times, depending on the server-side implementation. While an asynchronous command is executing, the user may be free to make further gestures and other tasks might be initiated. Asynchronous operations are normally delegated, as described in the "Business Delegates" section that follows. The `GetProductsCommand` of the Cairngorm Store is an example.

The Cairngorm Store contains several examples of synchronous and asynchronous commands, as described in the following subsections.

Synchronous Commands

A synchronous command usually locates a part of the application model, extracts some properties from its event parameter, then interacts with the model by setting properties or invoking methods. For example, the `FilterProductsCommand` of the Cairngorm Store first locates the Comparator object from the `Catalogue` model, through the `ShopModelLocator`. Then it extracts three property values from the event parameter and invokes three methods on the comparator:

```
public class FilterProductsCommand implements ICommand
{
    private var comparator:Comparator =
```

```
        ShopModelLocator.getInstance().catalogue.comparator;

    public function execute(event:CairngormEvent):void
    {
        var filterEvent:FilterProductsEvent = FilterProductsEvent(event);

        var filterOn:String = filterEvent.filterOn;
        var min:Number = filterEvent.min;
        var max:Number = filterEvent.max;

        comparator.addFilterRangeProperty(filterOn, min, max);
        comparator.filter();
        comparator.applyAlphaEffect();
    }
}
```

A private variable is used to store a reference to the Comparator object, for later use within the execute() method. The Comparator is located through the ShopModelLocator singleton. This private variable approach tends to create cleaner, more readable commands, rather than interacting with the model locator within the execute() method.

Inside the execute() function, the first line downcasts the event parameter to the concrete event type: FilterProductsEvent. Recall that the front controller performs the mapping from events to command classes, so ensures the correct type of event is passed in. This assumes, of course, that the commands have been registered correctly. If the wrong command has been registered for an event type, then a type coercion error is likely to occur at runtime.

With a local variable for the concrete event, the properties can be extracted in a type-safe manner. Here the filterOn, min and max properties, described earlier, are extracted to local variables. The final section of the implementation configures the filter on the comparator member variable, then performs the filtering operation and finally applies an alpha effect. This last method call causes each of the items in the catalog that don't match the filter criteria to be partially faded out of view.

Asynchronous Commands

Asynchronous commands are those that begin some action and then later complete it, upon receiving a result or fault message. An example might be a command that requests the latest news from a Web Service, that completes when the news data has been received and processed. The Cairngorm Store contains several asynchronous commands, including the GetProductsCommand, which fetches the catalog data from the server.

In addition to the ICommand interface, asynchronous commands implement the IResponder interface. This is the standard Flex interface for handling results and faults generated asynchronously. It defines two methods — result() and fault() — that are implemented to process result data or fault information. When the GetProductsCommand is executed, the implementation of the execute() function begins an asynchronous process to load the product data.

If this is successful, the result() method will be called. The role of the command is then to process the result data and update or interact with the model. Depending on the contents of the result data, this may involve extracting some strongly typed objects, perhaps parsing some XML, and passing new data into the model. The `GetProductsCommand` extracts a collection of product data, then sorts it by name, before updating the `Catalogue` model and setting the selected item.

```
public function result(data:Object):void
{
    varproducts:ICollectionView = ICollectionView(data.result);

    // sort the data
    var sort:Sort = new Sort();
    sort.fields = [ new SortField( "name", true ) ];
    products.sort = sort;
    products.refresh();

    // update the model
    model.catalogue.selectedItem = products[ 0 ];
    model.catalogue.products = products;
    model.workflow.workflowState = ShoppingWorkflow.VIEWING_PRODUCTS_IN_THUMBNAILS;
}
```

If a fault occurs while fetching the products, the `fault()` method will be called instead. In simple cases, an `Alert` dialog may be opened, but rich Internet applications provide the opportunity to do a lot better than that. A command may update the model to indicate that the products are temporarily unavailable, triggering a timer that will periodically retry by dispatching the `GetProductEvent` again. The view could then react by disabling product browsing features but allowing the user to continue using other aspects of the application.

Asynchronous commands provide the opportunity to handle errors elegantly by temporarily disabling features and attempting automatic recovery.

Result and fault handling has been explained but little has been said about initiating the asynchronous process that leads to these events. This is because service interactions are encapsulated within business delegate objects, which are explained in the next section.

Business Delegates

Most Flex applications interact with remote services of some kind, from making simple HTTP requests to consuming messages pushed out from the server. The various server-side components available in Flex are described in Parts VIII and IX of this book.

Cairngorm commands often perform actions involving service calls. In the Cairngorm Store, the `GetProductsCommand` fetches details of the product catalog from the server, while the `ValidateCredit CardCommand` sends credit card details to the server for validation. In commands like these, a further layer of abstraction is introduced with the Business Delegate pattern.

A business delegate performs business logic using the server side that cannot or should not be performed on the client side. Figure 62-7 shows two of the business delegate classes from the Cairngorm Store application. While Flex and ActionScript makes it possible to perform a considerable amount of business logic on the client, maintaining complex models and performing data processing, some business logic belongs on the server. When a shopper logs in to the Cairngorm Store, the latest catalog of products needs to be fetched from the server, and when the shopper has filled his or her basket with merchandise, credit card details need to be processed by the server. This logic belongs on the server side because it depends on the database and payment system.

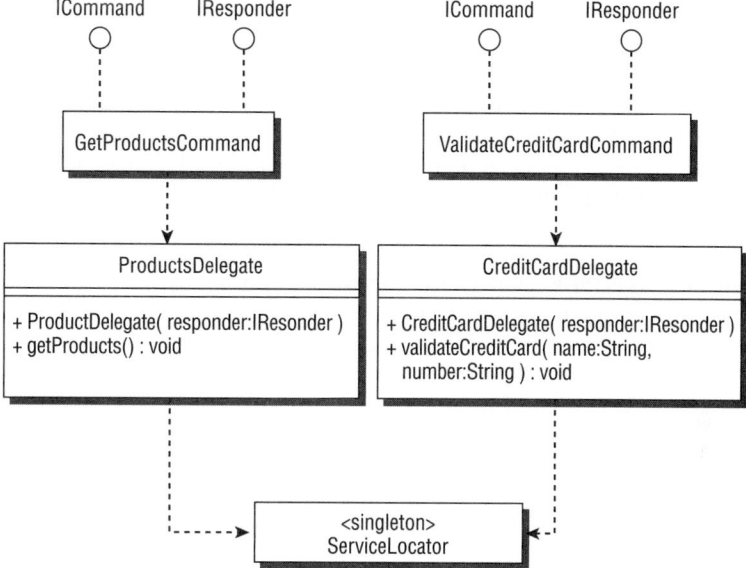

Figure 62-7

Using a Business Delegate in a Command

A business delegate is responsible for interacting with a server-side component, such as an `HTTPService`, `WebService`, or `RemoteObject`. It encapsulates the service interaction, hiding the command from the code that locates and invokes the service. The command instead creates a business delegate and calls a method on it to perform the business logic.

In the Cairngorm Store, the `GetProductsCommand` creates the `ProductsDelegate` and invokes the `getProducts()` method. Similarly, the `ValidateCreditCard` command creates the `CreditCardDelegate` and invokes the `validateCreditCard()` method, as follows:

```
public override function execute(event:CairngormEvent):void
{
    var cardEvent:ValidateCreditCardEvent = ValidateCreditCardEvent(event);
    var cardholderName:String = cardEvent.cardholderName;
    var cardNumber:String = cardEvent.cardNumber;

    var delegate:CreditCardDelegate = new CreditCardDelegate(this);
    delegate.validateCreditCard(cardholderName, cardNumber);
}
```

Notice that the `this` reference is passed into the constructor of the `CreditCardDelegate`. This is because the command acts as responder to the delegate operation. The `validateCreditCard()` method is asynchronous; it makes a request to validate the credit card, then calls back onto the `result()` or `fault()` method upon success or failure.

Creating a Business Delegate

A Cairngorm application may interact with a multitude of different services. The normal approach is to create a business delegate for each service, although the granularity is really left up to the developer. In some cases, a single service may be used in many different ways, so it might make sense to separate these concerns into different delegates.

There is no base class or interface defined by Cairngorm for a business delegate. A business delegate is just an object with a number of business methods defined on it. These methods are usually asynchronous, since they involve service interaction, so the constructor of a business delegate is parameterized with an `IResponder`. This is where the command passes itself in, so its result and fault handlers are hooked up to the service call.

The Cairngorm Store uses the Remote Object Service to perform business logic on the server. The implementation of the `ProductsDelegate` is:

```
public class ProductsDelegate
{
    private var responder:IResponder;
    private var service:RemoteObject;

    public function ProductDelegate(responder:IResponder)
    {
        this.responder = responder;
        service = ServiceLocator.getInstance().getRemoteObject("productService");
    }

    public function getProducts():void
    {
        var token:AsyncToken = service.getProducts();
        token.addResponder(responder);
    }
}
```

Two member variables are declared, one for the responder, the other for the service. A `responder` parameter is passed into the constructor and used to initialize the member variable of the same name. Next, the service is located using Cairngorm's `ServiceLocator` singleton. This provides a centralized point of access for all the services used by a Cairngorm application; more details will follow in the next section. The `getProducts()` method invokes a method on `service`, the `RemoteObject`, and attaches the responder.

This is the general pattern to follow when creating business delegates: define a constructor that initializes an `IResponder` and locates a service; define one or more methods that make service calls and attach the responder.

Stubbing the Service Layer

Since a business delegate encapsulates a set of server-side interactions, it provides a convenient place to stub the service layer of a Flex application. When the service layer is stubbed, the Flex application can be developed and demoed offline, which can be very convenient when server-side components are unavailable for one reason or another. However, it is recommended to develop as much as possible against real services rather than stubs so that integration problems are minimized.

The service layer can be stubbed by extracting an interface from the business delegate, then providing two implementations: one to really interact with the server side, the other to pretend. So in the Cairngorm Store, an IProductsDelegate interface would be extracted from the GetProductsDelegate. A second implementation, the GetProductsDelegateStub would be implemented. This would simply construct the expected result object and pass it back to the result handler on the GetProductsCommand.

Various approaches to stubbing the service layer are described in Chapter 63, "Advanced Cairngorm."

Service Locator

The service locator serves two purposes: it provides a centralized place to declare all of the services required by a Cairngorm application, and it provides a simple means of locating services for use by business delegate classes. It's another singleton because, in general, Cairngorm applications only need one instance of each service object (an exception is described later). Figure 62-8 shows the ServiceLocator class. The static getInstance() getter provides convenient access to the service locator wherever it's needed.

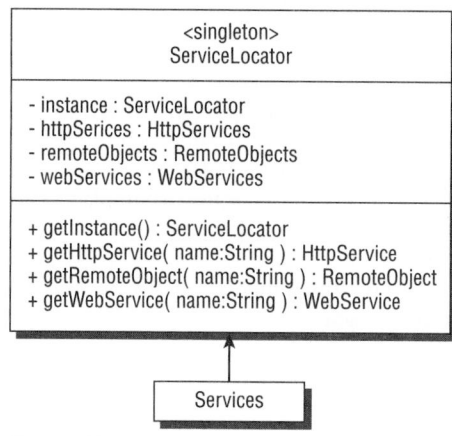

Figure 62-8

Creating a Service Locator

A Cairngorm application that interacts with services should declare those services in a Services.mxml file. This MXML component must extend from the ServiceLocator class provided by Cairngorm, so delegates can locate the services they need. In the Cairngorm Store, the Services.mxml file declares two RemoteObject services: the first for fetching the catalog of products; the second for validating credit card payments.

```
<cairngorm:ServiceLocator
    xmlns:mx="http://www.adobe.com/2006/mxml"
    xmlns:cairngorm="http://www.adobe.com/2006/cairngorm">

  <mx:RemoteObject
      id="productService"
      destination="productService"
```

```
        showBusyCursor="true"/>

    <mx:RemoteObject
        id="creditCardService"
        destination="creditCardService"
        showBusyCursor="true"/>

</cairngorm:ServiceLocator>
```

A service locator may equally well contain other service objects, such as `HttpService` and `WebService` instances. Each service object must be given a unique `id`, which can be used by a delegate for locating the service.

Once the `Services.mxml` file has been created, it is declared in the top-level application file. Like the front controller, the declaration requires a single line of MXML, normally placed below the script block but before the visual components. The relevant line of the `CairngormStore.mxml` application file is shown here:

```
<business:Services id="services"/>
```

Locating a Service

Earlier in the chapter, the Business Delegate pattern was explained, but one aspect was skirted around: the means of locating a service. The solution will come as no surprise, since it's very similar to locating a model with the `ModelLocator`. Once again, a static `getInstance()` method is used to access the single instance of the `ServiceLocator`. With this reference in place, various methods can be used for locating different types of service.

Returning to the `ProductsDelegate` implementation, the `RemoteObject` named `productService` is located in the constructor of the delegate:

```
private var service:RemoteObject;
private var responder:IResponder;

public function ProductDelegate(responder:IResponder)
{
    service = ServiceLocator.getInstance().getRemoteObject("productService");
    this.responder = responder;
}
```

It's as simple as that. The `productService` names must match the `id` of the `RemoteObject` service declared in the `Services.mxml` file. If this is not the case, Cairngorm will raise a "Remote object not found" runtime error.

The `ServiceLocator` defines methods for locating the following service types:

❑   getHttpService()

❑   getRemoteObject()

❑   getWebService()

Cairngorm Enterprise provides an extended `EnterpriseServiceLocator` class that defines a further three get methods for the service types available to LCDS and Blaze DS developers:

❑ `getDataService()`

❑ `getConsumer()`

❑ `getProducer()`

What about REST?

There is one common exception to the rule about maintaining a single instance of each service. That is the case of RESTful services, or more specifically, HTTP services that use URL parameters. For instance, a simple search service may be instructed with the following URL:

❑ `http://www.wroxsearch.com?query=flex`

Here a `query` parameter has been specific with the value `flex`. To search for a different topic, such as `AIR`, a different URL string would be required.

❑ `http://www.wroxsearch.com?query=AIR`

The Cairngorm `ServiceLocator` assumes that service URLs are static, which is not the case for RESTful interactions. There are two straightforward solutions:

❑ Extend the `ServiceLocator` class to support URL parameterization, as described in Chapter 63.

❑ Create the `HTTPService` instance with the required URL inside the business delegate instead of using the `ServiceLocator`.

Value Objects

One of the most basic principles of object-oriented programming is class separation — deciding how to structure code into separate classes with distinct responsibility and clear meaning. It's desirable for classes to represent aspects of the problem domain familiar to both developers and nondevelopers, since this helps communication. So the Cairngorm Store includes classes such as `Product` and `Catalogue` for representing the catalog or products available to purchase.

The Value Object (VO) pattern is a design pattern for transferring data in meaningful pieces between subsystems. It is also known as the Data Transfer Object (DTO) pattern, but when Cairngorm was created the term "value object" was more common. A value object (VO) encapsulates some business data but has no behavior except for the storage and retrieval of its own data. In strict terms, this means that a constructor is defined for passing in the required attributes of a class; these are stored in private member variables, and a number of getters are provided for retrieving the data again. However, in Flex, the member variables of a VO are usually defined as public and an empty constructor is used.

In the case of a Cairngorm application, VOs are normally used for two purposes: the first is transferring data in both directions between the client and a service; the second is storing data within the model that may be bound to the view. It may be that a business delegate invokes a method on a `RemoteObject` which returns a collection of VO instances. These might then be added to the model, causing the view to update through bindings. Figure 62-9 shows `ProductVO` class used for transferring product data in the Cairngorm Store application.

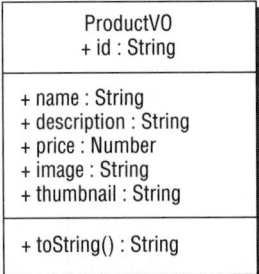

Figure 62-9

This is exactly what happens when the Cairngorm Store initializes. The `GetProductsEvent` is dispatched, leading the `ProductDelegate` to invoke the `getProducts()` method on the remote `productService`. In the responder, the `ProductVO` instances are extracted from the result data and set onto the `Catalogue` model. The `GraphicalProductList` and `TextualProductList` views both update through bindings.

Behind the scenes, the Remoting Service (on the server side) has accessed a collection of Java VOs. These have been serialized into AMF3 data and transferred over the wire to the Flex client. When the data is received it is serialized back into matching VOs on the Flex side. A mapping needs to be established between the Java and Flex implementations of each VO, as described in the next section. Here, it is the Value Object pattern that facilitates the transfer of data over the wire, providing a simple means of storing and retrieving the values that make up the VO.

Creating a Value Object

A value object (VO) in Flex can be nothing more than an ActionScript class with a number of public properties describing an aspect of the domain. A banking application may deal in Statement and Transaction VOs with properties such as date, amount, and balance, while the Cairngorm Store is more concerned with the name, description, and price of Product VOs. The essentials of the `ProductVO` from the Cairngorm store are as follows:

```
package com.adobe.cairngorm.samples.store.vo
{
    import com.adobe.cairngorm.vo.IValueObject;

    [RemoteClass(alias="com.adobe.cairngorm.samples.store.vo.ProductVO")]
    public class ProductVO implements IValueObject
    {
        [Bindable]
        public varid:Number;

        [Bindable]
        public varname:String;

        [Bindable]
```

```
        public vardescription:String;

        [Bindable]
        public varprice:Number;

        [Bindable]
        public varimage:String;

        [Bindable]
        public varthumbnail:String;
    }
}
```

Simple stuff. The class implements a marker interface, `IValueObject`, contained in the Cairngorm library. This marks the class as a VO but requires no methods to be implemented. Each of the properties that make up the `ProductVO` data are declared public and made bindable, so that they can be placed into binding expressions within the view.

```
[RemoteClass(alias="com.adobe.cairngorm.samples.store.vo.ProductVO")]
```

Above the class definition is a `[RemoteClass]` metadata tag that specifies the qualified name of the Java class that maps to this ActionScript class using the `alias` parameter. This is only required when working with `RemoteObject` services or `DataService` objects on the client. It provides Flex with the information necessary to automatically serialize and deserialize objects when transferring the value object/data back and forth between the client and server. The Java implementation is shown here:

```
package com.adobe.cairngorm.samples.store.vo;

public class ProductVO
{
    private int id;
    private String name;
    private String description;
    private float price;
    private String image;
    private String thumbnail;

    public intgetId()
    {
        return id;
    }

    public void setId(int id)
    {
        this.id = id;
    }

    ...
}
```

It is conventional in Java to define private member variables for the data together with public getter and setter methods. The getter and setter take the form `getVariableName()` and `setVariableName()` where `VariableName` corresponds to the ActionScript property `variableName`. This pattern is used for serializing and deserializing between Java and ActionScript objects.

Instead of writing ActionScript value objects by hand, they can also be generated automatically using the Java code generation tool XDoclet2.

Receiving Value Objects

Assuming that everything is going well, when a business delegate makes a service call, a result event will be generated and passed back into a Cairngorm command. Depending on the type of service, the result event may contain ready-made ActionScript objects or else loosely typed data in XML or dynamic objects. The command strips the data from the result event then updates the model, as described in the "Cairngorm Commands" section. If the data is loosely typed, it is good practice to translate it into strongly typed objects before passing the data into the model.

Sending Value Objects

As well as consuming data, many Flex applications also produce it, of course. The way in which data is sent depends on the service type. If the application is using data services or remote objects, there's very little to it: the framework performs translation automatically. If, on the other hand, HTTP services or Web Services are used, translation needs to be performed to manually convert the ActionScript objects into something suitable for the services, such as XML or a parameter string. This might involve some `e4x` or simple string concatenation.

Summary

In this chapter, each main part of Cairngorm was examined in detail, from the two locator classes for accessing services and the model wherever they're needed, to the `CairngormEvent` class and `ICommand` interface for responding to user gestures and executing actions.

The most crucial point is to minimize dependencies. Just because the model locator *can* be accessed from anywhere doesn't mean it *should* be accessed from anywhere! Instead, only the parts of the model that are required should be injected into lower-level view components, and the model itself should be refactored vigorously to always serve the needs of the view well.

The next chapter covers more advanced Cairngorm topics, including customization of the framework and its use in conjunction with the Presentation Model pattern.

63

Advanced Cairngorm

This chapter contains advice to help you build on the foundations of Cairngorm. It is targeted at developers with an understanding of traditional Cairngorm and consists of the best practices, anti-patterns to avoid, and useful customizations.

Although Cairngorm provides a framework on which to build a Flex application, the quality of the end result depends on many other factors, including:

- ❏ **Testability:** If code cannot be tested easily, how can a developer be sure that it works?
- ❏ **Organization:** When a project grows rapidly, how can the codebase be kept tidy and navigable?
- ❏ **Dependencies:** If dependencies are not minimized, software becomes difficult to maintain.

This chapter addresses these issues. The first section explains how to use Cairngorm in conjunction with the Presentation Model pattern to move view logic into a place where it can easily be unit tested. Guidance for organizing smaller and larger Cairngorm projects follows, before a number of known Cairngorm anti-patterns are exposed; these tend to occur in Cairngorm projects but are easily avoided with a little care and attention. Finally, the topic of customization is covered, including extending the front controller for various purposes, timing the execution of commands, and stubbing the service layer.

The Presentation Model Pattern

The Presentation Model is a design pattern for user interface programming that is particularly well suited to Flex, since it can take advantage of language features such as MXML bindings and inline event listeners. It can be used in conjunction with Cairngorm to support the development of large-scale enterprise applications. No changes are required to any Cairngorm class or interface, but rather, the way in which Cairngorm is used is altered slightly. Instead of dispatching Cairngorm events from view components, they are dispatched from inside model classes and a user gesture results in a method call.

In essence, a presentation model is a class that contains the state and logic required by a view. It exists to support the view, so that the code inside the view itself can be minimized. The Presentation Model design pattern seems to have its origins in Smalltalk, but it was described in detail by Martin Fowler and then analyzed with respect to Flex by Paul Williams:

❑   http://martinfowler.com/eaaDev/PresentationModel.html

❑   http://weblogs.macromedia.com/paulw/archives/2007/10/presentation_pa_3.html

The general purpose of the Presentation Model design pattern is to separate concerns, so that the state and logic required by a view are extracted into a supporting class, known as the presentation model. The view is responsible for rendering the presentation model, invoking operations upon it, and responding to changes in state. The view holds a reference to the presentation model, but the presentation model knows nothing at all about the view or the user interface controls that it is composed of. This allows the presentation model class to be unit tested in isolation.

Figure 63-1 shows a UML class diagram for simple login view and its associated presentation model. The LoginView is composed of two text fields for the username and password, and a login button. The view has a reference to the LoginPresentationModel, which contains two fields for storing the username and password state and a method for performing the login operation. The view code will be light, since all it needs to do is update the presentation model state and call the login() function.

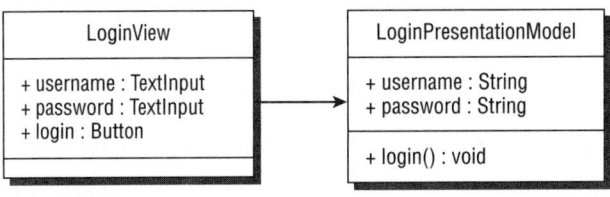

Figure 63-1

In Flex, the view code can be particularly light thanks to the language features of binding and inline event handlers. In many cases, the script block of a view component can be reduced to a single model property with no functions at all. The user interface controls within the view are bound directly to properties of the presentation model and any user gestures, such as a button click, result in a method call on the presentation model. The benefits to this are twofold: a simpler view with less logic to break, and a presentation model with behavior that is easy to unit test.

Using Cairngorm with Presentation Models

Using Cairngorm in conjunction with presentation models in straightforward, but there are two changes in responsibility:

❑   The logic for constructing and dispatching Cairngorm events migrates from the view into the presentation models. A user gesture results in a method call to a presentation model.

❑   A presentation model may pass itself into a Cairngorm event constructor, allowing the associated command to retrieve and interact with it.

Figure 63-2 shows a Cairngorm interaction involving a presentation model. As usual, the interaction begins with a user gesture, such as a click on a button. Inside the inline event handler for the button click, a method is called on the presentation model. In simple cases, this method will just perform some logic local to the presentation model and the view will be updated through bindings, without involving Cairngorm. In other cases, the presentation model will construct and dispatch a Cairngorm event, passing itself into the event constructor. As usual, this causes the front controller to execute the corresponding command. When the command completes successfully or fails, a callback is made onto the presentation model, so that it can update itself accordingly. The bindings in the view will execute and the user will see the outcome of their gesture.

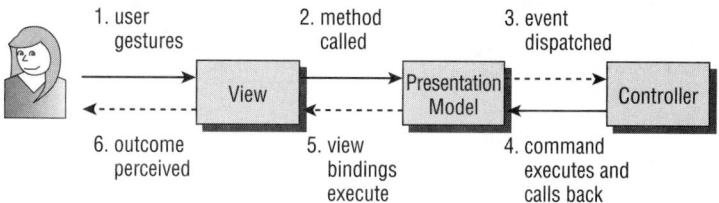

Figure 63-2

Sample Cairngorm Presentation Model Application

Paul Williams's series of blog posts on presentation patterns features a sample application for browsing albums. This application has been adapted for the purposes of this chapter, to demonstrate how Cairngorm can be used in conjunction with presentation models. The source code can be found in the `CairngormPresentationModel` project that accompanies this book.

Figure 63-3 shows the running application. When an album title is selected on the left, its details can be viewed, edited, and applied using the form on the right. Edits can also be canceled. Under the hood, the code contains a hierarchy of view components, starting with the application file, which contains an `AlbumBrowserView`, which contains an `AlbumFormView`. This hierarchy is reflected with a presentation model for both of the main views, as shown in Figure 63-4.

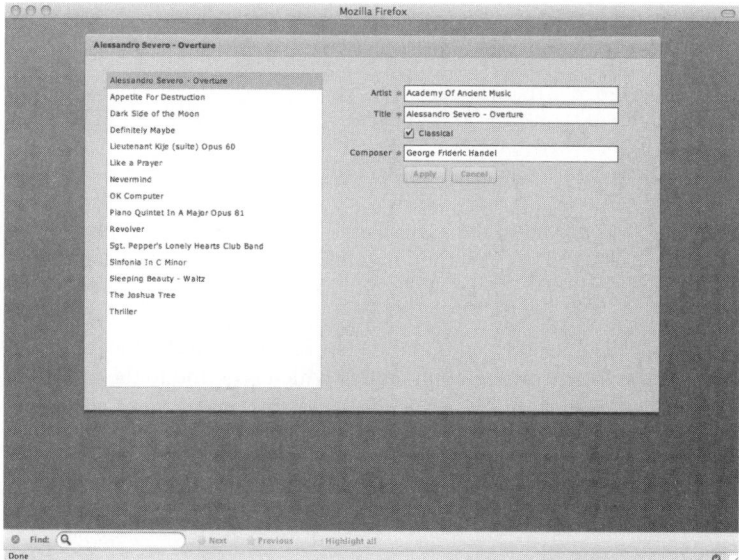

Figure 63-3

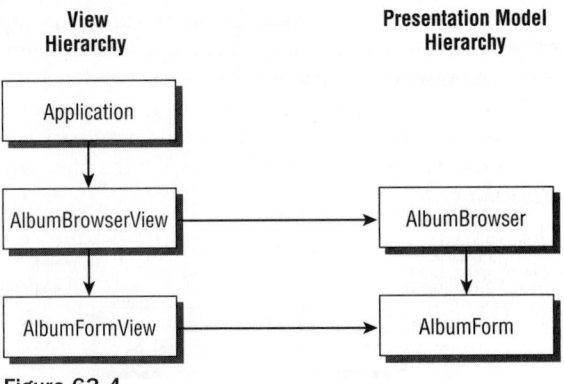

Figure 63-4

Nothing to Break

Moving into the code, the first thing to note is that there is very little code inside the views. The `AlbumFormView` contains nothing but a single `albumForm` property:

```
<mx:Script>
    <![CDATA[
        import com.adobe.ac.model.AlbumForm;

        [Bindable]
        public var albumForm:AlbumForm;
    ]]>
</mx:Script>
```

The user interface controls are bound directly to properties of the `AlbumForm` presentation model, while inline event handlers are used to invoke methods on the presentation model:

```
<mx:TextInput
    id="artist"
    width="300"
    text="{ albumForm.album.artist }"
    errorString="{ albumForm.artistError }"
    enabled="{ albumForm.canEdit }"
    change="albumForm.updateArtist( artist.text )"/>
```

Here the `text` property is bound to the `albumForm.album.artist` property chain. When the `text` input changes, the `updateArtist()` method is called to update the model. By this means, the view and model are kept synchronized.

The presentation model itself is injected into the view by its parent. So the top-level application file instantiates the `AlbumBrowser` presentation model, which is bound to the `albumBrowser` property of the `AlbumBrowserView`. Then at the next level down, the `albumBrowser.albumForm` property is bound to the `AlbumForm` view.

```
<view:AlbumFormView
    id="form"
    width="400"
    albumForm="{ albumBrowser.albumForm }"/>
```

There may not be *nothing* to break in the view, but there is at least very little. The code within binding expressions and event handlers is minimal and type-safe, so the compiler will catch basic errors. Logic and state is confined to the AlbumForm presentation model (and its children), where it can be easily unit tested.

Models Dispatch Cairngorm Events

So how does Cairngorm fit into the picture? Well, each of the presentation models dispatches a Cairngorm event. The AlbumBrowser model dispatches a GetAlbumsEvent in order to populate itself with a collection of Album objects, and the AlbumForm model dispatches an UpdateAlbumEvent in order to apply any edits made to an Album.

```
public function loadAlbums():void
{
    new GetAlbumsEvent(this, "title").dispatch();
}
```

This is the loadAlbums() method of the AlbumBrowser class. It is called on creationComplete in the application file. This creates and dispatches the GetAlbumsEvent, passing itself into the constructor along with the sort field name, "title". The normal Cairngorm process commences: the GetAlbums Command is executed, it invokes an AlbumDelegate to fetch the album data, and the data is passed back to the command.

Command Callbacks

Now things change a little. Instead of locating the model in the traditional Cairngorm manner, with a model locator, the command calls back onto the AlbumBrowser presentation model. Remember that this was earlier passed into the event constructor. The command retrieves it from the event and stores it in a model property, which it later interacts with inside the result or fault handler.

```
public class GetAlbumsCommand implements ICommand, IResponder
{
    private var model:AlbumBrowser;

    public function execute(event:CairngormEvent):void
    {
        var getAlbumsEvent : GetAlbumsEvent = GetAlbumsEvent(event);
        model = getAlbumsEvent.model;

        var delegate:AlbumDelegate = new AlbumDelegate();
        delegate.getAlbums(this, getAlbumsEvent.sortField);
    }

    public function result(data:Object):void
    {
        var albums:ICollectionView =
            ICollectionView(ResultEvent(data).result);
        model.handleGetAlbumsResult(albums);
    }

    public function fault(info:Object):void
    {
        model.handleGetAlbumsFault();
    }
}
```

The `execute()` function sets the model property to reference the presentation model, then calls the `getAlbums()` method of a business delegate. The result handler retrieves a collection of albums from the result event and passes them back to the model through the `handleGetAlbumsResult()` method. If a fault occurs instead, the command calls the `handleGetAlbumsFault()` method of the presentation model, allowing it to update itself to reflect the error:

```
public class AlbumBrowser
{
    ...

    public function handleGetAlbumsResult(albums:ICollectionView):void
    {
        this.albums = albums;
    }

    public function handleGetAlbumsFault():void
    {
        windowTitle = "Unable to load albums. Please try again later.";
    }

}
```

These callbacks are very simple. On a result, the `albums` collection is set and the view will automatically render them through bindings. Similarly for a fault, the `windowTitle` string is set to display an error message. Of course, the implementations for these callbacks could be more sophisticated, triggering effects and transitions in the view or error recovery processes.

The need for a command to notify a model when it completes or fails is a common one, but it can be implemented in several ways. The preceding example used the simplest approach, with the command calling methods directly on the model. However, this introduces a dependency between the command and concrete model class. If the same Cairngorm event is dispatched from various places in the application, the callback methods can be extracted onto an interface that each presentation model implements, or the Flex `IResponder` interface can be used. A third approach is to pass function references into the Cairngorm event, and then retrieve and invoke those in the command. This is the most flexible approach, but the resulting code is not strongly typed.

Domain Models

A presentation model exists to support a view. If several views present a feature of an application in different ways, they will most likely require different presentation model classes. A hierarchy of presentation models generally emerges that reflects the view hierarchy, to a degree. However, there are usually business or domain concerns of an application that are independent of the way they're presented on screen. These should be encapsulated within *domain model* classes that can be shared among the presentation models.

For example, a more elaborate version of the Album Browser application may allow users to rate their music and build up a profile that connects them to other users with similar tastes. We might expect the `Album` class to evolve from a simple VO into part of a domain model class with functions for applying ratings. Meanwhile, a `UserProfile` class may emerge that observes the ratings applied to albums and maintains a collection of related users. These domain concerns could be exposed in multiple ways by the user interface, so it is best to encapsulate them inside domain model classes, rather than mixing concerns inside presentation models.

Taking Things Further

The Presentation Model pattern provides a simple way to extract logic from view components to improve readability and better facilitate unit testing. The approach described previously is one way to apply the Presentation Model pattern in Flex. However, there are some interesting variations on this approach. For instance, you can declare presentation models in MXML to take advantage of binding expressions and inline event handlers, or you can use an inversion of control (IoC) framework to inject presentation models into views, instead of maintaining a hierarchy and injecting manually.

Organizing Cairngorm Projects

This section gives some guidelines for packaging Cairngorm projects. The first section describes a package structure suitable for smaller Cairngorm projects that perhaps involve a few different services and views, rather than many services and views. The second section describes a more scalable package structure that remains easy to navigate and understand even when there are hundreds of Cairngorm events and commands.

Small Cairngorm Projects

For small Cairngorm projects, it is conventional to organize the code by grouping classes of the same kind into the same package. So Cairngorm events are kept together, commands are kept together, delegates are kept together, and so on. The following package structure is used, where `root` is the root package for your own application:

- ❑ `root.control`
- ❑ `root.control.event`
- ❑ `root.control.command`
- ❑ `root.model`
- ❑ `root.model.vo`
- ❑ `root.view`
- ❑ `root.service`
- ❑ `root.service.delegate`
- ❑ `root.service.translator`

The front controller would be packaged in `root.control`, whereas all its events are in `root.control.event` and the corresponding commands are in `root.control.command`.

The `model` package should contain subpackages for grouping related parts of the application model. It is common to store value objects (VOs) in subpackages such as `root.model.vo`. Subpackages may be created for storing models that apply to different parts of the user interface. These may be divided into further `presentation` and `domain` subpackages to separate those models that contain state and behavior to support specific views from those that represent the business of the application independently to its presentation. The `model` packages may also contain normal Flex events, dispatched by model classes, which are usually packaged in an `event` subpackage.

The `view` package should be structured to reflect the view, so it may contain subpackages representing different areas of the application. Inside these packages are placed the MXML and ActionScript view components. Item renderers are often packaged in `renderer` subpackages, and similarly, any normal Flex events dispatched by view components are contained in `event` subpackages.

The service locator is packaged in the `base.services` package. Beneath this is a `delegate` package for storing the business delegates and often a `translator` package for storing any translator classes used to convert the data returned by services into strongly typed model objects or VOs. This may not be necessary if the BlazeDS Remote Object or LCDS Data Management Service is used, but for HTTP Service and Web Service clients, it is often required.

Large Cairngorm Projects

For large Cairngorm projects, a variation on the preceding package structure is called for. Instead of dividing into `model`, `view`, `control`, and `service` packages directly beneath the `root` package, the structure should be separated into functional areas first, where a "functional area" is a distinct part of an application with its own feature set. For example, a large Flex client may contain an instant messaging system, a dashboard showing an overview of sales activity, a news reader, and many other functional areas. The top-level package structure for such an application could be:

- ❑ `root.dashboard`
- ❑ `root.messaging`
- ❑ `root.news`

It is common for functional areas such as these to require their own backend services and thus delegates, as well as their own views, models, and control classes. So the typical Cairngorm structure for small projects is applied several times over for each functional area. This helps to keep related classes closer together so that functional areas can be understood in isolation, rather than by trying to extrapolate the relevant pieces from oversized centralized packages.

The next level of packaging for the Dashboard functional area would be:

- ❑ `root.dashboard.control`
- ❑ `root.dashboard.model`
- ❑ `root.dashboard.service`
- ❑ `root.dashboard.view`

Note that a functional area can have its own front controller, such as the `DashboardController`, which registers events and commands specific to that area. More about decentralizing the Front Controller pattern in this way is described in the "Customizing Cairngorm" section of this chapter.

Organizing larger projects in this way makes it easier to understand the codebase and easier to manage the dependencies that cross between different functional areas. This makes maintenance more straightforward and paves the way for modularization. Functional areas can be extracted into self-contained modules that can be developed, tested, and profiled in isolation.

Cairngorm Anti-Patterns

As frameworks go, Cairngorm is more prescriptive than restrictive. It makes recommendations for the ways in which concerns should be separated, but doesn't enforce them. This gives developers the freedom to use Cairngorm in their own way, picking and choosing certain parts of the framework, discarding others, or making their own customizations along the way.

Cairngorm is also fairly lightweight, providing the basic structure on which to build an application but not the finer details. A successful Cairngorm project still requires good software engineering and object-oriented design. Dependencies should be carefully managed and minimized, duplication of code should be avoided, a clear separation of concerns established, and thorough testing and profiling carried out throughout development. Despite these aspirations, issues of one sort or another always occur!

This section covers a number of known Cairngorm anti-patterns or misuses of Cairngorm that have been observed on Cairngorm projects. They're often easy to resolve, but developers who are aware of them can avoid them in the first place. If left unchecked, anti-patterns can start to negate the benefits of a good framework, resulting in an application that is difficult to maintain and extend.

The Fat Controller

This anti-pattern occurs when the incremental growth of an application has caused a front controller to become large and disorderly. Recall that one of the benefits of the Front Controller pattern is its self-documenting quality, providing a readable description of the functionality of a Cairngorm application. If 50 or 100 commands have been registered haphazardly within a single function, this benefit is lost. Instead, the controller becomes an impenetrable jumble of event and command names.

The solution requires simple refactoring. First, arrange the events and commands into logical groups, usually based on related functionality. For instance, those events and commands relating to accessing and updating a user's profile or those to do with managing and account. Next, extract a function for each of these event/command groupings.

Bad Practice

```
public class BankController extends FrontController
{
   public function BankController()
   {
      initializeCommands();
   }

   private function initializeCommands():void
   {
```

```
        addCommand(BankTransferEvent.BANK_TRANSFER, BankTransferCommand);
        // many, many more commands added in any old order
    }
}
```

In this example, all the commands are added within the initializeCommands() function, and their order is indicative only of when they were introduced to an application. A controller of this kind does not provide a clear overview of the functionality of a large Cairngorm application.

Good Practice

```
public class BankController extends FrontController
{
    public function BankController()
    {
        initializeCommands();
    }

    private function initializeCommands():void
    {
        addAccountManagementCommands();
        addHomeInsuranceCommands();
        addMortgageCommands();
        addUserProfileCommmands();
    }

    private function addAccountManagementCommands():void
    {
        addCommand(BankTransferEvent.BANK_TRANSFER, BankTransferCommand);
        // add other related commands
    }
    ...
}
```

The resulting class is orderly and can be read at a high level by scanning the initializeCommands() method, and then understood in detail by reading the specific addXCommands() methods. The self-documenting quality has been preserved and it's in good shape for further refactoring.

This refactoring can be taken further by extracting the command groupings into separate front controllers for different functional areas of an application. For example, an AccountManagementController could be created specifically for the account management area of the application. This decentralized approach is recommended for larger projects and particularly those involving multiple modules. It also helps when source code is stored under version control, since it minimizes the merge conflicts that occur when multiple developers introduce new events and commands concurrently. Decentralizing the front controller is discussed in detail later in the chapter in the "Customizing Cairngorm" section.

Model Locator Landfill

This anti-pattern occurs when Model Locator is used as the sole or primary model class, with many properties added to it in an ad hoc fashion as an application develops. The result is a large class with too many responsibilities that is not a good model of anything in particular. When using the model locator, it is important to remember the general principles of object-oriented software design — encapsulation, abstraction, inheritance, composition, and so forth — and to strive to create a coherent, comprehensible model, assembled from small parts with specific roles and duties that are representative of the application domain.

Bad Practice

```
public class BadBankModelLocator implements IModelLocator
{
    // …singleton code omitted…
    public var name:String;
    public var dateOfBirth:Date;
    public var address1:String;
    public var address2:String;
    public var country:String;
    public var zipcode:String;
    public var balance:Number;
    public var overdraftLimit:Number;
    public var transactions:IList;
    public var dateOpened:Date;
    // etc
}
```

This example contains a flat list of properties relating to different aspects of a bank application. In real-life applications, this list can grow very large if kept unchecked.

Good Practice

```
public class GoodBankModelLocator implements IModelLocator
{
    // …singleton code omitted…
    public var personalDetails:PersonalDetails = new PersonalDetails();
    public var currentAccount:Account = new Account();
}
```

In this example, groups of related properties have been refactored into smaller classes with more specific duties. This process of refactoring model classes does not end here; it should continue throughout development to ensure a clear and concise model without duplication or redundancy.

Chains of Dependency

This anti-pattern occurs when view or command code is polluted with excessive chains of dependency to the model. This harms code readability, and couples otherwise unrelated objects, making maintenance and refactoring more difficult and time-consuming.

The Model Locator pattern provides convenient global access to the application model, allowing it to be used by any view or command class that needs it. However, this simplicity and flexibility come at a price. Whenever the Model Locator pattern is used directly, a chain of dependency is established between the class that is using it and the structure of the model. Consider the following binding expression:

```
<mx:Label text="{ BankModelLocator.instance.personalDetails.address.country }"/>
```

Although the label is only interested in the country name string, the binding has dependencies on the BankModelLocator instance, down through the personalDetails and address models to the country property. If the structure of the model or any of the property names change, the binding expression will need to be updated. As well as introducing greater dependencies, long property chains like this are also more difficult to read than shorter binding expressions.

In many cases, a view component is only interested in a small part of the application model. When this is true, there is no benefit to accessing a model locator singleton, then navigating down through the entire model. Instead, the part of the model that is needed should be set as a property of the view component. This minimizes dependencies and improves code readability.

Bad Practice

```
<mx:VBox xmlns:mx="http://www.adobe.com/2006/mxml">
    <mx:Script>
        <![CDATA[
            import model.BankModelLocator;
        ]]>
    </mx:Script>
    <mx:Label text="{ BankModelLocator.instance.personalDetails.address.line1 }"/>
    <mx:Label text="{ BankModelLocator.instance.personalDetails.address.line2 }"/>
    <mx:Label text="{ BankModelLocator.instance.personalDetails.address.country }"/>
    <mx:Label text="{ BankModelLocator.instance.personalDetails.address.zipcode }"/>
</mx:VBox>
```

In this example, each binding expression creates a chain of dependencies, from the concrete BankModelLocator singleton, down to a property of the address. It would be difficult to reuse this view for rendering a different address and if the structure of the model was changed, there would be unnecessary consequences.

Good Practice

```
<mx:VBox xmlns:mx="http://www.adobe.com/2006/mxml">
    <mx:Script>
        <![CDATA[
            import model.personal.Address;

            [Bindable]
            public var address:Address;
        ]]>
    </mx:Script>

    <mx:Label text="{ address.line1 }"/>
    <mx:Label text="{ address.line2 }"/>
    <mx:Label text="{ address.country }"/>
    <mx:Label text="{ address.zipcode }"/>
</mx:VBox>
```

In this example, the model locator is not used directly. Instead, the view has a property of type Address. The view is only interested in rendering properties of the Address class, so it should not depend on any other classes. With this approach, the parent view is responsible for setting the address property. The result is more readable and has far fewer dependencies. It is not dependent on the structure of the model or on Cairngorm, and could be reused elsewhere in the application for rendering other Address objects.

Customizing Cairngorm

Cairngorm consists of a relatively small number of core classes and interfaces. There's the `FrontController` for handling Cairngorm events by executing commands, the `ServiceLocator` for looking up services, the `ICommand` interface for abstracting operations, and not a great deal more than that. This section explains various ways to extend and implement these classes and interfaces in order to customize the behavior of Cairngorm. This includes logging and timing the commands that are executed, stubbing service interactions, and decentralizing the Front Controller pattern to better encapsulate parts of a larger application.

Sample code for each of the customizations is contained in the `CustomizingCairngorm` project that accompanies the book. Since Cairngorm has now become open source, it's entirely possible that some of these customizations (or different solutions to the same problems) will become a part of the Cairngorm library itself in the future.

Logging Cairngorm Events and Commands

It can be interesting and useful to log the Cairngorm events that are heard and the commands that execute when an application is running. These often correspond to user gestures and can provide a profile of the way in which users are typically interacting with the application, showing which features are used most often, which are never used, and the order in which actions take place. In addition, the trail of events and commands can be useful for debugging purposes.

The Cairngorm `FrontController` class defines several protected methods that are invoked when an event is heard and a command is prepared for execution. These can be overridden in order to log the event type string and command class name.

- ❑ `executeCommand(event:CairngormEvent):void`—called when a Cairngorm event is heard
- ❑ `getCommand(commandName:String):ICommand`—called to retrieve the command class corresponding to the name retrieved from the Cairngorm event type

The Flex logging framework is used to issue the log statements, so that different Log targets can be configured. The logging framework is described in great detail in Chapter 74, "The Logging Framework," but in essence log statements can be filtered and directed toward different targets. They can be directed to the local Flash log file, the Flex Builder console, or even a remote server.

```
public class LoggingFrontController extends FrontController
{
    private static const LOG:ILogger =
        Log.getLogger("com.adobe.cairngorm.control.LoggingFrontController");

    override protected function executeCommand(event:CairngormEvent):void
    {
        LOG.info("Handling Cairngorm event: {0}", event.type);
        super.executeCommand(event);
    }

    override protected function getCommand(commandName:String):Class
    {
        var commandClass:Class = super.getCommand(commandName);
```

```
                LOG.info("Executing command: {0}", getQualifiedClassName(commandName));
                return commandClass;
        }
    }
```

When logging is enabled, a trail of log statements will be created, such as:

```
8/25/2008 10:58:55.856 com.adobe.cairngorm.control.LoggingFrontController
Handling Cairngorm event: getProducts
8/25/2008 10:58:55.858 com.adobe.cairngorm.control.LoggingFrontController
Executing command class: com.adobe.cairngorm.samples.store.command::GetProductsCommand
```

The simplest way to enable logging is to declare a `TraceTarget` in an application file. Full configuration details are given in Chapter 74.

```
<mx:TraceTarget
    includeCategory="true"
    includeDate="true"
    includeTime="true"
    level="{ LogEventLevel.DEBUG }"
    />
```

Timing Asynchronous Commands

The time taken to perform asynchronous actions, such as fetching data from a remote server, has an impact on the perceived performance of an application. For this reason, it is useful to measure and log the duration of asynchronous commands. If an application takes an unreasonable length of time to fetch some data for rendering, users will become frustrated. With timing and logging in place, it becomes easy to see whether performance bottlenecks exist in the service calls of a Flex client.

The easiest way to time command execution is to create a base class that implements `ICommand` and `IResponder` and perform the timing, then extend this for all asynchronous commands:

```
public class TimedCommand implements ICommand, IResponder
{
    private static const LOG:ILogger =
        Log.getLogger("com.adobe.cairngorm.command.TimedCommand");

    private var startTime:Number;

    public function execute(event:CairngormEvent):void
    {
        startTime = flash.utils.getTimer();
    }

    public function result(data:Object):void
    {
        logCommandDuration("result");
    }

    public function fault(info:Object):void
    {
```

```
        logCommandDuration("fault");
    }

    private function logCommandDuration(outcome:String):void
    {
        LOG.info(
            "Command executed: class={0}, outcome={1}, duration={2}ms",
            getQualifiedClass Name(this),
            outcome,
            flash.utils.getTimer() - startTime);
    }
}
```

The start time is recorded when the `execute()` method is first invoked. The duration is then calculated and logged when the `result()` or `fault()` handler is invoked. An asynchronous command then extends the `TimedCommand` class and invokes the super methods from `execute()`, `result()`, and `fault()`.

```
public class GetProductsCommand extends TimedCommand
{
    override public function execute(event:CairngormEvent):void
    {
        super.execute(event);
        //…etc…
    }

    override public function result(data:Object):void
    {
        super.result(data);
        //…etc…
    }

    override public function fault(info:Object):void
    {
        super.fault(info);
        //…etc…
    }
}
```

The resulting log shows the duration of any asynchronous commands that extend `TimedCommand`:

```
8/25/2008 11:18:22.527 com.adobe.cairngorm.command.TimedCommand Command executed:
class=com.adobe.cairngorm.samples.store.command::GetProductsCommand,
outcome=result, duration=126ms
```

Injecting Dependencies into Commands

The Chains of Dependency anti-pattern was mentioned earlier. An example showed how the Model Locator pattern can introduce many unnecessary dependencies to a view component if it is misused. This pattern can also introduce excessive dependencies to Cairngorm commands, since they often navigate down from the root of a model locator to a specific child model, introducing dependencies each step of the way. You can avoid this problem by customizing the `FrontController` class to inject dependencies into commands, either manually or using an IoC framework.

Manual Injection

To manually inject a specific model into commands, first define an interface for the commands requiring the model. For example, the `ICatalogueCommand` interface defines a setter for injecting the `Catalogue` model.

```
public interface ICatalogueCommand
{
    function set catalogue(value:Catalogue):void;
}
```

Next extend the `FrontController` class and override the `executeCommand()` method. When the command is created, check whether it implements the `ICatalogueCommand` interface, and if so, inject the `Catalogue` model.

```
public class InjectingController extends FrontController
{
    public var catalogue:Catalogue;

    override protected function executeCommand(event:CairngormEvent):void
    {
        var commandClass:Class = getCommand(event.type);
        var command:ICommand = new commandClass();
        if (command is ICatalogueCommand)
        {
            ICatalogueCommand(command).catalogue = catalogue;
        }
        command.execute(event);
    }
}
```

In this case, the `Catalogue` model has been stored in a public property of the `InjectingController` class. This property can be initialized in the MXML declaration for the controller, as follows:

```
<model:Catalogue id="catalogue"/>
<control:InjectingController id="controller" catalogue="{ catalogue }"/>
```

Framework Injection

Rather than injecting dependencies manually, a more sophisticated approach is to use an IoC framework to inject dependencies automatically. This can be taken further to inject business delegates as well as model classes into commands, thus further reducing dependencies and improving testability.

The customization process is the same: just extend the `FrontController` and override the `executeCommand()` method, adding the framework-specific details. For example, the following code shows how to inject dependencies into a command using the lightweight IoC framework Swiz:

```
override protected function executeCommand(event:CairngormEvent):void
{
    var commandClass:Class = getCommand(event.type);
    var command:ICommand = new commandClass();
    Swiz.autowire(command);
    command.execute(event);
}
```

The Swiz `autowire()` method will pick up any `[Autowire]` metadata from the command and then locate the dependent objects and inject them. A similar approach can be used with other IoC frameworks such as Parsley, Spring ActionScript, and Flicc.

Stubbing the Service Layer

Flex applications often interact with services of different kinds. These services can be developed by the same team that's building the Flex frontend, or they can be developed independently by a different team in a different time zone. For the sake of efficiency, it's important that Flex development is not hampered when services are temporarily unavailable.

This can be achieved by simulating or "stubbing" the service layer and providing a mechanism for switching between the real services and the stubs. With that in place, if the server-side team needs to restart its application servers to deploy a new service, Flex developers can simply enable their stubs and continue working. Similarly, if a network problem prevents access to the real services, Flex developers can switch on their stubs and develop against them until the issue is resolved.

Stubbing can be performed in various different ways. Some developers run their own local web servers containing stub service implementations so that the Flex client still makes service requests, but the stub services return simulated data instead of integrating with backend systems. However, it is often easiest to stub entirely on the client side, which can be achieved easily with Cairngorm.

Stubbing the Command, Business Delegate, or Service Locator

The following are three ways to stub a Cairngorm application:

❑ **Command**—Stub implementations of commands can be created that update the model directly, instead of invoking business delegates and services. A `Timer` can be used inside the commands to simulate the asynchronous nature of the real commands. The stub commands can be registered in a stub front controller that is declared instead of the real front controller when developing in stub mode.

❑ **Business delegate**—Stub implementations of business delegates can be created to mimic the effects of the real business delegates, by manually creating `ResultEvent` or `FaultEvent` objects and using a `Timer` to call onto the `IResponder` interface asynchronously. An interface can be extracted from the business delegate, then a factory used by the commands to instantiate business delegates. This can swap implementations, between the stub and real business delegates, depending on whether the services are available.

❑ **Service locator**—A set of stub services can be defined in a stub service locator, which is declared instead of the real service locator when developing in stub mode. The service definitions inside the stub service locator can reference stub services deployed to a local web server or else can be driven from local files. For instance, an `HTTPService` can be configured to load a local XML containing simulated data, or the `HTTPService` class can be extended to simulate more elaborate service behavior.

Of these three approaches, the first is the simplest, but it is somewhat limited. Enabling the stub commands only really allows development to continue on view and model code, since execution never reaches beyond the command. Stubbing the business delegates allows the real commands to be used and developed, as well as the views and models. Care must be taken to ensure the stubs create accurate result and fault events; otherwise, code developed against the stubs may not operate correctly against the real services. The third approach means development can continue on almost the whole codebase when the real services are unavailable. However, its suitability depends on the complexity of the services.

As well as the above techniques, a novel approach is described by Børre Wessel in the following blog post: http://www.borrewessel.com/?p=24. This is perhaps the simplest and least intrusive approach of all for applications driven by HTTP services.

Further Considerations

You can tweak and tailor the preceding approaches. For example, you can compile stub business delegates or commands into a module and load them only when the stubs are enabled, preventing them from being compiled into the main application SWF. To simplify enabling and disabling of stubs, use a URL parameter or Flashvar to switch between the stub and real implementations, on a global or service-by-service basis. And you can use IoC frameworks, such as Parsley or Spring ActionScript, for swapping real and stub implementations of commands, delegates, and services without needing to write factories or other helper classes by hand.

In addition to preventing development work from stalling, stub services have another benefit: they allow the application to be demoed without an Internet connection. This can be very convenient for presentations to clients or conference audiences, where last-minute network problems are almost guaranteed! However, the *real* service layer should always be used as much as possible during development, to minimize integration issues, and care must always be taken to ensure stub and real-service contacts do not diverge.

Decentralized Controllers

In a traditional Cairngorm application, there's a single front controller that registers all the Cairngorm commands supported by the application. This centralization is fine for smaller applications but can become undesirable for larger projects. Instead of providing a convenient overview of the application, the controller becomes overwhelming, presenting developers with more information than they need about different parts of the system, and resulting in many merge conflicts. To prevent this from happening, it's best to decentralize and declare separate controllers for separate functional areas.

Cairngorm supports multiple controllers out of the box, with the single caveat that all Cairngorm event names must be globally unique. Multiple controllers can be declared at the top level of the application, or encapsulated within child components, or contained in modules that are loaded at runtime. This works because each controller instance listens to the same CairngormEventDispatcher singleton that lies at the core of Cairngorm. So a Cairngorm event dispatched from anywhere in a Flex application can be processed by a controller anywhere in the application that has a suitable command registered.

Separating controllers in this way promotes encapsulation, so the distinct functional areas of a large Flex application can be developed more independently, and also provides a loosely coupled means of interaction between these areas. For example, consider an MP3 music store application that includes a Charts view displaying the top downloads, as well as a Compilations view where users can create and mix their own compilations, and Community area for chatting with other music fans. Such an application may define three separate controllers for these functional areas. The source code for the ChartsController is:

```
public class ChartsController extends FrontController
{
    public function ChartsController()
```

```
    {
        addCommands();
    }

    private function addCommands():void
    {
        addCommand(GetTopTenEvent.GET_TOP_TEN, GetTopTenCommand);
        addCommand(GetLatestReleasesEvent.GET_NEW_RELEASES, GetNewReleasesCommand);
        addCommand(GetRelatedUsers.GET_RELATED_USERS, GetRelatedUsersCommand);
    }
}
```

Because all Cairngorm front controllers listen to the same singleton `CairngormEventDispatcher`, Cairngorm event names must be globally unique. This can generally be achieved by prefixing them with the functional area, or for large portal-like applications, by fully qualifying them with the package name. An example of the former approach follows:

```
public static const GET_TOP_TEN:String = "charts.getTopTen";
```

With several controllers in place, Cairngorm events can be used to coordinate the functional areas. The developers of one part of the application can make available a set of events for other parts to use. For instance, the Compilations functional area might provide an `AddToCompilationEvent` that can be dispatched from within the Charts or Community functional areas to add a featured song to one of the user's compilations, as follows:

```
new AddToCompilationEvent(trackId).dispatch();
```

This approach is loosely coupled, confining the dependencies to a lightweight event class. The functional areas effectively offer services to one another and the details of the implementation are encapsulated.

Disposable Controller

The `FrontController` class maintains a `Dictionary` containing the registered command names and classes and listens to the `CairngormEventDispatcher` singleton for all events that match these commands. Although the APIs allow commands to be registered with weak references, so that the controller can be made eligible for Garbage Collection, it is sometimes preferable to deregister all the commands more determinately.

To understand why, consider the scenario of a front controller declared in a module that is being unloaded. If the module is made eligible for Garbage Collection, it may not actually be garbage collected immediately. If this module has registered its commands with weak references, the commands will remain registered until Garbage Collection takes place. If one of the corresponding events is dispatched, its matching command will still be executed, even though the controller is eligible for Garbage Collection. Therefore, it is necessary to remove registered commands explicitly prior to unloading a module. This can be achieved by a simple extension to the `FrontController`, as follows:

```
public class DisposableController extends FrontController
{
    public function dispose():void
    {
        for (var commandName:String in commands)
```

```
        {
            removeCommand(commandName);
        }
    }
}
```

The `dispose()` function simply iterates through the command names, registered in the protected commands dictionary, removing each one. The `removeCommand()` function provided by the `FrontController` deals with removing event listeners from the `CairngormEventDispatcher` singleton.

Summary

Cairngorm provides a solid framework for building Flex applications, but many decisions remain in the hands of developers. Decisions like how to test the logic that drives the views, how to minimize view-to-model dependencies, or how to develop efficiently without suffering whenever a remote service becomes unavailable. These decisions need to be made wisely for a project to be successful.

This chapter has covered various topics that elaborate on the basic Cairngorm story. If a development team has an understanding of the Presentation Model pattern, together with an awareness of the common pitfalls of Cairngorm projects, and the confidence to customize Cairngorm when necessary, they will be well placed to succeed.

Part XI: Application Development Strategies

64

Best Practices

Everyone has their own coding style. Different people have different thought processes, and each has his or her own interpretation of what is the "right" way to build an application. If you've ever had the experience of working on a project with multiple developers without predefined standards and best practices, then you have likely experienced the chaos of ambiguous naming and references, inconsistent standards and naming conventions, improper use of object-oriented principles, or excessive use of data bindings.

Beginning a project with standards and best practices in mind sets your team on the path to a successful project. The goal of this chapter is to help define best practices when developing Adobe Flex applications. This chapter will emphasize the importance of coding standards, proper uses of object-oriented principles, proper use of data binding, and component development.

Coding Standards

Clearly defined coding standards are possibly the best of the "best practices" that can help drive you toward a successful project. Coding standards help lay the foundation for what I refer to as the three C's of coding: consistency, clarity, and cleanliness.

Consistency

Consistency and standardization of coding practices helps you write code that is easier to understand and maintain because everything is done the same way. Functions are named consistently, variables are named consistently, classes are named consistently, and actions are invoked in familiar patterns.

Coding consistency often goes hand in hand with development frameworks and design patterns because they provide uniform and well-understood methods for accomplishing tasks.

Standards "set the stage" for your development. Adherence to coding to standards will ensure that your code will be consistent.

Clarity

Clarity is another extremely important factor when developing your applications. Not only should things be consistent, but they should be clear. Function names should be indicative of the action being performed, and variable names should be indicative of their content. Nothing is worse than trying to track down a variable simply named `z`, when it is actually a complex object instance.

It is typically best practice to name objects after their variable type. For instance, when naming a `TabNavigator` object, use a name like `mainTabNavigator`, rather than something nondescriptive such as `container`. Likewise, if you are using an `Event` object, simply name the object instance `event`.

As mentioned previously, function names should be indicative of the action being performed. Event handler functions should use either the form `onEventType` (so for a mouse down event, the handler would be named `onMouseDown`) or the form `eventTypeHandler`. In this case, a mouse down event handler would be `mouseDownHandler`. It is purely a matter of personal preference as to how you want to name your code, but in either case it should be consistent and clear.

Additionally, functions that perform a task should be named so that they indicate what task is being accomplished. An example of this would be a function that transforms data from XML to a strongly typed object. It is best practice to have an indicative name such as `xmlToUserObject` rather than an nondescriptive name such as `update`.

Clarity in function and variable naming is extremely important for maintenance reasons. Regardless of whether you are coming back to code you haven't seen in over a year or inheriting someone else's code, it is much easier to manage code that is clearly named than it is to decipher abbreviations and nondescriptive content.

Cleanliness

Consistency and clarity are only part of the battle. It is also very important to have clean code. Clean code is easier to read and easier to understand. Function and variable names should have the same case rules and code should be properly indented. Line breaks should be used appropriately to format code and prevent side-scrolling.

Naming Conventions

Naming conventions are extremely important for maintaining clean code. Proper naming conventions enable easier distinction between variables and classes. The Flex framework itself follows "camel case" naming conventions, and it is best practice to follow the same conventions in your own code so that there are not multiple naming styles within the same project.

In "camel case" naming style, there are no spaces, underscores, or special characters in variable names. The first character within each is indicated by a capital letter, thus providing the word divisions. For instance the phrase `ProfessionalFlex` is written using "camel case." In this example, you can see that there is no space between the words `Professional` and `Flex`, and the capitalization of the word `Flex` provides the logical word separation.

Namespaces

Namespaces should be named indicative of type of logic that they encompass. Namespace names match the project directory structure, and it is best practice to logically group similar functionality. Namespaces should always use the "camel case" naming style and should always begin with a lowercase letter.

Consider the following namespaces:

```
com.professionalFlex.model
com.professionalFlex.view
com.professionalFlex.view.controls
com.professionalFlex.view.itemRenderers
com.professionalFlex.events
```

You will notice that all the namespace package names begin with a lowercase letter and follow the "camel case" rules discussed earlier, which will match the directory structure. The namespace names indicate what kind of logical functionality is contained within those code packages. The com.professional Flex.model namespace would contain classes used within an application's data model. The com.professionalFlex.view namespace would contain classes used within an application's view/user interface.

These namespaces would actually match the following directory structure:

```
com
    professionalFlex
        model
        view
            controls
            itemRenderers
        events
```

Classes

Classes should also use "camel case" naming conventions, but the first letter of a class name should always be capital. The capitalization of class names helps differentiate between class instances and function or variable instances. These capitalization rules apply to both MXML and ActionScript classes. Notice in the following examples, both classes would be named MyCustomView. In ActionScript classes, it is easy to see the class name. In MXML files, it is important to keep in mind that the MXML filename is actually the class name.

The following ActionScript class, in a file named MyCustomView.as indicates a class called MyCustomView that extends from the Canvas class. We will be discussing more on inheritance later in this chapter.

```
public class MyCustomView extends Canvas {
}
```

In MXML, creating a file called `MyCustomView.mxml` would create a class called `MyCustomView`:

```
<mx:Canvas
    xmlns:mx="http://www.adobe.com/2006/mxml">
</mx:Canvas>
```

In this case, the `MyCustomView.as` and `MyCustomView.mxml` files would both create classes named `MyCustomView` and would contain identical functionality.

Variables and Functions

Variables and functions follow nearly identical naming conventions. Variable and function names should always follow "camel case" style, should always begin with a lowercase letter, and most importantly, should always be indicative of their action. Variable names should indicate what type of value is being stored within the variable, and function names should be indicative of the action being performed by the function.

Consider the following `UserManager` class, which is an example of a class that would be used to manage collections of `User` class instances:

```
public function UserManager()
{
    public var activeUsersCollection : ArrayCollection;
    public var inactiveUsersCollection : ArrayCollection;

    public function loadActiveUsers() : void {
    }

    public function loadInactiveUsers() : void {
    }

    public function loadUser( userId : int ) : void {
    }

    public function saveUser( user : User ) : void {
    }

    public function deleteUser( user : User ) : void {
    }
}
```

In this class, you can see that the class itself follows the class naming conventions described earlier. Reviewing the class, it is also evident that there are two data collections in this class: `activeUsers Collection` and `inactiveUsersCollection`. You can see that these variables (properties of the `UserManager` class) follow the naming conventions of camel case and use a lowercase first letter. Not only do they follow proper naming conventions, but the way that they are named also indicates what is actually contained within each collection. Descriptive naming allows for easier maintenance and cleaner code. Imagine attempting to maintain code that another developer wrote, where these collections were simply named a or i; you would need to actually dig into the class code to find out what is contained in these classes, rather than simply glancing at them and immediately understanding what they contain.

This example also shows function names that are descriptive of the action being performed. In this case, it is easy to identify that the `loadActiveUsers` function loads all of the active users into the `activeUsersCollection` ArrayCollection.

Another important factor regarding functions, beyond descriptive naming, is that functions should always have a return declaration. If the function returns a string, it should be indicated as the return value:

```
public function getFormattedDateString( date : Date ) : String {
}
```

In the case that the function has no return value, this should be indicated by using the void keyword, as shown in the following example:

```
public function deleteUser( user : User ) : void {
}
```

In most cases, and especially with function parameters, a variable name that generically describes the value passed in is the naming convention to use. In the first of the two previous code examples, you can see that the parameter `date` is passed into the `getFormattedDateString` function, which is of type `Date`. Using the name `date` helps keep your code simple and clean. It clearly defines what you are working with and helps avoid confusion. The same applies to the `deleteUser` function described previously. The parameter passed into the `deleteUser` function is named `user` and is of type `User`. This clearly denotes the user that should be deleted and results in clean and clear code. Also notice the use of capitalization and its role in differentiating between the `user` instance and the `User` class type.

Code Syntax

Naming conventions are not the only factor in producing consistent, clean, and clear code. Coding style and usage of syntax have just as much to do with readability of code. How you indent your code, where you place brackets, and using spaces around colons or semicolons are all personal choices. Different people prefer different styles. The key factors in syntax style are consistency and clarity. You will want to avoid having a specific loop format in one function and then, in another function, using a completely different style. You should also make sure that your syntax clearly shows the action that is occurring.

This may sound overly simplistic, but proper usage of brackets can go a long way in making your code clean and easy to understand.

Proper Indentation

Clear code using loops and conditional statements relies heavily on consistency of coding style. When using loops of conditional statements, you always want to use proper indentation, and ensure proper usage of brackets. Let's compare two loops that perform the exact same logic:

```
for each ( var user : User in activeUsersCollection ) {
    determineIfUserUpdated( user );
    if ( !user.isUpdated ){
        updateUser( user );
        notifyUserWatchers();
        publishChanges();
```

```
        }
    }

    for each ( var user : User in activeUsersCollection )
    {determineIfUserUpdated( user );
    if ( !user.isUpdated ){
    updateUser( user );
    notifyUserWatchers();
    publishChanges();}}
```

You will notice that both loops perform the exact same action; however, the first is significantly easier to comprehend than the second. The only difference between the two is indentation and spacing of brackets. Proper indentation helps to identify scope of code segments. Indentation and bracket placement helps to visually group the looped and/or conditional logic so that is immediately apparent what is being looped over and what the conditional actions are.

Ternary Operators

Ternary operators are a quick shorthand syntax for conditional (if- then-else) logic. They can be extremely helpful in writing clear code. Ternary operators use the following format:

```
( booleanCondition ) ? trueValue : falseValue;
```

Ternary operators can be use for assigning variable values, return statements, or can be used as shorthand if-then-else statements for executing code. Consider the following functions:

```
public function getUserIdentifier( user : User ) : String {
    if ( identifier == EMAIL ) {
        return user.email;
    }
    else {
        return user.guid;
    }
}

public function getUserIdentifier( user : User ) : String {
    return (identifier == EMAIL) ? user.email : user.guid;
}
```

Both functions perform the exact same action; however, the second function is much shorter and easier to understand because of the usage of ternary operators. Proper usage of ternary operators makes code cleaner and easier to understand; however, it is also very important to note that they can make code significantly more confusing. You should always avoid using complex or nested ternary operators.

```
public function getUserIdentifier( user : User ) : String {
    if ( identifier == EMAIL ) {
        return user.email;
    }
    Else if ( identifier == LAST_NAME ) {
```

```
            return user.lastName;
        }
        else
            return user.guid;
        }
    }

    public function getUserIdentifier( user : User ) : String {
        return (identifier == EMAIL) ? user.email : ((identifier == LAST_NAME) ?
            user.lastName : user.guid  );
    }
```

It is very easy to see in the previous code segment that nested ternary operators quickly get confusing. Although they may be shorter to type, they make the code very difficult to understand and, thus, more difficult to maintain.

Constant and Static Members

Constants are the only coding constructs in your applications that should not follow "camel case" naming conventions. While constants are accessed similarly to variables, they do not change; hence the term constant. When using constants they should always be written in uppercase, with word separations denoted by an underscore character. This follows the constant naming convention in the Flex framework. For example, Flex framework events use constants to define the event types: MouseEvent.MOUSE_UP, Event.RESIZE, EVENT.CREATION_COMPLETE. Constants should be used anywhere in your code that values do not change.

```
    public static const DOTS_PER_INCH : Number = 72;
```

Static members are functions or variables that exist on the class itself and are not tied to a particular class instance. It is very often the case that constants are static members on a class. Since static functions and variables do not require a class instance, they can be accessed directly on the class. Typically, static functions perform a specific action related to the class but do not rely on any class instance in particular, or they are used for utility functions.

The following example shows a utility class for conversion of temperatures from Fahrenheit to Celsius values. This is a common conversion that does not require instantiation of any classes, so it has been created as a public static function.

```
    public class TemperatureUtil {
        public static function fahrenheitToCelsus( temperature : Number ):Number {
            return ( temperature - 32) * 5/9;
        }
    }
```

Public static functions are available to any class and can be accessed by the format ClassName.staticFunction(). The previous temperature utility would be invoked as follows:

```
    private var celsiusValue : Number = TemperatureUtil.fahrenheitToCelsus( 32 );
```

Typed versus Dynamic Objects

One of the major changes from ActionScript 2 to ActionScript 3 was the addition of strongly typed objects. Strong-typing of objects enables superior application performance and should always be used. Dynamic objects can be helpful in some circumstances but, for the most part, should be avoided.

Strongly typed objects have clearly defined properties on them. You know that a `User` object has `firstName` and `lastName` properties. Dynamic or weakly typed objects do not have a clearly defined list of attributes. Attributes can be added or removed "on the fly" at any time during code execution.

When using dynamic objects, the Flash Player runtime must inspect your object to see if a particular property exists. When using strongly typed objects, the runtime automatically knows that properties exist, and this results in far superior runtime performance.

Consider two objects that contain the exact same data:

```
private var user1 : Object;
private var user2 : User;
```

Although both contain the same data, code utilizing the `User` object will always execute faster because the `User` object does not need to be inspected to first determine if it has the properties that you are trying to access. This becomes more apparent when looping or parsing over large data sets.

Dictionaries and Associative Arrays

Associative arrays are programming constructs that allow you to create key-value mappings of objects within memory. They are commonly referred to as *hash maps* in other programming languages, and when used properly they can enable amazing performance improvements in your application.

When developing your applications, you can use either a generic object or an array instance to create a map using string-based keys for object values. The following shows two examples creating maps, one using an `Object` instance and one using an `Array` instance:

```
var map : Object = new Object();
map[ key ] = value;

var map2 : Array = new Array();
map2[ key ] = value;
```

Functionally, these two statements are identical. There is little advantage to using one method over the other; it is a matter of personal preference. However, Adobe documentation recommends using `Array` as a hash map object. When accessing your object at runtime, you simply need to provide the key to retrieve the hashed value:

```
myValue = map[ key ];
```

It is important to keep in mind that results returned from these mappings are not returned as a specific type of object. It is extremely important that your code check the type of the returned object to ensure that it is actually the object type that you are expecting.

The `Dictionary` class is very similar to associative arrays; however, Dictionary objects are more powerful in that they allow you to create maps based on object instances as the keys for the key-value pairs. For example:

```
var dictionary : Dictionary = new Dictionary();

var key1 : Object = new Object();
var key2 : String = new String();
var key3 : Canvas = new Canvas();

dictionary[ key1 ] = value1;
dictionary[ key2 ] = value2;
dictionary[ key3 ] = value3;
```

Associative arrays and dictionaries provide huge performance benefits when dealing with look-up values in large data sets. Rather than looping over *N* iterations of a loop comparing objects to see if you have found the right one, you can perform the same look-up in a single line of code, without any looping. This can provide orders of magnitude differences in performance as opposed to array looping, as well as simplified code, as shown in the following example:

```
public function getUserById( id : String ) : User {
    return userMap[ id ] as User;
}

public function getUserById( id : String ) : User {
    for each ( var user : User in userCollection ) {
        if ( user.id == id )
            return user;
    }
}
```

Object-Oriented Principles

A solid understanding of object-oriented programming is absolutely essential for Flex development. ActionScript 3 is a fully object-oriented language, and the Flex framework takes full advantage of what the ActionScript language has to offer. Mastery of object-oriented principles and design skills will enable you to build better, more powerful applications, with less effort, and provide more reusable code.

Object-oriented programming is a development paradigm in which your code is organized into logical objects. Each object has properties and methods, and contains similar and/or related functionality. In object-oriented programming, your code is organized into classes that logically represent and logically organize their functionality. Object-oriented development heavily relies upon the concepts of encapsulation, inheritance, and polymorphism.

Encapsulation

Encapsulation is essentially information hiding and the logical organization of functionality. In object-oriented languages, the internals of a particular action are hidden from the rest of the program, and only the major "hooks" to the capability are exposed. This technique hides complex decision-making code, and also isolates code that may be subject to change.

Let's examine the concept of an automobile. The following Automobile class has a public function, drive. The concept of encapsulation hides all of the complex instructions to drive, which enables you to have programs that are easier to understand.

```
public class Automobile
{
    public function Automobile() { }

    public function drive() : void {
        //code to make the drive action happen will go here
    }
}
```

When you want your program to drive the Automobile class, you simply need to invoke the drive function on your Automobile instance. As the developer using the Automobile class, you don't need to know anything about what makes the drive function work.

```
myAutomobile.drive();
```

Now, let's examine more of a real-world development scenario. You have a Flex application that contains a DataManager class that is responsible for loading data from the server.

```
public class DataManager
{
    public var dataCollection : ArrayCollection = new ArrayCollection();

    public function load() : void {
        //code to load data from the server into the dataCollection ArrayCollection
    }
}
```

In order to load data from the server, you simply need to invoke the load method on your DataManager class instance:

```
myDataManager.load ();
```

No matter where you are calling this from, you know the action that will be performed; data will be loaded from the server. The details of how the data is loaded or the data format is irrelevant in this context. Inside the load method you could simply generate random stub data, load data from an XML file, load data from a RemoteObject call, or even retrieve and parse a .csv file. By hiding the internals of the load method, the code becomes both easier to understand and easier to use.

When to Use Public/Private/Protected/Final Functions

With the concept of encapsulation, it is important to understand variable scope. Variable scope is used to protect access of your variables from other classes. Variable scope determines what properties and functions of your class will be exposed externally and to descendant classes (we'll discuss descendant classes more in the next section regarding inheritance). It is an extremely important factor in encapsulation/information hiding and should always be specified on every property or function.

Public Functions

Public functions and methods are exposed to any class. They are accessible outside of your class and can be accessed by descendant classes. To declare a variable or function with public memory scope, you simply need to use the `public` keyword. The public keyword is used for all values that should be accessible outside of your class.

```
public var myPublicVar : String;
```

Private Functions

Private functions and methods are not exposed to any class. They are only accessible from within your class and cannot be accessed by descendant or derived classes. To declare a variable or function with private memory scope, you simply need to use the `private` keyword. If you have functions or variables that do not contain relevant information outside of your class, or you want to restrict access to those variables or functions, then you use the private variable scope:

```
private var myPrivateVar : String;
```

Protected Functions

Protected functions and methods are very similar to private functions and variables in that they are not accessible outside of the current class. The difference is that they are accessible in descendant classes, where private variables are not. To declare a variable or function with protected memory scope, you simply need to use the `protected` keyword:

```
protected var myProtectedVar : String;
```

Internal Functions

Internal functions and methods are similar to those of public classes, with one major difference. Rather than being exposed to all classes, they are only accessible to classes within the same package/namespace. To declare a variable or function with internal memory scope, you simply need to use the `internal` keyword:

```
internal var myInternalVar : String;
```

Inheritance

Inheritance is the method of creating new classes from classes that already exist. When a class inherits from another class, it takes on the traits and behaviors of the existing class. All of the public and protected functions of the existing class (referred to as the base class) are now functions of the inherited class. Thus, the child class can extend or alter the behavior of the base class. The class inheriting from the base class is often referred to as the child class or the descendant class.

In ActionScript, the `extends` keyword is used to denote that a class is extending from the base class. For instance, you can have a `SportsCar` class that extends from `Automobile`, and a `DumpTruck` class that extends from `Automobile`.

```
public class SportsCar extends Automobile {
    //code for SportsCar class goes here
}
public class DumpTruck extends Automobile {
    //code for DumpTruck class goes here
}
```

When instantiated, both are instances of the `Automobile` class; however, they can have very different methods describing how they drive and can posses very different capabilities.

In Flex, there are actually two ways to extend classes. You can use the ActionScript `extends` keyword as described previously, or you can create an MXML file. In MXML, the root node of the MXML file is actually the base class that your MXML class is extending. Now consider the following example, which would be in a file called `MyHBox.mxml`:

```
<?xml version="1.0" encoding="utf-8"?>
<mx:HBox xmlns:mx="http://www.adobe.com/2006/mxml">

    <mx:Button label="Button 1" />
    <mx:Button label="Button 2" />
    <mx:Button label="Button 3" />
    <mx:Button label="Button 4" />

</mx:HBox>
```

You can see that this MXML class consists of four buttons within an `HBox` component. Since the `HBox` is the root of the MXML, the MXML class extends the `HBox` class and inherits all of the properties of the `HBox` class. In the extension of the `HBox` class, this instance has augmented the capability of the parent HBox by adding the four child buttons. The logic used to position the buttons is actually that of the parent HBox class.

Regardless of whether you are using ActionScript or MXML to extend your base classes, all visible components extend from the `DisplayObject` class. Most visible MXML components actually extend the `UIComponent` class, which is a descendant of the `DisplayObject` class. Any time that you are changing the width or height of a Flex component, you are actually accessing capability exposed by the low-level base classes of the Flex framework.

It is also important to understand inheritance in terms of code reusability. Imagine that you need to create a series of classes that, while they all have different behavior, all have a subset of functionality that is exactly the same. In this case, you would create a base class that has all of the common functionality, and create individual classes that extend from the base class. Each individual class would handle the unique behavior, while all of the shared behavior is maintained in the base class.

Overriding Functions

In addition to inheriting the behavior of an existing class, one of the most important features of inheritance is the ability to override functions. When you override a function, you change its behavior. You can either extend its current behavior to add additional capabilities or you can completely change it altogether.

One of the first things you may notice when you extend an existing component is the use of the super()
function within your component constructor. The super() function actually invokes the constructor
from the parent class.

The FrameListenerPanel class in this example extends the existing Panel class, and augments its
behavior. It first uses the super() constructor and then adds its own event listener for the
Event.ENTER_FRAME event:

```
public class FrameListenerPanel extends Panel
{
    public function MyPanel() {
        super();
        this.addEventListener( Event.ENTER_FRAME, onEnterFrame );
    }

    private function onEnterFrame( event : Event ) : void {
        //do something here
    }
}
```

In any of your overridden functions, you can also use the super keyword to access functions of the base
class. For example, whenever you override the updateDisplayList function, you can invoke the parent
class's updateDisplayList function by using the super keyword:

```
override protected function updateDisplayList(w:Number, h:Number):void {
    super.updateDisplayList(w,h);
    //do something here to augment the capability
}
```

As mentioned earlier in this section, not only can you augment the capability of a function as shown
above, you can completely change the behavior of a method. It can still be invoked by the same function
call, but the behavior of the method is not at all related to the base class's behavior.

If you take the exact same example and do not use the super keyword, but instead create your own
behavior, you have completely altered the display behavior of the class without changing how it is
invoked. In this example, it simply clears the graphics of the current object and draws a red rectangle:

```
override protected function updateDisplayList(w:Number, h:Number):void {
    var g:Graphics = this.graphics;
    g.clear();
    g.beginFill( 0xFF0000 );
    g.drawRect( 0,0,w,h );
}
```

When to Use Getter and Setter Methods

Getter and setter methods are extremely helpful constructs within the ActionScript language that are
extremely helpful when developing your Flex applications. If you have not used them before, I strongly
advise picking them up.

Getter and setter methods allow you to write ActionScript functions that are treated as variables when developing your code, and when accessed by other components. Getter and setter methods allow you to alter the behavior of reading or setting a variable value.

Before we get into the details on why getters and setters are beneficial, let's examine what they are. When accessed, getter and setter methods are treated as variables. They can be public, protected, or private. In ActionScript code, you can set a value on getter/setter functions as follows:

```
userDetails.user = currentUser;
```

Or, you can read a value from a getter/setter function as:

```
currentUser = userDetails.user;
```

In MXML, you can apply data bindings to getters and setters as though they are public properties of your component:

```
<local:UserDetails id="userDetails" user="{ currentUser }" />
```

Even though the getter/setter functions are treated like public properties, they are in fact functions. Getter functions are identified by the keyword get, and setter functions are identified by the keyword set.

```
private var _user : User;

public function get user():User {
    return _user;
}

public function set user(value:User):void {
    _user = value;
}
```

Whenever you are using a getter/setter combination with a value stored in a local private variable, it is best practice that the private variable has the same name as the getter/setter functions, preceded by an underscore. In the preceding example, you can see that the user value is stored in the private variable _user.

Public Variables versus Getters/Setters

You may be wondering why you would want to use getter/setter functions instead of a simple variable. Getter/setter functions enable greater control over what happens when you set a value. You can use them to control read/write access to variables, to invoke methods when a value is set, to validate data before the value is set, to create variables that represent calculated values, and to create variables that can be overridden in descendant classes. If you don't need any of these features, then it is perfectly acceptable to use a public variable. Getter/setter variables do not provide any performance advantages.

Read/Write Access Control

Getter/setter functions always come in a pair if you want both read and write capability. However, having both a getter and a setter method is not required. If you only have a getter function, then the value will be read-only. If you try to write to your read-only value, your application will not compile; however, you can still access the value for read access.

The following example shows creating a read-only user property. You would use this technique if you have a class that maintains and exposes the read-only value for consumption, but you do not want any other code to be able to write to that value. Notice that there is no setter method in this case.

```
private var _user : User;

public function get user():User {
    return _user;
}
```

Enabling write-only access is just as simple as enabling read-only access. The only difference is that you will have a setter method but no getter method. You would use this technique in instances where you want other classes to be able to pass data into your class, but you do not want those classes to be able to access that data once it has been passed into your class.

```
private var _user : User;

public function set user(value:User):void {
    _user = value;
}
```

Functions Invoked when Treated as Variables

Another benefit of getter/setter methods is that they can act like functions, although they are treated as properties. This means that you can have code that reacts every time the getter/setter property is accessed. You can enable it to dispatch events, increment counters, or call any other function any time that a value is written to the setter method or retrieved from the getter method.

The following example shows how to use a getter method to dispatch an event and increment a counter:

```
public function get user():User {
    dispatchEvent(new Event(UserEvent.USER_GET));
    getCounter ++;
    return _user;
}
```

This code will be invoked any time that the user value is accessed; thus, it is a function that mimics the interaction of a property:

```
myUser = this.user;
```

Setter functions can handle the same type of interaction as getter functions. Any time a value is set, it will invoke the actions of that function. The following example shows a setter function that will dispatch an event and increment a counter any time that the user value is set.

```
public function set user(value:User):void {
    dispatchEvent(new Event(UserEvent.USER_SET));
    setCounter ++;
    _user = value;
}
```

This example would be invoked simply by setting the value of the `user` property:

```
this.user = myUser;
```

Perhaps one of the most common uses of getter and setter functions is to have the set function call the Flex component's `invalidateProperties()` or `invalidateDisplayList()` method to cause the component to re-validate itself using the new value:

```
public function set user(value:User):void {
    _user = value;
    this.invalidateProperties();
}
```

Data-Checking Values

Another advantage of using getter/setter variables is that you can validate data before setting private variables, or returning it. This is extremely useful if you want to protect data passed into your classes. One example where this is helpful is if you want to make sure that the values passed into your setter function meet specific criteria.

The following example shows a setter function that will only set the private variable `_positiveNumericValue` if the value passed into the setter method is actually a numeric value greater than zero. Negative values will be ignored, thus ensuring that the value of `_positiveNumericValue` is always a positive value.

```
private var _positiveNumericValue : Number = 0;

public function set positiveNumericValue(value:Number):void {
    if (value > 0)
        _positiveNumericValue = value;
}

public function get positiveNumericValue():Number {
    return _positiveNumericValue;
}
```

You can also use this same technique to prevent null values being set on objects that you don't want to ever be null. Additionally, you can have the getter function check the return value to prevent it from returning an invalid value. The following example shows a simple getter/setter pair that will prevent it from ever getting or setting a null value:

```
private var _user : User;

public function get user():User {
    if ( _user == null )
        return new User();
    return _user;
}

public function set user(value:User):void {
    if ( value != null )
        _user = value;
}
```

Calculated Values

Another common usage of getter and setter functions is that they can be used to set or return calculated values instead of simply returning the value of a private variable. The next example shows how you can use a getter method to return a calculated numeric value:

```
public function get halfHeight():Number {
    return height/2;
}
```

Although this example is using calculated number values, it is in no way limited to numbers. You can use a getter method with `if` or `switch` statements to have a conditional return value for the getter function. The following example shows a getter method that conditionally returns a temperature value based on its Fahrenheit or Celsius value:

```
private var _tempFahrenheit : Number = 0;
private var _isCelsius : Boolean = true;

public function get temperature():Number {
    if (_isCelsius)
        return (_tempFahrenheit - 32) * 5/9;
    else
        return _tempFahrenheit;
}
```

Variables That Can Be Overridden in Child Classes

One of the most important advantages of getter/setter methods is that they can be overridden in descendant classes. This is a very important factor. Standard variables, regardless of their public/private/protected scope cannot be overridden in descendant classes. Using getter/setter functions allows them to be overridden.

This is extremely helpful in a variety of situations. You would use this technique if you want to change the behavior of a getter or setter in a child class. You can have it transform the data, ignore the data, or pull data from a completely different source. One of the most common uses of overridden getter/setter functions is the usage of the public get/set "data" in all visual Flex components, and most importantly item renderers.

```
override public function set data(value:Object):void {
    super.data = value;
    trace( "I'm debugging, so trace my value: " + value.toString() );
}
```

Polymorphism and Interfaces

Polymorphism is the concept of using unrelated classes in similar functions through interfaces. Polymorphism allows you to have a variety of unrelated classes, which have nothing in common, that can be used interchangeably in various functions because of their implementation of interfaces.

Simply put, an interface is a set of "rules" that an object must adhere to. The rules are public function signatures that are specified by an interface class. A class implements an interface when it implements the functions specified by the interface class and uses the `implements` keyword to denote that the interface has been implemented.

When an interface is defined, in actuality you are just defining functions that will be created in classes that implement the interface rules. No code logic exists directly in an interface class.

The following example examines the `IAutomobile` interface. The `IAutomobile` interface simply creates the rule that any class that implements the `IAutomobile` interface must implement the public function `drive`.

```
public interface IAutomobile
{
    function drive() : void;
}
```

Implementation of this interface will allow a class to behave as an `Automobile` instance. All `Automobile` instances must have the `drive` method. They need not have anything else in common. This doesn't mean that they won't have anything else in common. It is very possible to have two unrelated classes that implement multiple interfaces, or extend from the same base class.

The following two classes show implementation of the `IAutomobile` interface. The `SportsCar` and `GoKart` classes have nothing in common other than implementing the `IAutomobile` interface, thus implementing the `drive()` function. How they each implement the `drive` method is completely determined inside of the class.

```
public class SportsCar implements IAutomobile
{
    public function drive():void
    {
        //logic to drive here
    }
}
public class GoKart implements IAutomobile
{
    public function drive():void
    {
        //logic to drive here
    }
}
```

The benefit to interfaces is that they allow unrelated items to be used as though they were the same type of item. The following loop shows how to invoke the `drive` method on a collection of automobiles. In this collection, you could have a number of `SportsCar` or `GoKart` instances, which are used interchangeably.

```
for each ( var auotmobile : IAutomobile in automobilesCollection ){
    automobile.drive();
}
```

Code Behind

A common approach to abstraction of code and the user interface is to use the "code-behind" programming methodology. It is not necessarily best practice to always use this method; the decision to use code behind is entirely based upon personal coding style and project requirements.

When using the code-behind approach, the code for the scripting or event handling is defined within a separate file as the actual user interface components themselves. This approach helps to keep the code clean and logically separated, and it enables separation of development tasks. The user interface developer can focus on programming logic in the code file, while the designer focuses on implementation of styling and skinning in the UI file.

As shown in the following example, the scripting functions and event handlers would be created in a class that extends from the base class which you would want to extend. In this example, the CustomPanelCode class extends from the base mx.container.Panel class.

```
package codebehind
{
    import flash.events.Event;
    import mx.containers.Panel;
    import mx.controls.Alert;

    public class CustomPanelCode extends Panel{

        public function onSubmitButtonClick( event : Event ) : void {
            Alert.show( "submit button clicked" );
        }

        public function onCancelButtonClick( event : Event ) : void {
            Alert.show( "cancel button clicked" );
        }

        public function onTextAreaChange( event : Event ) : void {
            Alert.show( "text area changed" );
        }
    }
}
```

You can see that all of the functions that will be used to handle input from the user interface are defined in the CustomPanelCode class. The following code segment shows the contents of the CustomPanelUI.mxml file. The CustomPanelUI.mxml file contains the entire MXML markup that is actually used to create the interface for the customized panel instance.

```
<?xml version="1.0" encoding="utf-8"?>
<CustomPanelCode
    xmlns="codebehind.*"
    xmlns:mx="http://www.adobe.com/2006/mxml"
    width="400" height="300"
    title="Custom Panel With Code Behind">

    <mx:TextArea
        change="onTextAreaChange( event )"
        width="100%" height="100%"/>

    <mx:HBox width="100%" horizontalAlign="right">

        <mx:Button
            label="Submit"
            click="onSubmitButtonClick( event )" />
```

```
                <mx:Button
                    label="Cancel"
                    click="onCancelButtonClick( event )" />

        </mx:HBox>

    </CustomPanelCode>
```

You may also notice that all of the event handlers in the `CustomPanelUI.mxml` file refer to the event handlers in the parent `CustomPanelCode` class. This shows the separation of logic mentioned earlier. Changes to the scripting will not affect the user interface and MXML, while changes to the MXML and user interface will not affect the related scripts.

When the custom panel is used within an application, you simply need to create an instance of the user interface class. The following code shows an example that implements the `CustomPanelUI` class in MXML:

```
<?xml version="1.0" encoding="utf-8"?>
<mx:Application
    xmlns:mx="http://www.adobe.com/2006/mxml"
    xmlns:codebehind="codebehind.*"
    layout="absolute" >

    <codebehind:CustomPanelUI />

</mx:Application>
```

Summary

Best practices are considered "best practice" for a reason. They are guidelines set forth to ensure that your code is easy to understand and easy to maintain. Code that is easy to understand and easy to maintain always has the following items in common:

❏ It is clean and easy to read. Code is properly indented and formatted so that it is easy to follow.

❏ It clearly identifies what it does. Variables and functions have descriptive names, and there is no need to dig into application logic to determine what something is or what a function does.

❏ It is consistent. Various application modules follow consistent coding techniques and formatting, and familiar coding paradigms are used when appropriate.

In the next chapter, we will review the details of the Flash Player's security model, which dictates what data or assets you are permitted to consume within your applications.

65

The Security Model

Understanding the Flash Player's security model is essential when building Flex-based rich Internet applications (RIAs). The security model dictates how your application interacts with the environment around it, both the local client machine and any servers that you may be accessing data from. The focus of this chapter is to explain the Flash Player's security model as it pertains to Flex applications.

Understanding the Security Sandbox

When speaking of the security model, we don't mean authentication against a server or application-level security. We are actually referring to the security levels of the Flash Player and what resources it can access.

It is easiest to think of a security sandbox this in the context of a web browser. No web pages that are loaded in the browser can automatically access resources or scripts on the local machine. They also cannot load and invoke scripts or data directly from other servers, although you can load images from other servers. You can load other web pages in Frame elements; however, each frame has its own sandbox.

In general, a security sandbox is a mechanism that allows you to execute programs in a controlled manner. The sandbox defines and controls what resources you can and cannot access. In the case of the Flash player, this controls whether or not you can access data or media files from remote servers or the local filesystem.

By default, each Flex application instance has its own security sandbox. Each SWF file loaded into memory has its own security sandbox instance. The access rules of the sandbox are determined by how the application is loaded, and they can be modified either with compiler arguments or through the use of cross-domain security policies.

As a point of clarification, the security sandbox rules discussed in this chapter apply only to Flex applications that are compiled as a SWF running within the Flash Player. Adobe AIR applications that are developed with Flex have unrestricted sandbox rules. Since AIR applications do not run within the browser, cross-site scripting and cross-domain rules (discussed later in this chapter) do not apply. AIR applications can call remote services and load resources from any server, regardless of the cross-domain policy on the servers hosting those resources.

What Is crossdomain.xml?

The most common use case for Flex applications is that they are loaded from a web server and access data from other servers. In this case, the Flex application is utilizing the remote sandbox. Without cross-domain policies, an application can only access resources and services that reside within the same sandbox, which would served by the same server instance.

As mentioned in the previous section, the access rules of the Flash Player's security sandbox can be modified based on cross-domain security policies. In most cases, this is controlled by an .xml file that is called crossdomain.xml. The contents of the crossdomain.xml file dictate which resources are exposed to other Flex or Flash applications.

If both the Flex application and the services used by that application reside on the same server, you will not need to specify a crossdomain.xml file. By default, the Flex application will be able to access any files or services exposed on the server instance that actually hosts the Flex application. If you are hosting the Flex application on one server and accessing data from another server or domain, then your application must use cross-domain security policies to enable access to the remote services; using the default security policy is not be sufficient.

The crossdomain.xml file controls access to data resources. Before getting into syntax of the security policy files, we will examine what it is that they actually do.

Consider a basic scenario with four servers. For simplicity, we will call them A, B, C, and D (see Figure 65-1). Server A is the home of the Flex application. The application resides on server A, and the Flex application can access any data files or service requests on server A without any custom security policies.

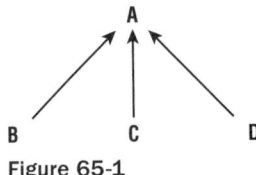

Figure 65-1

Server B provides graphical assets for the application hosted on server A. Servers C and D provide data services for the application hosted on server A.

Without any modified security policies, you cannot access any data from servers C and D. However, you will be able to access any images loaded from any of these servers using a mx:Image component. Since server B is our image server, the application will be able to load images from that server, however, usage of those images is limited. The default policy is that images are allowed to be loaded and displayed; however, you cannot access the underlying bitmap data for the image. Therefore, you cannot perform any kind of low-level manipulation on those image objects.

It is very important to remember that the `crossdomain.xml` file resides on the server that is hosting services or data files for the Flex or Flash application, not the server that is hosting the Flex application itself.

When a resource is requested from server B, the Flash player will first request a cross-domain security policy file for server B. If no security policy is found, the default security policy will be used. The cross-domain policy file for server B must identify any server that can access the resources that are hosted by server B.

The cross-domain policy works in a white-list type of manner; all applications that request images from server B will have the default security policy, unless full access is permitted to the requesting sever by server B's security policy. If the cross-domain policy for server B allows full access to server B from server A, then the application (and any other applications hosted by server A) will be able to access the assets served by server B without limitations.

Now let's consider servers C and D. When it comes to services, you will not be able to access anything without a modified security policy. The access to data is blocked regardless of the type of service (Web Service, XML over HTTP, text files, AMF Remoting, etc.) under the default security policy.

Both servers C and D provide data retrieval and persistence for the application hosted by server A. If there are no security polices specified for either server C or server D, then the application hosted on server A will not be able to access any of the services residing on servers C and D. If there is a cross-domain policy on server C allowing access from server A, but not on server D, then the application hosted by server A will be able to access data from server C but not server D. If both servers C and D have cross-domain policies that allow access from applications hosted on server A, then the Flex application will be able to access any data services that reside on servers C and D.

The `crossdomain.xml` file normally resides in the root of the server. If you were to try and access data from www.amazon.com, the Flash player would automatically check the root for a cross-domain policy at www.amazon.com/crossdomain.xml. This cross-domain policy would specify any domain that would have access to images or data hosted by www.amazon.com.

You can also have custom locations for `crossdomain.xml` files, but we will discuss that in detail later in this chapter.

Following you will find the contents of a sample `crossdomain.xml` file. In the next sections, we will analyze each of the components of this file and what they are used for. The XML Schema Definition (XSD) used to define the structure of `crossdomain.xml` files is publicly available from Adobe at www.adobe.com/xml/schemas/PolicyFile.xsd.

The root of a `crossdomain.xml` file is always a `cross-domain-policy` element. Within the root node, you can have `allow-access-from`, `allow-http-request-headers-from`, and `site-control` nodes. There can be multiple entries for each type, and each type performs a specific function.

```
<cross-domain-policy>
   <allow-access-from domain="*"/>
```

```
        <allow-http-request-headers-from domain="*" headers="SOAPAction"/>
        <site-control permitted-cross-domain-policies="master-only"/>
    </cross-domain-policy>
```

allow-access-from

The `allow-access-from` nodes within a cross-domain policy file define the servers and domains that are allowed to access services from the current server that is hosting the `crossdomain.xml` file. The following shows a sample `allow-access-from` policy file entry:

```
    <allow-access-from domain="*" to-ports="*" secure="true" />
```

In your cross-domain policy file you can have as many `allow-access-from` nodes as you see fit for your application. As mentioned earlier in this chapter, the default security policy is that a Flash-based application cannot retrieve data from a remote server that does not have a security policy applied to it. If you are hosting services, you can grant permission to any server, or a specific group of servers to have access to your services by creating a cross-domain policy and authorizing servers through the `allow-access-from` nodes.

The `domain` attribute is used to specify which domains are authorized to access your services. It is very important to keep in mind that this identifies the domain or server address that hosts the application that will utilize your services.

You can use an asterisk (*) value to denote wildcard values for the domain value. Using only a wildcard value, as follows, will open your services up to anyone. Any application hosted from any server will be able to access your services.

```
    <allow-access-from domain="*" />
```

You should be careful to only allow full access to your services if you actually want them to be publicly available to anyone in the entire world.

It is possible to have fine-grained control over any of the applications that access your services and/or data by specifying the full domain name or IP address of the server. You can have multiple `allow-access-from` entries in your cross-domain policy file, which allows you to define a specific set of servers that will be able to access your application. The following entries would allow applications hosted from `http://www.tricedesigns.com` or `http://65.135.118.70` to access services on the current/hosting server:

```
    <allow-access-from domain="www.tricedesigns.com" />
    <allow-access-from domain="63.135.118.70" />
```

When working with domain specification, it is important to recognize that `tricedesigns.com` and `www.tricedesigns.com` are not treated as equals in the cross-domain policy even if their actual DNS entries refer to the same physical server. If you would like both of these entries to have access to your services, you would need to include separate `allow-access-from` entries for each of the domain values, or you would use a combination of wildcard and non-wildcard values to specify an access group. The following entry would allow any server from within the `tricedesigns.com` domain to access the services hosted by the current server:

```
    <allow-access-from domain="*.tricedesigns.com" />
```

It is important to recognize that the security policy file does not only pertain to services and transactions that take place using a web server. The security file loaded from the HTTP server also dictates how data is accessed using raw socket connections to that server. The `to-ports` attribute of the `allow-access-from` entry allows you to identify specific port numbers or port ranges that can access socket connections on your server.

```
<allow-access-from domain="*.tricedesigns.com" to-ports="1080" />
<allow-access-from domain="*.tricedesigns.com" to-ports="1080,1083,1085" />
<allow-access-from domain="*.tricedesigns.com" to-ports="1080-2080" />
<allow-access-from domain="*.tricedesigns.com" to-ports="*" />
```

You can allow applications access to access a single port by entering only that port number in the `to-ports` field, or multiple specific ports by entering them as a comma-delimited list, or you can specify a range of ports by using a dash (-) to specify the numeric range of ports allowed for socket connections. Wildcards can be used in the `to-ports` attribute to allow access to any port number on the current server.

Last for the `allow-access-from` entry, but certainly not least is the `secure` attribute. The `secure` attribute is used to allow or disallow nonsecure applications that reside on non-SSL-enabled servers to access services on servers that have SSL encryption enabled. This only applies to services that are on a secure server (HTTPS). The default value for the `secure` attribute is `true`. When the `secure` attribute is `true`, applications from non-HTTPS servers are blocked from accessing data and services from the current HTTPS-enabled secure server.

```
<allow-access-from domain="*.tricedesigns.com" secure="false" />
```

When the `secure` value is set to `false`, requests from nonsecure servers are allowed to access the secure server. The decision to use a `secure` value of `false` should take consideration to the overall security of your application. Combining secure and nonsecure data and applications can potentially create holes in your security and open up your application to being compromised.

allow-http-request-headers-from

While the `allow-access-from` attribute governs which applications can access the hosting server, the `allow-http-request-headers-from` nodes within a cross-domain policy file define what custom headers can be attached to those requests from the Flash-based application. The following shows a sample `allow-access-from` policy file entry:

```
<allow-http-request-headers-from domain="*" headers="*" secure="true" />
```

Just as you can have multiple `allow-access-from` entries, you can also have as many `allow-http-request-headers-from` nodes as you see fit for your application.

The `domain` and `secure` attributes for the `allow-http-request-headers-from` entries function exactly as they do the `allow-access-from` entries. The `domain` attribute governs which domains can send requests to the current server that contain custom headers. The secure attribute allows you to send custom headers from applications residing on nonsecured servers to services on a secure server.

The `headers` attribute of the `allow-http-request-headers-from` entry allows you to specify custom headers that will be accepted from an application to the current server. The value of the headers attribute can either specify a single custom header name, a comma-delimited list of names, or a wildcard value. Wildcard values will allow any custom header to be passed from the application to the current server.

The following example shows various sample entries for the `allow-http-headers-from` node.

```
<allow-http-request-headers-from domain="www.tricedesigns.com"
    headers="SOAPAction" />
<allow-http-request-headers-from domain="*.adobe.com" headers="*" />
<allow-http-request-headers-from domain="www.wrox.com"
    headers="Header1,Header2,Header3" />
```

The first entry will only allow `SOAPAction` custom headers from the server `www.tricedesigns.com`. The second entry will allow any kind of custom header from any server in the `adobe.com` domain, and the third entry will allow `Header1`, `Header2`, and `Header3` custom header values to be sent from the applications residing on the `www.wrox.com` server.

site-control and Meta-Policies

The `site-control` entry is slightly different from the `allow-access-from` and `allow-http-request-headers-from` entries. The `site-control` entry controls meta-policies for the current server/domain. Meta-policies are policies that can restrict the usage/loading of additional cross-domain policies that can be loaded dynamically at runtime, which differ from the default cross-domain policy.

```
<site-control permitted-cross-domain-policies="all"/>
```

Meta-policies apply to the access of policy files that are not located in the site root; they could be located in any web-accessible directory on the server. The purpose of the site-control entry and meta-policies is to limit access to the cross-domain policy access. For example, it is theoretically possible for someone to upload a cross-domain policy to your server if you expose a service that allows users to upload files. If that user was able to successfully upload a cross-domain policy file and meta-policies in place did not restrict this, it could then be loaded as a meta-policy for the current server, even if it is not an XML file.

The `permitted-cross-domain-policies` attribute allows you to limit the files that can be used as meta-policies for the current server. The values supported in this attribute are: none, `master-only`, `by-content-type`, `by-ftp-filename`, and `all`.

A value of none would indicate that no cross-domain policies are allowed for the current server; this would limit all cross-domain access. The `master-only` value indicates that only the master cross-domain policy is allowed; no other meta-policies will be accessible for the current server. The `by-content-type` value indicates that only files served from the current server with a mime type `text/x-cross-domain-policy` are allowed to be loaded as cross-domain policy files. This value would prevent loading any other file type, including basic text or XML files. The `by-ftp-filename` value would indicate that only policy files that are actually named `crossdomain.xml` will be accepted as cross-domain policy files; attempts to load meta-policies from files of any other name will be ignored. A value `all` will allow any type file to be loaded as a cross-domain policy file, and a value of none indicates that no policy files are accepted for the current server. The value `master-only` is the default value for the site-control element.

The site-control entry limits the type of files that are accessible, using the `Secuirty.loadPolicyFile()` method to load a policy file that differs from the master policy file:

```
Security.loadPolicyFile
    ( "http://www.exampleServer.com/extendedPolicy/policy.xml" );
```

You may be wondering why or when you would use `Security.loadPolicyFile()`. To illustrate this case, let's consider a server located at `http://www.exampleServer.com`, whose master policy located at the root (`http://www.exampleServer.com/crossdomain.xml`) does not allow other servers to access its resources; however, it does permit meta-policies. Since it does not specifically grant access to server resources, you cannot access any media, data, or services from that server.

Now, let's load the policy file using `Security.loadPolicyFile()` as shown previously, and assume that the result of that file appeared as shown here:

```
<cross-domain-policy>
    <allow-access-from domain="*"/>
    <allow-http-request-headers-from domain="*" headers="*"/>
    <site-control permitted-cross-domain-policies="all"/>
</cross-domain-policy>
```

This new policy will allow an application from any server to access resources from the `www.example Server.com` server, with one major caveat. The additional policy file only applies to the directory that it was loaded from and any subdirectories of that directory. Therefore, a request to `http://www.example Server.com/extendedPolicy/myData.xml` would be successful, whereas a request to `http://www.exampleServer.com/myData.xml` would fail.

The implementation of multiple policy files allows you to have greater control of what assets and services are publicly exposed. You may have an API that is exposed to the public and open to everyone and also a private API that is only available to specific servers, and you can have them both reside on the same server. The limited or unlimited access would be controlled by the policy files based on the directory hierarchy.

Local Sandboxes

Whenever you access a SWF file from a server, the remote sandbox applies, as previously discussed in this chapter. On the contrary, different rules apply any time that you access the SWF file from the local filesystem. Since the application instance that runs locally has access to your entire machine, the sandbox for the application changes to limit what your application is authorized to do.

When you are developing your application, you can change the permissions of the local sandbox through compiler options to meet the needs of your application.

local-with-filesystem

The default for the local sandbox for Flex and Flash applications is the `local-with-filesystem` sandbox. Any time that you run a Flex application from your local machine without specifying any additional permissions, the `local-with-filesystem` sandbox is used. In this case, the SWF file can access any data or images residing on the local filesystem but cannot access any resources on the network.

This limitation is put into place for security reasons. Limiting the network access prevents unauthorized sharing of local data or media.

local-with-networking

While the default settings for locally run SWF files limit what your application is capable of for security reasons, you have the option to change the security settings at development time. When you develop an application and know that the target usage is through the local filesystem, you can allow access to the network using the `use-network` compiler option.

If you are using Flex Builder, you simply need to add the following to the compiler arguments setting for your project.

```
-use-network=true
```

If you are using command-line compilation, you simply need to add the `use-network` option to the command line parameters, as shown here:

```
mxmlc main.mxml -use-network=true
```

However, using the `local-with-networking` sandbox has its own limitations; it is essentially the opposite of the `local-with-filesystem` sandbox. Your application will be able to access resources across the network, although access to local data and assets has been restricted.

If you develop your application using the `local-with-networking` sandbox, it is important to recognize that you will still not be able to access any remote resources by default without first allowing access to the domains that host the services.

You can allow your local application to communicate with a specific server by either loading a specific policy file or using the `Security.loadPolicyFile()` or `Security.allowDomain()` functions:

```
Security.loadPolicyFile( "http://www.tricedesigns.com/extendedPolicy/policy.xml" );
Security.allowDomain( "www.tricedesigns.com" );
```

Additionally, you can enable access to any server from a SWF running on the local filesystem by invoking the `Security.allowDomain()` function with a wildcard as the domain:

```
Security.allowDomain( "*" );
```

Both the `local-with-filesystem` and `local-with-networking` sandboxes only apply to release versions of Flex applications. Debug-compiled Flex applications that are running within a Debug Flash Player have more lenient security policies; however, they also contain debugging code and are not optimized for runtime performance. You should always deploy your applications in Release mode for optimal performance.

local-trusted

In addition to the `local-with-filesystem` and `local-with-networking` sandboxes, the Flash player also supports a `local-trusted` sandbox. The `local-trusted` sandbox allows access to both local resources and network access regardless of security options at compilation. Unfortunately, you cannot automatically add a SWF file to the `local-trusted` sandbox through the application itself.

A SWF file or Flex application can only be added to the `local-trusted` sandbox by a user with administrative rights to the local machine. SWF files, HTML files referring to SWF files, or filesystem directories can be added to the `local-trusted` sandbox, and there is no limit on the number of SWFs that can be trusted.

For every Flash Player installation, there is a global trust directory. In that directory are text files that identify local files and folders that belong to the `local-trusted` sandbox. To add a SWF file to the local trust, you just need to create a text file for you application and add references to the trusted files or directories.

Inside the text file, you would simply list the directories or files that should be trusted. For example:

```
C:\Documents and Settings\atrice\My Documents\MyApplication\trustedDirectory\
C:\Documents and Settings\atrice\My Documents\MyApplication\trustedHtml.html
C:\Documents and Settings\atrice\My Documents\MyApplication\trustedSwf.swf
```

The global trust directory varies for different operating systems. Full details for identifying the global trust directory and adding trusted resources are available online in the Adobe Flex documentation at `http://livedocs.adobe.com/flex/3/html/help.html?content=05B_Security_03.html#143824`

Summary

A solid understanding of the Flash Player's security model is essential when building Flex-based RIAs. A comprehensive understanding of the security mechanisms is an important tool whenever you are architecting a Flex application, as it dictates how application and server components can interact with each other.

66

Modular Application Development

When building Flex applications, you may find it necessary to take a modular approach to the application architecture and components. If you're wondering what it means to have a modular application development approach, you're in luck. The goal of this chapter is to provide insight into what modular development is, why you would want to use it, and how it can be used in your Flex applications.

Overview

Modular development is an approach to software design and architecture that separates application components into separate logical components, or modules. Each module is a logical grouping of functionality, thus common logic and common tasks are bundled into the same module.

To get a better idea of what is meant by a module, consider an application used for software development and project management. The application could be composed of sections devoted to the following tasks:

❑ Tracking ongoing development tasks

❑ Requirements tracking

❑ Bug tracking

❑ Staff resourcing

❑ Reporting

❑ Administrative tasks

Each section of the application could be built into modules. They are self-sufficient and operate more or less independently of each other. A user could work in staffing and development work areas but never get into administrative or reporting tasks because the logic necessary to accomplish these logical tasks does not overlap.

For the portions of logic that do overlap, "common" code modules or libraries can be developed that contain logic that is shared throughout the application.

This should not be confused with Model-View-Controller (MVC) architectures, in which the application components are separated into three tiers: the data model, the user interface (view), and the controller, which controls application logic and behaviors. However, MVC often goes hand in hand with modular development. It is likely that each module would have its own MVC architecture internally that is used to perform the application logic for that specific module.

Why Modular Development?

Now that we've discussed the "what" of modular development, let's examine the "why." There are numerous reasons why you would want to use modular application development strategies, but they do not apply to all applications. Smaller applications, which perform only one specific task, do not necessarily need modular development strategies.

One of the biggest reasons to use modular development strategies is that they help you create logical groupings of functionality, which often leads to cleaner code with less cross-dependencies between components. This, in and of itself, is a huge bonus.

Additionally, Flex enables you to separate compiled SWF files for each application modules. You can load these SWF modules incrementally, as needed; you would not have to load all the application components from the server up front. Your application can be architected so that there is an application shell, which contains no business logic. Instead, it would be the main user interface and would be used to load in additional modules as needed.

This approach provides better startup performance because less has to be downloaded to start using the application. Because each module is loaded as it is needed, there may be cases where specific users never download components of an application that never get used.

In addition to helping with application startup speeds, this approach enables you to create tighter security policies for application components. In the preceding project management software example, if you have a user who does not have permission to view either the administrative or reporting modules, you can prevent those components from ever being loaded onto the user's system.

In addition to logical grouping, cleaner code, and better startup performance, modular application development also generally leads to building application components that are more generic and more reusable. Common visual components are typically built as generic components, and common pieces of logic are built into libraries that can be reused across multiple modules and in multiple scenarios.

Building Components

Modular development also comes into play when building custom components. In essence, a custom component is a very specialized module that serves one specific purpose. It should be built generically enough so that it can be used throughout numerous use cases; however, it is modular in that it is a black box: you drop it in your code, apply properties and styles, and it works.

Building custom components is an enormous aspect of building Flex applications in general. You can read more specifically about custom component development in Part IV, "Advanced Component Development" (Chapters 16–22).

Runtime Shared Libraries

Runtime shared libraries (RSLs) are compiled code libraries that can be used in many scenarios. They are typically common groups of logic that can be reused in multiple projects, and they can be cached on the client side to help make your applications smaller in compiled file size. You can have RSLs that contain utility classes and functions, data access code, the data model, common view components, or any combination of these topics.

There is no limitation to what you can put within a RSL. With modular application development strategies, you would use RSLs to encapsulate common logic that is shared across multiple projects or modules. You can read more detail regarding creating and using RSLs in your own Flex applications in Chapter 21, "Using Libraries," and Chapter 27, "Loading External Assets."

Using the Module and ModuleLoader Classes

Now it's time to focus on the meat of this chapter: the Module and ModuleLoader classes. Module and ModuleLoader are used together to allow you to build modular applications that can be downloaded incrementally as needed, rather than all at once.

When building modular applications, you still need to start out with a root Application class. When your application is first requested from the server, it will load the main application, which acts as a shell of sorts. It can contain business logic, UI components, a navigational interface, or any other component that you would like. It will also contain a ModuleLoader instance, which is used to download separate application modules as they are needed.

The ModuleLoader class is used to load separate application components at runtime rather than having all the components compiled into the same SWF file. When using the ModuleLoader class, you will specify a URL to a SWF file and then load it into memory.

Each of these separate SWF files will be based on a Module class instance. When developing modules, you treat the Module class as you would the Application class. The difference is that the Application class is used as the root of the application, whereas `Module` is the root of a module, which must be loaded into a running application.

This may seem confusing, so let's examine into a very basic example. Figure 66-1 shows a very simple (and empty) interface. There is a large blank area at the top, and at the bottom are buttons used to control the module instances. In the blank area is an instance of the `ModuleLoader` class, although it is not visible because no module has been loaded.

Figure 66-1

You can select a module to load from the combo box and then press the Load button to load it into memory of the running application. While the module is loading, you will see a progress bar in the bottom-right corner of the application.

Once the module loads, you will see contents of the module in the blank area. In this case, the module itself only contains a `Text` component with text "Module 1" (see Figure 66-2). Once the module is loaded, you can unload it from memory by clicking on the Unload Current Module button.

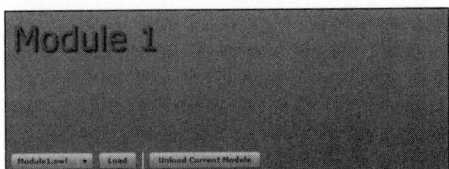

Figure 66-2

Although this scenario is very basic, it shows you everything that you need to load complex application modules incrementally as they are needed at runtime.

And now for the code that makes this work. The following code is used to render the module shown in Figure 66-2. It is simply a `Text` component with a `DropShadow` filter applied to it.

```
<?xml version="1.0" encoding="utf-8"?>
<mx:Module xmlns:mx="http://www.adobe.com/2006/mxml" layout="absolute">

    <mx:Text text="Module 1" fontSize="45" color="#FF0000" >
        <mx:filters>
            <mx:DropShadowFilter />
        </mx:filters>
    </mx:Text>

</mx:Module>
```

When compiled, this module will be in a separate SWF from the rest of the application. The compiled SWF file will be named exactly as the MXML file used to create the module. In this case, the MXML file is named `Module1.mxml` and is compiled into the `Module1.swf` file.

The following code is used to render the basic interface shown in Figure 66-1. You will see the buttons used to invoke the loading and unloading of modules, and most importantly, you will see the `ModuleLoader` instance that is used to load the separate module SWF instances. Most of the code in this example is actually used to show progress on the progress bar as the module is being downloaded.

```xml
<?xml version="1.0" encoding="utf-8"?>
<mx:Application xmlns:mx="http://www.adobe.com/2006/mxml" layout="absolute">

    <mx:Script>
        <![CDATA[
            import mx.controls.Alert;
            import mx.events.ModuleEvent;

            private function loadModule() : void
            {
                var target : String = moduleSelector.selectedItem.toString();

                if ( target != moduleLoader.url )
                {
                    progress.setProgress( 0,1 );
                      progress.visible = true;
                    addEventListeners();
                    moduleLoader.url = target;
                    moduleLoader.loadModule();
                }
            }

            private function unloadModule() : void
            {
                moduleLoader.url = "";
                moduleLoader.unloadModule();
            }

            private function addEventListeners() : void
            {
                moduleLoader.addEventListener( ModuleEvent.PROGRESS, onProgressEvent,
                  false, 0, true );
                moduleLoader.addEventListener( ModuleEvent.READY, onReadyEvent, false,
                    0, true );
                moduleLoader.addEventListener( ModuleEvent.ERROR, onErrorEvent, false,
                    0, true );
            }

            private function removeEventListeners() : void
            {
                moduleLoader.removeEventListener( ModuleEvent.PROGRESS,
                  onProgressEvent );
                moduleLoader.removeEventListener( ModuleEvent.READY, onReadyEvent );
                moduleLoader.removeEventListener( ModuleEvent.ERROR, onErrorEvent );
```

```
        }

        public function onProgressEvent( event : ModuleEvent ) : void
        {
           progress.setProgress( event.bytesLoaded, event.bytesTotal );
        }

        public function onReadyEvent( event : Event ) : void
        {
            progress.visible = false;
            removeEventListeners();
        }

        public function onErrorEvent( event : Event ) : void
        {
            progress.visible = false;
            removeEventListeners();
            Alert.show( "Error loading module:" + moduleLoader.url );
        }

    ]]>
</mx:Script>

<mx:ModuleLoader
    id="moduleLoader"
    bottom="40" right="10" left="10" top="10"/>

<mx:HBox bottom="10" left="10" >

    <mx:ComboBox
        id="moduleSelector">
        <mx:dataProvider>
            <mx:Array>
                <mx:String>Module1.swf</mx:String>
                <mx:String>Module2.swf</mx:String>
                <mx:String>Module3.swf</mx:String>
            </mx:Array>
        </mx:dataProvider>
    </mx:ComboBox>


    <mx:Button
        label="Load"
        click="loadModule()"/>

    <mx:VRule  height="22"/>

    <mx:Button
        label="Unload Current Module"
        click="unloadModule()"
        />
</mx:HBox>

<mx:ProgressBar
    id="progress"
```

```
                    mode="manual"
                    labelPlacement="center"
                    right="10" bottom="16"
                    visible="false"
                    />

    </mx:Application>
```

Using the `ModuleLoader` class itself is very easy. It is simply an empty container on the user interface. To load a module, you need only to specify a URL for the target module SWF and invoke the `loadModule()` function.

```
moduleLoader.url = target;
moduleLoader.loadModule();
```

You can unload modules from the current application simply by calling the `unloadModule()` function. You do not need to do anything else to the module to unload it from the current application. In this example, we are also setting the `ModuleLoader`'s URL to a blank string to allow us to reload the module if the Load button is clicked again (the URL value is being used to prevent reloading an already loaded module).

A very important thing to keep in mind here is that it is extremely important to keep track of event listeners using strong references between modules. Strong-referenced event listeners will prevent the Flash Player from unloading the modules properly. Weak-referenced event listeners should always be used in these cases.

You can read more details regarding the specifics of the `Module` and `ModuleLoader` classes directly from Adobe LiveDocs at `http://livedocs.adobe.com/flex/3/html/help.html?content=modular_5.html`.

Cross-Module Communication

Now that we've covered how to load a module, let's examine how to have separate modules communicate with each other. Your application and application modules are compiled using the same version of the Flex SDK, and run in the same Flash Player AVM virtual machine instance. Therefore, they have a shared memory space, and they can communicate directly with each other.

Typically, the best practice of having modules communicate with each other is through the use of events. You can use the Flash player's built-in event-dispatching mechanism to send event notifications between modules or to have different modules react to the same event.

There is one major caveat when working with modules and events: a module will respond to an event only if that module has been loaded into memory. If a module has not been loaded, it will not respond to any events, since it has not necessarily been downloaded to the running application or instantiated.

The next example demonstrates two different means of communication across modules, and that modules do not respond to events if they have not yet been loaded into the running application. The two types of event communication between modules in this example are dispatching events through the application's `systemManager` and dispatching events through a static event dispatcher.

Figure 66-3 shows this example in action. The application consists of two side-by-side panels. In each panel is a `ModuleLoader` instance, although neither module instance is loaded by default.

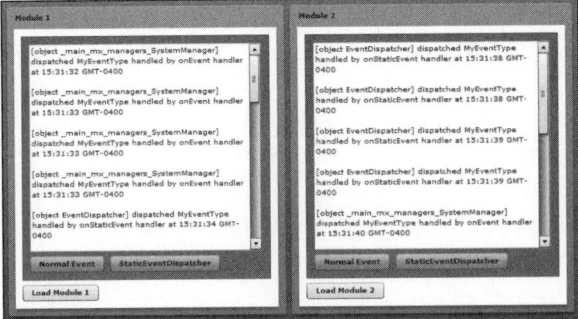

Figure 66-3

Each module instance consists of a text area and two buttons. One button is used to dispatch events through the application's `systemManger` instance, and the other is used to dispatch events through the static event dispatcher. Each time an event is received, a message is displayed in the text area.

Both modules will listen for the same events, and both will respond to the same event that is dispatched, regardless of which module it was dispatched from. If only one module is loaded, the second module will not respond to the events from the first. If both modules are loaded, both will respond to the same events. In Figure 66-3, you can see that the contents of the second module's text area are not the same as the first; this is because the second module was loaded after events had already been dispatched from the first module.

Now the code that makes all this work. First, we will examine the "shell" application. As you will see in the following code segment, there is very little to the shell application. It contains only two `Panel` instances containing empty `ModuleLoader` instances, and buttons that are used to load the modules into memory.

```
<?xml version="1.0" encoding="utf-8"?>
<mx:Application xmlns:mx="http://www.adobe.com/2006/mxml" layout="horizontal">

    <mx:Script>
      <![CDATA[

          private function loadModule1() : void
          {
             moduleLoader1.url = "EventModule.swf";
             moduleLoader1.loadModule();
          }

          private function loadModule2() : void
          {
             moduleLoader2.url = "EventModule.swf";
             moduleLoader2.loadModule();
          }

      ]]>
    </mx:Script>

    <mx:Panel
       width="100%" height="100%"
```

```
      paddingLeft="10" paddingBottom="10"
      paddingRight="10" paddingTop="10"
      title="Module 1">

      <mx:ModuleLoader
         borderColor="#FF0000"
         borderStyle="solid"
         id="moduleLoader1"
         width="100%" height="100%" />

      <mx:Button
         label="Load Module 1"
         click="loadModule1()" />

   </mx:Panel>

   <mx:Panel
      width="100%" height="100%"
      paddingLeft="10" paddingBottom="10"
      paddingRight="10" paddingTop="10"
      title="Module 2">

      <mx:ModuleLoader
         borderColor="#FF0000"
         borderStyle="solid"
         id="moduleLoader2"
         width="100%" height="100%" />

      <mx:Button
         label="Load Module 2"
         click="loadModule2();" />

   </mx:Panel>

</mx:Application>
```

Next up are the module contents. The module contains only a text area, two buttons, and the necessary script to dispatch and handle events. Both of the preceding panels load separate instances of the same module into memory, within separate `ModuleLoader` instances. When a module has been successfully loaded, the `creationComplete` event will be triggered, which adds event listeners to the `systemManager` instance and to the static event dispatcher. Whenever an event is received, the `appendOutput()` function is invoked, which displays details about the received event in the module's text area.

```
<?xml version="1.0" encoding="utf-8"?>
<mx:Module
   xmlns:mx="http://www.adobe.com/2006/mxml"
   layout="vertical"
   width="100%" height="100%"
   backgroundColor="#999999"
   paddingLeft="10" paddingBottom="10"
   paddingRight="10" paddingTop="10"
   creationComplete="onCreationComplete()">

   <mx:Script>
```

```
        <![CDATA[
            import mx.core.Application;

            private static const EVENT_TYPE : String = "MyEventType";

            private function onCreationComplete() : void
            {
                systemManager.addEventListener( EVENT_TYPE, onEvent );
                StaticEventDispatcher.addEventListener( EVENT_TYPE, onStaticEvent );
            }

            private function onEvent( event : Event ) : void
            {
                appendOutput( event, "onEvent" );
            }

            private function onStaticEvent( event : Event ) : void
            {
                appendOutput( event, "onStaticEvent" );
            }

            private function dispatchNormalEvent() : void
            {
                systemManager.dispatchEvent( new Event( EVENT_TYPE ) );
            }

            private function dispatchStaticEvent() : void
            {
                StaticEventDispatcher.dispatchEvent( new Event( EVENT_TYPE ) );
            }

            private function appendOutput( event : Event, source : String ) : void
            {
                output.text += event.target.toString() + " dispatched " +  event.type
                + " handled by " + source + " handler at " + new Date().toTimeString()
                + "\n\n";
            }

        ]]>
    </mx:Script>

    <mx:TextArea
        id="output"
        editable="false"
        width="100%" height="100%"/>

    <mx:HBox>

        <mx:Button
            label="Normal Event"
            click="dispatchNormalEvent()"/>

        <mx:Button
            label="StaticEventDispatcher"
```

```
                    click="dispatchStaticEvent()" />

        </mx:HBox>

    </mx:Module>
```

Whenever either button is clicked, an event is dispatched through the chosen event dispatcher. You can dispatch events either through the systemManager, which is the application's instance of a SystemManager class, or through a static event dispatcher instance.

The SystemManager class is one of the highest-level classes in a Flex application; it is even higher than Application.application, as the application instance resides in the systemManager. The systemManger itself is an event dispatcher instance, so you can dispatch events directly through it, as follows:

```
    systemManager.dispatchEvent( new Event( EVENT_TYPE ) );
```

An event dispatched through the systemManager can be received by every component within a Flex application; thus, it is a very effective mechanism for communicating between modules, or from a module to the shell application.

The second approach utilized in this example for cross-module communication is using a static event dispatcher class. Basically, a static event dispatcher class is a class that has static methods that are used to dispatch events and manage event listeners. You would use a static event dispatcher in any case where you don't want the event to be dispatched to every component in the Flex application. This would be a useful scenario if you only wanted a subset of components to be able to receive the event.

The following is the code used to create a static event dispatcher. All the actual event dispatching takes place through a private static EventDispatcher instance.

```
    package
    {
        import flash.events.Event;
        import flash.events.EventDispatcher;

        public class StaticEventDispatcher
        {
            private static var _ed : EventDispatcher = new EventDispatcher();

            public static function dispatchEvent( event : Event ) : void
            {
               _ed.dispatchEvent( event );
            }

            public static function addEventListener( type : String, listener : Function,
              useCapture : Boolean = false, priority : int = 0, useWeakReference :
              Boolean = true ) : void
            {
               _ed.addEventListener( type, listener, useCapture, priority,
                  useWeakReference );
            }

            public static function removeEventListener( type : String, listener :
```

```
        Function ) : void
    {
        _ed.removeEventListener( type, listener );
    }
  }
}
```

To add an event listener, you just need to call the addEventListener static method and specify the event type and event handler function.

```
StaticEventDispatcher.addEventListener( EVENT_TYPE, onStaticEvent );
```

When dispatching to the static event dispatcher, you call the static dispatchEvent() function with any kind of Event instance as a parameter.

```
StaticEventDispatcher.dispatchEvent( new Event( EVENT_TYPE ) );
```

Because the separate modules share the same memory space, the static methods in each module reference the same class declaration and the same static EventDispatcher instance. The static event dispatcher approach gives you fine-grained control over the components that dispatch and handle various events, and is also a common approach used in MVC-type frameworks.

Cross-Module Data Access

In addition to cross-module communication, you may also find it necessary to share data between separate module instances. As shown in the cross-module communication with events discussion previously, module instances within an application use the same memory space and AVM virtual machine instance as the parent application. Data sharing between modules can be easily accomplished either using singleton classes or static variable instances for data storage.

Just for clarification, static variables are variables that are associated with the class definition itself, not with any particular instance of a class. Therefore, you can access static variables directly on the class declaration, as follows:

```
ClassName.variable
```

Singleton classes are classes that have a single instance in memory. You can access that single instance through a static getter method, or static getInstance method of the singleton class, as follows:

```
ClassName.getInstance().variable
```

Before we dive into the code of how this works, let's take a look at what we are building. This example will use the exact same parent shell application as was used in the cross-module communication section. The difference is that the contents of the module demonstrate techniques used to access data that is shared across multiple module instances.

As shown in Figure 66-4, the application contains two panels, each containing a module. In each module are mx:List instances that are bound to static and singleton data sources. Next to each list is a button that is used to append data to the list. As items are added to each data source, you will notice that the data collections change in both modules, and the collections remain in synch. In fact, the lists in the separate modules are bound to the exact same data collection instance.

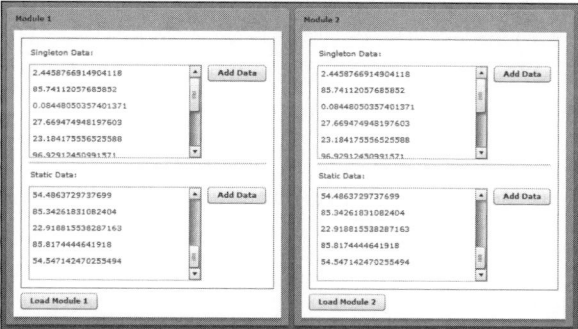

Figure 66-4

The following code segment shows you the shell application for the cross-module, data-sharing example. You can see that there is very little to the shell application, and in fact it is exactly identical to the shell application used in the previous example. It contains two `Panel` instances containing empty `ModuleLoader` instances, and buttons that are used to load the `Module` instances.

```
<?xml version="1.0" encoding="utf-8"?>
<mx:Application xmlns:mx="http://www.adobe.com/2006/mxml" layout="horizontal">

    <mx:Script>
      <![CDATA[

          private function loadModule1() : void
          {
             moduleLoader1.url = "DataModule.swf";
             moduleLoader1.loadModule();
          }

          private function loadModule2() : void
          {
             moduleLoader2.url = "DataModule.swf";
             moduleLoader2.loadModule();
          }

      ]]>
    </mx:Script>

    <mx:Panel
       width="100%" height="100%"
       paddingLeft="10" paddingBottom="10"
       paddingRight="10" paddingTop="10"
       title="Module 1">

       <mx:ModuleLoader
          borderColor="#FF0000"
          borderStyle="solid"
          id="moduleLoader1"
          width="100%" height="100%" />

       <mx:Button
```

```
                label="Load Module 1"
                click="loadModule1()" />

        </mx:Panel>

        <mx:Panel
            width="100%" height="100%"
            paddingLeft="10" paddingBottom="10"
            paddingRight="10" paddingTop="10"
            title="Module 2">

            <mx:ModuleLoader
                borderColor="#FF0000"
                borderStyle="solid"
                id="moduleLoader2"
                width="100%" height="100%" />

            <mx:Button
                label="Load Module 2"
                click="loadModule2();" />

        </mx:Panel>

    </mx:Application>
```

Each of the two `ModuleLoader` instances in this example load two separate instances of the same `Module` class, which you will find in the next code segment. Each module contains two lists: one list is bound to an `ArrayCollection` that is available from a singleton class, and one list is bound to an `ArrayCollection` that is available from a static variable instance.

Whenever the data changes, the contents of the modules will show the exact same data, regardless of when the module is loaded, because the data source is shared between the separate module instances.

```
    <?xml version="1.0" encoding="utf-8"?>
    <mx:Module
        xmlns:mx="http://www.adobe.com/2006/mxml"
        layout="vertical"
        width="100%" height="100%"
        paddingLeft="10" paddingBottom="10"
        paddingRight="10" paddingTop="10">

        <mx:Script>
            <![CDATA[
                import data.DataUtil;
                import mx.collections.ArrayCollection;
                import data.StaticModel;
                import data.SingletonModel;

                [Bindable]
                private var singletonData : ArrayCollection =
                    SingletonModel.getInstance().data;

                [Bindable]
```

```
        private var staticData : ArrayCollection = StaticModel.data;

        private function addSingletonData() : void
        {
            singletonData.addItem( DataUtil.generateDataPoint() );
        }

        private function addStaticData() : void
        {
            staticData.addItem( DataUtil.generateDataPoint() );
        }

    ]]>
</mx:Script>

<mx:Label text="Singleton Data:" />
<mx:HBox width="100%" height="100%">

    <mx:List
        dataProvider="{ singletonData }"
        width="100%" height="100%"/>

    <mx:Button
        label="Add Data"
        click="addSingletonData()" />

</mx:HBox>

<mx:HRule width="100%" />

<mx:Label text="Static Data:" />
<mx:HBox width="100%" height="100%">

    <mx:List
        dataProvider="{ staticData }"
        width="100%" height="100%"/>

    <mx:Button
        label="Add Data"
        click="addStaticData()" />

</mx:HBox>

</mx:Module>
```

The most important part of this example is shown in the next code segment. It is important to notice that the list instances are not directly bound to the singleton data or the static data instances. Instead, a local `Bindable` variable is created, which references the singleton or static data.

```
[Bindable]
private var singletonData : ArrayCollection = SingletonModel.getInstance().data;

[Bindable]
private var staticData : ArrayCollection = StaticModel.data;
```

This approach is used because static variables cannot be declared `Bindable`, since they are not a property of any particular class instance. Singleton instances can be `Bindable`, but since the context of this example does not require a `Bindable` class, it is not needed; only the local variable is `Bindable`.

In any instance of the module, it will always be referring to the exact same `ArrayCollection` instance, regardless of the number of module instances. Any change to the local `ArrayCollection` is actually a change to the singleton or static collection. This is all possible because the `Module` and the `Application` share the same memory space. In fact, this approach does not need more than one module. This approach can be used to share data between an application and a module, or between different components of the same application.

Now we will examine the actual code for the data structures that are used to share data between the two modules in this example. The first data structure is a singleton data model. This type of structure is referred to as a singleton because there is typically a single instance throughout an entire application.

The static `getInstance()` method of the `SingletonModel` class will always return the private static `_instance` value, no matter where it is called from. The public data `ArrayCollection` is a property of the `SingletonModel` instance. In essence, singletons provide the equivalent of a global variable; it is a variable instance that can be accessed from anywhere within the application.

```
package data
{
    import mx.collections.ArrayCollection;

    public class SingletonModel
    {
        private static var _instance : SingletonModel = new SingletonModel();

        public var appData : ArrayCollection = DataUtil.generateDataCollection();

        public static function getInstance() : SingletonModel
        {
            return _instance;
        }

    }
}
```

The static data structure, shown next, is a bit less complicated than the singleton data structure. In this case, there is a static `data ArrayCollection` as a property of the `StaticModel` class. All references throughout the application to `StaticModel.data` will always be referencing the exact same `ArrayCollection` instance, no matter where they are called from.

```
package data
{
    import mx.collections.ArrayCollection;

    public class StaticModel
    {
        public static var appData : ArrayCollection =
            DataUtil.generateDataCollection();
    }
}
```

Finally, there is the simple utility class that is used to generate data for this example. The `DataUtil` class just contains static methods that are used to populate data in this example. It is designed so that you can easily change all of the generated data in the example simply by modifying the `generateDataPoint()` function.

```
package data
{
    import mx.collections.ArrayCollection;

    public class DataUtil
    {
        public static function generateDataCollection() : ArrayCollection
        {
            var ac : ArrayCollection = new ArrayCollection();

            for ( var x : int = 0; x < 10; x ++)
            {
                ac.addItem( generateDataPoint() );
            }

            return ac;
        }

        public static function generateDataPoint() : Number
        {
            return Math.random() * 100;
        }

    }
}
```

Summary

Modular development is an approach to software design and architecture that separates application components into separate logical application components, or modules. The Flex framework provides everything that you need to build applications that take advantage of modular design principles, and enables you to create applications that perform well and are optimized to only download what they need as they need it. Part IV, "Advanced Component Development," discusses how adding modular design to application components can aid in your development efforts.

The next chapter focuses on strategies to optimize your application performance. This includes memory optimizations, coding tricks, and other helpful tips to make your applications fast.

Application Performance Strategies

There's no question about it — everyone wants their application to be the fastest. It should start up quickly, it should load data quickly, it should render data quickly, it should be able to crunch numbers quickly, and it should not use much memory. When developing your Flex applications, it is often easy to overlook simple pitfalls that can be detrimental to your application's performance. This chapter highlights strategies for building applications that perform well and identifies simple mistakes that can cause large impacts on application performance.

Understanding Object Creation Policies

One small change that can have a potentially disastrous affect on application startup performance is changing the creation policy of a container object. By default, all container objects use a deferred creation policy. This means that objects are only created as they are needed.

For example, consider a `TabNavigator` component. If `TabNavigator` contains multiple children, only the children of the first tab are actually created upon initialization of the tab navigator instance. In the following code snippet, only the children of the first canvas would be created upon initialization.

```
<mx:TabNavigator>

    <mx:Canvas label="Tab 1">
       <!-- various child components here -->
    </mx:Canvas>

    <mx:Canvas label="Tab 2">
       <!-- various child components here -->
    </mx:Canvas>
```

```
        <mx:Canvas label="Tab 3">
            <!-- various child components here -->
        </mx:Canvas>
    </mx:TabNavigator>
```

The children of the second and third tabs are only created when they are accessed. The default creation policy is the preferred creation policy in the vast majority of situations. Rarely, you may encounter a scenario where you change the `creationPolicy` value from `auto` (deferred instantiation) to `all`.

When the creation policy is set to `all`, all child objects of the container are created upon initialization. In the previous example, all three tabs, and all of their children, would be created when the `TabNavigator` instance is created. If there are very few children in each tab, the impact of this is minimal; however, if each tab contains complex components or complex nested components, this can have a dramatic effect on application initialization.

It is very easy to overlook this and set `creationpolicy` to `all`. In some cases simply setting this policy can cause the application to lock up for upwards of 15 to 30 seconds while the child components are being created, depending on their complexity. It is very important to only use the `all` creation policy under specific and limited use cases.

Structuring Data for Performance

Another extremely important factor in creating applications that perform well is the structure and complexity of the data that is used within the application. In general, a Flex user interface is designed to render data and provide a visual interface for the user to interact with. It is not designed to perform heavy number crunching or data transformations. Requiring a Flex application to perform major calculations and transformations of data will always result in an application that performs slower than an application that does not require any data processing. For this reason alone, it is extremely important to maintain high fidelity between the data and the visual interface.

Servers are orders of magnitude more efficient than the Flash Player at performing complex calculations and transformations, and should be used for those tasks whenever available. Data should always be transformed on the server and serialized to the Flex user interface in a format that is easy to consume and display. Any processing resources that are utilized transforming data on the user interface will not be spent rendering the interface or handling any events, thus yielding an application client interface that is less responsive.

Lazy Loading Data

The structure of the data is not the only factor that can impact how the performance of the application. How the data is loaded can have as big an impact on application performance as anything else. When I refer to how the data is loaded, I don't mean the serialization method (AMF remoting, XML over HTTP, or SOAP Web Services); this technique applies to all three serialization methods.

Lazy loading of data is the process of only loading data as you need it, as opposed to loading all data initially. Consider an application that loads thousands of records of data. Regardless of whether you are using AMF Remoting or XML, it will always be faster to return a minimal data set, rather than load every attribute o of every record, especially when all attributes of the data are not visible in the current view.

Consider an application that loads contact information for thousands of contacts and displays them in a data grid, although the data grid displays only the first, middle, and last names. Following are two separate versions of XML data that is used to populate the grid.

The first version of the XML contains all information regarding that contact. Each record contains the contact name, plus additional data that is not necessary to display within the grid.

```
<contact>
    <id>1</id>
    <first>John</first>
    <middle>Q</middle>
    <last>Doe</last>
    <email>johndoe@gmail.com</email>
    <home_phone>123-456-7890</home_phone>
    <work_phone>234-567-8901</work_phone>
    <mobile_phone>345-678-9012</mobile_phone>
    <address>1600 Pennsylvania Avenue</address>
    <city>Washington</city>
    <state>DC</state>
    <zip>20006</zip>
    <website>www.wrox.com</website>
</contact>
```

The following is a trimmed-down version of the same data. For each record, only the name values are loaded. Any time that you want to drill down into the data, the complete data for that record would be retrieved based on the contact ID.

```
<contact>
    <id>1</id>
    <first>John</first>
    <middle>Q</middle>
    <last>Doe</last>
</contact>
```

Multiply these XML records by thousands of records, and it's easy to see how lazy loading can make a difference. With the compacted data, the size of the data being transferred from the client to the server is reduced by more than half, thus reducing the overall data load and transfer time. Additionally, the data is less complex, so it can be parsed faster in the client interface, and it runs faster at runtime since the XML objects are simpler.

Impacts of Multiple Service Invocations

Another important factor to keep in mind when creating your Flex applications is how the data is loaded into the application. You will want to minimize the number of service calls required to load a particular data set. This should not be confused with the lazy loading of data. Lazy-loaded data should be used whenever possible.

Instead, this refers to using multiple service invocations to load a single data set. Consider the contact list discussed in the previous section. You would not want a scenario where you have to use multiple service invocations to load that list. For example, first you load information about the currently logged-in user, then load the user's permissions list, and finally load the contacts list based on the permissions list.

Instead, you would simply want to load the list in one service method. You should have a single service method that takes the ID of the current user, handles the permissions on the backend, and returns the contact list to the client interface.

Every additional service request causes latency as a result of server processing and network lag. The more chained requests, the larger the delay will be, and the slower your application will respond. The back-end services should always be structured to return the necessary data from a single service invocation.

Managing Event Listeners and Data Bindings

Data bindings and event listeners are found in every Flex application. They are an integral part of building Flex applications, and in most cases, they make your life significantly easier. However, there are some cases where event listeners and data bindings negatively impact your applications.

The following sections provide a few tricks that can help your applications perform at optimal levels.

Collection Events

Collections, whether ArrayCollections, XMLListCollections, or some other kind of collection, are the preferred objects to use when handling data within your Flex applications. This is because collections dispatch events any time an item is added, updated, or removed from the collection, or when the order of items in the collection has changed. The events that are dispatched by collections are what enables automatic data binding of components to the collection data. These events cause actions to occur when the data changes, such as changing the contents of item renderers, updating the position of objects, or triggering functions.

It is very important to remember that any time the collection is changed, these events are dispatched. In turn, this can invoke actions on objects that are listening for the collection events. Thus, rapidly changing the contents of a collection can trigger an excessive amount of event dispatching and unnecessary CPU usage.

Consider the basic scenario where a List is bound to an ArrayCollection. Whenever the Button instance is clicked, the addData() function is invoked, which adds numbers to the myDataCollection ArrayCollection.

```
<mx:Script>
  <![CDATA[
    import mx.collections.ArrayCollection;

    [Bindable]
    private var myDataCollection : ArrayCollection = new ArrayCollection();

    private function addData() : void
    {
```

```
            for ( var x : int = 0; x < 1000; x ++ )
            {
                myDataCollection.addItem( x );
            }
        }

    ]]>
</mx:Script>

<mx:List dataProvider="{ myDataCollection }"  x="10" y="10"/>

<mx:Button click="addData()"  x="180" y="10"/>
```

Upon each iteration of the loop, a collection event is dispatched, thus invalidating the properties of the List instance. This will cause 1000 collectionChange events to be dispatched. Since the List properties have been invalidated, the List component will follow the normal component life cycle, and then it will be revalidated. Although every collectionChange event will not directly invoke the component validation process, it is likely that the component will be validated multiple times during the processing of a loop.

You can drastically reduce the number of collectionChange events dispatched, improve runtime performance, and reduce the computational power necessary to update your components in a few simple steps. The improved performance is achieved by disabling collection events before processing the collection, and reenabling collection events upon completion of processing. The following snippet shows the usage of the disableAutoUpdate() and enableAutoUpdate() functions to achieve this goal:

```
private function addData() : void
{
    myDataCollection.disableAutoUpdate();

    for ( var x : int = 0; x < 1000; x ++ )
    {
        myDataCollection.addItem( x );
    }

    myDataCollection.enableAutoUpdate();
}
```

Calling the disableAutoUpdate() function on the collection instance causes collectionChange events not to be dispatched when the contents of the collection change. This applies to all actions on the collection: add, remove, update, and reorder. Once processing is complete, you can use the enableAutoUpdate() function to reenable collection events. This also causes a single collectionChange event to be dispatched, which will cause automatic updates to any components that are bound to the collection instance.

Using this technique, the simple loop processing now dispatches only one event, instead of 1000. In this case, the performance advantage is not immediately noticeable; however, complex applications with multiple data bindings and large data sets will see a significant performance improvement from this simple step.

Cleaning Up Unused Event Listeners

Another extremely important tip is to always be aware of your event listeners. Even though you may have components that are no longer visible, or have been removed from the display list, they can still respond to application events.

This is especially the case when you are dynamically setting event listeners on components that are added to or removed from the display list. This is also the case when using a global singleton or static event dispatcher instance. While your components or views may no longer be visible or "active," they maintain references to the event dispatcher and will still respond to events dispatched across these structures. This can add unnecessary processing to your application, can cause memory leaks, and can lead to degraded performance over time.

Weak Referenced Event Listeners

An easy way to prevent memory leaks and prevent extra events from firing is to use weak-referenced event listeners. The default action for adding an event listener is a strong-reference event listener, as follows:

```
eventDispatcher.addEventListener( "eventType", eventHandler );
```

I'm sure you recognize this syntax and probably think nothing of it. Strong-referenced event listeners maintain a reference between the event dispatcher and event handler. If your component is no longer used but has strongly referenced event listeners, the component and event handler will not be available to the Flash Player's Garbage Collector, and thus will consume unnecessary memory and may still respond to application events that are dispatched

Weakly referenced event listeners use optional parameters when adding the event handler functions. You can see this in the following code:

```
eventDispatcher.addEventListener( "eventType", eventHandler, false, 0, true );
```

The parameters of the addEventListener function are: eventType, eventHandler, capturePhase, priority, and useWeakReferences. The capturePhase parameter is set to false by default. Typically, you want to leave this as is. If you change capturePhase to true, the event handler is invoked in the capture phase, which occurs before the event bubbles to other components. The priority dictates the order in which event handlers are invoked. In most cases, you will not need to change this. A higher priority number for the event handler will be invoked before lower-priority event handlers. Last, but certainly not least, is the Boolean flag used to determine strong or weak references.

Strong references (false) are the default value. Setting a true value indicates that the event handler will use weak references. Weak references will not block the Flash Player's Garbage Collection, and should be used in most cases.

Cleaning Up Event Listeners Manually

When you are dynamically adding and removing components from your application, it is extremely important to be aware of event listeners, as they can quickly and silently add up and cause degraded performance. In most of these cases, it is very difficult to track down what is causing the undesirable performance or memory leak.

As a matter of practice, it is generally necessary to manually add event listeners when you need them and remove them when they are no longer necessary. One very easy way to do this is to add public functions to your components that add and remove all event listeners. The following sample shows how you can structure your code to create these functions:

```
public function addEventListeners() : void
{
    addEventListener( MouseEvent.CLICK, onClick, false, 0, true );
    addEventListener( MouseEvent.DOUBLE_CLICK, onDoubleClick, false, 0, true );
    addEventListener( MouseEvent.MOUSE_MOVE, onMouseMove, false, 0, true );
}

public function removeEventListeners() : void
{
    removeEventListener( MouseEvent.CLICK, onClick );
    removeEventListener( MouseEvent.DOUBLE_CLICK, onDoubleClick );
    removeEventListener( MouseEvent.MOUSE_MOVE, onMouseMove );
}
```

When your component is added to the parent container, and you want it to be interactive, you invoke the addEventListeners() function. The addEventListeners() function would add all event listeners that are necessary to make your component interactive: mouse events, keyboard events, Flex events, and so forth. The following example shows how you could invoke this function on an object instance (myComponent) before adding it as a child of the current object:

```
myComponent.addEventListeners();
this.addChild( myComponent );
```

When you are no longer using the component and want it to become inactive, you simply invoke removeEventListeners() to ensure that no arbitrary event handlers are left active:

```
myComponent.removeEventListeners();
this.removeChild( myComponent );
```

Manually controlling your event handlers might seem like additional work, or unnecessary; however, it is essential to minimizing resource consumption and maximizing application performance.

Associative Arrays and Dictionaries

One performance tip that is often overlooked is the use of associative arrays inside the client interface for faster data look-ups. Index-based arrays are your standard array structure. To find a particular item within an index-based structure, you would need to loop over the contents of the array and compare the properties of the array contents to a known value to determine if you have found the object that you are looking for.

The next example shows a function that will search an array of `Contact` items and find the appropriate object instance based on the `contactId` value.

```
public function getContactById( contactId : int ) : Contact
{
    for each ( var c:Contact in contacts )
    {
        if ( c.id == myId )
            return c;
    }
    return null;
}
```

In every case, the function must loop over a variable number of items in the contacts array to find the appropriate contact to return. If the first item in the array is found immediately, then the function returns immediately; however, if `Contact` instance you are searching for is the last item, it will take longer for the function to return. Multiple invocations of this method are not guaranteed to execute in the same amount of time, and this function can potentially take a long time on large data sets.

Associate arrays can make this faster. Associative arrays are key-value mappings of objects that can execute this type of look-up without any looping. Associative arrays, also commonly known as *hash maps*, are used to identify an object instance with a key string.

Associative arrays can be created from either `Array` or `Object` class instances. In either case, they both function in exactly the same way. To create an associative array, you simply need to create an object and populate its members.

```
var hashMap : Object = new Object();
hashMap[ key ] = value;
```

The key is simply a string value. The value being associated with the string can be any kind of object instance. When you want to access your object from the mapping, you just need to access the associative array instance with the appropriate key. There can be only one unique value associated with each key, so be careful not to accidentally overwrite your mapped values with nondistinct keys.

```
myRetrievedValue = hashMap[ key ];
```

You can apply this technique to dramatically improve performance of your application. Data look-ups that take multiples of seconds to execute with index based arrays can be performed in fractions of seconds using hash maps/associative arrays.

The following example examines the `getContactById()` function discussed earlier. The function has been reworked to use an `Object` instance as an associative array.

```
private var contactMap : Object;

private function createMap() : void
{
    contactMap = new Object();
```

```
    for each ( var c:Contact in contacts )
    {
        contactMap[ c.id.toString() ] = c;
    }
}

public function getContactById( contactId : int ) : Contact
{
    if ( contactMap == null )
        createMap();
    return contactMap[ contactId.toString() ];
}
```

In this case, you can see that the mapping is created by using the `createMap()` function if the map is null. In the `createMap()` function, the collection of contacts is looped over and a map is created based on the `id` attributes of the `Contact` object instances. The mapping is only created on the first invocation of this function, thus every subsequent invocation of this method returns immediately based on the mapping. No looping over arrays is required.

This technique can cause dramatic improvements on the speed of your application; however, you will also need to maintain your object mapping. If objects are deleted from your collection, they will also need to be deleted from your mapping. The opposite also applies: if objects are added to your collection, they will need to be added to your mapping as well.

The `Dictionary` class is another class within ActionScript that functions very similarly to associative arrays. The `Dictionary` class allows you to create mapping of key-value object pairs; however, the keys are not limited to string values, as they are when using `Array`- or `Object`-based associative arrays. Keys for `Dictionary` classes can be any type of class instance; they can be simple value objects or complex visual components. This enables you to have complex look-ups based on object instances, rather than strings. This is especially useful in situations where you have multiple object instances that may have the same properties, where string values would not be an acceptable key.

The following example shows how to use an object instance as a key in a dictionary map:

```
var dictionaryMap : Dictionary = new Dictionary();

var key : Object = new Object();
dictionaryMap[ key ] = value;
```

Any time that you want to access that value, you simply need to reference the `Dictionary` instance, using the object key:

```
myRetrievedValue = dictionaryMap[ key ];
```

It is also very important to note that, when using `Dictionary` class instances, you should always delete key or value references when they are no longer needed. These references leave the potential for memory leaks because they do not automatically release the memory references to either the key or value objects. Another option to help mitigate memory leaks with `Dictionary` class instances is to use the Boolean `weakKeys` constructor parameter. Using the `weakKeys` parameter creates all mappings using weakly referenced classes, which can be garbage collected.

Working with Graphics

One of the biggest advantages of using Flex and the Flash platform over traditional HTML-based development is the vast graphics capabilities and drawing API that are provided by the Flash Player. It is easy to see the graphics power once you start working with it. The following sections will provide you with a few tips that can maximize the graphical performance of your Flex applications.

Frame Rates

The frame rate of your Flex application determines how many times the graphics are rendered on-screen in a given period of time. The default frame rate of Flex applications is 24 frames per second. In many cases, this value is sufficient for a great user experience. However, it is important to keep in mind that this value can be changed and can lead to a smoother user experience.

A higher frame rate means that the graphics are rendered on-screen more often. This often means that animations are smoother, the user interface is generally more responsive, and things happen on-screen faster. It is also important to keep in mind that a higher frame rate means more processing power is required to render the screen more often. There is a delicate balance between frame rate, processing needs, and application performance. Trial and error is typically the best way to determine the frame rate that best suits your needs.

You can change the frame rate of a Flex application either by changing the `frameRate` attribute of the root `mx:Application` instances or by adding the `-default-frame-rate` compiler argument. The following is an example of how to change the frame rate through the `Application` tag:

```
<mx:Application
    xmlns:mx="http://www.adobe.com/2006/mxml"
    layout="horizontal"
    frameRate="30">
```

Using Bitmap Caching

Bitmap caching is a feature of the Flash Player whereby vector-based visual components can be cached in memory as bitmaps. When bitmap caching is enabled on a component, the vector-based content does not need to be re-rendered on-screen for every enter-frame event; The graphical content is only re-rendered when you instruct it to redraw via `invalidateDisplayList()` or when properties of the graphical object change (`width`, `height`, scale, etc.).

This feature enables greater application performance because graphics are only redrawn when there is actually a change. Bitmap caching greatly reduces the amount of processing necessary to render the entire screen and improves the performance of visual transitions and animations.

You can enable bitmap caching on a component simply by setting the `cacheAsBitmap` Boolean value on a `UIComponent` instance:

```
this.cacheAsBitmap = true;
```

Use bitmap caching with caution. In many cases, it greatly improves performance; however, in some cases caching vector graphics that are continually changing causes more work to render the graphics than would normally be necessary if the graphics were not cached. This can lead to extra processing and degraded application performance.

Managing External SWF Content

You may think nothing of loading a Flash animation by using a SWFLoader object, or embedding SWF-based content within your application so that it can be displayed at runtime. When the SWF animation is no longer visible, it is no longer taking up any CPU cycles or causing any screen redraws, right?

Wrong. You should be very careful when using embedded or dynamically loaded SWF-based content that has an endless-looping animation. As long as the content is still on the Flex application's display list, any animation that happens in embedded SWF content causes additional processing and causes a redraw to occur even if the object is not visible.

This applies to all content loaded via a SWFLoader or embedded content that is displayed as a skin. If you are running into mysterious CPU usage issues, try running your application within a debug version of the Flash Player and turn on the Show Redraw Regions option. If you have a constantly looping animation, you will notice a red outline showing the area being constantly redrawn by the Flash Player.

The only way to prevent the constant redraw cycle is to actually remove the SWF animated content from the display list:

```
this.removeChild( myAnimatedContent );
```

This does not in any way mean that you shouldn't use SWF-based animations in Flex applications. They can be used to achieve amazing and dramatic results. However, you should be careful to ensure that your animated content is not bogging down other parts of the application when it is no longer visible.

Object Caching and Recycling

Object caching and recycling is an advanced topic used for squeezing every last bit of performance out of your application.

You may already be familiar with how itemRenderer objects are used within the Flex framework for a List or DataGrid component. New renderers are not created for every object in the data collection that is being displayed in the grid. Instead, renderers are only created for what is visible on-screen. When you scroll through the grid, item renderers that once contained data which are no longer visible on the screen get recycled to display the new data that will be displayed on the screen. This behavior is made possible by the caching and recycling of item renderer components.

With object caching, you create a collection or cache of objects that are available for use within your application components. When you need a new object instance, you request one from the cache. If there are objects within the cache, the first available object is removed from the cache and returned so that it can be used within the application. If the cache is empty, then a new object is created and returned.

This technique is typically used with visual objects but can be applied to any ActionScript class. Object caching allows you to control object instances—how many objects are created, how many are currently in use, and how many are available to use. This often leads to better memory consumption because of the object instance reuse. Object caching can also lead to better performance and scalability, since the application is not constantly creating new objects; it creates a finite set of objects and reuses them.

Object caching can get very complex. The following example is a simple object caching class that will help to get you started:

```
public class ObjectCache
{
    private static var cache : Array = [];

    public static function get item() : UIComponent
    {
        if ( cache.length <= 0 )
            return new UIComponent();
        else
            return cache.shift();
    }

    public static function set item( o : UIComponent ) : void
    {
        if ( o )
            cache.push( o );
    }
}
```

In this example, the ObjectCache class contains an Array called cache, which will be used to maintain the managed collection of UIComponent instances. A UIComponent instance can be retrieved from the cache simply by retrieving the ObjectCache.item static property, which actually invokes the get item static getter method.

```
var renderer : UIComponent = ObjectCache.item;
this.addChild( renderer );
```

When this action is invoked, the ObjectCache class checks the contents of the cache Array. If there are objects available in the cache, the first one in the cache array is returned; otherwise, a new UIComponent instance is created and returned.

When you no longer need the object instance, you return it to the cache by calling the ObjectCache.item setter method:

```
ObjectCache.item = this.removeChild( renderer ) as UIComponent;
```

This example is very basic, but it illustrates the concept of object caching. It has everything you need to get started with this technique. In a real-world scenario, you probably will also want to implement an initialization routine for your cached items, and also a cleanup routine that can be used to clean up instances before they are returned to the cache.

Summary

Performance can be everything in the overall experience of an application. Poor performance directly leads to a poor user experience, and great performance is a contributing factor to a great user experience. As shown in this chapter, a properly architected data model and services layer, along with simple techniques used when building your application, can go a long way toward speeding up the entire application overall.

Long-term maintenance of an application or the creation of a public API not only need to be optimized properly, but people need to be able to quickly identify how everything works together. The next chapter covers project documentation with ASDoc, Flex's tool for generating documentation directly from your code.

Project Documenting with ASDoc

When developing for Adobe Flex, you may find it necessary to create reference documentation for your applications. Whether you are creating reference materials for application maintenance, or API documentation for a redistributable .swc file, the Flex framework provides the tools you need to automatically generate documentation based on your Flex project code.

This chapter will examine the ASDoc program that accompanies the Flex framework. The following sections will explain what ASDoc is, how to use it, and how to customize your generated documentation.

What Is ASDoc?

ASDoc is a tool that is packaged with the Adobe Flex Software Development Kit (SDK) that is used to generate reference documentation for your Flex applications. ASDoc scans your Flex and ActionScript code and generates HTML-based documentation based on your classes, their public properties and methods, their metadata attributes, and formatted comments within your code.

If you have ever seen the Flex API reference, then you have first-hand exposure to the generated HTML output of the ASDoc tool. The ASDoc tool outputs a series of HTML files that mimic the directory structure of your code. It also outputs a HTML frame-based interface for easy navigation, with an index of package structures, index of classes, and an alphabetized index of all the HTML content generated from your Flex project code. Figure 68-1 shows sample generated ASDoc documentation.

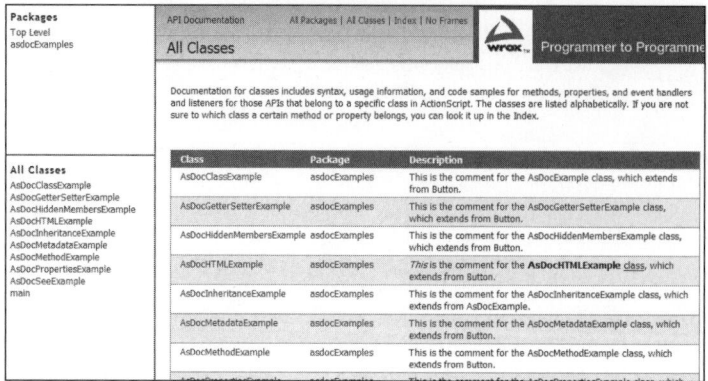

Figure 68-1

Using ASDoc

The ASDoc tool is invoked from the command line. To use the tool, you need to open a command prompt, and the directory containing the ASDoc executable must be in your system path variable. If you are using Adobe Flex Builder, the Flex Builder installer creates a shortcut for you. Just launch the Adobe Flex 3 SDK Command Prompt shortcut, and a command prompt will open with everything that you need to get started with ASDoc already in your system path.

Once you've got the command prompt open, invoking the ASDoc tool is straightforward. You simply need to invoke the `asdoc` function with the proper command-line parameters to target your Flex code. For example, the following input will instruct the ASDoc tool to generate documentation for the `main` class within the directory (source path) `C:\ProFlex3 - 68 - 01 AsDoc\src`:

```
asdoc -source-path "C:\ProFlex3 - 68 - 01 AsDoc\src" -doc-classes main
```

The preceding example uses only two of the available ASDoc command-line arguments to generate the documentation. There are additional arguments that can be used to specify documentation for namespaces, specific classes, and specific custom templates (among others). Full documentation of the command-line parameters can be found in the ASDoc API reference.

To generate documentation, the ASDoc tool will analyze all of the code of your application and extract specially formatted code comments to generate HTML-based reference documentation. In essence, your properly commented code *is* the documentation for your application.

The ASDoc tool will generate documentation for the `main` class and any public classes that are public children of the `main` class, and continues recursively on these children. Figure 68-1 shows the output ASDoc created with this instruction. You can see that it generated documentation for the `main` class, as well as `AsDocClassExample`, `AsDocGetterSetterExample`, and so forth.

Invoking the ASDoc tool from the command line is only half of what you need to properly take advantage of the tool. Commenting your code with a specific format, similar to the "Javadoc" format used in Java, will generate detailed comments and descriptions within the generated HTML documentation.

All public and protected methods and properties of a class will be included in the generated HTML documentation, unless they are directly identified for exclusion. Any class, variable, or function in an ActionScript class can be documented with ASDoc. In MXML files, only code inside of the `<mx:Script>` tag can be documented. ASDoc does not support documenting MXML files.

ASDoc formatted comments must adhere to the following format:

```
/**
 * Comment and/or description
 *
 * @tags tag text goes here
 */
```

The first line of the comment will be a forward slash, followed by two asterisks (/**). Every line within the comment should start with an asterisk (*), followed by a space, which is then followed by the comment text or tags. The comment should *always* be placed directly above the function/variable/class that the comment should apply to.

ASDoc Comments and Formatting

The text within the comment will be directly embedded within the generated HTML content output of the ASDoc tool. These comments are used to describe the action that a function performs or what a variable represents, so that it is meaningful within the generated documentation.

For example, the following code will be parsed by the ASDoc tool into meaningful, easy-to-read documentation:

```
/**
 * Returns the boolean status whether or not a
 * user is logged into the system.
 *
 * @return true if the user is logged in, false otherwise
 */
public function isUserLoggedIn() : Boolean
{
    return _loggedIn;
}
```

The generated HTML output will appear as shown in Figure 68-2 when viewed in the browser.

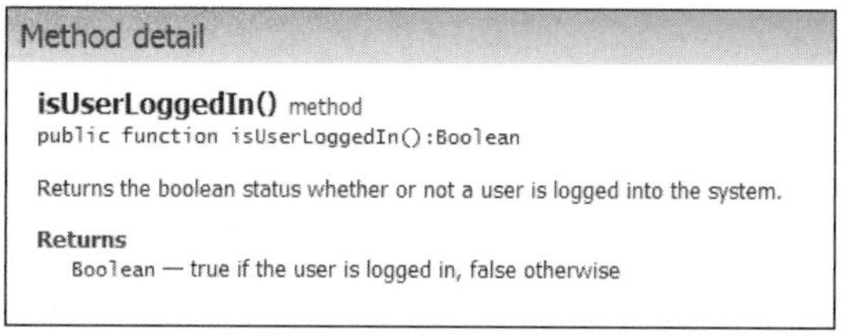

Method detail

isUserLoggedIn() method
`public function isUserLoggedIn():Boolean`

Returns the boolean status whether or not a user is logged into the system.

Returns
Boolean — true if the user is logged in, false otherwise

Figure 68-2

ASDoc Tags

You may have noticed that the comment in the preceding code also included the `@return` tag. Tags are used within comments to specify details or attributes for the target object. The following tags are the most commonly used when using the ASDoc. Note that these are not all the tags supported by the ASDoc tool. You can find a definitive list of all the tag options in the ASDoc API reference.

@return

The `@return` tag is used to describe the return output of a function. There can only be one return value per ASDoc comment, and the function being documented must return a value. The generated output of the `@return` tag will show the variable type and the description for the result as it was specified in the comment.

Sample output:

```
Boolean - true if the user is logged in, false otherwise
```

@param

The `@param` tag is used to describe the parameters of a function. There can be multiple `@param` statements in a comment if the function has parameters. The generated output of the `@param` tag will be the parameter name, followed by the type of the parameter and the description as it was specified in the comment. The `@param` string supplied must match one of the parameters in the function signature.

Sample Output:

```
username:String - The distinct username for the current user.
```

@see

The `@see` tag is used to add "See Also" links to your generated HTML documentation. They can allow you to add simple text, HTML links, or links to other areas within your documentation. You can have multiple `@see` tags per comment.

Sample Output:

```
See also
  http://www.wrox.com
  mx.controls.Button
```

@private

The `@private` tag is used to exclude a function or class from the generated HTML documentation. There can only be a single `@private` tag per ASDoc comment.

Classes

You can add class-level comments and descriptions to your source files by adding the ASDoc comment directly before your class definition. Note that adding the comment before the import statements will result in the comment description being omitted from your generated HTML documentation. The comment should be added directly before the class definition, after the import statements.

```
package asdocExamples
{
    import mx.controls.Button;

    /**
     * This is the comment for the AsDocClassExample class, which extends
     * from Button.
     */
    public class AsDocClassExample extends Button
    {
        /**
         * This is the comment for the AsDocClassExample constructor.
         */
        public function AsDocClassExample()
        {
            super();
        }

    }
}
```

Functions

You can also use ASDoc comments to provide helpful information about your public and protected functions. In these comments, you specify a meaningful description of what the function does.

Additionally, when documenting functions, you can use @param and @return tags to include more information about the expected inputs and outputs of each function. The following example shows how to add ASDoc comments to functions within your applications.

You will also notice that function comments that contain the @private tag will be omitted from the generated HTML documentation output.

```
package asdocExamples
{
    import mx.controls.Button;

    /**
     * This is the comment for the AsDocMethodExample class, which extends
     * from Button.
     */
    public class AsDocMethodExample extends Button
    {
        /**
         * This is the comment for the myFunction function.
         */
        public function myFunction() : void {}
```

```
    /**
     * This is the comment for the myFunctionWithReturn function.
     * @return A boolean value
     */
    public function myFunctionWithReturn() : Boolean
    {
        return true;
    }

    /**
     * This is the comment for the protected myFunctionWithParams function.
     *
     * @param value1 Is a string value.
     * @param value2 Is a number value.
     */
    protected function myFunctionWithParams( value1 : String, value2 : Number )
    : void {}

    /**
     * @private
     */
    public function myPrivateFunction() : void {}
    }
}
```

Properties

Similarly to functions, ASDoc comments can be specified to provide helpful information about your
public and protected variables. In these comments, you specify a meaningful description of what the
variable contains or represents.

Additionally, when documenting properties, you can use the `@default` tag to identify the default
value of that variable in the generated HTML output. The following example shows how to add ASDoc
comments to variables within your code. You will notice that variables whose comments contain the
`@private` tag will be omitted from the generated HTML documentation output.

```
package asdocExamples
{
    import mx.controls.Button;

    /**
     * This is the comment for the AsDocPropertiesExample class,
     * which extends from Button.
     */
    public class AsDocPropertiesExample extends Button
    {
        /**
         * The comment for public var myPublicVar1.
         */
        public var myPublicVar1 : String;

        /**
         * The comment for public var myPublicVar2.
```

```
     *
     * @default null
     */
    public var myPublicVar2 : String = null;

    /**
     * The comment for protected var myPublicVar3.
     *
     * @default abc123
     */
    protected var myPublicVar3 : String = "abc123";

    //this private variable will not show up in the generated AsDoc output
    private var myPrivateVar : String;
  }
}
```

Getters and Setters

Getter and setter functions follow similar conventions that are used with variables. The difference is that you only need to add the ASDoc comment to either the getter or the setter, not both. The other should be marked with a @private tag to prevent duplication. Another distinction with getter and setter methods is that getters that have no setter are automatically identified in the generated HTML output as "read-only" variables. The opposite also applies to setters, with no getter method; they are identified in the generated HTML output as "write-only" variables. Getter and setter methods will show up in the generated HTML documentation as either public properties or protected properties, depending upon the function scope specified for the getter/setter pair.

```
package asdocExamples
{
    import mx.controls.Button;

    /**
     * This is the comment for the AsDocGetterSetterExample class,
     * which extends from Button.
     */
    public class AsDocGetterSetterExample extends Button
    {
        /**
         * This is the AsDoc comment for the getter/setter methods "myGetterSetter"
         */
        public function get myGetterSetter():String { return "abc123" };

        /**
         * @private
         */
        public function set myGetterSetter(value:String):void {};


        /**
         * This is the AsDoc comment for the read-only getter
         * method "myReadOnlyGetter"
         */
```

```
                public function get myReadOnlyGetter():String { return "abc123" };

                /**
                 * This is the AsDoc comment for the write-only setter
                 * method "myWriteOnlySetter"
                 */
                public function set myWriteOnlySetter(value:String):void {};

                /**
                 * This is the AsDoc comment for the getter/setter
                 * methods "myPrivateGetterSetter".
                 * This comment will not be included in the generated AsDoc output
                 * @private
                 */
                public function get myPrivateGetterSetter():String { return "abc123" };

                /**
                 * @private
                 */
                public function set myPrivateGetterSetter(value:String):void {};

        }
    }
```

Metadata

ASDoc commenting and documentation is not limited only to functions and variables. You can use ASDoc to document metadata regarding your classes and components. You can use this approach to document the various effects, events, and styles that are exposed publicly on your components. These comments should be used to describe what the metadata is used for. For events, it should describe what the event represents and what triggers that event. For effects, it should describe what that effect is used for. For styles, the comment should describe what the style is used for and what type of value it should expect.

Additionally, any comments on bindable properties or functions will automatically be annotated with the phrase "This property can be used as the source for data binding" in the generated output.

```
    package asdocExamples
    {
        import mx.controls.Button;

        /**
         * This is the comment for the myEffect Effect metadata.
         */
        [Effect (name="myEffect")]

        /**
         * This is the comment for the myEvent Event metadata.
         * @eventType flash.events.Event
         */
        [Event (name="myEvent", type="flash.events.Event")]
```

```
/**
 * This is the comment for the myStyle Style metadata.
 */
[Style (name="myStyle")]

/**
 * This is the comment for the AsDocMetadataExample class, which extends
 * from Button.
 */
public class AsDocMetadataExample extends Button
{
    /**
     * This is the comment for the myBindableVar boolean variable.
     */
    [Bindable]
    public var myBindableVar : Boolean = false;
}
}
```

Formatting with HTML

ASDoc comments are not limited to plain text input. You can add rich formatting or images to your generated documentation using standard HTML markup in your ASDoc comments. This applies to both comments and descriptions associated with ASDoc tags.

When using HTML within ASDoc comments, it is important to remember two things. First, the HTML must be treated as valid XML markup. All opening tags require closing tags. The phrase `<b>This is bold` will fail because there is no closing `</b>` tag. The other important feature to keep in mind is that special characters must be HTML-encoded. Opening brackets (<) should be embedded as `&lt;` and closing brackets (>) should be shown as `&gt;`. ASCII characters can be referenced by their encoded ASCII value. For instance, the copyright symbol can be embedded as `&#169;`.

```
package asdocExamples
{
    import mx.controls.Button;

    /**
     * <em>This</em> is the comment for the <b>AsDocHTMLExample</b>
     * <u>class</u>, which extends from Button.
     * <p><em>This</em> is inside of a <code>&lt;p&gt;</code> tag</p>
     */
    public class AsDocHTMLExample extends Button
    {
        /**
         * <em>This</em> is the comment for the
         * <b>AsDocHTMLExample</b> constructor.
         */
        public function AsDocHTMLExample()
        {
            super();
        }
```

```
/**
 * <em>This</em> is the comment for myHTMLFunction() method,
 * which includes HTML formatting.
 *
 * @param value1 Is a string value.
 * @param value2 Is a number value.
 *
 * @return This will always return <code>true</code>;
 */
public function myHTMLFunction( value1 : String, value2 : Number ) : Boolean
{
    return true;
}
}
}
```

Referencing Outside Elements

You can also include external references in the generated documentation, under a "See Also" section using the @see tag. You would use the @see tag to refer to related information that is found in another location. For example, if you are discussing handling of objects in an array collection, you may want to include a reference to the ArrayCollection documentation. Likewise, you can provide a link to any URL that would contain a point of reference that will aid in the quality of your documentation.

These external references will be provided in addition to the ASDoc comment; they will not replace it.

```
package asdocExamples
{
    import mx.controls.Button;

    /**
     * This is the comment for the AsDocSeeExample class,
     * which extends from Button.
     */
    public class AsDocSeeExample extends Button
    {
        /**
         * This is the comment for the AsDocSeeExample constructor.
         * This comment utilizes the "@see"
         * tag to reference external content
         *
         * @see This is simple text
         * @see http://www.wrox.com
         * @see AsDocClassExample
         */
        public function AsDocSeeExample()
        {
            super();
        }
    }
}
```

Excluding Classes from Generated Output

Just as you can exclude functions or variables from the generated HTML output, you can also exclude entire classes from the generated documentation. Including the @private tag in the class-level ASDoc comment will instruct the ASDoc tool to ignore that class completely. It will not be included in the reference documentation, or generated indices of the code.

```
package asdocExamples
{
    import mx.controls.Button;

    /**
     * This is the comment for the AsDocHiddenClassExample
     * class, which extends from Button.
     * This class is marked "@private", so it will not
     * be included in the generated AsDoc output.
     * @private
     */
    public class AsDocHiddenClassExample extends Button
    {
        /**
         * This is the comment for the AsDocHiddenClassExample constructor.
         */
        public function AsDocHiddenClassExample()
        {
            super();
        }
    }
}
```

Applying Custom Templates

The ASDoc tool also allows you to apply custom templates to the generated HTML documentation. The easiest way to get started with custom templates is to copy the existing template provided with the ASDoc tool into another directory and begin customizing it. The existing templates can be found in the Flex SDK directory, under asdoc\templates directory. Editing the templates requires a knowledge of HTML and CSS as it applies to HTML documents.

To apply a custom template, you simply need to add a command-line argument when invoking the ASDoc tool. The following command line input will instruct the ASDoc tool to generate the same documentation as our previous example; however, it will apply the template located in the directory C:\ProFlex3 - 68 - 01 AsDoc\src\customTemplate. This template has been updated to include the Wrox logo from www.wrox.com (refer to Figure 68-1).

```
asdoc
-source-path "C:\ProFlex3 - 68 - 01 AsDoc\src"
-doc-classes main
-templates-path "C:\ProFlex3 - 68 - 01 AsDoc\src\customTemplate"
```

Summary

As you can see, the Adobe Flex framework provides you with everything necessary to automatically generate documentation for your applications, code libraries, or public APIs. The ASDoc tool provides the capability that you need to generate your API, and all that is required on the developer's end is to diligently maintain descriptive and relevant comments in their code.

In the next chapter, we will explore the deployment and distribution of desktop applications using Adobe AIR.

Desktop Deployment with AIR

With the long hours of hard work coding the application behind you, it's time to package it up as an AIR file and deliver it to end users. Before distributing an application, though, it'll need to be code signed with a certificate issued by a security authority, like VeriSign or Thawte. After acquiring a certificate, the AIR package will be code signed, allowing customers to verify who made and packaged the application. This is important because Adobe AIR applications execute with the same user privileges as native applications, allowing local filesystem access, including full file manipulation support, network connectivity, bitmap rendering, local data access, and so forth.

After code signing the AIR package, it can then be distributed to end users via a few different methods:

❏ By providing a link to download the AIR file package via a link on the Internet.

❏ By creating a Web-based installation with Adobe's AIR badge with one-click install, which will verify that the AIR runtime is installed on the user's machine and install your application, all from within a web page.

❏ By redistributing Adobe AIR runtime and the AIR application with a silent installation. This is useful for enterprise distribution where end users shouldn't be prompted with end-user license agreements (EULAs) and installation wizards.

Let's get started by signing an AIR Application code signing.

Code Signing and Certificates

Code signing an AIR application builds end-user confidence that what they're installing was created by a reputable software vendor, and that the package that was signed by the software vendor hasn't been tampered with during its life on the Internet. Users installing your application want to trust that you aren't going to do bad things to their machines. Since AIR accesses local files (for example, deleting all your images from last summer's family vacation, or grabbing all your QuickBooks data files and sending them out over the Internet to a nefarious organization in some unknown land) it's important for your users to feel secure running your software on their computer. By signing an AIR application with a certificate issued by a trusted authority, like VeriSign or Thwate, you assure users that the application they are installing was made by you (hopefully a reliable publisher) and hasn't been tampered with since you signed it (that third-party websites haven't been injecting evil bits into your application and distributing it on your behalf).

Users can't trust that the identity of the party who created the software they're installing is legitimate, but they can trust a certificate authority, who issued the certificate used to sign the application, to vouch that the code signer is who they claim they are. Certificate authorities are third-party organizations that will perform due diligence on anyone requesting a certificate to sign their AIR applications. As a result, there are some requirements that must be met by developers requesting certificates. These requirements are hard documents, such as articles of incorporation and tax forms, and because of this, acquiring a certificate isn't just a 10-minute task.

And, while trusted software vendors can still do bad things to your files and data, a signed application does promote a trail to recourse by end users of code-signed software. The certificate authority can revoke issued certificates.

Let's get started with code signing by acquiring a certificate.

Acquiring a Certificate

Code signing an AIR application requires using any class-3, high assurance certificate provided by any certificate authority (CA). VeriSign and Thawte are two of the more popular, and both are trusted by default (as root certificates) by the operating system on most end users' machines (OS X or Windows). Adobe AIR uses the native operating systems's keystore, which holds and manages these trusted certificates, and as a result, a certificate signed by VeriSign or Thawte will be trusted by Adobe AIR.

> *Your organization may already have a certificate for code signing applications. To use an existing certificate, you must get both the private key and the certificate into the right format: either a .P12 or .PFX file. Java has some command-line tools for creating the .P12 files. On Microsoft platforms, PFX is your goal, and you can use Microsoft's pvkimport tool to import a certificate into the windows keystore, and then, using Internet Explorer, export it as a PFX file. Using these tools is beyond the scope of this book, and if you already have a certificate, chances are you're already familiar with them.*

While it's possible to get a code-signing certificate from various sources, we're going to only discuss acquiring one from Thawte here. This is because they've worked with Adobe to optimize the process of procuring a certificate, and the directions are pretty simple, using the free cross-platform Firefox web browser, which provides support for both OS X and Windows.

Purchasing a Certificate from Thawte

The process of purchasing a certificate takes longer than you might think. So, don't wait until the night before you want to release your application. Plan ahead, with the knowledge that it might take a week to get a certificate. To purchase a certificate, perform the following steps:

1. Open Mozilla Firefox and navigate to www.thawte.com.

2. Find their product Adobe AIR Developer Certificates. Websites change often, but as of this writing you can navigate from Thawte's home page to Products ⇨ Code Signing Certificates ⇨ Click Here to Buy. A page listing several different code-signing certificates types should appear.

3. Select the Adobe AIR Developer Certificate, and then press Next.

4. Select either a one-year or two-year certificate. At the time of this writing, the default pricing is $299 for one year, and $549 for two years.

5. Fill out the rest of the required information, including all the proper contact and organizational information. This will all be validated by Thawte during an identity verification process that might require additional information. Be prepared to fax them information like corporate tax identity, articles of incorporation, VAT certificates, partnership papers, fictitious name certificates, and the like. This verification process can take some time.

6. Now you must wait for Thawte to finish the identity verification process. They'll contact you via email with a link to log back onto the Thwate website. It's important that you navigate back to the Thwate link with Firefox, as the certificate will then be installed in your Firefox keystore.

Now that you have a certificate, it's time to get it into a format usable by the AIR tools for code signing.

Personal code-signing certificates for AIR applications have recently been made available by Chosen Security. Personal certificates will allow individuals without a company shell to code sign their applications. Visit Chosen Security's website for more information: `http://chosensecurity.com/products/tc_publisher_id_adobe_air.htm`.

Exporting the Thawte Certificate from Firefox

To convert the certificate you just purchased from Thawte, open Firefox and perform the following steps:

1. Navigate to Tools ➪ Options ➪ Advanced.

2. Select the Encryption tab, as shown in Figure 69-1.

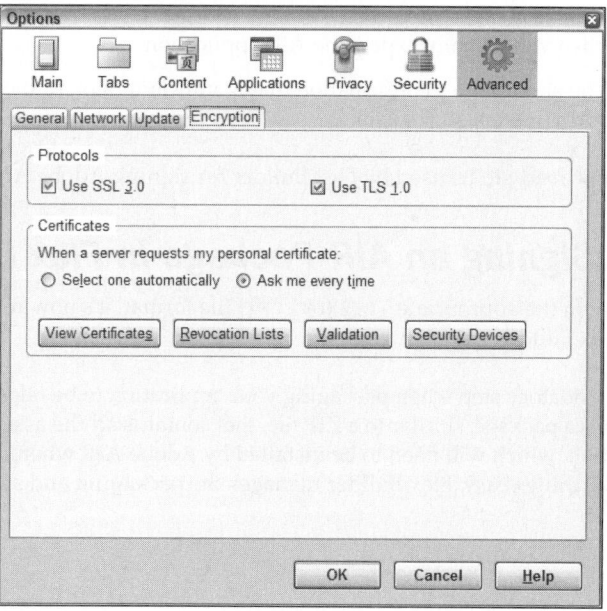

Figure 69-1

3. Click the View Certificates button to bring up the Certificate Manager window (see Figure 69-2).

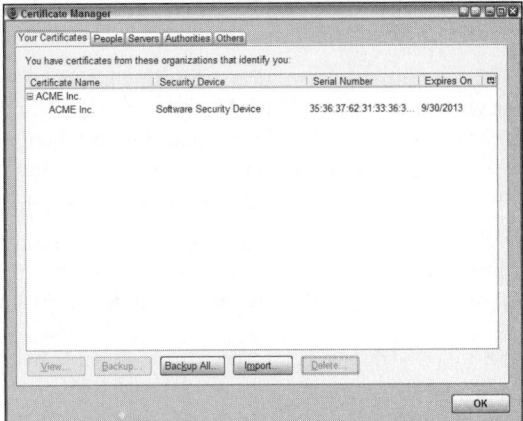

Figure 69-2

4. In the Your Certificates tab, select the certificate that you just purchased from Thawte (in this case, the ACME INC. certificate). Then click the Backup button to export the certificate from the Firefox keystore. Firefox will save your certificate and private key in a .P12 file (PKCS12 format) that is supported by the Adobe AIR code-signing tools, whether you're using the ADT.exe command-line tool or the Flex Builder 3 Export Wizard.

5. Save the .P12 file somewhere logical, such as the application directory. In this case, it's saved in the Chapter 69 source code as acme_cert.P12.

6. You'll be asked to create a password for the certificate. Don't forget it, as Flex Builder will ask you for it when you actually export the AIR application.

7. Click OK. You should see a confirmation dialog informing you of the successful backup of the certificate and private key. Shazam!

Your certificate is now ready to be used by Flex Builder for signing Adobe AIR applications.

Creating and Signing an AIR Package in Flex Builder

With your certificate in the appropriate .P12 (or .PFX) file format, it's now ready to sign an AIR application from within Flex Builder.

Code signing is a mandatory step when packaging your application to be released as an AIR application. An AIR application is a package, similar to a ZIP file, that contains all the assets, including the main SWF file of your application, which will need to be installed by Adobe AIR when the user goes to install your application. To make things easy, Flex Builder manages the packaging and signing of your application.

To export and sign an application, perform the following steps:

1.   In the Flex Builder menu, select Project ⇨ Export Release Build to bring up the dialog in Figure 69-3.

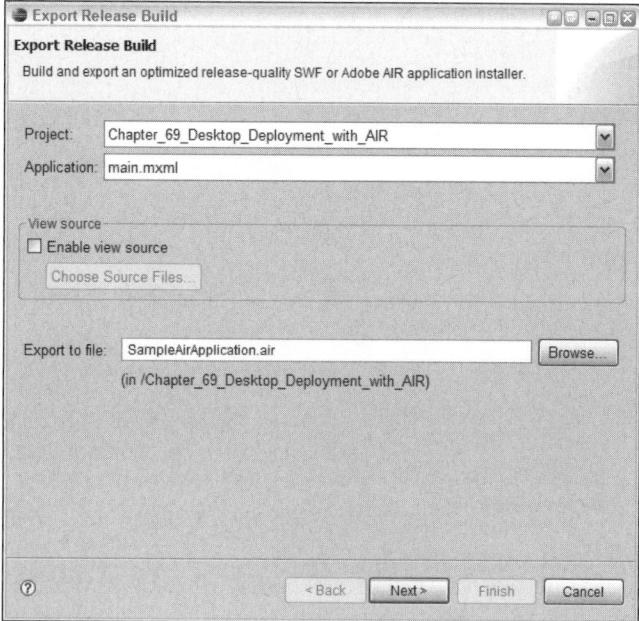

Figure 69-3

2.   If more than one Flex Builder project is open, select the project you want to export and the application you're exporting. Give your AIR application distribution file an appropriate name; in Figure 69-3 we named it `SampleAirApplication.air`. Click Next.

3.   With the Digital Signature window open (see Figure 69-4), it's time to browse to the saved `acme_cert.P12` file that you exported from Firefox. Browse to find the `acme_cert.P12` file.

4.   Enter the password you created in step 6 of the previous section for the certificate file. Optionally, you can check the Remember Password for This Session box, and every time you run Export Release Build during this Flex Builder session, you won't have to reenter the password (but if you reboot or close Flex Builder, you'll have to reenter the password). Also, if you don't want to sign the AIR file at the same time you're packaging everything, there's the option to Export an intermediate AIRI file that will be signed later. An AIRI file is an unsigned distribution package that can be signed later and converted into an appropriate AIR file for distribution. This might be useful in an organization where a special department is in charge of managing certificates.

5.   Next, select the files to include in the package, and click Finish. Files to include could be images, SQLite databases, custom XML files containing custom application settings, or any other data file your application expects for runtime execution.

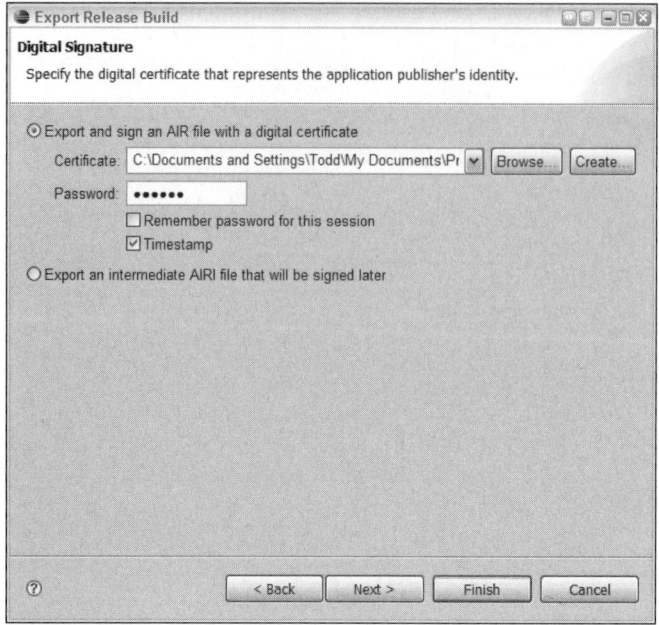

Figure 69-4

That's it! You've successfully created a signed AIR package that's ready for deployment. The following sections will discuss some deployment scenarios, but first let's discuss developer certificates.

Code Signing with a Developer Certificate

The preceding process to procure a valid certificate and sign an Adobe AIR application takes time and money. There's an alternative to this, though, called *self-signed certificates* (sometimes called *developer certificates*). Using one allows you to meet the AIR installer requirements for signing so that the AIR installer can install the application. However, when users of your application go to install the application, they'll be prompted with a big red caution screen, as shown in Figure 69-5.

The red warning and the publisher being identified as UNKNOWN should deter the end user from installing the application. Most users should be scared of installing such applications; however, whether or not to install it is left up to their judgment. They could be a regular customer, and you could be giving them a beta application that you haven't gotten around to signing yet.

Despite the warnings to end users, the developer certificate provides a way for open-source projects and individuals to distribute their applications without the cost of proper code signing. (How many people have installed beta Windows drivers from known companies that weren't signed?) Remember, the main point of signing applications is to really inform the user who's distributing the application; it does nothing to guarantee that the application won't harm their computer.

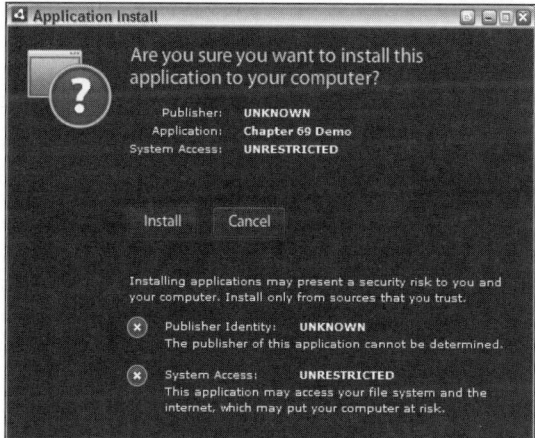

Figure 69-5

Creating a self-signed a certificate with Flex Builder is very simple. When you go to Export your AIR application, on the Digital Signature screen (see Figure 69-4), instead of browsing for the existing certificate, click the Create button. This will bring up the Create Self-Signed Digital Certificate window, as shown in Figure 69-6.

Fill out the publisher name and company name, give it a password, and then save the file somewhere convenient. None of the names here will be displayed to the users when they install the AIR application; they'll just see UNKNOWN as the publisher, since this isn't a valid, secured certificate.

That's it! You're ready to finish exporting your AIR application and test the installation on various operating systems.

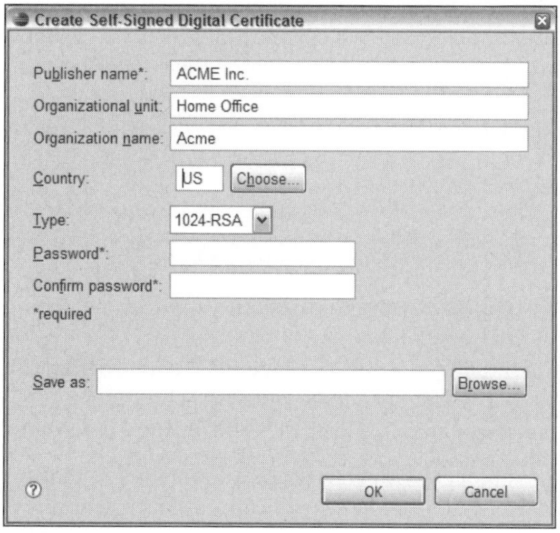

Figure 69-6

Packaging and Signing AIR Applications with the Command Line

We showed you how to package and sign AIR applications from within Flex Builder previously. The AIR SDK includes command-line tools to compile (mxmlc), and package and code sign (adt), an AIR application. These tools are useful if you're using a build server that controls the building and publishing of your applications, or if you prefer to code applications with your favorite text editor.

The first thing you'll need to do is acquire a certificate, whether from Thawte or a developer self-signed certificate, as shown previously. Although you can create a certificate from the command line (look up the adt -certificate option), we're only going to discuss signing and packaging here.

Next, make sure that /Flex SDK/bin is in the system path, so that the adt tool can be found when executing the following commands from the Windows command line or OS X shell. Usually, the Flex SDK is installed in a subdirectory of the main Flex Builder installation. Finally, in a command shell, execute the following command:

```
adt -package -storetype pkcs12 -keystore acme_cert.p12 -storepass 111111
        SampleAirApplication.air bin-debug/main-app.xml -C bin-debug main.swf
```

This executes the adt program, which on Windows is a .bat file, or a shell script on OS X that calls the native Java .jar file (called, surprise, surprise: adt.jar). The package command is in charge of packaging and signing the AIR file. There are other options available for the adt program, such as certificate (which creates a developer certificate) and prepare (which creates an unsigned AIRI package that must still signed — by the authorized person/group at your company — before distributing the application). Next, pass in information about the certificate, including the type of store, the certificate file, and the password that's protecting the certificate file. Next, tell adt the name of the packaged AIR file (SampleAirApplication.air, in this case) and the application descriptor (main-app.xml). The -C switch lets you change the current working directory so that you don't have to include more path information about the following assets that you want to include in the AIR package. Here, we've switched into the bin-debug directory, where our main SWF file resides. Finally, list any assets separated by white space. Our simple project only contains the main.swf file.

Executing this command creates the SampleAirApplication.air file, which is ready for distribution.

Distributing AIR Applications

Adobe AIR provides a few different ways to distribute applications to end users.

- ❑ End users can download your AIR package off the Internet and install it. The Adobe AIR runtime will have to be already installed on their machine, so most likely you'll link to the Adobe website where the user can download the AIR runtime before installing your AIR application.

- ❑ You can create a web page with an AIR installation badge that supports one-click installation of both the AIR runtime and your AIR application. This method is the easiest for end users, and also provides simple mechanisms for updating the application in the future.

❑   Silent installation of the AIR runtime and your application. This will require applying for a redistribution agreement from Adobe. But the benefits are for those who deploy applications in an enterprise environment will be able to do so silently, without EULA pop-ups, installation directory selection wizards, and so forth.

Let's delve deeper into the AIR badge installer.

Web Page Badge Installation

One of the exciting distribution methods of AIR applications is a one-click install from a web page. The Adobe AIR Install Badge SDK makes it really easy to embed a customizable installation experience on your website for AIR applications, allowing users to install your application from a web page, or on subsequent visits, launch the application.

To view examples of one-click AIR installation in action, visit the Adobe AIR Marketplace, at `www.adobe.com/cfusion/exchange/index.cfm?event=productHome&exc=24&loc=en_us`.

> *After you've completed your AIR application, get involved in releasing it at the Adobe Marketplace. It's a great way to promote your application.*

The AIR install badge installation will detect whether the user's machine has the AIR runtime installed. If the AIR runtime isn't installed, the AIR install badge will download the AIR runtime from Adobe's site and install it. Then it'll install your AIR application. This greatly simplifies the need for end users of your application to potentially download the AIR runtime separately.

The easiest way to get started with Web-based install is to download the AIR Install Badge SDK from Adobe (`www.adobe.com/devnet/air/articles/badge_for_air.html`).

> *Adobe has released a tool to simplify creating web page installs of AIR applications called Badger. Badger itself is an AIR application. More information, including the install, can be found at `www.adobe.com/devnet/air/articles/badger_for_air_apps.html`.*

The Flex SDK does include another sample badge installation process in the SDK/samples/badge folder to get you started with one-click badge install, but I find the AIR Install Badge SDK installer, which uses the SWFObject (to ensure the proper version of the Flash Player is installed on the user's machine) is the superior method for enabling one-click install. It provides all the necessary code for updating the end user's machine to the appropriate version of the Flash Player that will support the AIR one-click installation process (which is version 9.0.115). And it's simple and flexible to customize.

Using the Web Badge SDK

After downloading the AIR Install Badge SDK, unzip it to a folder. Included in the folder are various HTML, JavaScript, and SWF files. The `AIRInstallBadge.fla` and `AIRInstallBadge.as` files are for advanced use. Read the docs for other customizations that you might want to do. But the core of what we're going to do is copy some HTML code from the sample into a demo application, and then move all the appropriate files to a web server, modifying some JavaScript along the way.

Customizing the Installation

To use the AIR badge, you need to customize it for your application and then upload the files to the web server deploying the application.

1. Create an HTML file with the layout of your website. In the sample code, it's called `air_install_demo.html`.

2. Copy the JavaScript code from the `EmbedDemo.html` file that's included in the SDK. The code you copy should go into the target location of your web page. See both the `EmbedDemo.html` file and the `air_install_demo.html` file to see what code was copied over.

3. Make sure to include the JavaScript `include` for SWFObject code. This is important because all the JavaScript code relies on the included functionality that `swfobject.js` provides. Place the following script `include` directive in the HTML head:

    ```
    <script type="text/javascript" src="swfobject.js"></script>
    ```

4. Modify the JavaScript code in `air_install_demo.html` for the AIR application. The following properties must be customized.

    First, set the appropriate value for `airversion`. Setting this will ensure that the appropriate version of the AIR runtime is installed on the end user's machine.

    ```
    so.addVariable("airversion", "1.5");
    ```

    Next, set the `appname` parameter. This is the name of the application as it's displayed in the AIR installer badge. In our application, it's Sample AIR Application.

    ```
    so.addVariable("appname", "Sample AIR Application");
    ```

    Finally, and this is the most important part, set the URL. It must be fully qualified to point at the AIR package (`SampleAirApplication.air`) that was built above.

    ```
    so.addVariable("appurl", "http://www.yourwebsite.com/SampleAirApplication.air");
    ```

    Optionally, you can adjust the visual settings of the AIR installer, customizing it to promote your brand. The background image (`imageurl`), title color (`titlecolor`), button text (`buttonlabelcolor`), and application name color (`appnamecolor`) can all be tweaked. The following properties will affect the visual design of the install badge. There are a number of other options, too, so be sure to read the `Getting Started Guide.txt` file included with the SDK.

    ```
    so.addVariable("imageurl", "demoImage.jpg");
    so.addVariable("titlecolor", "#00AAFF");
    so.addVariable("buttonlabelcolor", "#00AAFF");
    so.addVariable("appnamecolor", "#00AAFF");
    ```

5. Upload all the files to a web server. Make sure that you copy the `AIRInstallBadge.swf`, `swfobject.js`, `expressinstall.swf`, `air_install_demo.html`, and `SampleAIR Application.air` files to an accessible folder on your web server.

6. Navigate to the URL where `air_install_demo.html` is located, and test your install. Figure 69-7 shows what the AIR Badge Installer looks like with these default settings.

Figure 69-7

That's all there is to it. When you have this working, and if you want users to be able to single-click launch your application from the web page, there are a couple of more steps, as described in the next section.

If there's the possibility that your users might be running an older version of the Flash Player — such as versions 6, 7, or 8 — make sure to upload the `expressinstall.swf` *to the installation directory on your web server and add the following JavaScript code to the* `air_install_demo.html` *file:* `so.useExpressInstall('expressinstall.swf');`. *This will make sure that the user's system is upgraded to the proper version of Flash (9,0,115,0) that is required for this seamless install.*

Launching Installed Applications from a Web Page

The AIR badge install also provides *Launch Now* functionality. For users with both the AIR runtime and the particular AIR application already installed, the AIR install badge will be a one-click launcher for starting the application. This will be very useful for intranet scenarios where you want to launch common tools from a portal control page.

In order to use Launch Now functionality, there are a few additional steps:

1. Edit the AIR application descriptor file. For the sample code, this is the `main-app.xml` located in the `src` directory of the project. Uncomment the `<allowBrowserInvocation>` node, and set it to `true`, as in the following code snippet:

```
<allowBrowserInvocation>true</allowBrowserInvocation>
```

2. Set the `appid` parameter in the JavaScript to match that of the `main-app.xml` descriptor file of the chapter. The JavaScript parameter code will look like this:

```
so.addVariable("appid", "Chapter-69-Desktop-Deployment-with-AIR");
```

3. Set the `pubid` in the JavaScript. This one's a bit tricky, because it's a hexadecimal string that's generated by the AIR runtime when the application was first installed to the user's machine. To get the `pubid`, you'll have to first package, including signing the AIR application, via Flex Builder's Project ⇨ Export Release Build, as shown previously, and then install the application on your local machine. The publisher identifier is a computed hash based on a lot of parameters from the certificate used to sign the application. All AIR applications signed with the same certificate will have the same publisher identifiers.

To find the publisher ID, just run the AIR application (after it has been installed through the AIR installer, not just running in the Flex Builder debugger). Then print out the `nativeApplication` `.publisherID` property.

```
Trace(NativeApplication.nativeApplication.publisherID);
```

The preceding code returns:

```
EDA4CEA82214C6831B38ABC925E4878B16C0B02E.1
```

This is your publisher identifier for every application you sign with the certificate created. Just take that identifier and assign it to the JavaScript `pubid` parameter:

```
so.addVariable("pubid", "EDA4CEA82214C6831B38ABC925E4878B16C0B02E.1");
```

Now, when a user returns to the web page with the AIR installer badge configured for that particular AIR application, and if the publisher ID and version number match, instead of being prompted to install, they'll see the badge in Launch Now mode that will launch the application when clicked, as shown in Figure 69-8.

Figure 69-8

Silent Installations

Web-based installation isn't for everyone. The need might arise to distribute an AIR application via a CD-ROM, or rolled out to thousands of users in an enterprise. For these optional scenarios, there's a redistribution license that offers an optional silent installation of both the AIR runtime and your AIR application.

A silent installation will enable the AIR runtime to be installed on end users' machines without the need for them to click through EULAs and prompts. Redistribution of the AIR runtime allows you to include it on a CD-ROM with your application. However, Adobe has rules on what you can do with this, so they require you to sign a redistribution agreement. With this distribution agreement, you won't be allowed to repackage the AIR runtime files for a customized installation experience; you'll be limited to either the silent installation or having users manually install the AIR runtime from a CD-ROM or your website.

Applying to redistribute the AIR runtime will involve a few minutes of paperwork. More information can be found at www.adobe.com/products/air/runtime_distribution1.html.

After you sign the redistribution agreement, Adobe will send you instructions on how to perform a silent installation of the AIR runtime and your AIR application. Silent installation is a necessity of corporate enterprise application deployment, and Adobe has an integrated solution to work with a variety of distribution methods.

Updating AIR Applications

After your application has been released, AIR provides a simple upgrade path for releasing new versions of the application. Whether your users are downloading the raw AIR file, or using the badge install process, they'll be prompted to replace the existing version. All this is provided without any application developer coding, only some tweaking of properties.

A few things you must change, though. For our sample application, we're going to upgrade from 1.0.3 to 1.0.4.

1. First, update the version number in the application descriptor file (main-app.xml). In our sample application, we increment:

```
<version>1.0.3</version>
```

to:

```
<version>1.0.4</version>
```

If all you're doing is having your users download the AIR file manually, then you are done. No need to perform steps 2 and 3 to update the AIR install badge on a web page. They will, however, see the same upgrade installation window as shown in Figure 69-10 when they run the AIR file on their local machine with a previous version of the application installed.

2. Next, if using the badge installer, update the JavaScript code to this new version. Change 1.0.3 to 1.0.4, so that it looks like this:

```
so.addVariable("appversion", "1.0.4");
```

3. Upload the new AIR package and HTML page to the website. When your user returns, the install badge will ask them if they want to upgrade, as shown in Figure 69-9.

Figure 69-9

When a user chooses to perform the upgrade, the AIR installer will display the current version of the AIR application, and the new version that will be installed. Figure 69-10 shows the upgrade that's about to occur from 1.0.3 to 1.0.4, asking the user if they want to replace the application.

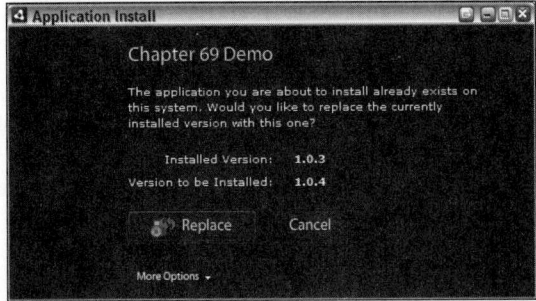

Figure 69-10

That's how simple it is. Just change a few version numbers, rebuild the application, and upload it to the website — all of which can be automated in a build process.

Signed AIR applications, whether they have a self-signed or official certificate for your company, can only be updated with a version of your application signed with the exact same certificate. Don't expect to sign with a developer certificate for betas and then release the application as version 1.0 signed with a production-ready certificate using AIR's automatic updating. Going this route will require users to uninstall the old version of application and then install a new version of application signed with the production certificate. After all, changing certificates changes the publisher's identity, on which this update process is dependent. However, this probably isn't a big deal, since end users are fairly used to uninstalling beta versions of demo software.

Summary

There was a lot of procedural material covered in this chapter. First, you'll have to code sign the application, whether with a self-signed or code-signing certificate purchased from a certificate authority. Remember, procuring a certificate from a CA will take some time, so schedule accordingly. Then you'll have to decide on a distribution method, whether it's one-click over the web or silently through your enterprise distribution tools, such as Microsoft SMS or IBM Tivoli. Getting desktop applications installed to an end user's machine has never been easier.

In the next chapter, we'll look at a strategy for creating a Flex application that can run both in a web browser or be distributed to the desktop as an AIR application, all from the same codebase.

70

Dual Deployment
for Flex and AIR

By now, you've got a handle on developing Flex applications for rich Internet applications (RIAs). You've also learned how the AIR runtime facilitates the creation of desktop applications. Now you might be thinking, how do I build an application from the same codebase targeting both the browser and the desktop? If so, this chapter is for you.

By its nature, AIR contains all the FLEX APIs, plus the AIR-specific APIs. Projects compiled for Web-based distribution don't include the AIR APIs, so if you try to compile an AIR project for the Web, you'll receive "Type was not found" compile errors. And if you're using Flex Builder, you won't even be able to import any of the AIR APIs because the `airglobal.swc` and `airframework.swc` files aren't included as build path libraries for Flex projects targeting the Web.

This chapter will show two different methods of writing software for both the Web and desktop. The first method will use a design-by-interface approach, combined with multiple Flex Builder projects to create software that can be run inside the web browser as a Flex application or on the desktop with AIR. The second method is the use of the new Flex compiler directives, which will be more of a chainsaw approach to coding but won't require the upfront effort that the design-by-interface approach requires.

Coding by Interface

The first solution to create both AIR and Flex applications involves creating a few projects in Flex Builder. One project will contain the Flex-based web application, one the AIR-based desktop application, and the final project will contain all the common application code, including the visual layout as an MXML component. The solution works by having the main application code call functionality that's exposed through a common interface that has very specific implementations for both the Flex and AIR version of the project. This allows the main application to be abstracted out from dependent APIs. Then, when the main application actually makes a call to the interface, either the Flex or AIR version returns the appropriate implementation of the function that is dependent on specific APIs compiled into the parent application.

Figure 70-1 shows a UML diagram of this strategy. It is fine not to understand exactly what's going on right now, as it'll all be explained as the chapter goes on. Use this as a point of reference as we start discussing the different elements needed. Don't worry — by the end of the chapter you'll understand it all.

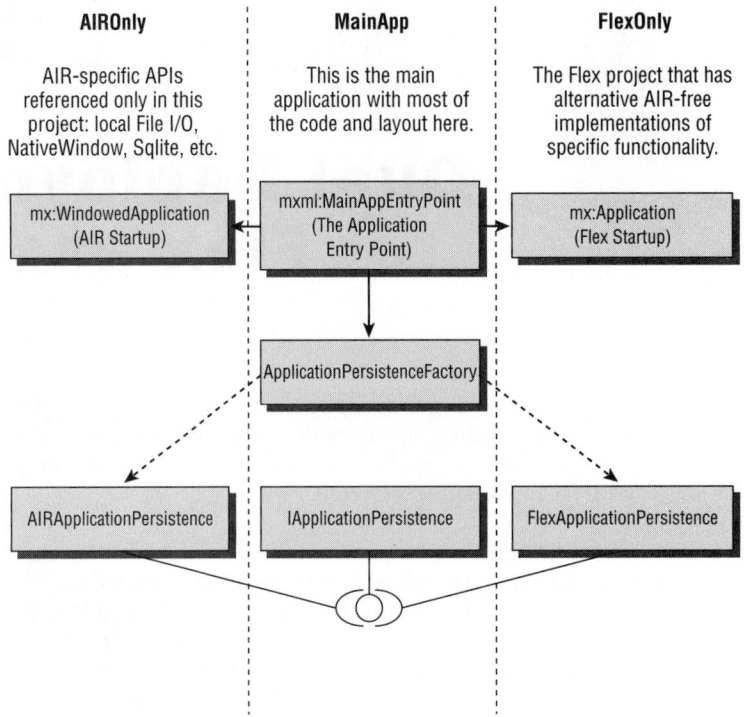

Figure 70-1

As you can see, there are three projects: `AIROnly`, `FlexOnly`, and `MainApp`. The `AIROnly` and `FlexOnly` projects link to the `MainApp` via a shared code path in Flex Builder. Think of the `AIRonly` and `FlexOnly` applications as containers (shells) that hold the `MainApp` and that compile for their specific targeted runtimes (Flex for the Web, AIR for the desktop).

The `MainApp` project contains the `MainAppEntryPoint.mxml` MXML component, which is really where all the action of the main application is. Think of this as the application itself. This component is then added to either the Flex-based `mx:Application` or the AIR-based `mx:WindowedApplication` declarations.

Next, the user will run the `AIROnly` or `FlexOnly` version of the application. They'll then execute a method in the `MainApp` that's been defined on an interface (`IApplicationPersistence`) that is shared and implemented in both the `FlexOnly` and `AIROnly` as `FlexApplicationPersistence` and `AIRApplicationPersistence`, respectively. For example, they press a button in the `MainApp`'s `MainAppEntryPoint` that calls `saveFile()`, which has different implementations for the Flex and AIR versions of the application. In AIR, `saveFile()` will bring up the file browser and allow the user to save the data locally. In Flex, this isn't possible, as the `flash.filesystem.File` API isn't accessible, so the user will need to either save the data to the server or proxy the file to the server, and then save it to their computer using traditional web download functionality. Thus, there is similar functionality but different implementations.

You might be wondering how `MainApp` knows which version of the interface to use. That's where the `ApplicationPersistenceFactory` comes into play. To get the specific implementation, you must use the `ApplicationPersistenceFactory`, which knows whether it's running in the AIR or Flex application. It's totally self-aware and returns an instance of the `IApplicationPersistence` interface with the appropriate implementation for either the Flex or AIR application. During compilation, only the `AIROnly` version will include the AIR implementation, and the `FlexOnly` application will include the Flex implementation.

The following is a quick example of what code looks like when the `MainApp` calls functionality has been abstracted out:

```
var appPersist:IApplicationPersistence;
appPersist = ApplicationPersistenceFactory.getInstance();
appPersist.saveFile();
```

First, declare the `IApplicationPersistence` interface. Second, get an instance of the interface (which will either be the `AIRApplicationPersistence` or `FlexApplicationPersistence`). Finally, call the `saveFile()` method, which has specific AIR or Flex implementation.

That's it for how we're going to be abstracting out functionality that will enable us to compile code into the application for both Flex and AIR distribution from the same codebase.

Before we start implementing this solution, let's look at some pros and cons.

Pros

❑   Provides better controlled design, with well-defined interfaces for abstracted functionality that needs different implementations for Web and desktop.

❑   There is very little duplicated code, as a majority of the application is created in a common component consumed by both the AIR and Flex projects.

❑   Provides hooks for selective functionality in the desktop versus web implementations. For example, you could have a message in the Flex-based version that tells the user to upgrade to the full desktop version to enable that feature. (The desktop version, of course, has a nominal fee.)

❑   Provides both online and offline versions for your application, and allows users to roam computers and still have access to their application data.

Cons

❑   Requires upfront design effort.

❑   Extra code required by using abstract interface classes is deemed overly complicated by some.

❑   Requires hard-coding of string literals that name dynamic classes to be created. This leads to errors not being recognized at compile time.

Setting Up the Flex Builder Projects

To get started with this, you'll need to create three projects in Flex Builder. Or, if you're looking at the sample code, you can import the three projects: Chapter_70_FlexOnly, Chapter_70_AIROnly and Chapter_70_MainApp.

1. The first project should be a Flex application (Chapter_70_MainApp). This project will need a main MXML component (MainAppEntryPoint.mxml) that's the container of your application. All visual aspects go here, as this is what will be rendered by either the AIR or Flex application. This project should never reference any AIR APIs (it won't be able to), as it's the lowest common denominator of both AIR and Flex functionality.

2. The second project is going to be the AIR application (or Chapter_70_AIROnly). This is the shell application that will eventually be compiled and packaged to a redistributable AIR application for end users to install on their desktop. During project creation (or from the project's properties window, shown in Figure 70-2), you'll be given the opportunity to add an additional source path. You need to browse on your filesystem to where the MainApp's src directory is and add that (see Figure 70-2 for what the path looks like when added).

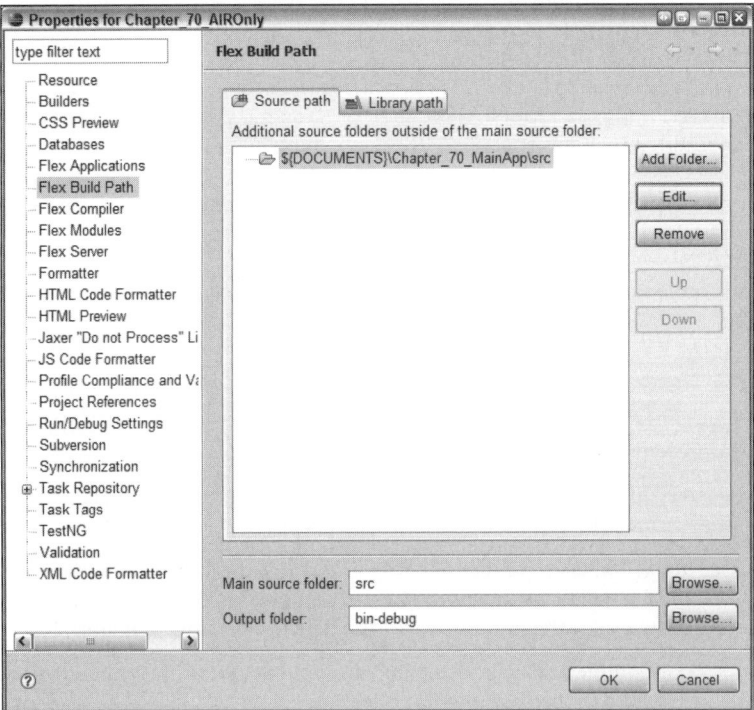

Figure 70-2

3. The third project is the Flex application (or Chapter_70_FlexOnly) that will be distributed via the Web. And just as in step 2, add the shared source path to the MainApp's src directory as an additional source path.

Referencing the MainAppEntryPoint Component

Both the Flex and AIR applications will be using the same user interface that has been defined as an MXML component in the MainApp (see Listing 70-1) which in turn has been shared with both projects. Perform most of your application development in the MainAppEntryPoint component, treating it as you normally would treat coding inside of the mx:Application.

Listing 70-1: The Main Application: MainAppEntryPoint.mxml

```
<?xml version="1.0" encoding="utf-8"?>
<mx:VBox xmlns:mx="http://www.adobe.com/2006/mxml"
.width="800" height="100%"
.borderStyle="solid" borderThickness="2"
.horizontalAlign="center"
.>
.<mx:Script>
    <![CDATA[
.    import mx.controls.Alert;
     [Bindable] public var messageFromContainer:String;

     [Bindable] private var xmlData:XML = …[truncated XML data, see sample code]

    private function saveFile():void
    {
.     try {
        var appPersist:IApplicationPersistence;
        ApplicationPersistenceFactory.getInstance();
        appPersist.saveFile();
.     }
.     catch (e:Error)
      {
        Alert.show("Unknown Error: " + e.message);
.     }
.   }

.   ]]>
 </mx:Script>
.<mx:Label text="The Main Application" fontSize="20" />
.<mx:Label text="{messageFromContainer}" fontSize="18" />
.<mx:Label text="This application is shared in both the FlexOnly and AIROnly
   Projects."
      fontSize="16" />

 <mx:Button click="saveFile()" label="Save File" />

 <mx:Button label="AIR Only Functionality"
    click="ApplicationPersistenceFactory.getInstance().airOnlyFunctionality()"/>

.<mx:ButtonBar>
    <mx:dataProvider>
      <mx:Array>
```

Continued

Listing 70-2: Adding the MainAppEntryPoint to the AIROnly Application *(continued)*

```
        <mx:String>Import Routes</mx:String>
        <mx:String>Find Routes</mx:String>
        <mx:String>Create Route</mx:String>
        <mx:String>Share Route</mx:String>
        </mx:Array>
      </mx:dataProvider>
  </mx:ButtonBar>
.<mx:DataGrid dataProvider="{xmlData.route}" width="100%"/>
</mx:VBox>
```

MainAppEntryPoint.mxml tries to create a simple user interface with some DataGrids binding to some data, a ButtonBar (no actual implementation on the buttons), and then a couple of Buttons (Save File and AIR Only Functionality). These buttons call into the common interface to execute the functionality.

Next, you need to add MainAppEntryPoint to both the AIRApp and FlexApp, as shown in Listing 70-2.

Listing 70-2: Adding the MainAppEntryPoint to the AIROnly Application

```
<?xml version="1.0" encoding="utf-8"?>
<mx:WindowedApplication xmlns:mx="http://www.adobe.com/2006/mxml" layout="absolute"
                        xmlns:local="*">
  <mx:Script>
    <![CDATA[
      private static const includeForCompilation:AIRApplicationPersistence = null;
    ]]>
  </mx:Script>

  <local:MainAppEntryPoint messageFromContainer="MainApp included in AIR
                                        WindowedApplication container." />
</mx:WindowedApplication>
```

As you can see here in the AIRApp's main MXML file, Chapter_70_AIROnly.mxml, the WindowedApplication is the top-level declaration of all AIR applications. First, you import the local namespace. Second, since a shared path that points to the MainApp's directory is included, you can reference the MainAppEntryPoint and add an instance to this AIR application. Now, when the AIR application starts, the MainAppEntryPoint.mxml component will be added as its main display object.

Note that there's some ActionScript code here declaring the includeForCompilation variable of type AIRApplicationPersistence. By default, the compiler will optimize and omit any type that isn't explicitly referenced by the application. Since the concrete implementations of the IApplicationPersistence interface are created dynamically at runtime, there's no way for the Flex compiler to know that they're needed. By including the includeForCompilation declaration, the compiler will compile the AIRApplication Persistence class into the application, where it will later be dynamically created by the Application PersistenceFactory. Without this declaration, there'll be a runtime error that the class (either AIRApplicationPersistence or FlexApplicationPersistence) can't be created.

Not being shown here is adding the MainAppEntryPoint code to the FlexApp. It's exactly the same as adding it to the AIROnly, except that it's being added to the mx:Application's display object hierarchy, instead of AIR's mx:WindowedApplication hierarchy. See the sample code for this chapter for the details.

Working with the IApplicationPersistence Interface

As discussed previously, any piece of functionality that requires an AIR-specific API call (such as saving data to SQLite, local file access, system tray notifications, etc.) needs to be abstracted out so that it isn't compiled into the FlexApp. You abstract out by using an interface. Any specific AIR functionality is *always* called through the IApplicationPersistence interface, which has a specific implementation for the Flex and AIR applications.

In the sample application, the IApplicationPersistence is defined as shown in Listing 70-3.

Listing 70-3: IApplicationPersistence Defined

```
public interface IApplicationPersistence
{
  function saveFile():void;
  function webOnlyFunctionality():void;
  function airOnlyFunctionality():void;
}
```

The IApplicationPersistence is defined in the MainApp since it's the MainApp's code that will always call the common functionality. This interface has a saveFile() method, that has specific implementations created for the AIR and FLEX versions. As previously discussed, the AIR method will save a file locally, and the Flex method will proxy the file through the web server that served up the Flex application for security reasons. Note, there's no actual code implemented, other than the fact that the AIR implementation brings up the File browser dialog box defined in the flash.filesystem.File class. The other functions, webOnlyFunctionality() and airOnlyFunctionality() just demonstrate supporting functionality that's only available in the AIR or Flex versions of the application — useful for building demo applications that have only a subset of the full application's capabilities.

Working with the ApplicationPersistenceFactory

The ApplicationPersistenceFactory is the key code in binding the specific AIR or Flex code to the MainApp's project. It roughly follows the factory object-oriented creational pattern, as it abstracts away the details of creating specific class implementations from the caller. The ApplicationPersistenceFactory is responsible for returning to the caller (always a component in MainApp in this case) an appropriate version of IApplicationPersistence for either the AIR or Flex applications (AIRApplication Persistence or FlexApplicationPersistence, respectively).

The ApplicationPersistenceFactory does this by knowing whether it's being called from an AIR application or a Flex application.

Let's look at the ApplicationPersistenceFactory code:

```
public class ApplicationPersistenceFactory
{
```

Next, we have the class generator method (getInstance()) that is called by the client seeking the appropriate implementation of IApplicationPersistence:

```
static public function getInstance():IApplicationPersistence
{
  var appPersistence:IApplicationPersistence;
  var cls:String = (isAir ? "AIRApplicationPersistence"
                          : "FlexApplicationPersistence");
  var clsToCreate:Object = getClassToCreate(cls);
  appPersistence = new clsToCreate();
  return  appPersistence;
}
```

First, we have some hard-coded string references to class names. Remember earlier when we had to declare variables that referenced the actual AIRApplicationPersistence and FlexApplication Persistence to trick the compiler to include them with the build? Well, these dynamic strings are the reason why. We can't really include the actual class names here, because then the compiler will want to include these classes and we will get compiler errors when certain AIR APIs can't be found while compiling the Flex version of the application. Remember that the MainApp has to remain free from AIR-specific APIs that aren't available to web applications. Next, we need to instantiate the class definition returned by the helper function getClassToCreate(), which will be discussed shortly. Dynamic object creation in Flex is as easy as calling new on an object that's holding a reference to the class definition. Here, we're setting appPersistence = new clsToCreate(), which is creating and assigning either an AIRApplicationPersistence or FlexApplicationPersistence object to appPersistence.

To inspect the runtime environment, we had to call the isAir() function:

```
static public function get isAir():Boolean
{
  return Security.sandboxType.toString() == "application" ? true : false;
}
```

This function does a simple check to see what Security.sandbox type the SWF file is currently being executed in. Here it's compared against the string "applicaton" because Flex applications don't have access to the constant Security.APPLICATION (which equals the "application" string) type, which is defined only in the AIR APIs.

Finally, the call to getClassToCreate() is a lightweight helper function that uses Flex's reflection APIs to search for an object based on a string representation of a class name:

```
static private function getClassToCreate(className:String):Object
{
  var someClass:Object = null;
  someClass = ApplicationDomain.currentDomain.getDefinition(className);
  return someClass;
}
}
```

First, declare a generic object (someClass) type to hold the created object of the className that we pass in. Next, find the definition of the object by calling getDefinition(), which searches all the classes defined in the SWF. This will return the definition of the class that will eventually be created.

When the appropriate class is created and returned from this factory, the MainApp is ready to call the function with an actual implementation behind it. Let's look at the AIRApplicationPersistence class, as shown in Listing 70-4.

Listing 70-4: The AIRApplicationPersistence Implementation of IApplicationPersistence

```
import flash.filesystem.File; //  NOTE: this is an AIR-only API, won't compile
                              //  in FLEX-only application.
import mx.controls.Alert;

public class AIRApplicationPersistence implements IApplicationPersistence
{
  public function saveFile():void
  {
    var f:File = new File();
    f.browseForSave("Set sample to save file as");

    //  There's no functionality to actually save the file here. I'm just
    //  displaying the browseForSave Dialog box that would start the process
    //  of saving a file.

  }

  public function webOnlyFunctionality():void
  {
    //
    //  This example shows throwing an ERROR for unsupported functionality.
    //
    throw new Error("Not Supported.");
  }

  public function airOnlyFunctionality():void
  {
    Alert.show("This is Air Only Functionality");
  }

}
```

The AIRApplicationPersistence.as is defined in AIRApp. The code in this class won't be available to the Flex application. The three functions, all defined in the IApplicationPersistence.as file located in the MainApp, have implementations here.

First, the saveFile() function uses standard AIR libraries to browse the local filesystem to save a file. The browseForSave() function is only available to AIR applications, never to Flex applications. In fact, if Flex tried to import and compile the flash.filesystem class, the fatal error message 1172: Definition flash.filesesystem could not be found would occur.

The webOnlyFunctionality() method only throws an error, informing the calling client that this functionality isn't yet supported. The airOnlyFunctionality() function only displays a message box for the time being. Both throwing the error and displaying alert boxes are useful techniques for stubbing out common interfaces that have a lot of methods declared on them that will take time to implement both the AIR and Flex versions. You can start by returning errors or alert messages that state that the functionality is coming soon.

Note that we're not discussing the implementation of the FlexApplicationPersistence because it's almost identical to AIRApplicationPersistence, except that it needs an alternative implementation for saveFile(). View the sample code for more information.

This completes the detailed explanation of the interface separation of specific functionality for both the AIR and Flex applications. Using this technique, you can decouple AIR-specific functionality into controlled libraries so that you can compile and release multiple versions of your application for both the Web and desktop environments.

Using Conditional Compilation

Another technique for including/excluding AIR functionality involves using conditional compilation. Anyone coming from a C/C++ background will be familiar with the #IFDEF and #DEFINE pre-processor directives that are used to conditionally include sections of code that are passed to the compiler for compilation. Flex 3 supports similar conditional compilation facilities.

Pros

- ❏ Requires simpler setup than the interface-based coding method, as there are only two projects.
- ❏ Easier to retrofit existing applications using this method than to redesign for interface-based coding.
- ❏ Managed build output is separate for each Flex and AIR builds. One for AIR desktop applications, including AIR packaging and signing; the other for Flex applications embedded in a web page.

Cons

- ❏ Chainsaw approach to code that is very easy to misuse, promoting spaghetti code in lazy hands.
- ❏ Must declare import statements inside of conditional declaration identifier scope. If you're swapping out only different versions of implemented functions, then any imports of AIR-exclusive APIs must be made inside that function.

Overview of the Conditional Compilation Approach

The sample project code for this chapter contains two projects that demonstrate this technique: Chapter_70_ConditionalCompilationAIR (hereafter called just the AIR project) and Chapter_70_ConditionalCompilationFlex (the Flex project). The crux to this solution involves performing the following four steps:

1. Create a file that will be shared with both an AIR and a Flex project. In this sample, it's called ApplicationPersistence.as and is declared in the AIR version of the project. There can actually be more than one class, depending on the size of your application.

2. Using conditional compilation, declare sections of code (or function signatures) within the desired scope of output. In our example, we'll be using CONFIG::AIR_ONLY to define the method signature for AIR and CONFIG::FLEX_ONLY to define the implementation included in the Flex application.

3. Reference the common code of AIR version from the Flex application. This is done the same way that shared code is imported into a Flex project (refer to Figure 70-2).

4. Configure the compiler for each the AIR and Flex application to include the appropriate code for desired output.

Looking at the ApplicationPersistence File

The heart of the conditional compilation solution is in the declaring a configuration namespace and variable in a code file. Listing 70-5 shows the ApplicationPersistence.as file, which is shared between two projects and defines the CONFIG namespace, and the AIR_ONLY and FLEX_ONLY variables.

Listing 70-5: The ApplicationPersistence implementation

```
public class ApplicationPersistence
{
   // The AIR Implementation
  CONFIG::AIR_ONLY
  static public function saveFile():void
  {
    import flash.filesystem.File;

    var f:File = new File();
    f.browseForSave("Save File");

  }

  //The Flex Implementation
  CONFIG::FLEX_ONLY
  static public function saveFile():void
  {
    Alert.show("Flex version the file through the server");

  }
}
```

The ApplicationPersistence class defines two functions with the exact same name, saveFile(). This is possible because of the CONFIG::FLEX_ONLY and CONFIG::AIR_ONLY declarations. At compile time, based on values set on the compiler, only one of the versions of saveFile will be compiled into the SWF. Notice that, for the AIR version of saveFile, we had to declare the import statement inside the function, instead of globally at the class level. This is because this import statement can't even exist at the Flex level.

The last step is to set up the Flex compiler to pass the appropriate values to determine whether to compile the Flex or AIR version of saveFile().

Configuring the Flex Compiler

To set the compilation options, you must right-click on the project name (`Chapter_70_Conditional CompilationFlex` or `Chapter_70_ConditionalCompilationAIR`) in the Flex Navigator Workspace Explorer. Select Properties from the drop-down menu to view the Project Properties dialog box, as shown in Figure 70-3. On the left side, select Flex Compiler. Finally, on the right side, add the following additional compiler arguments.

For the Flex version, add to your existing compiler arguments:

```
-define=CONFIG::AIR_ONLY,false -define=CONFIG::FLEX_ONLY,true
```

For the AIR version, add:

```
-define=CONFIG::AIR_ONLY,true -define=CONFIG::FLEX_ONLY,false
```

It's important not only to define the namespace and variable and set them to `true` but also to explicitly set to `false` the version that you don't want compiled. These definitions to the Flex compiler either include or exclude the sections of code defined in the appropriate namespace tag.

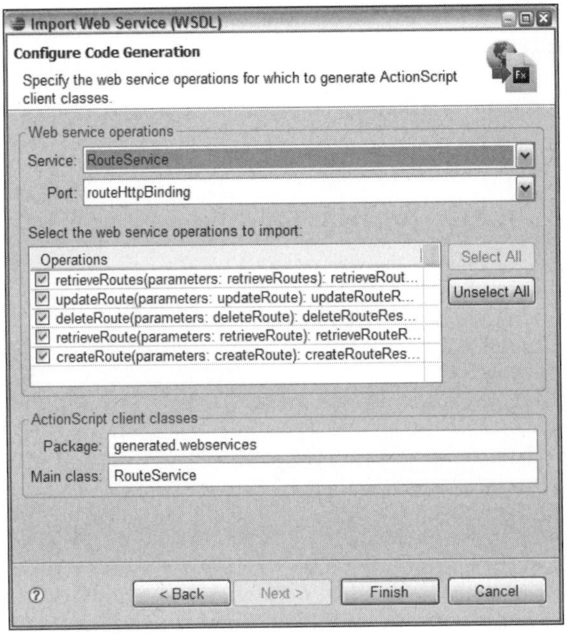

Figure 70-3

With the common `AppllicationPersistence.as` file shared between a Flex and an AIR project, and with the compilers set up appropriately in both projects, it's not hard to achieve support for both Flex and AIR from the same shared code.

Summary

Being able to distribute the same application to the Web and desktop is a compelling feature of Flex and AIR (in addition to cross-platform development). You can make a more feature-rich desktop application that integrates into the user's operating system and local data with AIR. At the same time, you can offer a Web-based application that users can access while roaming, giving users the best of both worlds.

This chapter introduced two techniques for separating the AIR and Flex functionality, whether by necessity (because AIR APIs can be neither accessed nor compiled into Flex applications) or to reduce complexity (you want certain features to be available in the desktop version but not the Web version or vice versa). It's up to you to decide which of the techniques your projects require. In some, it may be necessary to use both the conditional compilation directives and the interface implementation.

Coming up in the next section, Part XII, "Testing and Debugging," we're going to get into debugging and unit testing, logging, and automation, and cover the new profiler that can be used to fix all your application's memory leaks.

Part XII: Testing and Debugging

Debugging Flex Applications

Developers need an assortment of tools and techniques for debugging Flex applications. This chapter aims to cover a broad selection of them, beginning with the debugging features built into Flex Builder, touching briefly on its command-line counterpart, and then continuing with server-side debugging, monitoring tools, gathering diagnostic information through logging, and debugging bindings.

Overview

The influential Dutch computer scientist Edsger Dijkstra famously wrote, "If debugging is the process of removing bugs, then programming must be the process of putting them in." And many years later, the same can still be said. Even the most diligent of developers, with an extensive suite of unit tests and a green coverage report, will still write code with at least some bugs in it.

These bugs come in many shapes and sizes, from incorrect expressions and faulty algorithms to omitted code or dependencies on third-party libraries, which themselves contain bugs. There are even bugs within the Flex framework that surface from time to time to cause some mischief. It's because of the sheer variety of bugs and the various ways they reveal themselves that developers need to be equipped with many different tools and techniques for identifying and resolving them.

This chapter covers several approaches to debugging Flex applications, beginning with the Flex Debugging perspective built into Flex Builder, then covering a selection of complementary techniques from server-side debugging and the monitoring of Internet communications, to developing application-specific debuggers and resolving mysterious errors inside binding expressions.

Flash Debug Player

A debugger version of Flash Player is needed for debugging Flex applications. This is normally installed as part of the Flex Builder installation but can also be downloaded separately from `www.adobe.com/support/flashplayer/downloads.html`.

You can confirm that a Flex application is running in the Flash Debug Player by right-clicking to view the context menu. If the menu contains the Show Redraw Regions option, the Flash Debug Player is running. Further details about the player type can be determined by using the Capabilities class, as follows:

```
<mx:Application xmlns:mx="http://www.adobe.com/2006/mxml">
    <mx:Label
        text="{Capabilities.isDebugger ? 'Flash Debug Player' : 'Flash Player'}"/>
    <mx:Label text="{Capabilities.playerType} - {Capabilities.version}"/>
</mx:Application>
```

Figure 71-1 shows this application running.

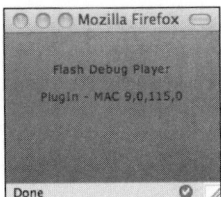

Figure 71-1

The Flex Builder Debugging Perspective

Flex Builder includes a debugging perspective to help you indentify bugs and better understand the behavior of your code at runtime. This perspective will show itself automatically during a debugging session, but you can open it manually from the top menu by selecting Window ⇨ Open Perspective ⇨ Flex Debugging.

The process of debugging with Flex Builder usually involves the following stages:

1. Placing breakpoints on specific lines of code
2. Launching the application in Debug mode
3. Stepping through part of the application code, line by line
4. Examining the application's state
5. Resuming or terminating normal execution

The following sections explain these steps and the other features of the debugging perspective.

Placing Breakpoints

A *breakpoint* is an indicator placed beside a line of executable code that tells Flex Builder to suspend execution. If a Flex application is running in Debug mode and one of these lines is reached, the application will be suspended automatically and the Flex Debugging perspective will be shown.

Breakpoints can be placed in several ways:

❑ By double-clicking in the marker bar margin of the ActionScript or MXML editor

❑ By right-clicking in the marker bar and selecting Toggle Breakpoint

❑ By pressing Ctrl+Shift+B (Windows) or Command+Shift+B (Mac)

A breakpoint is said to be "hit" when the corresponding line of code that it is attached to is about to be executed. Once a breakpoint has been hit, you can continue execution in a step-by-step manner, while observing the state of the application. Figure 71-2 shows a single breakpoint placed in the marker bar beside a line of code.

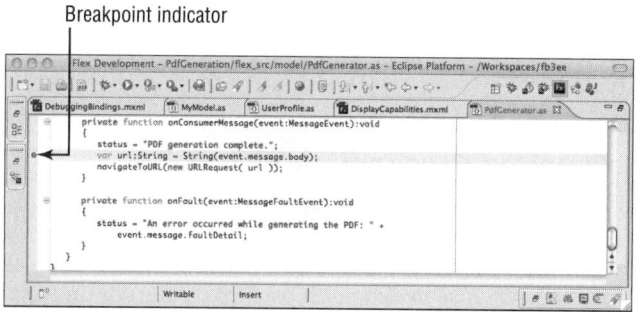

Figure 71-2

You can manage the breakpoints that have been placed using the Breakpoints View of the Flex Debugging perspective (see Figure 71-3). This view provides the following operations:

❑ To navigate to the line in the source file containing the breakpoint, double-click on a breakpoint label.

❑ To enable or disable a breakpoint, check or uncheck the checkbox beside the breakpoint, respectively. This also alters the appearance of the breakpoint in the margin of the ActionScript or MXML editor, from filled to hollow.

❑ To remove the selected breakpoints or all of the current breakpoints, right-click and select Remove or Remove All, respectively, from the context menu.

❑ To import or export the current set of breakpoints to and from disk, right-click and select Import Breakpoints or Export Breakpoints, respectively, from the context menu.

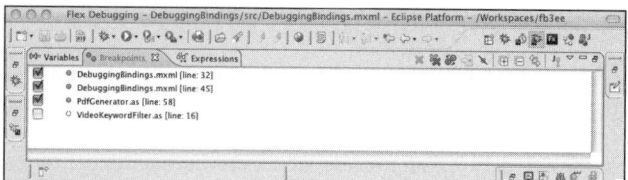

Figure 71-3

In addition to placing breakpoints inside application code, placing them inside Flex framework classes can be both useful and enlightening. These will suspend processing in the same way as any other breakpoints, allowing you to step through the Flex Framework source code, illuminating the inner workings of these classes. This does not extend to Flash Player classes, since unlike Flex, these are not open source.

Breakpoints in MXML

A breakpoint placed against a line of MXML applies to all the inline event handlers and binding expressions on that line of code. If this is not desired, it can be worked around by formatting the MXML so that attributes and inline event handlers are all placed on separate lines. For example:

```
<mx:Button
    label="{model.myProperty}"
    rollOver="rollOverHandler"
    click="clickHandler()"
    />
```

Conditional and Counting Breakpoints

At the time of writing, there is no support for conditional or counting breakpoints in Flex Builder, although these are expected in a future version of Flex Builder. Conditional and counting breakpoints are supported by the Java IDE, allowing Java developers to configure their breakpoints so that the debugger suspends execution only when a breakpoint is reached for the nth time or a certain condition is satisfied. Until these features are available in Flex Builder, a more primitive approach can be used.

The effect of counting and conditional breakpoints can be achieved in Flex by adding some simple logic to the class under test. An `if` statement can be introduced and a breakpoint placed inside the conditional block.

```
if (++counter == 5)
{
    trace("breakpoint"); // place breakpoint here in marker-bar
}
```

A `counter` variable is incremented and when it reaches 5, the condition will be satisfied, so the line of code containing the breakpoint will be reached. Instead of a simple counter, a more complex expression can be used to get the effect of a conditional breakpoint. Note that a line of executable code must be placed inside the conditional block, rather than a comment, because breakpoints can only be attached to executable lines; otherwise, Flex Builder will automatically move the breakpoint to the next executable line beyond the block.

Managing Breakpoints at Runtime

Breakpoints can be placed and enabled at runtime when an application has been launched in Debug mode. This can be particularly useful when debugging code that is executed under certain conditions within bindings. Sometimes bindings fire many times during initialization, so the breakpoint would catch repeatedly, making the debugging process laborious. In this case, the breakpoint might be enabled once the application is fully initialized, and then an action performed to cause the breakpoint to catch.

Alternatively, you can place the breakpoints before launching the application, and then temporarily disable them by selecting the Skip All Breakpoints button of the Breakpoints View. After initialization or at the required moment, they can be reenabled by deselecting the same button.

Launching an Application in Debug Mode

To begin debugging an application with Flex Builder, the application must be launched in Debug mode. This can be achieved in various ways:

❑ Right-click on an application file in the Flex Navigator, and then select Debug As ➪ Debug on Server or Debug As ➪ Flex Application from the context menu.

❑ Select an application file in the Flex Navigator, click on the Debug icon in the main toolbar, and then select Debug As ➪ Debug on Server or Debug As ➪ Flex Application from the drop-down menu.

❑ Select an application file in the Flex Navigator, and then select Run ➪ Debug As ➪ Debug on Server or Run ➪ Debug As ➪ Flex Application from the top menu bar.

❑ Select an application file in the Flex Navigator, and then hold down Shift+Alt+R to debug on the server or Shift+Alt+F to debug a standalone Flex application.

Debug configurations can be created with the Debug dialog, as shown in Figure 71-4. You can open this dialog using the context menu, the Debug drop-down menu, or the top menu bar. A debug configuration can be used repeatedly for launching an application in Debug mode with specific settings. Debug configurations are especially useful when different server environments are in use. For example, an enterprise may have development, user acceptance testing (UAT), and pre-production environments. The Debug dialog could be used to create debug configurations for launching the same application in each of these environments.

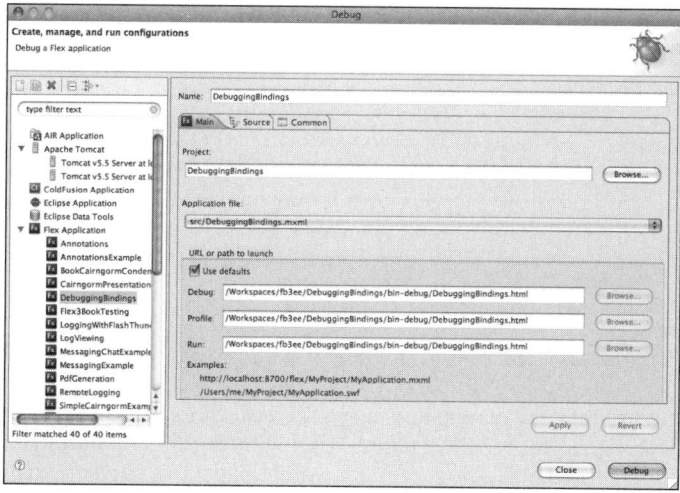

Figure 71-4

When an application is launched in Debug mode, Flex Builder runs a version of the application with debugging features enabled. Stack traces are captured to show the flow of execution through a program; the flow can be paused, resumed, and stepped through line by line; the `trace()` function can be used to write to the Flex Builder console; and the application state (objects and their properties) can be analyzed at runtime.

Stepping through Code

If an application is running in Debug mode, then as soon as a breakpoint is reached, Flex Builder will suspend execution and change to the Flex Debugging perspective. From there, you can step through the code in various ways:

❑ Stepping into a lower-level function

❑ Stepping over the lines of the current function, one by one

❑ Returning to the higher-level function that called the current function

The user interface controls for stepping over code are at the top of the Debug View within the Flex Debugging perspective, as shown in Figure 71-5. There are also convenient keyboard shortcuts for controlling a debugging session:

❑ F5 — Step into a function

❑ F6 — Step over a line of code

❑ F7 — Step return from a function

❑ F8 — Resume normal execution

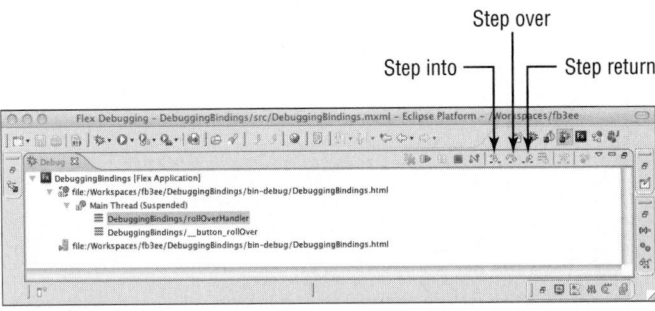

Figure 71-5

Step In (F5)

After the debugger has hit a breakpoint and suspended execution, the Debug View shows the current call stack, and the ActionScript or MXML editor highlights the corresponding line of code. If the line of code contains a function call (including a getter), the debugger can *step in* to that function. For example, in the following code, the debugger can step in from 1 to 2 and continue stepping through the implementation of the `updateButton()` function.

```
private function rollOverHandler(event:MouseEvent):void
{                          //
    updateButton();  // 1 --------------+   step-in
    updateImage();   //                 |
}                                    //  |
                                     //  v
private function updateButton():void//  2
{
    button.width += 10;
    button.height += 10;
    setBorderStyles();
}
```

The step-in operation is used to step deeper and deeper into the code, pushing entries onto the call stack shown in the Debug View. You can step all the way into the Flex framework classes and in this way gain an understanding of their workings. Figure 71-6 shows the Debugging perspective when execution has been suspended at the `updateButton()` function call.

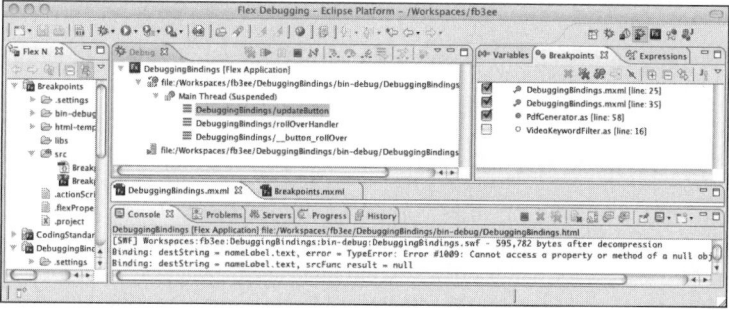

Figure 71-6

The debugger can also step in to property setters and getters, and in fact, will even step in to the implicit getters and setters for variables without defined accessors. When the last line of a function is reached, a step in returns to the next line of the calling function.

Step Over (F6)

The step-over operation proceeds from the current to the next line of the current function. It is used to observe the behavior of a function without examining its lower-level workings. Using the same example as above, a step-over from the line 1 will move to line 2.

```
private function onRollOver(event:MouseEvent):void
{
    updateButton();  // 1 --+ step-over
    updateImage();   // 2 <-+
}
```

During the move, the debugger will execute the `updateButton()` function in its entirety, rather than stepping through it incrementally. That is true unless there is an additional breakpoint placed inside `updateButton()`, which will cause the debugger to suspend execution as normal.

Step Return (F7)

Step return is the reverse of step in, instructing the debugger to execute the remaining code in the current function and return to the calling function. Back in the calling function, processing is again suspended, and debugging resumes.

```
private function rollOverHandler(event:MouseEvent):void
{                          //
    updateButton();  //  2 <------------+  step-out
    updateImage();   //                 |
}                                  //    |
                                   //    |
private function updateButton():void //  |
{                          //             |
    button.width += 10;   //              |
    button.height += 10;  //  1 ---------+
    setBorderStyles();
}
```

In this case, a step return from line 1 executes the rest of the code in the `updateButton()` function and returns to the end of line 2, back in the calling function, `rollOverHandler()`.

Examining Application State

Debugging with Flex Builder involves examining the state of an application while stepping through the code, looking for signs that something is wrong. For instance, the debugger might reveal that a property of an object is `null` when it's expected to have another value. The Flex Debugging perspective includes two views for this purpose — Variables and Expressions — as well as convenient tooltips in the ActionScript and MXML editors. Figure 71-7 shows the debug tooltip that appears when the mouse hovers over the `wrappedFunctionSuccessful` variable in the ActionScript editor during a debugging session.

During a debugging session, the value of a variable can be examined by hovering the mouse over the variable name in the ActionScript or MXML editor. A tooltip will appear containing the current value.

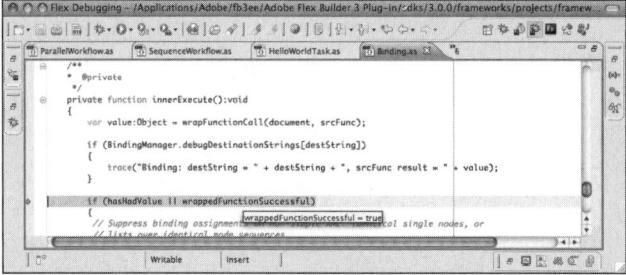

Figure 71-7

The Variables View

The Variables View displays the current state of the application. It lists all the visible variables for the selected frame of the stack trace. A tree is used to display the variables, with top-level nodes for the `this` object and any local variables. For simple types, the property value is shown, whereas for complex types, the reference is shown and the variable can be expanded to reveal the child properties. Different icons are used to distinguish between private, protected, public, and local variables.

Figure 71-8 shows the Variables View and its context menu. The Variables View is used mostly to inspect and change variable values at runtime. Inspection is carried out by navigating the variables tree or using the Find dialog. In many cases the number of visible variables is high, so the Find dialog is the easiest way to locate a particular variable.

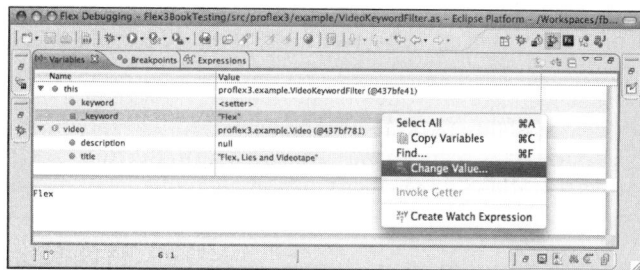

Figure 71-8

The Find Dialog

You can open the Find dialog, shown in Figure 71-9, either from the context menu by right-clicking on an entry in the Variables View and selecting Find or by using keyboard shortcuts: Ctrl+F (Windows) or Command+F (Mac). As the name of a variable is typed into the filter at the top, the list of visible variables will be reduced to those that match.

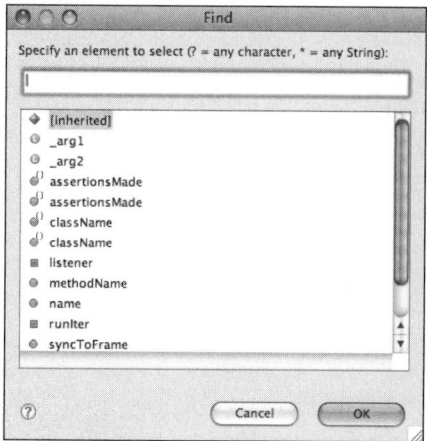

Figure 71-9

The Variables Menu and Other Options

The Variables menu is used to configure the Variables View. It is accessed by clicking on the menu icon of the Variables View. Options are provided to change the grouping of variables and show and hide constants, statics, qualified names, and inaccessible member variables. The Other Options dialog is also available from the Variables menu by selecting Flex ➪ Other Options. It allows further configuration of the visibility of hexadecimal values and mx_internal variables.

The Expressions View

The Expressions View is used to observe the value of selected variables and evaluate given expressions. There are two ways to select a variable for inclusion in the Expressions View:

❑   Right-click on entry in the Variables View and select Create Watch Expression.

❑   Right-click on a variable in an ActionScript or MXML editor and select Watch "variableName".

Whenever execution is suspended, the values of the selected variables are shown in the Expressions View, as long as they belong in the application being debugged. This provides a convenient way to view the values of variables outside the scope of the current frame in the call stack, since those are not shown in the Variables View. It also allows you to focus on a smaller number of relevant variables, rather than the larger quantity contained in the Variables View tree.

Adding and Editing a Watch Expression

As the name suggests, the Expressions View can also be used for evaluating expressions involving multiple variables. These *watch expressions* are evaluated whenever the debugger suspends execution and reevaluated when any of the variables contained in the expression change. This reevaluation takes place while stepping through the code with the debugger but not during normal execution.

Figure 71-10 shows the Expressions View and the Edit Watch Expressions dialog. A watch expression can be created or edited as follows:

❑   Right-click in the Expressions View and select Add Watch Expression.

❑   Right-click on an existing entry in the Expressions View and select Edit Watch Expression.

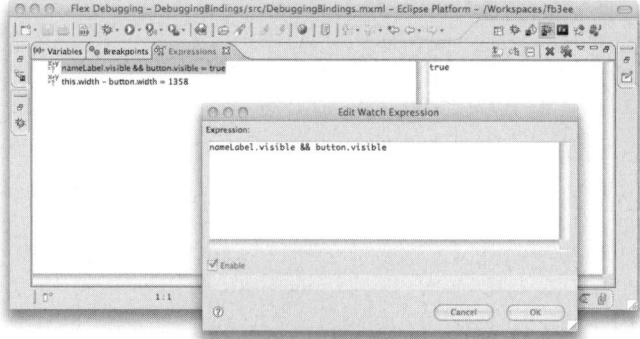

Figure 71-10

The Add Watch Expression and Edit Watch Expression dialogs enable you to define and edit watch expressions using a simple syntax. The following syntax rules apply:

❑ Properties and property chains can be used.

❑ Unary and binary operators can be used.

❑ Integer, Boolean, and String literals can be used.

❑ Floating point literals cannot be specified.

❑ Bracketing can be used to control the evaluation order.

When an error occurs while evaluating a watch expression, you can discover the cause of the failure by clicking on the expand icon beside the watch expression in the Expressions View.

The Command-Line Debugger

For those developers without access to Flex Builder and the die-hard few who prefer to code with text editors (and can still code without autocompletion), there exists a command-line debugger for Flex. This tool provides the same functionality as the Flex Debugging perspective of Flex Builder but exposes it through a minimalist command-line interface. Text entry commands are used to place breakpoints, step through code, and examine the application state.

The command-line debugger is described in detail in the official Adobe Flex 3 documentation, within a chapter of the "Building and Deploying Flex Applications" document.

Additional Debugging Techniques

This section describes additional debugging techniques to complement the Flex Debugging perspective of Flex Builder and its command-line counterpart. Since bugs can occur in many different places and take various forms, developers need an assortment of techniques for addressing them. The server-side code that a Flex client depends on may need scrutiny; logging may be applied to surface warnings and other information; web proxies can be used to analyze incoming and outgoing messages; and so on. In some cases it's possible to get Adobe to fix bugs for you through the Flex bug-base! All of these topics and more are covered here.

Debugging Java Server-Side Code

Because Flex Builder is built on top of Eclipse, you can take advantage of the debugging features of the Eclipse Java IDE and the many third-party extensions that are available. Furthermore, the Web Tools Platform (WTP) extension, included as standard with the Java EE distribution of Eclipse, provides features specifically for debugging Java server-side components.

The Java Debug Perspective

The Eclipse IDE includes a Debug perspective, which is very similar to the Flex Debugging perspective but offers greater functionality, including conditional breakpoints (see Figure 74-11). To show the Java Debug perspective, select Window ⇨ Open Perspective ⇨ Other... ⇨ Debug ⇨ OK.

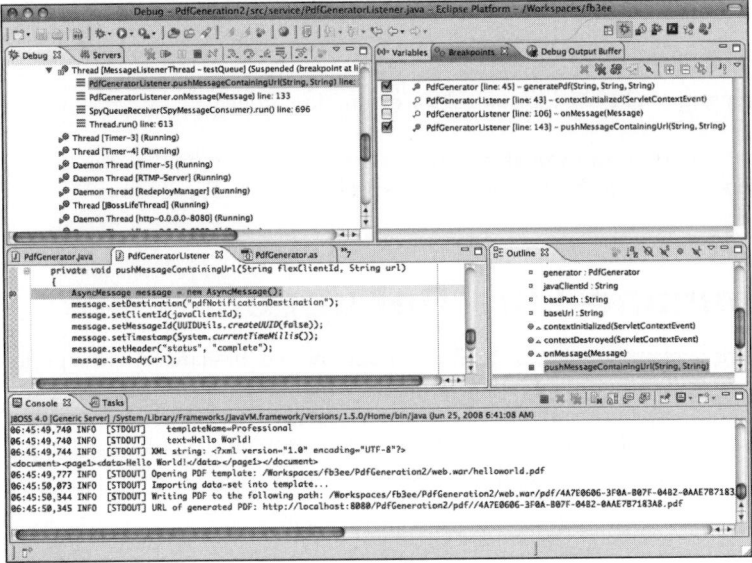

Figure 71-11

The Servers View

The Web Tools Platform (included with Eclipse for Java EE) includes the Servers View, which can be used for managing the deployment of Java server-side code and starting to debug that code (see Figure 71-12). To show the Servers View, select Window ⇨ Show View ⇨ Server ⇨ Servers ⇨ OK.

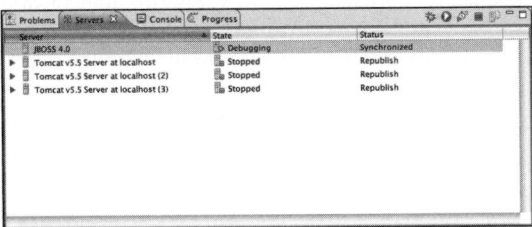

Figure 71-12

Using the Servers View, you can create new Web server instances and associate them with Flex or Java projects. You can then start the Web server instances in Debug mode. When the instances are running in Debug mode, any breakpoints that are reached in the server-side code will cause execution to be suspended and Eclipse to switch into the Debug perspective so that step-by-step debugging can proceed.

The Process of Debugging Server-Side Code

The process of debugging a server-side component of a Flex application, such as a remote object or a Data Management Service assembler, typically involves the following steps:

1. Place breakpoints at appropriate places in the server-side code. Breakpoints are managed in the same way as the Flex Debugging perspective, by double-clicking in the margin of the Java editor and using the Breakpoints View. (Refer to the earlier section "Placing Breakpoints.")

2. Start the Web server hosting the application in Debug mode. This can be achieved through the Servers View context menu or by clicking on the bug icon in the Servers View.

3. Run the Flex or AIR client application in order to call the server-side code so that the breakpoint will catch and debugging can commence.

When a breakpoint catches, you can control the flow of execution in the same way as with the Flex Debugging perspective. You can step into, over and return from executable statements, while inspecting variables and evaluating expressions, before resuming normal execution. Full documentation of the Java Debug perspective is provided in the Eclipse Help system, including details about managing conditional breakpoints and debugging code deployed to remote servers.

Monitoring Internet Traffic

Various tools are available to help you monitor the traffic sent between Flex applications and the Internet. These act as the middlemen, intercepting, examining, and recording the messages sent in both directions, before forwarding them onward to their destination. Monitoring tools tend to provide a user interface that shows the contents of all incoming and outgoing messages, allowing users to identify problems such as incorrect or unexpected data.

For example, a monitoring tool may reveal that an HTTP request that should have been sent with the POST method was actually sent with the GET method. In this case, a programming error may have occurred in the Flex client. Perhaps the method property of an HTTPService was not set to POST, or else no request data was provided, causing Flash Player to revert to the GET method. For messages traveling in the other direction, a monitoring tool may reveal an unexpected HTTP response code, which a Flex application interprets as a fault, or unexpected data that is not properly handled by the client.

Some of these tools provide richer functionality, such as the ability to throttle bandwidth to simulate slower Internet connections; the ability to record and replay sessions containing multiple requests and responses; and the ability to define breakpoints for debugging purposes, which catch certain messages and allow them to be modified before execution resumes. Charles and Service Capture are two rich, cross-platform monitoring tools with features tailored specifically to Flash and Flex development, including the ability to view the contents of binary AMF3 messages.

Using Charles to View AMF Message Details

Charles is a web debugging proxy for monitoring and debugging the messages sent to and from Internet applications. It is shareware, but a free trial version is available for download from www.charlesproxy.com/download.php.

Charles is written in Java and compatible with version 1.4 or above of Sun's Java Development Kit (JDK) and Java Runtime Environment (JRE). Three distributions are currently available: for Windows, Mac OS X, and Linux/Unix. From the same download page, a Mozilla Firefox add-on is also available, which auto-configures the proxy settings of the browser to communicate with Charles and adds a Charles folder to the Tools menu, from which monitoring can be enabled and disabled.

Installing Charles is straightforward. For Mac OS X, copy the Charles application to the Applications folder. For Windows, run the setup application. For Linux/Unix, unzip the compressed archive in an appropriate location. You can install the Mozilla Firefox add-on directly from the download page via Firefox, although it may be necessary to first grant permission for the browser to install the add-on from the Charles domain. More details are provided in the online documentation.

After Charles and the optional Firefox add-on are installed, monitoring and debugging can take place. Any requests and responses sent or received from the web browser, including embedded Flash and Flex content, or other Internet applications, will pass through the Charles web proxy. Messages will be captured automatically and can be viewed in the user interface.

Using Charles to monitor and debug a Flex application usually involves the following steps:

1. Launch Charles. A debugging session will begin automatically.

2. Load the Flex application and perform the desired actions.

3. View the requests and responses that have been made within Charles.

4. Optionally, save the session for later reference or replaying.

Figure 71-13 shows an example of the output produced by a Flex application that interacts with a remote object using AMF messaging. You can view the structure and contents of the AMF response message, including the property types and values. For further details about Charles, including more advanced features such as throttling and HTTPS monitoring, please refer to the documentation available from the Charles website.

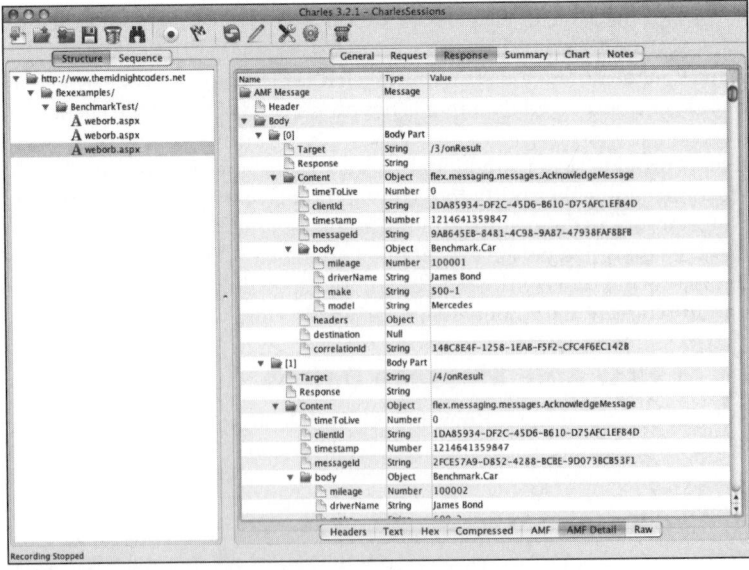

Figure 71-13

Application-Specific Debugging

All the techniques covered so far are general purpose, useful for debugging a broad range of Flex applications but not tailored to the needs of any particular project. For some Flex projects, it may be worth investing time in developing an application-specific debugger to complement these general techniques. Such a tool would be designed with an understanding of the distinct characteristics of the application under development, in order to simplify its debugging process.

An application-specific debugger can be integrated into a Flex application as a hidden view component that is revealed upon a key press or other user gesture. This approach can help you to identify application-specific bugs more quickly and often has the advantage of not freezing the browser in the same way as a Flex Builder debugging session. An application-specific debugger may also allow you to modify the application state at runtime so that you can observe the consequences immediately.

The developers of Adobe Buzzword (`https://buzzword.acrobat.com`), the collaborative online word processor, have incorporated an application-specific debugger into their Flex client. This allows members of the development team to view the object model representation of a Buzzword document while editing is underway. The changes that take place when, for example, a user selects a paragraph of text and applies formatting, can be observed. If the object model is not manipulated as expected, then a problem has been detected. In addition to viewing the document object model, developers can also make direct modifications to it, and observe the outcome in the main document area. Furthermore, the application-specific debugger allows editing sessions to be recorded, saved to disk, and later replayed, providing a form of automated functional testing.

In general, an application-specific debugger is not something to design up front, at the beginning of a project. It is more common to introduce one when the need becomes apparent. Perhaps the Flex Builder debugger is too laborious for a certain kind of debugging, or some part of the internal application state needs to be observed and altered at runtime. An application-specific debugger may be something as simple as a pop-up window for adjusting logging settings or something far more sophisticated like the Buzzword solution.

Making the Most of Logging

Logging is a simple yet vital tool for debugging Flex and AIR applications. By including log statements in your Flex application code, you can determine the flow of execution by reading the log files that are produced while the application is running. It is sometimes possible to identify bugs in these log files, or to better understand the behavior of complex sections of code, that can be awkward to analyze using the Debugging perspective.

In Flex and AIR, logging can be achieved by using the logging framework included as part of the Flex SDK and described in detail in Chapter 74. The logging framework makes it simple to write log statements and direct them toward different targets, from the local Flash log file to a remote Web Service. Log statements can be categorized according to their severity, from simple debugging messages to fatal error reports, and filtering can be applied to limit log output to specific parts of an application.

In addition to identifying bugs, logging can be useful for "passing the buck" and proving that a bug lies outside the Flex or AIR client and inside the server or network layer of an Internet application. Since the GUI is the part of an application that most users interact with, it often stands accused when something goes wrong, so it's important to be able to establish quickly that the client is not to blame, and move on to other parts of the system. If server-side code does not satisfy its contract, then dependent client code will have difficulty operating. By logging incoming and outgoing messages and the URLs used for service interactions, you can easily see when a client is not receiving the expected data. Defensive programming should still be applied to handle these situations as best as possible.

Logging Objects

You can use the `ObjectUtil` class in conjunction with the logging functions to describe the structure and property values of a complex object. This can be useful for debugging purposes, particularly when the object in question doesn't define its own `toString()` function.

```
Log.getLogger("my.package.MyClass").debug(
    "myObject looks like this: {0}", ObjectUtil.toString(myObject));
```

Here the logger for the class `my.package.MyClass` is retrieved from the `Log` class, and then the debugging function is called. A string is passed in containing a parameter `{0}`, and the value for that parameter is generated using `ObjectUtil.toString()`.

Debugging Bindings

Bindings are a notorious source of bugs, particularly because the binding mechanism is designed to silently swallow the errors that commonly occur when a binding expression is evaluated. The following table shows these errors.

Error Code	Cause
1006	Attempted to call an object that is not a function
1009	Attempted access of a property of a null object reference
1010	Attempted access of a property of an undefined object
1055	Attempted access of a property of an object that has no properties
1069	Attempted access of a nonexistent property with no default value

In most cases, this error swallowing is the desired behavior; for example, when properties in a binding chain are null because they've not yet been initialized. However, when genuine programming errors occur, they can be concealed. The effect of bugs in a binding usually surfaces in the user interface, when a view isn't updated as expected.

Luckily, there are several approaches to debugging binding-related code. The first approach uses the undocumented `BindingManager` class contained in the Flex SDK. The second approach uses the `Observe` (or `ObserveValue`) tag to reveal the errors that would otherwise have vanished inside the binding mechanism.

The BindingManager Class

The `BindingManager` class, which has existed since Flex 2 but is not officially documented, can be used to enable debugging output for bindings. To do so, pass a binding destination string to the static debugBinding() function. This normally takes place in a preinitialize event handler so that the destinations are registered for debugging before the bindings start to fire.

```
<mx:Application … preinitialize="preinitializeHandler()">

private function preinitializeHandler() : void
{
    BindingManager.debugBinding("nameLabel.text");
}
```

In this case, debugging output will be produced for any bindings with a destination that matches the string nameLabel.text. For example:

```
<mx:Label id="nameLabel" text="{model.userProfile.firstName}"/>
```

An inline binding has been used to bind the model.userProfile.firstName property chain to the destination text property of the nameLabel control. Note that the same result could be achieved using an MXML Binding tag instead:

```
<mx:Binding source="model.userProfile.firstName" destination="nameLabel.text"/>
```

In either case, if the userProfile property of the model object has not been initialized and remains null, then a TypeError will be shown in the output. This would otherwise have been silently handled by the internal binding mechanism.

```
Binding: destString = nameLabel.text, error = TypeError: Error #1009: Cannot access
    a property or method of a null object reference.
Binding: destString = nameLabel.text, srcFunc result = null
```

This output can be useful for establishing why bindings are not working as expected.

The Observe and ObserveValue Tags

The Adobe Consulting Observe tag and its sidekick, ObserveValue, can both be used for invoking a handler method when a property changes. This is in contrast to the MXML Binding tag, which calls a property setter and not a method. The other difference is in the approach to error handling. Whereas the MXML Binding tag swallows common errors, the Observe and ObserveValue tags instead catch any errors that occur while calling the handler function, then throw them onwards in a subsequent frame, via the callLater() queue.

Some good introductory material and downloads are available from the following blog posts:

❑ http://weblogs.macromedia.com/paulw/archives/2006/05/the_worlds_smal

❑ http://weblogs.macromedia.com/auhlmann/archives/2006/09/using_binding_s

❑ http://weblogs.macromedia.com/auhlmann/archives/ObserveUtility.zip

The Observe tag is used to invoke a handler function whenever a bindable property chain changes. You can use it as follows:

```
<util:Observe source="{model.myProperty}" handler="myFunction"/>
```

In this case, whenever a property changes in the `model.myProperty` chain, the handler function, `myFunction()`, will be invoked. If an error occurs inside the handler function, it will propagate in a subsequent frame.

The `ObserveValue` tag adds a little logic, so the handler function is only invoked when the `source` expression evaluates to a specified value. It can be used as follows:

```
<util:ObserveValue source="{model.myProperty}" value="{true}"
    handler="myFunction"/>
```

Here the handler function, `myFunction`, will be invoked when the property chain, `model.myProperty`, evaluates to `true`. Again, any errors that occur within `myFunction()` will be propagated.

Adobe Public Bug Database and Issue Reporting System

From time to time, Flex developers are faced with bugs in the Flex Framework, Flex Builder, or even the Flash Player and AIR runtimes. These can manifest themselves as compile-time or runtime errors, or they may affect the behavior of an application in more subtle ways. For example, a control may not operate exactly as the documentation suggests or an event may not be dispatched as expected. These issues may be the result of bugs in the implementation or shortcomings in the documentation. In either case, they can cause developers difficulty.

Thankfully, Flex is open source and Adobe has a public Bug and Issue Management System:

```
http://bugs.adobe.com
```

This can be used for reporting bugs and issues, making enhancement requests, and searching existing reports for Flex and related products, including Flash Player, Flex Builder, BlazeDS, ActionScript Compiler, Data Management and Visualization Components, and the Flex Test Automation Framework. The system allows users to vote for the bugs, issues, and enhancement requests that are of most importance to them. This provides an indication of the level of community interest in a particular report, which the Flex Management team can consider when planning improvements.

Registering and Logging In

To get the most out of the Bug and Issue Management System, you must register for an account and log in. This enables you to create new reports, add detail to existing reports, watch existing bug reports in order to be notified when they are updated, and participate in the community voting process. All users can visit their own profile page, which lists the bugs they are watching and the votes they have made, as shown in Figure 75-14.

Before Reporting a Bug

Before reporting a bug, always search the existing records, in case the bug has already been reported. In many cases, the bug will be well known and a workaround provided. If the bug is particularly important to you, vote for it. Bug reports are only viewed by the development team when they have received votes from the community.

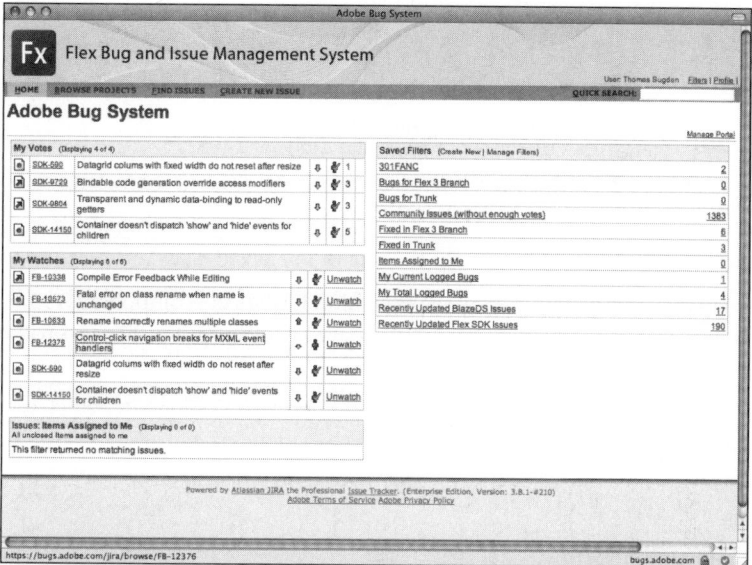

Figure 75-14

Creating a Good Bug Report

When reporting a new bug, it is important to provide a good account of the problem so that other users can find the report and vote for it, and Adobe can understand and potentially address the issue. A good bug report is clearly and concisely written, and most importantly, the bug is reproducible. If the bug cannot be reproduced, then it's unlikely to be resolved.

Try to isolate the issue and provide simple, step-by-step instructions for reproducing it. Any example code should be stripped down to the bare minimum, highlighting the problem without extraneous detail. For any example code, describe the actual results, the expected results if the bug were not present, and a known workaround, if one exists. When including source code, remember that the Bug and Issue Management System is a public resource, so do not submit any proprietary or confidential content.

Example Bug Report: Transition Flashes the Target State before Executing

This example bug report is taken from the Adobe Bug and Issue Management System documentation, with only minor modifications.

Steps to Reproduce

1.   Create a simple `TitleWindow` component with one state that changes the "height" property and one Resize transition defined.

```
<states>
    <State name="small">
        <SetProperty name="height" value="100"/>
```

```
            </State>
        </states>

        <transitions>
            <Transition fromState="*" toState="*">
                <Resize target="{this}" duration="1000"/>
            </Transition>
        </transitions>
```

2. With the attached example, change the size of the left `TitleWindow` using the `ComboBox`.

3. Notice that on every ~5th resize, the transition flashes the component in the final state just prior to playing the transition. It doesn't happen every time, but it's obvious when it does happen.

Actual Results

Transition flashes the target state before executing.

Expected Results

Transition should play smoothly.

Workaround

If the `SetProperty` is removed from the state and each state change is explicitly coded into the transitions, it works as expected. But this is too much extra code to be a scalable solution.

```
        <states>
            <State name="small"/>
        </states>

        <transitions>
            <Transition fromState="small" toState="">
                <Resize target="{this}" duration="1000" heightBy="500"/>
            </Transition>
            <Transition fromState="" toState="small">
                <Resize target="{this}" duration="1000" heightBy="-500"/>
            </Transition>
        </transitions>
```

Watching a Bug Report

You can watch an existing bug report by clicking on the "Watch it" link in the Operations box in the sidebar on the left (see Figure 71-15). A notification email will be sent to you whenever the content of the bug is updated — for example, if another user adds further details or a workaround, or if Adobe changes the status of the bug, perhaps deferring it for consideration in a later release.

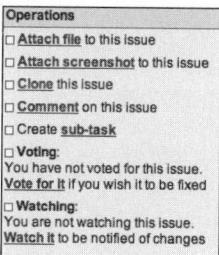

Figure 71-15

Summary

While developers always aspire to write code without bugs, and sometimes apply techniques such as unit testing and Test-Driven Development to systematically reduce them, a quantity of bugs always seems to remain. This chapter has covered many of the tools and techniques available for tracking down these bugs and eliminating them. The most important of these is arguably the Flex Debugging perspective of Flex Builder, but this alone is not sufficient. Developers need extra tricks up their sleeves, like the `BindingManager` class and `Observe` tag for dealing with misbehaving bindings, monitoring tools for scrutinizing Internet traffic, and logging statements for gathering diagnostic information. In some cases, an application-specific debugger can pay for itself many times over, providing the clearest view of state and behavior.

The next chapter covers the Flex Profiler, another important development tool included with Flex Builder to help you build applications that perform well. The Flex Profiler can be used to analyze the runtime performance and memory consumption of a Flex application, helping to identify and resolve performance bottlenecks and memory leaks.

72

Using the Flex Profiler

In the last chapter, you learned how to debug your Flex applications using the Flex Builder 3 Debugging perspective. This chapter builds on your application analysis toolset by discussing the Flex Builder 3 Profiling perspective that is only available in the Professional version of Flex Builder 3. The items that will be discussed are:

❑ Profiling basics

❑ Flex Builder 3 Profiling

❑ The Profiler in action

❑ Creating your own Profiler

Overview

The majority of this book discusses the tools and techniques that you need to build Flex 3 applications. However, as a developer it is your responsibility to try and build applications that make the best use of system resources and end-user attention spans. Here are some common situations that come up after a successful launch:

❑ The client is upset at the amount of system memory the application uses.

❑ The client is upset because the application doesn't run fast enough.

With the right knowledge coupled with the Flex Builder 3 Profiler, you will be able to deal with these situations.

Before You Get Started

The Flex Builder 3 Profiler is only available in the Professional version of Flex Builder 3. In other words, copies of Flex Builder 3 Standard will not have the Flex Profiler, a.k.a. the Flex Builder 3 Profiling perspective. If you're not planning to purchase Flex Builder 3 Professional, then you're welcome to skip to the next chapter.

It's worth noting that support for the Flex Builder 3 Profiler didn't exist in the Flash Debug Player until version 9.0.115, so you will need that version as a bare minimum. In addition, your SWF will need to be compiled with debugging information. In other words, using Export Release Build to output your SWF will render it useless with the Profiler.

Also, the Profiler uses a local port to connect to the runtime. By default it's 9999. You can change the port in the Profiler settings in Eclipse:

1. Open the Windows menu on a Windows system or the Eclipse menu on a Mac OS X system.

2. Select Preferences.

3. In the Preferences dialog box that opens, navigate to Flex ➪ Profiler ➪ Connections.

Keep in mind, if you change the port number make sure that the port number you choose isn't being blocked by a personal firewall or Internet security software. Also make sure the port number you choose is not already in use.

Profiling Basics

To be productive, it is worthwhile to understand some of the basics on profiling your applications. Although a deep dive into profiling and performance optimization theory is out of the scope of this book, key points will now be discussed.

Performance Profiling and Optimization Best Practices

In general, performance profiling and optimization is all about finding the bottlenecks in your application. Sometimes, the bottleneck is something you have no control over, as in the following:

❑   The database server is slow or overutilized.

❑   Network links have low bandwidth or are congested.

❑   The end-user system is underpowered or running too many processes.

In other cases, such as your application code, you are empowered to remove bottlenecks and if you get over zealous, performance profiling and optimization can become a potential time sink and eat into budget, hours, and resources allocated to your project. So before you get started, there are some things to keep in mind: remember stakeholder expectations, assess baseline performance, gather ample data, and get it right the first time.

Contrary to stakeholder expectations, as a developer it's easy to get absorbed and carried away by the task at hand. For instance, you might be working on a preload system that on average loads its application and all its assets in about 1–2 seconds. You are really into your code and you're spending a lot of time trying to get it to always load in less than a second.

In the previous scenario, it's time to step back and remember that the initial project specifications called for a preloader that would have the application loaded in less than 3 seconds. That being said, its time to halt your preloader profiling and optimizing effort and move on to the next task. This type of discipline will prevent more of your client's money from being wasted.

Another thing to remember when profiling is to profile early and often. The key thing to do is set some baselines on how certain sections of your application perform so that you know when the latest code starts to degrade the performance of the application below acceptable thresholds.

Also, without a baseline, there is no measurable way for you to know when optimizations that you've made actually help. As an example, assume that you are optimizing a loop algorithm in your application that is responsible for initializing some display children. You need a baseline to compare to and ample data to prove the validity of your efforts.

When gathering your data, at a bare minimum you'll need to make sure to run several test rounds and calculate averages based on your data sets. Otherwise you might be convinced that an optimization that you recently implemented was successful based on a testing anomaly. Another thing to keep in mind is if the algorithm you're trying to optimize requires input data, make sure to vary your input data.

For instance, there may be situations where the benefits of a particular algorithm might not be immediately obvious until you pass in a larger data set. If, however, your time is limited, one suggestion is to try to model the input data to represent what the real application would pass into the algorithm. Running multiple tests using various input data will help you to prove your optimization efforts, and as a value-add it will help your stakeholders realize that the time was well spent.

Before moving on, you should think about striving to get your code right the first time. As you gain experience and learn throughout your career, you start to pick up coding best practices such as knowing to do as little as possible in a looping algorithm by setting up as much as you can beforehand. Also, as you continue to profile and optimize your applications you will gain a tool belt full of not-so-obvious ways to optimize your applications: client-side data-caching logic, object pooling to manage instance reuse, and advanced display creation algorithms to name just a few.

During your career, there will be times when you have to build an application quickly, and you will be tempted to slap your code together as rapidly as possible regardless of performance requirements. Although this approach may result in a successful end product, in many cases it won't and will require much more code optimization to be performed during the tail end of the project when the stakeholders are getting antsy for launch and the remaining budget and hours are at risk. The other danger of leaving code optimization until the tail end of a project is introducing bugs into an application that may have already gone through the testing phase, prompting yet another round of testing.

Keep in mind that it's good not to optimize too much too soon. However, with your tool belt of optimizations you may already know that one particular code snippet is faster or better on resources than another. In cases like these, go for the better algorithm even if it means investing a little more time up front. In the same context, it's helpful to think the problem out before you start typing your code because it may make you realize that you need to spend a little extra time creating something such as an object pool or caching algorithm. Time and time again, getting it done right the first time will cost a little bit more up front, but in the grand scheme of the project, it will save much time in the long run.

Memory Profiling Basics

One of the key things to keep track of when it comes to how your application utilizes system resources is object instances. Object instantiation is a pretty expensive process, and if you're instantiating too often, it can bog down the speed of your application. Also, the object instances that have been created and not destroyed require memory, so more instances means more system memory being utilized.

The Memory Profiler in Flex Builder 3 is geared toward tracking down these object instances, where they came from, and how large they are. Having knowledge of this information will assist you with figuring out where you need to consider object reuse or tracking down memory leaks. Memory leaks are caused by objects that are thrown away by your application that have not been adequately dereferenced.

Although a thorough explanation of Garbage Collection is outside the scope of this book, the general concept is that when you are done using an object you need to make sure that all references to that object have been removed so that the Garbage Collection system in the Flash Player or AIR will know that it is safe to reclaim the memory being used by the object.

> *For more information on Garbage Collection, check out*
> `http://livedocs.adobe.com/flex/3/html/profiler_6.html#209189.`

Performance Profiling Basics

It was stated earlier that object instantiation is a pretty expensive process, meaning that it takes a good amount of system time for constructor methods and everything else involved in object instantiation to run. In that regard, performance profiling is all about finding the most expensive method calls in your application and trying to improve them or their surrounding logic so that the process becomes less expensive; in short, optimizing the process that these methods are involved in to be lighter on system time, and not so much of a bottleneck.

In performance profiling, there are a couple of different ways that an expensive method call can manifest itself. Sometimes you notice that the execution time of a method is extraordinarily long. In that case, you would look into optimizing the method itself or even one of the methods that it is responsible for calling. At other times, you notice that an excessive number of calls are being made to a particular method. If excessive calls are being made, that might indicate that you need to optimize the surrounding process that was responsible for invoking that method, rather than the method itself. In either case, the Flex Builder Performance Profiler will assist you by tracking method calls within your application and allow you to shed some light on the preceding scenarios.

Sampling Profiler Basics

The Flex Builder Profiler is a sampling profiler. Once every millisecond or so the Profiler will take a snapshot and utilize the collection of samples taken during the profiling session to generate the data you see in the Profiling perspective. The act of sampling can be both good and bad.

It's good that the Profiler samples rather than collecting data nonstop. If it were to do that, the Profiler would run so slowly that no one would want to use it. Luckily, the samples are collected once every millisecond or so, resulting in a Profiler that's fast enough to use and, in the grand scheme of things, more than adequate to get the job done.

However, since the sampler is only collecting information once every millisecond or so, there is a chance that particular method calls that complete in less than a millisecond will not be reported in any of the samples. Although this might be bad, if you really need the information on these methods, there is a zero-time method filter that will be discussed later that can be utilized to see these methods.

Flex Builder 3 Profiling

This section introduces the profiling features built into Flex Builder 3. There will be many screenshots throughout this section to keep you on track if you would like to follow along in Flex Builder while you read. Also, if you would like to follow along with the same application that was illustrated in the figures, open `ProfilingExample.mxml` from the Chapter 72 source code.

The Profiling Perspective

If you are an owner of Flex Builder 3 Professional, you are also a lucky owner of the Profiling perspective. Figure 72-1 shows a view of the Profiler perspective after a default profiling session launch.

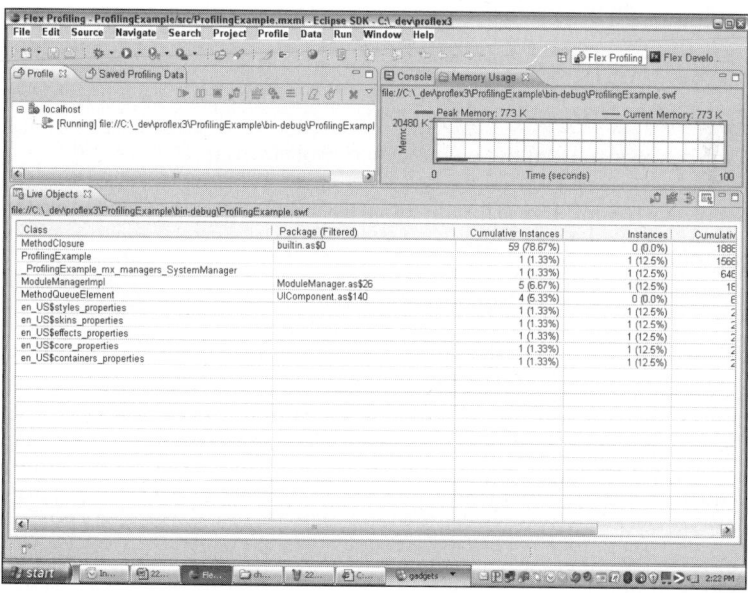

Figure 72-1

As of version 3, the Profiling perspective is new to Flex Builder. For those coming from Flex Builder 2, you will soon realize that the Profiling perspective is a much needed and welcome addition to the developer toolset.

The Profiler in Flex 1.x was taken out for the Flex 2.x release. If you're still supporting applications in Flex 1.x, see the following link for information about the old Profiler:
`www.adobe.com/devnet/flex/articles/profiler.html.`

Although the various views and dialogs that make up the Flex Builder 3 Profiler are well documented in the Adobe documentation, some of the less obvious details and things that you learn as you gather experience using the Profiler will be highlighted.

You can find the Flex Builder 3 Profiler documentation at
`http://livedocs.adobe.com/flex/3/html/profiler_1.html#205073.`

Before talking in more depth about the Profiler, you should know the various methods that can be used to launch the Profiler. It will be helpful to know how to launch the Profiler now so that you can follow along when the various Profiler Views and dialogs are discussed during this chapter.

Launching the Profiler

There are several different ways to initiate an application profiling session within Flex Builder 3:

- ❏ From the project
- ❏ From the Run menu
- ❏ Using keyboard shortcuts
- ❏ From the Flex Builder toolbar
- ❏ From an external application

Launching from the Project

To launch a profiling session from the project you're working on:

1. In the Flex Navigator, right-click on the project you'd like to profile.
2. Select Profile As.
3. Select the Flex Application option in the submenu (see Figure 72-2).

Launching from the Run Menu

To launch a new profiling session from the Run menu:

1. Highlight the project you'd like to profile in the Flex Navigator.
2. Open the Flex Builder Run menu.
3. Select Profile As.
4. Select Flex Application in the submenu (see Figure 72-3).

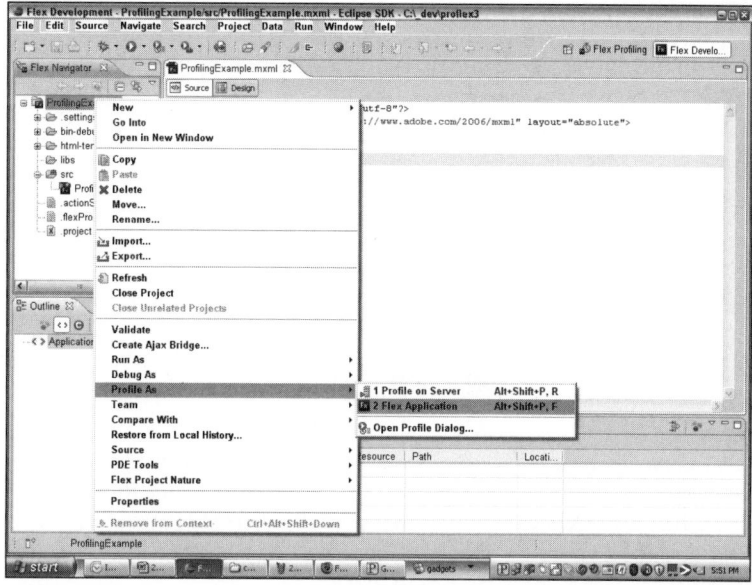

Figure 72-2

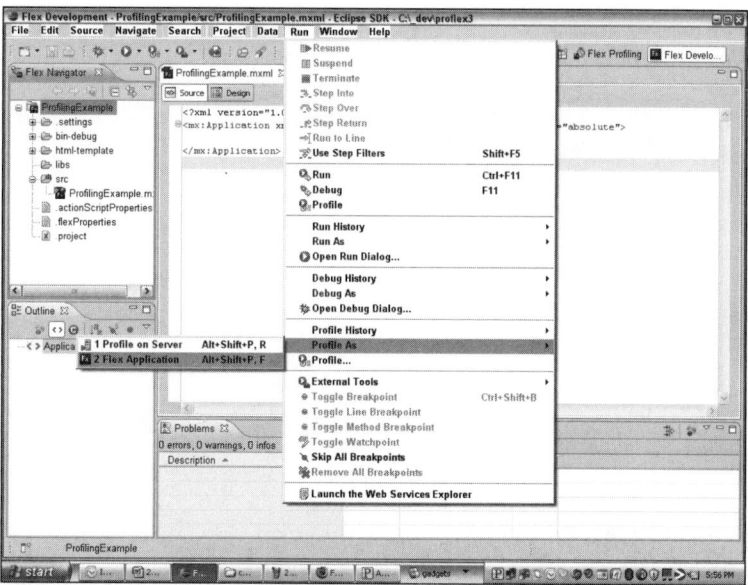

Figure 72-3

Launching from Keyboard Shortcuts

You can also launch a profiling session using keyboard shortcuts:

1. In the Flex Navigator, highlight the project you'd like to profile.

2. Press Alt+Shift+P to initiate the launch menu.

3. You will see a yellow launch menu asking for the next key. Press "F" for Flex application. Figure 72-4 shows a snapshot of the shortcut menu.

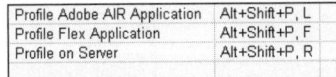

Profile Adobe AIR Application	Alt+Shift+P, L
Profile Flex Application	Alt+Shift+P, F
Profile on Server	Alt+Shift+P, R

Figure 72-4

Not only can you profile applications using this keyboard shortcut sequence, but you can also Run and Debug your applications using similar keyboard shortcuts. By default, the Run shortcut to get to the launch menu is Alt+Shift+X and the one for Debug is Alt+Shift+D.

Launching from the Flex Builder toolbar

To launch a profiling session from the Flex Builder toolbar:

1. Highlight the project you want to profile in the Flex Navigator.

2. Click on the Profile button in the Flex Builder toolbar (see Figure 72-5).

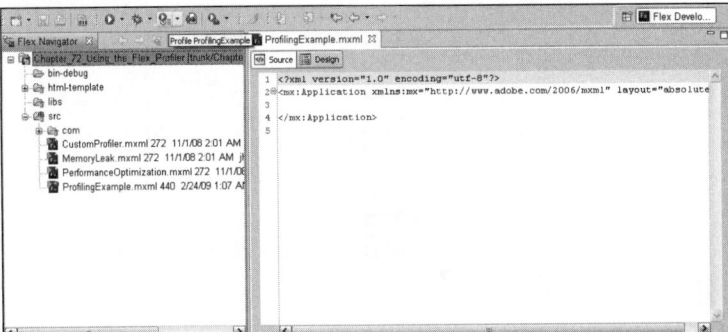

Figure 72-5

Launching External Applications

To profile an external application, you must first be in the Profiling perspective, and then:

1. Open the Flex Builder Profile menu.

2. Select the only option, Profile External Application (see Figure 72-6).

   The Profile External Application dialog appears, allowing you to profile an application using a predefined file path or URL, or manually launch one outside of Flex Builder (see Figure 72-7).

3. After making your selection, click the Launch button to start the profiling session.

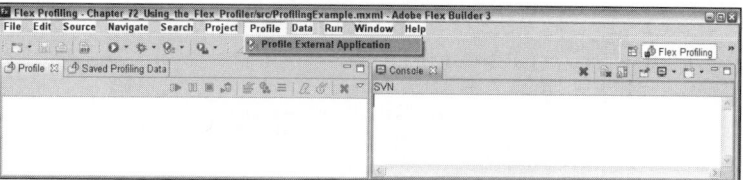

Figure 72-6

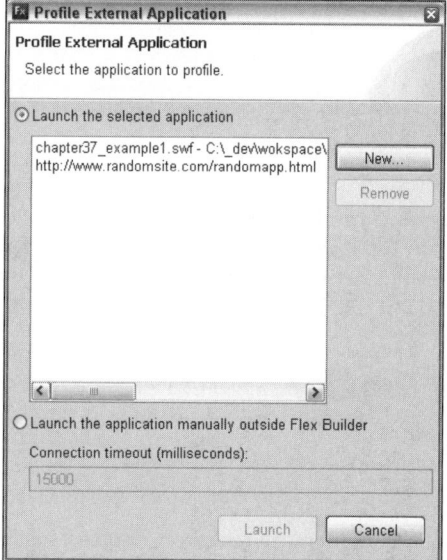

Figure 72-7

Once the profiling session starts, the application launches, and the connection is made between the Profiler and the runtime, Flex Builder will activate. At this point, you will see the launch dialog when you bring Flex Builder to the foreground. It is titled "Connection Established" and is illustrated in Figure 72-8.

The thing to note about the Connection Established dialog is the check boxes dictate what information is collected and available during a profiling session. For instance, the Memory Profiler's Usage Graph discussed in the next section will not have any data if you don't check the "Enable memory profiling" check box.

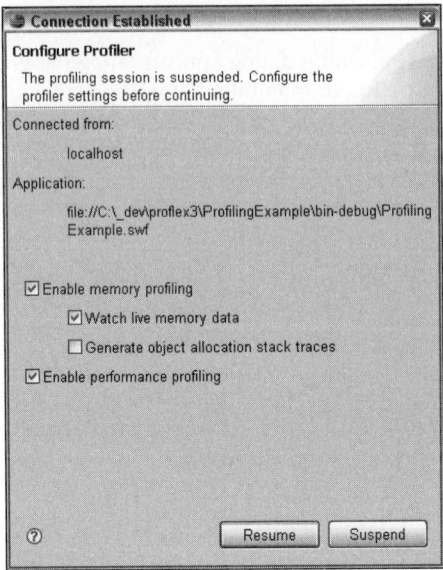

Figure 72-8

Although you may be tempted to check all the check boxes to ensure that the profiling data is available, this will end up slowing down the data collection process. In other words, check what you need and uncheck the rest. If you only need to profile performance, uncheck all the memory profiling check boxes, and vice versa.

Using the Memory Profiler

The Memory Profiler is used to:

❑ Learn how many object instances there are of the various classes in an application

❑ Learn the impact on system memory resources of object instances

❑ Learn which methods were responsible for allocating an object

❑ Obtain information about loitering objects when tracking down memory leaks

The following sections take a look at the pieces that make up the Profiler.

The Memory Usage Graph

Looking back at Figure 72-1, you will notice a graph in the top-right corner of the Profiling perspective. To utilize this graph, you just need to ensure that memory profiling is enabled when you start your profiling session.

The Memory Usage graph is pretty self-explanatory. It will track Peak and Current memory utilization over time. The units of measure are kilobytes for usage and seconds for time.

Many developers use Task Manager (Windows) or Top (Linux/Mac OS X) to assess the memory footprint of their Flex applications. The problem with these approaches is that these numbers are representative of the system memory impact of not only their Flex application but also the Flash Player and the web browser running the application. In this day and age of tabbed browsing, this method can be really unreliable.

Also, if you have used `System.totalMemory` to track memory usage, you will notice the numbers issued by this little snippet of ActionScript are much higher than what you will see in the Memory Profiler's Memory Usage graph. This is because `System.totalMemory` will report all memory being utilized by the Flash Player or AIR, including runtime overhead and all other running Flash Player or AIR applications, whereas the Usage Graph will only report the memory being utilized by the live objects in the application being profiled.

Compared to system utilities such as Task Manager, Top, and the ActionScript `System.totalMemory` call, the Memory Profiler's Memory Usage graph is currently the most accurate way to assess the impact and memory usage of a single Flex application.

Although the Memory Usage graph shows the memory footprint of a single application, it only accounts for live objects and not all of that application's process memory. In other words, an application may have memory allocated to it that is currently not in use. These pieces of "free" memory will not be reported in the Memory Usage graph.

Viewing Live Objects

If you've checked the Watch live memory data check box during launch, you will be able to watch live objects via the Live Objects View (see Figure 72-9). This is a very useful view that shows you the object instances and their impact on memory. The nice thing about the Live Objects View is that it's updated automatically throughout your profiling session. Note that any column that's "Cumulative" represents all instances since the application started, even if they've been destroyed and are no longer live.

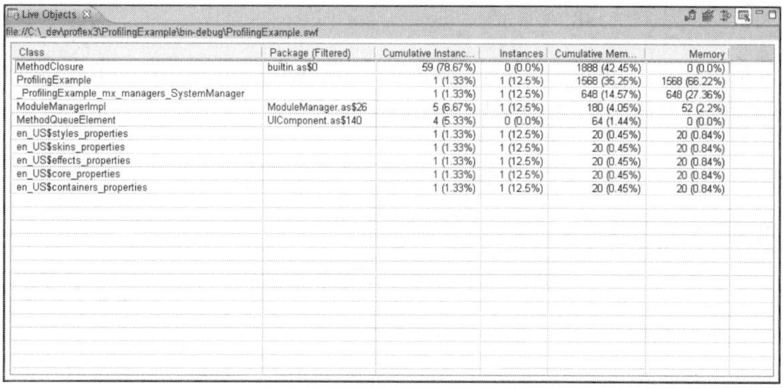

Class	Package (Filtered)	Cumulative Instanc...	Instances	Cumulative Mem...	Memory
MethodClosure	builtin.as$0	59 (78.67%)	0 (0.0%)	1888 (42.45%)	0 (0.0%)
ProfilingExample		1 (1.33%)	1 (12.5%)	1568 (35.25%)	1568 (66.22%)
_ProfilingExample_mx_managers_SystemManager		1 (1.33%)	1 (12.5%)	648 (14.57%)	648 (27.36%)
ModuleManagerImpl	ModuleManager.as$26	5 (6.67%)	1 (12.5%)	180 (4.05%)	52 (2.2%)
MethodQueueElement	UIComponent.as$140	4 (5.33%)	0 (0.0%)	64 (1.44%)	0 (0.0%)
en_US$styles_properties		1 (1.33%)	1 (12.5%)	20 (0.45%)	20 (0.84%)
en_US$skins_properties		1 (1.33%)	1 (12.5%)	20 (0.45%)	20 (0.84%)
en_US$effects_properties		1 (1.33%)	1 (12.5%)	20 (0.45%)	20 (0.84%)
en_US$core_properties		1 (1.33%)	1 (12.5%)	20 (0.45%)	20 (0.84%)
en_US$containers_properties		1 (1.33%)	1 (12.5%)	20 (0.45%)	20 (0.84%)

Figure 72-9

Taking Memory Snapshots

The Live Objects View is great to get a feel for how your application is utilizing memory, but the Live Objects View is not conducive to comparing one point in time with another. For example, suppose that you are trying to see the memory impact of loading and displaying 20 remote images in your application. It would be nice to take a snapshot before making the data call and then again after the images are displayed in your application. Taking a snapshot of an application being profiled is a two-step process:

1. In the Profile View, select the [Running] application that you'd like to take a snapshot of, as shown in Figure 72-10.

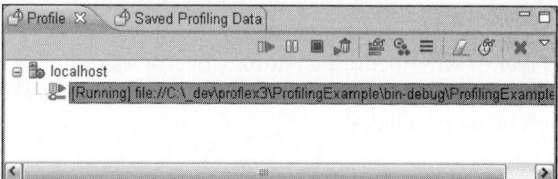

Figure 72-10

2. Once you have selected the application, click on the Take Memory Snapshot button in the Profile View toolbar, as shown in Figure 72-11.

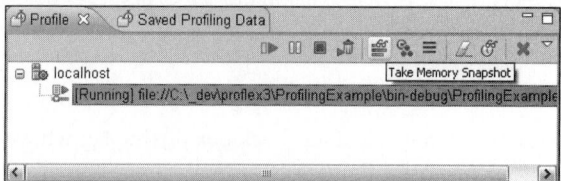

Figure 72-11

Later on, the Run Garbage Collector button will be discussed. The nice part of taking a memory snapshot is that it will run the Garbage Collector for you.

At this point, a memory snapshot will be generated and will appear in the Profile View as a child of the [Running] application (see Figure 72-12).

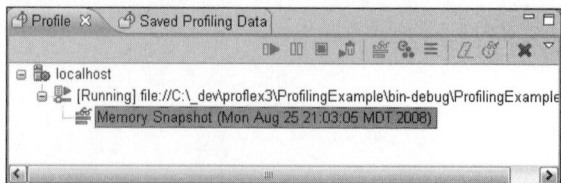

Figure 72-12

Now that you have a memory snapshot, you can double-click it in the Profile View. It will bring up a Memory Snapshot View (see Figure 72-13).

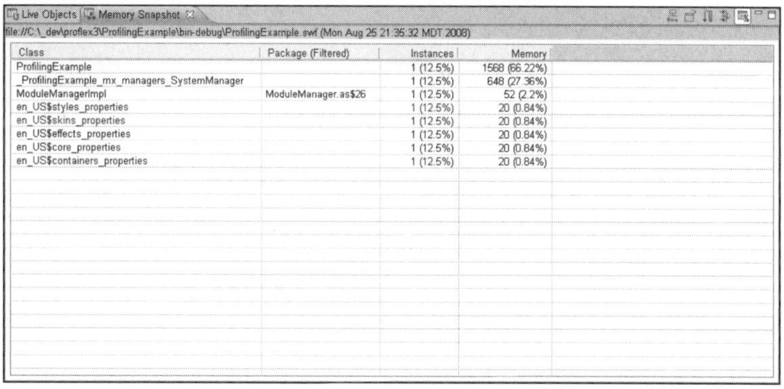

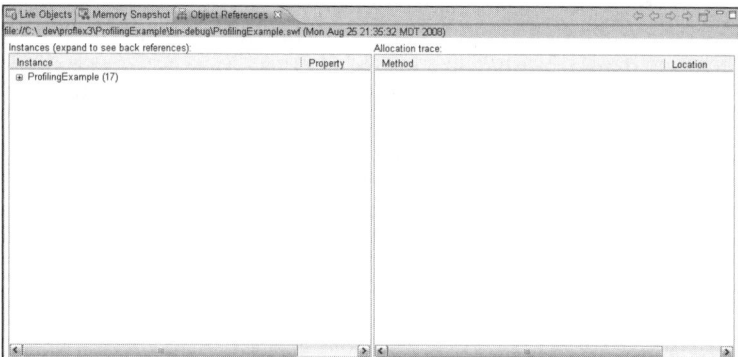

Figure 72-13

The Memory Snapshot View looks like the Live Objects View but lacks the two Cumulative columns (Cumulative Instances and Cumulative Memory). Also, unlike the Live Objects View, items in the Memory Snapshot View can be double-clicked to find out object reference details. As an added bonus, if "Generate object allocation stack traces" was selected when the profiling session was started, you can even view allocation trace details.

Examining Object References

As you're looking through the Memory Snapshot that you had generated, you may find a class that you'd like more information about. Double-click the row of the class you're interested in to bring up an Object References View (see Figure 72-14).

Figure 72-14

This view contains two panes. The one to the left shows the instance(s) you're looking at. Expand the tree for each instance to view the chain of back references leading up to that object. Figure 72-14 shows the number (17) next to the ProfilingExample instance. This is the number of references pointing to this object instance. If you expand the ProfilingExample tree, you will see that there's 17 items referencing ProfilingExample. Also, if you expand any of the objects that are referencing ProfilingExample, you'll see the objects referencing them (see Figure 72-15).

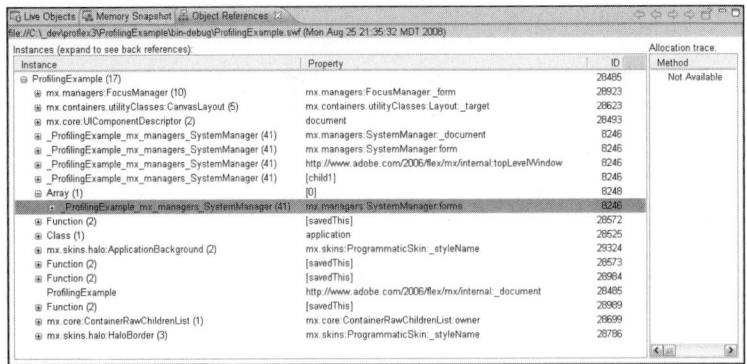

Figure 72-15

You can deduce the following:

1. `ProfilingExample` has 17 references pointing at it.

2. One of the 17 references is the property [0] of an Array.

3. The Array has 1 reference pointing to it. The reference is highlighted in Figure 72-15, and it is the `mx.managers:SystemManager:forms` property of `_ProfilingExample_mx_managers _SystemManager`.

4. If you drill down even further into the tree, you'll see that `_ProfilingExample_mx_managers _SystemManager` has 41 references pointing at it and the tree can be expanded to examine those references.

So far, only the left pane of the Object References View has been covered. There's also the right pane that details Allocation traces (refer to Figure 72-15). However, you must check "Generate object allocation stack traces" when you start profiling to utilize this feature. Allocation traces are illustrated in Figure 72-16.

The Allocation trace details the method that created the instance selected in the Instances table in the left-hand pane. In Figure 72-16, the selected instance is `ProfilingExample`, and by looking at the Allocation trace pane to the right you can see that:

❑ `_ProfilingExample_mx_managers_SystemManager:create()` is the method that instantiated `ProfilingExample`.

❑ `mx.managers:SystemManager:initializeTopLevelWindow()` is the method in the call stack that was responsible for calling the method that instantiated the `ProfilingExample` instance.

❑ If you inspect the call stack in the Allocation trace table from bottom to top, you will see the order of method execution.

Now that the Allocation traces feature has been discussed, it will be useful to find out more details on the origins of the object instances in your application.

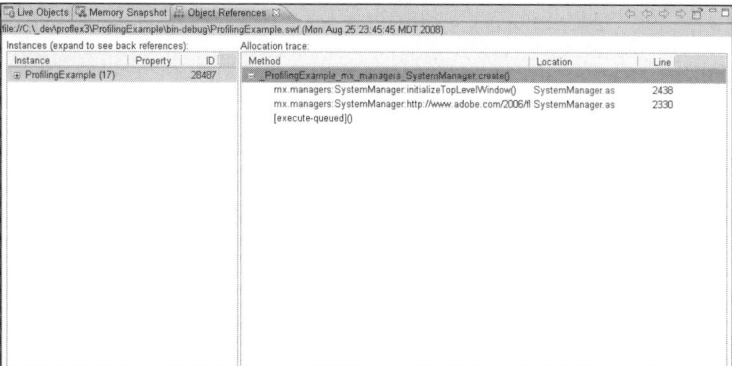

Figure 72-16

Inspecting the Cause of an Object Instantiation

The Allocation Trace View is used to view the various call stacks that were responsible for the object instances in your application. Once again, make sure that you checked "Generate object allocation stack traces" when you started the Profiler session. Figure 72-17 illustrates an Allocation Trace View for the `ProfilingExample` instance.

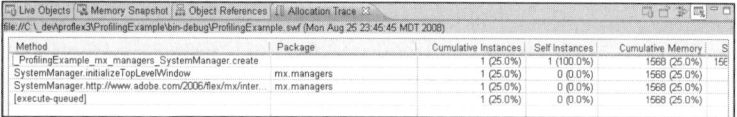

Figure 72-17

If you were following along and opened an Allocation Trace View with default Profiler settings, you would have seen two methods: `_ProfilingExample_mx_managers_SystemManager.create` and `[execute-queued]`. The reason this differs from what you see in Figure 72-17 is because in Figure 72-17 all package filtering had been turned off so that all the methods would be displayed. Package filtering will be discussed later on in this chapter.

If you compare Figure 72-16 with Figure 72-17, you will see that these are the same methods that were listed in the Allocation trace pane of the Object References View. However, the benefit of using the Allocation Trace View over the Allocation trace pane in the Object References View is that the Allocation Trace View will allow you to click the items to get additional data. To illustrate, Figure 72-18 shows what happens when you click on `_ProfilingExample_mx_managers_SystemManager.create`.

So, the Allocation Trace View is the gateway to the Object Statistics View. The Object Statistics View highlights some very granular data and is structured a little differently than the views you have looked at thus far.

The first thing you'll notice is that this view makes a distinction between cumulative values and self values, the values in this case being either instances or memory. Cumulative values have to do with all methods in the Allocation stack, and self values are a product of the method being detailed in the Object Statistics View. In the case of Figure 72-18, you will see that the cumulative and self values match, and therefore the method _ProfilingExample_mx_managers_SystemManager.create was the one responsible for the instance consuming 1568 bytes of memory.

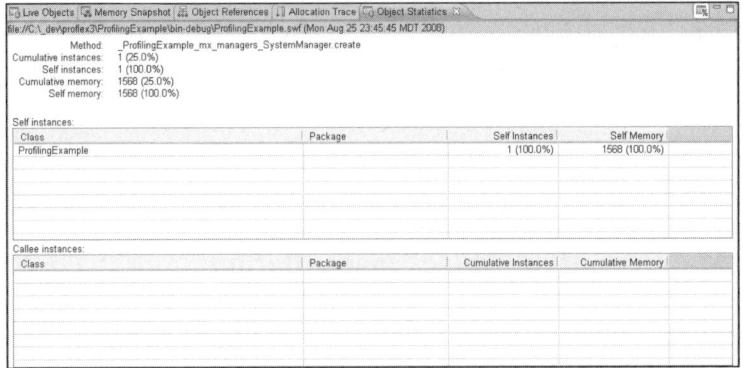

Figure 72-18

Also, if you remember the call stack earlier, there is a hierarchical chain of methods calling subsequent methods. Eventually, the chain will terminate at a final "Callee" method that is responsible for instantiating the instance. In Figure 72-18, you can see that the Callee instances table is empty and the ProfilingExample object instance is in the Self-instances table, once again verifying that _ProfilingExample_mx_managers_SystemManager.create was the final "Callee" method responsible for the creation of the object by invoking its constructor.

If you had gone down a level in the stack, actually to [execute-queued] at the very bottom of the stack, you would have seen that cumulative values are higher than self values and the ProfilingExample instance would be listed in the Callee instances table, as shown in Figure 72-19. In other words, [execute-queued] started the call stack, but it was not the method that instantiated the ProfilingExample instance.

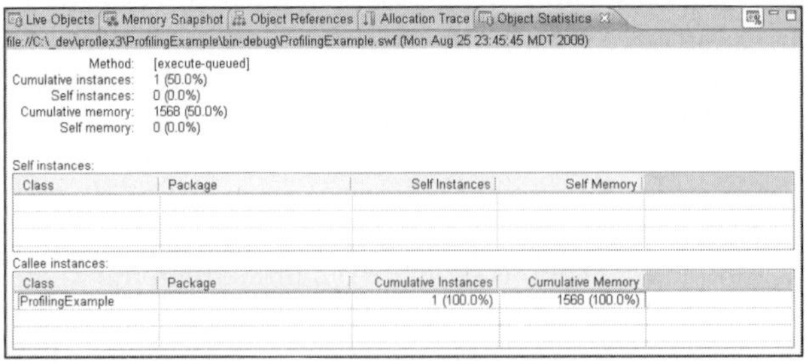

Figure 72-19

You can see that although there's only one Cumulative *instance, it has a (50.0%) next to it. This percentage is somewhat misleading. Basically, the percentage has to do with the number of call stack methods that are shown in the Allocation Trace View when you open the Object Statistics View. Since only the default package filters were on and only two methods were listed, you see 50%. If all the package filters had been turned off in the Allocation Trace View, the full call stack consisting of four methods would have appeared as illustrated in Figure 72-17, and when you click into the Object Statistics with the filters off, you would see (25.0%) instead.*

Views That Require Two Memory Snapshots

A couple things to examine before moving on to the Performance Profiler are the views that require two memory snapshots. Both of them are launched directly from the Profile View. One is the Loitering Objects View, and the other is an Allocation Trace View.

The Loitering Objects View and the Allocation Trace View each require two memory snapshots. When collecting the snapshots, you might decide to take a snapshot near the launch of the application and one near the termination. Alternately, you might decide to take two snapshots very close together and use those. The key thing to note is that as long as you have two snapshots, it does not matter how far apart they were taken while the application was running.

To open either of these two views:

1. Highlight the two memory snapshots that represent the period of time that you would like to analyze (see Figure 72-20).

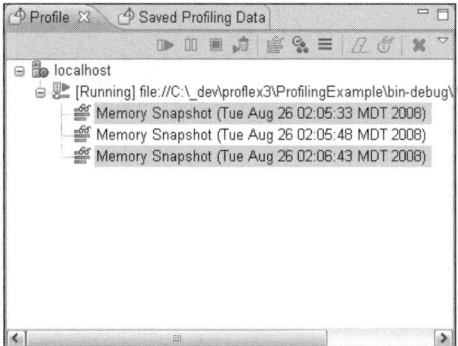

Figure 72-20

2. Click on either the Find Loitering Objects or View Allocation Trace button on the Profiler toolbar.

Now you will either see the Loitering Objects View (see Figure 72-21) or the Allocation Trace View (see Figure 72-22).

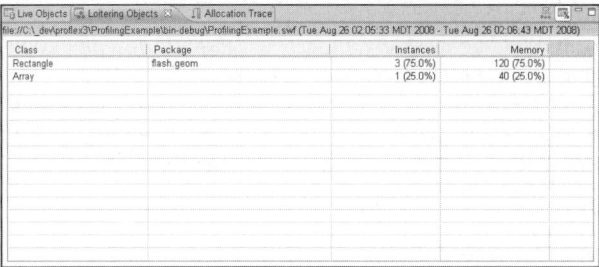

Figure 72-21

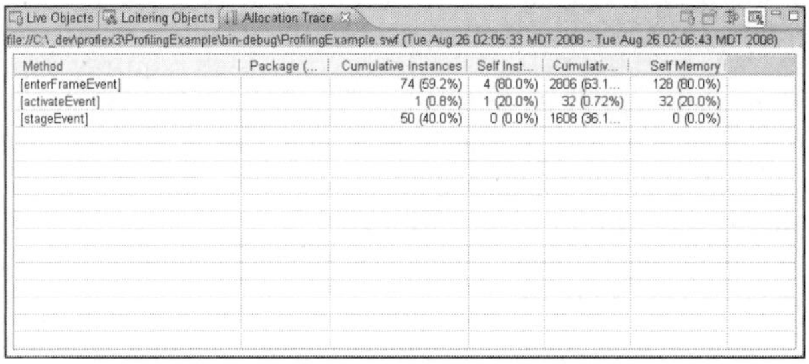

Figure 72-22

Earlier you saw the method [execute-queued] *when the Allocation Trace View was first being discussed. Now if you look at Figure 72-22 you see some more methods surrounded by brackets, such as* [enterFrameEvent] *and* [activateEvent]. *These methods are internal player actions. In other words, they're a view into what the Flash Player is spending its time doing: rendering, Garbage Collection, dispatching events, generating machine code, and so forth. Although you'll see more of them when you discuss performance profiling, here's a link to the Adobe LiveDocs if you would like to read more about them:* http://livedocs.adobe.com/flex/3/html/profiler_3.html.

Looking at the images, you will notice that the Loitering Objects View is similar to the Memory Snapshot View whereas the Allocation Trace View is the same as the Allocation Trace View that had been discussed earlier. Just remember that the data displayed in these cases is only the data collected between the first snapshot and the second snapshot.

That's about it in the world of Memory Profiler Views. Now it's time to check out the Performance Profiler Views.

Using the Performance Profiler

The Performance Profiler enables you to determine the following:

- ❑ Which method calls take the most time
- ❑ Which method calls happen most often
- ❑ Which method(s) was responsible for calling a particular method

❑   Which method(s) was called as a result of a particular method call

❑   The breakdown of time spent during a method call and all subsequent method calls

To use the Performance Profiler, check the Enable performance profiling check box when you launch your profiling session.

Taking a Performance Snapshot

Unlike the Memory Profiler that has a Live Objects View, the Performance Profiler doesn't have a live performance view. To view any of the performance data that has been collected, you will need to take at least one performance snapshot. To do this:

1.   In the Profile View, highlight the [Running] application that you would like to take a snapshot of.

2.   Once the [Running] application is selected, click the Capture Performance Profile button in the Profile View toolbar to take the snapshot (see Figure 72-23).

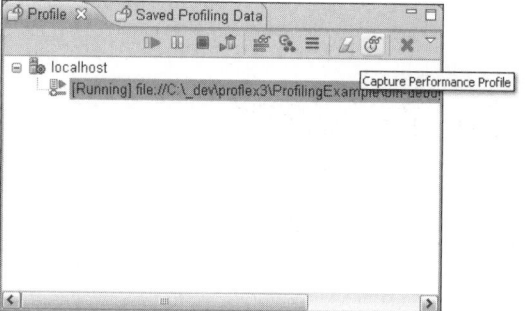

Figure 72-23

3.   Once the snapshot is available, it will show up as a child of the [Running] application in the Profile View (just like the memory snapshot did). Double-click Performance Profile to open the Performance Profile View, as illustrated in Figure 72-24.

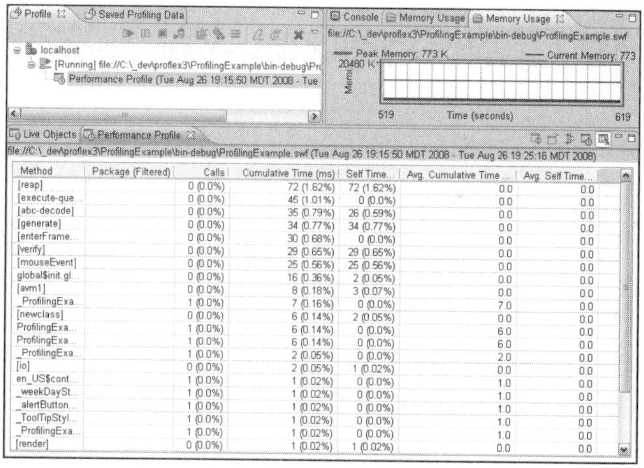

Figure 72-24

Looking at the Performance Profile View, the most important thing to keep in mind is the difference between Cumulative and Self Time. With the Performance Profile View you're looking at methods that can call other methods. Hence Cumulative Time is the time it takes a method and all its "Callee" methods to execute whereas Self Time refers to the time it takes for only that method to execute.

The other thing you'll notice from Figure 72-24 is that the Performance Profile View has an Average Cumulative Time and Average Self Time. Whereas the Cumulative and Self Times take into account every call to a particular method during a profiling timeframe, the Average Self Times are an approximation of how long individual calls took.

Viewing Method Statistics

If there are any methods listed in the Performance Profile View that are of particular interest to you, you can double-click them to pull up more data about them. The screen that will appear is the Method Statistics View, as shown in Figure 72-25.

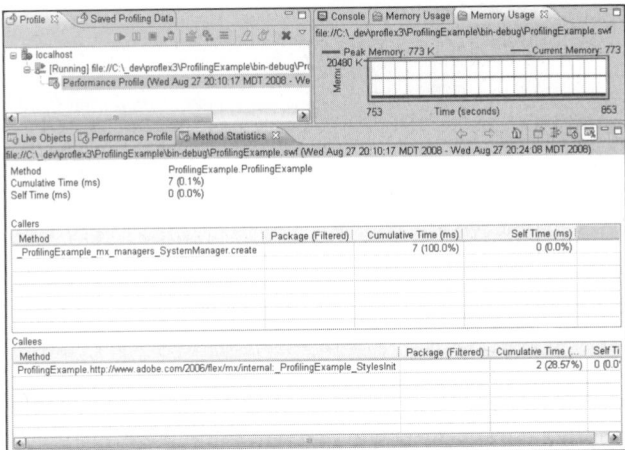

Figure 72-25

You can see the method statistics for `ProfilingExample.ProfilingExample` — in other words, the constructor for the `ProfilingExample` class. From looking at the Method Statistics View, you can tell the following:

- ❑ Based on Cumulative Time it took about 7 milliseconds for all calls to `ProfilingExample .ProfilingExample` to run.

- ❑ Out of those 7 milliseconds, 2 of them were used by the "Callee" method `ProfilingExample .http://www.adobe.com/2006/flex/mx/internal:_ProfilingExample_StylesInit`, and the other 5 milliseconds were from some other "Callees" that are in packages that are currently filtered from being displayed.

- ❑ By looking at the Caller table, you can see that `ProfilingExample.ProfilingExample` was invoked by `_ProfilingExample_mx_managers_SystemManager.create`, although there might have been more methods in packages that are currently filtered from being displayed that may have invoked `ProfilingExample.ProfilingExample`, too.

❑ Although the Cumulative Time for all calls to the `ProfilingExample.ProfilingExample` constructor was 7 ms, by looking at the Self Time, you can see that `ProfilingExample.ProfilingExample` itself took "0 ms," or at least was so quick that it didn't show up in any of the samples.

Clearing Accumulated Performance Data

When you launch a performance profiling session, Flex Builder will start accumulating performance data. There are going to be times when you're not going to want to view all data, but only data that was captured from one point in time to another. For instance, if you're testing one call to a particular algorithm, it would be nice to clear the data right before running the algorithm. Clearing data is very similar to taking a performance snapshot:

1. In the Profile View, highlight the [Running] application that you would like to clear the data from.

2. Once the [Running] application is selected, click the Reset Performance Data button in the Profile View toolbar to clear the data (see Figure 72-26).

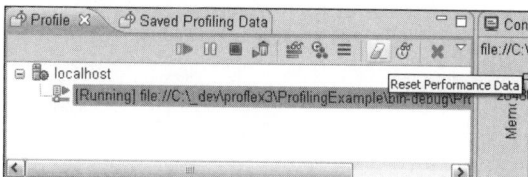

Figure 72-26

Filtering in the Profiler

This chapter has continually referred to filtered packages. By default, the Profiler filters packages in `flash.*.*` and `mx.*.*`. In addition, built-in items such as `Strings` are filtered out. This means that if you're profiling something and a successful outcome of your profiling session relies on `mx.controls.DataGrid` or `flash.text.TextField`, you will need to know how to change the inclusion/exclusion filters.

There are two places to change the inclusion/exclusion filters. The first is in the Eclipse preferences. The second is in each of the views that support package filtering. Keep in mind, if you decide to change the filters in the Eclipse preferences it will affect all the views in the Profiler unlike the per-view filter settings. The other thing to note is the filters work on packages and not class names.

To configure the per-view filters:

1. If the view you're in supports the inclusion/exclusion filters, you'll see the Filters button in the view's toolbar to the top right of the view (see Figure 72-27). Note that the Object References and Object Statistics Views don't have the Filters button.

Figure 72-27

2. After you click the Filters button, the Filters dialog will appear, as illustrated in Figure 72-28.

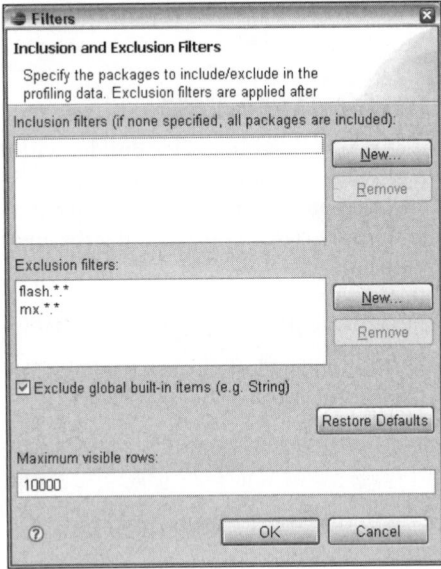

Figure 72-28

In this filter dialog, you can add and remove your filters. Exclusion filters are applied first. Don't worry about messing up the default filters because as you can tell, you can restore defaults by using the Restore Defaults button. Also, when you create various inclusion and exclusion filters for each package you would like to filter, the data collected remains the same. In other words, the filters are just filtering the view of the data and not the collected samples themselves.

As mentioned, filters are per view. In other words, if you created a custom filter on the Performance Profile View and then clicked on a method to enter the Method Statistics View, you would have to re-create your custom filters in that view, too. If you decide that there's a particular custom filter configuration that you'd like to apply across all views during your profiling session, you can configure the filter settings in the Eclipse preferences:

1. Open the Window menu on a Windows system or the Eclipse menu on a Mac OS X system.

2. Select Preferences.

3. In the Preferences dialog, navigate to Flex ⇨ Profiler.

4. From the Profiler settings you will see Exclusion Filters and Inclusion Filters. Although these views are broken into two screens they work the same as the dialog used in the per view settings. Also, just as with the per-view filters, if you screw up the filter settings you can restore them to default.

Saving and Loading Profiling Data

There will be times when you need to save the data you collected during your profiling session for later analysis. The Flex Builder 3 Profiler has built-in support for loading and saving the data collected during a profiling session.

To save your profiling data:

1. In the Profile View, select the profiling session you would like to save the data for.

2. Click on the drop-down arrow in the toolbar to the top-right corner of the Profile View.

3. Select the Save button, as shown in Figure 72-29.

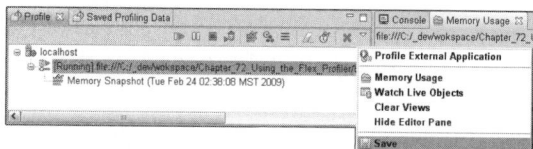

Figure 72-29

4. Once you've selected the Save button, you will be shown a folder browser window to select the location on disk that you'd like to save your profiling data.

5. Once the profiling data is saved, you will see a bunch of `flex-profiler*` files in the location that you had chosen. None of these files are human-readable, so they're really only useful in the Flex Builder 3 Profiler.

Now that you have some saved profile data, you can load it back into the Profiler using the following process:

1. Click on the Saved Profiling Data View. In a default Profiling perspective, it should be to the right of the Profile View.

2. Click on the Open button in the top-right toolbar of the Saved Profiling Data View. (The icon looks like an open folder.)

3. In the folder browser window that pops up, select the folder where you saved the profiling data. If you selected the correct folder, you'll see the saved profiling data show up in the view, as illustrated in Figure 72-30.

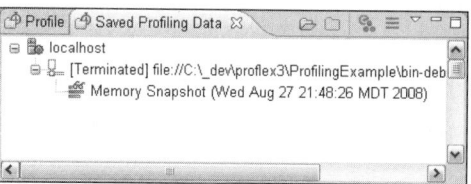

Figure 72-30

Other Useful Features

By now you should have a pretty good feel for how to use the Flex Builder 3 Profiler. Although it is still suggested to read through the Profiler documentation in the LiveDocs to reinforce the information you've learned thus far, here are a couple more highlighted features just in case you don't get around to reading the LiveDoc.

Profiler Preferences

If you get tired of continually turning the Memory Profiler or Performance Profiler on and off in the launch dialog when you start profiling sessions, you can modify the state of those check boxes in the Eclipse Preferences:

1. Open the Window menu on a Windows system or the Eclipse menu on a Mac OS X system.

2. Select Preferences.

3. In the Preferences dialog navigate to Flex ⇨ Profiler.

4. You will see the check boxes for "Enable memory profiling" and "Enable performance profiling." Check the check box you need and apply the changes and exit Preferences.

Running Garbage Collection Manually

Sometimes you don't necessarily want to take a memory snapshot but would like to manually run Garbage Collection. An example of such a scenario is when you're watching the Live Objects View and/ or the Memory Usage graph and would like to see if the memory utilization and the number of live instances will decrease after a Garbage Collection pass. To force Garbage Collection, click the Run Garbage Collector button in the toolbars of the Profile and Live Objects Views (see Figure 72-31).

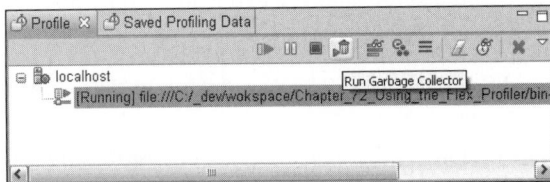

Figure 72-31

By default, this button is grayed out in the Profile View. If you want to enable the Run Garbage Collector button in the Profile View, you must first select a [Running] application, just as you would when taking memory snapshots.

Viewing Zero Time Methods

The Flex Builder 3 Profiler collects samples approximately every millisecond. There are times when methods will run so quickly that they won't show up in any of the samples. By default, these methods are filtered from the display. If you are in a view with a toolbar containing the Show Zero Time Methods button, such as the Performance Profile View, click it to see these zero time methods (see Figure 72-32).

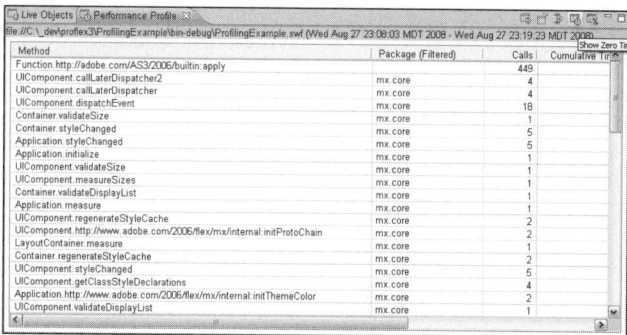

Figure 72-32

Viewing Source Code

If you have the source code available, some of the views support opening source code directly from the Flex Profiler — an especially powerful feature. If you're in a view that supports this functionality, such as the Performance Profile View or the Memory Snapshot View, and would like to open source code, just highlight one of the rows and click on the Open Source File button (see Figure 72-33). This button is shown in Figure 72-33.

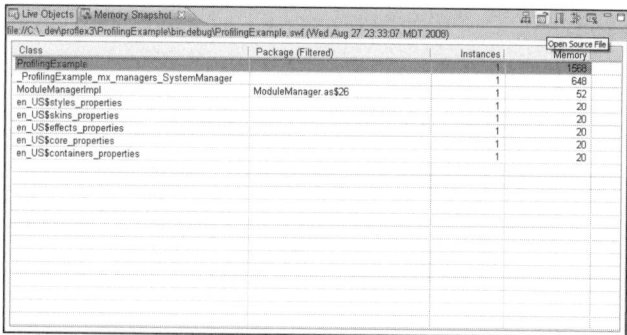

Figure 72-33

Navigating between Views

If you've been double-clicking "Callees" and "Callers" in the Method Statistics View to view different levels of a call stack, you can quickly navigate back, forward, and back home to the original method you opened in the Method Statistics View by using the same types of buttons you'd use in a web browser. These buttons will appear in the Method Statistics View toolbar, as shown in Figure 72-34.

Figure 72-34

The Profilers in Action

Now that you have a solid understanding of the features and functionality available in the Profiler and the reasoning behind them, two Profiler use cases will now be discussed. The first use case will give an example on how to track down a memory leak using the Profiler, and the second will illustrate how to use the Profiler to optimize an algorithm.

Using the Memory Profiler to Detect Leaks

During this use case, you will be running the `MemoryLeak.mxml` application available in the source code directory of the `Chapter_72_Using_the_Flex_Profiler` project. Start this use case by launching this application in a profiling session.

1. When you launch the profiling session make sure that "Enable memory profiling," "Watch live memory data," and "Generate object allocation stack traces" are all checked.

    Although you don't always need to enable all three of these check boxes, to refresh, "Enable memory profiling" enables memory profiling, "Watch live memory data" enables data in the Live Objects View, and "Generate object allocation stack traces" enables data in Allocation trace areas.

2. Let the application run for a minute and watch the Memory Usage graph. It will start to look like Figure 72-35. The first warning sign of a memory leak is when the Current Memory total rises along with the Peak Memory total with no sign of stabilization.

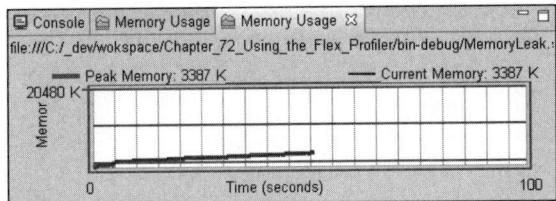

Figure 72-35

3. Now that you can see a leak, take a look at the Live Objects View such as the one illustrated in Figure 72-36. Watch the Live Object View for a couple minutes. What you're looking for is objects that continue to have an increasing number of live object Instances that have a value that stays on par with the number of Cumulative Instances. For instance, you can see that LeakyTitleWindow has 135 Cumulative Instances and 135 Instances. At the same time there are 135 Cumulative Instances of PopUpData and only 30 live object Instances. This means that PopUpData is probably being garbage collected properly whereas LeakyTitleWindow is not.

    If you don't see any Live Objects that look suspicious, remember that the view may be filtered. Click the filter button to make changes to the filter settings.

4. Since LeakyTitleWindow is suspicious, take a Memory Snapshot and open it. This will look similar to the Live Objects View, so no screenshot is provided here.

    Depending on how many objects there are, and how long you've been profiling, it may take a little while to open the memory snapshot. You can run it in the background and do other things if you like.

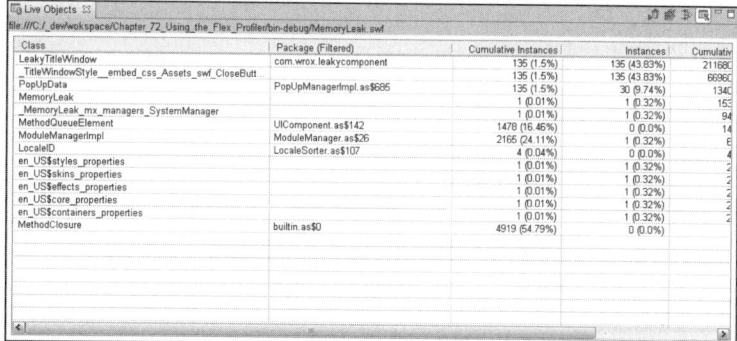

Figure 72-36

5. Double-click LeakyTitleWindow in the memory snapshot to open the Object References View. The first thing you see is the first object instance of LeakyTitleWindow has 22 back references. Expand the tree for the first LeakyTitleWindow back reference. If you look at the first two back references, you will see that they originate from the LeakyTitleWindow class itself (see Figure 72-37). This brings up a good point: not all of the object references shown will cause a leak.

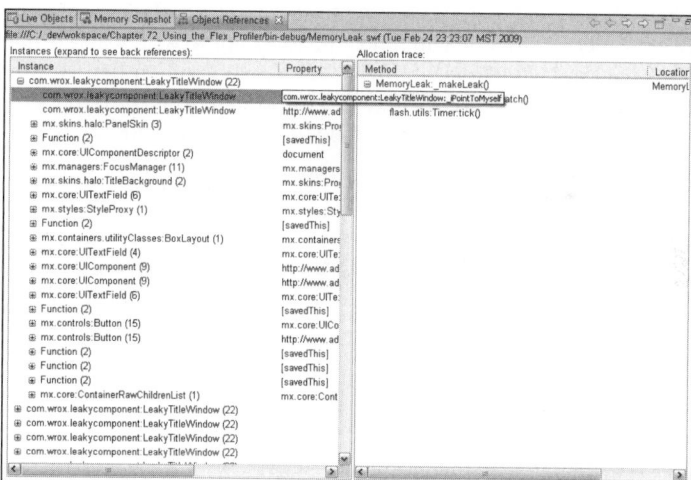

Figure 72-37

One thing to note is that the collected data may not necessarily show up in the same order all of the time. Pay particular attention to the figures in the book as you follow along so that you can match them up to what you see in your Flex Builder profiling session.

6. Start working your way down the list. Expand the back references to see where they end up. If you expand the back references labeled "Function (2)," you find one similar to the one detailed in Figure 72-38. Looking at this particular chain of back references you'll realize that it ends back up at the same LeakyTitleWindow instance. In other words, once LeakyTitleWindow is no longer reachable, this back reference chain won't matter to the Garbage Collector and therefore would not be of concern.

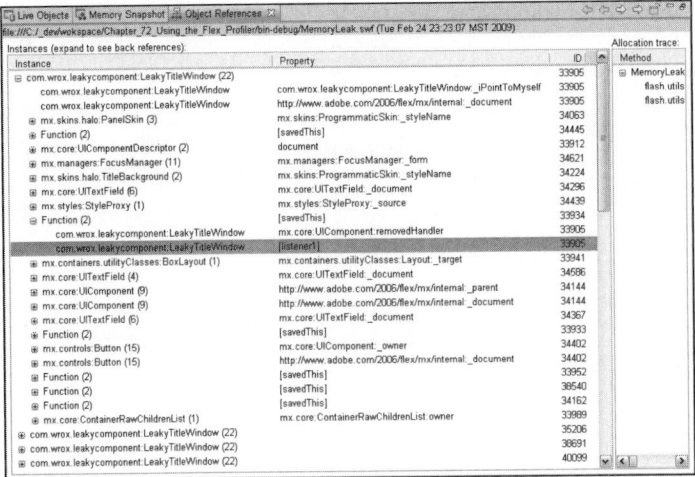

Figure 72-38

As you continue to look through the back references, pay particular attention for a back reference labeled "Function (2)" that appears similar to what's shown in Figure 72-39. Looking at this back reference chain, you can tell right away not to worry about the back reference to `Function` from the LeakyTitleWindow `_onEnterFrame` handler. However, `MemoryLeak` is the main application class and will hang around indefinitely; therefore the back reference to `Function` from `MemoryLeak` requires some further investigation.

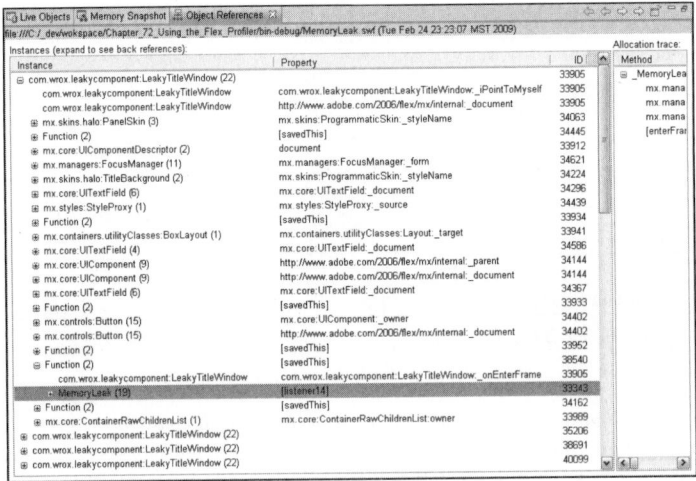

Figure 72-39

7. Go back and select the Function back reference again. Take a look at the right-hand Allocation trace pane, as illustrated in Figure 72-40. As you can see, this particular function was created in the `LeakyTitleWindow _onCreationComplete()` method. This gives us a starting point in the code to try to plug the leak.

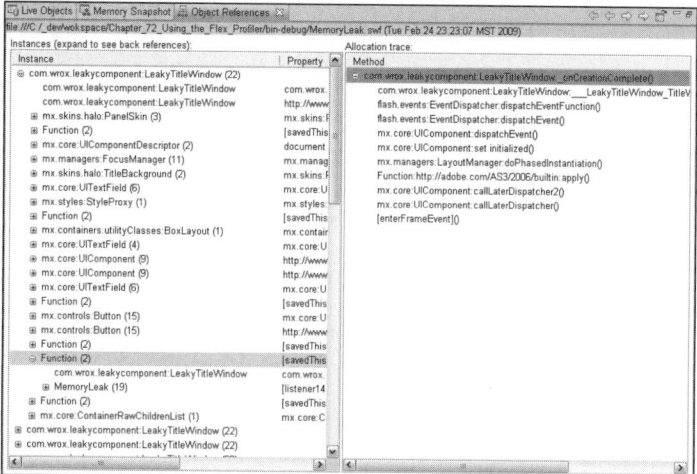

Figure 72-40

Taking a look at the code, you can see that there is a strong event listener that creates a reference from the application back into the `LeakyTitleWindow` component via the `_onEnterFrame` method:

```
private function _onCreationComplete( p_evt:FlexEvent ):void
{
 Application.application.addEventListener(Event.ENTER_FRAME,_onEnterFrame );
}
```

There are a couple of ways to resolve this issue:

❑ Get rid of the event listener completely. (In most cases this will not be an option.)

❑ Remove the listener when the `LeakyTitleWindow` is discarded.

❑ Make the listener weak.

8. Choose the option to make the listener weak, as shown in the following code:

```
Application.application.addEventListener( Event.ENTER_FRAME, _onEnterFrame, false,
0, true );
```

9. After making the code change, run another memory profiling session. Figure 72-41 is similar to what you will see in the Memory Usage graph and Live Objects View after waiting a little bit.

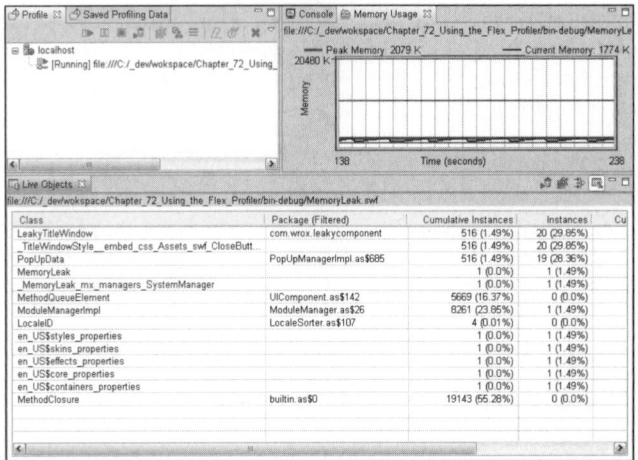

Figure 72-41

At this point you can feel pretty confident that the leak has been plugged. Here are some key indicators:

❑ The Memory Usage graph shows a pretty flat memory footprint. This means that the Flash Player has reached a good memory profile required to run the application under the current circumstances.

❑ The Memory Usage graph shows the Garbage Collector running. This is indicated with the dips in the graph of the Current Memory line.

❑ Looking at the Live Objects View, you can see that although there are 516 Cumulative Instances of LeakyTitleWindow, there are only 20 live instances. This indicates that the LeakyTitleWindow is now being properly garbage collected thanks to the modification of the Event.ENTER_FRAME event listener in step 8.

Although this was a pretty simplistic example of a memory leak, it should provide you with a pretty good workflow for memory profiling your applications.

Using the Performance Profiler to Optimize an Algorithm

During this use case, you will profile the PerformanceOptimization.mxml application available in the Chapter 72 source code. You can use the Performance Profiler to profile complete applications, which is something that you should be doing periodically throughout the development process of your Flex applications.

However, sometimes you may want to just profile a relatively self-contained algorithm. For instance, maybe you're trying to figure out if using strongly typed objects instead of generic objects is really going to help you. By taking a snippet out of the application and putting it into a sandbox, you can prevent any additional noise caused by the surrounding application code from degrading the accuracy of your test results.

The code in `PerformanceOptimization.mxml` was written to compare using a standard `for` loop to loop through an `ArrayCollection` versus using a `for each` loop. The general performance profiling process is to run this test several times until you have plenty of performance snapshots to feel comfortable about the results. Here are the steps:

1. Start profiling the application and make sure to select the "Enable performance profiling" check box in the launch dialog.

   During a performance profiling session, if you want to decrease the overhead of your profiling session, you can deselect all the memory profiling options at launch. If you're tired of unchecking check boxes at launch, an even better option would be to go into the Eclipse preferences and disable memory profiling for the duration of your testing.

2. If you disabled memory profiling, at this point, you will see the application listed as [Running] in the Profile View. Figure 72-42 shows the application running in the browser along with a view of the Flex Builder 3 Profiler perspective.

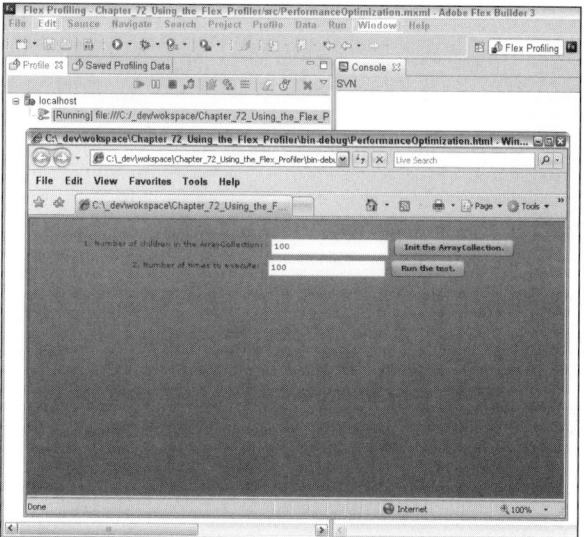

Figure 72-42

3. The next step is to use the Reset Performance Data button in the Profile View toolbar. This will start the profile data fresh, deleting any data that had been collected. If you don't remember this button, it's detailed in the "Clearing Accumulated Performance Data" section earlier in this chapter.

4. After you've reset the data, go back to your application (refer to Figure 72-42):

   a. Choose the number of children you'd like to have in your `ArrayCollection`.

   b. Click the Init the ArrayCollection button to set up the `ArrayCollection`.

   c. Decide on how many times you want the test to execute.

   d. Click the Run the test button to run the test.

5. The application will execute the test. During each iteration the `ArrayCollection` will be passed to each of the two algorithms at which time the algorithm will be executed. When the tests are complete an alert notification indicating that the "Test is Complete" will be displayed. When the alert is shown click the OK button to dismiss the notification and go back to the Flex Builder 3.

6. Now that you're back in the Flex Builder 3 Profiling perspective, you need to retrieve the collected performance data by clicking the Capture Performance Profile button on the Profile View toolbar. Refer to the section "Taking a Performance Snapshot" earlier in this chapter for more information on how to do that.

7. Open the Performance Profile that you created in Step 6. If you sort the "Package (Filtered)" column in descending order, you can view the results of running the methods right next to each other (see Figure 72-43).

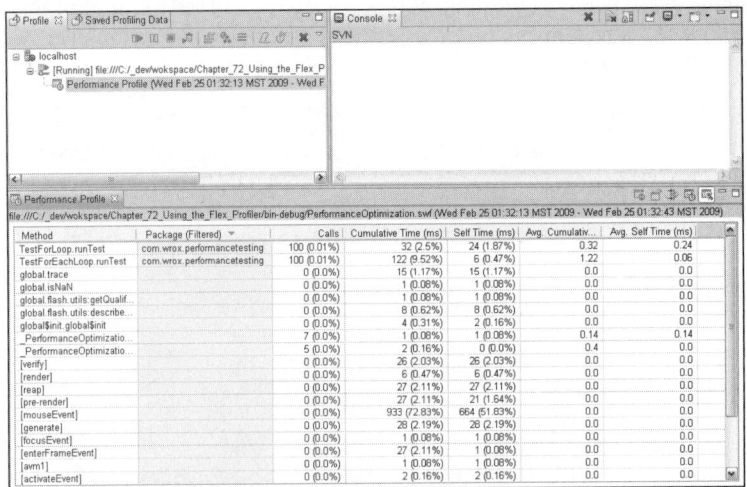

Figure 72-43

Looking at the round of results illustrated in Figure 72-43, you can see the following:

❏ Looking at the Self Time (ms) values, the call to `TestForLoop.runTest()` containing the `for` loop took four times longer to run than the calls to `TestForEachLoop.runTest()` containing the `for each` loop.

❏ In contrast, if you account for the initial call to the `runTest()` methods along with all subsequent calls, the call to `TestForEachLoop.runTest()` containing the `for each` loop took much longer: an Avg. Cumulative Time of 1.22 ms vs. 0.32 ms.

❏ In this case, you cannot prevent subsequent calls from firing, so you need to determine the outcome based on Cumulative Time and not just on Self Time. This means that if you had to use the code as is, you should choose the `for` loop code over the `for each` loop code, since executing all the supporting code was much faster.

At this point, in a real-world testing scenario, you still wouldn't be in the clear. To make an informed decision would require several more rounds of testing. To do this, you would perform Steps 3–6 over and over until you feel that you've collected enough snapshots.

Another thing is that it would be nice to run some tests with varied data to see if the number of children in the `ArrayCollection` affects the results. For instance, maybe the application you're using this for would only ever have 10 children in the `ArrayCollection`. After running several rounds of tests with that number of children in the `ArrayCollection`, you may find out that the performance data results aren't different enough to warrant a refactor.

> *Code readability is king. If you have competing algorithms that run similarly in the scenario in which they'd be used in your application, choose the one that's easiest to read and understand.*

Figure 72-44 shows a couple rounds of testing side by side. These tests indicate that with 100 children, looping through an `ArrayCollection` with `for` loops is much faster than doing it with a `for each` loop.

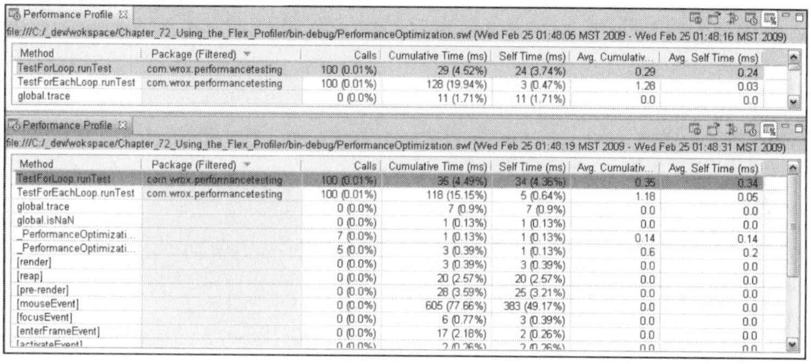

Figure 72-44

Although it is good to know when one algorithm is faster than another, it would be nice to know the methods involved that cause a particular algorithm to take a certain amount of time to run. Remember, you're looking at Cumulative Time and not Self Time and in the case of these method calls, the Cumulative Time is much larger than the Self Time. This means you need to drill down into the Method Statistics View to see which "Callee" method is the culprit. Refer to the section "Viewing Method Statistics" earlier in this chapter for help.

Because the `for each` loop-based algorithm `TestForEachLoop.runTest()` obviously took much longer, examine the Method Statistic View for it by double-clicking its row in the Performance Profile View. When you first open the view, the Cumulative Time of the "Callee" methods may not add up to the difference between the Cumulative Time and Self Time displayed. To see the other "Callees" that make up the remainder of the Cumulative Time will require you to turn off the package filters. Refer to the earlier section "Filtering in the Profiler" for assistance with that.

Now that the package filters are turned off, Figure 72-45 shows the other two methods that are causing the `for each` loop to run so slowly, `ListCollectionView.http://www.adobe.com/2006/action script/flash/proxy:nextValue` and `ListCollectionView.http://www.adobe.com/2006/actionscript/flash/proxy:nextNameIndex`.

Notice that the Self Time for each method is much smaller than the Cumulative Time. That means that if you drill into the Method Statistics View for either of them, you will see methods that they had called that make up the difference between their Cumulative Time and their Self Time.

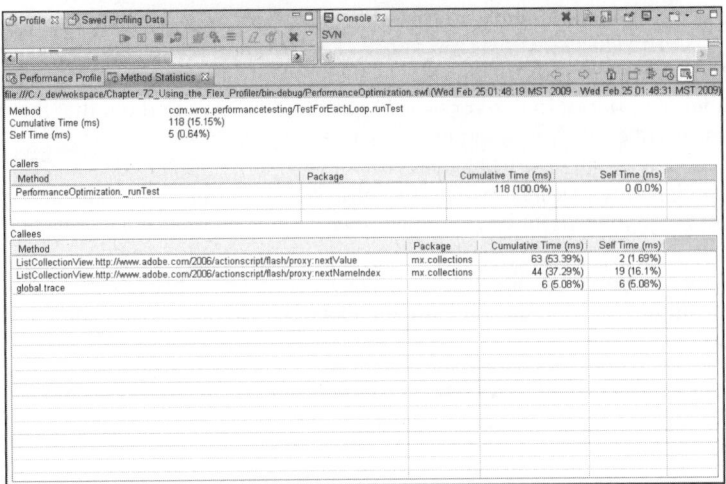

Figure 72-45

Now that you're armed with the knowledge of how to performance profile and memory profile your applications, the following section will give a very brief overview on what you can do if the Flex Builder 3 Profiler is not meeting your specific needs.

Creating Your Own Profiler

Although the Flex Builder 3 Profiler is a very robust profiling tool, there are a couple of drawbacks. The first is that it's not extremely customizable. For instance, you can only filter data based on package. Second, if you're not using Flex Builder 3 Professional, you don't have access to it. The good news is, the ActionScript classes that the Profiler uses to sample data are available for creating custom tools.

The ActionScript classes that are used by the Flex Builder 3 Profiler are the classes in the `flash.sampler.*` package. There are several things to keep in mind if you would like to attempt to create your own Profiler:

❑ You need to be running Flash Player Debug version 9.0.115 or later.

❑ For the time being, these classes are included in `playerglobal.swc` but not `airglobal.swc`. In other words, `flash.sampler.*` classes are not available in an AIR project. Here's a link to the bug in the Adobe public bug-base: `https://bugs.adobe.com/jira/browse/SDK-15731`.

❑ Flex Builder 3 uses a SWF called `ProfilerAgent.swf` to profile applications. When your applications are running in profiling mode, this SWF runs in the player parallel to your application. Accomplishing this requires configuring a setting in `mm.cfg` called `PreloadSwf`. You will need to keep this in mind if you want your custom Profiler to run as an agent.

For much more detailed information on utilizing the `flash.sampler.*` *classes to profile your applications, refer to the Adobe LiveDocs, at* `http://livedocs.adobe.com/flex/3/langref/flash/sampler/package-detail.html`.

Although building a custom Profiler is outside the scope of this book, you can see a very rudimentary custom Profiler by running the CustomProfiler.mxml application available with the Chapter 72 source code. Figure 72-46 shows this example Profiler in action.

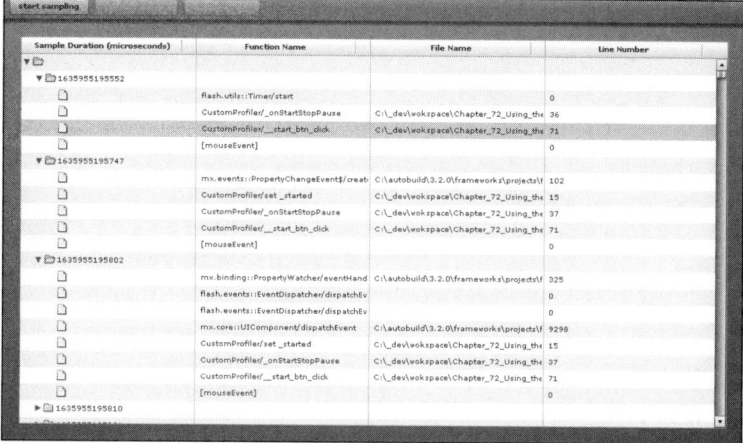

Figure 72-46

Summary

The Flex Builder 3 Profiler is a very powerful and welcome addition to the Flex Builder toolset. The Profiler enables you to optimize your application code, decrease excessive object instantiation, and even track down memory leaks. Although using the Profiler takes a little background knowledge and some practice, hopefully you've walked away from this chapter with the ability to start using the Flex Builder 3 Profiler effectively.

Up next, unit testing and Test-Driven Development will be discussed.

73

Unit Testing and Test-Driven Development with FlexUnit

This chapter covers the practice of unit testing and the best practice of Test-Driven Development (TDD), using FlexUnit, the open-source unit-testing framework for Flex. When practiced together, these techniques are invaluable, helping you to write more robust and better designed software with fewer dependencies and looser coupling between classes. You can catch bugs early, before they can enter production, when the cost of fixing them is much higher.

Overview

Unit testing is the practice of testing the small pieces of functionality that make up an application to ensure that they operate correctly. These small pieces are the *units*, and they are tested to ensure that each one satisfies its contract by returning the expected results, handling errors appropriately, and collaborating properly with dependent interfaces. If each unit of a system is deemed to be correct, one might infer that the system as a whole is correct. In reality, such a claim would be presumptuous, but unit testing does provide many benefits and reassurances.

TDD is a technique that takes unit testing to its logical extreme, by advocating that unit tests be written first, before the functionality that will actually be tested has even been implemented. Unsurprisingly, the unit test will initially fail, since the functionality has not been written, but when it does succeed, the developer knows that the code is correct. This process can seem back-to-front to newcomers, but its benefits can be quite remarkable, as this chapter aims to demonstrate.

This chapter covers both unit testing and TDD in detail, beginning with a discussion of the main benefits, before moving on to examine the open-source FlexUnit library available for unit testing Flex applications. Those readers already familiar with unit testing in other programming languages may wish to skip to the second half of the chapter, which contains practical examples and further topics, such as mock objects and event testing. The examples in this chapter are based on a simple video portal application.

Why Write Tests?

It is worth spending a little time understanding the motivation for unit testing and TDD, since we developers often prefer to hack away in darkened rooms, oblivious to the bugs creeping into our code. Why should we write unit tests and why on earth should we write them before the code that is to be tested?

Preventing Bugs in the First Place

A simple mistake in an algorithm can bring an application crashing to the ground. Perhaps an error message will be displayed or maybe the client will just stop responding. In any case, the user is disheartened and deterred from using the application again. The cost of fixing such a problem can be large, since the developer who wrote the original code may have jumped ship, and the fix itself could have unintentional consequences. By writing unit tests during development, many bugs like these can be caught before they have the chance to propagate in production code. This produces more robust, higher-quality software and reduces development time and costs.

Gaining the Confidence to Refactor

Making changes to a large application can be hair-raising. There could be hundreds or thousands of classes, each with its own properties and functions, and the documentation may be scarce or out of date. Understanding the full implications of a small change in one part of the system is a task fit for a computer, not a human. By writing unit tests and collecting these together to form test suites that can be run easily and repeatedly, you can gain the confidence to refactor and extend the system. You will be informed quickly of any side effects of your changes by a failing test case, allowing you to resolve the problem before committing new code.

Driving Improvements in Design

The process of writing the test case first, before the functionality under test has been implemented, prompts you to consider its behavior. In effect, by writing the test, you are trying out the API and will quickly notice if it is poorly designed. With the conventional approach of coding first and testing later, you are more likely to waste time coding something with a design flaw that will need to be scrapped or revised later. So TDD drives improvements in design and reduces unnecessary development effort.

Writing Testable Software

In order to write a unit test, you must devise an API that can be tested. So unit testing encourages you to design classes that can be easily tested. An analogy can be drawn with the manufacturing industry, where consumer products often incorporate design features that allow quality assurance tests to be performed automatically. More simplistically, think of a ballpoint pen with transparent casing. That design feature allows writers to see when the ink has run out. Class design decisions should be influenced by similar considerations of testability.

It is common to write a class that creates objects of another class internally and then collaborates with them. For instance, a Cairngorm command may create a business delegate object and call a function on it.

TDD tends to promote more loosely coupled designs, where collaborations take place through interfaces rather than concrete classes. These interfaces can be simulated or mocked for testing purposes, so the collaborating class can be tested in isolation without dependencies. This approach is known as *inversion of control* or *dependency injection*.

Happy Developers and Effortless Documentation

There are many more benefits to TDD discussed in various places. For instance, apparently developers receive a psychological boost every time they see a test success, thus sustaining long hours at the keyboard! In seriousness, test cases are a good measure of progress and they provide reassurance that functionality has been implemented correctly. Good test cases also provide a form of implicit developer documentation, describing in readable code the expected behavior of the classes under test.

Technology and Terminology

This section introduces the FlexUnit library and summarizes the basic terminology of unit testing, in preparation for the detailed examples that follow.

The FlexUnit Library

FlexUnit is the most established unit-testing framework available for Flex applications. It provides everything you need to begin writing unit tests and practice TDD. FlexUnit was originally based on JUnit 3 in Java, though a few features have been tailored specifically for Flex. There are plans to incorporate more advanced metadata-based test configuration, similar to more recent versions of JUnit, in the future. The latest version of FlexUnit includes an elegant Flex client for running unit tests and interpreting their results, known as the FlexUnit Runner, or simply the test runner, and shown in Figure 73-1.

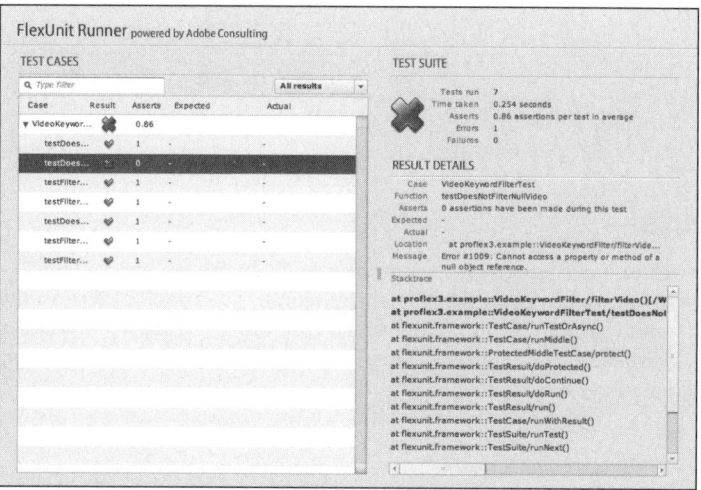

Figure 73-1

1305

Unit Tests, Test Cases, and Test Suites

In FlexUnit, a *unit test* is a function that tests the behavior of a class in some way. By convention, a unit test focuses on a small aspect of behavior, such as the operation of a function under certain conditions. There may be multiple unit tests for a single function that each test different aspects of its behavior, such as its response to normal parameters and boundary conditions as well as its error handling.

Multiple unit tests are grouped together to form *test cases*, and test cases are then aggregated to form *test suites*. These test suites are built into a composition containing all the test cases and unit tests for an entire project and this is known as the *AllTests suite*. Figure 73-2 shows a composition of unit tests, test cases, and test suites.

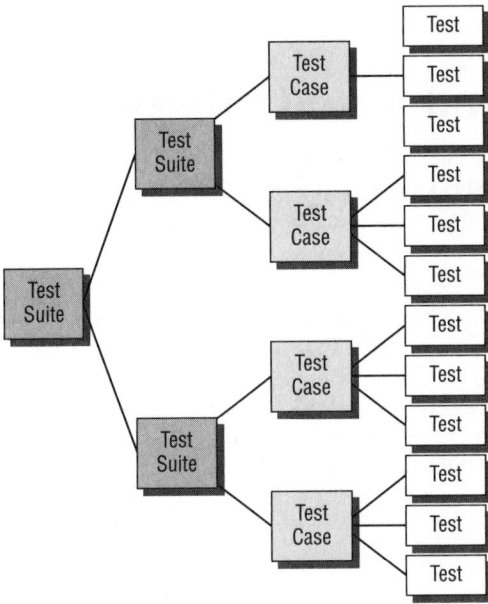

Figure 73-2

Running Tests

The FlexUnit test runner executes a test suite by recursively processing each test case and executing all the unit tests. When a unit test is performed, the outcome is recorded and presented by the test runner. The outcome of a unit test may be *success*, in which case the test completed without interruption; *failure*, in which case some specific but incorrect behavior was detected by the test; or *error*, in which case a problem unanticipated by the unit test occurred.

Test-Driven Development by Example

The most benefit is derived from unit testing when combined with TDD, so the examples in this section do precisely that. The example scenario involves creating a class for filtering video objects by keyword. The test cases will be created before the filter class, in order to reflect upon its design and ensure its testability, before expending effort on its implementation.

Preparing for Unit Testing

A Flex Builder or standalone project must be prepared for unit testing. This involves adding the FlexUnit library to the project build path and creating a source folder for storing test cases, test suites, and other related classes.

Download FlexUnit

FlexUnit contains the base classes for implementing and running unit tests. It is distributed as a ZIP archive that can be downloaded from `http://opensource.adobe.com/wiki/display/flexunit`.

The distribution contains a `flexunit` folder with the following contents:

- ❑ `license.txt` — Licensed under the terms of the New BSD License
- ❑ `bin/flexunit.swc` — The unit-testing framework library
- ❑ `docs/` — The AS3 documentation
- ❑ `src/` — The source code, should you need it

Adding the Library

To add the FlexUnit SWC to the build path of a Flex Builder project, copy the `flexunit.swc` file into the `lib` directory of the project. The build path can be viewed through the Project Properties dialog to verify that the `flexunit.swc` is included in the list of libraries.

If you are using the command-line compiler, you still must add the `flexunit.swc` to the build path. This is typically achieved through an Ant build script or compiler argument.

Creating the Test Folder

It is best to store unit tests in a different source folder from the main project code, but with a parallel package structure. This prevents the test cases from cluttering up the main source folder, but still makes them easy to locate. It also gives them access to internal properties of the classes under test, which can sometimes be useful.

To create a `test` source folder in Flex Builder, bring up the Project Properties dialog and select Flex Build Path ➪ Source Path ➪ Add Folder ➪ Browse ➪ New Folder.

Store test cases in a separate source folder with the same package structure as the main source folder.

Creating a Test Case

Imagine building a video portal that needs to filter videos based on a keyword. The filtering will simply match a keyword with the title of each video. This is already enough information to begin unit testing!

In FlexUnit, unit tests are specified in classes that extend `flexunit.framework.TestCase`. A unit test is defined in its own function, with a descriptive name starting with `test`. Here is an example of an initial test case for a class that will filter videos by keyword:

```
package com.wrox.video
{
    import flexunit.framework.TestCase;

    public class VideoKeywordFilterTest extends TestCase
    {
        // The object that will be tested
        private var filter:VideoKeywordFilter = new VideoKeywordFilter();

        public function testFiltersVideoWithMatchingTitle():void
        {
            fail("Unit test not yet implemented");
        }
    }
}
```

The class is named `VideoKeywordFilterTest` because it is going to test a class called `VideoKeyword Filter`. It is conventional to name a test case by appending `Test` to the end of the name of the class that will be tested.

At the top of the class, a private variable named `filter` is defined to reference the object that will be tested. Since the `VideoKeywordFilter` class doesn't actually exist yet, an empty class with this name must be created to successfully compile the test case.

A `testFiltersVideoWithMatchingTitle()` unit test is defined to test the behavior of the `Video KeywordFilter` class when filtering videos based on their titles. The implementation invokes the `fail()` function, inherited from the `TestCase` base class. This is to indicate that the filtering functionality has not yet been implemented. If the function body were left empty instead, the test would misleadingly report a success since, as you'll recall, a success is when a test case is completed without interruption.

> *Name test cases* `TestMyClass`, *where* `MyClass` *is the class under test.*
>
> *Give unit test functions descriptive names that begin with* `test`.
>
> *Call the* `fail()` *function from any unimplemented unit tests.*

Assembling a Test Suite

Before the simple test case can be run, a test suite must be assembled. Recall that a test suite collects together test cases to form a composition that can be processed by the FlexUnit test runner. In some programming languages, there is tooling to automatically generate test suites at runtime, but in Flex they are currently written by hand. This is straightforward, if somewhat tedious.

A test suite is defined in a class that extends `flexunit.framework.TestSuite`. In most cases, a test suite contains only a constructor, which invokes the inherited `addTest()` function repeatedly to assemble the test suite. A following is a simple test suite that adds the `VideoKeywordFilterTest`:

```
package com.wrox.video
{
    import flexunit.framework.TestSuite;

    public class AllVideoTests extends TestSuite
    {
        public function AllVideoTests()
        {
            addTest(new TestSuite(VideoKeywordFilterTest));
            // add further test cases here
        }
    }
}
```

Note that the test case class must be wrapped in a `TestSuite` object before being passed into the `addTest()` function.

Failing the Test!

With the test case written and the test suite assembled, the test can finally be run. Of course, a test failure is expected initially, since no filtering functionality has actually been written. This step is psychological; the disappointment of an initial failure makes a later success more rewarding! It also reassures us that the foundations are in place for TDD to begin in earnest.

The tests contained in a test suite can be run using the `TestRunnerBase` component of FlexUnit. This provides a user interface for viewing the progress of the tests as they run and interpreting the results afterwards. To use the `TestRunnerBase` component, a new MXML application should be created in the main source folder (not the test folder, since Flex Builder does not support this). It is conventional to name the application `TestRunner.mxml`. Here is an example:

```
<mx:Applicationxmlns:mx="http://www.adobe.com/2006/mxml"
    xmlns:flexunit="flexunit.flexui.*"
    creationComplete="creationCompleteHandler()">

    <mx:Script>
        <![CDATA[
            import com.wrox.video.AllVideoTests;

            private function creationCompleteHandler():void
            {
                testRunner.test = new AllVideoTests();
                testRunner.startTest();
            }
        ]]>
    </mx:Script>

    <flexunit:TestRunnerBase id="testRunner" width="100%" height="100%"/>

</mx:Application>
```

Here the `creationComplete` event causes the `creationCompleteHandler()` to execute. This function instantiates the `AllVideoTests` test suite and sets the test property of the `TestRunnerBase` component. This property is used to specify the test suite for the test runner to execute. The unit tests are then started by calling the `startTest()` method.

This example demonstrates one way to assemble a test suite and start the unit tests running. However, the FlexUnit APIs are flexible and provide various other ways to create test case classes and assemble test suites for running. In most cases, the simple approach described in this chapter is adequate.

Figure 73-3 shows the test runner with an initial unit test failure. With all the luck in the world, this test case would still have failed, but do not despair.

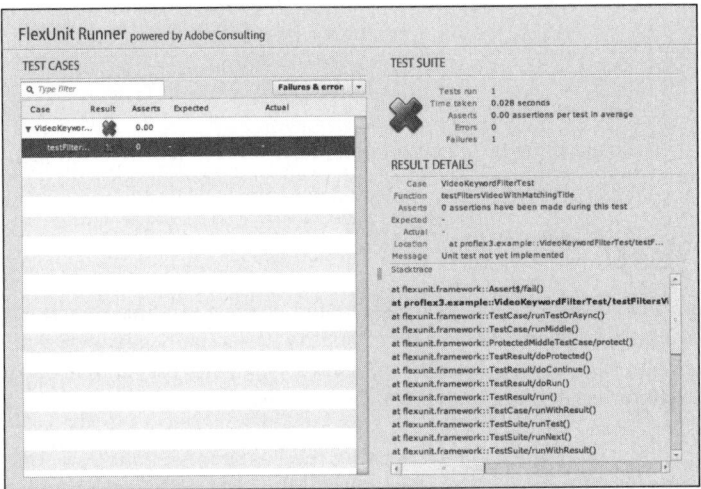

Figure 73-3

Prepare, Invoke, Assert

The skeletal test case needs to be fleshed out, and in doing so, the design of the `VideoKeywordFilter` class can be considered more deeply. A small design decision has in fact already been taken: the encapsulation of the video filtering behavior inside a class of its own.

A unit test usually has three stages:

1. **Prepare** — Setting up the objects involved in the unit test
2. **Invoke** — Calling the function that is being tested
3. **Assert** — Confirming that the correct behavior has taken place

The preparation code is usually nothing more than setting a few properties so that they are in the correct state for the test to begin. You will see later how preparatory code that is relevant to more than one test can be moved into a `setUp()` function.

Assertion Functions

FlexUnit includes a collection of `assert` functions for determining whether the expected behavior of a class took place. These are defined in the `flexunit.framework.Assert` class and inherited by `flexunit.framework.TestCase`. They are available in any test case that is created.

- ❑ `assertEquals( failureMessage, expectedValue, actualValue )`

- ❑ `assertFalse( failureMessage, actualValue )`

- ❑ `assertNotNull( failureMessage, actualValue )`

- ❑ `assertNotUndefined( failureMessage, actualValue )`

- ❑ `assertNull( failureMessage, actualValue )`

- ❑ `assertStrictlyEquals( failureMessage, expectedValue, actualValue )`

- ❑ `assertTrue( failureMessage, actualValue )`

- ❑ `assertUndefined( failureMessage, actualValue )`

Note that the initial `failureMessage` parameter is optional, but its use is recommended, as described in the "Failure Messages" section.

Examining Actual Values

An assertion function examines an `actualValue` to determine whether it satisfies a condition. For example, the `assertEquals()` function could be used to determine whether the expected value of 2 was actually returned by an `addNumbers()` function call when called with the parameters 1 and 1. Or the `assertNotNull()` function could be used to confirm that a `getName()` function does not return `null`. When an assertion function is unsatisfied, an error is deliberately thrown by FlexUnit to indicate a unit test failure. This error is handled by the FlexUnit test runner and presented to the user.

It is important to note the ordering of the `expectedValue` and `actualValue` parameters on the equality assertions. These can easily be muddled up, which causes the test runner to display misleading information, reporting that the expected result occurred rather than the actual result.

> *Ensure the expected value is specified before the actual value when using the* `assertEquals()` *and* `assertStrictlyEquals()` *assertions.*

Failure Messages

It is important to note the names and ordering of the parameters on the assertion functions, since these are not apparent from the FlexUnit ASDoc. The initial `failureMessage` parameter is optional, but its use is recommended. This message is displayed by the FlexUnit test runner whenever a unit test fails, so it should guide the developer towards fixing the broken test. The `failureMessage` parameter also enhances the self-documenting quality of a test case.

In the following example, the "Video title was not properly updated" failure message would display in the test runner if the unit test failed.

```
assertEquals(
    "Video title was not properly updated."
video.title );
```

Use the `failureMessage` *parameter to provide a concise yet descriptive failure message.*

Fleshing Out the Test Case

The test case can now be implemented, helping to drive out the design of the video filtering functionality. Since the class needs to filter based on keyword, there must be a way to specify that keyword. The simplest solution would seem to be a `keyword` setter on the `VideoKeywordFilter` class. With the keyword set, the filtering itself can be performed through a `filterVideo()` function that takes a `Video` parameter and returns `true` if the video should be filtered or `false` otherwise.

These decisions lead to the following unit test:

```
public function testFilterVideoWithMatchingTitle() : void
{
    var video:Video = new Video("Flex, Lies and Videotape");      // prepare

    filter.keyword = "Flex";

    var filtered:Boolean = filter.filterVideo(video);             // invoke

    assertTrue(
        "The filter should have detected a match in the video title",   // assert
        filtered);
}
```

The preparation stage involves creating a new `Video` object and setting a `keyword` property on the filter object (the `VideoKeywordFilter` object being tested). The title of the video contains the word "Flex," which is also used as the `keyword` property. The invoke stage is simply a call to a `filterVideo()` function on the `filter` object, and the assert stage involves checking that the video was correctly filtered using the `assertTrue()` function.

Before now, the `VideoKeywordFilter` was nothing more than an empty class. In the process of writing the unit test, a simple design for keyword and filtering functionality has emerged. And this design already has the merits of usability and testability, since we were able to write the unit test with ease.

Write unit tests first to guide the design of the class under test, ensuring usability and testability.

Some Real Coding

In order to compile and run the test case, the `keyword` setter and `filterVideo()` function need to be added to the `VideoKeywordFilter` class. At this stage, the initial implementation can also be written:

```
package proflex.model.video
{
    public class VideoKeywordFilter
```

```
    {
        private var _keyword:String;

        public function set keyword(value:String):void
        {
            _keyword = value;
        }

        public function filterVideo(video:Video):Boolean
        {
            return video.title.indexOf(_keyword) >= 0;
        }
    }
}
```

The value passed to the keyword setter is backed by the private _keyword property and the filter Video() function works by using the indexOf() function from the String class, called on the title property of the Video.

The project can now be rebuilt and the test runner launched again. See Figure 73-4 and cross your fingers. (Yes! Success at last.)

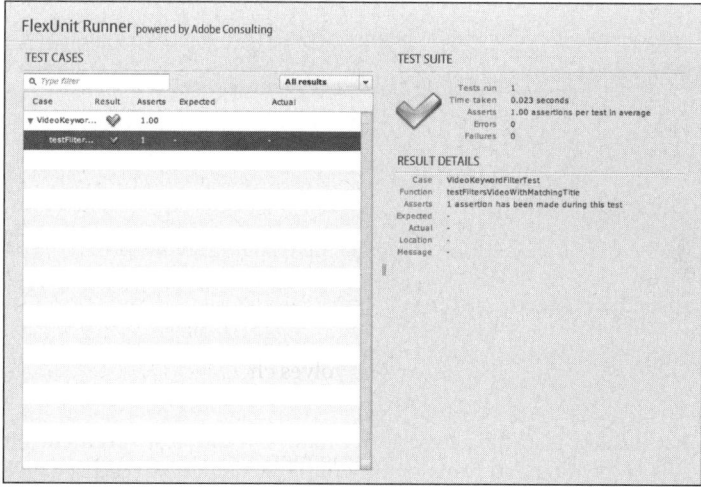

Figure 73-4

Happy and Unhappy Paths

The first test case tests "the happy path" through our filter class. That is, it tests the class under normal conditions, by passing a sensible parameter to the filterVideo() function and confirming that the expected behavior took place. However, this is not sufficient to consider the class complete. The test needs to be strengthened to consider the corner cases and boundary conditions.

Strengthening the Tests

A corner case is an unusual circumstance that may need to be handled specially, while a boundary condition is a value close to, on the edge, or just beyond the expected range of a parameter. The following are a number of additional unit tests for the VideoKeywordFilter class:

```
public function testDoesNotFilterNullVideo():void
{
    filter.keyword = "Flex";

    var filtered:Boolean = filter.filterVideo(null);

    assertFalse("A null video should not be filtered", filtered);
}

public function testDoesNotFilterVideoWithoutTitle():void
{
    var video:Video = new Video(null);

    filter.keyword = "Flex";

    var filtered:Boolean = filter.filterVideo(video);

    assertFalse(
        "A match should not have been found with a video that has no title.",
        filtered);
}

public function testFiltersAnythingWhenKeywordIsNull():void
{
    filter.keyword = null;

    var video:Video = new Video("Flexas Chainsaw Massacre");

    var filtered:Boolean = filter.filterVideo(video);

    assertTrue("All videos should match a null keyword", filtered);
}
```

Note first of all that the new tests have descriptive names. If the "test" prefix is removed, they can be read as descriptions of the intended functionality of the VideoKeywordFilter class. For example, the VideoKeywordClass "does not filter [a] video without [a] title."

Strengthening the Code

When the new, strengthened test suite is run again, the results reveal that the implementation of filterVideo() function is not yet robust. In fact, the corner cases of a null video and a null title have not been handled at all, resulting in errors that are reported by the test runner. These errors can be overcome by adding a pair of guard conditions to the filterVideo() function:

```
public function filterVideo(video:Video):Boolean
{
    if (hasNoKeyword()) return true;
```

```
        if (isInvalid(video)) return false;

        return video.title.indexOf(_keyword) >= 0;
    }

    private function isInvalid(video:Video):Boolean
    {
        return video == null || video.title == null;
    }

    private function hasNoKeyword():Boolean
    {
        return _keyword == null;
    }
```

When the `filterVideo()` function is called, a check is made to ensure there is a keyword. If not, then all videos should be filtered, so `true` is returned. Next the validity of the video is checked to ensure that it is not `null` and has a title. If the video is invalid, it cannot be filtered, so `false` is returned. If execution reaches beyond these two guard conditions, the existing algorithm is used to detect a match between the video title and keyword.

Enough Is Enough

Since a unit test case is normally concerned with the behavior of a specific class, it is usually easy to identify the corner cases and boundary conditions that need to be tested. However, it can be counter-productive to be obsessive about this. Instead of attempting to test every possible way of invoking any piece of functionality, prioritize the most plausible error conditions. Reflect on the complexity and importance of the behavior and decide what level of testing is required.

The Virtuous Cycle

When practicing TDD, the cycle of strengthening the test cases, detecting a weakness in the software, then responding by strengthening the code leads to ever more robust software. Even when bugs are reported in production software, they are fed back into the process. The first step is always to write a new unit test that reproduces the bug. Then effort can focus on fixing the issue, so the new unit test passes. The result is a stronger test suite that will prevent the same bug from occurring again.

Setting Up and Tearing Down

Although a test case can contain multiple test functions, each one is performed fresh, using a new instance of the test case. In other words, the test case class is instantiated, the first test is performed, then the instance is made eligible for garbage collection. This process is repeated for the remaining tests.

There are two intermediate stages in the life cycle of a test case: setup and teardown. The `TestCase` base class defines `setUp()` and `tearDown()` functions that may be overridden to perform initialization and cleanup before and after every test. The `setUp()` function is often used to prepare a number of member variables required by the unit tests, and these are known as the *test fixture*. The `tearDown()` function is used less often, for performing cleanup duties, such as resetting state on a singleton to prevent the outcome from one unit test interfering with another.

A unit test should run independently of any other unit test, and the order in which the unit tests in a test suite are run should not affect the success or failure of the test suite.

The UML sequence diagram in Figure 73-5 shows the life cycle of the `VideoKeywordTestCase`. For each unit test in the test case, a new instance of the `VideoKeywordTestCase` class is created. The `setUp()` function is called, then the next unit test function, followed by `tearDown()`, before the object is made eligible for garbage collection.

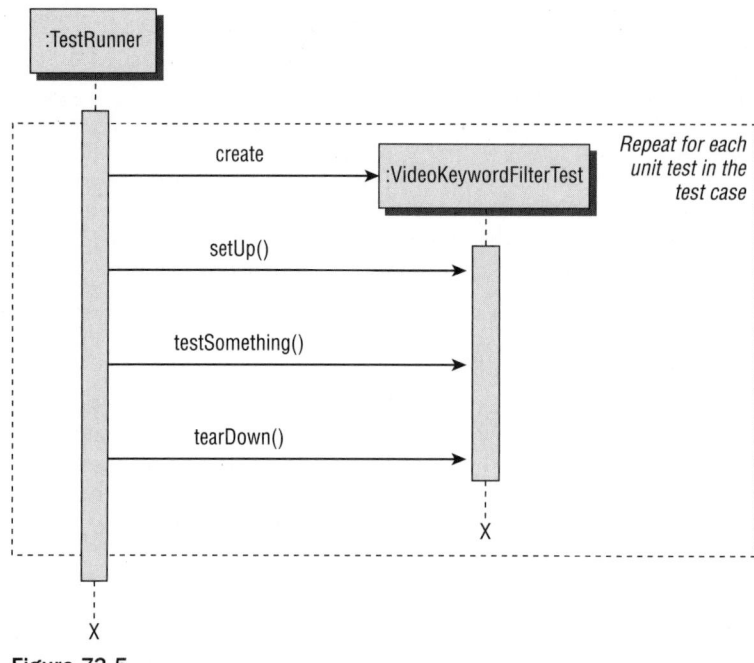

Figure 73-5

The `VideoKeywordFilterTest` can be refactored to take advantage of the setup phase and remove duplicate code. There is no need for teardown here, since the test will already clean up after itself by way of the Garbage Collector. Teardown is rarely needed, but one exception is any test that alters the state of a singleton, which may cause side effects in subsequent tests if not properly reversed. The refactored test case, including a `setUp()` implementation, is as follows:

```
public class TestVideoKeywordFilter extends TestCase
{
    private var filter:VideoKeywordFilter;
    private var video:Video;

    override public function setUp():void
    {
        filter = new VideoKeywordFilter();
        filter.keyword = "Flex";
        video = new Video("Flex, Lies and Videotape");
```

```
    }

    override public function tearDown():void
    {
        // no need for teardown here
    }

    public function testFilterVideo():void
    {
        var filtered:Boolean = filter.filterVideo(video);

        assertTrue(
            "The filter should have detected a match in the video title",
            filtered);
    }

    public function testFilterNullVideo():void
    {
        var filtered:Boolean = filter.filterVideo(null);

        assertFalse("A null video should not be filtered", filtered);
    }

    public function testFilterVideoWithNullTitle():void
    {
        video.title = null;

        var filtered:Boolean = filter.filterVideo(video);

        assertFalse(
            "A match should not have been found with a video that has no title.",
            filtered);
    }

    public function testFilterWithNullKeyword():void
    {
        filter.keyword = null;

        var filtered:Boolean = filter.filterVideo(video);

        assertTrue("All videos should match a null keyword", filtered);
    }
}
```

Don't write a `tearDown()` *function if the Garbage Collector will clean up automatically for you.*

If multiple test cases require the same test fixture, refactor this into a common base class and extend this when required.

White Belt in Testing

That brings the example to a close. It may have been a little simplistic, but it is the process that is most important to grasp. Put a test suite and test runner in place at the beginning of a project so that test cases can be written early enough to guide the design. Try out the various assert functions, make good use of failure messages, move preparation code into `setUp()` functions, and always apply descriptive names for test functions to enhance their self-documenting quality. When a project progresses in this way, through development, into production and beyond, its quality will continually improve.

Further Topics

This section provides some further guidance, including tips for organizing tests in larger projects and an example of the mock-object testing technique. The section ends with references for more information on continuous integration and event testing, and a high-level overview of two related subjects — behavior-driven development (BDD) and test coverage — both on the horizon for Flex and AIR developers.

Organizing Test Suites

For a small project, it may be sufficient to create a single test suite that aggregates all the test cases. For larger projects, it is better to create a hierarchical composition of test suites, with an `AllTests` suite at the root level. The following is an example of the root node of such a composition:

```
package proflex
{
    public class AllTests extends TestSuite
    {
        public function AllTests()
        {
            addTest(new AllVideoTests());
            addTest(new AllCommentaryTests());
            …
        }
    }
}
```

Each package within the test folder that contains test cases should have its own test suite. For example, a `proflex.model.video` package should have an `AllVideoTests` class.

Removing Dependencies with Mock Objects

When a class interacts with another class, it has a dependency on that class. And when that class interacts with yet another class, a secondary dependency exists. Perhaps the second class then performs some kind of service interaction, so a dependency exists beyond the Flex application into the service layer. This common scenario can make it tricky to unit test the original class, since the test case must understand the dependencies with other classes and external systems.

Dependencies like these introduce complexity and frailty to a test suite, but they can be overcome using what are known as *mock objects*. At its most simple, a mock object is an object that stands in for another object during testing, in order to eliminate or at least reduce dependencies. The mock object takes the place of the real object, and the unit test simply ensures that the correct actions are performed against the mock object. A mock object sometimes contains a small amount of logic to record the invocation that take place against it for later verification.

In some programming languages, there are libraries to make mock object testing very easy, by automating the creation of mock objects at runtime. There are some similar libraries for ActionScript, but they are currently somewhat limited, because of language constraints. For this reason, the following example uses a hand-coded mock object instead.

The Collaborating Class

The UploadVideoModel class uploads video files using a delegate to perform the actual uploading. There are two bindable status properties for indicating whether an upload is currently in progress and whether an error has occurred. The class implements the IResponder interface, since the delegate is expected to call back onto the result() or fault() functions, depending on whether the upload succeeds or fails. This is the class that will later be tested using a mock object:

```
public class UploadVideoModel implements IResponder
{
    [Bindable]
    public var uploading:Boolean = false;

    [Bindable]
    public var error:Boolean = false;

    private var delegate:IUploadVideoDelegate;

    public function UploadVideoModel(delegate:IUploadVideoDelegate)
    {
        this.delegate = delegate;
    }

    public function uploadVideo(videoFile:FileReference):void
    {
        uploading = true;
        error = false;
        delegate.uploadVideo(videoFile, this);
    }

    public function result(data:Object):void
    {
        uploading = false;
        error = false;
    }

    public function fault(info:Object):void
    {
        uploading = false;
        error = true;
    }
}
```

The Delegate Interface

Video uploading is delegated through the `IUploadVideoDelegate` interface, so the `UploadVideoModel` is decoupled from any specific uploading mechanism. The delegate interface is passed into the `UploadVideoModel` constructor, which is an example of the inversion-of-control or dependency injection pattern:

```
public interface IUploadVideoDelegate
{
    function uploadVideo(
        videoFile:FileReference,
        responder:IResponder):void;
}
```

The Real and Mock Implementations

There are two implementations of the `IUploadVideoDelegate` interface. The first is the real implementation, which actually streams the video file to a remote server. The second is a mock implementation that allows you to test the behavior of the `UploadVideoModel` class without concern for its server-side dependency. The `MockUploadVideoDelegate` contains simple logic to support testing:

```
public class MockUploadVideoDelegate implements IUploadVideoDelegate
{
    public var videoFile:FileReference;
    private var responder:IResponder;

    public function uploadVideo(
        videoFile:FileReference,
        responder:IResponder):void
    {
        this.videoFile = videoFile;
        this.responder = responder;
    }

    public function sendResult():void
    {
        responder.result(new ResultEvent(ResultEvent.RESULT));
    }

    public function sendFault():void
    {
        responder.fault(new FaultEvent(FaultEvent.FAULT));
    }
}
```

The mock object defines two public functions for sending result and fault events to the responder, which are passed in to the `uploadVideo()` function. These functions allow the mock delegate to be controlled from within a unit test, instead of being governed by the responses sent back from the server. They facilitate test cases for happy and sad paths through the `UploadVideoModel`.

Unit Testing with the Mock Delegate

The test case that makes use of the mock delegate follows. Some preparation is carried out in the `setUp()` function, where the `UploadVideoModel` is constructed. Here the mock delegate is injected into the constructor instead of the real delegate. Two tests are defined, one for testing a successful video upload and the other for testing a failed upload:

```
public class TestUploadVideoModel extends TestCase
{
    private var model:UploadVideoModel;
    private var mockDelegate:MockUploadVideoDelegate;
    private var videoFile:FileReference;

    override public function setUp():void
    {
        mockDelegate = new MockUploadVideoDelegate();
        videoFile = new FileReference();
        model = newUploadVideoModel(mockDelegate);
    }

    public function testUploadsVideo():void
    {
        model.uploadVideo(videoFile);
        assertUploadInProgress();
        mockDelegate.sendResult();
        assertUploadComplete();
        assertFalse(
            "An uploading error should not have occurred",
            model.error);
    }

    public function testHandlesFaultWhileUploadingVideo():void
    {
        model.uploadVideo(videoFile);
        assertUploadInProgress();
        mockDelegate.sendFault();
        assertUploadComplete();
        assertTrue(
            "An uploading error should have occurred",
            model.error);
    }

    private function assertUploadInProgress():void
    {
        assertEquals(
            "The video file was not passed into the delegate",
            videoFile,
            mockDelegate.videoFile);

        assertTrue(
```

```
            "The uploading should be in progress",
            model.uploading);
    }

    private function assertUploadComplete():void
    {
        assertFalse(
            "The uploading should be complete",
            model.uploading);
    }
}
```

Note that the preceding test case has two private functions containing assertions: `assertUpload InProgress()` and `assertUploadComplete()`. These are called from both the `testUploadVideo()` and `testHandlesUploadVideoFault()` tests. It is good practice to move repeated assertions into their own functions in this way, thus preventing duplication.

Move repeated assertions into their own functions with descriptive names.

Don't Make a Mockery of Your Unit Tests

Mock objects provide a powerful mechanism for unit-testing classes without dependencies on other classes or remote services. This can simplify some unit tests, by isolating the class under test from other parts of a larger system. However, it can also have the reverse effect, if the class under test has too many responsibilities or can be tested simply without mock objects.

The amount of code required to create and use a mock object should be small. If not, it may be time to step back and consider a simpler design. On the other hand, if the class is already simple and its dependencies can be prepared and tested easily, the argument for using mock objects becomes less convincing. The purist's approach of abstracting every dependency and testing each class in complete isolation is unlikely to be productive.

The technique of testing with mock objects is an important one, but it should be used with care. Mock objects are best used to isolated a class from more complex surroundings, therefore simplifying the unit test.

Continuous Integration with Ant and Maven

Continuous integration is the process of automating project builds and testing in order to identify and resolve integration issues early. This helps ensure that software remains correct and properly integrated throughout its development. There are several commercial and open-source continuous integration servers, including Cruise Control, Hudson, Team City, and Electric Cloud. These tend to integrate with source control repositories and execute Ant or Maven scripts in order to perform the builds and run the tests.

Peter Martin, of Adobe Consulting, developed the FlexUnit Ant task and a special Flex test runner for use in build scripts and continuous integration environments. This task and test runner work closely together. The Ant task launches the Flex test runner application and opens a socket for receiving the test results; the Flex test runner executes the tests and transmits the results to the Ant task through a local network connection.

You can download the Ant task, Flex test runner, and a sample project from the following blog post:

    http://weblogs.macromedia.com/pmartin/archives/2006/06/flexunit_ant.cfm

The open-source Flex-mojos project provides a collection of Flex plug-ins for Maven, including support for FlexUnit. Downloads and documentation are available from the project home page:

    http://code.google.com/p/flex-mojos

Eventful Test Cases

The events that a class dispatches form an important part of its contract with clients, yet for one reason or another they are seldom tested. Perhaps this is because event declarations are optional in Flex and specified as metadata, or perhaps it is because the FlexUnit assertions were mostly ported from JUnit and not tailored specifically to Flex. In either case, programming mistakes and design flaws in event logic can have far-reaching consequences, affecting dependent event listeners and the classes beyond.

A FlexUnit extension, known as EventfulTestCase, is included in the latest distribution of FlexUnit. This extension makes it simple to test event dispatching logic, including Cairngorm event dispatching.

Testing event dispatching logic involves three steps: recording the expected events, performing the function under test, and then asserting that the expected events actually occurred. The following is an example test that ensures a videoChange event is dispatched whenever a rating is added to a video:

```
public function testAddRating():void
{
    listenForEvent(video, VideoChangeEvent.VIDEO_CHANGE);

    video.addRating(5);
    assertEvents(
        "A change event for the video event should have been dispatched.");
}
```

For more details about testing events, read the following blog post, but note that the syntax has changed slightly since this extension was incorporated into the FlexUnit project:

    http://blogs.adobe.com/tomsugden/2008/01/post.html

The EventfulTestCase extension relies on the fact that most event dispatching in Flex is synchronous. However, it is sometimes desirable to write tests for truly asynchronous behavior, and FlexUnit provides a utility method for doing so: addAsync(). This is described in the following blog post:

    http://life.neophi.com/danielr/2007/03/asynchronous_testing_with_flex.html

Test Coverage

Test coverage is the process of analyzing the code that is executed while a test suite runs, in order to understand what code is really being tested and, more importantly, to identify any code that has been missed.

A test coverage report can be used to inform the development of new unit tests and to reassure developers and stakeholders that software is thoroughly unit tested. Test coverage is best incorporated into a project build process at an early stage, to encourage developers to build better tests, rather than toward the end when the results are likely to cause alarm!

Alex Uhlmann and Joe Berkovitz both developed test coverage tools for Flex in parallel without knowledge of each other's endeavors. Alex made use of the profiling instrumentation provided by Flash Player 9 to gather line coverage metrics as a test suite ran, while Joe extended the Flex compiler to provide a deeper level of instrumentation, tracking the conditional branch coverage. Joe's solution has now been released on Google Code under the name Flexcover, and the pair have begun collaborating on an enhanced test coverage client. For more information about Flexcover, visit the project web page:

```
http://code.google.com/p/flexcover
```

Behavior-Driven Development

Behavior-Driven Development (BDD) was created by Dan North in 2003 in response to TDD. Dan had witnessed confusion and misunderstanding whenever he attempted to teach TDD, so he set out to improve matters. What began as a simple rewording of TDD, placing greater emphasis on behavior than tests, evolved into a framework for end-to-end functional testing.

The first change suggested by BDD was that test function names should be rewritten as sentences in the language of the business domain. This could enhance their self-documenting quality to the point where a pretty-printed list of test function names made sense to business users, analysts and testers. From this change, it became apparent that BDD had the potential to provide a consistent vocabulary, or ubiquitous language, for application analysis in general, improving communications between analysts, developers, testers, and the business.

JBehave was the first Java framework for BDD that attempted to formalize acceptance criteria into structured scenarios that could be executed automatically. This framework defines various interfaces to represent small parts of these end-to-end scenarios. By implementing these interfaces, and assembling the parts in different combinations, a comprehensive suite of end-to-end functional tests can be assembled and executed automatically.

At the time of writing, there is no similar BDD framework for Flex. However, some of the best practices of BDD can also be applied to TDD and unit testing. In particular, you should always strive to write descriptive FlexUnit test cases using the domain language. Perhaps a BDD framework will soon emerge for Flex, but in the meantime, more details can be found at `http://dannorth.net/introducing-bdd`.

Summary

This chapter has tried to explain the benefits of unit testing and demonstrate through examples that it is a straightforward practice to learn and apply. Unit tests help to verify that the small parts that make up a system are operating correctly, providing the developer with reassurance that their code is correct. Developing a comprehensive suite of unit tests can prevent many bugs from occurring in the first place, while giving developers the confidence to refactor without fear of unintended consequences.

TDD takes unit testing to the extreme and brings with it greater benefits. In particular, it helps to improve software design by prompting developers to consider and use their classes before expending any effort implementing them. This can prevent bad ideas from getting into the code base, while ensuring that classes are testable by design from the outset.

Both unit testing and TDD are skills that need to be honed. It is easy to get started, but the same pitfalls exist as in normal software development. Care must be taken to write simple, structured, and readable tests that don't contain redundancies or duplication. As we develop more sophisticated Flex and AIR applications for the enterprise, testing becomes vitally important to ensure quality. After becoming comfortable with unit testing and TDD, many developers will insist upon it.

The next chapter covers the Flex logging framework, which can be used to gather diagnostic information about an application at runtime, to help locate bugs that slip the unit-testing net.

The Logging Framework

Flex includes a simple yet versatile logging framework that can be used for gathering diagnostic information while an application is running, and for reporting errors in deployed applications. This chapter begins by introducing the Flex logging framework and explaining how to use its main features, before moving on to look at customization, and then finishing with an assortment of further tips and tricks on the subject of logging.

Overview

Incorporating log statements into an application is preferable to using the global trace function, since log statements can be categorized and filtered based on their source and level of severity. Logs can also be targeted to different places, from the Flash log file or Flex Builder console to a remote Web Service. There are many ways to use logging, from the simple recording of diagnostic information that helps with debugging to creating detailed audit trails of the way a user interacts with an application.

This chapter begins by covering the basic logging framework classes and interfaces that are included with the Flex SDK. It explains how to create and configure a logger, issue log statements with different levels of severity, and apply filters. The second part of the chapter covers customizing the logging framework to send log statements to a remote server. The chapter ends with a collection of further tips, including some on logging to Firebug and removing log statements from production code.

To complement this chapter, you are encouraged to refer to the ASDoc for the mx.logging package in the *Flex Language Reference*. The official Flex documentation also includes a useful chapter on logging within the "Building and Deploying Flex Applications" document.

Using the Logging Framework

The logging framework consists of just two interfaces and a few classes, but these satisfy the general requirements for logging from Flex or AIR applications and also make customization straightforward. This section explains how to use the standard features of the logging framework.

Creating a Logging Target

The logging framework needs to be initialized before any log statements will be processed. This usually takes place during application startup, within a `preinitialize` event handler.

```
<mx:Application xmlns:mx="http://www.adobe.com/2006/mxml"
    preinitialize="initializeLogging()">
```

Initialization involves configuring and registering one or more logging targets. These receive log events whenever logging is used. A target may handle the log events it receives in any way it chooses. Flex includes the `TraceTarget` class, which handles log events by tracing their details with the global trace function, so the log messages appear in the Flex Builder console when an application is run in Debug mode or in the Flash log file. Here is some initialization code:

```
private function initializeLogging():void
{
    var target:TraceTarget = new TraceTarget();  // 1. create the logging target

    target.includeCategory = true;                // 2. configure the target
    target.includeLevel = true;
    target.includeDate = true;
    target.includeTime = true;

    Log.addTarget(target);                         // 3. register the target
}
```

See the "Configuring the Debugger Version of Flash Player" section in the "Building an Deploying Flex Applications" official Flex documentation for details about the configuration of Flash log files. These vary depending on operating system and Flash Player version.

In the example, a `TraceTarget` is created, configured to include category, level, date, and time descriptions, and then registered with the logging framework through the static `addTarget()` function of the `Log` class. The `Log` class is the real workhorse of the logging framework, storing and coordinating the logging targets, performing filtering and categorization duties, and providing access to loggers.

Getting the Right Logger

Log statements are issued through loggers, which implement the `ILogger` interface. The `Log` class provides access to categorized loggers with a static `getLogger()` function, as follows:

```
var logger:ILogger = Log.getLogger("my.category");
```

A logger category is basically a string identifier with some restrictions on what characters can be used. It is conventional to use qualified class names for logger categories, so the log statements for a class named `com.wrox.NuclearReactor` would be issued through a logger with a category of the same name.

```
private static const LOG:ILogger = Log.getLogger("com.wrox.NuclearReactor");
```

If a class performs logging in various places, it is often cleanest to declare the logger as a static member constant, instead of re-retrieving it each time it is needed.

Logging at Different Levels

When the right logger has been retrieved, log statements can be issued. All log statements have a level, which is an indication of their severity. As shown in the following table, the `ILogger` interface defines five methods for logging with specific levels.

Log function	Use for logging	Example
debug()	Low-level details about the progress of an application, intended for debugging purposes.	"Price before formatting: 12.35201", "Price after formatting: 12.35", etc.
info()	Higher-level details about a running application, for general information.	"Application initialized", "Sale completed", etc.
warn()	Problems that have been detected that will not stop the program operating but may lead to further errors.	"Memory usage has exceeded the normal bounds."
error()	Serious errors that have occurred that may restrict further use of the application.	"An error occurred while submitting a completed order to the Web Service."
fatal()	Errors that result in the complete failure of the application.	"The editor module cannot be loaded, so the application cannot begin."

Each function is parameterized with a message string and the `rest` parameter. The message string contains the message to be logged, which may include markers in the form {0}, {1}, {2}, and so on. These markers will be substituted with the string values of the `rest` parameters.

```
logger.debug("Simple message with no params");
logger.info("Message with multiple params: {0} / {1}", param1, param2);
```

The `ILogger` interface also defines a general-purpose `log()` method that requires the user to provide a numeric log level as a parameter. The `LogEventLevel` class defines the standard log-level constants. This approach is appropriate when the log level needs to be changed at runtime.

```
logger.log(LogEventLevel.FATAL, "Boom! A fatal error occurred");
logger.log(currentLevel, "A message with a dynamic log-level");
```

With the trace target configured to display the date, time, level, and category along with the message, the preceding log statements will produce output such as the following:

```
4/16/2008 22:22:44.701 [DEBUG] my.category Simple message with no params
4/16/2008 22:22:44.747 [INFO] my.category Message with multiple params: 226 / ABC
4/16/2008 22:22:45.783 [FATAL] my.category Boom! A fatal error occurred
4/16/2008 22:22:45.792 [DEBUG] my.category A message with a dynamic log-level
```

Recall that the trace target will produce output only if the application is run in the debugger version of the Flash Player.

Filtering Log Statements

You can filter log statements based on their level and the category of logger that produced them. This is achieved through properties of the registered logging targets.

The `level` property can be set to filter by the level of log event received. All log events of the specified level, or higher (more severe), will be handled.

```
var traceTarget:TraceTarget = new TraceTarget();
traceTarget.level = LogEventLevel.WARN; // log WARN, ERROR and FATAL events
Log.addTarget( target );
```

You can use the `filters` property to specify one or more filter expressions. These are patterns that are matched against the category of logger that produced a log event. The filter expression `com.wrox.service.MyService` will match only events dispatched by a logger with the same category, `com.wrox.service.MyService`. A wildcard can be specified at the end of a filter expressions; for example, `com.wrox.*` would match all log events dispatched by loggers with categories beginning with `com.wrox.`.

```
traceTarget.filters = [ "com.wrox.*", "mx.rpc.*" ];
```

Filtering by level and category provides a flexible way to control the number and type of log messages that are recorded. During development, the categories may be broad and the level low, to aid debugging, but in production they can be tightened so that only core components and the warnings or errors they produce are tracked.

Log Only When Necessary

Logging carries overhead, since the logging events that are generated are processed by the logging framework and directed to the registered logging targets. If none of the registered targets will handle a particular level of log event, this processing is redundant. The `Log` class includes a few Boolean functions for determining whether an event will be processed by a target. These can be used in guard conditions to prevent unnecessary processing when logging is disabled, as follows:

```
if (Log.isDebug())
{
    Log.getLogger( "example" ).debug(
        "This message will be processed by a target" );
}
if (Log.isInfo()) { … }
```

```
if (Log.isWarn())  { ... }
if (Log.isError()) { ... }
if (Log.isFatal()) { ... }
```

In the first example, the `if` statement checks whether log events with the debug level will be processed by any of the targets. If so, a debug-level log statement is made using the example logger. If not, there is no point in issuing a log statement, since it will not be directed at any target.

Using guard conditions is more verbose than simply logging without them, but it is much more efficient. This is particularly important when logging is taking place inside a loop or recursion, or when expensive log messages are created programmatically. Using guard conditions prevents unnecessary logging that could otherwise become a performance bottleneck.

Customizing the Logging Framework

Although the logging framework provides all the basic features for logging from Flex and AIR applications, there are situations where customization is required. The logging framework is designed with extensibility in mind, and it is quite straightforward to implement a custom logging target. Several examples are available online, including ThunderBolt, which forwards log events to Firebug and is discussed in more detail later in this chapter in the section "Logging to Firebug with ThunderBolt."

Other use cases for custom loggers include transmitting messages from distributed applications to a centralized logging service, and writing them to the local file system of an AIR application. This section concentrates on a simple example of a centralized logging service. We will walk through the implementation of a custom logger that sends log statements to a remote Java object on the server. The remote object passes these statements to Log4J, a popular logging framework for Java, which is then responsible for persisting them. In essence, we will translate Flex logging framework log statements on the client side into Java Log4J log statements on the server side. This process is shown in Figure 74-1.

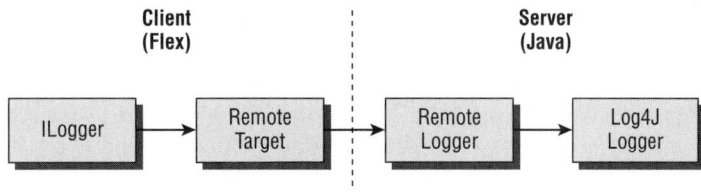

Figure 74-1

Implementing a Remote Logging Target

The most common way to customize the logging framework is to implement a new logging target. This is a class that receives log statements from the Flex logging framework and decides what to do with them. The standard Flex logging target simply traces log statements, but in this case we will implement a custom logging target that sends log statements over the wire to a remote object on the server side.

The Flex logging framework includes an abstract base class, `AbstractTarget`, to simplify the task of implementing a custom logging target. This handles the complexities of filter expressions and leaves only the `logEvent()` function to be implemented by a custom target. This function handles the log events that are generated when log statements are made. The following is the implementation for a `RemoteTarget`:

```
package log
{
    import mx.logging.AbstractTarget;
    import mx.logging.LogEvent;
    import mx.logging.LogEventLevel;
    import mx.rpc.remoting.RemoteObject;

    public class RemoteTarget extends AbstractTarget
    {
        private var remoteLogger:RemoteObject;

        override public function logEvent( event : LogEvent ) : void
        {
            if (remoteLogger == null)
            {
                remoteLogger = new RemoteObject("remoteLogger");
            }

            var message:String = event.message;

            switch (event.level)
            {
                case LogEventLevel.DEBUG : remoteLogger.debug(message); break;
                case LogEventLevel.INFO  : remoteLogger.info(message); break;
                case LogEventLevel.WARN  : remoteLogger.warn(message); break;
                case LogEventLevel.ERROR : remoteLogger.error(message); break;
                case LogEventLevel.FATAL : remoteLogger.fatal(message); break;
            }
        }
    }
}
```

The first time the target receives a log event, a remote object is instantiated to communicate with the server side. The message is then passed to a remote function of the remote object according to its level. So debug-level messages are passed to the remote `debug()` function, and so on. When subsequent log events are received, the remote object has already been instantiated, so the log messages are passed straight to the remote log functions.

Note that this is a very simple implementation of a remote logging target. It could be improved in various ways, such as introducing a buffer and then sending the log statements in batches, to improve performance by reducing the number of network calls made.

Implementing the Java Remote Logger

In this example, we are using a remote object to receive log events sent by the Flex client. This could also have been an HTTP service or a Web Service, but remote objects are usually quicker to implement and more straightforward to invoke from Flex using LCDS or BlazeDS. For an introduction to remote objects, see Chapter 59, "Using BlazeDS."

Our remote object implementation uses Log4J, the popular logging framework for Java, to persist the log statements it receives. The source code is:

```
package log;

import org.apache.log4j.Logger;

public class RemoteLogger
{
    private static final Logger LOG = Logger.getLogger(RemoteLogger.class);

    public void debug(String message)
    {
        LOG.debug(message);
    }

    public void info(String message)
    {
        LOG.info(message);
    }

    public void warn(String message)
    {
        LOG.warn(message);
    }

    public void error(String message)
    {
        LOG.error(message);
    }

    public void fatal(String message)
    {
        LOG.fatal(message);
    }
}
```

A static `final` property is declared (the Java equivalent of an ActionScript `const`) for the Log4J logger. It is standard practice for each class to declare its own logger in this way when working with Log4J. A log method is then defined for each log level and these pass their message parameters into the corresponding methods of the Log4J logger.

What happens after the Log4J logger has received log statements depends on its configuration. Log4J is highly configurable and supports filtering and categorization in a similar manner to the Flex logging framework, as well as message formatting and persistence. Log4J appenders are used to handle log statements as they occur, and several implementations are provided, including the `RollingFileAppender`, which writes the statements to a file until it reaches a certain size, and then archives the file and begins afresh.

One way to configure Log4J is to ensure that a `log4j.properties` file is contained on the Java class-path for the web application containing the remote object:

```
# Log all levels of messages using a rolling file appender by default.
log4j.rootLogger=DEBUG, ROLLINGFILE

# Log only error level messages for Apache classes.
log4j.category.org.apache=ERROR, ROLLINGFILE

# Configure the rolling file appender
log4j.appender.ROLLINGFILE=org.apache.log4j.RollingFileAppender
log4j.appender.ROLLINGFILE.Threshold=DEBUG
log4j.appender.ROLLINGFILE.layout=org.apache.log4j.PatternLayout
log4j.appender.ROLLINGFILE.layout.ConversionPattern=%-4r [%t] %-5p %c %x - %m%n
log4j.appender.ROLLINGFILE.File=/Users/tsugden/Servers/tomcat-5.5.26/logs/log4j.log
```

More information about remote objects is provided in Chapter 59, "Using BlazeDS," and further details of Log4J can be found online and in print.

Creating a Client that Logs Remotely

To use the new logging target, you must register it with the logging framework. The following is a simple Flex client that configures the logging framework and contains several buttons to send log statements to the target:

```
<mx:Application
    xmlns:mx="http://www.adobe.com/2006/mxml"
    creationComplete="onCreationComplete()">

    <mx:Script>
        <![CDATA[
            import log.RemoteTarget;
            import mx.logging.Log;
            import mx.logging.ILogger;

            private var logger : ILogger;

            private function onCreationComplete() : void
            {
                var category:String = "example";

                var target:RemoteTarget = new RemoteTarget();
                target.filters = [ category ];
                Log.addTarget(target);

                logger = Log.getLogger(category);
            }

        ]]>
    </mx:Script>

    <mx:HBox>
        <mx:Button label="debug" click="logger.debug('debug message')" />
        <mx:Button label="info"  click="logger.info('info message')"  />
        <mx:Button label="warn"  click="logger.warn('warn message')"  />
```

```
        <mx:Button label="error" click="logger.error('error message')" />
        <mx:Button label="fatal" click="logger.fatal('fatal message')" />
    </mx:HBox>

</mx:Application>
```

With the server up and running, clicking on the buttons of the Flex client should cause Log4J statements to appear in the log files of the server, as follows:

```
13416 [http-8080-Processor24] DEBUG log.RemoteLogger  - debug message
14183 [http-8080-Processor24] INFO  log.RemoteLogger  - info message
14928 [http-8080-Processor24] WARN  log.RemoteLogger  - warn message
15894 [http-8080-Processor24] ERROR log.RemoteLogger  - error message
16767 [http-8080-Processor24] FATAL log.RemoteLogger  - fatal message
```

Further Topics

This section contains some tips and tricks to help with logging in real projects. This includes sample code for viewing logs within a Flex or AIR application, logging the elapsed time between two events, enabling and disabling data service logging, logging to the Firefox Developer Extension, Firebug, and, finally, stripping log statements out of production code.

Embedded Log Viewer

During development, it is sometimes useful to be able to view log statements within a Flex or AIR application at runtime, rather than having to switch to the Flex Builder console or retrieve them from the Flash log file. You can achieve this by writing a custom logging target that buffers messages. Here is a simple example:

```
package log
{
    import mx.core.mx_internal;
    import mx.logging.targets.LineFormattedTarget;

    use namespace mx_internal;

    public class LogBufferingTarget extends LineFormattedTarget
    {
        [Bindable]
        public var messages:String = "";

        private var bufferSize:Number;

        public function LogBufferingTarget(bufferSize:Number = 20000)
        {
            this.bufferSize = bufferSize;
        }

        override mx_internal function internalLog(message:String):void
        {
            if (messages.length + message.length > bufferSize)
            {
                messages = messages.substr(bufferSize / 2);
```

```
            }

            messages += message + "\n";
        }
    }
}
```

The `LogBufferingTarget` extends `LineFormattedTarget`, which is a base class for logging targets that deal with formatted log message strings, including category, level, date, and time details. The constructor sets a `bufferSize` property to ensure the bindable `messages` string doesn't become too large. The `internalLog()` function from the `LineFormattedTarget` base class is overridden to handle the preformatted message string associated with a log event. In this case, the message is simply appended to the `messages` string. The length of the `messages` string is also checked and split in half if the `bufferSize` is reached.

The following is an MXML application that initializes the logging framework with the `LogBufferingTarget` and renders the log messages in a `TextArea`:

```
<mx:Application xmlns:mx="http://www.adobe.com/2006/mxml"
    preinitialize=" preInitializeHandler()">

    <mx:Script>
        <![CDATA[
            import log.LogBufferingTarget;
            import mx.logging.Log;
            import mx.logging.ILogger;

            private var logger:ILogger;

            [Bindable]
            private var target:LogBufferingTarget;

            private function preInitializeHandler():void
            {
                target = new LogBufferingTarget();
                target.includeCategory = true;
                target.includeDate = true;
                target.includeLevel = true;
                target.includeTime = true;
                target.filters = [ "example" ];

                Log.addTarget(target);
                logger = Log.getLogger("example");
            }

        ]]>
    </mx:Script>

    <mx:HBox>
        <mx:Button label="debug" click="logger.debug('debug message')"/>
        <mx:Button label="info"  click="logger.info('info message')"/>
        <mx:Button label="warn"  click="logger.warn('warn message')"/>
        <mx:Button label="error" click="logger.error('error message')"/>
        <mx:Button label="fatal" click="logger.fatal('fatal message')"/>
```

```
        </mx:HBox>

        <mx:TextArea id="logViewer" width="100%" height="100%"
            text="{ target.messages }"/>

    </mx:Application>
```

Initialization is performed in the `preInitialize` event handler. Then, whenever one of the buttons is clicked, a log statement is issued with a different level, depending on which button was clicked. The associated log event will be processed by the `LogBufferingTarget` and the formatted `message` string appended to the `messages` property, which is bound to the `text` property of the `TextArea`.

The idea of an embedded log viewer could be taken much further. A rich logging component might be developed that reveals itself upon a key press and includes functionality for searching and filtering the log messages. That task is left as an exercise for the keen reader!

Stopwatch Logging

Although the logging framework supports the timestamping of log statements, it can be useful to record the elapsed time between a series of events. For example, it may be interesting to record the duration between sending an HTTP request and receiving a response. Although you calculate this from a series of log statements containing timestamps, it is better to perform the calculation programmatically and then log the elapsed time.

The following is a simple utility class for this purpose:

```
package log
{
    import mx.logging.ILogger;
    import mx.logging.Log;

    public class StopwatchLogger
    {
        private static var id:uint = 0;

        private var logger:ILogger;

        private var startTime:int = -1;

        private var name:String;

        public function StopwatchLogger(category:String)
        {
            logger = Log.getLogger(category);
            StopwatchLogger.id++;
            name = "stopwatch-" + id;
        }

        public function start(message:String, … rest):void
        {
            startTime = flash.utils.getTimer();
            logger.info(message + " (" + name + " started)", rest);
        }

        public function stop(message:String, … rest):void
```

```
        {
            if (isUnstarted)
            {
                logger.warn(
                    message + " (" + name + " stopped without being started!)",
                    rest);
            }
            else
            {
                logger.info(
                    message + " (" + name + " stopped at " + elapsedTime + "ms)",
                    rest);
            }
        }

        private function get isUnstarted():Boolean
        {
            return startTime == -1;
        }

        private function get elapsedTime():int
        {
            return flash.utils.getTimer() - startTime;
        }
    }
}
```

The constructor of the `StopwatchLogger` class takes a `category` string that is used as the log category. The `start()` function records the current time and logs a start message with the info level. The `stop()` function ensures that the stopwatch was first started and then logs a stop message containing the elapsed time.

The `StopwatchLogger` class can then be instantiated wherever it is needed. The following is an example that logs the time taken to request a list of news stories from an `HTTPService`, receive the result data in XML, and convert it into a collection of strongly typed `NewsItem` objects.

```
package news
{
    import log.StopwatchLogger;

    import mx.collections.ArrayCollection;
    import mx.collections.ListCollectionView;
    import mx.rpc.events.ResultEvent;
    import mx.rpc.http.HTTPService;

    public class GetNewsService
    {
        private static const SERVICE_URL:String = "http://com.wrox/fetchNews";

        private var stopwatch:StopwatchLogger =
            new StopwatchLogger("news.GetNewsService");

        [Bindable]
```

```
public var items:ListCollectionView = new ArrayCollection();

public function getNews():void
{
    stopwatch.start("requesting news");

    var service:HTTPService = new HTTPService(SERVICE_URL);
    service.addEventListener(ResultEvent.RESULT, resultHandler);
    service.send();
}

private function resultHandler(event:Event):void
{
    for (var xmlItem:XML in event.result.items)
    {
        var item:NewsItem = new NewsItem();
        item.title = xmlItem.title;
        item.content = xmlItem.content;
        items.addItem(item);
    }

    stopwatch.stop( "received and converted news" );
}
}
}
```

When the getNews() function is called, the stopwatch logger is started, and then an HTTP request is sent. When the result of that request is received, the result data is converted into NewsItem objects, and then the stopwatch logger is stopped. This process causes log states similar to the following to appear in the console. The duration of the operation to fetch the news items can be seen to be 1044ms.

```
20:55:56.523 news requesting news (stopwatch-1 started)
20:55:57.566 news received and converted news (stopwatch-1 stopped at 1044ms)
```

Logging to Firebug with ThunderBolt

ThunderBolt is a custom logger that targets messages at Firebug, the popular development extension to the Firefox browser. It integrates seamlessly into the Flex logging framework via a ThunderBoltTarget trace target. When this trace target is registered, any log messages that are sent and match a filter will be displayed in the Firebug console, as shown in Figure 74-2.

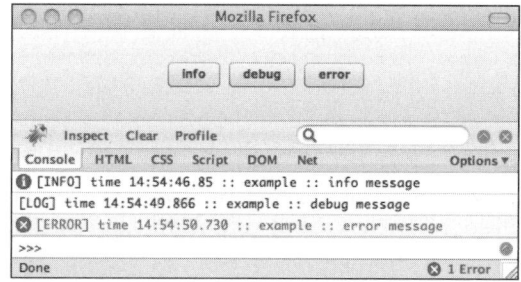

Figure 74-2

Both Firebug and ThunderBolt are free and open source. They can be downloaded from:

- ❏   www.getfirebug.com
- ❏   http://code.google.com/p/flash-thunderbolt

The ThunderBolt distribution includes a `lib` directory containing the compiled SWC for inclusion in your Flex projects. When working with Flex Builder project, simply add the SWC to your project library path in order to access the `ThunderBoltTarget` class in your code. The distribution also includes the source code, which provides a nice example of a customization of the logging framework, making use of the Flash `ExternalInterface` to communicate with Firebug.

The following is an example of an application that registers a `ThunderBoltTarget` and declares three buttons to issue info-, debug-, and error-level logs when they are clicked:

```
<mx:Application xmlns:mx="http://www.adobe.com/2006/mxml"
    backgroundColor="#FFFFFF"
    verticalAlign="middle"
    preinitialize="preinitializeHandler()">

    <mx:Script>
        <![CDATA[
            import org.osflash.thunderbolt.Logger;
            import mx.logging.ILogger;
            import mx.logging.Log;

            import org.osflash.thunderbolt.ThunderBoltTarget;

            private var logger:ILogger;

            private function preinitializeHandler():void
            {
                var target:ThunderBoltTarget = new ThunderBoltTarget();
                target.filters = [ "example" ];
                Log.addTarget(target);
                logger = Log.getLogger("example");
            }

        ]]>
    </mx:Script>

    <mx:HBox>
        <mx:Button label="info" click="logger.info('info message')"/>
        <mx:Button label="debug" click="logger.debug('debug message')"/>
        <mx:Button label="error" click="logger.error('error message')"/>
    </mx:HBox>

</mx:Application>
```

When you compile and launch this application in Firefox with the Firebug extension installed and enabled, log messages will appear in the Firebug console whenever the buttons are clicked.

There is a minor bug that occurs with some versions of Firebug on Mac OS X. If the browser URL has the prefix `file://localhost`, Firebug can't be enabled and, consequently, log messages can't be received. You can resolve this by specifying the full filesystem path to the application instead or by opening the application through the Open File dialog.

In addition to logging via the Flex logging framework, ThunderBolt also supports logging directly to Firebug through the static functions of a proprietary `Logger` class. This supports richer logging features, including memory snapshots, tree views of complex object structures, and disabling or enabling of logging at runtime. You should consider this approach if you are using Firebug as the primary log viewer and the additional features are beneficial to your project. The downside is that these features couple an application to ThunderBolt-specific APIs rather than to the generic logging framework.

Removing Logging from Production Code

Although it is simple to disable logging, there are sometimes reasons to remove logging statements altogether from code that is going into production. For instance, it may be possible to reduce the size of the compiled SWF or to increase performance by eliminating unnecessary function calls and the creation of message strings. Having said that, premature optimization should generally be avoided, and profiling could be performed to establish the real cost of logging prior to removing any log statements.

There are several ways to remove logging and trace statements from source files before they are compiled, including:

- ❑ **Conditional compilation** — You can use the conditional compilation feature of the Flex compiler to prevent log statements from being compiled into the resulting SWF when a certain compiler argument is specified.

- ❑ **Ant build script** — You can use an Ant build script to locate logging and trace statements in source files using regular expressions, and then to remove them before the files are compiled.

For more details about conditional compilation, refer to the "Using conditional compilation" section of the Flex LiveDocs. What follows is a description of the second process, removing logging statements using an Ant build script.

Removing Logging and Trace Using Ant

A target can be defined that makes use of Ant's regular expression task to match logging or trace statements within the source code, then replace them with empty strings or comment them out. The question then becomes how to identify these statements. Trace is easy to detect using the following regular expression:

```
trace(.*?\);
```

Logging statements are trickier because they can be expressed in many different ways. The easiest option is to apply a consistent approach during development, such as defining a private constant named `LOG` in any class that performs logging, and directing log statements through that. With this approach, you can use the following regular expression:

```
LOG.info.*?\);
```

The following is a simple Ant build script for removing log statements. The `remove-log` target first cleans up by deleting the temporary folder, then it re-creates a new temporary folder and copies all the source files into it; finally, it strips out the log statements from the copied source files using a regular expression:

```
<project name="MyProject" default="remove-log">

    <!-- Define properties -->
    <property name="src.dir" location="/path/to/source/folder" />
    <property name="tmp.dir" location="/path/to/temporary/folder" />

    <!-- Delete temp folder -->
    <target name="clean">
        <delete dir="${tmp.dir}" />
    </target>

    <!-- Copy source code into temporary folder -->
    <target name="copy" depends="clean">
        <mkdir dir="${tmp.dir}" />
        <copy todir="${tmp.dir}">
            <fileset dir="${src.dir}" />
        </copy>
    </target>

    <!-- Remove logging statements -->
    <target name="remove-log" depends="copy">
        <replaceregexp match="LOG.info.*?\);" replace="" flags="gs">
            <fileset dir="${tmp.dir}" includes="**/*.as" />
            <fileset dir="${tmp.dir}" includes="**/*.mxml" />
        </replaceregexp>
    </target>

</project>
```

You can extend this script to compile the processed files from the temporary folder, to produce a SWF or SWC with the logging removed.

Summary

The logging framework is a standard part of the Flex SDK that can be used to incorporate logging into Flex and AIR applications. It is generally preferable to using the global trace function, since log messages can be categorized and filtered based on their source and severity. The logging framework is easy to use and easy to customize, with several base classes provided to simplify the task.

The next chapter covers the automation framework, which supports functional testing for Flex and AIR applications. It provides the mechanism for recording and replaying user interactions that is used by various third-party functional testing tools.

75

The Automation Framework

The automation framework enables you to test Flex applications by recording user gestures and their results in a test script, and then playing back the script to verify that the expected behavior actually occurred. This chapter explains the technology, and then provides a simple example and pointers towards further information on the topic.

Overview

It's easy to write software that's crawling with bugs, but there's really no excuse. Testing can be conducted and automated throughout development and delivery, so that programming mistakes and integration issues are identified early and resolved before they have serious consequences. There are many tools available to help and many testing techniques to follow. A successful software project is most likely when testing is carried out continuously, at various different levels, from the smallest logical unit inside an ActionScript class, to the integrated whole. Chapter 73, "Unit Testing and Test-Driven Development with FlexUnit," covered the lower level; this chapter covers higher-level testing with the Flex automation framework.

The automation framework consists of a number of Flex libraries that are included in full with Flex Builder Professional and provided in limited form with Flex Builder Standard. These libraries serve various needs: they allow developers to test the round-trip behavior of their applications using third-party tools, they facilitate the development of these third-party tools by providing a means of recording and playing back interactions, and they enable custom component developers to instrument their own components so that they can be understood by automation testing tools.

Because the topic of Flex automation is quite broad, the focus of this chapter needs to be confined to a smaller region. The chapter aims to provide a quick introduction and enough guidance for you to begin automation testing for simple Flex applications. The first section explains the basics of the technology; the second section covers recording and replaying a test script for a simple sample Flex application, and the third section covers more advanced topics, but consists mostly of references to the official documentation provided by Adobe.

The Technology Explained

All the controls contained in the Flex framework support automation. This means that when buttons are clicked, text is typed, or items are dragged from one list to another, these gestures can be captured by automation tools, recorded into scripts, and then later replayed. The technology that facilitates this process is contained in the automation libraries provided with Flex Builder Professional.

Recording and Playback

Figure 75-1 shows the process of recording a user gesture in a test script. On the left is a Flex application that has been prepared for automation (more on this later). When the button is clicked, a click event is dispatched as usual. This event is heard by an automation delegate, which proceeds to dispatch an automation event describing the button click. All Flex controls have automation delegates, responsible for surfacing information about important user gestures, such as clicks and keyboard input. In this case, the automation event describing the button click is received by an automation agent, which communicates with an automation tool. The automation tool records the details of the user gesture into a script for later playback. There are various automation tools on the market, but Flex Builder Professional includes a plug-in for HP Quick Test Professional (QTP).

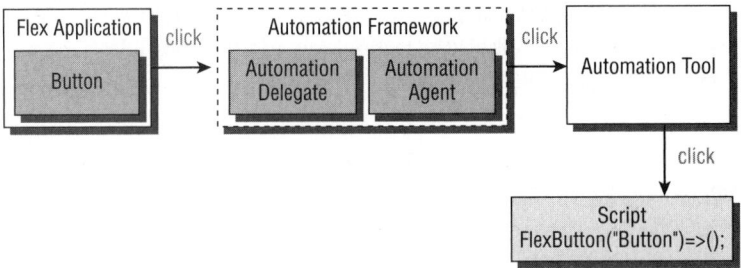

Figure 75-1

When a user gesture or series of gestures takes place, an action is normally performed that results in some change in application state. For example, when a row is selected in a data grid and then a Delete button is clicked, the selected row would be expected to disappear. Automation tools are able to examine application state via their automation agent and the automation delegates of the components that make up the user interface. A checkpoint can be added to a test script to verify that the expected behavior took place. The verification may involve comparing some properties of the user interface components or even comparing bitmap data.

Figure 75-2 shows the reverse process. After a script has been recorded, an automation tool such as QTP can play back the script and verify whether the application behaved correctly according to the checkpoints. In this example, the automation tool processes the button click described in the test script. It communicates with the automation agent, which invokes the automation delegate for the correct button in the Flex application. The automation delegate informs the button that it has been clicked, resulting in a normal mouse click event, which triggers the application to respond as though it had been physically clicked by a real user. After the click, the next step of the test script may be a checkpoint, causing the automation tool to examine the application state to verify the result of the gesture. If it is not as expected, the automation test will fail.

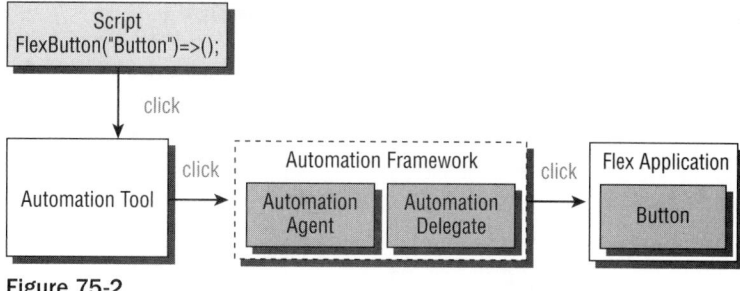

Figure 75-2

The Automation Libraries

Flex Builder Professional includes a set of automation libraries that enable automation testing and allow developers to instrument their own custom components and develop automation agents.

The automation libraries consist of the following:

- ❑ `automation.swc` — The automation delegates for the Flex framework components and the classes necessary for adding automation support to custom components

- ❑ `automation_dmv.swc` — The automation delegates for the Flex charting and `AdvancedDataGrid` classes

- ❑ `automation_agent.swc` — The generic automation agent mechanism, upon which third parties can develop their own automation agents

These SWC files can be found at the following location of the Flex Builder Professional installation:

```
sdks/3.0.x/frameworks/libs/
```

Also contained in this folder is the `qtp.swc` file, a specific library for HP Quick Test Professional (QTP). You can use this library to run automation tests on existing Flex applications or to compile Flex applications with built-in support for automation.

Runtime or Compile-Time Automation

There are two ways to prepare an application for automation: at runtime or at compile time (see Figure 75-3). The first approach requires the use of a wrapper SWF that contains the necessary automation libraries and loads the application SWF into itself at runtime. The wrapper contains the delegates and agent classes that are able to automate the components of the embedded application. The second approach compiles the automation libraries into the application SWF itself, so that it has built-in support for automation and can be automated independently.

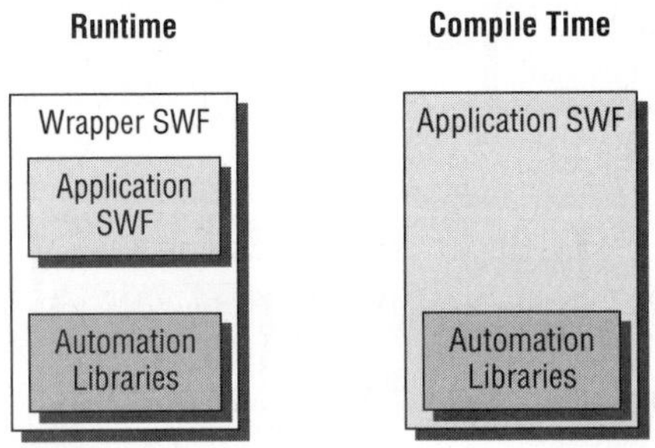

Runtime **Compile Time**

Figure 75-3

Component Identification

The components that make up a Flex application need to be identifiable if they are to be automated, so their automation events can be recorded and later played back through their automation delegates. For this purpose, an `automationName` property is defined on the `UIComponent` class, which is extended by all the Flex framework controls and containers. You can use this to give a descriptive name to any component that makes up part of a Flex application. These automation names will appear in a test script generated by an automation tool.

The precise rules by which different components or parts of a Flex application are identified depend both on the type of component and the automation tool in question. For example, with HP Quick Test Professional, a `Button` control is identified firstly by its `automationName` property; however, when this has not been explicitly set, the automation name is taken from the `Button`'s `label` property. Some other components will be identified by their `id` properties. This can have unexpected consequences if a button's label changes dynamically at runtime, so it is generally good practice to specify an `automationName` for any interactive component.

> You must be cautious with automation names, as any changes to them may affect preexisting test scripts. If a test script uses an old name that no longer exists, the test will fail, until the script is updated with the new name. Some testing tools provide special features to help keep scripts synchronized with an evolving code base.

Automating a Simple Application

A simple application that consists only of standard Flex components can be automated quite easily. This section contains an example, starting with the installation of an automation tool and ending with the running of two test scripts that verify the behavior of the application.

The sample application is contained in the `AutomationExample` Flex Builder project, accompanying this book.

The following steps are involved:

1. Installing an automation tool
2. Creating a testable application

3.   Compiling for automation

4.   Recording a test script

5.   Replaying a test script

Although the worked example uses the RIATest automation tool, the general process is similar for the other automation tools on the market. In particular, Adobe provides detailed documentation and sample applications for working with HP Quick Test Professional (QTP) at the following URLs:

- ❏   `http://livedocs.adobe.com/flex/3/testing_with_QTP_flex3.pdf`

- ❏   `www.adobe.com/devnet/flex/samples/custom_automated`

Installing an Automation Tool

You can download a 30-day evaluation version of RIATest from the following URL:

- ❏   `http://riatest.com/download-final.html`

RIATest runs on Windows and supports Firefox 2+ and Internet Explorer 6+ browsers. At the time of writing, there is no Flex automation tool available specifically for Mac OS X, although it may be possible to use FunFX, an open-source tool written in Ruby. Any of the Windows tools can run perfectly well on Mac OS X inside a Windows virtual machine.

After downloading the evaluation version, run the installer. This should create a shortcut to RIATest on the desktop and an entry in the Start Menu.

Creating a Testable Application

A testable application is one that supports automation. In other words, it is assembled from components that have automation delegates. All the standard Flex framework components have automation delegates and so support automation testing.

Automation tools need to be able to identify the components that make up an application so that they can record and replay interactions, as well as verify application state. As discussed earlier, the rules of identification depend on the type of component, but supplying a descriptive automation name is always a good idea. This avoids problems such as the dynamically changing button label and makes test scripts easier to read.

The `AutomationExample` sample application is shown in Figure 75-4. It consists of a data grid, two text inputs, and two buttons: one to add a new person to the data grid and another to remove the selected person. These components have all been given descriptive automation names:

```
<mx:DataGrid … automationName="namesDataGrid" … />

<mx:TextInput … automationName="firstNameInput" … />

<mx:TextInput … automationName="secondNameInput" … />

<mx:Button … automationName="addButton" … />

<mx:Button … automationName="removeButton" … />
```

These names will be used by the automation tool for identifying the components of the application.

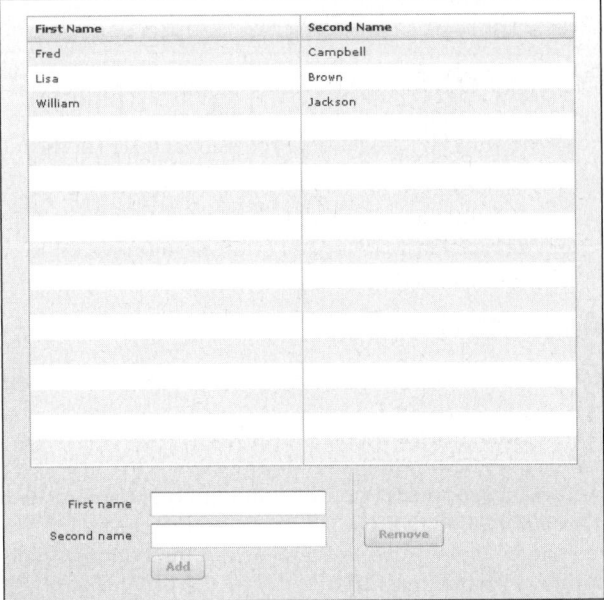

Figure 75-4

Compiling for Automation

This example uses compile-time automation rather than runtime automation. This means that the Flex automation libraries, provided in full with Flex Builder Professional, are compiled into the application. Furthermore, the automation agent for RIATest is also compiled into the application. This agent enables communication between the automation tool and the application. Other automation tools provide their own automation agents.

To compile the `AutomationExample` application, you need to use the `-include-libraries` compiler flag to ensure the automation and agent libraries are compiled into the application. To do so, open the Flex Builder Properties dialog for the project, and then select the Flex Compiler settings. In the "Additional compiler arguments" input, add the following:

```
-include-libraries

"\path\to\RIATest\agent\RIATestAgent.swc"
"\path\to\Adobe\Flex Builder 3\sdks\3.1.0\frameworks\libs\automation.swc"
"\path\to \Adobe\Flex Builder 3\sdks\3.1.0\frameworks\libs\automation_agent.swc"
"\path\to\Adobe\Flex Builder 3\sdks\3.1.0\frameworks\libs\automation_dmv.swc"
```

Make sure that the library paths are correct for your system, based on the installation location of RIATest and Flex Builder. The next time the project is built, these libraries will be embedded into the application SWF and automation support will be in place.

Recording a Test Script

The process of recording a test script varies for different automation tools, and some tools allow test scripts to be written by hand. In general, the process involves using the automation tool to start recording, and then interacting with the Flex application, placing checkpoints, and finally stopping the recording. During these interactions, the automation agent will be capturing data and passing it back to the automation tool, ready for replaying later. The RIATest agent includes a floating toolbar to assist with the test recording process, as shown in Figure 75-5.

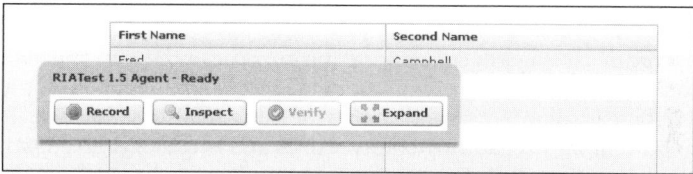

Figure 75-5

Recording the example test script with RAITest involves the following steps:

1. Create an RIATest project.
2. Create a test script.
3. Start recording.
4. Record checkpoints and interactions.
5. Stop recording.

Creating an RIATest Project

To create an RIATest project, perform the following steps:

1. Launch RIATest, and then create a new project by selecting File ⇨ New Project.
2. Configure the project options by selecting Project ⇨ Options.
3. Check all the boxes.
4. Specify the application URL or path. This needs to point to the application compiled earlier, containing the embedded automation libraries. For example:

    ```
    \path\to\AutomationExample\bin-debug\AutomationExample.html
    ```

5. Save the project by selecting File ⇨ Save As, name the project `AutomationExample.rtp`, and then click Save.

Creating a Test Script

Before recording can begin, you must create a new test script. A recording is saved in a test script, but the specific format of a test script depends on the automation tool. RIATest uses a simple language similar to ActionScript for storing test scripts, which makes them easy to read and edit by hand.

1. Select the AutomationExample project.
2. Select Project ➪ Add New Script.
3. Name the script `AddPerson.rts` and click Save.

This script will be used for testing the behavior of the application when a new person is added to the list of names.

Starting Recording

Before starting recording, it is worth considering the purpose of the test. The main intention is to verify that a new person can be added by typing their name into the two input boxes and clicking the Add button. However, there is some more subtle behavior that can also be verified. The Add button is initially disabled to prevent the user adding empty names and becomes enabled only when a first and second name have both been specified. This additional behavior may be tested in another test script or can be combined into one, as is the case here.

To start recording:

1. Select Run ➪ Launch Application.
2. Select Run ➪ Start Recording.

These steps should cause a browser to open containing the Flex application. The RIATest agent floating toolbar should be visible above the application with the status message "Recording." The RIATest automation tool should also display "Recording" in its title bar.

Recording Checkpoints and Interactions

First, generate some checkpoints to capture the initial application status. A checkpoint can be generated by holding down the Ctrl+Shift keys, then clicking on a component of the user interface. When Ctrl+Shift are held, a green border should be displayed around any component over which the mouse is hovered.

Generate three checkpoints:

1. Hold Ctrl+Shift, and click the `firstNameInput`.
2. Hold Ctrl+Shift, and click the `secondNameInput`.
3. Hold Ctrl+Shift, and click the `addButton`.

These checkpoints verify that the text inputs are initially empty and the add button is disabled. The script window the RIATest automation tool shows the following script:

```
var comp = FlexTextArea("First name:firstNameInput");
verifyEqual(comp=>text,      "");
```

```
verifyEqual(comp=>htmlText,  "");

var comp = FlexTextArea("Second name:secondNameInput");
verifyEqual(comp=>text,       "");
verifyEqual(comp=>htmlText,  "");

var comp = FlexButton("addButton");
verifyEqual(comp=>enabled,    false);
verifyEqual(comp=>label,      "Add");
verifyEqual(comp=>selected,  false);
```

Now add a new person by performing the following interactions:

1. Select the `firstNameInput`.

2. Type a first name such as "Sandy."

3. Press the Tab key to change focus to `secondNameInput`.

4. Type a second name, such as "Bull."

5. Click the `addButton`.

These interactions should be captured by RIATest in the following lines of test script:

```
FlexTextArea("First name:firstNameInput")=>textSelectionChange(0,0);
FlexTextArea("First name:firstNameInput")=>textInput("Sandy");
FlexTextArea("Second name:secondNameInput")=>textSelectionChange(0,0);
FlexTextArea("First name:firstNameInput")=>keyFocusChange();
FlexTextArea("Second name:secondNameInput")=>textInput("Bull");
FlexButton("addButton")=>click();
```

Finally, record some more checkpoints to verify the outcome:

1. Hold Ctrl+Shift, and click the "Sandy" item in the `namesDataGrid`.

2. Hold Ctrl+Shift, and click the "Bull" item in the `namesDataGrid`.

3. Hold Ctrl+Shift, and click the `firstNameInput` field.

4. Hold Ctrl+Shift, and click the `secondNameInput` field.

5. Hold Ctrl+Shift, and click the `addButton`.

These checkpoints ensure that the new name is appearing in the data grid and that the inputs have been cleared and the Add button disabled again. The following script should be generated by the RIATest tool:

```
verifyEqual(FlexListLabel("*Sandy* | Bull")=>automationValue,"Sandy");
verifyEqual(FlexListLabel("Sandy | *Bull*")=>automationValue,"Bull");

var comp = FlexTextArea("First name:firstNameInput");
verifyEqual(comp=>text,       "");
verifyEqual(comp=>htmlText,  "");

var comp = FlexTextArea("Second name:secondNameInput");
verifyEqual(comp=>text,       "");
```

```
verifyEqual(comp=>htmlText, "");

var comp = FlexButton("addButton");
verifyEqual(comp=>enabled,  false);
verifyEqual(comp=>label,    "Add");
verifyEqual(comp=>selected, false);
```

Stopping Recording

The test scenario is complete, so you can stop recording by selecting Run ⇨ Stop Recording.

To save the test script that has been generated, select File ⇨ Save.

Note that recording can be restarted again after having been stopped.

If no more recording is required, terminate the application by selecting Run ⇨ Terminate Application.

Replaying a Test Script

You can now replay the test script to verify that the application is still behaving correctly. Since the test script was only just recorded, a change in behavior is unexpected, but give a team of developers a day or two to work on new features and a regression could easily be introduced. The automation tests act as a safeguard to ensure that any breakage to previously working functionality is quickly detected and can be remedied.

To replay the AddPerson test script, select AddPerson.rts from the Project view, and then select Run ⇨ Run Without Debugging.

This should cause a browser to open containing the Flex application. Very quickly the interactions that were previously recorded will take place automatically, and then the browser window will close again. The RIATest tool will show the results of the test in its Messages view, as follows:

```
Launching C:\Program Files\Internet Explorer\IEXPLORE.EXE "C:\Documents and
Settings\Administrator\My Documents\Flex Builder 3\AutomationExample\
bin-debug\AutomationExample.html"
Application launched. Waiting for connection from agent…
Agent connection accepted. Application id=AutomationExample
Starting script C:\Documents and Settings\Administrator\My Documents\AddPerson.rts
Verification passed at line 2
…
Verification passed at line 36
Finished running script C:\Documents and Settings\Administrator\My Documents\
AddPerson.rts
Project execution finished.
1 script(s) succeeded
0 script(s) failed
Agent disconnected.
Terminated.
```

You can simulate regression by modifying the `AutomationExample.mxml` application file and rebuilding the Flex project. Comment out line 18 so that the value of the `firstNameInput` is used incorrectly as the second name of a new person. It's too easy to make a mistake like this!

```
person.secondName = firstNameInput.text;
```

If you rerun the `AddPerson` test script, it will fail with the following entries in the Messages View:

```
...
Cannot get property automationValue, Cannot find object by locator:
    FlexListLabel("*Sandy* | Bull") at line 22
Verification failed. Expected value: "Sandy", actual: null at line 22
Cannot get property automationValue, Cannot find object by locator:
    FlexListLabel("Sandy | *Bull*") at line 23
Verification failed. Expected value: "Bull", actual: null at line 23
...
0 script(s) succeeded
1 script(s) failed
Agent disconnected.
Terminated.
```

Further Topics

This section contains some pointers to more advanced topics that are covered in detail by the official Adobe documentation. They are beyond the scope of this book, but they are particularly important for developers who want to automate complex Flex applications with custom components, or for developers intending to create their own automation agents.

Automating Custom Components

In order to automate a Flex application, automation delegates are needed for each of the interactive components used in the application. The example in this chapter featured a simple application built only from standard Flex framework components. Automation delegates for all these components are provided in the Flex automation libraries, but this is not the case for custom components.

Rich Internet applications (RIAs) often require custom components, developed by extending the `UIComponent` base class. These might be needed for high-performance item renderers, custom data visualizations, or any number of other purposes. When you develop custom components, you need custom automation delegates in order to support automation. The Flex automation framework has been designed to make this task relatively straightforward. The process is described in the "Instrumenting Custom Components" section of the *Advanced Data Visualization Developer Guide*, available from `http://livedocs.adobe.com/flex/3/datavis_flex3.pdf`.

Creating a Custom Agent

For the more adventurous among us, the automation framework provides extensibility points that can be used to develop custom automation agents for various purposes. The most obvious use is communicating with an automation testing tool, but there are other reasons to want to control or observe a Flex application programmatically. For instance, you can use an automation agent to gather information about how an application is being used, how many times a certain button is clicked, and so on; or perhaps for supporting co-browsing, so customer support can assist a user by filling in a form on their application via the automation agent.

Various third parties have already used the automation APIs to develop their own Flex automation tools. Adobe provides comprehensive documentation of the APIs available to developers for building their own automation agents in the "Creating Custom Agents" chapter of the *Advanced Data Visualization Developer Guide*, available from `http://livedocs.adobe.com/flex/3/datavis_flex3.pdf`.

Summary

This chapter covered just a small part of the Flex automation framework, but hopefully the part of most immediate value to those of you unfamiliar with the topic: creating and running automated tests. Other parts were only touched upon, such as the delegate and agent mechanism that facilitates automation, the rules by which tools identify components, and the extensibility points provided in the automation libraries for the instrumentation of custom components and developing new agents. The foundations are laid for discovering more about Flex automation through the official Adobe documentation and the trial versions of various automation tools.

Automated functional testing is an important quality-control measure that complements other testing practices, such as unit testing and integration testing. For enterprise projects, automated functional testing provides a vital safeguard against regression — in other words, the situation where something that worked perfectly a few weeks earlier has mysteriously stopped working. A suite of automated functional tests can provide reassurance that existing functionality remains operational while other parts of a system grow and evolve. Functional testing with the automation framework should be an ongoing part of the software development process for Flex applications.

ActionScript Language Comparison

This appendix compares and contrasts a number of aspects of ActionScript, Java, and C++. The goal is to detail differences in three popular object-oriented programming (OOP) languages, since they're so widely used, and during your career as a programmer you may find yourself moving from one of these languages to another.

This appendix uses a structured format to describe the differences between ActionScript, Java, and C++. ActionScript 3, Java 6, and ANSI C++ will be used during this comparison since those are the current versions as of the writing of this book. The general format will be to present a topic and discuss how it is handled in each of the three languages.

Runtime Environment Concerns

Before discussing the languages themselves, some aspects of their runtime environments will need to be discussed to assist in putting this comparison in context.

Compilation

All three of these languages are compiled languages. ActionScript is compiled into `.swf` or `.swc` files that contain ActionScript bytecode. Java is compiled into `.class` files that contain Java byte-code. C++ is compiled into actual programs — for instance, on a Windows system you will end up with an `.exe` file.

Runtime Engines

ActionScript bytecode is run in the ActionScript Virtual Machine (AVM). In the case of ActionScript 3, the bytecode is consumed by a Just in Time (JIT) compiler and converted into machine-specific code. Java bytecode is run in the Java Virtual Machine (JVM). It is similar to

ActionScript, since it is also bytecode transformed by a JIT compiler. Whereas both Java and ActionScript run in some type of runtime engine, C++ does not. C++ programs are already compiled machine-specific code that runs directly on a host operating system without any runtime machine such as the AVM or JVM acting as a middleman.

Memory Management

Physical memory is a finite resource and unfortunately must be shared between all the processes running on a computer system. ActionScript, Java, and C++ each have their own approach to managing the memory consumed by programs written in these languages. The following is a quick comparison of some of the very high-level differences.

Automatic versus Explicit

Since the AVM and the JVM are modern runtime engines, they implement automatic Garbage Collection systems. For instance, in ActionScript, the AVM implements MMgc, which runs deferred reference counting and incremental mark and sweep algorithms to determine what can be deallocated and reclaimed by the system. Java also has an automatic Garbage Collector built into the JVM.

The key thing about automatic Garbage Collectors is that they remove the responsibility of object deallocation from the developer. Rather than having to worry about deallocating objects, the developer can rest assured that the Garbage Collector will periodically run when the runtime machine does not have enough memory to allocate new objects.

In contrast, C++ does not have a Garbage Collection system. This puts the full scope of memory management responsibility on the developer. In C++, explicit destructors are needed and have to be implemented in the code by the developer.

The Delete Keyword

Since C++ requires explicit memory management, the language implements a `delete` keyword for a developer to use whenever they need to deallocate an object. This means that developers need to be diligent and delete their objects when they are no longer needed; otherwise, their applications will contain memory leaks.

ActionScript 3 has a `delete` keyword, but it does not deallocate objects. In ActionScript 3, `delete` is used to `delete` dynamically added properties from a dynamic object. Java does not have a `delete` keyword.

You would think that ActionScript 3 and Java might not be prone to memory leaks like C++ since memory management is handled automatically. That assumption would be wrong, since the AVM and JVM use references and object reachability to decide when to deallocate. In other words, preventing memory leaks in ActionScript and Java requires the developer to manage object references.

Block-Level Scoping

Both Java and C++ support block-level scoping. Block-level scoping is being able to limit the scope of a variable to a code block — for example, an `if` statement within a function. In other words, if you defined a variable within an `if` statement when coding a Java or C++ application, that variable would only be available to the `if` statement and not to any of the surrounding code within the same function.

In contrast, ActionScript performs variable hoisting during compile time. In other words, all variables within a function are hoisted to the top of that function, whether they're defined in code blocks of that function or not. So in the previous `if` statement example, the variable declared in the `if` statement would be available to the rest of the function's code outside the `if` block.

The Notion of Global Variables

C++ supports global variables. In C++, you declare a variable outside of any function bodies, and that variable will become available to all parts of the program. If you need to access that global variable in a different file, you use the `extern` keyword.

In the same sense, ActionScript and Java do not have global variables. However, in both languages you can emulate global variables by creating a class that contains a `public static` variable. From that point forth, you can access that variable globally via a `<classname>.<variablename>` syntax.

Using Console Output

When you're debugging your application, it's great to have a mechanism to provide console output. All three languages provide methods for console output. In ActionScript, you run your application in the debug player and issue `trace()` statements. Java allows you to output to the console using `System.out.println()`. In C++, you would either use `stdio::stdout` or `iostream` methods.

Language Differences

Now that some of the environmental specifics have been established, some of the major syntax and language implementation differences between ActionScript, Java, and C++ will be covered.

Working with Data Types

All programming languages have various types available to a developer to represent data. The following sections contrast the various data types in ActionScript, Java, and C++, and describe how to cast and confirm them.

Simple Types

Primitives, as they are known in ActionScript and Java, and fundamental types, as they are known in C++, are the most basic and fundamental data type building blocks. Here are the lists of the simple types for each of the three languages:

- **ActionScript**—`String`, `uint`, `int`, `Number`, `Boolean`
- **Java**—`char`, `short`, `int`, `long`, `boolean`, `float`, `double`, `byte`
- **C++**—`char`, `short`, `int`, `long`, `bool`, `float`, `double`, `long double`, `wchar_t`

Appendix A: ActionScript Language Comparison

Complex Types

Whereas neither Java nor C++ have any complex data types as first-class types, ActionScript does. The complex types in ActionScript that are first-class are:

- ❑ Object
- ❑ Array
- ❑ Date
- ❑ Error
- ❑ Function
- ❑ RegExp
- ❑ XML
- ❑ XMLList

Constants

Constants enable you to define unchanging values in your application. In ActionScript and C++, the constant is qualified with the keyword const. In Java, the constant is qualified with the keyword final.

Undeclared

Both ActionScript and C++ enable you to use a type to indicate that the type is actually undeclared and will be determined at runtime. This feature becomes handy when you would like to implement a method but have no idea about what data type the method will be receiving as an input parameter.

To specify the undeclared type in ActionScript, you use the asterisk (*) as the data type, and in C++ you use void *. Unfortunately for the Java developer, there is no undeclared type.

Enumeration

In C++, there is a special enum data type that represents a list of named integer constants. For instance:

```
enum { MONDAY, TUESDAY, WEDNESDAY, THURSDAY, FRIDAY, SATURDAY, SUNDAY };
```

In the preceding code, going from left to right, the named constants represent the values 0–6. You can also explicitly set values such as in this example:

```
enum { ONECENTURY = 100, TWOCENTURY = 200, THREECENTURY = 300 };
```

Like C++, Java supports enumeration through a class; unlike C++, ActionScript does not.

The Object Data Type

In ActionScript, there is a notion that everything is an Object, including the primitives discussed earlier. This is in strict contrast to both Java and C++, where this is not the case.

All classes in both ActionScript and Java inherit from Object. There are a couple things about Object that need to be pointed out.

Runtime Type Checking

In ActionScript, you can type check an object at runtime. This is done via the `is` keyword. The nice thing is that you can keep your public interface relatively generic and flexible and then use the `is` keyword to create conditional code to run specific blocks based on the actual runtime object type. Neither Java nor C++ provide this runtime type checking.

Object Equality

ActionScript can compare two identical objects to establish if they are the same instance. This is accomplished via the strict equality operator (===), which is like an equality operator but with an additional equal sign. The easiest way to think about strict equality is that if two objects have the exact same data state, they will be considered equal if you use the standard equality operator. However, since there are two different object instances, running a strict equality comparison on them will evaluate to false. The strict equality operator is used only in ActionScript and is not available in either Java or C++.

Type Casting

Casting is the act of taking the data type of an object instance and representing it as a different but compatible data type. For instance, if you type method input parameters as interfaces inside the method itself, you could cast the object back into its original type.

ActionScript supports two different kinds of type casting. The first kind uses an `as` keyword and the second uses a constructor style syntax, as shown here:

```
// Method one: Using the as keyword
var tempVar:SomeVarType = inputParam as SomeVarType;
// Method two: Using constructor-stype syntax
var tempVar:SomeVarType = SomeVarType( inputParam );
```

Java supports upcasting from a child type to a parent type, and downcasting from a parent type to a child type:

```
// Method one: Upcasting from a subclass type to a parent class type
SomeParentType tempParent = someChild;
// Method two: Downcasting from a parent type to a child type
SomeChildType anotherChild = (SomeChildType) tempParent;
```

C++ type casting is also different. Here is an example:

```
someParent = (SomeParentType) someChild;
```

Declarations

The method of declaring your variables in the three languages is very different. Here is an example of a declaration in ActionScript:

```
public var someVar:int;
```

Here is the same declaration in Java:

```
public int someVar;
```

Here is the example yet again, in C++:

```
public:
    int someVar;
```

The key difference is that in ActionScript, the data type is defined at the end of the declaration in a style called *post-colon syntax*. Also note that the C++ example specifies the public access modifier on a separate line. This is because you can group multiple declarations with one access modifier, as in this example:

```
public:
    int someVar;
    short anotherVar;
    bool thirdVar;
```

Statement Termination

In ActionScript, putting the semicolon at the end of the line is optional when you only have one statement in a line. In both Java and C++, the semicolon is mandatory.

Regular Expressions

As of version 3, ActionScript has built-in support for regular expressions. Java also has built-in support for regular expressions. However, C++ does not have any built-in support.

OOP Differences

No comparison of three different OOP languages would be complete without discussing the differences in how they implement OOP.

Classes, Filenames, and Packages

ActionScript, Java, and C++ all have their own ways of dealing with class files and if applicable, the packages in which the class files are contained.

In ActionScript programming, a package is a folder within the source tree. For instance, if you had ClassA.as and ClassB.as located in {SRC_ROOT}\com\wiley\custom, the package would be com.wiley.custom, and the class in those files would be a part of that package. Notice that class was stated and not classes. That is because even though you can have multiple classes in a file, only one of them can be public and available to the package in ActionScript.

The other consideration to take into account with ActionScript is that the class that's available to the package must have the same name as the containing file. In other words, the ClassA.as and ClassB.as files would have a class in them with the same name ClassA and ClassB, respectively. Java uses packages similarly to the way that ActionScript uses them.

ActionScript packages allow you to place not only classes in a package but also interfaces, variables, functions, namespaces, and executable statements. Java limits you to just classes and interfaces.

In contrast to ActionScript and Java, C++ is a completely different beast; C++ does not have packages. In C++, you can name things however you like. Also, in C++ you can put as many class declarations in a single file as you'd like. This means that for a C++ developer there is really no set standard in this regard, although the convention is to create two files for each class.

When you create a class in C++, it's customary to create an .h header file and a .cpp implementation file. The header file can be thought of roughly as a blueprint file, since it is the definition of the class, and the implementation file is where the actual functional code exists. The benefit of this approach is that you can distribute the header file with a compiled .obj implementation file. That way, developers making use of your code can reference the definition of the class they're using without concerning themselves about the implementation details.

Polymorphism

In OOP, polymorphism is the ability for something to have multiple meanings. For instance, there may be several classes that implement a dance() method. Polymorphism ensures that you can call that dance() method safely on all the classes without knowing the exact type of each class or the specific implementation of their version of dance().

Method Polymorphism

The preceding example mentioned all classes containing a dance() method. The key thing with method polymorphism is that the dance() method of each class would be implemented a little differently.

In ActionScript, you can accomplish this in two different ways. The first would be to create an interface that declares the dance() method. (The next section discusses interfaces.) The second way is to implement the dance() method in a Dancer base class and then use the override keyword to implement a type-specific dance() in each of the subclasses. For instance, you could have something like HipHopDancer.dance(), BalletDancer.dance(), and SquareDancer.dance().

Like ActionScript, Java allows you to implement method polymorphism using both the interface approach and the override approach. However, unlike ActionScript, Java enables you to take polymorphism one step further with a technique called *method overloading*. Using this technique, you declare a method several times in a class and in each instance you can change the type of input arguments that the method receives. For instance, you can have dance(int partners) or dance(String type).

Like Java, C++ allows method overloading, but unlike ActionScript and Java, C++ does not have interfaces and the override keyword. Instead, C++ uses virtual classes in place of interfaces and has a virtual keyword to be used when needing to implement method polymorphism.

Abstract Classes and Interfaces

In ActionScript, interfaces allow you to implement method polymorphism. Additionally, the interface in ActionScript allows you to implement type polymorphism. For instance, if you had a wash() method and wanted to pass in various animal classes without knowing exactly which animal classes could be potentially passed in, you could create an interface IWashableAnimal that all the classes could implement using the implements keyword.

Java also uses interfaces. However, whereas ActionScript will only allow method declarations in an interface, Java allows `final` variables, too. Unlike ActionScript, Java does not just stop at interfaces. In Java there are abstract classes.

Abstract classes are classes in Java qualified by the `abstract` keyword, and unlike using an interface, you can flesh out some of the methods and properties while leaving some of the methods abstract by prepending their declarations with the `abstract` keyword, too. When you qualify a class in Java with the `abstract` keyword, you make that class uninstantiatable and force developers into creating and instantiating subclasses of that abstract class instead. The same goes for any of the abstract methods in that abstract class.

C++ also makes use of abstract classes, although with C++, abstract classes are actually called *pure virtual classes*. These should be used when you need type polymorphism in C++, since the language doesn't have interfaces.

Inheritance

Both Java and ActionScript have the notion of a base class that is an ancestor to all other classes. In both Java and ActionScript, this base class is `Object`. This differs from C++, which does not have an ancestral root in the inheritance tree.

Whereas C++ supports multiple inheritance, by design neither Java nor ActionScript do. When developing your Java and ActionScript applications, you can work around the lack of multiple inheritance by using interfaces and/or mixins.

Access Modifiers

In C++, there is no notion of access modifiers; in other words, all classes are essentially public. The workaround in C++ is to create an "inner" class, which effectively limits the scope of the "inner" class to the class in which it had been defined.

In contrast, both Java and ActionScript have access modifiers, such as `public`, `private`, and `protected`, to limit the visibility of classes. That being said, the way in which Java and ActionScript implement access modifiers is slightly different.

In Java, there is a notion of having private classes with private constructors. This is a very useful feature of Java, for instance, having private constructors makes implementing the Singleton design pattern pretty simple. On the other hand, although you can mark class members as private in ActionScript, there is no way to make your classes or their constructors private. The lack of private constructors in ActionScript makes implementing things such as the Singleton design pattern more difficult.

Dynamic Classes

Although ActionScript is a strongly typed language, one thing that sets it apart from both Java and C++ is the loosely typed notion of dynamic classes. In ActionScript, you can mark a class dynamic using the `dynamic` keyword. This enables you to add properties and methods to the class at runtime. As a matter of fact, some of the core classes are dynamic — `Object` and `Array`, among others.

Summary

As you can see, although there are similarities between ActionScript 3, Java 6, and ANSI C++, each language has its own way of implementing an OOP language. Unfortunately, there is really no way for us to discuss all the differences and specifics of each of these languages without writing several more volumes of *Professional Adobe Flex 3*.

If you want to learn more about any of these languages, here are some references:

- ❏ ActionScript 3:
  - ❏ `http://livedocs.adobe.com/flex/3/html/help.html?content=Part6_ProgAS_1.html`
  - ❏ `http://en.wikipedia.org/wiki/ActionScript`
  - ❏ `www.adobe.com/devnet/actionscript/articles/avm2overview.pdf`
- ❏ Java:
  - ❏ `http://java.sun.com/javase/reference/api.jsp`
  - ❏ `http://en.wikipedia.org/wiki/Java_(programming_language)`
  - ❏ `http://en.wikipedia.org/wiki/Java_virtual_machine`
  - ❏ `http://en.wikipedia.org/wiki/Java_bytecode`
- ❏ C++:
  - ❏ `www.cplusplus.com`
  - ❏ `http://en.wikipedia.org/wiki/C%2B%2B`

Also, here are a couple links to community blog posts that detail some of the comparisons:

- ❏ `http://blogs.adobe.com/kiwi/2006/05/as3_language_101_for_cc_coders_1.html`
- ❏ `http://flexblog.faratasystems.com/?p=115`

This concludes the book and an excursion through the world of Flex 3. Hopefully you have enjoyed the journey and have found the materials in this book beneficial in assisting you with your Flex development.

Index

development with Flex Builder and, 104

`Module` class and `ModuleLoader` class, 1173–1177

overview of, 1171–1172

reasons for, 1172

RSL (Runtime Shared Libraries) and, 1173

summary, 1187

`Module` **class, 1173–1177**

`ModuleLoader` **class, 1173–1177**

monitoring

Internet traffic, 1257–1258

network connections with AIR, 785–786

mouse events

composite components and, 356–357

event priority and, 373–374

`Move` **effect, built-in effects, 443**

MovieStar Flash Player

smart pause functionality, 873–874

updates for Flash Player, 514, 539

MP3s

accessing sound metadata, 526–528

embedding sound in MXML, 517

playing VOD (video on demand), 867

`Sound` class and, 520

streaming video and, 872

as usable media format, 514

MP4s, 866–867

MPEG-4

Flash Player supporting, 539

streaming video and, 865, 872

multiple files, managing, 808–810

MVC (Model-View-Controller) framework.

***See also* Cairngorm**

abstraction and, 1080

advantages of, 1079

as approach to component architecture, 1082

component reuse, 1080

components, 1077

controller, 1078–1079

distributed development, 1080–1081

maintenance and, 1081

models, 1077–1078

modular application development contrasted with, 1172

overview of, 1076–1077

summary, 1082

technologies for, 1081

views, 1078

`mx` **prefix indicating Flex classes, 222**

`<mx:AddChild>` **tag, 388–390**

`mx.binding`. **See data binding**

`mx.containers`. **See containers**

`mx.controls`. **See controls**

`mx.effects`. **See visual effects**

`mx.logging`. **See logging**

`mx.managers`. **See managers**

MXML

ActionScript and, 141, 147–148

ActionScript functions declared in, 145–146

benefits of Flex and, 12

breakpoints in, 1248

calling Web Services, 925

class naming conventions, 1143–1144

code assist and, 172

component tags, 133

core data type tags, 135

CSS and, 139

`CSSStyle` tag, 139–140

data binding and, 231–232

display hierarchy, 129

event listeners, 240

Flex application development and, 104

Flex based on, 3

as Flex source file, 218

form creation, 281

formatter classes and, 226

history of Flex and, 18

inline ActionScript, 141–143

inline CSS, 139–140

interpreted tags, 134–135

languages in Flex 3 ecosystem, 28

LCDS producers and consumers declared in, 986–987

linking external ActionScript, 146–147

linking external CSS, 140–141

local namespace, 132

metadata added to, 372–373

MXML tags, 133

namespaces, 129–130

namespaces and packages, 131–132

namespaces and URIs, 130–131

naming conventions, 128

O

X